SCIENTIFIC EVIDENCE IN CIVIL AND CRIMINAL CASES

By

ANDRE A. MOENSSENS
Professor of Law, University of Richmond
Wm. J. Maier, Jr. Professor of Law (Visiting 1993–95),
West Virginia University

JAMES E. STARRS
Professor of Law and Forensic Sciences
The George Washington University

CAROL E. HENDERSON
Professor of Law
Nova Southeastern University

and

FRED E. INBAU
John Henry Wigmore Professor of Law Emeritus
Northwestern University
First Director, Chicago Police Scientific
Crime Detection Laboratory

FOURTH EDITION

Library of Congress Cataloging-in-Publication Data

Scientific evidence in civil and criminal cases / by Andre A.
Moenssens . . . [et al.]. — 4th ed.
p.   cm.
Rev. ed. of: Scientific evidence in criminal cases / Andre A.
Moenssens, Fred E. Inbau, and James E. Starrs. 3rd ed. 1986.
Includes bibliographical references and index.
ISBN 1–56662–233–6
1. Evidence, Expert—United States.   2. Evidence, Criminal—United
States.   I. Moenssens, Andre A.   II. Moenssens, Andre A.
Scientific evidence in criminal cases.
KF8960.S39   1995
347.73'67—dc20
[347.30767]   94–42654

 TEXT IS PRINTED ON 10% POST
CONSUMER RECYCLED PAPER

 PRINTED WITH
SOY INK™

PREFACE

Most trial lawyers, legal scholars and students of the law know that legal proof is rapidly evolving into a multidisciplinary mosaic of law, science and technology As a consequence of our modern age, in which increasing specialization is being held out as a desirable means of solving difficult problems, a recognition of the functions of scientific evidence and expert testimony has become indispensable in the trial of civil and criminal cases.

The importance of expert testimony in the trial of all types of cases continues to increase, not only in the frequency of its use, but also in the new techniques and disciplines which find their way into the courtroom. We have seen, in past years, entire new disciplines springing up, sometimes out of existing fields of endeavor, and on other occasions as the result of a genesis of their own. For instance, we have witnessed the introduction in paternity suits and in criminal cases of deoxyribonucleic (DNA) evidence. In established disciplines, new tests are developed, the results of which find their way into the courtroom even before the novel tests have been validated, on the coattails of the recognition the discipline which spawned the tests had already achieved. In yet other cases, new theories have sprung up which give birth to "expert" evidence of a type that can hardly be called "scientific".

The term scientific evidence covers, of course, a range of opinion testimony varying widely in probative value, weight, and persuasiveness. Some disciplines allow the formulation of an opinion with near-mathematical certainty; others are less precise and are intermixed with art. The various sciences and techniques are allied, however, in at least one respect: their secrets are unlocked by specially trained experts. Data disclosed in the laboratory or testing facility has no real meaning in law until presented to the trier of fact. Lawyers must rely on expert testimony as a vehicle for communicating this data, and common sense teaches us that myopic presentation can be avoided only by maintaining an intelligible dialogue with the expert. Unfortunately, legal education and experience in the practice of law have, on the whole, failed to equip trial lawyers for this task. It often happens that both sides to a controversy fail to fully utilize, or to even adequately appreciate, the great potential of expert testimony as a courtroom technique for proving or disproving facts.

This book was written to assist trial lawyers in obtaining a concise understanding of the scope of the most commonly encountered types of expert testimony, and the nature of the results which may be expected from the specialists. As we explored both the potentialities and the limitations of various types of expert proof, we also gave consideration to the qualifications needed for expertise in these various professional disciplines. Furthermore, in addition to discussing the status of the law concerning the subjects covered in the book, suggestions are offered about the future development of the law as it pertains to some areas in which expertise or certainty of conclusion remains elusive.

Apart from the value which we believe our book has for trial lawyers, we feel that it will also greatly benefit legal educators as a tool in structuring courses in scientific evidence, in the nature of proof, or a source book for more sophisticated trial advocacy programs. The book also directs itself to students in the criminal justice area, for they, too, are in need of general information regarding various scientific and technical disciplines which may be expected to be used in criminal trials.

Although *Scientific Evidence in Civil and Criminal Cases* is not a technical treatise for the specialist in any given area, it does give the expert an overview of the legal status in that expert's specialty, and an opportunity to become acquainted with other sciences and techniques with which contact may be anticipated, both inside and outside the courtroom.

The decision as to what materials to cover in this book and which ones to omit was made largely on the basis of the authors' collective experiences with the spectrum of scientific proof most commonly encountered in civil and criminal cases. The depth, or lack of it, with which individual topics were treated required difficult decisions. Some topics may appear to be explored in too much detail, while others may seem to be inadequately covered, but we settled upon our own best judgment, consistent with such factors as single-volume space limitation and present professional needs.

The fourth edition on *Scientific Evidence in Civil and Criminal Cases* is not merely an updating of the third edition. The decision to add, to the treatment of criminal evidence upon which the previous editions focused, discussions on the applications of these same techniques to civil litigation and the addition of chapters dealing entirely with expert testimony offered only in civil cases forced the authors to devise a different framework within which to mold the various topics. Thus, the book is now divided into four main Parts.

In Part I, the first four chapters of the book deal with general concepts underlying the use of expert opinion testimony, with the use of real and demonstrative evidence, and with opinion testimony of the non-expert "skilled witnesses" who testify routinely in DUI and speeding cases. In Part II, a number of chapters deal with expert testimony based upon the physical sciences, including questioned document examinations in civil and criminal cases, firearms and toolmark evidence, arson and explosives testimony, fingerprint identification evidence, trace evidence, and voice spectrographic recognition investigations. A new chapter on accident reconstruction evidence is also included in Part II.

In Part III, we focus on the biological and life sciences, where chapters deal with forensic pathology, toxicological examinations of biological fluids, the identification of drugs, and forensic odontology. In this part is also contained the extensive and brand new chapter on DNA, as well as one on forensic anthropology. The final Part IV deals with expert testimony in the behavioral sciences, containing the two new chapters dealing with forensic psychiatry, psychology, and neurology, and with the proliferation of "syndrome" evidence offered by the behaviorists. Also discussed are issues such as the degree of reliability of eyewitness testimony. Many of the topics discussed in this part deal exclusively with expert psychiatric and psychological testimony in civil cases, among them custody determinations and civil commitment hearings. The concluding part also contains the chapter on the detection of deception.

In the preparation of legal materials and for research assistance, we were also fortunate to have the valuable help of a number of bright law students who acted as research assistants to the authors. We gratefully acknowledge the invaluable research assistance of the following persons while students at their respective law schools. At the University of Richmond Law School, Gloria Frey and Tracy Houck; at the West Virginia University College of Law, Teresa Postle and Christina Nehls; at the George Washington University National Law Center, Melissa K. Rashbaum, Mary Beth Malefyt, Edward Bedrosian, Jr., and George J. Farrugia; at the George Washington University Dept. of Forensic Sciences, Kendra Styers-Smith; at Nova Southeastern University, Eugene Bardakjy, Paul Ghougasian, Beth Leboff, Alphonso Peets, Anthony Scaletta, Timothy Schulz, and Brian Waxman.

The scope of the book was so extensive that the authors also needed the frequent advice and counsel of many specialists in various fields of forensic science. Two such specialists' work, that of Charles R. Midkiff and Kenneth E. Melson, was so extensive that it deserved special mention at the beginning of the chapters for which they were primary authors. We would specially like to thank the advice and counsel of Linda J. Hart, Clarence E. Phillips, and Todd Reeves. Many other forensic scientists gave us valuable advice, read parts of the manuscript, offered helpful suggestions, or furnished us with illustrations. None of the persons whose counsel we sought, nor any of the ones mentioned in the text, in footnotes, or through inclusion of their publications, should be faulted for any of the shortcomings of this book. That is a responsibility which rests upon the authors alone.

A.A.M.
J.E.S.
C.E.H.
F.E.I.

September, 1994

*

SUMMARY OF CONTENTS

PART III. EXPERT TESTIMONY IN THE BIOLOGICAL AND LIFE SCIENCES

TABLE OF CONTENTS

PART I. GENERAL CONCEPTS

CHAPTER 1. EXPERT EVIDENCE AND TESTIMONY

I. THE NATURE AND PURPOSE OF EXPERT EVIDENCE AND TESTIMONY

II. BASIC ELEMENTS IN THE SELECTION AND PREPARATION OF EXPERT TESTIMONY

III. DISCOVERY AND DISCLOSURE IN CRIMINAL CASES

VII. MISCELLANEOUS

CHAPTER 2. DEMONSTRATIVE EVIDENCE

I. INTRODUCTION

II. CASTS, MODELS, MAPS AND DRAWINGS

III. PHOTOGRAPHIC EVIDENCE

IV. PHOTOGRAPHIC EVIDENCE IN GENERAL

V. MOTION PICTURES AND VIDEOTAPE IN COURT

VI. COMPUTER ANIMATION AND SIMULATION

VII. MISCELLANEOUS

CHAPTER 3. CHEMICAL AND OTHER TESTS FOR ALCOHOLIC INTOXICATION

I. ALCOHOL INTOXICATION TESTING

II. EVIDENCE OF ALCOHOL INTOXICATION

III. MISCELLANEOUS

CHAPTER 4. SCIENTIFIC DETECTION OF SPEEDING

I. INTRODUCTION

II. RADAR SPEED DETECTION

III. VASCAR SPEED DETECTION

IV. LASER SPEED DETECTION

V. EVIDENCE OF SPEEDING

VI. MISCELLANEOUS

PART II. EVIDENCE BASED ON THE PHYSICAL SCIENCES

CHAPTER 5. QUESTIONED DOCUMENTS

I. INTRODUCTION

II. THE EXAMINATION OF QUESTIONED DOCUMENTS

IV. LABORATORY ANALYSIS

V. EVIDENCE OF ARSON AND EXPLOSIVES USE

CHAPTER 9. TRACE EVIDENCE—THE SOURCE IDENTIFICATION AND COMPARISON OF SMALL OBJECTS AND PARTICLES

I. INTRODUCTION

II. INSTRUMENTATION AND METHODS OF ANALYSIS

III. EXAMINATION OF HAIR

IV. FIBERS

V. PAINT

VI. GLASS

VII. MISCELLANEOUS PARTICLES

VIII. TRIAL AIDS

IX. MISCELLANEOUS

CHAPTER 10. SPECTROGRAPHIC VOICE RECOGNITION

I. INTRODUCTION

II. THE SPECTROGRAPHIC VOICE RECOGNITION PROCESS

III. EVIDENCE OF VOICE COMPARISONS BY SPECTROGRAMS

V. MISCELLANEOUS

CHAPTER 13. SEROLOGY AND TOXICOLOGY OF BODY FLUIDS

I. INTRODUCTION

II. TOXICOLOGY AND CHEMISTRY—IN GENERAL

III. THE INVESTIGATION OF BLOOD

IV. THE INVESTIGATION OF OTHER BIOLOGICAL MATTER

CHAPTER 14. DRUGS AND THEIR CONTROL

I. INTRODUCTION

II. DRUGS

CHAPTER 15. DETERMINING INDIVIDUALITY BY DNA

I. INTRODUCTION

TABLE OF CONTENTS

CHAPTER 17. FORENSIC ANTHROPOLOGY

I. INTRODUCTION

II. IDENTIFICATION

V. TRIAL AIDS

VI. MISCELLANEOUS

PART IV. BEHAVIORAL SCIENCE EVIDENCE

CHAPTER 18. PSYCHIATRY, PSYCHOLOGY AND NEUROLOGY

I. INTRODUCTION

II. FORENSIC PSYCHIATRY

III. FORENSIC PSYCHOLOGY

CHAPTER 19. SPECIFIC TYPES OF BEHAVIORAL EXPERT EVIDENCE

I. THE DEFENSE OF INSANITY AND RELATED CONCEPTS

IV. MENTAL HEALTH EVIDENCE IN CHILD CUSTODY CASES

V. MISCELLANEOUS

CHAPTER 20. THE DETECTION OF DECEPTION

I. INTRODUCTION

II. THE POLYGRAPH TECHNIQUE

TABLE OF CONTENTS

TABLE OF CASES

Principal cases are in italic type. Non-principal cases are in roman type. References are to Pages.

*

SCIENTIFIC EVIDENCE IN CIVIL AND CRIMINAL CASES

*

Part I

GENERAL CONCEPTS

The Nature of "Scientific" Evidence

In the first part of this text, we begin a discussion of the use of scientific evidence in the courtroom by dealing with some very general concepts that relate to the use of expert opinion testimony in court. In truth, much of the proof that is presented as "scientific" evidence involves very little science. Over the years, the term has come to be generically applied to a broad spectrum of expert opinion testimony that spans the sciences, the arts and all kinds of skilled professions. Even within a profession that rests on scientific underpinnings, in the sense that the discipline has definite rules and fixed concepts that govern its workings, the testimony offered by its specialists is frequently couched in terms of opinions, conclusions, and evaluations which, themselves, are not scientifically measurable.

Thus, an expert skilled in examining substances and determining their elemental composition is engaged in scientific analysis when testifying to the composition of a specimen, but is not offering scientific "fact" when testifying to a conclusion as to what the analysis means in the context of disputed issues before the court. Similarly, in fingerprint identification, it can be asserted that fingerprint classification is an applied science, because fingerprint pattern interpretation is subject to fixed rules, but when lawyers deal with its experts in court, they do not confront science! A fingerprint specialist who has examined a latent crime scene print and who has compared it to a known impression of the defendant is not engaged in science but is discussing instead the art of evaluating rather obvious visible differences between an incomplete and frequently partially blurred latent impression and a more crisp inked impression for the purpose of determining whether these prints, despite their obvious differences, are nevertheless made by the same digit or by different digits.

The first four chapters offer an introduction to expert testimony in general. In Chapter 1 we deal with legal concepts on expert testimony in general, such as standards for admissibility, discovery of expert findings, and some practical aspects of using experts in general. In Chapter 2 we move on to photographic and demonstrative evidence, because that type of proof is often used in conjunction with expert testimony or as an aid to understanding an expert's testimony. In Chapters 3 and 4 we deal with types of evidence often presented by non-scientist, skilled police officers who are using devices where there are definite scientific principles at work. For example, testimony on wheth-

1

er the driver of a vehicle was intoxicated (Chapter 3) is frequently presented by non-scientist police officers who have been trained in the proper use of breath-alcohol testing instruments and in conducting field sobriety tests.

Similarly, testimony of the speed of vehicles (see Chapter 4) is routinely offered by witnesses who have been trained in the proper use of radar and vascar devices, but who are not scientists themselves.

Thus, while the term "scientific" evidence is frequently misused in the forensic process, we will continue the generally accepted practice of using it for all types of opinion testimony, whether it is based on science, art, or taught skills.

Chapter 1

EXPERT EVIDENCE AND TESTIMONY

I. THE NATURE AND PURPOSE OF EXPERT EVIDENCE AND TESTIMONY

♦ II. BASIC ELEMENTS IN THE SELECTION AND PREPARATION OF EXPERT TESTIMONY

III. DISCOVERY AND DISCLOSURE IN CRIMINAL CASES

IV. DISCOVERY AND DISCLOSURE IN CIVIL CASES

I. THE NATURE AND PURPOSE OF EXPERT EVIDENCE AND TESTIMONY

§ 1.01 Scope of the Chapter

While civil litigation has, historically, made widespread use of expert opinion testimony in a great variety of areas, in criminal cases, by contrast, there is no aspect of effective pretrial and trial planning that is of greater consequence and yet more neglected than the effective use of scientific evidence and expert testimony. This creates, particularly in criminal cases, a needless gap between the potentialities and actual use. Perhaps this condition can be attributed to the voluminous litigation which currently besieges the criminal courts, the public prosecutor, and the defense attorney.

The criminal bar's neglect [1] in developing competent expert testimony in all but the high profile cases is undoubtedly caused by a great variety of factors, not the least of which is the seemingly ever-increasing caseload and its concomitant "speedy trial" pressure.

The material in this chapter provides the attorney with a frame of reference in dealing with the expert, a person facetiously described as one who continues to know more and more about less and less.[2] This chapter is designed to aid the practitioner in the following particulars:

(1) Advice is offered on the evidentiary predicate necessary to support expert testimony on any given subject;

(2) General sources for obtaining expert assistance in particularized instances are identified;

(3) Consideration is given to the attorney's role in preparing the expert for trial as well as to the minimal standards of preparation for adverse testimony from an opposition expert;

(4) The rights and obligations respecting disclosure and discovery of scientific evidence;

(5) An outline of inquiry on both direct and cross-examination of the expert is posited as a guide for questioning the witness, while separate attention is given to the hypothetical question; and

(6) Ethical considerations in the selection and use of experts are discussed.

Because the subject matter of this chapter is so broad in scope, no attempt will be made to exhaust it. By highlighting the basics, however, what we do present here should serve as a useful adjunct to subsequent parts of this volume dealing with specific fields of expertise. The trial lawyer who studies this chapter should be able to reduce the extent of

---

§ 1.01

1. McConville & Mirsky, "Criminal Defense of the Poor in New York City," 15 *N.Y.U.Rev.L. & Soc.Change* 581 (1986–87). The survey of a group of attorneys who are appointed to represent indigent clients in New York City showed that most did not avail themselves regularly of investigative and expert services permitted by statute: "Attorneys consulted with experts in only 17 percent of all homicide cases ... [and] claimed for expert consultation in only 2 percent of all other felonies, despite the importance of forensic evidence to the state's case." Id. at 764.

2. Another facetious description of the expert, sent anonymously to one of the authors, reads: "An expert is a person who passes as an exacting authority on the basis of being able to turn out with prolific fortitude infinite strings of incomprehensible formulae calculated with micromatic precision which are based on debatable figures taken from inconclusive experiments carried out with instruments of problematical accuracy by persons of doubtful reliability and questionable mentality."

his problems with the mechanics of expert testimony and to recognize areas warranting his closer attention.

§ 1.02 Theory of Admissibility of Expert Testimony

The general rule of evidence is that a witness may testify only to facts known to him. When a person testifies to a fact that can be perceived by the senses, he must have actually observed that fact.[1] A lay witness can make inferences, however, and state them in the form of an opinion based upon what he has observed. Consequently, ordinary observers are allowed to give their opinions on such matters as identity of persons, color of objects, distances and speed of vehicles.[2] The touchstone is that the lay witness' impression of physical facts is assayable against the background of ordinary experience.

Over the course of history, the courts have encountered issues which require analysis and explanation by persons having scientific or specialized knowledge or experience. This situation, associated with the expanding horizons of the arts and sciences, gave impetus to the evidentiary use of expert testimony at trial.

The earliest reported use of expert testimony in this country occurred when a certain Dr. Brown, testifying at a hearsay trial, ventured the "scientific" opinion that the victims had been bewitched by the defendant.[3] From that questionable beginning, the scope of expert opinion testimony in civil and criminal trials has expanded to include any relevant subject, so long as the factual inference about which the expert will venture an opinion is distinctly related to a generally accepted science, profession, business or occupation beyond the experience of the layman. The expert must be shown to the court to possess such skill, knowledge, or experience in the relevant field of endeavor to reasonably assure the court that his opinion or inference will probably aid the trier of fact in determining the truth regarding the matter at issue.[4] Finally, as a matter of predicate to opinion testimony, there must be a showing that the expert maintained control over the analysis, examination, observation or experiment and that any instrument or process used as an intermediate is trustworthy and reliable.

The issue, of course, must be a proper one for expert opinion testimony. The principal consideration is whether or not the opinion of

§ 1.02

1. McCormick, *Evidence,* § 10 (3d ed. 1984); 2 Wigmore, *Evidence,* §§ 650–670 (Chadbourn rev. 1979).

2. McCormick, *Evidence,* § 11 (3d ed. 1984); 7 Wigmore, *Evidence,* § 1919 (Chadbourn rev. 1978).

3. Howell, *State Trials,* 687 (1665).

4. The mode in which knowledge or skill must be acquired differs. Some courts hold that knowledge acquired solely through experience can qualify one as an expert. See,

State v. Garcia, 357 S.W.2d 931 (Mo.1962), and State v. Smith, 228 Or. 340, 364 P.2d 786 (1961). Other courts hold that knowledge derived from study alone suffices to establish expertise. See, English v. State, 85 Tex.Crim. 450, 213 S.W. 632 (1919). In ruling on the degree of expertise required, the court ought to keep in mind the qualifications imposed within a profession itself. Thus, in some fields of specialty, the profession imposes both study and experience before one can qualify as an expert. See, e.g., Ch. 8, § 8.11, on the qualifications of a fingerprint expert.

the expert will assist the trier of fact. Wigmore states the test to be as follows: "On *this subject* can a jury receive from *this person* appreciable help?"[5] If the subject of inquiry is one within the range of ordinary intelligence and observation, expert opinion evidence is unnecessary to prove or disprove the matter and is inadmissible.

Experts are employed (1) to assist the attorney in understanding the complexities involved in proving a fact and/or (2) to assist the attorney in preparing the cross-examination of the adversary's expert, and/or (3) to present a report to the attorney, and (4) when the results are favorable to the employing party, to testify at trial concerning that opinion and the basis for it.

The fact question put to an expert may be so objective that any expert with competent training who performed the examination with requisite skill would give the same opinion. On the other hand, the fact issue may be one upon which two qualified, competent experts may subjectively disagree, even though their examinations meet all recognized standards and show precisely the same objective results. For example, psychiatry is a discipline where experts of unquestioned integrity often differ. Divergent approaches or schools of thought may result in conflicting resolution of a particular issue. The less subjective an interpretation is, the more acceptance and credence it will receive from the court and trier of fact.

§ 1.03   Tests of Admissibility

An evidential question arises when an attempt is made to deduce expert opinion from a test that has not yet received widespread scientific recognition. The courts have met this problem by fashioning a variety of admissibility standards,[1] some of which will be discussed more extensively herein. The oldest of these standards has come to be known as the "Frye" test, or also the "general acceptance" test and draws from the oft-quoted language of the *Frye* case which dealt with the inadmissibility of "lie detector" test results:

> "Just when a scientific principle or discovery crosses the line between the experimental and demonstrable stages is difficult to define. Somewhere in this twilight zone the evidential force of the principle must be recognized, and while courts will go a long way in admitting expert testimony deduced from a well-recognized scientific

---

5. 7 Wigmore, *Evidence,* § 1923 (Chadbourn rev. 1978).

§ 1.03

1. See, McCormick, "Scientific Evidence: Defining a New Approach to Admissibility," 67 *Iowa L.Rev.* 879 (1982); 3 Weinstein & Berger, *Evidence,* Par. 702[03] (1982); Moenssens, "Admissibility of Scientific Evidence—An Alternative to *Frye,*" 25 *Wm. & Mary L.Rev.* 545 (1984).

Much of the extensive writing on the issue has been summarized or is referred to

in the written report of the 1983 Symposium sponsored by the National Conference of Lawyers and Scientists, published as "Symposium on Science and the Rules of Evidence," 99 F.R.D. 187 (1983) [hereinafter cited as "Symposium Report"]. Two of the current authors of this book (Moenssens and Starrs) were symposium participants in this as well as in the follow-up symposium held later and reported on in 101 F.R.D. 599 (1983).

principle or discovery, the thing from which the deduction is made must be sufficiently established to have gained general acceptance in the particular field in which it belongs." [2]

The sweeping principle enunciated in *Frye,* for which the court cited no authority, initially was given scant attention by other courts. For several decades it remained known only as the case that held lie-detector testimony to be inadmissible. In civil cases, *Frye* would not be cited as a guiding principle until 1984, and was mentioned in less than half a dozen civil cases.[3] In criminal cases, by contrast, *Frye* became the polestar to guide the admission of test results from dozens of widely varied techniques that poured out of the growing number of crime laboratories in the 1970s. Saferstein noted that in 1966 there were only 110 crime laboratories in the United States; ten years later, at the time of a national proficiency testing program, 240 active criminalistics facilities were identified. In 1992 there were 345 state, local and federal crime laboratories in the United States.[4]

A similar growth has been noted in scope of laboratory services and manpower employed.[5] The staggering "output" of these laboratories

2. Frye v. United States, 293 Fed. 1013, 1014 (D.C.Cir.1923).

Some authors suggest that Frye was probably innocent; e.g., McCormick, *Evidence,* § 203, footnote 5: "Years after the conviction another person confessed to the murder." (3d ed. 1984), citing a law review article. Strongly debunking this "myth." See, Starrs, "A Still-Life Watercolor: Frye v. United States," 27 *J.For.Sci.* 684 (1982). The polygraph technique itself is subsequently discussed in Chapter 20.

3. For an account on the path of Frye v. United States in both civil and criminal cases between 1923 and 1993, see, Chesebro, "Galileo's Retort: Peter Huber's Junk Scholarship," 42 *Am.U.L.Rev.* 1737, 1693–96 (1993).

4. Forensic Science Research and Training Center, FBI Laboratory, U.S. Dept. of Justice, Directory of Crime Laboratories (1992).

5. Saferstein, "Criminalistics—A Look Back at the 1970s, A Look Ahead to the 1980s," 24 *J.For.Sci.* 925 (1979)—the author is a highly respected forensic scientist.

The growth of crime laboratories has not been without problems. In the mid 1970s, the Forensic Sciences Foundation, Inc., on behalf of the American Academy of Forensic Sciences and crime laboratory directors, organized a proficiency testing program. It was believed that such a testing program would establish that crime laboratories performed at high levels of professionalism and obtained accurate results in their examinations—one author of this text (Moenssens)

participated as a member of the sponsoring organization in the formulation of the concept. The results showed that an appalling number of participating laboratories reported erroneous results in testing of blind samples. As many as 94 out of 132 laboratories participating in blood typing (or 71.2%) obtained "unacceptable results"; 34% could not match paint samples; 22% could not spot the differences between three metal samples; 50% could not identify dog hairs; 18% erroneously analyzed documents. Peterson, et al., Laboratory Proficiency Testing Research Program, Final Report of LEAA Grants 74NI–99–00048 and 76NI–99–0091, *Forensic Sciences Foundation,* June 1977. This appalling rate of error caused one prominent forensic scientist and officer of an association of law enforcement specialists to state that "crime laboratories flunk analysis." See, Mooney, President's Address at the 1978 Annual Meeting of the International Association for Identification.

Lowell Bradford, a respected forensic criminalist, in discussing the firearms results of the above proficiency testing program, said that "Participating Laboratories were sent three .25 caliber bullets, two of which had been fired by the same gun. Five laboratories incorrectly reported that the same gun had fired all three bullets. That no two bullets could have been fired by the same gun was the finding of three other laboratories. These results are especially frightening when it is realized that a criminal prosecution for first-degree murder may hinge entirely on a bullet compari-

has found its way in the courtrooms of this country and, with few exceptions, has been found to be "generally accepted" simply because crime laboratories use the techniques. While the *Frye* test supposedly represents essentially a conservative approach to admitting evidence based on newly developed scientific applications,[6] an approach deemed desirable because jurors are easily overawed by conclusions voiced in court by articulate experts with impressive credentials, actual experience has shown that "general acceptance" under *Frye* does not necessarily result in "reliability" of the test used.

In *Frye,* the court said that the "field" which was generally to accept the new polygraph in order to assure admissibility of the test results was one composed of the combined fields of physiology and psychology. Some novel forms of expert testimony are easily classified as to the field in which they belong,[7] but many are not as easily categorized. New developments sometimes are made by imaginative workers in a field that may be considered radical by their more conservative colleagues, who reject the new developments regardless of their worth. On the other hand, workers in a novel area sharing a common goal may develop a technique that furthers their professional aims and they may "generally accept" it regardless of its scientific validity, sometimes despite strong scientific denial of its underlying premises.[8] In the first case, admissibility may be denied to a reliable and scientifically provable technique

son identification." In commenting on the performance of crime laboratories generally, he said: "There is some remarkable topflight work to be found even in the least prestigious laboratories. On the other hand, gross errors, bad practices, inefficiencies, and ineffectiveness infiltrate the forensic science family like an endemic disease." Bradford, "Barriers to Quality Achievement in Crime Laboratory Operations," 25 *J.For. Sci.* 902 (1980). See also, Peterson et al., "The Capabilities, Uses, and Effects of the Nation's Criminalistics Laboratories," 30 *J.For.Sci.* 10 (1985).

In 1981, the American Society of Crime Lab Directors—Laboratory Accreditation Board was incorporated. The Board promulgates standards for the performance of most forensic functions, evaluates personnel in terms of education, training, and experience, reviews laboratory management practices, inspects facilities, and observes the operational methods and instruments used in a laboratory. The first eight laboratories were accredited in 1982. By 1993 101 laboratories were accredited.

6. People v. Kelly, 17 Cal.3d 24, 130 Cal.Rptr. 144, 549 P.2d 1240 (1976).

7. See, e.g., People v. Slone, 76 Cal. App.3d 611, 143 Cal.Rptr. 61 (1978), wherein the court determined that bitemark identification belongs in "the community of

dentistry." The court in *Frye* decided that the polygraph belonged in the fields of physiology and psychology, though neither field has claimed the technique. When a court decides in what field a new technique belongs, it can produce somewhat convoluted interdisciplinary interactions that might not be welcomed by the affected fields. In Cornett v. State, 450 N.E.2d 498 (Ind.1983) the court felt that the relevant scientific communities for spectrographic voice identification include linguistics, psychology, engineering, and voice spectrography examiners!

8. Joseph Nicol, a highly respected former crime laboratory director, forensic scientist, consultant to the Warren Commission that investigated the assassination of President Kennedy, and professor of criminal justice, commented that "Many novel techniques over the years have been touted as panaceas, only to be disproved later, and it takes time for the credibility of earlier methods to be eroded and for their use no longer to be considered reliable." See Symposium Report, supra note 1 at 221. Forensic scientists are quick to utilize these new methods and unproven techniques in actual cases, which then in turn requires them to offer testimony when the results are included in their investigative reports. Because of the general scientific illiteracy of the legal profession, most of this testimony

because the logical "field" in which it belongs refuses generally to accept it; in the other, admissibility may easily follow because a test is generally accepted in a field that was newly created for the express purpose of generally advocating its reliability.[9]

Also, as a group, lawyers display an appalling degree of scientific illiteracy,[10] which ill equips them to educate and guide the bench in its decisions on admissibility of evidence proffered through expert witnesses. This scientific illiteracy is shared by a large segment of the trial and appellate bench; many judges simply do not understand evidence based on scientific principles. Even more tragically, they overlook important attributes indicative of reliability of evidence that they reject, while ascribing positive properties to other evidence they accept which that evidence simply does not possess.[11]

Much of the disenchantment is the result of a mutual lack of understanding of the wide differences in approaches used by, on the one hand, "scientists" who seek to solve problems which they face in their disciplines, and, on the other hand, the method used by the law when a dispute ends up in court for judicial resolution.

Superficially, both the scientific method and the legal method employ similar processes to acquire and interpret information. In looking at facts and issues, both seek to use a systematic rational approach, and both also use the same inductive method in attempting to solve problems. The differences are therefore not methodologically oriented, but rather lie in the purposes each discipline has in mind in pursuing the conclusion to the problems presented to them.

The scientist seeks to use the information obtained in a generally neutral fashion for the purpose of providing the best available explanation for the data examined, so that by isolating variables, predictions may be offered for use in future events. Rarely does the scientific method focus on an individual, particular incident. The incident is important only insofar as it permits scientists to explain past occurrences and formulate general hypotheses on how to deal with similar events that are yet to occur.

The legal method, by contrast, seeks to determine what ought to be, rather than what is. After having explored and examined certain data, the legal system is interested in how the findings and conclusions drawn from the data impact on the individual case before the court. Rather than being necessarily interested in what the impact on other cases will be, lawyers are concerned with applying the results to the normative values upon which behavior in our society is conditioned. At the same time, the law may also be creating new norms and values for future behavior. When differing or opposing values are involved, the adversary

---

based on techniques not yet validated will be admitted without objection!

9. Moenssens, "Requiem for the 'General Acceptance' Standard in Forensic Science—Some Whimsical Thoughts on the Battle of Frye vs. The Federal Rules of Evidence," in *1982 Legal Medicine Annual* 275, 279–80 (C. Wecht, ed.)

10. Moenssens, op. cit. note 1, at 551–55.

11. Id.

system which is the hallmark of our judicial process casts each participant into a competing posture. Thus, a trial lawyer will be interested in advocating only the values that favor the side that retained him or her.[12]

The failure of each side to understand the different aims and purposes of the other results in a lot of friction. It causes lawyers to hold experts in some disdain because they believe experts are for hire and will come to almost any conclusion one needs. It causes scientists to feel estranged from the judicial process because of the loss of dignity and stature that they feel from having their professional worth and integrity challenged on cross-examination. They are sometimes driven to refusing to testify in court. Whatever the reasons for the friction, an increased understanding on both sides of the other's role will greatly enhance the effectiveness of lawyers in their use of expert witnesses. This requires lawyers to become more knowledgeable about how the scientific method differs from the legal method.

There have been some improvements made in forensic science education for lawyers and judges to combat their scientific illiteracy. At present, more than forty law schools teach law and science courses. The National Judicial College in Reno, Nevada offers a two-week forensic science curriculum for judges. There also have been many continuing legal education programs developed by state CLE groups throughout the United States to educate attorneys on the latest developments in forensic science and to assist them in using and opposing expert opinion evidence.

In analyzing the process of deciding the reliability of certain proffered evidence, one of the current authors outlined the logical progression that takes place—or ought to take place—in bringing a novel technique from concept to evidence. It is a progression wherein recognizable stages can be identified. These stages are:

Stage 1: A theory is postulated.

Stage 2: Experiments are designed to verify the validity of the theory.

Stage 3: If the theory's validity is not disproven after a searching inquiry and empirical testing, it is "proven" valid and a court then appropriately may take judicial notice of the theory. This result is unlikely to occur at this stage, however, because no vehicle exists for translating the theory into relevant evidence in a law suit.

Stage 4: A technique is devised, or an instrument is designed and built, that will permit the theory to be applied practically in a forensic setting.

---

12. On the differences between law and science generally, see, Channels, *Social Science Methods in the Legal Process* (1985); Nyhart & Carrow, *Law and Science in Collaboration* (1983); Loevinger, "Science, Technology and Law in Modern Society," 26 *Jurimetrics* 2 (1985–86); Goldberg, "The Reluctant Embrace: Law and Science in America," 75 *Geo.L.J.* 1341 (1987).

Stage 5: After devising a methodology, further tests must demonstrate a positive correlation between the results and the underlying theory. This stage is necessary to prove that the effects observed are not the result of some unidentified cause.

Stage 6: After the test has been shown to yield reliable results that are relevant to disputed issues in a law suit, a court then may admit these results properly into evidence, and a qualified expert may interpret the results before the jury.[13]

If one looks critically at techniques that came before courts and were the basis of admitted opinion testimony, it will be noted that often this six-stage progression is not followed. Courts admit opinion testimony based on techniques when only the first four stages are followed or, worse, where stages two and three—verification of the underlying theory—never occurred.

Not all courts followed the *Frye* principle. Since the enactment in 1975 of the Federal Rules of Evidence,[14] questions have been raised by many courts on whether the *Frye* concept of "general acceptance" within a discipline remained viable. During the past two decades, state and federal court decisions have divided into at least three groups on that issue: (1) jurisdictions that hold the Federal Rules (or its state evidence rule equivalents) have superseded Frye v. United States and that the Federal Rules' more flexible "relevancy" test permits use of scientific evidence which is not "generally accepted;" (2) jurisdictions that maintain *Frye* survived the enactment of the Federal Rules of Evidence and is complementary of Rule 702; and (3) jurisdictions that have neither adopted *Frye*'s general acceptance test nor have a rule comparable to Federal Rule 702.

All of these stepping stones in the development of legal theory relating to novel expert opinion testimony have become overshadowed by the 1993 United States Supreme Court decision in Daubert v. Merrell Dow Pharmaceuticals.[15] In that case, our highest tribunal squarely relegated *Frye* to history as far as federal civil and criminal trials are concerned, holding that the Federal Rules of Evidence superseded, and did away with, *Frye*'s general acceptance test for admission of novel scientific evidence. In its decision, the Supreme Court mandated that in the future, instead of proof of general acceptance, proof that establishes the "scientific reliability" of expert opinion evidence be produced, and set up the following mechanism for that determination:

13. Moenssens, "Admissibility of Scientific Evidence—An Alternative to *Frye,*" 25 *Wm. & Mary L.Rev.* 545, 556 (1984).

14. Federal Rule of Evidence 702 provides: "If scientific, technical, or other specialized knowledge will assist the trier of fact to understand the evidence or to determine a fact in issue, a witness qualified as an expert by knowledge, skill, experience, training, or education, may testify thereto in the form of an opinion or otherwise."

Federal Rule of Evidence 401 states: " 'Relevant evidence' means evidence having any tendency to make the existence of any fact that is of consequence to the determination of the action more probable or less probable than it would be without the evidence." Federal Rule of Evidence 402 further provides that all relevant evidence is admissible except when specifically held inadmissible by conflicting rules or laws.

15. 113 S.Ct. 2786 (1993).

"Faced with a proffer of expert scientific testimony, then, the trial judge must determine at the outset, pursuant to Rule 104(a), whether the expert is proposing to testify to (1) scientific knowledge that (2) will assist the trier of fact to understand or determine a fact in issue. This entails a preliminary assessment of whether the reasoning or methodology underlying the testimony is scientifically valid and of whether that reasoning or methodology properly can be applied to the facts in issue." [16]

To assist the trial court in making the legal decision on admissibility of proffered expert opinion testimony, the Court further suggested that the trial judge examine the following factors: (1) whether the type of evidence can be and has been tested by a scientific methodology; (2) whether the underlying theory or technique has been subjected to peer review and has been published in the professional literature, though specifically stating that peer review and publication are not a *sine qua non* of admissibility; (3) how reliable the results are in terms of potential error rate; and finally (4) " 'general acceptance' can yet have a bearing on the inquiry. A reliability assessment does not require, although it does permit, explicit identification of a relevant scientific community and an express determination of a particular degree of acceptance within that community." [17] The Supreme Court stressed that the new test is a flexible one, wherein not one factor is determinative, and expressed a confidence, not necessarily shared by many commentators, that the trial judges are able to fulfill this gatekeeping role.

While this decides the admissibility principle for federal cases only, civil as well as criminal, the ruling is nevertheless bound to have a great impact in states that have evidence codes based upon the Federal Rules of Evidence, and even on states that have previously followed the general acceptance rule of *Frye* in the absence of specific evidence rules or statutes similar to the federal rules. It is too early, at this writing, to report on how courts deal with the admission of novel scientific evidence after *Daubert*,[18] though a plethora of writings on that subject is expected soon.[19]

---

16. Id. at 2796.

17. Id. at 2797 (quoting from United States v. Downing, 753 F.2d 1224, 1238 (3d Cir.1985)).

18. At least three courts have already chosen to remain faithful, for now, to Frye v. United States and not to follow the *Daubert* rule: State v. Bible, 175 Ariz. 549, 858 P.2d 1152 (1993)—probability calculations to explain statistical significance of matching two DNA samples not generally accepted in relevant scientific field and therefore inadmissible; Flanagan v. State, 625 So.2d 827 (Fla.1993)—admission of psychologist's testimony concerning sexual offender profile evidence which did not meet the *Frye* was error, although harmless; People v. Mehlberg, 249 Ill.App.3d 499, 188 Ill.Dec.

598, 618 N.E.2d 1168 (1993)—leaving the decision of whether to abandon *Frye* and follow *Daubert* to state supreme court. A number of courts have already chosen to follow the *Daubert* rule: e.g. State v. Alberico, 116 N.M. 156, 861 P.2d 192 (1993)—on the issue of the admissibility of testimony regarding victims of sexual abuse who suffer post traumatic stress disorder, the proper inquiry is whether the expert's testimony is grounded in valid, objective science and whether the underlying scientific method is reliable.

19. Probably the first post-*Daubert* analysis of the new requirements may be found in the series of articles on the *Daubert* case contained in the first issue of *Shepard's Expert and Scientific Evidence*

To establish "scientific reliability" under *Daubert* will likely prove to be no easier task than establishing "general acceptance" under *Frye*. To explore this on the stand will call for resources in manpower and insight on the part of the attorney opposing use of the evidence that is not typical of the trial bar. In criminal cases, courts seldom become aware of deficiencies in this matter of insuring reliability and replicability of novel test results. In the course of our ordinary trial procedure, reliability of a technique and its general acceptance in the proper discipline is shown through expert testimony. Since, in most criminal cases, only the prosecutor produces expert witnesses, it becomes immediately obvious that the court, in making the *legal* decision of whether proffered evidence is *scientifically reliable*,[20] often will have only the prosecution expert's assessment of the soundness of the procedures before it. The expert, having made the technique in question part of his or her standard working procedure, obviously believes in it, or he would discard it otherwise. The substance of his evidence, then, becomes entirely predictable. Can we trust the expert to give to the court an unbiased as well as an informed view of how reliable a new technique really is? The answer to that question appears compelling. The expert will of course vociferously advocate the reliability and accuracy of the technique, even when colleagues have not yet had an opportunity to validate the conclusions, or sometimes despite the fact that peer evaluation has characterized the process as unproven.[21]

While most forensic scientists, whether prosecution or defense oriented in their practice, sanctimoniously state—and indeed believe—that they are objective in their scientific inquiries, practicing lawyers, judges, and even candid experts realize that once the battle is joined and they are aligned with one of the sides in the courtroom, it becomes impossible to be totally "impartial." It should further be recognized that many experts who testify in court are not scientists, but examiners.[22] They

Quarterly, Black, Klein & Brunette, eds., (Vol. 1 No. 1, July 1993) [successor journal to *Expert Evidence Reporter*].

20. For a graphic illustration as applied to the technique of identifying individuals' voices through sound spectrography, see, Chapter 10, infra.

It would indeed be far preferable to require proof of scientific reliability, in whatever form deemed appropriate by the court, than relying on a showing of a vague "general acceptance." In Harper v. State, 249 Ga. 519, 292 S.E.2d 389 (1982), the Georgia Supreme Court adopted proof of a "stage of verifiable certainty" as the test for admission of new scientific evidence. The holding also suggests that the trial court may make this determination from evidence presented at trial, or base its decision on exhibits, treatises or the rationale of cases in other jurisdictions.

21. For a rare case where an expert declined to testify on the results of a test he had conducted on the ground that the test had not been validated as a scientific identification technique, see, People v. Slone, supra note 7 at 622, 143 Cal.Rptr. at 67.

Dean Strong acknowledges that courts are generally "forced to accept" what the expert says he believes. See, Strong, "Questions Affecting the Admissibility of Scientific Evidence," 1970 *U.Ill.L.Forum* 1, 14.

22. For many decades, some "professional" associations in criminalistics fields had and have as the primary requirement for full membership that one be a law enforcement officer. In the past there were no educational requirements, not even a high school diploma; highly respected scientists with graduate degrees and recognized expertise were not eligible for membership if not employed in law enforcement, or, at best, they were eligible for associate membership only.

utilize techniques that were explained to them as reliable and as offering replicable results, but frequently have done no independent verifications and accept as blind truth statements made by colleagues who instruct them in their laboratory or lecture to them at professional meetings. Some experts have absolutely no educational background in science, and were educated for their position by on-the-job training. While they are earnest, hardworking, and dedicated, they are ill equipped to critically examine issues of scientific verification. Some courts have recognized wisely that proof of accuracy and reliability cannot be established by witnesses with that background, but requires the testimony of disinterested scientists—people who have not staked their careers on advocating reliability.[23]

A difficulty further confounding the effort of a court to create a full and complete record which can serve as the basis for an intelligent decision on the admissibility of novel opinion evidence, is the fact that experts, in their sworn testimony, frequently transgress into fields that are beyond their expertise. What chemist (who identifies chemical substances, poisons, and drugs) isn't regularly asked about the effects of drugs upon the human body or the effects of certain dosages—conclusions that are beyond the scope of a legitimate scientific background and training as a chemist?[24] What medical examiner hasn't been asked to describe the functioning of a gun or state an opinion on the caliber of a deformed bullet in a gunshot wound case?[25] This is ordinarily not the fault of the experts, but of the lawyers who ask questions without knowing that the subject is beyond the witness' discipline, and of opposing attorneys who never object on that ground, again because of their lack of scientific understanding. In one case, a qualified firearms examiner had examined a 12–gauge shotgun in a homicide case and had also noticed at some time that the defendant had a red mark under his right shoulder. He was thereupon permitted to offer his opinion that this red mark could have been caused by the recoil of firing a shotgun. It is hard to imagine how such a conclusion could come within the expertise of a firearms examiner![26]

23. People v. Kelly, supra note 6; Commonwealth v. Topa, 471 Pa. 223, 369 A.2d 1277 (1977); People v. Tobey, 401 Mich. 141, 257 N.W.2d 537 (1977). These three cases illustrate how three or four expert witnesses, who were the "pioneers" in the so-called "voiceprint" technique, traveled to countless states to testify to its reliability, creating precedent of "general acceptance" in at least twice as many jurisdictions than there were experts involved in the discipline.

24. It was held to be error to allow a chemist to testify that LSD "made people go as far as to tear their eyes right out of their sockets, chew off an arm, jump out of windows, do some really ... bizarre things," in Smith v. Commonwealth, 223 Va. 721, 292 S.E.2d 362 (1982). The reason for the court's holding was not that it was beyond the training of the chemist—which it is—but because that testimony was irrelevant to the charge of possession of a controlled substance.

25. Starrs, "In the Land of Agog: An Allegory for the Expert Witness," 30 *J.For. Sci.* 289 (1985). The author cites many cases where experts testified to opinions in areas that were probably beyond the scope of their expertise.

26. People v. Lauro, 91 Misc.2d 706, 398 N.Y.S.2d 503 (1977). The testimony apparently was never objected to, and was *not* an issue on appeal.

Many of the deficiencies in our fact-finding process on scientific issues are inherent in the adversarial system and result from factors other than the test for admissibility that a jurisdiction may use. Some courts already had rejected a strict adherence to the *Frye* decision.[27] In People v. Williams,[28] the court held that when a test was unknown in the medical profession generally, but accepted by a narrow specialty within medicine, that its results would be admissible.[29] Recognizing as this case did that medical specialization today makes it impossible for some tests to become widely known and accepted in the general field of medicine, the opinion left uncharted the path for the courts to take when dealing with experimental testing tailored to the requirements of a specific investigative problem. A Florida appeals court took the step to supply the missing link in Coppolino v. State,[30] decided in 1968.

The *Coppolino* case was replete with scientific evidence for both the defense and the prosecution. Most significant, however, was evidence of scientific tests which had been specifically devised by a pathologist to reveal the presence of a certain chemical in body tissue. The test was previously unknown among pathologists, and expert witnesses for the opposing side testified to its lack of proven reliability. The court nevertheless upheld the admissibility of the test results on the theory that novel test results, specifically devised to explore a given problem, are not necessarily inadmissible simply because the profession at large is not yet familiar with them, so long as the expert witness lays a proper foundation for his opinion and explains what accepted principles of analysis he used.

Sometimes, courts that were nominally bound by *Frye* just ignore its dictates when they feel that to follow the general acceptance test would produce an inappropriate result. In People v. Marx,[31] for instance, the California Court of Appeals for the Second District held admissible evidence of an identification of bitemark impressions as having been

---

27. See, Harper v. State, supra note 20. See also, People v. Hampton, 746 P.2d 947 (Colo.1987) (*Frye* is to be used only for polygraph evidence and not for behavioral science evidence—here rape trauma syndrome evidence, which was held admissible); State v. Hall, 297 N.W.2d 80 (Iowa 1980) (*Frye* rejected, mandating showing of reliability of the evidence on an *ad hoc* basis—admitting blood splatter analysis evidence); State v. Klindt, 389 N.W.2d 670 (Iowa 1986) (*Frye* again rejected when dealing with serologist, anthropologist, and statistician evidence); Jenkins v. State, 156 Ga.App. 387, 274 S.E.2d 618 (1980) (electrophoresis test on blood not subject to *Frye* test); United States v. Ferri, 778 F.2d 985 (3d Cir.1985) ("Cinderella analysis" of impressions found inside shoe). See further fn. 34, infra.

28. 164 Cal.App.2d Supp. 858, 331 P.2d 251 (1958). Wigmore long ago contended

that the test for receiving expert opinion should be whether additional light could be thrown on the issue by a person of skill in the subject: 7 Wigmore, *Evidence,* § 1917 p. 7 (Chadbourn rev. 1978).

29. The case involved the development, by a physician, of the Nalorphine (Nalline) pupil test to determine narcotic addiction. See, Grupp, "The Nalline Test I—Development and Implementation," 61 *J.Crim.L., C. & P.S.* 296 (1970); "The Nalline Test II—Rationale," 61 *J.Cr.L., C & P.S.* 463 (1970); and "The Nalline Test III—Objections, Limitations and Assessment," 62 *J.Cr.L., C. & P.S.* 288 (1971).

30. 223 So.2d 68 (Fla.App.1968), appeal dismissed 234 So.2d 120 (Fla.1969), cert. denied, 399 U.S. 927 (1970).

31. 54 Cal.App.3d 100, 126 Cal.Rptr. 350 (1975).

made by the defendant despite the fact that the field of forensic dentistry was not shown to have generally accepted the underlying reliability of such identifications. The reasons advanced by the court were that (1) the experts had termed this particular identification to be based on "one of the most definitive and distinct and deepest bitemarks on record in human skin," [32] (2) the experts had prepared enlarged photographic exhibits which permitted the court and jury to verify the accuracy of the expert's findings; and (3) in any event, neither the judge nor jury was bound to give the testimony any particular amount of weight.[33]

If a court is going to indulge in playing the game of ignoring inconvenient precedents that erect unworkable barriers to relevant evidence, is it not fairer to discard *Frye* and refuse to follow its criteria for admissibility of evidence? A majority of the Iowa Supreme Court took that approach in State v. Hall [34] when confronting the issue of admissibility of evidence of blood spatter analysis, a technique arguably not widely accepted in the scientific community. It rejected the general acceptance requirement and instead held that an ad hoc determination of reliability of the evidence should be substituted.[35]

As stated earlier, the United States Supreme Court's opinion in *Daubert* held that the now widely adopted Federal Rules of Evidence have abrogated *Frye.*

As to whether this abrogation means that the Court substituted a loose relevancy rule remains to be seen as the various courts attempt to

32. Id. For an account of the case, see, Vale et al., "Unusual Three–Dimensional Bite Mark Evidence In A Homicide Case," 21 *J.For.Sci.* 642 (1976).

33. Even though the *Marx* decision was clearly limited by the unusual facts, and recognized the lack of general acceptance of bitemark identification at that time, this did not prevent later courts from citing the case as having "generally accepted" bitemarks as a reliable means of identification. See, e.g., People v. Milone, 43 Ill.App.3d 385, 2 Ill.Dec. 63, 356 N.E.2d 1350 (1976); People v. Watson, 75 Cal.App.3d 384, 142 Cal.Rptr. 134 (1977).

A more extensive discussion on the subject of bitemark identifications can be found in Chapter 16, infra, dealing with forensic odontology.

34. 297 N.W.2d 80 (Iowa 1980). See also, State v. Brown, 470 N.W.2d 30, 32 (Iowa 1991) (reiterating its rejection of *Frye,* the court required "only that the evidence be established as reliable and meet the general test for admission of expert testimony").

Similarly, in Prater v. State, 307 Ark. 180, 188, 820 S.W.2d 429, 433 (1991), the Arkansas Supreme Court rejected *Frye* and stated that: "[N]ovel scientific evidence

coupled with evidence of mathematical probabilities should be admitted only when the proponent of that evidence makes a preliminary showing of reliability of both the novel scientific evidence and of the process underlying the calculations." In State v. Kim, 65 Hawaii 598, 645 P.2d 1330 (1982), "general acceptance" was seen as simply one aspect of reliability, and other "indicators of suitability for admission at trial" ought to be considered as well. Applying this principle in State v. Montalbo, 73 Hawaii 130, 828 P.2d 1274 (1992), the Hawaii Supreme Court rejected the idea that the *Frye* test governed the admission of novel scientific evidence, holding that the trial court properly admitted, in a rape prosecution, population frequency statistics calculated by the FBI to interpret the significance of DNA test findings.

35. For other suggestions on how the admissibility of novel scientific test results ought to be approached, see, Moenssens, op. cit. note 13 at 563 et seq. See also the comments by Chief Judge Howard Markey at the "Symposium on Science and the Rules of Legal Procedure," reported at 101 *F.R.D.* 599, 603–604 (1983). Judge Markey is a distinguished jurist and frequent commentator on the interactions between law and science.

apply *Daubert*'s "proof of reliability" factors. Certainly, a change to a mere relevancy criterion has not been favored by jurisprudents and scientists who have critically examined the problem of the admission of expert opinion testimony based on novel scientific techniques. In 1983, a group of lawyers and scientists met for the specific purpose of examining *Frye* and its possible alternatives in a workshop sponsored by the National Conference of Lawyers and Scientists. The participants [36] were asked to consider whether *Frye* ought to be retained, how judges ought to decide whether the test was satisfied, and, if the *Frye* test were not to be retained, what consequences would follow. Divided in three study groups working independently, the participants, without dissent, agreed that the *Frye* rule was unworkable and ought not to be retained.[37] All the participants further agreed that *Frye* should not be replaced by a wide-open relevancy requirement such as Rule 401 of the Federal Rules of Evidence is said to be,[38] and they also advocated that courts ought to take a more meaningful part in screening novel scientific evidence for reliability and replicability.[39]

In criminal cases, where an individual's freedom is at stake, courts certainly ought to be very cautious in admitting evidence based upon insufficiently tested or verified premises, especially when the evidence seeks to establish the ultimate issue in the case—the identification of the accused as the perpetrator of the offense. It would appear that when this is the issue, there may be occasions when the most exacting test should be followed.[40]

Some scientific techniques and tests have become so thoroughly recognized as to receive judicial notice of their reliability for courtroom usage. Fingerprint evidence is a prime example of this almost blanket acceptance.[41] At the other end of the spectrum are such tests as those involving so-called "truth-serum," the use of hypnosis or psychological stress evaluation of the voice to ascertain the truthfulness of a person's assertions. They have very little support as reliable means for making such a determination.[42] In between these two extremes is the polygraph ("lie-detector") technique. A number of specialists in the field accredit

---

36. Symposium Report, supra note 35 at 229.

37. Id. at 229–30.

38. Rule 401 defines relevancy as "evidence having any tendency to make the existence of any fact that is of consequence to the determination of the action more probable or less probable than it would be without the evidence." Fed.R.Evid. 401. If this test is literally applied, scientific evidence which has not been proven reliable but in the opinion of an expert witness is reliable would be relevant because the evidence satisfies the "more-or-less-probable" test.

39. Symposium Report, supra note 35. Also, Moenssens, op. cit. note 13, supra, at 567–574.

40. For a veritable catalogue of reasons why courts, regardless of the test for admissibility used in the jurisdiction, ought to be cautious in admitting novel scientific evidence, see, Moenssens, "Novel Scientific Evidence in Criminal Cases: Some Words of Caution," 84 *J.Crim.L. & Criminology* 801 (1993).

41. A discussion of fingerprint identification is presented in Chapter 8, infra.

42. The subjects of truth serum use for interrogations, hypnosis to refresh witness recollection, and the psychological stress evaluation are subsequently discussed in Chapter 20.

it with a high degree of reliability and advocate judicial approval of test results. Opposing views are held by a substantial number of psychiatrists, psychologists and other professed evaluators. Up to the present time admissibility of test results has generally been denied.[43]

Unless the general scientific recognition accorded any test involved in a particular case has been judicially recognized, an attorney seeking to offer test results in evidence should insure that his witness can provide the court with ample proof of its reliability. When there is a serious question concerning the usefulness of expert testimony, counsel should prepare a memorandum in advance of trial supporting his legal argument for or against admissibility. The memorandum should also articulate the state of the science or art and should reflect the experience and qualifications of the proposed expert. Attorneys who have become aware, through discovery, that an opponent is seeking to introduce expert evidence based upon a novel principle, ought to prepare a motion *in limine* so that the admissibility issue may be resolved prior to trial. Thus, a motion *in limine* may be used offensively or defensively to move the court to admit or deny the admissibility of scientific evidence.

§ 1.04 Criminal Cases—Experts for the Prosecution

Experts testifying as the prosecution's witnesses conventionally fulfill one of four purposes in the criminal trial, namely: (1) to identify through fingerprint identification, firearms identification, document examination, microbiological matching of blood, hair and semen and toxicological analysis of drugs, or other trace evidence, incriminating items which can be evidentially traced to the accused; (2) to prove by way of psychiatric evidence of sanity, toxicological evidence of blood alcohol, etc., that the accused was in a certain mental or physical condition at a given time; (3) to prove the criminal circumstances of unobserved or suspicious death by means of post-mortem autopsy examination; and (4) to impeach or rehabilitate witnesses.

The prosecution expert frequently is a full-time salaried employee of some division of the local, state or federal government. The expert's opinion sometimes determines whether or not an arrested person will be prosecuted. Although the state-salaried expert may have a tendency toward bias, at trial the nature of the job requires that his sincerity in conducting analyses and examinations be beyond reproach. In addition to his moral obligation, he realizes that if he evinces a credibility gap, his entire agency will be suspect, his job in jeopardy, and the defense encouraged to independently negate his findings. It follows then, as a general rule, that the prosecution expert is expected to be honest in his dealings with both the prosecution and the defense. Nevertheless, it is a conceptual and tactical mistake for the defense to always consider the state's expert to be an impartial witness at trial. However successful the expert's desire to avoid the taint of partiality, at trial he remains an

---

43. Chapter 20 contains a detailed discussion of the polygraph technique and its　legal aspects.

arm of the prosecution. An examiner ordinarily is appointed to the case not by judicial selection, but by a governmental agency addressing itself to law enforcement. Even though law enforcement agencies are viewed as servants of the people, the trial of a criminal case takes place in an arena governed by the spirit of the adversary system. The constant purpose of both prosecution and defense counsel is to win, and every expert who appears in court is partial to the extent that he has an expert opinion or explanation of a material fact in the dispute which he is asked to present and, if necessary, *advocate* by one side or the other.

§ 1.05　Experts for the Criminal Defendant

The defense expert functions on the same basis that he would in a civil suit. His allegiance is only for the one case. He is ordinarily selected by defense counsel and receives his fee from the defendant, or, if the defendant is indigent, out of governmental funds appropriated for that purpose. Unfortunately, the defense usually does not have the advice and guidance of crime laboratory specialists that is freely available to prosecutors. However, some laboratories and medical examiners' offices will discuss cases freely with defense counsel. Furthermore, some professional associations of criminal defense counsel, such as the National Association of Criminal Defense Lawyers, have created forensic evidence clearing houses and hotlines to provide support to their fellow defense counsel.

In years past, as a matter of general practice, the defense in a criminal case rarely presented its own expert testimony. Instead, defense counsel would engage the state's expert in a battle of cross-examination—frequently a hopeless cause, unless defense counsel's knowledge about the particular subject was almost as extensive as the expert's.

Only in recent years has there been any real incentive for the defense to employ its own experts. Formerly, whatever evidence of guilt the prosecution obtained and expected to use for expert opinion purposes was within the sole province of the prosecution; the defense had to wait until the time of trial to find out about it, or to inspect it. New rules have evolved, however, so that now, as will be discussed in detail later in this chapter, the defense is permitted to learn of the existence of such evidence and is accorded the right to have its own expert examination of it. Moreover, as regards indigent defendants, some jurisdictions have appropriated funds to defray the costs of such examinations and also for the expert's courtroom testimony based upon such examinations.[1]

---

§ 1.05

1. About half of the states and the federal government have specific provisions under which courts are authorized to provide for public compensation of defense experts. A number of other states have statutes which allow appointed counsel to recover his expenses, including, in some of these states, fees of experts. It is generally agreed that the courts have the inherent power to appoint and compensate impartial or "neutral" experts who render their opinion to the court and may be cross-examined by either party. A few states provide access to the state crime laboratory to defense attorneys. E.g., Va.Code 1950, § 32–31.7. The results of the analysis are also available to the prosecution. See, e.g., O'Dell v.

As with prosecution experts, there is the ever present factor of possible innate partiality by reason of the expert's selection and employment by the defense.

Whether there is a constitutional right to court appointed experts for the indigent is an issue that only recently received some attention by the Courts. In the 1985 case of Ake v. Oklahoma,[2] the defendant was charged with capital murder. Because his behavior at arraignment had been very bizarre, the trial court had ordered a psychiatric examination, as a result of which he was later declared incompetent to stand trial and committed. Thereafter, because defendant was being sedated with an anti-psychotic drug, he was declared competent and the trial started. His defense was insanity. His request for a court appointed psychiatrist was denied, and he was ultimately convicted. The Supreme Court, in a 7-to-2 decision, reversed and remanded, finding that the denial of his request for a court appointed expert in the field of psychiatry deprived him of due process of law. The Court held that where a defendant makes a preliminary showing that his sanity at the time of the offense with which he is charged is likely to be a significant part in his defense, the Constitution requires that a state provide access to a psychiatrist's assistance on that issue if the defendant is indigent.[3]

In determining whether, and under what conditions, a psychiatrist's participation is important enough to the preparation of an effective defense so that the state will be required to furnish an indigent defendant with access to a psychiatrist, the Court suggested three relevant factors to be considered: (1) the private interest that will be affected by the state's decision to grant or deny the request for expert assistance;

Commonwealth, 234 Va. 672, 364 S.E.2d 491 (1988), cert. denied 488 U.S. 871 (1988).

Note that many states have public defender offices that employ experts who are paid from the operating budget of the defender office rather than on the case-by-case method, as is done under appointed counsel systems. See the Criminal Justice Act of 1964, 18 U.S.C.A. § 3006A for the federal provisions concerning the payment of defense costs other than counsel fees; see also, "Construction and Application of Provision in Subsection (e) of Criminal Justice Act of 1964 Concerning Right of Indigent Defendant to Aid in Obtaining Services of Investigator or Expert", 6 A.L.R.Fed. 1007 (1971). Illinois is one of the states that allows indigents expert witness fees, but only in capital cases. Ill.Cr.Code, § 113–3. See, State v. Kegley, 175 Ill. App.3d 335, 125 Ill.Dec. 42, 529 N.E.2d 1118 (1988). For a survey of indigent expense provisions by states, see, Monahan, "Obtaining Funds for Experts in Indigent Cases," *The Champion,* Aug. 1989, at 10; Salnick, "Effective Counsel for the (Almost) Indigent: Making the State Coffer Up," *The Champion,* Jul. 1989, at 6. The NACDL Indigent Defense Committee has compiled pleadings and materials to aid defense counsel in obtaining funds for indigent defense: *Indigent Defense Handbook: A Manual for Obtaining Attorney's Fees and Costs for Supplemental Services and for Challenging State-assigned Counsel Systems,* 1989.

It is within the discretion of a trial judge to authorize the hiring of an expert or an investigator to prepare for trial, according to Watson v. State, 64 Wis.2d 264, 219 N.W.2d 398 (1974).

For further discussion on the subject, generally, see, Hartnett, "Should the Defense Have Crime Lab Privileges?," *Trial Mag.,* Aug. 1976, p. 42.

2. 470 U.S. 68 (1985).

3. For a discussion of problems encountered by the states in applying *Ake,* see, Harris, "*Ake* Revisited: Expert Psychiatric Witnesses Remain Beyond Reach for the Indigent," 68 N.C.L.Rev. 763 (1990) (citing Moenssens, Starrs & Inbau, *Scientific Evidence in Criminal Cases* (3d ed. 1986)).

(2) the state's interest affected if the request is granted; and (3) the probable value of the additional or substitute safeguards that are sought and the risk of an erroneous deprivation of the private interest—loss of freedom and punishment—if those safeguards are not provided. The Court held that defendant was also entitled to expert psychiatric assistance on the issue of his future dangerousness, which was a significant factor at the sentencing phase in this capital trial.

In Liles v. Saffle,[4] the Tenth Circuit, following *Ake,* found that the Oklahoma trial court had deprived defendant Liles of due process by denying his pretrial motion for state funds to employ a psychiatrist in aid of his defense. Despite the factual difference between the cases—in *Ake* the defendant presented an insanity defense even though the trial court had denied him assistance, whereas in *Liles* the defendant, after his similar pretrial request had been denied, chose not to proceed with an insanity defense at trial—the Tenth Circuit relied extensively on *Ake.* Pointing to *Ake*'s requirement that a criminal defendant be granted access to a competent psychiatrist to assist not only in preparing and presenting the insanity defense, but also in evaluating it, the court held that Liles was not precluded from asserting his due process challenge just because he did not put on an insanity defense at trial: "One of the functions of such a court-appointed expert ... is to assist the defense in determining whether an insanity defense is viable or warranted under the circumstances of a particular case."[5] Liles' first degree murder conviction and death sentence were vacated, underscoring the importance and breadth of the *Ake* decision's mandate that the defendant be granted such resources where necessary for his defense.

Do the *Ake* and *Liles* decisions suggest that in all criminal trials where the state seeks to use expert witnesses the accused, if indigent, is entitled to court appointed experts for the preparation of his defense? Clearly not.[6]

The Supreme Court had an opportunity to settle that very issue and did not seize it. The day before *Ake* was decided, the Court heard oral arguments in the case of Caldwell v. Mississippi, a capital case in which the state supreme court had rejected, among many others, defendant's argument that his constitutional rights were violated by the state's refusal to provide firearms and fingerprint experts for defense consultation or use.[7] At the oral argument, the special assistant attorney general conceded that the Mississippi Supreme Court has since held there *is* a constitutional right for the indigent to obtain the services of

---

4. 945 F.2d 333 (10th Cir.1991).

5. Id. at 340.

6. In O'Dell v. Commonwealth, 234 Va. 672, 686, 364 S.E.2d 491, 499 (1988), cert. denied 488 U.S. 871 (1988), the Virginia Supreme Court refused any expansion of *Ake* by defendant who argued entitlement to an ex parte hearing on the necessity of the Commonwealth's funding of experts to assist with his defense. Defendant "admits

none of the proposed experts would address the question of his sanity, as in [*Ake*]; they were all forensic scientists. O'Dell had no constitutional right requiring the Commonwealth to provide this type of expert assistance."

7. Caldwell v. State, 443 So.2d 806 (Miss.1983). For further case history, see note 48, supra.

experts at state expense, but only if the necessity for such services is shown.

The *Caldwell* case was taken up to the Supreme Court on another major issue, involving an allegation of improper prosecutorial comment at the sentencing stage of the trial. When the Supreme Court handed down its decision, the sentence was vacated, because it was found to be constitutionally impermissible to lead the sentencing jury to believe that the responsibility for determining the appropriateness of the death sentence rests elsewhere.[8] In footnote 1, the Court's majority opinion mentioned the issue which related to the request for state paid experts, and held that there was no deprivation of due process in denying defendant's request because he had "offered little more than undeveloped assertions that the requested assistance would be beneficial." The Court refused to decide in the *Caldwell* case what if any showing "would have entitled a defendant to assistance of" expert witnesses.[9]

There has been increasing recognition in recent years that indigent criminal defendants may be constitutionally entitled to expert assistance in areas other than psychiatry provided the proper showing of need for expert assistance is made.[10]

Underlying all the voluminous expert knowledge that the attorney may be able to inject into the trial, there is, however, the discomforting realization that the trier of fact may disregard all of the expert testimony and decide the case on the basis of other evidence or other considerations.[11]

---

8. Caldwell v. Mississippi, 472 U.S. 320 (1985).

9. Id.

10. See, BNA Crim.Prac.Man. 21:406–413 (1989) for a discussion of whether *Ake* applies to experts other than psychiatrists and a list of cases in which defense counsel have requested expert assistance. See also, Dunn v. Roberts, 963 F.2d 308, 314 (10th Cir.1992) (Defense entitled to assistance from psychologists on the "battered wife syndrome.") Note, "Expert Services and the Indigent Criminal Defendant: The Constitutional Mandate of *Ake v. Oklahoma*," 4 Mich.L.Rev. 1326 (1986). Comment, "Nonpsychiatric Expert Assistance and the Requisite Showing of Need: A Catch-22 in the Post–Ake Criminal Justice System," 37 *Emory L.J.* 995 (1988); Annot., Right of indigent defendant in state criminal case to assistance of fingerprint expert, 72 A.L.R.4th 874 (1989); Annot., Right of indigent defendant in state criminal case to

assistance of ballistics experts, 71 A.L.R.4th 638 (1989); Annot; Right of indigent defendant in state criminal case to assistance of chemist, toxicologist, technician, narcotics expert, or similar nonmedical specialist in substance analysis, 74 A.L.R.4th 388 (1989).

11. In a few rare cases, appellate courts have upheld fact determinations by the trier of fact which were shown to be untrue by uncontested or uncontradicted scientific evidence. For instance, in Berry v. Chaplin, 74 Cal.App.2d 652, 169 P.2d 442 (1946), the court permitted the jury to accept the testimony of the mother of a child who, so the mother claimed, was the daughter of defendant Charlie Chaplin, despite uncontradicted scientific tests which positively excluded Chaplin as the father.

Other examples are the verdicts in "mercy killing" cases, or those involving paramour killings. See, Inbau, "Scientific Reasoning and Jury Verdicts," 16 Post-graduate Medicine (Oct. 1954).

II. BASIC ELEMENTS IN THE SELECTION AND PREPARATION OF EXPERT TESTIMONY

§ 1.06 Selecting an Expert—Limitations on Availability

A single capable and persuasive expert witness may do his sponsor's cause more good than several mediocre ones. Depending on the nature of the subject, numerical strength may also be offset by an increase of contradiction probability.

It is elementary that an expert will be evaluated by the trier of fact as a whole person, not just upon an understanding of the subject of his expertise. It follows then, however unfortunately, that it is not axiomatic that the expert chosen must be the one with the most knowledge of the subject. Reputation for honesty, personal appearance, dignity, voice, modesty, even-temper, memory for facts without reference to notes, ability to communicate and availability for court appearances are all factors to consider. Also, the ability to teach and educate can be invaluable when technical evidence must be presented.

It is frequently difficult to obtain expert testimony. Many physicians, and others whose services are desired, cannot be persuaded to voluntarily testify in court, regardless of the circumstances. There are a number of understandable factors which account for this inhibition.

An expert can function in two capacities: first, as an investigator into matters of cause and effect, clinical diagnosis, and/or identity; and second, as a witness who gives an opinion based on the information uncovered by his investigation. The first role is not distasteful to most experts; the second is often undesired. Experts who are not trained in forensic science may not want to be cast in the role of a participant in a legal controversy. Moreover, as regards the expert for a criminal defendant, the stigma of testifying for an accused criminal is feared by many professionals in a society emphasizing respectability. This latter category of witness may be unavailable for that reason alone. Moreover—and the attitude prevails among experts generally—the expert disdains the possible humiliation of cross-examination. Then, too, if the witness does not practice forensics for a living, courtroom participation as a witness may actually interfere with the professional schedule. However, the inconvenience attendant to a court appearance may be alleviated somewhat in trial courts which permit the witness to remain "on call" rather than being required to attend the trial until testimony is desired. Other courts will permit an expert witness to be placed on the stand out of the scheduled regular order.[1] The appropriateness of either practice should, if possible, be clarified in advance of trial by arrangement with the presiding judge.

Both plaintiff/prosecutor and defense counsel must avoid, at all cost, the "quack" or otherwise incompetent or dishonest pseudo-expert. An

---

§ 1.06

1. This can be done by a motion which asks that the chronological scheme of the proceedings be interrupted in order to permit the movant to call the expert witness to the stand to testify for the movant. It should be alleged that the witness has interrupted his professional work in order to attend court and will be seriously inconvenienced if he cannot be called at the requested time.

inept performance or exposure of deception may tarnish the entire prosecution or defense, and may even result in the reversal of a jury verdict.[2] Likewise, if an expert is allowed to testify in areas beyond his expertise an appellate court may reverse and remand a conviction based on such unreliable, speculative testimony.[3] Unless an expert witness measures up to satisfactory standards, he should not be used.

§ 1.07 Requiring an Expert to Testify—Calling an Opponent's Expert

The majority of states hold that the expert may be subpoenaed to give a professional opinion based upon facts observed and opinions arrived at *prior* to being ordered to testify; even though he is not to be compensated with an expert witness fee.[1] However, he may not be required to engage in any additional study or preparation. In instances where special preparation is not required in order to enable the expert to arrive at an opinion, or when the expert has previously formed an opinion based upon facts within his knowledge, the opinion is treated as any other testimonial evidence. The theory, though in the authors' opinion a faulty one, especially as regards a private, professional forensic scientist, is that such an opinion is no more compensable than that of a lay witness.

Another view allows the expert to refuse to testify except to facts he has personally observed.[2] A third group of cases holds that an expert may be required to testify to facts and opinions in all circumstances even when compensated only as an ordinary witness.[3] Some states have passed legislation which provides for criminal sanctions and appropriate discipline for any person who misrepresents association with or academic

---

2. People v. Cornille, 95 Ill.2d 497, 69 Ill.Dec. 945, 448 N.E.2d 857 (1983).

3. Gilliam v. State, 514 So.2d 1098 (Fla. 1987).

§ 1.07

1. Flinn v. Prairie County, 60 Ark. 204, 29 S.W. 459 (1895); People v. Conte, 17 Cal.App. 771, 122 P. 450 (1912); People v. Speck, 41 Ill.2d 177, 242 N.E.2d 208 (1968); Ramacorti v. Boston Redevelopment Authority, 341 Mass. 377, 170 N.E.2d 323 (1960); In re Hayes, 200 N.C. 133, 156 S.E. 791 (1931); Nielsen v. Brown, 232 Or. 426, 374 P.2d 896 (1962); Summers v. State, 5 Tex.App. 365 (1879); Ealy v. Shetler Ice Cream Co., 108 W.Va. 184, 150 S.E. 539 (1929); State ex rel. Berge v. Superior Court, 154 Wash. 144, 281 P. 335 (1929); and Philler v. Waukesha County, 139 Wis. 211, 120 N.W. 829 (1909).

See also, Annot. 88 A.L.R.2d 1186 (1963) (right to elicit expert testimony from adverse party called as witness); Annot. 77 A.L.R.2d 1182 (1961) (compelling expert to testify).

2. Agnew v. Parks, 172 Cal.App.2d 756, 343 P.2d 118 (1959); Buchman v. State, 59 Ind. 1 (1877); Hull v. Plume, 131 N.J.L. 511, 37 A.2d 53 (1944); People ex rel. Kraushaar Bros. & Co. v. Thorpe, 296 N.Y. 223, 72 N.E.2d 165 (1947); Pennsylvania Co. for Insurances on Lives & Granting Annuities v. Philadelphia, 262 Pa. 439, 105 A. 630 (1918); Bradley v. Poole, 187 Va. 432, 47 S.E.2d 341 (1948). But see, c.f., Cooper v. Norfolk Redevelopment and Housing Authority, 197 Va. 653, 90 S.E.2d 788 (1956).

3. Ex parte Dement, 53 Ala. 389 (1875); Board of Comm'rs of Larimer County v. Lee, 3 Colo.App. 177, 32 P. 841 (1893); Dixon v. State, 12 Ga.App. 17, 76 S.E. 794 (1912); Dixon v. People, 168 Ill. 179, 48 N.E. 108 (1897); Swope v. State, 145 Kan. 928, 67 P.2d 416 (1937); and Barnes v. Boatmen's Nat. Bank, 348 Mo. 1032, 156 S.W.2d 597 (1941); See also, 8 Wigmore, *Evidence,* § 2203. (J. McNaughton Rev. 1961); 4 Jones, *Evidence,* § 879 (5th ed. 1958).

standing at an educational institution or makes false claims of academic degrees or titles.[4]

It should be remembered that the hostility engendered in the reticent expert who is subpoenaed into court to testify against his wishes and without expert compensation poses a great potential danger to his sponsor's case. Consequently, arrangements should be made for the expert's compensation. Then, too, if counsel deems it desirable to serve the witness with a subpoena—as a protective device against the consequences of the witness not appearing in court at the specified time—it should be served in a courteous, informal manner, coupled with an explanation that it evidences no distrust in the witness, but represents, rather, a necessary and customary precautionary measure.

Many of the cases dealing with compelling an expert witness to testify involve civil controversies.[5] Different considerations ought to apply when dealing with criminal cases. If, for example, a federal, state or local crime laboratory has made an analysis of evidence and furnished a report of its findings to the prosecutor, which report was obtained by the defense in the discovery process, to permit the defense to call the prosecution expert as a defense witness seems entirely within the spirit of our criminal justice system, wherein the function of the law enforcement-prosecutor team is not to convict, but to seek the truth. In Flores v. State,[6] for example, a crime laboratory director who had performed an examination refused to testify for the defense unless retained as its expert. Such a refusal seems unjustified and arbitrary when one considers that the expert is on the public payroll and has a duty, as an arm of the prosecution team, to seek justice. The Texas Court of Criminal Appeals held that the trial judge erred in refusing to instruct the witness to testify, under penalty of contempt if he refused, as to the examination he had already conducted, citing defendant's Sixth Amendment right to the compulsory process of witnesses. (However, the ruling of the trial court was considered harmless error in view of the particular circumstances.)

4. See, West's Fla.Stat.Ann. §§ 817.566, 817.567 (1993). See also, Or.Rev.Stat. 348.-885 (1989) (providing that misrepresentation of possession of an academic degree is fraudulent); Nev.Rev.Stat. 205.420 (1986) (use of false permit, license or diploma is misdemeanor).

5. In Gugliano v. Levi, 24 A.D.2d 591, 262 N.Y.S.2d 372 (1965), defendant's expert who had rendered a report that was favorable to plaintiff's position was then subpoenaed by plaintiff. In reversing, the New York Appellate Division called this an "improper trial tactic" inasmuch as plaintiff did not lack expert evidence to prove his own case. The court said: "The practice [of calling an opponent's consulting expert without a showing of difficulty in obtaining other expert testimony] thrusts the expert into the intolerable position of working for both sides, and into violation of his 'ethical obligation not to accept a retainer from the other side.' " Id. at 374.

By contrast, in Carter–Wallace, Inc. v. Otte, 474 F.2d 529 (2d Cir.1972), cert. denied 412 U.S. 929 (1973), held that the weight of authority permits federal courts to subpoena any expert at trial and require the witness to state his previously formed opinions. Accord: Kaufman v. Edelstein, 539 F.2d 811 (2d Cir.1976); Gilly v. City of New York, 69 N.Y.2d 509, 516 N.Y.S.2d 166, 508 N.E.2d 901 (1987)—there is no ethical dilemma when the expert is merely ordered to speak the truth! The issues in this section overlap those discussed further in the sections on discovery and disclosure in Parts III and IV of this Chapter, infra.

6. 491 S.W.2d 144 (Tex.Crim.App.1973).

A different attitude might conceivably be taken if the prosecution has consulted an expert who is not on the public payroll. To compel an independent expert *to perform services* for one side without compensation might well raise questions of involuntary servitude under the Thirteenth Amendment. This is different, however, from compelling a witness, albeit an expert witness, to testify as to knowledge already possessed as a result of previous labors.[7]

Ought not an expert retained by the defense be equally available as a witness for the prosecution? As to this question, entirely different considerations are at play and the answer is not as simple. On the one hand, it is true that one side cannot simply garner in its corner the most outstanding expert in a given field or discipline, simply to prevent the other side from hiring the expert. Moreover, since neither side "owns" its witness, it would seem to be entirely proper for the prosecution to contact an expert already consulted by the defense with the aim of asking the expert to do a new or different evidential examination for the prosecution.[8]

When, however, the defense has engaged an expert to examine prosecution evidence and advise the defense on the validity of that evidence, it would seem to be entirely improper for the prosecution then to subpoena the expert as a prosecution witness *when the prosecution's only purpose in doing so is to embarrass the defense* and show, to the fact finder, that defendant's own expert agrees with the prosecution's experts. If, for example, the defense has engaged the services of an independent fingerprint expert to check the validity of the prosecution fingerprint evidence, and that expert's conclusion agrees with the prosecution's own experts—who would know that this was likely to be the defense expert's conclusion—there could be no valid reason for the prosecutor to subpoena the defense's expert as a witness other than to embarrass the defense. Certainly, the prosecutor who needs a fingerprint or other crime laboratory expert witness has his choice of literally dozens of highly qualified public servants employed by local and state laboratory facilities. If none of these are available, a local prosecutor can still appeal, without charge to his jurisdiction, to the Federal Bureau of Investigation's laboratory services which will provide him not only with an evidentiary analysis but with an expert for court testimony as well. By contrast, the defense attorney may not have very many experts to call upon; the person he called may be the only one in the area available for defense work.[9]

7. People v. Speck, supra note 1, section 1.07.

8. Practice approved in People v. Speck, supra note 1, section 1.07.

9. In many fields of criminal evidence analysis, very few private practitioners are available to the defense. By the very nature of the discipline, there are not many private fingerprint experts, firearms examiners, toolmark experts, controlled drugs analysts, etc. Those who are not employed in governmental facilities are likely to have retired from public service. While there is a trend in the forensic science disciplines to encourage retired public servants to make themselves available for defense consultation, every criminal defense practitioner knows that although such retired law enforcement experts are quite willing to do consulting work, they lack the enthusiasm or interest to do so for criminal defendants!

For the prosecution to call the defense's expert as its witness, in the foregoing circumstances, appears to be a fundamentally unfair move which tends to inhibit the defense from seeking to explore the validity of the prosecution evidence by consulting independent specialists.[10]

A fundamental unfairness argument cannot be made, of course, when the expert was not one selected by the defense, but by the court itself, in which latter situation there should be freedom to either party to call the expert as a witness. Such practices tend to remove the expert witness from the adversary arena and cloak him with an aura of impartiality that may indeed be entirely misplaced.[11] Suggestions have

The partisan attitude of some law enforcement experts is so strong that it reflects itself in the technical literature. For instance, after attending, "undercover," a defense attorneys' continuing legal education seminar in forensic sciences, the director of a drug enforcement administration laboratory reported in writing on his experience and "noted with alarm" that the "D.E.A. Analytical Manual" and an FBI publication entitled "Handbook for Forensic Science" were being offered for sale to defense attorneys: Perillo, "A Report: National Institute on Forensic Science; Problems in Criminal Defense—Symposium," *Identification News,* Mar. 1976, p. 5. One might wonder why forensic scientists would be alarmed at the fact that criminalistics manuals are available to defense attorneys.

10. The dilemma is real and recognized by forensic scientists generally. See, e.g., Byrd & Stults, "The Dilemma of the Expert Witness," *Trial Magazine,* May, 1976, p. 59. A similar article, by the same authors, appeared under the title "The Expert Witness: A Dilemma," in 21 *J.For.Sci.* 944 (1976). See also, Tanay, "Money and the Expert Witness: An Ethical Dilemma," 21 *J.For.Sci.* 769 (1976).

For an argument that a forensic scientist-client privilege ought to be created, see: Hilton, "A New Look at Qualifying Expert Witnesses and the Doctrine of Privilege for Forensic Scientists," 17 *J.For.Sci.* 586 (1972).

11. The practice of "shopping" for an expert has been recognized as a problem for many years. It lead an early English court to state: "... the mode in which expert evidence is obtained is such as not to give fair result of scientific opinion to the Court. A man may go, and does sometimes to a half-dozen experts ... He takes their honest opinions, he finds three in his favor and three against him; he says to the three in his favor, 'will you be kind enough to give evidence?' and he pays the three against him their fees and leaves them alone; the other side does the same ... I am sorry to say the result is that the Court does not get the assistance from the experts which, if they were unbiased and fairly chosen, it would have the right to expect." Thorn v. Worthington Skating Rink Co., L.R. 6 Ch.D. 415 (Engl.1876).

To remedy this problem, it has been suggested that use be made of court appointed impartial expert witnesses. This is by no means a novel idea; it has engendered much controversy between lawyers and scientists, especially in the medico-legal field where it has been advocated, applied, and criticized. For one viewpoint on the issue, see: Moenssens, "'Impartial' Medical Experts: New Look at an Old Issue," in 1974 *Legal Medicine Annual* 355 (C. Wecht. Ed.).

The Federal Rules of Evidence recognize the concept. Rule 706 permits the court, on its own motion as well as at the request of litigants, to appoint experts who may be required to report directly to the court and are subject to call for testimony by either the court or the adversaries. The court determines the expert's "reasonable compensation" which is, in civil cases, paid by the litigants, and in criminal cases, paid from public funds. The court may, in its discretion, disclose to the jury that a witness was court appointed. Each side can, of course, also call its own expert.

Advocating the concept of a "meta-expert," as *amicus curiae,* to help the court when there was a battle of the adversary experts, see, Hanson, "Expert Testimony," 49 *A.B.A.J.* 254 (1963). Some proposals go even farther and, suggesting that the courts and juries are ill equipped to deal with complex technical or scientific issues, these issues of scientific controversy ought to be tried by a "science court." See: Kantrowitz, "The Science Court Experiment," *Trial Mag.,* Mar. 1977, p. 48. See also, "Twenty-Five Year Retrospective on the Science Court: A Symposium," in 4 *RISK—Issues in Health & Safety* 95–188 (1993), containing articles on the "science court" issue by

even been made that court appointed experts ought not be required to testify at all, but should simply send their report to the court and parties, which report ought to be admissible in lieu of testimony—a notion well known to European continental experts but shocking to attorneys steeped in the adversary system.[12]

§ 1.08   General Sources for Locating an Expert

The expert witness can be valuable not only for the facts and opinions he may reveal but also for the knowledge he can impart to the attorney who must, in the last analysis, determine the strategy of the entire case. An attorney who has his own expert is also in a position to insure against an adverse expert's opinion receiving more credit than it deserves.

Some cases do not require expert testimony even though they might be enhanced by scientific proof. It is common knowledge, however, that other cases absolutely require scientific analytical assistance.

An attorney is frequently puzzled as to just where he should start looking for an expert. The following suggestions may be helpful.

1. CIVIL CASES

In civil cases, there are many sources where suitable expert witnesses can be identified. In recent years, commercial expert locator services have sprung up which advertise in the classified pages of national as well as state bar journals. Some such compilations are even available on computer data bases.[1] Individuals also make their availability known in these same publications. Probably the most reliable source for finding expert witnesses is through other attorneys who have made use of their services. In such a case, one can obtain at the same time the benefit of a colleague's personal experience with the expert.

There are also more than 20,000 national and international associations listed in the Encyclopedia of Associations, available in most libraries. After identifying the permanent offices of professional societies, or their current elected officers, it may be possible to obtain referrals to specific members of the group who are available for consultation, or membership rosters may be obtained.

Kantrowitz, Cranor, Jacoby, Jasanoff, Mazur and Cavicchi.

12. Ploscowe, "The expert witness in criminal cases in France, Germany, and Italy," 2 *Law & Contemp.Prob.* 508 (1935); Schroder, "Problems Faced by the Impartial Witness in Court: the Continental View," 34 *Temple L.Q.* 378 (1961).

In Strelitz, "Certificates of Analysis," 3 *The Crim.Just.Quarterly* [1] 39 (1975), the author examines the practice of admitting as evidence reports of analyses done by law enforcement laboratories and considers the

Official Records Exception and the Business Records Exception to the Hearsay rule.

§ 1.08

1. TASA—The Technical Advisory Service for Attorneys is available through Westlaw and lists more than 12,000 experts in over 4,000 categories. The National Forensic Center publishes a Forensic Services Directory and The Directory of Medical Specialists are available on both Lexis and Westlaw. See, Carol H. Garcia, "How to Select a Forensic Expert," *Criminal Justice,* Fall 1989, p. 19.

Colleges, universities and research institutes, public and private, have among their faculty members outstanding specialists in the widest variety of topics. Many faculty in higher education are consulted as experts and frequently are asked to provide opinion testimony in civil litigation.

While most expert witnesses will furnish impressive looking resumes, it should be remembered that the duty to verify credentials and check claims made in biographical sketches rests squarely on the attorney retaining the expert. There have been many instances where expert witnesses have lied about their credentials, experience, and professional affiliations.[2] Often, these deceptions have come to light only accidentally, and it is to be assumed that such instances are widespread. At least one court placed the responsibility for verifying the credentials and experience of an expert witness squarely on the shoulders of the attorney calling that witness.[3]

2. PROSECUTORIAL FACILITIES

The F.B.I. Laboratories in Washington, D.C. and Quantico, Va., with a large staff of technicians and scientists, conduct examinations with the understanding that the evidence submitted is connected with an official investigation of a criminal matter and that its laboratory report will be used only for official purposes related to the investigation and the preparation of a criminal prosecution.

The F.B.I. Laboratory is equipped to perform document examinations, serological tests, hair, mineral and fiber analyses, metalurgical tests, general toxicological and chemical tests, and identification of tool marks, explosives, firearms, shoeprints, tireprints and fingerprints. Autopsies, however, are not performed by the F.B.I. Laboratory, but arrangements are sometimes made with the Armed Forces Institute of Pathology to have specimens pathologically analyzed. Skeletal remains are examined by anthropologists at the Smithsonian Institute in Washington. The F.B.I. will also provide the prosecution with expert testimony at trial, provided, however, there is no other expert in the same scientific field testifying for the state.

Many of the states have created a central "crime lab" to furnish scientific aid in criminal investigations and prosecutions.[4] Local police

---

2. See, Starrs, "Mountebanks Among Forensic Scientists," in *Forensic Science Handbook*, Vol. II (Saferstein, ed., 1988); Moenssens, "Novel Scientific Evidence in Criminal Cases: Some Words of Caution," 84 *J.Crim.L. & Criminology* 801 (1993); Kuzma, "Criminal Liability for Misconduct in Scientific Research," 25 U.Mich.J.L.Ref. 357 (1992); Starrs, "The Misbehaving Expert—The Law Turns Turtle," *Sci. Sleuthing Rev.*, Spring 1993, p. 1. See also, Garcia, "Expert Witness Malpractice: A Solu-

tion to the Problem of the Negligent Expert Witness," 12 *Miss.C.L.Rev.* 39 (1991).

3. People v. Cornille, 95 Ill.2d 497, 69 Ill.Dec. 945, 448 N.E.2d 857 (1983).

4. State crime lab reports and experts' notes regarding tests performed there may or may not be discoverable by the defense. See, e.g., Roberts v. State, 196 Ga.App. 450, 396 S.E.2d 81 (1990) (state not required to furnish defendant with its expert's notes, including internal documents and graphs,

and sheriffs' departments may also maintain such laboratories. Most of the specialists working in these crime laboratory facilities are available as expert witnesses on behalf of the prosecution. Additionally, and ever increasingly, prosecutors may call upon authorities in various fields who are not employed in a public agency in an attempt to surround the testimony with an aura of impartiality and academic respectability.

3. DEFENSE FACILITIES

In cases where scientific aids may be needed by the defense, it is frequently handicapped by inadequate resources, or by the unavailability of a capable expert to examine the evidence and render an opinion in court. Unless the defense is entitled to expert services as a matter of constitutional law as discussed previously, or until the means of selecting an expert becomes vested in the court through an "impartial" expert system, or until a system is developed whereby governmental experts and facilities are made available to both the prosecution and defense, the criminal defense must find and engage its own experts.

Considerable time and effort may be required to locate an expert to perform an examination for the defense. The task is not a hopeless one, however, since expert assistance in every field of scientific proof is available to the defense attorney who is sufficiently devoted to his cause to expend the time, effort, and money. It is necessary, of course, to know the type of expert needed as well as the various sources through which he may be located. The mechanics of the search for an expert will vary according to the subject of examination. For that reason, possible sources of expert assistance are included with each individual chapter of this book rather than cumulatively under this section.

————

III. DISCOVERY AND DISCLOSURE IN CRIMINAL CASES

§ 1.09 The General Purpose and Nature of Disclosure and Discovery

In recent years there literally has been an avalanche of statutes, court rules, and case decisions involving pretrial disclosure and discovery in criminal cases. This is partially the result of a trend toward accepting, in criminal matters, the general purposes of disclosure and discovery in civil actions: preventing surprise at trial; narrowing the issues to be tried; and speeding the administration of justice by encouraging settlement (e.g., plea bargaining) of those cases where both sides know the strength or weakness of the evidence. Pretrial discovery also provides a means whereby defense counsel is able to equalize the imbalance of

or data such as the crime lab's forensic drug chemist's tests).

resources available to the state.[1]

(The single word discovery will be used generally throughout this chapter as embracing both disclosure and discovery. Only in certain parts is a differentiation warranted.)

The discovery of scientific information is, in one sense, merely a part of the total discovery of a party's case and the same general purposes apply. However, special considerations arise with regard to expert discovery. The major reason given for expert discovery in both criminal and civil actions is the need for the opposing attorney to adequately prepare himself for cross-examination. The cross-examining lawyer himself often needs to have a very technical knowledge of the particular scientific field to put the expert's conclusions to a meaningful test. This is different from the cross-examination of a direct evidence witness (e.g., eye-witness), where the lawyer may draw from his own knowledge of the common fallibilities of sense perception and memory.[2]

Our attention will focus first upon the statutes and court rules regarding expert criminal discovery.[3] Thereafter, discovery in civil cases will be discussed.

Rule 16 of the Federal Rules of Criminal Procedure and the American Bar Association's recommended standards for criminal discovery will be discussed in some detail, since these provisions have been models for many revisions in state criminal discovery rules. After examining the laws of all fifty states, it becomes evident that a majority of states have adopted statutes and court rules that specifically allow some pretrial discovery of expert information for both prosecution and defense. Reference to these other sources will be given wherever possible. For those states that have not adopted specific rules, case law will be analyzed in an attempt to classify that state's approach to expert discovery.

As a prelude to the general model and state analysis, relevant constitutional considerations will be discussed. Following the federal and state section is an examination of the procedures relevant to expert criminal discovery as well as the problems surrounding disclosure at trial.

---

§ 1.09

1. As Justice Benjamin Cardozo stated in People ex rel. Fordham Manor Reform Church v. Walsh, 244 N.Y. 280, 291, 155 N.E. 575 (1927), "Disclosure is the antidote to partiality and favor." See also, State v. Kilgore, 771 S.W.2d 57 (Mo.1989), cert. denied 493 U.S. 874 (1989) (basic purpose of discovery process is to permit the defendant a decent opportunity to prepare in advance of trial and avoid surprise) and State v. Burnison, 247 Kan. 19, 795 P.2d 32, 37 (1990) (discovery is to be "as full and complete as is reasonably possible under the circumstances").

2. Additionally, the position of the expert in the discovery process should be con-sidered. Given the special role of the expert in litigation, the most recent rules and legislative enactments have addressed the questions of expert fees and the expert's dual position as both advisor and witness. Simon, "Pretrial Discovery Of Expert Information In Federal And State Courts: A Guide For The Expert," 5 *J.Pol.Sci. & Adm.* 247 (1977).

3. Where, however, a jurisdiction has not dealt directly with discovery of scientific information, as is the case with the several states which do not have discovery rules, an extrapolation from the pronouncements regarding general criminal discovery will be made. See infra § 1.11(2)(d).

§ 1.10 Informal Disclosure by the Prosecution

Until recently, informal discovery of the prosecution's evidence was encouraged as a means of circumventing the severe restrictions placed on pretrial discovery by the rules then in effect.[1] The need for such informal procedures has been lessened, however, by the liberalization of the federal and state criminal discovery rules. Today, informal discovery is common.[2] Depending upon defense counsel's working relationship with the prosecutors involved in a case, it is sometimes possible to obtain a considerable amount of discovery without resorting to formal discovery practice. In essence, the informal technique entails a conference with the prosecutor, coupled with a defense request that the prosecutor reveal the contents of his file. This informal procedure may be in lieu of or as an adjunct to the filing of formal motions for discovery.

Informal discovery at a pretrial conference has several advantages. First, it may obviate the necessity of preparing, filing and arguing tedious motions, thereby lessening the workload of defense counsel. Second, this approach can aid in establishing a positive relationship with the prosecutor's office because it also spares the prosecutor from preparing, filing and arguing his answer to a formal motion.[3]

The informal approach requires a cooperative prosecutor. A prosecutor may be quite willing to reveal a strong case, but reluctant to allow broad discovery in a weak one.[4] In metropolitan areas different assistant prosecutors may control various phases of the case, which complicates matters. Finally, it should be recognized that counsel who relies solely upon the informal approach sacrifices the preservation of error for failure of the prosecution to give him all that the law requires. The best guideline in this respect is to seek a happy medium between overzealousness in the name of the client and capitulation to the state. The greatest assets an attorney has at his disposal in seeking informal disclosure of his adversary's case are his common sense and personality.

It must be kept in mind that the use of informal disclosure is a strategic concept. Each attorney employing this method must judge for himself the desirability of its use on a case-by-case basis.

---

§ 1.10

1. 8 *Moore's Federal Practice* § 16.02[3].

2. See, United States v. Clevenger, 458 F.Supp. 354 (E.D.Tenn.1978) (parties should try to accomplish discovery themselves without the interference of a court). In State v. Klindt, 389 N.W.2d 670, 672 (Iowa 1986), the court noted the trend of cases and evidence rules pointing toward broadening the scope of admissibility of expert testimony.

3. United States v. Magaw, 425 F.Supp. 636 (E.D.Wis.1977) (open file policy of prosecutor satisfies discovery requirements of Fed.R.Crim.P. 16). But see, United States v. Deerfield Specialty Papers, Inc., 501 F.Supp. 796 (E.D.Pa.1980) (fishing expeditions into government's files are not cognizable under Brady v. Maryland, infra note 1, section 1.07, and its progeny, especially at the pretrial stage.

4. See, "Discovery in Criminal Cases," 33 F.R.D. 47, 116 (1963).

§ 1.11 Laws of Disclosure

1. FEDERAL CONSTITUTIONAL REQUIREMENTS

Certain federal constitutional provisions have a significant influence on criminal discovery even though there is no direct constitutional requirement for pretrial discovery in criminal cases.[1] These constitutional law cases have identified three important issues which indicate the minimum amount of defense discovery of prosecution evidence required in criminal actions. This section will address these constitutional issues in broad terms since constitutional considerations act upon the specific question of expert criminal discovery only in a general manner.

A. SCOPE OF DEFENDANT'S DUE PROCESS RIGHT TO DISCLOSURE

In 1935 the Supreme Court first recognized a constitutional duty in the area of disclosure.[2] Generally, a criminal defendant has a Fifth Amendment due process right which requires the prosecutor to disclose certain evidence. The issue as to what disclosures fall within the requirement was clarified by the Court in its opinion in United States v. Agurs.[3] Justice Stevens, speaking for a majority of seven members of the Court, cast the requirement in terms of *materiality*. Exculpatory information that is material must be disclosed and there are three standards of materiality, depending upon the factual circumstances of the particular case.[4]

The first circumstance is where undisclosed evidence demonstrates that the prosecution's case includes perjured testimony and the prosecution knew or should have known of the perjury. In such cases, the conviction will be set aside "if there is any reasonable likelihood that the false testimony could have affected the judgment of the jury."[5] The

---

§ 1.11

1. See Weatherford v. Bursey, 429 U.S. 545 (1977) (there is no general constitutional right to discovery in a criminal case). See also, Wardius v. Oregon, 412 U.S. 470 (1973) ("the Due Process Clause has little to say regarding the amount of discovery which the parties must be afforded."). Accord United States v. LaRouche, 896 F.2d 815 (4th Cir.1990), cert. denied 496 U.S. 927 (1990) (criminal defendants do not have a "general" constitutional right to discovery); Strickler v. Commonwealth, 241 Va. 482, 404 S.E.2d 227 (1991) (even where a capital offense is charged).

2. Mooney v. Holohan, 294 U.S. 103 (1935) (a criminal conviction procured by state prosecuting authorities solely by the use of perjured testimony known by them to be perjured and knowingly used by them in order to procure the conviction, is without due process of law and in violation of the Fourteenth Amendment).

3. 427 U.S. 97 (1976). Two of the most important questions answered by *Agurs* were noted in the first edition of this book: "Whether or not a request is mandatory to establish the constitutional duty to disclose is not yet certain" (p. 32), and "Unfortunately for the petitioner, the Supreme Court has yet to explicate the degree of prejudice which will warrant it to vacate a conviction and remand the cause for new trial." (p. 34).

4. 427 U.S. at 103.

5. Id. The Court described this as a "strict standard of materiality not just because [these cases] involve prosecutorial misconduct, but more importantly because they involve a corruption of the truth seeking function of the trial process." 427 U.S. at 104. Also, United States v. Hedgeman, 564 F.2d 763 (7th Cir.1977) (conviction upheld even though applying strict standard).

Thus, a conviction obtained by the knowing use of perjured testimony is "fundamentally unfair." Id. at 103. Also, United States v. Hedgeman, 564 F.2d 763 (7th Cir. 1977), cert. denied 434 U.S. 1070 (1978) (conviction upheld even though applying strict standard). Cf. United States v. Harrison, 679 F.2d 942 (D.C.Cir.1982) (absent a specific request by defendant, prosecution

leading case on this point is Miller v. Pate.[6] In *Miller,* the defendant was convicted of the rape-murder of a child with the aid of a pair of stained men's undershorts. A state chemist testified that the shorts contained blood stains of the same type as the victim. In a subsequent federal habeas corpus proceeding, evidence was introduced that the stains were found to be paint and the reversal of the conviction was ultimately upheld by the United States Supreme Court.[7]

The second situation where disclosure of "material" information is constitutionally required is where such evidence is favorable to the accused and the prosecution suppresses it after a request for disclosure by the defense. This was the holding of Brady v. Maryland.[8] There, the attorney for a defendant accused of murder asked to examine all statements of the defendant's companion. The prosecution disclosed all statements requested except the one in which his companion admitted doing the killing. The Supreme Court held the suppression to be a violation of the defendant's right to due process, irrespective of the good faith or the bad faith of the prosecution.[9] In this type of case, where there has been suppression of specifically requested material, *Agurs* characterized the evidence to be material if it might have affected the outcome had it not been suppressed.[10]

had no duty to disclose that interviews had taken place where the information elicited at such interviews did not indicate that a prosecution witness would perjure herself at trial).

6.   386 U.S. 1 (1967).

7. A subsequent investigation into the possible disbarment of the prosecutor found the Supreme Court erred in finding the prosecutor misrepresented the evidence since the stains were both blood and paint. See, "The Vindication of A Prosecutor," 59 *J.Crim.L., C. & P.S.* 335 (1968).

8.   373 U.S. 83 (1963). Although *Brady* held that disclosure in that case was constitutionally required, the Supreme Court in Weatherford v. Bursey, 429 U.S. 545 (1977) emphasized that *Brady* did not create a general constitutional right to discovery in a criminal case. United States v. Phillips, 664 F.2d 971 (5th Cir.1981) and State v. Brown, 214 Neb. 665, 335 N.W.2d 542 (1983) (defendant was denied a fair trial where prosecutor did not disclose pathologist's opinion, given after examining photographs of the victim's injuries, that the means used and manner in which the wounds were inflicted were not as victim had claimed).

9. Also see, to the same effect, Perkins v. LeFevre, 642 F.2d 37 (2d Cir.1981).

10.   427 U.S. at 105–06. One state court has held that the constitutional line of cases only forces the prosecution to disclose evidence which is "admissible and useful" for the defense. Anderson v. State, 241 So.2d 390 (Fla.1970), citing Giles v. Maryland, 386 U.S. 66 (1967). The qualification of "admissible" could eliminate from discovery the findings of experts which are considered to be inadmissible. An example would be the results of a Polygraph test. J.E. Reid & F.E. Inbau, *Truth and Deception: The Polygraph ("Lie–Detector") Technique* (2d ed. 1977) 343–48. Other courts have held, however, that inadmissible information, if exculpatory, must be disclosed under *Brady:* Emmett v. Ricketts, 397 F.Supp. 1025 (N.D.Ga.1975); Smith v. United States, 375 F.Supp. 1244 (E.D.Va. 1974); State v. Hall, 249 N.W.2d 843 (Iowa 1977). It is now firmly established that exculpatory information must be disclosed. Hicks v. Scurr, 671 F.2d 255 (8th Cir.1982), cert. denied 459 U.S. 968 (1982); Martin v. Blackburn, 521 F.Supp. 685 (E.D.La.1981), affirmed 711 F.2d 1273 (5th Cir.1983), rehearing denied 739 F.2d 184 (5th Cir.1984); United States v. Nix, 601 F.2d 214 (5th Cir.1979), cert. denied 444 U.S. 937 (1979). Still other courts have held that *Brady* requires not only the disclosure of material evidence in the sense of mitigation or exculpation, but also requires the prosecution to disclose evidence important or useful for impeachment purposes. See, e.g., United States v. Allain, 671 F.2d 248 (7th Cir. 1982); United States v. Gaston, 608 F.2d 607 (5th Cir.1979). The Supreme Court held that absent a showing of bad faith, the failure of police to preserve potentially ex-

The third standard of materiality is invoked by the factual situation in *Agurs* itself. In this case the defendant was convicted of murder despite her claim of self-defense. After the verdict, defense counsel moved for a new trial, claiming to have recently discovered that the victim had a criminal record for violent crimes which was not disclosed by the prosecution. In reasoning toward the conclusion that such a disclosure was not required, Justice Stevens first stated that there was no constitutional difference in the standard of materiality applied in cases where there had been no pretrial request by the defense (*Agurs*) and cases where there had been a general request for all "*Brady* material." [11] The Court found that:

> "The mere possibility that an item of undisclosed information might have helped the defense, or might have affected the outcome of the trial, does not establish, 'materiality' in the constitutional sense." [12]

However, materiality is established in the absence of a specific request "if the omitted evidence creates a *reasonable doubt* that it did not otherwise exist." [13] Where reasonable doubt exists, failure of the prosecution to disclose the material information is constitutional error.

There are, then, three relevant constitutional standards defining "material" evidence that must be disclosed on due process grounds: (1) strict materiality in false evidence cases (i.e., false evidence is material if it could have affected the case result); (2) specifically requested evidence which might have affected the outcome; and (3) evidence which would create a reasonable doubt as to the defendant's guilt even where there has been no request or merely a general request for exculpatory evidence. [14]

Defense counsel, in many cases, should not rely on a general request for all exculpatory evidence ("*Brady* material"); rather, there should be a specific request of the information desired in order to preserve the strongest constitutional claims to prosecution evidence. [15]

---

culpatory evidence did not constitute a due process violation in Arizona v. Youngblood, 488 U.S. 51 (1988). Discussing that case, see, Wecht, "A Comfort for the Bad Cop—A Challenge for the Good Forensic Scientist," 34 *J.For.Sci.* 525 (1989).

11. 427 U.S. at 107.

12. Id. at 109–10. The Court's analysis rejects the suggestion that the prosecutor has a constitutional duty routinely to deliver his entire file to defense counsel.

13. Id. at 112 (emphasis supplied). In determining whether the non-disclosure of evidence rises to the level of an unconstitutional denial of due process, some courts apply a strict standard of materiality. See, e.g., United States v. Beasley, 576 F.2d 626, 630 (5th Cir.1978), cert. denied 440 U.S. 947 (1979) (retrial is appropriate only if the withheld evidence requested "creates a reasonable doubt that did not otherwise exist as to the guilt of the accused").

14. By way of illustration, the *Agurs* opinion identified a fourth, and most difficult, test in the escalating standard of materiality. That would be a standard where evidence is material if it would create a *substantial likelihood* that the defendant would have been acquitted. This is the standard applied in Fed.R.Crim.P. 33 in determining whether a motion for a new trial on the basis of newly discovered evidence should be granted. 427 U.S. at 111, n. 9. See also, Comment, "Materiality and Defense Requests: Aids in Defining the Prosecutor's Duty of Disclosure," 59 *Iowa L.Rev.* 433, 445 (1973).

15. See the sample discovery request motion in § 1.19 infra.

B. FIFTH AMENDMENT LIMITATIONS ON PROSECUTORIAL DISCOVERY

It is generally accepted now that rules requiring the defendant to submit to limited pretrial discovery by the prosecution do not, by themselves, violate the Fifth Amendment. However, when Rule 16 of the Federal Rules of Criminal Procedure was amended in 1966 to allow for discovery of defense evidence by the prosecution as a condition to the defendant obtaining disclosure of government evidence, serious Fifth Amendment questions were raised which remain important for more than historical reasons. Justices Black and Douglas dissented from the promulgation of the new discovery rule by the Supreme Court.[16] Their dissents were directed toward the Fifth Amendment aspects of conditioning defense discovery upon reciprocal discovery being allowed the prosecution.[17] However, their arguments are presumably even stronger against nonreciprocal discovery where the prosecution has a right to discover defense evidence independent of a triggering defense request.

For present purposes, it is sufficient to note that limited discovery of defense evidence is constitutional.[18] Nevertheless, the Fifth Amendment right to be free from self-incrimination lingers behind all prosecutorial discovery.[19]

C. DEFENDANT'S RIGHT TO EQUAL DISCOVERY

A final constitutional consideration is found in Wardius v. Oregon.[20] There, the United States Supreme Court held unconstitutional a state law requiring a defendant to notify the prosecution if he intended to give an alibi defense, and to give the names of any witnesses that would be called to support such a defense. There was, however, no corresponding duty on the prosecution to give the defense the names of witnesses that would be called by the prosecution to rebut the defendant's alibi. The Court stated that "the Due Process Clause of the Fourteenth Amendment forbids enforcement of alibi rules unless reciprocal discovery rights

16. Transmittal of Amendments to Fed. Cr.Rules, 384 U.S. 1032 & 1092 (1966).

17. See, United States v. Fratello, 44 F.R.D. 444 (S.D.N.Y.1968); Comment, "Prosecutorial Discovery Under Proposed Rule 16," 85 *Harv.L.Rev.* 994 (1972). Under the current federal rule, no court involvement is required although a defense request to discover government evidence remains necessary to trigger prosecutorial discovery. See § 1.11(2) infra.

18. See, Williams v. Florida, 399 U.S. 78 (1970) (upheld constitutionality of state notice of alibi statute in the face of a fifth amendment claim). This acceptability rests on the theory that what is discoverable under the present rules is only nontestimonial evidence. ABA Standards Relating to Discovery and Procedures Before Trial, § 3.1 (Approved Draft, 1970). However, what is testimonial may not always be clear. See, Chimel v. California, 395 U.S. 752 (1969); n. 9 infra.

19. See, United States v. Ryan, 448 F.Supp. 810 (D.C.N.Y.1978), affirmed 594 F.2d 853 (2d Cir.1978), cert. denied 441 U.S. 944 (1979) (if a defendant demands discovery of the government, he waives protection against self-incrimination as far as documents are concerned although he is still free to refuse to testify and is entitled to the appropriate standard charge in such regard). While refusal to testify is constitutionally protected, trial strategy determination is not.

20. 412 U.S. 470 (1973).

are given to criminal defendants." [21]   In view of *Wardius,* it would seem that any prosecutorial discovery system, including discovery of scientific information, must also provide for similar discovery rights for the defendant.

2.   PRETRIAL DISCOVERY IN FEDERAL AND STATE COURTS

As previously stated, this section will examine the statutes, court rules, and case decisions dealing with the pretrial discovery of scientific evidence in criminal cases in the federal and state systems.   It should be noted that there is little procedural variation among those jurisdictions which have enacted statutes or adopted court rules dealing specifically with expert discovery.   Those systems provide for the release of tangible evidence held by one party so as to allow the opposing party to engage his own expert to test the evidence.[22]   There is also statutory resolution of the work-product privilege controversy which plagued both civil and criminal expert discovery.[23]   Most systems flatly state there is no work-product privilege available to protect expert reports from discovery.[24] Rather, these systems are designed to allow disclosure of specific scientific information.[25]

The emphasis of the following analysis will be on the discovery provisions concerning disclosure of reports of examinations and tests by experts.   This emphasis is appropriate since there is greater variation among these provisions, and also because discovery of the results

---

21. Id. at 472. The court further stated that "discovery must be a two-way street." Id. at 475.

22. See, e.g., Fed.R.Crim.P. 16(a)(1)(C) and (b)(1)(A). For example, where tangible objects are subject to discovery, the defense may require the state to produce things such as fingerprints, guns, bullets, cartridge cases, autopsy specimens, photographs, drug samples, documents and seminal or blood-stained clothing for analysis by a defense expert.

Statutes permitting discovery of scientific evidence sometimes require that the material be examined in the presence of a representative of the state. This is a rational rule, but it poses a logistical problem. Should the defense expert take the material to his laboratory in the company of a state expert or representative, or should the defense examination take place in one of the state's laboratories with a state expert in attendance? The latter procedure would appear to be more workable, in light of the excellent state-owned laboratory facilities available in most regions. However, competent defense experts usually have their own laboratories and equipment. If the court so ordered, a representative of the state could be assigned to deliver the object of evidence to the defense expert at a speci-

fied date and time where the defense analysis could be observed.

23. See the Advisory Committee Note for the 1970 amendments to Fed.R.Civ.P. 26 in 28 U.S.C.A. (1972). Originally, the attorney-client privilege was claimed to protect expert reports from discovery. This was directly refuted by Hickman v. Taylor, 329 U.S. 495, 508 (1947) ("the protective cloak of this privilege does not extend to information which an attorney secures from a witness while acting for his client in anticipation of litigation."). The rejection of the work-product privilege is subsequently explained below. See text accompanying note 36 infra.

24. See, e.g., Fed.R.Crim.P. 16(a)(2) and (b)(2); and Commonwealth v. Paszko, 391 Mass. 164, 461 N.E.2d 222 (1984).

25. Also of interest in this regard, is the rejection by Congress in the 1974 amendments to Rule 16 of a provision which would have mandated the disclosure of the names of party's witnesses three days before trial. Failure to approve this suggestion, proposed Rule 16(a)(1)(E) and (b)(1)(C), strengthen the overall scheme for predetermined disclosure of specific information, rather than civil type discovery.

reached by the opponent's expert from testing tangible evidence is often more helpful than the tangible evidence by itself.[26]

A. DISCOVERY IN FEDERAL CRIMINAL CASES

Currently, pretrial discovery in federal criminal cases is covered by Rule 16 of the Federal Rules of Criminal Procedure. Rule 16 has two separate provisions covering discovery of experts retained by the defendant and those experts retained or employed by the prosecution.[27]

The provision for defendant's discovery of expert information from the prosecution is contained in Rule 16(a)(1)(D).[28] Under this provision, discovery is activated by the "request" of the defendant. A new amendment to Rule 16, approved by the Supreme Court and submitted to Congress to take effect on Dec. 1, 1993, inserted subparagraph (E) and requires the government, upon defendant's request, to disclose "a written summary of [expert witness] testimony the government intends to use" in its case in chief, describing "the witnesses' opinions, the bases and reasons therefor, and the witnesses' qualifications."[29] A request is most often made and complied with extrajudicially; however, in the case of a dispute over discovery either party may make a motion to a court for an order denying, restricting, deferring or otherwise, discovery or inspection. Rule 16 grants courts the power to regulate discovery.[30]

26. Scientific reports and test results obviously are especially important to the defense since, in many cases, the defense does not have the resources to duplicate the scientific analysis of the state's expert by employing its own expert to examine the fingerprint, bullet, pistol, blood sample, hair or the deceased's body. Another problem is that some scientific examinations necessarily destroy or materially alter the specimen which is the subject of the test report. In these situations, to deny the defense pretrial access to the state expert's report is to deny it any pretrial discovery, for its experts have nothing to examine.

27. See, for an interesting aspect of expert categorization, United States v. Bel–Mar Laboratories, Inc., 284 F.Supp. 875 (E.D.N.Y.1968) (for purposes of Rule 16, experts who are government employees and experts who are retained by the government are treated alike).

28. Rule 16, 18 U.S.C.A. § 365 (1993). Discovery and Inspection.

(a) Disclosure of Evidence by the Government.

(1) Information Subject to Disclosure

. . .

(D) Reports of Examinations and Tests. Upon request of a defendant the government shall permit the defendant to inspect and copy or photograph any re-

sults or reports of physical or mental examinations, and of scientific tests or experiments, or copies thereof, which are within the possession, custody, or control of the government, the existence of which is known, or by the exercise of due diligence may become known, to the attorney for the government, and which are material to the preparation of the defense or are intended for use by the government as evidence in chief at the trial.

29. Fed.R.Crim.Proc. 16(a)(1)(E), 1993.

30. Rule 16(d). See also, United States v. Clevenger, 458 F.Supp. 354 (E.D.Tenn. 1978) (in view of language used in this rule, discovery should be accomplished by the parties themselves; only if there is a failure to comply should court have to interfere). Note also that in some jurisdictions, the government's failure to comply with a discovery request does not mandate the reversal of a conviction unless the defendant is able to show prejudice. See, e.g., United States v. DeWeese, 632 F.2d 1267 (5th Cir. 1980), cert. denied 454 U.S. 878 (1981), (absent showing of prejudice, defendant was not entitled to reversal of conviction due to claimed violation by government of its discovery obligations in failing to inform defendant until day before trial that specific expert would testify).

Once the defendant makes a request, the rule provides that the government shall permit the defendant to inspect or copy the results of reports of medical or scientific tests.[31] However, for the rule to apply, the expert information must be in the control of the government, the prosecution must know of its existence, and the information requested by the defendant must be material to the preparation of his defense or it must be intended to be introduced at the trial by the prosecution in the case-in-chief.[32] The final restriction is intended to prevent the defendant from conducting a "fishing expedition" through the voluminous reports of the government. It also protects the work efforts of the advisor-expert from disclosure, thus encouraging full case investigations by the prosecution.[33] Of course, the defendant will eventually receive expert information from the prosecution which is material and favorable to the defense under the *Brady* rationale, even if the expert is not expected to testify.[34] Nevertheless, neutral or other information not favorable to the defense, and which is not intended to be introduced, is not discoverable.

The provision for the prosecution discovering the expert information of the defense is contained in Rule 16(b)(1)(B).[35] Corresponding to the

31. See, United States v. Hearst, 412 F.Supp. 863 (N.D.Cal.1975) (reports of prosecution and defense psychiatrists to be exchanged between the parties). Despite the broad language of the statute, there are limitations on the scope and content of discoverable material. See, e.g., United States v. Orzechowski, 547 F.2d 978 (7th Cir. 1976), cert. denied 431 U.S. 906 (1977) (prosecution not required to produce internal memoranda of Drug Enforcement Administration relating to testing of alleged cocaine products since such reports had not been made in connection with any particular prosecution); United States v. Beaver, 524 F.2d 963 (5th Cir.1975), cert. denied 425 U.S. 905 (1976) (court did not err in permitting fingerprint testimony on the ground that the government, while furnishing defendant with a fingerprint report, failed to provide prior to trial the specific points of identification and the number of points).

What constitutes a "report" or "result" is often problematic. See, e.g., United States v. Dennison, 937 F.2d 559 (10th Cir. 1991) (psychiatrist's notes taken during discussion with defendant were not discoverable medical reports or results); United States v. Peters, 937 F.2d 1422 (9th Cir. 1991) (examination of Federal Rule 16(b) and Hawaii District Court Rule 345–1(b) where expert made no written findings of his review of photographs and medical records).

32. In United States v. Lambert, 580 F.2d 740 (5th Cir.1978), certain evidence was held to be outside the scope of the prosecution order since it was introduced not as part of the government's case-in-chief, but as impeachment evidence during cross-examination of the defendant. The distinction between the two rules was articulated in United States v. Kaplan, 554 F.2d 577, 579–80 (3d Cir.1977): "Where documentary evidence is exculpatory, it may be within both *Brady* and Rule 16, but nonexculpatory records are obtainable in advance of trial only by virtue of Rule 16. It is conceivable that some documents which are not covered by Rule 16, e.g., a Jencks Act statement, may be *Brady* material because of their content."

33. An "advisor-expert" is an expert who is retained to test and advise regarding the technical evidence but who is not intended to be called as a witness. In most cases, an expert who is retained to evaluate the tangible evidence begins as an advisor. At some point, the decision is made for the expert to remain an advisor or to be called as a witness.

34. Courts consistently distinguish between information discoverable under F.R.Crim.P. 16(a)(1) and that required to be disclosed under the *Brady* doctrine. See generally, Weatherford v. Bursey, 429 U.S. 545 (1977).

35. United States v. Countryside Farms, Inc., 428 F.Supp. 1150 (D.Utah 1977). See, e.g., United States v. Sherman, 426 F.Supp. 85 (S.D.N.Y.1976).

1993 duty imposed upon the government to disclose, upon request by the defense, information about its expert witness' opinions, the bases and reasons for such opinions, and the experts' qualifications, the 1993 amendment also imposed a like duty of disclosure upon the defense in the added paragraph now known as Rule 16(b)(1)(C). These provisions are nearly identical to those for discovery by the defense except that they contain a reciprocity clause. That is, the prosecution can discover the expert information of the defense only if the defendant first requests disclosure of similar information from the government.[36] If the defendant has triggered Subdivision (b)(1)(B), the prosecution may request the information it desires. However, the reports or test results which are sought must be within the control of the defense *and* there must be the intention to introduce such evidence at trial. Also, the prosecution may seek only the results or reports of medical or scientific tests that were made in connection with the case at hand, thus prohibiting possible oppression by a prosecutor requesting irrelevant expert information. But the prosecution may also discover information which was prepared by a person whom the defense intends to call as a witness, and this applies even though the reports or results themselves are not intended to be introduced as evidence. It is sufficient that they relate to the expert's testimony. At first glance, this latter provision appears to grant to the prosecutor an additional right which the defense does not have. However, it is evident that this merely involves the ability of the government to cross-examine defense witnesses which is also provided to the defense through its ability to discover information which is "material to the preparation of the defense" in Subdivision (a)(1)(D).

It is important to note that Rule 16 removes any possible work product claim to prevent discovery of expert information. Presumably this was the result of logic similar to that applied in the civil discovery rules: expert information is evidence in itself and is not merely an evaluation of evidence.[37] The report of a coroner or medical examiner, or of a firearms or fingerprint expert, can be crucial to linking or not linking the accused person to the crime. Overriding public policy considerations call for allowing the court to receive this information. The strong public interest in ascertaining the truth in criminal matters is evidenced by the tone of Rule 16.

---

36. 18 U.S.C.A. § 366 (1975):

(b) Disclosure of Evidence by the Defendant.

(1) Information Subject to Disclosure

. . .

(B) Reports of Examinations and Tests. If the defendant requests disclosure under subdivision (a)(1)(C) or (D) of this rule, upon compliance with such request by the government, the defendant, on request of the government, shall permit the government to inspect and copy or photograph any results or reports of physical or mental examinations and of scientific tests or experiments made in connection with the particular case, or copies thereof, within the possession or control of the defendant, which the defendant intends to introduce as evidence in chief at the trial or which were prepared by a witness whom the defendant intends to call at the trial when the results or reports relate to his testimony.

37. See, Friedenthal, "Discovery and Use of an Adverse Party's Expert Information," 15 *Stan.L.Rev.* 455, 485–86 (1962).

"Discovery" under Rule 16 is more aptly termed "disclosure" since, once certain conditions are met, specified information must be disclosed. This difference from the discovery methods in civil cases is further emphasized by the absence of provisions for depositions or other discovery methods in addition to what is required to be disclosed.[38]

B. American Bar Association Standards

Before discussing the various state provisions, it is important to realize that the American Bar Association Recommended Standards for Criminal Discovery,[39] together with Federal Rule 16, have formed the models for many recent revisions in state criminal discovery rules.

As with the federal rules, the Standards have provisions relating to the discovery of expert information by both the defendant and the prosecution. Also, as with the federal rules, "discovery" is not as accurate a description as "disclosure" for the purpose and scope of the Standards.

C. Discovery Rules of the States

From the foregoing discussion of the ABA Standards and Federal Rule 16, it is evident that these general models have three main elements which can be dealt with in different ways: (1) whether or not disclosure of expert information is available only upon motion and court order (the motion element); (2) whether or not there is a need for reciprocity—no prosecution discovery unless the defendant seeks similar discovery (the reciprocity element); and (3) whether or not the opposing party must intend to introduce the expert information at trial before it can be discovered (the intent element).

We will now consider the ways by which the states have dealt with the foregoing three elements, and also to the similarities and dissimilarities between state provisions and the federal and ABA models.[40] One

---

38. It is interesting to note that the question of fees for the time experts spend responding to discovery does not normally arise in federal criminal trials and thus no provision is made for expert fees in the rule. See, Fed.R.Civ.P. 26(b)(4)(C).

39. See, American Bar Association Standards for Criminal Justice (3d ed. 1992), dealing with Discovery and Procedure Before Trial.

40. While it is contended that whether or not intention to introduce expert information at the trial must be shown is an important element in the general models, this factor did not figure into the classification of what states followed which model. The states appeared to be largely in agreement that some form of intent was required. However, states which agree on other elements common to a model chose

separate versions of whose intention to introduce expert information was necessary.

Where intention to introduce need not be shown by one or both parties, whether there is a clause limiting discovery of expert information to that "material" to or "made in connection with" the current case can also become a very important element. For example, if the prosecution need not show the defendant intends to introduce the expert information sought and there is no materiality requirement, the prosecutor could harass the defendant by seeking every medical or scientific record in his possession. Thus, while the current classifications do not require the materiality element be a factor, such a limitation should be given consideration by experts working in a state which does not require an intent element.

must note that these three main elements may vary even within a given state as differing burdens are placed upon the prosecution and the defense. Also, while an attempt will be made to present the states examined under the heading of the general model they most nearly resemble, it should not be inferred that states so listed consider themselves as operating under that particular model. Nor is this an attempt to completely categorize the states following any particular model.

(i) State Provisions Patterned After Federal Rule 16

As already noted, federal Rule 16 conditions prosecution discovery upon reciprocal defense discovery; under it there is no need for a motion or court order to obtain discovery; however, discovery is only available if the expert information is material and/or is intended to be used as evidence.[41] The following categorization of states was determined essentially on the basis of whether or not two of the three elements were adopted. Specifically, if the state's provisions contained a reciprocity clause (defendant triggered) and no motion of the court was required to obtain discovery, then the state was considered to be following the current Rule 16.

Of the states surveyed, eleven have that particular combination of these two elements. They are Alabama, Delaware (Superior Court), Florida, New Jersey, North Carolina, North Dakota, Ohio, Rhode Island, South Carolina, South Dakota and Tennessee.[42] They do differ, however, as to whether or not intention to introduce must be shown. Rhode Island limits both the prosecution and defense to discovering expert information which the opponent intends to introduce at trial.[43] Dela-

41. Effective Jan. 1, 1991, Alabama adopted discovery rules modeled on current Federal Rule 16 but specifically chose to omit the defendant-triggered reciprocity element. The Committee Comments to Ala. R.Crim.P. 16.2 explain that it "is different from the federal rule in that it does not condition the state's right to discovery upon the defendant's request for discovery. It also eliminates the need for the state to prove that the objects sought are material." In discussing the mutual abilities of the parties regarding reports of examinations and tests, the Comment states: "Section (c) provides for discovery by the state similar to that allowed to the defendant.... The same reasoning applies. The state should have a pretrial opportunity to examine and challenge expert reports of the defendant which will be introduced into evidence."

42. Ala.R.Crim.P. 16 (effective 1991); Del.Sup.Ct.Crim.R. 16; West's Fla.Crim. R.Proc. 3.220; N.J.Crim.Prac.R. 3:13–3; N.C.Gen.Stat. § 15A–903(e) (amended effective 1983) & § 15A–905(b) (1987); N.D.R.Crim.P. 16; Ohio Crim.R.Proc. 16; R.I.Sup.Ct.R.Crim.P. 16; S.C.R.Crim.P. 5

(effective 1988); S.D.C.L. Ch. 23A–13 (added 1978) (1988 Revision); Tenn.R.Crim.P. 16.

In 1989, Delaware Superior Court Criminal Rule 16(g) was added, providing that the parties file with the court a "Notice of Service" containing (1) certification that request or response was served and (2) the date and manner of service. Cf. Rose v. State, 542 A.2d 1196 (Del.1988) (requirement of strict compliance with rule—motion not filed with court). See also, State v. Payne, 791 S.W.2d 10 (Tenn.1990) (no evidence of the state acting in bad faith or of prejudice to murder defendant where state did not learn of, or notify defendant of, drug paraphernalia found on defendant upon arrest, until a week and a half before trial; remedy for any non-compliance with Rule 16 is within the trial court's discretion, and its refusal to exclude evidence was not error).

43. For a Rhode Island case dealing with defendant's discovery of test results and scientific reports which the state has prepared, see, State v. Faraone, 425 A.2d 523 (R.I.1981).

ware, Ohio, North Carolina and Tennessee require that the defendant intend to use the information at trial before the prosecution may obtain discovery. South Carolina and South Dakota also impose this intent requirement on the prosecution, but the defendant too has a hurdle to overcome. Similar to current Federal Rule 16, the rules in these two states condition the defendant's right to inspect or copy results of examinations or scientific tests on the evidence being either material to the preparation of the defense or being intended for use by the prosecution as evidence in chief at trial.[44] South Dakota's reciprocity element is triggered by the prosecution's compliance with the defendant's request, not by the request alone.[45] In Florida and New Jersey neither the prosecution nor the defense is limited by the "intend to use" requirement.

Considering the practical consequences, two of the aforementioned states, North Carolina and Ohio, can be characterized as following the current Rule 16 mold with respect to not requiring motions for discovery. Although each one provides that upon motion of the other party, the court *"shall"* or *"must"* order disclosure, the court actually has no discretion to deny discovery.[46]

(ii) State Provisions Patterned After Pre–1974 Federal Rule

As previously noted, the main difference between the pre–1974 and the current federal Rule 16 is the need originally for a motion and court order to obtain discovery. Several states still follow the pre–1974 federal expert criminal discovery rule. Thus it is beneficial to view the motion and non-motion rules separately. Concentration will be upon those states which view the main elements of expert criminal discovery in a manner similar to the former Rule 16, which conditioned the prosecution discovery upon reciprocal defense discovery, but required a motion by the requesting party to obtain expert information before trial. In addition to these two characteristics, pre–1974 Rule 16 also had a requirement that only the prosecution had to show that the defendant intended to introduce the expert information at trial before it could be discovered. In contrast, the defendant had to indicate that the scientific or medical reports were "made in connection with the particular case" but did not have to show intent to introduce. Under the current rule, the defendant has an alternative showing to make—that the expert

---

44. South Carolina's Criminal Procedure Rule 5 (effective 9/1/1988) contains the language of S.C.Crim.Prac.R. 8, which is discussed in State v. Riddle, 291 S.C. 232, 353 S.E.2d 138 (1987) and State v. Patterson, 290 S.C. 523, 351 S.E.2d 853 (1986).

45. S.D.C.L. Ch. 23A–13–12 (1978). For a South Dakota case supporting liberal construction of discovery statute, see State v. Catch the Bear, 352 N.W.2d 640 (S.D. 1984).

46. The court may, however, refuse to order particular discovery despite motion by counsel; see, e.g., State v. Tucker, 329 N.C. 709, 407 S.E.2d 805 (1991) (approving trial court's refusal to issue order for hair samples of murder defendant's companion) and State v. Jones, 85 N.C.App. 56, 354 S.E.2d 251 (1987) (finding reversible error where trial court failed to conduct in camera inspection of "electronic surveillance" in prosecution's possession, prior to denying defendant's motion for such evidence).

information sought from the government is material to the preparation of his case or is intended to be introduced by the prosecution. Thus, while the current rule might be more restrictive in appearance, from a practical viewpoint the two versions of Rule 16 are similar on the element of intent to introduce. This is so because normally expert information, if made in connection with the case, will be material to the defense.

Eight of the states surveyed, with some minor language variations, have adopted the pre–1974 Rule 16. That is, those states require reciprocity, a formal motion for court ordered discovery, and a showing by the prosecution of the defense intent to introduce the scientific evidence before allowing expert criminal discovery. These states are Iowa, Kansas, Kentucky, Louisiana, Massachusetts, Nebraska, New York, and Wyoming.[47] Although most state rules provide that upon motion to the court the judge shall order discovery, the Iowa and the Massachusetts rules expressly state that granting motions for expert discovery is within the court's discretion.[48]

As with all discovery provisions, court interpretation can strongly influence what practice is followed under a given rule. For example, in Kentucky, the motion by a defendant for discovery of the prosecution's expert evidence should almost automatically be granted.[49] This follows from James v. Commonwealth,[50] where the Supreme Court of Kentucky chastised the prosecution for not releasing the reports of a chemist in a narcotics case. The court stated: "A cat and mouse game whereby the Commonwealth is permitted to withhold important information requested by the accused cannot be countenanced." [51] If similar logic applies to

47. Iowa Sup.Ct.Rules 13; Kan.Crim. Code & Code of Crim.Proc., § 22–3212 (Vernon) (1981); Ky.R.Crim.Proc. 7.24; L.S.A.–C.Cr.P. arts. 716–729.6 (added 1977); Mass.R.Crim.P. 14; Neb.Rev.Stat. §§ 29–1912 & 1916 (1943); N.Y.—McKinney's Crim.Proc.L. §§ 240.20 & 240.30 (1986); Wyo.R.Crim.P. 18.

48. Iowa Sup.Ct.Rule 13b: Discretionary discovery. Upon defense motion, the court may order the prosecution to permit the defendant to inspect physical medical evidence; Mass.R.Crim.P., 14a: "Upon motion of a defendant, the judge may issue an order of discovery ..."

The Iowa court has gone so far as to say that even in the absence of such statutory authority, courts have inherent power to compel disclosure of state's evidence when necessary in the interest of justice. State v. Gabrielson, 464 N.W.2d 434 (Iowa 1990). Further, the court has broad power to sanction where discovery orders are not complied with: State v. Longstreet, 407 N.W.2d 591 (Iowa 1987) (court has authority to continue trial and thereby retain defendants in jail indefinitely to compel compli-

ance with an order requiring handwriting exemplars).

49. Perhaps the nature of the case can affect the court's willingness to automatically grant such defense motions. In Gale v. State, 792 P.2d 570 (Wyo.1990), the charge was the taking of indecent liberties with a minor. The Wyoming court held the defendant was not denied a fair trial, and the trial court did not abuse its discretion in denying the defendant's motion to compel production of summaries of the testimony potential state expert witnesses might give at trial.

50. 482 S.W.2d 92 (Ky.1972).

51. Id. at 94. But see, for more recent explication of the Kentucky court's view as to the scope of the accused's entitlement, Bussey v. Commonwealth, 697 S.W.2d 139 (Ky.1985) (in prosecution for attempted sodomy of daughter, defendant was not entitled to disclosure of psychiatric files of defendant's son where psychiatrist's testimony was not based on the contents of those files) and Milburn v. Commonwealth, 788 S.W.2d 253 (Ky.1989) (defendant not

disclosure by the defense experts, then the discovery rule in Kentucky is more closely akin to the current Rule 16 which requires no court order.

Four of the surveyed states, while following the pre–1974 model in adopting reciprocity and the need for a motion, open discovery further than the former federal rule by deleting the requirement that the prosecution discover only what the defendant intends to introduce. These states are Arkansas, Delaware (Common Pleas), Nevada, and Virginia.[52] Although there is no intent requirement in Arkansas and Nevada, those states do require that the prosecution show the expert information sought is material to the preparation of the state's case.[53] Virginia, while adopting requirements similar to pre–1974 Rule 16, lists specific types of scientific tests and reports which may be discovered. This list includes autopsies, firearms identification tests, fingerprint examination, hand writing examinations, and blood, urine, and breath tests. The Virginia rule provides for an expansion of what may be discovered by the appendage of "other scientific reports."

(iii) State Provisions Patterned After the ABA Standards

Several states follow the expert criminal discovery procedure in the ABA Standards. The key difference between the Standards and federal Rule 16 is the absence in the former of prosecutorial discovery based upon reciprocity. Under the ABA type provisions, the prosecutor has a right to obtain discovery of defense expert information independent of what the defendant does. Also, in the Standards there is a need for only the prosecution to seek a court order to obtain discovery and neither the prosecution nor the defense must show that the other intends to introduce the expert information at trial to discover that material. Of the states surveyed, fourteen have adopted the key ABA element of no reciprocity. Among those there is a variety of viewpoints on the other elements.

Regarding the requirement that one or both of the parties move the court to obtain discovery, eight of these fourteen states follow the Standards in requiring a court order only with regard to prosecution discovery. These states are Alaska, Colorado, Illinois, Maine, Missouri, New Mexico, Vermont, and Washington.[54] Missouri's Rule 25 lists

---

entitled to advance notice of firearms examiner's testimony as far as its being consistent with certain findings in his report, where the report was made available to the defendant prior to trial, and where the opinion was drawn directly from the findings in the report).

52. Ark.Stats. § 43–2011.2 (Supp.1981); Del.Ct.Comm.Pl.Crim.R. 16; Nev.Rev.Stat. 174.235 and 174.255 (1986); Va.R.Sup.Ct. 3A: 14; Delaware's Superior Court Rules follow the current Fed.R.Crim.P. 16.

53. Arkansas cases dealing with the scope of required disclosure by the prosecution are Yates v. State, 303 Ark. 79, 794 S.W.2d 133 (1990) (state's obligation to disclose polygraph exam materials) and Alford v. State, 291 Ark. 243, 724 S.W.2d 151 (1987) (witness statements).

54. Alaska R.Crim.P. 16; Colo. R.Crim.P. 16; Ill.—S.H.A. ch. 110A, ¶¶ 412 and 413 (1934); Me.R.Crim.P. 16; Mo. R.Crim.P. 25.03 and 25.05; N.M.R.Crim.P. (Dist.Ct.) 27 and 28; Vt.R.Crim.P. 16; Wash.Crim.Rules (Sup.Ct.) 4.7.

For a history of Colo.R.Crim.P. 16, see, People v. Adams County Court, 767 P.2d 802 (Colo.App.1988). Several states, in-

general discoverable evidence which is available without a court order and further provides that upon a showing of good cause, either party can make a written motion asking the court to order other discovery. The Illinois provision is somewhat confusing since it says that the state shall disclose "upon written motion of defense counsel" but the motion apparently need only be directed as a request to the prosecution, not as a formal motion to the court. Also, in Illinois, for the prosecution to discover defense expert information, it must file a written motion with the court. However, once this motion is filed, the rule states the trial court *shall* require disclosure of that material. Thus, in practice, since there is no court discretion to refuse expert discovery, Illinois could be viewed as a state requiring neither side to obtain court approval for criminal discovery. This would be an expansion of the ABA Standards' language, although it might better accomplish the ABA's goal to ensure "the encouragement of full and free discovery applies equally to both sides of criminal cases." [55]

At least one state, Wisconsin,[56] seems to tighten the basic ABA approach by requiring both prosecution and defense to move the court to order discovery.

Five of the fourteen states following the ABA Standards' rejection of reciprocity require no motion for either side to obtain expert information. Four of these states are Arizona, Maryland, Minnesota and Oregon.[57] This is the furthest any jurisdiction has gone to date in adopting a system requiring disclosure of specific information as opposed to civil

cluding Washington, Maine and Missouri, provide that upon the prosecution's motion, the court can order the defendant to submit to various kinds of testing (e.g., voice exemplar, hair sample, line-up). For other general discovery, the prosecution need only make a written request to the defendant.

55. See, Standards, supra note 38 at 3 (Amending Supplement).

56. Wis.Stat.Ann. 971.23 (West) (1957). Subsections 971.23(4), (5) provide in part that: "On motion of a party" the court may order production of scientific evidence for inspection or testing "which is intended to be introduced at trial." Once a discovery scheduling order has been issued, the court has discretion in sanctioning for non-compliance. See, State v. Wild, 146 Wis.2d 18, 429 N.W.2d 105 (App.1988) (abuse of discretion where trial court excluded state medical evidence for failure to comply with terms of order in murder prosecution).

57. Ariz.R.Crim.P. 15.1, 15.2 (amended effective 1991); Md.R.Crim. Causes 4–263 (Michie's) (Supp.1992); Minn.R.Crim.P. 9.01, 9.02; Or.Rev.Stat. 135.815, 135.835 (1983).

The Arizona rule requires automatic disclosure by the state of specific information no later than ten days after arraignment; the defense has twenty days from arraignment to provide the state with the names of experts the defense will call, together with results and/or reports produced by the experts in connection with the case. While a request alone triggers disclosure obligations of the parties in Minnesota, a motion is required of the prosecution if it wishes the court to order the defendant to be examined or give bodily samples for testing. See note 53, supra. For recent Maryland cases construing Rule 4–263, see, Brown v. State, 85 Md.App. 523, 584 A.2d 164 (1991) and Parham v. State, 79 Md.App. 152, 556 A.2d 280 (1989). Subsections 4–263(b)(4) and (d)(2) deal specifically with reports or statements of experts. In State ex rel. Upham v. Bonebrake, 303 Or. 361, 736 P.2d 1020 (1987), the Oregon court discusses the automatic disclosure obligations of the prosecution.

The rejection of reciprocity, i.e., defendant triggered discovery, is permissible under Wardius v. Oregon, supra note 20, since the defendant's right to discovery remains equal to the prosecutor's.

type discovery. The fifth state, Idaho,[58] slightly modifies this version of the ABA Standards. The Idaho rule merely requires a written request to obtain general pretrial expert discovery of reports of examinations and tests or police reports.[59] However, if the defense has "substantial need in the preparation of the case" for additional material not otherwise covered by the rule, upon motion of the defendant, the court in its discretion can permit discovery of the material.

Regarding the intent element, although the revised ABA Standards deleted the need for the prosecution to show that the defendant intended to introduce the expert information at trial, nine of the fourteen states which agree with the ABA on the reciprocity element have retained or reinstated the intent element for prosecutorial discovery. These are Alaska, Arizona, Idaho, Maine, Minnesota, Missouri, New Mexico, Vermont, and Washington.[60] Two states, Wisconsin and Oregon, added requirements of intent to introduce as a condition for discovery by either defense or prosecution. This is even more restrictive than what the ABA originally proposed. Two states, Colorado and Illinois have not reinstated the intent element in the provision for expert discovery from the defense. Colorado adopted the revised standards verbatim.

(iv) Other State Provisions

Of the states surveyed, several did not fit the patterns of the general models. Four states allow discovery of expert information only by the defendant. They are Connecticut, Georgia, Texas, and West Virginia.[61] West Virginia has simply adopted one-half of the former Federal Rule 16.[62] Thus, upon motion, the court may order the prosecution to

58. Idaho R.Crim.Prac. and Proc. 16b and 16c.

59. For judicial interpretation of the scope of disclosure to ensue upon request, see State v. Thompson, 119 Idaho 67, 803 P.2d 973 (1989) (state failed to comply with Rule 16 by not turning over test results obtained by state's agents, employees or witnesses, as the defense had requested).

60. See footnotes 41–56, supra. Vermont adds that if the court orders discovery of the defendant's experts it should protect against disclosing the work product of the defendant's attorney or agents. V.R.C.P. 16.1(b). It does not appear that Vermont is attempting to resurrect the argument that the work product privilege applies to exclude expert information. Rather, it seems that the added phrase is merely to protect any collateral observations or advice the expert might have offered when examining the evidence.

The Washington Supreme Court addressed the give-and-take nature of its discovery rule and how the intent requirement helps to balance prosecutorial and defense

obligations in State v. Pawlyk, 115 Wash.2d 457, 800 P.2d 338 (1990) (disclosure of mental exam results was not required of defendant raising insanity defense where defendant did not intend to call the psychiatrist as a witness).

As above noted, this intent requirement should help protect information which might be covered by constitutional limitations.

61. Conn.Gen.Stat.Ann.   § 54–86a (1958); Official Code Ga.Ann. § 17–7–210 (1981); Vernon's Ann.Tex.Code Crim.Proc. Art. 39.14 (1979); W.Va.Code, 62–1B–2, 62–1B–4 (1989 Repl.Vol.).

62. For a West Virginia case showing the court's criteria in determining whether the state's delay in disclosure warranted exclusion of the expert evidence at trial, see, State v. Shugars, 180 W.Va. 280, 376 S.E.2d 174 (1988) (tests performed by state's accident reconstruction expert were properly admitted even though not disclosed to the defendant until one week before trial).

disclose expert information. The Texas rule provides that the state must produce documents and papers constituting material evidence upon a showing of good cause.[63] The Georgia rule states that the defendant is entitled to a copy of any written scientific report that the prosecution intends to introduce at trial [64], however, "written scientific report" has been given a fairly narrow interpretation.[65] The Connecticut rule allows discovery by the defendant, but only for medical reports.[66] However, the Connecticut rule adds that the court might allow a subsequent discovery motion upon a showing that the interests of justice will be served.[67]

The rules of five states allow some type of expert discovery to both the defense and prosecution but do so in a unique way. Indiana employs a system of reciprocal depositions which apparently may be used for discovery purposes.[68] The state and the defendant may take and use depositions of witnesses in accord with the Indiana Rules of Trial Procedure. Rule 35 provides particularly for discovery of court-ordered medical examinations and for discovery of the examining physician's

---

63. Interpreting the statutory requirements, see, Vasquez Garza v. State, 794 S.W.2d 530 (Tex.App.1990); Nowling v. State, 801 S.W.2d 182 (Tex.App.1990) (materiality requirement in a drug possession case—defendant's absolute right to an independent examination of the drugs); Crane v. State, 786 S.W.2d 338 (Tex.Crim.App. 1990) (once defendant's motion has been granted, disclosure obligation is a continuing burden).

64. The intent of the legislature to limit the scope of pretrial expert discovery in criminal cases may be seen in their rejection of a bill which provided much broader discovery rights for defendants. The rejected bill stated that the defendant was entitled to reports or statements of experts, including results of scientific tests, experiments or comparisons. See, Hartley v. State, 159 Ga.App. 157, 282 S.E.2d 684 (1981). But see, Taylor v. State, 172 Ga. App. 408, 323 S.E.2d 212 (1984) (court committed error where it permitted defense counsel only five minutes to read report of polygraph test, where defendant had objected to allowing the evidence since a timely request had been made and no report of the results had been furnished).

65. See, e.g., Conklin v. State, 254 Ga. 558, 331 S.E.2d 532 (1985), cert. denied 474 U.S. 1038 (1985) (a death certificate is not a scientific report which the state must furnish the defendant pursuant to Section 17–7–211); Johnson v. State, 174 Ga.App. 579, 330 S.E.2d 791 (1985) (operating record for a photoelectric intoximeter not a scientific report); Griffin v. State, 183 Ga.App. 386, 358 S.E.2d 917 (1987) (latent fingerprint card which had to be interpreted by a testifying police officer in order to attain signifi-

cance not a scientific report); Conyers v. State, 260 Ga. 506, 397 S.E.2d 423 (1990) (emergency room record containing a physician's notes of defendant's inculpatory statement did not constitute a scientific report subject to discovery); but see, Paggett v. State, 188 Ga.App. 174, 372 S.E.2d 504 (1988) (emergency room report is a "written scientific report" though not specifically mentioned in the statute).

66. For a Connecticut case addressing "discovery" of court-appointed psychiatric expert evidence and whether such a psychiatrist acts as an agent of the state, see, State v. Johnson, 14 Conn.App. 586, 543 A.2d 740 (1988), cert. denied 209 Conn. 804, 548 A.2d 440 (1988).

67. See, State v. Whitaker, 202 Conn. 259, 520 A.2d 1018 (1987) (discussing lack of prosecutorial discovery, as well as the constitutional and societal interests affecting the criminal discovery process).

68. West's Ann.Ind.Code 37–4–3 (effective 1982); see, e.g., Gossmeyer v. State, 482 N.E.2d 239 (Ind.1985) (trial court properly ordered deposition of confidential informant by defense counsel). In Hutchinson v. State, 477 N.E.2d 850 (Ind.1985), the court had discretion to order a handwriting exemplar where it determined that such would aid the handwriting expert in testifying, even though there may have been other samples of the defendant's handwriting available. For a case discussing the three major criteria a court should consider in deciding questions regarding the scope of discovery by a criminal defendant, see, Rowe v. State, 262 Ind. 250, 314 N.E.2d 745 (1974).

written report. Montana allows either party to request production of all documents, papers, or other materials which either party intends to introduce into evidence.[69] The statute states that if the evidence refers to scientific tests or experiments, the opposing party may observe the examination and inspect the results, if practicable. In Pennsylvania, prosecutorial and defense discovery of expert testimony is governed by different standards.[70] Discovery by the defendant is mandatorily imposed upon the prosecution, while prosecutorial discovery is discretionary with the court. Upon request by the defendant, the state must disclose results or reports of scientific tests, expert opinions, or other physical or mental examinations subject only to any protective orders obtained by the state. Upon motion by the state, the court may allow discovery of the defense expert's information if he will be a witness at trial. Moreover, there is a reciprocity requirement: before the prosecution can obtain expert discovery, the defense must have requested the same.[71]

Mississippi's Criminal Rules of Circuit Court Practice 4.06 also has a reciprocity requirement with an unusual twist. Upon the defendant's written request, the prosecution must allow discovery of expert reports or statements; once this request is made by the defendant, his reciprocal duty automatically arises, and no request is required of the prosecution. Rule 16 of the Utah Rules of Criminal Procedure provides that the prosecution, upon the defendant's request, shall disclose, among other things, any item of evidence "which the court determines on good cause shown should be made available to the defendant in order for the defendant to adequately prepare his defense."[72]

D. States Without Statutory Discovery Rules

Five states, while not enacting statutory systems of expert criminal discovery, have allowed such discovery in varying degrees by court decision. They are: California, Hawaii, Michigan, New Hampshire and Oklahoma. The courts of those states reason that "Legislative silence on criminal discovery, ... means that it has left to the courts the adaptation of common law concepts."[73] The degree of expert discovery

---

69. Mont.Code Ann. 46–15–301, 302, and 303 were replaced in 1985 by Sections 46–15–321 through 46–15–329. The new law retains the substance of the repealed law but provides for expanded and expedited discovery. See also, Section 46–15–332. For a case upholding the constitutionality of Montana's reciprocal pretrial discovery statutes, see Carkulis v. District Ct., 229 Mont. 265, 746 P.2d 604 (1987).

70. Pa.R.Crim.P. 305.

71. See Rule 305(C)(2)(a), (b). See also, Commonwealth v. Miller, 385 Pa.Super. 186, 560 A.2d 229 (1989) (requirement that defendant first request item of information desired under mandatory discovery provi-

sions) and Commonwealth v. Faulkner, 528 Pa. 57, 595 A.2d 28 (1991) (ordering defendant to turn over to the prosecution defense psychiatric expert's reports before trial was reasonable where defendant had refused to be examined by the prosecution's psychiatric expert).

72. See, Cannon v. Keller, 692 P.2d 740 (Utah 1984) (state itself provided "good cause" necessary).

73. See, for example, Pitchess v. Superior Court, 11 Cal.3d 531, 536, 113 Cal.Rptr. 897, 900, 522 P.2d 305, 308 (1974). See also People v. Luttenberger, 50 Cal.3d 1, 265 Cal.Rptr. 690, 784 P.2d 633 (1990) (re-

allowed by the courts of these states varies from discovery being allowed routinely, to state courts which recognize discretionary discovery in theory but have rarely allowed such motions.

Oklahoma is apparently the most liberal of the states allowing discretionary expert discovery. In Wing v. State,[74] the court directly addressed the question of discovery of scientific reports and enunciated the following rule:

> As to pre-trial discovery and inspection of articles in the possession of prosecuting authorities, this Court has held there should be disclosure of technical reports, [and] an alleged death weapon with reports concerning same . . .[75]

The courts in California are somewhat less liberal in allowing criminal discovery, requiring the defendant to make a showing of need. In Pitchess v. Superior Court,[76] the court set forth the general standard used for criminal discovery by the defendant: "an accused in a criminal prosecution may compel discovery by demonstrating that the requested information will facilitate the ascertainment of the facts and a fair trial." [77] California also recognizes that pretrial discovery in criminal cases "should not be a one-way street" and has allowed the prosecution to discover expert reports of the defendant where expert evidence is intended to be introduced.[78] In 1981, in Holman v. Superior Court of Monterey City, a California court asserted that upon a showing that the information is "reasonably necessary," and in the absence of contrary legislation, the court has the power to order criminal discovery.[79] Thus, the court granted a motion seeking discovery of names and addresses of experts, and expert scientific and medical reports. The courts of Michigan and New Hampshire have employed similar reasoning.[80] Hawaii has

---

jecting federalization of state criminal discovery procedures) and Izazaga v. Superior Court, 54 Cal.3d 356, 285 Cal.Rptr. 231, 815 P.2d 304 (1991) (interplay between state constitutional privilege against self-incrimination and state constitutional provisions for reciprocal discovery). Due to the scarcity of case law in these states, portions of the following analysis are based upon cases which deal with criminal discovery generally rather than expert criminal discovery specifically.

74. 490 P.2d 1376 (Okl.Crim.App.1971), cert. denied 406 U.S. 919 (1972).

75. Id. at 1382 (footnotes omitted). Accord Hamm v. State, 516 P.2d 825 (Okl. Crim.App.1973) (lower court improperly denied defendant's pretrial motion to inspect ballistics report); Layman v. State, 355 P.2d 444 (Okl.Crim.App.1960); Amoco Production Co. v. Lindley, 609 P.2d 733 (Okl. 1980). See also, Allen v. District Ct., 803 P.2d 1164 (Okl.Crim.App.1990) (setting forth items state and defendant are required to disclose as well as sanctions available to court for non-compliance) and

Moore v. State, 740 P.2d 731 (Okl.Crim. App.1987) (prosecution's duty to disclose reports or statements made by expert, including results of examinations and scientific tests).

76. Pitchess v. Superior Court, supra note 73.

77. Id., 113 Cal.Rptr. at 901, 522 P.2d at 309; See also, People v. Municipal Ct., City and Cty. of San Francisco, 89 Cal. App.3d 739, 153 Cal.Rptr. 69 (1979).

78. Jones v. Superior Ct., 58 Cal.2d 56, 22 Cal.Rptr. 879, 881, 372 P.2d 919, 921 (1962). See also, In re Misener, 38 Cal.3d 543, 213 Cal.Rptr. 569, 698 P.2d 637 (1985) (factors for determining whether a particular demand for prosecutorial discovery should be allowed).

79. 29 Cal.3d 480, 174 Cal.Rptr. 506, 629 P.2d 14 (1981).

80. *Michigan:* People v. Maranian, 359 Mich. 361, 368, 102 N.W.2d 568, 571 (1960): "Discovery will be ordered in all criminal

also allowed the trial court to grant some pretrial discovery.[81] However, the Hawaii Supreme Court has been restrictive in allowing pretrial discovery to the defendant and has broadly excluded all discovery of prosecution witnesses.[82]

§ 1.12 Procedures Relevant to Discovery

As already noted, the federal system and most states have adopted provisions specifically dealing with pretrial discovery of expert information. These rules and statutes contain their own procedures for obtaining discovery which normally consist of written request to the other party or motions to the court. However, for some of the discovery rule states, and for all of those following a case-by-case approach, pretrial procedures which have traditionally involved discovery are relevant.

1. DEPOSITIONS

Virtually all modern criminal discovery rules do not allow civil type depositions of an opponent's expert witness. Rather, specific disclosure of test results and reports is mandated. Such a system is intended to

cases, when, in the sound discretion of the trial judge, the thing to be inspected is admissible in evidence and a failure of justice may result from its suppression." Accord: People v. Brocato, 17 Mich.App. 277, 169 N.W.2d 483 (1969); Commonwealth v. Lewinski, 367 Mass. 889, 329 N.E.2d 738 (1975); People v. Lynn, 91 Mich.App. 117, 283 N.W.2d 664 (1979); People v. Graham, 173 Mich.App. 473, 434 N.W.2d 165 (1988).

New Hampshire: State v. Superior Court, 102 N.H. 224, 229, 153 A.2d 403, 406–07 (1959): "We do not hold the Court to be without power, in the exercise of reasonable discretion and to prevent manifest injustice, to require the production of specific objects or writings for inspection under appropriate safeguards and at a time appropriately close to the time of trial, if it should appear that otherwise essential rights of the respondents may be endangered or the trial unnecessarily prolonged ... Justice might be thought to require that a respondent be permitted to inspect the corpse of a victim or an autopsy report." Also see, State v. LaRose, 127 N.H. 146, 497 A.2d 1224 (1985) (trial court has authority to exercise its sound discretion in matters relating to pretrial discovery); State v. Miskell, 122 N.H. 842, 451 A.2d 383 (1982) (though control of discovery is within trial court's discretion, court must be careful to protect legitimate interests of the prosecutrix as embodied in the rape-shield statute); State v. Sargent, 104 N.H. 211, 182 A.2d 607, 609 (1962) (plea must be entered before "motions to take depositions or for discovery may be entertained. What justice may then re-

quire is ordinarily a question for the court which tries the case."); and State v. Osborne, 119 N.H. 427, 402 A.2d 493, 498 (1979) (the trial court afforded "ample pretrial discovery including a motion for mental observation, a motion to take depositions of prosecution witnesses and a motion to produce photos and physical evidence.")

81. State v. Kahinu, 53 Hawaii 536, 498 P.2d 635 (1972), cert. denied 409 U.S. 1126 (1973). See also, State ex rel. Marsland v. Ames, 71 Hawaii 304, 788 P.2d 1281 (1990) (interpreting Penal Procedure Rule 16) and State v. Townsend, 7 Hawaii App. 560, 784 P.2d 881 (1989) (under Rule 16 governing disclosure, discovery is automatically available in felony cases, but in misdemeanor cases discovery is only available by the grace of the court's discretion, upon a showing of materiality and reasonableness).

82. Chung v. Lanham, 53 Hawaii 617, 620, 500 P.2d 565 (1972). The *Chung* majority felt constrained to strictly interpret Hawaii R.Crim.P. 17(h) as precluding discovery of prosecution witnesses before they testify at trial. This rule is a replica of the federal Jencks Act, 18 U.S.C.A. § 3500 (1970). The overlap of this act with discovery is discussed in § 1.13 infra. It is sufficient at this point to say that the Hawaii ruling was overbroad since Hawaii R.Crim.P. 16 permitted discovery of documents, books, etc. that were material to the defense. See pre–1966 Fed.R.Crim.P. 16. This overreaction was noted at 53 Hawaii 617, 621–22, 500 P.2d at 568–69 (Levinson, J. concurring and dissenting).

relieve experts from the burden of attending time consuming discovery sessions by instead making the basic information freely available.[1] At the same time, most jurisdictions having specific discovery provisions allow for witnesses to be deposed for the purpose of *preserving* their testimony rather than for discovery. These statutes and rules allow one party to depose a potential witness who is expected to be unavailable for trial because of death, infirmity, or absence from the jurisdiction.[2]

Florida, Iowa, Indiana, Nebraska, and possibly Missouri[3] seem to allow for discovery depositions of experts in addition to the specific information to be disclosed under the rules. Allowing full depositions raises the possibility that experts will be required to spend substantial amounts of time preparing for and undergoing discovery without reimbursement. This problem could be much more acute with experts who are retained by a defendant, since government experts are normally regular employees or at least in a position to request and obtain further fees for the extra time involved. Thus, experts for defendants, particularly experts appointed to assist indigent criminal defendants, may be subjected to economic harassment by a prosecutor seeking discovery depositions. If the expert were unable to be guaranteed reimbursement for discovery response time from the defendant, or from the court if appointed, experts might be reluctant to accept criminal defense work. In this regard, it should be pointed out that Florida and Missouri allow additional oral depositions for *defendants* only, whereas Iowa and Indiana allow depositions by the prosecution conditioned upon reciprocity. Thus, defense counsel in Iowa and Indiana should consider the effects of reciprocal discovery before moving to discover the prosecution's experts by deposition. Nebraska, however, allows either prosecution or defense to request the court to allow additional discovery by deposition if the pretrial oral examination would assist in the preparation of the case.

2. SUBPOENA DUCES TECUM

If permitted as part of the procedure accompanying the filing of a pretrial discovery motion or request for commission to take the deposition of a witness, counsel may require, by the service of a subpoena duces tecum, that an expert called to testify at the hearing on the motion or by deposition bring with him specified books, papers, documents or other things in his possession which are desired as evidence. The documents or objects sought by the subpoena duces tecum should be

§ 1.12

1. The hardship to a retained expert who must submit to extensive depositions and interrogatories is much greater than that on a lay witness who does not expect to be compensated for his time.

2. See, for example, Fed.R.Crim.P. 15; Vernon's Ann.Mo.Stat. § 545.380 (1987); 22 Okla.Stats.Ann. § 761 (1969), § 762 (eff. July 1, 1983). The 1983 Oklahoma statute expanded coverage of the rule from the previous one, which only allowed the defense to depose a potentially unavailable witness, to the present one which allows either side to depose any *material witness* who may potentially be unavailable.

3. West's Fla.Stats.Ann., Crim.Rule 3.220(d); Burns' Ann.Ind.Code, 35–37–4–3 wr971); 56 Iowa Code Ann. § 813.2, Rule 12 (1979) (amend. eff. July 1, 1985); Mo. R.Cr.P. 25.12 (West 1992); Neb.Rev.Stat. § 29–1917 (1979).

particularly described in it. Also, a party should be prepared to make a showing of materiality and relevance of the requested items. These latter requirements may be difficult to fulfill if the subpoenaing party is unaware of the contents of the requested item.

In jurisdictions with modern expert discovery provisions, the subpoena duces tecum will be of little use since those rules specifically state books, papers, reports, and other documents may be otherwise obtained. Thus, while there is often a subpoena duces tecum provision in those jurisdictions, such as Rule 17(c) of the Federal Rules of Criminal Procedure,[4] it is unlikely that the provision was intended to be used to expand upon the specific disclosure scheme set up in another part of the same document.

Some states, while not having adopted specific disclosure rules, do not allow a subpoena duces tecum to act as an expert discovery device. This refusal stems from a reluctance to allow discovery in criminal cases where none existed at common law and from a corresponding lack of legislative guidance.[5]

3. PRELIMINARY HEARING

In some jurisdictions the preliminary hearing offers the defense the first opportunity to discover the prosecution's case. Although the federal system is not such a jurisdiction, Rule 5(c) of the Federal Rules of Criminal Procedure is an example of a rule which allows the defendant to cross-examine witnesses against him and to introduce evidence in his own behalf during a preliminary hearing.

The burden at preliminary hearings is on the prosecution to introduce enough evidence to satisfy the examining court that there are reasonable grounds for believing that an offense has been committed by the accused.[6] This degree of proof is commonly referred to as probable cause. When present, it authorizes the examining court to hold the accused for grand jury consideration or further judicial proceedings.

Ordinarily, the preliminary hearing provides the defense with only a minimal opportunity to confront[7] and cross-examine prosecution witnesses.

Many jurisdictions are reluctant to allow the preliminary hearing to become a viable discovery device. In fact, courts indicate that the preliminary hearing is not intended to provide defendants with pretrial discovery, its primary purpose being to determine whether or not continued custody of the accused is justified by the facts. Thus, one state supreme court, while recognizing "that complete cross-examination and the opportunity to present affirmative defenses were crucial and neces-

---

4. See, United States v. Nixon, 418 U.S. 683, 698 (1974); Bowman Dairy Co. v. United States, 341 U.S. 214, 220 (1951).

5. State v. Superior Court, 102 N.H. 224, 153 A.2d 403 (1959).

6. Ex parte Schuber, 68 Cal.App.2d 424, 156 P.2d 944 (1945).

7. See, Pointer v. Texas, 380 U.S. 400 (1965).

sary to effectuate a true probable cause standard,"[8] refused to take the further step and hold that "the discovery and impeachment functions [of the preliminary hearing] are ends in themselves."[9]

4.　BILL OF PARTICULARS

The purpose of a bill of particulars is to apprise the defendant more specifically concerning the charge filed against him. Some degree of particularity in the charging instrument is required in order to enable him to prepare his defense, prevent surprise at trial, and protect him from being placed in double jeopardy for the same offense. Rule 7(f) of the Federal Rules of Criminal Procedure authorizes the trial court, at the defendant's request, to direct the government to file a bill of particulars. The power to order the filing of the bill is generally regarded as discretionary and not mandatory.[10] In addition to its discovery benefits, the bill of particulars restricts the government to the area prescribed in the bill.[11]

Some state jurisdictions have statutes which authorize the trial court to order the prosecution to furnish the defense with a bill of particulars containing information requested by the accused.[12] Other states do not recognize the bill of particulars.[13]

At its best, the bill of particulars does not provide the accused with a summary of the prosecution's evidence. The bill is discretionary, restricted in scope, and is generally limited to clarifying ambiguities in the indictment. Thus, it is unlikely that a significant amount of scientific evidence could be discovered through such a procedure.

§ 1.13　Disclosure at Trial

Of possible use in evaluating an expert's technique or prejudice is to obtain by motion the disclosure of any statements given to the government by the expert after his direct examination.

The Jencks Act[1] controls the federal procedure at the trial stage for the examination by the defendant of witness statements gathered by the government.[2] Under this rule, discovery is postponed until the govern-

---

8. Lataille v. District Court, 366 Mass. 525, 320 N.E.2d 877, 880 (1974).

9. 320 N.E.2d at 881. See also, Chung v. Ogata, 53 Hawaii 395, 495 P.2d 26 (1972).

10. See, Will v. United States, 389 U.S. 90 (1967). See also Annot. "Right of Accused to Bill of Particulars," 5 A.L.R.2d 444.

11. See, United States v. Murray, 297 F.2d 812 (2d Cir.1962), cert. denied 369 U.S. 828 (1962).

12. See, Fed.R.Crim.P. 7(f); 56 Iowa Code Ann. § 813.2, Rule 10(5) (eff. Jan. 1, 1978) (Supp.1984); A.L.M.Mass.R.Crim.P. 13(b) (eff. Jan. 1, 1979) (Supp.1984).

13. See, Annot., "Right of Accused to Bill of Particulars," 5 A.L.R. 444.

§ 1.13

1. 18 U.S.C.A. § 3500 (1976).

2. See, Palermo v. United States, 360 U.S. 343 (1959) upholding the constitutionality of the Jencks Act. See also, Scales v. United States, 367 U.S. 203 (1961), rehearing denied 366 U.S. 978 (1961).

ment witness has testified on direct examination.[3]

The test for examination of the witness statement under the Jencks Act is met by a showing that the statement relates to the subject matter about which the witness testified. The statute provides for a determination by the trial court of the relevancy of the document.[4] If the government chooses to withhold the witness statement in the public interest, the testimony of that witness is stricken from the record.[5] Whether or not the action should be dismissed is left to the trial court's discretion.

Some states have adopted a practice similar to the Jencks Act in governing the disclosure of witness statements.[6] Others leave the matter to the trial court's discretion.[7] The defense is still denied pretrial access to witness statements secured by investigators of the state,[8] but it may under proper circumstances gain access to the statements at trial.

After a state's witness has testified on direct examination, the defense attorney makes immediate demand on the prosecutor for all prior written statements of the witness for the purpose of determining their value for impeachment as prior inconsistent statements.[9] If the prosecutor indicates that he has no knowledge of such a statement, the witness may be asked if he ever made a written or oral statement or notes about the matter in question.

The test for disclosure in such instances may be more restrictive than the Jencks Act in that there may be a burden of showing inconsistencies between the pretrial statement and the trial testimony. This burden is sometimes dealt with by providing for an *in camera* inspection by the trial court to determine the existence of relevant inconsistencies.[10]

§ 1.14 Post–Trial Disclosure

In those jurisdictions which utilize a presentence investigation report as an aid in determining sentence, counsel should be aware of the practice regarding presentence discovery of such reports. Medical or

3. When successful in gaining disclosure of material during trial, it is a wise practice to approach the bench and ask the court for time to read the material and to make notes from it. Ordinarily, the court will require that the disclosed document be returned to the state before cross-examination resumes. Rather than trusting to memory in cross-examining the witness about the document, counsel may wish to record salient parts of it. Documentary evidence may be sought at trial by motion to produce and disclose made after the *direct* examination of the opposing witness.

4. 18 U.S.C.A. § 3500(b) (1976).

5. 18 U.S.C.A. § 3500(d) (1976).

6. Stout v. State, 244 Ark. 676, 426 S.W.2d 800 (1968), appeal after remand 246 Ark. 479, 438 S.W.2d 698 (1969), appeal after remand 247 Ark. 948, 448 S.W.2d 636 (1970); Ortega v. People, 162 Colo. 358, 426 P.2d 180 (1967); State v. Maluia, 56 Hawaii 428, 539 P.2d 1200 (1975); State v. Rosario, 9 N.Y.2d 286, 213 N.Y.S.2d 448, 173 N.E.2d 881 (1961); People v. Consolazio, 40 N.Y.2d 446, 387 N.Y.S.2d 62, 354 N.E.2d 801 (1976), cert. denied 433 U.S. 914 (1977).

7. See, State v. Jones, 202 Kan. 31, 446 P.2d 851 (1968).

8. See, Mattox v. State, 243 Miss. 402, 139 So.2d 653 (1962); Brenner v. State, 217 Tenn. 427, 398 S.W.2d 252 (1965).

9. See, 3 Wigmore, *Evidence,* §§ 1017–1046 (3rd ed. 1940); McCormick, *Evidence,* §§ 34–39 (1954).

10. See, State v. White, 15 Ohio St.2d 146, 239 N.E.2d 65 (1968); Moore v. State, 384 S.W.2d 141 (Tex.Crim.App.1964).

other expert reports might be relevant in the sentencing decision and counsel may want to have access to that information to prepare an argument for the court.

Rule 32(c)(2) of the Federal Rules of Criminal Procedure provides that the court may disclose to the defendant or his counsel, all or part of the material contained in the report of the presentence investigation. On its face, this rule makes disclosure discretionary rather than mandatory.[1]

There is considerable variation among the states. In some states presentence investigation reports are required in all felony cases. In others, it is left to the court's discretion whether to use a presentence report.[2] In some states the statutes provide for the mandatory use of the report in connection with certain dispositions such as probation cases, and the discretionary use of it in other cases.[3]

The constitutional issue of non-disclosure of the report has not been squarely decided.[4] Thus, the practice will vary according to the particular jurisdiction. Some commentators feel that the right of confrontation should be applied to the sentencing process and that, accordingly, a policy of disclosure should be adopted.[5]

IV. DISCOVERY AND DISCLOSURE IN CIVIL CASES

§ 1.15 General Considerations

Since the adoption by the Supreme Court of the Federal Rules of Civil Procedure in 1937,[1] and throughout its amendments, discovery has become an important part of the civil litigation process. It replaced pleadings as the primary means by which parties learned of some factual information and formulated issues in the case. When it comes to discovery of experts, and information held by them, two opposing views have traditionally been advocated. The first view is that which favors liberal discovery, leading to a narrowing of the triable issues prior to trial and the avoidance of surprise at the trial. The opposing view regards the retention and consultation of experts by an attorney as part

---

§ 1.14

1. See, United States v. Crutcher, 405 F.2d 239 (2d Cir.1968), cert. denied 394 U.S. 908 (1969); United States v. Weiner, 376 F.2d 42 (3d Cir.1967); Roeth v. United States, 380 F.2d 755 (5th Cir.1967), cert. denied 390 U.S. 1015 (1968); Hoover v. United States, 268 F.2d 787 (10th Cir. 1959).

2. E.g., Minn.R.Crim.P. 27.02(3).

3. See, Ohio Rev.Code § 2951.03 (1975) and Ohio Crim.Rules 32.2(c)(1).

4. See, Williams v. New York, 337 U.S. 241 (1949); but see, Townsend v. Burke,

334 U.S. 736 (1948). See also Woodson v. North Carolina, 428 U.S. 280 (1976).

5. See, Lehrich, "The Use and Disclosure of Presentence Reports in the United States," 47 F.R.D. 225 (1969).

§ 1.15

1. The rules first went into effect in 1938. See, McLaughlin, "Discovery and Admissibility of Expert Testimony," 63 *Notre Dame L.Rev.* 760 (1988), for discussion of the historical developments leading to the current rule affecting experts.

of a professional and competent pre-trial preparation that should be kept confidential; to do otherwise would be to reward the incompetent and less resourceful advocate. Adherents of this latter view suggest various rationales for prohibiting discovery of information in the possession of the expert: (1) an expert who is consulted in preparation of trial gains knowledge about the case that should be covered by the attorney-client privilege; (2) even if the expert's knowledge is not within the evidentiary privilege, it should nevertheless come under the "work product" rule; and (3) to permit an opponent to discover information collected at great expense and with considerable resourcefulness is unjust.

The modern view, exemplified by the Federal Rules of Civil Procedure provisions on discovery, have taken the position favoring discovery, and have sought to prevent abuses and exploitation by provisions permitting the courts to issue protective orders and direct the demanding attorneys to make payment of fees and expenses to the party retaining the expert. In 1993 the discovery rules were further amended to require voluntary disclosures about experts and others without a prior demand at a very early stage in the pre-trial period. Most state discovery rules are patterned upon the federal rules.[2] For that reason, only the federal rules will be covered herein.

§ 1.16 Scope of Expert Witness Discovery in Civil Cases Under Federal Rule 26

Significant and massive changes in Federal Rule 26 and other Rules of Civil Procedure occurred when the United States Judicial Conference, last year, recommended a new version of, inter alia, the discovery provisions that apply to expert testimony. On April 23, 1993, the United States Supreme Court's majority sent these recommended amendments to Congress, without suggesting further changes. Since Congress did not act to override these changes by December 1, 1993, the rules automatically became effective on that date.

To summarize the most important change, it should be noted that as of December 1, 1993, litigants must disclose to their opponent, without being asked to do so, three types of essential information about the pending litigation: (1) disclosures that must be made initially; (2) disclosures related to experts involved in the case; and (3) other pre-trial disclosures.

The new Rule 26 provides:

"Rule 26. General Provisions Concerning Discovery; Duty of Disclosure

(a) Required Disclosures; Methods to Discover Additional Matter.

---

2. At least, they were patterned upon Federal Rule 26 as it existed prior to the 1993 amendments. For a list of states with identical or similar discovery provisions relating to expert witnesses as the rule exist- ed until 1993, see Note, "Rule 26(b)(4) of the Federal Rules of Civil Procedure: Discovery of Expert Information," 42 *U.Miami L.Rev.* 1101 (1988).

(1) Initial Disclosures. Except to the extent otherwise stipulated or directed by order or local rule, a party shall, without awaiting a discovery request, provide to other parties:

(A) the name and, if known, the address and telephone number of each individual likely to have discoverable information relevant to disputed facts alleged with particularity in the pleadings, identifying the subjects of the information;

(B) a copy of, or a description by category and location of, all documents, data compilations, and tangible things in the possession, custody, or control of the party that are relevant to disputed facts alleged with particularity in the pleadings;

(C) a computation of any category of damages claimed by the disclosing party, . . .

(D) for inspection and copying as under Rule 34 any insurance agreement . . .

Unless otherwise stipulated or directed by the court, these disclosures shall be made at or within 10 days after the meeting under subdivision (f). A party shall make its initial disclosures based on the information then reasonably available to it and is not excused from making its disclosures because it has not fully completed its investigation of the case or because it challenges the sufficiency of another party's disclosures or because another party has not made its disclosures.

(2) Disclosure of Expert Testimony.

(A) In addition to the disclosures required by paragraph (1), a party shall disclose to other parties the identity of any person who may be used at trial to present evidence under Rules 702, 703, or 705 of the Federal Rules of Evidence.

(B) Except as otherwise stipulated or directed by the court, this disclosure shall, with respect to a witness who is retained or specially employed to provide expert testimony in the case or whose duties as an employee of the party regularly involve giving expert testimony, be accompanied by a written report and signed by the witness. The report shall contain a complete statement of all opinions to be expressed and the basis and reasons therefor; the data or other information considered by the witness in forming the opinions; any exhibits to be used as a summary of or support for the opinions; the qualifications of the witness, including a list of all publications authored by the witness within the preceding ten years; the compensation to be paid for the study and testimony; and a listing of any other cases in which the witness has testified as an expert at trial or by deposition within the preceding four years.

(C) These disclosures shall be made at the times and in the sequence directed by the court. In the absence of other directions from the court or stipulation by the parties, the disclosures shall be made at least 90 days before the trial date or the date the case is to be ready for trial or, if the evidence is intended solely to contradict or rebut evidence on the same subject matter identified by another party under paragraph (2)(B), within 30 days after the disclosure made by the other party.   The parties shall supplement these disclosures when required under subdivision (e)(1).

(3) Pretrial Disclosures.   In addition to the disclosures required in the preceding paragraphs, a party shall provide to other parties the following information regarding the evidence that it may present at trial other than solely for impeachment purposes:

(A) the name and, if not previously provided, the address and telephone number of each witness, separately identifying those whom the party expects to present and those whom the party may call if the need arises;

(B) the designation of those witnesses whose testimony is expected to be presented by means of a deposition and, if not taken stenographically, a transcript of the pertinent portion of the deposition testimony; and

(C) an appropriate identification of each document or other exhibit, including summaries of other evidence, separately identifying those which the party expects to offer and those which the party may offer if the need arises.

Unless otherwise directed by the court, these disclosures shall be made at least 30 days before trial.   Within 14 days thereafter, unless a different time is specified by the court, a party may serve and file a list disclosing (i) any objections to the use under Rule 32(a) of a deposition designated by another party under subparagraph (B) and (ii) any objection, together with the grounds therefor, that may be made to the admissibility of materials identified under subparagraph (C).   Objections not so disclosed, other than objections under Rules 402 and 403 of the Federal Rules of Evidence, shall be deemed waived unless excused by the court for good cause shown.

(4) Form of Disclosure; Filing.   Unless otherwise directed by order or local rule, all disclosures under paragraphs (1) through (3) shall be made in writing, signed, served, and promptly filed with the court.

(5) Methods to Discover Additional Matter.   Parties may obtain discovery by one or more of the following methods: depositions upon oral examination or written questions; written interrogatories; production of documents or things or permission to enter upon land or other property under Rule 34 or 45(a)(1)(c), for inspection and other purposes; physical and mental examinations; and requests for admission.

(b) Discovery Scope and Limits

* * *

(2) Limitations. By order or by local rule, the court may alter the limits in these rules or the number of depositions and interrogatories and may also limit the length of depositions under Rule 30 and the number of requests under Rule 36. The frequency or extent of use of the discovery methods otherwise permitted under these rules and by any local rule shall be limited by the court if it determines that: (i) the discovery sought is unreasonably cumulative or duplicative, or is obtainable from some other source that is more convenient, less burdensome, or less expensive; (ii) the party seeking discovery has had ample opportunity by discovery in the action to obtain the information sought; or (iii) the burden and expense of the proposed discovery outweighs its likely benefit, taking into account the needs of the case, the amount in controversy, the parties' resources, the importance of the issues at stake in the litigation, and the importance of the proposed discovery in resolving the issues. The court may act upon its own initiative after reasonable notice or pursuant to a motion under subdivision (c).

* * *

(4) Trial Preparation. Experts.

(A) A party may depose any person who has been identified as an expert whose opinions may be presented at trial. If a report from the expert is required under subdivision (a)(2)(B), the deposition shall not be conducted until after the report is provided.

(B) A party may, through interrogatories or by deposition, discover facts known or opinions held by an expert who has been retained or specially employed by another party in anticipation of litigation or preparation for trial and who is not expected to be called as a witness at trial, only as provided in Rule 35(b) or upon a showing of exceptional circumstances under which it is impracticable for the party seeking discovery to obtain facts or opinions on the same subject by other means.

(C) Unless manifest injustice would result, (i) the court shall require that the party seeking discovery pay the expert a reasonable fee for time spent in responding to discovery under this subdivision; and (ii) with respect to discovery obtained under subdivision (b)(4)(B) of this rule the court shall require the party seeking discovery to pay the other party a fair portion of the fees and expenses reasonably incurred by the latter party in obtaining facts and opinions from the expert."

It will be noted that the rule continues to deal with experts who are expected to be called as witnesses differently from those who are merely consulted for assistance in preparing the case. If the purpose of discovery is to prevent surprise and promote effective pre-trial preparation, then lawyers need access to the experts who will be witnesses at the earliest possible opportunity. It is for that reason that, under the rule, a party is now required to disclose the substance of the anticipated testimony of an expert at an early stage.

When a witness has been retained in anticipation of litigation but is not expected to testify as a witness for the retaining party, such as a consulting expert, discovery can be had only upon showing a special need. An exception is made for Rule 35 physical and mental examinations of persons.[1] Rule 26 does not address the expert witness who is an occurrence witness by virtue of having participated in the transaction that is the subject of the litigation. Such an expert would be treated as an ordinary occurrence witness.

§ 1.17 Discovery Based on the Expert's Role

It is clear from the rules discussed in the previous section that discovery rights depend upon the role the experts have played in the case prior to the request for discovery. According to Professors Wright and Miller,[1] an expert's involvement in litigation may be characterized as falling in one of four different categories: (1) experts who are expected to be called as witnesses by the opposing party; (2) so-called consulting experts who are not expected to testify at trial; (3) experts who are informally consulted prior to trial but not formally retained; and (4) experts who obtained information about the case independent of pre-trial preparation by a litigant.

1. EXPERTS TO BE CALLED AS WITNESSES

Experts retained by a party who are expected to testify as expert witnesses are compelled to reveal the nature of their anticipated testimony, and much other information about them, in the pre-trial voluntary disclosure process. This includes testimony about the facts known or made known to the expert, the opinions deduced therefrom, and a summary of the grounds for each opinion. Furthermore, the attorney retaining them must also furnish to the opponent the list of cases in which the experts have testified during the last four years and the qualifications of the experts. The purpose of the 1993 amendments was to get this most crucial information disclosed at the earliest possible

---

§ 1.16

1. Rule 35 provides, in part: "When the mental or physical condition (including the blood group) of a party, or of a person in the custody of or under the legal control of a party, is in controversy, the court in which the action is pending may order the party to submit to a physical or mental examination by a suitably licensed or certified examiner or to produce for examination the person in the party's custody or legal control. The order may be made only on motion to show cause and upon notice to the person to be examined and to all parties and shall specify the time, place, manner, conditions, and scope of the examination and the person or persons by whom it is to be made." The rule further provides that the detailed report of the examiner shall be made available to all parties.

§ 1.17

1. 8 Wright & Miller, *Federal Practice and Procedure* § 2029 (1970).

stage. Further discovery as it existed before the 1993 changes, such as by interrogatories may also be had. Under the old rule, discovery by interrogatories was often considered to reveal only the bare-bones of what a litigant would like to know, and its effectiveness was called into question.[2]

Rule 26(b)(4)(A) represents the potential second step of the discovery process. Discovery through depositions and motions to compel production is entirely subject to the discretion of the court and requires both a motion for further discovery and an affirmative act by the court. Yet, considering the shortcomings of discovery by interrogatory, the step may be a necessary one for a litigant.

Under the pre-Dec. 1, 1993 rule, there certainly seemed to be a trend toward more liberally allowing additional discovery by deposition, though scant case law exists on the issue, since discovery orders are interlocutory and ordinarily not appealable until final judgment. There is, of course, no case law as yet under the current amendments. The parties can, of course, agree otherwise, and as a practical matter, many litigants agree, by stipulation, to mutual depositions of the experts for each side.

Motions to compel production utilized to obtain disclosure of the expert's report and data relied upon by the expert will no longer be needed, since this information must now be voluntarily disclosed by each litigant. The foundational materials utilized by the experts in arriving at their opinions, whether forming the basis thereof or rejected by them, should also be included in the information turned over to opponent.

2. NON–WITNESS CONSULTING EXPERTS

Disclosure of information and discovery from an expert who was retained solely as a consultant to assist in the preparation of the trial, including the possible cross-examination of an opposing expert, is far more restricted than that allowed for the preceding category of expert. Here, no voluntary disclosure is required and discovery is permitted only if certain conditions are met. First, the demanding party must show exceptional circumstances demonstrating that the demanding party cannot discover the facts or information by other means in a practical way.[3] The courts will have to flesh out the types of exceptional circumstances which would require the granting of additional discovery privileges. Among the exceptional circumstances which ought to warrant discovery

2. Note, "Treating Experts Like Ordinary Witnesses: Recent Trends in Discovery of Testifying Experts Under Federal Rule of Civil Procedure 26(b)(4)," 66 *Wash. U.L.Q.* 787, 788 (1988).

3. It is not clear whether this provision the Rule permits a demanding party to discover the identity of consulting experts, though some courts discussing the pre–1993

rule have so held. E.g., Sea Colony v. Continental Insurance Co., 63 F.R.D. 113 (D.Del.1974); Ager v. Jane C. Stormont Hospital, 622 F.2d 496 (10th Cir.1980). See also, Emerick, "Discovery of the Non–Testifying Expert Witness' Identity Under the Federal Rules of Civil Procedure: You Can't Tell the Players Without a Program," 37 *Hastings L.J.* 201 (1985).

are: (1) where the only known expert in the field has been retained by the opposing party; (2) where the expert retained by the opposing side has made an investigation which now, due to a change in the circumstances, can no longer be duplicated by a different expert, as where an analysis has consumed the substance to be analyzed, or materially altered it; and (3) where the information is available through effective discovery but only by the expenditure of excessive time and money and where a significant delay of the trial would be caused.

The rule does not specifically address whether a litigant may discover the name of an expert who has been retained or specially employed but who will not be called as a witness at trial. In deciding the pre–1993 rule, courts have differed in their approach to the issue. In one case, the court held that the identity of a non-witness retained expert was discoverable without showing "exceptional circumstances." [4] By contrast, another court required a showing of exceptional circumstances even to discover the names and identities of experts.[5] The former rule is clearly the better one, when one considers that it may be difficult to conduct effective discretionary discovery of non-witness experts without knowing even their existence.

It may at times be difficult to determine whether an expert belongs in the first or second category. An expert may have been initially retained by an attorney who hoped to call that same expert as a witness, but the opinion rendered by the expert makes it undesirable to call the specialist at trial so that the status is changed to that of a consultant. Which rule applies in that instance? The conclusion reached by such an expert, as well as the data reviewed, ought to be privileged from discovery. To do otherwise would be to discourage lawyers from seeking to gain as much information about a pending case as they can gather. However, if the expert had formed an opinion on the case or held knowledge of the facts of the case, prior to being retained, such opinions and facts would not be shielded from disclosure under Rule 26.[6] Furthermore, an expert may sometimes straddle both categories, so that some of the facts and opinions are discoverable, and other aspects are not.[7]

---

4. Sea Colony v. Continental Insurance Co., 63 F.R.D. 113 (D.Del.1974). This is also the view advocated in Wright & Miller, *Federal Practice and Procedure* § 2032 (1970). The court in *Sea Colony* suggested, in dictum, that the "exceptional circumstance" requirement would have to be satisfied with respect to the discovery of reports prepared by retained non-witness experts.

5. Perry v. W.S. Darley & Co., 54 F.R.D. 278 (E.D.Wis.1971).

6. Inspiration Consol. Copper Co. v. Lumbermens Mutual Casualty Co., 60 F.R.D. 205 (S.D.N.Y.1973).

7. Employees who are also experts may be asked opinions to assist their employer in pending litigation. The courts are in conflict on whether such information was protected by old Rule 26(b)(4)(B). Contrast Virginia Electric & Power Co. v. Sun Shipbuilding & Dry Dock Co., 68 F.R.D. 397 (E.D.Va.1975) with Seiffer v. Topsy's International, Inc., 69 F.R.D. 69 (D.Kan.1975). See also, McDonald "The In–House Federal Expert Witness: Discovery Under the Rules of Civil Procedure," 33 *S.Dak.L.Rev.* 283 (1987–88).

3. EXPERTS INFORMALLY CONSULTED BUT NOT RETAINED

It is not uncommon for attorneys to telephone an expert and ask off-the-cuff opinions on some aspect of a pending case. Sometimes, these conversations result in the expert being retained, which then would put the expert in one of the two categories already discussed. At other times, however, the conversation will not result in a retainer, even though the expert has been told some of the essential facts of the case. Rule 26 does not address itself expressly with the discovery of experts informally consulted but not retained. However, the advisory committee note to the pre–1993 version of Rule 26 suggested that Rule 26(b)(4)(B) "precludes discovery against experts who are informally consulted in preparation for trial, but not retained or specially employed." [8]

4. EXPERTS WHO OBTAINED INDEPENDENT INFORMATION

If an expert gained information about the pending case prior to being retained by a party, whether as part of the expert's regular employment and not in anticipation of litigation or by being a participant or witness to an occurrence which becomes the focus of later litigation, such knowledge will not be shielded from discovery. [9] The expert, here, will be treated as any ordinary witness would be, for purposes of discovery, and discovery of any information possessed should be freely allowed.

§ 1.18 Additional Discovery Ought to Be Liberally Allowed

Judge Joseph M. McLaughlin, in a brief but eloquent article on discovery of experts, [1] contrasted the broad and permissive Federal Rules of Evidence as they apply to expert testimony with the narrowness of the earlier version of the civil discovery rules. He concluded that this contrast results in a "major collision" that is at odds with the liberal-discovery-approach the Federal Rules of Civil Procedure set out to accomplish a half a century earlier. [2] He concluded that while the Rule itself was well understood, its application to discovery from experts "remains enshrouded in obscurity." [3] He further advocates recasting the rule entirely so that discovery from experts becomes the rule, rather than the exception. Perhaps the amendments to the Rules which went into effect on December 1, 1993, accomplish the purpose he advocated.

---

8. Fed.R.Civ.P. 26(b)(4), Advisory Committee Note, 48 F.R.D. 487, at 502. Ager v. Jane C. Stormont Hospital, 622 F.2d 496, 501 (10th Cir.1980), identified four factors to help the court decide the particular status of an expert in a given case. The court should (1) make a determination of the manner in which the consultation was begun; (2) identify the nature of the information provided to the expert; (3) ascertain the duration and intensity of the relationship; and (4) identify the terms of the relationship, including whether payment of a fee was made or demanded.

9. See, Day, "The Ordinary Witness Doctrine: Discovery of the Pre–Retention Knowledge of a Nonwitness Expert," 38 *Ark.L.Rev.* 763 (1985).

§ 1.18

1. McLaughlin, "Discovery and Admissibility of Expert Testimony," 63 *Notre Dame L.Rev.* 760, 765 (1988).

2. Id. at 765.

3. Id. at 769.

V. TRIAL AIDS

§ 1.19 Pretrial Criminal Defense Motion/Request for Discovery

Herein we suggest a sample motion, or request for discovery. The reader is cautioned, however, to consider it as a general guide only, since it must always be tailored to the peculiar facts of the case. Note also that, while a similar format is advisable to insure particularity, under many discovery rules now in effect counsel need only *request* his opponent to disclose certain scientific information rather than filing a motion with the court.

The pretrial motion for discovery must be sufficiently particular to avoid characterization as a blanket request for all statements, documents and evidence in possession of the state.[1] The essence of a motion is the showing of "good cause." The motion should evidence the materiality of the items sought, the fact that the evidence sought is nonprivileged, the reasonableness of the request, and the fact that the items sought are within the possession or control of the opposing side.

1. SAMPLE DEFENSE MOTION/REQUEST

"Comes now the Defendant in the above-styled and numbered cause, by and through his attorney of record, ..., and respectfully [moves this Honorable Court for an order requiring] *or* [requests] the state's attorney of [county, state] and his agents, associates and assistants to produce certain evidentiary material for the Defendant's inspection, examination, analysis and use. Under the provisions of [insert applicable discovery statute] and the procedural and substantive rights guaranteed to the Defendant pursuant to the Fourth, Fifth, Sixth and Fourteenth Amendments to the United States Constitution, pretrial discovery is requested of the following articles:

Evidentiary Items

"Any and all statements taken from the Defendant or a Codefendant by the State or any of its agents, including tape recorded statements, written statements or indicia of oral statements.

"Any and all objects or specimens of physical evidence including [here specify relevant items such as blood, urine or hair samples, drugs, letters, weapons, fingerprints, etc.] removed from the person and/or property of the Defendant after he became a suspect in this cause.

"Any and all objects or specimens of physical evidence including [here list specific relevant items such as bullets, cartridge cases, pistols, revolvers, knives, clothing, fingerprints, maps, charts, drugs, semen stains, tape recordings, letters, blunt instruments, checks, hair, blood

---

§ 1.19

1. See, Ballard v. Superior Court of San Diego County, 64 Cal.2d 159, 49 Cal.Rptr. 302, 410 P.2d 838 (1966); United States v. Crisona, 271 F.Supp. 150 (D.C.N.Y.1967).

stains, dirt samples, photographs, etc.] obtained by the [name] Department [or insert other applicable state agency], or their agents or employees, or the agents and/or employees of any state investigative agency, as a result of which the Defendant became a suspect herein, regardless of the location of the physical evidence or the process by which it was obtained.

"Any and all objects or specimens of physical evidence the disclosure of which is favorable or exonerative to the accused and is material either on the issue of guilt or punishment.

Scientific Reports of Experts

"Any and all scientific reports of analysis or examination conducted by the [name] Police Crime Laboratory or the [name] Sheriff's Department [or insert name of applicable state crime laboratory], or the Federal Bureau of Investigation Laboratories, or by any other analytical source such as hospitals, physicians or private laboratories, on specimens removed from the person and/or property of the Defendant or by examination of his person on or after the time he became a suspect in this case, including [here specify relevant expert reports such as psychiatric reports, neurological reports, psychological reports, firearm identification reports, fingerprint identification reports, toxicological analysis of alcoholic content of blood or urine or drug sample, microbiological analysis of hair, blood or semen, handwriting analysis, etc.].

"Any and all scientific reports of analysis and/or examination conducted by the [name] Police Crime Laboratory or the [name] Sheriff's Department [insert name of applicable state crime laboratory], or the Federal Bureau of Investigation Laboratories, or by any other analytical sources such as hospitals or physicians, on specimens, the basis of which contributed to the Defendant becoming a suspect in this case, regardless of the location of the specimens examined or the process by which they were obtained for analysis including [here, specify the relevant expert reports such as microbiological tests of sperm, seminal fluid, hair and blood, chemical and toxicological tests for blood, alcohol, drug and poison identification, firearm identification and ballistics reports, autopsy reports, psychiatric report of witnesses, fingerprint report, questioned document report, etc.].

"Any and all scientific reports favorable to the accused and material on the issue of guilt or punishment.

Items for Scientific Testing

"Any and all specimens or objects of physical evidence including [here specify the objects or specimens sought] which are presently in the possession or control of the state or its agents, for analysis and testing by a defense employed expert, to-wit: [here, specify the expert's profession].

"The Defendant requests the [court] or [prosecutor] to specify the time, place and manner of making the above examination, inspection, analysis [2] and copying, and submits that scientific analysis by a defense expert will allow the Defendant to adequately prepare for trial rather than being limited to cross-examination of the state's expert at trial concerning vital determinative facts which may be deduced from scientific analysis."

[The motion may continue, of course, to request other information such as the names of witnesses, record of prior convictions of prospective witnesses, investigative reports, as well as an omnibus request for any and all other evidence in the control or possession of the state which is favorable to the Defendant or which is material to the guilt or punishment of the Defendant.]

"This [Motion] or [Request] is made in good faith and is not intended for the purpose of delay or to engage in a general exploratory fishing expedition. The items and reports requested exist and are in possession and/or control of the State of ... and are not otherwise procurable by the Defendant even with the exercise of due diligence [and cannot be properly examined prior to trial other than by order of this Honorable Court]. The items sought are material to the defense because [give reasons].

"[The materiality and necessity of the items sought and their evidentiary relevance in affording the Defendant an adequate defense to the charge of ... will be further shown at the hearing on this Motion and upon the hearing of the other Motions filed by the Defendant.] The matter requested in this Motion is not privileged from pretrial disclosure. This request is being filed far enough in advance to make it reasonable. In fact, the failure to obtain disclosure of the requested matter at an early date in advance of trial will deny the Defendant the right to properly prepare for trial and failure to obtain the requested matter in advance of trial may unduly serve to delay the trial of this cause.

"WHEREFORE, premises considered, the Defendant [prays this Honorable Court order] *or* [requests] the State's Attorney of ..., the Sheriff of [county, state], and the Police Department of the City of ..., and all other authorities involved in this case in an investigatory or analytical capacity to appear herein and, as requested, to bring the requested evidentiary matter for this Defendant's copying and analysis in order that this Defendant may realize the rights guaranteed him by the Fourth, Fifth, Sixth and Fourteenth Amendments to the United States Constitution and to enter any and all appropriate orders to carry out the foregoing matters enumerated in the Motion for Discovery, and for such other and further reasons as may appear at oral pretrial hearing

---

2. If independent scientific analysis by a defense employed expert is sought, the court may order it done at the offices of the state employed expert and under his supervision. The defense's right to participate in scientific tests of the state's evidence can make the difference between conviction and acquittal. See United States v. Taylor, 25 F.R.D. 225 (E.D.N.Y.1960) for a narcotic case allowing independent defense analysis of suspect drug sample at the office of the government chemist and under government supervision.

of this Motion and for such other orders as the Court may deem proper and appropriate."

Respectfully [submitted],

_____

Attorney for Defendant

2. PROSECUTION MOTION/REQUEST

With the foregoing sample of defense counsel's motion or request for disclosure and discovery before him, a prosecutor should encounter no difficulty in preparing his own—by following the appropriate statutory provisions. Absent such guidance, recourse is available to the general case law upon the subject. Not to be overlooked, of course, are the constitutional limitations with respect to defense disclosure and discovery.

In instances where insanity may be reasonably anticipated as a defense, and where such a defense need not be specially pleaded, the prosecution should attempt to have the defense disclose whether or not an insanity defense will be raised.

§ 1.20 Pretrial Preparation for Expert Testimony

1. WRITTEN REPORTS OF EXPERT

Prior to conferring with the expert about his testimony, the attorney should obtain a full written report of the expert's findings. Although this may entail some further expenditure, it is beneficial in preparation for the pretrial conference and trial. The report may also be instrumental in bringing about a negotiated settlement of the charge.

2. COUNSEL'S PRETRIAL CONFERENCE WITH EXPERT

At some time prior to trial it should be every attorney's practice to schedule a conference with his expert. It may be that the expert has testified in hundreds of cases and is acquainted with the local rules of practice as well as with what he may expect in the courtroom. This is especially true if he is a forensic expert employed by the state, such as a police chemist or a county psychiatrist. However, in some instances, the expert may be unfamiliar with the courtroom procedures and understandably apprehensive about being on the witness stand. Further, he may be psychologically unprepared for the occasional slashing cross-examination with attacks upon his character and motives as well as his logic. Failure of the attorney to communicate with his expert witness, at the pretrial stage, may result in a lost case.

At the pretrial attorney-expert conference, the attorney can explain to the witness exactly what he intends to prove by the witness' testimony and how he intends to prove it.[1] This serves to focus the scope of the expert's attention to the relevant facts and insures that he is aware of the evidentiary theory of his testimony. The conference also gives the attorney an opportunity to ask any questions based upon the expert's previously submitted written report. Documents, photographs, and tangible objective evidence intended as exhibits can be reviewed to assure that the identification can be proved as a predicate to the introduction of the exhibit at trial. Demonstrative evidence such as models, charts or diagrams can be examined and discussed. A suggestion ought to be made that the expert acquaint himself with recent, scientific literature relevant to the issues involved in his testimony. Experts should be prepared to deal with cross-examination based upon any books, articles or treatises expressing views contrary to those expressed by the expert. The expert should also be thoroughly familiar with any of his own publications. In some instances, when the expert has written on the subject, these earlier writings may contain an opinion which suggests a conclusion different from the one he will state on the witness stand. This change in opinion is of little impeaching value if the expert frankly admits the existence of the prior contradictory opinion. Indeed, the change in opinion may be used advantageously if the expert can relate facts about his field demonstrating how technological advances led to the formation of his new opinion. At the least, this is indicative of an open mind susceptible to change based on the progress of science.

3. FRAMING QUESTIONS FOR DIRECT AND CROSS–EXAMINATION

To get an intelligent answer, one must ask an intelligent question. Pretrial advice from the expert on the precise wording of the questions he will be asked on direct examination can be of great assistance. His expertise may also be used to design revealing cross-examination questions that may be asked of an opposing expert. If the results of the opposing expert's inquiry have been determined through pretrial disclosure or discovery practice, they should always be made available to one's own expert. This data may disclose material error and miscalculation obvious only to one sophisticated in that field of endeavor.

Complex explanatory terminology can be rephrased and simplified into layman's language for more understandable presentation to the trier of fact. Above all, the attorney who is familiar with the expert's field can satisfy himself that the expert has done a complete and

---

§ 1.20

1. An attorney may suggest that the expert read some of the following books or articles to acquaint himself with courtroom expectations and demeanor: Feder, *Succeeding as an Expert Witness—Increasing Your Impact and Income,* 1991; Kogan, "On Being a Good Expert Witness In a Criminal Case," 23 *J. Forensic Sci.* 190 (1978); Poynter, *The Expert Witness Handbook,* 1987; Ludwig & Fortune, "Effect of Witnesses' Expertness and Manner of Delivery of Testimony on Verdicts of Simulated Jurors," 42 *Psychological Reports* 681 (1979).

accurate examination and is reasonably certain about his opinion based on the examination.

4.　COUNSEL'S ADVICE TO THE EXPERT WITNESS

The following are offered as basic explanations to be given to the expert at the pretrial conference:

1.　Expect to be vigorously cross-examined as to your qualifications, your scientific findings, and perhaps your character. Do not be drawn into antagonism merely because your examiner expresses a doubtful attitude about your opinion. Keep your temper.

2.　Do not talk down to your examiner or to the jury, but try to synthesize your technical concepts to thoughts understandable by laymen.

3.　If you are asked a question the answer to which you honestly do not know, tell the examiner you do not know; you are not expected to know everything. Likewise, if you are unable to answer a question "yes" or "no", tell your examiner that you are unable to do so. There is no compulsion to make you answer in a way contrary to your beliefs. If you can answer, do not say "I assume so," "I believe so" or "I think so"; be positive.

4.　If you are asked whether you are receiving a fee or not, do not hesitate to admit it.

5.　If you are asked whether or not you discussed this case with the attorney who called you in the case or with anyone else, admit it. It is expected that the attorney will go over your testimony so that he will know in advance how you are going to testify. You may have talked to your colleagues and to investigators and other persons, without any impropriety whatsoever. If there is an insinuation that someone talked to you in an attempt to influence your opinion, voice an emphatic denial.

6.　If you want to explain your answer to a cross-examiner's "yes" or "no" question, ask the judge if you can explain your answer. This will alert counsel even if the judge refuses to allow you to explain it.

7.　Do not volunteer comments or answers to questions you think should have been asked of you. Answer only the questions asked without trying to interject other material even though you think it will be helpful.

8.　If you are cross-examined from treatises, books or pamphlets, do not admit the existence or authority of the writing unless you are in fact familiar with it.

After conferring with his own expert, defense counsel may wish to discuss certain areas of uncertainty with the state's expert in advance of trial. The defense attorney may find, much to his surprise, that the state expert does not object to an informal pretrial conference with him.

This is especially true when the expert knows that formal procedures exist for forcing him to give the information that the defense attorney seeks. It is a simple matter to determine the expert's position by writing or phoning him. If he refuses to agree to an informal meeting, one can proceed formally by filing a motion for discovery, and/or a request to take his deposition accompanied by a subpoena duces tecum for his reports, notes, sketches and photographs.

VI. THE EXPERT AT TRIAL

§ 1.21 Direct Examination

1. QUALIFYING PROCEDURES

An expert witness is permitted to testify not only to facts but also to his opinions and conclusions drawn from the facts. As a predicate to opinion testimony, however, it must be demonstrated by proof that the witness is qualified from observation, study, or actual experience to speak as an expert.[1]

Before the expert testifies, his knowledge and experience should be tested by questions producing answers from which the trial judge may determine the witness' competency. This discretionary judgment is made after the court has heard the witness recite his qualifications. The scope of this discretion is quite broad.[2] Nevertheless, even after the trial judge rules that the witness is competent to testify as an expert, the trier of fact (jury or judge) may weigh paltry credentials against the witness' credibility.

It has been suggested that the trial judges typically permit any witness who is shown to have had some experience or background in a field of specialty to qualify as an expert, suggesting that any weaknesses in the competence may be brought out on cross-examination as going to credibility. This is at times quite frustrating to an opposing expert or opposing counsel who is convinced that the other expert is either a fake or a person totally incompetent in the area in which he is prepared to testify.[3]

---

§ 1.21

1. Upon the subject generally, consult 31 Am.Jur.2d (Expert and Opinion Evidence) §§ 26–32. See also, Rosenthal, "The Development of the Use of Expert Testimony," 2 *Law & Contemp.Prob.* 403 (1935). Federal Rule 702 provides that an expert witness is one qualified "by knowledge, skill, experience, training, or education." In Wheat v. State, 527 A.2d 269 (Del.1987), a clinical social worker was held sufficiently qualified to testify as a state expert in intrafamily sexual abuse, despite the fact she was not a psychiatrist or a psychologist. (Reversed because the witness went beyond describing general principles.)

2. McCormick, *Evidence,* § 13 (3d ed. 1984).

3. Hilton, "A New Look at Qualifying Expert Witnesses and the Doctrine of Privilege for Forensic Scientists," 17 *J.For.Sci.* 586 (1972). But Judge David L. Bazelon of the U.S. Court of Appeals for the District of Columbia Circuit, speaking to an Atomic Industrial Forum conference in Washington, expressed the view that much litigation pertains to matters "on the frontiers of science and technology," and that it makes no sense to have judges, who lack scientific

Qualifying questions should be tailored to the individual expert. The sample group of questions offered at the end of this section should be reviewed with the witness and altered to suit his particular background. If the witness' credentials are impressive, it is unwise to accept opposing counsel's offer to stipulate to his expertise. His true motive, under the guise of saving the court's time, is quite often to minimize the consideration the jury might attribute to imposing qualifications. An attorney cannot be forced to stipulate his witness' qualifications and ordinarily should not do so.

In practice, the process of establishing the qualifications of a witness is very much routine. Frequently based on a resume furnished by the expert, trial lawyers in the past have seldom verified the information contained in experts' resumes. Yet, they may be remiss in their professional obligations in not doing so, since not infrequently experts exaggerate their qualifications, claim experience they did not have, and indeed claim to possess academic degrees which were never awarded to them.[4] It is not hard to imagine the embarrassment of a trial lawyer who, without having verified qualifications, puts before the court the testimony of an apparently eminently qualified expert, only to see the qualifications proved a sham and a fraud on cross-examination. A careful examination of the claimed qualifications, academic degrees, and experience, prior to trial, by the lawyer who seeks to utilize the services of an expert, is required to demonstrate minimum competence under the state's Code of Professional Responsibility or Rules of Professional Conduct.[5]

Once the witness' qualifications have been accepted by the court, direct examination on the substance of his investigation commences. The witness should first specify the data which he considered, or the

expertise, decide these issues when the experts themselves disagree on either the underlying principles, facts, or implications to be drawn from the facts. In Hooten v. State, 492 So.2d 948 (Miss.1986) the trial court had, after hearing extensive evidence, held that a graphoanalyst (a person studying character traits from handwriting) and not familiar with any of the standard texts in questioned document examination, was not qualified to testify as a document expert to determine genuineness or forgery of a writing. A divided Supreme Court reversed. The dissenting opinion of Presiding Justice Hawkins critically examined the qualifications of this pseudo-expert, characterized her as a "quack" and said it was an "astonishing indictment to the gullibility of lawyers and judges that this person had been able to testify in over 300 cases as an expert in questioned document analysis."

The problem of dishonest and incompetent expert witnesses in civil as well as criminal cases is one that has proved to be far more widespread than long suspected.

It is addressed elsewhere in this Chapter. See also: Jonakait, "Forensic Science: The Need For Regulation," 4 *Harv.J.Law & Technology* 109 (1991); Moenssens, "Novel Scientific Evidence in Criminal Cases: Some Words of Caution," 84 *J.Crim.L. & Criminology* 801 (1993), and sources cited therein. Despite its title, the latter article applies to civil litigation as well.

See, in this regard, the comments made in notes 8 through 27, section 1.03 and accompanying text, supra.

4. See, e.g., Starrs, "Mountebanks among Forensic Scientists," *Forensic Science Handbook* Vol. II (Saferstein, ed., 1983); State v. Caldwell, 322 N.W.2d 574 (Minn.1982) and commentary by Starrs, "A Miscue in Fingerprint Identification: Causes and Concerns," 12 *J.Pol.Sci. & Admin.* 287 (1984).

5. People v. Cornille, 95 Ill.2d 497, 69 Ill.Dec. 945, 448 N.E.2d 857 (1983). See also, Model Rules of Professional Conduct, Rules 1.1 and 3.3 (1993).

examinations he made, after which he gives his opinion. The weight to be given to his substantive testimony is for the trier of fact.[6]

Ordinarily, counsel will not wish to write out verbatim the word-for-word questions which he will ask his expert witness; however, when the questions are highly technical, it is quite appropriate to question an expert from prepared notes. The following is a general outline of questions which may be used to qualify the expert so that the court may determine competency:

Q: I am going to ask you a few preliminary questions about yourself, your work, and your experience, so the jury will know just who you are, what you have done, and your qualifications to speak in the field about which you have been called to testify.

Q: What is your present title?

Q: What position do you hold?

Q: You are a (chemist, pathologist, etc.), is that correct?

Q: Will you briefly describe, please, the subject matter of that specialty?

Q: And do you specialize within that field?

Q: What is your subspecialty?

Q: What is that concerned with?

Q: Are you also certified as a specialist in the field of ...?

Q: What does that certification involve?

Q: How long have you been so certified?

Q: Concerning your formal education, will you state what colleges and universities you attended, if any, and what degrees you may have received?

Q: Was that degree in any major field?

Q: What field was that?

Q: Are you licensed as a ... in the state of ...?

Q: How long have you been licensed?

Q: How long have you been in practice in that specialty?

Q: Will you tell us, please, what positions you have held since the completion of your formal education, and the number of years in each?

Q: You said [with respect to prior important work] you were at ...; will you tell us what you did there?

Q: What are the duties and functions of your present position?

---

6. Clark v. United States, 293 Fed. 301 (C.C.A.5 1923).

In Delaware v. Fensterer, 474 U.S. 15 (1985), the Court held that the inability of the state's expert witness to recollect a scientific basis for his conclusion that an evidence hair specimen had been forcibly removed did not present a constitutional confrontation issue, but merely went to the weight, not the admissibility, of the testimony.

Q: How long have you held that position?

Q: In the course of your work, have you had occasion to conduct examinations of (specifying sort involved here)?

Q: How many such examinations have you conducted?

Q: Have you done any teaching or lecturing in the field of ...?

Q: When and where?

Q: Have you published any works in the field of ...?

Q: What are the titles of those works?

Q: Are you a member of any professional associations?

Q: Do you hold any special positions therein? [As to this, of course, a cross-examiner may inquire as to whether the only qualification for membership is dues payment. If that is the case the question should be omitted.]

Q: Have you previously testified as an expert witness in court?

Q: And has that been on a number of occasions?

A: Yes.

[At this point counsel may begin to inquire about the matter which was the subject of the expert examination or consideration, although opposing counsel is entitled to first cross-examine the witness regarding his qualifications. In fact, in some states he must do so at this stage; otherwise he will be considered as having waived any right to attack the witness' qualifications after the witness has testified about the matter in issue.] [7]

2. LEGAL IMPEDIMENTS TO EXPERT TESTIMONY

There are several areas where the attorney may encounter problems with the admissibility of expert testimony. To some extent the following rules of evidence may impede the use of expert testimony.

A. Ultimate Issue Doctrine

It is a general rule that an expert who testifies as to cause and effect from his analysis of the facts must state his conclusion in the form of an opinion rather than as absolute fact. This rule has been extended by a line of cases indicating the inadmissibility of testimony from an expert witness in the form of an opinion or inference which embraces the ultimate issue or issues to be decided by a jury. The ultimate issue rule, therefore, prohibits any witness, including an expert, from giving an opinion on the ultimate issue in the case. The rationale underpinning the ultimate issue rule is that expert opinion should not be permitted to

---

7. State v. Owens, 167 Wash. 283, 9 299 Ill. 393, 132 N.E. 477 (1921).
P.2d 90 (1932); contra People v. Sawhill,

invade the province of the jury.[8]

The problem regarding the ultimate issue limitation is simply that in complex cases involving issues beyond the abilities of laymen, a jury may need an expert's opinion on the ultimate issue in order to reach a fair verdict. Opinion on the issues of identity, value, insanity, and intoxication, for instance, all border on what would be considered ultimate fact issues, yet they are generally held admissible.[9]

Intoxication and insanity as defenses to criminal responsibility involve mixed questions of law and fact, and for that reason some jurisdictions refuse to allow ultimate issue opinion testimony as to those conditions. A review of the cases indicates a severe erosion in the strictured subject matter of the ultimate issue doctrine. Reportedly, at least 37 states have abandoned the rule that an expert witness may not testify as to the ultimate facts in issue.[10] Rule 704 of the Federal Rules of Evidence flatly rejects the ultimate issue doctrine:

> Testimony in the form of an opinion or inference otherwise admissible is not objectionable because it embraces an ultimate issue to be decided by the trier of fact.

Abolishing the ultimate issue rule does not mean, however, that all expert opinions become admissible. Rules 701 and 702 require that opinions be "helpful" to the trier of fact in order to be admissible.[11]

It must also be noted that not all courts facing the issue in recent years have followed the pattern of rejection of the ultimate issue rule. In Bond v. Commonwealth,[12] the Virginia Supreme Court refused to

---

8. Shreve v. United States, 103 F.2d 796 (9th Cir.1939); but see, United States v. Johnson, 319 U.S. 503 (1943), rehearing denied 320 U.S. 808 (1943). Also, upon the subject generally: 2 Underhill, *Criminal Evidence* § 307 (1956 ed.); 31 Am.Jur.2d (Expert and Opinion Evidence), § 22, State v. Hull, 45 W.Va. 767, 32 S.E. 240 (1899).

9. See, 7 Wigmore, *Evidence*, §§ 1920–1921 (Chadbourn rev. 1978); McCormick, *Evidence*, § 12 (1984); see, Kennedy v. United States, 4 F.2d 488 (9th Cir.1925); Atles v. United States, 50 F.2d 808 (3d Cir.1931), (taste, sight, smell of liquor); Hopson v. State, 201 Tenn. 337, 299 S.W.2d 11 (1957) (identity); and Farnsworth v. State, 343 P.2d 744 (Okl.Crim.App.1959) (intoxication). In Gantt v. State, 81 Md. App. 653, 569 A.2d 1220 (1990), a narcotics investigator was allowed to testify that defendant "was actually selling drugs," despite the fact the testimony embraced the ultimate issue, because it "assisted the trier of fact."

10. Bond v. Commonwealth, infra note 12.

McCormick states that today "in a majority of state courts an expert may state his opinion upon an ultimate fact, provided that all other requirements for admission of expert opinion are met." McCormick, *Evidence*, § 12 (at p. 30) (3d ed. 1984).

11. For an illuminating discussion of the interplay between Federal Rules 701, 702 and 704, see, United States v. Theodoropoulos, 866 F.2d 587 (3d Cir.1989) (expert, an F.B.I. agent trained in code breaking, was properly allowed to testify regarding drug trafficking conversations conducted in Greek and using names of household objects to stand for drugs, e.g., four "blue" steaks; crypt analysis was helpful to jury).

12. 226 Va. 534, 311 S.E.2d 769 (1984): see also, Callahan v. Commonwealth, 8 Va. App. 135, 379 S.E.2d 476 (1989) (citing Moenssens, Inbau & Starrs, Scientific Evidence in Criminal Cases (3d ed. 1986) in discussion of Virginia's refusal to adopt the majority view.) The traditional Virginia view was reinforced in Llamera v. Commonwealth, 243 Va. 262, 4141 S.E.2d 597, 598 (1992), where the trial court had permitted a police officer who qualified as an expert in the sale, distribution, marketing, packaging, and effects of narcotics, to testify that in his opinion the cocaine seized from defendant

follow the "unmistakeable trend" of authority and retained the ultimate issue prohibition:

> We are not prepared to reject the ultimate issue prohibition ... in a criminal case such as this where life or liberty often turns upon inferences raised by circumstantial evidence. The process of resolving conflicting inferences, affected as it is by the credibility of the witnesses who supply such evidence, is the historical function of a jury drawn from a cross-section of the community. We are unwilling to entrust that function to experts in the witness box.[13]

The court stressed the inequality of resources between prosecution and defense in the matter of obtaining expert assistance and testimony:

> True [if the ultimate issue rule were rejected] jurors would still be free to disregard an expert's opinion and to resolve conflicts when experts disagree. But ... the services of an expert witness are expensive. Drawing upon the public fisc, the prosecution can afford to finance a duel of experts; an indigent defendant cannot.[14]

B. HEARSAY

A hearsay question arises when the expert bases his opinion on information given to him by someone else. Hearsay evidence is defined as testimony or written evidence of a statement made out of court, whenever such a statement is offered for the truth of the matters asserted therein, and thus resting for its value upon the credibility of the out of court declarant. As a general principle of law, all hearsay evidence is inadmissible unless the hearsay falls within one of the long list of recognized exceptions to the hearsay rule—exceptions that have been carved out because of necessity or because the hearsay was uttered under circumstances which evidence some guarantee of trustworthiness.

At common law, in criminal cases where the forces of the state seek to take the life, liberty, or property of the accused, the trial courts demanded strict proof of the foundation facts of the case without relaxation of the hearsay rule. Thus, state experts might be prohibited from testifying to an opinion based in whole or in part upon what others have told him.[15] But as with the ultimate issue rule, there has been a

was packaged in a way that "suggested that the owner of the cocaine was a person who sold cocaine." The Supreme Court rejected the prosecution's view that the expert's use of the word "suggest" was a qualification, not a statement of fact on the ultimate issue: "We consistently have held that the admission of expert testimony upon an ultimate issue of fact is impermissible because it invades the function of the fact finder."

Also holding that expert testimony improperly invaded the province of the fact finder, see, e.g. Corbett v. Weisband, 380 Pa.Super. 292, 551 A.2d 1059 (1988). While Federal Rule of Evidence 704 permits ultimate issue evidence, this does not include merely telling the jury what result to reach. Montgomery v. Aetna Cas. & Sur. Co., 898 F.2d 1537 (11th Cir.1990).

13. Id. at 538, 311 S.E.2d at 772.

14. Ibid.

15. A Virginia case discussing and reaffirming this view is McMunn v. Tatum, 237 Va. 558, 379 S.E.2d 908 (1989). The court stated: "We now hold that Code § 8.01–401.1 does not authorize the admission in evidence, upon the direct examination of an expert witness, of hearsay matters of opinion upon which the expert relied in reach-

gradual erosion in the prohibition against testifying on the basis of information obtained from others, culminating in a partial rejection of the prohibition in the Federal Rules of Evidence.

Rule 703 provides that an expert may give opinion testimony based on facts and data, including reports by others, even though this information may be inadmissible, provided the information is "of a type reasonably relied upon by experts in the particular field in forming opinions or inferences upon the subject."

It must be recognized that in criminal cases because of the constitutional right of confrontation guaranteed in the Sixth Amendment,[16] evidence that may be admissible under a recognized hearsay exception may still violate the confrontation right.[17]

A slightly different situation is presented when the expert formulates an opinion derived from the operations of technicians working under his orders. The hearsay rules are frequently adjusted to allow an expert under whose control and supervision a test is made to testify at trial and to give his expert opinion based on the factual results of the test, even though the test was actually conducted by another. Although the hearsay objection may not be sufficient against expert testimony regarding the results of an analysis made under the supervision of the witness, the witness generally should not be permitted over a hearsay objection to testify as to the conclusion reached by an assistant.

As indicated above, under Rule 703 of the Federal Rules of Evidence, an expert may base his opinion upon facts or data "perceived by or made known to him *at or before the hearing*. If of a type reasonably relied upon by experts in the particular field in forming opinions or inferences upon the subject, the facts or data need not be admissible in evidence." (Emphasis added.) This would seem to justify use of hearsay by the expert in reaching his opinion, as long as others in his chosen field do likewise. It could apply to reports of investigators, laboratory analyses, and information from other persons peripherally involved with crime detection. Some courts have held that although the evidentiary rule states an expert witness is entitled to render an opinion based on inadmissible evidence when the facts and data are of a type reasonably relied upon by experts, the witness may not serve merely as a conduit for the introduction of otherwise inadmissible evidence,[18] or to parrot the corroborative opinions solicited from non-testifying colleagues.[19]

---

ing his own opinion, notwithstanding the fact that the opinion of the expert witness is itself admissible, and notwithstanding the fact that the hearsay is of a type normally relied on by others in the witness' particular field of expertise." Id. at 566, 379 S.E.2d at 912.

16. The confrontation clause was held applicable to the states in 1965 in Pointer v. Texas, 380 U.S. 400 (1965).

17. E.g., California v. Green, 399 U.S. 149, 155–156 (1970); United States v. Puco, 476 F.2d 1099 (2d Cir.1973).

18. Riggins v. Mariner Boat Works, Inc., 545 So.2d 430 (Fla.App.2d Dist.1989); Kurynka v. Tamarac Hosp. Corp., 542 So.2d 412 (Fla.App.4th Dist.1989).

19. Bong Jin Kim v. Nazarian, 216 Ill. App.3d 818, 159 Ill.Dec. 758, 576 N.E.2d 427 (1991).

Expert opinion may be predicated on the facts contained in hospital records properly admitted in evidence under state business or hospital records statutes. This reasoning would, for example, hold true in the case of a medical examiner who testifies to his own conclusion formed on the basis of an autopsy conducted under his supervision and control. A different question is whether or not an opinion on cause of death, contained in an autopsy report, may be admitted into evidence. Ideally, the autopsy report should be an admissible document under a state statute.[20]

Again, the Federal Rules of Evidence, in Rule 803(6), exempt from exclusion as hearsay any records of regularly conducted activity which may be contained in memoranda or reports kept in the regular course of a business, institution, association, profession, occupation or calling of any kind.[21]

C. Proof of Chain of Custody of Tangible Evidence

The chain of custody rule provides that the party seeking to introduce into evidence the results of an expert analysis has the burden of proving that the specimen or object analyzed was, in fact, derived or taken from the particular person or place alleged. This proof, which is of particular importance in criminal cases, is customarily adduced by testimony which traces the location and custody of the specimen from the time it was secured by law enforcement officers or agents of the state until it is offered in evidence. The chronicle of custody includes (1) the initial possession of the specimen or object by an officer, (2) the journey to the laboratory, (3) the method of storage at the laboratory prior to analysis and (4) the retention, whenever feasible, of the unused portion of the specimen or the object after analysis and up to the time of trial.[22] It must also be established, as a prerequisite to admissibility of the evidence specimens, that they were in fact the same ones taken from the place or person in question, so that not only unbroken possession, but also the original source, can be established with certainty.[23]

---

20. See, e.g., Va.Code 1950, § 19.2–188: "Reports of investigations made by the Chief Medical Examiner or his assistants or by medical examiners, and the records and reports of autopsies made ... shall be received as evidence in any court or other proceeding, ... when duly attested by the Chief Medical Examiner or one of his Assistant Chief Medical Examiners...." But see, Bond v. Commonwealth, supra note 12, excluding the cause of death information on the reports as inadmissible evidence upon the ultimate fact in issue.

21. For extensive treatment of the case law and literature on the admissibility of certificates of analysis by crime laboratories, see, Strelitz, "Certificates of Analysis," 3 *The Crim.Just. Quarterly* 1 39 (1975).

22. Rodgers v. Commonwealth, 197 Va. 527, 90 S.E.2d 257 (1955). See also, Williams v. Commonwealth, 10 Va.App. 636, 638, 394 S.E.2d 728, 729 (1990): "In light of this principle, [Virginia] Code § 18.2–268(G) provides: 'Adequate portions of the blood samples so withdrawn shall be placed in vials * * * *which containers shall be sealed so as not to allow tampering with the vial.'* " [Emphasis in court's opinion.]

23. Failure to establish that a comparison hair of supposedly known origin was taken from the deceased homicide victim resulted in a reversal in Kuntschik v. State, 636 S.W.2d 744 (Tex.App.1982).

For a comprehensive discussion of admissibility attacks on testimony by chain of custody witnesses and weight attacks on

Chain of custody is an essential quantum of proof in any case involving such materials as bullets, cartridge cases and weapons, finger-prints, hair, stained clothing, drugs, and blood specimens. In most cases the chain of custody can be sufficiently proven by the testimony of the investigator who secured the specimen or object and the analyst who examined it. The investigator's conduct reflects that he took the exhib-it, identified it and placed it in a sealed container which he also marked for identification, and that the exhibit remained in his custody until he placed it in the mail or in the laboratory receptacle such as a lock box. The expert proceeds to remove the specimen or object from the mail or laboratory receptacle and to analyze it. Tangible objects which are not consumed in the analysis are marked for identification by the analyst and secured until the time of trial so that they will be admissible in addition to testimony concerning the analysis. For example, in the case of blood specimens from a D.W.I. suspect, there must be legal proof that the specimen taken by a physician, nurse or laboratory technician was the same specimen analyzed by the expert. However, when specimens of blood or objects such as bullets are removed from the body by a specialist, it is customarily unnecessary that the specialist be produced to testify so long as the officer who does testify was present, observed the removal of the object and took possession of it. The defense, of course, must also be prepared to demonstrate a proper chain of custody concern-ing analytical test specimens which are the subject of a defense expert's testimony.

Whenever a break exists in the chain of custody of a specimen which was linked by scientific analysis to the defendant in an inculpatory fashion, it will be reversible error to admit the opinion testimony that is based upon the analysis.[24] It is important to determine in each case whether the break affects the possible validity of the expert's findings. However, the practicalities of proof may not require a party offering certain evidence to negative the remotest possibility of substitution or alteration; all that need be established is a reasonable certainty that there has been no substitution, alteration, or tampering with the speci-men.[25]

the chain of custody, see, Imwinkelried, *The Methods of Attacking Scientific Evidence,* 2d ed. (1992).

24. In Robinson v. Commonwealth, 212 Va. 136, 183 S.E.2d 179 (1971), panties, a blouse and some pubic hair specimens were collected from a rape victim by a registered nurse at the hospital. The officers who received the evidence from the nurse and those who analyzed it testified at the trial, but the nurse was not called as a witness. The court held that the chain of custody was fatally defective and the expert testimo-ny should not have been admitted. (Two Justices dissented, however.)

25. When there is no evidence that a technician improperly tested a blood sample in an involuntary manslaughter prosecu-tion, the fact that the doctor testified he could not remember whether he took the blood sample of the defendant or whether it was taken by someone else in his presence does not affect the admissibility of the spe-cimen, but goes only to its weight: Beck v. State, 651 S.W.2d 827 (Tex.App.1983).

Similarly, taking what has become the rather generally recognized flexible ap-proach to the necessity for an intact chain of custody, see, People v. Mascarenas, 666 P.2d 101 (Colo.1983).

§ 1.22   Cross–Examination

1.   ATTACK UPON THE EXPERT'S COMPETENCY

It is clear that each side has the right to cross examine the opposition's expert as to his competency as an expert and as to matters which may impeach the credibility of the expert's opinion. Cross-examination is also an effective way to test an opinion or assertion. Its efficacy, however, depends upon the skill, experience, and quality of the cross-examiner's preparation, as well as the caliber and preparedness of the opposition's expert.

It is impossible to plan the entire cross-examination of an opposition expert in advance of trial, but the general scheme as well as a number of specific questions should be constructed as part of the pretrial preparation. It is also most certainly helpful to have authoritative legal citations prepared in support of any cross-examination questions to which an objection may be anticipated.

Whenever counsel, either for the prosecution or the defense, has advance knowledge that a certain expert witness will appear for the other side, an effort should be made to learn as much as possible about him.[1] A good source or lead, of course, is the expert whom the cross-examiner intends to use in the presentation of his own case. Experts in the same specialty are the ones who best can appraise the competency and integrity of the one who is to testify. Checking with appropriate scientific associations or organizations may also be productive. By checking with the professional associations, an attorney may discover whether an expert has been sanctioned by the association for ethics violations. Most professional associations have codes of ethics and ethics committees to investigate and sanction instances of unethical professional conduct. An attorney should also consult with bodies that certify the various forensic sciences to see whether an expert has failed to be certified, or has been decertified or, where periodic re-credentialing is mandated, has allowed his certification to lapse.[2] A search should be made of possible publications authored by the anticipated expert witness. Whatever he has written should be read, especially the material pertaining to the particular subject of his testimony.

§ 1.22

1. For example, learning about specific prior conduct of the expert when he or she testified in other cases can provide ammunition for attacking credibility. See, Navarro de Cosme v. Hospital Pavia, 922 F.2d 926 (1st Cir.1991).

2. Such certifying bodies include the various medical boards, and also the American Board of Forensic Anthropology, the American Board of Forensic Document Examiners, the American Board of Forensic Odontology, the American Board of Pathol-ogy, the American Board of Forensic Psychiatry, the American Board of Forensic Toxicology, the California Association of Criminalists, the American Board of Criminalistics, and the International Association for Identification.

See also, Blum, "Propriety of Questioning Expert Witness Regarding Specific Incidents or Allegations of Expert's Unprofessional Conduct or Negligence," 11 A.L.R.5th 1 (1993).

As previously stated, whenever an attack is to be made upon an expert witness' qualifications, the time to do it is at the end of opposing counsel's voir dire examination of the witness. Two reasons support this recommendation. First, in some states unless it is done at this point, a waiver will be affixed upon a later attempt to attack the witness' qualifications. Secondly, if the witness is in fact unqualified, or if his credentials are weak, the jury should learn of this *before* the witness gives testimony about the matter at issue.

When a trial lawyer faces the prospect of possibly cross-examining an opposing expert witness whom he believes to be incompetent or with very weak credentials, an effort should be made to prevent there from being any evidence from the witness at all, by a pretrial motion *in limine* to exclude the proffered expert's testimony. At a hearing on such a motion, the moving party should present evidence that the expert proffered by the opposing side is disqualified from giving opinion testimony for lack of the required qualifications.

It is quite common for experts to exceed the scope of their training and expertise when testifying. Medical doctors are ordinarily permitted to give opinion evidence on any matter dealing with a health related issue. Thus, even an ordinary family doctor is permitted to opine on mental health issues, though the opinion may not be given the same weight by an astute fact finder as that of a specialist in the subject area. Similarly, a psychiatrist may give opinion testimony on physical ailments, on the theory that the psychiatrist was a medical doctor before specializing in behavioral medicine. Yet, even in medicine, there are limits. Thus, an allopathic physician was not held to be qualified to give opinion testimony on the proper standard of care in osteopathic medicine.[3] In criminal cases, drug chemists often testify as to dosages or as to the effects of chemical substances, although they are ordinarily not qualified by training to do so, unless they establish possessing a background in pharmacology. Graphologists who make a study of character as revealed in handwriting have been permitted improperly to testify as to the authorship of disputed documents, a subject matter altogether beyond their "training" as graphologists.[4] Medical examiners frequently give opinions on gun calibers and firearms identification data when testifying about gunshot wounds, even though they never studied firearms and ammunition identification techniques in medical school.[5] Sim-

---

3. HCA Health Services v. Hampshire, 206 Ga.App. 108, 424 S.E.2d 293 (1992): "in order to be an expert competent to testify, the expert either must be a member of the same professional school as the defendant or, if from a different professional school, must state the particulars how the methods of treatment are the same for the different schools ..."

4. See, Hooten v. State, 492 So.2d 948 (Miss.1986). A dismayed dissenting opinion noted that the witness had vaunted she never "bothered to read any books on fo-

rensic document work, said she did not intend to, and already knew all she needed to know," thus exemplifying, in the words of the dissent, "the one sure sign of a quack: contempt for recognized authority." Id. at 958 (Hawkins, J. dissenting).

5. In Lee v. State, 661 P.2d 1345, 1354 (Okla.Crim.App.1983), however, the court allowed a forensic pathologist to testify on bullet caliber from a gunshot wound examination because this was within the expert's area of "professional experience." By contrast, a pathologist's testimony that "live-in

ilarly, firearms identification technicians, without medical training, ought not to be permitted to give opinions on paths of bullets through the body, or on bruises and contusions on the body being caused by the recoil of a rifle.[6]

2. IMPEACHMENT OF THE EXPERT

In addition to attacks on the scientific basis of the expert's opinion and his basic experience and ability in drawing scientific opinions from facts, there are a number of impeachment stratagems which should be known to every trial attorney when preparing or questioning an expert. These techniques should be used tactfully as weapons to enlighten and to expose bias, perjury, intentional dishonesty and incompetency, but not to assassinate character. Some outline examples follow:

Faulty memory as indicated by reliance on prior conversational experiences or documents to refresh memory:

Q: Have you talked to anyone about this case? [If the witness answers "no", ask him to explain how he happened to be called as a witness.]

Q: To whom have you talked about this case?

Q: When did you talk to him?

Q: When did you first learn that you were to be a witness in the case?

Q: Have you refreshed your memory [concerning the matter in question] by examination of your notes, reports, sketches, diagrams or any other documents?

Q: Did this enable you to recall facts about which your unaided memory was unclear?

Q: Have you made any written statements [concerning the matter in question]?

Then question the witness concerning events before and after the transaction to see if he recalls in detail those incidents. Ask him about the effect of time on his memory. Also, examine the documents used to refresh his memory and cross-examine him on any prior inconsistent statements contained therein.

Opinion as speculation:

In some fields of expertise, the opinion an expert might likely offer to the court has less probative value than in other fields. It is important

or babysitting boyfriends" of single mothers are most likely to be implicated when child abuse occurs, was held beyond the witness' expertise in State v. Steward, 34 Wash.App. 221, 660 P.2d 278 (1983), and the forensic pathologist's testimony that knife wounds were more characteristic of those made by a woman than those made by a man was deemed to be exceeding the witness' compe- tence in Fisher v. State, 361 So.2d 203 (Fla.App.1978).

6. Cf. People v. Lauro, 91 Misc.2d 706, 398 N.Y.S.2d 503 (1977). See the tongue-in-cheek article by Starrs, "In the Land of Agog: An Allegory for the Expert Witness," 30 *J.For.Sci.* 289 (1985), on experts straying beyond their expertise.

to explore this prior to trial. DNA evidence, for example, is generally deemed to be very precise when it comes to matching biological material with known samples, in issues involving paternity as well as when matching crime scene evidence to a particular individual. Experts have been permitted to testify to mathematical probabilities that defy chances of error, as will be seen in the chapter on that topic. By contrast, when it comes to psychiatric evidence, courts know that on issues such as "competency" or "sanity" or "impairment," contradictory expert opinions are commonplace. Thus, it is important to consider the extent to which a particular discipline is able to predict the accuracy and reliability of its results.

When a microanalyst testifies about having compared hairs found on the clothing of a rape victim with hair samples taken from the defendant, he is likely, on direct examination, to express his opinion as being that "these hairs match in all microscopic detail." To the uninitiated— the jury, court, and attorneys—this may sound as if the expert determined that the hairs found on the victim positively came from the defendant. Yet, the expert can make no such assertion. The following might be typical questions to ask on cross-examination:

Q: You didn't mean to say that you could actually tell that these hairs found on Miss X actually came from the defendant, isn't that a fact?

Q: Isn't it a fact that you have no idea how many people in the City of ... also would have hair that matches these samples in all microscopic detail?

Q: In fact, isn't it true that there might be people in this courtroom whose hair could match these samples?

Q: Isn't it true that some of the jurors' hair could conceivably have the same matching microscopic characteristics?

Q: You really don't know at all, do you, whether these hairs did come from any particular person?

Q: So, in expressing your opinion, as you did earlier, you were really just guessing and not talking about a scientifically reliable identification? [7]

Crime laboratory experts freely use statistics to justify their opinions on the low probability of innocent duplication of test results. Yet, they frequently are ignorant of the data upon which the calculations are

---

7. Should an opinion, the scientific basis for which the expert cannot recall, be admissible at all? Finding no confrontation issue where the state's expert had testified that a hair had been forcibly removed, even though he could not articulate a reason for such conclusion, the Supreme Court in Delaware v. Fensterer, 474 U.S. 15 (1985), held that the "memory lapse" went to the weight, not the admissibility of the testimony. The Court's summary reversal of the Delaware Supreme Court's decision fails to address some significant factors brought out in the state court opinion: (1) that the expert was a Special Agent of the FBI and that such a person "can appear to be a highly credible person to the average lay jury"; and (2) that the witness testified to finding that two hairs "bore *similar* characteristics" to the victim's hair, which the court then interpreted as meaning that the agent had *identified* the hairs as being the victim's. See, Fensterer v. State, 493 A.2d 959 (Del.1985).

made (having simply read the statistics in a professional journal), if indeed there is empirical data. An exploration of the premises upon which statistical results are postulated may reveal that the authors of the statistics have no background in the proper formulation of statistical calculations. Very seldom will an expert have independently verified the validity of the "statistics" used to support an opinion.[8]

List of authorities, one of which is false:

Q: Have you familiarized yourself with the subject of (e.g., document examination) by reading the following books: [Then cite the title and author of several books, one of which is wholly non-existent; if the witness answers that he is familiar with the book, then ask him whether he has it in his library, or at home. If he says yes, ask the court to require him to produce it, explaining to the court that there is no such book.] [9]

This stratagem should be reserved for the witness whom the cross-examiner knows to be a "quack" or quite unintelligent or uninformed in his purported field of expertise. It may boomerang if otherwise used.

Expert witness questioning interrogator:

Q: You are the witness, sir. My role is to ask questions; yours is to answer them. I ask that you answer my last question. If you don't remember it, I'll ask the reporter to read it back to you.

Repeat of hypothetical question:

Q: [If the cross-examiner has reason to believe that opposing counsel and his expert have not conferred prior to trial, and a long, complex hypothetical question was put on direct.] You indicated in response to counsel's hypothetical question that you were of the opinion that ...; will you please repeat the question upon which you based your answer?

Probing to determine if the expert is a professional witness and biased for money motives:

Q: You spend about one-half of your time in the courthouse testifying in cases, do you not?

8. On the topic of probability theories as used by experts, generally, see, Brook, "The Use of Statistical Evidence of Identification in Civil Litigation: Well–Worn Hypotheticals, Real Cases, and Controversy," 29 *St. Louis U.L.J.* 293 (1985). See also, Jaffee, "Of Probativity and Probability: Statistics, Scientific Evidence, and the Calculus of Chance At Trial," 46 *U.Pitt.L.Rev.* 925 (1985); Tribe, "Trial by Mathematics: Precision and Ritual in the Legal Process," 84 *Harv.L.Rev.* 1329 (1971); Kaye, "The Laws of Probability and the Law of the Land," 47 *U.Chi.L.Rev.* 34 (1979); George, "Statisti-cal Problems Relating to Scientific Evidence," in *Scientific and Expert Evidence* (Ed. Imwinkelreid, 2d ed. 1981); Callen, "Notes on a Grand Illusion: Some Limits on the Use of Bayesian Theory in Evidence Law," 57 *Ind.L.J.* 1 (1982); Callen, "A Brief Word On the Statistical Evidence Debate," 66 *Tul.L.Rev.* 1405 (1992), referring to several other recent sources.

9. For an interesting case in which a professed "handwriting expert" was impeached in this manner, see, State v. Owens, 167 Wash. 283, 9 P.2d 90 (1932).

Q: You have testified for the [defense, plaintiff, etc.] in a large number
     of cases, have you not?

Q: How many times in the last two years?

Q: In that same period you have been consulted by [the defense,
     plaintiff, etc.] in many other cases that did not come to trial, haven't
     you?

Q: How much pay do you receive for your services in the cases where
     you testify in court, and in the other cases in which you are
     consulted but in which you did not appear in court?

Q: How much are you being paid for your testimony here today? [10]   [As
     a final ploy, the cross-examiner may ask the witness whether or not
     his fee is contingent upon the outcome of the case.] [11]

Cross-examination from a book:

     There are two rules concerning the use of books or written authori-
ties on cross-examination to impeach or discredit an expert witness
where the authorities are in fact contrary to the witness' testimony.
The first rule allows an expert to be questioned in regard to his
knowledge of an authority's teaching if it can be demonstrated that the
witness relied upon the written authority.[12]   The more liberal rule
permits cross-examination when the expert admits that the particular

10.   The court allowed cross-examination regarding the amount an expert witness earned annually for the two years pri-
or to testifying and on the number and
frequency with which the proffering attorney offered him as an expert in Trower v.
Jones, 121 Ill.2d 211, 117 Ill.Dec. 136, 520
N.E.2d 297 (1988). In Plitt v. Griggs, 585
So.2d 1317 (Ala.1991), the court allowed
discovery of the identity of an expert's ac-
countant to determine the income earned
from expert witness fees to demonstrate
bias.   In Navarro de Cosme v. Hospital
Pavia, 922 F.2d 926 (1st Cir.1991) it was
not error to cross-examine expert on inflated invoices for fees filed in other cases.
Some state evidence codes allow an adversary party to inquire into the compensation
and expenses paid to an expert by the party
calling him. See, e.g., West's Ann.Cal.Evid.
Code art. I § 772(b) (1993).

11.   An agreement for expert compensation contingent on the outcome of a case is
contrary to public policy since such an
agreement is likely to be an inducement to
fraud or perjury.   E.g., Ojeda v. Sharp Ca-
brillo Hospital, 1 Cal.App.4th 1556, 2 Cal.
Rptr.2d 767 (1991); Dupree v. Malpractice
Research, Inc., 179 Mich.App. 254, 445
N.W.2d 498 (1989): expert's 20% contingent fee in medical malpractice case held
repugnant to public policy—also unethical

for lawyer to share fees with non-lawyer.
Cf. Person v. Association of the Bar of the
City of New York, 414 F.Supp. 139
(E.D.N.Y.1976).

12.   Willens, "Cross–Examining the Expert Witness with the Aid of Books," 41
J.Crim.L.C. & P.S. 192, 193–95 (1950).

See, e.g., West's Ann.Cal.Evid.Code art. I
§ 772(b) (1993).

    (b) If a witness testifying as an expert
testifies in the form of an opinion, he may
not be cross-examined in regard to the
content or tenor of any scientific, technical, or professional text, treatise, journal,
or similar publication unless:

        (1) The witness referred to, consid-
    ered, or relied upon such publication in
    arriving at or forming his opinion; or

        (2) Such publication has been admit-
    ted in evidence.

One nationally prominent psychiatrist, at
a meeting of the Section on Forensic Psychiatry of the American Academy of Forensic Sciences attended by one of the present
co-authors (Moenssens), gave advice to psychiatrists on how to deal with cross-examination on the basis of textbooks.   He said,
"I never recognize a textbook as authoritative.!"

book offered is a standard authority. The latter rule [13] allows the expert to be cross-examined and impeached from standard books, pamphlets and articles in his field even though the expert did not rely on the particular book in reaching his opinion. The predicate for cross-examination from a book requires that the book be authenticated as authoritative. If the expert does not so acknowledge it, the examiner may wish to call his own expert to do so.

In many jurisdictions the book itself is not admissible as substantive evidence. Excerpts from it are limited for impeachment purposes. The data recited is not offered for the truth of the matter contained therein; hence, it is not deemed hearsay. In a number of jurisdictions, learned treatises may be used as substantive evidence in direct examination as well as impeaching evidence on cross-examination.[14] The theory of such a rule is that reliable writings, as with basically reliable oral testimony, should be considered admissible as evidence.[15]

The objections against the admissibility of learned treatises as substantive evidence are that the facts or opinions contained therein are hearsay since there is no opportunity to evaluate the credibility of the author, and confrontation is denied. Other objections may be that a treatise is outmoded, that passages may be extracted which convey a false impression and that the raw, unexplained material may be confusing to the jury. In those jurisdictions admitting the learned treatise as substantive evidence, a foundation is laid by proof that the work is authoritative. The foundation may be established by an expert or by judicial notice.

The rule against the admission as substantive evidence of learned treatises has been criticized in the legal literature. Rule 803(18) of the Federal Rules of Evidence lists learned treatises among the recognized exceptions to the hearsay rule. It provides:

> "The following are not excluded by the hearsay rule, even though the declarant is available as a witness:

* * *

> "(18) Learned treatises—To the extent called to the attention of an expert witness upon cross-examination or relied upon by him in direct examination, statements contained in published treatises, periodicals, or pamphlets on a subject of history, medicine, or other science or art, established as a reliable authority by the testimony or admission of the witness or by other expert testimony or by judicial notice. If admitted,

13. See, Darling v. Charleston Community Memorial Hospital, 50 Ill.App.2d 253, 200 N.E.2d 149 (1964), affirmed 33 Ill.2d 326, 211 N.E.2d 253 (1965).

14. See, Lewandowski v. Preferred Risk Mutual Ins. Co., 33 Wis.2d 69, 146 N.W.2d 505 (1966); State v. Nicolosi, 228 La. 65, 81 So.2d 771 (1955); Stoudenmeier v. Williamson, 29 Ala. 558 (1857); Kan.Code of Civil Procedure, § 60–401 (1964); S.C.Code, § 26–142 (1952); and Uniform Rules of Evidence, Rule 63(31).

15. Legal writers have generally been in favor of abandoning the prohibitions of the common law doctrine prohibiting admissibility of treatises. See authorities collected in Redden & Salzburg, Federal Rules of Evidence Manual, 1975, at pp. 295–96.

the statements may be read into evidence but may not be received as exhibits."

The federal rule does not require that the expert rely on the text or even recognize it as authoritative. Its rationale is founded on the case of Reilly v. Pinkus,[16] where the Supreme Court pointed out that testing of professional competence of a witness would be incomplete unless there was an opportunity to explore the witness' attitude toward the authoritative or generally accepted textbooks in his field.

Rule 803(18) makes even more sense when one reads it in conjunction with Rule 703, which also departed from the common law in permitting an expert to express an opinion based on facts or data which are not admissible in evidence, or upon data received by the expert from books. If the witness may rely thereon, it makes sense that such authorities may be independently used as evidence by a cross-examiner.

When cross-examination from scientific texts is contemplated, the lawyer sponsoring the witness should caution him beforehand not to admit the authority of any book with which he is not sufficiently familiar to make that judgment. The opposition is thus put to the proof of showing its authenticity from other sources. Experts should be advised to ask to examine the book, its date of publication and edition before conceding it to be authoritative.

Cross-examination based upon a text should proceed in most jurisdictions roughly as follows:

Q: In reaching your opinion, did you rely upon any authority?

Q: Is your opinion in this case corroborated by authorities in the field of [the witness' specialization]?

Q: I have here a copy of ... by ... entitled.... The author is a recognized leader in his field, isn't he?

Q: Isn't it true that this book is currently used as an authoritative source in the field of [witness' specialization]?

Q: Have you read this book?

Q: Do you rely in part upon the teachings or views of [author of learned treatise] in reaching your opinion?

[or in lieu of the foregoing six questions:]

Q: I have here a copy of ... by ... on the subject of [witness' specialization]. Are you familiar with this book?

Q: Is it considered a standard authority in your field?

Q: In fact, it is an authority contained in the library of many other specialists in your field, isn't it?

16. 338 U.S. 269 (1949). See also, Delaware v. Fensterer, supra note 7.

Then proceed as follows:

> [Read the helpful passage to the witness and ask if he agrees; or hand him the book; point out the contradicting passage and have him read it.]

Q: Does this support your opinion or is it inconsistent with your opinion?

§ 1.23 The Hypothetical Question

When an expert bases his testimony on personal knowledge, it is relatively simple to lay an evidentiary foundation. He is asked to detail the facts he relied upon in forming his opinion, and then he gives his opinion based upon those facts. However, when he has no firsthand knowledge of the facts at issue or has made no investigation of them, his scientific skill may be drawn upon by asking him to *assume* certain facts disclosed by the evidence and to give his opinion in answer to a question based upon those assumptions. Ordinarily the assumptions are based upon the testimony of other witnesses. The question usually assumes those disputed facts which are consistent with the examiner's theory of the case.

A hypothetical question may also be used in the cross-examination of testifying experts in order to seek a contradictory opinion by the assumption of facts otherwise in evidence but unknown to the testifying witness.

The weakness of the hypothetical question as an effective tool of evidence lies in its artificial nature. In practice, it does not accurately portray the whole panorama of facts. Attorneys are permitted to slant their questions and to ignore significant facts. Consequently, a misleading answer may be adduced when an expert is forced to answer the question in the context in which it is framed.

Some latitude is permitted in framing the hypothetical facts. Although most jurisdictions require that undisputed relevant facts must be included in the question even though they favor the opposition, the question does not have to include all material facts, since they may be supplied by the opposition on cross-examination; but the hypothetical question must not include a situation having no foundation in the facts presented.

Mechanically, the witness is asked to assume the recited facts to be true, and he is asked whether or not he is able to form an opinion from the assumed facts, and, if so, to state that opinion.

Cross-examination of an expert on his answer to a hypothetical question may follow one of several tracks, namely: (1) supplementing the hypothesis with additional facts in evidence and asking for an opinion on the modified hypothesis; (2) substituting a different hypothesis based on the examiner's theory of the case; or (3) showing the witness based his opinion on hypothetical facts not in evidence.

The following questions may be utilized as a predicate for expert opinion based on a hypothetical set of facts:

Q: Please assume the following set of facts to be true and correct. [State facts.]

> Assuming those facts to be true and correct, can you express an opinion with reasonable certainty as an expert whether [state the problem]? [The witness then answers in the affirmative.]

Q: What is that opinion?

Q: Will you explain to the jury the reasoning upon which you base this opinion?

Q: I have just asked you to assume certain facts, which I related in detail, and to give the court your opinion based upon them. Is this the first time the facts I just recited for you to assume have been brought to your attention?

Q: Had you previously been given this same hypothetical set of facts for study and examination? When? Who gave it to you?

Q: What did you do with this statement when it was given to you?

Q: Was the opinion you gave today the result of your serious study of the assumed facts previously given to you?

There are some jurisdictions, in certain types of case situations, which permit an expert lacking first-hand knowledge of the facts to give his opinion without embodying the question in a hypothetical form.

§ 1.24 Court Instructions on Expert Testimony

Jury instructions, similar to those that follow, might be requested in appropriate cases. These samples are intended only as guides and will require revision to fit the facts of the particular case.

1. LIMITING IMPORT OF EXPERT OPINION

Sample: "There has been introduced the testimony of certain witnesses who purport to be skilled in their line of endeavor. Such witnesses are known in law as expert witnesses. An expert witness is one who is skilled in any certain science, art, business, or profession, and possesses peculiar knowledge acquired by study, observation and practice. You are instructed that you may consider the testimony of these witnesses and give it such weight and value as you think it should have, but the weight and value to be given their testimony is for you to determine. You are not required to surrender your own judgment to that of any person testifying as an expert, for the testimony of an expert, like that of any other witness, is to be received by you and given such weight and value as you deem it is entitled to receive."

Sample: "During this trial the jury has heard the testimony of expert witnesses. Such evidence is admissible where the subject matter involved requires special study, training, or skill not within the realm of the ordinary experience of mankind, and the witness is qualified to give an expert opinion. However, the fact that an expert opinion is given does not mean that it is binding upon the jury, or that the jury is obligated to accept the expert's opinion as to what the facts are. It is the province of the jury to determine the credibility and weight that should be given to the expert opinion in the light of all the evidence. Although the jury may not arbitrarily disregard the testimony of an expert witness, if the jury finds that his opinion is not based on the facts, or is contrary to the evidence, the jury should disregard it." [1]

2. UNCONTRADICTED EXPERT OPINION

Sample: "A person who by education, study, and experience has become an expert in an art, science or profession and who is called as a witness may give his opinion as to any such matter in which he is specially qualified and versed and which is material to the case. The opinion of an expert should be considered and weighed by you like other evidence in the case. You are not bound by it if the facts upon which the opinion is based have not been established by the evidence, beyond a reasonable doubt; however, you should not reject the opinion of a qualified expert if it is uncontradicted and not inherently unreasonable."

3. CONFLICTING EXPERT OPINION

Sample: "If, in this case, you find that there has been a conflict in the testimony of the expert witnesses, then by considering and weighing the credibility and qualification of the respective experts who have testified, the logic of the reasons given in support of their opinion and the other evidence in the case which favors or opposes a given opinion, and by using your own experience and good judgment as reasonable and intelligent people, you must resolve that conflict and determine which, if either, of the opinions to accept as accurate."

§ 1.25　Ethical Considerations

1. THE EXPERT'S ETHICAL OBLIGATIONS

When selecting, preparing, and presenting expert testimony, an attorney must be aware, throughout the process, of his own ethical obligations as well as of the ethical constraints upon an expert's behavior. It is important to become aware of the expert's ethical obligations under the ethics codes of certifying bodies or professional associations.[1]

§ 1.24

1. See, Manual on Jury Instructions, 33 F.R.D. 523, 595 (1964).

§ 1.25

1. E.g., National Association of Medical Examiners Bylaws, Article Ten, Ethics (1992) which provides that members of N.A.M.E. shall conform to the published ethics of the American Medical Association; The National Society of Professional Engineers Code of Ethics (1990) sets forth fundamental canons, rules of practice, and professional obligations; The American Board of Criminalistics has promulgated rules of professional conduct which must be complied with by applicants and diplomates: Bylaws, Article IV.5 (1992).

For example, members of the American Academy of Forensic Sciences (AAFS) are prohibited from making material misrepresentations of their education or of the data upon which their professional opinions are based.[2] If an AAFS member is found to have violated the code, an ethics committee may impose sanctions, such as censure, suspension, or expulsion from the organization.[3]

Some courts have sanctioned experts for their unethical behavior. In Schmidt v. Ford Motor Co.[4] the court banned the plaintiff's accident reconstruction expert from testifying in federal court in Colorado because he had conveyed intentionally misleading information in depositions and informal conversations with defense expert. The expert also concealed his knowledge from the defendant that one of the plaintiffs had tampered with the evidence.

2. ATTORNEYS' ETHICS IN DEALING WITH EXPERTS

Attorneys' ethical obligations are contained in each state's Rules of Professional Conduct or Code of Professional Responsibility. While no specific rule deals directly with attorneys and expert witnesses, some of the American Bar Association Model Rules of Professional Conduct are applicable. The Model Rules have been adopted in a majority of states.[5] Some of the model rules which impact upon an attorney's use of expert witnesses are the following:

Rule 3.3 (Candor Toward the Tribunal) requires the attorney to investigate the background of expert witnesses to avoid putting on perjurious testimony regarding their credentials.

Rule 3.8 (Special Responsibilities of a Prosecutor) specifies that the prosecutor's role as a "minister of justice" requires him to make timely disclosure of evidence or information that will negate evidence of guilt or mitigate guilt. Therefore, if fraud is uncovered relating to the expert's acts or knowledge it must be disclosed.

Rule 5.3 (Responsibilities Regarding Nonlawyer Assistants) applies to experts as well as paralegals, and extends to situations where the lawyer is in essence ratifying the unethical conduct of the expert.

Rule 8.3 (Reporting Professional Misconduct) requires the prosecutor to report unethical conduct of other attorneys. Therefore, if the opposing party's counsel knowingly uses an expert discovered to be a fraud, counsel is obligated to report the other lawyer to the grievance committee. If counsel doesn't report, he is himself in violation of the rule.

Rule 8.4(c) (Misconduct) states that it is professional misconduct to violate the Model Rules, commit a criminal act that reflects adversely on

---

2. The American Academy of Forensic Sciences Bylaws Code of Ethics and Conduct, Art. II, Section 1 (1993).

3. Id. at Art. II, Section 2.

4. 112 F.R.D. 216 (D.Colo.1986).

5. By November 1993, 37 states and the District of Columbia and the Virgin Islands had adopted the Model Rules.

a lawyer's honesty, trustworthiness or fitness; engage in conduct involving dishonesty, fraud, deceit or misrepresentation or engage in conduct that is prejudicial to the administration of justice.

Additionally, an attorney shall not fabricate evidence or counsel or assist a witness to testify falsely or offer an inducement to a witness that is prohibited by law or make frivolous discovery requests or intentionally fail to comply with a legally proper discovery request.[6] A lawyer shall not make false statements of material fact or law to a third person, such as an expert witness.[7]

Model Rules 1.1 (Competence) and 1.3 (Diligence) require an attorney to seek out expert services, if needed by the client. Failure by a defense counsel in a criminal case to obtain the services of expert witnesses may later be deemed by courts to have resulted in the ineffective assistance of counsel.[8]

A lawyer may not promise an expert a fee contingent on the outcome of the case,[9] nor may an attorney share fees with an expert.[10] An attorney has been held to have an ethical obligation to pay an expert's fees unless he gives an express disclaimer of responsibility.[11]

Attorneys have been sanctioned by the bar for abusing an expert witness on cross-examination. A prosecutor was suspended from the practice of law for thirty days for improperly eliciting irrelevant testimony from the defense's expert witness, a psychiatrist. The prosecutor insulted the witness, ignored the court's rulings on defense objections which were sustained, and inserted his personal opinions on psychiatry and the insanity defense into his questioning.[12]

It should also be noted that Rule 11, Federal Rules of Civil Procedure, provides for sanctions to punish a knowing filing of a false and misleading pleading. Courts have held that failure to disclose a contrary expert opinion alone is an insufficient basis for imposing Rule 11 sanctions.[13] In Coffey v. Healthtrust, Inc.[14] the defendant moved for Rule 11 sanctions against a plaintiff's attorney claiming that when the lawyer filed an economic study, expert's affidavit and accompanying brief supporting plaintiff's position that the hospital did not have competitors in its geographic market, the study's authors had told him that the expert's use of the study to support plaintiff's position would be misguided. The Tenth Circuit reversed, noting that while the attorney lied at

---

6. Model Rules of Professional Conduct, Rule 3.4 (1993).

7. Model Rules of Professional Conduct, Rule 4.1 (1993).

8. Proffitt v. United States, 582 F.2d 854 (4th Cir.1978), cert. denied 447 U.S. 910 (1980); Moore v. State, 827 S.W.2d 213 (Mo.1992)—counsel ineffective for failing to request serological test.

9. Dupree v. Malpractice Research, Inc., 179 Mich.App. 254, 445 N.W.2d 498 (1989).

10. Sharing fees with nonlawyers violates ABA Model Rule 5.4(1), Model Rules of Professional Conduct (1993).

11. Copp v. Breskin, 56 Wash.App. 229, 782 P.2d 1104 (1989)—the court cited ABA Model Rules of Professional Conduct 1.8(e) and 4.4 as authority.

12. The Florida Bar v. Schaub, 618 So.2d 202 (Fla.1993).

13. Schering Corp. v. Vitarine Pharmaceuticals Inc., 889 F.2d 490 (3d Cir.1989).

14. 1 F.3d 1101 (10th Cir.1993).

the Rule 11 hearing regarding whether the study's authors talked with him, it may be a disciplinary matter but not a subject for Rule 11 sanctions.

The court reasoned that an attorney must be allowed to reasonably rely on an expert's opinion as the basis of the client's position without fear of punishment for the expert's errors in judgment. The court found that the attorney's reliance on the expert's opinion had been reasonable because (1) the expert had sworn to his position in his affidavit, (2) the trial court had accepted the witness's expert status, and (3) the expert had held his position even when confronted with the contradictory conclusions of the study's authors. The court noted that opposing counsel had the opportunity and the duty to expose weaknesses in evidence.

The American Bar Association standards relating to the Administration of Criminal Justice also set forth standards for prosecutors and defense counsel to follow when working with expert witnesses in criminal trials. The standards provide that the attorney should respect the expert's independence, not dictate the formation of the expert's opinion, and that paying excessive or contingent fees is unprofessional conduct.[15]

§ 1.26 Liability of the Expert Witness For Malpractice

1. EXPERT MALPRACTICE—A PROBLEM OF NATIONAL SCOPE

In recent years, the law has been developing a new cause of action designed to hold expert witnesses, like doctors and lawyers, responsible for their negligent professional behavior. The law of expert witness negligence has developed largely in response to a recent recognition that such negligence is not uncommon.[1] Erroneous conclusions have been reported even within well-accepted scientific techniques such as fingerprint identification. In 1987, federal and state officials had to review 159 criminal cases in North Carolina after local authorities discovered what they determined to be questionable fingerprint identifications.[2] A similar situation arose in 1993 in New York.[3] Also in 1993, in the

---

15. American Bar Association Standards Relating to the Administration of Criminal Justice, Standards 3–3.3 and 4.4.4 (3d ed. 1992).

§ 1.26

1. Hilts, "Misconduct in Science Is Not Rare, a Survey Finds," *The New York Times* [Nat. ed.] Nov. 12, 1993, at A–13; Starrs, "In the Land of Agog: An Allegory for the Expert Witness," 30 *J.For.Sci.* 289 (1985)—Professor Starrs cites numerous instances of erroneous expert testimony. See also, Moenssens, "Novel Scientific Evidence in Criminal Cases: Some Words of Caution," 84 *J.Crim.L. & Criminology* 801 (1993)—this article contains numerous re-

cent instances of expert incompetence, negligence, and intentional fraud.

2. Bowden & Barret, "Fingerprint Errors Raise Questions on Local Convictions," *Fayetteville Times*, Jan. 15, 1988, at 1A. The review was prompted by a fingerprint misidentification that resulted in the dismissal of two murder charges by the district attorney's office.

3. The negligence that may have bordered on intentional misconduct of several fingerprint technicians of the New York State Police was disclosed on the CBS program *60 Minutes*. See, Moenssens, op. cit. supra n. 14, at 816. On these cases, see also, Kutz, "Guest Editorial—A Mill Stone,

aftermath of the reversal of a rape conviction based largely on a serologist's evidence that was shown to be in error,[4] a state supreme court mandated an investigation of the effect the expert's potential errors might have had on other cases in which the expert witness had testified. At the conclusion of the inquiry, the judge assigned to investigate the conduct of the expert rendered a detailed report to the Supreme Court of West Virginia concluding that:

> "The overwhelming evidence of a pattern and practice of misconduct by Zain [the state police serologist] completely undermines the validity and reliability of any forensic work he performed during his tenure in the serology department of the state police crime laboratory. If the information which is now available concerning the pattern and practice of misconduct by Zain had been available during the prosecution of cases in which he was involved, the evidence regarding the results of serological testing would have been deemed inadmissible.[5] "

Within the last year, pathologists have either been shown to have faked hundreds of autopsies,[6] or committed grievous errors [7] in determining the cause of death.

At present, the law does little to regulate the quality of expert testimony.[8] Solutions offered by the scientific and legal communities to

Not a Milestone," 43 *J.Forensic Identification* 1 (1993).

4. State v. Woodall, 182 W.Va. 15, 385 S.E.2d 253 (1989).

5. In The Matter of an Investigation of the West Virginia State Police Crime Laboratory, Serology Division, Civil Action No. 93–MISC–402, Report by The Hon. James O. Holliday, Senior Judge [hereinafter Report]. The report's recommendations included that statement that "[d]ue to the undisputed nature of the overwhelming evidence of misconduct on the part of Zain, ..." that prisoners and parolees in whose cases the serologist testified be permitted to file petitions for post-conviction habeas corpus. This applies to defendants in potentially 134 cases. Zain left the state police in 1989 and took a position as serologist with the Bexar County Criminal Investigative Lab in San Antonio, Texas. He was fired from that job for similar irregularities. "West Virginia Invalidates Blood Test Results in Crimes," *The New York Times* [Nat. ed.], Nov. 12, 1993, at A12; "Texas investigator says Zain more than careless," *The Dominion Post*, Nov. 7, 1993, at 4–A.

6. Fricker, "Pathologist's Plea Adds to Turmoil," *A.B.A.J.*, Mar. 1993, at 24. The cases may result in the review of numerous convictions. In a related story, the pathologist was reported to have a "reputation for

providing the type of forensic evidence prosecutors needed," though his conclusions were later deemed "impossible" by qualified reviewing medical examiners. See, Fricker, "Reasonable Doubts," *ABA J.*, Dec. 1993, 38, at 44.

7. Nordheimer, "New Jersey Autopsy Misses Two Bullets in a Man's Head," *The New York Times* [Nat. ed.], Oct. 20, 1993, at A1. The article mentions autopsies by county medical examiners in two different New Jersey counties, and quoted the pathologist who had discovered the errors as stating that bad forensic medicine in New Jersey is more commonplace than the average citizen would dare imagine. It also mentions cases where a pathologist described bullet entrance and exit wounds, its track through the brain, in a case where it was later established that death was due to "blunt force injury" and that no evidence of a bullet wound existed. Further noted was a case where a medical examiner concluded that a woman died from alcohol poisoning and exposure, when a later autopsy at the request of the family established the woman had been strangled and raped—a homicide.

8. Peterson & Murdock, "Forensic Science Ethics: Developing an Integrated System of Support and Enforcement," 34 *J.For.Sci.* 749 (1989).

curb expert abuses include: capping expert witness fees,[9] pre-screening experts, using only court-appointed experts, adherence to a strict code of ethics,[10] peer review,[11] and a science court.[12] Additionally, it has been suggested that fraudulent experts be prosecuted,[13] and that the principal safeguard against errant expert testimony is the opportunity for opposing counsel to cross-examine.[14] The reality is that most lawyers do a woefully inadequate job in cross-examining experts.[15] One reason for this is improper preparation. Another may be that lawyers are often reluctant to incur the risks involved in challenging experts in their own fields. Many lawyers do not even avail themselves of the assistance of experts in preparing for cross-examination and are therefore unable to effectively challenge statements made by experts. Finally, the vast majority of civil and criminal cases are settled or plea bargained prior to trial so that the expert may never be subjected to rigorous questioning during the adversary process.

To date, none of the solutions offered to curb expert abuses have succeeded in accomplishing their goal. Arguably, attempts at monitoring expert testimony may serve to deter some expert negligence and also result in experts being held personally accountable. However, such steps do not necessarily provide for compensation to individuals harmed by an expert's negligence.

2. THE NEW TORT OF EXPERT MALPRACTICE

In view of the inadequacy or unavailability of the solutions to expert negligence and/or intentional professional misconduct, and that professional sanctions against an expert do not make whole a person injured as a result of such misconduct, tort actions for damages against experts and their employers are being resorted to more and more frequently. In the West Virginia serologist's case, a civil action for damages filed against the State resulted in a $1,000,000 settlement.[16]

---

9. Florida Senate Bill 380 (1990), proposed capping expert fees at $250 an hour.

10. National Forensic Center Summarized Code of Professional and Ethical Conduct, 1992.

11. Burack, "Of Reliable Science: Scientific Peer Review, Federal Regulatory Agencies and the Courts," 7 *Va.J.Nat.Resources L.* 27 (1987).

12. See, "Twenty–Five Year Retrospective on the Science Court: A Symposium," in 4 *RISK—Issues in Health & Safety* 95–188 (1993), containing a series of articles by advocates and detractors of the science court, including one by its "inventor." See, Kantrowitz, "Elitism vs. Checks and Balances in Communicating Scientific Information to the Public," 4 *RISK—Issues in Health & Safety* 101 (1993).

13. Report, supra n. 17.

14. Trower v. Jones, 121 Ill.2d 211, 117 Ill.Dec. 136, 520 N.E.2d 297 (1988); Sears v. Rutishauser, 102 Ill.2d 402, 80 Ill.Dec. 758, 466 N.E.2d 210 (1984).

15. Dowd, Book Review on Anderson & Winfree, "Expert Witnesses: Criminologists in the Courtroom," [1987], 14 *N.Eng.L. on Crim. & Civ.Confinement* 169, 171 (1988).

16. Report, op. cit. at note 18, at 2. The Report discloses that the filing of the civil law suit by the released Woodall resulted in the preliminary discovery that the serologist's errors and other misconduct were a matter of common practice, and induced the state insurance carrier to recommend settlement for the policy's limit. This settlement then led to the mandate by the state supreme court to investigate all the past cases wherein the serologist gave expert testimony.

Only an expert witness malpractice cause of action will protect and compensate injured individuals, as well as deter future misconduct. It will ensure "quality control" of expert opinions by encouraging experts to be careful and accurate. The four elements of the expert witness malpractice action are: (1) the existence of a duty owed to the plaintiff arising out of the relationship between the expert and the plaintiff; (2) a negligent act or omission by the expert in breach of that duty; (3) causation; and (4) damages.[17]

The premise of the expert witness malpractice cause of action is that, first of all, expert witnesses owe a duty to their clients. However, the duty does not end there. Expert witnesses also owe a duty to any foreseeable plaintiff who may be affected by the expert's conduct and who are likely to suffer damages due to a negligently rendered opinion. These duties based upon their professional knowledge and skills are similar to those duties owed by a doctor to a patient and a lawyer to a client.

The standard of care for a forensic scientist is that of the reasonably prudent practitioner in the relevant scientific field. Standards of professional practice and ethical codes as promulgated by the discipline may be used to help define the duty of care. Most disciplines within the forensic sciences have adopted such standards of conduct. In order for a plaintiff to prevail, it must be determined that the expert did not adhere to the standard of a reasonably prudent expert in either rendering an opinion, conducting an examination, or giving testimony. Ordinarily, an independent evaluation by a disinterested expert skilled in the same field will be required to determine whether an expert deviated from the required standard of care.

A crucial element of the tort of malpractice is causation. Causation tests whether the defendant's actions were in fact connected by physical events to the plaintiff's injury, and whether the connection was close enough to allow compensation to the injured party. As stated by Richard S. Frank, a past president of the American Academy of Forensic Sciences, "[t]he impact of the forensic scientist's conclusions affords no room for error, because such an error may be the direct cause of an injustice." [18] In some cases, it will be readily apparent that an expert's testimony alone "caused" the wrong. This is especially true when the expert evidence is the only determinative evidence presented in the litigation. Many studies have demonstrated that, despite jury instructions to the contrary, jurors give expert testimony greater weight than other evidence.[19] Thus, it is clear that financial injury to a potential plaintiff, or conviction and incarceration of a potentially innocent indi-

17. Keeton et al., *Prosser and Keeton on the Law of Torts* § 30, at 164–165 (5th ed. 1984).

18. Frank, "The Essential Commitment For a Forensic Scientist," 32 *J.For.Sci.* 5 (1987).

19. Ludwig & Fontaine, "Effect of Witnesses' Expertness and Manner of Delivery of Testimony on Verdicts of Simulated Jurors," 42 *Psychol.Rep.* 955 (1978).

vidual who is prosecuted on the basis of an expert's opinion evidence,[20] are reasonably foreseeable consequences of negligence, incompetence, or intentional misconduct by an expert.

Where a claim of expert witness malpractice is proved to have occurred in civil litigation, the measure of direct damages could include: the difference between a full verdict of proved loss and the reduced verdict resulting from the expert's testimony; the difference between a full settlement and the reduced settlement that resulted from the expert's misconduct; and/or the cost in experts' and investigators' and attorneys' fees for responding to the expert's testimony and in proving the misconduct.

Expert witness malpractice causes of action are gaining momentum. Courts in New Jersey,[21] Texas,[22] California,[23] and Missouri [24] are among the growing number of jurisdictions that have allowed plaintiffs to sue experts for their malpractice. Only one jurisdiction, Washington,[25] has clearly granted immunity to expert witnesses, stating that experts ought to be accorded absolute immunity and should be shielded through the testimonial privilege. Such limitations are rare, however, and the general recognition that such actions will be recognized by courts have induced defendants in malpractice suits to agree to settlements in many cases.

While no courts have been found who shield erring expert witnesses from perjury charges for willful deceptions, or from damage actions where the expert's conduct involved intentional or grossly negligent conduct, a few courts have shielded experts from civil liability for damages in ordinary negligence cases. The courts have arrived at that result in one of two ways: (1) by holding that negligent mistakes or inaccuracies do not constitute perjury; or (2) by holding that testimony and reports provided to courts are privileged.[26] Some courts hold that the expert witness who gives opinion evidence is the court's witness, and therefore enjoys immunity against all post-trial damage claims whether sued by a party or non-party to the action.[27] Two cases addressing such issues arose in California and Missouri. In Mattco Forge, Inc. v. Arthur

---

20. Courts have awarded plaintiffs damages of a certain amount per month for illegal confinement due to legal malpractice, rejecting the argument that estimating the value of a person's loss of liberty is speculative. E.g., Geddie v. St. Paul Fire and Marine Ins. Co., 354 So.2d 718 (La.App. 1978). See also, Holliday v. Jones, 215 Cal.App.3d 102, 264 Cal.Rptr. 448 (1989), awarding damages for emotional distress as a result of wrongful incarceration due to professional malpractice.

21. Levine v. Wiss & Co., 97 N.J. 242, 478 A.2d 397, 399 (1984).

22. James v. Brown, 637 S.W.2d 914 (Tex.1982).

23. Mattco Forge, Inc. v. Arthur Young & Co., 5 Cal.App. 4th 392, 6 Cal.Rptr.2d 781 (1992).

24. Murphy v. A.A. Mathews, 841 S.W.2d 671 (Mo.1992).

25. Bruce v. Byrne–Stevens & Assoc. Engineers, Inc., 113 Wash.2d 123, 776 P.2d 666 (1989).

26. Saks, "Prevalence and Impact of Ethical Problems in Forensic Science," 34 J.For.Sci. 772 (1989)—containing a summary of some cases involving litigation against expert witnesses.

27. Bailey v. Rogers, 631 S.W.2d 784 (Tex.App.1982); Clark v. Grigson, 579 S.W.2d 263 (Tex.App.1978).

Young & Co.,[28] the court held that the litigation privilege in the California Civil Code does not protect a negligent expert witness from liability to the party who hired the witness. In so holding, the court stated "applying the privilege does not encourage witnesses to testify truthfully; indeed by shielding a negligent expert witness from liability, it has the opposite effect." [29] The case went to trial and, in July 1994, the jury returned a verdict of $14,200,000 in compensatory damages and $27,680,000 in punitive damages against the expert witnesses for their negligence.[30] Also, in Murphy v. A.A. Mathews,[31] the Missouri Supreme Court held that witness immunity does not bar an action against a professional who agrees to provide litigation-related services for compensation if the professional is negligent in providing the agreed services. The court stressed, however, that its holding would not subject an adverse expert to malpractice liability because the expert owes no professional duty to the adversary. The court also stated that an expert retained by the court, independent of the litigants, would not be subject to malpractice liability. The *Matthews* holding is limited to pre-trial, litigation support activities.

Witness immunity is an exception to the general rules of liability. The rule is traditionally limited to defamation cases and is extremely narrow in scope. Immunity was not meant to bar a suit against a professional who negligently performs services. The complaint is not with the testimony provided in court, it is with the out-of-court work product which was negligently produced. By testifying, the expert is merely publishing his negligence in court. Therefore, no absolute immunity should be afforded experts; they are neither judges nor their adjuncts, but merely third party participants in litigation. And the courts, the legal profession, and the forensic disciplines recognize that the trend is firmly toward permitting claims for damages resulting from negligent testimony by experts.

Some concern may be voiced over whether the growing recognition of a cause of action for expert malpractice will have a chilling effect on the willingness of persons to serve as forensic experts in litigation. The emergence of such a cause of action may in fact result in the disappearance of some experts who are habitually negligent or incompetent, but this is of course a salutary by-product of the legal trend. But even if the existence of a cause of action for expert malpractice has an effect on the availability of a number of experts, or results in an increase in the fees charged for their services, these results are not so compelling as to justify a public policy against recognizing causes of action for expert witness malpractice. The very existence of the cause of action will ensure that experts are held accountable for their opinions. The full and accurate development of evidence in civil and criminal litigation is

28. 5 Cal.App. 4th 392, 6 Cal.Rptr.2d 781 (1992).

29. Id. at 788. The court stated, however, that the California litigation privilege would still shield experts that are court appointed, and would also shield expert witnesses from suit by opposing parties. (At 789.)

30. *The Expert Witn. J.* 1 (July 1994).

31. 841 S.W.2d 671 (Mo.1992).

not served by protecting the negligent, incompetent, or dishonest expert witness. The justice system as a whole benefits when such causes of actions are permitted. The forensic sciences themselves will enjoy greater respect and admiration when it is known their practitioners are accountable for misdeeds and that the professions favor eliminating the unworthy among them.[32]

VII. MISCELLANEOUS

§ 1.27 Bibliography of Additional References

Books and articles footnoted in the text are ordinarily not repeated here.

Anonymous:

"Locating Scientific and Technical Experts," 2 Am.Jur.Trials 293 (1964).

"Selecting and Preparing Expert Witnesses," 2 Am.Jur.Trials 585 (1964).

Annotations:

"Sanctions Against Defendant in Criminal Cases for Failure to Comply with Discovery Requirements," 9 A.L.R.4th 837 (1981).

"Exclusion of Evidence for Failure of Prosecution to Comply with Discovery Requirements," 27 A.L.R.4th 105 (1984).

"Rights of Accused in State Courts to Have Experts Inspect, Examine or Test Physical Evidence in the Possession of the Prosecution— Modern Cases," 27 A.L.R.4th 1188 (1984).

Articles and Books:

Carlson, "Policing the Bases of Modern Expert Testimony," 39 *Vanderbilt L.Rev.* 577 (1986).

Carter, "Scientific Liberalism, Scientistic Law," 69 *Ore.L.Rev.* 471 (1990).

Cohn, "Tort and Other Remedies for Spoliation of Evidence," 81 *Ill.Bar J.* 128 (1993).

Conrad, "The Expert and Legal Certainty," 9 *J.For.Sci.* 445 (1964).

---

32. The President of the International Association for Identification wrote a letter to CBS' *60 Minutes* after the program about the New York State Police fingerprint experts who fabricated evidence aired on March 28, 1993. In it, he states, *inter alia:* "The IAI strongly condemns the manipulation of any type of physical evidence or sworn testimony which influences the fair outcome of an investigation or legal proceeding. Nothing undermines the integrity of scientific evidence more severely than fabrication [of evidence] by an individual." The writer also assured CBS that the organization scrutinizes very carefully all cases where any examiner's misconduct or incompetence is questioned and said "the forensic disciplines are quick to discipline and criminally prosecute those responsible." See, "Letter from President Shane to CBS '60 Minutes'," [reprinted in] *Chesapeake Examiner,* Aug. 1993, at 20.

Ehrhardt, "The Conflict Concerning Expert Witnesses and Legal Conclusions," 92 *W.Va.L.Rev.* 645 (1990).

Forinash, "Analyzing Scientific Evidence: From Validity to Reliability With A Two–Step Approach," 24 *St. Mary's L.J.* 223 (1992).

Garcia, "Legal and Ethical Considerations in Using Expert Witnesses in Litigation," 1 *Shepard's Exp. & Scient. Ev. Q.* 717 (1994).

Giannelli & Imwinkelreid, *Scientific Evidence* 2d ed. (1993).

Graham, "Expert Witness Testimony and the Federal Rules of Evidence: Insuring Adequate Assurance of Trustworthiness," 31 *Tr.Law Guide* 1 (1987).

Guttmacher, "Problems Faced by the Impartial Expert Witness in Court: The American View," 34 *Temp.L.Q.* 369 (1964).

Harbour, "Increasing Judicial Scrutiny of Expert Testimony in Toxic Tort Cases," 30 *Washburn L.J.* 428 (1991).

Herasimchuk, "A Practical Guide to the Admissibility of Novel Expert Evidence in Criminal Trials Under Federal Rule 702," 22 *St. Mary's L.J.* 181 (1990).

Imwinkelreid, *The Methods of Attacking Scientific Evidence* (1982).

Imwinkelreid, "Judge versus Jury: Who Should Decide Questions of Preliminary Facts Conditioning the Admissibility of Scientific Evidence," 25 *Wm. & Mary L.Rev.* 577 (1984).

Imwinkelreid, *Evidentiary Foundations* (2d ed. 1989).

Imwinkelreid & Blumoff, *Pretrial Discovery: Strategy & Tactics,* [Callaghan's Trial Practice Series] (1986).

Imwinkelreid & Scofield, "The Recognition of an Accused's Constitutional Right to Introduce Expert Testimony Attacking the Weight of Prosecution Science Evidence: The Antidote for the Supreme Court's Mistaken Assumption in *California v. Trombetta,*" 33 *Ariz. L.Rev.* 59 (1991).

James, "Fryed Expert Witnesses: The 5th Circuit Takes Charge of Scientific Evidence," 12 *The Rev. of Litigation* 171 (1992).

Jasanoff & Nelkin, "Science, Technology, and the Limits of Judicial Competence," 214 *Science* 1211 (1981).

Lederer, "Rules of Admissibility of Scientific Evidence," 115 F.D.R. 79 (1987).

Lee, "Court–Appointed Experts and Judicial Reluctance: A Proposal to Amend Rule 706 of the Federal Rules of Evidence," 6 *Yale L. & Pol'y Rev.* 480 (1988).

Lewis, "The Expert Witness in Criminal Cases," *Criminal Defense,* Jan. 1976, p. 4.

Lucas, "The Ethical Responsibilities of the Forensic Scientist—Exploring the Limits," 34 *J.For.Sci.* 729 (1989).

Massaro, "Experts, Psychology, Credibility and Rape: The Rape Trauma Syndrome Issue and Its Implications for Expert Psychological Testimony," 69 *Minn.L.Rev.* 395 (1985).

McLaughlin, "Discovery and Admissibility of Expert Testimony," 63 *Notre Dame L.Rev.* 760 (1988).

Moenssens, "Polygraph Test Results Meet Standards for Admissibility as Evidence," in *Legal Admissibility of the Polygraph,* Ansley, Ed., 1975.

Nyharet & Jones, "What You Don't Know about Technology Can Hurt You," 69 *A.B.A.J.* 1667 (1983).

Peterson, *et al., Crime Laboratory Proficiency Testing Research Program,* 1978.

Peterson & Murdock, "Forensic Science Ethics: Developing an Integrated System of Support and Enforcement," 34 *J.For.Sci.* 749 (1989).

Plotkin, *"Brock v. Merrell Dow Pharmaceuticals, Inc.* What Is the Court's Role in Evaluating Expert Testimony?" 64 *Tulane L.Rev.* 1263 (1990).

Riesel, "Discovery and Examination of Scientific Experts," 32 *Practical Lawyer* 59 (Sept.1986).

Saks, "Expert Witnesses, Nonexpert Witnesses, and Nonwitness Experts," 14 *L. & Human Behavior* 291 (1990).

Strong, "Language and Logic in Expert Testimony: Limiting Expert Testimony by Restrictions of Function, Reliability, and Form," 71 *Ore.L.Rev.* 349 (1992).

Tanford, "A Political Choice Approach to Limiting Prejudicial Evidence," 64 *Ind.L.J.* 831 (1989).

Wilton & Campbell, "The Admissibility of Prior Testimony of Out-of-Court Experts," 39 *Rutgers L.Rev.* 111 (1986).

Zuch, "Discovery of Facts Known and Opinions Held by Experts," 58 *Florida B.J.* 225 (April 1984).

Law Review Notes and Comments:

" 'Helpful' or 'Reasonably Reliable'? Analyzing The Expert Witness's Methodology Under Federal Rules of Evidence 702 and 703," 77 *Cornell L.Rev.* 350 (1992).

"Competency of Medical Expert Witnesses: Standards and Qualifications," 24 *Creighton L.Rev.* 1359 (1991).

"Rubanick v. Witco Chemical Corp.: A New Admissibility Standard for Controversial Scientific Evidence in Toxic Torts—Leaving Science to the Experts Will Not Open the Courts to 'Junk Science'," 14 *Geo. Mason U.L.Rev.* 447 (1991).

"Scientific Evidence in Wisconsin: Using Reliability to Regulate Expert Testimony," 74 *Marquette L.Rev.* 261 (1991).

"Arizona v. Youngblood: Does the Criminal Defendant Lose His Right to Due Process When the State Loses Exculpatory Evidence?," 5 *Touro L.Rev.* 309 (1989).

"The Admissibility of Expert Witness Testimony: Time to Take the Final Leap?" 42 *U.Miami L.Rev.* 831 (1988).

"Cross–Examination of Expert Witnesses: Dispelling the Aura of Reliability," 42 *U.Miami L.Rev.* 1073 (1988).

"Scientific Evidence and the Question of Judicial Capacity," 25 *Wm. & Mary L.Rev.* 675 (1984).

"Seeing Can Be Deceiving: Photographic Evidence in a Visual Age—How Much Weight Does It Deserve?" 25 *Wm. & Mary L.Rev.* 705 (1984).

"Rape Trauma Syndrome and Inconsistent Rulings on Its Admissibility Around the Nation: Should the Washington Supreme Court Reconsider Its Position In State v. Black," 24 *Willamette L.Rev.* 1011 (1988).

Chapter 2

DEMONSTRATIVE EVIDENCE

I. INTRODUCTION

I. INTRODUCTION

§ 2.01　Scope of the Chapter

The modern world is increasingly oriented toward visual stimuli. The media and computers have changed the way society gets and gives its information and its expectations of communication. "It has been estimated that upon graduation, the average high school student has completed 11,000 hours of classroom education while viewing over 15,-000 hours of television."[1] Studies have shown that people retain 87% of the information presented to them visually but only 10% of what they hear.[2] Therefore, in order to effectively communicate to judges and jurors, lawyers and experts must give considerable thought to the types of exhibits they wish to use at trial. The exhibits available will be in one of two categories of evidence, real evidence or demonstrative evidence. Real evidence is evidence furnished by things themselves, as distinguished from a description of them through a witness' testimony.[3] The suspected murder weapon and a bullet retrieved from the decedent would be real evidence presented in a homicide case, while the plaintiff's damaged vehicle and the exhibition of his scars due to the injuries he suffered in the automobile crash would be real evidence in a personal injury case. Demonstrative evidence illustrates, demonstrates or helps explain oral testimony.[4] Examples of demonstrative evidence include models, diagrams, charts, drawings, and computer simulations and animations.

Demonstrative evidence can be used to highlight salient points of an expert's testimony; increase the jurors' comprehension; illustrate information difficult to comprehend; permit the jury to digest large amounts of data; recreate or reconstruct critical events in an evidentiary chain, and add traumatic effect to oral testimony.[5] To be most effective an attorney needs to know what key parts of the expert's presentation will benefit from the use of demonstrative evidence, what kinds of exhibits are available and finally how to introduce such evidence.

To be admitted, demonstrative evidence must illustrate or explain a relevant issue in the case. Generally, courts require substantial similari-

---

§ 2.01

1. Seltzer, "Demonstrative Exhibits: A Key to Effective Jury Presentations," 387 P.L.I. 371 (1990).

2. Id.

3. *Black's Law Dictionary* (6th ed. 1990), at 1264.

4. Id. at 432.

5. Dombroff, *Dombroff on Demonstrative Evidence* (1983), at 4.

ty before admitting demonstrative evidence.[6] The admissibility of demonstrative evidence is within the court's discretion and will only be overturned if the court abused its discretion. In determining the admissibility of such evidence the court must weigh the probative value against any prejudicial effect the evidence might cause.

The use and presentation of various types of real and demonstrative evidence is the subject of many treatises and law review articles.[7] This chapter is not an exhaustive treatment of all types of demonstrative evidence, but an attempt to introduce the reader to frequently used demonstrative evidence and the legal concerns one may face in utilizing such evidence.

II. CASTS, MODELS, MAPS AND DRAWINGS

§ 2.02 Use of Casts and Models as Evidence

It is often useful in court to utilize three-dimensional representations of objects in addition to or in lieu of photographic evidence. The best type of evidence in this category is the plaster cast or mold. It consists, essentially, of a reproduction in plaster or some other substance of an imprint that is discovered at a crime scene. The imprint may be a tire impression in mud, wet soil, or snow; a shoe impression; or an impression of any other object which contains characteristic marks. Certain plastics, resins and materials such as those employed by dentists in making mouth impressions for dentures can also be used to make casts and models. The selection of the proper casting material is usually determined by the circumstances under which an imprint has been made.

Plaster casts are relatively easy to make, provided a good grade of plaster is used and the technician has had some experience working with it. The plaster should be mixed in water until it becomes creamy, after which it is poured over the entire surface to a thickness of about ½ inch. At that time, some reinforcing wire or sticks should be added, and then more plaster is poured into the mold. After the plaster has set—a process that ordinarily takes 10 to 20 minutes—the cast can be removed. It is then marked on the reverse side as to the place it was taken, the date, and by whom.

Special techniques may be needed when the impression is in sand or loose soil or snow, since ordinary pouring of wet plaster may destroy the fine characteristics of the imprint. Among these techniques are strengthening of the marks with a plastic spray, shellac or some other quick-drying fixative. In all such situations, however, before any attempt is made to make a plaster cast of an imprint, the impression should be photographed, to guard against the contingency of any of its details being obliterated by the casting process.

---

6. Carson v. Polley, 689 F.2d 562 (5th Cir.1982); Lopez v. City Taxing Assoc., Inc. 754 S.W.2d 254 (Tex.App.1988).

7. See, Bibliography at end of this chapter for such references.

Another type of demonstrative evidence often employed during a trial is a scale model of a place or a building. The type of model used at trial is only limited by the attorney's imagination (and a client's resources).[1] It can be used in court to help the jury to obtain a clearer image of where and how an incident occurred. It is essential, of course, that the model be built exactly to scale and this calls for extremely accurate measurements and a great deal of skill in reconstructing minute details. One outstanding example of how such a model was used effectively occurred in a notorious Illinois case where eight student nurses had been murdered in a townhouse. The prosecution, in preparation for the trial of the accused killer, had constructed a scale model of the townhouse where the girls lived and where the crime occurred. The model of the townhouse is shown in Figure 1.

Courts have allowed the use of models or skeletons to assist in the explanation of a radiologist's X-ray findings.[2] Courts have also upheld the admission at trial of styrofoam models of heads,[3] replicas of signs,[4] and models of mechanical equipment.[5] Most recently courts have permitted the use of anatomically correct dolls to aid a victim's testimony in sexual abuse and rape cases.[6] In some jurisdictions their use is allowed by statute. For example, Alabama, Connecticut, Michigan, New Hampshire, New Jersey, New York, Pennsylvania, West Virginia, and Wyoming have statutes which allow the use of anatomically correct dolls in certain cases.[7]

§ 2.02

1. See, e.g., Roland v. Langlois, 945 F.2d 956 (7th Cir.1991) (Life-size models of amusement rides admitted into evidence); Martinez v. W.R. Grace Company, 782 P.2d 827 (Colo.App.1989) (Scale model of asphalt bump in a parking lot over which plaintiff tripped properly admitted).

2. Webb v. Angell, 155 Ill.App.3d 848, 108 Ill.Dec. 347, 508 N.E.2d 508 (1987).

3. See, State v. Shaw, 839 S.W.2d 30 (Mo.App.1992) (Court upheld admission of styrofoam head with a pencil inserted to show wound location, bullet path and orientation of the murder weapon. Court also held the model did not have to be made to scale as long as it did not mislead the jury.); Vollbaum v. State, 833 S.W.2d 652 (Tex. App.1992) (Styrofoam model of a woman's head to assist the jury in understanding medical examiner's testimony was properly admitted; Brown v. State, 550 So.2d 527 (Fla.App.1989) (The use of a styrofoam head as demonstrative evidence was allowed with a knife to demonstrate the injuries to the victim in an aggravated battery case.)

4. Cravens v. County of Wood, Ohio, 856 F.2d 753 (6th Cir.1988) (replicas of signs admissible when original sign no longer existed, the replica matched photographs

of the original sign and a cautionary instruction was given).

5. Hoffman v. Niagra Machine and Tool Works Co., 683 F.Supp. 489 (E.D.Pa.1988) (Mechanical model of foot pedal of punch press properly admitted in products liability action, even though it was not identical to the original, as long as the jury was not misled into believing it was an exact replica).

6. See, e.g., State v. Hood, 18 Kan. App.2d 1, 846 P.2d 255 (1993); State v. Ball, 733 S.W.2d 499 (Mo.App.1987); State v. Watson, 484 So.2d 870 (La.App.1986); Vera v. State, 709 S.W.2d 681 (Tex.App. 1986).

7. Ala. Code § 15–25–5 (1993); Conn. Gen.Stat.Ann. § 54–869 (1993); Mich. Comp.Laws Ann. §§ 600.2163a, 712A.17b; 38.104a, 24.275a (West 1993); N.H.Super.Ct.Rule 93–A (1992); N.H.Dist. & Mun. Cts.Rule 1.24; N.J.Stat.Ann. 2A:84A–16.1 (West 1993); N.Y.–McKinney's Crim.Proc. Law § 60.44 (1993); N.Y.–McKinney's Exec.Law § 642–a (1993); 42 Pa.Cons.Stat. Ann. § 5987 (Purdon 1992); W.Va. Code 61–8–13; 61–8B–11; 61–8C–5 (1993); Wyo. Stat. § 7–11–408 (1993).

Most statutes state that the use of the doll is permitted when the witness or victim is under a certain age. For example, the

Fig. 1. The scale model illustrated here was used to show the exact location of the murder victims as well as the layout of the premises and the sequence in which the accused slayer proceeded through the premises. *Courtesy: William Martin, Chicago.*

Casts and models are ordinarily admissible in evidence at the discretion of the judge, if it assists the jury, is relevant to a matter at issue and fairly and accurately represents the item it seeks to portray as long as its probative value is not outweighed by prejudice.[8]

§ 2.03 Maps, Diagrams and Sketches

Another supplement to photography is the use of maps, diagrams and sketches. While it is necessary to record photographically all of the detail of a crime scene, photographs often fail to show important data that cannot be effectively transmitted without the use of sketches or

New York statute permits persons less than sixteen years old to use such dolls. However, one New York court has held that an elderly sodomy victim may also use such a doll to aid in his testimony. People v. Herring, 135 Misc.2d 487, 515 N.Y.S.2d 954 (1987).

8. State v. Mitchell, 751 S.W.2d 65 (Mo. App.1988) (Model or replica of gun, properly admitted when actual weapon was unavailable); People v. Pike, 131 A.D.2d 890, 517 N.Y.S.2d 246 (1987) (model "stun gun" admissible). A scale model may be properly excluded if the danger of unfair prejudice outweighs any probative value of an exhibit. For example, a scale model of an accident scene was properly excluded by the trial court since the jury's primary impression of the scene would have been that it was very dark, when there was a dispute over the visibility and brightness conditions at the scene. Tritt v. Judd's Moving & Storage, Inc., 62 Ohio App.3d 206, 574 N.E.2d 1178 (1990). The use of a specially constructed scale model of the home where multiple murders were committed served as a useful adjunct to the testimony of a surviving eyewitness and was not unduly prejudicial: People v. Speck, 41 Ill.2d 177, 242 N.E.2d 208 (1968). See also, Annos., Propriety in Trial of Criminal Case of Use of Skeleton or Model of Human Body or Part, 83 A.L.R.2d 1097 (1962); McGraw, "Casting, Another Means of Identification," 29 J.For.Sci. 1212 (1984). See also, Chapter 12, supra, on admissibility of medical sketches and drawings. In Lackey v. State, 215 Miss. 57, 60 So.2d 503 (1952), the court held admissible large medical drawings showing the relative location of organs of the body, used by a pathologist-expert witness to explain medical and anatomical evidence.

diagrams.   When viewing photographs of a room where a homicide
occurred, for instance, the pictorial evidence may appear as a series of
overlapping pictures.   Only a detailed sketch, with all dimensions accurately marked and drawn to scale, can give an overall view of the room's
layout.

Even a drawing of a building alone might not be completely satisfactory.   It may need to be supplemented by a sketch of the building in
relation to the street, the paths through the garden, the location of a
garage or shed, or the location of trees and shrubbery that might have
made it impossible to observe from the street what happened inside or
what objects might have provided shelter for the criminal as he left the
premises.   Again, photographs can best record details of the surrounding
location and accurately portray views from certain directions, but only
when a map—or perhaps an aerial photograph—of the entire surroundings is shown can everything be viewed in its true perspective.

In automobile accident cases, photographs are extremely important,
but so is a sketch showing the precise location of the vehicle(s) in
relation to the curb, the intersection, the center of the road, and traffic
signs.   Drawings and sketches, as well as maps, must record the exact
location and relationship of all the important pieces of evidence at the
crime scene.   This does not require the special talent of a draftsman or
artist; in fact, police officers, even lawyers, can do it if they take the
time to record accurate measurements.

Sometimes it is useful to use professionally drawn maps of certain
districts or towns, particularly when an accused or witness is reported to
have traveled from one location to another, and then on to a third
location, or when it becomes necessary to explain exactly what routes he
followed and the length of time he took to reach different locales.   Such
maps may be obtained from various city departments where they are
used to assist in traffic planning, designing zoning areas, laying out and
repairing sewage and utility lines, or dividing areas into school districts,
election precincts, or census tracts.   Larger cities have a special department of cartography which prepares such maps, and evidence can be
procured from these sources.

The admission of diagrams, maps and sketches into evidence is
generally within the discretion of the trial judge.[1]   The judge's decision

---

§ 2.03

1.   Map made by surveyor properly admitted.   Blair v. Preece, 180 W.Va. 501, 377
S.E.2d 493 (1988).

No abuse of trial court's discretion to
admit diagram of murder victim's torso depicting location of wound and bullet trajectory.   State v. Lindsey, 543 So.2d 886 (La.
1989);   State map showing where fires occurred properly admitted on state's behalf
in action by landowners alleging negligence
in combating forest fire.   Jacobsen v. State,
236 Mont. 91, 769 P.2d 694 (1989).

Gordon v. United States, 438 F.2d 858
(5th Cir.1971), cert. denied 404 U.S. 828
(1971), denied 404 U.S. 960 (1971), charts;
United States v. Brickey, 426 F.2d 680 (8th
Cir.1970), charts;   United States v. Kane,
450 F.2d 77 (5th Cir.1971), cert. denied 405
U.S. 934 (1972), charts;   State v. Jones, 51
N.M. 141, 179 P.2d 1001 (1947), blackboard
drawing;   Holding v. State, 460 S.W.2d 133
(Tex.Crim.App.1970), diagram.

Where a sketch was made on a blackboard by a witness to illustrate part of his
testimony, the fact that it was not pre-

to admit or exclude such evidence is not ordinarily disturbed on appeal unless a clear abuse of discretion is shown.[2] In some cases maps have been admitted for other than demonstrative purposes.[3] The fact that drawings are not strictly accurate or drawn to scale does not make them inadmissible per se, although it may have a significant impact on the judge's decision as to admissibility.[4] An official map may be admitted as an official document, without the necessity of calling as a witness the individual who drew the map or the head of the office who supervised the drawing of maps.[5] If a witness testifies to the correctness and accuracy of a map, or plat, or drawing as properly representative of the thing it purports to show, the map, plat, or drawing is deemed properly authenticated for courtroom purposes.[6]

§ 2.04 Artist Drawings and Composite Photographs

When witnesses to or victims of a crime are interviewed after the event, they are frequently able to furnish the police with a fairly detailed description of the unknown offender. From these descriptions, law enforcement agencies have attempted to prepare pictorial likenesses of the offenders for the purpose of disseminating these likenesses to investigating officers or newspapers as an aid in locating the fugitives. Such likenesses may be prepared by a police artist in the form of a drawing, or

---

served and could not be transmitted to the appellate court was not error. United States v. Skinner, 138 U.S.App.D.C. 121, 425 F.2d 552 (1970). Accord: Byrne v. State, 482 P.2d 620 (Okl.Crim.App.1971).

2. See, e.g., State v. McElrath, 322 N.C. 1, 366 S.E.2d 442 (1988): nonadmission of map found in murder victim's personal effects indicating possible scheme to burglarize defendant's home prejudiced defendant and warranted a new trial. The map cast doubt on the State's evidence that the defendant (victim's father-in-law) was the killer and suggested an alternative theory for the victim's death.

3. State v. Thomas, 256 N.J.Super. 563, 607 A.2d 997 (App.Div.1992) (Map indicating crime of possession of cocaine with intent to distribute was committed within 1000 feet of a school was sufficient to create a permissive inference the school was used for school purposes. Therefore, there was sufficient evidence to support the conviction); Lockwood v. State, 795 S.W.2d 323 (Tex.App.1990) (Maps and photographs of a crime scene have been admitted to rehabilitate a victim's testimony after impeachment during cross-examination); People v. Williams, 44 Cal.3d 1127, 245 Cal.Rptr. 635, 751 P.2d 901 (1988) (Map outlining escape plans drawn by incarcerated defendant

awaiting murder trial was admitted in the guilt phase of his trial as evidence of flight).

4. Lake Street El. R. Co. v. Burgess, 200 Ill. 628, 66 N.E. 215 (1903), involving an inaccurate pencil drawing. On the other hand, if the drawing presents a distorted view, there is no abuse of discretion in denying admission: People v. Hampton, 105 Ill.App.2d 228, 245 N.E.2d 47 (1969).

5. Such maps are, in many jurisdictions, presumptive evidence in themselves of the facts set out thereon: City of Marshfield v. Haggard, 304 S.W.2d 672 (Mo.App.1957), appeal transferred 300 S.W.2d 419.

6. State v. Furlough, 797 S.W.2d 631 (Tenn.Crim.App.1990) (Drawing of murder scene by detective admitted); Scheble v. Missouri Clean Water Commission, 734 S.W.2d 541 (Mo.App.1987) (Maps from the Department of Natural Resources admissible in action alleging violation of state clean water law where engineer testified maps were drawn to scale and markings on maps fairly and accurately represented locations where water samples were taken); See also, 44 Am.Jur.Proof of Facts 2d "Foundation" § 3 (1986); Clarke County School Dist. v. Madden, 99 Ga.App. 670, 110 S.E.2d 47 (1959). Cf., Swiney v. State Highway Dept., 116 Ga.App. 667, 158 S.E.2d 321 (1967).

by one of several mechanical devices.[1]

1. ARTIST DRAWINGS

The method of producing likenesses of fugitives or missing persons by artist drawings is self-descriptive. The witness or victim describes the unknown offender to an artist who, on the basis of the description, makes sketches and keeps altering these sketches until one is produced that is deemed to be an accurate likeness by the witness or victim.

A proper foundation must be laid before a composite drawing may be admitted. "The moving party must present a witness or witnesses with firsthand knowledge of how the composite was prepared and of how accurately it portrays that which it is intended to depict."[2] If there is no testimony from an eyewitness that the sketch is accurate, then the sketch is irrelevant and inadmissible.[3] It must be a representation prepared at the direction of the witness and the witness, after viewing the completed sketch, adopted it as an accurate portrait of the suspect.[4] The procedures in drafting the composite sketches may not be overly suggestive.[5] If the prosecution fails to disclose the existence of a composite sketch upon defendant's discovery motion, it is a discovery violation and suppression of the sketch has been held to be an appropriate sanction.[6]

Sketches or composite pictures produced by a police artist and based upon eyewitness' descriptions are generally regarded as hearsay evidence and therefore inadmissible to support or corroborate the eyewitness'

---

§ 2.04

1. If a witness, without police intervention makes a sketch of a person he had seen, later identified as defendant, it is not a composite sketch. People v. Ross, 186 A.D.2d 1006, 588 N.Y.S.2d 463 (1992). A general discussion of sketches and some composite picture techniques as related to police investigative procedures may be found in 20 Am.Jur.Proof of Facts 539.

2. State v. Weidenhof, 205 Conn. 262, 533 A.2d 545, 551 (1987).

3. State v. Patterson, 103 N.C.App. 195, 405 S.E.2d 200 (1991) (Admission of the sketch was irrelevant and hearsay, however the error was harmless).

4. People v. Yates, 98 Ill.2d 502, 75 Ill. Dec. 188, 456 N.E.2d 1369 (1983).

5. State v. Dorisio, 189 W.Va. 788, 434 S.E.2d 707 (1993) (The procedures used in drafting composites of a convenience store robbery suspect were not overly suggestive where none of the witnesses providing description knew the defendant when the composites were made and the detective, who knew the defendant, independently matched the defendant with the composite); People v. Bullock, 154 Ill.App.3d 266, 107 Ill.Dec. 380, 507 N.E.2d 44 (1987) (A composite sketch of two victims' assailant was admissible and held not to be suggestive even though the sketch was produced by the first victim and shown to the second, since both victims independently concurred that the composite accurately represented their attacker. The second victim did suggest adding some wrinkles to the sketch before she agreed to its likeness to her attacker); In States v. Romanosky, 162 Ariz. 217, 782 P.2d 693 (1989), the court considered the admissibility of a composite sketch developed through a limited description by the murder victim's wife and by a suspect's description given by witnesses to an unrelated crime committed on the same day. The court held that the sketch's admission into evidence was harmful error because the jurors could have believed that the descriptions had been provided by the witnesses to the murder, rather than by the witnesses to the unrelated crime.

6. State v. Browning, 321 N.C. 535, 364 S.E.2d 376 (1988).

testimony on the issue of identity.[7]　However, some courts have held composite sketches not to be hearsay.[8]　Sketches have been held admissible in a few instances as coming within an exception to the hearsay rule. Thus, where an eyewitness' testimony identifying the accused was attacked as a "recent fabrication," a sketch by a police artist based on a description supplied by the witness was held properly admitted as a prior consistent statement on the issue of identity.[9]

2. IDENTI–KIT

Identi–Kit is a method of producing a visual likeness of an unknown person from a verbal description furnished by a witness or victim. The likeness is produced without the use of photographs or an artist, by combining transparent slides, each of which bears a facial characteristic.[10]

The kit consists of hundreds of transparent celluloid overlays which can be assembled into a composite overlay "sandwich." The investigator selects each individual characteristic from the verbal description given by a witness or victim. After the basic likeness is completed, the victim or witness may suggest changes.

The different printed overlays represent a variety of human facial characteristics: hairlines, eyes, noses, lips, chin lines, age lines, etc. Each individual characteristic is numbered so that a composite which has been assembled will also indicate a row of numbers that can be transmitted by wire or telephone. This enables distant law enforcement

7. People v. Turner, 91 Ill.App.2d 436, 235 N.E.2d 317 (1968); People v. Jennings, 23 A.D.2d 621, 257 N.Y.S.2d 456 (1965); Commonwealth v. Rothlisberger, 197 Pa.Super. 451, 178 A.2d 853 (1962). Formal rules as to admission of documentary evidence are also applied to sketches and composite pictures: Kostal v. People, 160 Colo. 64, 414 P.2d 123 (1966), cert. denied 385 U.S. 939 (1966). But in Rowe v. State, 262 Ind. 250, 314 N.E.2d 745 (1974) the court said that the police sketch was not inadmissible hearsay where the person furnishing the description to the officer was present and a witness in the case.

For an exhaustive look at the legal aspects of composite drawings, see the Note, "Hearsay and Relevancy Obstacles to the Admission of Composite Sketches in Criminal Trials," 64 *Boston U.L.Rev.* 1101 (1984). The article lists many recent cases and a plethora of other legal literature.

8. United States v. Moskowitz, 581 F.2d 14 (2d Cir.1978), cert. denied 439 U.S. 871 (1978); Harrison v. Commonwealth, 9 Va. App. 187, 384 S.E.2d 813 (1989); Commonwealth v. Thornley, 400 Mass. 355, 509 N.E.2d 908 (1987); State v. Packard, 184 Conn. 258, 439 A.2d 983 (1981).

9. Lay v. State, 752 P.2d 823 (Okl.Crim. App.1988); People v. Coffey, 11 N.Y.2d 142, 227 N.Y.S.2d 412, 182 N.E.2d 92 (1962), on remand 36 Misc.2d 67, 232 N.Y.S.2d 545 (1962), affirmed 18 A.D.2d 794, 236 N.Y.S.2d 1021 (1963), affirmed 12 N.Y.2d 443, 240 N.Y.S.2d 721, 191 N.E.2d 263 (1963), remittitur amended 13 N.Y.2d 726, 241 N.Y.S.2d 856, 191 N.E.2d 910 (1963); People v. Peterson, 25 A.D.2d 437, 266 N.Y.S.2d 884 (1966). See also, State v. Lancaster, 25 Ohio St.2d 83, 267 N.E.2d 291 (1971). Sketch or composite picture of person described by witness was held admissible under res gestae exception to the hearsay rule in People v. Bills, 53 Mich. App. 339, 220 N.W.2d 101 (1974), cause remanded 396 Mich. 802, 238 N.W.2d 29 (1976).

10. See, "New Kit 'Builds' Photographs of Criminal Suspects," *Finger Pr. & Id. Mag.,* Oct. 1959, p. 3; "New Identi–Kit Addition 'Type Casts' Criminals," *Finger Pr. & Id. Mag.,* May, 1963, p. 3. The system is marketed by: Smith & Wesson Identi–Kit Co., 2100 Roosevelt Ave., Springfield, Mass. 01102.

agencies to duplicate the composites within minutes. This speed of assembly and transmission is one of the major assets of Identi–Kit. A trained operator can construct a composite within a few minutes.

Identi–Kit was developed after a detailed study of the principles of physiognomy and the comparison of hundreds of thousands of photographs of arrested individuals. It is claimed that because of certain consistencies in the structure of human likenesses, only four factors are necessary to construct the basic composite: age, height, weight, and one of 49 different hairlines. Other characteristics which may be added simply expand the versatility. The use of Identi–Kit composites such as are illustrated in Figure 2 has resulted in arrests and identifications in many criminal cases.

The Smith & Wesson (S & W) Identi-Kit Company is marketing, in conjunction with Infotec Development, Inc., the Identi-Kit III, which is their latest product in computer composite imaging. It is completely compatible with Identi-Kit II, which is S & W's current manual composite system. The process used to question a witness and to develop the new Identi-Kit III composite is the same for both systems. Identi-Kit III's software program allows the user to create a better likeness by employing computer controlled printing, blending, erasing, moving and sizing functions. The recommended hardware is a fast portable computer with a 486 processor, which enables the trained operator to render the composite at witness' homes, crime scenes, or at any other location.

Several cases have dealt with Identi–Kit composites. In 1969, the court declared in Commonwealth v. McKenna,[11] that a composite made by a police officer with the aid of Identi–Kit at the direction of a witness

---

11. 355 Mass. 313, 244 N.E.2d 560 (1969). In Commonwealth v. Balukonis, 357 Mass. 721, 260 N.E.2d 167 (1970), defendant maintained that admission of a composite picture violated the best evidence rule in that it was not authenticated. The court held that composite pictures do not come within the ambit of the rule.

Identi-Kit
Thu Sep 23 18:32:52 1993

File # 3646876LKR
Date: 9/27/93
Agent: TOPOR
Operator: SMITH

Fig. 2. *Courtesy: Identi-Kit Co., Inc.*

could have been used to refresh the witness' recollection but was inadmissible as evidence. In Butler v. State,[12] the court held that after an officer had testified that he was trained in and familiar with the use of Identi–Kit, it was proper to allow him to testify as to the operation of the kit, which had been used to prepare the composite of a robber. Also in State v. Ginardi,[13] the court held that a composite prepared by a police officer using Identi–Kit was admissible into evidence under the New Jersey Rules of Evidence. These rules provide that where identity is in issue, a prior out-of-court identification of a party is admissible if it was made by a person present in court as a witness, if it would have been admissible as part of the witness' testimony at trial and if it was made under circumstances which preclude unfairness and unreliability.

In Commonwealth v. Weichell,[14] the Massachusetts Supreme Judicial Court held that a composite drawing prepared by a police officer and a witness using an "Identikit" may be introduced as substantive evidence of identification if two conditions are met: (1) the witness is available for cross-examination, and (2) the procedures used in preparing the drawing were not unduly suggestive. On the other hand, in People v. Tyllas,[15] the defendant failed in his attempt to persuade the reviewing court that the trial judge committed error in excluding a police composite sketch, not because the sketch was inadmissible, but because failure to admit it was deemed harmless error. In People v. Johnson[16] the court held that appellate counsel's failure to challenge on appeal the trial court's refusal to admit an Identi–Kit composite sketch was not ineffective assistance of counsel.

3. COMPUTERIZED IDENTIFICATION PROGRAMS

Computers have had an impact on personal identification and have resulted in the development of programs such as Compu Sketch, E Fit, and Mac–A–Mug, to assist law enforcement in creating composite sketches from victims' and witnesses' descriptions of perpetrators of crimes. The FBI has recently put in place a computerized software database developed by QMA/Infotech.[17] It has a template and a paint program. The system is presently being used in Atlanta, Ga., Chicago, Ill., and at FBI headquarters in Washington, D.C. The database contains both hand-drawn facial features and photographic facial features from the FBI's Facial Identification Catalog. An investigator in the field interviews the witness or victim, then asks the person to select facial

---

12. 226 Ga. 56, 172 S.E.2d 399 (1970).

13. 111 N.J.Super. 435, 268 A.2d 534 (1970), affirmed 57 N.J. 438, 273 A.2d 353 (1971). Contra, People v. Griffin, 29 N.Y.2d 91, 323 N.Y.S.2d 964, 272 N.E.2d 477 (1971).

14. 390 Mass. 62, 453 N.E.2d 1038, 34 Cr.L. 2071 (1983), cert. denied 465 U.S. 1032 (1984). The dissent would hold the evidence of the sketch inadmissible.

15. 96 Ill.App.3d 1, 51 Ill.Dec. 211, 420 N.E.2d 625 (1981). See also, People v. Slago, 58 Ill.App.3d 1009, 16 Ill.Dec. 392, 374 N.E.2d 1270 (1978): not error to exclude Identi–Kit picture, such being inadmissible hearsay.

16. 154 Ill.2d 227, 182 Ill.Dec. 1, 609 N.E.2d 304 (1993).

17. QMA/Infotech, 1420 Springhill Road, Suite 205, McLean, VA 22102.

features from the catalog which match those of the suspect.   The investigator then inputs those features into the computer and sends the image by modem to FBI headquarters where a forensic artist "fine-tunes" the sketch.   It is then sent back to the field by modem.   Photographs can be scanned into the system and then retouched in the computer.   See Fig. 3.   QMA/Infotech has also developed PhotoSketch which is used by the National Center for Missing and Exploited Children.   That program can age a photograph taken at the time the child was missing, so it portrays the child's present features.

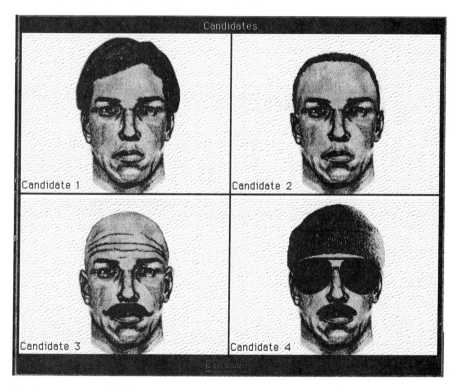

Fig. 3. Illustration of the FACEKIT computer composite system. *Courtesy: Infotec Development Inc.*

III.   PHOTOGRAPHIC EVIDENCE

§ 2.05   Photography as an Aid in Communication

In order to convey ideas, we normally use speech, that is, a verbal description of what we seek to communicate.   If we want to explain the type of a car that was involved in an accident, we can describe the car by make, model, year, color of the body and interior, placement of the radio antenna, license plates, and other such details.   This is not too hard to do when we are talking about a new car, because most people have either actually seen such a car, or have looked at reproductions of a similar car in magazines or newspapers.   It is fairly easy, then, to build up a mental picture simply on the basis of a verbal description because the description will agree with a mental picture which we already possess. Things are different, however, when we are dealing with something of which we know nothing. The car was in an accident, let's say, and severely damaged. A description of the dent in the fender, the ripped-off side rear-view mirror, will conjure up in our mind some mental picture, but it is not likely to be highly accurate. In order to accurately convey what we have in mind some other means must be sought. We can accurately communicate the condition of the car by exhibiting it, showing the actual damage, or we could show photographs of it, taken from several angles, or we could conceivably use a smaller model of the same car with the damage to the original carefully imitated on the model.

If we go this route, then, we are simply implementing the age-old adage that a picture is worth a thousand words. The "picture," whether in the form of a photograph, model, or diagram assists the viewer in creating in his mind a mental representation of the actual conditions which are described. The description is still necessary, of course; in fact, it is indispensible. Showing a photograph or model of a damaged car is meaningless unless accompanied by a story of the circumstances under which the damage was inflicted. The picture, then, illustrates the details of a story we are attempting to outline verbally.

§ 2.06 History of Legal Photography

In civil as well as criminal cases, photography provides probably the most potent tool in conveying facts to a jury. In criminal trials, photography plays an extremely important role for the police and prosecutor and can play the same role for the defense. Invented in 1839 by Daguerre, photography was used as early as 1843 to provide pictures of arrested persons—what we now call *mug shots*—in Belgium. These early pictures were on metal plates, called daguerreotypes. See Figure 4. The use of mug shots to identify individuals has survived to this day.

At a very early stage, photographs were also used to record scenes of crimes and accidents, of bodies and wounds, of suspect documents and checks and of other items of evidence. As early as 1860, courts were confronted with photographic enlargements of questioned documents in criminal cases and by 1871 post mortem photographs were widely used in court to establish the identity of victims of crimes. Shortly thereafter, courts were looking at stereoscopic photographs, photomicrographs and photomacrographs, and X-rays.[1]

As photographic techniques became more sophisticated, still photographs were made through a microscope of hairs, fibers, paint chips, tool marks, and other minute items of trace evidence. The advent of color photography, stereophotography, and infrared and ultraviolet picture

---

§ 2.06

1. Moenssens, "The Origin of Legal Photography," *Finger Pr. & Ident. Mag.,* Jan. 1962, at 3.

taking, sometimes in conjunction with the use of a microscope, also permitted the taking of photographs of small details that the human eye could not distinguish.

Because of the wide uses of photography by the public generally it is probably the one type of evidence that is best understood by all people, including police officers, lawyers and judges. Most anybody has used a simple camera, and a good many people can operate quite elaborate pieces of photographic equipment. All but the smallest law enforcement agencies possess photographic laboratories as well as a wide array of specialized and general-purpose photographic instruments.

Fig. 4.   One of the early daguerreotype mug shots used in Belgium in 1843. The illustration is one of a series of four which constitute the oldest documented use of identification photography in the world.

§ 2.07 Basic Principles of Photography

Since photography is so widely used, and provides the most accurate means for recording the maximum of information in the shortest possible time, it is important for the lawyer to understand at least the most basic principles.

Stripped of all its complexities designed to make the process of picture taking more efficient, a camera is essentially a light-tight box with an opening through which light can be admitted by the release of a shutter. If the shutter is opened, light entering the camera passes through the lens, which acts much like the human eye, and focuses on the inside of the back panel in the camera box. The back panel is removable in modern cameras and in its place there is a device which holds the photographic film, so that light entering through the lens focuses on the film. In some cameras, the film is contained in a roll film holder, in others, the film is on a circular disk, in yet other models the film may be placed in special cartridges or other devices. On the outside of most cameras there is a device which permits the photographer to know how many pictures have been taken on the film that is contained in the camera.

Film comes in many types—sheet film, perforated roll film, film pack, disk film, cartridges containing film, and the like. Film consists basically of a sheet of celluloid, glass, or other base that is coated with an "emulsion" of smooth particles of silver halides suspended in gelatin. This emulsion is capable of retaining an invisible image when light coming through a lens strikes the emulsion, because the silver salts are sensitive to light. When the camera shutter is opened to let in the light that will expose the film, the image of the scene toward which the camera is pointed fixes itself into these salts. At that time, however, the image is still invisible, or latent. Only upon "development" do the exposed silver halides transform into black metallic silver. After fixing the image in place a "negative" is produced. The negative is a piece of film on which the image appears reversed and on which the light areas of the subject appear dark and the dark areas light. The development of most film must be done in a darkroom to prevent light from affecting the emulsion before the image is firmly fixed.

After development, the film is usually passed through a "stop bath," which simply arrests further development; then the film is placed in a "fixing bath," which removes all unexposed and undeveloped silver. After the film has passed through the fixing stage, the negative is no longer sensitive and can be viewed in bright light.

In order to obtain a photographic print on paper, a similar process is used. In contact printing, the emulsion (dull) side of the negative is placed against the emulsion side of photosensitized paper (coated with light-sensitive materials) and light is permitted to pass through the negative so that it reaches the sensitized paper. During this print-making process the technician may operate with a "safelight"—usually red or yellow—rather than in complete darkness. The image is then developed by passing the paper through a developer, a stop bath and a fixer. This process results in a "print" in which the image appears the same as it did when it was first viewed by the camera; that is, black areas in the subject matter again appear black in the print.

Often it is desired to enlarge the image appearing on the negative. This is done with the aid of an instrument called an enlarger, which is the reverse of a camera. Again, however, light passes through the negative to a lens, which projects the image on photosensitized paper, which is developed and fixed the same way as contact prints. The enlargement may be adjusted to whatever scale desired.

In the manufacture of emulsions for film, several stages are involved. Each of these stages gives rise to special properties of the emulsion. Through the selection of proper combinations of stages and treatments, photographic emulsions of a distinct type can be manufactured. Emulsions can be prepared with selected sensitivity (orthochromatic, infrared, color) or emulsions may be sensitized to respond to the whole color spectrum in equal proportions (panchromatic).

Developing papers vary according to (1) type of emulsion (chloride, bromide, etc.), (2) contrast range (soft, hard, normal) and (3) physical properties (thickness, finish, color, texture, etc.). Most developing papers consist of silver chloride or silver bromide, or a combination of the two, which determines the sensitivity and image tone. Developing papers for color prints are usually of two types: positive and reversal. The positive paper is used to make color prints from color negatives, whereas the reversal paper is used to make color prints from color transparencies. Color developing papers are sensitized to blue, green, and red light, and they contain complementary color couplers that record the colors of the negative.

Regardless of the characteristics of the film, developer and paper used, the appearance of the final picture may still be affected by the use of filters, either on the camera or during development; in fact, it can be affected even by the length of time of exposure or development or by the use of a great number of compensating factors such as reducers or intensifiers. The degree of accuracy with which the picture portrays the original can be affected by a number of other factors as well.

§ 2.08 Use of Photographs in Evidence Collection

Because of the frequent need for photographic evidence, law enforcement agencies use photographers who are highly skilled in their field, and who have a thorough understanding of cameras, lenses, light-sensitive materials, processing chemicals, etc. In final analysis, however, "evidence photography" is not a branch of photography which requires extensive special training; it only requires knowledge of the special requirements. Any skilled professional photographer or advanced amateur can do evidence photography work once instructed in its special requirements. In fact, amateur photographers often know as much about it as the "pros" and are distinguished from them only in that their equipment may be less costly and photography is not their occupation.

Evidence photographs of individuals, crime scenes, accidents and minute particles found must be absolutely honest and stark. The prime directive is to produce a photograph that accurately portrays the person or subject photographed. Commercial photography, on the other hand, seeks to enhance certain details in a picture through the use of special lenses, sensitive materials, filters, lighting and so forth. If the desired effect is not achieved to the satisfaction of the commercial photographer, either the negative or the enlargement can be retouched. No enhancement or retouching of any kind is permitted in photographs taken of crime scenes or for personal identification. Observe, for example, the degree of detail with which the condition of a murder victim's body is reproduced in Figure 5.

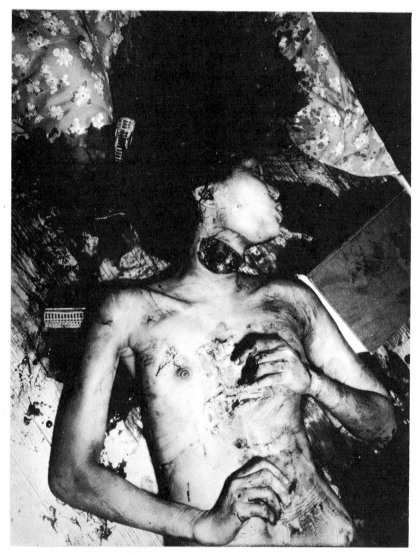

Fig. 5. One of a series of photographs admitted into evidence in a murder trial, over objections of gruesomeness, to show the condition of the victim.

Crime scene photography and mug shots are only two of the areas with which evidence photographers are concerned. They also have to assist in the photographic needs of all the other specialists in scientific crime detection. Almost every phase of criminalistics depends to a large extent on photography for investigation, analysis, or demonstration. The fingerprint expert requires photographs of latent impressions, inked impressions, or court exhibits. So does the examiner of questioned documents. Examples of the type of photographic exhibits used by those specialists were shown in Chapters 8 and 5. Both of these specialists, and others as well, may require the use of special techniques to make evidence visible that may otherwise be poorly discernible or invisible to the naked eye. Some latent fingerprints can be made visible and photographed when exciting the inherent luminescence of some substances contained in human perspiration by the use of laser lighting. See Chapter 8 for a description of this technique.

The use of infrared light-sensitive emulsions or ultraviolet lighting may produce evidence of fine detail that is invisible to the eye, as in documents altered by erasures, overwritings, or tracings. X-ray photography may reveal the presence of a bullet and its precise location inside such objects as door jambs or the wooden post of a table or the sole of a shoe, as well as the presence of lead in loaded dice. The application of the microscope to photography, in order to produce photomicrographs, may show detail that is too refined to be visible without the use of the great magnification provided by such optical equipment. Examples of photomicrographs are illustrated in Chapters 9 and 6.

The extensive use of photographs of accident and crime scenes permits one to present, in pictorial form, all of the facts and physical circumstances of a case; it aids in preserving available evidence; it permits the consideration of certain types of evidence that cannot be brought into court easily because of their size or form; it permits reconstruction of past events at some later date; and generally it assists in accurately revealing the conditions prevailing at a past event. In addition, a good photographic record also reveals physical evidence that might otherwise be easily overlooked and constitutes an excellent refresher for the witness who must testify in court about some event that happened months earlier.

Evidence photographers are told that a crime scene should be photographed as soon as possible, because the longer the delay the greater the likelihood that some changes may be made that would reflect on the accuracy of the crime scene photograph. Before anything is touched or moved, therefore, the investigator should complement his own observations and notes by making a photographic record of the entire area, viewed from every conceivable angle, with close-up photographs of all objects or items that may play an important role in solving the crime. Whenever possible, crime scene photographs should not include officers or observers.

Whenever violent deaths are involved, photographs of the scene should include the body. The victim should be photographed from all angles to show his or her relationship to other articles in the area and also to enable identification of the victim. If any wounds or marks are visible on the body, close-ups are also necessary.

The "scene" includes the whole area surrounding the place where an event, accident, or crime occurred. If a crime was committed in one room inside an apartment, adjoining rooms must be photographed as well. The building itself should be photographed, including close-ups of places where the perpetrator might have gained access, such as windows or doors. In addition, suspect tire marks or foot impressions should be recorded photographically. In certain instances, aerial photographs of the general scene can be very helpful.

During this whole process, the photographer must keep a careful record of each photograph taken, including details concerning date, time, other officers present, location described with particularity, type of film, camera and lens used, exposure, lens opening and any other relevant information. After development and printing, the photographer will be able to complement the photographic record with information about the types of chemicals, papers, and equipment used in the darkroom. All of the information must ultimately be marked on the back of each photographic print or enlargement, as well as on the envelope containing the negatives. The negatives should also preferably contain a number referring to the case, either written or stamped in a corner so that it does not interfere with or obliterate parts of the negative image. All negatives should be preserved, even those that "did not come out" because of faulty exposure or other circumstances. Since properly taken color photographs convey more accurate information than black-and-white photographs, color film should be used whenever possible or practical.

§ 2.09 Special Photographic Techniques

As the most powerful tool in the arsenal of the scientific crime investigator because of its wide range of applications, photography can be used or misused to produce misleading evidence—misleading in the sense that the pictures may be made to appear different from what the eye observed. We have just stated that in evidence photography absolute honesty of reproduction is required, and retouching is prohibited. In the laboratory, though, it is sometimes necessary to call on special photographic techniques in order to render visible details that can be recorded by a camera but are invisible to the naked eye. A great number of these special processes are available. The selection of the one that is best suited for a particular job depends upon the type of evidence involved and the result sought. A few of the most important techniques can be discussed briefly here.

1. FILTERS

Filters are usually made up of colored discs of glass, plastic or gelatin. They stop some light, which means that the color of the light that passes through any filter is thereby changed. Filters are used to correct color, to brighten or darken colors for certain effects, to change the color temperature of light in color photography, and to enable pictures to be taken by light of a single color. They are also used in photography with polarized light.

Sunlight, which is usually referred to as white light, is actually made up of rays of light composed of all the colors in the rainbow in exactly the same proportions as they appear there. The rainbow constitutes the visible spectrum of light. When it is broken down into its components—by being passed through a crystal, for example—the colors range from red on one side of the spectrum to violet on the other side. In between are orange, yellow, green and blue.

By the proper use of filters it becomes possible to emphasize some colors and suppress others. When the color of a filter is the same as one of the colors in the image, that color will turn out lighter in the photograph than it actually is, and the colors of the opposite side of the spectrum will appear to be darker in the photograph. Considering that black-and-white photographs depict a scene in varying shades of gray, a red object may be made to appear to be quite light in a black-and-white photograph by placing a red filter over the lens. By contrast, blue objects are made to appear to be dark or even black when a red filter is used. A blue filter would lighten a blue object but would also make any red portions of it appear to be black or dark gray. This happens only, of course, if the type of film used is one that records all colors in the same degree as the human eye sees them—panchromatic film. Some films are made with emulsions that are not able to "see" certain colors, such as orthochromatic film which does not register red light. A red object photographed on orthochromatic film will therefore appear black or dark in the photograph even though no filters were used.

In a laboratory, then, filters can be of great value when it is necessary to either lighten or darken certain portions of a photograph, a process referred to as "varying the contrast." This is well illustrated in the two pictures shown in Figure 6. On the left is a photograph of a postage stamp as it appeared to the naked eye, nearly obliterated by heavy, red pencil marks. The photograph was taken without a filter on regular (panchromatic) film. On the right is a photograph of the same postage stamp, but this time a red filter was placed over the lens, and that lightened the red pencil marks so much that they are hardly visible. This procedure revealed that the stamp had been previously used and cancelled by the post office.

The use of filters to alter the contrast is of great importance to both the fingerprint technician and the questioned document examiner. The fingerprint technician may use it to photograph a latent fingerprint developed on a multicolored surface, such as a magazine cover. By using a filter of essentially the same color as the background (magazine cover illustration), he can make that background appear to be white or light gray, so that the fingerprint developed with black powder stands out more clearly and can be studied with greater care.

Fig. 6.

The document examiner, too, has frequent use for contrast filters, as when it comes to photographing endorsement signatures on cancelled checks. Blue or red bank stamps are often placed over portions of signatures, making it difficult to study the fine detail of the handwriting. By using contrasting filters to blot out (lighten) such stamps, a photograph may be produced which makes the check appear as if it were free from stamps. In that fashion, the examiner can properly examine all of the fine detail of the signatures.

Other types of filters may at times be used, not always to vary tonal quality, but to correct the image that would be imperfectly recorded on the film if no filters were used. This is particularly true of color photographs taken under artificial lighting. Considering that not all light sources emit light rays that have the qualities of sunlight—that is, a combination, in equal proportions, of all the colors of the rainbow—it may sometimes be necessary to compensate for deficiencies in available light by using filters that will render colors accurately.

There are also "neutral density filters," which absorb an equal percentage of all colors. This requirement is desirable for taking photographs in bright sunlight with a high-speed film. The camera may not be equipped with a fast enough shutter or a small enough lens opening, or both, to prevent overexposure. Using a neutral density filter reduces the intensity of the light striking the film so that a normally exposed photograph can be obtained.

Polarizing filters are used in both black-and-white and color photography to eliminate unwanted reflections of stray light, such as are produced when the light source is reflected from glass, polished metal or other highly reflective surfaces. The use of a polarizing screen in color photography can assist in increasing color saturation.

2. INFRARED PHOTOGRAPHY

In our discussion on filters, we talked about the visible spectrum of light and stated that sunlight is made up of a combination in equal proportions, of rays of light of all the colors of the rainbow. It is the wavelength of a ray of light that determines its color. In the visible spectrum, red rays have the longest wavelength and violet rays have the shortest. There are various ways of expressing wavelengths—in millimeters, centimeters, cycles, kilocycles—depending upon the types of radiation. When we are discussing visible light, however, the most frequently used is the Angstrom. An Angstrom (A) is one ten-billionth of a meter. Visible light ranges from about 4,000 A (violet) to about 7,700 A (red).

The visible spectrum is but a small part of a much broader whole, the electromagnetic spectrum, which includes alternating current on the one extreme (very long waves) and cosmic rays on the other (extremely short waves). In between we find ordinary radio waves near the longwave end of the electromagnetic spectrum and X rays and gamma rays near the shortwave end. Visible light, then, differs from other types of radiation only in the length of the waves. Figure 7 shows the electromagnetic spectrum with wavelengths expressed in mathematical units, rather than Angstroms.

At the longwave end of the visible spectrum there exists a band of radiation waves from 7,700 A (nearest to visible light) to 5,000,000 A. The waves in that band are called infrared waves. One of the characteristics of infrared waves is that they are readily absorbed and converted into heat energy. But they are not heat waves. The radiant energy felt as heat is a result of molecular thermal agitation, which is a surface phenomenon of a hot object, such as a lamp filament, emitting rays. Any object that gives off electromagnetic radiation gives off some waves in the infrared region as long as the object has a temperature above absolute zero. The temperature of the object determines the quantity of infrared radiation. The hotter an object is, the more infrared waves are emitted.

Infrared waves cannot be seen by the human eye and they are not actually red. The word "infrared" indicates that type of radiation which adjoins the red rays of the visible spectrum. While infrared radiation cannot be "seen" by the human eye, photographic emulsions can be made which are sensitive to them. And that is what makes infrared radiation particularly useful to the evidence photographer, especially to the examiner of questioned documents.

Since most infrared plates of films are also sensitive to the visible portions of the spectrum, it is customary to use a filter on the camera lens that screens out all visible light but permits the infrared "picture" to pass and be recorded. In that fashion, a photographer may be able to discover erasures on documents, and sometimes he can even reveal what was originally written underneath other words. Infrared photography can also distinguish among inks and reveal blood stains and powder burns on cloth and clothing. Snooperscopes and hidden cameras equipped with infrared lenses are used to observe people in the dark and to photograph intruders.

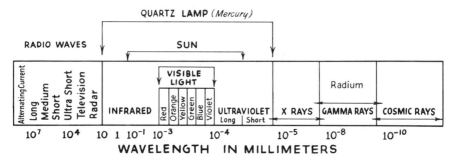

Fig. 7. The Electromagnetic Spectrum.

3. ULTRAVIOLET PHOTOGRAPHY

Immediately outside the other end of the visible light spectrum is the ultraviolet band (see again Figure 7). Since this band occupies quite a wide spread of wavelengths, it is divided into shortwave and longwave ultraviolet rays. The longwave ultraviolet rays lie next to the visible light spectrum (from 4,000 A to 3,500 A); the shortwave rays are closer to the X-ray band (from 3,500 A to 2,500 A).[1]

Because it emits rays in the invisible region of the electromagnetic spectrum, ultraviolet light is often referred to as black light, although more technically the term "black light" is limited to the longer wave ultraviolet rays. The usefulness of ultraviolet light in evidence photography stems from the fact that many substances fluoresce or give off visible light when exposed to ultraviolet rays. This fluorescence occurs because such substances have the power to receive radiant energy of a certain (invisible) wavelength and to convert portions of that energy into a longer wavelength within the visible light range, resulting in a visible glow that can be clearly seen when all ordinary visible light is blocked off, as in a darkened area.

---

§ 2.09

1. Actually, the ultraviolet region adjoins the visible spectrum (Violet) at about 4,000 A and extends all the way to about 140 A where it merges into the X-ray region of the electromagnetic spectrum. For the purpose of photography, however, only the portion from about 4,000 A to 2,500 A is used.

A frequent use of ultraviolet light in crime detection is in the identification of people who have committed petty thefts. There are a great number of powders that fluoresce, and they come in many colors. Some are green; some are a buff color approximating the color of skin. When thefts occur in offices, plants or schools, some of the powder can be placed in the coat pockets or money boxes from which thefts have occurred. This powder is so tenacious than even a vigorous washing of the hands will not immediately remove all traces of it. By requesting suspects to pass their hands under an ultraviolet lamp, officials can detect the guilty.

Invisible crayons and pens permit the secret marking of money, works of art and other valuables for easy identification, and, in the intelligence field, the writing of secret messages between the lines of seemingly innocuous letters. Using fluorescent powder on multicolored surfaces that are dusted for fingerprints may render them visible under ultraviolet light without distracting backgrounds. Bodily secretions such as urine, semen, perspiration and pus often glow when illuminated with ultraviolet rays, thus permitting the detection of otherwise invisible traces on clothing. In the questioned document field, again, obliterated writings can often be rendered visible by exposure to ultraviolet rays.

Unlike infrared photography, ultraviolet photography does not require specially prepared emulsions because most panchromatic films are sensitive to ultraviolet radiation as well as to visible light. Any light source that emits ultraviolet rays will do for ultraviolet photography. A quartz lamp with a filter over the lens, screening out all infrared and visible light rays, is all that is needed in addition to standard photographic equipment.

4. X–RAY PHOTOGRAPHY

In addition to the infrared and ultraviolet bands of the electromagnetic spectrum, a third band of rays can be useful in police work. They are X-rays, discovered by Wilhelm von Roentgen in 1895. X-ray photography requires special generating equipment: a vacuum tube, through which an electric current is passed, is needed to produce X-rays that can affect photographic plates.

X-rays have the property of being able to penetrate objects that appear to be opaque to the naked eye. If an object is placed between a photographic plate and a source of X-ray emission, the photographic plate will record, in varying degrees of black and white, the density of the object. The densest objects appear white; the least dense, black.

5. PHOTOMICROGRAPHY

Microscopic vision differs from photographic enlargement in a number of ways, but for our purposes we note these differences. A microscope enlarges a very small portion of a larger whole. The greater the power of magnification of the microscope, the smaller the portion of an object being enlarged. While we can obtain the same result with a photographic enlarger, that is, to enlarge only a portion of a negative and "blow it up," a photographic enlargement also permits us to enlarge an entire photographic image, simply by the use of larger paper than the size of the photographic negative that is used. When a camera is fitted to a microscope and an object is filmed, the result is called a photomicrograph. Examples of such photomicrographs and the uses of this technique in criminalistics are illustrated in the chapters on firearms identification and comparative micrography, and microanalysis. Most cameras can be fitted to take photographs through a microscope, although some require special attachments.

6. PHOTOMACROGRAPHY

Photo*macro*graphy is the photographing of an object at initial magnification on the negative without the use of a microscope. In photo*mi*crography, on the other hand, the enlargement on the negative is obtained by photographing through a microscope. In photomacrography, only the camera or a special lens is used to obtain a detailed view on the negative which appears there larger than it does in actuality. This may be done by the use of extension bellows on certain press cameras, view cameras or other specially designed professional cameras, or by the use of special macro or supplementary and diopter lenses placed in front of the regular camera lens. For practical reasons, the initial magnification in photomacrography is limited to twenty power. To obtain a greater initial enlargement, it is generally necessary to utilize a microscope in connection with the camera.

7. MICROPHOTOGRAPHY

Microphotography is the opposite of photomicrography. In photomicrography, pictures are taken of extremely small portions of an object or of detail that could not be seen by the naked eye. In microphotography, a photograph is made of a large area that can readily be seen on an extremely small piece of film. Microphotography, commonly called microfilming, is frequently used to reproduce extensive files onto small negatives to save storage space. Many letter-size pages can be reproduced onto one 8mm negative. In espionage work, microphotographs the size of a pinhead may contain several pages of text.

§ 2.10 Motion Pictures and Videotape

Videotape technology has been embraced by the courts as a useful courtroom tool and as a source of evidence. Videotaped depositions are becoming common, as are videotaped confessions.[1] Abused children

---

§ 2.10

1. A nationwide survey by the National Institute of Justice found that one-sixth of all U.S. police and sheriffs' departments video tape confessions or interrogations. As the severity of the crime increased so did the likelihood of videotaping. Geller, "Police Videotaping on Suspect Interrogations

have been allowed to testify via one-way closed circuit video hook-ups [2], videotaped lineups are routinely used and some states even provide for arraignment via audio visual device.[3] Some administrative agencies are permitted to use videotape as part of their investigations.[4]

Videotaped evidence has been used as demonstrative evidence in the form of re-enactments and as "real" evidence of criminal activity when taken from security cameras or recording drunk drivers under arrest. Today, some courts are permitting the admission of crime scene videotapes.[5] Courts have even admitted videotapes of the crime taken by the defendants during the perpetration of the crime.[6] In civil cases so called "day-in-the-life" videos of an injured person can be powerful evidence for a trial lawyer presenting a compelling liability or damages case.

Videotape has inherent credibility associated as it is with its similarity to television.[7]

The practice of making motion pictures of persons arrested on drunk driving charges started in Fresno, California, about 1945 with an amateur 8mm camera. The practice spread fairly rapidly. Over the years, a number of departments obtained color-sound motion-picture cameras with which they recorded the condition, behavior and speech of persons arrested for driving while intoxicated. The adoption of this technique resulted in a dramatic increase in the conviction rate, up to 85–95% in many cases. Most of these convictions are obtained on guilty pleas after a private viewing of the film by the defendant's attorney.

Today videotape is commonly used as a substitute for sound motion pictures. Videotape differs from movies in that the picture and sound are recorded on magnetic tape rather than on film.

A few additional factors are to be considered with respect to sound motion pictures. The sound track of a movie can be made in two ways. The first method employs the use of a magnetic tape or wire recorder. In this process, the audio portion of the movie is separately recorded and later magnetically transferred to the film strip. Tapes or wires that are

---

and Confessions: A Preliminary Examination of Issues and Practices," cited in N.I.J. Research in Brief (March 1993).

2. See, Maryland v. Craig, 497 U.S. 836 (1990).

3. See, e.g., Fla.R.Crim.Proc. 3.160(a) (1994).

4. In re Establishment Inspection of Kelly–Springfield Tire Co., 13 F.3d 1160 (7th Cir.1994) (Court held that OSHA has the authority to inspect an employer's premises for hazards associated with ergonomics and compliance officers may videotape the working environment as part of their investigation.)

5. People v. Pride, 3 Cal.4th 195, 10 Cal.Rptr.2d 636, 833 P.2d 643 (1992); Peo-

ple v. Turner, 50 Cal.3d 668, 268 Cal.Rptr. 706, 789 P.2d 887 (1990); State v. Kingsley, 252 Kan. 761, 851 P.2d 370 (1993); State v. Hummel, 483 N.W.2d 68 (Minn.1992); State v. Russo, 243 N.J.Super. 383, 579 A.2d 834 (App.Div.1990); Stamper v. Commonwealth, 220 Va. 260, 257 S.E.2d 808 (1979); See also, Curriden, "Crime–Scene Video," *A.B.A.J.* May 1990, at 32 (describes Cobb County, Georgia cases).

6. See, "Motion to View Videotape of Crime Denied for Victim's Privacy Rights, People v. Colon and Cardona, Supreme Court, Justice Cowhey." *N.Y.L.J.*, June 30, 1992, at 21.

7. Dombroff, *Dombroff on Demonstrative Evidence,* § 6.9 (1983).

prepared in this manner can be altered or cut almost without detection and certainly without affecting the visual portion of the film.

The second process by which the audio portion of a movie can be recorded is through the use of optical recording; that is, a device on the camera transforms the sound into optical patterns and records them directly on the film alongside the visual portion. Since optical sound records cannot be erased or modified, motion pictures making use of this process have been freely admitted, provided the other requirements for admissibility are met. These other requirements include some expanded form of testimony on authenticity. Because of the greater possibility of exaggeration by control of camera speed and editing, courts often require testimony to establish the following facts:

1. The circumstances surrounding the taking of the film, including the competence of the operator, the types of camera, film and lens, weather conditions or lighting arrangements, and the speed at which the film was taken.

2. The manner and circumstances surrounding the development of the film, including proper chain-of-custody evidence.

3. The manner of film projection, including the speed of projection and the distance of the projector from the screen.

4. Testimony by someone who was present at the time the film was taken to establish the accuracy with which the filmed scene depicts the actual events that were filmed.

Together, these requirements establish that the motion picture presents a true and accurate reproduction of the scene or event.

The recent proliferation of VCRs (videotape cameras and recorders) has seen a significant switch away from motion pictures to the use of videotape. Its widespread adoption in the legal field is further discussed at § 2.18, infra.

§ 2.11 Techniques of Altering Photographs

No photographic representation is completely accurate unless in color and in three dimensions.[1] Misrepresentation of the subject may be achieved at one of two stages, namely: (1) at the time the photograph is taken; and (2) during the developing or printing process.

At the time the photograph is taken, the angular placement of the camera governs its point of view. Even if there has been no tampering with a photograph, the placement of the camera can make a significant difference in the accuracy of the subject depicted. The closer the camera is placed to the subject, the farther apart objects will appear insofar as depth perspective may be perceived in the developed photograph. Dis-

---

§ 2.11

1. Even then the photograph cannot be said to be totally accurate since the human eye can perceive at least 10,000 distinct shades, although it is said that the visible spectrum contains 100 to 150 named and discernible shades of colors. See, e.g., Snyder & Varden, "Is True Color Reproduction Possible?," *Identification News*, Aug. 1967, p. 4.

tortion may occur if a lens of proper focal length is not used. If a telephoto lens is used, depth perspective will be distorted to make objects appear closer together. Elongation in breadth may be caused by the use of a wide angle lens.

The distance at which photographs are viewed, too, may give an impression of distortion. It is said that "if a photograph is made with a camera having a between-the-lens shutter, there will be absolutely no distortion in the photograph regardless of the focal length of the lens used. If a photograph does not appear normal, it is viewed in improper perspective." [2] Determining the correct viewing distance of a photograph requires knowledge of the focal length of the lens, and the making of an enlarged print of a size that will conform to the normal viewing distance for most individuals. This relationship is illustrated in Figure 8.

EXAMPLE OF VIEWING DISTANCES

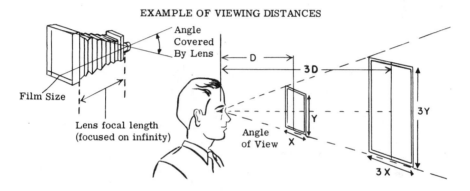

Fig. 8. To view a photograph in proper perspective, the same angular relationship must be maintained between the eye and print in viewing the photograph as occurred between the lens and film when the negative was made. *Courtesy: Harris B. Tuttle, Sr., Rochester, N.Y.*

The normal viewing distance of an object for persons with normal eyesight is fifteen inches. If a picture was taken with a 4 × 5 camera using a 7½ inch focal length lens, a contact print of the negative (4″ × 5″) would have to be viewed at a distance of 7½ inches from the eyes to have a correct perspective. In order to provide a correct visual impression of the photograph for viewing at the normal viewing distance of 15 inches, the photograph would have to be enlarged two times (2 × 7½ = 15) or to 8″ × 10″ size.

False lighting can also cause a misleading representation. Filters are used to add or subtract different colors of light from the subject. If a

2. Tuttle & Conrad, "Photographs for   June 1965, p. 3, at 6.
Use in Court," *Finger Pr. & Ident. Mag.,*

photographer wishes to lighten the intensity of a color, he can place a filter of the same color over the lens, as discussed earlier in § 2.09(1). A filter may be used to eliminate objects entirely in the photograph, as was illustrated earlier in Figure 6. If the camera is carefully positioned, an expert may be able to depict two images on one area of film by double exposure.

There are more than 3,000 different film types on the commercial market; each will react differently to light and colors. For example, fast films need less light than regular films to produce a picture; panchromatic film shows the relative degree of brightness and contrast between the objects depicted in a photograph far better than other types of film. A person who is aware of the difference in film can determine to some extent the nature of the resultant print made from it. With the proper combination of film and filter, it is possible to radically alter appearances. For an example of this, see Figure 9.

The final method of altering a photograph is to etch or paint the print or negative. Etching involves the use of a sharp knife to remove layers of the transfixed silver on the negative. This allows for the entire removal of things otherwise appearing on the negative or, phrased differently, the increase in darkness of areas of the print by decreasing density of areas of the negative. The altered negative can then be printed. The print will, of course, reflect the altered view. Additions can be made to a photograph by painting it with an airbrush, using opaque flour-water paint as a medium. The air brush is a device attached to a tank of CO_2 which can simulate the grain structure of the photograph. After this is done, it is a simple matter to photograph and print the painted photograph.

A reversal of horizontal direction (right-left) can be accomplished by printing the negative from the flip side. If the negative faces the wrong way when the print is made, a reverse print will then result (see Figure 10). An upside down alteration of the photograph without a frame of reference can be accomplished by printing an inverted negative.

After taking the photograph, it may also be altered during the process of developing a negative by varying the type of chemical developer used. For example, a soft developer will produce low contrast; a high contrast developer will produce more graphic contrast. After the negative has been developed, the print may be altered by the photographer holding back a certain amount of light which would otherwise pass through the negative to the print paper. By using his hands to selectively block light (dodging), he can turn white what would otherwise have been a dark area on the print. The less light reaching the print paper, the whiter it will be. The more light passing through the negative to the print paper, the darker the print. Even the type of print paper (glossy or matte) used can affect the definition of the photograph.

It is foolhardy for an attorney to depend solely on cross-examination to challenge the accuracy of a photograph. The adverse witness who has falsely testified that the photograph is a correct representation will stick to his story. The danger of photographic misrepresentation or tampering can be minimized by pretrial preparation. First, if possible, the attorney can visit the scene depicted in the photograph and cause photographs to be taken of it. If the opposition attempts to introduce misleading photographs, accurate photographs can be introduced in rebuttal. Second, the attorney can seek discovery of the negative of the opposing side's photograph so that an expert can make a new print thereof and determine if the negative has been altered or is a copy shot.

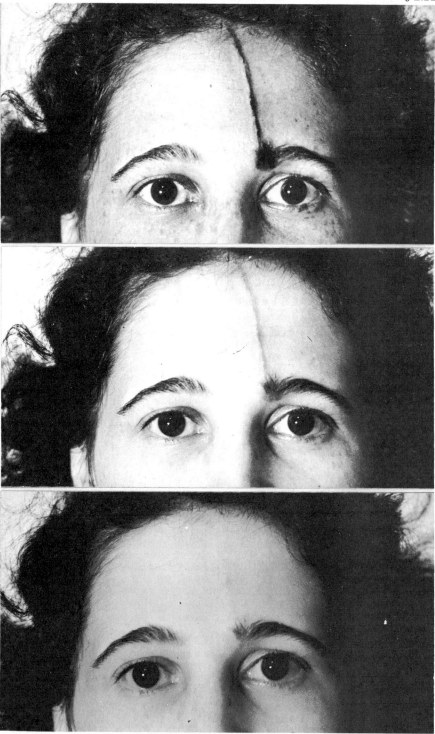

Fig. 9.　　Result of using filters when photographing the same subject.　Top panchromatic film, no filter; middle, panchromatic film with X–2 filter; bottom, panchromatic film with F filter.　(Fig. 281. in Scott, *Photographic Evidence*, 2d Ed. [1969]). *Courtesy: Chas. C. Scott, Kansas City, Mo.*

Fig. 10. The effect of proper and improper printing from the same negative. Top, emulsion side of negative facing the sensitized paper; bottom, emulsion side of the negative away from the paper.

Considering the many ways in which photographs may be altered or distorted, even though no retouching has taken place, the trial attorney against whom photographs are being used should carefully explore whether any such alteration or distortion has occurred so as to errone-ously depict a scene on the photograph. It is easy to create visual illusions on photographs which do not correspond to the visual impressions which were received when viewing the actual scene. A room shot through a wide-angle lens, for example, can appear to be larger or roomier than it really is. Conversely, a telephoto lens causes an object in a photograph to appear to be much closer to the camera than it would appear to a viewer looking at the object from the point where the photograph was taken.

Other real or apparent distortions can be obtained by very simple techniques that do not involve retouching or altering the negative. A dramatic illustration is provided in Figure 11, which appears to depict a road at the crest of a mountain ridge. Actually, this photograph is printed upside down. By turning the book upside down the correct visual impression is conveyed, namely that of a river (the Snake River) flowing through canyons. It is obvious then, that eliciting information about the camera, lens, film, filters, developing processes, as well as all other relevant information concerning the taking of a photograph, may be a crucial part of the cross-examination of a witness who seeks to illustrate testimony by the use of photographs.

Fig. 11.

New technologies are emerging which may cause one to question whether one can ever take a photograph at face value. Electronic photographs may be made by one of three methods: computer imaging, still video camera and image synthesis. Computer imaging digitizes the photo then processes the image. Colors can be adjusted and elements can be erased or added to the image on the computer. A still video camera records light as a series of digital impulses on magnetic computer disks. The data on such disks can be hooked up to a T.V., printer or fed into a digitizer and then into a personal computer where it can be manipulated. Image synthesis creates an image mathematically from information entered into the computer that describes the object to be depicted. With these new techniques, computers can alter a photograph and detection is nearly impossible.[3]

§ 2.12 Color Photography

At various occasions in the previous sections we have made allusion to color photography, but without elaboration on the special processes involved. It is important for the attorney, however, to have a basic understanding of color photography, since much of the photographic evidence adduced in trials is of that variety.

Color photography may be defined as the creation, by photographic means, of a picture in the brain of the observer that approximates as closely as possible the picture he would have experienced in observing the colored subject directly.

There are two basic kinds of color film. The first type is called "reversal" film. It is a film which, after development, produces a transparent image of positive colors, just as the eye perceives them. The film is used as a transparency for exhibition in a light box or as a slide suitable for projection onto a screen. The second type of color film produces, after development, a color negative on which the image photographed appears in colors complementary to its true colors. From this negative, color prints can be made on specially prepared photographic paper.

White light (noon sunlight) is a combination of all colors in equal proportions. When white light is passed through a prism, the light is broken down in its component colors and shows all of the colors of the rainbow. In § 2.09, supra, we discussed the electromagnetic spectrum and pointed out that light differed only from other forms of radiation in its wavelength. When discussing infrared and ultraviolet radiation, we measured them in Angstrom (A). The visible portion of the electromagnetic spectrum, that portion we call light, ranges from approximately 3900A to 7700A. Individual colors within that spectrum can also be identified by their wavelengths, as follows:

Violet	3900A to 4550A
Blue	4550A to 4920A
Green	4920A to 5770A
Yellow	5770A to 5970A
Orange	5970A to 6220A
Red	6220A to 7700A

---

3. Guilshan "A Picture is Worth a Thousand Lies: Electronic Imaging and the Future of the Admissibility of Photographs Into Evidence," 18 *Rutgers Computer & Tech. L.J.* 365 (1992).

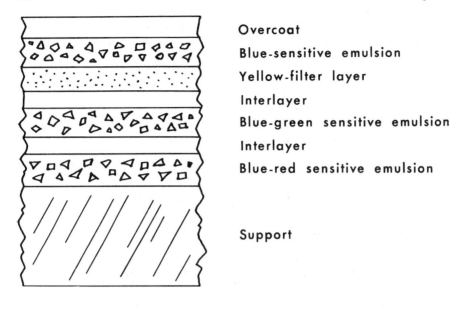

Overcoat

Blue-sensitive emulsion

Yellow-filter layer

Interlayer

Blue-green sensitive emulsion

Interlayer

Blue-red sensitive emulsion

Support

Fig. 12. Artist drawing of a typical cross-section of a three-color film.

For the purpose of color photography, the visible spectrum may be broken down into three primary colors: red, green, and blue.[1] We see an object in color because when white light is directed toward it, the object will absorb some of the component rays of sunlight and reflect others. If an object illuminated with sunlight absorbs the green and blue rays and reflects the red rays of the light, the object appears red to our eye. If an object appears to be blue, that means it has absorbed the red and green parts of white light and is reflecting the blue rays. An object appears black when it absorbs all colors and reflects none; it appears white when it reflects all colors.[2]

When using a typical color film (See Fig. 12), to photograph a multi-colored object that is illuminated with white light, the areas of the object which reflect white (containing of course all three primary colors in equal proportions) will affect all three emulsion layers. The parts of the object that are red, reflect red rays only; they will register only in the bottom emulsion layer (red-sensitive). The same thing happens to the green and blue areas of the object respectively.

In the chemical process of development of the emulsion layers, the interaction of the color couplers which form complementary color dye images in each layer, using the unexposed silver halides as color formers, and the bleaching out of the silver, ultimately will produce a positive or a negative color film, depending upon the characteristics of the film used.

By the variance of components within the emulsions, or development processes, color films can be produced which will reproduce faithful colors under varying lighting conditions (daylight or artificial light films), or those which are more or less sensitive to light intensity (fast or slow films).

The incorrect use of color films, through inaccurate exposure time, incorrect lens opening, or inappropriate lighting, to name but a few, will produce color images which do not faithfully portray the objects depicted. Development processes can, to some extent, compensate for these color deficiencies, but the person processing the film can obviously do this only when he has observed, and correctly remembered, the colors of the object he photographed. It behooves the attorney, then, to carefully explore the circumstances of photography and development, when confronted with color photographs wherein the precise hues and shades may be important to the resolution of factual disputes.

Properly made color photographs give the jury a much better understanding of the issues than they might get from black-and-white photographs. In fact, it is frequently stated that if color photography had been invented before black-and-white photography, it would be next to impossible to get a court to admit a black-and-white photograph today; without colors, it would be said to portray its subject inaccurately because everyone with normal vision sees things in color.

IV. PHOTOGRAPHIC EVIDENCE IN GENERAL

§ 2.13 Admissibility of Photographs

1. IN GENERAL

An early mention of photographs as evidence dates back to 1859 and involves photographs of questioned and known samples of handwriting in a dispute about the signature on a land grant. A photographer was interrogated and he attached to his deposition photographs of original documents, of impressions of genuine seals, and of the signature on the disputed document. This is probably the first recorded case where photographs were presented in court. We can imagine the curiosity of the court when examining this novel type of evidence:

> "We have ourselves been able to compare these signatures by means of photographic copies and fully concur, from evidence *oculis subjecta fidelibus,* that the seal and signatures of Pico are forger-

ies." [1]

A few years later, an Alabama court undertook to define daguerreo-typist and ambrotypist, the names then given to photographers,[2] whom it compared to a photographic painter. The court stated that a person who was not an expert could testify whether a photograph was a good likeness. In describing the functions of the specialists, the court stated:

> "The ambrotypist or daguerreotypist, whatever title he may give himself, is rather an artisan, than an artist. His labor is more manual than mental. He works more by rules, than under the inspiration of genius. The process by which he accomplishes his undertaking, is mainly mechanical; and success in vocation demands, not creative power, but dexterity, contrivance, and the skillful application of fixed rules. He follows an art, but not one of the fine arts...." [3]

The first important criminal case involving photographic evidence was Udderzook v. Commonwealth,[4] decided in 1874. Not only was it one of the earliest criminal cases, but in it the court also took judicial notice of the principles of photography.

William E. Udderzook was indicted for the murder of his brother-in-law and another man of unknown identity. The brother-in-law had obtained a large life insurance policy of which Udderzook's wife was the beneficiary. One day, defendant's brother-in-law's shop was destroyed by fire and among the ruins were found the remains of a body, identified by Udderzook to be that of his brother-in-law. Later, the remains of another man's body were found in a woods, and the state contended that it was that of defendant's brother-in-law, and that the body in the shop was of someone else. A photograph was introduced in evidence and shown to witnesses. After Udderzook's conviction for murder of his

---

§ 2.13

1. Luco v. United States, 64 U.S. (23 How.) 515 (1859). It seems that several of the earliest photography cases dealt with questioned documents with the photographer acting as the document "expert." In Marcy v. Barnes, 82 Mass. (16 Gray) 161, 77 Am.Dec. 405 (1860), a comparison of a questioned signature with admitted genuine signatures was testified to by the photographer on the basis of enlargements he had prepared. The court opined that a photographer who is accustomed to compare handwriting in connection with his business is qualified to give an expert opinion on the genuineness of a disputed signature. The court did not find it objectionable that the witness' opinion was based in part on enlarged photographs, which he had testified to be accurate copies, except as to size and color.

2. The Daguerreotype process consisted originally of a mirror-polished silver plated copper sheet, treated with iodine fumes which converted its surface into a thin coating of silver iodide. After the plate had been exposed in a bulky camera, which required a long exposure, the plate was developed with a vapor of metallic mercury, which forms an amalgam in proportion to the light and shades of the original subject. Washing in sodium thiosulphate removed the unaffected silver iodide, and a rinse in water completed the operation.

The Ambrotype process was also an early photographic process that had but a short life. It consisted of a glass negative which had a whitish deposit to represent the highlights that appeared positive when backed by black. The method died in the 1860s.

3. Barnes v. Ingalls, 39 Ala. 193, 201 (1863).

4. 76 Pa. 340 (1874).

brother-in-law, the Supreme Court of Pennsylvania, in ruling on the admissibility of the photograph, declared:

> There seems to be no reason why a photograph, proved to be taken from life and to resemble the person photographed, should not fill the same measure of evidence. It is true the photographs we see are not the original likenesses; their lines are not traced by the hand of the artist nor can the artist be called to testify that he faithfully limned [Sic.] the portrait. They are but paper copies taken from the original plate, called the negative, made sensitive by chemicals, and printed by the sunlight through the camera. . . .

> It is evident that the competency of the evidence in such a case depends on the reliability of the photograph of a work of art, and this, in the case before us, in which no proof was made by experts of this reliability, must depend upon the judicial cognisance we make of photographs as an established means of producing a correct likeness. The Daguerrean process was first given to the world in 1839. It was soon followed by photography, of which we have nearly a generation's experience. . . . We know that its principles are derived from science; that the images on the plate, made by the rays of light through the camera, are dependent on the same general laws which produce the images of outward forms upon the retina through the lenses of the eye. The process has become one in general use, so common that we cannot refuse to take judicial cognisance of it as a proper means of producing correct likeness.[5]

Since those early days, it has become well settled that photographs are admissible, provided what they depict is relevant to the issues of the case.[6] This applies to photographs of objects,[7] crime scenes,[8] and victims

5. Id. at 342. Luke v. Calhoun County, 52 Ala. 115 (1874), also dealt with identification photographs in a murder case. A murdered man's widow prior to, and at her husband's death, resided in Canada. Her murdered husband's sojourn in Alabama preceded his death by a few months. The photograph she offered the police had been taken in Alabama and was sent to her by her husband, with the endorsement of his handwriting. The court took judicial notice that photography is an art of reproducing *facsimiles* or representations of objects by the action of light on a prepared surface.

6. Courts tend to be rather relaxed in the foundational requirements for the admission of photographs. Presence of the photographer is not necessary. All that is required is that a testimonial sponsor, usually a witness, testify that he or she is familiar with the scene or object depicted in the photograph, and that it fairly and accurately portrays that which it purports to portray.

7. Rodriguez v. People, 168 Colo. 190, 450 P.2d 645 (1969): stolen property.

8. State v. Wheeler, 187 W.Va. 379, 419 S.E.2d 447 (1992): Photographs showing trail of blood left by shooting victim not so gruesome as to render their admission reversible error in malicious wounding, attempted murder and murder prosecution. Fair v. State, 198 Ga.App. 437, 401 S.E.2d 626 (1991): Admission of photos of robbery crime scene, stolen automobile and of defendant taken on day of crime not reversible error; People v. LaClere, 157 A.D.2d 473, 549 N.Y.S.2d 397 (1990): Introduction of crime scene photographs depicting blood on the sidewalk was not reversible error in attempted murder prosecution. Hampton v. People, 171 Colo. 153, 465 P.2d 394 (1970); People v. Speck, 41 Ill.2d 177, 242 N.E.2d 208 (1968); Daniels v. State, 257 Ind. 376, 274 N.E.2d 702 (1971). Even photographs of mock-ups of crime scenes have been admitted. Willis v. State, 309 Ark. 328, 829 S.W.2d 417 (1992): No prejudice in admission of photograph of mock-up of crime scene of possession of cocaine with intent to deliver even though sack used in mock-up was larger than actual sack in

of crime.[9]   Photographs of the victim may be shown to prove the corpus delicti, corroborate other evidence establishing the cause of death and to prove positive identification of the victim.[10]

Photographs may also be shown to prove an essential element of a crime, such as the swollen condition of a robbery victim's face to prove the use of force.[11]   In People v. Tolbert,[12] it was held proper to admit into evidence photographs of a murder victim to show the condition of the body and refute the defendant's claim that death was the result of a lover's quarrel and not a sexual attack.   A picture of a victim with a knife wound in the neck was deemed material in proving death and that such death was not due to natural causes, since these were the contested issues at trial.[13]   It is also important to make a clear record at trial regarding which photographs or other demonstrative aids are objected to [14] or the precise ground for an objection [15] in order to perfect the record for appeal.

which pill bottle with cocaine was found. Trial court ruled that prosecutor had to explain the discrepancy in the sack size to the jury, which he did.

9.   State v. Day, 866 S.W.2d 491 (Mo. App.1993): Photos of victim's injuries admissible; State v. Devlin, 251 Mont. 278, 825 P.2d 185 (1991): Photographs of aggravated assault victim and of crime scene properly admitted; State v. Campbell, 562 So.2d 37 (La.App.1990): Crime scene photographs of victim of shooting were properly admitted to prove corpus delicti, corroborate other evidence of manner in which death occurred, establish location, severity and number of wounds and to establish the identity of the victim. Nowels v. People, 166 Colo. 140, 442 P.2d 410 (1968): photographs of various poses of nude young girls and a notebook which referred to these girls, of whom the defendant was charged with taking indecent liberties; People v. Tolbert, 70 Cal.2d 790, 76 Cal.Rptr. 445, 452 P.2d 661 (1969); People v. Robinson, 106 Ill.App.2d 78, 246 N.E.2d 15 (1969); People v. Frank, 31 Mich.App. 378, 188 N.W.2d 95 (1971); State v. Conklin, 54 N.J. 540, 258 A.2d 1 (1969); Snake v. State, 453 P.2d 287 (Okl.Cr.1969); State v. Mathers, 3 Wash.App. 639, 477 P.2d 34 (1970): photographs of victim and bloodsheet held admissible, even though defendant offered to stipulate that a deceased person was found in the cabin, but he refused to stipulate that an assault occurred.

10.   State v. Hosford, 572 So.2d 242 (La. App.1990).

11.   People v. Smith, 264 N.E.2d 232 (1969).

12.   Supra n. 9. No error to admit photographs of murder victim showing his amputated genitals stuffed in his mouth: Peo-

ple v. Lindgren, 79 Ill.2d 129, 37 Ill.Dec. 348, 402 N.E.2d 238 (1980).

13.   People v. Brannon, 14 Mich.App. 690, 165 N.W.2d 903 (1968). Photograph of deceased victim taken at the morgue revealing knife wound above left breast held admissible to corroborate doctor's testimony that victim had died from a stab wound: Jackson v. State, 231 So.2d 839 (Fla.App.1970).

14.   To understand the importance of a clear record, see, e.g., Roland v. Langlois, 945 F.2d 956, 963 (7th Cir.1991), in which the court criticized counsel for failing to make such a record:

> The plaintiffs' argument consists solely of a one-paragraph assertion, without legal citation, that the plaintiffs were prevented from introducing photographic evidence that would have highlighted the inaccuracy of the defendants' life-size model. What is more, the argument at no point identified a single photograph that was offered but not admitted. It is asking too much, we believe, to expect this court to comb through the volumes of transcripts in order to identify which of the 157 photographs in this record are implicated and then raise, research, and resolve all possible arguments involving those photographs. An appellate court reviews arguments, it does not construct them.

15.   In Irving v. Commonwealth, 13 Va. App. 414, 412 S.E.2d 712 (1991), a panel of the intermediate appeals court reversed and remanded because of the trial court's admission of a "mug shot" as possibly suggesting evidence of other crimes; however, on rehearing *en banc*, an equally divided

Photographs of the charred body of a murder victim,[16] of a dismembered victim as substantiating evidence that the victim's murder was so planned,[17] of a badly decomposed dead body lying beside a cement block which was attached to the body,[18] have all been held admissible in evidence. The photograph of a victim's liver was held relevant to supplement and corroborate the testimony of doctors in explaining the mechanism of death, which was in issue because of the time interval between the assault and the resulting death.[19] It has been held not to be error to introduce the photo of a victim's brain during autopsy.[20] Just because such photographs might depict the nude body of a victim, they are not rendered inadmissible if otherwise relevant.[21]

Likewise, in civil cases, photographs will be admitted if they are relevant and probative and not overly prejudicial. In Washburn v. Beatt Equipment Co.,[22] where plaintiff suffered burns over 70% of his body of which over 50% were third degree burns that completely destroyed the entire epidermis so that the skin could not regenerate, it was held not an abuse of discretion for the trial court to admit 78 photographs sequentially showing the course of plaintiff's treatment over 16 months. Such photographs were relevant to damages, illustrated the testimony of the treating physicians and were probative of the plaintiff's emotional and psychological problems and pain and suffering.

The defendant cannot, by offering to stipulate facts shown in evidence photographs, preclude the prosecution from introducing these photographs, assuming their relevance to a fact the prosecution would have had to prove in the absence of a stipulation.[23] In Bullard v. State,[24]

---

court affirmed the trial court's admission because counsel had failed to state a proper reason for his objection. See, Irving v. Commonwealth, 15 Va.App. 178, 422 S.E.2d 471 (1992).

16. State v. Raymond, 258 La. 1, 245 So.2d 335 (1971).

17. Schmidt v. State, 255 Ind. 443, 265 N.E.2d 219 (1970), rehearing denied 256 Ind. 218, 267 N.E.2d 554 (1971); State v. Winston, 105 R.I. 447, 252 A.2d 354 (1969).

18. People v. Krogol, 29 Mich.App. 406, 185 N.W.2d 408 (1971).

19. State v. Wilbur, 186 Neb. 306, 182 N.W.2d 906 (1971). Autopsy photographs showing points of entry and exit of gunshot wounds and the powder burns surrounding the wound were unquestionably of substantial aid to the jury: Cottrell v. State, 458 P.2d 328 (Okl.Cr.1969). See also, New v. State, 254 Ind. 307, 259 N.E.2d 696 (1970). But in People v. Turner, 17 Mich.App. 123, 169 N.W.2d 330 (1969), it was held prejudicial error to admit into evidence autopsy pictures that were needlessly gruesome.

20. Ladner v. State, 868 S.W.2d 417 (Tex.App.1993).

21. Green v. State, 265 Ind. 16, 349 N.E.2d 147 (1976); Commonwealth v. Schroth, 479 Pa. 485, 388 A.2d 1034 (1978); Irving v. State, 228 So.2d 266 (Miss.1969); State v. Blackwell, 184 Neb. 121, 165 N.W.2d 730 (1969). There was no abuse of discretion in allowing into evidence a photograph of the nude body of a child victim laying face down in the water: People v. Miller, 71 Cal.2d 459, 78 Cal.Rptr. 449, 455 P.2d 377 (1969). But in Whaley v. State, 367 S.W.2d 703 (Tex.Cr.App.1963), photographs of nude body of deceased and automobile with pools of blood were held inadmissible where they did not serve to illustrate a disputed fact issue.

22. 120 Wash.2d 246, 840 P.2d 860 (1992).

23. Peterson v. Commonwealth, 225 Va. 289, 302 S.E.2d 520 (1983).

That facts depicted by photographs are not contested does not necessarily render them inadmissible: State v. Fryer, 243 N.W.2d 1 (Iowa 1976). See also, State v. Tharp, 27 Wash.App. 198, 616 P.2d 693 (1980).

24. 263 Ga. 682, 436 S.E.2d 647 (1993).

the court held the trial court properly admitted photographs of dismembered victim's body parts, which illustrated, among other things, chopping incisions on the bones, as probative and relevant to the charge of concealing the death of another and whether the defendant acted with malice, when he killed the victim. In State v. Kingsley,[25] the court held the autopsy photographs of the murder victim were admissible as was the photograph of burnt matches in the victim's pubic hair to show the attempt to burn the body.

It has been held, on the other hand, that a photograph which depicts the victim *after autopsy incisions are made* or after the state of the body has been changed by the police or medical examiner, will not be admissible unless it is necessary to show some material fact which becomes apparent only because of the autopsy. In Brown v. State,[26] the court recognized that a photograph which shows mutilation of a victim resulting from the crime against him may, however gruesome, have relevancy to the trial of his alleged assailant. The necessary further mutilation of a body at autopsy has no such relevance, said the court, and may cause confusion, if not prejudice, in the minds of the jurors.

The photograph of a defendant, who had fallen asleep after committing a rape, at the time of his arrest showing the fly of his trousers undone and his privates exhibited was held admissible as portraying the accused as he was found at the crime scene in a condition from which it could be inferred that he had engaged in sexual intercourse and possibly rape.[27] Photographs of an accused showing scratches on his face are admissible,[28] as are photographs of a defendant taken at the reenactment of the crime,[29] if otherwise relevant. It might be properly said that photographs of anything a witness can describe in words are competent evidence.[30] On the other hand, if the fact to be evidenced by the photograph is itself not admissible, it cannot be proved by a photograph.[31]

Photographic evidence of a demonstrative nature is widely used by experts to illustrate their findings and to facilitate the jury's understanding of the reasons for the experts' opinions. Thus, the firearms and toolmark experts use photomicrographs of striations on bullets or tools; fingerprint experts use enlargements of the known and latent print on which the matching ridge characteristics are marked; questioned document experts use enlargements of cut-outs of letters from the exemplars and disputed writings. Such photographs are freely admitted by the

25. 252 Kan. 761, 851 P.2d 370 (1993).

26. 250 Ga. 862, 302 S.E.2d 347 (1983).

27. Johnson v. Commonwealth, 472 S.W.2d 695 (Ky.1971).

28. Leaver v. State, 250 Ind. 523, 237 N.E.2d 368 (1968), cert. denied 393 U.S. 1059 (1969). The admission of the picture of defendant, taken at time of arrest, was not inadmissible as an attack on his character because of his "hippy" appearance: State v. Blakely, 445 S.W.2d 280 (Mo.1969).

29. United States v. Daniels, 377 F.2d 255 (6th Cir.1967); Pollack v. State, 215 Wis. 200, 253 N.W. 560 (1934), affirmed 215 Wis. 200, 254 N.W. 471 (1934).

30. Hampton v. People, supra n. 8.

31. United States v. Daniels, supra n. 29.

courts because the fields of expertise to which they relate have been given credence by the courts.

Photographs in aid of a science or technique not yet judicially accepted, nor proven reliable, would not be entitled to admission in evidence. Thus, in United States v. Tranowski,[32] an expert astronomer sought to establish by means of an examination of the shadows on a photograph, that the picture could only have been taken on April 13 or August 31. The expert arrived at his opinion by calculating the angle and attitude of the sun from shadows in the photographs, and then comparing the finding with an astronomical "sun chart." The Court of Appeals reversed a conviction obtained, in part, on this evidence, noting that the procedure of interpreting photographs in the manner done by this expert had never been performed by other experts. No data was available, said the court, to verify the accuracy of the chart; there had also been no verification of the accuracy of the witness' methods through possible camera distortion, imprecision, or other factors that admittedly might affect the results. The court concluded that the technology of interpreting photographs as done in this case was not generally accepted in the field, and admonished: "The trial court should not be used as a testing ground for theories supported neither by prior control experiments nor by calculations with indicia of reliability."[33]

2. LAYING THE FOUNDATION

The predicate for introduction of a photograph requires proof of its accuracy as a correct representation of the subject at a given time, in addition to its material relevance to a disputed issue. The authentication of a photograph as a true and correct representation of what it purports to depict does not require that the photographer himself testify. It is not even necessary that the authenticating witness was present at the time the photograph was taken, as long as he is able to testify to the accuracy of the conditions or circumstances portrayed.

3. COLOR PHOTOGRAPHS

Since color photographs are more accurate representations of a person, object, or scene, than black-and-white pictures, they should be admissible in any circumstance where black-and-white photographs would be admitted into evidence.

Green v. City & County of Denver,[34] a 1943 case, is the first appellate case involving the issue of admissibility of a color photograph. It involved a charge of violating a health ordinance prohibiting the offering for sale to the public of putrid meat—in this case, wieners and

---

32. 659 F.2d 750 (7th Cir.1981).

33. The dissenting judge suggested that what was involved was not a brand new technique but rather a new application of old principles, which should be admissible since margins of error had been provided and the so-called inaccuracies were at most possibilities rather than probabilities.

34. 111 Colo. 390, 142 P.2d 277 (1943).

liver. The prosecution offered in evidence color photographs of the putrid meat placed alongside similar fresh meat. One of the photographs had been underexposed and therefore its colors were not truly representative, but the photographer candidly explained to the jury that the colors of the one print were too dark due to underexposure, and he testified that the others did portray the evidence accurately. The Colorado Supreme Court found no error. Since then, reviewing courts have readily accepted color photographs in criminal cases. In fact, even though it may appear paradoxical, color photographs have been more readily admitted in criminal cases than in civil cases, although there really is no logical reason for a differentiation.

It has become well settled that color photographs are admissible, provided (1) what they depict is relevant to the issues in the case; (2) they have been shown to be true and accurate representations; and (3) their probative value is not outweighed by gruesomeness or inflammatory character. (On that point, see § 2.14, infra.)

Thus, color photographs have been admitted to show the wounds of the victim of the crime,[35] even though they depicted a considerable amount of blood,[36] or were taken at the morgue before or after an autopsy,[37] or to show the condition in which the victim's body was found.[38] "Gruesome" color photographs have also been held properly admitted at the first stage of a capital sentencing hearing even though the photographs simply depicted what witnesses had already orally described.[39]

In what was called a "borderline" case, the Nebraska Supreme Court nevertheless upheld the admissibility of two color photographs of a homicide victim taken during the autopsy, depicting the size and location of the wound by folding back part of the flesh over the left chest, shoulder, and neck with a forceps inserted through the wound in the

---

35. State v. Mohr, 106 Ariz. 402, 476 P.2d 857 (1970), showing several gaping neck wounds and blood; State v. Conte, 157 Conn. 209, 251 A.2d 81 (1968), cert. denied 396 U.S. 964 (1969), to show location and direction of bullet wounds; People v. Eddington, 23 Mich.App. 210, 178 N.W.2d 686 (1970), detailing condition of bodies of victims as police found them to show malice.

36. State v. Mohr, supra n. 35; Brown v. State, 252 Ind. 161, 247 N.E.2d 76 (1969); Shuff v. State, 86 Nev. 736, 476 P.2d 22 (1970).

37. Sleziak v. State, 454 P.2d 252 (Alaska 1969), cert. denied 396 U.S. 921 (1969); People v. Arguello, 65 Cal.2d 768, 56 Cal. Rptr. 274, 423 P.2d 202 (1967); State v. Hanna, 150 Conn. 457, 191 A.2d 124 (1963); State v. Bucanis, 26 N.J. 45, 138 A.2d 739 (1958), cert. denied 357 U.S. 910 (1958); State v. Atkinson, 278 N.C. 168, 179 S.E.2d

410 (1971); State v. Iverson, 187 N.W.2d 1 (N.D.1971), cert. denied 404 U.S. 956 (1971): ten color pictures taken prior to internal probing by pathologist in the course of the autopsy; Walle v. Sigler, 329 F.Supp. 1278 (D.C.Neb.1971).

38. Brown v. State, 252 Ind. 161, 247 N.E.2d 76 (1969): pool of blood on floor of grocery store where killing occurred; Alcala v. State, 487 P.2d 448 (Wyo.1971), body found in lake, tied to a cement block.

39. People v. Simms, 143 Ill.2d 154, 157 Ill.Dec. 483, 572 N.E.2d 947 (1991): "demonstrative evidence may be clearer and more persuasive than oral testimony." See also, People v. Shum, 117 Ill.2d 317, 353, 111 Ill.Dec. 546, 559, 512 N.E.2d 1183, 1197 (1987): it is not an abuse of discretion to allow the jury to consider photographs which may be characterized as "disgusting."

neck.[40] In restating the general rule that in determining the relevancy the trial court is to weigh and balance the probative value of the picture against its possible prejudicial effect, the court stated:

"The State has the burden of going forward with the evidence. It cannot anticipate the nature of the defense which will be subsequently advanced by the defendant and which it will be required to meet. It must prove all elements of the crime charged beyond a reasonable doubt and also combat all possible defenses. Under such circumstances, evidence is frequently advanced which appears unnecessary after the trial has been concluded. Nevertheless, if such evidence were to be omitted, it could well leave an opening for a successful defense on the part of the defendant. This is true in most criminal prosecutions and this case was not an exception."[41]

In Wright v. State,[42] however, three of the eight color pictures introduced were held to have been erroneously admitted because they were considered grossly inflammatory and unnecessary to explain or elucidate any portion of the state's case. The three pictures were, (1) a photograph depicting the nude body of the 8-year old victim at the gravesite but in a different position than where it was found; (2) a photograph taken at the morgue after removal of the body from the grave, which picture showed a deep stab wound on the left top side of the head, another wound in the left breast, and other lacerations in the abdominal area; and (3) a morgue picture showing the deceased victim laid out on her right side in a horizontal position taken from the rear, showing several stab wounds and a gashing type of wound in her upper buttocks.

It was also held to be prejudicial error to permit the jury to consider, "accidentally," 90 photographs of the crime scene not admitted in evidence. About half of the photographs were duplicates or different angle shots of the photographs admitted in evidence, and the other half were of irrelevant and immaterial subject matter surrounding the crime scene, such as a doorway, wall, bedroom, utility area, and the like. Nevertheless, the court held that jurors may not properly receive any evidence other than what has been admitted at trial, and such admission is prejudicial. The test, the court said, was not whether the jurors were

40. State v. Robinson, 185 Neb. 64, 173 N.W.2d 443 (1970).

41. Id. at 68, 173 N.W.2d at 446.

42. 250 So.2d 333 (Fla.App.1971). On the other hand, in Albritton v. State, 221 So.2d 192 (Fla.App.1969), the same court held admissible photographs which showed the nude body of a 16-month old victim with bruises, blemishes, abrasions, lacerations and wounds from beating and burning on practically every part of her body, in addition to heavy surgical wrappings from a skull operation, even though they might inflame and arouse to a high degree the minds of otherwise impartial jurors. The

photographs were considered proper demonstrable visual evidence of the extent and severity of the child's injuries.

See also Commonwealth v. Garrison, 459 Pa. 664, 331 A.2d 186 (1975), holding that admission of some 11 color slides in a matricide case was error. Five of the slides were of the deceased in her bedroom, two of the bedroom and bedding covered with blood, two of deceased's head showing blood and fragments of bone tissue, and one frontal view of deceased nude from the waist up and a view of the lacerated side of the deceased's head in a pool of blood.

actually prejudiced by the extraneous matter, but whether they might have been so prejudiced.[43]

The fact that pictures are in color, then, does not determine their admissibility or inadmissibility. Color in itself is not the test; the test lies in the effect of the photographs, whether in color or in black-and-white.[44]

4. SLIDES

Color or black-and-white slides, even though they require darkening of the courtroom to permit their projection on a screen, are just as admissible as ordinary photographs. Thus, colored slides of injuries, taken by the medical examiner at the autopsy, and an 8″ × 10″ color enlargement of the victim in a shallow grave, which the medical examiner used to illustrate his testimony, were held properly admitted in Wasley v. State.[45]

Similarly, in detailing the rules as to admissibility of photographic evidence, the court held, in State v. Adams,[46] that the use of autopsy slides by the pathologist for the purpose of illustrating his testimony is proper in the discretion of the court. The fact that death was clearly caused by a criminal agency did not relieve the state of its obligation to prove the elements of the crime by the best means available to it. To this end, the slides were found to have clear and relevant probative value.

§ 2.14 Gruesome and Inflammatory Photographs

In the previous section we stated that the admissibility of photographs rests in the discretion of the judge, who determines the relevancy

43. Brittle v. Commonwealth, 222 Va. 518, 281 S.E.2d 889 (1981).

44. State v. Duguay, 158 Me. 61, 178 A.2d 129 (1962). Cf., State v. Joy, 452 A.2d 408 (Me.1982).

45. 244 So.2d 418 (Fla.1971); State v. Danahey, 108 R.I. 291, 274 A.2d 736 (1971).

In the celebrated case of State v. Sheppard, 100 Ohio App. 345, 128 N.E.2d 471 (1955), affirmed 165 Ohio St. 293, 135 N.E.2d 340 (1956), cert. denied 352 U.S. 910 (1956), rehearing denied 352 U.S. 955 (1956), colored slides of victim's wounds were projected on a 6′ × 6′ screen. Defendant's claim that the projection exaggerated the size of the wounds and unfairly emphasized the cause of death was rejected.

46. 76 Wash.2d 650, 458 P.2d 558 (1969), also admissible were pictures of the victim's body and the interior of her home as discovered during the police investigation. See also, Commonwealth v. Chasten, 443 Pa. 29, 275 A.2d 305 (1971), where color slides depicting various wounds on the deceased's nude body were admissible to explain to the jury how the wounds were inflicted.

Other cases admitting color slides as an aid to the pathologist's testimony include: People v. Moore, 48 Cal.2d 541, 310 P.2d 969 (1957); Commonwealth v. Makarewicz, 333 Mass. 575, 132 N.E.2d 294 (1956); State v. Collins, 242 La. 704, 138 So.2d 546 (1962), cert. denied 371 U.S. 843 (1962); People v. Gill, 31 Mich.App. 395, 187 N.W.2d 707 (1971); State v. Little, 57 Wash.2d 516, 358 P.2d 120 (1961). State v. Jackson, 22 Utah 2d 408, 454 P.2d 290 (1969). In Koonce v. State, 456 P.2d 549 (Okl.Crim.App.1969), it was held proper to show a picture of deceased prior to autopsy through the use of a photographic slide and a mechanical viewer.

But where slide was not relevant to pathologist's testimony, it was error to introduce it: People v. Coleman, 116 Ill.App.3d 28, 71 Ill.Dec. 819, 451 N.E.2d 973 (1983).

of the evidence. An overriding policy of the law, founded in the principle of fundamental fairness and a concern for the rights of a person accused in a criminal trial, requires the trial judge to exclude otherwise relevant photographs if their probative effect is far outweighed by their gruesomeness and inflammatory nature. A claim of gruesomeness arises with particular frequency in homicide cases where color photographs or slides showing extensive wounds and profuse bleeding are offered in evidence.

As early as 1882, a court was confronted with photographs of a gruesome nature, which it described as follows:

"The throat of the deceased was cut; the character of the wound was important to elucidate the issue; the man was killed and buried, and a description of the cut by witnesses must have been resorted to; we cannot conceive of a more impartial and truthful witness than the sun, as its light stamps and seals the similitude of the wound on the photograph put before the jury; it would be more accurate than the memory of witnesses, and the object of all evidence is to show the truth, why should not this dumb (mute) witness show it?" [1]

Since then, it has been generally held that gruesome photographs become inadmissible only when they are not relevant, or where the probative value is outweighed by the prejudicial effects, or where the principal effect of the photograph is to arouse the passions and prejudices of the jury.[2] The mere fact that photographs portray in a vivid manner the details of a shocking crime, or incidentally tend to arouse passion or prejudice, does not render gruesome pictures inadmissible.[3] In State v. Duguay,[4] the court said:

"Surely the average man and woman is not so far removed from pain and sorrow, from gruesomeness, from scenes of death and violence and the like, that [color] photographs such as these would turn the reasoning mind [of the jurors] into dislike or prejudice against an accused defending himself in the halls of justice." [5]

Thus, three photographs which could be classified as gruesome were held relevant and properly admitted in connection with witness testimony for the purpose of establishing the cause of death, the identity of the

---

§ 2.14

1. Franklin v. State, 69 Ga. 36, 39 (1882).

2. State v. Rowe, 210 Neb. 419, 315 N.W.2d 250 (1982); Dick v. State, 246 Ga. 697, 273 S.E.2d 124 (1980); People v. Love, 53 Cal.2d 843, 3 Cal.Rptr. 665, 350 P.2d 705 (1960). In Pennington v. State, 57 Ala. App. 655, 331 So.2d 411 (1976), a trial for indecent molestation of a female child, the court failed to see the relevancy of two nude photographs of the victim with her mother and sister and also with her mother, sister, and stepfather (the defendant), since the

pictures did not depict a crime. However, the reviewing court found the error "innocuous."

See generally, Note, "Admission of Gruesome Photographs In Homicide Prosecutions," 16 *Creighton L.Rev.* 73 (1982).

3. State v. De Zeler, 230 Minn. 39, 41 N.W.2d 313 (1950). Peterson v. Commonwealth, supra note 23, section 2.13.

4. 158 Me. 61, 178 A.2d 129 (1962).

5. Id. at 65, 178 A.2d at 131. Accord: State v. Long, 195 Or. 81, 244 P.2d 1033 (1952).

deceased, and to refute the claim of self-defense.[6] One of the color pictures showed the victim's body lying on the stairway as it was discovered; another showed the deceased's back exposing knife wounds; and the third one showed the upper portion of the victim's body with the head partially severed and a pantyhose wrapped around the neck.

Photographs of victims of crime have been readily admitted in evidence over claims that they were gruesome, inflammatory, and prejudicial, even though they were taken in the morgue before, during, or after the autopsy. Thus, the introduction of gruesome pictures showing the deceased's mangled body in the morgue were held properly admitted,[7] as were color slides of the victim's wounds showing evidence of severe blows to the head and face, to support the explanation of the autopsy surgeon.[8]

Even when the relevancy to disputed issues is marginal, courts have upheld the trial judge's discretion in admitting gruesome photographs. Thus, hideous and grotesque pictures which displayed the nude, blood-stained body of a homicide victim, were held admissible as aiding in some fashion to the understanding of the medical testimony.[9] In Young v. State,[10] the victim of a homicide had survived for a short time after the infliction of severe head wounds. In an effort to save the victim's life, the doctor shaved the head and stitched the wounds after applying mercurochrome. Photographs were made after the stitches were removed; creating a ghastly appearance of the wounds which was enhanced by the shaved head and the mercurochrome. The medical witness explained the reason for the appearance and the Arizona Supreme Court held that the pictures were not inadmissible merely because they might have had a tendency to arouse passion and resentment against the defendant in the minds of the jurors.

---

6. Henninger v. State, 251 So.2d 862 (Fla.1971). See also, People v. Seastone, 3 Cal.App.3d 60, 82 Cal.Rptr. 907 (1969), photographs revealed brutally inflicted wounds on the body of an infant, including the face and genital area; Daniels v. State, 257 Ind. 376, 274 N.E.2d 702 (1971); State v. Hall, 256 La. 336, 236 So.2d 489 (1970).

7. Johnson v. Commonwealth, 445 S.W.2d 704 (Ky.1969); People v. Ford, 39 Ill.2d 318, 235 N.E.2d 576 (1968).

8. People v. Gardner, 71 Cal.2d 843, 79 Cal.Rptr. 743, 457 P.2d 575 (1969).

For additional cases, see also § 12.13, supra.

In Hewlett v. State, 607 So.2d 1097 (Miss.1992), the trial court did not admit morgue photos of the charred victims of a vehicular manslaughter, but did admit photos of them at the scene. In upholding the admission, the appellate court noted the photographs depicted the bodies as they were viewed at the scene by the medical

examiner. Such photographs supplemented and clarified his testimony and were not so gruesome, hideous or nauseating as to be inflammatory and prejudicial.

Photograph of nude body of victim, for identification purposes, admissible when surgical marks in abdominal area were covered: Green v. State, 265 Ind. 16, 349 N.E.2d 147 (1976).

9. People v. Terry, 2 Cal.3d 362, 85 Cal. Rptr. 409, 466 P.2d 961 (1970). See also, Freshwater v. State, 2 Tenn.Crim.App. 314, 453 S.W.2d 446 (1969), cert. denied 400 U.S. 840 (1970): while the picture of the deceased lying on a slab in the morgue had little probative value, it was not the type of a photograph that would likely inflame the passions of the jury.

10. 38 Ariz. 298, 299 P. 682 (1931). See also, Commonwealth v. Sheppard, 313 Mass. 590, 48 N.E.2d 630 (1943), cert. denied 320 U.S. 213 (1943).

Reviewing courts have tended to find an abuse of discretion in admitting gruesome photographs when their inflammatory character was overemphasized and their probative value minimal. Thus a photograph of a disemboweled body of a victim as it appeared after the autopsy was deemed "repulsive" beyond description and therefore erroneously admitted.[11] Another reason for finding an abuse of discretion may be when an inordinate number of gruesome pictures have been shown. Thus, it was held to be reversible error to introduce some twenty-two photographs showing all or portions of the victim's partially decomposed torso.[12]

A few courts have held that when a pathologist is fully able to explain his testimony without the use of photographs, it would be error to use any that might arouse the jury.[13] The showing of an autopsy picture of a victim with open chest cavity, a tangled mass of bloody hair, bloody scalp, laboratory pan, and surgical instruments was held irrelevant and highly inflammatory.[14]

It has also been held to be error to dwell unnecessarily long on the photographic evidence during a trial. In one trial, the medical examiner used gruesome color slides, projected on a screen, of the wounds of the deceased. The trial lasted four and one-half days; the medical examiner's slides were exhibited on the screen during one-half day. In reversing on other grounds, the court gave this advice to the judge on retrial:

> "Since the case will be remanded, we are constrained to suggest that the pictures should not, if used, be put before the jury for so long a time. . . . Although they were subjected to medical explanation, we regard the duration of their view as excessive. Such pictures may be used as a fine point of demonstration but not as a bludgeon for winning the case." [15]

§ 2.15   Identification Photographs

Photographs are generally admissible for the purpose of identifying the defendant in a criminal case. Identification photographs may be of several kinds.

11. People v. Burns, 109 Cal.App.2d 524, 241 P.2d 308 (1952), hearing denied 242 P.2d 9 (1952); Commonwealth v. Rogers, 485 Pa. 132, 401 A.2d 329 (1979).

12. Young v. State, 234 So.2d 341 (Fla. 1970). But see, State v. Jells, 559 N.E.2d 464 (1990) (Admission of gruesome photos of badly decomposed victim of homicide, while of a repetitive and cumulative nature, was harmless error).

13. E.g., State v. Bischert, 131 Mont. 152, 308 P.2d 969 (1957). Where there was no controversy concerning the commission of the homicide, it is improper to admit gruesome photographs of the victims (defendant's wife and two children): State v. Makal, 104 Ariz. 476, 455 P.2d 450 (1969), cert. denied 404 U.S. 838 (1971).

14. People v. Turner, 17 Mich.App. 123, 169 N.W.2d 330 (1969). Commonwealth v. Garrison, 459 Pa. 664, 331 A.2d 186 (1975).

15. Commonwealth v. Johnson, 402 Pa. 479, 483, 167 A.2d 511, 513 (1961). Justice Musmanno, concurring in result, would exclude the color slides altogether, "unless they supply an indispensable link in the chain of evidence inculpating a defendant." Cf., Shaffer v. State, 640 P.2d 88 (Wyo. 1982).

1. "MUG SHOTS"

Probably the best known type is the so-called "mug shot"—a photograph taken at a police station upon arrest on a criminal charge, or at a prison or detention facility. "Mug shots" ordinarily show a defendant from the chest on up, in full face and profile, and they also frequently include a little plaque near the bottom of the photograph with the name of the department or agency and a number. Today, many agencies take identification photographs in color; some types of mug shots show three views, full face, profile, and full length.

Mug shots are frequently affixed to the back side of fingerprint cards and/or filed in the police department's criminal history files of individual arrestees. Another frequent use of mug shots is for exhibition on "wanted" posters of the type commonly seen in the United States Post Office branches throughout the country.

The law of evidence ordinarily prohibits the prosecution from introducing in its case in chief evidence tending to show the bad character of the defendant for the purpose of convincing the jury of defendant's guilt on the present charge.[1] Even when a defendant takes the stand on his own behalf, and may therefore be impeached on cross-examination or through the introduction of rebuttal witnesses, his character itself is not in issue; only usable are those character traits which reflect on his credibility as a witness.

The admissibility of identification photographs of the type that might conceivably impart knowledge to the jury that the defendant has a prior criminal record, depends in large measure on the reasons for offering the photographs in evidence. If mug shots are offered to prove an extrajudicial identification of the defendant by a witness, the courts generally admit the photographs. Identification of the defendant is almost always an issue, and courts, as a rule have rejected the contention that use of such photographs is unduly prejudicial,[2] even if the photographs bear a legend identifying them as coming from police files.[3]

Identification photographs are particularly relevant when the appearance of a defendant has changed between the time of the commission of the crime and that of trial, by, for example, shaving off a mustache,[4] or changing of hair style and dress.[5] A photograph of the

---

§ 2.15

1. Rider v. Commonwealth, 8 Va.App. 595, 383 S.E.2d 25 (1989).

2. E.g.: United States v. Amorosa, 167 F.2d 596 (3d Cir.1948); Dirring v. United States, 328 F.2d 512 (1st Cir.1964), cert. denied 377 U.S. 1003 (1964), rehearing denied 379 U.S. 874 (1964).

3. E.g.: People v. Bracamonte, 253 Cal. App.2d 980, 61 Cal.Rptr. 830 (1967), front and side views with police department number and a booking number; People v. Purnell, 105 Ill.App.2d 419, 245 N.E.2d 635 (1969), photograph bearing legend "Police

Department, Maywood, Ill.," and a number; People v. Maffioli, 406 Ill. 315, 94 N.E.2d 191 (1950); State v. Childers, 313 S.W.2d 728 (Mo.1958). But see, People v. Murdock, 39 Ill.2d 553, 237 N.E.2d 442 (1968); People v. Hawkins, 4 Ill.App.3d 471, 281 N.E.2d 72 (1972).

4. People v. Bracamonte, supra note 3, State v. Moran, 131 Iowa 645, 109 N.W. 187 (1906).

5. In State v. Mordecai, 83 N.M. 208, 490 P.2d 466 (App.1971), a three-pose mug shot taken at the time of arrest showed the defendant's "hippie" hairstyle and mode of

accused from which a complainant makes an identification is almost always admissible,[6] provided the identification process itself was fairly conducted and not so suggestive as to constitute a violation of constitutional due process.[7]

Some courts have held that mug shots which purport to disclose the existence of a criminal record by showing a law enforcement agency legend, or which show a date much earlier than the date of arrest for the crime for which the defendant is on trial, were improperly admitted as revealing the existence of prior arrests and possible convictions.[8] Other courts have held that the mug shots are irrelevant when the witness identification in court is positive, and therefore the photographs are without probative value.[9]

Prejudicial error has been found where the photograph also bore a description of a record of criminal arrests and/or convictions, since the record itself was inadmissible as hearsay.[10]

2.   SNAPSHOTS

Courts ordinarily permit into evidence snapshots or candid photographs for the purpose of identifying the defendant.   In Simmons v.

dress. At the time of trial he was dressed conservatively.

6. People v. Purnell, supra note 3.

7. See, Simmons v. United States, 390 U.S. 377 (1968), on remand 395 F.2d 769 (7th Cir.1968), appeal after remand 424 F.2d 1235 (7th Cir.1970), where the United States Supreme Court held that in-court identifications based upon earlier viewing by eye witnesses of snapshots from which they had identified the defendant prior to his arrest were admissible in evidence provided the photographic identification procedure had not been "so impermissibly suggestive as to give rise to a very substantial likelihood of irreparable misidentification" (at 384). This requires, ordinarily, that the witnesses be shown a series of photographs which fit the general descriptions given by them to the police, from which they can select the offender, if he is among them, without prompting or suggestions on the part of the police. See, e.g.: Rech v. United States, 410 F.2d 1131 (10th Cir.1969), cert. denied 396 U.S. 970 (1969), where each witness was separately shown several groups of mug shots, each group containing six pictures portraying males of similar age and physical characteristics; United States v. Baker, 419 F.2d 83 (2d Cir.1969), cert. denied 397 U.S. 971, 976 (1970), where the witness was shown fifteen photographs, one of which was of defendant.

It might be suggested that the police keep a record of precisely which pictures were shown to a witness, so that it will be possible to explore, at a later date, whether the identification process was fairly conducted.

8. United States v. Fosher, 568 F.2d 207 (1st Cir.1978). In Matters v. Commonwealth, 245 S.W.2d 913 (Ky.1952), the court held that where the photograph bore an identification number, the trial court should have admonished the jury that the picture was admissible only for the purpose of identifying the defendant as one of those participating in the crime charged.

People v. Cook, 252 Cal.App.2d 25, 60 Cal.Rptr. 133 (1967), photograph disclosed it had been made seven years earlier and therefore contained inadmissible hearsay declarations; the court, however, did not find prejudicial error.

People v. West, 51 Ill.App.3d 29, 9 Ill.Dec. 532, 366 N.E.2d 1043 (1977), held the admission of police photographs to be reversible error where the information was displayed linking the defendant to an earlier offense. Accord: Richardson v. State, 536 S.W.2d 221 (Tex.Cr.App.1976).

9. E.g., Blue v. State, 250 Ind. 249, 235 N.E.2d 471 (1968).

10. United States v. Harmon, 349 F.2d 316 (4th Cir.1965); Anno., "Admissibility, and Prejudicial Effect of Admission, of 'Mug Shot,' 'Rogues' Gallery' Photograph, or Photograph Taken in Prison, of Defendant in Criminal Case," 30 A.L.R.2d 908, explores the cases which have resulted in reversals of convictions. Cf., State v. West, 192 Conn. 488, 472 A.2d 775 (1984).

United States,[11] the United States Supreme Court held that due process was not violated when witnesses were shown several snapshots, mainly group photographs, from which they identified the offender. Similarly, in Bunk v. State,[12] the Florida Appellate Court held that the defendant in a rape case was properly identified from a Polaroid snapshot taken by the victim at a party both attended.

Courts have quite generally held that the identification was improperly done as impermissibly suggestive when a witness was shown one or more photographs of the defendant only, or when the *Simmons* guidelines were not obeyed.[13]

3. SURVEILLANCE PHOTOGRAPHS

In the past few decades, the use of surveillance cameras in business, industry, banks, and public institutions has increased dramatically. Surveillance cameras are basically of two types. One type automatically takes photographs of a given area at regular time intervals, from 2 to 10 seconds, on a large roll of motion picture film. The film is developed only in the event an intrusion or theft has occurred. An example of such a photographic series of time-interval pictures is illustrated in Figure 13. The six shots show the intruder entering the storage area (top row, left) through a ceiling trap door. In the fourth and fifth frames (bottom row, left and center), the intruder is looking directly at the camera; the final frame shows him leaving the area in somewhat of a hurry after having spotted that he had been photographed.

11. Supra note 7, including comments and additional cases cited there. In *Simmons,* the photographs themselves were not offered in evidence; the prosecution relied on the in-court identifications. The Court explored the many abuses which can result from photographic identification and suggested a series of guidelines to follow.

12. 231 So.2d 39 (Fla.App.1970).

13. E.g.: Mason v. United States, 134 U.S.App.D.C. 280, 414 F.2d 1176 (1969); United States v. Sutherland, 428 F.2d 1152 (5th Cir.1970); United States v. Cunningham, 423 F.2d 1269 (4th Cir.1970).

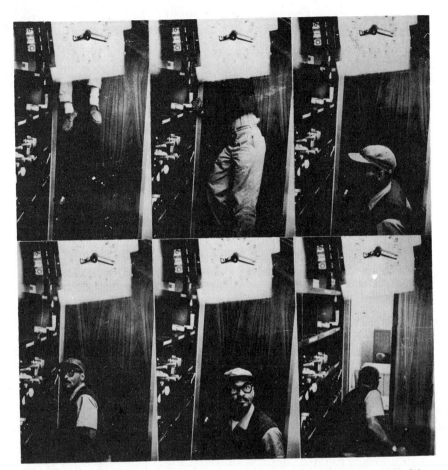

Fig. 13. These six frames were recorded by a surveillance camera installed in an airline's liquor stockroom at one-second intervals as an intruder gained access through the ceiling, started to select his favorite refreshment, finally heard the click of the mechanism which controlled the hidden camera, and then bolted out the door. *Courtesy: Cameras for Industry, Inc., Los Angeles, Calif.*

The other type of surveillance photograph is one that is triggered from a remote place when a need for the photograph arises. They are typically used in banks where tellers are able to activate the camera by a hidden foot switch in the event of a holdup. Photographs of that type have been shown frequently in newspaper accounts of bank robberies.

In United States v. Hobbs,[14] a robbery picture taken at a bank when the teller activated an automatic camera, was held admissible for the purpose of identifying the defendant. In so holding, the court recognized that admission of such a photograph required a relaxation of stringent admission requirements of the past, but deemed justified in

14. 403 F.2d 977 (6th Cir.1968). See also, Commonwealth v. Balukonis, 357 Mass. 721, 260 N.E.2d 167 (1970); State v. Pulphus, 465 A.2d 153 (R.I.1983). Admitting surveillance movies, see, State v. Tillinghast, 465 A.2d 191 (R.I.1983).

doing so by a recognition of the increasing degree of sophistication of modern photographic equipment.

In United States v. Cairns,[15] the court permitted an FBI photographic identification specialist to compare a rather unclear photograph taken during a bank holdup with one of the defendant taken ten days prior to trial. The specialist concluded his testimony by stating that the general characteristics of the individuals in both photographs were the same, and he based his opinion upon a comparison of the nose, mouth, chin line, hair line, ear contours, inner folds of the ears, etc.

There are other kinds of surveillance photographs. One of these is the night-time photograph taken with an infrared snooperscope, or with sophisticated equipment such as laser-television (see Figure 14). Some infrared light sources used for police surveillance work can take a clear photograph of a subject 1,500 feet away from the camera in total darkness by using an 800,000 candlepower searchlight with infrared filters to screen out all of the visible light.

Fig. 14. Night surveillance photograph taken with a laser TV system which scans subjects by rapidly moving narrow lines of red laser light of an intensity well below the level which might endanger the vision of human subjects. *Courtesy: Perkin-Elmer Corporation, Norwalk, Conn.*

15.   434 F.2d 643 (9th Cir.1970).

Another special type of photograph is that taken of check cashers at supermarkets or currency exchanges. Cameras of that type ordinarily take a photograph of the person who presents a check for cashing, and of the check itself, as illustrated in Figure 15. Photographs of this kind have only infrequently been the subject of discussion in the opinions of reviewing courts.

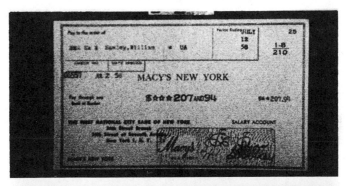

Fig. 15. A model poses in front of a Regiscope camera with a sample check to demonstrate how the subject and document are both photographed on the same film. *Courtesy: Regiscope Division, Radiant Manufacturing Corp., Morton Grove, Ill.*

In Sisk v. State,[16] the Maryland Court of Appeals reversed a conviction of obtaining money by false pretenses, holding that a "Regiscope" identification photograph was improperly admitted in evidence. The admissibility of such a photograph, the court said, should be governed by the same principles as those governing the admissibility of ordinary photographs, that is, that they serve to illustrate the evidence given by a testimonial sponsor who can independently testify that the photograph accurately portrays what it purports to represent.

This is obviously an impossible requirement with respect to Regiscope photographs, and an unnecessary one. The cashier at a bank or supermarket who activates the camera at the time a check is cashed, has no particular reason to suspect any one individual of fraud. If a fraud has in fact occurred, this will not be discovered until after hundreds of similar photographs have been routinely made, and the cashier will not recall the particular individual involved. This is one of these rare instances where the rules of admission for ordinary photographs should be somewhat modified, since we are not dealing with an "ordinary" photograph. All that should be required as foundation for the admission of a Regiscope photograph, is that the testimonial sponsor be able to state that the apparatus was in proper working order at the time the photograph was taken, that the film was developed and printed in the normal process of photographic development and printing process, and that no changes have been made to the negative or print to in any way alter the appearance of what is shown in the photograph. Since the Regiscope picture is being introduced for the purpose of identifying the subject of the photograph, any dispute as to whether or not it depicts a defendant in a criminal case can be resolved by the fact finder by a visual comparison of the photograph with the features and physical appearance of the defendant. No more should be required.

16.	232 Md. 155, 192 A.2d 108 (1963).

§ 2.16 Evidence Resulting From Special Photographic Techniques

Ordinarily, to be admissible in evidence, photographs must portray accurately what they purport to depict. Whenever special photographic techniques are used, the resulting photograph is likely *not* to depict that which can be observed by the naked eye. For example, a photomicrograph—one taken through a microscope—will reveal detail where the naked eye sees nothing. Nevertheless, courts have been extremely receptive to the type of photographic evidence where special techniques were used or where purposeful distortion has been induced. The only requirement, other than relevance, is that the techniques be adequately explained and the purpose for using the special techniques is a legitimate one.

Stereoscopic views, photographs creating an illusion of depth, seem to have been made very early in the history of photography. As far back as 1863, the famed American pioneer in this field, Oliver Wendell Holmes, developed a skeleton-type viewer for his "stereographs," which replaced the awkward box-type stereo viewer. In spite of this early start, only two early cases have been found where "relief" pictures were offered as evidence. In 1881 an Illinois court held that, when a town was sued for damages sustained from a defective highway, a stereoscopic view of the scene where plaintiff was injured when a horse pulling his sleigh became frightened and ran off the embankment, was properly admitted for inspection by the jury with the aid of a stereoscope. The court decided, ". . . that the process of taking stereoscopic views was the same as in photography." [1] Also, in Iowa, a stereoscopic view of water damage to property after a flood was accepted to show the condition of the premises.[2]

In 1887, it was held that photomacrographs and photomicrographs were admissible whenever it would be proper for the jury to examine the original subject with a magnifying glass or a microscope.[3] The Taylor Will Case[4] in 1871, which held differently, should not be considered authority because it was decided before the art of photography was perfected to such an extent as to offer proper guarantees of accuracy. In Fields v. State,[5] the court held admissible a color stereoslide depicting the scene of a murder, and in State v. Thorp,[6] it was held that the trial court properly admitted into evidence a photograph taken by ultraviolet light showing the defendant's footprint in blood on a linoleum floor.

As for the use of X-rays, the court accepted, in 1897, an X-ray showing the overlapping bones of one of the legs of plaintiff, broken by an injury for which a suit was brought. It was taken by a physician and

§ 2.16

1. City of Rockford v. Russell, 9 Ill.App. 229 (1881).

2. German Theological School v. City of Dubuque, 64 Iowa 736, 17 N.W. 153 (1883).

3. Rowell v. Fuller's Estate, 59 Vt. 688, 10 A. 853 (1887).

4. 10 Abb.Prac., N.S. 300 (N.Y.1871).

5. 284 P.2d 442 (Okl.Cr.App.1955).

6. 86 N.H. 501, 171 A. 633 (1934).

surgeon familiar with fractures, who also testified that he was familiar with the process of taking such photographs and that the X-ray in evidence accurately represented the condition of the leg.[7] The acceptance of the X-ray was no ground for reversal.

A few years later, a court ruled that photographs taken by the aid of X-rays should be treated in the same fashion as the use of ordinary photographs in a trial; it afforded a better understanding by the jury of the evidence and the merits of the case.[8] Here, the court stated that every new discovery, when it shall have passed beyond the experimental stage, must necessarily be treated as a new aid in the administration of justice.

There seems to have been no objection, ever since this early period, to the admittance in evidence of photographs of any kind, provided the accuracy and relevancy of them were duly established.[9]

With respect to the status of X-rays of human beings today, it must be shown that (1) the type of X-ray equipment used is of acceptable quality; (2) it was in good operating condition when used; (3) the operator was qualified in the use of the equipment; (4) the X-ray picture is identified as being one of the person whose condition is under inquiry; (5) the condition of the person at the time the X-ray was taken was the same as it was at the time in issue in the case; and (5) the X-ray picture is interpreted for the judge and jury by a competent specialist.[10] While the foundation for the admission of X-ray pictures would ordinarily require the testimony of the technician who operated the equipment, it is fairly well settled that their interpretation requires the testimony of a physician or surgeon.[11]

In criminal cases, X-ray pictures have been admitted to demonstrate the effect on the skull of blows struck by the defendant,[12] to show the injury to the nose of a complaining witness in an assault and battery

---

7. Bruce v. Beall, 99 Tenn. 303, 41 S.W. 445 (1897).

8. Mauch v. City of Hartford, 112 Wis. 40, 87 N.W. 816 (1901).

9. Johnson v. State, 27 Ala.App. 5, 165 So. 402 (1935), cert. denied 231 Ala. 466, 165 So. 403 (1936); Phillips v. Wilmington & Phila. Traction Co., 1 Del. 593, 117 A. 241 (1922); Kramer v. Henely, 227 Iowa 504, 288 N.W. 610 (1939); Howell v. George, 201 Miss. 783, 30 So.2d 603 (1947).

10. E.g., United States v. La Favor, 72 F.2d 827 (9th Cir.1934).

11. Lamb v. Moore, 178 Cal.App.2d 819, 3 Cal.Rptr. 507 (1960). In Butler v. Armour Fertilizer Works, 195 N.C. 409, 142 S.E. 483 (1928), the interpretation was by an osteopathic doctor; in Jerobek v. Safeway Cab Co., 146 Kan. 859, 73 P.2d 1097 (1937), by a chiropractor; and in Schairer v. Johnson, 128 Or. 409, 272 P. 1027 (1929), a dentist interpreted the X-rays of the teeth and jaw. But see, in Harrison v. Sears, Roebuck and Co., 981 F.2d 25 (1st Cir. 1992), where the court found no abuse of discretion in permitting defendant's engineering expert to use an x-ray during his testimony. The expert had read x-rays of hand and body parts involved in accidents on numerous occasions, had consulted with doctors concerning this interpretation of x-rays, and he testified that x-rays were often interpreted and relied upon by experts in his field. The record demonstrated that the trial judge was within his discretion in determining that the engineer possessed sufficient knowledge, skill, experience and training to utilize the x-ray to support his testimony. The record also indicated that he used the x-ray to determine the location and angle of the cuts to the plaintiff's fingers and not for a medical diagnosis.

12. State v. Casey, 108 Or. 386, 213 P. 771, 217 P. 632 (1923).

prosecution,[13] and to explain that a gunshot "hole" shown on an X-ray corresponded to the hole in that same location in the lower leg of a deceased who had suffered a gunshot wound.[14]

V. MOTION PICTURES AND VIDEOTAPE IN COURT

§ 2.17 Admissibility of Motion Pictures as Evidence

The courts have quite readily admitted into evidence, as an aid in explaining a witness' testimony, sound as well as silent motion pictures, in black and white as well as in color, provided the proper foundation is laid. Before motion pictures may be admitted in criminal cases it must be shown that they are relevant to contested issues in the case; [1] if they are, they are admissible in the discretion of the judge,[2] provided a proper authentication has been presented.[3] Authenticating testimony will ordinarily be presented by the person who operated the motion picture camera; this, however, is not an absolute requirement because whenever a competent witness is able to state that the movies accurately portray the action captured on them, the authentication requirement is satisfied.[4]

When dealing with sound motion pictures, the visual portion of the movie has been treated as a series of still photographs; [5] consequently, the rules of admissibility of photographs are quite frequently applied to the pictures. The audio portion, however, requires an independent foundation, since it may not be as easily authenticated.

As already noted, the sound track of a sound movie can be made in either of two ways. The first method employs the use of a magnetic tape or wire recorder. In this process, the audio portion of the movie is separately recorded and later transferred to the film strip magnetically. Tapes or wires, prepared in this manner, may be altered or edited almost without detection and certainly without affecting the visual portion of the films, as may be fully appreciated by anyone who has seen a "dubbed-in" foreign sound movie. The second process by which the audio portion can be recorded is through the use of so-called optic recording. In this process, a device transforms the sounds to be recorded into optic patterns and it records them on the film alongside and simultaneously with the recording of the visual images. With optic

---

13. State v. Coleman, 96 W.Va. 544, 123 S.E. 580 (1924).

14. Cantrell v. State, 129 Tex.Cr.R. 240, 86 S.W.2d 777 (1935).

§ 2.17

1. Lanford v. People, 159 Colo. 36, 409 P.2d 829 (1966); Carpenter v. State, 169 Tex.Cr.R. 283, 333 S.W.2d 391 (1960).

2. Johnson v. United States, 362 F.2d 43 (8th Cir.1966).

3. People v. Porter, 105 Cal.App.2d 324, 233 P.2d 102 (1951). See also, Model Code of Evidence, Rule 105(j).

4. Kortz v. Guardian Life Ins. Co., 144 F.2d 676 (10th Cir.1944), cert. denied 323 U.S. 728 (1944); People v. Bowley, 59 Cal.2d 855, 31 Cal.Rptr. 471, 382 P.2d 591 (1963); Gulf Life Ins. Co. v. Stossel, 131 Fla. 127, 179 So. 163 (1938).

5. Heiman v. Market St. Railway Co., 21 Cal.App.2d 311, 69 P.2d 178 (1937).

recording, the audio recordings cannot be erased or altered without detection.[6] It is because of this distinction that courts have held that magnetic sound recordings are not admissible because of their susceptibility to alteration, while optic sound tracks are admissible.[7]

If foundation requirements are met, motion pictures are freely admitted: to show a relevant link in the chain of evidence,[8] to prove the circumstances surrounding the making of a confession,[9] to show the robbing of a bank and to identify the robber,[10] to depict the reenactment of a crime,[11] and to illustrate the nature and extent of wounds inflicted upon a murder victim.[12]

Another area in which motion pictures have known wide acceptance is in the prosecution of cases of driving under the influence of intoxicating liquor, usually referred to as D.W.I. (driving-while-intoxicated) cases. In the D.W.I. area, motion pictures of drivers arrested serve primarily the function of obviating trials. Many a defendant, charged with driving under the influence, vehemently denies intoxication, but when he and his attorney are afforded an opportunity to privately view the motion pictures taken on such occasion, quietly withdraws his not guilty plea and changes it to guilty. On the other hand, some drivers who may well be intoxicated nevertheless succeed in giving a fairly good performance in the movie; in such a case, the prosecutor may be inclined not to press the charges, or, if he does, a not-guilty verdict may well be the result.

Ordinarily, D.W.I. movies should be admissible to depict the demeanor, appearance, and mannerisms of the defendant upon arrest as in any other criminal case. Many courts have so ruled. An example of this approach is illustrated in Lanford v. People,[13] where the Colorado Supreme Court held that moving pictures and their sound, when relevant, which show the demeanor and condition of a defendant charged with driving under the influence of either alcohol or drugs, taken at the time of the arrest or soon thereafter, are admissible in evidence, even though they show the defendant refusing to take sobriety and coordination tests, as long as they are offered for the purpose of showing the defendant's demeanor, conduct, and appearance, and to show why sobriety tests were not given. The trial judge must give a limiting instruction to that effect to the jury. Similarly, it has been held that the use of sound motion pictures of a defendant, taken while he was undergoing tests to determine the degree of impairment of his physical faculties, did not violate the privilege against self-incrimination, and that the moving

6. People v. Hayes, 21 Cal.App.2d 320, 71 P.2d 321 (1937); Commonwealth v. Roller, 100 Pa.Super. 125 (1930).

7. People v. Hayes, supra note 6.

8. Jones v. State, 151 Tex.Cr.R. 519, 209 S.W.2d 613 (1948); State v. Tillinghast, supra n. 76.

9. People v. Dabb, 32 Cal.2d 491, 197 P.2d 1 (1948); Sutton v. State, 237 Ind. 305, 145 N.E.2d 425 (1957); State v. Perkins, 355 Mo. 851, 198 S.W.2d 704 (1946).

10. Mikus v. United States, 433 F.2d 719 (2d Cir.1970).

11. People v. Dabb, supra note 7; People v. Kendrick, 56 Cal.2d 71, 14 Cal.Rptr. 13, 363 P.2d 13 (1961).

12. People v. Lindsey, 56 Cal.2d 324, 14 Cal.Rptr. 678, 363 P.2d 910 (1961), cert. denied 368 U.S. 916 (1961).

13. Supra note 1.

pictures were competent as illustrating the statements of the officer regarding his observations of the defendant.[14]   Such movies do not constitute testimonial evidence so as to invoke the protection afforded by the fifth amendment.[15]

Some jurisdictions do not permit the introduction of sound motion pictures showing the defendant's refusal to submit to chemical intoxication or other sobriety tests, on the theory that to do otherwise would constitute a denial of the constitutional right to freedom from compulsory self-incrimination.[16]   An analogy has been inaccurately drawn between evidence of refusal to take a sobriety test and the impermissible comment on a defendant's failure to testify,[17] though other jurisdictions have rejected this analogy and permit evidence of the refusal.[18]

§ 2.18 Admissibility of Videotapes in Court

At present the Federal Rules of Evidence do not provide specific guidelines for the admission of videotaped evidence.   Such evidence now falls within the definition of "photographs."[1]

The cases that have addressed the issue of admissibility have been uniform in suggesting that the same rules apply for the admission of videotapes as exist for photographs and motion pictures.[2]   As with motion pictures, there is no absolute requirement that the cameraman or photographer be the one to present the foundation testimony or authenticate the video and audio portions of the tape;   all that is required is that a witness can testify that the tapes clearly and accurately portray that which they purport to represent.[3]   A judge's decision will only be overturned for an abuse of discretion.[4]

14. State v. Strickland, 5 N.C.App. 338, 168 S.E.2d 697 (1969), reversed 276 N.C. 253, 173 S.E.2d 129 (1970).

15. Id. Accord: Housewright v. State, 154 Tex.Cr.R. 101, 225 S.W.2d 417 (1949); Carpenter v. State, supra note 1.

16. People v. Knutson, 17 Ill.App.2d 251, 149 N.E.2d 461 (1958); Duckworth v. State, 309 P.2d 1103 (Okl.Cr.App.1957); Spencer v. State, 404 P.2d 46 (Okl.Cr.App. 1965); Ritchie v. State, 415 P.2d 176 (Okl. Cr.App.1966). But in Stewart v. State, 435 P.2d 191 (Okl.Cr.App.1967), the court limited its constitutional objections to the sound portion of the film.

17. State v. Benson, 230 Iowa 1168, 300 N.W. 275 (1941).

18. State v. Durrant, 55 Del. (5 Storey) 510, 188 A.2d 526 (1963) and cases cited at note 1. Some states mandate evidence of the refusal be admitted. See, e.g., West's Fla.Stat.Ann. § 316.1932 (1993).

§ 2.18

1. Fed.R.Evid. 1001(2) (1993) states " 'Photographs' include still photograph, x-ray films, video tapes, and motion pictures."

2. Videotape recordings of fencing or bribery operations conducted by undercover police officers in sting operations have featured prominently in many cases. See also, People v. Childs, 67 Ill.App.3d 473, 24 Ill. Dec. 380, 385 N.E.2d 147 (1979); People v. Banks, 70 Ill.App.3d 1045, 27 Ill.Dec. 365, 389 N.E.2d 177 (1979); People v. Teicher, 73 A.D.2d 136, 425 N.Y.S.2d 315 (1980)— videotape of court-ordered surveillance; Palmer v. State, 604 P.2d 1106 (Alaska 1979)—videotaped sobriety tests; State v. People, 60 N.C.App. 479, 299 S.E.2d 311 (N.C.App.1983)—videotape of hypnosis session.

3. People v. Mines, 132 Ill.App.2d 628, 270 N.E.2d 265 (1971).

4. Commonwealth v. Hindi, 429 Pa.Super. 169, 631 A.2d 1341 (1993) (Held no abuse of discretion to exclude freeze frame and slow motion versions of videotape in criminal mischief prosecution).

Videotaped evidence is generally admissible. Crime scene videotapes have been held admissible [5] unless particularly gruesome.[6] Videotaped reenactments have been admissible [7] unless found to be prejudicial.[8] Courts have also admitted videotapes of drug transactions [9] and have allowed videotaped interviews to be admitted for impeachment purposes.[10]

In some jurisdictions, the reviewing courts have upheld the use of videotapes as evidence of the defendant's statements and confessions,[11] as long as they are relevant.[12] In State v. Lusk,[13] the Missouri Supreme Court approved the introduction at trial of the videotape of a defendant's murder confession, stating that once the issue of voluntariness of the confession has been determined by the trial court, the presentation to a jury of a properly authenticated videotape of the confession does not infringe any constitutional right asserted by the defendant.

5. Price v. State, 870 S.W.2d 205 (Tex. App.1994); Swann v. Commonwealth, 247 Va. 222, 441 S.E.2d 195 (1994); State v. Williams, 227 Conn. 101, 629 A.2d 402 (1993); State v. Van Tran, 864 S.W.2d 465 (Tenn.1993); State v. Martin, 607 So.2d 775 (La.App.1992).

6. State v. Van Sickle, 90 Ohio App.3d 301, 629 N.E.2d 39 (Ohio App.1993) (Error to admit videotape of body burned beyond recognition). But see, Bullard v. State, 263 Ga. 683, 436 S.E.2d 647 (1993) (The admission of the videotape of the recovery of a dismembered victim's body parts was not error); People v. Sims, 5 Cal.4th 405, 20 Cal.Rptr.2d 537, 853 P.2d 992 (1993) (The court upheld the admission of a videotape of a crime scene which showed the coroner lifting the body out of a bathtub and cutting away a pillowcase to reveal the victim's face and gag in his mouth. That it was in part cumulative did not mandate its exclusion. The court noted that if a videotape is more graphic, gruesome and potentially prejudicial than static photos it should be excluded).

7. People v. Sims, 5 Cal.4th 405, 20 Cal.Rptr.2d 537, 853 P.2d 992 (1993) (Admission of the videotape recreation of a crime scene was held not an abuse of the trial court's discretion when the defense "opened the door" during cross examination by asking a state witness about the videotape and the circumstances under which it had been made. The court had previously granted the defense's motion in limine to exclude the videotape); State v. Billings, 104 N.C.App. 362, 409 S.E.2d 707 (1991) (Videotaped reenactment of a confrontation between a witness and the defendant on the day of the crimes was admissible); State v. Wilson, 135 N.J. 4, 637 A.2d

1237 (1994) (Admission of unauthenticated crime scene videotape filmed three days after the crime to show relative positions of the victim and witnesses in the store on the day of the attempted armed robbery and murder held to be harmless error).

8. Lopez v. State, 651 S.W.2d 413 (Tex. App.1983), reversed on other grounds 664 S.W.2d 85 (Tex.Crim.App.1983) (The court reversed Lopez's conviction for aggravated delivery of marijuana because the trial court admitted a videotape recreation of the offense. The appellate court held that the videotape posed too great a danger of prejudice).

9. Brooks v. Commonwealth, 15 Va.App. 407, 424 S.E.2d 566 (1992).

10. State v. King, 183 W.Va. 440, 396 S.E.2d 402 (1990) (A videotaped interview with a defense witness (the defendant's daughter) in which she admitted she and her sisters had sex with their father in an incest prosecution was admissible as a prior inconsistent statement).

11. Williams v. State, 626 So.2d 315 (Fla.App.1993): Videotape of accused in cell after his arrest showing he was in a rage and refused to give statement to police was not relevant and should have been excluded in prosecution for battery on a law enforcement officer.

12. Paramore v. State, 229 So.2d 855 (Fla.1969); State v. Hendricks, 456 S.W.2d 11 (Mo.1970).

13. 452 S.W.2d 219 (1970). See also, People v. Heading, 39 Mich.App. 126, 197 N.W.2d 325 (1972)—videotape of a lineup; State v. Kidwell, 199 Kan. 752, 434 P.2d 316 (1967)—reenactment of crime shown on videotape.

The 1988 Supreme Court decision in Coy v. Iowa[14] has caused several states to rework, modify or reconsider laws concerning the use of videotaped testimony in child sexual abuse cases.[15] In *Coy*, the defendant was charged with sexually assaulting two 13–year–old girls. Pursuant to statute, the trial court, upon the state's motion, approved the use of a large screen that was placed between the defendant and the witness stand during the girls' testimony. The Court held that the use of the screen was unconstitutional, stating that it was difficult to imagine a more obvious or damaging violation of the defendant's right to a face-to-face encounter. But the Court expressly left open the question whether any exceptions to the right to face-to-face confrontation exist.[16]

VI. COMPUTER ANIMATION AND SIMULATION

§ 2.19 Computer Technology as a Visual Aid

The advent of computer technology has revolutionized many areas of the law, from computerized legal research to the storage of documents on laser discs for retrieval at trial.[1] Within the past few years, computer generated animations and simulations have become almost commonplace in civil litigation,[2] and have recently begun to appear in criminal cases.[3]

---

14. 487 U.S. 1012 (1988).

15. Compare, State v. Vincent, 159 Ariz. 418, 768 P.2d 150 (1989), upholding the constitutionality of the videotape statute, which requires a finding that face-to-face testimony would so traumatize a child witness as to prevent the child from reasonably communicating (conviction reversed on ground statute was unconstitutionally applied); Perez v. State, 536 So.2d 206 (Fla. 1988), hearsay statute upheld; Glendening v. State, 536 So.2d 212 (Fla.1988), application of hearsay and videotape statutes held constitutional; State v. Davis, 229 N.J.Super. 66, 550 A.2d 1241 (1988), closed circuit television procedure upheld. But see, State v. Eastham, 39 Ohio St.3d 307, 530 N.E.2d 409 (1988), closed circuit television procedure held unconstitutional in the absence of particularized findings concerning necessity of procedure; and Lam v. State, 860 F.2d 873 (8th Cir.1988), admission of videotaped testimony of burglary victim held unconstitutional where reason for victim's absence from trial was vacation trip (error held harmless). See also, People v. Bastien, 129 Ill.2d 64, 133 Ill.Dec. 459, 541 N.E.2d 670 (1989), voiding statute permitting use, in a child-sexual abuse case, of videotapes of pretrial proceeding in which prosecution interviewed the child-witness but the defense was not permitted to cross-examine. Even though the statute permitted cross-examination at trial, the court said the constitution requires contemporaneous cross-examination.

16. Coy v. Iowa, 487 U.S. at 1021.

§ 2.19

1. See, "21st Century Courtroom Demonstrated at Law School," *Trial* (November 1993), at 86.

2. Reagan, "The Admissibility of Computer Simulations as Novel Scientific Evidence: An Analysis Under the Frye and Relevancy Standards," 1991 WL 330753. Computer animations and simulations have been introduced in aviation litigation, personal injury cases, product liability cases, patent infringement cases and environmental litigation.

3. While People v. McHugh, 124 Misc.2d 559, 476 N.Y.S.2d 721 (N.Y.Sup.Ct.1984), is the only reported appellate decision dealing with computer animation or simulation in a criminal case, such evidence has been admitted in trial courts in Florida, California and Arizona. State v. Pierce, No. 92–19316CF10A (Cir.Ct. Broward County, Florida, 1993) (Computer animation proffered by prosecution to show how the vehicular manslaughter occurred); State v. Mitchell, 12462 (Super.Ct. Marin Co., Calif.1992) (One minute computer animation

The increase in the use of this type of evidence is due in part to the public's increased expectation of visual stimuli [4] in court, as well as the decrease in the expense of creating computer generated animations and simulations.[5]

Computer animation is a series of still images created on a computer, which are then recorded one at a time onto videotape. When these frame by frame illustrations are viewed at playback speed, the result is a moving picture or animation. In contrast, a computer simulation combines the computer's capabilities for animation with its capabilities for computation. A simulation is a projection of possible outcomes mathematically predicted by a computer program.[6] (See Fig. 16.)

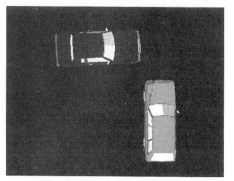
Vehicle Positions Prior to Impact

An Eye Witness View

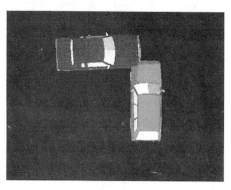
Impact

Vehicle Trajectories after Impact

Fig. 16. Simulation of a traffic accident. *Courtesy: FMC Corporation, Forensic Engineering Group*

proffered by prosecution to demonstrate victim's position and timing proved the killing was deliberate and premeditated.); Arizona v. Phillips, 87–365 (Super.Ct. Jilo Co.1988) (Prosecutor used an animation to show an entrance wound was caused by a gun held against a victim's head, not fired from a distance.); See, Frazer, "The Ultimate Expert Witness," *Barrister* (Fall 1992), at 24.

4. See discussion supra at page 105, sec. 2.01.

5. In 1990, the cost of forensic animation was $1500 to $3000 per second. Today, that cost has dropped to approximately $150 per second. Suchocki, "Forensic Animation, the 21st Century Eyewitness," *National Trial Lawyer* (November 1993), at 21.

6. Vanyo, "Communicating with 'Post-Literate' Jury: Advanced Graphic Exhibits in Patent Trials," 349 PLI/Pat 409 (Nov.–Dec. 1992).

For example, in an accident reconstruction simulation known facts about the accident are entered into the computer and the computer analyses the data and generates conclusions based upon the assumptions contained in the software being used.[7] Alternative scenarios may also be evaluated, e.g., what the outcome would have been had the person been wearing a seatbelt.[8] The simulation is then converted to a graphic animation that can be stored on a videotape or a laser disc.[9] The evidentiary standards that computer generated visual evidence must meet depends on whether it is presented as demonstrative evidence to illustrate testimony, or as scientific evidence forming the basis of the expert's opinion.[10] Animations are most often used as demonstrative evidence while simulations are more often used as a basis of expert opinion and thus must meet the test for admissibility of scientific evidence.

When presenting an animation to the court, an attorney should qualify the animation expert, the computer hardware and software, and the source of the input data, as well as qualify the computer animation calculation accuracy and the accuracy of the presentation media.[11] If offering an animation as a demonstrative aid it must be relevant, help explain a witness' testimony, be substantially similar to the event it is portraying and its probative value cannot be outweighed by prejudice.

If offering a simulation as scientific evidence, its proponent must meet either the *Daubert*[12] or *Frye*[13] test depending upon the relevant test for admissibility in the jurisdiction.[14]

Even under the more stringent *Frye* test a computer simulation should be admitted after the court determines the relevant field or science into which the principle or theory falls and then determine whether the principle or technique on which the evidence is based has achieved general acceptance within that scientific community. Therefore, a computer simulation should be admitted if it is shown the simulation is based upon recognized theories based on the laws of physics and the principles upon which it relies are generally accepted in the scientific community of forensic engineers or accident reconstructionists, for example. One must also argue that the simulation is relevant and its probative value outweighs any prejudice. One may even argue a simulation is the type of underlying data reasonably relied upon by experts in the fields of forensic engineering and/or accident reconstruction to support their opinions.

---

7. O'Connor, "Computer Animations in the Courtroom: Get with the Program," *Fla.B.J.* (November 1993), at 22.

8. Id.

9. Id.

10. Menard, "Admission of Computer Generated Visual Evidence: Should There Be Clear Standards?" *6–APR Software L.J.* 325 (April 1993).

11. Jones, Muir & Groo, "Computer Animation–Admissibility in the Courtroom," Society of Automotive Engineers # 910366.

12. Daubert v. Merrell Dow Pharmaceuticals, Inc., 113 S.Ct. 2786 (1993).

13. Frye v. United States, 293 Fed. 1013 (D.C.Cir.1923).

14. See discussion regarding admissibility in Chapter One at § 1.03.

The majority of appellate cases which have addressed computer animation and simulation involve civil litigation. As of 1993 there was only one reported criminal appellate case. People v. McHugh,[15] was a prosecution for manslaughter and intoxicated driving. The defendant claimed he was neither drunk nor speeding and sought to introduce a computer reenactment of his version of the accident.[16] The prosecutor moved pre-trial for a *Frye* hearing. The court held that a *Frye* hearing was not required and the computer reenactment may be introduced at trial provided defense counsel laid the proper foundation and qualified the expert.[17] The court stated that the evidence sought to be introduced was like a chart or a diagram.

> Computers are simply mechanical tools—receiving information and acting on instructions at lightening speed. When the results are useful, they should be accepted, when confusing they should be rejected. What is important is that the presentation be relevant to a possible defense, that it fairly and accurately reflect the oral testimony offered and that it be an aid to the jury's understanding of the issue.[18]

Computer animation and simulation was first offered in airline litigation.[19] Since then the majority of appellate cases which discuss animation and simulation involve accident reconstruction. In Starr v. Campos,[20] the court held that, upon remand, the trial court should determine whether evidence derived from computerized analysis of an accident was generally accepted by scientists in the relevant fields.

The court noted it is not sufficient that any one expert relies on the technique in question or that the technique is "widely used," unless that widespread use is without significant objection from the relevant scientific community.[21] There need not be universal agreement, but scientists in the relevant field must agree the procedure has a sound scientific basis and is capable of rendering a practicable result with awareness of any limitations, for scientific purposes.[22]

In Schaeffer v. General Motors Corporation,[23] the appellate court reversed the trial court's decision to admit computer simulation evidence. In doing so the court set out a standard to be followed when the case was retried. The court stated that it was first up to the trial judge to determine whether the simulation technique has achieved sufficient reliability and acceptance to warrant its use in judicial proceedings.[24]

---

15. 124 Misc.2d 559, 476 N.Y.S.2d 721 (1984).

16. Id. at 722.

17. Id.

18. Id. at 722–723.

19. Dombroff, *Dombroff on Demonstrative Evidence* §§ 9.7–9.8 (1983).

20. 134 Ariz. 254, 655 P.2d 794 (App.2d 1982).

21. Id. at 796.

22. Id.

23. 372 Mass. 171, 360 N.E.2d 1062 (1977).

24. Id. at 1067.

In Deffinbaugh v. Ohio Turnpike Comm.,[25] the appellate court found that the trial court properly admitted into evidence a computer simulation used for purposes of accident reconstruction. The simulation depicted the motion of a tractor trailer striking the guard rail and bridge. In creating this simulation the expert witness in accident reconstruction used known facts such as the weight of the trailer, its physical dimensions, and the surface friction coefficient to generate the computer simulation.[26] The court observed that the computer simulation was based on data which was routinely relied upon and the computer simulation assisted the trier of fact in determining how the accident occurred.[27]

In Commercial Union v. Boston Edison,[28] the Massachusetts Supreme Court held computer simulation evidence admissible under the *Frye* test. Admissibility of the computer simulation is conditioned on a "sufficient showing that: (1) the computer is functioning properly; (2) the input and underlying equations are sufficiently complete and accurate (and disclosed to the opposing party, so that they may challenge them); and (3) the program is generally accepted by the appropriate community of scientists."[29]

In Commercial Union, the Court stated that the function of the computer is to rapidly and accurately execute a series of computations. Therefore, if experts are permitted to base their testimony on calculations performed by hand, there is no reason to prevent them from performing the same calculations with far greater rapidity and accuracy.[30]

In Kudlacek v. Fiat S.p.A., an accident reconstruction expert used a computer simulation in a product liability case to show the path of an automobile prior to collision.[31] The expert relied on physical evidence from the accident scene which included skid marks, road exit speeds, and the angle exiting the road to formulate the computer simulation.[32]

The Nebraska Supreme Court found that the simulation met the requirements necessary to be admissible as a demonstrative aid. "Evidence relating to an illustrative experiment is admissible if a competent person conducted the experiment, an apparatus of suitable kind and condition utilized, and the experiment was conducted fairly and honestly."[33] The court noted that the computer program used was generally relied upon by experts in the accident reconstruction field.

In Bledsoe v. Salt River Valley Water Users' Assn.,[34] which involved a bicycle accident, the court held that the evidentiary use of computer

25. 67 Ohio App.3d 692, 588 N.E.2d 189 (1990).
  26. Id. at 194.
  27. Id.
  28. 412 Mass. 545, 591 N.E.2d 165 (1992).
  29. Id. at 168.

30. Id.
31. 244 Neb. 822, 509 N.W.2d 603 (1994).
32. Id. at 618.
33. Id. at 617.
34. ___ Ariz. ___, 880 P.2d 689 (App. 1994).

simulations was generally permissible so long as it satisfied the usual foundation requirements for demonstrative evidence.

Not all courts have admitted computer simulations. In Pino v. Gauthier,[35] the appellate court upheld the lower court's exclusion of a computer simulation on the basis that "it was not necessary for the jury to view a computer simulation to understand how a vehicle might lose control during a lane change maneuver." [36]

In Perma Research & Dev. Corp. v. Singer,[37] a breach of contract action, the appellate court held the trial court did not abuse its discretion in allowing testimony by plaintiffs' experts relating their opinion that the device that was the subject of the contract was perfectible based upon the results of a computer simulation. The court noted, however, the better practice would have been to provide opposing counsel with the underlying data and forms employed in the computer simulation in advance of trial in order to avoid an unnecessary discussion of highly technical tangential issues at trial.

The dissenting opinion in *Perma Research* voiced its concerns about computer simulation. These included the computer's ability to package hearsay and erroneous or misleading data in a persuasive format; that errors may be introduced in data processing; or that the computer may inaccurately display the data or display it in a biased manner.[38]

VII. MISCELLANEOUS

§ 2.20 Selected Sources, Bibliography, and Additional References

The Dade County (Miami) Florida Medical Examiner Department's Forensic Imaging Bureau conducts comprehensive Forensic Photography Workshops every year. Methods of discovery and documentation relating to death investigation, crime scene and general photography are covered along with biomedical and forensic photography techniques.

The Forensic Imaging Bureau serves the needs of the University of Miami Medical School, local hospitals, county and state departments of health, police and federal agencies such as the D.E.A., B.A.T.F., Customs and the Secret Service. They have one of the few high speed photography facilities in the United States.

Barry University in Miami Shores, Florida offers a Bachelor of Arts degree in Biomedical and Forensic Photography through their Department of Fine Arts.

The Association of Professional Investigative Photographers (P.O. Box 479, Charlestown, West Virginia 25414) produces a newsletter. A magazine, *Law Enforcement Photography,* is available by writing to 445 Broad Hollow Road, Melville, New York 11747.

35. 633 So.2d 638 (La.App.1993).   **38.** Id. at 125.
36. Id.
37. 542 F.2d 111 (2d Cir.1976), cert. denied 429 U.S. 987 (1976).

Books and articles footnoted in the text are not repeated here:

Belli, "Demonstrative Evidence: Seeing is Believing," 16 *Trial*, July 1980, at 70.

Belli, "Demonstrative Evidence: Seeing is Believing," 1981 *Pers.Inj.Ann.* 858.

Brain & Broderick, "The Derivative Relevance of Demonstrative Evidence: Charting Its Proper Evidentiary Status," 25 *U.Cal.Davis L.Rev.* 957 (1992).

Brandes, "Consider Videotape," *Fair$hare,* May 1981, p. 6.

Bronstein, "Leading Federal Cases on Computer Stored or Generated Data," ABA Section of Science and Technology Scientific Evidence Review, Monograph No. 1 (1993), at 92.

Chaney, "Computer Simulations: How They Can Be Used at Trial and the Arguments for Admissibility," 19 *Ind.L.Rev.* 735 (1986).

Cobo, "A Strategic Approach to Demonstrative Exhibits and Effective Jury Presentations," 395 PLI/Lit 359 (July 1990).

Colvin, *Photography and the Lawyer* (1983).

Cox, *Photographic Optics* (13th ed. 1966).

Dombroff, *Dombroff on Demonstrative Evidence* (1983).

Donoghue, "Demonstrative Exhibits: A Key to Effective Jury Presentations," 349 PLI/Pat 369 (Nov.–Dec. 1992).

Dorion, "Photographic Superimposition," 28 *J.For.Sci.* 724 (1983).

Duckworth, *Forensic Photography* (1983).

Fadely, "Use of Computer–Generated Visual Evidence in Aviation Litigation: Interactive Video Comes to Court," 55 *J.Air & Com.* 839 (1990).

Feller, "Photographic Evidence: More Than Meets the Eye," 8 *Me.B.J.* 372 (1993).

Gibson, "Review: Applications of Luminescence in Forensic Science," 22 *J.For.Sci.* 680 (1977).

Givens, *Demonstrative Evidence* (1989).

Hamlin, *What Makes Juries Listen* (1985).

Hansen, "Unfettered Filming—Court bars defense lawyers from set of day-in-life video," *ABAJ* Feb. 1992, p. 32.

Hempling, "The Applications of Ultraviolet Photography in Clinical Forensic Medicine," 21 *Med.Sci.Law* 215 (1981).

Hocking, "Videotape in the Courtroom—Witness Deception," *Trial Mag.* Apr. 1978, p. 52.

Houts, *Photographic Misrepresentation* (1964).

Joseph, "Real and Demonstrative Videotape Evidence," in *Modern Visual Evidence* (1992).

Kraemer, "The Polaroid Identification System and Its Misuse," 26 *J.For.Sci.* 99 (1981).

Levkov, "A Rapid, Inexpensive Method of Obtaining Infrared Images," 23 *J.For.Sci.* 539 (1978).

Morgan & Morgan, *The Morgan & Morgan Dark Room Book* (1980).

Neblette, *Photography: Its Materials and Processes* (6th ed., 1962).

O'Connor, "Computer Animations in the Courtroom," 67 *Fla.Bar J.* 20 (Nov. 1993).

Panian, "Truth, Lies and Videotape: Are Current Federal Rules of Evidence Adequate," 21 *S.W.U.L.Rev.* 1199 (1992).

Practicing Law Institute, *Using Demonstrative Evidence in Civil Trials* (1982).

Reagan, "The Admissibility of Computer Simulations as Novel Scientific Evidence: An Analysis Under the Frye and Relevancy Standards," 1991 WL 330753.

Roberts, et al., "Enhancement of Latent Images on Backing Sheets of Polaroid Photographs," 19 *J.For.Sci.* 220 (1979).

Scott, *Photographic Evidence* (2d ed. 1969).

Siemer, *Tangible Evidence, How to Use Exhibits at Trial* (2d ed. 1989).

Turley, "Effective Use of Demonstrative Evidence: Capturing Attention and Clarifying Issues," *Trial* (Sep. 1989).

Tuttle & Conrad, "Photographs as a Mode of Communicating Testimony," 7 *J.For.Sci.* 82 (1962).

Warton, "Litigators Byte the Apple: Utilizing Computer–Generated Evidence at Trial," 41 *Baylor L.Rev.* 731 (1989).

Law Review Notes and Comments:

"Have Juries Gone to the Movies?—The Use of Videotape in the Courtroom," 12 *Am.J.Trial Adv.* 141 (1988).

"Let's Go to the Videotape: The Second Circuit Sanctions Covert Video Surveillance of Domestic Criminals," 53 *Brooklyn L.Rev.* 469 (1987).

" 'Day in the Life' and Surveillance Videos: Discovery of Videotaped Evidence in Personal Injury Suits," 97 *Dickinson L.Rev.* 305 (1993).

"The Use of Videotaped Testimony of Victims in Cases Involving Child Sexual Abuse: A Constitutional Dilemma," 14 *Hofstra L.Rev.* 261 (1985).

"Televised Testimony vs. the Confrontation Clause ... The Use of Videotapes In the Prosecution of Child Sexual Abuse," 23 *Houston L.Rev.* 1215 (1986).

"Admissibility of Video-taped Testimony: What is the Standard After *Maryland v. Craig* and How Will the Practicing Defense Attorney be Affected?," 42 *Mercer L.Rev.* 883 (1991).

"Videotaped Prior Identification: Evidentiary Considerations For Admissibility," 50 *Mo.L.Rev.* 157 (1985).

"Computer Simulations and Video Reenactments: Fact, Fantasy and Admission Standards," 17 *Ohio N.U.L.Rev.* 145 (1990).

"Does the Child Witness Videotape Statute Violate the Confrontation Clause?" 17 *Tex.Tech L.Rev.* 1669 (1986).

"Constitutionality of Admitting The Videotape Testimony at Trial of Sexually Abused Children," 7 *Whittier L.Rev.* 639 (1985).

Chapter 3

CHEMICAL AND OTHER TESTS FOR ALCOHOLIC INTOXICATION

I. ALCOHOL INTOXICATION TESTING

I. ALCOHOL INTOXICATION TESTING

§ 3.01 Alcohol in the Human Body

There are a number of different alcohols, i.e., wood alcohol (methyl), rubbing alcohol (isopropyl), and consumable alcohol (ethyl). The last named type is the alcoholic ingredient contained in alcoholic beverages. The terms "ethyl alcohol," "alcohol," and "ethanol" will be used throughout this chapter as synonymous. Alcohol is volatile, with a low

176

boiling point, colorless, and practically odorless.[1]

When alcohol reaches the stomach, it is not "digested." In fact, the stomach acts as a holding tank and as long as the alcohol is in the stomach, it cannot show up in blood/breath/urine tests and no physical impairment occurs. Only a small percentage is "absorbed" into the bloodstream through membranes in the stomach. At some time after consumption, the alcohol passes from the stomach to the duodenum and into the intestinal tract. It is only at this point the bulk of the alcohol begins to be absorbed into the bloodstream at a fairly constant rate, but the degree and rate of absorption of alcohol is governed by several factors, such as the quantity of alcohol (ethanol) ingested, and the nature and quantity of diluting and membrane coating in the stomach. Obviously, alcohol consumed on an empty stomach will pass into the intestinal tract fairly rapidly, since it requires no digestion, and will thus have a faster absorption rate than alcohol taken with or after a meal. Some foods, such as fatty and oily substances, sugar, and milk, are among the substances which, if still in the stomach in whole or in part at the time alcohol is being ingested, may retard significantly absorption into the blood stream. Carbohydrates in beer retard absorption, which is why the alcohol in beer will be less rapidly absorbed than a like concentration of alcohol in water. After eating, the maximum blood alcohol concentration after ingestion of ethanol may not occur until 30 to 150 minutes later. (For a graphic description of the difference occasioned by the factor of an empty or full stomach, see Figure 1.) As long as a person is still in the absorptive period, arterial blood containing alcohol that has been freshly absorbed from the digestive system is slightly higher in BAC than venous blood. The two will tend to equalize, however, in the post-absorptive stage.

When the alcohol passes through the duodenum into the intestinal tract and to the liver, the ethanol is eliminated from the body tissues into harmless metabolites by being oxidized to energy, carbon dioxide and water. Much of this metabolism occurs in the liver where, on the first passage, 90–95% of the alcohol is eliminated.[2] Only 5–10% of the alcohol ingested will get into the general circulation and spread throughout the entire body, where it will cross the blood/brain barrier. It is in

---

§ 3.01

1. Breath odor of a person who has been drinking alcohol in its usual available forms is actually the odor of the congeners or other ingredients inserted into the beverage, and this varies from one beverage to another. There is supposedly no breath odor from pure alcohol consumed in water, although some chemists contend that they can detect ethyl alcohol by smell.

It is precisely because ethanol itself is odorless, that police officers are taught to say, on the witness stand, that upon approaching the driver of a vehicle they "de-

tected the odor associated with alcoholic beverages about his person."

2. If, through disease or otherwise, the chemical detoxification system of the liver is impaired, so that the bulk of the alcohol consumed is not being eliminated on its first passage, physical impairment due to the ethanol would demonstrate itself unusually fast and at an unusually high rate. This would be true (not false) impairment. Some prescription medicines, notably common ulcer medications, cripple the detoxification mechanism of the liver.

the deep lung tissue that the ethanol is exchanged from the blood into the air (breath).

Absorbed alcohol does not undergo chemical change; it remains alcohol. Once absorbed into the bloodstream, alcohol is distributed throughout the body in a constant proportional relationship to the water content of the various tissues. For example, the alcohol concentration in urine bears approximately the same relationship to the alcohol concentration of the blood as the water content of the urine bears to the water content of the blood. Urine and blood plasma are richer in alcohol than bone or fat. In fact, very little alcohol will be found in the bones or in fatty tissue. Some of the alcohol, however, will be found in other body fluids such as perspiration, spinal fluid, saliva, and tears. The higher the concentration of alcohol in the blood, the higher the relative proportion of alcohol excreted in the urine and breath. The percentage of alcohol excreted by the kidneys, as urine, or by the lungs in the breath varies in approximate proportion to the concentration of alcohol in the blood. During the interval when blood alcohol concentration is decreasing, the urine alcohol concentration may be up to one and one-half that of blood alcohol. The concentration of blood alcohol is approximately 2100 times as much as that of the same unit volume in the deep, alveolar breath. The rate of elimination varies from person to person, but it is reasonably constant according to body size, i.e., the average 150 pound man can eliminate ⅓ ounce of pure alcohol per hour. Transposed, this equals ⅔ ounce of 100 proof whiskey per hour or one beer per hour.[3]

---

3. Beer ferments to an alcohol concentration of approximately 3 to 6 percent. A 12–ounce bottle of 3% beer contains about ⅓ ounce of alcohol; 4% beer would contain ½ ounce of alcohol. Wine ferments to an alcohol concentration of 12 to 14 percent; however, some wines have alcohol added to increase concentration up to 20%. Alcohol percentages of "hard" liquor can be determined by dividing the "proof" by 2, i.e., "100–proof" whiskey contains 50% alcohol.

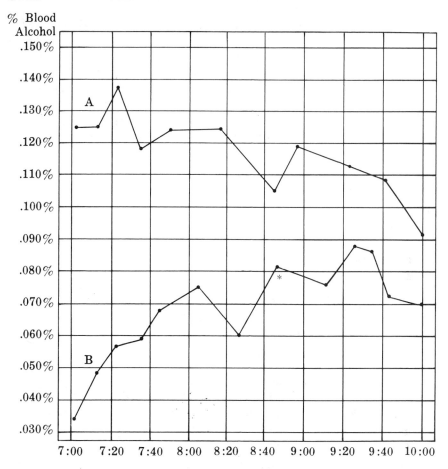

Fig. I. A graphic description of a test series performed on two subjects, A and B, by Richard B. Hall before a group of circuit court judges in Illinois.

SUBJECT A
(Weight 180 lbs.)
Drank 300 cc of 86 proof alcohol while stomach *empty*; started at 6:05 p.m., stopped at 6:35 p.m.

SUBJECT B
(Weight 170 lbs.)
Drank 300 cc of 86 proof alcohol while stomach *full*; started at 6:05 p.m., stopped at 6:35 p.m.

* At this stage of the experiment, Subject B consumed an additional 25cc of alcohol.

Concerning the effects of alcohol on the body, it is most important to understand that it is not the amount of alcohol consumed that governs the degree of impairment but rather the amount of alcohol that is absorbed into the blood and carried to the central nervous system. Contrary to popular notions, alcohol acts not as a stimulant but as a depressant to the responses of the central nervous system which is composed of the brain, spinal cord and spinal nerves. The alcohol-rich blood courses over the brain through the vascular system, imparting a depressing effect to the brain tissue until the alcohol disappears from the blood. Its primary blunting effect, in low concentrations, occurs in the cerebral areas of the brain which control the higher functions. There are consequent reductions of judgment, response to stimuli and self-restraint. At higher concentrations, blood alcohol causes a noticeable loss of muscular control with a lengthening of reaction time, confusion, and disturbance of sensory perception such as hearing and vision, decreased pain sensitivity, staggering gait and slurred speech. These deteriorations in functions occur as a result of the weakened effectiveness of nerve impulse transmissions. At even higher concentration, stupor approaching paralysis results. Finally, at maximal sublethal concentration the individual lapses into unconsciousness, with attendant depression of reflexes and impairment of circulation.

Despite the fact that statutes which prohibit driving with a blood alcohol concentration over a certain level assume that every one is impaired in the same manner at the same BAC, manifestations of alcoholic influence are not uniform. There are some persons who can consume comparatively large amounts of alcohol without seeming to be seriously impaired: This results from (1) less alcohol going into the bloodstream because of different consumption tolerances of absorption, distribution and elimination, and (2) the constitutional tolerance involving a variable susceptibility to alcohol in the nerve cell. At certain blood alcohol concentrations, however, everyone is impaired to a significant degree. A number of studies have shown that the drunken driver precipitates many motor vehicle accidents, and excessive dosage of drink is a proximate cause of many highway casualties, with approximately 40 to 55 percent of drivers fatally injured in traffic accidents having blood alcohol concentrations (BAC) in excess of the legal limit in most states.[4]

§ 3.02 General Nature of Chemical and Other Tests for Blood–Alcohol Concentration (BAC)

Since impairment of a person's faculties is, in a general sense, proportioned to the BAC, the scientific determinant as to whether an individual is "intoxicated" or "under the influence" of alcohol is the amount, if any, that has coursed through the blood vessels of the brain. Theoretically, therefore, a test for alcohol within those vessels (or in the spinal fluid) would afford the most accurate information respecting questions concerning alcohol. The big difficulty with any such test, of course, is its impracticability, except with respect to dead bodies. Moreover, for medico-legal purposes, there is less data available regarding the correlation between the brain alcohol concentration and a person's conduct and behavior than there is regarding alcohol in the blood within extremities (e.g., the arm), or within the urine or in the breath. The latter sources, therefore, offer the only practical alternatives for ascertaining the absence or presence of alcohol within a living person's system, and, if present, the approximate amount thereof.

4. Ruschmann, Joscelyn, Greyson and Carroll, *An Analysis of the Potential Legal Constraints On the Use of Advanced Alco-*hol–Testing Technology* (U.S. Dept. of Transp., Final Report, April 1980), p. 3.

Of all the tests, the simplest and most socially acceptable one, which has been accepted by the courts as scientifically valid as well, is the test of a specimen of breath. Expelled "deep lung" or "alveolar" air will reflect with a reasonable degree of accuracy that which a blood test itself might reveal. Usually, however, a blood test renders slightly higher readings than a breath test.

The available scientific literature regarding the various BAC tests is voluminous, and it is not feasible in a portion of any text to do more than discuss some of the basics of testing in terminology understandable to lawyers and law students who do not have, nor who are expected to possess, the knowledge of human physiology, chemistry and toxicology required for an in-depth appreciation of the relevant scientific principles and test procedures. For those practitioners who are confronted with actual cases requiring more extensive information the references herein cited will be of assistance.[1] The legal aspects, of course, can and will be presented in a manner and form that should meet adequately the practitioner's needs.

§ 3.03 Limitation Factors and General Value of Tests

It was at one time assumed that if an individual tested by any of the previously mentioned procedures had a certain amount of alcohol in his system, a retrograde extrapolation could be made to ascertain what the alcoholic content had been during a preceding period—for example, twenty, thirty, forty minutes, or one or more hours prior to that time. This extrapolation theory, subsequently to be discussed in detail, no longer possesses the full validity it was once thought to possess.[1] Nevertheless, what has remained inviolate is the well-confirmed fact that a scientific determination can be made as to (a) whether alcohol is present in a tested person's system *at the time of the test,* and (b) the appropriate percentage of alcohol present at that time in terms of blood volume content.

§ 3.02

1. Extremely valuable and technical information upon the subject of chemical tests for alcoholic intoxication is contained in (a) Mason and Dubowski, "Alcohol, Traffic and Chemical Testing in the United States: A Resume and Some Remaining Problems," 20 *Clinical Chemistry* 126–140 (1974), and (b), with regard to breath tests, the article by the same authors in 21 *J. Forensic Sci.* 9–42 (1976). At the conclusion of each article there is an extensive bibliography—139 references in (a) and 159 in (b).

See also, Gullberg, Variations in Blood Alcohol Concentration Following the Last Drink, 3 *J. Police Sci. & Admin.* 289 (1982); A.M.A. *Alcohol and the Impaired Driver: A Manual on the Medicolegal Aspects of Chemical Tests for Intoxication with Supplement on Breath Alcohol Tests,* 1972.

§ 3.03

1. One authority, Richard W. Hall, is firm in the conviction that "a person's sobriety can only be accurately determined from a blood alcohol test result at the time of the occurrence or from one obtained immediately thereafter." Hall adds, however, "the test result is admitted in evidence insofar as it may tend to render the issue of DUI more or less probable. For these reasons, the blood alcohol and physical coordination tests are considered corroborative evidence of other facts that establish the corpus delicti. The tests help to elevate other evidence to the required level of proof (beyond a reasonable doubt in criminal cases)." See Chapter 6 of the Illinois Institute for Continuing Legal Education's 1978 publication *Misdemeanors And Moving Traffic Violations.*

Experiments have indicated that the percentage of alcohol in a person's blood, urine, or breath, is a fairly dependable indication of the "extent of intoxication," in the context, for instance, of a person's control of his faculties sufficiently well to properly operate or control a vehicle.

One of the principal values of the tests for alcohol is the means afforded for ascertaining whether a person's questionable conduct may be attributed to alcohol, or whether it may be accountable by some other non-alcohol factor, i.e., a diabetic's erratic conduct, or the ketone odor of his breath due to the diabetes, and especially when he is in a state of insulin deficiency, or a narcotic such as heroin or cocaine.[2]

Contrary to an assumption that is often made, support for an allegation that alcohol was responsible for a person's conduct at the time of a particular event cannot rest solely upon the results of chemical tests in driving under the influence (DUI) cases, even if there should be an acceptance, complete or partial, of the extrapolation theory. There must be corroborative evidence based upon such factors as visual observations of conduct at the time of, or very soon after, the occurrence in dispute.

§ 3.04 Blood and Urine Tests

Chemical determination of blood alcohol concentration by analysis of blood or urine is quite complicated. Even when the test is valid and accurate in principle, error is possible whenever the analyst is careless or incompetent, or if the specimen was contaminated at the time it was taken, or subsequently. Contamination of a blood specimen is less likely than a urine sample since blood samples usually are, or must be taken under controlled medical circumstances.

The result of a laboratory analysis of urine alcohol is converted to blood alcohol by virtue of the known relationship between alcohol content of urine as compared to alcohol content of blood. Urine contains about 1.3 times as much alcohol as blood. Urine alcohol concentration, of course, has no direct effect on the brain; it is merely a device by which a scientific inference of blood alcohol concentration can be made.

Urine alcohol analysis, when converted, yields the average blood alcohol concentration during the time the urine was accumulating in the bladder. To pin it down to a particular time, the researchers advise that the bladder be emptied and that a test specimen be collected 30 minutes later. There is some authority to the effect that the urine test is sometimes unfavorable to the defendant, in that the blood alcohol figure calculated from analysis of the urine exceeds the actual value determined directly from blood analysis. Another view is that the urine test does not prejudice the defendant because alcohol in the bladder is absorbed

---

2. At least sixty pathological conditions may produce symptoms in common with those of alcoholic intoxication. Consult Donigan, *Chemical Tests and the Law* (1966) 300–307, published by Northwestern University Traffic Institute. It covers not only the scientific aspects, as of that date, but also the law governing the admissibility of test results in evidence. As to the law upon the subject, pocket supplements have been published with court decisions and statutes.

through the bladder membrane, resulting in the calculated blood alcohol figure being lower than the true blood alcohol.[1] Because of the problems with urine testing, the Committee on Alcohol and Drugs, of the National Safety Council, has discouraged the use of such tests.

One of three methods is typically used to remove the alcohol from a blood or urine specimen, namely: (1) chemical methods; (2) biochemical methods; or (3) gas chromatographic methods. The gas chromatographic methods are now the most widely used methods. They can be used for simultaneous identification and quantification of not only alcohol, but also ketones and aldehydes. The type of qualitative and quantitative analysis may vary from one laboratory to another.

As noted, urine analysis suffers from very serious drawbacks. The relationship between the alcohol concentration in urine to that of blood is rather complicated. Since the collection of a quantity of urine in the bladder takes time, the higher concentration of alcohol will occur at a later time in urine than in blood. Except for a short peak period, the alcohol concentration in the blood changes constantly; it is either rising or falling. In urine, the same curves do not work out that way. For these reasons, urinalysis is not nearly as widely used as the blood test, or, for that matter, the breath tests discussed in the next section. Urinalysis also requires the use of a sophisticated laboratory for analysis, and it is also encumbered by additional factors.

The results of a urine test may be affected by the bladder condition before or after the consumption of alcohol. If alcohol is consumed with a full bladder the tests would inaccurately underestimate the degree of blood-alcohol content. Conversely, if the individual consumed alcohol with an empty bladder some time prior to the test and had not voided himself recently, the results could easily overestimate the amount of alcohol in the blood at the time of the test. Alcohol in the bladder is not an active agent in causing symptoms of intoxication and, like the test of estimating the amount of alcohol ingested, probably not as reliable an index for determining the degree of intoxication. (Two specimens taken at 30 minute intervals would, it is conceded, greatly augment the reliability of the urine test.)

If the specimen to be analyzed is blood, it should be obtained as soon after the traffic stop as possible. Because ordinarily the blood is extracted only once, even when a statute requires that two samples be collected in order to afford the motorist to have an analysis done at a laboratory of his choice, the BAC result may nevertheless not properly demonstrate the accused's blood-alcohol concentration at the time he was driving. Furthermore, a number of possibilities for inaccuracies or error are inherent in the entire analysis process, as will be addressed infra in § 3.09.

§ 3.04

1. See also report of a study on whether urine samples can be compromised by endogenous ethanol production, in, Lough & Fehn, "Efficacy of 1% Sodium Fluoride As a Preservative in Urine Samples Containing Glucose and *Candida albicans*," 38 *J.For. Sci.* 266 (1992).

§ 3.05 Breath Tests

As previously stated, of the various chemical tests for alcoholic intoxication, the preferred one, considered in the context of practicability, is the one which seeks to make the determination from breath specimens.

Breath tests for alcoholic intoxication are based upon the assumption that breath specimens are saturated with alcohol vapor at the temperature of the normal respiratory tract. Alcohol breath tests, then, constitute an indirect means of establishing blood-alcohol content, one that is inherently less reliable than the blood analysis for alcohol content. Other than possible errors in operation, calibration, or inspection of the instruments, which are addressed in § 3.09, infra, there are some serious questions about the underlying principles upon which breath-alcohol determinations are based.

This presents an attorney who seeks to challenge breath test results with a serious evidentiary problem. First of all, judges have been accepting breath test results for decades, and they certainly don't like hearing an attorney say that the technique is unreliable. Second, a defense attorney who seeks to cross-examine the operator of breath testing equipment is in for an exercise in frustration. In breath testing school, the operator, who is not a scientist, is taught only that which the designers of the instrument feel it is necessary for the officer to know and which they feel he can understand and relate to others. A lot is left out. The operator typically does not have enough scientific knowledge to answer probing questions about the physiology of the digestive and respiratory systems, as well as the weaknesses of the scientific instrument itself, and the cross-examiner will quickly be perceived as trying to discredit an honest, hard working police officer with some irrelevant scientific nonsense. Third, even if the defense has a qualified scientist on the stand, there still is no certainty that the judge is even willing to seriously consider scientific explanations that seem to fly in the face of long-time acceptance by the courts of breath testing to determine alcohol impairment.

Clearly, the breath testing instruments measure fairly accurately the *breath* alcohol by weight by volume, but it is in converting the breath/alcohol concentration into a blood/alcohol concentration figure that uncertainties creep in. The possible rates of error are not formidable, but they are nevertheless significant in close cases. Since the breath test instrument reading will be a close approximation of the true BAC of a subject, there is not much to be gained by seeking to attack a test result showing a BAC of .15 percent by weight/by volume, or higher, by the presentation of competent scientific experts in a jurisdiction where the presumption of intoxication starts at .10 percent.[1] Any inherent inaccuracies are unlikely to permit the challenger to demonstrate that

----

§ 3.05

1. See § 3.08, infra, for the standards of intoxication.

the true BAC was below the statutory level of .10 percent. But where the test result was at or only slightly above the presumptive intoxication level, then the issue of whether the person truly was above .10 becomes questionable. In truth, the accurate result may just as well be below .10 as it may be above that level.

The exchange of the alcohol that is in blood into the breath occurs in the alveolar sacs (deep lung tissue), which is the site of the gas exchange in the lungs. There is, of course, much less alcohol that is transferred to the breath than is in the blood. The rate, or proportion, of alcohol-in-blood to alcohol-in-breath, is known as the partition rate. Since 1950, it has been generally accepted that the ratio is approximately 1 to 2,100.[2] Highly renowned and respected forensic toxicologists have suggested in more recent years that the rate is not constant, and indeed may fluctuate greatly between 1 to 1,100 to 1 to 3,200.[3] Yet, though it was never intended to be anything but an approximation, the 1 to 2,100 ratio has been enshrined as an "absolute." [4]

For the lawyer and law student readership of the present text the authors' description of one such instrument and its operation should suffice. It is the Breathalyzer (Model 1000), which was an improvement over its predecessors in that, primarily, its operation is much more automatic, thereby decreasing the amount of manipulation previously required of the operator.[5] (See Figures 2, 3 and 4.)

2. Harger et al., "The Partition Ratio of Alcohol Between Air and Water, Urine and Blood: Estimation and Identification of Alcohol in Those Liquids from Analysis of Air Calibrated with Them," 183 *J. Biological Chem.* 197 (1950); Harger et al., "Estimation of the Level of Blood Alcohol from the Analysis of Breath," 36 *J.Lab.Clin.Med.* 306 (1950).

Dr. R.N. Harger developed, in 1938, the first breath testing instrument, which he called the Drunkometer. Other early instruments were the Intoximeter, developed by Glenn Forester, and the Alcometer, developed by Prof. Leon Greenberg, both in 1941. See, Gerstenzang, *Handling the DWI Case In New York* 180 (1987).

3. State v. McGinley, 229 N.J.Super. 191, 201, 550 A.2d 1305, 1310 (1988), recognizes the research on that issue of Dr. Stanley Broskey, forensic toxicologist of the New Jersey State Police, and other scientists. R. Mumford, a California criminalist, estimates that the true ratio varies between 1 to 1,550 and 1 to 2,700. See, People v. McDonald, 206 Cal.App.3d 877, 880, 254 Cal.Rptr. 384, 386 (1988). Dr. Kurt Dubowski, of the University of Oklahoma Medical School, is probably the most eminent scientist who has devoted a lifetime researching, writing, and teaching on breath/alcohol issues. He had originally concluded that the 1-to-2,100 ratio caused

greater than true BAC readings in 14% of the cases, but has now revised his research. His more recent work, quoted in State v. Downie, 117 N.J. 450, 462, 569 A.2d 242, 248 (1990), concludes that "[i]n only 2.3% of the cases does the breathalyzer materially overestimate the blood-alcohol level potentially to the detriment of the accused," but adds that the 2.3% figure is subject to question. The *Downie* court did not believe this to present a problem and continued to place its stamp of approval on breath testing devices.

4. The National Highway Traffic Safety Administration has formulated specifications for breath testing equipment which define BAC to be the "Blood alcohol concentration, expressed in percent weight by volume (% w/v) based upon grams of alcohol per cubic centimeters of blood or per 210 liters of breath ..." 49 Fed.Reg. 48857 (1984). Similarly, the Committee on Alcohol and Other Drugs, National Safety Council, specifies that 1-to-2,100 is the accurate ratio to determine BAC from breath tests. 49 Fed.Reg. 48855 (1984).

5. Even so, in a study of 90 Breathalyzer Model 1000s, the instruments "produced a significant number of test results which exceeded normally expected scientific deviation." See, Caplan, et al., "An In Vitro Study of the Accuracy and Precision

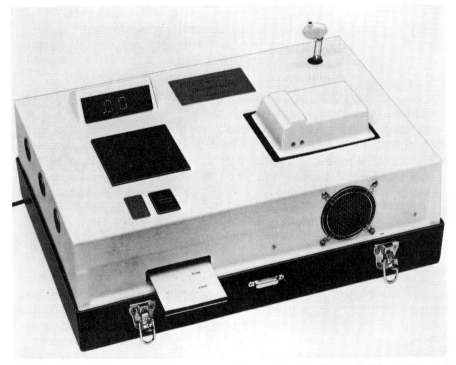

Fig. 2. Breathalyzer Model 1000, as manufactured by the Smith & Wesson/General Ordinance Equipment Co., Springfield, Mass. [6]

Although the prevailing view, as indicated before, is to convert a breath quantity to a blood concentration of ethyl alcohol for forensic purposes, two authorities, Mason and Dubowski, have recommended that this conversion procedure be abandoned and that "the offense of driving while under the influence should be statutorily defined in terms of the concentration of alcohol found in the breath." [7]

In the testing process the subject blows with force through the mouthpiece. Electrically activated valves permit a piston-cylinder to collect and discard at least the first 400 ml of delivered breath. Then the remaining 56.5 ml is warmed and collected in an additional piston-cylinder and 55.2 ml of this is bubbled through an ampoule containing potassium dichromate, sulfuric acid and silver nitrate as a catalyst. The initial photometric absorbance is established by equalizing the filtered "blue light" absorbance of a reference and test ampoule, using the

of Breathalyzer Models 900, 900A, and 1000," 30 *J.For.Sci.* 1058 (1985).

6. On July 10, 1984, National Draeger, Inc., of Pittsburgh, Pa., acquired the Breathalyzer Division of Smith and Wesson, but not the manufacturing rights to Model 1000. Draeger is continuing the manufacture of the two predecessor models to Model 1000, Models 900 and 900A. Smith and Wesson no longer manufactures Model 1000, but that instrument is serviced by National Draeger. Models 900 and 900A are less sophisticated devices that do not have a multicopy printer.

7. Mason and Dubowski, 21 *J.Forensic Sci.* 33 (1976).

Bunsen principle. The change in absorbence on analysis of breath appears as a digital readout and a printed record of the presumed blood-alcohol concentration, based on an assumption of a blood-breath ratio of 2100:1. (Adapted from a description of the instrument by Mason & Dubowski in supra note 7 at p. 15.)

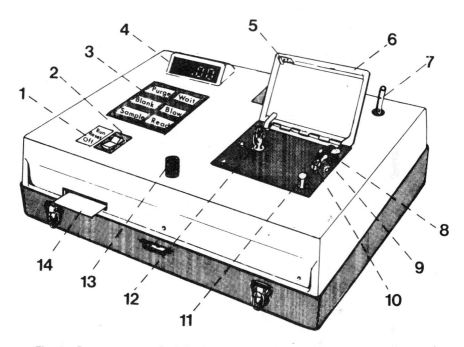

Fig. 3. Instrument panel of the Breathalyzer Model 1000 pictured in Fig. 2.

1. Mode Selector Panel
2. Mode Selector Switch
3. Program Indicator Panel
4. Digital Electronic Display
5. Ampoule Cover Latch
6. Ampoule Cover
7. Sample Collection Tube
8. Rubber Extension Sleeve
9. Rubber Extension Sleeve Holder
10. Test Ampoule
11. Test Ampoule Release Knob
12. Comparison Ampoule
13. Ampoule Gauge
14. Multicopy Printer Card

In recent years devices have appeared that utilize the infrared absorption theory. They are based upon the principle that the alcohol in breath absorbs specific wavelengths of infrared light.

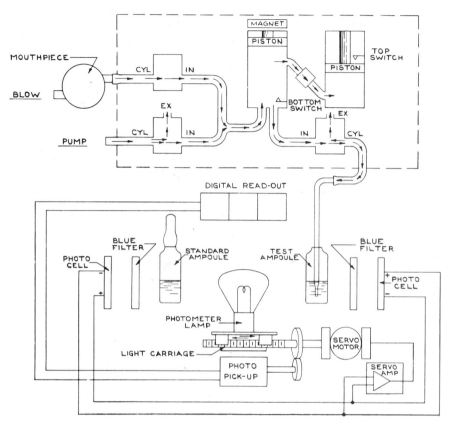

Fig. 4. Operational diagram of Figures 2 and 3. (*Courtesy of Smith & Wesson/General Ordnance Equipment Co.*)

Another such device that has appeared on the market is the BAC Verifier manufactured by Verax Systems, Inc., pictured in Fig. 5. Among the features of the BAC Verifier is an acetone reading if acetone is present, an optional second sample collection capability, and a radio frequency interference detector (RFI). In recent years it has been claimed that some breath testing devices can give distorted readings if they are unknowingly subjected to radio waves in the environment. The BAC Verifier is said to monitor the immediate environment for any radio frequency interference (RFI) which might invalidate the results. The instrument will not proceed with testing if RFI is detected. This is done by using an external antenna and an internal sensor circuit. An audible alarm, warning display and printed message confirms the presence of RFI, or if RFI is not present in the environment, a message to that effect appears on the printout with the BAC and acetone reading.

The relative advantages and disadvantages attending the utilization of breath testing procedures have been set forth as follows: [9]

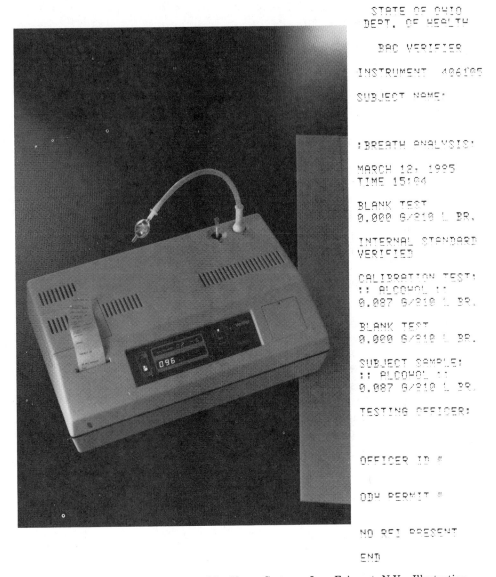

Fig. 5. BAC Verifier manufactured by Verax Systems, Inc., Fairport, N.Y. Illustration at right shows information appearing on hard copy printout after each test.

Advantages

(1) The result of a breath alcohol analysis, expressed in terms of the blood-alcohol concentration, is obtainable within a few minutes of the start of the analysis.

---

9. From the publication, *Alcohol and the Impaired Driver* 95–96 (National Safety Council, Chicago, Ill.1970).

Item 5 under Disadvantages is a recent development.

(2) Breath as the analyzed material accurately reflects the actual pulmonary arterial blood-alcohol level at the time of the test, without lag or overrun.

(3) When breath samples are obtained, the problem of positively identifying the specimen donor, and most of the collection, identification, preservation, transportation, and evidentiary safeguard problems common to other body materials are eliminated, as is the need for specially qualified collection personnel, special collection facilities and containers, and most of the precautions outlined in detail in the section on "Application of Laboratory Procedures."

(4) Since breath analysis eliminates certain difficult steps in analyses of body fluids, requirements for technical background and skill of the analyst are greatly reduced, and adequate supervision considerably simplified.

(5) Required test facilities can be minimal and need include only the self-contained, breath-alcohol apparatus. Costs per test after acquisition of the necessary equipment are, therefore, lower than for comparable laboratory analysis.

(6) There is usually less objection by the subject to collection of a breath sample than to the body penetration required to obtain a blood specimen. Generally less cooperation and considerably less time are required than for collection of adequate saliva or urine specimens. Replicate, and serial alcohol determinations at frequent brief intervals are practical because of the rapidity and relative simplicity of the on-the-spot breath analyses and the rapid nontraumatic sampling of breath specimens. This allows accurate determination of the directional trend of the blood-alcohol curve, and many analyses on a given subject.

Disadvantages

(1) It is difficult to preserve entire breath specimens for a later replicate or independent confirmatory analysis, although the alcohol from a measured volume of breath can be collected and preserved for later analysis.

(2) Some cooperation is required from the tested subject for collection of an adequate breath specimen, the extent varying with the nature of the required breath sample (alveolar air, mixed-expired air, or rebreathed air) and the collection apparatus (for example: balloon, or sample chamber of apparatus).

(3) Most breath alcohol methods are inapplicable to unconscious or completely uncooperative subjects.

(4) A period of approximately 15 min. after the last ingestion of alcohol, or its regurgitation, must elapse before the sample is obtained to insure elimination of the possible effects of any residual mouth alcohol.

(5) Some breath testing devices may give distorted readings if they are set up in an environment where radio frequency interference from a foreign source is present (RFI). The RFI is said to be common where breath testing devices are located inside buildings having equipment or machines producing radio waves. The legal implications of this are discussed infra in § 3.12.

(6) Some substances other than ethanol may have been present in the subject's breath which were responsible, either for the producing of an apparent ethanol concentration, or for elevating the true ethanol concentration.[10]

§ 3.06 Preliminary Breath Tests

Thus far, we have discussed breath tests that measure the presence and quantity of alcohol in a person's blood. Such tests are commonly referred to as "evidentiary tests" because the results are considered sufficiently reliable to be admitted at a civil or criminal trial on the disputed issue of BAC. Under the "Implied Consent" laws of the various states, evidentiary tests for BAC are administered *after* a person has been arrested for driving under the influence of intoxicants. Therefore, probable cause for the arrest must exist *before* an evidentiary test is administered. Even when probable cause is present, the arresting officer cannot administer the test unless the driver consents to it. If the driver refuses to consent, the test cannot be administered; however, if that occurs, provisions of the applicable implied consent law allow for a suspension or revocation of the arrestee's license to drive.

The evidentiary test is considered a "search" within the meaning of the Fourth Amendment protection against unreasonable searches and seizures. This is because the test requires "entering" a person's body to extract a fluid or deep lung air sample as evidence of BAC that would not otherwise be accessible to the police.

In recent years, another type of breath test has appeared that is sometimes referred to as a "roadside screening device" or "preliminary breath testing" (PBT) device. PBTs are portable devices, usually hand-held and the size of pocket calculators, that detect the presence of consumable alcohol in a driver's breath. Some devices also approximate the quantity of detected alcohol.

Common devices include the Alcolmeter, the Alcolyzer, which utilizes chromate salt in acid and gives an indicator response of color

---

10. In a study by Cowan, McCutcheon and Weatherman, "The Response of the Intoxilyzer 4011AS–A to a Number of Possible Interfering Substances," 35 *J.For.Sci.* 797 (1990), it was found that isopropanol, toluene, and methyl ethyl ketone, could "reasonably interfere with the [breath] test," by producing "a slight additive effect to a breath alcohol concentration near the level required for prosecution," but the researchers nevertheless found the instrument used to be "an effective way of determining the ethanol concentration in human

change; the A.L.E.R.T.[1] Model J3A, which utilizes a Taguchi Mos conductor and causes a "pass," "warn" or "fail" indicator light to glow; and the Alco–Sensor, which uses a fuel cell and gives a digital readout response. Some of these devices are calibrated at a particular BAC, such as .05% or .10%. They are said to give a "pass-fail" reading in the sense that the indicator response is below or over a calibrated setting. Some devices, like the Alco–Sensor shown in Fig. 6, give a numerical BAC reading, but this is not as accurate as the numerical BAC reading of instruments used for evidentiary tests. These PBT devices require a person to blow in a disposable plastic tube connected to the device for the collection and measurement of deep lung air. Since the person must perform an act—blowing into a tube—these devices are sometimes referred to as "active" devices, as opposed to the "passive" devices described in the next section.

Unlike evidentiary tests, the results of PBTs are *not* admissible in court on the factual issue of BAC under a DUI statute. The devices are used for screening purposes, that is, to determine whether a driver has consumed alcohol, and his *approximate* BAC. The results of the PBT, along with other objective facts known to the officer, such as erratic driving behavior, slurred speech, obvious alcohol breath, etc., may give the officer probable cause to make an arrest and the right to request that the driver participate in an evidentiary test under an implied consent statute. Thus, although the result of the PBT will not be admissible at trial as evidence of the driver's BAC, it may be admissible at a preliminary hearing or motion to suppress where the issue is not guilt or innocence of driving under the influence, but whether the officer has probable cause to make an arrest. A fuller discussion of the legal issues raised by the use of the PBT is presented in Section 3.12, infra.

breath for purposes of evidence." Id. at 811.

§ 3.06

1. "Alcohol Level Evaluation Roadside Tester." Results are inadmissible in evi-

dence: State v. Ifill, 574 A.2d 889 (Me. 1990).

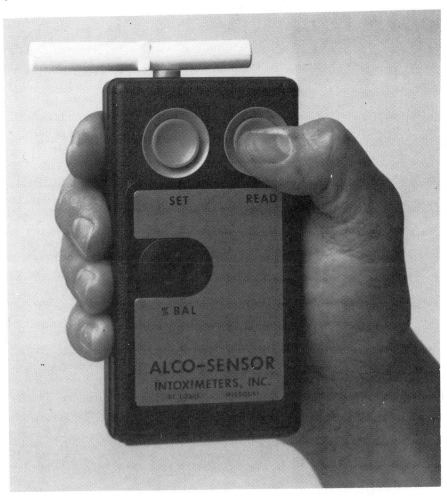

Fig. 6. Alco-Sensor manufactured by Intoximeters, Inc., St. Louis, Mo. The manufacturer previously marketed a device called the Alco-Sensor II. The device shown above has replaced the Alco-Sensor II devices still on the market.

§ 3.07 Passive Alcohol Screening Devices

Passive alcohol screening devices (PASD) represent the frontier of alcohol detection devices of the preliminary screening variety. PASDs will be used to detect the presence of ethyl alcohol in the breath of a person simply by sampling the air around the person which includes air exhaled by the person. In this sense, such a device may be referred to as "passive" since it does not require the person suspected of being under the influence of intoxicants to perform an act, such as giving a sample of a body fluid (blood or urine) or blowing into a tube to produce a sample of deep lung air. Although the procedure may require the person to stay in a particular place while the sample of air is taken, which may raise certain legal questions to be dealt with in Section 3.12, infra, in its ordinary use the person to be tested remains passive and undisturbed.

The PASD that was first experimentally tested was based on the Lion Passive Alcolmeter,[1] built into a police flashlight casing so as to allow an officer to conduct night time tests easily, and incorporated "an electrochemical fuel cell sensor together with a pump that draws the expelled breath over the sensor."[2]   The instrument contains three switches, one which is used to operate the flashlight; the second to activate the pump for 5 seconds to draw in the breath sample; and the third to turn on the sensor circuitry. The maximum reading is obtained in approximately 10 seconds, and discharge, to ready the unit for new use, takes 30 seconds. The early tests established that several of the officers participating in the test, who had received only one hour of training, clearly needed more rigorous training in the proper operation of the device than had been provided.

Use of the device is becoming more widespread, but still on an experimental basis. Since it may never be accurate enough to do more than affording probable cause, evidentiary challenges are more likely to be delayed. Its chief utility will be similar to that of the PBT, that is, as a screening device producing information which, when taken with other facts known to the police officer, may give probable cause for an arrest and for an evidentiary breath or blood test.

Its legal implications center around the issue whether to compel a person to submit to a PASD constitutes a "search" under the Fourth Amendment, and, if so, what level of cause will be required for its use— probable cause sufficient for an arrest, or reasonable suspicion as in a stop and frisk.[3]

Robert V. Voas, an early researcher on the PASD, described the device in these terms:

> The Passive Sensor is a simple but highly sensitive alcohol detector. It has the appearance of a large flashlight. The fan in the front end pulls expired air from the driver (mixed with some of the external air) past a sensor which is specially designed to react to alcohol. Power for the device comes from four D-cell batteries which are stored in the handle. Only one control is provided—an "on" button which starts the fan and heats the Sensor. The presence of alcohol is shown by the activation of a red light.[4]

The same report gives this diagram and description of the device:

§ 3.07

1. Built by Lion Laboratories Ltd., Barry, South Glam. CF6 3BE, United Kingdom.

2.   Jones & Lund, "Detection of Alcohol-Impaired Drivers Using a Passive Alcohol Sensor," 14 *J. of Pol.Sci. & Admin.* 153, 159 (1986).

3. Manak, "Constitutional Aspects of the Use of Passive Alcohol Screening De-

vices as Law Enforcement Tools for DWI Enforcement," 19 *The Prosecutor* 29 (1986); Fields and Hricko, "Passive Alcohol Sensors—Constitutional Implications," 20 *The Prosecutor* 45 (1986).

4. Voas, *Reports on Passive Sensing Research*, Report No. 8 (National Public Services Research Institute, Alexandria, Va.1983).

PASSIVE ALCOHOL SENSOR

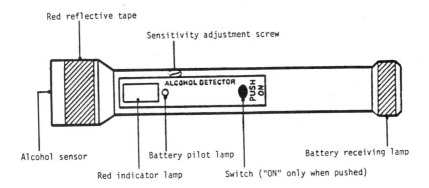

PASSIVE ALCOHOL SENSOR (PAS)

When held four to six inches in front of the face, this sensor at maximum sensitivity will collect expired air and determine whether the individual has been drinking heavily (enough alcohol to bring the blood alcohol content to 0.05%).

BEFORE USING THE PAS

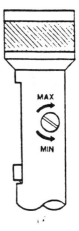
Sensitivity adjustor

    1)   Check batteries:

        Push "On" button. Make sure GREEN battery pilot light comes on and that the fan is operating. If pilot light does not come on, change batteries.

    2)   Adjust sensitivity:

        a)   Push "On" button—run for 10 seconds.
            With GREEN pilot on—fan running;

        b)   Turn the sensitivity adjustor screw (using a coin) counterclockwise until it comes to a stop.

        c)   Reverse direction and turn sensitivity adjustor clockwise until RED indicator lamp comes on.

        d)   Turn the sensitivity adjustor in the counter-clockwise direction until the RED indicator lamp goes out.

    The Sensor is now at its most sensitive setting.

    Always adjust sensitivity shortly before use. If tempera-ture varies significantly between time or place of adjustment and time or place of use, the PAS device will not operate correctly.

TO USE THE PAS

    a) Push "On" button. Start fan five seconds before use.

    b) Hold the PAS sensor 4" to 6" in front of the person's mouth.

    c) If RED indicator comes on, withdraw sensor but keep fan operating until RED light goes off.

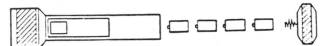

[D7648]

About the accuracy of the PASD and its sensitivity to alcohol in general and consumable (ethyl) alcohol in particular, Voas explains:

A great part of the value of the PAS device is that it is simple, easy and rapid to use and because it is not designed to make precise measurements for use in court, and therefore does not have to have extremely high accuracy. Its purpose is simply to take the first step towards the apprehension of a drunk driver. It provides evidence that the suspect *has been drinking heavily* (e.g., BAC greater than 0.05%). Even though the results of the PAS test would not be presented in court as evidence that the individual was impaired by alcohol, the use of the test would come up in the testimony of the police officer. When the police officer states that he relied upon the PAS detector for the initial evidence that the individual "had been drinking" the defense will undoubtedly challenge the accuracy of the PAS device. This accuracy is dependent upon two factors: First, the sensitivity to the detection of ethanol in the driver's breath and second, the extent to which the PAS detector reacts to other substances than alcohol . . .

The principal limitation in the sensitivity of a passive detector is the mixing of external air with the expired breath of the suspect. The active tester avoids this by having the individual blow directly into the device so that there is no mixing with outside air. Mixing is reduced in the passive operation by bringing the device closer to the face of the subject. The mixing of the expired air with the external air means that a passive device will always be less accurate than the active device given that the sensor elements themselves are equally sensitive. The mixing of the expired air with the outside air will be increased if there is a strong wind or a breeze. Therefore, a measurement taken outdoors in a wind or inside in the draft of a fan, air conditioner or heating unit will be less accurate than one taken in still air. A third factor which will affect the sensitivity is the external air temperature. Where the air is cold the temperature of the mixture of environmental with expired air will lower the sample temperature, and the PAS device will be less sensitive to alcohol.

The important feature of all of the sensitivity issues that arise with regard to the passive detector are that they operate in the favor of the suspect since they will tend to result in a failure to detect alcohol where it is actually present. Such a failure to detect alcohol where it is actually present is classified as a *"false negative"* result in contrast to the situation in which a positive reading is obtained when no drinking has occurred. . . .

Because the expired air from the subject is mixed with the environmental air it is possible for the substances which set off the sensor light to be from the environment rather than from the subject himself. Potential contaminants include gasoline or carbon monoxide leaks from the automobile exhaust system into the driving compartment and open bottles of alcohol and/or heavy drinking passengers in the vehicle. To check for this possibility, the officer should ask the driver who has just given a positive PAS test result to step out of the car. The officer should then place the PAS tester at about the position formerly occupied by the driver's head and take a second sample of the vehicle air. If the PAS tester lights again, then there is evidence that the vehicle environment contains a contaminate to which the sensor reacts. If this is the case, the police officer should immediately retest the driver himself outside the car to determine whether he still provides a positive result ...

A remote but possible contaminate to be eliminated is the presence of perfume, aftershave or hair oil containing alcohol which might be producing the PAS result. To determine that this is not the case, the officer should request the driver to turn his head and look over his shoulder while the officer operates the PAS close to the cheek and hair. If the sensor is picking up aftershave lotion or hair oil then the sensor reading should be positive. However, if the positive result was from the expired breath, a negative reading should appear because the PAS detector will not be in the line with the expired air. Thus, the fact that the passive alcohol sensor can make repeated tests quickly and easily can be used to prove the validity of the sensor and avoid the problems associated with environmental contaminants.[5]

§ 3.08 Standards of Intoxication

The District of Columbia and all of the states have statutes providing for chemical tests for intoxication in traffic related incidents. Moreover, the states must conform to federal testing standards or run the risk of loss of federal funds for highway construction.[1]

In most chemical test statutes the following presumptions are prescribed:

1. A subject whose blood alcohol content was less than 0.05% was presumed not to be under the influence of alcohol.

2. Where the alcohol content was in excess of 0.05% but less than 0.10%, there was no presumption either way.

---

5. Voas, *Reports on Passive Sensing Research*, Report No. 4 (National Public Services Research Institute, Alexandria, Va., 1983).

§ 3.08

1. In the Commercial Motor Vehicle Safety Act of 1986, 49 App. U.S.C.A. § 2707(f)(4) (Supp.1994), the Dept. of Transportation seeks to lower the blood-alcohol content level at which commercial drivers are deemed to be intoxicated from .10% to as low as .04%. Congress, in § 2708(a)(3), then requires the states to adopt the level set pursuant to § 2707(f)(4). After September 30, 1992, § 2710(a) permits the federal government to withhold 5% of the state's federal highway funds for fiscal 1993 for a non-complying state, with withholding increased to 10% for subsequent years. If a state has funds withheld for failing to comply with this legislation after September 30, 1995, these funds will become permanently unavailable to the offending state. 49 App. U.S.C.A. § 2710(c)(1)(B) (Supp.1994).

3. A level of 0.10% or higher gave rise to a presumption of being under the influence.

Experiments within the past several years have shown, however, that a person's driving ability may be significantly impaired by a lesser concentration than the 0.10% previously adopted. According to a 1971 report of the committee on Alcohol and Drugs of the National Safety Council, where there is an 0.10% blood alcohol concentration in the driver of a vehicle his relative risk of being involved in an accident increased by a factor of about 6. In recognition of such a risk, some states have settled upon a presumption of influence at 0.08%, and the *Uniform Vehicle Code* (UVC), which is a model for most states, adopted the 0.08% presumption. The UVC presumptions are as follows:

Upon the trial of any civil or criminal action or proceeding arising out of acts alleged to have been committed by any person while driving or in actual physical control of a vehicle while under the influence of alcohol, the concentration of alcohol in the person's blood or breath at the time alleged as shown by analysis of the person's blood, urine, breath, or other bodily substance shall give rise to the following presumptions:

1. If there was at that time an alcohol concentration of 0.05% or less, it shall be presumed that the person was not under the influence of alcohol.

2. If there was at that time an alcohol concentration in excess of 0.05% but less than 0.08% such fact shall not give rise to any presumption that the person was or was not under the influence of alcohol, but such fact may be considered with other competent evidence in determining whether the person was under the influence of alcohol.

3. If there was at that time an alcohol concentration of 0.08% or more, it shall be presumed that the person was under the influence of alcohol.[2]

The UVC has also developed a statute, making it illegal "per se" for a person to drive or be in actual physical control of a motor vehicle while "... [t]he alcohol concentration in his blood or breath is 0.08% or more ..."[3] While most states that have followed the UVC model of enacting "illegal per se" statutes initially used a standard of 0.10%, more and more now follow the 0.08% standard adopted by the UVC in 1984.

Once again the authors want to make clear that the amount of alcohol within a person's system at the time of the test is not by itself proof of what the content was at the time of an occurrence prior thereto. This does not render test results irrelevant, of course. Moreover, some experts are willing to express an opinion based upon a retrograde extrapolation *provided* they are permitted to clarify their opinions with

---

2. *Uniform Vehicle Code and Model Traffic Ordinance*, Sec. 11–902.1(b), Supplement IV (1984).

3. *Uniform Vehicle Code and Model Traffic Ordinance*, Sec. 11–902(a)(1), Supplement IV (1984).

an explanation of certain relevant factors. One of them is that there must be an assumption that at the time of the test all of the consumed alcohol has been absorbed. For this purpose it is necessary to know when the drinking started and the past absorptive interval of time. Also, the fact finder (judge or jury) should be advised that individuals vary as to their rates of absorption or their tolerance of alcohol; in some it is intrinsically greater than the "mean," whereas in others it is less. Once these and certain other qualifications are attached to the opinion founded upon the extrapolation, the risk of error on the part of the fact finder may be considerably diminished. Moreover, rather than merely permit judges or juries to hear testimony as to the alcohol within a person's system at the time of a test and leave it up to them to draw their own inferences as to what it may have been at the time of an occurrence, it seems preferable to have the expert testimony reveal the assumptions required for retrograde extrapolations.

The courts have not been sympathetic to our suggestion that evidence of extrapolation be used. The majority of jurisdictions provide that, in drunken driving prosecutions, where the defendant has submitted to a blood, breath or urine test, there is no need for the prosecution to "relate back" the resulting BAC percentage to the time of driving, at least not when the test has been administered within a reasonable time after the defendant was either stopped or arrested. Thus, in Miller v. State,[4] the testing, which occurred one hour and twenty minutes after the stop, revealed a BAC of .14%. Since defendant refused to tell police when he had his last drink, the state's toxicologist admitted it was impossible to determine with reasonable certainty the blood-alcohol level at the time defendant was driving, and admitted that "it was scientifically possible the blood-alcohol level was below the legal limit of 0.10% at the time defendant was driving." The Florida Supreme Court decided to follow what it found to be the "weight of authority" and held that the prosecution need not present evidence relating back the BAC at testing to the BAC at the time defendant was driving. The inability to "relate back" is only a question of credibility of the evidence, and is not a bar to admissibility.[5] One state even barred the defendant from presenting extrapolation evidence to show that the defendant's BAC at the time of

4. Miller v. State, 597 So.2d 767 (Fla. 1991) [Breathalyzer test].

5. Id. at 770. Accord, e.g.: State v. Lusi, 625 A.2d 1350 (R.I.1993); Ransford v. District of Columbia, 583 A.2d 186 (D.C.App.1990); State v. Kubik, 235 Neb. 612, 456 N.W.2d 487 (1990) [Intoxilyzer Model 4011AS breath test reading of .139]—state is not required to demonstrate conclusive nexus between test result and BAC at time of driving, though when the delay is substantial, the test results may become nonprobative of the accused's impairment or BAC while driving; State v.

Taylor, 132 N.H. 314, 566 A.2d 172 (1989) [Intoximeter test showed BAC level of .13 after mandatory 20 minute waiting period following arrest]; Livingston v. State, 537 N.E.2d 75 (Ind.App.1989) [Intoxilyzer result of .13 29 minutes after driving]; Commonwealth v. Speights, 353 Pa.Super. 258, 509 A.2d 1263 (1986), appeal denied 517 Pa. 594, 535 A.2d 83 (1987) [Breathalyzer test result of .12 obtained 2 hours 45 minutes after driving]; People v. Kappas, 120 Ill. App.3d 123, 76 Ill.Dec. 1, 458 N.E.2d 140 (1983) [Breathalyzer test showing .11, given 38 minutes after arrest].

driving was only .07%.[6]

Not all courts agree on this issue. In Desmond v. Superior Court,[7] the Supreme Court of Arizona held that the state's inability to relate back defendant's BAC at the time of testing rendered inadmissible the numerical test result at the time of testing. The court would permit evidence showing that at the time of testing the defendant tested positive for alcohol, provided the jury was also told that such evidence was admitted for the limited purpose of showing that the defendant had alcohol in the blood at the time of the test, and that such evidence standing alone is not sufficient to show either that the defendant was impaired or had an unlawful BAC level at the time the car was being driven.[8]

As a result of the difficulties in providing the nexus between the BAC at testing and the BAC while driving, the legislative trend has been to change the statutes to read that possession of a BAC level above the stated level shall be unlawful, thus obviating the need for relation-back opinion evidence.

The foregoing statutory presumptions, it is important to note, are limited to cases involving charges of driving while under the influence of alcohol (or intoxicated). As will be subsequently discussed (in § 3.13), they do not apply in cases where, for instance, a determination is to be made whether a person was or was not intoxicated at the time of a murder, or at the time a confession was made to a crime, etc. In such instances, of course, an expert witness may consider chemical test results in arriving at an opinion of intoxication or non-intoxication; the only restriction is the inapplicability of *the presumptions* specified in the motor vehicle statutes.

As noted, in an effort to obviate some of the difficulties encountered by the presumption statutes, most states have enacted laws based on the UVC model which simply make it an "absolute" or "per se" offense to drive a motor vehicle when the driver's blood alcohol content is at a certain concentration, for example 0.10 percent or over. In other words, proof of impairment of driving ability is not required under such statutes.

---

6. State v. Tischio, 107 N.J. 504, 527 A.2d 388 (1987) [Breathalyzer test result of .11%. Defense expert testified defendant's BAC when driving was .07%. Court concluded that "interpretation of the statute which would permit extrapolation evidence would frustrate and impede" the strong and consistent legislative revisions designed to make it easier to convict in drunken driving cases. Dissenting opinion would admit extrapolation evidence in close cases, as this one certainly was].

7. 161 Ariz. 522, 779 P.2d 1261 (1989).

8. Since the decision was handed down, the legislature changed the definition of the crime to ".10 or more within two hours of

driving or being in actual physical control of the vehicle." Ariz. R.S. § 28–692(B) (Supp.1990). Prior to this change, the question arose whether the BAC percentage could be testified to if, as *Desmond* requires, the state presented relating-back opinion evidence? In State ex rel. McDougall v. Albrecht, 168 Ariz. 128, 811 P.2d 791 (App.1991), the court said: No! But, in State ex rel. Romley v. Brown, 168 Ariz. 481, 815 P.2d 408 (App.1991), the same court, in a case of first impression, held that the *Desmond* restriction does not require a prosecutor to relate back a defendant's BAC in a prosecution for reckless manslaughter, nor does it prohibit the state from proving the actual BAS test result.

§ 3.09 Sources of Error in Chemical Tests Themselves

Apart from some of the weaknesses alluded to earlier, there are a number of disruptive influences which may cause the results of the chemical tests for intoxication to be misleading. In blood removal, if the solution used to disinfect the syringe or the skin area of blood removal contains alcohol (iodine, ether, disinfecting alcohol, or carbolic acid) the sample may be mildly contaminated to indicate a deceptively high alcohol content, or, at least, defense counsel may be able to lead a jury to such a belief. A blood sample taken as a result of a postmortem examination, while otherwise just as viable for analytical purposes as blood taken from a living person, is rendered useless if the body has been previously embalmed. The formaldehyde will react to show a false positive for alcohol. Laboratory instruments, or the containers used to transport the specimen, may be contaminated with foreign substances. Some labs may even clean and dry their glassware with ether, alcohol or acetone. If distillation (boiling off alcohol) is used to qualitatively remove alcohol from the test specimen, foaming may occur, with consequent entrapment of impurities into the distillate which may be falsely calculated as alcohol.

Leaving the flask containing a urine or blood specimen exposed to air containing dust and vapors of oxidizable organic materials in the lab or at the time it was taken can cause an increase in the apparent alcohol. Exposure to air for a sufficient period of time for putrefaction to occur can result in formation of organic material falsely attributable to alcohol. In the absence of preservatives (sodium fluoride or mercuric chloride) added to the sample, putrefaction begins in a matter of hours. Conversely, a sample that is exposed to the air for an hour or so may give a falsely low test result due to the volatile alcohol evaporating. But even when various preservatives are added, alcohol does not remain in the blood sample indefinitely, and it may fluctuate.[1]

In order to determine the percentage of alcohol in a sample, the dichromate oxidation method of determining alcohol content of blood or urine measures the unconsumed amount of dichromate or the chromic sulfate formed when alcohol is present in the test system, as compared to when it is not. When the dichromate oxidation method of quantitative analysis is used to determine the percentage of alcohol in the sample, another possible error arises. The sulfuric acid reagent used with the dichromate as an ingredient in the test, if left exposed to the air for 24 hours, or if exposed to prolonged sunlight or heat, may oxidize the dichromate and cause a reduction in the dichromate remaining or the chromic sulfate formed, either of which could be falsely attributable to the presence of alcohol.

§ 3.09

1. See, e.g.: Glendening & Waugh, "The Stability of Ordinary Blood Alcohol Samples Held Various Periods of Time Under Different Conditions," 10 *J.For.Sci.* 192 (1965); Bradford, "Preservation of Blood Samples Containing Alcohol," 11 *J.For.Sci.* 214 (1966).

Ketones present in the blood and urine of severe diabetics may be wrongly associated with high alcohol values if the test does not have a safeguard to winnow out these misleading substances. (This extraneous factor will not, however, produce any false positives in breath testing.)

In any testing of blood or urine specimens there should be two tests made at spaced intervals. The omission to do so makes it possible for an accused person to contend that sobriety at the time of the event in question was possible even though a subsequent single test might show a high alcohol blood (or urine) content at the time of the test. Moreover, if a person had consumed an inordinate amount of alcohol very soon before his detention or arrest, it is entirely possible that its presence or quantity might not have been revealed by a test administered shortly thereafter. On the other hand, if a second specimen is obtained sometime later, the blood alcohol may have reached a certain percentage to indicate intoxication.

Breath tests which utilize potassium permanganate as a chemical reagent are potentially misleading if this reagent is not fresh. It is very unstable and will decompose to form brown manganic oxide, which acts as an accelerating catalyst for increased decomposition; hence, more color change and a false apparent increase in breath alcohol. The chemical decomposes when exposed to organic compounds, dust, lint or an acid medium.

To argue that there be a showing that the chemicals, simulator solutions, and ampoules be shown to be of proper quality is not an exercise in excess zeal, as the experience of the late 1980s with one manufacturer of law enforcement supplies proves. The prime manufacturer of simulator solutions and ampoules for law enforcement agencies in Michigan, New York, Oklahoma, Pennsylvania, South Carolina, and Virginia was a company called Systems Innovation, Inc. (SII). A worker dismissed from SII after participating in the production for 14 months revealed to the Auditor General of Pennsylvania in 1987 that manufacturing conditions at his former employer's "plant" were anything but according to scientifically accepted practices. Mixing sulfuric acid solutions was done in 5-gallon jugs from which about 5000 ampoules could be filled; the same batch numbers were assigned to solutions mixed in different 5-gallon jugs. As many of 35 to 40 different batches resulting from different mixings would receive the same lot number before being shipped to law enforcement agencies all over the country. During the ensuing ten-month investigation by the Auditor General of Pennsylvania, it was discovered, inter alia, that the "plant" where SII manufactured its law enforcement supplies was located in the back room of a Radio Shack store in Hallstead, Pennsylvania.[2]

> "The manufacturer was found to be preparing the simulator solution from alcohol purchased from a local liquor store which was then mixed with filtered city water, instead of using pure, absolute ethyl

2. Much of the background of this investigation was restated in Commonwealth v. Brosnick, 530 Pa. 158, 607 A.2d 725 (1992) and in the cases cited in footnote 5, infra.

alcohol. There were no written instructions given to employees concerning the production of the solution, nor were there any notes for the employees concerning the contents of the solution.

"It was also discovered that the State Police received shipments of the solution in bottles without expiration dates and without content certification certificates from independent testing laboratories. All of these deficiencies in the certification process led the investigators to conclude that the accuracy of certificates of simulator solution was unreliable." [3]

The employee of SII who actually mixed the solutions lacked education, training, and prior experience as a chemist. The Auditor General found SII to be an unprofessional "laboratory" lacking adequate record-keeping and quality controls. The Pennsylvania Supreme Court saw the report as casting "a serious cloud of uncertainty upon the accuracy of the simulator solution and on the accuracy of the tests performed on the Breathalyzer machine," when that test result is the only evidence of intoxication.[4] It caused a number of courts in New York to reject breathalyzer results on the grounds that ampoules and simulator solutions were scientifically unreliable.[5]

Breath tests, too, are subject to errors not only due to faulty operator usage, but the instruments themselves need standardization procedures using equilibrator solutions. Furthermore, care must be taken to aerate a breathalyzer machine to remove moisture and any minimal traces of air from prior tests. It would even be advisable to make a test of room air to determine whether any pollutant in the air might affect the chemical reagents used. Quite frequently, even modern police departments omit these standardization and equilibration tests.

In addition to the advisability of two tests of either blood or urine at spaced intervals, two breath tests should be conducted at appropriate intervals as a safeguard against the false positive that may have been produced by such a simple occurrence as a "burp" on the part of the

---

3. Commonwealth v. Brosnick, 530 Pa. 158, 163, 607 A.2d 725, 728 (1992).

4. Id. at 165, 607 A.2d at 729.

5. In People v. Serrano, 142 Misc.2d 1087, 539 N.Y.S.2d 845 (Crim.Ct.1989), the court, *in limine,* found: that the New York Police Department ordered 5,000 ampoules at a time approximately every six months from SII for the past 3 years, and ordered simulator solutions in quantities of 50 to 100 bottles every few months "because of its relatively short life"; that a 55–gallon drum which was used for the simulator solution was also used to make coffee and kool-aid and to draw drinking water; after recounting numerous instances of sloppy lab work, the court concluded that the results of the breathalyzer tests were inadmissible. In People v. Ruiz, et al., 146 Misc.2d 825, 552 N.Y.S.2d 496 (Crim.Ct. 1990), motions to suppress in eight consolidated cases were granted, the judge asking, rhetorically, "Why then should the Courts relax and revise traditional evidentiary standards for the admission of Breathalyzer results simply to accommodate a sloppy and deceitful manufacturer and a state prosecutor who, in my judgment, has failed to investigate adequately SII's operation after so much time has elapsed since these problems were exposed?". Based on similar records, the reviewing court in People v. Uruburu, 169 A.D.2d 20, 571 N.Y.S.2d 965 (1991), and in People v. Colon, 180 A.D.2d 876, 580 N.Y.S.2d 95 (1992), reversed convictions because of the erroneous admission of breath test results, and upheld the suppression of breath test results in People v. Sperber, 177 A.D.2d 725, 577 N.Y.S.2d 94 (1991).

subject at the time of the first test. Such an expulsion of "stomach gas" could result in a showing in a breath test of a higher alcoholic reading than is warranted by the actual fact regarding blood alcohol ("alveolar" air) content.

Another problem with breath tests that has surfaced is the susceptibility of such test to radio frequency interference (RFI), particularly, though not exclusively,[6] the Breathalyzer instrument. The effect of RFI is described by the Supreme Court of New Jersey in Romano v. Kimmelman:[7]

> [R]adio frequency interference (sometimes designated herein as "rfi") describes the effect on an electronic instrument of a radio wave or current that it is not designed to pick up. If a particular breathalyzer, as an electronic instrument, were susceptible to rfi, then the measurement of the light distance obtained when the operator balances the meter might not be an accurate indication of the amount of alcohol in the breath sample. Instead, the light distance might reflect, in part, a deflection in the meter needle caused by a stray current induced by radio waves in the surrounding environment.
>
> In order for radio frequency interference to affect a susceptible breathalyzer instrument in a way that would lead to an erroneous reading, certain conditions must occur. The coalescence of these conditions has been referred to as the "window of susceptibility." First, because each instrument exhibits different degrees of susceptibility to rfi, the radio frequency source would have to be transmitting at a frequency to which the particular instrument was sensitive. Second, this source would have to be powerful enough to affect the instrument. Third, the proximity and direction of the breathalyzer in relation to the source of radio frequency transmission would have to allow radio frequency energies of sufficient strength to affect the instrument. Fourth, such radio frequency transmission would have to be present while the meter and light are activated in order for it to affect the instrument. (The activation of the meter and light occurs only when the operator balances the machine, which balancing is done twice during each test for a period of about ten seconds.) A final condition is that the needle fluctuation caused by the interference would have to be imperceptible to the operator.

Despite the fact that the maker of the instruments had recalled its Models 900, 900A, and 1,000,[8] the New Jersey court however, did not consider the RFI problem to be sufficiently serious to warrant barring the use of test results in court. The *Romano* court ruled that models 900 and 900A of the Breathalyzer are scientifically reliable for purposes of determining BAC, with a narrow qualification as to admissibility of

6. Freed, Radio Frequency Interference with the Model 1000SA Alco–Analyzer Gas Chromatograph, 28 *J.Forensic Sci.* 985 (1983).

7. 96 N.J. 66, 474 A.2d 1, 10 (1984).

8. See, "Breathalyzer Recall," Trial, June 1983, pp. 62–63.

test results because of the possible effects of RFI. The results of the 900 model can be received in evidence without further proof establishing any additional conditions for admissibility relating to RFI, if hand-held transmitters were banned from the area in proximity to the Breathalyzer at the time of its use. The results of the 900A model can also be received in evidence if the test consists of two readings within a tolerance of 0.10 percent of each other, or the instrument has been found not to be RFI-sensitive, or, if sensitive, it is shown that in the administration of the instrument it was protected from transmitters and radio frequency.[9]

Following the lead of *Romano,* the Supreme Judicial Court of Massachusetts has ruled that the admissibility of test results obtained from a Model 900A for determining the blood-alcohol concentration of a drunk driving suspect is contingent on presentation by the prosecution of an adequate foundation establishing that the instrument was not so susceptible to RFI as to create a significant risk that the result was inaccurate. The recommended procedure to establish a foundation is to conduct a second corroborative test of the driver's breath after a correct simulator reading, although a second test is not required. At a minimum, the prosecution should be prepared to demonstrate that RFI testing procedures recommended by the manufacturer in a customers' advisory have been followed. These procedures consist of two testing programs, one designed to measure susceptibility to RFI and the other to check the effects of radio frequencies transmitted by environmental sources at the police department.[10] Thus, although the potential for RFI induced error exists, it would appear that adequate preventive measures can be taken, and are now being taken by manufacturers to minimize the danger of inaccurate test results due to RFI.[11]

§ 3.10　Horizontal Gaze Nystagmus Test

The horizontal gaze nystagmus test, referred to alternatively as HGN, alcohol gaze nystagmus, lateral nystagmus, or, simply, Nystagmus, is not truly a scientific test in that it does not measure the level of intoxication, but may give an indication that intoxication may be what caused the observed phenomenon in a defendant. That certain types of nystagmus can be caused by alcohol intoxication is not a new concept. Early medical research observed the correlation between intoxication

---

9. 474 A.2d at 10–12.

10. Commonwealth v. Neal, 392 Mass. 1, 464 N.E.2d 1356 (1984). A Canadian RCMP test for susceptibility to RFI of Breathalyzer Models 900 and 900A found Model 900 to be unaffected, but Model 900A to be affected by transmissions from transceivers positioned in close proximity to the instruments, but believed the risks of inaccurate readings to be, for practical purposes, nonexistent. See, Samija, Shajani & Wong, "Radio Frequency Interference (RFI) Effects on Evidentiary Breath Testing Using the Breathalyzer Models 900 and 900A," 18 *J.Canadian Soc.For.Sci.* 211 (1985).

11. For example, according to the present manufacturer of the Breathalyzer, Model 900A, National Draeger, Inc., of Pittsburg, Pa., the device is now built with a protective shield that prevents RFI from affecting it. The BAC Verifier illustrated and described at Figure 5, supra, has instrumentation indicating RFI presence, and will not give a BAC reading if RFI is present.

and lateral nystagmus.[1] The test was first popularized by law enforcement in California in the 1960s, and rapidly spread nationally as an adjunct to other physical coordination and sobriety tests. HGN is now used in all 50 states. Ordinarily, the HGN test is used to establish probable cause for an arrest of a suspected drunk driver, but prosecutors have attempted to use it as evidence of intoxication as well, as will be seen herein.

HGN is based on the observation of three different physical manifestations which occur when a person is under the influence of alcohol: (1) the inability of a person to follow, visually, in a smooth way, an object that is moved laterally in front of the person's eyes; (2) the inability to retain focus and the likelihood of jerking of the eyeball when a person has moved his or her eye to the extreme range of peripheral vision; and (3) the reported observation that this "jerking" of the eyeball begins before the eye has moved 45 degrees from forward gaze if the individual's BAC is .10% or higher.[2] If HGN is a reliable technique, it would be very important in DUI cases, since HGN is said to appear only when the BAC of the subject is over a certain threshold, and disappears when there no longer is alcohol in the blood.[3]

Nystagmus, a physiological phenomenon, thus, is a term used to describe the "involuntary rapid oscillation of the eyeballs in a horizontal, vertical, or rotary direction,"[4] and the inability of the individual to maintain visual fixation on an object as the eyes turn from side to side or move from center focus to the point of maximum deviation at the side while attempting to observe the object as it is slowly moved from side to side.[5] This phenomenon is described as a motor disorder, which may be "congenital or due to a variety of conditions affecting the brain, including ingestion of drugs such as alcohol, barbiturates, palsy of lateral or vertical gaze, disorders of the vestibular apparatus and brainstem and cerebellar dysfunction,"[6] which motor disorder is characterized by a

§ 3.10

1. See, e.g., Ashan, et al., "Positional Nystagmus in Man During and After Alcohol Intoxication," 17 *Q.J. Studies on Alcohol* 381 (1956); Howells, "Nystagmus as a Physical Sign in Alcoholic Intoxication," 6 Brit.Med.J. 1405 (June 16, 1956); Goding & Dobie, "Gaze Nystagmus and Blood Alcohol," 96 *Laryngoscope* 713 (1986). For the types of nystagmus documented in medical literature, and their causes, see, Tharp, Burns & Moskowitz, Development and Field Test of Psychophysical Tests for DWI Arrest, at 79, U.S. Dept. of Transportation, DOT HS–805–864 (March 1981); McClintic, Basic Anatomy and Physiology of the Human Body, at 309 (1975); Goldberg, "Behavioral and Physiological Effects of Alcohol on Man," 28 *Psychosomatic Med.* 570 (1966).

2. U.S. Dept. of Transportation, *DWI Detection and Standardized Field Sobriety Testing: Student Manual,* page VIII–3 (March 1990) [hereinafter *Student Manual*].

3. Goldberg, op. cit. supra note 1 at 581.

4. 3, Schmidt's Attorneys Dictionary of Medicine, N–102 (1991); Stedman's Medical Dictionary 1074 (25th ed. 1990); *The Merck Manual of Diagnosis and Therapy,* 1359 (15th ed. 1987).

5. State v. Garrett, 119 Idaho 878, 881, 811 P.2d 488, 491 (1991); People v. Buening, 229 Ill.App.3d 538 (1992); " 'Jittery' Eyes Give Away Drunk Driving," *American Optometric Association News,* Mar. 1, 1986.

6. People v. Buening, supra note 5 at 539, quoting from *The Merck Manual of Diagnosis and Therapy* 1980 (14th ed. 1982). In State v. Witte, 251 Kan. 313, 328, 836 P.2d 1110, 1119 (1992), the court noted the many conditions other than alco-

slow drift, usually away from the direction of gaze, followed by a quick, involuntary jerking of the eyeball back in the direction of the gaze.

The HGN test as it is routinely performed by law enforcement personnel for the detection of intoxication, requires a suspected drunken driver to cover one eye and focus the other on an object such as a finger or pen held approximately twelve to fifteen inches from the subject's face. The subject is then asked to keep the head facing straight ahead, while following with the uncovered eye the object as it is moved laterally along a horizontal plane to the periphery of the subject's vision. If the subject is wearing contact lenses, it has been suggested they first be removed since they could impede lateral movement of the eyeball, though some texts suggest that while the presence of contact lenses should be documented for the court, their removal is not necessary and does not significantly interfere with the test.[7] If the test is administered at night, the subject's eye movement will be observed by shining a flashlight in the face. As the officer administers this first part of the test, called "smooth pursuit," if the subject's eyeball jerks involuntarily and fails to follow the object smoothly, a first clue of intoxication has been observed.

While the officer holds the object at the extreme left or right of the subject's peripheral vision for a short period of time, an intoxicated person will also have a distinct, and involuntary, jerking of the eye. This is a second indicator of intoxication. And finally, the officer observes at what point in the movement of the object away from straight ahead the jerking commences. This third stage seeks to measure the degree from center at which the jerking first occurs, to derive therefrom an approximation of the level of the subject's BAC.[8] Three separate tests are ordinarily conducted to seek confirmation of data obtained during prior attempts.

The National Highway Traffic Safety Administration (NHTSA) conducted a field study in 1983 to evaluate the effectiveness and accuracy of three different sobriety tests it had previously developed: the one-leg-stand test, the walk and turn test, and the horizontal gaze nystagmus test. In the study, officers were given one day of training and were thereafter required to administer all the standard sobriety tests over a three-month period prior to administering preliminary breath test devices. The research data suggested that HGN was the most powerful of

hol consumption that may cause nystagmus.

7. *Student Manual,* supra note 2, at VIII–4.

8. See, Thorp, "Gaze Nystagmus As a Roadside Sobriety Test," Alcohol Gaze Nystagmus Fact Sheet, California Highway Patrol (1984). The Fact Sheet asserts that by estimating the angle of onset, an officer can estimate the BAC to within ± .02%, and that the test is 96% effective. It further states that the relationship of the angle of onset to BAC is as follows:

1. 40 degrees = .10%
2. 35 degrees = .15%
3. 30 degrees = .20%

But see, Lehti, "The Effect of Blood Alcohol Concentration on the Onset of Gaze Nystagmus," 13 Blutalkohol 411 (1976), stating that with a BAC of .10%, HGN would occur at about 51 degrees, while with a BAC of .20%, gaze nystagmus would occur at about 29 degrees.

the three if only one test was being used, but the combination of all three presented the best opportunity for discriminating between subjects whose BAC was above or below .10%.[9]

§ 3.11　Legal Literature and Court Decisions on HGN

The legal writings have alerted attorneys to the HGN test's weaknesses.[1] In State v. Witte,[2] the court said that in addition to intoxication, nystagmus can be caused by many other factors:

> " 'Nystagmus can be caused by problems in an individual's inner ear labyrinth. In fact, irrigating the ears with warm or cold water ... is a source of error. Physiological problems such as certain kinds of diseases may also result in gaze nystagmus. Influenza, streptococcus infections, vertigo, measles, syphilis, arteriosclerosis, muscular dystrophy, multiple sclerosis, Korsakoff's Syndrome, brain hemorrhage, epilepsy, and other psychogenic disorders all have been shown to cause nystagmus. Furthermore, conditions such as hypertension, motion sickness, sunstroke, eyestrain, eye muscle fatigue, glaucoma, and changes in atmospheric pressure may result in gaze nystagmus. The consumption of common substances such as caffeine, nicotine, or aspirin also lead to nystagmus almost identical to that caused by alcohol consumption.' "[3]

The procedures for conducting the test have also come under criticism, especially those that seek to determine the degree of intoxication based on the angle at which the onset of nystagmus is first observed. Since, like the California Highway Patrol Fact Sheet,[4] the NHTSA 1981 study[5] declares that the expected angle of onset for a BAC of .10% is 40.2 degrees for the right eye and 40.1 degrees for the left eye, and that

9. Anderson, Schweith & Snyder, Field Evaluation of a Behavioral Test Battery for DWI. U.S. Dept. of Transportation, DOT HS–806–475, Sep. 1983. As a result of this study, NHTSA recommends the use of all three tests. See *Student Manual*, supra Note 2, in Part VIII. See also the testimony of Dr. Marcelline Burns who conducted two large-scale NHTSA studies, in State v. Hill, 865 S.W.2d 702 (Mo.App.1993).

§ 3.11

1. E.g., Tarantino, Defending Drunk Drivers (2d. ed. 1990); Busloff, "Can Your Eyes Be Used Against You? The Use of the Horizontal Gaze Nystagmus Test in the Courtroom," 84 *J.Crim.L. & Criminology* 203 (1993); Erwin, Defense of Drunk Driving Cases, (3rd ed. 1985); Pangman, "Horizontal Gaze Nystagmus: Voodoo Science," 2 DWI J. 1, 3–4 (1987); Rouleau, "Unreliability of the Horizontal Gaze Nystagmus Test," 4 *Am.Jur Proof of Facts* 3d 439 (1989); Cowan & Jaffe, "Proof and Disproof of Alcohol–Induced Driving Impairment Through Evidence of Observable Intoxication and Coordination Testing," 9 *Am.Jur. Proof of Facts* 3d 459 (1990); Halperin & Yolton, "Is the Driver Drunk? Ocularmotor Sobriety Testing," 57 *J.Am.Optometric A.* 654, 657 (1986); 1 Erwin, Defense of Drunk Driving Cases §§ 8A:06, 8A:08 (3d ed. 1992); 2 Nichols, Drinking/Driving Litigation § 26.01 (1992 Supp.).

2. 251 Kan. 313, 326, 836 P.2d 1110, 1119 (1992).

3. Quoting from Pangman, op. cit. supra note 1.

4. See, Thorp, op. cit. supra note 8, section 3.10.

5. See, Tharp, Burns & Moskowitz, op. cit. supra note 1, section 3.10; See also, "Improved Sobriety Testing," National Highway Traffic Safety Administration, DOT–HS–806–512, (1984 NHTSA Study).

"A score of six points is possible, three for each eye. According to NHTSA, if a driver scores four or more points, the driver's BAC is above .10." State v. Witte, Supra note 2 at 317, 836 P.2d at 1113.

if nystagmus is observed at a 45–degree angle, a BAC of .10% can be estimated correctly 78 percent of the time, it also follows that "22 percent of the time it is wrong."[6] Pangman observes, however, according to one authority, 50–60 percent of sober individuals will exhibit horizontal gaze nystagmus when moving their eyes more than 40 degrees to one side that cannot be distinguished from alcohol gaze nystagmus, and according to a different authority individuals with a BAC reading of .10% do not exhibit nystagmus until the eye is deviated from center to a 51–degree angle.[7]

When a prosecution-oriented California group conducted its own research on the correlation between highly trained police officers' estimation of BAC based on nystagmus and the BAC measured by chemical testing of the blood (which analysis was done by a different technician), it found there was virtually no correlation, though it found there was a correlation between breath testing conducted by the officers themselves and estimates based on the onset of nystagmus. The study concluded that this discrepancy was caused by the very subjective nature of the nystagmus test, and by the fact that the same officers who already knew the breath test BAC reading were influenced by it in determining the angle of onset of nystagmus.[8]

A further criticism of HGN is that the nystagmus can be caused by drugs other than alcohol. Where this is suspected, the administration of a Preliminary Breath Test for alcohol, which will give an approximate BAC reading, can detect whether nystagmus was caused by alcohol or by some other condition. If probable cause for an arrest exists, the suspect may be required to undergo a blood test at the police station to determine the category of drug(s) that causes the nystagmus.

Faced with the issue of admitting or denying admission of the results of HGN tests, the courts have taken a variety of approaches. . The clear majority of courts have held that HGN was a form of scientific evidence that needed to meet the *Frye* test of general acceptance,[9] and

---

6. State v. Witte, supra note 2 at 326, 826 P.2d at 1119.

7. Op. cit. supra note 1 at 2. In this regard, the *Witte* decision, supra note 2, quoted: "An individual's circadian rhythms (biorhythms) can affect nystagmus readings—the body reacts differently to alcohol at different times of the day. One researcher has suggested that because of this, the angle of onset should be decreased five degrees between midnight and 5 a.m. A number of driving under the influence arrests occur after midnight, which 'would seem to indicate that sensitivity of HGN to alcohol is enhanced during the hours of the day when the greatest number of drunk driving arrests occur.' " [Citations omitted.]

8. State v. Witte, supra note 2: "Simply put, the cops fudged the horizontal gaze

nystagmus determination to correspond with the already known correct answer determined by the breath test result." 251 Kan. at 329, 836 P.2d at 1120.

9. The "general acceptance" test of Frye v. United States, 293 Fed. 1013 (D.C.Cir.1923), once the mainstay of the courts for the admission of novel scientific evidence, was discussed extensively in Chapter 1, supra. The *Frye* test is now giving way to the recent test enunciated by the United States Supreme Court (under the Federal Rules of Evidence) in Daubert v. Merrell Dow Pharmaceuticals, 113 S.Ct. 2786 (1993), which focuses more on proof of "reliability" of the technique and places the onus of determining such reliability upon the "gatekeeper"—the trial judge.

Holding that HGN is "scientific evidence," see, Ex parte Malone, 575 So.2d

that the technique had not reached the stage where it was generally recognized as reliable.[10] By contrast, a few courts held that HGN has achieved general acceptance within the behavioral science community and test results are therefore admissible to prove intoxication.[11]

In State v. Superior Court,[12] the Arizona Supreme Court held that the administration of road-side, performance-based sobriety tests does not require probable cause. Furthermore, evidence which forms the basis for probable cause does not require the existence of reasonable suspicion. The court also held that HGN need not be tested under the *Frye* principle of "general acceptance," and held that HGN test results, when administered by a trained police officer, are sufficiently reliable to establish probable cause of DUI, and are also sufficiently reliable to "corroborate or attack, but not to quantify, the chemical analysis of the accused's blood alcohol content.[13] Thus, some courts have taken the approach to admit HGN test results for the limited purpose of generally indicating the presence of alcohol, but not to testify to a specific BAC as proven by chemical testing.[14] Assuming the test is properly conducted

106 (Ala.1990); State v. Superior Court, 149 Ariz. 269, 718 P.2d 171 (1986)—while citing extensive scientific data, no *Frye* hearing was said to be required; reaffirmed in State ex rel. Hamilton v. City Court, 165 Ariz. 514, 799 P.2d 855 (1990)—evidence admissible when test conducted by properly trained officer, but no correlation to specific BAC permitted; People v. Williams, 3 Cal. App.4th 1326, 5 Cal.Rptr.2d 130 (1992); State v. Garrett, 119 Idaho 878, 811 P.2d 488 (1991); State v. Witte, 251 Kan. 313, 836 P.2d 1110 (1992); State v. Armstrong, 561 So.2d 883 (La.App.1990), writ denied 568 So.2d 1077 (La.1990); State v. Wheeler, 764 S.W.2d 523 (Mo.App.1989); State v. Borchardt, 224 Neb. 47, 395 N.W.2d 551 (1986); People v. Torrey, 144 A.D.2d 865, 534 N.Y.S.2d 807 (1988); State v. Reed, 83 Or.App. 451, 732 P.2d 66 (1987); Commonwealth v. Apollo, 412 Pa.Super. 453, 603 A.2d 1023 (1992); Commonwealth v. Moore, 430 Pa.Super. 575, 635 A.2d 625 (1993); State v. Barker, 179 W.Va. 194, 366 S.E.2d 642 (1988).

10. People v. Leahy, 34 Cal.Rptr.2d 663, 882 P.2d 321 (1994)—*Frye* rule retained; HGN evidence not admissible until general scientific acceptance can be shown. One of the first cases was People v. Loomis, 156 Cal.App.3d Supp. 1, 203 Cal.Rptr. 767 (1984)—holding that California's equivalent of the *Frye* test was not met in that neither the reliability of HGN nor the qualifications of the testifying officer as an expert were established. In Commonwealth v. Moore, supra note 9, the officer testified that while HGN was accepted in the optometric and police science communities, ophthalmologists and medical people differed in their assessment of HGN reliability.

11. State v. Hill, 865 S.W.2d 702 (Mo. App.1993). See also, State v. Klawitter, 518 N.W.2d 577 (Minn.1994), holding that a determination that nystagmus test for drug use satisfied *Frye* standard for admission of scientific evidence was not clearly erroneous, though trial court should give appropriate cautionary instruction when requested.

12. 149 Ariz. 269, 718 P.2d 171 (1986). The record was replete with scientific and police expert testimony and contained extensive references to the medical and behavioral literature. See also, Lusk, "Horizontal Gaze Nystagmus," *Ariz.Bar J.*, p. 27 (Dec/Jan. 1988).

13. Id. at 280, 718 P.2d at 182. The court had held that *Frye*'s "general acceptance" was established, a conclusion with which commentators take issue. However, the holding was reaffirmed in State ex rel. Hamilton v. City Court, 165 Ariz. 514, 799 P.2d 855 (1990).

14. Whitson v. State, 314 Ark. 458, 863 S.W.2d 794 (1993); People v. Loomis, 156 Cal.App.3d Supp. 1, 203 Cal.Rptr. 767 (1984); State v. Murphy, 451 N.W.2d 154 (Iowa 1990); State v. Clark, 234 Mont. 222, 762 P.2d 853 (1988); Richardson v. State, 766 S.W.2d 538 (Tex.App.1989); Finley v. State, 809 S.W.2d 909 (Tex.App.1991). A conviction was reversed when the officer had testified that defendant's BAC was .15 or .16 based solely on HGN in Middleton v. State, 29 Ark.App. 83, 780 S.W.2d 581 (1989), even though the court did not consider HGN to be "novel scientific evidence" requiring a preliminary hearing for its admission. Proper training of police officer sufficient foundation to admit HGN evi-

by a well trained individual—questions which are not easily answered, this view represents perhaps the best compromise to the judicial use of HGN.

The approach which puts HGN in a "non-scientific evidence" category, for which therefore no expert testimony is required,[15] ignores the fact that the "testing" is done by a police officer who purports to be specially trained in administering this procedure for determining intoxication which is radically different from standard physical coordination tests. The witness, though not necessarily college trained, will nevertheless be considered an "expert"[16] whose testimony on the so-called physical testing will be in the form of opinion evidence of a type radically different from other "observations" during coordination tests for sobriety. In the view of the jury, the opinion of the witness is likely to carry some exaggerated notion of the accuracy of a technique called by the "pretentiously scientific name"[17] of horizontal gaze nystagmus. This is the more critical since precious little training[18] is required to become a skilled witness in the entirely subjective "measurement" of angles of onset of nystagmus—a process found to be unreliable by prosecution-friendly research.[19]

Even assuming that the onset of nystagmus has been correctly observed and the angle accurately measured—an assumption for which little support is to be found outside police-oriented texts,[20] the limited training of the operators, and the dispensing with true scientific expert testimony, severely restricts the ability of cross-examiners to explore the physiological bases for determining the reasons for nystagmus. Most trial lawyers have experienced that the less education and training a

dence as circumstantial evidence of intoxication only: Fargo v. McLaughlin, 512 N.W.2d 700 (N.D.1994).

15. See, State v. Bresson, 51 Ohio St.3d 123, 129, 554 N.E.2d 1330 (1990): "The HGN test cannot be compared to other scientific tests ... since no special equipment is required in its administration. Thus the only requirement prior to admission is the officer's knowledge of the test, his training, and his ability to interpret his observations. The admission of the results of the HGN test is no different from any other field sobriety test, such as finger-to-nose, walk-and-turn, or one-leg stand." Accord: State v. Edman, 452 N.W.2d 169, 170 (Iowa 1990): "Because the test may be easily administered and its results objectively recorded by a properly trained officer, it is unnecessary to establish a foundation for such evidence through scientific testimony." See also, Whitson v. State, supra note 14.

See also, People v. Sides, 199 Ill.App.3d 203, 145 Ill.Dec. 160, 556 N.E.2d 778 (1990) wherein the Fourth District Appellate Court held no *Frye* hearing was required to

admit HGN evidence. However, the Second District, in People v. Dakuras, 172 Ill. App.3d 865, 122 Ill.Dec. 791, 527 N.E.2d 163 (1988), held HGN evidence inadmissible on the ground that the statute authorized analysis only of "blood, urine, breath or other bodily substance," and noted that HGN test results, which fall not into any of these categories, "are derived from the subjective interpretation of the police officer administering the test."

16. Of the "skilled witness" type.

17. State v. Murphy, 451 N.W.2d 154, 156 (Iowa 1990).

18. According to the testimony of Dr. Marcelline Burns, a NHTSA validation expert, "At least eight hours of training on the use of the HGN test is recommended." See, State v. Hill, 865 S.W.2d 702, 704 (Mo.App.1993).

19. Supra, text at note 8.

20. The NHTSA instructs officers to "estimate" the 45–degree angle: State v. Witte, supra note 9 at 328, 836 P.2d at 1119.

"skilled witness" has, the more steadfast the witness is in advocating the reliability, if not near infallibility, of tests the witness has been told to perform. Assertions by such witnesses that nystagmus due to alcohol can be easily distinguished from nystagmus caused by other physiological or medical conditions will be the purest of hearsay based on nothing more than having read such a statement in a police training manual.

It is clear, therefore, that the approach taken by the majority of jurisdictions, which hold that "the horizontal gaze nystagmus test draws its convincing force from the supposed scientific principle that alcohol affects the smooth pursuit mechanism of the human eye." [21] and which classifies HGN as a scientific test for which the proper foundation must be laid by proof of reliability of the underlying premises, has much to commend itself.

II. EVIDENCE OF ALCOHOL INTOXICATION

§ 3.12 Legal Aspects of Chemical Tests

Before the advent of chemical testing technology the only means by which the prosecution could prove a violation of a statute making it a criminal offense to drive a motor vehicle upon a public road while "intoxicated", generally referred to as a DUI offense, was to produce the testimony of police officers or lay witnesses that the accused (a) behaved or looked like he was drunk (e.g., he staggered, he talked incoherently, he had blood shot eyes or a flushed face), and/or (b) had the "odor of alcohol" on his breath. Although we may conclude with a reasonable degree of certainty that in most instances the accused who exhibited these "symptoms" was actually intoxicated and in no condition to safely drive a vehicle, it is a fact, as previously stated, that factors other than alcohol intake could account for the same symptoms. Indeed, one authority, Robert L. Donigan, has disclosed that well over 60 pathological conditions could produce such symptoms.[1]

At the present time, however, reliance is placed primarily upon the results of chemical tests. All fifty states and the District of Columbia have statutes which either (a) prescribe presumptions based upon the percentage of alcohol in the blood, determined directly from tests of the blood itself or indirectly from tests of the urine or breath,[2] or (b) they provide that it is an "absolute" or "per se" offense to operate a vehicle

---

21. State v. Witte, 251 Kan. 313, 321, 836 P.2d 1110, 1116 (1992), quoting Rouleau, "Unreliability of the Horizontal Gaze Nystagmus Test," 4 *Am.Jur.Proof of Facts* 3d, § 10, p. 458 (1989). See also, People v. Leahy, supra note 10.

§ 3.12

1. Supra, note 2, section 3.04.

2. See supra section 3.06 for the prescribed presumptions specified in the Uniform Vehicle Code, which has served as a

while there is a certain amount of alcohol within the blood of the driver.[3]

In a single chapter of a manageable size book on scientific evidence in litigation it is obviously impossible to adequately discuss all of the various state statutes and all or most of the many legal issues that have arisen in the courts regarding chemical tests for intoxication. Moreover, new statutes have been enacted and the original ones have been subjected to revisions. Consequently, in the present text only the major legal aspects will be discussed. For the ones of lesser significance—even though of importance in a particular case situation—the reader is referred to current case reporting services.[4]

1. THE SELF–INCRIMINATION PRIVILEGE, DUE PROCESS, SEARCHES AND SEIZURES, AND IMPLIED CONSENT LAWS

It is well settled that the Fifth Amendment self-incrimination privilege is limited to testimonial compulsion and is inapplicable to the procurement of physical evidence such as blood, urine, or breath specimens,[5] and that the due process clause of that Amendment has applicability with regard to such evidence only when in the procurement process the police resort to procedures that offend "a sense of justice," or, stated another way, procedures that are "shocking to the conscience" of the courts.[6] It is also clear that the Fourth Amendment offers protection only against searches and seizures without probable cause—in other words, "unreasonable" ones.[7] Nevertheless, a simple legislative expedient has been devised, and adopted in all jurisdictions, whereby there is an almost complete avoidance of any of the foregoing constitutional issues, as well as an avoidance of possible citizen disapproval of police compulsion conduct. It is a law known as an "implied consent statute," which has as one of its effects the encouragement of consensual relinquishment of the desired specimen. The initial underlying principle in support of such legislation was that the use of the streets and highways by a motorist is a privilege rather than a right and consequent-

---

model for most of the statutes upon the subject.

3. Not only have such absolute offense statutes been upheld as to their constitutionality, but, in states having both an absolute offense statute as well as a presumption one, each has been held to be separate and distinct; neither one is inclusive or exclusive of the other.

4. E.g., *The National Traffic Law News*, published by Donald H. Wallace, Warrensburg, Mo., and the *Criminal Law Reporter*, published by the Bureau of National Affairs, Inc., Washington, D.C. The former publication covers all DUI legal issues.

5. Schmerber v. California, 384 U.S. 757 (1966); South Dakota v. Neville, 459 U.S. 553 (1983).

6. For the basic principle, see, Rochin v. California, 342 U.S. 165 (1952) (stomach pump used by physician in a hospital at request of police, but over the arrestee's protest, to secure narcotic capsules swallowed by arrestee was found by the Court to offend a sense of justice.)

7. See, *Schmerber*, supra note 5, at 766–772, wherein the Court stated that after an arrest upon probable cause for DWI, the procurement, over an arrestee's protest, of a blood specimen in a reasonable manner (i.e., by a physician using accepted medical procedures) did not constitute a Fourth Amendment violation.

ly reasonable conditions can be appended to the government's grant of that privilege. One such condition was that a motorist, who has been lawfully arrested, impliedly consented to submit to a scientific test as to whether he was "intoxicated" or "under the influence of alcohol". In the event of a refusal to submit to a test, the motorist incurred the risk of having his driver's license suspended or revoked.

The "driving privilege" concept has undergone certain modifications. The first was the requirement, either by decisional law or statute, that before a driver's license would be suspended or revoked he was entitled, as a matter of due process, to an opportunity for a hearing by an appropriate administrative agent such as a commissioner of motor vehicles.[8] Since these early cases, it appears that at least under some circumstances a suspension or revocation may precede an administrative hearing without incurring a due process violation.[9] The "important public interest in safety on the roads and highways, and in the prompt removal of a safety hazard" seems to outweigh the private interest of continuing to drive until a full administrative hearing.

In *Schmerber,*[10] the Court also recognized that the Sixth Amendment right to counsel does not apply to the taking of physical evidence from the body of the accused. Therefore, there would be no federal constitutional right to the presence of an attorney at the taking of a blood sample. State law may, however, provide such a right, either by statute or state constitutional provision. Thus, for instance, in Sites v. State,[11] the Maryland Court of Appeals concluded that the state constitution as well as the 14th Amendment's due process clause provided a DUI suspect with a limited right to consult with counsel prior to deciding whether to submit to breath testing, when such consultation will not substantially interfere with the "timely and efficacious" conduct of state breath testing. Also, the majority of the Minnesota Supreme Court, interpreting its own constitution, held that a demand to submit to a breath test was a "critical stage" in a DUI proceeding at which the suspect had a right to counsel.[12] In Vermont, a state statute permitting a motorist to consult with an attorney prior to deciding whether to submit to a DUI test, provided the consultation take place within 30 minutes from the initial attempt to contact counsel, was held to limit unfairly a suspect's right to counsel if, despite repeated attempts, the public defender could be located within the 30–minute time limit.[13]

---

8. Beatty v. Hults, 22 A.D.2d 740, 253 N.Y.S.2d 327 (1964). Also, with respect to a related problem, see, Bell v. Burson, 402 U.S. 535 (1971).

9. Mackey v. Montrym, 443 U.S. 1 (1979), affirmed in Illinois v. Batchelder, 463 U.S. 1112 (1983).

10. Supra note 5.

11. 300 Md. 702, 481 A.2d 192 (1984). See also, Brosan v. Cochran, 307 Md. 662, 516 A.2d 970 (1986): "[T]he decision

whether to submit to the State test is of the most fundamental importance in determining the ultimate resolution of the suspect's case." But, rejecting the 14th Amendment right to counsel analysis over one dissent, see, McCambridge v. State, 778 S.W.2d 70 (Tex.Crim.App.1989).

12. Friedman v. Commissioner of Public Safety, 473 N.W.2d 828 (Minn.1991).

13. State v. Garvey, 157 Vt. 105, 595 A.2d 267 (1991).

2. WARNINGS TO PERSON TO BE TESTED

Since the self-incrimination privilege applies only to testimonial compulsion and not to the procurement of physical evidence, no self-incrimination warning need be issued to the person about to be given a chemical test for intoxication.[14] If, however, he is under custodial arrest for a DUI related offense and the police want to interrogate him, for example, as to the cause of an accident, Miranda v. Arizona mandates the issuance of the Supreme Court's prescribed warnings.[15]

Most states, in their implied consent statutes, require that before a motorist is asked to submit to a test he must be told of the possible suspension or revocation consequences of a refusal. Confusion may result from the "overlap" between chemical test statutory requirements of warnings as to the consequences of a test refusal (license suspension or revocation) and the *Miranda* requirements with respect to the interrogation of a motorist who has been taken into custody. For instance, upon the arrest of a motorist whom the police plan to subject to a chemical test as well as interrogate about the offense, if the jurisdiction requires a suspension/revocation warning and the arrestee is also advised of his *Miranda* rights, he may not understand the difference between the two, and particularly where he is, indeed, intoxicated. As a matter of fact, even if only the *Miranda* warnings are given he might still assume he had a right to refuse to be tested, equating refusal with the right to remain silent. In any such instances, therefore, the police should make every reasonable effort to explain the difference; in other words, make clear to him that he has a right to refuse to talk about the accident, but that he has no right to refuse to submit to a chemical test.[16]

3. EVIDENCE OF REFUSAL TO SUBMIT TO CHEMICAL TEST

Under the implied consent statutes, evidence of refusal to submit to a chemical test is obviously admissible at a hearing to determine whether a driver's license or permit is to be revoked or suspended. What, however, is the status of a refusal to submit if the driver is being prosecuted for a DUI offense? May evidence of the refusal be offered at trial to suggest that his refusal was tantamount to an admission of intoxication? May the prosecutor comment upon the refusal in his closing argument to the jury?

The case law has been in conflict, but appears now to have been settled by the United States Supreme Court in the case of South Dakota v. Neville,[17] where the Court held that a driver's refusal to take a blood-alcohol test may be used against him at his DUI trial without offending

---

14. See, *Schmerber,* supra note 5.

15. Berkemer v. McCarty, 468 U.S. 420, (1984).

16. Scores of "confusion" cases are collected in *The National Traffic Law News,* supra note 4, under the topic heading, "Al-cohol Related Offenses—Implied Consent—Evidence of Refusal—Confusion with Miranda."

17. 459 U.S. 553 (1983).

On remand, the South Dakota Supreme Court again excluded the refusal to take the

the Fifth Amendment's privilege against compelled self-incrimination. The refusal involves no impermissible coercion on the part of the government or its agents and, therefore, is not shielded from admissibility by the Fifth Amendment privilege. The Court did *not* hold that the refusal is nontestimonial, but simply took the position that the refusal involved no governmental coercion of the type the framers of the Constitution sought to avoid. Under *Schmerber* a state may actually force a suspected drunk driver to take a blood-alcohol test, because it is, in essence, a search incident to arrest. Instead of using such constitutionally permissible compulsion, many states have chosen a less stringent alternative: they have enacted Implied Consent laws which, among other things, give suspects the right to refuse testing. The Court reasoned that adding a penalty to the exercise of this right of refusal, such as its use in evidence, does not constitute impermissible coercion, and the admission of such evidence also does not violate due process principles.

Again, state law may of course alter these principles. Thus, in Farmer v. Commonwealth,[18] the admission of evidence of defendant's refusal to submit to a preliminary breath test permitted without violating the federal constitution under South Dakota v. Neville, was held to violate the state constitutional right against self-incrimination. Also, while the fact an accused refused to take a test for blood-alcohol content is admissible into evidence, the actual statements of refusal may not be admissible if the driver was not given the required Miranda warnings.[19]

4. SPECIAL PROBLEMS WITH PRELIMINARY BREATH TESTS AND PASSIVE ALCOHOL SCREENING DEVICES [20]

One of the major legal issues surrounding the use of preliminary breath testing devices (PBTs) is whether their use constitutes a "search" for Fourth Amendment purposes, or merely a less intrusive investigatory step analogous to a "frisk." If it is the former, absent consent by the driver, the police officer would have to possess the full measure of "probable cause" before requiring the suspected driver to take the PBT. If it is the latter, then the lesser standard of "reasonable suspicion" articulated in the stop-and-frisk decisions would suffice.[21] A third legal alternative is that the PBT fits neither the search nor the investigatory stop models, and is more analogous to gathering evidence already in plain view.

chemical test on state constitutional grounds. See, State v. Neville, 346 N.W.2d 425 (S.D.1984). Thereafter, however, the court changed its mind and overruled *Neville* in State v. Hoenscheid, 374 N.W.2d 128 (S.D.1985), stating that evidence of a refusal to cooperate with field sobriety testing was not testimonial in nature, but rather physical evidence not protected by the privilege against self-incrimination.

18. 10 Va.App. 175, 390 S.E.2d 775, 781 (1990).

19. State v. Beaton, 516 N.W.2d 645 (N.D.1994).

20. See Sections 3.06 and 3.07 supra for a description of the technology involved in these instruments.

21. Terry v. Ohio, 392 U.S. 1 (1968).

No definitive answer can be given to this legal issue, because to date few courts have considered the use of PBTs. However, it is possible that the third alternative may be rejected because the use of the device requires a person *to do something,* i.e., blowing air into a tube, thereby amounting to an intrusion into an area of constitutionally protected privacy safeguarded by the Fourth Amendment. Nevertheless, a balancing of the important governmental interest in detecting alcohol impairment in drivers against the relatively minor invasion of a driver's right of privacy, may warrant an acceptance of the PBT as a relatively unintrusive process requiring no more than "reasonable suspicion" for its use—the same standard used for an investigatory stop and frisk. The act of blowing into a tube attached to a small, hand-held device, a process which lasts but a few seconds, is certainly far less intrusive than an ordinary pat-down of the outer clothing such as is permitted in an ordinary stop and frisk.

A majority of states have passed PBT laws setting forth explicit guidelines for their use. Although most of these statutes establish a *probable cause* rather than *reasonable suspicion* standard for their use, it is likely that the courts will ultimately decide that the federal constitutional standard only requires the lesser standard. This would permit states now having the probable cause standard to amend their laws to adopt the lower standard, should they desire to do so. In 1984, the *Uniform Vehicle Code* adopted the lower standard, using the words "articulable grounds" as the equivalent of "reasonable suspicion".[22] It is reasonable to expect that a number of states in the years ahead will use the following UVC provision as a model:

> **Preliminary Screening Test.** When a law enforcement officer has articulable grounds to suspect that a person may have been violating Sec. 11–902(a), he may request the person to submit to a preliminary screening test of his breath to determine his alcohol concentration using a device approved by the (State Department of Health) for that purpose. In addition to this test, or upon refusal to submit to testing, the officer may require further testing under Sec. 6–205.1.[23]

With respect to the Fourth Amendment issues surrounding the use of passive alcohol screening devices (PASD), their resolution is wholly speculative at this time because such devices will not likely be used with any frequency by police departments until the late 1980s. However, one of the first commentators to examine the legal issues involved in the use of PASD has focused upon its "inactive" nature,[24] and has compared it to other law enforcement techniques such as the use of drug sniffing

---

22. United States v. Cortez, 449 U.S. 411 (1981).

23. *Uniform Vehicle Code and Model Traffic Ordinance,* Sec. 11–903.3, Supplement IV (1984).

24. See Section 3.07 supra.

dogs [25] and sensory enforcement devices [26] which the United States Supreme Court has held do not involve Fourth Amendment "searches." The commentator concluded that its use will ultimately be declared by the courts to have either no Fourth Amendment search implications at all, or if it does involve protected privacy interests, that it is a limited search requiring no more than reasonable suspicion.[27]

§ 3.13 Restricted Application of Statutory Presumptions

Due to the legislative intent, the prescribed presumptions usually apply only to DUI case prosecutions. Many states have not followed the recommendations of the Uniform Vehicle Code that the presumptions should be prescribed for utilization in *any* criminal or civil action or other proceeding arising out of acts alleged to have resulted from the use of a motor vehicle by an intoxicated person. It would seem that there is no logical reason for legislative confinement of the presumptions to DUI cases, and especially in homicide prosecutions of a motorist for the recklessness of his conduct due to intoxication.

It is clear, of course, that the presumptions are inapplicable to nonvehicular case situations. For instance, they may not be invoked in cases such as prosecutions for theft, where specific intent is an element of the offense and intoxication is interposed to support a defense of lack of intent.[1] Another illustration is a case where a confession is used against a person accused of a criminal offense and the contention is made that he was so intoxicated he did not know what he was saying.[2] Here, again, the statutory presumptions are of no avail per se.

Regardless of the nature of the case, however, an expert may render an opinion upon an intoxication issue by adopting, as his own standards, the same ones stated in the presumption statutes.

§ 3.14 Intoxicated *Per Se* Statutes—Constitutionality

In recent years, the states have passed statutes containing so-called "mandatory rebuttable presumptions" which permit jurors to presume that a driver is under the influence of alcohol if it is shown that the driver has a blood-alcohol concentration of 0.10 or more.[1] Even if a statute provides that such presumption is rebuttable, the constitutionality of such provision remains in doubt in the light of United States

---

25. United States v. Place, 462 U.S. 696 (1983); United States v. Jacobsen, 466 U.S. 109 (1984).

26. Texas v. Brown, 460 U.S. 730 (1983).

27. Manak, "Constitutional Aspects of The Use of Passive Alcohol Screening Devices As Law Enforcement Tools for DWI Enforcement," 19 The Prosecutor — (1986).

§ 3.13

1. Donigan, supra n. 6 at pp. 166–171 and supplements.

2. Donigan, supra n. 6 at pp. 42–43, and supplements.

§ 3.14

1. The states adopted the presumption of intoxication to fulfill federal highway funding requirements. See 23 U.S.C.A. § 408(e)(1)(C); 23 C.F.R. § 1204.4, Highway Safety Program Guideline No. 8, IB.

Supreme Court decisions on the impermissible uses of presumptions as burden-of-proof-shifting devices in criminal cases.[2] A permissive presumption does not violate due process so long as a rational connection exists between the predicate and presumed fact. A mandatory presumption, on the other hand, may or may not be constitutional depending on its type and function.[3] A mandatory rebuttable presumption is generally just as unconstitutional because it commonly shifts the burden of persuasion to the defendant.[4] Most jurisdictions which have considered such jury instructions have held that jury charges based on the statutory language create mandatory presumptions unless the language of the inference is unambiguously permissive.[5] While the United States Supreme Court has held that mandatory rebuttable presumptions which shift the burden of persuasion to the defendant are constitutional,[6] the Court has not, as of this writing, determined whether burden-of-production shifting presumptions violate due process.

In State v. Leverett,[7] the defendant was charged with negligent homicide after his car struck a pedestrian who died the next morning of injuries. Following the accident, Leverett underwent field sobriety tests and a breath test. The breath test registered his blood alcohol content at .121. Upon appeal from his conviction, the Montana Supreme Court reversed, holding that the jury instructions on the presumption of intoxication that were given were unconstitutional, but the court did not reach the statute itself, because by its plain language the relevant portion of the statute created a mandatory rebuttable presumption.

Wilhelm v. State[8] came to a similar result. The issue there was the validity of an instruction that if the jury found that defendant had .10% or more by weight of alcohol in his blood, prima facie evidence was established that the defendant was under the influence of alcoholic beverages to the extent that his normal faculties were impaired. This was held to create an unconstitutional mandatory rebuttable presumption. The court said, in part:

2. See, e.g. Mullaney v. Wilbur, 421 U.S. 684 (1975); Patterson v. New York, 432 U.S. 197 (1977); Sandstrom v. Montana, 442 U.S. 510 (1979); Francis v. Franklin, 471 U.S. 307 (1985); McMillan v. Pennsylvania, 477 U.S. 79 (1986).

3. State v. Leverett, 245 Mont. 124, 799 P.2d 119 (1990).

4. Francis v. Franklin, supra note 2.

5. E.g., State v. Dacey, 138 Vt. 491, 418 A.2d 856 (1980); State v. Vick, 104 Wis.2d 678, 312 N.W.2d 489 (1981); Barnes v. People, 735 P.2d 869 (Colo.1987) [saving the constitutionality of the statute by reading indisputably mandatory language as permissive]; State v. McDonald, 421 N.W.2d 492 (S.D.1988). Virginia's statute that makes it a crime to drive with a BAC of .10 or greater is not a *per se* statute, since the accused is entitled to rebut the presumption: Davis v. Commonwealth, 8 Va.App.

291, 381 S.E.2d 11 (1989). Reaching a contrary conclusion on similar statutory language, see, State v. Rollins, 141 Vt. 105, 444 A.2d 884 (1982). See also, Commonwealth v. DiFrancesco, 458 Pa. 188, 329 A.2d 204 (1974) and Hillery v. State, 165 Ga.App. 127, 299 S.E.2d 421 (1983).

6. This type of presumption involves the affirmative defenses where defendant is required to meet some enumerated degree of persuasion to overcome the presumption. Such defenses do not violate due process if they do not replace the traditional elements of the offense with which a defendant is charged. See, Martin v. Ohio, 480 U.S. 228 (1987): affirmative defense of self defense; Leland v. Oregon, 343 U.S. 790 (1952) requiring defendant to prove his insanity.

7. Supra note 3.

8. 568 So.2d 1 (Fla.1990).

" 'Prima facie' is a technical legal term without a common meaning for the lay person. Confronted with such a term in the jury instructions, and provided with no definition, a reasonable juror would be forced to guess as to its meaning from the context in which it was used. In this case, that context is an explanation in the jury instructions of what the jury can and cannot 'presume.' Further, there was no language in the instruction immediately following that challenge which instructed the jury that evidence of blood-alcohol content as it related to intoxication could be rebutted by the defendant. Although such language would not have cured the instruction, its absence makes it possible that the jury understood the instruction not only as a mandatory presumption, but one which is irrebuttable." [9]

It seems clear from these decisions that the solution to due process problems when the jury is charged in terms of "presumptions" is to make them unambiguously permissive.

§ 3.15 Qualifications of Witness and Courtroom Testimony

In view of the presumption standards specified in the various chemical test statutes there obviously is no need to establish the validity of the standards by means of expert testimony.

Where a breathalyzer has been used for the chemical testing, and especially where the instrument produces a digital display and a printout of the test result, the witness need not be a chemist or other type of scientist. It is necessary, however, that the witness (e.g., a police officer or police laboratory technician) received proper training in the usage of the instrument and with respect to the conditions under which the test should be conducted, and he must conduct the test in conformity with prescribed procedures mandated by the relevant statute or the ones established by the jurisdiction's designated agency (e.g., the state board of health).

Although the breathalyzer operator must have a rudimentary knowledge of the chemicals required for instrument function, and also know where and how to insert the appropriate chemical ampoules, a knowledge of the internal intricacies of the instrument itself is not a requisite.

In many jurisdictions only those persons who have passed state board examinations are considered qualified to testify in court regarding breathalyzer test results. The permit issued by the state readily satisfies the court that the witness is qualified.[1] Of course, competence in

---

9. Id. at 3.

§ 3.15

1. As regards the permit to establish the witness' qualifications, compare State v. Batiste, 327 So.2d 420 (La.1976) and State v. Jones, 316 So.2d 100 (La.1975) (test results inadmissible unless operator physically produces official certification of a valid permit because official certificate is best evidence of operator's qualifications), with Davis v. State, 541 P.2d 1352 (Okl.Crim.App.1975) (testimony of operator that he possessed a valid permit is sufficient without introducing permit).

administering the test cannot save its admission if it is established that the operator falsified breathalyzer results. Thus, in New Jersey, an undercover officer posing as a motorist caught a breathalyzer operator in falsifying test results and extorting money from DUI arrestees. Thereafter, the Supreme Court of New Jersey held that persons convicted of drunk driving offenses on the basis of tests administered by the same officer were entitled to new trials, at which the state would have the burden of demonstrating that its BAC test evidence is free from the taint of the officer's misconduct.[2]

As is generally required in cases where opinions are based upon the revelations of scientific instruments, the breath instrument operator must testify that the instrument he used is a generally accepted one for test purposes, and that it was in proper working order at the time of the test.[3]

Where the chemical test is made of blood or urine, the witness must, of course, be a person with the credentials of a scientist (e.g., a chemist).[4]

As previously mentioned, since chemical tests can only establish the alcohol content of the blood at the time of the test, some experts will attempt to extrapolate this result back to the time of the alleged offense and thereby estimate the blood alcohol content present at the prior time.[5] However, such extrapolation estimates are not necessary prerequisites to the introduction of the test results, although the lack of extrapolation testimony may be considered in determining the weight to be given to the evidence presented by the witness.[6]

§ 3.16 Preservation of Evidence

Although methods are available for the preservation of additional specimens of blood or urine that had been subjected to a chemical test for alcohol, a real problem is presented with respect to breath specimens.

Scientists in the field of breath testing were of the general view that it is not feasible to preserve the breath test ampoules for a check upon

2. State v. Gookins, 135 N.J. 42, 637 A.2d 1255 (1994) reversing 263 N.J.Super 58, 621 A.2d 968. That such occurrences are not rare, see Moenssens, "Novel Scientific Evidence in Criminal Cases: Some Words of Caution," 84 *J.Crim.L. & Criminology* 1, at 15–17 (1993). See also, In re Investigation of the West Virginia State Police Crime Laboratory, 190 W.Va. 321, 438 S.E.2d 501 (1993).

3. Owens v. Commonwealth, 487 S.W.2d 897 (Ky.1972); People v. Krulikowski, 60 Mich.App. 28, 230 N.W.2d 290 (1975); Romano v. Kimmelman, supra note 6, section 3.09; People v. Todd, 79 Misc.2d 630, 360 N.Y.S.2d 754 (1974); State v. Hood, 155 W.Va. 337, 184 S.E.2d 334 (1971).

4. Such an expert will also be needed in breath test cases not covered by the pre-

sumption statute (e.g., a manslaughter prosecution).

5. As disclosed in § 3.08 supra, the value of such extrapolation is not fully supported scientifically, nor do courts necessarily permit such extrapolation.

6. State ex rel. Williams v. Tucson, 15 Ariz.App. 229, 487 P.2d 766 (1971); State v. Sutliff, 97 Idaho 523, 547 P.2d 1128 (1976); People v. Kozar, 54 Mich.App. 503, 221 N.W.2d 170 (1974). But see, State v. Hughes, 713 S.W.2d 58 (Tenn.1986), and Note, "Right of Confrontation—Right of DUI Defendant to Cross–Examine a Laboratory Technician," 54 *Tenn.L.Rev.* 525 (1987).

the accuracy of the results reported by the police breathalyzer operator. Since being compelled to do so by some courts, as is discussed hereafter, methods have been developed that can accomplish the objective. Silica gel and magnesium perchlorate adsorption techniques have shown to be effective.[1] The silica gel method utilizes a glass tube containing silica gel crystals, which are highly absorbent and attract and capture moisture.[2]

Courts disagree on whether police must preserve breath test ampoules as a prerequisite to the admissibility of test results. In People v. Hitch,[3] the California Supreme Court held that since it was feasible to store the test ampoules and later re-testing would produce accurate results, police had a duty to preserve them. Failure to do so would result in the suppression of future test results. However, the *Hitch* decision has not been met with general acceptance. Some courts have rejected it completely, claiming that the basic premise of *Hitch,* that preservation of test ampoules was feasible and would produce accurate results upon retesting, was incorrect.[4] Other courts placed the burden on defendant to show that something of value for the defense would be discovered before objections to the destruction of the ampoule would be entertained.[5] The Colorado Supreme Court,[6] by contrast, went as far as to require the prosecution to preserve a sample of the *breath* itself for defendant to analyze later, as did a California Court of Appeals,[7] relying on the Hitch case which dealt with ampoules.

The Arizona Supreme Court, having earlier adopted a *Hitch*-type view, reaffirmed the duty of the state to capture and retain breath samples in State v. Velasco,[8] despite evidence of three state experts who agreed that the silica gel method of preservation is not as accurate and reliable as the Intoxilyzer instrument which had been used. The *en banc* court declared, "Under the present state of scientific knowledge, the silica gel preservation method to capture a DUI defendant's breath specimen and preserve it for independent testing is not so unreliable that its use violates due process."[9]

§ 3.16

1. See, Goldberger, Caplan & Zetti, "A Long-Term Field Experience With Breath Ethanol Collection Employing Silica Gel," 10 *J.Analytical Tox.* 194 (1986), concluding that satisfactory results were obtained after preservation of breath samples that were from 1 to almost 3 years old.

2. State v. Velasco, 165 Ariz. 480, 799 P.2d 821 (1990).

3. 12 Cal.3d 641, 117 Cal.Rptr. 9, 527 P.2d 361 (1974). See also, Note, "The Right to Independent Testing: A New Hitch in the Preservation of Evidence Doctrine," 75 *Colum.L.Rev.* 1355 (1975).

4. State v. Shutt, 116 N.H. 495, 363 A.2d 406 (1976); State v. Teare, 135 N.J.Super. 19, 342 A.2d 556 (1975). See also, Lauderdale v. State, 548 P.2d 376, 379–80 (Alaska 1976) ("Apparently, at the present time, it is not possible to rerun a test and obtain accurate results.")

5. People v. Godbout, 42 Ill.App.3d 1001, 1 Ill.Dec. 583, 356 N.E.2d 865 (1976).

6. Garcia v. District Court, 197 Colo. 38, 589 P.2d 924 (1979).

7. People v. Trombetta, 142 Cal.App.3d 138, 190 Cal.Rptr. 319 (1983).

8. 165 Ariz. 480, 799 P.2d 821 (1990). (En Banc.)

9. Id. at 489, 799 P.2d at 830.

Since the *Hitch* decision rests on the Brady v. Maryland [10] principle that the prosecutor is bound to disclose only favorable material evidence to the defense, some courts have refused to suppress test results unless the defendant can show a high degree of prejudice by the destruction of the ampoule; in other words, the defendant must establish a reasonable possibility, based on concrete evidence, that a re-test would be favorable to his case.[11]

Federal constitutional considerations do not require the result reached in *Hitch*. The United States Supreme Court has held that at least for those states that do not choose to apply the *Hitch* rule on the basis of independent state grounds, the prosecution saving of ampoules of breath samples is not a due process requirement.[12] The Court so decided in a sweeping unanimous opinion written by Mr. Justice Marshall. The argument was rejected that the Fourteenth Amendment Due Process Clause requires police and prosecutors to preserve breath samples of suspected drunk drivers tested on chemical breath-alcohol measuring devices such as the Intoxilyzer or Breathalyzer. The Court adopted the rule that any duty the states may have to preserve evidence is limited to evidence that possesses an exculpatory value that is apparent before its destruction and that is unobtainable by the defendant by other reasonable means. In the case of breath samples saved for defense use, they would almost always confirm the results obtained by the state, and any inaccuracies in the state's results could be shown by other means, such as cross-examination or independent tests obtained by the defendant after taking the state's chemical test. Thus, even if the police use a device that saves a breath sample they have *no constitutional duty* to retain it and make it available to the defendant.

III.　MISCELLANEOUS

§ 3.17　Bibliography of Additional References

Anonymous

Breath Alcohol Operator's Training Manual, Virginia Bureau of Forensic Science, 1984. Rev'd 1988.

"Horizontal Gaze Nystagmus Test—Myth or Magic?" *Liquor Liability J.* (Sep. 1984) p. 3.

10. 373 U.S. 83 (1963). A California appellate court so construed *Hitch* on the remand of Trombette v. California, infra note 12. Also see, United States v. Agurs, 427 U.S. 97 (1976). See also, Arizona v. Youngblood, 488 U.S. 51 (1988), holding that due process only requires the prosecution to collect, preserve, and present to the defendant evidence that has actual and apparently exculpatory value, and not evidence that is only potentially exculpatory.

11. People v. Godbout, supra note 5; State v. Reaves, 25 Or.App. 745, 550 P.2d 1403 (1976); State v. Michener, 25 Or.App. 523, 550 P.2d 449 (1976).

12. California v. Trombetta, 467 U.S. 479 (1984). On remand a California appellate court held that neither due process, nor equal protection, nor the informed consent statute required preservation, which was a step beyond the U.S. Supreme Court's due process holding: 173 Cal.App.3d 1093, 219 Cal.Rptr. 637 (1985).

Articles and Books:

Anderson, et al., *Field Evaluation of a Behavioral Test Battery for DWI* (U.S. Dept. of Trans. Report No. DOT–HS–806–475, Sep. 1983.

Biasotti, "The Role of the Forensic Scientist in the Application of Chemical Tests for Alcohol in Traffic Enforcement," 29 *J.For.Sci.* 1164 (1984).

Campbell, et al., *Defense of Speeding, Reckless Driving & Vehicular Homicide* (1984).

Carper & McCamey, "Gaze Nystagmus: Scientific Proof of DUI?" *Ill. Bar J.* (Nov. 1988), p. 146.

Chang & Kollman, "The Effect of Temperature on the Formation of Ethanol by *Candida Albicans* in Blood," 34 *J.For.Sci.* 105 (1989).

Cowan, et al., "The Response of the Intoxilyzer 4011AS–A to a Number of Possible Interfering Substances," 35 *J.For.Sci.* 797 (1990).

Erwin, *Defense of Drunk Driving Cases* [Multi-volume set] (1993).

Feldman & Gutman, "A Study of DUI Law Enforcement Practice Based on EBT Data from Five Precincts in Mass. and Cal.," 29 *Jurimetrics J.* 221 (1989).

Fitzgerald & Hume, "The Single Chemical Test for Intoxication: A Challenge to admissibility," 24 *Mass.L.Rev.* 23 (1981).

Fitzgerald & Hume, *Intoxication Test Evidence: Criminal & Civil* (1987).

Frajola, "Blood Alcohol Testing in the Clinical Laboratory: Problems and Suggested Remedies," 39 *Clin.Chem.* 377 (1993).

Frajola, "Evidentiary Standards for Blood Testing," W.Va. C.L.E. Seminar on Representing the DUI Defendant, Nov. 19, 1993.

Goldberger, Caplan & Zetti, "A Long–Term Field Experience With Breath Ethanol Collection Employing Silica Gel," 10 *J.Analytical Tox.* 194 (1986).

Goldberger & Caplan, "Infrared Quantitative Evidential Breath–Alcohol Analyzers: In Vitro Accuracy and Precision Studies," 31 *J.For.Sci.* 17 (1986).

Goldberger, et al., "A Long–Term Field Experience With Breath Ethanol Collection Employing Silica Gel," 10 *J.Analytical Tox.* 194 (1986).

Harding, et al., "Field Performance of the Intoxilyzer 5000: A Comparison of Blood– and Breath–Alcohol Results in Wisconsin Drivers," 35 *J.For.Sci.* 1022 (1990).

Hume & Fitzgerald, "Chemical Tests for Intoxication: What Do the Numbers Really Mean?" 57 *Anal.Chem.* 876A (1985).

Jones, "How Breathing Technique Can Influence the Results of Breath–Test Analysis," 22 *Med.Sci.Law* 275 (1982).

Jones & Jonsson, "Food Induced Lowering of Blood-Ethanol Profiles and Increased Rate of Elimination Immediately After a Meal," 39 *J.For. Sci.* 1084 (1994).

Jones & Lund, "Detection of Alcohol–Impaired Drivers Using a Passive Alcohol Sensor," 14 *J.Police Sci. & Admin.* 153 (1986).

Lewis, "The Individual and the Estimation of his Blood Alcohol Concentration from Intake, with Particular Reference to the 'Hip-flask' Drink," 26 *J.For.Sci.Soc.* 19 (1986).

Lewis, "Blood Alcohol: The Concentration–Time Curve and Retrospective Estimation of Level," 26 *J.For.Sci.Soc.* 95 (1986).

Misna, "Public Outcry v. Individual Rights: Right to Counsel and the Drunk Driver's Dilemma," 69 *Marq.L.Rev.* 278 (1986).

Rose, "Factors Influencing Gastric Emptying," 24 *J.For.Sci.* 200 (1979).

Robertson, "Discretion and the Intoximeter," *Crim.L.Rev.* (Nov.1986), p. 726.

Saferstein, ed., Forensic Science Handbook, Vol. I (Chapter 12), 1982.

Samuels, "Drunk Driving: Challenging the Blood or Urine Analysis," 20 *Med.Sci.Law* 14, 1980.

Sapir & Kling, "Cross–Examination of Breath Alcohol Machine Operators," 13 *So.Ill.U.L.J.* (1988).

Senkowski & Thompson, "The Accuracy of Blood Alcohol Analysis Using Headspace Gas Chromatography When Performed on Clotted Samples," 35 *J.For.Sci.* 176 (1990).

Tarantino, *DWI Defense Forms and Checklists* (1984, 1988 Supp.).

Tarantino, *Defending Drunk Drivers* (2d ed. 1990).

Tarantino, exec. ed., *DWI Journal: Law & Science* (since 1983).

Taylor, *Drunk Driving Defense* (1981—Supplemented).

Thompson, "Determining Blood/Alcohol Concentration: Two Methods of Analysis," 46 *Mont.L.Rev.* 365 (1985).

Wade, "DUI Statistics Often Don't Add Up," *Crim. Justice* (Spring 1990), p. 16.

Winek & Carfagna, "Comparison of plasma, serum and whole blood ethanol concentrations," 11 *A.Anal.Tox.* 267 (1987).

Law Review Notes and Comments:

"In Vino Veritas: The Truth About Blood Alcohol Presumptions in State Drunk Driving Law," 64 N.Y.U.L.Rev. 141 (1989).

"Driving With 0.10% Blood Alcohol: Can The State Prove It?" 16 *U.San Francisco L.Rev.* 817 (1982).

"The Continuing Search for Solutions to the Drunken Driver Tragedy and the Problem of Social Host Liability," 82 *NW.U.L.Rev.* 403 (1988).

"Is DUI DOA?: Admissibility of Breath Testing Evidence in the Wake of Recent Challenges to Breath Testing Devices," 20 *SW.U.L.Rev.* 247 (1991).

Chapter 4

SCIENTIFIC DETECTION OF SPEEDING

I. INTRODUCTION

§ 4.01 Scope of Chapter

Almost everyone is familiar with the enormous toll in human lives and property damage that automobile accidents take every year. Because of the great number of motor vehicles which crowd the nation's roads, it is inevitable that accidents will occur. The causes are many; some are preventable, others are not. Among the causes are driver intoxication, fatigue, negligence and mechanical failure, to name but a few. Another significant one is excessive speed.

Once an accident has occurred and it becomes necessary to determine at what speed the driver was driving, there are a variety of means whereby the speed may be proved, though many of them are recognized as being highly subjective.　One would be simply by eyewitness estimate; another might be by the testimony of a driver who was following or passed by the vehicle involved in the accident; and yet another might be a calculation of the speed of the vehicle involved in the accident by a study of the skid marks—a technique which affords considerable accuracy as to the speed a vehicle was going when the brakes were first applied.

In order to prevent accidents and to protect the motoring public and pedestrians alike, a number of means have been devised or adapted which are designed to catch speeders and prosecute them criminally for violations of the motor vehicle codes.　Again, speed may be established by the trained observation of a traffic police officer, by police pursuit in a car so that the speed of the pursued vehicle can be established by reference to the police vehicle's speedometer, and by various mechanical devices, one of which consists of a rubber tube stretched across the highway which is connected to a box that measures speed on the basis of the interval elapsing between front wheel and rear wheel passage over the tube, and by airplane.　The most effective means of speed detection, however, have been scientific ones, primarily radar speed detection, VASCAR, and laser.

————

II.　RADAR SPEED DETECTION

§ 4.02　Principles of Radar Speed Detection

The radar speedmeter is probably the most common automatic speed detector currently used.　Contemporary units were developed as an offshoot of military radar utilized during World War II to measure the height, speed and distance of various objects.　The word "radar" is an acronym for Radio Detection And Ranging, and is applied to both the technique and the equipment used.　A radar unit is essentially composed of a transmitter and a receiver of radio waves.

The "pulse" type of radar, developed and used by the military, sends out a beam of radio microwaves in regular intervals which are reflected or bounced back to the receiver by the object detected.　The waves move in both directions at the speed of light, which is a constant factor.　Thus a computation of the time elapsed between the time of sending out the pulse wave and receiving it gives the distance of the object under surveillance.

The radar speedmeter operates in a distinct but similar manner to military radar.　The components also include a transmitter-receiver, coupled to a specially designed voltmeter calibrated on a scale in mile-per-hour equivalents, and an optional graph recorder.　The transmitter sends out a cone-shaped stream of radio wave crests continuously in the direction the speedmeter is pointed.　The number of wave crests is constant, being the frequency of the radio wave.　When the beam strikes an object, some of the beam is reflected back to the receiver part of the speedmeter. The reflection is called the "echo."

If the object is stationary, the frequency of the echo is identical to the frequency of the original transmitter beam. If the object is moving toward or away from the transmitter, the echo has a different frequency and the change in frequency varies directly with the speed of the moving object off which the echo is reflected. This change in frequency is part of an effect that Christan J. Doppler called attention to in 1842.

Everyone has observed the Doppler effect when driving past a car whose horn is blowing, or when standing still at a railroad crossing while a train passes by giving the crossing signal. The pitch or frequency appears to change in both situations, moving from a high pitch to a lower pitch just as one passes the car or as the train passes. So the Doppler effect is an apparent change in the frequency of a vibration which occurs when there is relative motion between the source of the vibration and the receiver of the vibration.

The Doppler effect is particularly suitable for measuring the speed of motor vehicles. When a car is moving along a road toward a radar speedmeter, it runs into some wave crests emitted by the speedmeter that it would not have run into until the next microsecond or so had it been standing still. To the car, the frequency of the transmitter seems to be higher than it actually is. In reflecting these waves toward the receiver of the radar speedmeter, the car becomes a moving source of waves of this slightly higher frequency. The receiver picks up the waves of the transmitter and the waves sent back by the car, thus forming a "beat" wave similar to the one produced by striking two piano keys simultaneously. By means of a simple formula calculated within the machine, the difference in the frequencies of the beat wave is determined to be directly proportional to the velocity of the car. The velocity is recorded in mile-per-hour equivalents on the meter face for the control officer's evaluation and record.

Originally, the technique of using radar speedmeters involved two police cars. One was equipped with the radar unit and parked alongside a road. The other was parked a distance down the road so that it was in a position to apprehend violators. When a speeding car passed the radar car, the controlling officer communicated by radio with the "catch" car. A description of the offender, the license number and the speed registered were transmitted, so that the "catch" car operator could stop the motorist and issue a summons for the violation.

Today, a technique involving the use of "moving radar" is most commonly used. One advantage is that it requires only one police car. Another is that speeders can be detected even when the radar equipped police vehicle is cruising on the highways. The moving radar device operates on the same scientific principles as does stationary radar, but the instrument is a little more sophisticated. It can also be held in the hand of an officer in a stationary vehicle and pointed toward oncoming traffic.

In a typical "moving radar" unit, the police car's own speed, if moving, appears on the right hand side of the dashboard radar unit. On the left side, a digital reading of the target vehicle will appear. The figure on the left side changes continuously as vehicles enter the range of the radar's instrument. For instance, the unit will register the speed of the closest vehicle, then, as the car leaves the range or the cone of transmitted radar waves, the unit will register the speed of the next vehicle. When a number of cars are moving toward the radar unit, the speed reading device may change several times in a split second as it registers the speed of each successive car. Only if a car is "blocked" from the reach of the radar waves by another car, will the radar unit fail to register its speed. If there are no oncoming cars, the unit will register the speed of a car moving away from it.

Moving radar units also transmit a sound that increases in pitch and loudness as the target vehicle approaches. By correlating the tone signal, the digital reading of the speed on the unit, and the visual observation of traffic, the police officer can determine which vehicle is speeding, and pursue the violator. As a standard operating procedure, if the radar operator is even slightly in doubt as to which of several vehicles has been registered as speeding on the unit's display, he is prohibited from issuing a summons to either or any of the drivers.

In the wake of widespread expansion of the use of radar by law enforcement authorities, technology has developed a "countermeasure" used by motorists to detect the use, by police, of a radar unit in the vicinity while driving on the highways. The unit, popularly referred to as a "Fuzzbuster," or, more prosaically, a "radar detector," warns motorists who have the unit installed in their cars of the presence of radar speed detectors so that they may, presumably, lower their speeds to avoid being caught exceeding the speed limit.[1] As of this writing, the use of radar detectors is legal everywhere except in Virginia,[2] the District of Columbia, and Connecticut, although, from time to time, lobbying occurs in other states to change the laws so as to prohibit the use of the detectors.[3]

§ 4.03 Factors Affecting Reliability

The principles of the radar speedmeter are scientifically sound. Yet, the practical use of these devices may create problems. As with any mechanical device operated by human beings, either mechanical failure, or human error, or both, may result in an erroneous determination of the true speed of a targeted car.

§ 4.02

1. Many models of radar detectors have been marketed; full-page ads touting the merits of the devices can typically be found in airline magazines.

2. E.g., Virginia Code 1993, § 46.1-198.1 makes it a misdemeanor to operate a motor vehicle in the state while a radar detector is installed in the car. The device will be impounded as evidence upon arrest for violation of the law.

3. See § 4.05, infra.

Any factor that impacts upon the propagation of radio waves at or near the frequencies used by radar units can affect speed readings recorded by police. Some of the factors may be said to result from operational error, others may be the result of technical defects which can develop in the radar unit itself. Whether classified as operational or technical, among the most important factors that affect the accuracy of radar speed readings to varying degrees we note:

1. The inability to distinguish among targets.

Police radar does not supply the officer operating the unit with target identification, nor can it calculate the range of the target. These are perhaps the most important shortcomings of police radar. The more range a radar set has, the greater the potential for error.

The waves transmitted spread into a cone-shaped pattern that rapidly embraces a broad area. One of the units built a few years ago that was designed to be operated in a portable, stationary, or moving fashion,[1] has an operational range of one-half mile. With a transmitting beam of eighteen angular degrees, the beam would be about eight lanes wide at its normal range. Within this cone-shaped beam, only one speed will be printed out, though any metallic object can return echoes to the set. Ordinarily, if the suspect vehicle is the only moving target, the reading can be fairly accurate. But if multiple moving vehicles are present in the cone, the officer typically chooses, subjectively, which vehicle to stop and cite.[2] This inability to designate which specific vehicular unit is speeding is true of stationary units as well the so-called "moving radar."

Manufacturers sometimes assert that the closest object will be responsible for the echo received, which is true only if all of the vehicles in the beam are of the same size and reflective capabilities; at other times, they assert that the fastest, or the largest, or even the closest vehicle among the various ones caught in the cone will be selected by the radar unit. This, too, is not always true when looking at other environmental factors. If one considers the rather skimpy training received by most radar operators,[3] to interpret the result shown by the radar unit, which only makes a selection based on the intensity of the returning echoes it receives. Since the radar unit does not exhibit judgment, and does not compute the range of the subjects reflecting echoes, it does not

---

§ 4.03

1. The MR-7, built by Kustom Signals.

2. Most radar sets have an adjustable range. At the extreme ranges, the receiver is particularly susceptible to picking up, erroneously, a non-speeding vehicle because the range at which cars or trucks are detected varies depending upon the size, the shape, and the type of construction of the vehicle.

3. A state trooper-law student, who wrote a research paper on the subject for a "Scientific Evidence" class, and who was interviewed thereafter, stated he received less than an hour of training on the radar set before being expected to write citations. He also asserted that most of the information he did receive was erroneous or incomplete. He was told, for instance, that the radar always selects the largest or fastest vehicle, which is not true. Many states have no certifying authority, or "standards" for training. In practice, any county, town or city can buy a set and go into business the same day!

identify a target, but operates purely on the basis of which target is the most radio-reflective among the targets that are "hit" within the beam of the transmitting unit. There are a great number of factors that affect radio-reflectivity. Larger vehicles will ordinarily reflect more energy and can therefore be detected at a greater distance. More streamlined vehicles, on the other hand, present a smaller area from which waves will be reflected. Plastic and fiberglass vehicle bodies are much less reflective. The result is described by R.B. Fitzgerald, Jr., in his paper "Countermeasures," [4]:

> "Consider the common situation of a large truck following a smaller car operating on the highway. If the truck is speeding, and if they are both in the beam at the same time, and if the officer believes that the radar reports on the *closest* vehicle, he will cite the car for any violation suggested by the radar. It is entirely possible that the truck, being both larger and more nearly perpendicular to the beam, is the culprit. For the sake of fairness, consider the situation in which the car in the example is the true violator, but the officer believes that the radar always displays the speed of the *largest* vehicle. The speeder would get away, the innocent driver would get the citation, and the court would certainly convict. The radar is prima facie evidence of the speed of the target, and the officer is the sole authority as to which target he thinks the radar is reporting."

When "moving radar" is utilized, more complex problems arise. With stationary radar, the only "speed" the radar unit is asked to measure is that which intersects its frequency beam transmitted. If installed in a moving patrol car, however, the computer within the unit must first calculate the speed of the police vehicle on the basis of the constant return of echoes received when the beam bounces off stationary objects along the path of the police car. When another vehicle enters the beam, the frequency shift of the radar's transmissions will reflect the "closing" speed, which includes the speed of the target vehicle. Thus, the unit must instantly subtract what it has determined to be the patrol car speed from the perceived closing speed to only display the difference, which should be the speed of the target.

When moving radar units were first used, the entire calculation was done within the unit itself and only the speed of the target vehicle was displayed. More recently manufactured units, however, have two displays, one of which shows the patrol car speed, and the other the speed of the target. Theoretically, this would allow the officer to verify whether the unit at least reads the patrol car speed accurately by a quick look at the police vehicle's certified speedometer. In practice, however, this seldom happens, and, in fact, the operation of the unit may produce an inaccurate reading referred to as a "bumping error." When the

4. Privately printed. Copyright 1982. Portions reprinted here with permission of the author.

Most of the possible errors are also mentioned in Engineering Report on Traffic Ra-

dar, Cincinnati Microwave, 1988 (referring to the Texas Department of Public Safety Manual which catalogues situations that can produce erroneous speed readings.

officer observes a suspect vehicle that appears to be traveling at a rate of speed higher than the speed limit and in response thereto abruptly slows down to begin a turn around, thus "dampening" the patrol speed, the control unit may subtract the now already slower speed of the patrol vehicle, which causes the target vehicle to read as traveling at a higher rate of speed than its actual speed.

Fitzgerald [5] also describes "shadowing error" as one related to the moving radar:

> "In a typical scenario, the patrol car is faster than the general traffic, and is passing traffic going in the same direction, especially on the multi-lane highway. The 'best' radar target in the beam could be a nearby and large vehicle being overtaken. When the target appears from the opposite direction, the rate of closing between the target and the patrol car is compared not to the patrol car's ground speed but to the rate at which the patrol car is closing upon the car it is passing, which is necessarily less than the patrol car's true speed. By accurately reading the closing speed, and subtracting an incorrect patrol speed, the target is reported as having both its own speed and the speed of the error. If this error is rather small, and if the officer cannot or did not know that the computer was confused, he will undoubtedly swear that the radar was operating accurately, and the defendant will be found guilty."

Some units have a "locking" feature where the operator inputs a given speed which, if exceeded by a vehicle within the cone of transmissions, will sound an audible alarm and freeze the speed on the unit's read-out. This feature permits the operator to be less attentive in observing traffic. It also impedes target identification because it prevents an adequate tracking history from being obtained wherein it becomes impossible to correlate, visually, changing speeds of various vehicles moving within the cone of transmissions.

To overcome the lack of target selectivity of police radar, operators are supposed to observe the traffic within the beam and visually estimate the speed of a vehicle suspected of speeding,[6] and then compare it with the reading obtained by the radar unit.

2. Cosine, or Angle Error.

Assuming proper targeting and vehicle identification, a properly maintained and functioning radar unit will produce an accurate reading of the speed of the suspect vehicle if the transmitting radar unit is either directly in front or directly behind the target. This scenario rarely occurs on the highway and there is nearly always a difference between the angle of the radar beam's path and the path of the suspect vehicle.

---

5. Supra note 4.

6. According to the National Highway Traffic Safety Administration's *Basic Training in RADAR Speed Measurement: Training Instruction Manual,* at 3–15, a police officer can be trained to be able to visually estimate the speed of vehicles more or less reliably, and should be able to testify that a vehicle was traveling faster than the speed limit even without a radar reading.

This difference may result in an error that either favors the suspect car or overestimates the speed of it. To take account of this directional difference, speed can be determined by use of a mathematical cosine formula.

A related problem occurs when the radar waves are bounced back off a metallic billboard or other highly reflective surface. Under those circumstances, the unit may calculate the patrol speed as being less than it is in actuality. This will automatically increase the reported speed of the target above its actual speed.[7] The possibility of angle error is one that should be carefully considered.

3. Batching Error.

Batching error, again, is a problem common to moving radar, and can result from sudden accelerating or decelerating of the patrol vehicle, with which the older radar units had difficulties keeping up.[8] If the patrol vehicle suddenly accelerates, the radar unit may actually read the police car's speed at the slightly lower rate it was before sudden acceleration. Since its true speed is greater than that which is measured by the radar unit, it will also calculate a speed for the suspect vehicle that is higher than its actual speed. Of course, if the patrol car were suddenly decelerating, the same batching error would favor the suspect's vehicle whose speed would be recorded as lower than it actually was. Newer radar units use processors that react fast enough so that batching error no longer is likely to be a problem. Even with the older units, such errors will be avoided if the officer is aware of the potential problem and regards the results obtained upon sudden acceleration with suspicion.

4. Shadow Error.

Shadow error is a condition that may produce a temporarily incorrect speed reading when a police car in pursuit of a possible speeder passes a slower moving vehicle. At the time of passing, the unit that measures the patrol car's speed may be temporarily focused upon the slower moving vehicle, especially if it is of much larger size. As a result, the radar unit will display a patrol car speed that is less than its actual speed, which would cause the speed of the suspect vehicle to be overestimated. If the officer is aware of this potential problem, such shadowing error can be anticipated and disregarded.

7. For discussion on the subject, see, Trichter & Patterson, "Police Radar 1980: Has the Black Box Lost Its Magic?," 11 *St. Mary's L.J.* 829, 834 (1980); Dujmich, "Radar Speed Detection: Homing in on New Evidentiary Problems," 48 *Fordham L.Rev.* 1138, 1146 (1980); N.H.T.S.A., U.S.D.O.T., *Basic Training in RADAR Speed Measurement,* reprinted in Defense of Speeding, Reckless Driving & Vehicular Homicide (Matthew Bender), 1992; Goodson, "Technical Shortcomings of Doppler Traffic Radar," 30 *K.For.Sci.* 1186, 1186 (1985); Incantalupo, "A Candid Picture of Speeding—Gotcha!." *Newsday,* Mar. 19, 1990 at p. 6.

8. People v. Ferency, 133 Mich.App. 526, 351 N.W.2d 225, 232 (1984). Batching error was more common in the older units.

5. The condition of the radar unit.

Another significant factor in the accuracy of the radar reading is the age and condition of the radar set used. When a set is old, and/or has been improperly maintained and calibrated, erroneous readings can result. These requirements are addressed in § 4.04, *infra.*

6. The presence or absence of electrical or electromagnetic transmissions.

The presence of electrical transmission wires, especially high-voltage lines, can produce interference that results in "ghost" readings or other effects that distort the accuracy of the radar reading,[9] as can the presence of other transmitters in the area, such as airport surveillance radar. It is also suggested that other sources of interference, such as other police or Citizens Band radio signals, neon lights, the police automobile's ignition system, mobile telephones, garage door openers and other sources of microwave radiation may produce interference.

Also, when operating hand-held equipment, if the radar antenna is inadvertently directed toward a mechanical device within the patrol car, such as the whirring blades of the heater or cooling fan, a "panning error" may be induced. This may also occur when the antenna is pointed toward the control head or other electronic equipment, such as the car's radios, or even a radar set operated within the same vicinity by another officer. Though less likely to occur when radar is used in a stationary mode, panning error can occur when the officer fails to adjust the set in order to diminish or eliminate the interference.

A different form of panning error occurs when a hand-held unit is swung around by the officer using it to follow a car passing by. In such a case, the speed of the motion of the hand-held antenna is added to the speed of the suspect vehicle to produce a higher readout than the car's actual speed.[10]

7. Other potential sources of error.

Among the other potential errors which have been reported are: (a) "Doubling," when the ground radar of a moving patrol vehicle focuses on a large metallic stationary object such as a metal shed or barn or billboard, harmonics within the electronics of the radar set may result in the reflected signal appearing as a multiple of the frequency of the transmitted signal; (b) Auto-lock errors due to a feature on some radar units that will cause the highest speed detected over a set speed limit to remain displayed on the unit and "locked in." Once the speed has been locked on, the unit will not record decreases in speed, but only increases. An officer who is momentarily distracted may, when alerted to the beep of the locked-in signal, attribute that speed to a motorist currently

---

9. The popular literature tells of a tree clocked at 85 mph, or a house travelling at 35 mph. These ghost readings result from electromagnetic interferences with the ra-dar unit, and are less likely to result in erroneous convictions!

10. See, Trichter & Patterson, supra note 7, at 848.

passing the patrol vehicle when the speeder has already passed the patrol car [11]; and (c) power surges which may produce an erroneous speed reading when, in order to avoid being spotted by radar detectors, the officer keeps the radar unit switched off until they spot a likely speeding vehicle, at which point the radar unit is suddenly activated. The momentary power surge can cause an inaccurate reading which overestimates the speed of the target vehicle. This possible error is eliminated in modern units which can remain powered on without emitting radar waves until a switch is thrown.

Largely as a result of public concern over the accuracy of traffic radar, the International Association of Chiefs of Police engaged in a comprehensive testing program of twenty-four different models of police traffic radar during the period of June 1983 to January 1984. The report, published in April, 1984, concludes that after manufacturers had followed some of the suggestions for improvement made by the Law Enforcement Standards Laboratory (LESL) of the National Bureau of Standards (NBS), "definitive improvements in radar devices that will be available in the future," may be expected. The study also recommended that every agency procuring radar units require that the manufacturer comply with the Model Performance Specifications for Police Traffic Radar Devices recommended by the National Highway Traffic Safety Administration, and that the unit appear on the consumer products list approved by the International Association for Chiefs of Police.[12] It is difficult to ascertain the extent to which the purposes of this testing program have been obtained and the impact it currently has on accuracy of radar devices presently in service.

§ 4.04 Required Testing of Equipment

The radar speed detector is also subject to error if it is not operated properly, which includes sufficient testing to ensure accuracy. This is very important because many courts hold that untested radar equipment readings standing alone are insufficient to convict for speeding. What the proper testing requirements are varies with the equipment used, and also with the requirements various states impose. Most states have requirements for testing; some require approval of the unit by state officials and periodic testing, as often as once every thirty days. The three basic methods of testing a radar unit for accuracy are internal tests, tuning fork tests and road tests using a vehicle with a calibrated speedometer.

The internal tests must be performed by an electronics technician and involve checking the oscillation input of the device. As has been alluded to, an extremely small variation in this input can produce a significant error in the speed reading. Based on the proposition that an

---

11. The locked-in speed may, in rare cases, even be a ghost speed reading which may be assigned by the previously inattentive operator to a vehicle currently in the vicinity.

12. *Testing of Police Traffic Radar Device,* Vol. I (Test Program Summary); Vol. II (Test Data), International Association of Chiefs of Police, Research and Development Division, 1984.

oscillation variation of .1% produces a speed error of two miles per hour, it can readily be seen that an error in oscillation of a mere one percent produces a speed error of 20 miles per hour, an error that would most assuredly render the device useless as a means of enforcing speed laws.

Field-testing the radar speedmeter is a necessary verification of accurate operation. Two tests are used for this purpose. One is to run a vehicle with a calibrated speedometer past the radar unit and compare the speedometer reading in the "drive through" vehicle with the reading obtained on the radar meter. The second most commonly used test of accuracy requires the use of an external tuning fork. Since the unit measures the Doppler effect, which is in turn a measurement of reflected frequency of vibration, any given frequency corresponds to a given speed as it would be recorded in the speedmeter. Tuning forks are available that are calibrated in almost all speeds from 15 mph to 100 mph in multiples of 5 mph. By holding several different tuning forks in front of the speedmeter and observing whether the recorded speed corresponds with that for which each tuning fork was designed, the field accuracy of the radar unit may be established. A number of states made such a testing procedure mandatory before and after use.[1]

III. VASCAR SPEED DETECTION

§ 4.05 Principles of VASCAR Speed Detection

VASCAR is an acronym for Visual Average Speed Computer And Record. It originated as a relatively simple device patented in 1958 in West Virginia by Arthur N. Marshall. The original device was purely mechanical and allowed for the measurement by a pursuit vehicle of the distance traveled by a suspect vehicle by simply having the pursuit vehicle travel the same distance while the device measured that distance. At the same time, a stopwatch measured the time it took the suspect vehicle to travel the known distance. The device offered a crude improvement on the conventional speedometer-odometer combination but left much to be desired. The officer still had to compute the speed of the suspect vehicle using time-distance information obtained from the device and the stopwatch, and he was forced to observe two instruments while attempting to watch the suspect vehicle at the same time.

When the Federal Sign and Signal Corporation assumed the manufacturing and marketing responsibility in 1967, VASCAR quickly developed into a sophisticated and highly refined electronic digital computer. Acceptance and use of the device grew tremendously since that time. VASCAR was at one time in use in over 30 states and Puerto Rico. It remains in use in a number of states.

§ 4.04

1. Vercammen, "How to Win When Your Client Has a Speeding Ticket," 20 *Barrister* 47, 48 (Spring, 1993). For court opinions on the requirement of equipment testing, see § 4.11, infra.

VASCAR operates on the simple and scientifically proven formula that average velocity equals the distance traveled divided by the time taken to travel that distance, or, as expressed in a formula,

$$AV = \frac{D}{T}.$$

So it should encounter no difficulty meeting court standards. Three modules make up the VASCAR device: the odometer module, the control module with its readout portion and the computer module.

The odometer module measures distance and is inserted in the odometer cable at the transmission. It is the only part of the instrument that needs a mechanical connection to the police vehicle that is using the equipment. It consists of a photosensitive diode, an exciter lamp and a light-interrupter disk driven by the speedometer cable.

The control module is used by the operator to activate the distance and time measuring device. It has two single-pole, double-throw switches for controlling time and distance inputs, a black momentary contact switch for resetting to zero, a red momentary contact switch to control the distance-storage function, and a multi-turn screw potentiometer for calibration adjustments. The control module is mounted on a rigid stand between the driver's seat and the front passenger's seat of the police car (see Figure 1). The readout portion consists of three seven-line digital displays utilizing 25 MA tungsten filament lamps, a lamp to indicate speeds in excess of 99.9 mph and continuously lighted decimal point.

The computer module, which is generally located under the front seat on the driver's side, consists of electrical circuitry to store time and distance information, to provide an accurate time base, to compute average velocity and to provide switching for the digital display of the readout portion of the control module.

The operator of the device can measure distance by turning on the distance switch when the police car reaches a predetermined point on the highway; he turns off the same switch when he reaches another predetermined point farther down the road. The time element can be stored in the computer by turning on another electrical switch when the target vehicle reaches the first of the same points, and the switch is

Fig. 1. The control module and visual readout portion of the VASCAR Unit are within easy reach of the police officer. *Courtesy: Federal Sign & Signal Corp., Chicago, Ill.*

turned off when it reaches the second point.   The only component of the unit which the operator is concerned with during field use is the control module.   A switch on the left of the operator is for measuring distance, which is always measured by the police car; a switch on the right is for time, and is always measured on the target vehicle.

§ 4.06   Operating Procedure

When the violator's vehicle reaches a certain location or reference point on the road, such as a painted line across the pavement, the time switch is turned on, thus activating the time circuitry in the computer. When the police car equipped with VASCAR reaches the same point, the operator turns on the distance switch, activating the distance circuitry to record the distance being measured by the police car through the odometer module connected to the speedometer cable.   As the target vehicle reaches a second point, such as another line across the road, the time switch is turned off.   The time that it has taken the target vehicle to travel between the two points has been measured and put into the computer.

As soon as the police vehicle reaches the same second point, the distance switch is turned off, and the distance between the same two points has then been measured and put into the computer.   The speed of the violator's vehicle is electronically computed and instantly displayed on the control module readout in miles per hour.   It is not necessary for the officer to take his eyes off the road at any time during the clocking procedure except to glance at the resulting readout speed.   This speed will remain on the readout portion until the officer clears the computer by pushing the reset button.   This method of clocking results in an average speed calculation; the average speed is never higher than the peak speed the vehicle reached.

The reference points an officer can use as location markers are many and varied: shadows being cast by stationary objects along the highway, guard rails, beginnings of crossovers and intersections, rural roadside mailboxes and so forth.   The unit can be used in sunlight, on overcast days and even at night when driving requires the use of headlights.

The accuracy of the combined modules is tested by the manufacturer to a maximum variation of one-tenth of one percent before they are shipped.   This test is based on an average velocity of 100 mph.   Installation is purely mechanical with the odometer module being attached to the speedometer cable.   There is no need to tamper with the mechanical operation of any of the modular units.   If one of the units is damaged by being dropped the whole device will fail.   There will be no possibility of an error; it simply will not work.   The readout portion will read 00.1 and will continue to do so until repairs are made and the device is recalibrated.   This same figure, 00.1, remains on the digital display until the unit has had sufficient time to warm up.   The warm-up period is important since the most sensitive portion of the device, the oscillator, must be maintained at a constant temperature in its case.   If the temperature varies, the figure 00.1 will appear on the digital display, indicating an error. If the operator tries to feed in either time or distance twice during the same computation, the device will again read 00.1, indicating the error. The maximum capacity of the computer is 6.5 minutes and 5.5 miles.

While the VASCAR method has not been used as extensively as radar, some renewed interest is shown in its adoption as a relatively simple means of speed detection by the use of traffic helicopters equipped with the device. In at least one state, the legislature was asked to authorize use of VASCAR in police helicopters.

All VASCAR operators must be certified before they are allowed to use the device. The certification process involves classroom training of about one day, training on the road and the equivalent of one-half day of instruction in nighttime operation of the device. The student operator then spends approximately thirty days using the device, during which time he may issue warnings to motorists who, on the basis of his operation of the device, appear to be speeding. At the conclusion of his training period the operator is tested by his instructor, using a different vehicle, and must undergo a new series of examinations.

IV.   LASER SPEED DETECTION

§ 4.07   Speed Detection by Laser

Law enforcement has recently found a new technology to combat speeders in an adaptation of laser technology. Admired for its pin-point accuracy in locating targets in the Gulf War, this adaptation of laser aiming devices to the detection of speeders may well replace radar and Vascar speed detectors in the future.[1] Because it is a relatively new application, only limited information is available about the performance, reliability, and pitfalls, if any develop, of laser speed detection devices.

LASER is an acronym for Light Amplification by Stimulated Emission of Radiation. Unlike the electromagnetic radiation generated by radar units, lasers use light energy instead. As a result of the pioneering work of scientists Schawlow, Townes, and Maiman, a host of solid state and other types of lasers have been developed.[2] Laser techniques have seen many applications in everyday life beyond the military uses alluded to earlier. Thus, we find it used in the gun sights of some hunting rifles, in printing processes, in compact disc players, in surgical instruments, in holography, in communications, and even at grocery store check-out stands.

---

§ 4.07

[1] Koziol, "Speeders, You Better Watch Out for Lasers," *Chicago Tribune*, Nov. 28, 1991, at M3.

[2] On the pioneering work with Masers and Lasers, see the topic "Maser," in Van Nostrands' *Scientific Encyclopedia*, 4th ed., 1968, at pp. 1081–1085.

Essentially, the laser beam is produced when a material within a cavity that is partially mirrored is stimulated by electrical or light energy. As the material becomes stimulated, a chain reaction of sorts begins, wherein the energy emitted by the material itself further excites the material. When the energy built up is of a sufficient intensity, it passes through the mirror as a narrow, straight, and intense beam of monochromatic and coherent light.[3] Its application to the detection of speeders on the highway relies on invisible light waves that are emitted at frequencies which allow the laser beam to be focused onto a very narrow target. Thus, while the beam of a radar transmitter spreads out in a cone which, at one mile from the transmitter, may be as wide as 550 feet, the cone of invisible light emitted from the laser at that same distance would be only 19 feet wide.

Even though the first use of laser guns for the detection of speeders supposedly emerged in 1986, and its more general use did not commence until the 1990's, by late 1992 more than 600 laser "guns" were reported to be in use in 31 states and in Canada.[4] Florida was the first state to take legislative action approving the use of laser guns,[5] and presumably permitting into evidence such speed measurements, provided the statute's requirements are satisfied. Several other states,[6] introduced bills in 1993 aimed at permitting the detection of speeders by laser devices, but the fate of said bills was not determined at year's end.

§ 4.08   Operating Procedure and Limitations

Early use of the laser speed detection device by law enforcement agencies was in the testing mode. The popularity of the device has been growing as the officers utilizing it gave the laser speed gun rave reviews. The primary benefits of the device over traditional radar enforcement are the ease in target selection because of the narrow beam width,[1] and that no known countermeasures exist. Radar detectors obviously do not detect laser beams.

The greatest advantage laser has over the ever broadening radar cone with its difficulties in target selection when multiple targets are present, is the narrow band-width of laser that supposedly permits an officer to select a target out of a cluster of targets. However, the

---

3. National Highway Traffic Safety Administration, U.S.D.O.T., "Law Enforcement Bulletin; Laser Speed Measurement Devices," Feb. 9, 1993. See also, "Shedding Some Light On Lasers," *R.A.D.A.R. Reporter* (June, 1992). This monthly newsletter about radar, radar detectors, and automotive transportation issues is published by Radar, Inc., Tipp City, Ohio.

4. Libow, "Speed-limit Enforcement Turning to High–Tech Tools," *The Hartford Courant*, Oct. 1, 1992, at C1; UPI Newswire, "Illinois State Police Using Lidar to Trap Speeders," Oct. 1, 1992; Beasley, "Laser Guns '10 Times Better Than Radar'," *Atlanta Constitution & Journal*, May 19, 1992 at A1.

5. West's Fla.Stat.Ann. § 316.1906(1), (2) (1992), amending the definition of radar to also include "any laser-based or microwave-based speed measurement."

6. Among them, Maine, Maryland, Virginia, and Rhode Island.

§ 4.08

1. The PRO LASER–5000, manufactured by Kustom Signals, Inc., Overland Park, KS, manufacturer's literature states that the beam width is 4.5 feet at 1000 feet.

advantage may not be as great as first supposed. The early models of laser guns featured firearms-type sighting through which to aim, complete with detachable shoulder stock or with vehicle dash mounts for better targeting. These units require traffic law enforcers to be marksmen! Also, current models can be used only in a stationary mode and are not adapted to mobile use, though such development ought to be anticipated. With the sighting system as is currently in use, the officer using the device can only hit the intended target if (1) the sighting system is properly aligned in accordance with the officer's own style of aiming; and (2) the officer can maintain the sight picture while pulling the trigger to activate the laser. Even the addition of cross-hair telescopic sights[2] may not meaningfully make the task of finding and tracking a traffic offender easier.

Most traffic police officers are not trained in SWAT–type sniper shooting; they are not adept in the art of shooting long-range rifles, since their training in the use of firearms concentrates on handguns (revolvers and pistols) and shotguns. Their proficiency in the use of laser guns will therefore require additional training and a skill only some will acquire.

Furthermore, each laser gun's sighting system will have to be adjusted to the individual officer, since all persons using a sighting system, whether mechanical or optical, sight in differently.

It will also become important to develop procedures for verifying the accuracy of the electronic components, and for the testing of the speed measuring device as well. The most expedient field method might well be calibrating the Laser device by measuring the speed of a second patrol vehicle that has a calibrated speedometer, though this may cause evidentiary problems involving hearsay when seeking to lay the necessary foundation for admission of the evidence.

A serious limitation on the use of lasers is its inability to function effectively in poor weather conditions. The coherent light waves are either dispersed or reflected by anything that is in their path, so that rain, hail, and snow will have a limiting effect upon use of the laser as a detector of speeding. To what extent the weather conditions will play a role remains to be established.

Some questions that have not been satisfactorily proved to date involve the potential of the danger that the laser beam poses to human beings. If a laser light beam is concentrated enough to hit a target at 2000 feet and produce a measurable beam of light 2000 feet in the opposite direction, can it hurt a motorist whose eyes are inadvertently hit by the beam while the laser is transmitting? The manufacturers dismiss this as a non-issue, though independent testing will be required to determine not only the safety of the laser device newly placed in service, but its continued safety while in daily use as well.

---

2. The LTI–20–20, manufactured by Laser Technology, Inc., uses the "red-dot" type of sighting system that is probably not known for pin-point accuracy at the 1000–2000 feet distances at which the laser is supposed to be used.

The cost of the units, at twice that of radar speed measuring devices, is likely to be a further impediment in the widespread displacement of radar in favor of laser speed measurement.

———

V. EVIDENCE OF SPEEDING

§ 4.09 Non-scientific Evidence of Speeding

The courts have accepted, as proof of the speed of a moving motor vehicle, non-scientific evidence of a variety of types. It has been stated that the excessive speed of an automobile can be established by the opinion of eye-witnesses.[1] This type of opinion may be viewed as a matter of common observation, not calling for a witness endowed with expert qualifications. It may be easily discredited, however, as being in the realm of speculation and conjecture.

A person who, while not an expert in the true sense of the word, nevertheless possesses some qualifications not ordinarily had by the common man, may at times be permitted to testify to the speed, in miles-per-hour, of a vehicle on the basis of sound alone. In Kuhn v. Stephenson,[2] for instance, an automobile mechanic with twelve years' experience in his trade was permitted to state that a car was going 45 miles per hour based on the sound of the motor only, since he had not seen the vehicle as it passed by. Other courts have not been willing to permit the introduction of such evidence, however, where the witnesses lacked special experimental qualifications to judge speed by auditory perception only.[3] Sometimes, courts have admitted testimony which used the less definite terms of "fast," "very fast," or "at a high rate of speed," based on sound alone, but again, there is no uniformity among the jurisdictions and the cases appear to be decided pretty much on an *ad hoc* basis, depending on a totality of the facts and circumstances of a particular case.[4]

Markings painted on the highway at pre-measured intervals permit law enforcement agencies to measure the speed of vehicles from the air. A number of states use airplanes, and the airborne officer uses a stopwatch to measure the time it takes for a targeted vehicle to cover the

§ 4.09

1. E.g.: Hastings v. Serleto, 61 Cal. App.2d 672, 143 P.2d 956 (1943); Horton v. State, 119 Ga.App. 43, 166 S.E.2d 47 (1969); Heacox v. Polce, 392 Pa. 415, 141 A.2d 229 (1958).

2. 87 Ind.App. 157, 161 N.E. 384 (1928). Accord: Pierson v. Frederickson, 102 N.J.Super. 156, 245 A.2d 524 (1968).

3. Challinor v. Axton, 246 Ky. 76, 54 S.W.2d 600 (1932); Bernardini v. Salas, 84 Nev. 702, 448 P.2d 43 (1968); Meade v. Meade, 206 Va. 823, 147 S.E.2d 171 (1966).

4. Admitting such testimony are, e.g.: Pierson v. Frederickson, supra n. 2; Marshall v. Mullin, 212 Or. 421, 320 P.2d 258 (1958); Hauswirth v. Pom–Arleau, 11 Wash.2d 354, 119 P.2d 674 (1941).

Holding the evidence inadmissible: Carstensen v. Faber, 17 Wis.2d 242, 116 N.W.2d 161 (1962); Bernardini v. Salas, supra n. 3. See also, Anno., 33 A.L.R.3d 1405.

distance between the two lines. That time can then be compared to a chart to determine the speed of the tracked vehicle.[5] Never long in devising countermeasures, a company markets a device called the "Skybuster" to alert motorists to the possible presence of police aircraft by detecting the transponder in the aircraft as well as the airport's FAA radar reflections of the plane.[6]

Expert qualifications of a different kind will permit testimony on the speed of motor vehicles on the basis of the length of skidmarks. That type of evidence ordinarily calls for testimony by a traffic accident reconstructionist (infra, Chapter 11), who need not have witnessed the car at the time of speeding and the resulting accident.[7] No special qualifications are required, however, to testify to the speed of a vehicle on the basis of a "Prather" speed device consisting of two rubber hoses stretched across a highway at a known distance which activate a measuring device connected to the hoses, provided it is shown, by a proper foundation, that the apparatus was properly tested and utilized.[8]

A relatively new device on American highways is the Photo–Radar device, imported from Europe where it has known wide use for years. A narrow-beam traffic radar is mated to a camera in such a way that the camera's shutter is tripped and a photograph is taken of the car, license plate, and its driver's face as well, when the radar unit registers a vehicle passing by at a pre-set speed. The photograph also contains the time and date, as well as the monitored speed. Presence of the device, if advertised, offers a deterrent to speeding that is especially valuable in areas where traffic congestion is high and enforcement made more difficult on account of it.

Photo–Radar can be placed at a location that is unmanned, i.e., mounted on a utility pole, or installed in the back of a van or other utility vehicle.[9] Police personnel regularly visit the site where the Photo–Radar is set up to check on the calibration of the unit and insure that the device has not been damaged by unfavorable weather conditions or vandalism,[10] and to retrieve exposed film and reload the camera. After development, the names and addresses of suspected drivers caught in the photo-trap are obtained from motor vehicle department files, and

5. Sherman & Nadel, "Speeders Beware," *Popular Science Mag.*, Sep. 1990, p. 66.

6. Jensen, "Eye On The Sky," *Autoweek*, May 29, 1989, p. 28.

7. E.g.: Hann v. Brooks, 331 Ill.App. 535, 73 N.E.2d 624 (1947); People v. Zimmerman, 12 Mich.App. 241, 162 N.W.2d 849 (1968), affirmed 385 Mich. 417, 189 N.W.2d 259 (1971); Grapentin v. Harvey, 262 Minn. 222, 114 N.W.2d 578 (1962).

8. Carrier v. Commonwealth, 242 S.W.2d 633 (Ky.1951).

9. Some of these units may be managed by private security companies under contract with counties or municipalities and may be paid a flat rate per ticket issues or a percentage of the tickets paid. See, Baker, "'Photocop' didn't play in Peoria," *Chicago Tribune*, Mar. 21, 1991, at DuPage p. 1. Even when operated by public agencies, the profit motive in collecting fines to run local government remains a factor.

10. Smith & Cole, "Giving Big Brother the Birdie," *Car and Driver*, Aug. 1989, at 103, mention that in some areas the device had to be placed in a bullet-proof casing.

citations are issued.[11] If more than one vehicle is shown in a photograph, no citations are issued.

No significant legal opinions dealing with the device have been noted, though some of the most pressing legal questions arising from the use of Photo–Radar have been discussed in the literature.[12]

§ 4.10 Admissibility of Radar Speed Readings

When radar evidence was first sought to be introduced, the courts required that technical testimony be offered to demonstrate the scientific principle underlying the technique of detecting the speed of motor vehicles by radar.[1] Courts have taken judicial notice of the fact that radar is a reliable means of measuring speed.[2] This does not, however, benefit the many different types of devices that are on the market, some of them of questionable accuracy. Thus, in City of Seattle v. Peterson,[3] the court said that the accuracy of a particular model of radar unit is not a proper subject of judicial notice. Therefore, in the absence of evidence that shows the unit utilized in the case at bar has been determined to be reliable, readings from the device ought not to be admitted. The court added that if "the validity of a scientific principle is a prerequisite to its admission into evidence, then consistency requires that evidence of the ability of a machine to employ that scientific principle reliably must also precede admission of the machine's results into evidence."[4] Thus, in United States v. Fields,[5] the court, on the basis of the expert testimony presented by the prosecution in this speeding case—not the defense—rejected evidence of a radar device called the Speedgun Eight, because, the court found, it cannot be operated in a scientifically reliable manner.[6]

11. In its use in the Washington, D.C. area, the photograph was not mailed to the person cited, but is kept as proof of the violation. See, Fehr, "RADAR–Photo Speed Device Gets Test-drive on Beltway," *The Washington Post,* Jul. 21, 1990, at B–1.

12. Grab, "Photo–RADAR Enforcement: Is it Constitutional?," *Los Angeles Lawyer,* Dec. 1989, p. 22.

§ 4.10

1. People v. Torpey, 204 Misc. 1023, 128 N.Y.S.2d 864 (1953). See also, Anno., 49 A.L.R.2d 469.

2. Everight v. City of Little Rock, 230 Ark. 695, 326 S.W.2d 796 (1959); People v. Maclaird, 264 Cal.App.2d 972, 71 Cal.Rptr. 191 (1968); State v. Tomanelli, 153 Conn. 365, 216 A.2d 625 (1966); People v. Abdallah, 82 Ill.App.2d 312, 226 N.E.2d 408 (1967); State v. Dantonio, 18 N.J. 570, 115 A.2d 35 (1955); People v. Magri, 3 N.Y.2d 562, 170 N.Y.S.2d 335, 147 N.E.2d 728 (1958); City of East Cleveland v. Ferell, 168 Ohio St. 298, 154 N.E.2d 630 (1958).

Myatt v. Commonwealth, 11 Va.App. 163, 165, 397 N.E.2d 275, 276 (1990) held that "expert testimony is not admissible to contest the reliability of the use of radar," for the detection of speeding.

3. 39 Wash.App. 524, 693 P.2d 757 (1985).

4. Id. at 758. See also, State v. Doria, 135 Vt. 341, 376 A.2d 751 (1977).

5. 30 Cr.L. 2459 (DCS Ohio 1982).

6. In an earlier case dealing with the MR–7 moving radar, the Ohio Court of Appeals, in State v. Shelt, 46 Ohio App.2d 115, 75 O.O.2d 103, 346 N.E.2d 345 (1976), saw no reason for treating it differently from stationary radar. The court held that a person may be convicted solely upon MR–7 evidence upon (1) testimony by an expert on the construction of the device and how it works; (2) evidence that the unit worked properly; and (3) evidence that the officer using the MR–7 was properly qualified in its use. A concurring judge, however, would extend judicial notice to the underlying principles, requiring a showing only of

The Missouri Supreme Court, on the other hand, held that testimony from an experienced highway patrol officer and a highway patrol communications specialist concerning the use of the "Speed Gun Eight" provided enough foundation for the belief that the device is sufficiently reliable to be admitted into evidence as proof of the speed of a moving vehicle.[7] When a court relies on "the public record" and other decided cases, it is not always possible to determine whether sources relied on pertain to the same device, or another instrument. In view of the fact that radar devices differ greatly in their specifications as well as in the intricacy of their circuitry and design, the fact that one particular unit is proved to be highly reliable hardly benefits a different unit manufactured to different specifications. Yet, courts do not always distinguish the "sources" relied upon.

Some states also have passed statutes that provide for the admissibility of radar evidence without requiring expert testimony of the radar principle. These statutes, in effect, make the evidence of speed obtained through radar detection devices prima facie evidence of actual vehicle speed, subject to a showing of the proper operation and testing of the instrument and subject to having a qualified operator.

Many states regulate radar speed detection by statute in a wide variety of ways. No comprehensive attempt to deal with each state's statutory enactments pertaining to radar is here attempted. To illustrate the wide diversity of such statutes, however, we note that a North Carolina statute admits radar evidence only as corroborating the opinion of the officer as to the speed of a vehicle based on visual observation.[8] California prohibits use of evidence to establish speeding if the evidence is based on a "speed trap," which includes use of radar in some locations.[9] Pennsylvania prohibits use of radar to issue citations for speeding in speed zones unless the violation is in excess of six mph over the posted speed limit, and also prohibits use of radar by anyone not a state police officer.[10] While the Florida statute provides that radar evidence is not admissible unless certain conditions have been fulfilled, the enumerated conditions do not include a requirement that the device be properly calibrated or regularly tested for accuracy.[11]

Litigators should keep in mind that police officers who issue citations for speeding are not always "disinterested" individuals who are "merely" enforcing the law, as prosecutors tend to portray them. They

---

items (2) and (3) above. See also, People v. Donohoo, 54 Ill.App.3d 375, 12 Ill.Dec. 49, 369 N.E.2d 546 (1977) holding admissible evidence based on a radar "speed gun," when the instrument is properly calibrated, the operator trained in its operation, and proper use in a particular instance.

7. State v. Calvert, 682 S.W.2d 474 (Mo. 1984).

8. N.C.Gen.Stat. § 8–50.2(a) (1994). A 1994 amendment broadened the statute to apply to laser speed detection as well.

9. West's Ann.Cal.Veh.Code § 40802 (1994).

10. 75 Pa.C.S.A. § 3368 (1994).

11. West's Fla.Stat.Ann. Title 13 § 316.1906(2) (1990). This statute was amended in 1992 to also permit detection of speeding by "any laser-based or microwave-based speed-measurement system."

may, indeed, be "interested" in the outcome since most police agencies keep detailed statistics on the number of citations each officer issues, and, in fact, may evaluate the officer's effectiveness in part by the number of citations issued. While the goal of ridding the highways of speeders because of the danger to human lives they cause is laudable, it should also be kept in mind that some jurisdictions have the ulterior motive of revenue generation via traffic fines for speeding.[12] If, in fact, the goal of enforcing the speed limit statutes is to enhance safety on the highways by lowering the speeds at which drivers travel, then unmarked police cars, stealthily hidden in nooks and crannies along the highways, do not present the visible and impressive deterrence that clearly marked police cars present.

Although evidence of a radar speedmeter is now generally allowed into evidence, a proper foundation for its admission must be laid. In a jurisdiction which has not judicially noted the accuracy of the underlying scientific principles, this would require, (1) a showing, by expert testimony, on how the apparatus is constructed, functions and operates; (2) a showing that the operator of the device had the requisite training; (3) that the apparatus had been properly calibrated, checked and tested after it was set up at a site; (4) that the operator had observed the speed of defendant's car on the apparatus as it broke the radar beam; and (5) that he could positively identify the defendant's car as the one which was responsible for the speed reading the officer is testifying to.

Where the court has taken judicial notice of the scientific principles underlying speed detection by radar, the first step may be omitted, but all of the remaining steps must be shown.

§ 4.11   Testing of Radar Speed Detectors

There are at least three different ways in which the accuracy of radar apparatus readings can be checked. The first one consists of internal checks by a trained electronics specialist in a shop. This type of testing is done before the unit is sold to a law enforcement agency, and barring breakdowns requiring more frequent checks, the testing is repeated on the average of once every six months.

The second testing method requires the use of two patrol cars. After the radar car has been placed at the location where it is to be used, a second patrol car, equipped with a calibrated and certified speedometer, drives through the radar beam at a prearranged speed so that the radar operator can verify whether the instrument properly records the speed of the passing vehicle.

The third method involves the use of tuning forks, described earlier in § 4.04. Modern radar units now have a tuning fork calibrated at a given speed, e.g., 60 m.p.h., as an integral part of the unit. The fork is hermetically sealed in a box insulated against shock and against temper-

---

12. Commonwealth v. Martorano, 387   (Johnson, J., dissenting).
Pa.Super. 151, 563 A.2d 1229, 1235 (1989)

ature variations from 40 degrees below zero to 170 degrees above zero Fahrenheit. The instrument can thus be tested for accuracy immediately before and immediately after a car's speed is recorded merely by pushing a button on the radar unit.

Even when proper tuning forks have failed to reveal any problem, it is still possible for the radar unit to operate incorrectly, since the tuning fork test only proves that the timebase which converts the Doppler frequency into a digital reading works properly. The tuning fork test itself does not determine that the generator of radar waves operates on the correct frequency.[1]

Testing of the unit is an absolute prerequisite if the radar reading is the only evidence of speeding. In State v. Gerdes,[2] the Minnesota Supreme Court held that a speeding conviction cannot be predicated solely upon evidence of speed derived from a radar device which had not been subjected to external testing, whether by use of a reliably calibrated tuning fork, or by an actual test run with a police car.[3]

Some courts have held that external testing with a tuning fork alone is insufficient, and that additional proof of accuracy is required,[4] but this added proof would appear to be unnecessary with the models currently in use. Of course, some courts have held that a reading from an untested radar device, or from an untested speedometer, is admissible but not sufficient in itself to support a conviction; the deficiency can be supplied by the observations about the speed of the vehicle by the trained police officer who is shown to have experience in judging speed.[5]

Whatever the method of supplying proof of accuracy, it is well settled that the radar unit must be shown to have been tested both before and after it has been set up.[6] The fact that a jurisdiction has

§ 4.11

1. Godson, "Technical Shortcomings of Doppler Traffic Radar," 30 *J.For.Sci.* 1186, 1189 (1985).

2. 291 Minn. 353, 191 N.W.2d 428 (1971).

3. Also, Hardaway v. State, 207 Ga.App. 150, 427 S.E.2d 527 (1993); Brooker v. State, 206 Ga.App. 563, 426 S.E.2d 39 (1992).

4. E.g.: Cromer v. State, 374 S.W.2d 884 (Tex.Crim.App.1964); Biesser v. Town of Holland, 208 Va. 167, 156 S.E.2d 792 (1967), reversing a conviction of driving at 48 m.p.h. in a 35 m.p.h. zone. However, in Honeycutt v. Commonwealth, 408 S.W.2d 421 (Ky.1966), the court held that accuracy of the radar may be established by tuning fork alone. See also, People v. Stankovich, 119 Ill.App.2d 187, 255 N.E.2d 461 (1970). In City of Ballwin v. Collins, 534 S.W.2d 280 (Mo.App.1976), the court held that a dual test is required before a court can accept radar speedometer evidence. Testing the radar unit with a tuning fork, with-

out a showing of the accuracy of the tuning fork itself, is insufficient to support a conviction.

On the other hand, the fact that no witness could testify that either the tuning fork or the police car speedometer was certified as mechanically perfect was held not to bar use of the testimony on radar recorded speed but only to go to the weight of the evidence in State v. Shimon, 243 N.W.2d 571 (Iowa 1976).

5. People v. Fletcher, 30 Misc.2d 468, 216 N.Y.S.2d 34 (Cty.Ct.1961). In City of St. Louis v. Boecker, 370 S.W.2d 731 (Mo. App.1963), a speeding conviction was reversed where the officer testified that he tested the radar device prior to the defendant's arrest, but did not specify when or where.

6. E.g.: Everight v. Little Rock, supra note 2, section 4.10; State v. Graham, 322 S.W.2d 188 (Mo.App.1959); People v. Skupien, 33 Misc.2d 908, 227 N.Y.S.2d 165 (Cty.Ct.1962); Farmer v. Commonwealth,

judicially noted the Doppler–Shift principle upon which radar units are constructed does not relieve the state of its burden of proof in this regard. "Judicial notice does not extend to the accuracy or efficiency of any given instrument designed to employ the principle. Whether the instrument itself is accurate and is accurately operated must necessarily be demonstrated to the satisfaction of the trier [of fact]." [7] This is true even if the jurisdiction has a statute which makes radar checks prima facie evidence of speed.[8]

When the test of accuracy of the unit has been made by running a test vehicle at a known speed through the zone covered by the radar apparatus, other requirements may have to be met. When the machine was tested by one police officer driving through the radar zone at various speeds while another officer read the radar meter, it was held hearsay for the officer who drove through the radar zone to testify as to what the reading was on the radar machine, since the radar readings were observed by the other officer out of the presence of the witness.[9]

And, of course, it would seem just as essential that, when proof of testing of the radar unit is done by running a patrol car through the radar zone, it must be shown that the automobile's speedometer is accurate.[10] Lack of such proof was held not to bar admission of the radar speed evidence,[11] although it would make the evidence insufficient to support a conviction for speeding without additional evidence.[12]

§ 4.12 Speed Signs, Radar Detectors, and Other Factors

In some states, statutes prohibit the use of a radar device within a certain number of feet of a speed sign in the defendant's direction.[1] The intention of the legislature, in providing for such signs, is to give a driver ample time to adjust to a speed limit reduction before subjecting him to radar detection.[2]

The advent of the "Fuzzbuster" and a whole host of other radar detection devices has provoked a legislative response in some states, which have outlawed use of the devices on the highway. Such a statute was upheld as against constitutional attack in Smith v. District of

---

205 Va. 609, 139 S.E.2d 40 (1964). See also, Sweeny v. Commonwealth, 211 Va. 668, 179 S.E.2d 509 (1971).

7. State v. Tomanelli, 153 Conn. 365, 371, 216 A.2d 625, 629 (1966).

See also text, supra, at notes 3 and 4, section 4.10.

8. Crosby v. Commonwealth, 204 Va. 266, 130 S.E.2d 467 (1963).

9. Id.

10. People v. Tiedeman, 25 Misc.2d 413, 207 N.Y.S.2d 95 (City Ct.1960).

11. Farmer v. Commonwealth, supra note 8, section 4.09.

12. People v. Johnson, 23 Misc.2d 11, 196 N.Y.S.2d 227 (Cty.Ct.1960); People v. Fletcher, supra note 7, section 4.09.

§ 4.12

1. E.g., Ill.Rev.Stats.1972, C. 95½, § 11–604.

2. Cases decided under the statute include: People v. Johannsen, 126 Ill.App.2d 31, 261 N.E.2d 551 (1970), affirming a conviction; and People v. Russell, 120 Ill. App.2d 197, 256 N.E.2d 468 (1970), reversing a conviction.

See also, Darden v. Rapkin, 148 Ga.App. 127, 251 S.E.2d 94 (1978).

Columbia,[3] and other cases,[4] though the Virginia Supreme Court held that a provision of the statute which held that presence of a radar detector in an automobile was prima facie evidence of an intent to violate the statute, without requiring the state to prove that the device was in an operable condition, was an unconstitutional use of a burden of proof shifting presumption.[5]

Legislative attempts to curb the use of radar detectors have largely failed. Their use is legal, as of this writing, in every state except Connecticut, Virginia, and the District of Columbia.

Despite the persistent and heavy marketing effort by the manufacturers of radar warning devices and radar detectors, these instruments' effectiveness is limited. The development of "instant-on" (pulse) radar speed meters, and the electronic radar detector spotters do much to diminish the effectiveness of popular radar detectors as a countermeasure against police radar. Perhaps the more effective countermeasures are based on the same methods used by the U.S. Air Force in developing stealth aircraft that are near-invisible to radar: use of fiberglass, plastic and other non-metallic materials in the construction of car bodies, especially in conjunction with radar absorbent materials that are contoured and fitted to the car's exterior. Thus, there are products on the market such as vehicle "bras" which absorb most of the radar waves that strike the vehicle and thus give the car a low signal return impeding efforts to get a "lock" on the vehicle's speed.[6]

There are occasions when more than one speed detection device is used and the results conflict. Thus, in People v. Barbic,[7] the Illinois Appellate Court held that where there was testimony of speeding as observed on a radar unit, and evidence of no speeding through the "Tachograph" attached to the truck driven by defendant, the trier of fact's decision as to the conflicting evidence will be upheld.

§ 4.13 Evidence of VASCAR

Because of the less frequent use of the device, few significant court cases have been handed down, although testimony of speeding based on VASCAR readings has been admitted in over a dozen states, initially usually after the foundation for admissibility was laid by experts from the manufacturer who explained to the court and jury the workings of the VASCAR device and testified to its scientific reliability.

3. 436 A.2d 53 (D.C.App.1981).

4. E.g., Bryant Radio Supply, Inc. v. Slane, 507 F.Supp. 1325 (D.W.Va.1981), affirmed 669 F.2d 921 (4th Cir.1982). Also, State v. Anonymous, 35 Conn.Sup. 659, 406 A.2d 6 (1979).

5. Crenshaw v. Commonwealth, 219 Va. 38, 245 S.E.2d 243 (1978). See also, Leeth v. Commonwealth, 223 Va. 335, 288 S.E.2d

475 (1982). See also, Tolchin, "U.S. Acts to Ban Radar Detectors In Millions of Commercial Trucks," *The New York Times,* Nov. 12, 1993, at A1.

6. "Stealth technology hides cars from speed traps," *Machine Design,* Apr. 6, 1989 at p. 26.

7. 105 Ill.App.2d 360, 244 N.E.2d 626 (1969).

In State v. Schmiede,[1] the trial court found that VASCAR units were scientifically accurate and held that testimony based upon it is admissible provided it is shown that the unit was checked for proper calibration, and the operator trained in its use. In this case, the state trooper operating the unit had received one day's training in its use and had then employed it for one month under the supervision of a qualified supervisor who administered a series of 30 tests to the witness which he passed with the greatest deviation being ⁷⁄₁₀ths of a mile and the average being .229 miles. It is interesting to note that the court, prior to issuing its ruling on admissibility, went out on the road with the trooper to permit him to demonstrate his familiarity with the VASCAR unit's operating principles and calibration.

Contrast the laying of the foundation in the *Schmiede* case with that in People v. Leatherbarrow,[2] where no testimony was offered concerning the theory and operation of the unit or of the scientific facts and principles upon which it was founded. The two police officers who testified to a reading of 94.3 miles per hour in a 55 mph speed zone had not proffered an opinion on the device's reliability, nor had it been shown that they possessed sufficient familiarity with its operation to allow such an opinion. Consequently, the county court reversed the conviction of speeding, even though the court, based on its own research, believed the unit was undoubtedly an accurate speed measuring device. Since the operating principles and the accuracy of VASCAR are not yet widely known, the court felt that proof of accuracy and reliability could not yet be dispensed with.

Because the technique simply amounts to a method of timing the speed of a vehicle over a known distance, the principle is unassailable, and judicial notice was not long in coming. Thus, barely two years after the State v. Schmiede case, the New Jersey Superior Court took judicial notice of the scientific reliability of VASCAR in State v. Finkle.[3] While VASCAR still is used less frequently than radar speed detection, its use is sanctioned by statute in several states, either explicitly or by implication.[4] Courts seem to have had little difficulty in admitting evidence based on VASCAR speed measurements, provided the operator was properly qualified and the instrument tested.[5] In State v. Chambers,[6]

§ 4.13

1. 118 N.J.Super. 576, 289 A.2d 281 (1972). See also, State v. Finkle, 128 N.J.Super. 199, 319 A.2d 733 (1974).

2. 69 Misc.2d 563, 330 N.Y.S.2d 676 (1972).

3. 128 N.J.Super. 199, 319 A.2d 733 (1974). In 1977, it was held that the "key to demonstrating VASCAR accuracy was proof of proper testing" in City of St. Louis v. Martin, 548 S.W.2d 622, 623 (Mo.1977).

4. E.g., N.C.Gen.Stat. § 8–50.2(a) (1994): "The results of the use of radio, microwave, laser, *or other speed-measuring instruments* shall be admissible . . ." [Emphasis supplied.]

5. E.g., State v. Lomack, 238 Neb. 537, 471 N.W.2d 441 (1991), VASCAR evidence admissible, but no effective objections were made to either testing of the unit or the officer's qualifications; State v. Reynolds, 133 Wis.2d 474, 394 N.W.2d 920 (App.1986) [Unpublished opinion], conviction on basis of VASCAR speed measurement admissible despite mathematical errors by operator; State v. Dobrofsky, 146 Wis.2d 866, 431 N.W.2d 327, (App.1988), VASCAR enjoys presumptive accuracy; Commonwealth v. Smolow, 364 Pa.Super. 20, 527 A.2d 131 %3(3)5F

6. See note 6 on page 252.

however, the court held that testing the accuracy of VASCAR by means of radar, and vice versa, was insufficient to establish the accuracy of the VASCAR unit.

§ 4.14 Evidence of LASER Speed Detection

Because of its recency, there are no appellate decisions which explore the LASER speed measuring technique and set standards for admission of its results. In two unpublished intermediate appellate court decisions as of this writing, results of the LASER "gun" readings have been held properly admitted.[1] Because of the potential for error in the focusing and use of the device, a more complete record than was presented in these two cases is expected in future cases.

Probably in an attempt to forestall some of the objections made in radar and VASCAR cases, some states have rushed to amend traffic statutes to include LASER devices as proper instruments to measure speed.[2]

VI. MISCELLANEOUS

§ 4.15 Bibliography of Additional References

Articles and books listed in the footnotes are not necessarily repeated here.

Anno., "Proof by Means of Radar or Photographic Devices, of Violation of Speed Regulations," 47 A.L.R.2d 822.

Anno., "Possession or Operation of Device for Detecting or Avoiding Traffic Radar As Criminal Offense," 17 A.L.R.4th 1334.

(1987), VASCAR evidence admissible; Commonwealth v. Vishneski, 380 Pa.Super. 495, 552 A.2d 297 (1989), testimony on VASCAR–PLUS unit speed timing supports conviction. But see, Commonwealth v. Martorano, 387 Pa.Super. 151, 563 A.2d 1229 (1989), no proper foundation of compliance with statutory requirements for VASCAR evidence, and officer's uncorroborated testimony as to vehicle speed insufficient for conviction.

6. 241 Nev. 60, 64, 486 N.W.2d 219, 222 (1992), police witness testified he used his B36 radar to test the accuracy of his VASCAR unit and he tested his radar in the manner in which he was trained. The court said the state failed to prove compliance with the statute: "Without some proof of reliability in the device used to test for accuracy in a primary device, a test for accuracy of the primary device is a meaningless exercise." Court also held that radar is not a testing device normally recog-

nized and used to verify the accuracy of VASCAR.

§ 4.14

1. State v. Collins, 1994 WL 68496 (Ohio App.1994)—no challenge at trial to use of LASER evidence justifying traffic stop which then resulted in speeding and DUI convictions; State v. Moell, 1994 WL 159551 (Ohio App.1994)—no challenge at trial to officer's qualifications to operate LASER speed measuring device.

2. E.g., N.C.Gen.Stat. § 8–50.2(a), amended, first extra session of 1994, to include "laser" among the speed measuring instruments admissible as evidence of speed of an object in any criminal or civil proceeding; West's Fla.Stat.Ann.Title 13 § 316.1906(2), amended by Laws 1992: " 'radar' means law enforcement speed radar, *any laser-based* ... speed-measurement system employed by a law enforcement agency to detect the speed of motorists."

Anon., "Shedding Some Light On Lasers," *R.A.D.A.R. Reporter* June 1992.

Note, "Radar Detectors, 24 *N.Engl.L.Rev.* 1 (1989).

Bedard, "Jamming Police Radar," 25 *Car and Driver* 47 (Nov. 1982).

Bedard, "They Have Lasers," 30 *Car and Driver* 87 (Apr. 1987).

Ciccone, Goodson & Pollner, "Radar Detectors and Speeds in Maryland and Virginia," 15 *J.Pol.Sci. & Admin.* 277 (1987).

Cincinnati Microwave, *Engineering Report on Traffic Radar* (1988).

Fehr, "RADAR–Photo Speed Device gets test-drive on beltway," *The Washington Post,* Jul. 21, 1990, p. B–1.

Goodson, "Technical Shortcomings of Doppler Traffic Radar," 30 *J.For. Sci.* 1186 (1985).

Incantalupo, "A Candid Picture of Speeding—Gotcha!." *Newsday,* Mar. 19, 1990, p. 6.

Kopper, "The Scientific Rule of Radar," 36 *N.C.L.Rev. 352* (1958).

National Highway Traffic Safety Administration, U.S.D.O.T., *Law Enforcement Bulletin; Laser Speed Measurement Devices,* Feb. 9, 1993.

Raynal & Edsall, "Does Big Brother have his eye on you?", *Autoweek* Feb. 5, 1990, at 10.

Ross, "Police Gaining on Speeders Again," *The New York Times,* Mar. 1, 1989 p. D–6.

Schroeder, "Do Laser Detectors Work", *Car and Driver,* Dec. 1992, p. 133.

Sherman & Nadel, "Speeders Beware: It's the photo and laser cops," *Popular Sci. Mag.* p. 66 (Sep. 1990).

Smith & Cole, "Giving Big Brother the Birdie," 32 *Car and Driver* 66 (Sep. 1990).

Tomerlin, "Spurious Signals," *Road & Track,* May 1981, p. 69.

Vercammen, "How to Win When Your Client Has a Speeding Ticket," 20 *Barrister* 47 (Spring, 1993).

*

Part II

EVIDENCE BASED ON THE PHYSICAL SCIENCES

Chapter 5

QUESTIONED DOCUMENTS

I. INTRODUCTION

I. INTRODUCTION

§ 5.01 Scope of the Chapter

Literally for centuries, courts have been faced with the problem of determining the genuineness of handwriting and of documents generally. The scientific examination of questioned documents, however, did not develop into a distinct profession until about 1870, even though prior to that time certain legal photographers had made an attempt to discover forged writings by the use of photography. Around the 1860s, a few photographers pretended to be document examiners because the use of photographic enlargements, a then novel process, gave them a hitherto unknown means of studying and visually displaying minute portions of handwritings and signatures.[1]

The Frenchman Alphonse Bertillon, whom we will mention in Chapter 8 as the inventor of anthropometry, was also a master photographer who fancied himself as a great document expert as well. With false modesty, he disclaimed expertise in handwriting comparisons, but he nevertheless frequently proceeded to give opinions on the genuineness of documents. These opinions, coming as they did from the renowned head of the French identification service, carried great weight. It was Bertillon, the photographer and anthropometrist, who gave part of the damning evidence in the famous "Affaire Dreyfus" (which resulted in Emile Zola's famous manifesto *J'accuse*), by testifying that Alfred Dreyfus had written the document which served as the basis for his conviction for treason and his subsequent banishment. Later, of course, Dreyfus' innocence was established, as well as Bertillon's error in testifying that Dreyfus wrote the incriminating document.

Bertillon's mistaken opinion was the result of lack of expertise in the comparison of handwritings, and demonstrates probably more dramatically than any other example that a photographer is not a person qualified to give opinions on the identity of handwritings—not even a photographer who is also experienced in making minute and accurate measurements of insignificantly appearing trace evidence, as Bertillon was.

§ 5.01

1. Moenssens, "The Origin of Legal Photography," *Finger Print & Ident. Mag.,* Jan. 1962, p. 3.

Over the years, then, the examination of questioned documents developed into a profession all its own, and it came to be recognized that special skills and special training are required before a person achieves competency to give an opinion on the genuineness or fraudulent nature of documents. Rather than photographers being handwriting experts, it has come to be established that questioned document examiners need to utilize photography as an adjunct to their profession.[2]

As scientific progress made its influence felt in all human endeavors, so did document examiners begin to apply sophisticated techniques in their job. Today, the competent questioned document examiner has knowledge of and uses various sciences, including chemistry, microscopy, and photography, in the determination of the genuineness or non-genuineness of a document. He also requires the use of or access to an extensive laboratory which will permit him to make practical use of these sciences.

It is important to distinguish questioned document examinations and graphology; the two have hardly anything in common. Unfortunately, many lawyers are not aware of the differences between the fields. The most striking example of this lack of knowledge is the 1992 American Jurisprudence *Proof of Facts* article[3] on questioned document examination, which was to replace the twenty-five-year-old article by James V.P. Conway. The 1992 article was written by a graphologist and contained much erroneous information.[4] Efforts are being made by the questioned document community to publish an accurate article.[5] Handwriting is the end result of a long process that starts with the imitation of penmanship models, a process wherein the brain sends to the moving hand and fingers instructions through a complex muscle and nerve system. Initially, these writing efforts are very crude, but as the dynamic interplay between brain instructions and hand and finger movements becomes smoother, people begin to shape their handwriting by very slight deviations from the penmanship models used to instruct in the writing process. Questioned document examiners study these individual characteristics of handwriting and, by comparing the detail of such individual characteristics discovered in a document of disputed authorship with the individualistic marks of documents of known authorship, can arrive at a conclusion of common authorship, or lack of it. Questioned document examiners, then, basically study two sets of documents for the purpose of determining whether they were written by the same author.

---

2. For a further view of the development of the discipline, see, Hilton, "History of Questioned Document Examination in the United States," 24 *J.For.Sci.* 890 (1979).

3. Lehman, "Questioned Document Examination—Identification of Handwriting on Document," 15 *Am.Jur.Proof of Facts* 3d 595 (1992).

4. For a thorough review and critique of the article, see, Dillon, "A Review of Questioned Document Examination—Identification of Handwriting on Document," 16 *Sci. Sleuthing Rev.* 7 (1992).

5. Wenderoth, "Forensic Document Examination: An Introduction and Over-

By contrast, graphologists work only with one document, or with several documents known to be authored by the same person. By a study of certain characteristics of penmanship, graphologists then arrive at a conclusion that the writer of the document possesses certain personality traits or character markings. This assessment is made on the basis of the principle, advocated by graphologists, that people who share certain personality traits also exhibit these characteristics in their handwritings. The characteristics looked for by graphologists, then, are class characteristics, rather than the individual characteristics sought to be detected by questioned document examiners. The latter seek to determine whether one person was, or was not, the author of a particular document, to the exclusion of all other persons. By contrast, graphologists seek to discover traits in a writing that are shared by many others with similar personality characteristics who possess these same traits.[6]

The field of document examination is not without its critics. The authors of a 1989 University of Pennsylvania Law Review article questioned whether handwriting identification "expertise" existed.[7] They criticized the field of questioned document examination for a lack of standards and classification systems and a lack of empirical testing and validity studies. The authors discussed, among other things, the results of five Forensic Science Foundation studies from 1975 to 1987 and concluded that in 45% of the reports the examiners reached the correct result, in 36% they erred partially and in 19% they were unable to draw conclusions.

Since 1987, the Forensic Sciences Foundation has conducted and analyzed two other tests.[8] Another document examination proficiency test was conducted in 1992 which compared the expertise of a group of document examiners from the FBI against a control group of graduate students in the areas of engineering and business.[9] The results indicated that handwriting expertise does exist as the professional document examiners performed significantly better than members of the control group.

Questioned document examination should also be distinguished from forensic stylistics.[10] Stylistics is the study of individual or group charac-

---

view," *Am.Jur. TRIALS* (forthcoming 1995).

6. It may be noted that if a graphologist attempts to determine individual authorship of a document by a study of graphological detail—as many do—there is a serious risk of error, since graphologists look for characteristics that are common among certain types of people, rather than looking for the type of detail that individualizes a particular writer. The differences between the two fields are explored further in the section of expert's qualifications, infra at § 5.21.

7. Risinger, Denbeaux & Saks, "Exorcism of Ignorance as a Proxy for Rational Knowledge: The Lessons of Handwriting Identification 'Expertise'," 137 *U.Pa.L.Rev.* 731 (1989).

8. Collaborative Testing Services, Inc., Crime Laboratory Testing Program, Reps. No. 89–5, 1989; No. 92–6, 1992; Questioned Document Analysis.

9. Kam, Wetstein & Conn, "Proficiency of Professional Document Examiners in Writer Identification," 39 *J.For.Sci.* 5 (1994).

10. See, McMenamim, *Forensic Stylistics* (1993), for a comprehensive treatment of the subject.

teristics in written language. In forensic stylistics, writing style is examined to determine author identification and semantic interpretation. The characteristics of style include document format, spelling capitalization, abbreviations, punctuation, word choice, syntax (phrasing, grammar) and content.

§ 5.02 Use of Document Examinations

Document examinations play an important role in the criminal justice process. The issue of genuineness of documents presents itself in nearly all forgery prosecutions, kidnapings involving ransom notes, confidence games and embezzlements, and gambling offenses with policy slips. Apart from these, however, questioned document evidence may occur in nearly every other type of crime as well, including homicides, thefts, robberies, arson, burglaries, and art forgery.[1]

Document examiners find an even greater field in civil cases; many document examiners are not connected with law enforcement agencies and their practice is almost exclusively in civil cases. The issue of genuineness of documents presents itself there, too, in will contests, suits on notes and contracts, professional malpractice actions, stock fraud, copyright disputes, and divorce actions.

The function of the document examiner is not limited to determining whether some specimen of handwriting or typewriting has been made by a suspected individual. The examiner is also concerned with other facets of forgery detection. Among them are the authentication and dating of documents; the decipherment of erased, obliterated, charred, and water damaged documents; and the restoration of faded or chemically erased writings. Related problems he deals with involve the sequencing of a great number of writings or documents; a study of additions, interlineations and interpolations; rubber stamp and seal impressions; fluid ink and ball-point pen ink analysis; pencil markings; indented writings; suspected substitution of pages; the study of paper watermarks and of printing, copying and duplicating processes; and the detection of alterations.

The ever-expanding use of microcomputers and word processors which can be coupled to an infinite variety of printers, whether dot-matrix, "letter quality" printers of the daisy wheel or laser variety, and even newer advances in word processing, present new and challenging problems to questioned document examiners.

Competent document examiners own or work with sophisticated laboratories equipped with stereoscopic microscopes and other general and specialized optical instruments; varying types of light sources or illumination, including "invisible" light techniques to be discussed in the chapter on demonstrative evidence; and expensive calibrating and mea-

§ 5.02

1. See, Hanna, "Art Forgery: The Role of the Document Examiner," 37 *J.For.Sci.* 1096 (1992).

suring apparatus. The laboratory must include complete photographic facilities for the reproduction of documents, using the most up-to-date techniques, as well as equipment for the production and mounting of court exhibits and other modern visual aids for court use. An extensive reference library usually complements the laboratory facilities.

The qualified document examiner may be asked to resolve a great number of issues concerning the validity of a document. In civil and criminal cases, three main issues may present themselves:

(a) Did the person who supposedly wrote (or the machine that supposedly typed) a questioned document actually do so? (b) When was a disputed document executed? (c) Have any alterations or erasures been made on the document in question?

Although lay opinion may still be used in some cases to determine the genuineness of handwriting, it is often impossible for a layman to determine the age of a document or to detect a well-executed forgery, a clever alteration, or a deft erasure. A questioned document examiner approaches the task with far more experience and expertise than the layman, and with adequate laboratory aids that are more conducive to the truth. Hence, if the authenticity of a document is a possible issue in a case, the conscientious attorney will consider the necessity of submitting it to a competent examiner for an expert opinion.

II. THE EXAMINATION OF QUESTIONED DOCUMENTS

§ 5.03 The Nature of Questioned Documents

The term "questioned document," refers to any type of paper, cardboard, or other object, on which there may appear any signature, handwriting, handprinting, typewriting, printing, or other graphic markings, the authenticity of which is in dispute or doubtful. Although the questioned document examiner is involved mostly in the study of paper documents, use of the word "document" may at times be misleading when a message is conveyed on material other than paper.[1] The study of questioned documents involves, of course, messages of all kinds contained in letters, but it also includes such items as checks, telephone messages, telegrams, ledger entries, hotel or motel registration slips, drivers licenses, wills, birth certificates, passports, application forms, examination books or papers, diplomas, lottery or gambling slips, shipping or addressograph labels, and even newspapers. In addition, however, the examiner of documents may well be called in to study writings, printing, or other markings made on boxes, on the walls of washrooms,

---

§ 5.03

1. See, Taylor & Hnilica, "Investigation of Death Through Body Writing," 36 *J.For. Sci.* 1607 (1991), for a unique case in which the examiner concluded the writings on the decedent's body were, in essence, a suicide note.

the wood of doors, the walls of buildings in the street, and even writings in lipstick on bodies of homicide victims.

In questioned document work, a document is "questioned" whenever there arises any doubt as to its authenticity, whether as a whole, or as to a small, perhaps even insignificant, part of it. The doubt may center around authorship of a letter, but could just as well be concerned with whether a minute change has been made to an otherwise genuine document, such as the erasure of a name or the dollar amount on a check, or the substitution of a different name and a higher, or lower, amount.

Since documents are handled by individuals, it also may be important to determine whether there are fingerprints on it. That job is usually not within the expertise of the document examiner, and he would have to seek the cooperation of a fingerprint technician. This imposes upon both the fingerprint technician and the questioned document examiner a duty to conduct their examinations in such a manner as not to interfere with or make impossible the other's work effort.

Questioned documents should be handled as little as possible and with the utmost care. In the handling that is necessary, examiners ordinarily use tweezers. Otherwise, the writer's fingerprints, if present thereon, might be obliterated; or decipherable indentations or other markings of value to the document examiner may be damaged. Field investigators in criminal cases are advised to use plastic envelopes, if available, for the transportation of documents, and to use envelopes of such size that no folding of the document will be required. They are also generally advised not to make any markings on the document, not even to identify the document, but to make their marks on the outside of the envelope instead.

§ 5.04 Standards of Comparison

1. HANDWRITING

When the issue is one of establishing the identity of the writer of a document, or the genuineness of it, the examiner needs to compare it with other documents of known origin. Such documents are called standards, exemplars, or known specimens. A standard writing requires that the origin of the document can be positively established. This origin may be established by having the suspected writer give a sample of his writing in the presence of the examiner, or by having that person acknowledge authorship of other letters and documents written by him. It also may be done by the testimony of witnesses who actually saw a writing executed, or by persons familiar with the writing, or the very nature of the specimen may serve to authenticate it as a standard. For instance, writing on an employment application, or in a letter responding to someone else's communication, would be examples of self-authenticating documents. Pre-existing standards should be writing specimens of an age as near as possible to the date on which the questioned writing was supposed to have been executed.

It is usually said to be a good practice, when obtaining a request writing, to have the subject write the text of the disputed document by dictating the text to him. Supplementary request writings may be obtained by dictating different copy as well.

After a number of years of experimentation, the Chicago Police Scientific Crime Detection Laboratory (now officially designated as the Crime Laboratory) adopted the practice of having the suspected writer fill out the form reproduced on the next page, as Figures 1A & 1B. Its principal designer, Document Examiner David J. Purtell, who thereafter entered private practice, suggests that it is also a good practice to supplement the handwriting standard form with additional dictated specimens more comparable to the material in question.[1]

In check forgery cases, Purtell recommends using for standard purposes a check form printed on "safety" paper similar to that used for regular check purposes, but with the word "STANDARD" or "EXEMP-LAR" appearing in the place where a bank name normally appears. The latter will allay the fears of someone who may think he is being tricked into committing a real check forgery. The "safety" paper avoids a technical photography problem when courtroom exhibits are prepared.

§ 5.04

1. When printing such a form, Purtell recommends using colored ink, preferably light blue, for the inner lines on the form, so that they can be filtered out photograph-ically later on for making courtroom handwriting comparison exhibits: Purtell, "Handwriting Standard Forms," 54 *J.Crim. L., C. & P.S.* 522 (1963).

NAME		DATE	
ADDRESS	CITY & STATE		PHONE
MARRIED OR SINGLE	NAME OF SPOUSE		
CITY & STATE OF BIRTH		DATE OF BIRTH	
NAME OF PERSON LIVING WITH		RELATIONSHIP	
OCCUPATION (IF STUDENT LIST SCHOOL)		SOCIAL SECURITY NUMBER	
NAME OF EMPLOYER OR FORMER EMPLOYER		SALARY	
ADDRESS OF EMPLOYER		PHONE	
NAME OF NEAREST RELATIVE		RELATIONSHIP	
ADDRESS OF NEAREST RELATIVE		CITY & STATE	

WRITE THE FOLLOWING	WRITE THE FOLLOWING
ALBERT JOHNSON	DONALD O'CONNOR
EDWARD YOUNGBERG	ROBERT OLSEN
MICHAEL SMITH	PETER FISHER
CHARLES QUINN	JACK KOWALSKI
GEORGE KELLY	U. X. ZIMMERMAN
DAVIES MCINTYRE	ELIZABETH VAUGHN
WILLIAM BROWN	FRANKLIN PATRICK
RAYMOND TAYLOR	LAWRENCE HARRISON
THOMAS NOVAK	YOUR SIGNATURE

CHICAGO POLICE DEPARTMENT CRIME LABORATORY

NAT S B X R

RACSCDNANSHDRLYMSL

LAB NO   NAME

Fig. 1A.

WRITE THE FOLLOWING	
NAME	DATE
6739 N. FOURTH AVE.	LAKE PARKER, WASHINGTON
4256 S. INDIANA BLVD.	MANCHESTER CITY, VIRGINIA
6125 W. KILPATRICK RD.	BLACK WOODS, NEW JERSEY
8030 E. 47TH ST.	ANDERSON HILL, GEORGIA

| FIFTY | SEVEN | DOLLARS | AND | THIRTY | TWO | CENTS | $ 57.32 | JUNE 24, 1967 | 19__ |
| ONE | HUNDRED | EIGHTY | NINE | DOLLARS | & | NO CENTS | $ 189.00 | DEC. 30, 1958 | 19__ |

HANDPRINT THE FOLLOWING MESSAGE ABOVE THE WORDS SHOWN

THE MONEY IN DOLLARS WHICH DICK ZASS RECEIVED FROM VIRGINIA MCLONG WAS PLACED IN HER AUTO WITHOUT ANY TROUBLE. IT WAS LAYING COVERED BY A SLICK CAPE AND WITH LUCK WOULD NEVER BE FOUND BUT A PUSSY JUMPED ON THE SEAT AND KILLED THE OBNOXIOUS TRICK

USE THIS SPACE FOR DICTATED MATERIAL

SIGNATURE	WITNESSED BY

CPD-34.535 (REV.11/63)

INSTRUCTIONS TO INVESTIGATOR IN OBTAINING REPRESENTATIVE WRITING SPECIMENS: 1. To complete this form, all the writer at a desk provided with a normal lab foundtal pen. Instruct him to answer every question in handwriting or handprinting using no abbreviations. 2. ADDITIONAL STANDARDS should be obtained by duplicating the original paper and writing, instrument and dictating at least 3 times, selected portions of the questioned document without adding in spelling or punctuation. 3. Also obtain driver's license, applications, personal letters, etc. 4. Offer obtaining standards will check, 3. Also obtain driver's license, applications, personal letters, etc. 4. Offer obtaining standards will see that every line is completed and then sign as witness.

Fig. 1B.

Other than request writings, standards may be obtained from a variety of sources. One document examiner, Donald Doud, has suggested the following as possible sources of standard writings, including signatures:

1.	Letters, personal and business	23.	Petitions
2.	Post cards	24.	Leases
3.	Manuscripts	25.	Transcribed (signed) testimony
4.	Memoranda		Applications for:
5.	Occupational writings	26.	Lights
6.	Checks	27.	Power
7.	Endorsements on checks	28.	Water
8.	Withdrawal slips (savings accounts)	29.	Gas
9.	Bank deposit slips	30.	Steam
10.	Bank signature cards	31.	Telephone
11.	Drafts	32.	Credit accounts
12.	Deeds	33.	Positions
13.	Contracts	34.	Memberships (clubs, orders, etc.)
14.	Notes	35.	Insurance
15.	Complaints (legal)	36.	Gasoline, tires, auto, etc. (government)
16.	Administrator's reports	37.	Passports
17.	Agreements	38.	Surety bonds
18.	Wills	39.	Bank and trust co. loans
19.	Mortgages	40.	Marriage license
20.	Affidavits	41.	Dog licenses
21.	Bills of sale	42.	Business licenses
22.	Partnerships		

From this discussion it becomes obvious that in obtaining standards it is important first to examine the questioned writing so that a standard may be obtained which will afford maximum similarity to the conditions under which the questioned one was executed. For instance, if the questioned one was on unruled paper, the dictated standard should be on unruled paper of the same color, thickness and quality. For similar reasons, the writer of the standard should be supplied with the same type of writing instrument used for the questioned document, e.g., pencil, ballpoint pen, regular fountain pen, crayon, brush, etc. Furthermore, the same general kind of writing should be requested; in other words, if the questioned document was handprinted, handprinting should be requested. Under no circumstances should the writer be told how to spell certain words, even if he asks a question to that effect.

2.   TYPEWRITING

Where the origin, identity, or genuineness of a typewritten document is at issue and it becomes necessary to establish whether it has been typed on a particular typewriter, the only standards would be samples of the type produced by the suspected typewriter so that these samples may be compared with the questioned typescript. It is important that the typescript standard contain all of the machine's characters and several copies of the questioned typing.

When a writing pad or a stack of typing paper is available as a preexisting standard, the whole pad or stack should be handed over to the document examiner, not just a few sheets of it.

The more standards the examiner has to work with, the more likely it becomes that he will be able to reach a conclusion on the basis of his various comparisons.

§ 5.05 The Comparison of Handwritings

The comparison of handwriting is classed among the topics of scientific evidence because the document examiner makes use of many scientific principles and uses technological processes to aid him in his investigation, examination, and evaluation. The theory upon which the document expert proceeds is that every time a person writes he automatically and subconsciously stamps his individuality in his writing. Through a careful analysis and interpretation of the individual and class characteristics, it is usually possible to determine whether the questioned document and the standards were written by the same person.

A great number of factors are considered when examining handwritten materials, although a forger usually acts on the false assumption that writings differ only in the design of the letters. A specimen of handwriting may have from 500 to 1,000 different individual characteristics. Individuality is determined by a consideration of such factors as form, movement, muscular habits, skill, instrument use, pen position, line quality, shading, retraces, proportions, connections, spacings, terminals, slant, alignment, punctuation, embellishments, and various other factors as well.

The basic principles involved in the identification of handwriting were well stated in the early and great text upon the subject, *Questioned Documents*,[1] by its famous author, Albert S. Osborn:

> One of the first of these principles is that those identifying or differentiating characteristics are of the most force which are most divergent from the regular system or national features of a particular handwriting under examination.

> The second principle, perhaps more important than the first, is that those repeated characteristics which are inconspicuous should first be sought for and should be given the most weight, for these are likely to be so unconscious that they would not intentionally be omitted when the attempt is made to disguise and would not be successfully copied from the writing of another when simulation is attempted.

> A third principle is that ordinary system or national features and elements are not alone sufficient on which to base a judgment of identity of two writings, although these characteristics necessarily have value as evidence of identity, as stated above, if present in sufficient number and in combination with individual qualities and characteristics.

§ 5.05

1. The first edition appeared in 1910; the second in 1929.

Any character in writing or any writing habit may be modified and individualized by different writers in many different ways and in many varying degrees, and the writing individuality of any particular writer is made up of all these common and uncommon characteristics and habits. As in identifying a person, as we have already seen, it always is the *combination* of particulars that identifies, and necessarily the more numerous and unusual the various elements and features the more certain the identity.

The identifying significance of handwriting qualities depends somewhat upon their origin and that subject should be considered. It is impossible to discover how all the strange qualities and characteristics of handwriting came to be developed, and regarding most of them the writer himself cannot enlighten us. In many cases it almost seems that there must be some peculiar mental twist that produces the curious physical twists.

As in our speech and in our gestures, we do many wholly unaccountable things in our writing. To us, though, they are not peculiar and we do not put them in as a means of identifying what we do. About as satisfactory an explanation as we can make regarding them is that we do as we do because that is our way of doing it. The Englishman asks, 'Why do you say five by seven?' and in reply the American asks, 'Why do you say seven by five?'

An individual characteristic in a handwriting may be the survival of an error overlooked by the teacher when writing was learned. There are writers who make certain letters the wrong way around because they never were corrected. With the most careful teaching it is impossible, even if it is desirable, to make all children write alike. Another one of the fruitful sources of various individual qualities in handwriting is the conscious or unconscious influence of the writing of others that we frequently see.

Many characteristics are the outgrowth of admiration of a peculiar design that at some time attracted attention and was copied. These adopted forms may have high identifying quality in a handwriting as they often belong to an entirely different system or to no system. This unconscious influence no doubt accounts for about ninety-nine per cent of the alleged heredity theory regarding handwriting. We inherit handwriting as we inherit speech by imitating what we often hear and see.[2]

Figure 2 presents a good illustration of what the document examiner looks for when he compares two specimens of writings. Each one of the fifteen specimens of "and", written by fifteen different writers, contains individual characteristics—characteristics which differ from those found in the writings of other individuals. Subsequent illustrations serve to demonstrate how the comparisons are made and the manner in which the evidence is presented in court.

2. Id., 250–253.

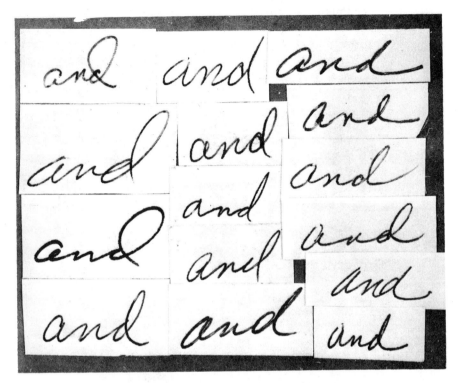

Fig. 2. The word "and" as written by fifteen different persons. A comparison of any one "and" with the other fourteen will reveal not only differences in the total formation of the word but also differences in the individual letters composing it. Note, for instance, the various ways in which the "a" is started.

One of the most noteworthy document cases ever to be brought before an American jury involved the kidnapping and subsequent killing of the infant child of the famous aviator Charles Lindbergh in 1932. The prosecution rested its case against Bruno Hauptmann primarily upon the testimony of handwriting experts who determined that the fifteen ransom notes sent to the Lindbergh family came from Hauptmann's hand.

The eight document examiners in the Hauptmann case were all unanimous in the opinion that Hauptmann had written the fifteen ransom letters, and also the addresses on the envelopes in which they had been mailed, as well as the address on the wrapper of the package containing the sleeping suit of the baby which the kidnapper had sent to Colonel Lindbergh to prove that he was dealing with the person who had the child.

The conclusion of one of the experts, the late Clark Sellers of Los Angeles, was based on a great number of factors. He illustrated his findings by referring to some of the details visible in selected words and numerals. One of these exhibits, shown in Figure 3, which incidentally also illustrates the type of demonstrative evidence generally used by questioned document examiners in court, relates to the manner and varied forms in which the word "the" was written. One of the unique forms in these documents, according to Sellers, is the writing of the word "the" so that it appears (in *A*) to be "Ue." There is no hump on the "h". Still another form (in *C*) is in making the "t" with an upstroke and crossing it at the bottom, giving it the appearance of being a capital letter "S". A rare variation of the word "the" (in *D*) was the oddity of transposing the "h" and the "t", so that the word appears to be "hle". This varied combination of form in the writing of the word "the" was of great identification value. Such a combination of variations makes it difficult, if not absolutely impossible, for a writer to successfully imitate the writing of another, and practically precludes the possibility of two writers accidentally adopting the same form.

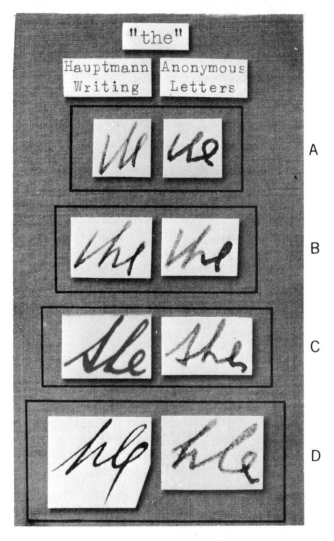

Fig. 3.

Numerals used in a questioned document also have a high identification value. In the court exhibit illustrated as Figure 4, Sellers illustrated that Hauptmann had developed certain divergencies of his own from the copy book style of writing numerals which was evident in the anonymous letters as well.

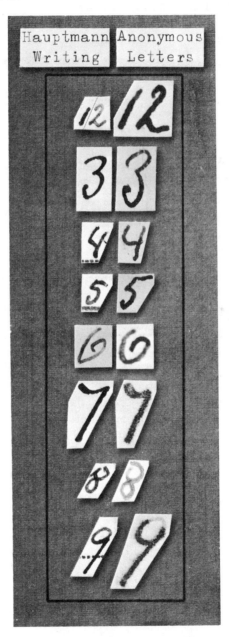

Fig. 4.

Since the ransom notes did not contain Hauptmann's signature, Sellers, in concluding that Hauptmann might nevertheless just as well have signed his name to the anonymous letters, illustrated this finding by displaying Hauptmann's signature as written on one of the known standards (see Figure 5) and piecing together Hauptmann's name with letters cut out from the anonymous letters. The "signature" thus reconstructed shows a surprising similarity with the known signature of Bruno Hauptmann.

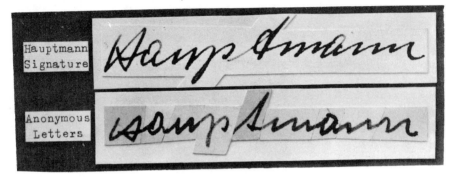

Fig. 5.

Dissimilarities in handwriting specimens are just as important as similarities since they may tend to prove that the questioned writing was *not* written by the same individual who furnished the exemplar.

Dissimilarities in the formation of capital letters usually are less indicative of non-identity than dissimilarities in forming small letters. Capital letters occur less frequently and the forger or anonymous writer usually pays particular attention to totally changing the appearance of the capital letters. He attempts to do the same with small letters, of course, but because there are many more of those, and because they admit of less variation, he is less successful in disguising his handwriting or imitating someone else's writing. The forger's handwriting does not flow smoothly and naturally over the paper. This is true whether the forged instrument was created by tracing or by freehand imitation. The forger's mind concentrates on guiding his hand and not necessarily on the subject matter of the document. As a result, the writing may often contain breaks and tremors indicating the slower than normal and uncertain motion of the forger's hand.

Comparison of signatures must be done with great care, since a signature is so personal to its author and outside influences may have a substantial effect on the writing. People usually have three different types of signatures: the formal, proper, complete signature used on an important document; the signature used for routine correspondence and documents; and the hurried scribble used for the quick note to a family member. Other circumstances will affect the signature also, such as a strained or cramped hand, an unusual writing position, excitement or hurry, heavy medication, intoxication, or missing eyeglasses. All of these influences must be considered along with the degree of consistency and naturally fluid movement that indicates an authentic signer. Yet, the differences between two handwritings of the same person, caused by some of the extraneous circumstances mentioned above, sometimes lead graphologists to misidentify signatures, or to fail to identify writings by the same author.

§ 5.06 Degree of Certainty of Expert's Conclusions

The question of the certainty of a document examiner's conclusions with respect to the genuineness of suspect handwriting are might be more properly explored by considering whether document experts frequently disagree. As a rule, equally competent document examiners infrequently disagree on the genuineness of documents. This assumes, initially, that the witnesses be truly expert in their field. There are a great many persons holding themselves out as experts in handwriting identification, whose qualifications are subject to serious attack. If they are proficient in their calling, we must examine what constitutes a disagreement.

Obviously, when expert *A* states that *X* wrote a document, and expert *B* asserts that he did not, the witnesses reach diametrically opposed opinions. Such instances are rare, though they have occurred. In 1972, news accounts writing about the purported autobiography of billionaire-recluse Howard Hughes revealed that a prestigious firm of document examiners had unqualifiedly authenticated certain disputed signatures as having been made by Howard Hughes. A few weeks later the firm retracted that opinion to admit that the signatures were forgeries,[1] thereby substantiating opposite opinions which had been previously rendered by other highly competent examiners. In another case, a handwriting expert whose decisions had been accepted as correct by the courts for over a quarter of a century publicly confessed having committed an erroneous identification which resulted in sending the wrong man to prison on a check forgery charge.[2] It is because of the ever present possibility of mistake that attorneys frequently have their own expert make an independent examination of document evidence introduced in a trial.

There are disagreements between experts of a less drastic nature. It may happen that a qualified expert has positively identified the author of a given document, and that another qualified expert concludes that no such positive identification is possible. There may be a perfectly logical explanation for this divergence of opinion; the experts might have had different standard specimens upon which to base their conclusions, or in

§ 5.06

1. "The Forgery Sleuths," *Newsweek,* Feb. 21, 1972, p. 113.

2. "Admits Mistake in Wrong Man Case—Writing Expert's 'Error'," *Los Ange-*

les Herald & Express, Sep. 10, 1959, p. A–3. See also, Cabanne, "The Clifford Irving Hoax of the Howard Hughes Autobiography," 20 *J.For.Sci.* 5 (1975).

different quantity. In such a case, each expert might have reached the same conclusion of the other expert, had he possessed the same material with which to work. This type of a case, then, does not really constitute a "disagreement". And even when both experts use exactly the same questioned and standard writings, the disagreement really hinges on the quantum of proof that each expert requires before coming to a positive conclusion; some experts may be more conservative in reaching decisions on identity or non-identity than others. One document examiner, addressing himself to that point, stated that "disagreements among Document Analysts are not more frequent than those among other professions. When they occur they are likely to involve borderline judgments, or a difference in the degree of certainty with which they are expressed." [3] The issue is tied somewhat to the degree of certainty with which experts express their opinions. Does a finding of common authorship have to be expressed "positively," or may it be expressed in terms of various degrees of probability?

The need for some standardization in the choice of terminology used in reporting opinions has long been recognized. Studies have shown that from 82 to 90% of document examiners use qualified opinions.[4] The terminology used in reporting qualified opinions was both divergent and confusing. In order to bring some order out of the chaos, the Questioned Document Section of the American Academy of Forensic Sciences and the American Board of Forensic Document Examiners adopted recommended guidelines for terminology in reports and testimony.[5]

§ 5.07 The Decipherment of Indented Writing, Charred Documents and Evidence of Alterations

Photography, ultraviolet light, and occasionally infrared rays, and more sophisticated methods,[1] such as digital image processing,[2] are

3. Shulenberger, "Do Document Experts Frequently Disagree?," *Identification News,* Mar. 1961, p. 5, at p. 6. See also, Todd, "Do Experts Frequently Disagree?" 18 *J.For.Sci.* 455 (1973); McAlexander, "The Meaning of Handwriting Opinions," 5 *J.Pol.Sci. & Admin.* 43 (1977).

Courts have held that a handwriting expert need not testify that his identification is "positive," but may express an opinion that a defendant in a criminal case "most probably," or "probably," or "very probably" made the signatures. See, e.g., State v. McGann, 132 Ariz. 322, 645 P.2d 837 (App.1981); Parker v. United States, 449 A.2d 1076 (D.C.App.1982). See also, Perry v. Leeke, 832 F.2d 837 (4th Cir.1987) (within trial court's discretion to allow expert to testify he "had a high degree of belief" as to the author of the handwriting. An expert opinion need not be based on absolute certainty.)

4. See, Decker, "A Study of Handwriting Terminology Used by Document Exam-

iners As Well As the Relationship Between Qualified Opinions and Years of Experience," Thesis, University of San Francisco, San Francisco, CA, Jan. 1982; Leung & Cheung, "On Opinion," 42 *For.Sci.Int'l.* 1 (1989).

5. McAlexander, Beck & Dick, "The Standardization of Handwriting Opinion Terminology," Letters to the Editor, 36 *J.For.Sci.* 311 (1991).

§ 5.07

1. See, e.g., Riordan, "Detection of Non-visible Writings by Infrared Luminescence and Ultraviolet Fluorescence," 36 *J.For.Sci.* 466 (1991). Noblett, "The Use of a Scanning Monochromator as a Barrier Filter in Infrared Examinations of Documents," 27 *J.For.Sci.* 923 (1982); Waggoner & Spradlin, "Obliterated Writing—An Unconven-

2. See note 2 on page 273.

valuable aids to the document examiner in such matters as indented writing, charred documents, and suspected documentary alterations.

When something is written on a piece of paper underneath which there are other papers, the underlying sheet may contain indentations which, if deciphered, may reveal what was on the top sheet. Such decipherments can be of inestimable value to the police investigator. For instance, a person who writes down a telephone number or other notation on a telephone pad may leave indented writing on an underlying sheet. That information, if deciphered, could lead to the identity of a criminal or to other evidence permitting the solution to a crime. Even what represents an original document, as, for instance, an extortion note, may have indentations on it of investigative or evidentiary value. The standard technique the document examiner uses in such cases is to photograph the piece of paper under oblique lighting so as to capitalize on the shadowing effect which frequently will permit decipherment. See Figures 6A, B, C.

tional Approach," 28 *J.For.Sci.* 686 (1983), also detailing the conventional methods; Hilton, "Special Considerations in Deciphering Erased Writing," 13 *J.Pol.Sci. & Admin.* 93 (1985).

2. See, Houde, "Image Enhancement for Document Examination Using the Personal Computer," 38 *J.For.Sci.* 143 (1993); Black, "Application of Digital Image Enhancement Software with the Macintosh Computer to Questioned Document Problems," 37 *J.For.Sci.* 783 (1992); Behren & Nelson, "Additional Applications of Digital Image Processing to Forensic Document Examinations," 37 *J.For.Sci.* 797 (1992); Wenderoth, "Application of the VSC-1/Atari 1040ST Image Processing System to Forensic Document Problems," 35 *J.For. Sci.* 439 (1990).

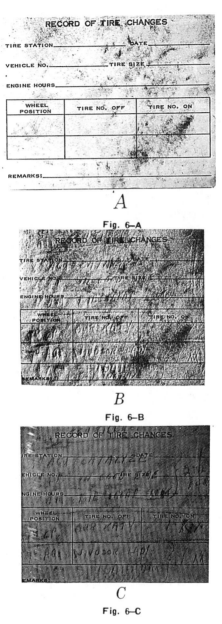

Fig. 6–A

B

Fig. 6–B

C

Fig. 6–C

Fig. 6. *A* is a document photographed in ordinary light. *B* is a photograph of the same document under oblique light. *C* was photographed with oblique light and a "Ronchi ruling plate," which serves to diffuse the light and render the indentations more discernible.

The ESDA (Electrostatic Detection Apparatus) is an electrostatic detection instrument developed in England, which provides document examiners with a superior instrumental method of deciphering indented writings, especially where faint indentations on rough paper surfaces are concerned.

The document examiner places the document on a porous brass plate and covers the document with a thin mylar film. The examiner then creates an electrostatic charge over the surface by moving a corona (a thin wire) above the surface. The examiner then spreads a toner over the surface by aerosol or by a cascading method. The procedure shows printed text or pen writings as clear areas in contrast to the black rendering of indentations.[3] Impressions of pencil and ballpoint pen have been developed by use of an ESDA on documents fifty or sixty years old.[4]

Photography can be used in many instances to decipher the writing on a document that has been charred in a fire, as shown in Figure 7.

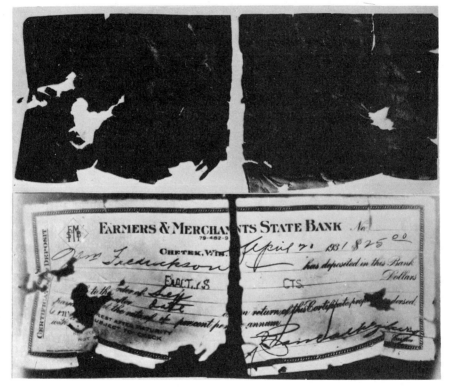

Fig. 7. Charred document decipherment. The upper portion of the illustration shows the condition of a document burned in a fire. The lower photograph illustrates its decipherment by a special photographic process.

3. Riebling & Kobus, "Some Parameters Affecting the Quality of ESDA Results," 39 *J.For.Sci.* 15 (1994); Giles, "Extending ESDA's Capability: The Determination of the Order of Writing and Impressions Using the Technique of Electrostatic Detecting," 59 *For.Sci.Int'l.* 163 (1993); Tolliver, "The Electrostatic Detection Apparatus (ESDA): Is It Really Non–Destructive to Documents?" 44 *For.Sci.Int'l.* 7 (1990); Hart & Hart, "Photographically Subtracting Interfering Images from ESDA Print," 34 *J.For. Sci.* 1405 (1989); Moore, "The Electrostatic Detection Apparatus (ESDA) and Its Effects on Latent Prints on Paper," 33 *J.For.Sci.* 357 (1988); Noblett & James, "Optimum Conditions for Examination of Documents Using an Electrostatic Detection Apparatus (ESDA) Device to Visualize Indented Writings," 28 *J.For.Sci.* 697 (1983); Baier, "Application of Experimental Variables to the Use of the Electrostatic Detection Apparatus," 28 *J.For.Sci.* 901 (1983).

4. Horan & Horan, "How Long After Writing Can an ESDA Image Be Developed?," 39 *For.Sci.Int'l* 119 (1988).

Charred documents must be handled with the utmost care by investigators who want to know and be able to prove its written contents. New developments such as the polyester film encapsulation technique are being used to preserve charred documents.[5]

Whenever suspicion arises as to whether writing has been obliterated by the use of ink eradicators, the document may be subjected to ultraviolet light and the disclosure photographed, as is shown in Figure 8. In that case, the original ink writing above a genuine signature had been removed with an ink eradicator and a different, typewritten, message inserted in its place. Observe how ultraviolet light reveals the original writing and consequently disclosed the fraudulent nature of the typewritten instruction.

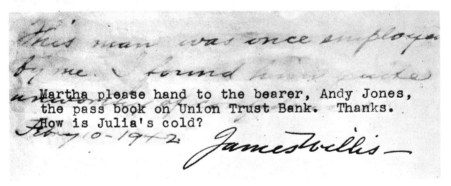

Fig. 8. Decipherment of a forgery by ultraviolet photography.

Infrared light may also be used effectively on documents suspected of being traced forgeries, as is shown in Figure 9. In that illustration, *A* is a genuine signature; *B* is the questioned one. *C* is an infrared photograph of *B* and discloses an underlying pencil (carbon) tracing of the signature over which the inked copy was made. A tip-off that *B* may have been a traced forgery appears in the uneven flow of the writing, particularly the *Jr* at the end.

5. Maldonado, "Polyester Film Encapsulation in Charred Document Cases," Presentation at the 46th Annual Meeting of the American Academy of Forensic Sciences, San Antonio, Texas, February 18, 1994.

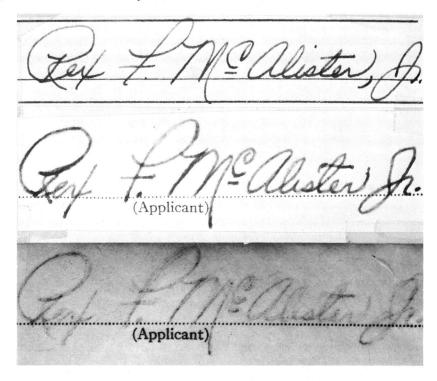

Fig. 9.

The development of digital image processing has opened the door to many new uses by document examiners. A document examiner may use an optical scanner or videocamera to scan the document into the computer. Then the software can be used to digitally alter or enhance the image. This has proven useful in deciphering indented writings and making fracture match comparisons on a typewriter ribbon with a questioned typewritten document.[6]

§ 5.08 Special Consideration in Handwriting Comparisons

While the multitude of factors alluded to earlier are extremely important in studying questioned documents, the examiner cannot neglect to consider the influence of additional environmental factors which may have played a role in the production of the questioned samples. While there are many such possible extraneous factors influencing writings, only a few are discussed here by way of example.

1. WRITING WITH THE UNACCUSTOMED HAND

The normally right-handed person might write an anonymous letter with his left hand, and vice versa. Usually it is quite easy for the document examiner to spot writing with an unaccustomed hand, because the lack of muscular control is ordinarily quite evident. Such writings

---

6. See, Behren & Nelson, "Additional Applications of Digital Image Processing to   Forensic Document Examinations," 37 *J.For.Sci.* 797 (1992).

exhibit angularity in letter form, especially at the base and top of the letters, and they are indicative of slow speed in writing. They also often appear vertical, or with a backhand slant, and evidence poor line quality, characterized by tremor and ragged line edge.[1]

Even when the opposite hand has been used in an attempt to disguise one's writing, the writer will very likely display his individual writing characteristics to such a degree as to permit an identification. In all such instances, of course, it is highly desirable to obtain from the suspect specimens of his opposite-hand writing.

2. EFFECT OF HEALTH AND AGE ON WRITING

Another consideration that must be taken into account is the writer's health at the time a writing is produced.[2] This is especially true when it is necessary to determine if a writing, allegedly written by an individual at a time he was in ill health or dying—as in a will contest case—is genuine or one written by another interested party. Writings executed when one is of advanced age or in ill health, or intoxicated, often appear erratic; and they may be so poorly written as to give the appearance of a forgery when in fact the writing is genuine. Problems of this kind tax the skill and experience of the examiner. The examiner may at times be required to qualify his opinion, though in other instances he may be able to arrive at a precise and definite conclusion. A very important factor in deciding the issue hinges on the availability of standards of comparison which are written when the person was in the same condition which prevailed at the time the questioned document was written. If such standards are available, identification is not likely to present any consequential problems. Most frequently, however, the only known standards of writing available are those which the purported writer executed at a much earlier time, when his health was good and his writing ability unimpaired. It is here that the task of the document expert becomes exceedingly difficult and, at times, he may be unable to arrive at a definite conclusion.

The effect of a person's age on handwriting can manifest itself in a number of ways. While it is not unusual for the writing of an individual

---

§ 5.08

1. See, Dawson, "Brain Function and Writing with the Unaccustomed Left Hand," 30 *J.For.Sci.* 167 (1985) for a description of characteristics of handprinting done with the unaccustomed left hand.

2. Writings produced by the aged or ill pose special problems to questioned document examiners. There is a wealth of information available to aid examiners, with articles covering the topic in a rather general way, to studies dealing with very specific infirmities. See, e.g., Behrendt, "Alzheimer's Disease and Its Effect on Handwriting," 29 *J.For.Sci.* 87 (1984).

For a reference to other factors that may influence writing quality, see, Masson, "The Effect of Fiber Tip Pen Use on Signatures," 53 *For.Sci.Int'l* 157 (1992); Morgan & Zilly, "Document Examinations of Handwriting with a Straightedge or a Writing Guide," 36 *J.For.Sci.* 470 (1991); Masson, "A Study of the Handwriting of Adolescents," 33 *J.For.Sci.* 167 (1988); Galbraith, "Alcohol: Its Effect on Handwriting," 31 *J.For.Sci.* 580 (1986); Masson, "Felt Tip Pen Writing: Problems of Identification," 30 *J.For.Sci.* 172 (1985); Hilton, "Effects of Writing Instruments on Handwriting Details," 29 *J.For.Sci.* 80 (1984); Morton, "How Does Crowding Affect Signatures?," 25 *J.For.Sci.* 141 (1980).

to remain nearly identical throughout life, there are a great number of individuals whose writing abilities and writing habits change throughout the years. This sometimes happens simply because a person changes to a job where a lot of writing must be done in very little time; in developing speed, form is sacrificed and handwritings executed several years apart may look quite different. Other persons are more fastidious and constantly work at perfecting the writing style they use. Some have adopted the habit of writing their signatures in one way and then suddenly, at one point in their life, decide to adopt a totally different form of signature. The appearance of a writing may also vary, depending upon the position of the writer (sitting, standing, or leaning), the writing instrument used (pencil, fountain pen, ballpoint pen), the writer's mood (excited or depressed emotionally), and other factors. In obtaining standards, therefore, it is important to attempt to secure exemplars executed as close as possible in time to the date of the questioned writing, and written under as similar circumstances as practicable.

If sufficient comparison data are available, many of these extraneous conditions may be minimized. However, when the questioned sample is meager in content, such as the single questioned signature appearing as an endorsement on a check, identification becomes much more difficult and equally competent experts have been known to differ in their conclusions, or at least in the degree of certainty that they ascribe to their findings.

§ 5.09   The Comparison of Typewritings

As with firearms identification, an appreciation of typewriter identification necessitates some understanding of the processes involved in the manufacture of typewriters.

In manufacturing type-bar typewriters, the characters ultimately appearing in the finished product that print out the message are placed on type "slugs" by pressing soft metal into a matrix or die containing the standard type design for a particular machine. Initially, the type matrix or die is machine-engraved from a large drawing made by the type face designer and, as with automobiles and other manufactured products, each type manufacturer has his own ideas about styles and shapes. Consequently, each manufacturer's products will differ from the others.

In former times, all typewriter companies in the United States designed and manufactured their own type. This made it possible for the examiner to identify the make and model of machine used in the preparation of a questioned document. (See Figure 10). Today, however, many domestic and foreign companies purchase type from outside sources, and, as a consequence, different brands of typewriters may use identical type style. This, in turn, limits the document examiner to an identification only of the manufacturing source of the particular type.[1]

---

§ 5.09

1. For an extensive, illustrated discussion of the identification problems presented by this development in the typewriter manufacturing process, see, Crown, "The Differentiation of Pica Monotone Typewriting," 4 *J.Police Sci. & Adm.* 134 (1976).

Periodically, manufacturers of type make minute, or substantial, changes in the letter designs, and in some instances, may discontinue one font and substitute another. This may be helpful in establishing the backdating of a document.

In order to be able to ascertain the source of the type, the make and the model of the instrument that typed a particular document, the document examiner must have at his disposal a reference collection of literally thousands of known type samples, and he must continue to keep this collection current by adding the type face samples of newly introduced machines as they become available.

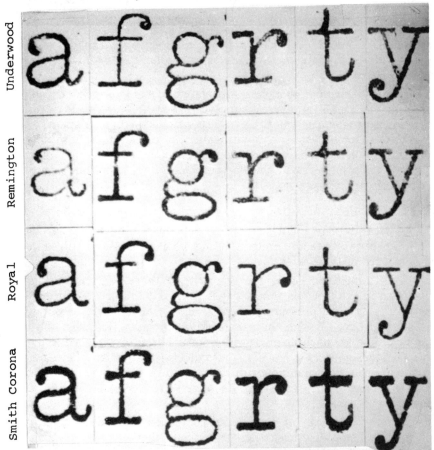

Fig. 10. Specimens of letters typed on four different makes of typewriters. Note the differences in the manufacturers' conceptions of what the letters should look like.

Once the manufacturing source of the type that produced a disputed type sample has been determined, it usually becomes possible to identify the specific machine by a study of the *individual characteristics* peculiar to that specific machine.

Typewriters usually develop, through usage, individual characteristics due to wear of certain parts, bending of the type bars, the chipping of small fragments from the typeface characters, and other factors.

The collective factors that contribute to the individuality of a particular typewriter may be stated as follows: the vertical and horizontal alignment of characters with respect to the horizontal base line of the writing; the variance of impression from top to bottom of particular type impressions resulting from maladjustment of the plane of the typeface and that of the paper surface; the condition of each typeface with respect to defects or damage; the relative weight of impression of a character as compared to other characters on the key board. For an example of typewriter identification by individual characteristics, see Figure 11.

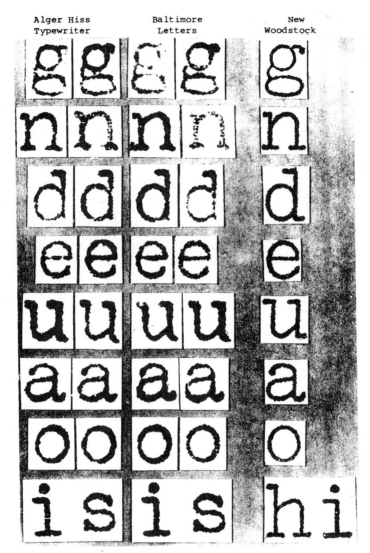

Fig. 11. An illustration of how typewriter defects which are the results of wear and tear may serve to identify a typewriter as being the one used to type a questioned document.

Alger Hiss, who was a high U. S. governmental official, was accused by a defector from the communist party of having supplied the Russians with secret military information. The above evidence convincingly established that the documents in question (the so-called "Baltimore letters" had been typed on Hiss' well-worn Woodstock typewriter).

Observe, on the right, how various letters appeared on a new Woodstock typewriter. Then notice the evidence of the scarring and faulty alignment of the keys of the typewriter that produced the "Baltimore letters" and the similarity to Hiss' typewriter.

§ 5.10   Special Typewriter Identification Problems

1. "SELECTRIC" TYPEWRITERS

We have been referring, up to now, to the ordinary and common shift key typewriters. In 1961, a new type of machine was introduced by IBM which does not use typebars, namely the "Selectric" typewriter. Other manufacturers have since come out with typewriters of a similar design. In this type of machine, the writing is produced by a "golf ball" typehead consisting of a ball of nickle-plated plastic bearing eleven rows of typeface, each row having four different faces. Unlike ordinary typewriters, the carriage of machines does not move from right to left in the course of typing; instead, the carriage remains stationary and the type head moves, whirling to strike the ribbon and impress the characters on the paper, as with the common shift key machines. Nevertheless these various new instruments develop individual characteristics. Among their defects are: typeface imperfections; vertical misalignment caused by a defective tilt mechanism; horizontal misalignment caused by defective centering mechanism; uneven impressions caused by head or roller that are out of alignment; and improper line spacing. One important feature about "Selectric" typewriters is that the type heads are also interchangeable from one machine to the other. Ordinarily, this interchangeable feature will create no problems for the document examiner so long as comparison specimens are available covering the periods of use of the different type heads. In the absence of such specimens, the use of a different ball on the same machine, or the same ball on a different machine, may render it impossible for the examiner to reach a definite opinion.[1]

2. TOY TYPEWRITERS

Over the years a number of anonymous letters have turned up which were written on "toy" typewriters. These cases include poison-pen letters, anonymous, threatening, and obscene documents. Identification data on toy typewriters had been scarce for quite a long time. In recent years, however, document examiners have accumulated much data on the subject, including information on type sizes and styles, inconsistency engendered by crude mechanical parts, and the effect on

---

§ 5.10

1. In addition to the article by Crown, cited supra note 1, section 5.09, see, Miller, "An Analysis of the Identification Value of Defects in IBM Selectric Typewriters," 29 *J.For.Sci.* 624 (1984); Hilton, "Some Practical Suggestions for Examining Writing From the Selectric Typewriter," 3 *J.Pol.Sci. & Admin.* 59 (1975); Casey & Purtell, "IBM Correcting Selectric Typewriter: An Analysis of the Use of the Correctable Film Ribbon in Altering Typewritten Documents," 21 *J.For.Sci.* 208 (1976). Among other problems produced by typewriting or special novel typewriters, consider: Hilton, "Problems in the Identification of Proportional Spacing Typewritings," 3 *J.For.Sci.* 263 (1958); Hilton, "The Effect of Interchanging Segments Between Two Typewriters: A Unique Criminal Defense Defeated," 19 *J.For.Sci.* 841 (1974). See, also: Crown, "Class Characteristics of Foreign Typewriters and Typefaces," 59 *J.Crim.L., C. & P.S.* 298 (1968); Gupta et al., "An Assessment of the Interpol Typewriter Classification System," 1 *J.Pol.Sci. & Admin.* 409 (1973).

the quality of impression as influenced by various kinds of defective rollers.

3. WORD PROCESSORS

The proliferation in the use of word processing equipment has introduced an entirely different set of problems for the forensic document examiner. Rather than producing a text directly on a typewriter, the material is first seen on a television-like screen where corrections, additions, and even shifting of entire paragraphs can be made. At the press of a few keys, the inkjet or laser printer, which is usually a separate unit, automatically types the entire text of the document at the astonishing rate of ten pages per minute, or even faster.

The output of a word processor, whether it be a dedicated unit suitable for word processing only, or a microcomputer loaded with a word processing program, usually produces almost errorless typewriting, which may be a clue in itself to the use of word processing equipment, as is the presence of justified right hand margins.

Similar in some ways to the IBM Selectric ball, dedicated word processor printers use single element typeheads, including daisy wheels, thimbles, dot matrix and jet printing heads. While the identification of typing produced by a word processing printer is certainly more difficult than the type bar machines of earlier days, it appears likely that, through wear and damage to the print producing mechanism, individualities will develop to enable document examiners to establish the identity of a text executed with a particular type element.[2]

As was mentioned in Section 5.09, a document examiner must have at his disposal a reference collection of known type styles to ascertain the source of the type on the questioned document. The F.B.I. has such a database which includes typebars, printwheels and elements. The F.B.I. also has an office equipment file which includes information on copiers and facsimile machines.

The most current and comprehensive typestyle database is the Dr. Philip D. Bouffard Typewriter Typestyle Classification Program. Dr. Bouffard based his computerized typewriter classification database in part on the Haas Atlas of typewriter styles as well as other collections of type wheels, typebars, and "Selectric" typeheads.

§ 5.11 The Comparison of Printed Matter

The analysis of printed matter for the purpose of differentiating originals from reproductions, or to establish the source of a printed

---

2. Allen & Hardcastle, "The Distribution of Damage Defects Among Characters of Printwheel Typing Elements," 47 *For. Sci.Int'l* 249 (1990). Behrendt, "Class Defects in Printwheel Typescript," 33 *J.For. Sci.* 328 (1988); Behrendt & Muehlberger, "Printwheel Typescript Variations Caused by the Manufacturing Process," 32 *J.For. Sci.* 629 (1987).

The forensic questioned document examiner societies actively exchange information on the most recent technological advances in word processing and microcomputer technology. See, e.g., Godown, "Technology That Affects You," *ASQDE Newsletter,* Spring, 1984, p. 6, describing the various types of characters produced by printers for microcomputer use.

document, is also within the document examiner's competence. This presupposes knowledge and familiarity with the printing process, movable type and linotype systems of typesetting as well as the modern techniques of "cold-type" typesetting, the kinds of presses used, including offset lithography and letterpress systems, the quality of professional workmanship, and type faces available to the printing trade.[1]

§ 5.12   The Analysis of Inks

A number of techniques exist to determine the kind of ink which was used to produce a writing. "Paper chromatography, thin-layer chromatography, electropheresis, chemical spot tests, gas chromatography, high performance liquid chromatography, and Fourier transform infrared spectroscopy have all been used for ink comparison."[1] Thin layer chromatography remains the most widely used procedure.[2]

Determinations of the precise age of ink are not easy to make, and they are very seldom positive, although it is frequently possible to determine that the ink used to write some words or characters is of a different type and age than that of the remainder of the writing on a document. Extensive scientific literature exists on the sophisticated techniques which have been developed for the examination and identification of inks.[3]

A new development in the study of inks in document examinations resulted from the advent of the ballpoint pen, introduced in this country in 1945. In a ballpoint pen, a rotatable ball approximately one millimeter in diameter is held in place in a small socket which permits the ball to freely revolve at the base of a pen-like instrument. Inside the pen is contained the "ink" consisting of coloring materials such as dyes or pigments dispersed in oil or another organic liquid. The ink flows down to the socket in which the ballpoint revolves. During writing, the rotating ball receives the writing fluid from the ink supply and deposits it on the paper.

Ballpoint pen inks can be analyzed by document examiners using a variety of techniques, among them thin layer chromatography, spectrophotometry and infrared luminescence photography.[4] Other writing

§ 5.11

1. See, e.g., Beck, "Printed Matter as Questioned Documents," 12 *J.For.Sci.* 82 (1967); Cromwell, "A Method of Indicating the Manufacturer of Courier Style Type Fonts," 1 *J.Pol.Sci. & Admin.* 303 (1973).

§ 5.12

1. Brunelle, "Inkdating—The State of the Art," 37 *J.For.Sci.* 113 (1992) (citations omitted) (The article traces the development of ink dating techniques from the 1930's to 1990).

2. Id.

3. As of this publication, the standard text on the topic is, Brunelle & Reed, *Forensic Examination of Ink and Paper,* 1984.

4. Merrill & Bartick, "Analysis of Ballpoint Pen Inks By Diffuse Reflectance Infrared Spectrometry," 37 *J.For.Sci.* 528 (1992); Horton & Stewart, "An Evaluation of the Use of Laser–Induced Infrared Luminescence to Differentiate Writing Inks," 36 *J.For.Sci.* 838 (1991); Stewart, "Ballpoint Ink Age Determination by Volatile Component Comparison—A Preliminary Study," 30 *J.For.Sci.* 405 (1985).

Black, "Identifying Ball Pens by the Burr Striations," 61 *J.Crim.L., C. & P.S.* 280 (1970); Kelly, "Spectrofluorometric Analysis of Ball Point Ink," 1 *J.Pol.Sci. & Admin.* 175 (1973).

traces, such as those produced by lead pencils or fiber brush tips can also be examined by the experts.

Richard Brunelle, formerly of the Bureau of Alcohol, Tobacco and Firearms (ATF) established the first comprehensive standard writing ink reference collection in the United States in 1968. The collection became known as the Bureau of Alcohol, Tobacco, and Firearms (ATF) Standard Ink Library. In 1985 the ink library was transferred. It is now maintained by the U.S. Secret Service Forensic Laboratory. At present it contains approximately 7000 different ink standards from all over the world.[5] The Internal Revenue Service has a duplicate library.

The object of the library is to establish that the specific ink used on the questioned document was not commercially available on the date that appears on the document. An Ink Tagging Program was developed at ATF between 1975 and 1979. Ink manufacturers volunteered to add unique chemicals (tags) to their inks and to change the tag each year. When the tags are detected in questioned inks the year of manufacture can be pinpointed.

§ 5.13   The Examination of Papers and Watermarks

The study of papers is a fundamental part of the document examiner's training, since the types and grades of paper are endless, going from ordinary writing paper, with its multitude of different qualities, to wrapping paper, wax paper, cardboard, and newsprint, to name but a few.

Investigations involving paper may answer the question whether the substance is in fact paper and of what quality or type.[1] Identity of one piece of writing paper with that of a stack of pages may be determined by general composition, form dates, and sometimes even by a microscopic comparison of the cutting marks on the edge, as well as by the thickness of the paper.

Watermarks are designs incorporated into paper during manufacture to identify the producer. On official documents, stamps, currency, identity cards, etc., they are used to discourage counterfeiting. On bogus instruments the watermark may be simulated by printing or other methods. Simple surface printing can be detected by observation of relief under angled illumination or by ultraviolet fluorescence of the ink. Sandwich-type counterfeits are much less readily detected.[2]

---

5. The Secret Service also maintain standards of inks from computer printers and color copiers, as well as maintaining a computer database of 22,000 watermarks.

§ 5.13

1. A recent article suggests that one may identify papers as coming from a common source by utilizing a ph Pen to determine the papers' acidity or alkalinity. Blackledge & Gernandt, "The ph Pen—A Means of Comparing Paper Products," 38 *J.For.Sci.* 134 (1993).

2. They are made by laminating two or three sheets, one or more of which contains a printed simulation of the watermark. For a description of a system to classify counterfeit documents containing watermarks and to aid in the determination of common origin of fraudulent copies, see, Clements, et al., "Counterfeit Watermarks on False French Identity Documents," 334 *Inter.Crim.Pol.Rev.* 2 (1980).

Some manufacturers change their watermarks yearly, and this practice affords a means by which the date of the paper's production may be ascertained. In many instances this fact alone can establish the invalidity of a document. For instance, if a will dated June 1, 1960 is written on paper which bears a watermark establishing that it was not produced until 1970, the will is obviously invalid, for that reason alone.

While most of the techniques involved in the examination of paper require special knowledge, elaborate instrumentation, and extensive experience, even the observant investigator, untrained in questioned document investigations, can often learn important facts from the study of a paper itself. In one case, for example, a serious credibility question was raised when a witness had told the police officer that she had written down certain facts on a piece of paper in 1965, although the date code stamped at the bottom of the sheet indicated it had not been placed in circulation until 1969.

Another example of the use of many different techniques in the analysis of paper involved the Hitler Diary investigation. An examination of the volumes consisted of a series of tests, including a breakdown of paper, ink and binding material. Ultraviolet light was used to reveal a white "glow" on the paper, a characteristic typical of certain brightness used in paper since the 1950s. Authenticity had to be questioned since the diaries were dated 1934, 1941, and 1943. The presence of the brighteners was proved by a chemical separation process. In addition, infrared spectroscopy revealed an adhesive component and synthetic fibers that were not used until after World War II. Another test proved that the diaries were written in an ink that had been manufactured only two years before the diaries came to light.

§ 5.14 The Examination of Imprinting or Stamping Machines

Questioned document examiners deal with many imprinting devices or marking machines which may be misused for fraudulent purposes. Since the increase in the use of fraudulent checks, examiners have developed techniques to examine and identify checkwriters or "checkprotectors"—machines which print the amount of a check onto paper by perforating or shredding part of the paper so that the amount cannot be changed without damaging the check. Besides identifying specific machines used to imprint a given check, examiners of questioned documents can sometimes use the imprints to date documents when a number of different impressions are available for comparison. Classification systems have also been devised for such machines.[1]

§ 5.14

1. See generally, Jackson, "Identification of a Checkwriter Based On Ink Deposit Pattern," 36 *J.For.Sci.* 257 (1991); Vastrick, "The Examination of Notary Seals," 27 *J.For.Sci.* 899 (1982); Kraemer & Voorhees, "The Manufacture and Examination of Hand–Operated Custom–Design Punches," 28 *J.For.Sci.* 273 (1983); Levin-son & Perelman, "Examination of Cachet Impressions," 28 *J.For.Sci.* 235 (1983); Jones, "A Case Involving the Identification of an Adding Machine," 21 *J.For.Sci.Soc.* 43 (1982); Hargett & Dussak, "Classification and Identification of Checkwriters," 4 *J.Pol.Sci. & Admin.* 404 (1976); Miller, "Role of Check Protector Identification in Law Enforcement Exemplar and Compari-

IBM keypunch machines can frequently be identified from the printed product that is produced by the machine.[2] Even oil delivery imprint machines, which measure the amount of oil pumped from a tanker truck and simultaneously print out the data on a delivery ticket when the oil flow is stopped, can often be identified from their printouts.[3]

§ 5.15 Photocopiers and Facsimiles

Other office equipment may leave distinctive impressions that can be analyzed by a document examiner. The examination of a photocopy machine to determine whether or not it was the source of a questioned photocopied document is conducted in the same manner as other examinations by the document examiner. First the document examiner observes the class characteristics of the photocopier such as the type of photocopy process, the method of fixing the toner to the page and its magnetic properties, enlargement and reduction capabilities, direction of feed, paper sizes and margins, roller marks, distinctive brand markings, gripper and sorter indentations, analog or digital image, toner color, and the chemical properties of toner.[1]

Once the class characteristics of the questioned document are determined to be consistent with a particular photocopier, an examination of the identifying or individual characteristics is undertaken. Wear and tear, dirt, debris and scratches produce "trash marks," streaks, smudg-

son Problems," 3 *J.Pol.Sci. & Admin.* 259 (1975).

2. Curvey & Eaton, "Identification of IBM Keypunch Machines by Their Printed Products," 21 *J.For.Sci.* 949 (1976).

3. Hilton, "Individualizing Oil Delivery Imprints," 21 *J.For.Sci.* 213 (1976).

Other new techniques or devices which call for study by qualified document examiners include the device known as Telenote, which, by the use of an electronics system, permits a person to actually sign a document in a different city, over the telephone. Document examiners may have to determine, in the future, whether a writing is a human made original or a machine-made image produced simultaneously with its original in another location. See, Flynn, "Forgery By Phone," 4 *J.Pol.Sci. & Admin.* 326 (1976). The color duplicating machine, manufactured by Xerox, has spawned a wave of counterfeit money orders, payroll checks, stock certificates, U.S. and foreign currencies, and other negotiable documents. Contrary to most opinions, these counterfeits are readily detectible and offer no problems to the document examiner.

§ 5.15

1. Gerhart, "Identification of Photocopiers from Fusing Roller Defects," 37 *J.For. Sci.* 130 (1992); see also, Chang, Huang & Giang, "An Improvement on Pyrolysis Gas Chromotography for a Differentiation of Photocopy Toners," 38 *J.For.Sci.* 843 (1993); Shiver & Nelson, "Nondestructive Differentiation of Full–Color Photocopies," 36 *J.For.Sci.* 145 (1991); Mazzella, Lennard & Margot, "Classification and Identification of Photocopying Toners by Diffuse Reflectance Infrared Fourier Transform Spectroscopy (DRIFTS): I. Preliminary Results," 36 *J.For.Sci.* 449 (1991); Mazzella, Lennard & Margot, "Classification and Identification of Photocopying Toners by Diffuse Reflectance Infrared Fourier Transform Spectroscopy (DRIFTS): II. Final Report," 36 *J.For.Sci.* 820 (1991); Crown, "The Differentiation of Electrostatic Photocopy Machines," 34 *J.For.Sci.* 142 (1989); James, "The Classification of Office Copy Machines from Physical Characteristics," 32 *J.For.Sci.* 1293 (1987); Osborn, "Fraudulent Photocopy of a Promissory Note," 32 *J.For.Sci.* 282 (1987); Zimmerman, Mooney & Kimmett, "Preliminary Examination of Machine Copier Toners by Infrared Spectrophotometry and Pyrolysis Gas Chromotography," 31 *J.For.Sci.* 489 (1986).

es, speckles, lines of toner and white fuzzy lines on a photocopy.[2] The photoconductor drum or belt, the imaging system, the copy glass, the cover, corona wires and fusing rollers all produce distinctive characteristics. A questioned photocopy can be definitely associated with a machine if it and the exemplars taken from the suspect photocopier exhibit the same distinctive flaws in the form of toner particles fixed to the page in a particular pattern and location in sufficient detail and abundance for an examiner to conclude this could not have occurred by chance.[3]

The F.B.I. is developing a database of copy toners. Data is being collected to aid in the identification of color photocopies by optical and chemical techniques.[4] Studies are also being undertaken to determine the age of photocopies by classifying the copier toner by infrared spectroscopy and pyrolysis gas chromatography and by measuring the level of oxidation.[5]

A document examiner may be able to identify a questioned document as a facsimile by the notched or stepped effect of the printing; the paper, if thermal paper is used; or the substance left by thermal ribbon transfer.[6] Laser fax printing is recognized by the fine, shiny, grimy particles of toner forming the images.[7]

III. EVIDENCE OF QUESTIONED DOCUMENT EXAMINATIONS

§ 5.16 Admissibility of Standards of Comparison

Before a document or writing may be admitted into evidence as a known specimen, or standard writing, for comparison with allegedly forged documents, the genuineness and authenticity of the document must be established to the satisfaction of the court.[1] The authenticity may be proved in several ways. For example, the document may be shown to be genuine by testimony of witnesses who were present when the standard was being written,[2] or who were familiar with a purported

2. Gerhart, supra note 1, at 131.

3. Id.

4. Mazzella & Roux, "The Identification of Color Photocopiers by Optical and Chemical Techniques," Paper presented at the 13th Meeting of the I.A.F.S. Düsseldorf, Germany, August 24, 1993.

5. Lyter, "Determination of the Age of Photocopies: A Preliminary Study," Paper presented at the 13th Meeting of the I.A.F.S. Düsseldorf, Germany, August 24, 1993.

6. Owens, "A Look into Facsimile Transmission," 35 *J.For.Sci.* 112 (1990).

7. Id.

§ 5.16

1. Citizens' Bank & Trust Co. of Middlesboro, Ky. v. Allen, 43 F.2d 549 (4th Cir.1930); People v. Pilkington, 199 Misc. 667, 103 N.Y.S.2d 66 (1951). An impressive body of case law in civil litigations exists on the issue of questioned document examinations. United States v. Ortiz, 966 F.2d 707 (1st Cir.1992); Stuckey v. Northern Propane Gas Co., 874 F.2d 1563 (11th Cir.1989).

2. Bowers v. United States, 244 Fed. 641 (9th Cir., 1917); Carter v. State, 135 Tex.Cr.R. 457, 116 S.W.2d 371 (1937), appeal dismissed 305 U.S. 557 (1938).

There is, however, no requirement that the writing of known origin, admittedly

maker's writing,[3] or by any kind of satisfying circumstantial evidence.[4]

When genuineness is admitted by the party against whom the document is sought to be used, authenticity is deemed shown without the necessity for further proof.[5] Courts have also admitted, as a standard, a writing signed by the plaintiff wherein he gave his counsel a power of attorney.[6]

In some states, the admissibility of exemplars is governed by statute, but genuineness of the document must still be established to the satisfaction of the court before it may be admitted as a standard.[7]

In admitting into evidence known specimens of handwriting, courts seem to prefer documents signed or written prior to trial in the ordinary course of business or daily life. Some authorities have suggested that a specimen writing that is made for the occasion of trial and *post litem motam* may not be used for comparison by the party making it. Modern court decisions have generally abandoned the prohibition against *post litem motam* exemplars. Even where retained, the rule is subject to the exception which permits a cross-examiner to demand and use an exemplar obtained in open court.[8]

There is certainly no scientific reason why the known specimen of handwriting made after the dispute arose is less valuable to the expert than an older document. In fact, experts prefer to have a wide variety of documents of known authenticity to serve as exemplars for comparison with the questioned document, but most of these should be writings executed as close as possible to the date of execution of the questioned writing. It is for that reason that most standards, today, are the so-called "request writings," (at least in criminal cases) made in the presence of the document examiner and for the precise purpose of having a handwriting example of unquestioned origin. The method in which exemplars are prepared goes to the weight to be given to the evidence, not to its admissibility.[9]

Compelling an arrestee to submit a specimen of his handwriting has been held not to violate his privilege against self-incrimination, nor is there any requirement that an attorney be present when the specimen is

genuine, be relevant to the proceedings at bar: DiPietro v. State, 31 Md.App. 392, 356 A.2d 599 (1976).

3. People v. Molineux, 168 N.Y. 264, 61 N.E. 286 (1901). But see, Inbau, "Lay Witness Identification of Handwriting," 34 *Ill. L.Rev.* 433 (1940) on the unreliability of such testimony.

4. People v. Davis, 65 Cal.App.2d 255, 150 P.2d 474 (1944). United States v. Echeverri, 982 F.2d 675 (1st Cir.1993).

5. Bowers v. United States, 244 Fed. 641 (C.C.A.9, 1917).

6. Moore v. United States, 91 U.S. (1 Otto) 270 (1875).

7. People v. Davis, supra note 4. Before an exemplar may be offered in evidence, opposing counsel ought to be afforded an opportunity to inspect it.

8. People v. Hess, 10 Cal.App.3d 1071, 90 Cal.Rptr. 268 (1970).

9. People v. Davidson, 160 Ill.App.3d 99, 112 Ill.Dec. 621, 514 N.E.2d 17 (1987). (The defendant had been told what to write and how to space the words on the exemplars. The expert conceded it was not good practice, however, other evidence indicated the defendant was the author of the questioned documents. Therefore, any error in the admission of the exemplars was harmless.)

obtained.[10] It is equally well settled that compelled handwriting exemplars violate no legitimate Fourth Amendment interest since handwriting is repeatedly shown to the public and there is no expectation of privacy in the physical characteristics of a person's script.[11]

Proof of genuineness of a standard writing may also be established by a showing that the document qualifies as an ancient writing,[12] although the value of such a writing in a comparison with a recently executed questioned writing is of doubtful value to a document examiner.

It is generally agreed that opinion evidence by an expert cannot establish the genuineness of a standard by comparing it with another exemplar. Courts have said that the standard should be proven by direct positive evidence, not by the opinion of an expert.[13] If the government fails to provide discoverable handwriting evidence that tends to exculpate the accused of forgery charges, the accused is entitled to a new trial.[14] However, the government's failure to provide the defendant's handwriting exemplar to the defense has been held not to be reversible error.[15]

§ 5.17 Evidence of Handwriting Comparisons

At common law, evidence of a comparison of the handwriting on one document with that on another was inadmissible, inasmuch as the only acceptable proof of one's handwriting was deemed to be the testimony of its author.[1] Over the years, however, this rigid view has been generally abandoned. Today, expert testimony, and lay testimony to some extent, is quite generally admissible to establish authorship of a questioned writing.

10. Gilbert v. California, 388 U.S. 263 (1967).

In re Special Federal Grand Jury Impanelled October 31, 1987, 809 F.2d 1023 (3d Cir.1987) (The court upheld a finding of civil contempt against a person who refused to provide exemplars in a backhand slant pursuant to a Federal grand jury order to give the exemplar.)

Some courts have held a prosecutor's comment in closing argument regarding an accused's refusal to provide a handwriting exemplar was not a comment on the appellant's right to remain silent and was not fundamental error. Wilson v. State, 596 So.2d 775 (Fla.App.1992).

11. United States v. Mara, 410 U.S. 19, 21 (1973). Also, compulsion of handwriting exemplar is not a 5th Amendment violation. Refusal to give exemplar is evidence of consciousness of guilt and is admissible and not violative of the accused's Sixth Amendment rights.

12. Generally, a document more than thirty years old. McCormick, *Evidence,* § 323 (3d ed. 1984). Rule 803(16) of the

Federal Rules of Evidence provides that statements in documents in existence twenty years or more fall under the hearsay exception.

13. Archer v. United States, 9 Okl. 569, 60 P. 268 (1900). In Rauenzahn v. Sigman, 383 Pa. 439, 119 A.2d 312 (1956), the court said that in order to permit a comparison of the handwritings, the genuineness of the specimen offered as a standard for comparison must be established, and nothing short of evidence by a person who saw the party sign the standard, or an admission, is sufficient.

14. State v. Stone, 869 S.W.2d 785 (Mo. App.1994).

15. United States v. Glover, 846 F.2d 339 (6th Cir.1988)—the court noted that appellant did not request a continuance or recess to obtain the exemplar, but only requested that the government's document expert be stricken.

§ 5.17

1. Rogers v. Ritter, 79 U.S. 317 (1870).

Since the United States Supreme Court's decision in Daubert v. Merrell Dow Pharmaceuticals,[2] some courts may require those parties proffering document examination evidence to lay an appropriate foundation by establishing the scientific reliability of document examination, before admitting expert opinion evidence based upon it.[3]

1. LAY TESTIMONY

If a lay witness is familiar with the disputed handwriting or signature, he will ordinarily be allowed to testify with respect to authorship.[4] If the witness' familiarity with the purported writer's handwriting was acquired for purposes of the litigation, the writer's testimony should not be allowed.[5] In Commonwealth v. Ryan,[6] a lay witness who had worked in the same office with the defendant for more than three years was permitted to testify regarding defendant's handwriting. Lay witness competency to testify depends on the extent of his association with the defendant's handwriting. Thus, where a witness was not particularly familiar with deceased's signature and had seen him write his name perhaps once in the past, the witness will not be allowed to give his opinion as to the genuineness of a signature in dispute.[7]

In Hickory v. United States,[8] the reviewing court held that the trial court could properly make a comparison of the disputed writings with a standard produced in court, even without the aid of an expert witness. Similarly, juries have been permitted to make their own comparisons, both as to identity on the basis of a comparison of handwriting charac-

---

2. 113 S.Ct. 2786 (1993). See discussion of *Daubert* in Chapter 1 at Sec. 1.03.

3. See, Wenderoth, "The Impact of *Daubert v. Dow* [sic.] on Forensic Document Evidence," Paper presented at the 46th Annual Meeting of the American Academy of Forensic Sciences, San Antonio, Texas, Feb. 19, 1994. See also, People v. Michallow, ___ A.D.2d ___, 607 N.Y.S.2d 781 (1994) (mem. op.)—erroneous admission, without showing of scientific reliability, of expert's testimony that spray painting on vehicles was written by defendant was harmless error in light of other evidence including handwriting analysis of notes found on the cars linking the defendant to the crimes of criminal mischief.

4. Lay opinion testimony may be an adequate basis under Federal Rule of Evidence 901(b) to connect a signature or record to a party. See, e.g., United States v. Tipton, 964 F.2d 650 (7th Cir.1992); United States v. Whittington, 783 F.2d 1210 (5th Cir.1986), cert. denied 479 U.S. 882 (1986); United States v. Barker, 735 F.2d 1280 (11th Cir.1984), cert. denied 469 U.S. 933 (1984); United States v. Mauchlin, 670 F.2d 746 (7th Cir.1982) (prison file documents sufficiently authenticated by a prison official who had seen defendant write on six occasions).

5. People v. Cepeda, 851 F.2d 1564 (9th Cir.1988).

6. 355 Mass. 768, 247 N.E.2d 564 (1969). Other laypersons who have been permitted to testify about authenticity of writings include: bankers, Stone v. Hubbard, 61 Mass. 595 (1851); post office clerks, State v. Sysinger, 25 S.D. 110, 125 N.W. 879 (1910); and public records custodians, Fenias v. Reichenstein, 124 N.J.L. 196, 11 A.2d 10 (1940).

7. Noyes v. Noyes, 224 Mass. 125, 112 N.E. 850 (1916).

8. 151 U.S. 303 (1894). Cf.: United States v. Ranta, 482 F.2d 1344 (8th Cir. 1973). The better view is expressed by Smith v. State, 489 S.W.2d 920 (Tex.Cr. App.1973), holding that the state may not prove the identity of defendant as the person who was previously convicted through the use of handwriting samples from which the jury alone is requested to make comparisons with signatures appearing on conviction records.

teristics,[9] and on the basis of language use and misspellings in the known and unknown documents.[10]

2. EXPERT TESTIMONY

When the genuineness of a document is a material issue in a case, opinion testimony by a qualified document examiner is generally held competent evidence. Such an examiner may develop and explain reasons for his findings in the presence of the jury,[11] but this is not necessarily a requirement. The testimony of a document examiner that handwriting on certain documents of questioned authorship and certain exemplars of handwriting were all written by the same persons should be properly admissible even if the expert gives no reasons for the opinion.[12] The failure to do so, however, may cause the expert to run afoul of a remnant of the "ultimate issue" rule.[13] For example, in Carlos v. Murphy Warehouse Company,[14] where the expert testified as to the relative times in which typewriting and a signature were placed on a document, the court admonished the jury that this testimony was an opinion only. The expert apparently had not stated the reasons for his conclusion. Given the factual and scientific basis for the expert's finding, the court might well have considered the evidence properly one of a factual observation, rather than opinion testimony, since it was quite apparent that the court labored under the misapprehension that questioned document testimony was *always* in the nature of some sort of speculation. The court did not draw the distinction between opinions of identity between two documents on the basis of handwriting characteristics, and testimony by an expert on whether a signature was written before or after the overlapping typewriting was produced—a fact that can be demonstrated rather unequivocally as a physical fact.[15]

The failure to state the reason for an expert opinion has been held not to strip it of its probative value. Such an omission affects the weight of the evidence, rather than its admissibility or sufficiency. In State v. Willey,[16] the expert failed to explain differences between sample and questioned documents after stating his opinion that they were written by

9. State v. LeDuc, 306 N.C. 62, 291 S.E.2d 607 (1982). This actually is a far more reliable method for lay witness participation in the handwriting identification process than reliance upon a memory comparison. Inbau, supra note 3, section 5.16.

10. United States v. Clifford, 704 F.2d 86 (3d Cir.1983).

11. Fenelon v. State, 195 Wis. 416, 217 N.W. 711 (1928), rehearing denied 195 Wis. 416, 218 N.W. 830 (1928).

12. The law does not require that reasons for an expert's opinion are given, although their absence would indeed make the expert's testimony less credible and less persuasive.

13. For a discussion on the origins and development of the ultimate issue rule, see Chapter 1, § 1.21(2)(a), supra.

14. 166 Ga.App. 406, 304 S.E.2d 439 (1983).

15. The court stated, rather unequivocally, that "the forensic science of questioned document examination lies in the field of opinion rather than scientific fact." This is certainly true for some aspects of handwriting identification, but other aspects of the discipline, discussed earlier, require instrumentation or scientific analyses resulting in rather precise and uncontrovertible findings of fact.

16. 171 N.W.2d 301 (Iowa 1969); accord: People v. Allen, 212 Cal.App.2d 857, 28 Cal.Rptr. 409 (1963).

the same person. When defense expert pointed out the differences, the state's witness was permitted to offer explanations or rebuttal. The court determined that such testimony was proper rebuttal.

The value of an expert's opinion will, of course, depend on the clearness with which he demonstrates the correctness of his opinion. This, in turn, depends largely on how well he explains the grounds on which he bases it. A lack of reasoning may make his opinion of little evidential value.

The weight to be given to the testimony is always a function of the jury (or the judge in a bench trial), which must give due consideration to the opinion of experts, although without any obligation to follow that opinion. On the other hand, it has been held, in a civil case, that the testimony of handwriting experts that a will is a forgery is sufficient to overturn oral testimony of subscribing witnesses that the will was duly executed, although in other jurisdictions a less confident viewpoint prevails and expert testimony will not offset subscribing witness testimony.[17]

Courts have been rather equivocal, at times, on the value of handwriting identification by an expert. Most courts agree that handwriting expertise is of great value in assisting the jury to reach a proper verdict.[18] In Estate of Sylvestri,[19] the handwriting expert's testimony that the signature on a will was not genuine was directly contradicted by the testimony of three disinterested, credible, attesting witnesses. The trial court believed the document expert. On appeal, it was contended that such expert testimony ought not to be able to outweigh the direct evidence of disinterested and credible witnesses. The Court of Appeals of New York affirmed, recognizing that in a given case, the testimony of a well qualified document examiner may be more convincing than that of attesters. "This possibility," said the court, "is one of the results of the modern scientific study of handwriting.... [I]t cannot now be said to be so inherently suspect, weak or unreliable as, ipso facto, to call for classification as evidence having an impaired or restricted probative worth." [20]

The worth of any expert's opinion lies in the extent of his qualifications and in the manner of presenting his testimony. This applies with equal force in the field of questioned document examination. Probably many of the less favorable court pronouncements about the reliability of handwriting comparisons by experts are due to the fact that this is a field in which many pseudo experts operate, especially in civil litigation. If the expert is truly qualified, his opinion is based upon a very high

---

17. In re O'Connor's Estate, 105 Neb. 88, 179 N.W. 401 (1920), cert. denied 256 U.S. 690 (1921). In Clark v. Lansford, 191 So.2d 123 (Miss.1966), the court held that an expert's testimony that a signature was forged was sufficient to overcome that of the notarizing officer. Cf., Jones v. Jones, 406 Ill. 448, 94 N.E.2d 314 (1950).

18. E.g., Murphy v. Murphy, 144 Ark. 429, 222 S.W. 721 (1920); Baird v. Shaffer, 101 Kan. 585, 168 P. 836 (1917), Clark v. Lansford, supra n. 17.

19. 44 N.Y.2d 260, 405 N.Y.S.2d 424, 376 N.E.2d 897 (1978).

20. Id.

degree of probability and deserves considerably more weight than the courts of the past have been willing to attribute to it. The worth of any questioned document examiner's opinion is also directly related to the type of examination conducted. An opinion can, in some cases, be expressed with scientific near-certainty ("positive"), while in other cases the opinion may be expressed in terms of being "highly probable," "probable," "possible," [21] "not a basis for identification," or "negative." [22]

§ 5.18   Evidence of Typewriting Identifications

As with the comparison of handwritings, the technique of proving the identity of typewriting is based upon a comparison of at least two writings, a questioned one and one or more exemplars. Here, too, it is well settled that the jury may be assisted in this task by an expert witness.[1] In fact, the relevancy of typewriting identification testimony was recognized as early as 1893.[2]

In People v. Risley,[3] an attorney was prosecuted for offering into evidence as genuine a will while knowing it to have been forged and fraudulently altered by insertion of two typewritten words. Specimens of typewriting made on a machine in the defendant's office two days subsequent to the commission of the alleged offense were held properly admitted as standards of comparison. The expert testified that his experience encompassed examination of some 20,000 typewriters, and that he had never encountered one that was in perfect alignment. He stated that the alignment was the "heart" of the machine, and that the spacing, keys, lever, carriage and roll all center around the alignment. He also stated that a machine cannot be manufactured so that the alignment will be perfect.

In State v. Swank,[4] the court recognized the propriety of permitting an expert to testify that in his opinion an authenticated note and a questioned note in a forgery prosecution had been signed by the same individual and also typed on the same typewriter. The reviewing court dwelt on the clarity of the expert testimony, the analytical and convinc-

---

21. Evidence held insufficient to convict defendant of offering a fraudulent voter registration card where the state's handwriting expert testified it was only "possible" that defendant signed card: State v. Nelson, 436 S.E.2d 308 (W.Va.1993).

22. There exists a controversy among document examiners whether opinions as to a "possible" identification ought to be given. For one view on that issue, see, Alexander, "The Meaning of Handwriting Opinions," 5 *J. of Pol.Sci. & Admin.* 43 (1977). See also discussion at § 5.06, supra, regarding standardization of terminology.

§ 5.18

1. E.g.: People v. Risley, 214 N.Y. 75, 108 N.E. 200 (1915), after extensive explo-

ration of the testimony and issues, the court also held that a university professor of mathematics had been improperly permitted to testify that according to the laws of probabilities the likelihood that the particular typescript was made on a different typewriter was one in 4,000,000,000. See also: Hartzell v. United States, 72 F.2d 569 (8th Cir.1934), cert. denied 293 U.S. 621 (1934).

2. Levy v. Rust, 49 A. 1017 (N.J.1893). Apparently, the earliest judicial expression on the point was in a Canadian case in 1886: Scott v. Crerar, 14 Ont.App.Rep. 152 (1886).

3. Supra note 1.

4. 99 Or. 571, 195 P. 168 (1921).

ing manner of his presentation, and the conciseness of the language with which he framed his opinion. In the case of In re Bundy's Estate,[5] the court's decision was held to have been properly based solely upon the testimony of a questioned document expert who testified that a will offered in probate was a forgery.

In another case, a study of type samples established that a document relating to attorney's fees, purportedly submitted by the attorney as a charge against an estate he represented, was a forgery, by testimony to the effect that the particular typewriter type face used on the document had not been put into use by the manufacturer until several years after the death of the purported writer of the document.[6]

In Hawksby v. New York Hospital,[7] a medical malpractice action, the appellate court held that the plaintiff was entitled to discover the typewritten exemplars of the text of the operative reprint, produced on the typewriter of the physician who operated on the patient to determine whether the report was recently fabricated.

It is a jury question whether typewritten notes were materially and fraudulently altered.[8]

In cases dealing with typewriter identification, some courts have admitted the suspect typewriter into evidence and have allowed the jurors to experiment with it.[9]

The credibility accorded the typewriting expert's testimony is a function of the impression the credentials and the testimony of the expert make upon the mind of the factfinder. The background and integrity of the expert will not only determine the admissibility of the evidence but will also affect its impact.

§ 5.19 Evidence of Other Questioned Document Examinations

In a few cases reviewing courts have been confronted with the admissibility of expert testimony relating to document examinations along with other issues in addition to the genuineness of handwriting or typewriting. In Duffin v. People,[1] for instance, the court held that it was proper to admit into evidence a photographic copy of a forged note on which the ink had faded so that the original had become illegible. The restoration of faded inks involves, of course, a relatively simple photographic process only.

5. 153 Or. 234, 56 P.2d 313 (1936).

6. Lyon v. Oliver, 316 Ill. 292, 147 N.E. 251 (1925).

7. 162 A.D.2d 179, 556 N.Y.S.2d 312 (1990).

8. Zions First National Bank v. Rocky Mountain Irrigation, Inc., 795 P.2d 658 (Utah 1990) (error for trial court to enter summary judgment for lender and bank president).

9. State v. Ulvestad, 414 N.W.2d 737 (Minn.App.1987) (no abuse of discretion for trial judge to permit jury to experiment with typewriter introduced into evidence by prosecution as instrument used to alter mileage readings on documents in theft by swindle case).

§ 5.19

1. 107 Ill. 113 (1883). In State v. Wetherell, 70 Vt. 274, 40 A. 728 (1898), a rape prosecution, expert testimony was held admissible to aid the jury in deciphering incriminating letters written by defendant.

Different problems are encountered when dealing with more complex examinations, such as those of ink analyses. In United States v. Bruno,[2] the government sought to prove that the ball point ink with which one of the defendants had signed a questioned document was of a type which had not been manufactured until May of 1967, and that the document therefore could not have been signed in 1965, the date appearing thereon. The expert testimony was based upon chromatograms made of the ink, a process whereby the ink separates into its component dyes. Considering that the comparison "ink library" of the witness was rather incomplete, and that the expert conceded to the existence of a number of variables which might influence the results, the court concluded that "the art in this field of ink identification is not yet sufficiently advanced to be reasonably scientifically certain that an ink of unknown composition is the same as a known ink."[3] The state of the art has, of course, progressed significantly, as discussed supra in § 5.12.

In Commonwealth v. Johnson,[4] a 1990 case, the appellate court held it was an abuse of discretion for the trial court in a perjury case to grant a motion in limine banning expert testimony based on results of ink analysis which indicated notes were not written in the year the appellee testified they were written.

§ 5.20 Use of Demonstrative Evidence

Ordinarily, the use of demonstrative evidence before the jury is within the sound discretion of the trial judge. This concept applies to questioned document examinations as well. Ordinarily, expert witnesses in this field will be permitted to use photographic enlargements, charts with photographic cut-outs of key portions of the writings, or slides, to illustrate the reasons for their opinions and to assist the trier of fact in understanding the basis for the testimony.[1] It has been said, however, that handwriting demonstrations and tests are not permitted to be conducted in the courtroom.[2] On the other hand, this rule would not necessarily apply to questioned document experiments other than handwriting tests. In State v. Gear,[3] for example, a demonstration before the jury in the use of water-soluble paper such as the defendant was

---

2. 333 F.Supp. 570 (E.D.Pa.1971).

3. United States v. Bruno, supra note 2 at 48. The court tested the admissibility of the evidence to the Frye v. United States, 54 App.D.C. 46, 293 Fed. 1013 (1923) "general acceptance" standard and found it wanting. The court also found that the expert had not vouched for the correct administration of the test. See also, United States v. Wolfson, 297 F.Supp. 881 (S.D.N.Y.1968), affirmed 413 F.2d 804 (2d Cir.1969), rejecting as insufficiently reliable ink analysis by a chemist and examination of watermark evidence.

4. 399 Pa.Super. 266, 582 A.2d 336 (1990).

§ 5.20

1. E.g.: United States v. Ortiz, 176 U.S. 422 (1900); State ex rel. Crooks v. Cummins, 56 S.D. 439, 229 N.W. 302 (1930); Adams v. Ristine, 138 Va. 273, 122 S.E. 126 (1924); Fenelon v. State, 195 Wis. 416, 217 N.W. 711 (1928), rehearing denied 195 Wis. 416, 218 N.W. 830 (1928).

2. People v. White, 365 Ill. 499, 6 N.E.2d 1015 (1937).

3. 115 N.J.Super. 151, 278 A.2d 511 (1971).

purportedly using at the time of his arrest for a gambling offense was held to be within the trial court's discretion.

There is, of course, no requirement that the expert use demonstrative aids. His opinion alone is sufficient. In one case, the use of photographic aids of one kind, but the non-use of such aids on another point, caused the court to reject as unreliable the testimony of the expert.[4] The expert had shown a slide on which three chromatograms of the same ink showed entirely different results, a fact considered by the court to be proof of the unreliability of the test. In the same case, however, the court criticized the expert for *not* producing exhibits of chromatographic plates of slides displaying the ink from the questioned document alongside samples of ink of known origin believed to be similar.

§ 5.21   Qualifications of the Expert

Because of the considerable number of incompetent or poorly trained document examiners who profess to be expert witnesses in civil and criminal cases, the worth of document investigation evidence can best be measured by the credibility of the witness. Therefore, attorneys should explore, in great depth, the extent of training and experience of a witness who purports to be an expert in document examination.

Although many courts have stated that a person may be qualified to testify as an expert either by study without practice, or by practice without study,[1] those in the questioned document examination profession who have evidenced a high degree of skill contend that this rule should not apply in their field. They contend, as do the fingerprint examiners, that both study and experience are imperative.

Over the years there have been few formal courses of instruction at colleges or universities which qualify one to become a questioned document examiner, and consequently expertise can be achieved only by a study of the available textbooks, and the quite extensive technical literature in periodicals and journals, plus an internship training under an experienced examiner. This should, in most instances, be supplemented by training in chemistry, physics, microscopy, or other such subjects taught in colleges and universities. Expertise as a document examiner is not something which can be achieved through study alone.

Penmanship instructors,[2] bank tellers,[3] and photographers,[4] all of whom have at times been permitted to testify as experts in the courts,

---

4. United States v. Bruno, supra note 2, section 5.19.

§ 5.21

1. In State v. Evans, 247 Mont. 218, 806 P.2d 512 (1991), it was held that the trial court did not abuse its discretion in allowing a detective who had taken a two-week questioned document course, had worked on approximately 20 cases as a handwriting expert and was spending 25 percent of his time on the examination of documents to testify as an expert.

2. See, supra, § 5.17(1).

3. Stone v. Hubbard, 61 Mass. 595 (1851); Savage v. Bowen, 103 Va. 540, 49 S.E. 668 (1905).

4. The earliest cases admitting photographic evidence involved photographers who were permitted to testify as experts on

are really not qualified to perform the types of examinations and make the kind of determinations which have been referred to in the earlier part of this chapter.

Just as the court decisions have failed to make the distinction between self-styled experts and truly competent questioned document examiners, even the legal literature seems to indicate, erroneously, that there are two classes of "experts" in document work. For example, an A.L.R. Annotation advises attorneys to use a traditional "handwriting expert," for the ordinary document problems and to hire a "questioned document examiner" or a "criminalist" if the lawyer is convinced "that he must use an expert with more exalted qualifications than those of a 'handwriting expert.' " [5] There simply are no such distinctions in the field. The truly qualified "handwriting expert" is precisely the questioned document examiner described in this chapter.

A distinction should also be made between the professional document examiner and the practitioner of graphology,[6] be he called a graphologist, graphoanalyst,[7] graphometrist, or graphoreader. Persons claiming skills in graphology engage in the study of such things as character analysis and personality assessment based upon a study of a person's handwriting. Graphology and its related branches is an art which, at least to date, lacks general acceptance by the courts and the scientific community; in fact, its very premises are still seriously challenged.[8] The only thing that graphology and questioned document examination have in common is that they both deal with handwritings, but their aims are widely divergent. The former deals with assessing character traits from writings based on general forms of letters and writings; the latter is concerned with determinations of the genuineness of writing on the basis of a comparison of minute details in writings of questioned and of known origin. The individual having studied graphology or any one of its related systems lacks the qualifications and training required for professional document examinations of the type needed in civil and criminal investigations and the establishment of courtroom proof on document genuineness or forgery. If the graphologist or graphoanalyst seeks to qualify as a questioned document examiner, his graphology training is totally irrelevant and he should be required to

document examinations from a study of their enlarged photographs.

5. Anno., "Admissibility of Expert Evidence to Decipher Illegible Document," 11 A.L.R.3d 1015, at 1017–1018.

6. About "graphology," the 1965 ed. of *Encyclopedia Britannica* notes that the question of its ultimate scientific value is as yet unanswered. The same reference tool also lists graphology under the heading of "Fortunetelling."

7. "Graphoanalysis" is a term coined by the International Graphoanalysis Society of Chicago. It is not defined in the standard dictionaries, nor was it defined by the witness who sought to qualify as an expert in handwriting analysis through graphoanalysis, according to the court in Carroll v. State, 276 Ark. 160, 634 S.W.2d 99 (1982).

8. It must be noted that, while graphology is claimed to be an invaluable adjunct to psychology, American colleges and universities have not seen fit to add its study to the psychology curricula. In Europe, on the other hand, many universities teach graphology as a required course for psychologists. See also, Beck, "Handwriting Identification and Graphology," 9 *J.For.Sci.* 477 (1964).

show that he has the training and experience of the competent questioned document examiner.[9]

Many appellate courts have upheld trial courts' exclusion of graphologists or graphoanalysts' testimony.[10] However, some courts have held the use of graphologists as document examiners to be merely harmless error.[11] Other courts have held it to be reversible error to have excluded graphologists' testimony.[12]

In view of the misapprehension on the nature of expertise in document work which the courts have evidenced in the past, the fact that a person has previously testified as a handwriting expert in court is not in itself a badge of competence. It behooves the attorney seeking to employ a questioned document examiner, or who is confronted with one in court, to determine that the expert's competency and experience extends to the type of work outlined in this chapter. In the following section, attorneys are given some advice as to how they can insure that examiners they may contact are truly qualified.

In 1977, the leading members of the questioned documents section of the American Academy of Forensic Sciences met to form the American Board of Forensic Document Examiners. That board initiated the process of certification, including the formulation of standards and tests. It may be expected that such board certification will become the standard by which examiners' competence will be measured. In fact, some courts have already referred to the American Board of Forensic Document Examiners in case decisions which upheld the trial courts' refusal to admit a proffered witness' testimony on document examination,[13]

---

9. Cf. Carroll v. State, supra note 7.

10. United States v. Bourgeois, 950 F.2d 980 (5th Cir.1992)—the proffered expert in this case stated that he had studied Egyptology, psychology, hypnosis and religion; claimed to hold a doctorate in metaphysics and religion which he completed by correspondence; stated he practiced graphology at the Universal Mind Spa which he operated for eight years; and he also practiced forensic document examination. In Graves v. State, 547 N.E.2d 881 (Ind.App.1989), the trial court was held not to have abused its discretion in determining proffered expert was not qualified as an expert since the record was devoid of identifiable standards for membership in any organization to which the proffered witness belonged (the International Graphoanalysis Society and the World Association of Document Examiners) and no explanation was offered as to how the witness' graphoanalyst training enabled her to determine whether the author of a known signature was the author of the questioned signature.

11. State v. Knerr, 426 N.W.2d 654 (Iowa App.1988)—court held it was harmless error for the prosecution to use a gra-

phologist in jury selection, but denounced the practice.

12. 1st Coppell Bank v. Smith, 742 S.W.2d 454 (Tex.App.1987) [this court held that the same witness who has been excluded in United States v. Bourgeois, supra note 10, was properly allowed to testify]; Hecklar v. State, 503 So.2d 269 (Miss.1987); Hooten v. State, 492 So.2d 948 (Miss. 1986)—the dissent stated: "If this witness has indeed testified over 300 times as an expert on discovering spurious handwriting as she has claimed, it is an astonishing indictment on the gullibility of lawyers and judges, ... Indeed, it takes remarkable ignorance or gall, one or the other, for any lawyer to offer her as an expert on the subject." (Id. at 958).

13. See, United States v. Bourgeois, 950 F.2d 980 (5th Cir.1992) (Court rejected testimony of proffered handwriting examiner whose training was completed through a correspondence school with a strong emphasis on graphoanalysis and who was not certified by the American Board of Forensic Document Examiners); State v. Livanos, 151 Ariz. 13, 725 P.2d 505 (App.1986)

upheld a request for exemplars [14] and upheld a denial of a motion claiming handwriting comparisons were unreliable.[15]

IV. TRIAL AIDS

§ 5.22 Locating and Engaging the Expert

The field of questioned document examination is one in which the attorney has no difficulty locating qualified experts. Since disputed documents are involved in as many, or more, civil law suits than criminal cases, there exists a fairly large group of qualified and highly skilled document experts outside those found in the crime laboratories and law enforcement agencies. In fact, many of the reputable private questioned document examiners have a wider experience and background than a number of their colleagues who work for small law enforcement agencies since they established themselves as private experts after a long career in governmental employ as document examiners.

A number of the highly qualified experts advertise in the classified columns of national legal publications such as the *American Bar Association Journal,* but it must be borne in mind that that journal and most others do not screen their advertisers; ads are accepted from all, the unqualified as well as the qualified. Others can be located through their professional organizations. Lawyers should be aware that there are dozens of professional associations, relating to document examination; however, only a few are composed of certified questioned document examiners, while many others' membership consists of graphologists.

The best known established professional association of document examiners is the American Society of Questioned Document Examiners, Inc., an Illinois not-for-profit corporation with nationwide membership.[1] Most reputable experts also belong to the questioned document section of the American Academy of Forensic Sciences.[2]

In 1977, partly in response to requests by attorneys and the judiciary for some means of measuring the qualifications of forensic document experts, a new voluntary organization was created to provide peer review of the abilities of those who hold themselves out as experts in questioned document examinations. The group is called The American Board of

(Court rejected testimony of graphologist not certified by American Board of Forensic Document Examiners); People v. Tidwell, 706 P.2d 438 (Colo.1985) (Court upheld trial court's refusal to admit testimony of a witness who gave only a vague explanation of her qualifications, no identifiable standards for membership in organizations to which she belonged and was not certified by the American Board of Forensic Document Examiners).

14. Buoni v. Browning Ferres Industries, 219 N.J.Super. 96, 529 A.2d 1044 (1987).

15. United States v. Buck, 1987 WL 19300 (S.D.N.Y.1987) (mem.)

§ 5.22

1. Its 1994 president is Gideon Epstein, I.N.S. Forensic Document Lab., 8000 W. Park Drive Suite 325, McLean, VA 22102.

2. Its 1994 chairperson is: John S. Gencavage, Hunter Lane Box FA57 Road # 3, Harrisburg, PA 17112.

Forensic Document Examiners.[3] The purpose, function, and organization of the ABFDE is analogous to the certifying boards in various other medical and scientific fields. Certification is based upon the candidate's personal and professional record of education, training and experience as well as on the results of formal written and oral examinations. Recertification is required every five years, the requirements for recertification being continuing education in the discipline, research efforts, and the preparation of scientific papers for discussion at professional meetings or for publication.

There are, of course, qualified experts who belong to neither of these two organizations; membership in one of the above groups, however, is some assurance of competence, since the groups are reputed to maintain high standards of proficiency and exact from their members continuing contributions to the advancement of knowledge in their profession. Other identification organizations exist which may number qualified document examiners among their members. Lawyers should be aware that some organizations offer membership on little more than completion of a correspondence course or payment of yearly dues without competency criteria. Therefore, a thorough investigation of each professional association is essential.

V. MISCELLANEOUS

§ 5.23 Bibliography of Selected References

1. BOOKS

ASTM "E1422–91 Standard Guide for Test Method for Forensic Writing Ink Comparison." ASTM Annual Book of Standards Vol. 13.01 (1992).

ASTM "E444–93 Standard Guide for Description of Scope of Work of Forensic Document Examiners." ASTM Annual Book of Standards Vol. 14.02 (1994).

Brunelle & Reed, *Forensic Examination of Ink and Paper* (1984).

Caputo, *Questioned Document Case Studies* (1982).

Conway, *Evidential Documents* (1959).

Hilton, *Scientific Examination of Questioned Documents* (1981). This is a revision, published by a different publisher, of the earlier seminal text by the same author.

----

3. Its 1994 president is: Dan C. Purdy, R.C.M.P. Forensic Document Laboratory, P.O. Box 8885, Ottawa, Ontario, Canada K1G3M8. At present there are approximately 200 diplomates.

McMenamin, *Forensic Stylistics* (1993).

Poulin & Ghirotto, *The Royal Canadian Mounted Police Questioned Document Bibliography,* (2d ed. 1990).

Osborn, *Questioned Documents* (1929).

Osborn, *The Problem of Proof* (1926).

Osborn, *The Mind of the Juror* (1931).

Smith, *Principles of Forensic Handwriting, Identification and Testimony* (1984).

2. ARTICLES

Articles cited in the footnotes are not included in this listing.

Aginsky, "Some New Ideas for Dating Ballpoint Pen Inks—A Feasibility Study," 38 *J.For.Sci.* 1134 (1993).

Anthony, "Examination of Magnetic Ink Character Recognition Impressions," 29 *J.For.Sci.* 303 (1984).

Armistead, "A Paradigm of Fraudulent Medical Prescriptions," 13 *J.Pol. Sci. & Admin.* 111 (1985).

Behrendt, "The Status of Training of Questioned Document Examiners in the United States," 34 *J.For.Sci.* 366 (1989).

Bertocchi, "Carbonless Paper Systems," 18 *J.For.Sci.* 309 (1973).

Bertocchi, "Envelope Association Through Manufacturing Characteristics," 22 *J.For.Sci.* 815 (1977).

Black, "Fiber Tipped Pens," 57 *J.Crim.L., C. & P.S.* 521 (1966).

Brunelle, et al., "Comparison of Typewriter Ribbon Inks by Thin–Layer Chromatography," 22 *J.For.Sci.* 807 (1977).

Cain, "Laser and Fiber Optic Photographic Analysis of Single–Edge Paper Striations," 29 *J.For.Sci.* 1105 (1984).

Cain & Winand, "Striation Evidence in Counterfeiting Cases," 28 *J.For. Sci.* 360 (1983).

Carney, "Fraudulent Transposition of Original Signatures by Office Machine Copiers," 29 *J.For.Sci.* 1209 (1984).

Carney, "A Charred Document Case Made Simple," *Fire & Arson Inv.* Dec. 1984, p. 17.

Casey, "Alteration of Pari–Mutuel Tickets," 62 *J.Crim.L., C. & P.S.* 282 (1971).

Caywood, "Decipherment of Indented Writings—A New Technique," 1 *J.Pol.Sci. & Admin.* 50 (1973).

Crown, "Class Characteristics of Foreign Typewriters and Typefaces," 59 *J.Crim.L., C. & P.S.* 298 (1968).

Crown & Shimaoka, "The Examination of Ideographic Handwriting," 2 *J.Pol.Sci. & Admin.* 279 (1974).

Crown, "The Differentiation of Pica Monotone Typewriting," 4 *J.Pol. Sci. & Admin.* 134 (1976).

Dalrymple, "Visible and Infrared Luminescence in Documents: Excitation by Laser," 28 *J.For.Sci.* 692 (1983).

Davis & Lyster, "Comparison of Typewritten Carbon Paper Impressions," 27 *J.For.Sci.* 424 (1982).

Doud, "Chromatographic Analysis of Inks," 3 *J.For.Sci.* 486 (1958).

Eldridge, et al., "The Dependence Between Selected Categorical Measures of Cursive Handwriting," 25 *J.For.Sci.Soc.* 217 (1985).

English, "Dye Composition of Typewriter Inks as an Indication of Date of Typing," 6 *J.Pol.Sci. & Admin.* 74 (1978).

Epstein, "A National Survey of Laboratory Questioned Document Reexaminations—Are They Being Done?", 22 *J.For.Sci.* 819 (1977).

Evett & Totty, "A Study of the Variation in the Dimensions of Genuine Signatures," 25 *J.For.Sci.Soc.* 207 (1985).

Faxon, "Demonstrative Evidence and Handwriting Testimony," 1957 *Trial Lawyer's Guide* 39.

Foley & Kelly, "Guided Hand Signature Research," 5 *J.Pol.Sci. & Admin.* 227 (1977).

Godown, "Forgeries Over Genuine Signatures," 14 *J.For.Sci.* 463 (1969).

Grantham, "Identification of Indented Typewritten Entries with Characters Present on a Lift–Off Correction Ribbon," 37 *J.For.Sci.* 1610 (1992).

Guineau, "Microanalysis of Painted Manuscripts and of Colored Archeological Materials by Raman Laser Probe," 29 *J.For.Sci.* 471 (1984).

Hilton, "Effect of Writing Instruments and Handwriting Details," 29 *J.For.Sci.* 80 (1984).

Hilton, "How Individual are Personal Writing Habits?", 28 *J.For.Sci.* 683 (1983).

Hilton, "Identification of the Work from an IBM Selectric Typewriter," 7 *J.For.Sci.* 286 (1962).

Hilton, "Consideration of the Writer's Health in Identifying Signatures and Detecting Forgeries," 14 *J.For.Sci.* 157 (1969).

Hilton, "Identifying the Typewriter Ribbon Used to Write a Letter," 63 *J.Crim.L., C. & P.S.* 137 (1972).

Hilton, "The Complexities of Identifying the Modern Typewriter," 17 *J.For.Sci.* 579 (1972).

Hilton, "The Evolution of Questioned Document Examination in the Last Fifty Years," 33 *J.For.Sci.* 1310 (1988).

Hilton, "Special Considerations in Deciphering Erased Writing," 13 *J.Pol.Sci. & Admin.* 93 (1985).

Kelly, Significant Dates of Modern Typing Methods. Monograph, Am.Bd.For.Doc.Examiners (1993).

Kelly, Classification and Identification of Modern Office Copiers. Monograph, Am.Bd.For.Doc.Examiners (1983).

Kelly & Haville, "Procedure for the Characterization of Zinc Oxide Photocopy Papers," 25 *J.For.Sci.* 118 (1980).

Kraemer, "Identification Cards and Systems That Incorporate Instant Films," 27 *J.For.Sci.* 412 (1982).

Leung, Cheng, Fung & Poon, "Forgery I—Simulation," 38 *J.For.Sci.* 401 (1993).

Leung, Cheng, Fung & Poon, "Forgery II—Tracing," 38 *J.For.Sci.* 413 (1993).

Löfgren & Andrasko, "HPLC Analysis of Printing Inks," 38 *J.For.Sci.* 1151 (1993).

Maldonado & Sierra, "Crayon Obliteration Over Ballpoint Pen Writing," 37 *J.For.Sci.* 1679 (1992).

Masson, "Felt Tip Pen Writing: Problems of Identification," 30 *J.For. Sci.* 172 (1985).

Miller, "An Analysis of the Identification Value of Defects in IBM Selectric Typewriters," 29 *J.For.Sci.* 624 (1984).

Moon, "Electrophoretic Identification of Felt Tip Pen Inks," 25 *J.For. Sci.* 146 (1980).

Noblett & James, "Optimum Conditions for Examination of Documents Using and Electrostatic Detection Apparatus (ESDA) Device to Visualize Indented Writings," 28 *J.For.Sci.* 697 (1983).

Osborn, " 'Explainable' Differences Revealed By Supplementary Typewriting Standards," 5 *J.Pol.Sci. & Admin.* 393 (1977).

Purtell, "Effects of Drugs on Handwriting," 10 *J.For.Sci.* 335 (1965).

Risinger, Denbeaux & Saks, "Exorcism of Ignorance as a Proxy for Rational Knowledge: The Lessons of Handwriting Identification 'Expertise'," 137 *U.Penn.L.Rev.* 731 (1989).

Schroeder, "Checlass—A Classification System for Fraudulent Checks," 16 *J.For.Sci.* 162 (1971).

Shaneyfelt, "Obliterations, Alterations, and Related Document Problems," 16 *J.For.Sci.* 331 (1971).

Slawinski, "New Approaches In Counterfeit Check Techniques," *Identification News,* Mar. 1982, at 7.

Stangohr, "Comment on the Determination of Nationality from Handwriting," 16 *J.For.Sci.* 343 (1971).

Taylor, "Intersecting Lines as a Means of Fraud Detection," 29 *J.For. Sci.* 92 (1984).

Totty & Roberts, "The Use of 'Calflex' Infrared Reflecting Mirrors to Enhance Infrared Luminescence," 21 *J.For.Sci.* 359 (1981).

Throckmorton, "Disappearing Ink: Its Use, Abuse and Detection," 35 *J.For.Sci.* 199 (1990).

Throckmorton, "Erasable Ink: Its Ease of Erasability and Its Permanence," 30 *J.For.Sci.* 526 (1985).

Vastrich, "A Nondestructive, Preliminary Test for the Determination of Page Insertion of a Multipage Questioned Document," *Identification News,* Aug. 1983, p. 5.

Wichmann, "A Photographic Technique for Identifying a Paper–Cutting Knife By a Single Sheet of Paper," *Finger Pr. & Ident.Mag.,* p. 14 (Aug.–Sept. 1976).

3.   NEWSLETTERS

ABFDE News, Quarterly Newsletter of the American Board of Forensic Document Examiners, Inc.; ABFDE, Administrative Offices, 7887 San Felipe, Suite 122, Houston, Texas 70063.

Chapter 6

FIREARMS IDENTIFICATION AND COMPARATIVE MICROGRAPHY

I.   INTRODUCTION

§ 6.01   Scope of the Chapter

This chapter is designed to provide the criminal trial attorney with an abbreviated, yet fundamental, understanding of the role of the firearms examiner in marshalling and presenting evidence concerning the identification of firearms and ammunition. In order to promote a meaningful dialogue between attorney and expert, a short glossary of firearms terminology has been included as a preface to a brief description of various classes of ammunition and guns. Although definitions may be considered unnecessary by the sportsman-attorney who is familiar with sporting firearms, this material may even be useful to him in attempting to prove a matter which requires a basic understanding of firearms to a juror who has never had any experience with guns.

The heart of the chapter deals with the firearms identification process and the theories underpinning it. Material is also included, however, on other tasks which are frequently part of the firearms examiner's duties or which developed under his direction, such as the restoration of serial numbers on firearms, gunshot residue tests, and toolmark identification.

§ 6.02   Definition of Common Terms [1]

Automatic pistol: Although commonly used to describe a self-loading pistol, which should be termed a semiautomatic or self-loader, since

---

§ 6.02

1. See, Glossary of the Association of Firearm and Toolmark Examiners, 3d ed.

1994, available Business Printing Inc., 1519 So. State St., Chicago, IL, 60605.

the trigger must be pressed anew for every shot fired, a truly automatic firearm is a self-loader which continues to fire until empty as long as the finger continues to depress the trigger.

Antimony: Metallic element with the chemical symbol of Sb, atomic number 51, and atomic weight of 121.75 alloyed with lead to harden the bullet; used in the modern non-corrosive primer compound as an oxidizing agent.

Ballistics: Study of the motion of a projectile.

Exterior Ballistics: Study of the motion of the projectile after it leaves the barrel of the firing weapon.

Interior Ballistics: Study of the motion of the projectile within the firearm from the moment of igniting of the primer until the projectile leaves the barrel.

Terminal (Wound) Ballistics: Study of the effect of a projectile's impact on the target.

Barrel: Tube that guides the bullet or projectile (shot charge); interior passage rifled in rifles and handguns, smooth in shotguns of American manufacture.

Barium: Metallic element with the chemical symbol of Ba, atomic number of 56 and atomic weight of 137.34 found in the primer compound.

Bearing Surface: Part of the bullet that comes in contact with the lands and grooves as it moves through the barrel; that portion of the bullet that mirrors the engraving of the rifling in the barrel.

Bolt: Generally a sliding rod that pushes a cartridge into the firing chamber as it closes and locks the breech in a breech loading rifle.

Bore: Diameter of the barrel; in a rifled firearm, the bore diameter measured from opposing land to opposing land; measurement is expressed in hundredths or thousands of an inch in weapons of American and British manufacture or in millimeters in weapons of other manufacturers.

Breech Block: Whether as a bolt, slide or cylinder that part of the firearm that blocks and locks the breech of the firearm before firing.

Bullet: Projectile of a pistol or rifle; one of the parts of the cartridge; term accurate only when referring to the projectile; composed of lead hardened by an alloy of tin and antimony. Sometimes semi-jacketed or full-jacketed with an outer layer of hard metal, usually a copper-zinc alloy; style variable, e.g., boattail, flat nose, hollow point, round nose, spire point and wad cutter.

Burning Rate: Relative speed at which smokeless powder burns when confined within the firearm.

Caliber: Ideally, the bore diameter expressed in hundredths or thousands of an inch or in mm.; practically, caliber often used in designating the name of the firearm or cartridge, regardless of its being slightly different from the bore diameter.

Cannelure: Groove or depression rolled into the cartridge case or bullet; sometimes used to hold lubricant or to crimp the end of the cartridge case to hold the bullet at the correct depth.

Cartridge: One unit of ammunition composed of cartridge case, primer, powder and bullet; sometimes referred to as one round of ammunition.

Cartridge Case: Metal cup generally made of brass; may be nickel-plated and can be made of steel (best example of steel case is .45 ACP made in World War II); holds the primer, powder and bullet in a waterproof container; three basic shapes, straight, tapered and bottlenecked; head of the case will be rimmed, semi-rimmed, rimless, rebated rimless or belted.

Chamber: Special enlarged area at the breech of the barrel where the cartridge fits when it is loaded and fired.

Choke: Constriction of the barrel diameter of a shotgun at, or near the muzzle to concentrate the pattern of shot; the more the choke the more concentrated the pattern; shotguns are made with the following chokes: improved cylinder, modified, or full choke; double-barrel shotguns generally have a different choke for each barrel; devices available that can be placed on the end of a shotgun barrel to adjust the choke from shot to shot as the shooter wishes.

Class Characteristics: Those unvariable characteristics of a particular make firearm or ammunition, e.g., number of lands and grooves in rifling, direction of the twist of the rifling. Class characteristics are not sufficient to identify a particular weapon as having fired a specified bullet or cartridge case.

Clip: Mechanical device for holding cartridges to speed the loading of a magazine; commonly mistaken by the layman for the magazine.

Crimping: Compressing of the cartridge case mouth to hold the bullet in place.

Deterrent Coating: A chemical coating used on smokeless powder particles to control combustion rate.

Drift: The lateral deviation of a bullet in flight from its trajectory.

Ejector: Part of the firearm action that kicks out or ejects the cartridge case from the firearm after firing or when the action is operated by hand.

Erosion: Removal of metal from the inside of the barrel by friction of bullet and from action of the voluminous high temperature gases; generally first seen in the "throat" of the rifle (the junction of the mouth of the cartridge case and the barrel); will make some changes in individual characteristics.

Extractor: Part of the action of the firearm that pulls or withdraws the cartridge case from the chamber.

Firing Pin: Part of the weapon that transmits the blow which detonates the primer.

Flash Hole: Aperture through the web of a centerfire case from the primer pocket through which primer flame passes to ignite the powder.

Foot-pound: Energy required to lift one pound one foot; unit of measure used to express the energy or power of a cartridge.

Forcement: Energy necessary to drive a bullet through the bore.

Gauge: Size designation of a shotgun; based on the number of pure lead balls per pound a particular gauge would take, e.g., 12 gauge would have bore diameter of a lead ball $\frac{1}{12}$ of a pound in weight—20 gauge, $\frac{1}{20}$ of a pound, etc.; only exception is the .410 shotgun where bore size is .41 inch.

Grain: Standard unit of weight for bullet weight and weight of powder charge; 7,000 grains to a pound.

Gram: Metric unit of weight; one gram equivalent to 15.4324 grains.

Groove: Spiral cuts or impressions inside a barrel which, together with the lands, rotate the projectile and stabilize its flight.

Groove Diameter: Diameter of a bore measured from depth of groove to depth of opposite groove.

Hair Trigger: Trigger requiring only a light touch or slight pressure to discharge the firearm; measurable as a force by a trigger pull dynamometer, a simple spring scale, or a force gauge.

Hammer: Part of the weapon that strikes the primer or moves the firing pin forward causing it to strike the primer.

Handgun: Short firearm intended to be aimed and fired from one hand. Three types:

　Automatic Pistol (semiautomatic): Automatic is common terminology for a self-loading handgun which fires, ejects the empty cartridge, reloads and cocks itself each time the trigger is pulled; accurate designation for this type firearm is semiautomatic since the fully automatic weapon will continue firing as long as trigger is held back and ammunition lasts.

　Derringer: Small, easily concealed handgun; may have one, two, or four barrels; fires a single shot from each barrel.

　Revolver: Repeating handgun with a revolving cylinder chambered to hold the cartridges; cylinder may contain as few as five chambers or as many as twelve, most common number being six. Two types:

　　Single Action: Hammer must be cocked manually each time before firing.

Double Action: Trigger pull alone will cock and fire, although hammer may be cocked manually as well.

Heel: Edge of base of bullet.

Individual Characteristics: Those characteristic markings or details of a firearm which serve to distinguish it from all other firearms, including those of the same caliber, make and model.

Keyhole: Shape of wound caused by bullet not striking nose or point first; caused by loss of gyroscopic stability (spin) of bullet.

Land: Original part of the bore left as raised ridges after rifling grooves are formed.

Lead: Metallic element with the chemical symbol of Pb, atomic number 82 and atomic weight of 207.19 main ingredient of the bullet and in jacketed bullet—of bullet core; generally considered too soft to be used in non-jacketed bullets without some hardening element being added, although pure lead is used for all flint and percussion weapons, as well as by some handloaders seeking maximum expansion at low velocities; alloy of lead, tin and antimony used as hardening agents in most unjacketed bullets; also found in the primer compound.

Leading: Deposit of lead in the bore of a rifle or pistol when lead bullets are fired; when extensive, positive bullet identification is difficult if not impossible.

Magazine: Holder for cartridges in a repeating firearm from which cartridges are automatically chambered; some detachable magazines (semiautomatic pistols, etc.) commonly, though inaccurately, referred to as clips.

Magnum: Cartridge of increased power than earlier standards for the same caliber; also firearms with the capacity to use magnum cartridges; manufacturers sometimes use word for glamour, not the increased power.

Metal Fouling: Depositing in bore of metal from bullet or jacket.

Millimeter: 1 mm. equals .03937 inch; to convert millimeters to inches, multiply by .03937 or divide by 25.4; to convert inches to millimeters, multiply by 25.4 or divide by .03937.

Muzzle Energy: Amount of energy of the bullet at the muzzle given in foot pounds (Ft. lbs.).

Muzzle Velocity: Speed of the bullet or shot at the muzzle expressed in feet per second (F.P.S.); measurement thereof customarily made a few feet away from the muzzle using a chronograph.

Pantascopic Camera: Photographic equipment that permits a photograph of entire longitudinal surface of bullet.

Penetration: Usually expressed in the number of ⅞ inch white pine boards that a bullet will pass through when fired from a specified barrel length, important when defense seeks to prove that a bullet may have ricocheted.

Pressure: The force in pounds per square inch exerted in the chamber by the powder gases of the cartridge at the time of discharge.

Primer: Small metal cap holding compound that is detonated by blow from either the hammer or the firing pin; replaceable in center-fire cartridges; compound variable but customarily contains some or all of following: antimony, barium, lead, mercury and potassium.

Powder: Two basic types:

> Black powder: Mixture of 10 parts sulfur, 15 parts charcoal and 75 parts potassium nitrate by weight; presently used in muzzle loading rifles and shotguns and cap and ball pistols; ignitable by shock, friction or spark.

> Smokeless powder: High energy chemical compound which requires a high kindling temperature for ignition; does not ignite from shock or friction; grains usually ball or tubular shaped; burns rather than explodes; rate of burn increases with confinement.

> Two types:

>> Single base smokeless powder—composed of nitrocellulose.

>> Double base smokeless powder—composed of nitroglycerin absorbed in nitrocellulose.

Proof Marks: Distinctive stamp placed upon firearms by manufacturers, indicating arm will withstand a stated pressure over that normally expected.

Pump: Repeating rifle or shotgun in which the mechanism is activated manually by means of a slide.

Range: Maximum distance a bullet will travel, e.g., maximum range at muzzle elevation between 29° and 35°: .22 long rifle with 40 grains of powder—1500 yards; .45 ACP with 234 grains of powder—1640 yards; .30 cal. M1 with 152 grains of powder—3500 yards; also, distance that a bullet traveled from muzzle to target.

Recoil: "Kick"; backward motion of gun when fired.

Revolver: Rifled pistol with a cylinder of several chambers, as few as five or as many as twelve; chambers arranged to revolve on an axis and discharge the shots in succession; see handgun.

Ricochet: Glancing shot.

Rifle: Firearm designed for and intended to be fired from the shoulder and held by both hands. Several types:

> Autoloading Rifle: Rifle in which part of the energy of the fired shell is used to operate the action to extract, and eject the spent shell and chamber a live shell while cocking for the next shot (semiautomatic rifles and automatic rifles).

Repeating Rifle: Rifle which will fire repeatedly without reloading until ammunition is exhausted; energy to operate the action supplied by shooter (pump rifle, lever-action rifle, some bolt-action rifles).

Manually Loaded Rifle: Includes single shot rifle, some bolt-action rifles, and double barreled rifles which must be manually reloaded after shot is fired.

Carbine: Originally a rifle made short enough to be easily carried on horseback, now a loose term applying to a short barreled rifle (18″ to 20″).

Rifling: Parallel cut, spiral grooves cut or engraved on the inner surface of the barrel; sometimes formed by forcing a tungsten carbide steel button in the negative image of the rifling through the bore by hydraulic pressure; primarily to impart to bullet a rotation or spin around its own axis in order to keep it gyroscopically straight or point first, and, secondarily, to retain the bullet in the barrel to await more complete combustion of the propellant; a class characteristic.

Rim Fire Cartridge: Cartridge in which the primer compound is positioned in the hollow rim of the cartridge case.

Shot Balling: Clumping of several shot pellets into a single mass forming a projectile which has greater range than the pellets individually; caused either by faulty wadding that permits hot gases to fuse pellets or by soft shot pellets.

Shotgun: Firearm with a smooth bore designed to fire a charge of shot (small, round pellets) but may shoot a slug.

Sight: Aiming device on a gun.

Squib Load: Defective load which does not impart full velocity to the bullet or shot charge.

Striker: Firing pin or part of the weapon which strikes the firing pin found in hammerless firearms.

Tin: A metallic element with the chemical symbol of Sn, atomic number 50 and atomic weight of 118.69; used in alloy with lead in the making of bullets.

Trajectory: Path of bullet in air over a long distance as determined by velocity, air density, gravity and the projectile rotation.

Velocity: Speed of a projectile in feet per second (fps); important in determining trajectory, stopping power and extreme range; low velocity for bullet fired from a rifled firearm is from 600 to 1750 fps; high velocity from 1750 to over 3000 fps; usually expressed in terms of muzzle velocity.

Yaw: Deviation between the long axis of the bullet and the axis of the path of the bullet; can cause keyhole entry wound; two types:

Nose Yaw: Nose of bullet spinning around the axis of flight; variable causes such as defect in bullet; imperfect seating of bullet in case, etc.; tends to increase in flight, eventually causing bullet to tumble.

Base Yaw: Base of bullet spinning around the axis of flight; variable causes as excessive velocity, wrong combination of rifling twist and bullet weight.

II. BASICS OF FIREARMS AND AMMUNITION

§ 6.03 Weapons

The variety of firearms is considerable. Among the different types are the semiautomatic pistol, the truly automatic pistol, the revolver, the single-shot pistol, the repeating rifle, the semiautomatic rifle, the automatic rifle, and the shotgun. Differences in mechanical design are apparent between the muzzle loader and the breech loader and between the smooth barrel and the rifled barrel. Further differentiation in mechanical as well as aesthetic design is imparted by the particular arms manufacturer who creates a firearm.

The discussion which follows considers the four classifications of firearms most commonly appearing as evidence in criminal prosecutions. Weapons comprising the first three classifications are rifled arms. Their size is denoted by caliber, roughly the diameter across two opposite lands. Firearms of the final classification have smooth bores. Their size is designated principally by gauge. One important factor in many firearm investigations is the ease with which a firearm discharges. The difference might mean that a victim was shot accidentally rather than intentionally. While some firearms readily discharge upon being dropped, others rarely do. One of the major factors to be considered is safety and trigger design. Furthermore, although testing can demonstrate with some reliability a weapon's sensitivity to shock, examination of the safety or trigger design may provide a better indicator of the shock sensitivity.[1]

1. SEMIAUTOMATIC PISTOL

The semiautomatic pistol is a rifled handgun which generally loads itself from fresh cartridges contained in a vertical magazine located in the hollow handle grip. There is no cylinder. The trigger must be pressed for every shot fired. The misnomer "automatic" is often used to describe this gun. Although the Mauser Arms Company of Germany did

§ 6.03

1. Lipscomb & Harden "Evaluating Trigger Sensitivity to Shock", 17 A.F.T.E. J. 4 (Oct.1985).

at one time manufacture a truly automatic pistol which continued to fire as long as the trigger was held back, the "automatic" pistol is virtually nonexistent. The semiautomatic pistol utilizes the powder gas recoil and backward movement of the sliding breech block (slide) upon discharge in order to remove the fired cartridge case from the chamber, and, by its forceful contact with the ejector groove, to cock the hammer in readiness for the next shot. When the trigger is pulled, the firing pin is pushed forward by the hammer, striking the primer of the cartridge which then discharges the bullet. The firing pin returns to its floating position by a spring. The slide is pulled forward by another spring, and the bolt strips the cartridge from the magazine and places it into the chamber. A spring-activated magazine follower forces fresh cartridges up in the magazine as others are expended.

2. REVOLVER

The revolver is a repeating pistol with a rifled barrel. The grip is solid and the weapon is designed as a handgun. It is distinguished from other handguns by the presence of a revolving cylinder containing multiple firing chambers, each accommodating a single cartridge. The spent shell is not automatically ejected in a revolver.

Revolver design is typically of three types. In the first, the barrel is fixed to the frame and the revolving cylinder is swung out to the side for loading and unloading. In the second, the barrel is hinged to the frame with the revolving cylinder exposed by releasing the barrel latch and swinging the barrel and cylinder forward on the hinge. The third design is a solid frame with a detachable cylinder that is removed by withdrawing a pin. A single-action revolver must be cocked each time it is to be fired. A double-action revolver can be cocked by hand or by prolonged pulling of the trigger.

The basic distinctions between a semi-automatic pistol and a revolver are illustrated in Figure 1.

3. RIFLE

A rifle is a firearm with a rifled barrel, designed for use with two arms and for firing from the shoulder. Rifles come in a variety of styles: lever action, bolt action, pump and self-loaders.

4. SHOTGUN

A shotgun is a smooth-bored shoulder weapon. The term "smooth bored" means that the inside of the barrel is smooth from end to end. Shotguns are available in a number of designs: self-loaders, pumps, single shot, or manually loaded double barreled. A shotgun may have a choke which is a contraction of the muzzle designed to produce a concentration of shot. The degree of choke may be constant or variable. The manufacturer determines whether or not the choke will be full,

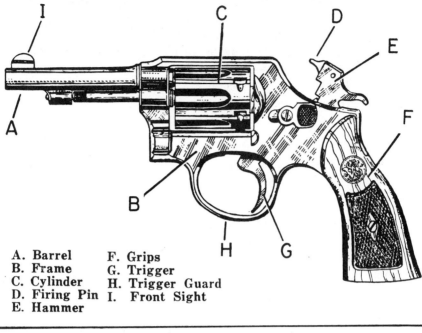

A. Barrel   F. Grips
B. Frame   G. Trigger
C. Cylinder   H. Trigger Guard
D. Firing Pin I. Front Sight
E. Hammer

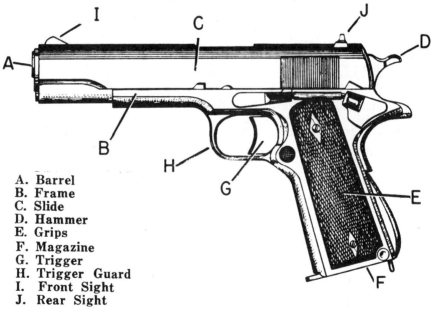

A. Barrel
B. Frame
C. Slide
D. Hammer
E. Grips
F. Magazine
G. Trigger
H. Trigger Guard
I. Front Sight
J. Rear Sight

Fig. I. Drawings of a typical revolver (above) and semi-automatic pistol (below).

improved cylinder or modified. A variable choke (polychoke) is a device that may be added to the muzzle to allow the shooter to adjust the choke as desired. The influence of the choke on shot pattern becomes increasingly marked the farther the muzzle is from the target. The range of a shotgun is comparatively short, due to the lightness of the shot; however, the cone-like spreading effect of the shot, coupled with their large number, improves the chances of hitting a particular target at moderate range.

The size of large-bore shotguns is expressed by the number of spherical balls of pure lead, each exactly fitting the inside of the bore, which together make a pound. For example, a 12 gauge shotgun would accommodate a lead ball weighing $\frac{1}{12}$ of a pound.

The most commonly used gauges of shotguns are the 10, 12, 16, 20 and .410. The .410 caliber is expressed in hundredths of inches. The following chart reflects the bore diameter of the more common gauges of shotguns.

Bore Diameter

Gauge No.	Inches	Millimeters
10	.775"	19.68 mm
12	.729"	18.52 mm
16	.662"	16.81 mm
20	.615"	15.62 mm
.410	.410"	10.41 mm

§ 6.04 Bullets, Shot and Wadding

A bullet, which is mounted on a cartridge case as shown in Figure 2–A, is the projectile propelled by the firearm. It is important to remember that the bullet is only one component of the complete cartridge. Bullet diameter is usually somewhat larger than the bore diameter of the weapon from which it is intended to be fired. This is necessary in order to permit the rifling of the barrel to grasp the bullet and impart a spin to it. Attorneys should be aware that the caliber of the bullet does not conclusively indicate the caliber of the weapon that fired it, since a sub-caliber bullet may be fired through a larger sized barrel.

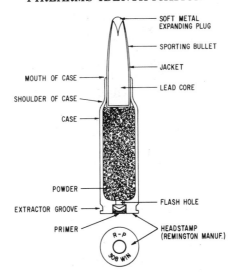

RIMLESS BOTTLENECKED CENTERFIRE
.308 WINCHESTER

Fig. 2–A

Bullets are of lead composition hardened with alloys of tin, antimony, etc., or encased in an envelope of hard metal. Expanding nose bullets having a mushrooming or fragmenting effect are prohibited by the Geneva Convention from use in warfare but are commercially manufactured for sport and law enforcement uses. If expanding bullets are used in the commission of a crime, it may be difficult for a firearms examiner to link them with a suspected weapon if the bullet does expand to the point that striae are obliterated.

1. BULLETS

Bullets are of several types; such as

(1) Full jacketed non-expanding: the lead slug is fully encased with a one-piece metal jacket open only at the base.

(2) Lead alloy: the lead slug is unjacketed but is alloyed with other hard metals to increase the bullet hardness.

(3) Round nose, soft point, expanding or mushrooming bullets: an area of lead is exposed at the tip and a metal jacket covers the base and side of the bullet.

(4) Open, hollow point, expanding bullet: the base and side of the bullet are enclosed by a one-piece jacket which has been intentionally weakened by nicking near the nose of the bullet. If it is designed to fragment rather than mushroom, the bullet is constructed similarly except that the metal jacketing is thinned to insure maximum fragmentation.

Bullets used in crimes will often be distorted. Lead bullets, because of their softness, tend to display pronounced impressions of the barrel surface through which they are fired. This same softness, however, may result in distortion through contact with a hard surface or object, or even when exposed to the air long enough to result in a coating of lead oxide, for which reason care must be exercised in the recovery and handling of evidence bullets.

The degree of hardness of lead will, of course, vary with the alloy used. Jacketed bullets reflect opposite traits. Jacketed bullets are more resistant to external distortion than lead bullets, although the metallic jacketing may flake off.

Expanding rifle bullets are commercially available. These include the Winchester silvertip, the Remington round nose, soft point, the Remington Bronze point, the Hornady pointed, soft point, expanding bullet and the Remington open, hollow point.

2. SHOT

Shot are small lead balls or pellets contained in a shotgun cartridge. See Figure 2-B. They emerge from the barrel with a typical muzzle velocity of approximately twelve hundred feet per second. Classification of shot is according to numbers, each number indicating a special size. They are measured by diameter and by weight in grains. Shot are composed of lead combined with a small percentage of antimony. The weight of the shot in the charge is indicative of the type of cartridge used. However, weight alone is insufficient to establish gauge of the gun from which it was fired. An elongated hollow rifled slug may also be fired from a shotgun. The slug is loaded in a shotgun cartridge and has an effective range much greater than any size of shot. The shock power of the rifled slug is tremendous.

The following charts demonstrate the comparative number of pellets that are contained in different shot sizes as well as the actual diameter of the pellets of the various shot sizes. Notice that for all shot sizes under no. 1, the shot number can be determined by subtracting the diameter of the pellets from 17. Subtracting the shot size from 17 will give the pellet diameter.

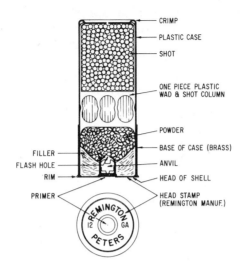

CRIMP

PLASTIC CASE

SHOT

ONE PIECE PLASTIC
WAD & SHOT COLUMN

POWDER

BASE OF CASE (BRASS)

FILLER

FLASH HOLE

RIM

ANVIL

HEAD OF SHELL

PRIMER

HEAD STAMP
(REMINGTON MANUF.)

CENTERFIRE SHOT SHELL

Fig. 2–B

Shot Size	Pellets in Charge Weight of Charge in Ounces				
	½	¾	⅞	1	1½
9	292	439	512	585	—
8	—	308	359	410	—
7½	175	263	—	350	—
6	113	169	197	225	338
5	85	128	149	170	—
4	68	101	118	135	203
2	—	—	—	90	135

Shot Size	Pellet Diameter	
9	.08″	
8	.09″	
7½	.095″	
7	.10″	
6	.11″	
5	.12″	
4	.13″	
2	.15″	
1	.16″	
BB	.18″	
00 Buck	.33″	(Buckshot is molded round shot about the size of a pea)

3. WADDING

Although not projectiles, the wad in a shotgun cartridge is blown out with the fired shot. The wad is a piece of greased felt between the powder and the shot. It acts to seal the bore, to keep gases from escaping and to protect the projectile from the ignition. An increasing number of manufacturers use a shot collar rather than wads to contain the shot. The collar is a polyethylene sleeve with slits at the side. The shot collar or sleeve typically opens when it reaches 24 inches from the muzzle. The position of the wads or the shot collar when discovered at the crime scene is sometimes useful to the expert in establishing the position and or range of the shotgun at time of discharge. Wads, more than pellets, can identify the manufacturer of the shot and even the specific lot in which it was made.

§ 6.05 Cartridge Cases

A cartridge case holds the ignition cap, the powder and the missile in the form of a single bullet or a charge of shot. Together, each of these components, the case, the ignition cap, the powder and the projectile, form the cartridge. The case is usually made of brass for use in rifled arms and plastic and brass or paper and brass for use in shotguns or other smooth bore arms. Cartridge cases may be stamped at the factory to indicate type and make. In ammunition made for semiautomatic pistols the base of the cartridge case is characteristically "rimless." There is only an indented extractor groove running around the circumference immediately above the base. Revolver and shotgun ammunition is usually rimmed because the design of these weapons requires that the cartridge case be anchored; however, some manufacturers make revolvers which will accommodate semiautomatic pistol cartridges. Examples are the Colt and Smith & Wesson .45 caliber revolver. It is also possible for a 7.65 mm pistol cartridge to be fired from a .32 caliber revolver.

The cartridge case from a semiautomatic weapon is more likely to be found at a crime scene than one from a revolver. This is attributable to the fact that the semiautomatic automatically ejects spent cartridges while the revolver retains them in the cylinder. Hence, cartridge cases will be more recurrent as evidence in criminal trials involving the use of a semiautomatic. The design of the semiautomatic pistol also results in more potentially identifiable marks being imprinted on the cartridge case as it comes in contact with the firing pin, the breech block, the extractor and the ejector. For an example of how firing pin impressions may mark ammunition differently depending on the type of weapon used, see Figure 3.

§ 6.06 Primer and Powder

The primer is a small charge which is detonated by the crushing blow of the firing pin or hammer. The flame produced by the ignition of the primer ignites the main powder charge. This is the sole purpose of the primer.

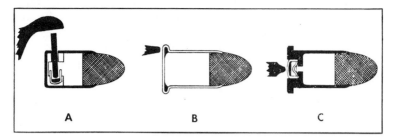

A. **Pin fire cartridge.** When the hammer strikes the firing pin, the priming is crushed between the bottom end of the pin and the priming cap.

B. **Rim fire cartridge.** In this type, the priming is around the circumference of the rim and the blow of the firing pin anywhere on the rim crushes the priming between the rear and front faces of the rim.

C. **Center fire cartridge.** The firing pin must strike in the center to crush the priming between the primer cup and the little anvil inside the primer cup.

Fig. 3. Firing pin impressions may mark ammunition differently depending on the type of weapon used.

Priming is of two types. Rim fire priming involves the positioning of the primer in the fold of the cartridge case rim and over the inner surface of the cartridge head; the primer is ignited when the firing pin strikes the rim. Rim fire cartridge design is commonly found in .22 caliber ammunition. The center fire primer is a small metal cup containing the primer compound. It is placed in the center of the cartridge case in a recess behind the powder charge. When the hammer or firing pin strikes the anvil in the primer, the primer composition between the two is crushed and ignition occurs.

The combustion of cartridge powder produces gases which propel the missile from the cartridge and through the barrel toward the target. Pressure emanating from the expanding powder gases within the cartridge case is sufficiently violent to force the case against the breech face and the chamber walls. The characteristics thus imprinted on the cartridge case are the basis of identification of a suspect weapon. Obviously, the strength, condition and amount of powder present in a given cartridge will have significant influence on the force with which the case is hurled against the breech and chamber walls.

In the past, black powder was the propulsion agent for bullets. It was composed of 75% potassium nitrate, 10% sulfur and 15% charcoal. Black powder proved unsatisfactory because its combustion produced a great deal of black smoke and resulted in fouling of the inner barrel. A more powerful substance, smokeless powder, was introduced around 1886 and is used in all modern ammunition. It produces a comparatively small amount of smoke and does not markedly foul the firearm. There are two types of smokeless powder: single based smokeless

powder is composed of nitrocellulose with additives; double based powder is composed of nitrocellulose and nitroglycerin with additives.

III. PRINCIPLES OF FIREARMS IDENTIFICATION *

§ 6.07 Rifle Barrel Manufacture

Understanding how bullets and shells can be identified as having
come from a certain type and make of weapon, or from a specific weapon,
depends upon some knowledge of how firearms are manufactured, especially the manufacture of pistol and rifle barrels.

First, a hole is bored through a cylindrical bar of steel of the desired
diameter for the particular weapon. That diameter determines the
caliber of the weapon and is expressed in hundredths or thousandths of
an inch, or in millimeters. Therefore, a weapon with a bore diameter of
forty-five hundredths of an inch would be a "forty-five" (.45") caliber
gun. Likewise, a weapon of foreign manufacture possessing a bore
diameter of nine millimeters is said to be a nine-millimeter (9 mm)
caliber gun.

In earlier days, after the hole had been bored, a "cutter" was used
to scrape out twisting grooves, the "rifling" contour of the interior,
which produced higher rotational velocity to a fired bullet, giving it
greater gyroscopic stability and consequently greater accuracy, range
and energy impact whereas a bullet fired through a smooth-bore barrel
would travel in an end-over-end fashion. For an illustration of the
twisting appearance of the interior of a rifled barrel, see Figure 4B.

Cutters have been replaced by what is known as a "broach," a long,
hard, cylindrical, segmented tool that in one operation produces all of
the twisting grooves desired by the manufacturer, or a "button" method.
As shown in Figure 4C, some manufacturers prefer four grooves, others
five or six; and they may twist either to the right or to the left. The
way in which the bullets themselves are affected is illustrated in Figure
4D and in Figure 5.

---

* For a brief and cogent primer see, Meyers, "Firearms and Toolmark Identification:
An Introduction," 25 A.F.T.E. J. 281 (Oct.
1993).

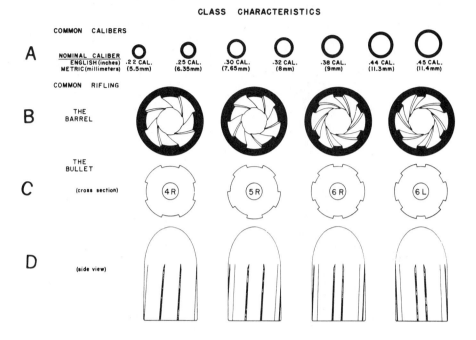

Fig. 4. Manufacturers' specifications for barrel making greatly influence the "class characteristics" left on the bullet after it has been fired through a barrel. *Courtesy: Albert Biasotti, San Jose, Calif.*

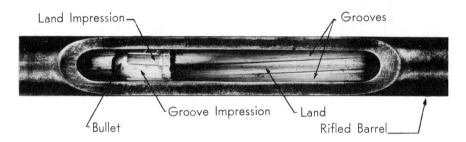

Fig. 5. Barrel section showing interior of barrel and bullet. Observe the twist in the grooves and in the projecting interspaces (the lands). Also note the groove and the land impression on the bullet, which has been pushed through the unsectioned portion of the barrel to its present position. *Courtesy: Charles M. Wilson (deceased), Madison, Wis.*

Regardless of the type of instrument used to produce the rifling within a barrel, each barrel inevitably acquires minute marks, called striations or striae, primarily through minor accidental occurrences in the rifling process. They are not the same for any two barrels, even though manufactured one right after the other. The magnified photograph of a bullet in Figure 6 shows the kind of marks transmitted to the bullet by the structural characteristics of a barrel's interior.

Fig. 6.

The individuality of each rifle barrel can best be appreciated by observing, in Figure 7, how great the differences are within the same barrel between its own grooves and between its own lands. A and B are two identical photographic prints, made from the same negative, of the entire circumference of a bullet fired from a barrel that was made by the original "cutter" process. The difference in appearance upon a first look at A and B is due to the fact that one of the prints has been shifted over one position, so that each land impression can be compared with the one adjacent to it. For instance, the photograph of groove 1 (G_1) in B is the same as groove 1 (G_1) in A, but it has been placed beneath groove 2 in order to more vividly demonstrate the difference between 1 and 2. The same is done for the other lands and grooves. Thus, it may be observed how distinct the striations on each groove and on each land impression are from those on the adjoining grooves and lands. This comparison demonstrates that even within the same gun barrel there is no significant duplication of the characteristics on the various lands and grooves. Since that is true of every barrel, it may be appreciated how unlikely it would be to find two gun barrels (even though of successive manufacture in the same factory) that contain identical characteristics throughout their interiors.

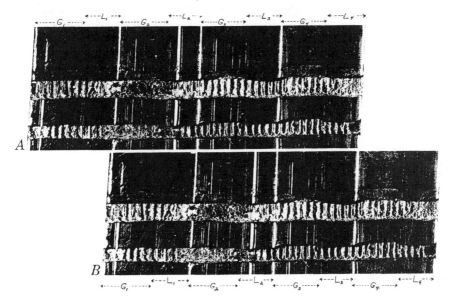

Fig. 7.

§ 6.08   Bullet Identification

Because of manufacturers' different concepts concerning the preferred structure of the interior of a rifled barrel (for example, six grooves instead of four, or a twist to the left instead of to the right), a fired bullet may reveal to the expert the make of the gun from which it was fired. However, there are indications that computerization of the rifling measurements can help in the identification process.[1] Sometimes precise measurements of the lands and grooves are needed to obtain such a clue, and there are of course instances when the expert can only exclude certain possibilities rather than point to a particular make. This is especially so with regard to some cheaper, foreign made products.[2]

Since there is no practical way of making a comparison directly between the imperfections and irregularities within a barrel and the reverse impressions on a bullet, the firearms examiner fires a series of test bullets[3] from the suspected weapon and then uses them instead of the gun barrel itself for comparison. In order to secure a comparison

§ 6.08

1. Jauhari, Rao, & Pal, "A Scheme for the Computerization of Rifling Specifications of Firearms," 34 *For.Sci.Internat'l.* 183 (1987).

2. The so-called "Saturday Night Specials" (inexpensive .22 Caliber revolvers) may be very poorly constructed. Because of this, two bullets may be fired concomitantly, misfires occur frequently, and malfunctions are the rule rather than the exception.

See, e.g., Schmidt–Orndorff et al., "Peculiarities of Certain .22 Caliber Revolvers (Saturday Night Specials)," 19 *J.For.Sci.* 48 (1974).

3. Test cartridges should reasonably correspond to the essentials of the evidence bullet. Finding the manufacturer of ammunition therefore becomes essential. Nennstiel, "The Determination of the Manufacturer of Ammunition," 31 *For.Sci.Internat'l.* 1 (1986).

test bullet without damaging its individual characteristics or distorting its shape, the test bullet is fired into a specially constructed box filled with some soft material such as cotton waste. This is called a "bullet trap." The test bullet might also be fired into a water container, called "bullet recovery tank."[4] After making a preliminary examination consisting of determining the test bullet's various class characteristics (lands, grooves, etc.), and if he finds them the same as those on the evidence bullet, the technician proceeds with a microscopic examination of the individual characteristics of both bullets.

He uses a binocular comparison microscope[5] (see Figure 8), which is an instrument consisting essentially of two separate microscopes mounted side by side and fitted with a comparison bridge in which there is an arrangement of lenses and prisms that produces the effect of using the images of objects as they appear in the field of each microscope. The evidence bullet is placed under one microscope and the test bullet under the other. The bullets are mounted horizontally by means of a plastic substance on cylindrical adjustable holders.

After the two bullets are mounted, the usual practice is for the examiner to scrutinize the entire surface of the rotating bullet at relatively low magnifications for the purpose of locating the most prominent group of striations. Once such marks are located on the evidence bullet, that bullet is permitted to remain stationary. Then the examiner rotates the test bullet in an attempt to find a corresponding area with individual characteristics that match those on the evidence bullet. If what appears to be a match is located, the examiner rotates both bullets simultaneously to determine whether or not similar coincidences exist on the other portions of the bullets. A careful study of all of the detail on both bullets ultimately permits him to conclude that both bullets were or were not fired through the same barrel. However, corrosion or other damage to a bullet shell or to a weapon's bore might necessitate an inconclusive finding by an examiner.[6] In preparing an evidence bullet for analysis the firearms examiner in an AIDS anxious world will cleanse and sterilize the bullet. This can have the deleterious effect of obliterating bullet striae.[7] Typically, firearms examiners do not require a prede-

4. Water is a much preferred medium for test firings over fibrous materials, such as cotton, saw dust, etc. since the projectile suffers less polishing in water. See, Bradford, "Problems and Advantages of Test Firing Weapons into Water," 6 *J.For.Sci. Soc.* 97 (1966).

5. The inventor of the comparison microscope is said to be Alexander von Inostranzeff. See, Thornton, "Some Historical Notes on the Comparison Microscope," 10 A.F.T.E.J. 71 (Mar. 1978); Beck, "Alexander von Inostranzell and the Technical Development of Optical Comparison Systems," 21 A.F.T.E.J. 317 (Jan. 1989).

6. Although corrosion, abrasion and oxidation do affect the ability of the examiner to identify a bullet, Arnold of the Maine Crime Laboratory reports a positive identification of striae on a bullet after it had been buried over ten years. Arnold, "Identification of Striae on Bullet Buried over 10 Years," 20 A.F.T.E.J. 168 (1988). Criminals have been known to attempt to prevent striation matching of a bullet by a prefiring scoring of the bullet, all to no avail. Dodson & Stengel, "Bullets, Marked Before Firing," 24 A.F.T.E.J. 354 (Oct. 1992).

7. Schubert, "Disinfecting Bullets with Bleach Solution and Its Effects on Striations," 21 A.F.T.E.J. 618 (1989), Smith, Berryman & Symers, "Detrimental Effect of Cleansing or Sterilization on Bullet Striations," 22 A.F.T.E.J. 129 (1990).

termined number of points of similarity between the evidence and the test bullets. Figure 9 illustrates how two bullets fired through the same barrel appear when viewed through the comparison microscope. The photographs show portions of the evidence and test bullets side by side, separated by a fine hairline in each illustration, with characteristics on both bullets in matching positions.

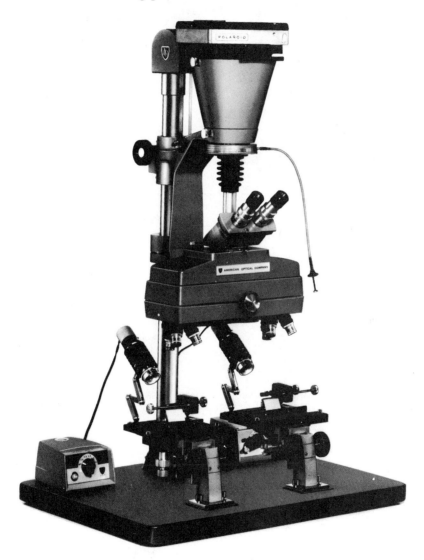

Fig. 8. A binocular comparison microscope used by firearms examiners. Note the Polaroid camera mounted above the microscope for producing photomicrographs. *Courtesy: American Optical Co., Buffalo, N.Y.*

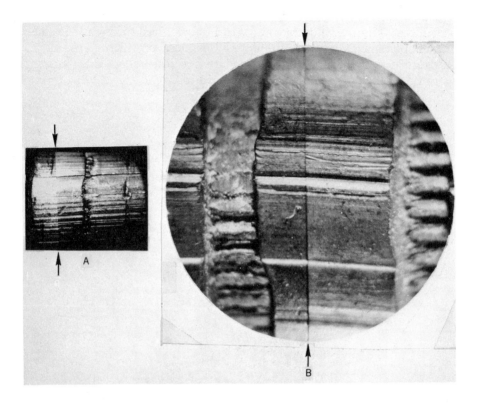

Fig. 9. A is a photomicrograph showing two bullets in match position at relatively low magnification. B illustrates the match position of only a small portion of the same bullet at higher magnification.

Since a comparison microscope consists essentially of two separate microscopes with different and individual optics, a perfect matching of the striations on an evidence and test bullet fired from the same gun will be possible only if the optics of the two microscope tubes are perfectly matched. This is ordinarily assured by the manufacturer of the instrument, but the firearms examiner can verify and demonstrate this matching of the optics by switching the evidence and test bullets to the opposite stages. If the striations can still be made to match, the optics must of necessity be matched as well. This process is called "calibration" of the microscope. Many a firearms examiner who is asked by a cross-examiner whether he had calibrated the microscope is at a loss to explain this very simple process.

To reduce the time and tedium necessary for comparison microscope striation matching, an automated system, using photography and computer technology, is in the experimental stage.[8] Similarly photography

8. Uchiyama, "Automated Landmark   (July 1993).
Identification System," 25 A.F.T.E.J. 172

of toolmarks utilizing fiber optic video-microscopy has been in the process of development.[9] In order to expedite the time for analysis and courtroom preparation, efforts are also afoot to produce a system for scanning electron microscopy that will substantially reduce its cost and encourage firearms examiners to capitalize on its depth of field, high magnification and imaging advantages.[10]

Even if bullets were fired in succession from the same weapon, not all individual characteristics would be identical. There would be some striations caused by powder residues, rust, corrosion and pitting, sand or dirt, and other surface factors or fugitive materials which of course are not likely to be duplicated on all bullets fired through that particular barrel. Moreover, there might be other striations on the bullets which would have no relationship to the interior of the barrel through which they were fired. For instance, there might be marks on metal-cased bullets due to imperfections on the interior of the sizing die used in the fabrication of the bullet. Likewise, fired bullets might contain crimp or burr impressions left there by the mouth of the cartridge case or shell. Obviously, the presence or absence of such marks, whether duplicated or not, must be discounted by the firearms identification technician.

The caliber of the bullets affects the quality of the identification, or, indeed, the ability of the examiner to make an identification. .22 caliber bullets are much harder to identify than .38s. If a series of, say, twenty bullets of .22 caliber are fired from the same gun, not all of these will show matching striations. When dealing with .22 lead bullets, there may be only one chance in six that an identification will be possible, even when the gun that fired the lead bullets is available.

All of the foregoing assumptions presuppose that the examiner has available an evidence bullet and a test bullet obtained by firing from a suspect weapon. This is not possible when there is no evidence gun that can be linked to the defendant, or else retrieved bullets previously fired from a gun known to have been possessed by the defendant. In a few cases where a defendant, upon arrest, has in his possession unspent bullets, it may be possible to compare them chemically or by instrumental analysis with the evidence bullets. "Identical elemental composition is usually taken as evidence that the bullets may have the same origin; that is, they may have come from the same box or lot." [11] A procedure

---

9. Hueske, "The Application of Fiber Optic Videomicroscopy to Firearm and Tool Mark Examination—A Further Look," 25 A.F.T.E.J. 132 (Apr. 1993).

10. Mann & Espinoza, "Firearms Examinations by S.E.M.: Observations and an Update on Current and Future Approaches," 24 A.F.T.E.J. 294 (July 1992).

11. Haney & Gallagher, "Differentiation of Bullets by Spark Source Mass Spectrometry," 20 *J.For.Sci.* 484 (1975). For other modern sophisticated examination techniques not yet routinely employed by

firearms examiners, see, e.g., Judd, et al., "SEM Scanning Electron Microscope Microstriation Characterization of Bullets and Contaminant Particle Identification," 19 *J.For.Sci.* 798 (1974).

It must be noted that in Easley v. State, 529 S.W.2d 522 (Tex.Cr.App.1975), a "chemical similarity" between the bullets removed from the deceased's body and two of the bullets found on the premises where the defendant had lived was insufficient to prove guilt to a "moral certainty."

has been developed capable of matching up to six elements of bullet lead which can help experts identify similar lots.[12]

Every now and then a firearms expert will come up with a novel method of identifying a bullet. In a unique Florida case, a murder suspect either shot himself or was shot by his partner in the ankle during the murder. He limped to the airport and took a plane to New York to have the bullet removed, presumably to avoid suspicion in Florida. The Florida firearms expert was able to use the X-ray of the bullet in the suspect's ankle to match the bullet to the murder weapon. The expert was able to match the "shadow" the bullet cast in the X-ray to a similar shadow from one of the bullets recovered from a victim.[13]

§ 6.09 Identification of Bullet Fragments

While distorted or smashed evidence bullets often make identification difficult,[1] they do not invariably preclude an identification of the weapon through which they were fired. Figure 10 illustrates such a case. On the left is a bullet fragment removed from a victim's body. The bullet had previously penetrated the sheet metal hood of an automobile, the metal partition between the driver's compartment and the motor, and the dashboard. The bullet in the center is a test bullet fired from the suspected weapon. The bullet fragment and the test bullet were photographed at the same scale. To the right is shown a photomicrograph showing a matching of the striations on the evidence bullet (left portion of the photomicrograph) with those on the test bullet. Due to the bent and twisted condition of the evidence bullet fragment, not all of the land impressions were in focus when the photomicrograph was taken, which accounts for the blurred area on the lower left portion of the picture.

12. Peters, Havekost & Koons, "Multi-element Analysis of Bullet Lead by Inductively Coupled Plasma–Atomic Emission Spectrometry," 15 *Crime Lab Dig.* 33 (1988). (Article is a good review of scientific attempts to resolve the question of connecting an evidence bullet to a manufacturer's batch.) An assessment of varying lead isotope ratios in commercially manufactured bullets has also been proposed. Andrasko et al., "Lead Isotope Ratios in Lead Smears and Bullet Fragments and Application in Firearm Investigations," 38 *J.For. Sci.* 1161 (1993).

13. Hart, "Identification of a Bullet to an X-ray Shadow," 21 A.F.T.E.J. 605 (1989).

§ 6.09

1. The examination of battered bullets is said to be "the most difficult task" of the firearms examiner. Booker, "Examination of the Badly Damaged Bullet," 20 *J.For.Sci. Soc.* 153 (1980) where many criticisms of the "subjectivity" of a firearms analysis are lodged.

Fig. 10. Identification of a bullet fragment.

Since bullets are cylindrical and since a bullet that has entered or gone through a body has fewer defined barrel impressions on it than the one previously shown in Figure 6, many firearms experts are unwilling to use comparison microscope photographs when testifying in court. The out-of-focus areas are hard to explain to jurors, and defense attorneys frequently harp on this deficiency in an effort to discredit the witness; hence the usual reliance upon opinion testimony by the expert, unaided by photographs.

§ 6.10 Cartridge Case Identification

Identification of a cartridge case and primer as having been fired in a particular firearm is dependent upon the same principles of probability as govern bullet identification. In many instances the cartridge case is more easily identifiable than the bullet. Recoil pressure of the powder gases forces the brass cartridge case against the steel breech block or bolt with the result that the striation irregularities present on the steel surface are imprinted onto the base and sides of the cartridge case as if they had been intentionally die stamped. The face of the cartridge case is relatively hard, while the primer cap is made of more malleable material and will take an impression more readily than the case material. The quality of the impression is also dependent on the pressure developed by the load. A low pressure load is less likely to result in markings on the case.

The striations of the breach face are produced by hand filing of the breech surface. Also during the manufacturing process, individual marks are acquired on a gun's firing pin and on its ejector and extractor. (See Figure 11 for an illustration of the location of these parts and for an indication of the mechanics involved in the firing of a cartridge in an automatic weapon.) A firing pin, either by static contact or through a sliding action which produces scrape marks, leaves distinctive and indi-

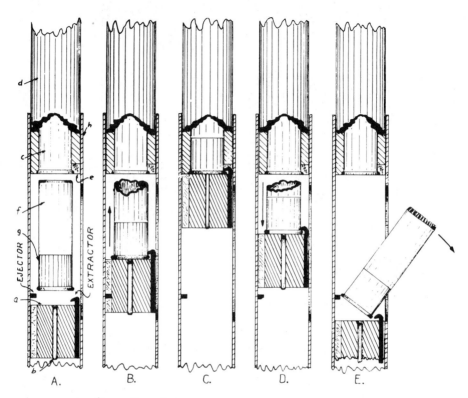

Fig. 11. An illustration of the action involved in the firing of a cartridge in an automatic weapon. In A, the small *a* identifies the face of the breech block; *b* the firing pin. The vertical labels identify the ejector and extractor. In B, the breech mechanism carrying the hook (extractor) pushes the shell forward into the chamber. In C, the breech is closed and locked in firing position. D shows the extractor engaged with the shell head and the breech traveling to the rear after firing. E illustrates how the left side of the shell strikes the ejector, casting the shell to the right and out of the action. *Courtesy: Charles M. Wilson (deceased), Madison, Wis.*

vidual striations on the cartridge case which may be used to identify a particular gun as having fired a particular cartridge case.[1]

The shape of the indentation caused by the firing pin or hammer is a characteristic peculiar to the firearm. It can be of aid in identifying a particular gun but is not always conclusive. The firing pin on center fire firearms is customarily round. One exception is the rectangular shaped firing pin which is found on a few center fire firearms. The depth of the indentation is not considered particularly useful in firearms identification. (For an illustration of gun identification by means of firing pin marks, see Figure 12.) But attempts to improve its usefulness have been suggested through more accurate measurements of firing pin "indents".[2]

All cartridges do not behave in the same manner. The pressure produced by the discharge of a cartridge may vary. The type and concentration of powder, the force of the firing pin and the load are variables. Humidity and age can also cause powder to deteriorate with the result that the pressure produced in the firing chamber is decreased. Therefore, the attorney who wishes to introduce evidence of a cartridge comparison experiment conducted on a suspect weapon must be prepared to prove that the expert exercised great care to duplicate the same conditions present at the time of the criminal act.

Although constituting valuable evidence in some cases, shell identification is not nearly as useful as bullet identification, for two reasons. First, unless the shell was ejected or discarded at or near the scene of the crime, its identification as coming from a particular gun is of little or no probative value. Second, even if a shell found at or near the scene is identified as having been fired from a suspect's weapon, that fact does not establish, as does a bullet removed from a victim, that it was the gun used in the offense.

The machining marks detectable in the headstamp of a cartridge case may connect an evidence cartridge case to the same lot or batch from which a test shell originated. Caution however must be exercised in this area since the studies of headstamp toolmarks are still highly experimental.[3]

Another technique sometimes used in the identification of fired cartridge casings is comparing the microscopic imperfections in the headstamp.[4] With such a technique the headstamp of evidence shells can be matched with cartridge cases found in the possession of the suspect.

§ 6.10

1. Sharma, "The Importance of Firing Pin Impressions in the Identification of Firearms," 54 *J.Crim.L., Criminol. & P.S.* 378 (1963), Sharma, "Firing Pin Scrape Marks and the Identification of Firearms," 57 *J.Crim.L., Criminol. & P.S.* 365 (1966).

2. Frazier, "Firing Pin Impressions—Their Relation to Hammer Fall Condi-

tions," 21 A.F.T.E.J. 589 (1989); Frazier, "Firing Pin Impressions—Their Measurement and Significance," 21 A.F.T.E.J. 584 (1989).

3. Schrecker, "The Identification of Cartridge Case Headstamps," 11 *Crime Lab Digest* 51 (1984).

4. Ibid.

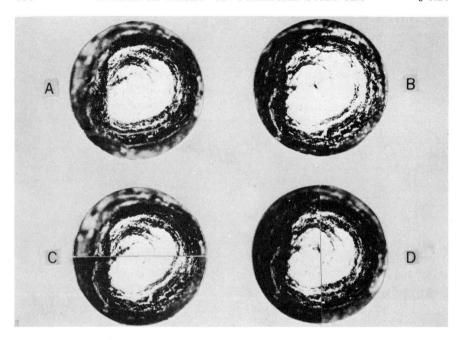

Fig. 12. A shows the firing pin impression on an evidence shell; B shows the impression on a test shell. C and D show the coincidence of the impressions as half of A and half of B are placed alongside of each other.

Although distinct differences are observed in casings made with different bunter tools, (the instrument which creates the headstamp), sample casings made at intervals using the same "bunter tool" possess significantly distinct microscopic characteristics to show that they were products of the same production run. Even though a single production run can produce over 1.7 million pieces, identifying characteristics are retained throughout the run. There is, of course, the problem that a multitude of casings would have the same microscopic markings, and thus detract from the individualized significance of the comparisons.

It is also possible to identify the shell used in a shotgun. One problem frequently encountered, however, is that in order to obtain definitive markings suitable for comparison with those of the evidence shotgun shell, high pressure loads must be used. This is particularly troublesome with old or improvised firearms.

By covering the brass head of a shotgun shell with a thin layer of lead, good markings can be obtained from a homemade pistol where previous normal loads did not provide extractor marks suitable for comparison with the shell from the crime scene.[5] With this method, the powder charge can be substantially reduced and usable marks still obtained.

5. Sinha, "Test Extractor Marks Under Low Pressure on Shotgun Cartridges", 27 *For.Sci.Internat'l* 227 (1985).

§ 6.11　Determining Muzzle to Target Distance

Differentiating among accident, self-defense, suicide, and criminal homicide in a shooting may hinge on an expert determination of the distance between the gun muzzle and the first surface of the target (victim's clothing or skin). Besides the shot or bullet, other important elements are projected from the muzzle of the gun at the time of firing. Depending upon the kind of ammunition used, partially burned and unburned powder, and primer residues are thrown out for distances varying with each component's physical properties and with air resistance. The pattern observed may represent a composite of some or all of these factors.

A gunshot wound may result from three different kinds of shootings: a distant shot, a close range shot and a contact shot. A distant shot does not deposit residues on the target. Close range shots are those wherein residues are found around the wound, causing tatooing or stippling. A contact shot burns where the weapon's muzzle is held against the surface of the target. In such an event, hardly any gunshot residues will be found around the entrance hole. The residues will be discerned along the bullet track in the underlying tissues through which it has passed.

At close range, say from zero to two inches, gases hot enough to scorch and sear belch from the muzzle. A microscopic examination of the region around the wound will disclose the effects of this phenomenon. Fibers of cloth will show thermal changes; hair may be blistered and the skin itself burned.

At distances farther away, scorching ceases and a black smudge composed of burned and unburned powder particles and fine metal particles can be seen. The velocity of the fine material rapidly diminishes at greater distances, approximately six to ten inches, and this material does not contact the skin or clothing with sufficient force to stick; it simply disperses into the air. At this range, only the larger, heavier, powder grains, fair-sized particles of metal and grease continue on to end up on the surface surrounding the bullet hole. Of course, in each preceding stage, the pattern possesses all of the elements not eliminated by distance; in fact, the particles capable of distant projection possess the ability to penetrate at closer distances and can be found embedded in clothing or skin.

Finally, a point is reached at which the velocity of all except the projectile has diminished so much that the gunshot residue will not adhere to or reach the surface surrounding the bullet hole. It is this limiting distance that is most crucial. If it can be established that the maximum distance for powder deposit exceeds the reach of the arms of the victim, then the absence of a powder pattern clearly indicates that the shooter and victim were outside the range of physical contact when the shot was fired. Although other mitigating circumstances might indicate otherwise, such an established fact usually eliminates suicide or an accidental discharge during a struggle.

To determine the distance from muzzle to surface cannot be reduced to a formula or table; in fact, what actually occurs is only an approximation.[1] Although the cloud of gaseous discharge forms a roughly cone-shaped figure, the spread, shape, and density of the pattern depend on many factors which require, for proper evaluation, extensive experience and experimentation. Different combinations of gun and ammunition influence the pattern at any given distance. Any factor or variable which affects the burning rate and pressure characteristics of gun powders may result in a powder pattern variance. Thus variations in the length of the barrel, the gap between cylinder and barrel, and the fit of the bullet in the barrel may change the pattern even though the weapon tested is of the same make and model as that which produced the crime pattern. In fact, even ammunition of the same make but of different manufactured lots can produce variations in spread and density of the pattern, even when fired from the same gun. Consequently, evidence of this nature must be accepted with caution.[2]

When a victim displays a powder pattern on the skin, the pattern should be photographed with a scale or ruler placed in the plane of the powder pattern at the edge of the field of view. This will permit later reproduction of the pattern full size for comparison with test patterns. Failure to detect a substantial visible pattern should lead to the use of

§ 6.11

1. Somewhat novel mathematical formulations have been reported in the effort to give greater definition to the muzzle to target distance assessment. Deinet & Leszlynski, "Examinations to Determine Close–Range Firing Distances Using a Process Control Computer," 31 *For.Sci.Internat'l.* 41 (1986). A very comprehensive survey of "Methods for the Determination of Shooting Distance" is presented by Lichtenberg in 2 *For.Sci.Rev.* 35 (June 1990).

2. On the subject generally, see, Jauhari, "Determination of Firing Distance in Cases Involving Shooting Through Glass," 54 *J.Crim.L., Criminol. & P.S.* 540 (1963);

Krishnan, "Determination of Gunshot Firing Distances and Identification of Bullet Holes by Neutron Activation Analysis," 12 *J.For.Sci.* 112 (1967); Krishnan, "Firing Distance Determination by Atomic Absorption Spectrophotometry," 19 *J.For.Sci.* 351 (1974); Lundy & Midkiff, "Determination of Weapon Caliber From Firearms Discharge Residue Levels," *Identification News,* June 1974, p. 6; McLaughlin & Beardsley, Jr., "Distance Determinations in Cases of Gun Shot Through Glass," 1 *J.For.Sci.* 43 (1965).

For a discussion of one court's view of the atomic absorption test, see, Chatom v. State, 348 So.2d 838 (Ala.1977).

infrared photography and chemical detectors. In extreme cases, skin surrounding the wound can be removed during the autopsy and examined by soft X-rays.

When a suspected gun is obtained, as well as ammunition of the same type and brand as was used to produce the shot pattern on the victim,[3] a series of firings can produce test patterns for comparison purposes, as shown in Figure 13. By comparing the test patterns with the pattern found on the victim or on some other object, an examiner may find a similarity in pattern formation that may enable him to approximate the distance at which the shot was fired.

Several studies have concluded that the distance from the muzzle to the target in shotgun firings can be determined by examining the spread patterns of the pellets. In one such study, using a 12 gauge shotgun with 00 and 0 buckshot, firing tests were made at varying distances while averages and standard deviations of the spread patterns were made. The standard deviation was 50–60 percent for mean values of distance between buckshot (DBB) and 20–30 percent for mean values of pattern diameter (PD). The study also showed evidence of poor test results when only a few holes of the spread pattern are available.[4]

By examining the spread of pellets and the burn patterns created from short-range firings, an expert can also determine whether the firearm was of a traditional manufacture or homemade.[5] If powder burning is incomplete it is usually a sign of a short barrel and loose fitting ammunition which causes abnormally low pressures in homemade firearms. In addition, when improvised shotguns are fired, the pellet patterns resemble a more conventional firearm at greater range. Thus the combination of widespread patterns for shot and a strong powder pattern may indicate the use of improvised firearms. In determining the muzzle to target distance by using the amount of certain trace elements deposited on the target and originating from the primer, such as barium, antimony or lead, one of the factors to be considered is the type of ammunition used. For most calibers lead is detectable at six inches but at twelve inches is insignificant. When barium and antimony were present, tests gave low trace readings at three inches for .22 caliber primers and at six inches for larger calibers. Copper gives minimal readings at about three inches and six inches from jacketed projectiles. In addition, zinc has been determined to be of no value in estimating firing distance.[6]

3. Barnes and Helson, "An Empirical Study of Gunpowder Residue Patterns," 19 *J.For.Sci.* 448 (1974).

4. Alfonsi, et al., "Shooting Distance Estimation for Shots Fired by a Shotgun Loaded with Buckshot Cartridges", 25 *For.Sci.Internat'l.*, 83 (1984). Other studies have developed mathematical formulas to help determine the muzzle to target distance by the dimensions of the spread pattern. Chugh, "Mathematical Analysis of Dispersion of Pellets Fired From a Shot Gun," 32 *For Sci.Internat'l.* 93 (1986); Nag & Lahiri, "An Evaluation of Distribution of Pellets Due to Shotgun Discharge," 32 *For.Sci.Internat'l.* 151 (1986).

5. Modi, Nigam and Kumar, "Improvised Firearms Versus Regular Firearms", 26 *For.Sci.Internat'l.*, 199 (1984).

6. Stone and Fletcher, "Primer Residue Study", 18 A.F.T.E. J. 49 (April 1986).

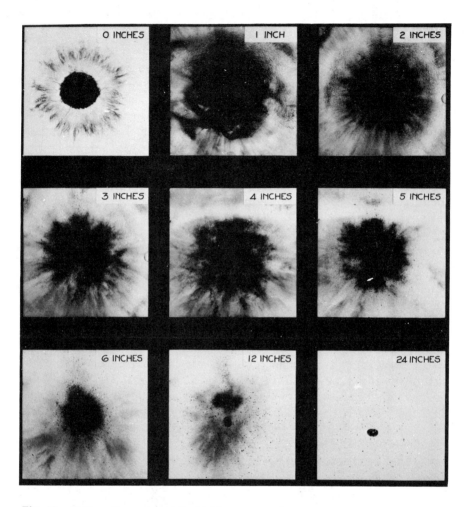

Fig. 13. Shot patterns on white blotting paper. (As to the approximation of shot pattern distances from powder patterns, the reader should consult the treatment of this subject in the next chapter.)

§ 6.12   Gunshot Residue on the Hands: Tests

Many times it would be extremely helpful if a determination could be made, by means of a scientific examination of a suspect's body, and particularly of his hands, of whether or not he had recently fired a gun. In 1933 Theodoro Gonzalez of Mexico announced that he had developed a test that could provide such evidence. It was known as the "diphenylamine paraffin test" (or dermal nitrate test) and consisted of making a paraffin cast of one or both of a suspect's hands and then treating the inside area of the cast with drops of a chemical (diphenylamine in a concentrated solution of sulphuric acid). If a reaction occurred in the form of dark blue pinpoint specks, it was considered evidence of recent gun firing. The theory behind the test was that the results established the presence of particles of nitrates deposited on the hand by the gases of a discharged cartridge. The flaw in this theory was, however, that similar reactions could result from the presence of other, innocently acquired substances containing nitrates, as was disclosed by controls conducted in various criminalistics laboratories.

Research discovered that many people who had never fired a gun but whose profession, occupation, or happenstance brought them in contact with nitrates can be expected to yield positive reactions to the test. Among them are photographers, engravers, match workers, farmers and gardeners handling fertilizers, etc. Other substances which may be expected to yield positive tests include bleaching agents, chemicals, cosmetics, explosives, certain types of foodstuffs, tobacco, and urine. At the first seminar on scientific aspects of police work conducted by the International Criminal Police (Interpol) in 1963, the participating experts of the several countries unanimously rejected the dermal nitrate test as without value, not only as evidence in court, but even as furnishing workable investigative leads to the police.[1]

Another color test, much more specific than the dermal nitrate test, was suggested by Harrison and Gilroy.[2] In their test, analysis is made for antimony, barium and lead rather than for the presence of nitrates. The reliance is placed on testing for primer residues and lead rather than for gunpowder residues, as has been the more recent vogue among crime laboratories in other instrumental analyses of more modern cognizance. It is, therefore, inappropriate today to speak of gunpowder residues since the heavy metals in primer residues and lead are the main area of current analytical consideration. The primer composition of firearms ammunition needs to be understood for gunshot residue analy-

---

§ 6.12

1. Note. *Internat.Crim.Pol.Rev.*, Jan. 1964, p. 28. See also, Turkel & Lipman, "Unreliability of Dermal Nitrate Test for Gunpowder [Sic]," 46 *J.Crim.L., Criminol. & P.S.* 281 (1955). On the other hand, Conrad, "Evidential Implications of the Dermal Nitrate Test," 44 *Marq.L.Rev.* 500 (1961), is pro-admissibility.

2. Harrison & Gilroy, "Firearms Discharge Residues," 4 *J.For.Sci.* 184 (1959). But see, Pillay, "New Method for the Collection and Analysis of Gunshot Residues as Forensic Evidence," 19 *J.For.Sci.* 769 (1974).

sis to be intelligently conducted and reported upon. A history of primers and their composition is provided by Matty,[3] as well as a discussion of current primer compounds. Except for .22 rimfire cartridges, antimony sulfide is found in all cartridge primers as is barium nitrate and lead styphnate.

While many of the gunshot residue tests are now concentrating on detecting barium and antimony, some studies have suggested that a varied proportion of the two elements occur in a variety of different cartridges.[4] The studies question whether threshold levels of barium and/or antimony on the hands of a suspected shooter are warranted. In addition some cartridges have been found not to contain any traces of barium at all while others show no trace of antimony.

The Harrison–Gilroy test has not gained general acceptance among crime laboratories mainly since its detection levels are not sufficiently low to make it adequately sensitive to detect the tenths of a microgram amounts of gunshot residues. In addition, the colors developed tend to be unstable and interference has been encountered in the color reactions of the three elements when tested simultaneously.[5]

Various chemical tests for gunshot residues as well as for indications of a bullet having struck an object or a person are in common use among firearms examiners. The Griess test is seen as being specific for nitrates.[6] The sodium rhodizonate test detects the presence of lead.[7] The rubeanic acide/dithiooxamide reagent is valuable in detecting traces of copper.[8]

Other methods have been developed in recent years which offer a more reliable test for gunshot residues. Among these newer techniques, the foremost are neutron activation analysis (NAA),[9] flameless atomic absorption spectrophotometry (FAAS)[10] and the scanning electron microscope (SEM).[11] Others have been proposed as well, some based on X-

3. Matty, "Primer Composition and Gunshot Residue," 19 A.F.T.E. J. 8 (Jan. 1987).

4. Booker, Schroeder, and Propp, "A Note on the Variability of Barium and Antimony Levels in Cartridge on Primers and Its Implication for Gunshot Residue Identification", 21 *J.For.Sci.Soc.* 81 (1984).

5. Krishnan, "Detection of Gunshot Residue: Present Status," in Saferstein, ed., *Forensic Science Handbook* 573, 574 (1982).

6. Dillon, "A Modified Griess Test: A Chemically Specific Chromophic Test for Nitrite Compounds in Gunshot Residues," 22 A.F.T.E. J. 243 (Oct. 1990).

7. Dillon, "Sodium Rhodizonate Test: A Chemically Specific Test for Lead in Gunshot Residues," 22 A.F.T.E. J. 251 (Oct. 1990).

8. Haag, "A Microchemical Test for Copper–Containing Bullet Wiping," 13 A.F.T.E. J. 23 (July 1981).

9. Palacios, Lugarzo et al, "Examination of Gunshot Residue by Neutron Activation Analysis," 324 *Inter.Crim.Pol.Rev.* 7 (1979); Krishnan, "Detection of Gunshot Residue: Present Status" 574 in Saferstein, ed., *Forensic Science Handbook* (1982).

10. Newbury, "The Analysis of Gunshot Residues for Antimony and Barium by Flameless Atomic Absorption Spectrophotometry," 13 *Can.Soc.For.Sci.J.* 19 (1980); Newton, "Rapid Determination of Antimony, Barium and Lead in Gunshot Residue via Automated Atomic Absorption Spectrophotometry," 26 *J.For.Sci.* 302 (1981).

11. Andrasko & Maehly, "Detection of Gunshot Residues on Hands by Scanning Electron Microscope," 22 *J.For.Sci.* 279 (1977); Wolten, Nesbitt, et al., "Particle Analysis for the Detection of Gunshot Resi-

ray fluorescence, which meet the need for accuracy and specificity in gunshot residue analysis.[12]

Another relatively new method of testing for gunshot residues is testing for indications of organic compounds from the powder.[13] A major advantage of this approach is that the compounds to be detected are more readily associated with firearms and/or explosives than are metals from the primer. In addition, these compounds are unlikely to be attributable to environmental contamination and are thus indicative of recent firearms discharge.

In this method diphenylamine (DPA) is used as a stabilizer for the nitrocellulose in smokeless powder and traces may be deposited in the hands of the shooter during firing. Cotton swabs soaked in cyclohexane are used to collect the DPA and the swabs are then examined by liquid chromatography with electrochemical detection using a mobile phase of acetone and phosphoric acid.

Even though SEM has the ability to detect barium and antimony which can be pinpointed by their distinctive morphology as deriving from gunshot residues as opposed to other non-firearm related sources for those inorganic elements, still its excessive cost and its time-consuming nature have all but priced it out of the market in crime laboratory testing for gunshot residues.[14] SEM is like other tests for gunshot residue in that a finding of the trace metals does not necessarily mean the suspect has fired a gun. Handling a weapon, loading or unloading a

dues. I Scanning Electron Microscopy/Energy Dispersive X–Ray Characterization of Hand Deposits from Firing," 24 *J.For.Sci.* 409 (1979); Kee & Beck, "Casework Assessment of an Automated Scanning Electron Microscope/Microanalysis System for the Detection of Firearms Discharge Particles," 27 *J.For.Sci.Soc.* 321 (1987).

12. Bosen & Scheuing, "A Rapid Microtechnique for the Detection of Trace Metals from Gunshot Residues," 21 *J.For.Sci.* 163 (1976); Canfield & De Forest, "The Use of the Gandolfi Camera as a Screening and Confirmation Tool in the Analysis of Explosive Residues," 22 *J.For.Sci.* 337 (1977); DeHaan, "Quantitative Differential Thermal Analysis of Nitrocellulose Propellants," 20 *J.For.Sci.* 243 (1975); Jones & Nesbitt, "A Photoluminescence Technique for Detection of Gunshot Residue," 20 *J.For.Sci.* 231 (1975); Kilty, "Activity After Shooting and Its Effect on the Retention of Primer Residue," 20 *J.For.Sci.* 219 (1975); Krishnan, "Detection of Gunshot Residues on the Hands by Trace Element Analysis," 22 *J.For.Sci.* 304 (1977); Midkiff, "Barium and Antimony for the Detection of Firearms Discharge Residue," *Identification News*, May 1973, p. 9; Midkiff, "Detection of Gunshot Residues: Modern Solutions for an Old Problem," 3 *J.Pol.Sci. & Admin.* 77 (1975); Nag & Mazumdar, "Detection of Firearm

Discharge Residues in Blood–Stained Articles By Fluorescence," 5 *J.For.Sci.* 69 (1975); Nesbit, et al., "Evaluation of a Photoluminescence Technique for the Detection of Gunshot Residue," 22 *J.For.Sci.* 288 (1977); Price, "Firearms Discharge Residues on Hands," 5 *J.For.Sci.* 199 (1965); Seamster, et al., "Studies of the Spatial Distribution of Firearms Discharge Residues," 21 *J.For.Sci.* 868 (1976); Stone, "Examination of Gunshot Residues," 19 *J.For.Sci.* 784 (1974); Tassa, Keist, and Steinberg, "Characterization of Gunshot Residues by X–Ray Diffraction," 27 *J.For. Sci.* 677 (1982); Sen et al., "Application of Protein–Induced X–Ray Emission Technique to Gunshot Residue Analyses," 27 *J.For.Sci.* 330 (1982); Steinberg et al., Spectrophotometric Determination of Nitrites in Gunpowder Residue on Shooters' Hands, 29 *J.For.Sci.* 464 (1984).

13. Dahl, Slahck, and Lott, "Gunshot Residue Determination by High Performance Liquid Chromatography with Electrical Detection", 31 *Microchemical J.* 145.

14. Krishnan, "Detection of Gunshot Residue on the Hands by Trace Element Analysis," 315, 338 in Imwinkelried, ed., *Scientific Evidence and Expert Evidence* (2nd Ed.1981).

cartridge or magazine or even the throwing up of one's hands as a defensive gesture could account for the presence of that which is provably gunshot residue.

Furthermore, even assuming that a suspect admits having fired a weapon on an earlier occasion, it may still be necessary to establish whether the gunshot residues on his hands originated from that earlier firing or from the shooting in the case under investigation or prosecution. A leading researcher [15] has ascertained under laboratory conditions that "significant residue deposits" can be detected up to twenty-four hours after a firing. The circumstances in an actual shooting incident may reduce this time considerably, but it is still impossible to state with certainty how long gunshot residue will persist on hands that have not been thoroughly washed with soap and water since having fired a weapon.

NAA and FAAS are the principal techniques in use today for gunshot residue analysis. Even though NAA cannot detect lead in a ready fashion, it and FAAS are alike in being capable of quantitative measurement of the trace metals barium and antimony at microgram and nanogram levels. Whereas contamination of the sample is a constant concern in FAAS analysis and not in NAA, FAAS' short turn around time makes it more expedient for busy crime laboratories. But FAAS, unlike NAA, is handicapped by its inability to perform multi-element analyses simultaneously. This obstacle will in no sense compromise the results obtained by FAAS testing, however.

In recent years, an electrochemical technique known as anodic stripping voltammetry, which has had an established usage in environmental [16] and other non-forensic applications,[17] has emerged as a method for the detection of gunshot residues.[18] The technique results in a voltammogram which registers the peaks of the trace metals in the substance under analysis. The peaks, of course, require the interpretation of an expert.

The proponents of anodic stripping voltammetry for gunshot residue analysis point to its many advantages over atomic absorption and neutron activation analysis. It is said to involve instrumentation whose cost is within manageable limits. It can conduct simultaneous qualitative and quantitative testing. Highly trained personnel are not a precondition to its operation. Not only is the technique fast but it is specific for the particular trace metals in gunshot residues and it is highly sensitive at concentration levels in the microgram range.

15. Id.

16. Ferren, "Analyses of environmental samples by means of anodic stripping voltammetry," 10 Am.Lab. 52 (1978).

17. Vydra, Stulik and Julakova, Electrochemical Stripping Analysis (1976).

18. Liu and Lin, "The Application of Anodic Stripping Voltammetry to Forensic Science, Part 1," 16 For.Sci.Inter. 43 (1980); Liu, Lin and Nicol, "The Application of Anodic Stripping Voltammetry to Forensic Science, Part 2" 16 For.Sci.Inter. 53 (1980); Brihaye, Machiroux and Gillain, "Gunpowder Residues Detection by Anodic Stripping Voltammetry," 20 For.Sci.Inter. 269 (1982).

However, the major drawback to the use of anodic stripping voltammetry is its present inability to detect barium, a constituent of primer compounds and its consequent reliance upon antimony to prove the existence of gunshot residues. Apparently for this reason, no crime laboratory outside the state of Missouri is known presently to be using anodic stripping voltammetry in preparation for courtroom testimony.[19] Indeed, one of its most ardent advocates has written that its most valuable use is as "investigational assistance"[20] and that interpretation problems have resulted in laboratory reports couched in the language of "consistent with," a most equivocal phrasing.

§ 6.13   Trace Metal Detection Tests

Operating on the exchange principle by which it is hypothesized that when two objects come into contact, there is a transfer of traces of one object to the other, tests have been developed to detect the existence and pattern of metal ions transferred from metallic objects, like guns, to the hands or other parts of the body of a person or even to articles of clothing or other fabrics. Unlike gunshot residue determinations, trace metal detection tests (TMDT) in firearms cases are concerned not with establishing whether a firearm has been discharged, but whether it has been handled, or otherwise been in touch with an individual.

The TMDT, as originally formulated,[1] involved four separate steps. The person or object to be examined must be sprayed with a reagent. Next, the sprayed site must be observed under ultraviolet light to search for distinctive colors. Third, the reaction resulting in varying shades of fluorescent colors should be noted, sketched and photographed. Fourth, the fluorescent patterns displayed should be compared to standard handgun or other metallic object patterns or to a recovered weapon to identify the source of the fluorescent pattern.

The test, as first proposed,[2] employed a 0.1–0.2% solution of 8–Hydroxyquinoline in isopropanol as a reagent. A later development envisaged the use of the reagent ferrozine or PDT[3] since its results would be visualized under normal light and, consequently, were more readily photographed. A later proposal[4] suggested the use of the

---

19. Not only the co-existence of barium and antimony but the levels of each are significant parameters. See, Cowan et al., "Barium and Antimony Levels on Hands: Significance as Indicator of Gunfire Residue," 15 *J.Radioanal.Chem.* 203 (1973). In United States v. Barton, 731 F.2d 669 (10th Cir.1984), the Director of the Albuquerque Police Department Crime Lab testified that only the presence of both barium and antimony on the hands would permit him to conclude one has fired (or handled) a firearm.

20. Briner, "An Interesting Gunshot Residue Pattern," 30 *J.For.Sci.* 945 (1985).

§ 6.13

1. LEAA, *Trace Metal Detection Technique in Law Enforcement* (G.P.O. Oct. 1970). And see, Stevens & Messler, "The Trace Metal Detection Technique (TMDT): A Report Outlining a Procedure for Photographing Results in Color, and Some Factors Influencing the Results in Controlled Laboratory Tests," 19 *J.For.Sci.* 496 (1974).

2. Id. at p. 15.

3. Goldman & Thornton, "A New Trace Ferrous Metal Detection Reagent," 21 *J.For.Sci.* 625 (1976).

4. Glass & Grais, "A New Trace Metal Detection Reagent," 24 *J.For.Sci.* 247 (1979).

compound 2–nitrose–1–naphthol since it, unlike PDT, was commercially available.

TMDTs are simple in operation and require no laboratory analysis. Consequently, the tests were most frequently supervised by police officers who lacked background in the scientific underpinnings for the test. False positives could result if an officer failed to recognize that the patterns of guns could be distorted by innocuous metallic objects like handles, door knobs, keys, etc., depending on the duration and intensity of one's holding such objects. In addition, a number of metallic objects may have patterns so similar that a gun pattern may be mistaken for a crowbar or other object. An ill-trained police officer could also misread the distinctive colors produced by the reagent so that the purple color of brass could be misinterpreted as the blackish purple for steel.[5]

The possibility of contamination, particularly from the hands of police officers or from handcuffs, although a less tangible objection, was some cause for concern. For these reasons, after a flurry of initial interest in TMDT, many law enforcement agencies have become more conservative in its use.

§ 6.14 Restoring Obliterated Serial Numbers

The serial number of a firearm is an important investigative tool. In tracing the manufacture and sale of a firearm, one of the most valuable resources in a criminal investigation can be the Bureau of Alcohol, Tobacco and Firearms of the Treasury Department. The Bureau's capability allows an investigator to trace a weapon found at the crime scene directly from the manufacturer to a seller and then to the owner. In some instances, the Bureau has been used to link the firearm directly to a suspect, while in other instances the Bureau can help identify the firearm as being stolen, leading to the firearm's return to its rightful owner. In addition, one of the most important aspects of tracing has been in the investigation and prosecution of narcotics trafficking by Organized Crime Drug Enforcement Task Forces.[1] Investigators sometimes encounter firearms from which the serial numbers have been filed off to make tracing the guns more difficult. Sometimes a false number may have been stamped in as a replacement. It is occasionally possible, through various chemical or other techniques, to reveal the number that has been eradicated.[2] In Figure 14, for example, the left portion of the illustration shows how a gun appeared to the naked eye after the serial number had been removed. The right portion of the

---

5. Op.Cit. note 1 at p. 3.

§ 6.14

1. A good discussion of the Bureau's tracing abilities can be found in Hill, "Firearms Tracing: A Crime Fighting Weapon," *FBI Law Enf. Bull.*, 23 (July 1985).

2. Wilson, "Restoration of Erased Serial Identification Marks," 52 *Police J.* 233 (July–Sept. 1979): Cook & Rhodan, "Training Manual for the Restoration of Obliterated Stamped Markings," (Colo.Bur.Inv., N.C.J.R.S. 051869).

photograph shows how the number was revealed after an etching process.[3]

A magnetic means of restoring serial numbers exploits the fact that the magnetic properties of deformed metal are different from that of the unworked surrounding metal. After polishing the surfaces, a suspension of magnetic particles is applied to the object. It is then magnetized by directly applying a large magnet. The surface is then subjected to vibration and the restoration occurs instantly.[4]

One chemical process for restoring obliterated serial numbers requires cleaning the area with fine emery paper and then swabbing it with a strong acid solution composed of 40 cc of concentrated hydrochloric acid, 30 cc of distilled water, 25 cc of ethyl alcohol and 5 grams of copper chloride, which is rubbed onto the surface already wet with the solution. As a last resort, a nitric acid solution may be used.

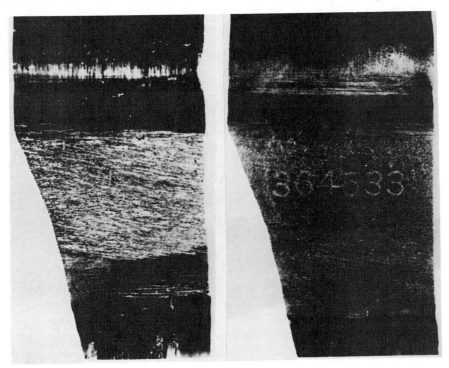

Fig. 14.

3. Thornton et al., "The Mechanism of the Restoration of Obliterated Serial Numbers by Acid Etching," 16 *J.For.Sci.Soc.* 69 (1976). See also, Cook, "Chemical Etching Reagents for Serial Number Restoration," 7 A.F.T.E. J. 80 (July 1975).

4. Turley, "Restoration of Stamp Marks on Steel Components by Etching and Magnetic Techniques," 32 *J.For.Sci.* 640 (1987); Wolfer et al., "Application of Magnetic Principles to the Restoration of Serial Numbers," 50 *J.Crim.L.Criminol. & P.S.* 519 (1960); Cook, "Obliterated Serial Numbers," 7 A.F.T.E. J. 27 (Mar. 1975); Polk & Giessen, "Metallurgical Aspects of Serial Number Recovery," 7 A.F.T.E. J. 37 (July 1975).

Similar techniques exist for the restoration of serial numbers on aluminum, a material increasingly used in the manufacture of engines, power tools, and even firearms. The standard reagents used in etching on iron and other metal provide too vigorous a reaction with aluminum, resulting in pitted metal and blurred results. For that reason, special dilute solutions are applied to aluminum surfaces, using metallic mercury as a catalyst.[5]

A modern technique uses an ultrasonic vibrator which generates very high frequency vibrations in water which create millions of microscopic bubbles. These cavitation bubbles, which impact upon the metal plate bearing the obliterated serial numbers at thousands of pounds per square inch, may restore the invisible numbers.[6]

Many methods used to obliterate a serial number can severely hamper, or completely frustrate the recovery of the serial number. One very simple method is overstamping. A counterfeit serial number is restamped over the area in which the filed or ground original serial number was located. If the counterfeit serial numbers are not located directly over the original numbers, recovery of the original numbers is still possible.

IV. COMPARATIVE MICROGRAPHY

§ 6.15 Origin and Nature of the Technique

The field of toolmark comparisons, also called comparative micrography, uses techniques and decision making criteria quite similar to that used in firearms identification. The methods of comparison originated with firearms technicians. For this reason, comparative micrography is often combined with firearms identification work in smaller and medium-sized criminalistics laboratories.

The beginning of a good toolmark case is a proper collection and preservation of the initial mark at the crime scene. Tools or other implements used for cutting metal or for turning or prying objects apart have edges with ridges and hollows created either in the process of manufacture or by wear in the use of the tool. Those often leave impressions on the material to which they are applied, which can be termed either negative impressions, because a stamp of the marks on the tool will be implanted into another surface, or striae, caused by the scratching movement of one surface over another. The obvious gross impressions may only indicate the nature of the tool or implement used, but minute microscopically discernible impressions may also be left which can be of great value in determining whether or not they were made by a particular tool.

---

5. Chisum, "A Catalytic Process for Restoration of Serial Numbers in Aluminum, 6 *J.For.Sci.Soc.* 89 (1966).

6. Young, "The Restoration of Obliterated Stamped Serial Numbers by Ultrasonically Induced Cavitation in Water," 19 *J.For.Sci.* 820 (1974).

The term comparative micrography may be applied to almost any type of case in which a hard object is applied to a softer object that is capable of absorbing marks on the harder one. For instance, if a metal implement is used on wood with a protective coating, or perhaps even in the grain line area of raw wood, it may be possible to identify the implement that was used. But the greatest potential for comparative micrography is where hard implements such as tools are applied to other metals, as so frequently happens in burglary cases.

§ 6.16 Toolmark Identification

The results of comparisons with test marks and the evidence marks will be given in the same range and with the same degree of certainty as might be rendered in any other area of opinion testimony. The opinion may be positive, negative, or inconclusive. Comparative micrography has found its widest application in burglary investigations.

An excellent illustration of the type of case in which the expert in comparative micrography can be of great assistance to the prosecution is a case in which bolt cutters have been used in the course of a burglary to remove a window bar or cut a chain or other such object. For the purpose of determining whether or not a bolt cutter found in the suspect's possession was the tool used, a piece of lead is cut with the suspected cutter in order to obtain a specimen of the characteristics of its cutting edge. The severed end of the bolt or the cut link of a chain, or whatever else may have been cut, is then placed under one barrel of a binocular comparison microscope and the cut area of the lead plate is placed under the other barrel, as is shown in Figure 15. If a number of impressions converge, as is shown in the photograph taken through the comparison microscope illustrated in Figure 16, the conclusion can be drawn that the suspected instrument was the one used in the burglary.

Fig. 15.

Fig. 16. **Left** portion: bolt; right portion: test lead plate. *Courtesy: Arthur R. Paholke, Criminalistics Division, Chicago Police Department.*

The proper interpretation of what is shown in a photomicrograph must be left to the expert, for laymen looking at the photograph are easily confounded by what appear to be dissimilarities. In Figure 16, for instance, the seeming dissimilarity in the lower part of the picture is due to the curved surface of the cut end of the bolt and the consequent lack of identical lens focus upon it and the lead plate.

Crowbars frequently leave impressions on metal objects that permit a determination to be made as to whether or not a suspected crowbar was responsible for those impressions. Such a case is graphically illustrated in Figure 17, in which A is a photograph of a jimmied door, and B is a suspected crowbar. The marks on the strike plate that is attached to the white area of the wall are clearly observable in A. Figure 18 is a photomicrograph of the results of a comparison between the impressions of the strike plate and those made by the suspected crowbar on the test lead plate.

Although certain match areas in Figure 18 do not appear to be clear to the novice, the skilled technician has no doubt that the same crowbar was used in both instances. The areas in the picture which seem to reveal a nonmatch of the impressions are due to the fact that the laboratory lead specimen was obtained as a result of a continuous stroking of the edge of the crowbar on the lead plate, whereas the marks left on the strike plate were caused by uneven pressure and by a bending of the metal, hence showing some void areas in the left center portion of the photograph. This again illustrates why many comparative micrography experts, like many firearms identification experts, do not always use photomicrographs as demonstrative evidence when they are called upon to testify in court. Instead, they explain the test procedures they have followed and the conclusions they have reached, without using illustrative exhibits.

A   B

Fig. 17. *Courtesy: Arthur R. Paholke, Criminalistics Division, Chicago Police Department.*

Fig. 18. The left portion is the strike plate; the right portion is the test lead plate. *Courtesy: Arthur R. Paholke, Criminalistics Division, Chicago Police Department.*

Other telltale impressions found at crime scenes which may be compared with recovered suspected implements are screwdriver marks or drills used to open a lock on burglarized premises. In a unique Louisiana murder investigation, a suspect was connected to a crime scene through the striae on his car's battery terminal caused by jumper cables connected to the victim's car. The evidence made the suspect less a good samaritan than a murderer.[1] Toolmarks may also be used to compare cut or torn objects, such as pieces of cut hose from automobile engines or the cut ends of wires.[2] However, saws, files and grinding wheels leave marks which are not ordinarily traceable to the instruments which produced those marks. But foreign deposits of paint or metal on a suspected tool may be helpful in connecting it to a crime scene.

§ 6.17　Fingernail Matching

Although of infrequent occurrence, it has happened on occasion that part of a fingernail has been left at a crime scene. The finding of such evidence has naturally led to an attempt to match the segment discovered at the crime scene to a suspect. Assuming no alteration in the suspect's fingernails since the crime was committed, it might be possible to engage in a physical matching of the fragment of a fingernail to the

§ 6.16

1. Lane, "Toolmarks on Battery Terminals," 20 A.F.T.E. J. 151 (1988).

2. Singh and Aggarwal, "Identification of Wires and the Cutting Tool by Scanning Electron Microscopy," 26 *For.Sci.International* 115 (1984).

fingernail of a particular person. In such a case, microscopic examination would not be essential to an opinion that the fingernail segment was severed from the fingernail of a suspect.

Fingernails may also be compared based on their longitudinal striations, which are most prominent on the underside. These striations are a function of the creation of the fingernail in the nail bed. Studies [1] have indicated that the patterns in the nail bed are so significantly dissimilar from individual to individual that the longitudinal striations on the fingernails of an individual can be said to be distinct from everyone else's fingernail striations.

Short and long term [2] studies have established that fingernail striations do not undergo significant change. Even identical twins [3] have been shown to have detectably different fingernail striations. Even though the human fingernail grows at a rate of three mm. per month, which would result in the replacement of the entire nail in from five to six months, the striations remain constant on each individual's fingernails.

The most effective system for the comparison of fingernail striations is the comparison microscope. Analytical methods, such as atomic absorption spectroscopy, of the trace elements in fingernails or in their composition have not been successful in identifying a fingernail segment to its source.

Fracture matching can be made from fingernail fragments and a victim's fingernails. In one instance, red painted fingernail fragments were found on the clothing of a homicide suspect. After matching the fingernail polish with polish found at the victim's apartment, the victim was exhumed and her fingernails removed. The nails were then cleaned and fracture matching of the fragments was made. The striation marks on each nail appeared to be unique, and three of the fragments could be matched.[4]

V. EVIDENCE OF FIREARMS AND TOOLMARK EXAMINATIONS

§ 6.18 Bullet Identification Evidence

§ 6.17

1. Stone & Wilimovsky, "Evidentiary Basis for Fingernail Striation Association," 12 *J.Pol.Sci. & Admin.* 201 (1984). Stone, "Fingernail Striations: An Unusual Toolmark," 20 A.F.T.E. J. 42 (Oct.1988).

2. Mann & Given, "Human Nail as a Means of Personal Identification," *Ident. News* 3 (Mar.1981); MacDonell & Bialousz, "Evaluation of Human Fingernails as a Means of Personal Identification," *Legal Med. Annual* 135 (1973); Thomas and Baert, "A New Means of Identification of the Human Being: The Longitudinal Striation of the Nails," 5 *Med.Sci. and the Law* 39 (1965).

3. Haag, "The Comparison of Fingernail Striae of Identical Twins," 14 A.F.T.E. J. 23 (1982).

4. Boehm, "Fingernail Comparisons: A Case Study," 16 A.F.T.E. J. 94 (July 1984).

A Virginia case decided in 1879, Dean v. Commonwealth,[1] is the first in which an appellate court approved of testimony regarding the similarity between fatal and test bullets—although weight, rather than any characteristic markings, constituted the basis for comparison. Moreover, it was held proper to introduce evidence to the effect that of all the guns in the community none were found which had the same bore or which could carry precisely the same ball. Two or three only, out of a large number examined, were even "nearly" of the same bore, so that only they "might have" carried the same type ball as that removed from the body of the deceased, and all of those were accounted for, with the exception of the defendant's gun.

Another interesting feature of this early case concerned the impressions upon a fence, presumably made when the murderer rested his rifle upon a rail in order to fire at the deceased who was working in his garden at the time. The evidence disclosed the fact that on top of the rail there was a distinct impression, and a "peculiar" notch made on the edge of the rail. By actual experiment, "made by some of the witnesses", the defendant's gun, when laid upon the same rail and drawn back, left "a similar square impression and a similar notch, made by the small piece of iron which was fastened to the barrel near the muzzle."

Although the evidence in the *Dean* case was of a conjectural nature, the Virginia Supreme Court held it admissible in proof of a first degree murder charge.

The first semblance of firearms identification evidence as we know it today, was presented in the 1902 Massachusetts case of Commonwealth v. Best.[2] In it, a test bullet was obtained from the defendant's rifle by "pushing" it through the barrel, after which photographs were taken of that bullet and the fatal bullets for the purpose of comparison. The defendant objected to the admission of the evidence pertaining to their similarity, mainly on the ground that "the conditions of the experiment did not correspond accurately with those at the date of the shooting, that the forces impelling the different bullets were different in kind, that the rifle barrel might be supposed to have rusted more in the little more than a fortnight that had intervened...." To these arguments, the Massachusetts Supreme Court replied:

> "We see no other way in which the jury could have learned so intelligently how that gun barrel would have marked a lead bullet fired through it, a question of much importance to the case. Not only was it the best evidence attainable but the sources of error

---

§ 6.18

1. 73 Va. (32 Gratt.) 912 (1879). See, in general, Anno: "Expert Evidence to Identify Gun from Which Bullet or Cartridge was Fired," 26 A.L.R.2d 892.

2. 180 Mass. 492, 62 N.E. 748 (1902).

Between the *Dean* and *Best* cases, three other relatively inconsequential firearms identification cases were decided, which we note here only for their historical interest: State v. Smith, 49 Conn. 376 (1881); People v. Mitchell, 94 Cal. 550, 29 P. 1106 (1892); and State v. Hendel, 4 Idaho 88, 35 P. 836 (1894). For the full details of the many cases upon the subject which reveal its historical development up to 1933, see, Inbau, "Scientific Evidence in Criminal Cases," 24 *J.Crim.L. & Criminol.* 825 (1933).

suggested were trifling. The photographs avowedly were arranged
to bring out the likeness in the marking of the different bullets and
were objected to on this further ground. But the jury could correct
them by inspection of the originals, if there were other aspects more
favorable to the defense." [3]

It is of interest to note that the judge who wrote the opinion was Oliver
Wendell Holmes, then Chief Justice of the Massachusetts Supreme
Court, and subsequently a Justice on the Supreme Court of the United
States.

Obviously, the best scientific techniques were not used in the
foregoing case, but at that time there was not available the instrumentation which is available today, nor the firearms identification sophistication that currently exists. Nevertheless, the witness must have presented some rather impressive evidence to incur the favorable opinion
expressed by Justice Holmes.

Holmes' decision was not immediately followed by a flood of case law
heralding this new scientific development. In fact, the 1923 Illinois
Supreme Court case of People v. Berkman [4] went so far as to label as
"preposterous" the suggestion that distinctive markings were impressed
upon bullets fired from different pistols of the same caliber and make.
Nevertheless, the trend towards judicial recognition of the validity of
firearms identification continued in spite of cases like *Berkman*.

Beginning with Jack v. Commonwealth, [5] a Kentucky case decided in
1928, expert testimony concerning firearms identification began to receive a truly objective appraisal by appellate courts. The extended
discussion devoted to the subject in that opinion represents the first
satisfactory treatment of this comparatively new phase of circumstantial
evidence, even though there was a reversal of the trial court's conviction
because of other evidentiary deficiencies. A year later, this same court,
in Evans v. Commonwealth, [6] rendered the first exhaustive opinion
treating firearms identification as a science, and sanctioning its use for
the purpose of establishing the guilt of the accused.

Shortly after these Kentucky cases, firearms identification evidence
was readily admitted in an Ohio case, Burchett v. State, [7] and in an
Illinois case, People v. Fisher. [8] The *Fisher* case represents an about-face
from the view expressed in *Berkman*, [9] in that the court recognized
firearms identification as trustworthy. It also indicated, in an exhaustive opinion, what expert qualifications were needed to render this type
of evidence admissible in a capital case.

At the present time, the accuracy of firearms identification is

3. 62 N.E. at 750.

4. 307 Ill. 492, 139 N.E. 91 (1923).

5. 222 Ky. 546, 1 S.W.2d 961 (1928).

6. 230 Ky. 411, 19 S.W.2d 1091 (1929).

7. 35 Ohio App. 463, 172 N.E. 555 (1930).

8. 340 Ill. 216, 172 N.E. 743 (1930).

9. Supra note 4.

common knowledge,[10] and ample case law upholds the admissibility of such evidence when presented by a qualified expert.[11] As with other expert testimony, the witness is permitted to testify that in his opinion a particular bullet was fired from a certain weapon.[12] The expert's testimony is confined, of course, to the area or areas within his special knowledge; for example, a witness whose expertise concerns only the identification of bullets through their microscopic markings, would not be permitted to testify upon the issue as to whether a certain wound was caused by a particular weapon.[13]

In situations where bullets are so mutilated that identification is impossible,[14] or where the condition of the weapon itself is such that a suitable comparison bullet cannot be fired from it,[15] an expert may still be permitted to testify as to other relevant matters. For instance, even though the condition of fatal bullets may preclude an identification of the evidence weapon, an identification is permissible on the basis of cartridge case breech face imprints, firing pin impressions, or ejector and extractor markings.[16]

Class characteristics, in the absence of a positive identification through individual markings on a bullet, may be helpful to the jury and are, therefore, relevant and admissible evidence. A firearms expert may be able to identify only the class characteristics of a badly mutilated bullet. In State v. Bayless,[17] the expert testified that the fatal bullets were so mutilated that he could not determine whether they were fired by the gun taken from the accused but he could say that the bullets were fired from a gun having characteristics similar to those of a gun obtained from the accused which had physical characteristics like those on bullets

10. State v. Hackett, 215 S.C. 434, 55 S.E.2d 696 (1949).

11. Cummings v. State, 226 Ga. 46, 172 S.E.2d 395 (1970), King v. State, 456 P.2d 121 (Okl.Cr.1969), cert. denied 397 U.S. 1049 (1970), and Pickens v. State, 450 P.2d 837 (Okl.Cr.1969), where spent bullets from the deceased's body were admitted over defense claims that they were ghastly; Ward v. State, 427 S.W.2d 876 (Tex.Cr.App.1968); State v. Sneed, 76 N.M. 349, 414 P.2d 858 (1966), appeal after remand 78 N.M. 615, 435 P.2d 768 (1967); People v. Sustak, 15 Ill.2d 115, 153 N.E.2d 849 (1958); and Le Marr v. State, 165 Tex.Crim.R. 474, 308 S.W.2d 872 (1957). General treatments of the subject can be found in 2 Wharton, *Crim.Evid.* 542 (1955), and 23 C.J.S. Crim. Law 868. Also see, Kukla, "Ballistics Evidence," *Trial Lawyer's Guide* 31 (1958).

12. State v. Martinez, 52 N.M. 343, 198 P.2d 256 (1948). See, Lackey v. State, 41 Ala.App. 46, 123 So.2d 186 (1960), cert. denied 271 Ala. 699, 123 So.2d 191 (1960), for a case where a mass of lead pried from the heel of a shoe was identified by a sheriff (not an expert) as a .22 caliber bullet in an attempt to prove that the defendant had fired a gun during an altercation.

13. State v. Varner, 329 S.W.2d 623 (Mo.1959), cert. denied 365 U.S. 803 (1961). This is the field of wound ballistics, usually the province of a forensic pathologist. But see, Commonwealth v. Snyder, 282 Mass. 401, 185 N.E. 376 (1933), affirmed 291 U.S. 97 (1934). Here a firearms expert was permitted to testify concerning the approximate path of the bullet through the victim's anatomy. Frequently experts are qualified to testify both on matters of fire arms ballistics and wound ballistics.

14. Dominguez v. State, 445 S.W.2d 729 (Tex.Cr.App.1969).

15. Williams v. State, 169 Tex.Crim.R. 370, 333 S.W.2d 846 (1960).

16. Id. 2 cartridge shells found at the crime scene were identified as having been fired in the defendant's gun, although identification of bullets was impossible.

17. 48 Ohio St.2d 73, 357 N.E.2d 1035 (1976).

in the accused's gun. And, in State v. Benson,[18] the Missouri Court of Appeals allowed a shotgun found in the possession of the defendant to be admitted into evidence although the prosecution only produced evidence showing that the victim was shot with number six shot and that the defendant's gun contained number six shot.

Although the general rule is to admit testimony even if it is only nominally probative, testimony solely concerning class characteristics, in absence of any further positive identification, may be too tenuous to be admitted into evidence. In People v. Giuliano,[19] the defendant, who was convicted of first-degree manslaughter, challenged the admission of testimony concerning "ballistics" reports, as the bullets tested could have belonged to any number of guns.

Where only bullet fragments exist, the firearms expert may be called upon to identify whether the fragments belong to one bullet or to many bullets. The bullet pieces in the John F. Kennedy assassination were examined for such a purpose but the results were at first inconclusive. A later reexamination using the more modern process of neutron activation analysis established, particularly through the levels of antimony and silver, that the bullet fragments could be attributed to only two bullets.[20]

Although the most frequent use of firearms identification evidence occurs with regard to the identification of the defendant's weapon as being the one which fired a particular shot, this is not always the case. In Doss v. State,[21] a bullet removed from the defendant's non-fatal head wound was identified as having been fired from a policeman's gun. This evidence was sufficient to prove that the defendant was present in a truck that was fired upon as it attempted to flee from the scene of a crime.

The prosecution may be selective in the introduction of its firearms identification evidence. In Cook v. State,[22] for instance, the bullet which killed the deceased was not offered into evidence, but the bullet which wounded a witness to the incident was both offered and received.

---

18. 574 S.W.2d 440 (Mo.App.1978). See also, Collins v. State, 266 Ind. 430, 364 N.E.2d 750 (1977) where an inconclusive ballistics test was held to be admissible, since it was for the jury to determine its weight.

19. 65 N.Y.2d 766, 492 N.Y.S.2d 939, 482 N.E.2d 557 (1985).

20. Guinn, "J.F.K. Assassination: Bullet Analysis," 51 Anal.Chem. 484 (1979). Wound ballistics experts can sometimes determine the number of bullets which have struck a victim by examining the entrance and exit wounds. See, Colbert v. State, 268 Ind. 451, 376 N.E.2d 485 (1978) where the defendant claimed that while he struggled with the victim his pistol discharged, but the victim then moved away and a second and fatal shot (not fired by the defendant)

hit the victim. Witnesses collaborated this claim, but a pathologist testified that the wounds in the victim's arm and chest were caused by a single bullet.

21. 256 Ind. 174, 267 N.E.2d 385 (1971). Similarly in State v. Grady, 38 N.C.App. 152, 247 S.E.2d 624 (1978) after a parking lot argument where several persons were shot, a bullet removed from defendant's back was tested to verify that it was not fired from a gun in the possession of one of the victims. The defendant claimed his gun had gone off accidentally and shot the victim while the victim was attacking him. This self defense argument was partially refuted when the bullet in defendant's back proved to be from a gun not possessed by the victim.

22. 269 Ala. 646, 115 So.2d 101 (1959).

§ 6.19　Shell Identification Evidence

Identification based upon a comparison of breechface imprints, firing pin impressions, and extractor and ejector marks, achieved recognition by the courts concurrent with the identification of bullets. State v. Clark,[1] an Oregon case decided in 1921, appears to be the first one approving of identification by means of markings upon fatal and test shells. "A peculiar mark on the brass part of the primer" of the shell was used as the identifying characteristic.

During the same year in which the previous decision was rendered, a conviction was obtained in State v. Vuckovich,[2] a Montana case, partly upon the evidence that "a peculiar crimp" on an empty shell found at the scene of a murder corresponded with a similar mark on shells fired from the defendant's pistol. Evidence was also introduced to show that "the firing marks made by the lands and grooves of the barrel of the pistol were the same" on both test and fatal bullets. Thus, this appellate decision represents an approval of both methods of identification, shells as well as bullets. The shell identification, however, was based on a class characteristic.

Now that judicial acceptance is the rule rather than the exception, cartridge casings can be used to supplement the identification of bullets,[3] and in many cases they provide the sole connection with a particular weapon. The latter may occur when a questioned bullet is unavailable or is too mutilated for a comparison.[4] In Edwards v. State,[5] breechface markings were the only possible means of identification since the defendant had made a bullet comparison impossible by removing much of the rifling within the barrel by the use of steel wool.

In cases involving shotguns, the absence of lands and grooves in the barrel obviously makes the comparison of shell markings a preferred means of identification.[6]

§ 6.20　Shotgun Wadding and Pellets Evidence

The firearms expert may present evidence other than that which tends to identify a bullet or shell as having been fired from a particular

§ 6.19

1. 99 Or. 629, 196 P. 360 (1921). See, in general, Anno.: "Expert Evidence to Identify Gun From Which Bullet or Cartridge was Fired," 26 A.L.R.2d 892.

2. 61 Mont. 480, 203 P. 491 (1921).

3. People v. Sustak, supra note 10, section 6.18, and State v. Lane, 72 Ariz. 220, 233 P.2d 437 (1951); State v. Gonzales, 92 Idaho 152, 438 P.2d 897 (1968).

4. Williams v. State, supra note 15, section 6.18. For cases involving shell comparison without bullets see, People v. Appleton, 1 Ill.App.3d 9, 272 N.E.2d 397 (1971); and Norton v. Commonwealth, 471 S.W.2d 302 (Ky.1971). In State v. Michael,

107 Ariz. 126, 483 P.2d 541 (1971), the trial court was permitted to let an expert testify on the basis of photographs even though the spent casings were lost prior to trial.

5. 198 Md. 132, 81 A.2d 631 (1951), reargument denied 198 Md. 132, 83 A.2d 578 (1951).

6. Sebastian v. Commonwealth, 436 S.W.2d 66 (Ky.1969). In this case, firing pin impressions were of significance. For a case involving the identification of a weapon by fitting it to broken grips left at the scene of a crime, see, United States v. Rees, 193 F.Supp. 849 (D.Md.1961), habeas corpus denied 341 F.2d 859 (4th Cir.1965). The handgrips were separated from the weapon while it was being used to beat the deceased on the head.

weapon. In Brown v. Commonwealth,[1] shotgun wadding taken from the head wound of the deceased was admitted into evidence after having been compared with wadding taken from unfired shells found in the defendant's father's home. In Patrick v. State,[2] shotgun pellets were admitted into evidence over defense objections that they could not be identified as having been fired from a particular weapon. The defense also objected to admission of the pellets on the theory that they were not the cause of death since the pellet which produced the fatal wound was not recovered during the autopsy. The court ruled that this fact only affected the weight of the evidence and not its admissibility, and that the evidence gave logical support to the state's theory that the defendant had killed the deceased with a shotgun.

§ 6.21 Trace Element Analyses of Bullets

The use of various instrumental techniques to analyze the trace elements in bullet lead has enabled an expert to identify a bullet as having come from a particular batch of bullets. If bullets having trace elements similar to a crime bullet are found in a defendant's possession, this may be significant circumstantial evidence of guilt. Such was the situation in People v. Riser,[1] where factory made bullets taken from the defendant's car were of the same weight and shape as those found at the crime scene, and in which handloaded bullets found in his car and at the crime scene were subjected to spectroscopic analysis which showed both sets of bullets as probably poured from the same batch of metal.

In Medley v. United States,[2] bullets found in the defendant's possession and bullets removed from the body of the deceased all had similar scrapes on their noses. Spectroscopic analysis of the bullets, as well as of metal scrapings found in the teeth of a file in the accused's possession, demonstrated the common source of all.

It must be noted that an analysis of the trace elements in an evidence bullet which links it to the batch from which a known bullet

---

§ 6.20

1. 275 S.W.2d 928 (Ky.1955). In Smith v. State, 235 Ga. 620, 221 S.E.2d 41 (1975), an expert identified wadding in the deceased's body as coming from either a 16 or 20 gauge shotgun. Based on this testimony, the court allowed the defendant's 20 gauge shotgun to be admitted into evidence, even though the weapon could not be positively identified as the murder weapon.

2. 245 Ark. 923, 436 S.W.2d 275 (1969).

§ 6.21

1. 47 Cal.2d 566, 305 P.2d 1 (1956), appeal dismissed for want of a federal question, 358 U.S. 646 (1959). See also, State v. Ware, 338 N.W.2d 707 (Iowa 1983); Brock v. State, 54 Md.App. 457, 458 A.2d 915 (1983) and Krummacher v. Gierloff, 290 Or. 867, 627 P.2d 458 (1981). Even without scientific analysis of the composition of any

part of firearms ammunition, the courts have allowed an inference of guilt to arise from the accused's possession of the same type of ammunition as that used in the offense. In People v. Rivera, 126 A.D.2d 579, 510 N.Y.S.2d 698 (1987) the court convicted the defendant of second degree murder based on evidence that was wholly circumstantial. On his arrest the defendant was found to have a round of .25 caliber ammunition in his jacket pocket. Although the firearm used in the murder was not recovered, two .25 caliber bullets were removed from the body of the victim during an autopsy. The court concluded that this evidence, along with the corroborative circumstantial testimony of various witnesses was sufficient to establish guilt.

2. 81 U.S.App.D.C. 85, 155 F.2d 857 (1946), cert. denied 328 U.S. 873 (1946), rehearing denied 329 U.S. 822 (1946).

was made may be given undue weight by a jury. The size of the batch is important as is the distribution of it in the marketplace in determining how closely the evidence bullet can be tied to the person in possession of the known bullet. The size of the sample of the bullets which is analyzed will also be a relevant factor in assessing the value of the conclusions to be drawn from the analysis.

Although tin, lead and antimony are the major constituents of bullet lead, impurities, such as arsenic, silver and copper may be of greater import to a firearms examiner in conducting a trace element analysis. Such impurities are found in insignificant amount in pure lead but scrap lead, from which bullets are often produced, has measureably larger amounts.

Emission spectrography is the simplest and least costly method for the analysis of trace elements in bullets.[3] However, it is not the system of preferred use for quantitative analysis of those trace elements. Atomic absorption spectroscopy is more suited to quantitation of the test results but its inability to test for more than one element at a time makes it inefficient. The method of choice for trace element analysis of bullet lead is neutron activation analysis,[4] but it is, for most laboratories, a prohibitively expensive operation.

§ 6.22 Evidence of Firing Distance Determination

Firearms identification experts may also be called upon to determine the approximate distance from the gun muzzle to the point of impact, using shot patterns, penetration tests, and powder burn analysis.[1] Shot patterns will be more dispersed as the distance from the muzzle increases. In Williams v. State,[2] shot dispersal experimentation was admitted when it was shown that the test was a standard comparison of the shot dispersed in the wound with experimental patterns obtained by using cartridges and loads similar to the ones found in the defendant's shotgun which was recovered at the scene of the crime.

Firing distance determination, along with other evidence, can strongly suggest an accidental, as opposed to homicidal shooting, and in doing so, the evidence can substantiate an homicide accused's claim as to his position at the time of the shooting. In Guerrero v. State[3], the appellate court reversed a murder conviction finding that there was a

3. Ceccaldi, "Examination of Firearms and Ammunition," in Lundquist, ed., *Methods of Forensic Science*, Vol. I (1962).

4. Lukens & Guinn, "Comparison of Bullet Lead Specimens by Nondestructive N.A.A.," 16 *J.For.Sci.* 301 (1971); Guinn, "N.A.A. of Bullet–Lead Specimens in Criminal Cases," 72 *J.Radioanal.Chem.* 645 (1982).

§ 6.22

1. In general, see, Anno., "Admissibility, in homicide prosecution, of evidence as to tests made to ascertain distance from gun to victim when gun was fired," 11 A.L.R.5th 497.

2. 147 Tex.Crim. 178, 179 S.W.2d 297 (1944). Also see, State v. Tourville, 295 S.W.2d 1 (Mo.1956), cert. denied 352 U.S. 1018 (1957).

The F.B.I., on the contrary, recommends using only "the same type of ammunition" for shot pattern determinations. F.B.I., *Handbook of Forensic Science* 54 (G.P.O., Mar.1984).

3. 720 S.W.2d 233 (Tex.App.1986).

reasonable possibility that the death was caused accidentally. Testimony revealed a small powder burn on the victim's index finger and also that the gun used to kill the victim was discharged while in contact with her face. Given the contact firing and the fact that the appellant had not a trace of blood spattered on him, the court concluded that an accidental shooting was a real possibility. The lack of gunshot residue on either the accused's or the victim's hands was also meaningful.

Pellet penetration will be greater the closer the target is to the muzzle.[4] In State v. Blair,[5] it was held to be reversible error to have excluded the penetration tests offered by the defendant in an attempt to corroborate his story. Here, too, the tests must be conducted under circumstances reasonably similar to those of the questioned shots.

Evidence of powder burns on flesh, clothing, and other target surfaces may be admitted into evidence along with tests conducted to show at what distance from the muzzle a target must be in order for the particular weapon in question to deposit similar powder residue and burns.[6] As with dispersal and penetration tests, powderburn tests must be conducted under conditions sufficiently similar to those present during the questioned discharge;[7] for instance, in State v. Atwood,[8] the

4. In shotguns the range of the shot will depend largely on the weight of the shot. The approximate maximum range of # 12 shot (.05 caliber) is 110 yards, whereas the approximate maximum range of 00 Buckshot (.32 caliber) is 750 yards.

5. 147 Mont. 87, 410 P.2d 450 (1966). The trial court had refused to admit the test results because the shot giving rise to the criminal complaint had been fired through bushes, while the test shots had not. The reviewing court found that since one pellet recovered from the injured party bore none of the scratches or marks that would have been present had it come into contact with twigs and branches, the test results should have been admitted and the absence of bushes should have gone to the weight of the evidence.

6. Opie v. State, 389 P.2d 684 (Wyo. 1964); McPhearson v. State, 271 Ala. 533, 125 So.2d 709 (1960); Straughn v. State, 270 Ala. 229, 121 So.2d 883 (1960); and Washington v. State, 269 Ala. 146, 112 So.2d 179 (1959). For a discussion of early powder burn cases see, 8 A.L.R. 41.

7. State v. Jiles, 258 Iowa 1324, 142 N.W.2d 451 (1966); and Commonwealth v. Snyder, supra note 13, section 6.18.

8. 250 N.C. 141, 108 S.E.2d 219 (1959). A piece of pork into which a bullet was fired was offered into evidence without objection but was later excluded.

For a case where test results were admitted in spite of dissimilar conditions, see, Douglas v. State, 42 Ala.App. 314, 163 So.2d 477 (1963), reversed on other grounds 380 U.S. 415 (1965). Here the court seems to have admitted the evidence solely because it felt the witness was a qualified expert. Also see, State v. Truster, 334 S.W.2d 104 (Mo.1960). Here, testimony of a sheriff that a gun blazes about 6–8 inches from the barrel at night and therefore that would be the approximate limit of powder burns, was admitted. Also admitted were two swatches of test cloth, one similar to the clothes worn by the decedent and one dissimilar. About the dissimilar one the court remarked that it would have been more likely to show burns than the clothes actually worn by the decedent (it was lighter in color) and therefore would have been favorable to the defense had powder burns appeared.

In State v. Goins, 24 N.C.App. 468, 211 S.E.2d 481 (1975), the court did not abuse its discretion in accepting the expert's experimental evidence on shot patterns even though the expert had used specially treated paper in making test firings of weapons rather than using portions of a shirt worn by the victim. In People v. Carbona, 27 Ill.App.3d 988, 327 N.E.2d 546 (1975), firearms and microanalysis testimony was based on shot patterns and firearms residues; a pathologist, using the above testimony as a basis for his own testimony, then concluded to a reasonable medical certainty that the wounds could not have been self inflicted.

tests were conducted with the same weapon and similar ammunition, and consequently the sheets of blotting paper used in the test were admitted into evidence.

When conditions are not sufficiently similar the test results will be declared inadmissible. Such was the ruling in Done v. State,[9] in which a sheriff conducted powderburn tests by nailing a towel to a tree. In Miller v. State,[10] test results were barred because of variations in atmospheric conditions, bullet weight, condition of weapons, and ammunition type. In Jorgenson v. People,[11] the victim's shirt was tested for powder residue six months after the shooting. No evidence was offered to explain that the elapsed time would probably have little effect upon powder residue, and the state failed to show either that the test shot was fired at an angle similar to that of the questioned shot, or that the angle would make little difference with regard to powder deposits (other than shape). These omissions, coupled with the use of different cloth and different cartridges, led to the inadmissibility of the test results.

In State v. Bates,[12] cardboard targets were used to conduct tests of the spread of shotgun pellets. The tests, showing that the shot had come from a distance of four feet, refuted a defense contention that the gun had gone off during a struggle with the victim over the gun's possession. The defendant claimed the cardboard was dissimilar to the crime situation since the victim wore several layers of clothing and had a pack of cigarettes in his breast pocket. Rejecting this claim, the court concluded that such factors would affect the penetration but not the spread pattern of the shot.

Photographs of the victim's wounds which are displayed to the jury with the test patterns to demonstrate the similarity between them are often challenged by the defense since the explicit nature of the photos might inflame the jury. In State v. Castagna,[13] the court allowed the prosecution's expert to show such photos over the defense's objections.

§ 6.23 Time Factor and Chain of Custody

As with all evidence presented by the state, the chain of custody of weapons, shells, bullets, and other items of significance must remain unbroken.[1] Long periods of time may elapse, however, between the time

9. 202 Miss. 418, 32 So.2d 206 (1947). Here the defendant claimed his pistol discharged accidentally when it fell from the glove compartment of his automobile.

10. 250 Ind. 656, 236 N.E.2d 585 (1968). Gun condition was different since the original weapon was unrecovered. Ammunition differed in that the murder bullet was commercially loaded while the test bullets were handloads.

11. 174 Colo. 144, 482 P.2d 962 (1971). Also see, Rhea v. State, 208 Tenn. 559, 347 S.W.2d 486 (1961), where test results were not admitted because the powder used in the test might have been different from the unidentified powder firing the fatal bullet.

12. 48 Ohio St.2d 315, 358 N.E.2d 584 (1976).

13. 170 Conn. 80, 364 A.2d 200 (1976).

§ 6.23

1. Johnson v. State, 121 Ga.App. 281, 173 S.E.2d 412 (1970). Here the weapon was stored in the city hall safe prior to trial. Also see, People v. Appleton, supra note 4, section 6.19. Here, although a .45 caliber shell was stored in a drawer accessible to a police sergeant not called to testify, the

shots are fired and the time the bullets or shells are collected, without affecting admissibility. In State v. Boccadoro,[2] a bullet fired into the ground a year or two prior to the commission of the murder under investigation was recovered and identified as having been fired by the murder weapon. In State v. Lane,[3] shells dropped into a river during target practice months before their recovery were admitted. The time spent under water was to be considered when assigning weight to the evidence, but it was not detrimental to admissibility. Bullets that had been fired into an oak tree four months prior to the homicide were recovered and matched, in Commonwealth v. Ellis,[4] to the bullets found at the scene of the crime. A 1969 Federal case, Ignacio v. People of the Territory of Guam,[5] held to be admissible a bullet recovered from unsecured ground two days after the victim was found. Here too, the delay went only to the weight to be given to the evidence but not to admissibility.

Changes and alterations in items of firearms evidence will not preclude admission of the item if the change is reasonable and does not affect the evidentiary value of the specimen. Clipping the ends of shotgun shells to reduce the powder charge was permitted in Sebastian v. Commonwealth,[6] where the intent was to avoid bursting the barrel of a test weapon that was in poor condition, although the firing pin impressions (which was the aspect under examination) were unaffected by the general condition of the weapon.

shell was admitted. Also see, State v. Vuckovich, supra note 2, section 6.19, where the secret removal of a bullet from the victim's body didn't affect its admissibility.

2. 105 N.J.L. 352, 144 A. 612 (1929).

Here the defendant was suspected of having shot and killed the occupant of a home while in the act of committing burglary. In an effort to determine the defendant's whereabouts at the time of the murder, his common law wife was questioned as to her knowledge of the affair. She finally informed the investigators that on the particular night in question the defendant told her that he had fled from the scene of a burglary and had disposed of his pistol by throwing it away as he ran from the scene of the crime. The weapon was never located.

About a month prior to the murder, another home in the community had been burglarized, and among the articles stolen were some jewelry and a hammerless revolver. For some reason the owner became involved in the present investigation and he identified as his stolen property some jewelry in possession of the defendant's wife. The evidence indicated this had been given her by the defendant. It was inferred,

therefore, that if the defendant had stolen the jewelry he also was guilty of the theft of the revolver. Consequently, if there were any means of connecting that particular weapon with the murder in question, this would constitute a material factor in establishing his guilt.

It so happened—and herein is the strange feature of the case—that the owner of the stolen weapon had fired a bullet from it into the ground near his home, as part of a holiday celebration some year or two previous to the theft. It was suggested that this be retrieved for the purpose of comparison with the fatal missile, since there was no evidence weapon from which a test bullet could be obtained. Fortunately it was found, and an expert was permitted to testify at the defendant's trial that this old bullet and the fatal bullet were fired from the same pistol. This evidence the appellate court considered sufficiently reliable to sustain a conviction of first degree murder.

3. 72 Ariz. 220, 233 P.2d 437 (1951).

4. 373 Mass. 1, 364 N.E.2d 808 (1977).

5. 413 F.2d 513 (9th Cir.1969), cert. denied 397 U.S. 943 (1970).

6. Supra note 6, section 6.19.

The disturbance inflicted by transit through the mails upon a shirt bearing powder burns did not prevent its introduction into evidence in Hedges v. State.[7] The expert witness in that case testified that he was experienced in handling and testing disturbed garments and that he had made due allowance for the disturbance in his test results.

Where there is no reasonable probability of tampering, a break in the chain of custody is not error. In Van Meter v. State,[8] the court concluded that tampering with the weapon was highly unlikely if not totally improbable, where such tampering would have had to cause the weapon to score the test cartridge cases so as to correspond identically with those found at the crime scene. Moreover, it is not necessary to account for every hand-to-hand transfer of the evidence between the time it is obtained and its introduction at trial if the court is satisfied that the condition of the exhibit remains the same. In State v. Starr,[9] the court ruled that a proper chain of custody was established between a highway patrolman who used "gunshot residue kits" to test the defendant for traces of gunpowder and the chief of police who delivered the kits to the crime laboratory, since the trial testimony made the possibility of alternation in the gap between the patrolman and the chief highly unlikely.

In State v. Brooks,[10] a cocked weapon was brought to a police station property room. Instructions were left that the weapon was not to be touched until it was dusted for fingerprints. However, an unknown person uncocked the weapon, presumably for safety reasons, prior to the treatment for latent prints. Nevertheless, the magazine of the weapon, untouched in the process of uncocking, yielded a thumbprint of the defendant which was admitted into evidence.

In State v. Griffith,[11] the defense objected to the introduction of a pistol allegedly used in a robbery on the grounds that its condition had changed while in police custody. The complaint was that at the time of seizure the weapon could only be fired by thumbing the hammer. What happened was that while the officer who confiscated the weapon was making out his report, a second officer picked up the gun, found a loose screw which he tightened, and thereupon rendered the weapon capable of double action firing. The court ruled that the weapon was admissible since its ability to fire at the time of the crime was not at issue, nor was it contended that the defendant ever actually discharged it. The gun was offered solely to show that the victim relinquished his money because he feared he would be shot, and the alterations therefore did not affect its evidentiary value.

7. 165 So.2d 213 (Fla.App.1964), reversed on other grounds 172 So.2d 824 (1965).

8. 30 Md.App. 406, 352 A.2d 850 (1976).

9. 676 S.W.2d 311 (Mo.App.1984).

10. 3 Wash.App. 769, 479 P.2d 544 (1970). Also see, State v. Foust, 258 N.C. 453, 128 S.E.2d 889 (1963), where a test by a police chief to determine whether a certain weapon could have been fired accidentally was excluded because no evidence was offered to show that the weapon was in the same condition as it was while in the defendant's possession, or to show whether or not the safety was engaged.

11. 94 Idaho 76, 481 P.2d 34 (1971).

The chain of custody must be proved from the time the evidence comes into the possession of law enforcement personnel. In Love v. State,[12] a knit hat had helped to convict a defendant who claimed he had fired a shot when the victim grabbed for his gun. The bullet hole in the hat showed a lack of gunpowder residues. The shot had come from beyond arm's reach. The victim had been wearing the hat when he entered the tavern where he was hot, but its location during the ambulance ride afterwards and until it was turned over to the police by a doctor at the hospital was uncertain. The defendant unsuccessfully argued that the ambulance attendant was an "agent of the state," and therefore there was a break in the chain of custody.

The destruction of ballistics evidence before the defendant has an opportunity to conduct his own tests may be a violation of a defendant's constitutional rights to due process or confrontation. Where the destruction is inadvertent, the courts have been unsympathetic to such claims. The state had made such an inadvertent destruction of the evidence in People v. Triplett,[13] where the alleged murder weapon and bullets were destroyed. The defendant contended that this destruction denied him his right to confront the state's firearms expert with his own expert's analysis of the physical evidence. The court rejected this assertion refusing to take an absolutist view of the confrontation clause.

Although the retention of evidence over an extended period of time is of obvious importance to the defense, many courts will not deem the inadvertent destruction or loss of evidence to be a violation of a defendant's confrontation rights, absent demonstrable prejudice. Thus, in People v. Lawrence,[14] the defendant, who fled the state after being charged with murder, returned eleven years later to face criminal charges. At the time the crime was committed a "ballistics" expert found that two of the four bullets used to kill the victim came from the firearm used by the defendant. However, by the time of trial eleven years later, this evidence had been accidentally lost. Notwithstanding, the court admitted testimony alluding to the lost bullets, maintaining that at cross-examination the defendant failed to inquire if an independent examiner might have reached a different conclusion had the bullets been available.

§ 6.24 Testimonial Conditions

The testimony of a firearms expert need not be accompanied by the introduction of the test bullets.[1] If the test bullets are produced, the

12. 178 Ind.App. 497, 383 N.E.2d 382 (1978).

13. 68 Mich.App. 531, 243 N.W.2d 665 (1976).

14. 172 Cal.App.3d 1069, 218 Cal.Rptr. 345 (1985).

§ 6.24

1. People v. O'Neal, 118 Ill.App.2d 116, 254 N.E.2d 559 (1969); Roberts v. State, 164 So.2d 817 (Fla.1964); and State v. Wojculewicz, 140 Conn. 487, 101 A.2d 495 (1953). In State v. Michael, 107 Ariz. 126, 483 P.2d 541 (1971), an expert testified as to the possibility of a certain wound being inflicted based on characteristics of ammunition such as that fired from a casing that was found in the murder weapon. The shell was lost prior to trial but the oral evidence was admitted. In this case a pho-

jury may be permitted to examine them through a comparison microscope.[2] The wisdom of this practice is questionable, however, since the microscope must be focused for each individual juror's eyes and the expert has no way of knowing whether or not the juror has focused correctly. Proper focusing is complicated by the fact that the curvature of the bullet prevents much of the area from being in focus at any one time. Photographs of the matching bullets and shells are not required; [3] the oral opinion testimony of the expert is considered to be sufficient.

The tests performed by a firearms expert need not be conducted in the presence of the accused.[4] It was held to be error in Johnson v. State,[5] however, to admit prosecution evidence in a case where the fatal

to of the casing was available, however. Also see, State v. Richardson, 321 S.W.2d 423 (Mo.1959). Here the defendant threw his weapon into a river from which it was never recovered. The state introduced what it called a similar weapon (a .45 automatic) to demonstrate that the weapon's trigger had to be pulled once for every shot fired, (the defendant claimed the weapon just kept firing) and that it fired the same type of bullets as those found at the crime scene. This evidence was received despite the lack of proof that the weapon discarded by the defendant was a .45 automatic. In addition, the court mentions a full magazine of ten bullets when in fact a .45 automatic magazine holds only seven. The court also seemed to be unaware of the fact that the disconnector of an automatic pistol can be altered so that one pull of the trigger will fire all the bullets in the magazine (the weapon thus operating as a machine pistol).

2. Cantu v. State, 141 Tex.Crim.R. 99, 135 S.W.2d 705 (1939), cert. denied 312 U.S. 689 (1941); Macklin v. State, 64 Okl. Cr. 20, 76 P.2d 1091 (1938); and Evans v. Commonwealth, 230 Ky. 411, 19 S.W.2d 1091 (1929). Contra, Commonwealth v. Newsome, 462 Pa. 106, 337 A.2d 904 (1975).

3. McKenna v. People, 124 Colo. 112, 235 P.2d 351 (1951); People v. Buckowski, 37 Cal.2d 629, 233 P.2d 912 (1951), cert. denied 342 U.S. 928 (1952), where photos were taken but not introduced; Higdon v. State, 213 Ark. 881, 213 S.W.2d 621 (1948); State v. White, 321 So.2d 491 (La.1975); Commonwealth v. Ellis, 373 Mass. 1, 364 N.E.2d 808 (1977). See also, State v. Schreuder, 712 P.2d 264 (Utah 1985). At the preliminary hearing an expert witness testified as to the similarity between striations made by a test bullet passing through the bore of the defendant's gun and those striations found on a bullet recovered from the body of the victim. The defendant objected to the admission of this testimony on the grounds that the expert was unable to

give an exact description of the striations, and that he had not produced photographs of the bullets. The court, however, deemed the testimony properly admitted, maintaining that the expert did not have to furnish photographs where he was able to form an opinion based on his own personal observations of the bullets in question. Neither the Utah rules requiring an expert's opinion to be based on facts known to him, nor the accused's right to confrontation were violated by the lack of photomicrographs of the bullets.

4. United States v. Rees, supra note 6, section 6.19, Goodall v. United States, 86 U.S.App.D.C. 148, 180 F.2d 397 (1950), cert. denied 339 U.S. 987 (1950); and State v. Aiken, 72 Wash.2d 306, 434 P.2d 10 (1967), reversed in so far as death penalty was imposed 403 U.S. 946 (1971). In Richardson v. State, 481 N.E.2d 1310 (Ind.1985) the defendant who had been charged with murder, robbery, and with being an habitual offender, objected to the admission of testimony of the State's firearms expert on the ground that the defendant was not present during the testing which was conducted at a trial recess. The Indiana Supreme Court decided that the defendant had no right to be present at firearms tests conducted by the prosecution during a trial recess at least where no prejudice was demonstrated.

5. 249 So.2d 470 (Fla.App.1971).

The State's obligation to give the defense pretrial access to its firearms evidence varies from state to state. But even where the State has such an obligation, it usually requires a motion to that effect from the defense, which motion may have to be quite specific in its request for discovery. Such was the case in Clemons v. State, 491 So.2d 1060 (Ala.Cr.App.1986) where the defendant, charged with manslaughter, objected to the admission into evidence of a shotgun and a shotgun shell which were given to the

bullet was not made available for an examination by the defense. But when the bullet (or shell, weapon, etc.) is made available for an examination by an independent defense expert, it is reasonable to condition the test upon the presence of a state expert. The court in State v. Nutley [6] held that since firearms identification is a relatively exact science with a common methodology, no prejudice to the defense is incurred by prosecution representation.

Furthermore, the defense may properly be denied funds to hire a "ballistics" expert unless such evaluation is necessary to a real defense. Thus in Moore v. State,[7] such a request was denied since the State's expert had merely indicated the fatal bullets were "consistent with having been fired by (the accused's) gun." The court characterized that testimony as "neutral" and inconclusive and otherwise not particularly damaging to the accused.

Courtroom demonstrations of firearms matters have been permitted. In one example of such a demonstration a Missouri court allowed a police officer to demonstrate the process and time necessary for reloading a handgun without first proving that the gun used in the demonstration was similar to the one used at the crime scene.[8]

The prosecution felt the demonstration was important since the defendant had engaged in a gun battle with the victim, (over a game of craps) and fired seven shots in all. Two of the shots hit and killed the victim while the victim's girlfriend was the fortunate survivor of five bullet wounds.

The prosecution in pressing for a deliberate homicide conviction produced a firearms expert who, using his service .38 caliber revolver, demonstrated in court the process and time necessary for reloading such a revolver. The Missouri appellate court upheld the defendant's capital

---

police shortly after the shooting by the defendant. The defense's objection was predicated on the failure of the State to produce those items pursuant to a pretrial discovery order requiring the production of books, papers, and tangible objects. The appellate court affirmed the trial court's holding that the State had no duty under the discovery order to produce the shotgun and shell since they were not specifically requested.

6. 24 Wis.2d 257, 129 N.W.2d 155 (1964), cert. denied 380 U.S. 918 (1965). In State v. Archambeau, 333 N.W.2d 807 (S.D. 1983), it was gratuitously said to be "highly unlikely that any expert ... would have reached any conclusions regarding the fingerprints (on the murder weapon) or gunpowder residue that would have been different from (the prosecution expert's) finding." In State v. Vincik, 398 N.W.2d 788 (Iowa 1987) the defendant submitted a pretrial motion for an order permitting him to have experts perform "ballistics" tests on evidence within the custody of the State.

He specifically asked, moreover, for a protective order preventing police officers from being present during the experiments. The appellate court affirmed the trial court's decision to grant the defendant's discovery motion without granting his request to perform the tests outside the presence of the state. The court reasoned that the prosecution's interest in safeguarding its physical evidence did not prevent the defendant from discussing the evidence and the test results with his attorney at a later time out of the State's presence and, thereby, did not deprive the defendant of his attorney-client privilege.

7. 736 P.2d 161 (Okl.Cr.1987).

8. State v. Price, 719 S.W.2d 801 (Mo. App.1986), withdrawn by publisher, appeal after remand 763 S.W.2d 286 (Mo.App. 1988). See also, Com. v. Hollihan, 388 Pa.Super. 525, 566 A.2d 254 (1989). Expert allowed to dry fire murder weapon in court to demonstrate that it would not accidentally discharge as alleged.

murder conviction despite claims by the defendant that the prosecution failed to show that the defendant's gun and the gun used by the expert were essentially similar. The court found no error in the courtroom demonstration arguing that whether to allow the demonstration was a matter for the trial court's discretion.

The police, in obtaining physical evidence necessary for laboratory analysis, either for the presence of gunshot residue or for the presence of metallic ions from a weapon, may run afoul of Fourth Amendment constitutional concerns as to the suspect's right to privacy. The question, at bottom, is whether the suspect has such a reasonable expectation of privacy as to require the police to secure a search warrant prior to swabbing or otherwise obtaining trace evidence from the suspect's person. In a 1986 case from the Colorado Supreme Court [9] the requirement of a search warrant as a prerequisite to an ultraviolet examination of a suspect's hands was upheld, even though most other state's courts have decided to the contrary. In addition, a correct interpretation of the evanescent evidence rationale for a warrantless taking of evidence as enunciated in Cupp v. Murphy,[10] would permit the warrantless swabbing of hands or other similarly non-intrusive means of obtaining very evanescent trace evidence for laboratory analysis.

This review of the case law regarding firearms identification evidence clearly refutes the judicial attitude once expressed in People v. Berkman [11] which, as previously noted, characterized firearms identification as "preposterous."

§ 6.25 Evidence of Gunshot Residue Tests

The first reported case deciding the question of admissibility of the results of a dermal nitrate test for gunpowder residues was Commonwealth v. Westwood,[1] decided in 1936. In it, the Pennsylvania Supreme Court held that the testimony of experts who had administered the test, and who had concluded that the specks on the paraffin mold taken from defendant's hand were gunpowder residues, was admissible, even though a chemist who testified for the defense stated that the chemical test would give an identical reaction with thirteen other materials, including tooth powder, cigar ashes, cigarette ashes, and different kinds of matches. The court said that the unexplained presence of specks of partially burned gunpowder on defendant's right hand, a few hours after the shooting, was "significant."

Thus, a precedent was set that was to survive, without serious challenge, for some 26 years. It took eighteen years before another

9. People v. Santistevan, 715 P.2d 792 (Colo.1986).

10. 412 U.S. 291 (1973).

11. Supra note 4, section 6.18.

§ 6.25

1. 324 Pa. 289, 188 A. 304 (1936). In general see, Anno., "Admissibility in criminal case, of results of residue detection test to Determine Whether Accused or Victim Handled or Fired Gun," 1 A.L.R.4th 1072.

reviewing court had occasion to explore the paraffin test. In Henson v. State,[2] a state chemist had concluded that the test showed the defendant had soon prior to the test fired a gun. In holding the evidence admissible, the court observed that the test was not inherently unreliable. In fact, the court equated the test to footprint and fingerprint tests. Demonstrating that once the test had gained a firm foothold in the courts, judges were bound to unequivocally equate a positive test reaction with conclusive proof that gunpowder residue was present, the North Carolina court, also, affirmed a conviction based on this type of evidence.[3]

Despite these decisions scientific investigators had become greatly disturbed by the many possible false reactions, indistinguishable from those made by gunpowder residues, which many substances had shown when they were found on the hand. An article by two respected scientists suggested that the test's evidentiary value was close to nil, because the lack of specificity and the possibilities of gross errors.[4] It was largely on the basis of this article that the Colorado Supreme Court, in the 1959 case of Brooke v. People,[5] reversed a conviction obtained on the testimony of a police "ballistics" expert who had been permitted to testify that the defendant had refused to take a paraffin test. In view of the fact that the test enjoys no particular reputation for accuracy, the court held this testimony to be prejudicial error.

After the Colorado decision in *Brooke,* a number of courts had occasion to review the admissibility of the test. The *Brooke* decision was followed, and admissibility of paraffin tests rejected, largely on the ground of unreliability, by the Oklahoma courts in Born v. State,[6] and in Tennessee in Clarke v. State.[7] In the meantime, Interpol had also condemned the paraffin test as unreliable and had reported that the test was not only without value as evidence, but should not even be used as an investigative lead.[8]

2. 159 Tex.Crim.R. 647, 266 S.W.2d 864 (1954).

3. State v. Atwood, 250 N.C. 141, 108 S.E.2d 219 (1959).

4. Turkel & Lipman, "Unreliability of Dermal Nitrate Test for Gunpowder (Sic.)," 46 *J.Crim.L., C. & P.S.* 281 (1955). Conrad condemned the article in no uncertain terms: "In my opinion, the Turkel and Lipman research does not conform to the minimum requirements of scientific methodology, and I have gained the impression that the authors want us to accept their findings that the test is unreliable solely upon the strength of their own opinion...." Conrad. "Evidential Implications of the Dermal Nitrate Test," 44 *Marq. L.Rev.* 500, 513 (1961).

5. 139 Colo. 388, 339 P.2d 993 (1959). Conrad, supra note 4, also condemned this court for its holding: "It seems to me that the Colorado Supreme Court, without any

adequate basic research, acted arbitrarily in condemning the use of the Dermal Nitrate Test ... by reference to one single isolated authority in the technical literature and ignoring the viewpoint of eminent criminologists such as Dr. Mathews and others." Conrad, op. cit. note 4, at 514. The viewpoint of Dr. Mathews, referred to by Conrad, was expressed in: Mathews, "The Paraffin Test," *The American Rifleman,* Feb. 1954, p. 20. But even Mathews concedes in the same article, that the dermal nitrate test is not specific for gunpowder residues.

6. 397 P.2d 924 (Okl.Cr.1964), cert. denied 379 U.S. 1000 (1965).

7. 218 Tenn. 259, 402 S.W.2d 863 (1966), cert. denied 385 U.S. 942 (1966).

8. Note, *International Criminal Police Review,* Jan. 1964, p. 28: "The (First Interpol Seminar on Scientific Aspects of Police Work) did not consider the traditional pa-

Nevertheless, several courts have since that time admitted evidence of gunpowder residues, distinguishing the *Brooke* holding,[9] or even simply ignoring it.[10] These decisions are clearly erroneous! Evidence which is so untrustworthy that the technical literature suggests it not be used, could not possibly meet the test of relevancy.[11]

The more recently developed Harrison–Gilroy test for gunshot residues (see, supra, § 6.12), which tests for the presence of antimony, barium and lead, rather than for nitrates and nitrites, initially received more favorable acceptance in the forensic sciences. The test was deemed far more reliable. Yet, it is stated that "Because of the limitations in the sensitivity of the colorimetric reactions to detect Ba, Sb, and Pb, there was no widespread adoption of ... [the Harrison–Gilroy test]." [12] Judicial acceptance, therefore, is and should be slow in coming, to avoid the admission into evidence of test results which are clearly meaningless—as was the case with the old fashioned dermal nitrate test—and yet have a significant prejudicial impact on the fact finder. Few cases, however, have dealt with the test. In Commonwealth v. Farrior,[13] decided December 20, 1971, the Pennsylvania Supreme Court upheld a conviction of voluntary manslaughter, largely based on evidence of two "criminologists" who had used the "Harrison Residue Test" to determine whether defendant had recently fired a gun. The court held that the test results were properly admitted in evidence. Unfortunately, the Pennsylvania high court based its opinion upon erroneous grounds. As authority for the admissibility of the Harrison–Gilroy test results, the court cited Commonwealth v. Westwood,[14] the case dealing with the nitrate test that has been so resoundingly criticized for its unreliability, as previously discussed. In so doing, the court was apparently unaware of the decisions in other states rejecting dermal nitrate tests, and appeared equally unaware of the fact that the Harrison–Gilroy test is one which determines the presence of residues of lead and barium on the hand, and not of nitrates and nitrites, as was the case in *Westwood*. We have a fairly typical example, then, of a case possibly correctly decided but on an incorrect premise.

raffin test to be of any value, neither as evidence to put before the courts, nor even as a sure indication for the police officer. The participants were of the opinion that this test should no longer be used."

9. State v. Fields, 434 S.W.2d 507 (Mo. 1968).

10. Harris v. State, 239 Ark. 771, 394 S.W.2d 135 (1965), cert. denied 386 U.S. 964 (1967); People v. Simpson, 5 Mich.App. 479, 146 N.W.2d 828 (1966).

11. Turkel & Lipman, op. cit. n. 103. See also, Cowan, "A Study of the 'Paraffin Test'," 12 *J.For.Sci.* 19 (1967), reporting on an extensive study project affirming the Turkel & Lipman findings of unreliability

and confirming the Interpol (see note 2, section 6.21) opinion.

12. Pillay, "New Method for the Collection and Analysis of Gunshot Residues as Forensic Evidence," 19 *J.For.Sci.* 769 (1974). Scientists search for a quantitative test because "the existing techniques ... are found to be unsatisfactory ...": Krishnan, "Detection of Gunshot Residue on the Hands by Neutron Activation and Atomic Absorption Analysis," 19 *J.For.Sci.* 789 (1974).

13. 446 Pa. 31, 284 A.2d 684 (1971). The Harrison–Gilroy study is referred to in note 2, section 6.12.

14. Supra note 1.

Of the newer techniques for gunshot residue analysis, anodic stripping voltammetry has had three challenges [15] in the appellate courts, all in Missouri, and has survived on each occasion. In all three cases, the defense argument in opposition to anodic stripping voltammetry was the same, viz. the technique had not been accepted in the scientific community. None of the decisions indicates that any expert testified in support of the defense position. On the contrary, the self-serving declarations of acceptance by the prosecution's experts seem to have been taken at face value. In none of the decisions did the Missouri appellate courts define the relevant scientific community within which one should look for acceptance of anodic stripping voltammetry. Certainly, in the field of firearms examiners, anodic stripping voltammetry is not nearly as accepted as it is in toxic waste and other environmental affairs. Probably this is accounted for by the inability of anodic stripping voltammetry to detect barium, as well as antimony, a significant deficiency in the technique not mentioned in any of these three Missouri opinions.

The use of the scanning electron microscope coupled with an X-ray analyzer for gunshot residue analysis of particles from the hands has been approved in People v. Palmer.[16] Even though the state's criminalist who did the analysis was the only person to affirm the technique's acceptance within the relevant scientific community, the California appellate court was persuaded that the test results were deservedly admissible. Similarly, neutron activation analysis [17] and atomic absorption spectrophotometry [18] for the detection of gunshot residues on the hands have received widespread judicial approval.

Florida has now joined the states that have accepted neutron activation analysis as a valid form of gunshot residue testing. In Mills v. State,[19] the victim awoke after hearing noises and upon investigation was shot and killed with a shotgun carried by one of the two intruders. Two hours after the shooting, the two defendants were detained and the police "conducted gunshot residue tests on them." The results of the test showed that one of the defendants had traces of antimony on his hands but apparently no traces of barium. The other defendant, who tested positively for both antimony and barium, attempted to exclude the test results stating that the use of neutron activation analysis was "not

15. State v. Walker, 654 S.W.2d 129 (Mo.App.1983); State v. Williams, 659 S.W.2d 309 (Mo.App.1983); State v. Cooper, 691 S.W.2d 353 (Mo.App.1985).

16. 80 Cal.App.3d 239, 145 Cal.Rptr. 466 (1978).

17. State v. Spencer, 298 Minn. 456, 216 N.W.2d 131 (1974); State v. Jackson, 566 S.W.2d 227 (Mo.App.1978).

18. Chatom v. State, 348 So.2d 838 (Ala. 1977); State v. Chatman, 156 N.J.Super. 35, 383 A.2d 440 (1978); State v. Crowder, 285 N.C. 42, 203 S.E.2d 38 (1974), vacated in part on other grounds 428 U.S. 903 (1976). See, in general, Anno.: "Admissibility, in Criminal Case, of Results of Resi-

due Detection Test to determine Whether Accused or Victim Handled or Fired Gun," 1 A.L.R.4th 1972 (1980).

19. 476 So.2d 172 (Fla.1985). For a good discussion as to the current status and uses of neutron activation analysis see, Katz, "Neutron Activation Analysis", *Amer. Lab.*, 16 (June 1985). In addition, neutron activation analysis is used by the F.B.I. Laboratory to detect elevated levels of barium and antimony on hands; Kilty, "A Review of the FBI Laboratory's Gunshot Primer Residue Program", 13 *Crime Lab Dig.*, 54 (April 1986).

scientifically accepted in general" and too inconclusive to be reliable. The defendant's arguments were rejected by both the trial court and the Florida Supreme Court. While stating that neutron activation analysis was a valid form of gunshot residue testing, the court did err in relying upon the Nebraska decision in State v. Journey,[20] where trace metal detection technique was used and not neutron activation analysis.

Although the results of a Harrison–Gilroy test may be admissible, modifications in its procedure may render the results unacceptable. In State v. Smith,[21] a murder conviction was reversed when a police officer had altered the Harrison–Gilroy test by using filter paper to collect the sample instead of cotton swabs and by not testing for antimony. The test itself was held to be reliable, but the alteration from its methodology rendered the results unreliable.

While evidence of gunshot residues is commonly used to show that the person tested had actually fired a gun, in one case large traces of gunshot residue were actually used to prove that a victim did not fire a gun. In a North Carolina case [22] the victim was apparently shot by his friend while his friend was sitting just two feet away. The North Carolina Court of Appeals rejected the defendant's explanation that the victim accidentally shot himself and based their reasoning largely on the testimony of a forensic chemist who interpreted gunshot residue sample taken from the victim's hands.

According to the expert, the gunshot residue test revealed a high concentration of residue on the palms of the victim's hands which would be inconsistent with the amount and location of residue found on the hands of someone who had recently fired a gun. The expert suggested that the residue could have most likely gotten onto the victim's hands if the victim brought his hands up in a defensive way between himself and the gun prior to the gun being fired. While the gunshot residue tests showed that the victim most likely could not have fired the gun, the tests taken of the defendant were inconclusive. The expert suggested that the amount of time between the shooting and the tests (roughly three and a half hours), was sufficient to create the inconclusive results. In addition, there was also evidence that the gun had been fired a distance of 22 to 26 inches from the victim's head and the prosecution was allowed to show via a courtroom demonstration that the victim, due to his size, could not have shot himself in the head from that distance.

Another instance in which gunshot residue evidence, or rather the lack of it, was used in a novel manner by the prosecution occurred in a Florida case in which the defendant's refusal to allow police to test his hands for gunshot residue could not be put in evidence as an indication of his guilt.[23]

20. 201 Neb. 607, 271 N.W.2d 320 (1978).

21. 50 Ohio App.2d 183, 362 N.E.2d 1239 (1976).

22. State v. Benjamin, 83 N.C.App. 318, 349 S.E.2d 878 (1986).

23. Herring v. State, 501 So.2d 19 (Fla. App.1986). Compare South Dakota v. Neville, 459 U.S. 553 (1983). Contra Com. v.

§ 6.26 Trace Metal Detection Tests

The reported decisions demonstrate that TMDT has had a variety of uses in the trial of criminal cases. In Commonwealth v. Massart,[1] the defendant was convicted of using a hammer to kill his wife. On the trial of the charge, the prosecution introduced the opinion of a "criminologist," based on a TMDT, that a piece of sailcloth found in defendant's possession had been wrapped around the murder weapon at some previous time. On appeal, the expert's testimony was upheld.

In Knott v. Mabry,[2] a toxicologist testified that TMDT and other tests indicated that the defendant's hands had been in contact with a metal consistent with the metal bucket used to carry an accelerant to the scene of an arson. The Federal court in the habeas petition did not review the legitimacy of this testimony. And in People v. Level,[3] a table leg had been used to bludgeon the deceased to death. TMDT revealed traces of metal on the accused's hands. The reviewing court did not pass on the propriety of this testimony.

The decisions addressing the admissibility of the results of TMDT are few and are in dispute. In a one paragraph explication of the admissibility issue in State v. Daniels,[4] the police officer's testimony that TMDT indicated defendant had "recently fired a gun" was sustained, in spite of the officer's saying the defendant had fired a gun. But in State v. Snyder,[5] the New Jersey court took pains to review the police's conscientious handling of the TMDT and to approve the testimony as to its results.

On the contrary, in State v. Lauro,[6] a jeweler's homicide conviction was reversed where a police officer had handcuffed the defendant and then performed a TMDT. The court's rejection of the officer's testimony was probably motivated largely by the officer's gross ignorance of the literature and the scientific basis for a TMDT. Similarly, in Esquivel v. State,[7] a police officer's carelessness resulted in a denial of TMDT results. The officer had first sprayed the accused's bloody hands and upon obtaining a negative reaction, he had held the gun confiscated from the accused and sprayed his own hands. Once again the findings were negative, but the officer sought to explain this result by noting that the pistol was coated and that its metal did not show through. The Texas reviewing court was disturbed by the officer's failure to use a spray on his own hands comparable to the one he used on the accused's hands.

Monahan, 378 Pa.Super. 623, 549 A.2d 231 (1988).

§ 6.26

1. 469 Pa. 572, 366 A.2d 1229 (1975).

2. 671 F.2d 1208 (8th Cir.1982).

3. 162 Cal.Rptr. 682 (1980), opinion withdrawn and vacated sub nom. California v. Level, 449 U.S. 945 (1980).

4. 37 Ohio App.2d 4, 305 N.E.2d 497 (1973).

5. 190 N.J.Super. 626, 464 A.2d 1209 (1983).

6. 91 Misc.2d 706, 398 N.Y.S.2d 503 (1977).

7. 595 S.W.2d 516 (Tex.Cr.App.1980), cert. denied 449 U.S. 986 (1980).

Probably the most confused judicial reaction to TMDT occurred in State v. Journey.[8] In this case the Nebraska high court upheld a police officer's testimony that his "tests proved conclusively that the defendant had fired a gun." The test utilized by the policeman was denominated a "gun particle residue test" by the court. The court's juxtaposition of TMDT and gunshot residue tests is understandable in light of the officer's trial testimony that he had sought "to get a blow back of gunpowder on the hand and wrist" by seeking to discover "little flakes, metallic flakes" under ultraviolet light. Not only did the court accept the test results, whatever the true nature of the test conducted might have been, but it also indicated, in an aside, that the officer need not have stated the nature of his testing as a foundational requirement for the admissibility of his opinion since the Nebraska rules of evidence did not impose such a restriction upon an expert's testimony.

§ 6.27   The Law on Comparative Micrography

The comparison of an object and an impression allegedly made by the object was admitted as evidence in a criminal case as early as 1879 in Dean v. Commonwealth.[1] In that case, the distinct square impression and a "peculiar" notch left on a fence rail, presumably when the defendant rested his weapon in order to fire at the deceased, were examined by several witnesses. These markings were found to correspond with impressions made when the defendant's gun was laid upon the same rail and was drawn back. The lack of expertise on the part of those testifying did not preclude the admission of this evidence.

Seven years later, in Passmore's Appeal,[2] the jury was allowed to consider whether some questioned sheets of paper had originally been attached in a certain book. The court disposed of the need for expert testimony, saying:

> Expert testimony cannot be of any use in helping, and is improper to be used in preventing, a jury from drawing conclusions for themselves from every day appearances open to the judgment of any intelligent observer.[3]

In State v. Baldwin,[4] a case decided the same year as *Passmore,* the value of comparative micrography was demonstrated, along with the need for expert testimony in its support. In this case, a panel had been cut out of the door of the house where a crime had been committed. The defendant was a carpenter, and when arrested he had a knife in his possession. The court allowed experts to testify concerning the items of evidence, and said of the witnesses:

> These men were skilled workers in wood, and their experience enabled them to judge, from the marks and impressions left upon

8. 201 Neb. 607, 271 N.W.2d 320 (1978).

§ 6.27

1. 73 Va. (32 Gratt.) 912 (1879).

2. 60 Mich. 463, 27 N.W. 601 (1886).

3. Id. at 466, 27 N.W. at 603.

4. 36 Kan. 1, 12 P. 318 (1886), writ of error dismissed for want of jurisdiction 129 U.S. 52 (1889).

the door by the tool used, whether it had been cut with a knife, chisel, or saw; whether it had been cut by a thick or a thin bladed knife; whether it had been cut by one accustomed to the use of tools; and the marks or traces made upon the wood by the knife would indicate to the trained eye whether it had been cut from the outside or the inside. The manner in which the cutting was done, and the effect of the tools upon the wood, involve skill and experience to judge of, and are not within common experience.... [5]

At the present time, the use of comparative micrography and the need for qualified expert testimony is generally accepted by the courts and has been compared to the science of fingerprint identification.[6] For instance, the Washington Supreme Court remarked, "The edge on one blade differs from the edge of another blade as the lines on one human hand differ from the lines on another." [7]

Widespread exposure to the science of comparative micrography was given during the notorious Lindbergh–Hauptmann kidnapping case.[8] There, the wood in the ladder used to abduct the Lindbergh baby was traced to a particular sawmill by examination of the cutter marks on the rails. Markings on the ladder made by a dull hand plane matched the markings found on a piece of lumber in the defendant's garage. Comparison of the growth rings and individual characteristics of portions of the ladder disclosed that the board had once been joined to lumber in the attic floor of the defendant.[9] This case, therefore, is a clear example of the evidentiary value comparative micrography can have in a criminal prosecution or investigation.

1. TOOLMARKS LEFT AT THE CRIME SCENE

Toolmarks left at the scene of a crime are typically found in burglary cases. A sizeable body of case law provides precedent for the

---

5. Id. at 324.

6. People v. Perroni, 14 Ill.2d 581, 153 N.E.2d 578 (1958), rehearing denied 359 U.S. 1005 (1959). This case involved tool mark comparison. But see, Glasgow Ice Cream Co. v. Fults' Administrator, 268 Ky. 447, 105 S.W.2d 135 (1937), where the court regarded the use of expert testimony to identify a fragment of a coat as permissible but not necessary.

7. State v. Clark, 156 Wash. 543, 287 P. 18 (1930). Here the defendant admitted using his knife to cut three cedar boughs. The markings on these boughs compared with the marks made on fir saplings used to construct a blind which hid the assailant prior to the rape in question. But see, State v. Fasick, 149 Wash. 92, 270 P. 123 (1928), affirmed 149 Wash. 92 (1929), where the knife in question and branches that were used to hide the body of the deceased were held inadmissible. The court felt that the marks made by a hand

held knife did not deserve the same weight that would be accorded to a fixed tool. The court in Clark distinguished this case because in Fasick the cuts were not shown to be similar.

8. State v. Hauptmann, 115 N.J.L. 412, 180 A. 809 (1935), cert. denied 296 U.S. 649 (1935).

9. Koehler, Technique Used in Tracing the Lindbergh Kidnapping Ladder, 27 *J.Crim.L., C. & P.S.* 712 (1937). A re-evaluation of Koehler's work fifty years later has confirmed his findings. Haag, "The Lindbergh Case Revisited: A Review of the Criminalistics Evidence," 28 *J.For.Sci.* 1044 (1983).

Similar techniques were used in Commonwealth v. Fugmann, 330 Pa. 4, 198 A. 99 (1938), to show that wood used in a bomb carrying cigar box and wood found in the defendant's cellar were of a common origin.

admission of a vast array of tools and tool markings. Drills have been matched with the holes bored in a safe.[10] Screwdrivers and crowbars are routinely matched with prymarks on doors,[11] window sashes,[12] and safes.[13] Car tools and tire irons have left their marks on door moldings,[14] and doorknobs,[15] in one case, a tire iron was shown to have been used to puncture the gas tank of a burned automobile containing a corpse. This evidence countered the defendant's claim that his wife was killed when their car ran off the road and "accidentally" caught fire.[16]

A hammer has been matched with the markings on the spindle of a safe,[17] and a taper punch with impressions left on a safe's lock pin.[18] Bolt cutters can be connected to a criminal offense when they have been used to gain entry or to disconnect merchandise which is the object of a theft, such as copper tubing.[19] The distinctive marks left by pliers have also been used to associate an individual with a crime.[20]

2.　REASSEMBLING PARTS OF A WHOLE

Often, a criminal investigation or prosecution will depend upon the fitting together of a number of pieces that together make a complete object. This area of scientific evidence is particularly well suited to hit-and-run cases, where materials left at the accident scene can be physically connected to the suspect vehicle when it is located. A typical example of this application is People v. Leutholtz,[21] where a disk shaped radiator emblem found at the accident scene fitted perfectly into the radiator of the defendant's automobile. In another case, a radio antenna found at the scene of an accident under investigation fitted perfectly onto the broken antenna base on the car of the accused.[22]

Homicides that may or may not have been vehicular related have also been solved by fitting together various fragments. In State v.

---

10. Starchman v. State, 62 Ark. 538, 36 S.W. 940 (1896).

11. State v. Wade, 465 S.W.2d 498 (Mo. 1971); State v. Brown, 291 S.W.2d 615 (Mo. 1956); State v. Eickmeier, 187 Neb. 491, 191 N.W.2d 815 (1971).

12. State v. Brown, supra note 11.

13. People v. Perroni, supra note 6.

14. Adcock v. State, 444 P.2d 242 (Okl. Cr.1968).

15. State v. Smith, 156 Conn. 378, 242 A.2d 763 (1968).

16. State v. Harris, 241 Or. 224, 405 P.2d 492 (1965).

17. State v. Olsen, 212 Or. 191, 317 P.2d 938 (1957).

18. State v. Montgomery, 175 Kan. 176, 261 P.2d 1009 (1953).

19. Souza v. United States, 304 F.2d 274 (9th Cir.1962). Here the marks made by the tool in question were identical to the marks on tubing found in the possession of the dealer purchasing the stolen tubing and with tubing still on the owner's property.

For a case where a stolen coin collection was identified through a record of the mint marks on the coins, see, Jenkins v. United States, 361 F.2d 615 (10th Cir.1966).

20. Mutual Life Ins. Co. of Baltimore, Md. v. Kelly, 49 Ohio App. 319, 197 N.E. 235 (1934). Here an insurance company defended its nonpayment on a life insurance policy on the ground that the insured had been engaged in illegal conduct when he was killed by a spring gun.

21. 102 Cal.App. 493, 283 P. 292 (1929). The defense argued that the emblem may have been planted but the court found that this claim only went to the weight of the evidence.

22. Castleman v. State, 378 S.W.2d 315 (Tex.Cr.1964).

Rowe,[23] a number of metal pieces found near the body of the deceased fitted exactly into the running board of the defendant's automobile. No explanation of how the pieces were broken off was offered, but the evidence nevertheless placed the accused's car at the scene and tended to implicate him.

A malicious mischief charge was substantiated when pieces of brick thrown through a broken shop window matched pieces of brick found in defendant's car.[24] Moreover, the rubber in a slingshot found on the ground at the scene matched the ends of an inner tube also found in the defendant's vehicle. The matching of the torn end of a piece of tape on a package of narcotics with the end of a roll of tape found in the accused's locker helped lead to another conviction.[25]

When an offender breaks a tool or other instrumentality of a crime during the commission of the act, the piece left at the crime scene often provides damaging circumstantial evidence (similar to hit-and-run cases) if the rest of the tool is ultimately located. In State v. Walker,[26] a piece of metal lodged in the door of a burglarized safe was found to be the broken end of a long-handled screwdriver found in defendant's possession. In another burglary prosecution, a knife and its broken point were admitted into evidence.[27] A pistol and the grips that once had been attached were admitted in United States v. Rees.[28] Here the grips, which had been dislodged during a beating of the victim, were left at the scene and were later identified as having once been attached to the gun found in the home of defendant's parents.

3. GLASS FRAGMENTS

The fitting together of glass fragments usually occurs during automobile cases or in burglary prosecutions. Glass from the scene may be matched with the defendant's headlight,[29] reflectors,[30] or windshield.[31]

23. 203 Minn. 172, 280 N.W. 646 (1938).

24. Smith v. State, 215 Ind. 629, 21 N.E.2d 709 (1939).

25. United States v. Massiah, 307 F.2d 62 (2d Cir.1962), reversed on other grounds 377 U.S. 201 (1964). For a case involving the matching of torn sheets of paper from a book, see, Passmore's Appeal, supra note 2, section 6.27. Also see, Koehler, supra note 9, concerning the wood in the Lindbergh kidnapping ladder.

26. State v. Walker, 6 N.C.App. 447, 170 S.E.2d 627 (1969).

27. Tripi v. State, 234 So.2d 15 (Fla. App.1970), cert. denied 238 So.2d 110 (Fla. 1970). Both the knife and the broken point were found at the burglary scene.

28. 193 F.Supp. 849 (D.Md.1961), habeas corpus denied 341 F.2d 859 (4th Cir. 1965).

29. Rolls v. State, 35 Ala.App. 283, 46 So.2d 8 (1950), and McIntyre v. State, 26 Ala.App. 499, 163 So. 660 (1935).

30. State v. Marcus, 240 Iowa 116, 34 N.W.2d 179 (1949).

31. Castleman v. State, supra note 22. Also helpful in hit and run cases is the examination of impressions left upon the auto body by the fibers in the clothes of the victim. People v. Ely, 203 Cal. 628, 265 P. 818 (1928), and People v. Wallage, 353 Ill. 95, 186 N.E. 540 (1933). In Wallage, microscopic analysis of the dent in the vehicle showed 31 minute scratches to the inch. Examination of the victim's shirt showed 31 raised threads to the inch.

A different approach was taken in Patalas v. United States,[32] involving a conviction for unauthorized use of a motor vehicle. The auto was found damaged and abandoned. A thorough examination disclosed some pieces of broken glass under the steering wheel. These pieces matched perfectly the broken lens of a pair of glasses found in the defendant's pocket.

4. MARKS ON BODIES

The imprints made on flesh or bone may be received in evidence along with the article making the impression. A cleaver, and testimony that marks on the victim's skull could have been made by such a cleaver, were admitted in Commonwealth v. Bartolini.[33] But in Ramirez v. State,[34] against all the evidence and against the undisputed testimony of all scientists in the field,[35] the Florida Supreme Court reversed a conviction where the state's expert testified the impression in the deceased victim's rib cartilage was caused by the defendant's knife to the exclusion of all others. The Florida court decided that there was an insufficient predicate for that allegedly "self-serving" opinion. On a retrial four experts appeared for the prosecution in support of the knife's causing the impression and none testified to the contrary. A second conviction was returned, which has been appealed.[36]

In another case, the court allowed expert testimony which claimed that two small puncture marks on an abortion victim's cervix could only have been inflicted by a particular instrument, a tenaculum.[37] In a homicide prosecution, the marks on the deceased's legs were compared with the pattern of the floor mats used in the model of vehicle driven by the accused.[38]

Forensic odontologists, utilizing techniques found acceptable in the identification of bitemarks, have been permitted to testify that scratch marks on a child strangulation victim's neck were caused by the accused's fingernail.[39] The Pennsylvania reviewing court, however, completely failed to recognize that the class characteristics of the fingernail

---

32. 87 U.S.App.D.C. 379, 185 F.2d 507 (1950).

33. 299 Mass. 503, 13 N.E.2d 382 (1938), cert. denied 304 U.S. 565 (1938). A knife was connected to marks on a homicide victim's sternum in State v. Churchill, 231 Kan. 408, 646 P.2d 1049 (1982).

34. 542 So.2d 352 (Fla.1989). The Ramirez opinion is analyzed critically in Garcia, "Are 'Knife Prints' Reliable Evidence: An Analysis of Tool Mark Evidence and Ramirez v. State," 25 A.F.T.E. J. 266 (Oct. 1993).

35. Kilty, "Court Presentation of Toolmarks Identified in Stab Wounds," 17 A.F.T.E. J. 66 (Apr. 1985); Galan, "Identification of Knife Wound in Bone," 18 A.F.T.E. J. 72 (Oct. 1986).

36. Supra note 34 at 269. See, in general, Anno, "Admissibility of Expert Opinion Stating Whether a Particular Knife was, or Could Have Been, the Weapon Used in a Crime," 83 A.L.R.4th 660.

37. People v. Johndrow, 71 Ill.App.2d 75, 218 N.E.2d 25 (1966).

38. People v. Kirkes, 243 P.2d 816 (Cal. App.1952), vacated 39 Cal.2d 719, 249 P.2d 1 (1952). The evidence was admitted but the court felt expert testimony was unnecessary.

39. Commonwealth v. Graves, 310 Pa.Super. 184, 456 A.2d 561 (1983). See the analysis of this case in Starrs, "Procedure in Identifying Fingernail Imprint in Human Skin Survives Appellate Review," 6 *Am.J.For.Med. & Path.* 171 (1985).

and the scratch marks, although similar, lacked the necessary individual markings to tie the accused's fingernail to the scratch marks on the victim to the exclusion of all others.

5. FINGERNAIL MATCHING

The admissibility of the identification of a fingernail found at a crime scene to a particular individual as its source through striation matching is finding favor among the courts, in spite of two negative appellate court opinions.[40]   Clearly such matching has probative value on the issue of guilt or innocence and will, therefore, be of assistance to the fact finder.   And where the standard of admissibility is the general scientific acceptance of the method, the unanimous approval in the scientific literature of the validity of fingernail striation matching indicates this standard too has been met.[41]   Nor should it be possible to challenge the use of the comparison microscope in such matching since that technique is of longstanding acceptance in other, comparable areas of scientific testing.

6. TESTIMONIAL CONDITIONS

As with other areas of scientific evidence, photographs can be introduced to aid the jury in their determination of fact,[42] although they are not required as a matter of law.   It also has been held permissible for a court to allow a witness on the stand to demonstrate the piecing together of fragments in the presence of the jury.[43]

Evidence of the type we have been discussing must follow the chain of custody requirements; it must not undergo any substantial change between the occurrence of the act complained of and its presentation in court.   However, the use of shellac to protect a series of scratches, for example, is a permissible change.[44]

Any tests must be conducted under circumstances reasonably similar to those present during the act in question.[45]   When the foregoing

---

40. People v. Wesley, 103 Mich.App. 240, 303 N.W.2d 194 (1981) rejects fingernail matching by striations but State v. Shaw, 124 Wis.2d 363, 369 N.W.2d 772 (App.1985) accepts it. See also, Anno., "Admissibility of Evidence of Fingernail Comparisons in Criminal Cases," 40 A.L.R.4th 575 (1985).

41. Op. cit. supra notes 1–3, section 6.17.

42. People v. Adams, 259 Cal.App.2d 109, 66 Cal.Rptr. 161 (1968). See further, Chapter 2, supra, on the admissibility of photographs.

43. Rolls v. State, supra note 29 and State v. Marcus, supra note 30. It was error, however, to allow the jurors to view the exhibit in separate panels of three, in McIntyre v. State, supra note 29.

44. People v. Wallage, supra note 31.

45. See, Mutual Life Insurance of Baltimore, Md. v. Kelly, supra note 20, section 6.26, where the beneficiary sought to show that the deceased's pliers did not make the marks alleged to have been made during an illegal entry. The court remarked that it was an easy matter to squeeze the tool differently to purposely produce different marks, and, consequently, excluded the results of these particular tests. See also, People v. Ely, 203 Cal. 628, 265 P.2d 818 (1928), where tests of cloth pressed against an automobile bumper were excluded as having been conducted under dissimilar conditions.

standards are followed, the science of comparative micrography can provide a great deal of valuable evidence.

An expert should not be permitted to testify to opinions beyond his professional abilities or that of his profession. Firearms examiners are regularly reminded not to express an opinion on the intent or state of mind of a shooter at the time of the firing of a firearm.[46] But the New Hampshire high court in State v. Aubert[47] found the refusal of the trial court to allow the defendant's firearms expert to state his opinion on the intent of the wife when she shot her husband to be error requiring a reversal of the wife's conviction for attempted murder.

§ 6.28   Evidence of Alteration of Serial Numbers

There should not be any evidentiary problems of undue magnitude when it comes to admitting evidence of restored serial numbers which have been criminally altered or removed. The techniques are simple and straightforward and, when relevant to triable issues, it is proper to admit such expert testimony.[1]

§ 6.29   Expert Qualifications

Since there are no formal training courses to prepare one to become a firearms examiner, the training and experience of the expert is usually acquired through a study of the quite extensive literature, supplemented by practical work in law enforcement crime laboratories, firearms manufacturing plants, military service, or firearms testing laboratories. Usually, a number of years of work, under proper supervision, in comparing and examining weapons and ammunition is required before attaining the degree of proficiency in the work required to make a determination of identity or lack of it.[1] A thorough familiarity with the technical literature, optical equipment including the comparison microscope, standard laboratory measuring techniques, and photography would also be required.

An experienced and highly regarded toolmark comparison expert has proposed[2] fifteen essential qualifying questions for a witness who pro-

46. Garrison, "Intent Behind the Bullet," 25 A.F.T.E. J. 294 (Oct. 1993).

47. 120 N.H. 634, 421 A.2d 124 (1980). On the retrial a second conviction was returned. See, Aubert v. Aubert, 129 N.H. 422, 529 A.2d 909 (1987) and Allstate Insurance Company v. Aubert, 129 N.H. 393, 529 A.2d 915, 916 (1987).

§ 6.28

1. See, e.g., People v. Snow, 21 Ill. App.3d 873, 316 N.E.2d 216 (1974).

§ 6.29

1. Allegations by the defense in questioning an expert's competence to testify about firearms evidence must be weighed against that expert's experience and edu-

cation in the field of firearms identification. In a trial for armed robbery and attempted manslaughter, the Louisiana Court of Appeals upheld the determination of the lower court that the expert employed to identify bullet fragments found in the car door and those in close proximity to the victim in the hospital's x-ray room, was qualified to testify. The expert's education included a B.S. in Zoology and an M.A. in organic chemistry. His other credentials consisted of two years training in firearms, and studying firearms journals. State v. Jones, 457 So.2d 110 (La.App.1984).

2. Murdock, "Some Suggested Court Questions to Test Criteria for Identification Qualifications," 24 A.F.T.E. J. 69 (Jan. 1992). Additional questions, of a more in-

fesses to be expert in the field of toolmark comparisons. These questions boil down to two crucial concerns. Is the expert's opinion that there is an identification based upon standard criteria in the field? The answer which is suggested is that there are no real standards recognized by the profession. There are instead individual "standard criteria" built up in the examiners' mind's-eye.[3] Such subjectivity might well be challenged as impermissibly speculative and, as such, unscientific. This same writer is a strong proponent of the necessity for the examiner to gain credibility by "deliberately" comparing toolmark impressions known to be made by different tools. He, therefore, recommends that the expert be queried whether such comparisons have been made in the training he has received.[4]

In *Bell v. State*,[5] the court held qualified as a ballistics expert a witness who had received training through reading text books, working under the supervision of the chief of the police identification division, working with a Department of Public Safety firearms examiner and who had over three years of experience.[6]

Gunshot residue tests may be conducted to determine the existence of nitrates on the periphery of a bullet hole, to determine the firing distance or to detect gunshot residues on the hands of a suspect. The determination of the firing distance through test firings is a duty frequently delegated to firearms identification personnel and is ordinarily within the scope of such a person's training. The firearms examiner who is not knowledgeable in matters of chemistry and instrumental analysis should not be competent to testify to gunshot residue detection on the hands nor to the presence of traces of gunpowder or the other byproducts of a firing around a bullet hole. Such opinion testimony requires the participation of one with expertise of a different order from that of the firearms examiner in general practice today.

Toolmark examiners ordinarily can qualify as experts on the same basis as firearms examiners.

Since the overwhelming majority of firearms identification experts in criminal prosecutions testify for the prosecution, the courts have been fairly lenient in qualifying expert witnesses on the assumption that if the crime laboratories feel the witness is competent to work in the field, he ought to be competent to qualify as an expert—an assumption that may

---

trospective nature, but still important as qualifying criteria, have been recommended by a crime laboratory manager. See, Smith, "Who Me ... Biased? or 'We Have Met the Enemy, and He is Us!'", 25 A.F.T.E. J. 260 (Oct. 1993). A sound basis for qualifying questions also appears in the A.F.T.E. Code of Ethics adopted in 1980. See, A.F.T.E. Code of Ethics, 25 A.F.T.E. J. IX (Jan. 1993).

3. Murdock supra note 2 at 70.

4. Id. at 71–72.

5. 442 S.W.2d 716 (Tex.Cr.App.1969).

6. A true "ballistics" expert, as opposed to a firearms examiner, will have skills distinct from those utilized in identifying a projectile or firearms. In an Indiana case, a police officer having considerable investigative experience with homicide crime scenes was deemed competent to give his opinion on the trajectory of a fatal bullet and the position of the victim when shot. Van Orden v. State, 469 N.E.2d 1153 (Ind. 1984).

have some well-founded basis in most of the cases, but not in all.[7] Thus, a state toxicologist was permitted to give an opinion that a weapon required "more than an average pull on the trigger" and that "it would be difficult for it to be fired accidentally."[8]

On the other hand, in one case an employee of the crime lab was not permitted to testify that another employee of the same lab had made certain ballistic comparisons of bullets, as such would be patent hearsay.[9]

VI.   FIREARMS LITIGATION—THE CIVIL SIDE[1]

§ 6.30   Civil Liability—In General

Gun control is not a matter of legislation alone. The impact of judicial decisions permitting persons involved in the manufacture, importation and sale of firearms to be sued in damages for the injuries sustained from the use or misuse of firearms can be a telling form of gun control. United States District Court Judge Penn took due note of this possibility in his decision denying relief against a gun manufacturer in an action by three of those injured in the attack of John Hinckley upon then President Reagan. As he candidly put it, "what is really being suggested by plaintiffs, and indeed by many citizens, is for this Court, or courts, to indirectly engage in legislating some form of gun control"[2] under the guise of compensation to those injured by firearms.

1.   SUITS AGAINST FIREARMS' MANUFACTURERS

It is most particularly in damage actions against firearms manufacturers, both domestic and foreign, that the refrain of "a handgun ban by judicial fiat"[3] has been recited by the courts as a cautionary admonition

---

7. The decision to allow a witness to offer an opinion is left to the discretion of the trial judge and may be based more on the helpfulness of such testimony to the jury than on the witness' education and experience. In Dudley v. State, 480 N.E.2d 881 (Ind.1985) one of the arresting officers was permitted to give testimony concerning bullet paths and powder burns existing on the car used by the accused, over the objection of the defense that he was not a firearms expert. The Indiana Supreme Court held that the officer, although not a firearms expert, was more knowledgeable than the average juror and, therefore, the trial judge did not abuse his discretion in admitting the opinion.

8. Boswell v. State, 339 So.2d 151 (Ala. Cr.App.1976).

9. State v. Ceja, 113 Ariz. 39, 546 P.2d 6 (1976).

§ 6.30

1. See generally, Miller, "A Call to Arms: Trends in Firearms Litigation," *Trial* 24 (Nov. 1993).

2. Delahanty v. Hinckley, 686 F.Supp. 920, 930 (D.D.C.1986). See also, Perkins v. F.I.E. Corporation, 762 F.2d 1250, 1269 (5th Cir.1985) citing Note, "Handguns and Products Liability," 97 *Harv.L.Rev.* 1912, 1925 n. 78 (1984) and Santarelli & Calio, "Turning the Gun on Tort Law: Aiming at Courts to Take Products Liability to the Limit," 14 *St. Mary's L.J.* 471, 474 (1983).

3. Martin v. Harrington & Richardson, Inc., 743 F.2d 1200, 1204 (7th Cir.1984).

against countenancing an expansion of the traditional remedies in tort against firearms manufacturers. Clearly manufacturers of firearms like manufacturers of other products can be held liable for the consequences of their negligent acts. However the difficulties in establishing unreasonable behavior on the part of firearms manufacturers as well as in proving the necessary causal link between a manufacturer's breach of duty and the injuries to a remote person long after the manufacture and sale of a firearm have forced lawyers to look outside the bounds of the tort law of negligence to strengthen the claims of their firearms-injured clients.

Well-entrenched legal doctrines permit damage actions in tort on a theory of strict liability, a liability which is not predicated on proof of the negligence of an alleged wrongdoer, but such actions are authorized only in certain limited and exceptional situations. The liability of common carriers to their passengers and innkeepers to their guests have been rooted in strict liability due to the nature of the relationship between the parties. By a similar line of reasoning firearms manufacturers have been alleged to be strictly liable in tort either because

> 1. the manufacture and distribution of firearms is an ultra-hazardous undertaking in view of the lethal potential of firearms or

> 2. the manufacture and distribution of a product designed to be used as an instrument with fatal results is the loosing on the market of a product in a defective condition with the potential of unreasonably injurious consequences.

The first theory essentially states the ultra-hazardous activity doctrine of the common law which is incorporated in the Restatement of Torts (Second) sections 519 and 520. In an unbroken series of cases the courts have consistently refused to permit the enlargement of the ultra-hazardous activity doctrine to include the manufacturers of firearms.[4] It is not that firearms are not ultra-hazardous. Quite the contrary. It is that the courts never reach the point of deciding on that issue since the ultra-hazardous activity doctrine has been limited both at common law and under the Restatement of Torts to the owners or users of land whose actions create abnormally dangerous risks to others.

The second possible theory for strict liability in tort suits against firearms manufacturers is the defective product doctrine, deeply rooted as it is in the restructured common law and in the Restatement of Torts (Second) section 402A. Section 402A provides, in relevant part, that "One who sells any product in a defective condition unreasonably dangerous to the user or consumer or to his property is subject to liability for physical harm thereby caused to the ultimate user or consumer . . ." It is further stated that it is no defense to the seller that he "has exercised all possible care in the preparation and sale of his product."

---

4. Perkins, supra note 2; Delahanty, supra note 2 and Kelley v. R.G. Industries, Inc., 304 Md. 124, 497 A.2d 1143 (1985).

The courts have given short shrift to the frequent efforts to bring the defective product doctrine to bear upon persons in the manufacturing or marketing of firearms where there is no defect in the design or manufacture of the firearm. If a firearm is to be considered to be a defective product simply because it is capable of inflicting harm either in its criminal or its lawful use then the door of court access will be thrown open to all and sundry who can claim firearms injuries under a myriad of diverse circumstances. The courts have steadfastly refused to heed the call to go even one step in that direction, recognizing its cataclysmic effect upon the firearms marketing chain. Viewed even from the perspective of the firearms consumer, the defective product doctrine is totally maladroit in the context of the run-of-the-mill firearms injury. The routine expectation of a firearms purchaser is that the item bought will be "dangerous by its very nature" [5] and that it will "have the capacity to fire a bullet with deadly force." [6]

The courts have given credence to the defective product claim in firearms litigation only when the firearm is defective in its design or manufacture according to the meaning of defective in common parlance. So a firearm which is not "drop safe" (which will discharge a chambered round if the firearm is dropped) or, more arguably, a semi-automatic without a magazine safety [7] (which will discharge a chambered round if the trigger is pulled even in the absence of the magazine) may be deemed to be defective in manufacture. Manufacturers have been held liable for accidental injuries due to the lack of safety devices, the absence of specified handling warnings and the malfunctioning of the gun.

None of the most artful strategies of lawyers, save one, has sufficed to render the manufacturers and suppliers of firearms generally liable in tort to injured persons. And the result in Kelley v. R.G. Industries, Inc.,[8] the so-called Saturday Night Special decision, may be more properly seen as a triumph of judicial creativity rather than the acumen of lawyers. The Kelley case involved a damage action filed in the Maryland courts by the victim of a grocery store armed robbery who was shot during the hold-up. He sued Rohm Gesellschaft, a German corporation, which had designed and marketed the firearm, a .38 special revolver, from which the bullet was fired injuring Kelley. Joined as a defendant in the action was R.G. Industries, a Florida-based corporation, which assembled and sold the firearm to a retailer. After the litigation had been removed to a Federal court, a series of questions were propounded to the Maryland Court of Appeals on the state of Maryland's law on the relevant issues of the defendants' liability. In responding, the Maryland high court discredited Kelley's ultra-hazardous activity and defective product claims as unfounded under Maryland law. But in its reformulation of the Federal court's certified questions the Maryland court asked:

5. Kelley, supra note 4 at 1148.

6. Ibid.

7. Berg, "Magazine Safeties: Important Safety Design," 25 A.F.T.E. J. 301 (Oct. 1993).

8. Supra note 4.

"Is the manufacturer or marketer of a particular category of small, cheap handguns, sometimes referred to as 'Saturday Night Specials,' and regularly used in criminal activity, strictly liable to a person injured by such handgun during the course of a crime?"[9]

The Maryland court gave a definite but highly controversial affirmative response to this query. In doing so it established for the first time anywhere a tort cause of action against a manufacturer or marketer of a "Saturday Night Special" when and only when the so-styled firearm caused injuries while used in the commission of a crime. The injuries must be to one other than the perpetrator of the crime and the firing of the firearm must be by a perpetrator of a crime and not one who is a victim of the crime or who is seeking to prevent it.

Much was said but much was also left unsaid by the *Kelley* court. Whether the .38 special involved in this very litigation was a Saturday Night Special was for the jury to decide, said the court. There was every intimation, however, on the part of the court that it should be so characterized by the jury. Even though the court recognized that there is "no clear-cut, established definition of a Saturday Night Special,"[10] it proposed certain "relevant factors" to define the borders within which such a firearm could be denominated. Such criteria included "the gun's barrel length, concealability, cost, quality of materials, quality of manufacture, accuracy, reliability, whether it has been banned from import by the Bureau of Alcohol Tobacco and Firearms and other related characteristics."[11]

The consequences of the Kelley decision have not been as draconian as might have been expected at the time of its announcement in 1985. As early as 1986 it was rejected as an authority of any value for the District of Columbia.[12] Subsequently the District of Columbia did enact legislation[13] providing strict liability in actions against the manufacturers, importers and sellers of assault weapons where persons were injured in the discharge of these weapons but assault weapons, no matter how elusive their definition, are not Saturday Night Specials.

Other state courts have not followed the lead of the *Kelley* court[14] and Saturday Night Specials have not been broadened to include assault weapons or BB guns.[15] For all intents and purposes, the Kelley decision is to firearms litigation what the Saturday Night Special is to firearms— the flotsam and the jetsam on the waters of the law.

With the exception of the limited and the isolated instance of the Kelley case, the manufacturers of firearms are not greatly at risk of tort actions when they design and produce firearms fit for the purpose for

9. Supra note 4 at 1146.

10. Supra note 4 at 1159.

11. Ibid.

12. Supra note 2.

13. D.C.Code § 6–2391 (Supp.1992). See, Ratten, "Corrective Justice and the D.C. Liability Act," 19 *J.Legis.* 282 (1993).

14. Richardson v. Holland, 741 S.W.2d 751 (Mo.App.1987).

15. Addison v. Williams, 546 So.2d 220 (La.App.1989), cert. denied 550 So.2d 634 (La.1989); Koepke v. Crosman Arms Co., 65 Ohio App.3d 1, 582 N.E.2d 1000 (1989).

which they are intended. The retailers of firearms are in a much more vulnerable legal posture, however, for the reason that they are more directly regulated through licensing by the Gun Control Act of 1968 [16] in their sale of ammunition and firearms and because the direct contact they have with firearms purchasers will often give them knowledge of the dangerous propensities of the purchaser in a particular instance, giving rise to a duty of care that may result in liability for their negligent response to that duty.

2. SUITS AGAINST FIREARMS' RETAILERS

Damage actions against the retailers of firearms have had greater success than such actions against manufacturers, but only when the suits are founded on the negligence of the retailers rather than strict liability. The basis for a sizeable number of actions against retailers has been their violation of a statutorily mandated duty of care constituting negligence per se. The governing statute from which these cases have sprung is the Federal Gun Control Act of 1968. Section 922(b) of the act prohibits the sale of handgun ammunition to anyone under the age of 21 and any firearm or ammunition to anyone under the age of 18. Section 922 lists several classes of people who are not permitted to purchase firearms including indicted or convicted felons, drug users, adjudicated mental incompetents, illegal aliens and fugitives from justice. Under the Federal regulations implementing the act, the retailer is directed to have the buyer complete Firearms Transaction Accord Form 4473. The form lists those ineligible to purchase a gun and requires the prospective purchaser to certify that he does not fall into any of the proscribed categories.

As the Federal gun control statute is subdivided into ammunition purchase and firearms purchase situations, so the negligence cases have followed a similar categorization. Retailers are rarely held liable for injuries ensuing from the sale of ammunition. The Federal statutory duty of retailers selling ammunition or firearms is not to sell to individuals under the prescribed ages. In other sales the duty of the retailer is one of ordinary care. In a Michigan case,[17] a K–Mart clerk sold shotgun ammunition to McKay who was intoxicated at the time. McKay was over the required age of 18 and there was no evidence that he had behaved in a manner which would have signalled to the K–Mart sales clerk that he was intoxicated. After leaving the store, McKay shot the plaintiff. The Michigan court held that K–Mart had not violated its Federal statutory duty in the ammunition sale. Ammunition sales, unlike firearms transactions, are not off limits to intoxicated persons. The legitimacy of a purchase depends solely upon the buyer's age. A duty of ordinary care would have been breached by K–Mart if McKay had acted in a minatory or incompetent manner in the store, but there

16. 18 U.S.C.A. §§ 921–922 (Supp. 1993).

17. Buczkowski v. McKay, 441 Mich. 96, 490 N.W.2d 330 (1992).

was no evidence indicating he had done so. Without a breach of some duty, K–Mart could not be held liable.

In another suit, stemming from an ammunition sale in Texas,[18] a convicted felon purchased ammunition from a Winn–Dixie store. The purchaser then used it to commit four murders. The Texas court, in deciding for Winn–Dixie, reasoned that the duty of ordinary care of a retailer does not encompass a duty of inquiry as well. While a retailer is prohibited under the Gun Control Act from selling ammunition to a person it knows or has reason to believe is a convicted felon or mentally unstable, the retailer is not required by law to ask the purchaser if he fits these categories or for what purpose he intends to use the ammunition.

The retailer must, however, heed the purchaser's statements. For example, a 19 year old, under Federal law, can purchase ammunition for a rifle or shotgun, but not for a handgun. In another suit against K–Mart,[19] it was proved that a 19 year old purchased .357 magnum ammunition and told the clerk it was for use in a rifle. Three days later, the 19 year old killed a man with a handgun containing the .357 magnum ammunition. Since the ammunition could be used in a rifle and the purchaser had stated that that was his intent, K–Mart avoided liability.

Retailers are more routinely found liable in damages to injured persons where a gun purchase contravenes Federal law. In a Florida damage claim,[20] a K–Mart sales clerk sold a gun to a man named Knuck. The clerk filled out form 4473 himself without asking Knuck if he fit into any of the listed categories. Knuck claimed at the trial that, if asked, he would have told the clerk he was a convicted felon and a user of marihuana. Both would have made Knuck ineligible to purchase a firearm. Knuck loaned the gun to his brother who also fit into several of the prohibited categories. The brother shot the plaintiff, Keller. K–Mart admitted it was negligent in selling the weapon, but claimed it was not liable due to the unforeseeable transfer of the firearm to Knuck's brother and his shooting Keller.

The Florida court deferred to the United States Supreme Court's interpretation of the legislative purpose of the Gun Control Act. The high court had previously declared that the main objective of the federal statute was to keep firearms out of the hands of those too irresponsible to possess them because of age, criminal background or incompetency.[21] Therefore a jury could find the shooting to be within the risk designed to be prevented by the statute. The fact that the recognizable danger was achieved in an unanticipated way did not relieve K–Mart of liability for its negligence. The occurrence of a harm was foreseeable as happening

18. Bryant v. Winn–Dixie Stores, Inc., 786 S.W.2d 547 (Tex.App.1990).

19. Phillips v. K–Mart Corp., 588 So.2d 142 (La.App.1991).

20. K–Mart Enterprises of Florida, Inc. v. Keller, 439 So.2d 283 (Fla.App.1983).

21. Huddleston v. United States, 415 U.S. 814 (1974).

in some form and Knuck's transfer of the gun to his brother did not change the nature of the risk created by K–Mart's statutory breach.[22]

Retailers may also be held liable when they sell firearms to people who appear to be incompetent. For example, a retailer may be found liable for the purchaser's intervening acts if a jury decides the retailer sold the firearm to a visibly intoxicated person and that the sale was the proximate cause of the injury.[23] Sellers have been held liable for injuries resulting from any purchase where the buyer appeared to be a danger to himself or to others.[24] Such people are recognized by the Gun Control Act as incompetent to purchase firearms.

Retailers cannot avoid liability when guns are purchased by a straw person if they are on notice or reasonably should be alert to this subterfuge. Courts have held retailers accountable for injuries consequent upon sales that circumvent the Gun Control Act. In such cases, the actual purchaser or "straw man" has no legal impediment to purchasing a firearm. The straw person buys the gun for another person who is usually too young or otherwise statutorily disabled from buying firearms. The illegal owner uses the gun to inflict injuries. To be liable to the injured person, the retailer must know or have reason to know it is helping an unqualified individual obtain a gun through a straw person. For example, the retailer may be held liable when a legal purchaser merely accompanies an underage person who picks out the firearm and gives the purchaser the money for the gun,[25] all in the presence and to the knowledge of the retailer.

3. SUITS AGAINST FIREARMS' OWNERS

Another subset of firearms litigation embraces suits against the owner of a gun which is used to do harm. The theory of such suits is grounded in the Restatement of Torts 2d, § 308:

> "It is negligence to permit a third person to use a thing or to engage in an activity which is under the control of the actor, if the actor knows or should know that such person intends or is likely to use

---

22. Supra note 20. Failing to have the purchaser fill out Form 4473 himself, while a violation of federal gun regulations, is not enough to prove the legal cause of injury necessary to hold the retailer liable. In Phillips v. Roy, 431 So.2d 849 (La.App. 1983), the retailer filled out Form 4473 for the purchaser who turned out to be mentally incompetent and dangerous. The court remanded the case for trial to a jury to decide if the purchaser had displayed any signs of mental incompetence when buying the gun. If so, the retailer would be liable.

23. Bernethy v. Walt Failor's, Inc., 97 Wash.2d 929, 653 P.2d 280 (1982).

24. Jacoves v. United Merchandising Corp., 9 Cal.App.4th 88, 11 Cal.Rptr.2d 468

(1992). See also, Angell v. F. Avanzani Lumber Co., 363 So.2d 571 (Fla.App.1978).

25. Failey v. Snug Enterprises, Inc., No. CL 89–2047 (Va.2d. Jud.Cir.Ct., Oct. 4, 1990). See also, Hoosier v. Landa, 17 Cal. Rptr.2d 518 (Cal.App.1993)—opinion later withdrawn.

Manufacturers have no duty to prevent the sale of their handguns to persons likely to cause harm to the public. That is the duty of the retailer. Linton v. Smith and Wesson, 127 Ill.App.3d 676, 82 Ill.Dec. 805, 469 N.E.2d 339 (1984). Manufacturers are not liable when a retailer of its firearms is held accountable for failing to properly check the identification of a buyer. Franco v. Bunyard, 261 Ark. 144, 547 S.W.2d 91 (1977).

the thing or to conduct himself in the activity in such a manner as to create an unreasonable risk of harm to others."

The official comment to this rule notes that it most frequently applies where the injuring party is a member of a group known to be likely to misuse the item in question. Specifically, the comment illustrates the meaning of section 308 in referring to the act of negligence in placing "loaded firearms ... within the reach of young children or feebleminded adults." [26]

Much of the owner-type litigation involves suits against the parent of a child who caused injuries with his parent's gun. The fundamental common law rule that a parent is not liable for the tort of his child does not apply in these cases since it is the parent, not the child, who is being sued for his own carelessness in allowing his child to have access to a firearm.[27] There is nothing on the order of vicarious liability here.

In Jacobs v. Tyson,[28] the defendant's twelve year old child took a loaded pistol from an unlocked bedroom dresser drawer to show to the plaintiff's twelve year old child. The defendant's parents were unaware that their son knew where to find the gun. The gun accidentally discharged and the plaintiff's son suffered a fatal injury. The boys were without adult supervision at the time of the tragedy. The Georgia court held that a loaded firearm may be considered an inherently dangerous instrument for which one must take exceptional precautions to prevent the very foreseeable acts of children playing with the gun and causing it to accidentally discharge.

Other owner cases also make the duty of the owner and the foreseeability of the injury the linchpin of accountability. For example, in Dick v. Higgason,[29] an employer kept an unloaded gun behind his desk and the ammunition in the back of a drawer. An employee occasionally brought his son to work but the child had never previously gone into the employer's office. One day, while unsupervised by his father, the boy entered the office, found the gun, searched for the ammunition, loaded the gun, and went outside to do target practice during which he caused the injuries for which this suit was brought. The employer was held not to be negligent since the plaintiff's injury was not a foreseeable consequence of the manner in which the employee stored his gun.

Regardless of their liability for their own negligence, the owners of firearms are not liable in damages to persons injured subsequent to the theft of their firearms. Absent some demonstrable negligence making the theft more likely, criminal wrongs are not answerable in damages by the gun owner whose stolen firearm was used to inflict the injury. The

26. A.L.I. Restatement of the Law 2d Torts 100 (1965).

27. Spivey v. Sheeler, 514 S.W.2d 667 (Ky.1974).

28. 200 Ga.App. 123, 407 S.E.2d 62 (1991).

29. 322 S.W.2d 92 (Ky.1959). Contra: Palmisano v. Ehrig, 171 N.J.Super. 310, 408 A.2d 1083 (App.Div.1979), cert. denied 82 N.J. 287, 412 A.2d 793 (1980).

owner in Thomas v. Borkelman [30] permitted an ex-convict relative, who had never been involved in a firearms-related crime, to live in his home. The ex-convict stole one of the owner's three rifles and committed a homicide. The Nevada court did not find the event sufficiently foreseeable to hold the owner liable. Merely keeping a gun in a home creates no foreseeable risk of harm which would establish a duty by the gun owner toward a person injured by the intervening acts of minors or criminals. [31]

4. SUITS AGAINST MAGAZINE PUBLISHERS

Another category of firearms litigation involves suits against the publishers of magazines. A leading case in which the publisher was found liable for money damages for injuries due to a firearm is Braun v. Soldier of Fortune Magazine, Inc. [32] The defendant magazine ran an advertisement titled "Gun for Hire" which went on to describe the qualities and the availability of the advertiser as a mercenary. A business man hired the mercenary to kill his business partner. Upon the completion of the contract the murder victim's children sued the publisher for damages for their loss. The Federal court held that a publisher could be liable since the advertisement on its face would have alerted a reasonably prudent publisher to a clearly identifiable risk of harm to the public posed by the ad. The court further observed that imposing liability under such circumstances does not impinge upon the publisher's First Amendment freedoms. A publisher does not have an immunity under the First Amendment precluding a court from holding it liable for injuries resulting from advertisements it publishes in its magazine. [33]

However, the fact that an advertised product might be used illegally does not mean the magazine publisher loses all protection under the First Amendment's commercial speech doctrine. [34] For example, advertising an illegal activity like a notice of the readiness of a murderer for hire as in *Braun* is not constitutionally protected while advertising guns, which can be used illegally, is protected.

These Soldier of Fortune decisions establish that a magazine publisher does not have a duty to investigate and to refuse publication to any suspicious or ambiguous ads that might conceivably cause harm.

---

30. 86 Nev. 10, 462 P.2d 1020 (1970).

31. In Romero v. National Rifle Ass'n of America, Inc., 749 F.2d 77 (D.C.Cir.1984), a gun was stolen from the N.R.A. offices in Washington, D.C. The gun had been locked in a closet and the key to the closet was left in a desk drawer. Burglars broke into the office, stole the gun, and used it to fatally shoot someone during a street-side robbery several days later. The N.R.A. had no liability because it had no extended duty beyond the normal locking of the building against theft. The owner was not liable either. There was no violation of any D.C. statutory provision concerning the proper storage of guns. See, D.C.Code 6.2372 and 6.2347(a).

32. Braun v. Soldier of Fortune Magazine, Inc., 968 F.2d 1110 (11th Cir.1992).

33. Norwood v. Soldier of Fortune Magazine, Inc., 651 F.Supp. 1397 (W.D.Ark. 1987).

34. Eimann v. Soldier of Fortune Magazine, Inc., 880 F.2d 830 (5th Cir.1989).

Such a duty would be too rigorous and too onerous. The exclusive duty is not to publish ads whose language clearly indicates a real and substantial possibility of illegal or harmful activity flowing from it. Furthermore, even the use of the words "Gun for Hire" in an advertisement does not suffice for liability. The entire advertisement must be scrutinized to see if it reveals an identifiable offer to commit crimes.

VII. TRIAL AIDS

§ 6.31 Locating and Engaging the Expert

Most states have central crime laboratories with facilities and staff for firearms identification procedures to assist in the prosecution of cases where toolmark comparisons are to be made. The metropolitan police departments also maintain excellent laboratories staffed by qualified technicians. In the event that neither of these sources is available, resort may be had, but only by Law enforcement, to the FBI laboratory in Washington, D.C. The prosecutor, then, should not encounter any difficulty in securing the analytical and forensic services of qualified experts.

Even the defense, however, should not encounter any significant problems in locating specialists qualified to examine firearms evidence and give expert testimony in court from sources unconnected with law enforcement. The great number of hunting accidents, and the civil suits brought yearly against firearms manufacturers for defective guns and ammunition, have contributed to the growth of a profession of private firearms experts. Most private and police experts belong to professional organizations, among them: the International Association for Identification, P.O. Box 90259 Columbia, SC, 29290; and the Association of Firearms and Tool Mark Examiners.[1] This group, formed to facilitate the exchange of technical information related to the examination of firearms and toolmarks, is heavily assisted by technical advisors from among the members of the firearms industry, the ammunition industry, and the physical security industry. This association has given intense study to the certification of its members by examination and other means. While the matter has attracted some support from toolmark examiners, it has not been endorsed by the membership of the Association.[2]

A number of highly qualified firearms experts also belong to the Criminalistics Section of the American Academy of Forensic Sciences,

---

§ 6.31

1. The association elects officers annually and maintains no fixed headquarters address. Contacts with the organization may be made through its officers or through the editor of its quarterly journal, Billy J. Hornsby, USACIL—CONUS, Ft. Gillem, Ga. 30050–5000. Phone 404–362–3489.

2. Kopera, "Summary of the Study of the Feasibility of Certification—September 10, 1991," 24 A.F.T.E. J. 84 (Jan. 1992).

which has its headquarters at 410 North 21 Street, Suite 203, Colorado Springs, CO, 80904–2798.

A private, commercial venture entitled the Forensic Services Directory, which is a Westlaw data base, gives descriptive information on firearms experts who pay a fee to be listed.

Although there are gunsmiths who may be qualified to testify about the functions of firearms, it cannot be overemphasized that a knowledge of guns is only one of the requisites of a firearms examiner. Unless gunsmiths have training and experience in comparing fired bullets and cartridges, they cannot qualify as firearms identification experts.

———

VIII. MISCELLANEOUS

§ 6.32 Bibliography of Additional References

(Books and Articles cited in the footnotes are not repeated here.)

Anno., "Expert Evidence to Identify Gun From Which Bullet or Cartridge Was Fired," 26 A.L.R.2d 892.

"Firearms Identification," 5 *Am.Jur.Proof of Facts* 113 (1960); 29 *Am. Jur.Proof of Facts* 65 (1972).

Anderson, "Military Rifle and Light Machine Gun Identification," 10 *J.For.Sci.* 294 (1965).

Ayers & Stahl, "The Ballistic Characteristics and Wounding Effects of a Tear Gas Pen Gun Loaded with Ortho–Chlorobenzalmalononitrile," 17 *J.For.Sci.* 292 (1972).

Basu, "Formation of Gunshot Residues," 27 *J.For.Sci.* 72 (1982).

Bellemore, "Ammunition: Manufacturing vs. Identification," 5 *J.For. Sci.* 148 (1960).

Biasotti, "The Principles of Evidence Evaluation as Applied to Firearms and Tool Mark Identification," 9 *J.For.Sci.* 428 (1964).

Bonte, "Tool Marks in Bones and Cartilage," 20 *J.For.Sci.* 315 (1975).

Braverman, *The Firearms Encyclopedia* (1960).

Burd & Gilmore, "Individual and Class Characteristics of Tools," 13 *J.For.Sci.* 390 (1968).

Burd & Greene, "Tool Mark Examination Techniques," 2 *J.For.Sci.* 297 (1957).

Burd & Kirk, "Toolmarks—Factors Involved in Their Comparison and Use as Evidence," 32 *J.Crim.L. & Criminol.* 679 (1942).

Davis, *An Introduction to Tool Marks, Firearms and the Striagraph* (1958).

DiMaio, "Injury by Birdshot," 15 *J.For.Sci.* 396 (1970).

DiMaio, "Gunshot Wounds—Practical Aspects of Firearms, Ballistics, and Forensic Techniques." (1985).

Drake, "Shotgun Ballistics—Part 1," 2 *J.For.Sci.Soc.* 85 (1962).

Drake, "Shotgun Ballistics—Part 2," 3 *J.For.Sci.Soc.* 22 (1963).

Goddard, "Scientific Identification of Firearms and Bullets," 17 *J.Crim.L. & Criminol.* 254 (1926).

Goddard, "The Unexpected in Firearm Identification," 1 *J.For.Sci.* 57 (1955).

Goddard, "A History of Firearms Identification to 1930," 25 A.F.T.E. J. 214 (July 1993).

Goddard, "The Identification of Projectiles in Criminal Cases," 19 A.F.T.E. J. 393 (Oct. 1987).

Graham, et al., "Forensic Aspects of Frangible Bullets," 2 *J.For.Sci.* 507 (1956).

Grove, et al., "Evaluation of SEM Potential in the Examination of Shotgun and Rifle Firing Pin Impressions," 19 *J.For.Sci.* 441 (1974).

Guerin, "Characteristics of Shotguns and Shotgun Ammunition," 5 *J.For.Sci.* 295 (1960).

Gunther, *The Identification of Firearms* (1935).

Gunther & Gunther, *Identification of Firearms* (1950).

Hatcher, *Hatcher's Notebook* (1962).

Hatcher, Jury & Weller, *Firearms Investigation, Identification and Evidence* (1957).

Hoffman, "A Simplified Method of Collecting Gunshot Residue for Examination by Neutron Activation Analysis," *Identification News*, Oct. 1968, p. 7.

Jauhari, "Determination of Firing Distance in Cases Involving Shooting Through Glass," 54 *J.Crim.L., Criminol. & P.S.* 540 (1963).

Jauhari, "Approximate Relationship between the Angles of Incidence and Ricochet for Practical Application in the Field of Criminal Investigation," 62 *J.Crim.L., Criminol. & P.S.* 122 (1971).

Jauhari, et al., "Statistical Treatment of Pellet Dispersion Data for Estimating Range of Firing," 17 *J.For.Sci.* 141 (1972).

Joling and Stern, "An Overview of Firearms Identification Evidence for Attorneys I: Salient Features of Firearms Evidence," 26 *J.For.Sci.* 153 (1981).

Joling and Stern, "An Overview of Firearms Identification Evidence for Attorneys II: Applicable Law of Recent Origin," 26 *J.For.Sci.* 159 (1981).

Joling and Stern, "An Overview of Firearms Identification Evidence for Attorneys III: Qualifying and Using the Firearms Examiner as a Witness," 26 *J.For.Sci.* 166 (1981).

Joling and Stern, "An Overview of Firearms Identification Evidence for Attorneys IV: Practice and Procedures When Using the Firearms Examiner and Demonstrative Evidence," 26 *J.For.Sci.* 171 (1981).

Jones, et al., "Ballistic Studies and Lethal Potential of Tear Gas Pen Guns Firing Fixed Metallic Ammunition," 20 *J.For.Sci.* 261 (1975).

Koffler, "Zip Guns and Crude Conversions—Identifying Characteristics and Problems," 61 *J.Crim.L., Criminol. & P.S.* 115 (1970).

Lukens & Guinn, "Comparison of Bullet Lead Specimens by Nondestructive Neutron Activation Analysis," 13 *J.For.Sci.* 301 (1971).

Mathews, *Firearms Identification* (1962).

Mattoo, "Evaluation of Effective Shot Dispersion in Buckshot Patterns," 14 *J.For.Sci.* 263 (1969).

McLaughlin & Beardsley, Jr., "Distance Determinations in Cases of Gun Shot Through Glass," 1 *J.For.Sci.* 43 (1965).

Moulton, *Methods of Exterior Ballistics* (1962).

Munhall, "Firearms Identification Problems Pertaining to Supplemental Chambers, Auxiliary Cartridges, Insert Barrels and Conversion Units," 5 *J.For.Sci.* 319 (1960).

Ogle & Mitosinka, "The Identification of Cut Multistranded Wires," 19 *J.For.Sci.* 865 (1974).

Principe, et al., "A New Method for Measuring Fired Bullets Employing Split–Image Analyzer," 4 *J.Pol.Sci. & Admin.* 56 (1976).

Rowe, "Firearms Identification," 2 *Forensic Science* (R. Saferstein ed. 1988).

Handbook 393 (R. Saferstein ed. 1988).

Sinha & Kshettry, "Pellet Identification," 63 *J.Crim.L., Criminol. & P.S.* 134 (1972).

Sinha, et al., "Bullet Identification By Non–Striated Land and Groove Marks of Abnormally Undersized Barrels," 4 *Forensic Sci.* 43 (1974).

Sinha, et al., "Direct Breech Face Comparison," 4 *J.Pol.Sci. & Admin.* 261 (1976).

Sinha, et al., "Misleading Firing Pin Impressions," *Identif.News*, Nov. 1976, p. 6.

Stahl, et al., "Forensic Aspects of Tear–Gas Pen Guns," 13 *J.For.Sci.* 442 (1968).

Starrs, "Once More unto the Breech: The Firearms Evidence in the Sacco and Vanzetti Case Revisited," 31 *J.For.Sci.* 630 (1986) (part I); 31 *J.For.Sci.* 1050 (1986) (part II).

Stebbins, *Pistols—A Modern Encyclopedia* (1961).

Townsend, "Identification of Rifled Shotgun Slugs," 15 *J.For.Sci.* 173 (1970).

Van Amburgh, "Common Sources of Error in the Examination and Interpretation of Ballistics Evidence," 26 *Boston U.L.Rev.* 207 (1946).

Wilbur, *Ballistic Science for The Police Officer* (1977).

Wilson, "The Identification of Extractor Marks on Fired Shells," 29 *J.Crim.L. & Criminol.* 724 (1939).

Wolten and Nesbitt, "On the Mechanism of Gunshot Residue Particle Formation," 25 *J.For.Sci.* 533 (1980).

Chapter 7

ARSON AND EXPLOSIVES*

I. INTRODUCTION

II. BASICS OF ARSON AND EXPLOSIVES INVESTIGATIONS

III. INVESTIGATIVE ASPECTS

IV. LABORATORY ANALYSIS

* The authors express their appreciation to John J. Lentini of Applied Technical Services, Inc., for his comprehensive assistance, and Charles R. Midkiff, Jr., for his unstinting advice and review of this chapter.

397

I. INTRODUCTION

§ 7.01 Scope of the Chapter

The trial of an arson prosecution as well as one relating to the criminal use of explosives are alike in their considerable reliance on both investigative details and the analytical procedures of the forensic laboratory. Circumstantial evidence plays a larger role in such prosecutions than almost anywhere else in the criminal law. The reality of the destruction wrecked by fire and explosives presents unique problems in organizing both the prosecution and the defense of trials resulting from such, often catastrophic events.

Fire and explosions are allied in a number of ways. Both may occur accidentally or by criminal design. A fire may cause an explosion and an explosion may result in a fire. Crimes committed through the device of fire or explosives tend to be surreptitious in nature, frequently happening without the presence or the survival of witnesses.

This chapter is designed as a primer for the trial attorney to the law and science of fire and explosives investigations and trials. Materials have also been drawn from the civil side since many of the applicable legal principles are equally relevant in civil trials, particularly those involving insurance claims where the defense is arson.

This chapter is subdivided so that the novel terminology of arson and explosives is addressed first, followed by an explanation of the rudiments of fire and explosives. The complex myth-laden tasks of the fire investigator are surveyed prefatory to an elaboration on the varied services of the crime laboratory in supporting these investigative efforts. In recognition of the real potential that death may ensue from fire or explosives or that the cause and manner of death may be masked in such a case, a section is devoted exclusively to the role of the forensic pathologist and supporting professionals in piecing together the puzzles arising from the discovery of a body at a fire or explosion scene. The subsection headed "Evidence of Arson and Explosives" is not duplicated in any other single volume in the legal literature. It analyzes problems arising from ambiguous and confusing statutory phraseology, the incessant quest for a solution to the search warrant requirement in arson and explosives investigations and the proper function of the expert witness at the trial of an arson or explosives charge.

§ 7.02 Glossary of Arson and Explosives Terminology

1. ARSON

Accelerant: A material used to initiate or promote the spread of a fire. Flammable liquids are the most common accelerants.

Alligatoring: Large, shiny blisters of char which may indicate a fast moving, rapidly burning fire. See checkering.

Backdraft: An explosion or rapid burning of heated gases resulting from the introduction of oxygen, such as when air is admitted to a building heavily charged by smoke from a fire which has depleted its oxygen content.

Burning rate: The rate at which the surface of a pool of burning liquid recedes. (Gasoline has a burning rate of about one-quarter inch per minute.)

Char depth: (Depth of charring) The depth to which the pyrolysis action of fire has converted an organic material (wood) to its volatile fractions and charcoal.

Checkering: Small, dull blisters of char which may indicate a slow burning fire. See alligatoring.

Combustion: Occurs when a combustible material (one that can be burned) and a supporter of combustion (one that can stimulate burning) are brought together and the temperature raised to the point of ignition.

Conflagration: A major fire usually covering a wide area and which has the capacity to cross fire barriers such as streets.

Exothermic: Occurs when more heat is generated by a chemical reaction than that necessary to break the molecular bonds. An endothermic reaction is the reverse.

Fire load: The amount of combustible material in a room on a per square foot basis.

Fire, (flame, or ignition) point: The lowest temperature at which the vapors from a volatile liquid will ignite and burn continuously. American Society of Testing and Materials standard.

Flash point: The lowest temperature at which the vapors from a volatile liquid will ignite momentarily in the presence of a flame. American Society of Testing and Materials standards should control.

Flaming fire: One in which a flame is evident, such as where gas is burning. See glowing fire.

Flashback: Occurs when the fire from a flammable liquid returns from the source of ignition back to the flammable liquid container.

Flashover: A stage in the development of a contained fire in which all exposed surfaces reach ignition temperature at or about the same time causing the rapid spread of the fire.

Gas Chromatography: A laboratory method for the separation of complex mixtures by an instrument called a gas chromatograph to produce a chromatogram, which by comparison with ASTM chromatogram standards, enables tentative identification of a suspect sample.

Ghost marks: Localized spalling on floor tiles left by the partial dissolution of tile adhesives by flammable substances.

Glowing fire: One which is characterized by the absence of any flame but the presence of very hot materials on the surface of which combustion is continuing. Example a charcoal or wood fire.

Ignition temperature: The temperature at which a fuel will ignite on its own without any additional source of ignition.

Petroleum distillates: By-products of the refining of crude oil. Various types exist:

low boiling: very volatile mixtures of hydrocarbons.

Examples: petroleum ether, gasoline, cigarette lighter fluid, Naphtha.

medium boiling: some flammable liquids such as paint thinners, charcoal starters.

high boiling: combustible liquids, like fuel oils.

Examples: Kerosene, fuel oil, diesel fuel.

Plant: An intentional means of starting a fire with or without delayed ignition mechanisms.

Pyrolysis: The chemical decomposition of matter into new compounds through the action of heat.

Spalling: Chipping or crumbling of a concrete or masonry surface that may be caused by the effects of heating, by mechanical pressure, or a combination of them.

Trailers: Paths of rapidly combustible materials, such as toilet paper or film, used by an arsonist to spread a fire rapidly throughout a structure.

Vented itself: Occurs when a fire has destroyed windows or burned an opening in the roof or walls or otherwise gained a source of oxygen from outside the burning structure.

2. EXPLOSIVES

Binary: A mixing of two substances to form an explosive. The substances may be both non-explosive, explosive or a combination of the two.

Blast pressure effect: Occurs in an explosion when expanding gases exert pressure on surrounding atmosphere, rushing away from the point of detonation in a circular pattern, smashing and shattering objects in its path, until it diminishes to nothing at a distance.

Blasting agent: A chemical mixture, insensitive to shock, friction or impact, usually ammonium nitrate and a fuel such as oil. They are detonated when initiated by a booster.

Bomb: Combines an explosive with a fusing or detonating device, such as a blasting cap.

Booster: (Also called a primer) An explosive which provides the detonation link in the explosive train between the sensitive primary explosive (blasting cap) and the comparatively insensitive main charge (high explosive).

Brisance: A shattering shock effect of very rapidly detonating thermal decomposition. Explosives are sometimes rated as to the intensity of their brisance. Plastic explosives and nitroglycerin have high brisance.

Combustion: Rapid oxidation that generates heat and light but does not generate sufficient gases to produce a pressure wave.

Deflagration: A very rapid oxidation producing heat, light, and a pressure wave that can have a disruptive effect on the surroundings. This is an oxidation process that takes place at the surface of the reacting fuel (whether vapor or solid). This process can proceed at speeds of up to 1,000 meters per second.

Detonating cord: Acts to detonate a charge of high explosives in the same manner as a blasting cap. The detonating cord with its high explosive core may be tied around, threaded through, or knotted inside explosives to cause them to detonate.

Detonation: An extremely rapid reaction that generates very high temperates and an intense pressure/shock wave that produces violently disruptive effects. This process occurs through the reacting material at speeds in excess of 1,000 meters per second, as the shock wave is transmitted at supersonic speeds.

Explosion: The sudden and rapid escape of gases from a confined space, accompanied by high temperature, violent shock and loud noise. Classified as diffuse or concentrated.

Explosive: A chemical material which produces an explosion or detonation by means of a very rapid, self-propagating transformation of the material into more stable substances, accompanied by the liberation of heat and the formation of gases.

Explosive Train: A series of explosives specifically arranged to produce a desired outcome, usually to proceed from a fuse initiated system to initiation of an insensitive high explosive.

Griess test: A chemical test for nitrogenous compounds involving diazotization (nitrogen addition) of sulfamic acid and coupling with alpha-napthylamine to form a red water soluble azo-dye.

Infernal machine: A bomb, disguised as some innocuous object, rigged to detonate at a certain happening (the opening of a package) or at a certain time.

Safety fuse: Detonates explosives non-electrically by transmitting a flame at a continuous and uniform rate to a non-electric blasting cap.

———

II. BASICS OF ARSON AND EXPLOSIVES INVESTIGATIONS

§ 7.03 The Arson and Explosives Problem

1. ARSON

The United States has seen a startling upsurge in the incidence of arson and in its cost to the American public. In 1991 alone, a total of 86,147 arson offenses were reported nationwide to the F.B.I.'s Uniform Crime Reports averaging $11,980 per incident. The property value damaged by arson totaled $8.32 billion. During 1991, the estimated number of arson arrests totaled 20,000. Arson is predominantly a crime committed by white males, with 87% of all arrestees in 1991 being males and 77% being white.[1]

Arson is the most recent addition to the F.B.I.'s Crime Index, permanently categorized as the eighth Index crime when Congress passed the Anti–Arson Act of 1982. DeHaan[2] has estimated that 40% of all fires in structures are caused by arson, requiring a much greater degree of diligence in the investigation of all fires in buildings or other structures.

The increase in the commission of arson is outdistancing its arrest and conviction rates. Nationwide, the arson arrest rate was but 17% of offenses reported in 1984. Arson investigations are difficult to conduct since typically no witnesses to the crime exist. In addition, it is not always possible to establish a motive, victim, or sometimes even the occurrence of a crime, when initially dealing with suspicious fires. Moreover, investigation is hampered by the destruction caused by a fire and the damage occasioned in extinguishing it. Common sense indicates that flammable liquids, the major tool of arson, will evaporate if an investigation is not performed promptly and with due circumspection. The confusion about the investigative jurisdiction of police and fire officials, and the special prosecutorial problems engendered by the need to rely on circumstantial evidence combine to frustrate efforts to effectively investigate fires and explosions of suspicious origin. Arson reporting immunity laws, together with a model statute from the alliance of American insurers are intended to encourage greater reporting from insurance companies to law enforcement agencies so as to develop all the available facts for investigative purposes.[3]

One of the aids available to arson investigators is a computer-based arson information management system (AIMS) developed by the US Fire

§ 7.03

1. United States Department of Justice, *Sourcebook of Criminal Justice Statistics 1992* (1993).

2. DeHaan, "Training of Arson Investigators: Common Sense from the Laboratory," 28 *J.For.Sci.* 824, 825 (1983).

3. Icove & Gilman, "Arson Reporting Immunity Laws," *FBI Law Enf.Bull.* 15 (June 1989).

Administration and the International Association of Arson Investiga-tors.[4] The system can provide instant access to many pertinent facts important in an arson investigation, i.e., insurance information, property history and name files. The AIMS is designed to run on a variety of microcomputers. In addition, an AIMS Users Manual is available which can be combined with a suitable data base manager to allow implementa-tion of AIMS in other computers.

The problem of juvenile arsonists is a noticeable phenomenon re-flected in arson statistics. 45.3% of all arson arrests in 1991 involved persons under the age of 18, over 65% involved persons under 25.

2.   EXPLOSIVES

The use of explosives has been a favorite of persons who wish to terrorize. In 1881, Tsar Alexander II of Russia was torn apart by a bomb thrown at his feet. In the capitals of Europe near the end of the nineteenth century, anarchists made several bomb throwing attempts on heads of state. In 1892, following an explosion in the attempted assassi-nation of the State Prosecutor of Paris, Alphonse Bertillon's anthropo-morphic system of identification enabled the police to arrest the perpe-trator, a man named Koenigstein who pretended to be one Ravachol.

Lately, explosives have become the stock in trade of revolutionary groups who claim to have political justification for their wantonly terrorist acts. The I.R.A., the Red Brigade, Black September have all maintained a political campaign while using explosives to kill and maim. Letter bombs, book bombs and similar infernal machines have been the scourge of those who are the enemies of these revolutionaries.

Others too, motivated less by political concerns than by other interests, have employed explosives for their perfidious purposes. In 1949, Albert Guay and his two accomplices blew a Quebec Airways DC–3 out of the air killing twenty-three passengers among whom was Guay's heavily insured wife. In 1955, John Gilbert Graham killed his mother and forty-three other passengers on a United Air Lines plane out of Denver to repay her for refusing to remain with him during Thanksgiv-ing. Both Guay and Graham paid the ultimate penalty.

George Metesky, the "Mad Bomber" of New York City, put that city under siege in 1956 when his homemade bombs exploded in theaters, subways and other public places, quite fortuitously not killing anyone. His rampage sought vengeance against the firm that had fired him in 1931.

Most recently, we have seen the use of explosives in the New York bombing of the World Trade Center in early 1993. This was one of the first cases of waged terrorism of this magnitude taking place in the United States.

---

4. Sege, "The USFA–IAAI Information Management System," 35 *Fire & Arson*   *Inv.* 5 (Dec. 1984).

Explosives serve multiple, invidious purposes in criminal hands. They kill randomly and in large numbers. And they put the community of law abiding citizens in a state of panic.

The most detailed, national statistics on the problem of explosive use in criminal incidents are provided by the annual reports of the Treasury Department's Bureau of Alcohol, Tobacco and Firearms. Its 1991 report indicates that explosives were implicated in the deaths of seventy-five persons that year and in the injury of 695 persons nationwide. Property damaged by explosives was estimated to be in excess of twenty-seven million dollars. The total number of bombing incidents for 1991 numbered 1585 with California, Florida and Illinois being ranked highest among the states.

Overall the total number of criminal bombings reported in 1991 increased 24.3 percent from those of 1990, while deaths increased seventeen percent as well as notable increases in the amount of personal injuries and property damage from 1990.

The A.T.F. figures may be misleading because the number of unreported incidents may well outdistance the total reported. This possibility arises from the fact that the reporting is entirely voluntary.

§ 7.04　The Fundamentals of Fire

Although arson is one of the most expensive and troublesome crime problems in the United States today, the action of fire is still poorly understood or even misunderstood by many people, including some firefighters and fire investigators. Fire or combustion consists of a number of simultaneous chemical reactions involving the oxidation process. The three primary factors necessary for sustained combustion, as represented in the fire triangle,[1] are oxygen, fuel, and heat. Oxygen is added to a combustible compound or fuel which, in the presence of heat, breaks down and recombines with the oxygen to form new compounds. Fire is generally viewed by non-experts as a destructive phenomenon, but from a chemical point of view it is a transformation process.

The term combustion encompasses any exothermic (heat producing) reaction in the presence of oxygen but it is often erroneously considered as synonymous with fire. The kinds of combustion properly known as fire are rapid oxidations which take the form of flaming fires or glowing fires. Other types of oxidation are much slower processes, such as the rusting of iron and the drying of oxidizing oil paints.

The existence of flames shows that the combustion of a gaseous fuel is taking place. A flaming fire can therefore, only occur with a gaseous fuel. Consequently, a liquid must be vaporized or volatilized to a gas before it can burn with a flame. If during a fire the volatilization is

§ 7.04

1. The fire triangle is a basic concept in arson investigation. Some writers have proposed a fire tetrahedron whose fourth side would be a self-sustaining chain reaction.

stopped, the flaming combustion will cease.[2] An important and measurable property of liquid fuels is the flash point, the lowest temperature of the liquid at which enough volatilization will take place to produce an ignitable vapor near its surface.

Solid fuels, such as wood, cannot be volatilized, but when a solid fuel is heated and pyrolysis occurs, the fuel necessary for flaming combustion is produced. Pyrolysis is a process whereby a solid fuel, when heated to elevated temperatures, experiences irreversible chemical changes resulting in decomposition of the solid and the creation of new compounds which did not exist in the unheated sample.[3]

Glowing fires occur when solid fuels cannot be pyrolyzed to produce a sufficient quantity of flammable gases to sustain a flame. The reaction takes place at the surface of the solid, continuing until the fuel is exhausted. The reaction rate is limited by the surface-to-volume ratio of the fuel and the availability of oxygen. Pyrolyzable solid fuels such as cloth, wood, and paper may undergo glowing combustion when, for example, access to air is limited. This sort of glowing fire is often called smoldering. If the smoldering fire gains access to a better supply of oxygen the reaction rate can increase, producing more heat, which may be sufficient to allow for flaming combustion.

Each fuel has an associated ignition temperature, indicating the degree of heat needed to initiate combustion. The ignition temperature is always much higher than the flash point. The ignition temperature of gasoline varies up to 495 degrees F., whereas its flash point is about $-40°$ F. But fuel, even at the right temperature, and in the presence of an ample supply of oxygen will not suffice for combustion without a source of energy adequate to ignite the fuel. Igniters used by arsonists to create the necessary heat source include electrical devices left in the "on" position, timers connected to heating devices, cigarettes, matches, candles and incendiary devices, like a Molotov cocktail.

The heat given off during a fire is known as the heat of combustion which, being higher in temperature than the heat required for ignition, adds enough energy so that the fuel continues to overcome the internal energy holding the molecules together allowing the fuel to break down and recombine with oxygen forming new compounds and producing more heat. The reaction continues to regenerate itself indefinitely in this manner as long as fuel and oxygen are available.

2. This may be illustrated in several ways. Recently this was observed with the combination of granular swimming pool chlorine and brake fluid. See, Kirkbride & Kobus, "The Explosive Reaction Between Swimming Pool Chlorine and Brake Fluid," 36 *J.For.Sci.* 902 (1991).

3. Traces of flammable or combustible compounds are sometimes left as the result of pyrolysis and are not necessarily indicative of arson, confusing the investigative process. For example, wood after being burned may leave traces of turpentine. Another example of "innocent accelerants" is the residue of kerosene or diesel-like compounds detectable in asphalt products. Lentini & Waters, "Isolation of Accelerant-Like Residues from Roof Shingles Using Headspace Concentration," 6 *Arson Analysis Newsltr.* 48 (May 1982).

The fuel in an ordinary fire is an organic compound, often a hydrocarbon. Fires of carbonaceous materials always produce carbon dioxide, CO_2. Other combustion products are carbon monoxide, CO, and oxides of sulfur and nitrogen, SO and NO. Additionally, plastics which contain nitrogen, such as polyurethane will produce hydrogen cyanide gas, HCN, and plastics containing chlorine, such as PVC, will produce hydrogen chloride, HCL, and phosgene, COCL. As an organic material such as wood, paper, gasoline, or oil is consumed, a large volume of these gases is formed. These products of combustion should not be confused with the gases produced by heat alone, which are the source of the flame.

If a fire is to continue to burn, the fire triangle must continue to exist and the heat must be transferred to new fuel sources while an oxygen supply is maintained.[4]

§ 7.05 The Chemistry of an Explosion

A chemical explosion results in a very rapid transformation of unstable compounds or mixtures into stable substances accompanied by the liberation of gas and of energy in the form of heat. An explosive, as that term is used in this chapter, cannot be self-initiating. It must be caused to explode generally either by heat or by shock. While an explosive must not be self-initiating, it must be self-sustaining, so that its action will continue throughout the entire explosive charge once it has been initiated at any point within it.

The chemistry of an explosion is akin to that of a fire. Just as is the case with the burning of fuel oil or gasoline, an explosion is predicated on the oxidation of hydrogen, nitrogen and sulfur in a two-tiered reaction. But the process would be too slow to have the blast effect of an explosion without either a mixing of substances, as in the case of gunpowder, which have carbon, hydrogen and an oxidant which will upon decomposition, release oxygen or by a combination of the fuel and oxidizer into a single compound like nitroglycerin or TNT.

Chemical explosions, as with fire, require fuel, oxygen and initiation.[1] This explosion triangle is the equivalent of the fire triangle, but unlike the burning of a combustible in a fire, an explosive contains its own oxidizer. The potassium nitrate in black powder is such an oxidizing agent as is ammonium nitrate in ANFO. In the manufacture of explosives, the mixing of compounds is designed to release and realign oxygen so as to enable it to be used as an oxidizing agent. For example, nitroglycerin is produced by treating glycerin with nitric acid (HNO_3) in the presence of sulfuric acid (H_2SO_4). Acids rich in oxygen are also used in the manufacture of TNT and RDX.

---

4. Heat may be transferred by conduction, convection, or radiation, or by combination of the three. Heat is transferred to objects with which it is in contact by conduction. Transfer by the movement of hot gases is known as convection. The radiation of heat waves from hot objects or flames will heat other objects at a distance.

§ 7.05

1. Not all explosives require oxygen, however. For example, heavy metal azides or acetylides do not require oxygen.

Once the fuel and the oxygen have been added to an explosive, upon initiation, the third leg of the triangle is complete. Heat or shock will detonate an explosive. Gunpowder, for example will explode when confined under the influence of a heat-producing spark, but dynamite, TNT and RDX, being much less sensitive, require detonation by shock.

§ 7.06 Types of Explosives

A vast assemblage of explosives exists. The 1985 scheduling of regulated explosives by the Treasury Department's Bureau of Alcohol, Tobacco and Firearms lists hundreds of them.[1] They can be classified in a number of different ways. According to the source of their manufacture, explosives can be considered to be commercial, military or improvised (also known as homemade). In crimes involving the use of explosives, improvised explosives outstrip all the rest by a wide margin.

1. LOW EXPLOSIVES

When an explosive reaction is initiated, the speed of the reaction will vary depending on the explosive used. Although there is no precise line of demarcation, if the reaction occurs at a rate of up to 3500 meters per second, the explosive is described as a low explosive which is said to deflagrate rather than to detonate. If the speed of the reaction is greater than 1000 meters per second, the explosive is termed a high explosive which is said to detonate rather than to deflagrate.

The low explosives that are usually involved in criminal enterprises use black or smokeless powders. Black powder, usually combining the oxidizing agent potassium nitrate with much smaller quantities of sulfur and charcoal, can be confined in a pipe or other container and detonated by a fuse or a blasting cap as is illustrated in Fig. 1. Smokeless powder may be either single base, involving nitrocellulose only or double base, adding 30 to 40% nitroglycerin to nitrocellulose. A criminal desiring to use this more potent smokeless powder in improvised bombs can easily obtain it by cracking open shotgun shells, or by purchase of containers of powder for reloading purposes and inserting it into a pipe which is closed at both ends and to which a fuse is attached.

Another low explosion can result from the ignition of gaseous fuels in combination with atmospheric oxygen. Natural gas leaks, whether intentional or unintentional, can result in such explosions. Other combustible gases can produce a similar explosive effect as long as the gas to air mixture is within the upper and lower explosive limits of the particular gas when ignited. Similarly, many solids which have poor burning power or none at all in a solid state will explode when diffused into the air as minute, dust-like particles, so long as the right air-particle mixture obtains and ignition occurs. Coal, aluminum, magnesium, grain and flour have this capacity when in the form of dust.

---

§ 7.06

1. 53 Fed.Reg. 52561–52562 (12/28/88) effective 1/1/89. This list is not all inclusive, but does include blasting agents and detonators, which are within 18 U.S.C.A. § 841(c).

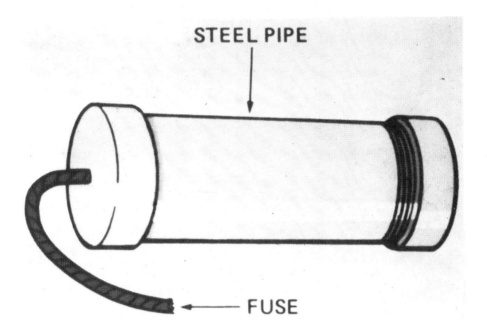

Fig. 1. Drawing of an improvised pipe bomb with two capped ends and fused from one end. A bomb of this type would ordinarily be made with black or smokeless powder.

An explosion which leaves no trace of a crater signals an explosion of a gaseous nature. The blowing out of walls on all sides and the equal distribution of explosive forces on all sides are other signs of a gaseous explosion.

2.   HIGH EXPLOSIVES

High explosives can be subdivided into those that are so insensitive to heat, friction and shock that they require initiation by another, more sensitive explosive either contained in a blasting cap, a primer charge or in a fuse-like detonating cord. Such explosives are called secondary explosives and include dynamite, TNT, PETN and RDX. The primary explosives are those which initiate the secondary explosive. In this category are lead azide, lead styphnate, silver azide, nitrogen triodide and mercury fulminate. The sensitivity of these explosive charges makes them exceedingly dangerous to use in improvised bombs. Based upon the functions performed by them, the ingredients in multi-component explosives are classed as explosive bases, combustibles, oxygen carriers, antacids and absorbents. Combustibles and oxygen are added to achieve oxygen balance, whereas the explosive base releases heat energy upon detonation by heat or shock. The antacid stabilizes an explosive while in storage and an absorbent absorbs a liquid explosive base. See Figure 2. Some of these high explosives of the secondary type are:

Fig. 2. An improvised pipe bomb containing dynamite with an electrically operated blasting cap.

A. DYNAMITE

Dynamite, derived from the Greek word for power, was first commercially produced by Alfred Nobel, who later established the Nobel Prizes. The composition of dynamite has changed markedly from what it was when produced by Nobel in the late 19th century. Then it was essentially nitroglycerin and an inert filler such as kieselguhr (diatomaceous earth). As commercially produced today, dynamite is more heavily reliant upon ethylene glycol dinitrate (EGDN) than NG since EGDN is less sensitive, and therefore easier to handle than nitroglycerine. Moreover, cold weather problems arise in using NG but the addition of EGDN reduces the freezing temperature of dynamite to give it a more all-climate use.

Straight dynamite is today's equivalent of the kieselguhr dynamite of Alfred Nobel. It has high brisance and contains sodium nitrate as an oxidizer for a combustible material on which the NG/EGDN is absorbed. If ammonium nitrate replaces part of the NG and sodium nitrate, the dynamite is called ammonia or "extra" dynamite. Ammonia dynamite is widely used commercially and has lower detonation velocity and is less sensitive than straight dynamite.

Straight dynamite is classified according to an equivalence to dynamite containing only a percentage of NG as the explosive. It is usually manufactured in weight strengths of from 20 to 60 percent. A 60 percent grade contains nearly three times as much NG as a 20 percent grade. But the blasting strength of a 60 percent grade is only one and a half times that of a 20 percent grade, in view of the sodium nitrate and carbonaceous fuel added to it.

Gelignite is a European generic name for a type of gelatin dynamite, used in underground mining which is a spongy-type gelatinous mixture of nitrocellulose, known as guncotton, and nitroglycerin. Gelatin dynamites are much more water resistant than straight dynamite. Blasting gelatin is the most powerful of commercial dynamites.

Dynamite is generally packaged in round cartridges of wax-coated paper or cardboard. The NG is sometimes seen to exude through the dynamite cylinder as the dynamite ages. Being an oil, NG can be readily absorbed by the skin and will cause a headache upon contact with it. Dynamite can be desensitized if the oxidants, such as sodium nitrate and ammonium nitrate, which it contains absorb water. Industry standards require at least 12 percent NG for it to deserve the label dynamite. The detonating velocity of dynamite can be up to 7700 meters per second.

B. RDX

RDX,[2] first synthesized by Henning for medical purposes, was developed by the British for military uses during World War II. RDX, also known as hexogen or cyclonite, belongs to the nitramines, in which a nitro group is bonded to a nitrogen atom. It is a very powerful explosive, second only to NG in strength among commonly used explosives. RDX mixed with motor oil and filler/binder materials becomes a plastic putty-like material known in the U.S. military as Composition C–4. The consistency allows C–4 to be molded around an object and therefore more effective for demolition than rigid explosives like TNT. The inhaling of RDX dust may cause symptoms analogous to epilepsy and amnesia.

C. TNT

TNT (2, 4, 6–trinitrotoluene) is a nitro compound which is derived from toluene, a petroleum product, which has many legitimate uses. When TNT is mixed with RDX, it is known as cyclotol. When a desensitizer is added to the mixture, it becomes Composition B. TNT was a widely used explosive, alone and in combination with other explosives, in the munitions produced during World War II.

In view of its stability in storage and under varying temperature conditions, it is a widely used military explosive. Moisture does not affect it. Its detonation velocity is about 6900 meters per second, which gives it a high brisance. TNT is an ingredient in explosive mixtures like pentolite and composition B, a mixture of RDX and TNT with the

2. A British acronym for Research De-   Explosive.
partment Explosive or Royal Demolition

addition of 1% wax. It is also used in primer charges for use with blasting agents.

D. PETN (PENTAERYTHRITOL TETRANITRATE)

PETN, a nitrate ester,[3] is an ester of tetrahydroxylic alcohols. When combined with TNT, it is called pentolite and is used by the military in small caliber projectiles and grenades. It is used as a priming compound for detonators, as a base charge in blasting caps and as the core for detonating cord, commercially known as Primacord. Its rapid action in a detonating cord enables it to be used to detonate a number of separate, but interconnected, explosions almost simultaneously. It can be formed into flexible, waterproof explosive sheets, such as Du Pont's Detasheet, and used as a booster in blasting caps. Like most organic explosive compounds, PETN is soluble in acetone.

E. BLASTING AGENTS

In the mid–1950's, with the development of AN–FO (ammonium nitrate mixed with fuel oil) dry blasting agents came of age and AN–FO began to overtake the use of dynamite in many commercial applications. In the 1960's, a denser slurry blasting agent was forthcoming and this too has made inroads on dynamite usage.

A blasting agent is defined as any material or mixture, containing a fuel and an oxidizer and in which none of the ingredients is classified separately as an explosive. To be a blasting agent, the finished product cannot be susceptible to detonation by a No. 8 test blasting cap.[4] The constituents of blasting agents are generally inorganic nitrates (i.e. ammonium nitrate) and carbonaceous fuels but may also contain powdered aluminum or ferrosilicon. AN–FO is customarily mixed in proportions of 94 percent ammonium nitrate and six percent fuel oil.

Blasting agents, being very insensitive to heat or shock (thus not cap sensitive) must be detonated by a primer charge of a high explosive. Where the charge diameter is six inches or more, dry blasting agents can reach a confined detonation velocity of more than 12,000 feet per second. Blasting agents are economical when compared to other explosives and are safe during storage, handling or transportation. But the presence of ammonium nitrate prevents them from being moisture proof, unless they are packaged in protective plastic bags.

Dry blasting agents have been supplemented by the production of slurries or water gels. These contain high proportions of ammonium nitrate, some of which is in an aqueous solution. Slurry blasting agents contain non-explosive sensitizers or fuels like carbon, sulfur or aluminum and are not sensitive to blasting caps. When a slurry contains any

---

3. Op. cit. supra note 1.

4. A No. 8 blasting cap is one containing the equivalent of two grams of a mixture of 80 percent mercury fulminate and 20 percent potassium chlorate.

of several types of sensitizers, it can be initiated by a # 8 cap and is referred to as a cap-sensitive slurry. These are usually packaged in cartridges as direct replacements for dynamite. More significant today are cap-sensitive emulsions, also water based. They are blowing dynamite away. There is only one dynamite plant operating today in the United States and Canada.

In view of ammonium nitrate's widespread use in farming as a fertilizer as well as in blasting agents, an analytical procedure which reveals ammonium nitrate traces has not necessarily proved its use as a blasting agent.

3. EXPLOSIVES' ACCESSORIES

A. BLASTING CAPS

Blasting caps, being composed of sensitive explosives, are used to detonate less sensitive high explosives with a greater detonation velocity than that of the blasting cap. An electric blasting cap, either with a detonating fuse or inserted directly into an explosive cartridge, is commonly used in the commercial application of explosives. The electric blasting cap has two insulated leg wires connected to a bridge wire.

When current is applied to the leg wires, the bridge wire gives off heat igniting a flash charge of heat-sensitive explosive. The primer charge is set off by the flash charge which then detonates a base charge of high explosives. The primer and flash charges are sometimes combined. The initiation of the base charge detonates a detonating fuse or explosive. In an electric blasting cap, a delay mechanism calibrated to provide a time lapse, sometimes is used between the bridge wire and the primer charge.

A blasting cap and fuse combination can be used, in lieu of an electric blasting cap, to set off a high explosive. The cap contains a sensitive explosive, like PETN, while a safety fuse consists of a core of black powder covered by a water proofed textile shell.

Minute fragments of a blasting cap might be located among the explosive residues at the scene. Analysis has been effectively conducted by SEM.[5]

B. DETONATING FUSE

Detonating fuse, sometimes called detonating cord, has a core of high explosives, like PETN, in a waterproof plastic sheath. It can be detonated by a blasting cap. It is very insensitive to shock and impact. Detonating fuse performs satisfactorily even under wet conditions. Delay mechanisms can be employed to control its initiation. It is used to link a series of charges and provide essentially simultaneous initiation while using one cap.

5. Ueyama & Ishiyama, "The Characterization of Fragments from Electric Blasting Cap After Detonation by Scanning Electron Microscopy," 35 *For.Sci.Internat'l.* 219 (1988).

4.   THE MOLOTOV COCKTAIL

The Molotov cocktail is an incendiary device rather than a bomb or explosive since there is no chemical explosion when the bottle container is broken and the gasoline spreads and ignites.   Thus it is technically incorrect to call a Molotov cocktail a fire bomb as many states' statutes do.   On the other hand, a mechanical explosion may result from throwing a Molotov cocktail.

Molotov Cocktails are simple in design and execution.   A wick is placed through the opening of a frangible bottle which contains gasoline or other flammable filler.   The device is thrown after the wick is ignited and the breaking of the bottle spreads the gasoline over the combustible surface which the burning wick sets on fire.   A Molotov cocktail will work in air if the bottle is broken by an M–80 or M–100.   Ignition is essentially instantaneous with any type of Molotov cocktail.

The fillers used in a Molotov cocktail need not be limited to gasoline. Gasoline is sometimes mixed with fuel oil to give the burning greater staying power.   If a soap is added to gasoline, the mixture becomes what is known as napalm.   The inclusion of sulphuric acid with gasoline as a filler precludes the need for a wick since if the bottle is wrapped with a cloth saturated with potassium chlorate and sugar, the hypergolic reaction of the sulfuric acid with the potassium chlorate and sugar upon the bottle's breaking will produce a flame.   The flame will then ignite the gasoline vapor.

Another type of self-igniting incendiary device was developed in England during World War II.   At first known as a self-igniting phosphorus grenade, since the contents included white phosphorus, it later became more familiar as the No. 76 grenade.   Like a Molotov cocktail, the No. 76 grenade employed a glass bottle which, upon being broken, released the white phosphorus, benzine and water combination which would spontaneously ignite.

III.   INVESTIGATIVE ASPECTS

§ 7.07   Expert Qualifications

An expert witness in a criminal trial involving the use of explosives must have a basic grounding in the chemistry of explosives.   More than that, the expert must understand the materials used in the formation of explosives as well as the various ways in which explosives are interrelated and initiated.   The explosives expert should also have access to a library of explosive exemplars in order to have a standard reference to determine the exact nature of the explosive in question.[1]

Explosives experts are generally of two types, those who are attached to the bomb squad of the local police force or those whose regular employ is in the forensic laboratory, ordinarily as a chemist. In both cases, the expert should not merely be a theorist, but rather one whose capabilities include actual experience in the handling of explosives. Unlike the expert in the crime laboratory, the bomb squad's experts must be able to make a bomb scene secure from any further dangers from an exploded or unexploded bomb. In conjunction with this activity, this expert must be schooled in the procedures for locating, packaging and preserving evidence.

The expert witness in an arson case is one whose function determines his expertise. There are firefighters who are competent to testify on their observations when combatting a blaze. Their experience may enable them to express opinions on the causative features of the fire. Fire and arson investigators should be persons with more specialized talents than firefighters. Routinely, state fire marshals and local fire departments have trained specialists in both arson and fire investigations. However, police departments also have a distinct section defined as an arson investigations' squad or some similar appellation. Although the activities of the police and the fire departments in investigating the causes of fires may overlap and result in jurisdictional disputes on occasion, the National Fire Protection Association has recommended against the consolidation of the two forces.

The number of long term, full curriculum educational programs for fire and arson investigators, is few, but the National Fire Academy at the Federal Management Agency's National Emergency Training Center in Emmitsburg, Maryland has trained some 50,000 fire fighters, 10,000 of these in resident short courses at its site in Emmitsburg, Maryland and 40,000 in field training programs. The field training programs are supervised and supported by a fire training agency located in every state's government. A fire investigator's completion of such a training course augurs well for his expertise.

Affiliation with various organizations of persons knowledgeable in arson investigations is also some sign of an expert having a foundation for the expression of an opinion. The International Association of Arson Investigators,[2] the National Fire Protection Association,[3] the International Association of Fire Fighters[4] and various fire insurance companies have provided fire investigators with background reports, studies and other learning opportunities to sharpen their skills as experts. The various Batelle[5] institutes and centers have been in the forefront in

§ 7.07

1. *"The Detonator,"* a quarterly journal of the International Association of Bomb Technicians and Investigators, 1270 Friendship Lane West, Colorado Springs, Colo. 80904 provides much valuable information.

2. 5616 Bardstown Rd., P.O. Box 91119, Louisville, KY 40921.

3. Batterymarch Park, Quincy, Mass. 02269.

4. 1750 New York Avenue, N.W., Washington, D.C.

5. Battelle Memorial Institute.

developing programs to train arson investigators. To be truly expert, fire investigators should be at least on notice of these organizations and activities and, preferably, sharers in them and others like them.[6]

Specialized skills may be required in some arson investigations which will require the talents of persons who have more in depth understanding on a particular subject than the usual fire investigator possesses. Questions of electrical and mechanical engineering not uncommonly arise in the context of many fires. Fire investigators, although trained to have a broad based knowledge of all aspects of a fire investigation, are generally not sufficiently well schooled to express an opinion on coplex engineering or other specialized disciplines involved in the assessment of a particular fire.

Laboratory personnel who test the debris from a fire scene must have the academic and experiential training in chemistry sufficient for the instrumental and chemical tasks they perform. They must, therefore, be skilled in the recognition of the patterns on the chromatograms of gasoline, fuel oil and other flammable liquids which they are called upon to analyze and should follow recognized ASTM procedures in their analyses. Optimally, they should be acquainted with the processes by which petroleum products are refined for use as flammable hydrocarbons. These manufacturing processes are sufficiently well-documented for ready reference.[7]

§ 7.08 Arson Indicators

As circumstantial proof of the incendiary origin of a fire, arson investigators rely most heavily upon a rather amorphous group of so-called burn or arson indicators. Some of these indicators are observed during the course of the fire, such as the sight of black smoke spewing forth from a burning object. Black smoke is said to result from the burning of hydrocarbons.[1] A fire with a flame that is blinding white is said to demonstrate not only intense heat up to 1500 degrees C. but that the intense heat was fueled by an accelerant.[2] When a firefighter finds a blaze to be hotter than normal or to require an extraordinary amount of time to extinguish, this may also be considered as evidence that the fire was fueled by accelerants, either naturally on the premises or present with an incendiary intent.[3] Most arson signs, on the other hand, are not visible until the fire is under control. In this category are trailers, alligatoring of wood, depth of char and spalling, among many others.

The Center for Arson Prevention, Training and Analysis.
505 King St.
Columbus, Ohio 43201

6. Ferrall, "Arson Information: Who, What, Where?" 50 *FBI Law Enf.Bull.* 16 (May 1981).

7. Bland and Davidson, editors, *Petroleum Processing Handbook* (1967).

§ 7.08

1. People v. Brown, 104 Ill.App.3d 1110, 433 N.E.2d 1081 (1982).

2. Berry, "Characteristics and Behavior of Fire," 34 *Def.L.J.* 243 (1985).

3. Waters v. State, 174 Ga.App. 916, 331 S.E.2d 893, 895 (1985).

A few arson indicators need little explanation from an expert for the jury to comprehend their meaning. The removal of a householder's personal effects from the scene of a fire shortly before the fire occurs, although ambiguous, can be read as a sign of an incendiary intent on the part of the homeowner.[4] That a refrigerator in an occupied house which has been burned is found to be empty is also said to be, if not satisfactorily explained, evidence of arson.[5]

Other discoveries by a fire investigator may require the testimony of an expert to enlighten the jury as to their significance to a charge of arson. In this category are freshly drilled holes in the floors and the roof of a burned building which represent evidence of an effort to vent a fire by providing a ready upward route of travel for the fire which will increase the rapidity of its spread.[6] An untutored jury, left to its own devices, might not appreciate the import of such circumstantial evidence. This section is concerned with those arson indicators that tend to appear with greatest frequency among the cases and which seem to require some expertise by the witness who elaborates upon them.

1. ODOR

That many liquid accelerants and some solids do have recognizable odors cannot be gainsaid. Ammonia, for example, which arsonists may use to mask the aroma of other accelerants used by them, is readily detectable by its odor. The arson expert's problem comes in attempting to identify the traces of one or more accelerants as having been smelled at the fire scene and then, from the smell, to hypothesize one or more causes for the fire.

The olfactory sense is a most unreliable indicator of the suspicious nature of a fire or of the specific accelerant consumed in it. Gasoline, kerosene and other liquid accelerants do have a distinctive odor, but the odor of one accelerant can be mistaken for that of another, kerosene, say, for paint thinners. The error-prone nature of investigating the cause of a fire through recourse to the sense of smell was revealed in one case[7] during a courtroom demonstration on the cross-examination of a firefighter who claimed to have smelled ammonia and chloride of sulfur while he was combatting a fire. The defense attorney was permitted to test the firefighter by producing four containers which the witness was asked to smell and identify in turn. Shrewdly, the defense attorney had the witness inhale from the ammonia filled container first. This inhalation momentarily so dulled his sense of smell that the witness was disabled from identifying the contents of the other three containers. Concededly the demonstration was staged to benefit the defense but it

---

4. People v. Freeman, 135 Cal.App.2d 11, 286 P.2d 565 (1955).

5. Waters v. State, supra note 3.

6. Rogers v. State, 161 Tex.Crim.R. 536, 279 S.W.2d 97 (1955).

7. Gamm, "Defense Vs. Offense" or "The Bad Guys Vs. The Good Guys," 35 *The Fire and Arson Investigator* 33, 43 (1984).

also disclosed one of many serious flaws in type-casting liquid accelerants through the odors they produce.

The sense of smell can have meaningful investigative value in pinpointing the location where accelerants remain in the debris at the fire scene.   The human nose appears to be highly sensitive to the aromatic hydrocarbons, in gasoline and other vapors.   However, the nose suffers a loss of sensitivity due to olfactory fatigue after an extended exposure to a particular odor or to a variety of pungent odors.   Some persons might also have temporarily lost the ability to detect certain categories of odors, a condition known as hyposmia.   Another problem in using the human nose in investigating a fire arises from its inability to reach inaccessible locations where an examination might be fruitful.

In fire scene investigations, the nose is sometimes supplemented by a variety of instrumental flammable vapor detectors of a portable nature. These detectors, sometimes called sniffers,[8] operate on principles of catalytic combustion, flame ionization, thermal conductivity, infrared spectrophotometry or ultraviolet fluorescence.   These detectors cannot be considered as providing positive proof that a fire was ignited by accelerants and, in some cases, the instrument may only respond to a vapor, which might not be the vapor of a flammable liquid.[9]

2. BURN PATTERNS

In seeking the cause of a fire, the first concern is to locate its point or zone of origin.   Then the investigator will look for a plausible ignition source at that point or in that zone.   Burn patterns are the "linchpin of all fire investigation," and will alert the investigator to the point or zone of origin.[10]   These indicators may also provide a footing for an opinion concerning the speed of development, temperature and duration of the fire and its time of occurrence.   They may be helpful in demonstrating the presence of flammable liquids as well.

These signs, albeit often invaluable as leads, may be misleading. The ventilation in a room, the activities of firefighters, the falling of debris and the glowing (smoldering) nature of a fire before or after its extinguishment are factors which effect any decision on the point of a fire's origin and its cause.

Despite claims that the type of flammable liquid can be determined by the burn pattern, in a series of controlled tests involving both hardwood and sealed plywood flooring, it was found often difficult to obtain any pattern from the use of a flammable liquid alone.[11]   The

8. Burd, "Detection of Traces of Combustible Fluid in Arson Cases," 51 *J.Crim. L., Criminol. & P.S.* 263 (1960).

9. Juhala and Birr, "An Added Note of Caution on the Use of the Combustible Gas Detector (Sniffer)," 5 *Arson Analysis Newsletter,* 55 (Jan.1981).

10. Sandburg–Schiller v. Rosello, 119 Ill.App.3d 318, 74 Ill.Dec. 690, 456 N.E.2d 192 (1983).

11. Taylor, "Flammable and Combustible Liquid Characteristics in Certain Types of Fires," 37 *Fire & Arson Inv.* 45 (Sept. 1986).

study suggested that a major source of "pour patterns" might be plastic materials which melt and drip onto the surface. Burning of the plastics produces a char pattern which may appear to be due to the pouring of a flammable liquid.

According to the experience of one fire investigator, in some instances investigators have improperly hypothesized fire causes which have led to lawsuits and the escape of arsonists.[12] Misdiagnoses can occur when speculations are given as to the cause of a fire, but which are proved inaccurate when subject to controlled conditions. Examples of misdiagnoses are said to be using blistered wood as an indicator of the use of accelerants and using the color of the smoke as an indicator of the presence of a petroleum product.

Although the presence of burn patterns attributed to flammable liquids is frequently an indicator of arson, in tests on carpeting, patterns were observed which could erroneously be attributed to burns caused by flammable liquids.[13] In addition, the detection of "traces of hydrocarbons" is considered meaningless unless the hydrocarbons are specifically identified.

Among fire investigators some burn patterns are given more credence than others. The following discussion includes a number of most frequently encountered burn patterns.

A.   DEPTH OF CHAR; ALLIGATORING

Fire investigators in reconstructing a fire scene may consider the depth of charred wood and the alligatored appearance of it as indications of the point of origin of a fire and the fact that an accelerant was used. Such conclusions, drawn from depth of charring and alligatoring alone, are highly suspect.

Alligatoring is the description of the checkered or blistered pattern on the surface of partially burned wood which is caused by heat and burning. When the blisters are large and shiny, investigators will sometimes conclude that the fire was a fast-spreading fire, typical of an accelerant-fueled fire as in Fig. 3. If the blisters appear dull and baked, then the fire is said to have been slow-developing. Such findings are an unsafe method to determine the cause and spread of a fire. The size of the blistering is an unreliable sign because rapid burning sometimes produces the same blistering encountered by slow burning fires.[14] Adjoining boards in the same room have been shown to have had markedly different degrees of blistering under the influence of the same fire.

---

12. Ettling, "Are We Kidding Ourselves," 34 *Fire & Arson Inv.* 19 (June 1984).

13. Taylor, "Carpet, Wood Floor and Concrete 'Burn Patterns' Often Are Not From Flammable Liquids ... Are a Highly Misunderstood Aspect of Fire Investigation," 35 *Fire & Arson Inv.* 32 (March 1985).

14. Ettling, "Are We Kidding Ourselves," 34 *The Fire and Arson Investigator* 19 (June 1984).

Fig. 3. Alligatoring with distinct line at edge between burned and unburned areas typical of a fast burn from accelerants.

The char depth of burned wood is said to be a more accurate yardstick to the reconstruction of a fire scene than alligatoring. The char depth is the depth to which an organic compound (generally wood) has been converted into charcoal by the pyrolysis action of fire. The char rate of wood is quoted to be approximately one inch every forty-five minutes, but wood does not pyrolyze at a uniform rate. As charring occurs, the char itself forms an insulating barrier for the subsurface wood from the action of the fire, requiring progressively longer periods to char the wood at deeper levels.

Char depth can be easily measured using a gauge for that purpose. Since wood will shrink under the impact of heat and some char may flake off, it is imperative to take into account the original dimensions of the wood, not the charred remains alone. Measurements should be taken and charted at the same level throughout the room. The cautious fire investigator will take char depth measurements in the same room at a number of different levels, say at a waist high level, floor level and near the ceiling. In theory, the point of deepest charring can be assumed to be the low point of the fire and possibly also its place of origin.[15]

The depth of char has also been seen as evidence of the duration of a fire, giving an investigator a method of assaying how long a fire has been burning and the time when the fire was ignited. Extreme care must be exercised in making such assertions from char depth alone. Char depth can be used only as a guide to the duration of a fire, allowing ranges or approximations to be developed. A number of factors must be consid-

---

15. But to say the "depth of char will determine the exact origin" of the fire over-states its evidentiary value. See, Carroll, *"Physical and Technical Aspects of Fire Investigation,"* 95 (1979).

ered in weighing the value of char depth measurements. The amount of ventilation, the species of wood and its age (moisture content), the temperature of the fire, the presence of readily combustible materials at the point of deepest charring, the efforts of firefighters to extinguish a fire which skirted the area of deepest charring and whether paint or lacquer finishes have been applied to the wood are all matters that can have a direct effect on the char depth. The only really useful measurements of char depth are those in which the same species of wood in the same configuration are measured and compared.

The combustibility of wood is sometimes said to be in direct proportion to its moisture content. This is just another myth in the field of fire investigation. The moisture content of wood will vary from season to season and from place to place. The combustibility of wood varies with the species of the wood as well as its physical dimensions and shape. Moisture content is, except in rare instances, not a noteworthy factor in determining the combustibility of wood. Heat can, however, depending upon its duration and intensity cause a transformation of wood into pyrophoric carbon which, having an affinity for oxygen, will self-ignite.

B. Flashover—Flashback

A flashover must be distinguished from a flashback. A flashover occurs when a flaming fire's radiant heat becomes so intense that the ignition temperature of distant combustibles is reached—causing them to ignite. To the observer it would appear that the fire has leap-frogged from one place to another. A flashback occurs when the flaming fire has been extinguished and the debris and remnants are smoldering. During this period of glowing combustion, combustible gases are still being produced and if the circumstances are right and the ventilation adequate, the fire will re-ignite. It is often said that flashbacks are indicative of fires fueled by accelerants, but all fires are susceptible to such a response.

C. Multiple Fires

Multiple fires in different locations which are flaming simultaneously on the same premises are said to be a classic illustration of an incendiary fire. The assumption underlying such a position is that the multiple fires (sometimes denoted plants) were either separately ignited or were ignited from one source and spread to other sites using trailers. In either event, an incendiary act is indicated.

However, multiple fires can arise accidentally, for example, as a result of a flashback. When an accelerant is spilled and flows from one room into another where there is a source of ignition, as there is in a kitchen, the ignition in one room may cause the flame to flash back to the source of the spill creating two apparently separate fires in two different locations. Further, the falling of flaming debris in different locations during a fire may be misinterpreted as proof of multiple fires with an incendiary source.

D. TRAILER

A trailer, in the idiom of fire investigators, is a continuous path of highly flammable material directing a fire from one place to another to promote its rapid spread. Flammable liquids, newspaper, sawdust, toilet paper, black powder, motion picture film, string or rope soaked in oil, crepe paper, cotton batting and other flammables may be used. Signs that trailers have played a role can be seen on carpets and wooden floors where the burning of the trailer will leave a characteristic mark which can sometimes be traced to the source.

E. POUR PATTERN

When a fluid accelerant is poured on a floor, the burning of its vapors will leave a discernible outline on the floor around the outer edges of the liquid spill area. This outline, when observed after a fire has been controlled, is often called a pour pattern. This pour pattern is said to be a characteristic signature of an accelerant induced fire. See Fig. 4.

An accelerant which is poured on carpeting may leave a ring around the outside while leaving the pile of the inner part untouched, that is if the fire is extinguished before the carpet is consumed. The arsonist who is convicted in part on the evidence of a pour pattern probably is unaware that a liquid accelerant may protect the floor covering rather than damage it and that if the fuel does not raise the temperature of the floor covering to its ignition temperature, the floor on which the accelerant has been poured may suffer little or no damage from the fire.

F. V (INVERTED CONE) PATTERN; INVERTED V PATTERN

Usually fire burns upward spreading outward creating a V pattern. When the fire reaches a horizontal obstruction, it flows along it burning back downward towards its point of origin, being preceded by a smoke stained area followed by the fire charred portion. Furniture and chairs and similar wooden objects which are in the path of the upward thrust of the fire will evidence on their undersides, rather than their tops, a charring indicating that the fire was proceeding upward from beneath them. In this respect, wooden furniture will have a similar deflecting effect on the fire as the ceiling of a room.

Fig. 4. Pour patterns on floor of fire damaged premises.

The V formed by the upward movement of the fire will be wider at the topmost portion in the case of an accidental or naturally initiated fire, whereas the V will be substantially narrower when an accelerant is used to fuel the flame. The ventilation of the fire can drastically affect the width of the V. No exact standards exist to determine what width signifies an accelerant fueled fire as opposed to any other kind of fire.

The apex of the V pattern is sometimes erroneously assumed to be the point of origin of a fire. A ceiling light fixture, for example, which ignites dripping flaming material onto the floor below it may create a burned area in the floor which will flame upward enveloping and destroying the light fixture, masking the true origin of the fire.

An inverted V reflected on a wall is often taken as evidence of downward burning, demonstrating the ignition of the vapors of an accelerant which flashed downward scoring the wall.

Some fire investigators wrongly believe that fire propagates upward because it is searching for oxygen. For the same reason, when fire is observed to evacuate through an open window, the search for oxygen is said to be the reason. In truth, fire rises for the very simple reason that the hot gases generated by a fire, being lighter than the surrounding air, will progress upward. As these gases ascend, air is aspirated below them creating an oxygen rich environment below the hot gases. Any claimed expert who speaks of a fire's searching for oxygen as it rises gives good cause to doubt his credentials as an expert.

G. Low Burns

Heavy burning or charring at low points in a room or building is said to be unexpected in accidental fires since the thermodynamics of fire would be most likely to produce the most severe burning as the fire took its natural course and climbed upward. The discovery of low burns, therefore, is said to be evidence of an accelerant fueled fire as well as the fire's point of origin.

However, collapsing debris could just as readily be the basis for such low burns. Fiery drapes which fall on carpeting, lighting fixtures, particularly those with polystyrene light diffusers, which send fire to the floor in unanticipated and random locations and ignitable plastic plumbing pipes could just as readily be the source of low burns. Indeed, floor level burns are well-known to be produced by the effect of heat radiating floorward from intense fires in the ceiling areas of a room. In any event, the textbook action of a fire is a far cry from the reality of a fire scene where, fuel, wind and numerous other unpredictable factors play a significant role.

H. Spalling

Spalling can be described as the chipping or similar erosion of the surface of cement or masonry which is evidenced by a patched or crater-like appearance and which results from concrete's reaction to stress. Fire investigators routinely assert that spalling reflects the use of accelerants and that it occurs because the moisture within the concrete reacts violently to the intense heat produced by the ignition of accelerants at the site of the spall. Neither assertion has the force of scientific truth and, indeed, what limited scientific studies there are contradict these axiomatic refrains of fire investigators.

Smith's studies [16] are some evidence that wood can cause spalling even more assuredly than accelerants. That was not unforeseen since the most intense heat in an accelerant fueled fire is in the vapors above the fluid pool. And in a solid fuel fire the heat is directed downward. Canfield,[17] like Smith, found that under laboratory conditions, accelerants did not cause spalling. Using gasoline, kerosene, ethanol and methanol as accelerants he was unable to produce spalling of concrete even after preheating it with a propane torch and after dousing the fire with ice water—in an unsuccessful effort to induce stress.

Canfield [18] postulated that the type of aggregate in the concrete, not the heat from accelerants, caused spalling. A disagreement among experts exists, at least where the concrete is covered by, say, floor tiles. The aggregate which can be igneous, siliceous or calcareous, comprises 75 percent of concrete. Canfield said that the thermodynamic reaction, which is called spalling, is most likely to happen with calcareous aggregate but least likely to result from the igneous type. Until the necessary research data is forthcoming, it would seem that spalling depends upon a number of variables to a degree which is as yet unknown. The type of aggregate, the covering of the concrete (if any), the age of the concrete, the intensity of the heat (the source of which may be accelerants or falling debris) and, lastly, the moisture content of the concrete all seem to be instrumental in creating spalling.

The presence or absence of spalling is of little significance in and of itself. Most experts would concede that spalling is caused by heat, and therefore, spalling in some type of pattern may be significant. A trail of spalling on concrete may be just as informative as a trail of burning on carpet or wood. It is the pattern which is important, not the mere existence of spalled concrete.

§ 7.09   Electricity as a Cause of Fire

A fire may be ignited by electrical means when sufficient electrical energy exists to cause sustained ignition in a particular environment. For example, small areas of overheated wire or small arcs and sparks are of little consequence in the ignition of a solid material with a high ignition temperature, whereas the smallest discernible spark is a serious hazard in a case of a combustible gas or vapor.

Ignition by electrical means is caused by overcurrent, sparks, or arcs. The current a conductor should carry is limited so that minimal amounts of heat are generated. When these limiting currents are exceeded and a conductor is overloaded, the generation of heat becomes a hazard and over time the temperature of the conductor will rise, the rate of temperature increase depending on the degree of overcurrent. The

---

16. Smith and Mitchel, "Concrete Spalling Under Controlled Conditions," 32 *The Fire and Arson Investigator* 8 (1981). But one expert has attacked just about every aspect of the Smith and Mitchel study. See, Lentini, "A Documented Case of Ac-

clerant–Induced Concrete Spalling," 33 *The Fire & Arson Inv.* 30 (Dec. 1982).

17. Canfield, "Causes of Spalling Concrete at Elevated Temperatures," 34 *The Fire and Arson Investigator* 22 (June 1984).

18. Id.

temperature will rise to the conductor's melting point and when melting occurs the wire will sever and an arc will momentarily occur at this point.

Electric sparks and arcs are very hot and the temperature is very localized. A spark can be defined as the flow of electric current through a gas, as distinguished from an arc which is an electric current flowing through a vapor. A spark may cause a short circuit when, for example, a segment of electrical wiring is replaced with telephone wire. Once the switch is turned on and there is a current flow, sparks will occur causing a short circuit and, possibly, a fire.

When electrical failure is detected at the scene of a fire, it is exceedingly difficult to determine whether it was the cause or result of the fire. When an investigator locates the point of origin of a fire as being adjacent to a heating appliance in an area containing several electrical circuits, he cannot assume that either the appliance or electrical wiring was the source of ignition. Neither can it be assumed that evidence of a short circuit near the fire's point of origin indicates that the short circuit is the cause of the fire.[1] Tracking the location of short circuits in a fire scene can, however, aid in the determination of the point of origin, since once an arc occurs in a circuit, additional downstream arcing is unlikely.[2]

IV. LABORATORY ANALYSIS

§ 7.10 Explosive Traces From the Person

Organic explosive residues may be transferred to the hands in detectible amounts by the handling of explosives. The recovery of such residues from the hands is usually achieved with a cotton swab soaked in a solvent such as ether or acetone. To avoid loss of nitroglycerin (NG) from evaporation the used swabs should be placed immediately in a sealed container. Studies[1] have shown that the use of ether or acetone as a solvent results in raising the level of NG detectability since the extract tends to be contaminated by other materials removed from the hands. Ethanol or cyclohexane remove less of these extraneous materials and produce much better results than ether or acetone in recovering NG from the hands.

§ 7.09

1. It is more likely that the fire itself caused the short circuit to occur by burning away the insulation around the wires and allowing them to come into contact with each other. See also, Anderson, "Surface Analysis of Electrical Arc Residues in Fire Investigation," 34 *J.For.Sci.* 633 (1989).

2. See the elucidation of tracking the progress of a fire in a circuit or an appliance through the arcs in Lentini, "Appliance Fires: Determining Responsibilities," 39 *Fire & Arson Inv.* 52 (June 1989).

§ 7.10

1. Twibell, et al., "Assessment of Solvents for the Recovery of Nitroglycerine from Hands Using Cotton Swabs," 27 *J.For.Sci.* 792 (1982).

Once explosive residues have been successfully removed from the hands for testing, several analytical techniques are available for detection and identification. Early research efforts [2] resulted in the championing of gas chromatography with electron capture detection in view of its low range of detectability. Clean up procedures to separate out the interfering materials from hand swabs were proposed.[3] More recent studies have revealed that low nanogram and sub-nanogram levels of NG can be detected using capillary column gas chromatography with electron capture detection [4] and gas liquid chromatography with thermal energy analyzer detection.[5] Thermal energy is more suitable than electron capture detection since it is specific for the nitro (NO_2) group whereas electron capture responds to any electro-negative group such as chlorine.

The persistence of explosive residues on the hands has been a source of much scientific scrutiny. That commercial explosives of the nitrate ester class, like NG, are absorbed into the skin and not entirely removed by daily activities or mere handwashings is well recognized. Attempts have been made under controlled conditions to define precisely how long explosives will last on the hands. According to Twibell,[6] persistence, at the outset, depends upon whether the explosive handled was well-encased, sweating or simply in its raw form. If well-wrapped, little NG is transferred to the hands and detectable time will only be a few hours. Sweating explosives may leave traces detectable up to twelve hours after handling. In the case of raw explosives, a thirty hour period of persistence would not be unexpected. On the other hand, military explosives, like TNT and RDX, being less volatile than NG, will remain on the hands for longer periods than is the case with NG.[7] But TNT and RDX, being solids, will wipe off more readily than NG oil.

When NG is detected in the extract from a hand swab, there is still the potential that the source of the NG was not an explosive, such as dynamite, but other substances of a less criminal disposition. Double base smokeless gunpowder, for example, combines nitrocellulose with a range of 15 to 40 percent nitroglycerin. Firearm enthusiasts who hand load their own ammunition might conceivably show traces of NG on their hands. So too might the sufferers from angina pectoris who are on

2. Twibell, et al., "Transfer of Nitroglycerine to Hands During Contact with Commercial Explosives," 27 *J.For.Sci.* 783 (1982) which reports on a 1977 study.

3. Lloyd, "Clean-up Procedures for the Examination of Swabs for Explosive Traces by High–Performance Liquid Chromatography with Electrochemical Detection at a Pendent Mercury Drop Electrode," 263 *J.Chromatogr.* 391 (1983).

4. Douse, "Trace Analysis of Explosives in Handswab Extracts Using Amberlite XAD–7 Porous Polymer Beads, Silica Capillary Column Gas Chromatography with Electron–Capture Detection and Thin–Layer Chromatography," 234 *J.Chromatogr.*

415 (1982). See, Tranthim–Fryer, "The Application of a Simple and Inexpensive Modified Carbon Wire Adsorption/Solvent Extraction Technique to the Analysis of Accelerants and Volatile Organic Compounds in Arson Debris," 35 *J.For.Sci.* 271 (1990).

5. Douse, "Trace Analysis of Explosives at the Low Picogram Level Using Silica Capillary Column Gas Chromatography with Thermal Energy Analyser Detection," 256 *J. Chromatogr.* 359 (1983).

6. Op. cit. supra note 2 at page 789.

7. Twibell, et al., "The Persistence of Military Explosives on Hands," 29 *J.For. Sci.* 284 (1984).

a pharmaceutical regimen of nitroglycerin based tablets. That NG, in measurable quantities, can be transferred from cardiovascular tablets to the hands has been established.[8] In recognition of this fact, the finding of NG on the hands of a suspect is only presumptive, highly non-specific evidence of his handling an explosive, until all the circumstances for the presence of the NG are taken into account.

§ 7.11 Fire Scene Evidence

The laboratory analysis of fire debris for the presence of accelerants is of major importance in determining the cause of a fire. One study[1] indicated that in 62% of arson cases a flammable liquid accelerant was used and that, on laboratory analysis, gasoline was detected in 80% of 5758 arson cases. The crime laboratory, of necessity puts major emphasis upon seeking traces of such flammable fluids. That residues of flammable fluids will survive a fire, even a fire which totally destroys the premises, has been established.[2] Porous substances are ideal absorbents of flammable liquids. Soil will also retain traces of such liquids.[3] The purpose of laboratory analysis is to locate the residues of any flammable liquids, to assess the type of such fluid and to trace it to a particular manufacturer, where possible.

A dispute exists in the scientific community whether gasoline can be identified by manufacturer or by its grade, as premium or regular. The early literature stated the ability of the crime laboratory to accomplish these objectives.[4] But Midkiff[5] has more recently argued, quite convincingly, that the marketing of petroleum products within the industry, where for example a BP dealer might buy from a Shell distributor, makes the likelihood of accurately tracing the manufacturer of a gasoline an uncertain and unreliable undertaking. Where gasoline manufacturers include colored dye additives, however, gasolines may be distinguished by brand using a thin-layer chromatographic separation technique, that is if the dyes are distinctive to a particular manufacturer. Once the gasoline has been poured onto a surface and exposed to a fire, characterization beyond identifying the residue as gasoline is nearly impossible. A more recent study suggests alternatives for identifying different types of gas to their refineries of origin.[6]

The first order of laboratory business in the analysis of fire debris is the separation of the accelerant residues from the ashes, carpeting and

8. Lloyd, "Transfer of Nitroglycerin from Cardiovascular Tablets to Hands," 23 *J.For.Sci.Soc.* 307 (1983).

§ 7.11

1. Boudreau, *Arson and Arson Investigation* 62–63 (1977).

2. Nicol, "Recovery of Flammable Liquids from a Burned Structure," 114 *Fire Engineering* 550 (1961).

3. Rajeswaran and Kirk, "Identification of gasolines, waxes, greases, and asphalts by

evaporation chromatograph," 6 *Microchemical J.* 21 (1962).

4. Lucas, "The Identification of Petroleum Products in Forensic Science by Gas Chromatography," 5 *J.For.Sci.* 236 (1960).

5. Midkiff, "Brand Identification and Comparison of Petroleum Products—A Complex Problem," 26 *The Fire and Arson Investigator* 18 (1975).

6. Hirz, "Gasoline Brand Identification and Individualization of Gasoline Lots," 29 *J.For.Sci.Soc.* 91 (1989).

the like from the fire scene. It is widely recognized that it is the separation technique which will determine how small an amount of flammable or combustible liquid residue a laboratory will be able to detect. Problems can be encountered when the substrate itself contains hydrocarbon-based products such as plastics, rubber, and carpeting.[7] It has been shown that approximately 75% of all substrate material analyzed in a sample size of 3823 arson cases involved flooring, rugs, and upholstery.[8] This finding is significant since these substances themselves often contain hydrocarbons.

A number of different methods exist for the preparation of debris for laboratory analysis.[9] The ASTM has published five standard methods for separating and concentrating volatile components from a sample of fire debris.[10]

Steam distillation (ASTM E 1385–90) was, at one time, the most regularly used separation procedure in laboratories conducting arson analysis. This procedure is time-consuming, but theoretically, quite simple to explain, unlike some of the more sensitive separation techniques.

The theory of steam distillation is that two immiscible liquids will exert their own vapor pressures independently of each other. This concept allows the vaporization of a sample under heat in the presence of a suitable volatile liquid (in this instance, water), and the transfer of it to a condenser, followed by the separation of the two liquids. The distillation under heat should not be prolonged, for heating may produce pyrolysis products which may lead to confusion in the subsequent analysis. A disadvantage exists in trying to recover small amounts of an accelerant without a solvent wash. (see Figure 5).

For this reason, the steam distillation method is best applied only to samples with a high concentration of accelerants, as detected by odor. Despite its inconveniences, steam distillation has the distinct advantage of providing a visible quantity of extract, which itself can be a convincing exhibit for a jury.

---

7. The medium used as a container for fire debris suspected of containing accelerants might itself create problems if as in the case of KAPAK bags, it contains a petroleum distillate. Henderson, "Problems Facing Insurance Carriers in Investigating Fire Losses," 8 *The National Fire & Arson Report* 8, (No. 3, 1990); Diet & Mann, "Evidence Contaminated by Polyester Bags," 12 *Sci.Sleuth.News.* 5 (No. 3, 1988).

8. Op. cit. supra note 1 at p. 64.

9. The quickest method to obtain testable vapors is to withdraw them from the head space of the evidence container without pre-withdrawal preparation and then to inject the vapors into a gas chromatograph. See, State v. Burtchett, 165 Mont. 280, 530

P.2d 471 (1974). This procedure is acceptable for screening purposes, but it can result in false negatives in the case of the less volatile flammable fluids. In general, see Midkiff, "Arson and Explosive Investigation" in Saferstein, *Forensic Science Handbook* 222, 230–233 (1982). Also Stafford, "Fire Investigation, Part II: Laboratory Investigation," 14 *Crime Lab Dig.* (1987).

10. Midkiff, "Separation and Concentration of Flammable Liquids in Arson Evidence," 2 *Arson Analysis Newsletter* 8 (1978); Yates, "Recovery and Identification of Residues of Flammable Liquids from Suspected Arson Debris," in Davies, *Forensic Science* 108 (1975).

Solvent extraction (ASTM E 1386–90) is another method of separating flammable liquids from fire scene evidence. A volatile solvent, such as carbon disulfide, diethyl ether, or n-pentane, is used for the extraction. After extraction, controlled evaporation is used to reduce the volume of the extracting solvent. The interpretation of a chromatographic pattern rendered after solvent extraction can be complicated by the nature of the substrate materials from which the extraction was made. Solvent extraction is a very sensitive technique, but the unintended dissolution of background materials makes it an unsuitable method for many samples. Solvent extraction is best applied to very small samples of debris and to uncomplicated samples such as empty containers.

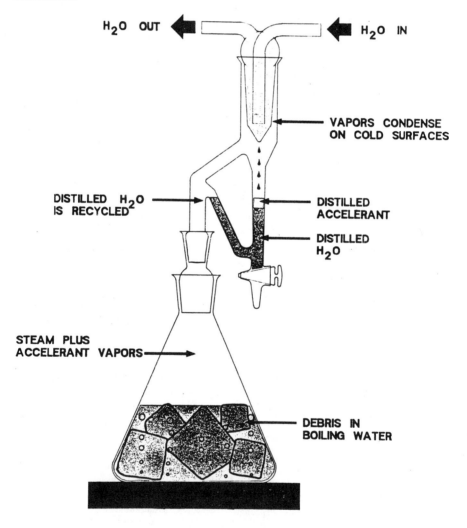

H$_2$O OUT   H$_2$O IN

VAPORS CONDENSE ON COLD SURFACES

DISTILLED H$_2$O IS RECYCLED

DISTILLED ACCELERANT

DISTILLED H$_2$O

STEAM PLUS ACCELERANT VAPORS

DEBRIS IN BOILING WATER

Fig. 5. ASTM E—1385 Steam Distillation Apparatus. *Courtesy: John J. Lantini, Applied Technical Services, Inc.*

In the heated headspace method (ASTM E 1388–90), a small portion of the vapor above a sample is taken from a heated evidence container and injected directly into a gas chromatograph. This method has been reported to be the favorite method of sample preparation among laboratories undertaking arson investigations,[11] but it has drawbacks, in that it over-emphasizes the most volatile components of a mixture and precludes distinguishing one heavy hydrocarbon, like kerosene, from another, like fuel oil.

The purge and trap, or adsorption/elution, method (ASTM E 1412–91) has gained wide acceptance as a separation technique during the 1980's. In this system, the sample is heated, while an inert gas or air is either pushed or pulled through the sample. The volatile components are adsorbed, either onto charcoal, Florisil, or a similar solid medium. Elution from the adsorbant is done with a small amount of carbon disulfide or other suitable solvent. The eluted material is then injected into the gas chromatograph. Adsorption/elution methods are widely regarded as the most sensitive available, and are easily capable of isolating 0.1 microliter, or one five-hundredth of a drop of common accelerant from a gallon of charred debris.

The separation technique which has gained the most acceptance lately is the passive adsorption method (ASTM E 1413–91). This method involves the use of a highly selective adsorbant package, such as charcoal impregnated teflon tape, which is placed in the sealed container while the debris is heated. This method involves almost no sample preparation time, is as sensitive as the more complicated dynamic headspace, and has the added advantage of being almost completely non-destructive. The sample is thus available for additional testing by the defense, if required.

Gas chromatography is the most widely used, and the only widely accepted analytical technique for determining the presence of flammable or combustible liquid residues. Its sensitivity, moderate cost, and relatively uncomplicated operation commend it to laboratories. It operates on a principle of separation resulting from the vaporization of a sample and its being carried through a suitably packed or capillary column of the gas chromatograph by an inert carrier gas, usually helium or nitrogen. The speed of a compound's passage through the column is largely a function of its molecular weight. A detector, generally a flame ionization detector, charts the component peaks on a chromatogram as they emerge from the end of the column. (See Figure 6).

Although it is often loosely said that the gas chromatograph enables the analyst to identify a compound, in reality, the chromatograms, such

---

11. Loscalzo, DeForest and Chao, "A Study to Determine the Limit of Detectability of Gasoline Vapor from Simulated Arson Residues," 25 *J.For.Sci.* 162 (1980). Other modifications to improve the technique have also been reported. Kobus, Kirkbride & Maehly, "An Absorption Sampling Method Combined with Capillary Column Gas Chromatography and Cryogenic Focusing for Trace Analysis of Volatile Organic Compounds," 27 *For.Sci.Soc.* 307 (1987).

as those shown in Figures 5 and 6, present a pattern which must be recognized by the analyst. It is not strictly correct, therefore, to say that identification results from gas chromatographic analysis. Even pattern recognition is contingent upon a reference library of samples, both fresh and weathered. ASTM E 1387–90 requires that a chromatogram exhibit certain characteristics before an identification of a particular class of flammable or combustible liquid can be made.

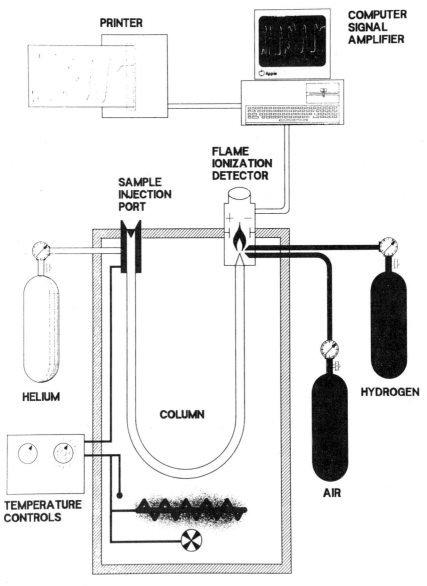

Fig. 6. Schematic of Gas Chromatography System. *Courtesy: John J. Lantini, Applied Technical Services, Inc.*

When a mass spectrometer is coupled with a gas chromatograph, measuring the molecular weight of the unknown compound by ionizing it and passing it through a magnetic field, then each compound can be identified as it elutes from the chromatographic column. This is a very powerful analytical tool, but it is capable of being misused. Many petroleum based plastics produce compounds which are common to petroleum distillates upon burning. Thus, the finding of toluene or xylene in a complex mixture of hydrocarbons need not indicate the presence of gasoline. The mass spectrometer may be used as an adjunct technique to gas chromatography, but if the chromatogram fails to reveal a pattern meeting the criteria of ASTM E 1387, the identification of the flammable or combustible liquid residues would be highly suspect.

In order to avoid the possibility of erroneous results, some experts [12] have recommended the use of more than one analytical tool, such as infrared spectroscopy, energy dispersive x-ray, or nuclear magnetic resonance to confirm the first analysis by the gas chromatograph. Since the adoption of the ASTM standards, however, the interpretation of gas chromatograms has improved, and if the gas chromatography has been done properly, these additional methods can only confirm the initial results. None of the methods listed in addition to gas chromatography, other than GC/MS, are suitable for the identification of complex mixtures of hydrocarbons.

The purge and trap or solid adsorption method [13] which seems to be preferred at present is another separation technique. In this system vapors from the sample are drawn off from the evidence container and the volatile components are adsorbed either to charcoal, Florisil or a similar solid medium. Elution from the adsorbent is done with a small amount of carbon disulfide or other suitable solvent. The eluted material is then injected into the gas chromatograph. Flammable fluids are distinguishable from each other under this system. This is the method of choice today.

Contradicting several studies which reported huge sensitivity improvements when purge and trap techniques are used for sampling compared to the heated headspace technique, a controlled study showed that while overall purge and trap is decidedly superior, for material such as gasoline in containers of reasonable size, the purge and trap technique does not excel as suggested by some of the studies.[14] The study concluded that headspace analysis continues to be a responsible screening technique.

In another study in which five techniques for the separation/concentration of flammable liquids in arson evidence were compared, a com-

---

12. Kirk's *Fire Investigation* 285 (De Haan, ed. 1991).

13. Chrostowski and Holmes, "Collection and Determination of Accelerant Vapors from Arson Debris," 3 *Arson Analysis Newsletter* 1 (1979).

14. Kurz, Jakacki, and McCaskey, "Effects of Container Size and Volatility on Relative Detectability of Accelerants by Purge and Trap versus Heated Headspace Method," 8 *Arson Analysis Newsletter*, 1 (Jan.1984).

mercial sorbent trap/thermal desorption system gave recovery values nearly twice as high as a charcoal tube method.[15] The researchers did encounter operational problems with the commercial system, however. In addition, no usable results were obtained with steam distillation.

The gas chromatograph is the most widely used analytical technique for examining even small samples from fire debris for the presence of liquid accelerants. Its sensitivity, moderate cost and relatively uncomplicated operation commend it to forensic laboratories. It operates on a principle of separation resulting from the vaporization of a sample and its being carried through the suitably packed or capillary column of the gas chromatograph by an inert carrier gas. The speed of a compound's passage through the column in the mobile phase is determined by its individual characteristics. A detector, generally a flame ionization detector, charts the component by its peaks on a chromatogram as it emerges from the gas chromatograph.

Although it is often loosely said that the gas chromatograph enables the identification of a compound, in reality the chromatogram as in Figs. 7 & 8, presents a pattern which must be recognized by the analyst. It is not strictly correct, therefore, to say that identification results from gas chromatographic analysis.[16] Products formed by pyrolysis, particularly of plastic type materials such as carpet, tile and floor covering complicate gas chromatographic examination.[17] Even pattern recognition is contingent upon a reference library of samples, both fresh and aged.

However, when a mass spectrometer is coupled with a gas chromatograph, measuring the molecular weight of the unknown compound by ionization and passing it through a magnetic field, then identification of the compound can be expected but not as a petroleum distillate. But a determination of the existence of an accelerant after gas chromatographic analysis may be misleading since the accelerant identified might be a pyrolysis product of the fire or one found naturally in the material from the fire scene, such as the terpenes in wood. In order to avoid the possibility of erroneous results in such a case, some experts [18] have recommended the use of more than one analytical tool, such as infrared spectroscopy, energy dispersive X-ray or nuclear magnetic resonance,[19] to

15. Nowick and Strock, "Comparison of Fire Debris Analysis Techniques," 7 *Arson Analysis Newsletter,* 98 (September/November 1983). For a less technical overview of four of the methods to discover concentrations of residual accelerants, (Heated head space, steam distillation, solvent extraction and vapor concentration) see Byron. "Arson Analysis for the Nonscientist," 35 *Fire and Arson Inv.,* 6 (Sept.1984).

16. "The greatest weakness of chromatography: It does not provide unique identification data." Stafford, Op. cite supra note 8, page 140 at p. 12.

17. DeHaan & Bonarius, "Pyrolysis Products of Structure Fires," 28 *For.Sci. Soc.* 299 (1988).

18. Stone and Lomonte, "False Positives in Analysis of Fire Debris," 34 *The Fire and Arson Investigator* 36 (1984).

19. Bryce, Stone and Daugherty, "Analysis of Fire Debris by Nuclear Magnetic Resonance Spectroscopy," 26 *J.For.Sci.* 678 (1981). See also, Karkkainen, Seppala & Himberg, "Detection of Trace Levels of Gasoline in Arson Cases by Gas Chromatography–Mass Spectrometry with an Automatic On-line Thermal Desorber," 39 *J.For. Sci.* 186 (1994).

confirm the first analysis by the gas chromatograph.   Microwave plasma detection has been found especially useful.[20]

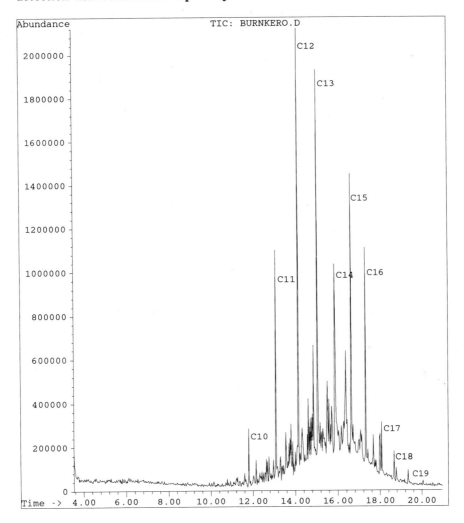

Fig. 7.   Chromatogram of Partially Evaporated (Aged) Kerosene. *Courtesy: John J. Lantini, Applied Technical Services, Inc.*

20. Holzer & Bertsch, "Recent Advances Toward the Detection of Accelerants   in Arson Cases," *Amer.Lab.* 15 (Dec.1988).

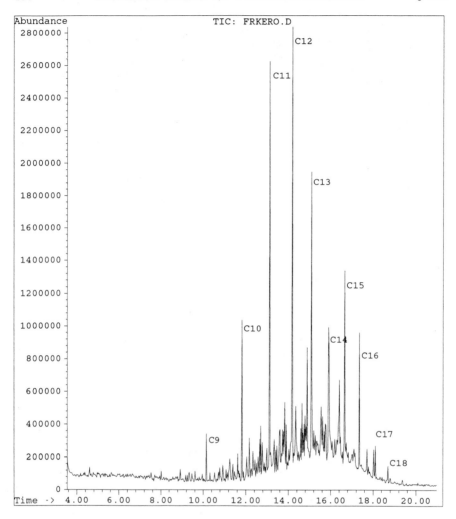

Fig. 8. Chromatogram of Fresh Gasoline. *Courtesy: John J. Lantini, Applied Technical Services, Inc.*

§ 7.12 Explosives' Residues

Laboratory analysis of explosives' residues is aimed at identifying the explosive which was used, its manufacturer as well as providing any other clues not immediately observable to the bomb scene investigator. Examination of the debris through a low power stereomicroscope is the first order of business. The examiner, through the microscope, is usually able to detect the presence of black or smokeless powder in view of their distinctive morphology. Other explosives require other, more exacting analysis.

Microscopic identification of black or smokeless powder is followed by the separation of the particles of the explosive from the rest of the debris. A fine-pointed probe is used for this purpose. Suspected black and smokeless powder can be ignited to test its burning characteristics. Some authors believe that no further confirmation is needed for black and smokeless powder, other than its recognition microscopically and by its burning characteristics.[1]

On rare occasions, some laboratories will minimize the time consumed in microscopic examination by a preliminary screening using a vapor trace analyzer or explosives' sniffer (a special purpose gas chromatographic detector). This analyzer is very sensitive to small amounts of explosive and can discriminate among the different types. It uses an electron capture detector which is acutely sensitive to the nitro group found in most explosives.

After a microscopic study of the debris, extraction may be necessary to separate the explosive residues from the non-explosive substrate.[2] Acetone is usually sufficient to make most organic high explosives soluble. Cold water is the best medium for the extraction of water soluble inorganic substances like the nitrates and chlorates. The acetone mixture is filtered and permitted to air dry which will reveal the explosive residues. Heating to hasten the drying time is not recommended since it might also cause the explosives' particles to decompose.

1. COLOR TESTS

After extraction screening of the extracted residue may be accomplished by color tests using various reagents.[3] These tests, it must be emphasized, are not specific for explosives but are only presumptive, not confirmatory, evidence of the presence of explosives' substances. The Griess and diphenylamine reagents are two of the most commonly used reagents. When spotted with the Griess reagent, NG will demonstrate a pink to red color, whereas a blue color for NG will appear after application of the diphenylamine reagent. However, the same color reactions also will appear in the presence of both RDX or PETN. Consequently, although a positive color reaction will indicate that an explosive substance may be present, and will narrow the field to a few types of explosives, the exact nature of the explosive will still need to be determined by further tests.

A failure of the Griess or diphenylamine or other reagent to cause a reaction can also be instructive. TNT, for example, will show no color change when spotted with the Griess or diphenylamine reagents as does PETN, RDX and NG. But the absence of a reaction is no guarantee of the presence of TNT, since chloride and perchlorate will not react either.

§ 7.12

1. Hoffman and Byall, "Identification of Explosive Residues in Bomb Scene Investigations," 19 *J.For.Sci.* 54 (1974).

2. See, Trimpe, "Turpentine in Arson Analysis," 36 *J.For.Sci.* 1059 (1991).

3. Parker, "Analysis of Explosive and Explosive Residues: Part 1. Chemical Tests," 20 *J.For.Sci.* 133 (1975).

2. INSTRUMENTAL ANALYSES

A vast diversity of instrumental techniques exists for the analysis of bomb debris for the existence of explosives' residues. Some depend on whether the analyst is seeking to discover the presence of organic or inorganic compounds or whether the substance is in a crystalline form or not. Others depend upon the state of the art in a particular laboratory. Among the analytical techniques employed in such laboratory analyses are high performance liquid chromatography, X-ray diffraction, thin-layer chromatography, ion chromatography, infrared spectroscopy, ion mobility spectrometry, mass spectrometry and gas chromatography. In this section, only some of these techniques, those commonly utilized, will be given separate attention.[4]

A. THIN-LAYER CHROMATOGRAPHY

Thin-layer chromatography, (TLC), is a rapid, inexpensive and sensitive method which is widely used to identify traces of explosives in extracts from the debris from an explosion scene. As in the case of other applications of TLC, the plate to be employed in the testing should be spotted with both the known and the unknown sample. This procedure will eliminate the possibility of variations resulting from differences in the plate or solvent used or the analytical conditions under which they are used. TLC, being primarily a separation technique, should be used prudently and cautiously in the identification of compounds.

Different solvent systems exist for the separation of compounds by TLC. Some systems are preferred over others because they overcome the interference with the analysis caused by contaminants in the debris. A system involving four parts of chloroform to one part dichloroethane as a solvent is commonly used. A modified Greiss reagant is sprayed on the dried plate to visualize the migration. Air drying of the plate is preferred to drying under heat since the residues of explosives may decompose under heat. Exposure to ultraviolet light, where the plate contains a fluorescent pigment, will result in luminescence except where spots are present containing UV absorbing compounds. The R_f (rate of flow) values of the compound in contrast to the developing solvent on the plate will be measured to gauge the nature of the compounds present.

Smokeless powders have been analyzed using TLC with a solvent system suitable for the separation of nitrocellulose from nitroglycerine which is also capable of distinguishing propellant grade nitrocellulose from non-propellant grade nitrocellulose, which is used in some inks, films and lacquers.

---

4. For a more extended treatment, the reader is referred to: 22 *Am.Jur.Proof of Facts* p. 385; Yinon and Zitrin, *The Analysis of Explosives* (1981); and Urbanski, *Chemistry and Technology of Explosives,* Vol. I (1964), Waters & Palmer, "Multiple Analysis of Fire Debris Samples Using Passive Headspace Concentration," 38 *J.For. Sci.* 165 (1993).

The identification of explosives' sensitizers by TLC can be of tremendous advantage not only in detecting the type of explosive used but also in identifying the commercial manufacturer of the particular explosive.[5] Methylamine Nitrate (MAN) is used by DuPont in its tovrex and ethanolamine nitrate (EAN) is used by Hercules. A TLC system to separate out these sensitizers has been described.[6]

B. INFRARED SPECTROSCOPY

Infrared spectroscopy (IR) is one of the most regularly used techniques in the crime laboratory analysis of the organic components and many of the inorganic components of explosives. IR operates on the principle that an element or compound can be identified by the type and amount of infrared radiation which it absorbs. IR has a unique ability to distinguish among complex molecular structures. It is predicated upon a recognition that the infrared spectrum comes between the red end of the visible and the short end of the microwave segments of the electromagnetic spectrum. IR uses the middle sections of the infrared spectrum from about 2.5 to 15 microns. (a micron is about $\frac{1}{50,000}$ of an inch long.) Samples in aqueous solutions are not suitable for IR analysis since water is highly absorbent of wavelengths in excess of 1.5 microns. Extracting inorganic substances with water, therefore, makes them inappropriate for IR testing while in that aqueous state.

IR spectra for a considerable number of explosive ingredients are available in the literature,[7] so that the existence of adequate reference spectra make identification a reality in many instances. When analysis is conducted of a solvent, a control of a pure solvent should be tested at the same time. The non-destructive nature of IR permits the recovery of the sample which has been tested for later testing by TLC or other techniques or by the defense, if the legal circumstances permit.

Developments in IR have progressed to the point that small samples, even in the milligram range, may be tested using two diamonds or sapphires as a holder. A dual beam IR spectrophotometer is then used to obtain a well-defined spectrum of the sample.

One of the newest systems of IR examination of explosives is the fourier transform IR (FTIR). This technique permits the computerized processing of multiple spectra resulting in a composite spectrum. The size of the sample is not a deterrent to FTIR. FTIR will inevitably play an important role in the crime laboratory, particularly in light of current efforts to couple it to a variety of chromatographic systems.

5. Peterson et al., "Identification of Explosives Containing Aklylammonium Nitrates by Thin–Layer Chromatography," 28 *J.For.Sci.* 638 (1983).

6. Yinon, "Identification of Explosives Mixture by Tandem Mass Spectrometry (MS/MS)," 21 *Can.Soc.Forens.Sci.J.*, 46 (1988).

7. Pristera et al., "Analysis of Explosives Using Infrared Spectroscopy," 32 *Anal.Chem.* 495 (1960).

C. Ion Chromatography

Inorganic explosives are analyzed by most laboratories through chemical spot tests [8] and X-ray powder diffraction. (XRD). Many commercial manufacturers have begun using inorganic compounds to a significant degree in their water gel or slurry explosives. Ammonium nitrate has begun to replace nitroglycerine in many commercial preparations. Ion chromatography (IC) has been developed as a rapid method to assay the inorganic ions in bomb debris after extraction using deionized water.[9] The F.B.I. laboratory has had acceptable results in the use of IC in the analysis of post-blast debris from black powder pipe bombs and from the detonation of commercial slurry explosives.[10] A variation on IC which emphasizes high performance liquid chromatography (HPCL) and an ultraviolet (UV) detector is in use in the F.B.I. laboratory.[11] IC has become a significant part of a forensic laboratories protocol for black powder and pyrodex residues.

Even though IC has the potential to become a useful tool in the examination of bomb debris, its limitations must be recognized. Artifacts may arise, for example, when the suppressor column becomes depleted. Advanced instrumentation and improved analytical procedures may shortly resolve such problems in the use of IC.

D. X-ray Diffraction

X-ray diffraction (XRD) is a non-destructive and reasonably quick means of identifying elements and compounds which occur as crystalline solids. It is highly specific for such solids and requires only a minimal sample to be used effectively. The sample material, for satisfactory results, should be extracted to as near a pure form as possible. Otherwise there will be interpretative problems in the results of the analysis. X-ray diffraction is not the method of choice for quantitative analysis but it will provide excellent qualitative findings by identifying the chemical state of the sample as well as its crystalline form. However, polymorphic compounds, which have more than one crystalline structure, may give a number of different diffraction patterns. An experienced analyst who has access to a computer data file of standards will be able to overcome the difficulties created by such polymorphic compounds.

§ 7.13 Fire or Explosion Fatalities

When death results from a fire or an explosion, the cause and the manner of death are issues that summon the special talents of the pathologist. The presence of bodies or parts of them among the re-

---

8. The chemical spot tests may also assist in the detection of match use in causing an explosion. See, Glattstein, Landau & Zeichner, "Identification of Match Head Residues in Post–Explosion Debris," 36 *J.For.Sci.* 1360 (1991).

9. Rudolph, "The Characterization of Some Low Explosive Residues by Ion Chromatography," *Proc.Inter.Sym.Anal.Det. Expl.* 213 (1983).

10. Reutter, et al., "Ion Chromatography in Bombing Investigations," 55 *Anal. Chem.* 1468A (1983).

11. Bender, "Indirect Photometric Detection of Anions for the Analysis of Low Explosives," 16 *Crime.Lab.Dig.* 78 (1989).

mains of a fire or an explosion is not always a matter where the cause of death is obvious. Individuals have been known to use fire or an explosion with homicidal intent [1] or in careless disregard for the safety of persons who may be found at the fire or explosion scene. And a fire or an explosion may just be a cover for a homicide occurring by some other means.[2] Even where there is no homicide, a body may be planted to fabricate an accidental death by fire or explosion to defraud a life insurance company. Of course, persons have been known, either by accident or by design to kill themselves through the medium of a fire or an explosion.[3]

The investigation of a fire or explosion, where a dead person has been found, requires close cooperation between the firemen, police, forensic pathologist and forensic toxicologist. Only when all of the facts, medical and non-medical resulting from this team effort, have been evaluated can a well-considered opinion be developed on the cause and manner of death of the fire or explosion victim.[4] Once it has been determined that a body has been discovered among the remains of a fire or an explosion, the forensic pathologist's task is two-fold: to determine the identity of the victim and to assess the cause and manner of death. A complete autopsy is essential to the proper performance of these functions. Despite the fact that extensive damage has occurred to the body of the victim, an autopsy can often provide many important facts relevant to the pathologist's activities. Total destruction of the human body by fire, at least in household fires, is rare, as a great deal of heat and fuel is necessary to turn a body into ash, due to its high water content, but an infant's body may be more readily consumed by fire.

1. THE IDENTIFICATION OF THE VICTIM

Obviously the extent to which the body is destroyed by the fire or explosion affects the ease with which the body may be identified. The height and weight of the remains of a fire victim are unreliable indicators of the size of the decedent during life since desiccation of the tissues, skeletal fractures and pulverization of the intervertebral discs due to heat may significantly alter the dimensions of the body.[5] But formulae to reconstruct the lifetime height of a fire victim, resulting in an accuracy of +/− one inch are available.[6] As a result of the effects of

§ 7.13

1. Neal v. State, 55 Cal.2d 11, 9 Cal. Rptr. 607, 357 P.2d 839 (1960); Commonwealth v. Stickle, 484 Pa. 89, 398 A.2d 957 (1979); Green v. United States, 218 F.2d 856 (D.C.Cir.1955); Stevenson v. State, 299 Md. 297, 473 A.2d 450 (1984); People v. Lippert, 125 Ill.App.3d 489, 80 Ill.Dec. 824, 466 N.E.2d 276 (1984).

2. People v. Carlson, 79 Ill.2d 564, 38 Ill.Dec. 809, 404 N.E.2d 233 (1980); People v. Ciucci, 8 Ill.2d 619, 137 N.E.2d 40 (1956), affirmed 356 U.S. 571 (1958); Smiley v. State, 376 So.2d 813 (Ala.Cr.App.1979);

State v. Wardwell, 158 Me. 307, 183 A.2d 896 (1962).

3. James, "Suicide by Burning," 6 *Med., Sci., and the Law* 48 (1966).

4. Sopher, "The Role of the Forensic Pathologist in Arson and Related Investigations," 34 *The Fire and Arson Investigator* 27, 30 (June 1984).

5. Spitz and Fisher, eds., *Medico–Legal Investigation of Death* 254 (2nd Ed.1980).

6. Fisher, "How the Pathologist Can Aid the Arson Investigator," 35 *The Fire and Arson Investigator* 19, 21 (Mar.1985).

heat, body length may be shortened by several inches and weight loss may reach 60 percent. The skin, if any remains, may be tightened and contracted, thus changing the features of the victim. Peculiarities on the body surface such as moles, tattoos, and scars may be destroyed, though evidence of a scar may be deduced by other autopsy findings, such as a missing appendix.

Despite the potential lack of clues as to the identity of the body, a great deal can be learned from x-rays of the victim, revealing old fractures, bodily abnormalities or even rings on fingers too charred for the naked eye to see the jewelry.

The sex of the body can be determined by an examination of the reproductive organs of the deceased. Additionally, the prostate and uterus with their thick muscular structure and well protected pelvic locations are quite likely to survive intact.

The race of the victim may be determined by looking at the remains of the skull,[7] which in the Negroid race tends to be longer and not as high as in Caucasians, or to patches of intact skin. Skin may be preserved under tight clothing, or on areas of the body touching a floor or wall. The gums of the victim may be of assistance, as in Negroids they are brown or mottled.

Fingerprints may be recovered from the body. Often, in a burn victim, fluid will collect between the layers of skin. This may lead to the skin coming off the hands like a glove. Either this glove or the remaining hand may be used to obtain fingerprints. Obviously, in a severely charred body it will be impossible to recover fingerprints, but the clenched fist (pugilistic pose) characteristic of many fire victims may serve to protect the friction ridges of the fingers from obliteration.

The teeth of the victim must be examined extremely carefully, as often they will provide the only means of identifying the victim. The teeth tend to be remarkably heat resistant, and with the help of dental charts it may be possible to identify a victim otherwise burned beyond recognition. Indeed, it was by identification of Adolf Hitler's teeth that he was discovered to be dead.[8]

Any remaining hair may also prove helpful to identification. But heat can affect the color of hair. Gray hair turns brassy blond at about 250 degrees F. and brown hair develops a reddish hue after ten to fifteen minutes at 400 degrees F. Black hair does not change color when exposed to heat.

An examination of the internal organs may aid in shedding light on the identity of the victim by showing evidence of operations or known abnormalities. The internal organs of the body are often remarkably

7. Holland, "The use of the Cranial Base in the Identification of Fire Victims," 34 *J.For.Sci.* 458 (1989).

8. Bezymenski, *The Death of Adolf Hitler: Unknown Documents from Soviet Ar-* chives (1968); Sognnaes, "Dental Evidence in the Postmortem Identification of Adolf Hitler, Eva Braun, and Martin Bormann," in Wecht, ed., *Legal Medicine Annual* 173 (1976).

preserved, even when the rest of the body is badly charred, due to the high water content of the body.

2. THE CAUSE OF DEATH

In seeking the cause of death, it is inevitable that the pathologist will be asked his opinion on whether death ensued from the fire or explosion or whether the victim predeceased it. Murderers have been known to kill their victims and then to use fire or explosions to attempt to conceal the evidence of their crime.[9] In addition a victim may be rendered defenseless by a blow or sedative prior to the fire, as an apparent accidental cause of death. Furthermore, the ravages of a fire or explosion may mask the fact that the death was precipitated by a natural calamity, such as a heart attack or alcohol misuse. A pathological examination of a fire victim is incomplete without a blood and tissue analysis for the presence of alcohol or drugs.[10] The pathologist will be asked to find evidence in support of one or more of these possibilities.

An examination of the bones may show that death occurred prior to the fire or explosion due to severe head injuries. Yet the victim may evidence a beating, even though death was caused by fire or an explosion. With injuries to the bones care must be exercised to assure that the injuries were not caused by falling beams and other debris in the wake of the fire or explosion, or that the injuries to the bones did not occur as a result of fracturing from the heat of the fire. In assessing injuries to the bones, and when they occurred, x-rays can prove invaluable.

A victim should always be examined for knife wounds or bullet holes. X-rays will show any previously undetected metallic items in the body, such as bullets.

The soft tissue around the neck should be carefully examined for evidence of strangulation, keeping in mind that a tight fitting shirt collar can lead to burned neck tissue which looks like strangulation.

An examination of the internal organs of a fire victim will help to clarify whether shock or cardiovascular collapse, triggered by the extreme heat of the fire or otherwise, played a role in causing the death. Finally, when investigating an unknown gas explosion death, it is important for the pathologist to examine the victim's blood in determining the explosion causing agent.[11]

Death could have been caused by burns sustained in a fire, or by the inhalation of carbon monoxide or soot. Fire can also lead to delayed death some hours or days later due to pulmonary edema, (where the victim drowns in respiratory tract secretions produced by smoke and gas inhalation), laryngeal edema (airway obstruction due to inhalation of hot

---

9. Op. cit. supra note 2.

10. Op. cit. supra note 6 at p. 24.

11. Lowry, Gamse, Armstrong, Corn, Juarez, McDowell, and Owens. "Toxicolog- ical Investigation of Liquid Petroleum Gas Explosion: Human Model for Propane/Ethyl Mercaptan Exposures," 36 *J.For.Sci.* 386 (1991).

air, gases or flames), shock, pneumonia, acute hemolytic anemia (marked red blood cell destruction), or sepsis (blood poisoning from bacterial infection of burns).

3. THE TIME OF DEATH

Two of the most important factors to consider in deciding whether the victim died before or after the fire or explosion occurred are the carbon monoxide level of the blood and whether there are carbon particles (soot) in his airways.[12]

Smoke contains dangerous amounts of carbon monoxide, a colorless, odorless gas, which can lead to loss of consciousness and death within minutes. The carbon monoxide supplants the oxygen carried by the hemoglobin of the blood, which oxygen is essential to sustain life. The carbon monoxide results in a chemical change to carboxyhemoglobin. Carbon monoxide only enters the blood through respiration. Therefore it will not be absorbed after death through the skin. If a fire victim's hemoglobin or bodily tissues contain a 10 percent or greater saturation of carbon monoxide, the victim was probably alive during the fire.[13] Carbon monoxide levels may range from 40 to 70 percent (depending on age and physical condition) in a person whose death is cause by smoke inhalation.

But it must be kept in mind that a lethal concentration of carbon monoxide in the blood does not positively prove that the victim died in the fire under investigation. The victim may have been asphyxiated somewhere else (say from automobile exhaust fumes) and then moved to the site of the fire. In addition, a low level of carbon monoxide is not certain evidence of a pre-fire death since death, under the impact of an explosion or intense heat, may occur very nearly instantaneously.

A high carbon monoxide content in the body will cause the blood to appear cherry red. The skin of the victim, if visible, will also be cherry red. Even if the cherry red color of the skin is not apparent due to charring, it will become so when the body is opened on autopsy and the musculature, viscera, mucous membranes and blood are observed.

The presence of carbon particles on the mucus membranes which line the larynx, trachea, and bronchi is evidence that the victim was breathing during the fire. A victim may attempt to cough the carbon particles out of his air passages and in the process swallow them. Therefore, carbon particles found in the esophagus and stomach are also evidence that the victim was alive during the fire. Carbon particles found in such superficial areas as the nostrils and mouth do not carry the same diagnostic significance as carbon found in the more distal portions of the respiratory tract, as they may have settled there even

---

12.   Water-filled blisters and hemorrhages beneath the endocardium of the left ventricle are two other, far less specific, indicators that death occurred in the fire. See, Adelson, "Role of the Pathologist in Arson Investigation," 45 *J.Crim.L.Criminol.* & *P.S.* 760, 764 (1955).

13.   Op. cit. supra note 4 at p. 31.

though the victim was already dead. It must be noted that the absence of carbon particles in the airways does not irrefutably prove that the victim was dead prior to the fire, since the victim may have died extremely rapidly in a very hot fire or explosion. In such a case the larynx, glottis, epiglottis, trachea, and large and small bronchi should be examined for evidence of inhalation of flames, hot air or gases.

Evidence can be gathered that the victim was alive during the fire by examining the burns on the body to see if they are ante mortem burns.[14] Burns that occur prior to death show the presence of vital reaction, which is evidenced by redness or hyperaemia around the burned area. If the victim was alive during the fire, blisters on the body will contain a fluid rich in protein, which will become solid upon heating.

With post-mortem burns to the body there is no vital reaction, and, instead of the areas surrounding the burns being red, they will be hard and yellow.

An examination of any bone fractures suffered by the victim can assist in the pathologist's tasks. Exposure to very high heat can cause unique curved fractures to develop. Such fractures are only caused by high temperatures and are an artifact of fires. Prolonged exposure to the heat of a fire may also cause the bones to become brittle, so that they are easily fractured while being moved or examined. Characteristic of fractures occurring after death is the lack of hemorrhaging present in the tissue surrounding the fracture. In an ante mortem fracture there would be hemorrhaging.

If the head of the victim is exposed to sufficient prolonged heat, intracranial steam pressure can develop to the extent that the skull will suffer a linear fracture. Upon first glance such a fracture could be misapprehended as evidence of foul play. However, on closer scrutiny, it will be noted that the injury will usually be accompanied by gaping holes or wide margins in the skull and no hemorrhaging.

In some cases where there has been a prolonged post-mortem heating of the head, blood will extrude between the dura and the inner table of the skull creating an artificial post-mortem epidural hematoma. In an ante mortem epidural hematoma, the clots will customarily be unilateral. The blood in a post-mortem epidural hematoma will be a light chocolate color, with a tinge of pink if there has been as appreciable saturation of the victim's blood with carbon monoxide. The clot will not be solid, but rather will have a honeycomb appearance caused by bubbles of steam being created when the blood was boiled by the external application of heat. The finding of a subdural hemorrhage, however, is always indicative of an ante mortem injury.

When a dead body is subjected to the extreme heat of a fire, the skin will char, causing contractions which lead to post-mortem heat rupture or skin splits. While these injuries may look like they were inflicted by a

---

14. Fisher reports considerable disagreement among pathologists on this issue. Op. cit. supra note 6. Accord: Benz, "Thermal Deaths," in Curran et al. *Modern Legal Medicine, Psychiatry, and Forensic Science* 269, 276 (1980).

sharp instrument, they can be distinguished from ante mortem injuries. In a post-mortem skin split there is no hemorrhaging, as the heat has coagulated the blood in the vessels. Also a post-mortem skin split will generally be found in areas of the body extensively damaged by fire, be irregular, show an absence of bruising or vital reaction, and sometimes the blood vessels and nerves will be intact on either side of the skin split.

Occasionally a burn victim will be found with an apparently mutilated abdomen. If such an injury, manifested by the protrusion of the large and small intestines, was caused by extreme heat there will be no evidence of either internal or external hemorrhaging, and the victim may therefore be determined to have been dead prior to receiving the abdominal dislocation.

Aside from identifying the victim and aiding in establishing the cause of death, the forensic scientist may provide evidence on subsidiary issues as well. In a bomb explosion, the discovery of bomb residues may enable an interpretation to be made as to the location of the bomb relative to the victim at the scene of the explosion [15] or whether the victim handled the explosive. The detection of minute traces of foreign materials, either radiopaque or radiolucent, such as electrical wiring, imbedded in the body or clothing of a victim, may give some clue as to the cause of the explosion.[16] Similarly, the nature of the explosive used may be evidenced from the analysis of bodily tissues or clothing.

V.   EVIDENCE OF ARSON AND EXPLOSIVES USE

§ 7.14   The Law of Arson

Under modern arson statutes, three elements are often stated to be the essential elements of proof by the prosecution to establish the crime of arson. It must be demonstrated that there was a fire or an explosion; that it was incendiary in origin, by which is meant that it resulted from a willful act rather than through an accident or natural causes and that the accused's agency was responsible for the fire or explosion.[1]

Since arson is generally a crime of stealth, the elements of the crime are customarily proved by circumstantial evidence alone. In establishing the incendiary nature of a fire or explosion, a prosecutor in many jurisdictions must introduce sufficient evidence to overcome a presump-

---

15. Spitz, Sopher and Dimaio, "Medicolegal Investigation of a Bomb Explosion in an Automobile," 15 *J.For.Sci.* 537 (1970).

16. Laposata, "Collection of Trace Evidence from Bombing Victims at Autopsy," 30 *J.For.Sci.* 789 (1985).

§ 7.14

1. State v. Harris, 639 S.W.2d 122, 125 (Mo.App.1982). The status of arson at common law and in its modern statutory dress is extensively and comprehensively analyzed in Poulos, "The Metamorphosis of the Law of Arson," 51 *Mo.L.Rev.* 295–449 (1986).

tion that the event resulted from an accident or natural causes.[2] The very real likelihood that arson, unlike other crimes of similar gravity, will occur from causes other than criminal ones has been cited as the basis for this long-standing presumption.[3] In some instances, an explosion or a fire might be unexplainable due to a paucity of facts or other reasons. In that event, it is more correct to infer the incident was occasioned by unknown causes [4] than that the failure to find a natural or accidental cause signifies a criminal act of arson.[5]

Once the prosecution has demonstrated a criminal cause for the explosion or the fire, it still remains to connect a particular suspect to the wrongdoing. The decisions reveal the difficulty that a prosecutor sometimes encounters in convincing a court that the circumstantial evidence points unerringly to the defendant as the culprit. In People v. Marin,[6] for example, the conviction of Luis Marin, an apparently disgruntled employee of Stouffer's Inn in New York, was set aside for the insufficiency of the evidence to prove anything more than his presence at the scene of the fire which claimed the lives of twenty-six persons, his fear of an imminent dismissal from Stouffer's employ for his being an illegal alien and his falsehoods subsequent to the event. The verdict of the jury was deemed speculative when predicated on this circumstantial evidence of Marin's culpability.

The Missouri statutes [7] typify the modern trend in the statutory definition of arson. Both fire and explosions can be the wrongful instrumentalities for the commission of the crime of arson in Missouri. The crime is divided into degrees, providing more severe punishments for the higher, more grievous, forms of arson. The knowing damaging of any building which recklessly causes a danger of death or serious bodily harm to persons on the premises or to those who are nearby is classified as arson in the first degree.[8] Arson in the second degree lacks the ingredient of jeopardy to the welfare of an individual and is plainly a prohibition against setting a fire or an explosion in any building.[9] Where the fire or explosion occurs not intentionally but recklessly or only negligently the crime is mitigated in severity.[10] The most heavily punished offense in the category of fires or explosions is that which has the catastrophic result, by the design of the offender, of causing death or serious bodily harm to ten or more people or has a similar large scale effect.[11] Of course, to seek to defraud an insurance company through

---

2. Jenkins v. Commonwealth, 216 Va. 838, 223 S.E.2d 880 (1976); State v. Brown, 308 N.C. 181, 301 S.E.2d 89 (1983); Borza v. State, 25 Md.App. 391, 335 A.2d 142 (1975); Baxter v. State, 160 Ga.App. 181, 286 S.E.2d 460 (1981); Bray v. State, 12 Ark.App. 53, 670 S.W.2d 922 (1984).

3. Perkins and Boyce, *Criminal Law* 276 (1982).

4. Baxter, "Proof of Cause and Origin of Fire," *For the Defense* 8, 14 (Sept.1982).

5. Kennedy, *Fire-Arson Explosion Investigation* 631 (1977).

6. 102 A.D.2d 14, 478 N.Y.S.2d 650 (1984). As to an explosion, see, State v. Thoe, 565 S.W.2d 818 (Mo.App.1978).

7. Vernon's Ann.Mo.Stats. §§ 569.030, 569.040, 569.050, 569.060, 569.065, 560.067 and 569.070.

8. Id. at § 569.040.

9. Id. at § 569.050.

10. Id. at §§ 569.060, 569.065, 569.067.

11. Id. at § 569.070.

the medium of destructive fires or explosions is also interdicted.[12]

The Missouri statutory scheme and that of most states is a far cry from the restrictive view of arson which prevailed at the common law. At the common law, arson was the malicious burning of the dwelling house of another.[13] The crime had four integral parts: the malice; the burning; the dwelling house; the possessory interest in the dwelling of a person other than the arsonist. Each of these elements of the common law definition has been broadened in modern statutes throughout the states. The impetus to do so was to some extent stimulated by the proposals of the Model Penal Code for the revision and recodification of the offense of arson.[14]

At the common law, the malice necessary to the crime of arson required evidence of a deliberate, fixed intent to set fire to another's dwelling. Just acting recklessly or negligently would not suffice to establish the requisite malice. The Model Penal Code has jettisoned the concept of malice and substituted for it the requirement of purposeful conduct in the setting of the fire. Some states, following the Model Penal Code, have eschewed the word malice and stated a preference for a number of more intelligible terms to connote the mental element of culpability in arson.[15] Others have retained the common law phrasing but have interpreted it more broadly than at the common law.[16]

The common law element of burning was freighted with confusing distinctions between a scorching and a burning, the former not constituting arson while only the latter would do so. In today's statutory world, arson often occurs upon the mere setting of a fire or the starting of an explosive train,[17] steps which the common law would have considered too preparatory to be punishable as the completed offense of arson.

Common law arson was an offense against the habitation and not against property in general and certainly not against the endangering of a person's safety, except as ancillary to the burning of the dwelling. In an early Indiana decision, Simmons v. State,[18] the dwelling place was construed strictly, in accord with the common law, so as not to include the burning of a house trailer. Under current arson statutes, the dwelling place has been expanded to include almost any and all buildings or structures, regardless of whether they are occupied at the time or not. Occupancy or the lack of it is relevant only to the punishment for the offense.[19] In some jurisdictions even the burning of vegetables, crops

---

12. Id. at § 569.030.

13. Perkins and Boyce, *Criminal Law* 273 (3d Ed.1982).

14. Model Penal Code, T.D. # 11, p. 33, sec. 220.1 (1960).

15. Colo.Rev.Stat.Ann. § 18–4–102 (1973).

16. D.C.Code § 22–401 (1973).

17. Mass.Gen.Laws Ann. c. 266, § 1 (1977); Wis.Stat.Ann. 943.02 (1958). But

see, Anno. "What constitutes 'burning' to justify charge of arson," 28 A.L.R.4th 482 for cases on the continuing definitional controversy.

18. 234 Ind. 489, 129 N.E.2d 121 (1955). The current statute still uses the word dwelling to define the subject of arson. West's Anno.Ind.Code 35–43–1–1–14.

19. N.Y.—McKinney's Penal Law § 150.00 et seq. (1975).

and timber will constitute arson.[20]   The Rhode Island statute is unique in punishing as arson the use of fire or explosives to place a person in jeopardy of death or great bodily harm even where no building is at hazard.[21]

More commonly, the knowing placing of a person in physical jeopardy combined with the burning of property constitutes the most grievous form of arson.   Issues of statutory interpretation have been a regular feature in the trial of these newly minted statutes.   In a Connecticut case,[22] for example, the accused argued that he had not endangered "another person" within the meaning and language of the arson statute since his accomplice could not be the other person contemplated by the statute.   The argument was rejected.

The final element of common law arson that has been statutorily reworked in recent years is the need to prove that the dwelling which was burned was that of some person other than the arsonist.   In modern times legislators have regarded the risks to personal safety in the setting of fires or explosions to be of such serious moment that whether one burns or blows up one's own property or not is in most instances irrelevant to a finding of culpability for the act of arson.   Certainly the distinct and separate modern crime of arson to defraud an insurance company can be committed regardless of who actually owns or has a possessory interest in the property set ablaze.

The more legislation extends the scope of arson as known to the common law, the more such legislation chances being constitutionally flawed.   Arson statutes, like other criminal statutes, must meet the measure of being rationally related to a legitimate legislative purpose.   As a consequence, if a statute outlaws behavior which may be innocent in its nature, that statute will be in violation of the constitutional precepts of due process of law.   An Illinois aggravated arson statute fell afoul of due process when it proscribed any person's burning a building which causes injury to a fireman at the scene in the line of duty.   The statute would make an aggravated crime out of even an owner's burning of his own shed, say, where a fireman is accidentally injured in fighting the blaze.   The statutory reach was said to be overbroad in penalizing such conduct and in doing so more severely even than a burning with an unlawful purpose, where no one is injured.[23]

§ 7.15   Terminological Quagmires

Definitional problems have plagued the enforcement of the Federal statutes prohibiting the possession or use of explosives, and incendiary or destructive devices more than has been the case in the state courts. But the states have had their share of difficulty in elaborating a

20. Mass.Gen.Laws Ann. c. 266, § 5 (1994).

21. R.I.Gen.Laws 1956, § 11–4–2. A similar provision appears in the Model Arson Law, section 100.1.   See, *1984 Fire Almanac* 398 (N.F.P.A.)

22. State v. Pellegrino, 194 Conn. 279, 480 A.2d 537 (1984).

23. People v. Wick, 121 Ill.App.3d 94, 76 Ill.Dec. 587, 458 N.E.2d 1387 (1984).

consistent understanding of terms, like explosives, fire bombs and incendiary devices, which commonly appear in their statutes.

1. FEDERAL

Infernal machine, explosive, explosive or incendiary device, destructive substance, inflammable materials and destructive device are the sometimes disparate, often duplicative and always befuddling terms used in the Federal statutes to prohibit causing damage or injury through fire or explosion.

The Organized Crime Control Act of 1970 (Explosive Control Act) separates explosives into three categories [1]: 1) articles like gun powder and blasting materials that are commonly used as explosives; 2) explosive or incendiary devices within the meaning of 18 U.S.C.A. § 232(5); and 3) chemical compounds or mixtures that may cause an explosion when ignited. An annual list of explosives is compiled by the Bureau of Alcohol, Tobacco, and Firearms, of the Department of the Treasury.[2] Controversies over the meaning of the term "explosive" under the act generally focus on definitional categories (2) and (3) above.

The decisions from most Federal circuits agree that uncontained gasoline is not an incendiary device under the Explosive Control Act,[3] although natural gas contained in a closed room and then exploded by an automatic timer attached to an open coil hot plate in the room has been held to be an incendiary device.[4] The Ninth circuit has also held that pouring gasoline along the walls and on the floors of a building with a

---

§ 7.15

1. 18 U.S.C.A. §§ 841–848.   Anno., "Meaning of term 'explosive' within 18 U.S.C.A. § 844(i) Prohibiting Damage or Destruction of Property used in Interstate Commerce by Means of Explosive," 61 A.L.R.Fed. 899.

§ 844(j) defines "explosives" for purposes of those sections criminalizing their intentional misuse.   The term "explosive" means gunpowders, powders used for blasting, all forms of high explosives, blasting materials, fuses (other than electric circuit breakers), detonators, and other detonating agents, smokeless powders, other explosive or incendiary devices within the meaning of paragraph (5) of section 232 of this title, and any chemical compounds, mechanical mixture, or device that contains any oxidizing and combustible units, or other ingredients, in such proportions, quantities, or packing that ignition by fire, by friction, by concussion, by percussion, or by detonation of the compound, mixture, or device or any part thereof may cause an explosion.

§ 232(5) further provides that the term "explosive or incendiary device" means (A) dynamite and all other forms of high explosives, (B) any explosive bomb, grenade, missile, or similar device, and (C) any incendiary bomb or grenade, fire bomb, or similar device, including any device which (i) consists of or includes a breakable container including a flammable liquid or compound, and a wick composed of any material which, when ignited, is capable of igniting such flammable liquid or compound, and (ii) can be carried or thrown by one individual acting alone. Explosives, without definition, are prohibited from the mails in 18 U.S.C.A. § 1716.

2. See, 49 Fed.Reg. 50492 for the 1985 list.

3. See, e.g., United States v. Gere, 662 F.2d 1291 (9th Cir.1981). Contra: United States v. Beldin, 737 F.2d 450 (5th Cir. 1984). And see the Anti–Arson Act amendments of 1982 (P.L. 97–298) which bring fire within the Act.

4. United States v. Neary, 733 F.2d 210 (2d Cir.1984).

delay fuse added was not setting an incendiary device.[5] A molotov cocktail, it is generally agreed, is an incendiary device.[6]

It should be noted that an incendiary device under the Explosive Control Act is also, by definition, an explosive and that such a device may also be a "destructive device" under the National Firearms Act.[7]

In United States v. Ragusa [8] the court, in upholding a conviction for possession of a destructive device in violation of the National Firearms Act, concluded that six trash bags, each holding a five gallon container of gasoline, suspended in various parts of a building, connected by overlapping paper towels trailing through out the building, and intended to be ignited by matchbooks fastened to cigarettes was both a destructive device and an incendiary device. A molotov cocktail is also a destructive device.[9] As a consequence, the prosecution has a choice, in a case involving a molotov cocktail, to proceed under the Explosive Control Act or National Firearms Act.

Commercial blasting materials have sometimes been held to constitute a destructive device [10] and sometimes just considered as a "familiar industrial blasting charge," [11] usually depending on whether wires and blasting caps are attached and whether the intended use is antisocial.

A pipe bomb would be a destructive device as well as an explosive permitting the government to choose whether to prosecute under the Explosives Control Act or the National Firearms Act.

Prior to the amendment of the Explosive Control Act by the Anti–Arson Act of 1982,[12] a recurring question, reflected in the cases, was whether the ignition of the fumes of gasoline, methane, or naphtha or similar combustibles which could cause an explosion was within the Federal prohibition. In United States v. Xheka [13] the court held that gasoline and gasoline soaked towels, which exploded when ignited, fell within the Federal statute.[14] In support of its theory that gasoline vapors constituted a chemical compound which was a proscribed explo-

---

5. United States v. Reed, 726 F.2d 570 (9th Cir.1984).

6. See, e.g., United States v. Davis, 313 F.Supp. 710 (D.Conn.1970); See, in general, Anno., "Possession of bomb, Molotov cocktail, or similar device as criminal offense" 42 A.L.R.3d 1230.

7. 26 U.S.C.A. § 5845(f). See also, the Omnibus Crime Control and Safe Streets Act 18 U.S.C.A. § 921(a)(4) which contains the same definition of a "destructive device" as the National Firearms Act (26 U.S.C.A. § 5845(f)). Anno., Validity, Construction, and Application of Provision, A National Firearms Act (26 U.S.C.A. § 5845(f)) and Omnibus Crime Control and Safe Streets Act (18 U.S.C.A. § 921(a)(4) Defining "Destructive Device" 25 A.L.R.Fed. 344. A "destructive substance" under 18 U.S.C.A. § 31, 18 U.S.C.A. § 921(a)(4) prohibiting damaging an air-craft or motor vehicle, includes "any explosive substance."

8. 664 F.2d 696 (8th Cir.1981), cert. denied 457 U.S. 1133 (1982).

9. See, e.g., United States v. Cruz, 492 F.2d 217 (2d Cir.1974), cert. denied 417 U.S. 935 (1974).

10. United States v. Greer, 404 F.Supp. 1289 (W.D.Mich.1975) where the court concluded that the intended use of the commercial blasting materials was irrelevant.

11. United States v. Curtis, 520 F.2d 1300 (1st Cir.1975).

12. Pub.L. 97–298, 96 Stat. 1319 (1982).

13. 704 F.2d 974 (7th Cir.1983).

14. See, op. cit. supra note 1—chemical compound which could cause an explosive.

sive, the government presented expert testimony that gasoline is a chemical compound capable of causing an explosion. The court gave a broad reading to the statutory definitions of explosive after analyzing the legislative history of the act, and concluded that simple devices using common substances could be used to create an explosive within the meaning of the act. Most Federal appellate courts have held similarly, particularly where an expert gave an opinion that the substance was within the statutory language.[15] Both methane [16] and naphta [17] have been found within the act's prohibition.

Other courts have concluded that uncontained gasoline is not an explosive.[18] In United States v. Gelb [19] defendant burned a commercial building. Gasoline was used as a means of creating a hot, spreading, and all-consuming fire, but no explosion occurred. The court found that the ignition of gasoline which had been spread inside a building did not constitute an explosive air-fuel mixture under the act.

Identifying fires caused by explosives is technically difficult but the 1982 amendments prohibit damage and destruction caused by both explosives and fire, thus eliminating the necessity for the awkward inquiry as to whether gasoline is an explosive air-fuel mixture.[20]

The Interstate Commerce Clause is the jurisdictional prerequisite for a prosecution of a Federal explosives crime. In United States v. Belcher [21] defendant moved to dismiss alleging that the building that had burned was closed for repair and thus not used in interstate commerce. The court rejected this argument after concluding that the building was only temporarily closed. The Federal circuits are not in agreement as to how expansively the interstate commerce requirement should be read. For example, some circuits hold that if the property involved is residential then jurisdiction is precluded under the act while others conclude that a dwelling house which is owned and rented to tenants is a business property involved in interstate commerce.[22]

15. See, United States v. Paulos, 667 F.2d 939 (10th Cir.1982); United States v. Lorence, 706 F.2d 512 (5th Cir.1983). The Anti-Arson Act of 1982 by adding "fire or" to explosives has evidently brought gasoline etc. within the sweep of title 18 sec. 844.

16. United States v. Hepp, 656 F.2d 350 (8th Cir.1981).

17. United States v. Agrillo–Ladlad, 675 F.2d 905 (7th Cir.1982), cert. denied 459 U.S. 829 (1982).

18. See, op. cit. supra note 3; United States v. Birchfield, 486 F.Supp. 137 (M.D.Tenn.1980).

19. 700 F.2d 875 (2d Cir.1983).

20. See, H.R.Rep. No. 678, 97th Cong., 2nd Sess. reprinted in 1982 U.S.Code Cong. and Adm.News 2631, 2632.

21. 577 F.Supp. 1241 (E.D.Va.1983).

22. Compare United States v. Russell, 738 F.2d 825 (7th Cir.1984) with United States v. Mennuti, 639 F.2d 107 (2d Cir. 1981).

Very little more than substantial firefighting experience is necessary to qualify a firefighter as an expert in determining the cause of a fire. In State v. Garrett, 682 S.W.2d 153 (Mo.App.1984) a fire chief's twenty-five years of experience coupled with his training in fire control, combat of fires and arson investigation at a local university were sufficient credentials to qualify as an expert in determining where the fire has initiated.

2. STATES

Among the states, no standard formula seems to be observed in defining explosives for the possession or use of which criminal sanctions can be imposed. Some states limit the definition of explosives to chemical compounds or mixtures which are capable of producing destructive effects and do not deal specifically with incendiary devices or address a general category of blasting materials.[23] The Wisconsin statutes apparently do not define the term explosive at all but do prohibit the manufacture, purchase, transportation, possession, or transfer of any explosive compound.[24]

In some states the subject of explosives appears in both the health and safety and the criminal codes [25] while other states regulate explosives as part of their natural resources statutes [26] or other type of legislation.[27]

A few states proscribe the possession of flammable substances, without explaining what are flammable and what are not.[28] However, a flammable liquid, under the New York General Business Law [29] is defined as "any liquid which has a flash point of seventy degrees Fahrenheit, or less, as determined by a Tagliabue or equivalent closed cup test device." Connecticut divides flammable liquids into three classes according to whether the liquid has a high or low flash point.[30] A turn of the century Connecticut decision [31] saw flammability in terms of a liquid's ignition temperature rather than its flash point.

A number of states define a fire bomb as what is commonly understood to be a molotov cocktail.[32] In People v. Dorris,[33] a molotov cocktail was held to be an incendiary device even though the state's expert witness rejected such a conclusion since the device did not contain any sulfuric acid. A wick was deemed essential to a molotov cocktail in People v. Owens [34] even though the more generic term, incendiary device, did not require a demonstration that a wick had been used. An unusual statute in California,[35] in defining a fire bomb, includes only "breakable" containers which contain a flammable liquid having a flash point of 150 degrees Fahrenheit or less. It is understood that the trial courts in California require proof in each case that the flammable liquid identified by laboratory testing is established by testing to have the required flash point. This requirement would seem to be unnecessary

23. Mont.Code Ann. 50–38–101 (1983); Va.Code 1950, § 18.2–85(a)(ii).

24. Wis.Stat.Ann. 941.31 (1957).

25. West's Ann.Cal.Health and Safety Code § 12000 et seq. (1939); West's Ann.Cal.Penal Code § 453, § 12301 et seq.; West's Colo.Rev.Stat.Ann. § 9–7–101 et seq., 18–12–109 (1973).

26. Ill.Rev.Stat. ch. 96½, § 4801 (1975).

27. West's Fla.Stat.Ann. § 552.081 et seq. (1941)—trade and commerce chapter; N.Y.—McKinney's Labor Law § 451(1).

28. West's Ann.Cal.Penal Code § 453.

29. Section 308.

30. Conn.Gen.Stat.Ann. § 29–62.

31. State v. Boylan, 79 Conn. 463, 65 A. 595 (1907).

32. West's Ann.Cal.Penal Code § 453(b); Wis.Stat.Ann. 943.06 (1957); Md. Code 1957, Art. 27, § 139A; Code of Va. § 18.2–85 (1994).

33. 95 Mich.App. 760, 291 N.W.2d 196 (1980).

34. 670 P.2d 1233, 1237 (Colo.1983).

35. West's Ann.Cal.Penal Code § 453(b).

since standard references for a known liquid's flash point do exist. The use of such well-settled data should not occasion hearsay problems.

In People v. Sullivan,[36] a charge that kerosene, housed in a bottle stuffed with a wick, constituted an explosive substance was deemed ill-founded, but the court did construe it to be an incendiary device under the meaning of another subdivision of the New York Penal Law.[37] What is or is not a molotov cocktail is not properly the subject of expert testimony in Delaware[38] since Delaware juries are thought to be adequately schooled to decide the matter under the instructions of the court. Such instructions should include a judicially devised definition of a molotov cocktail which states it to be "a makeshift incendiary bomb made of a breakable container filled with flammable liquid and provided with a wick composed of any substance capable of bringing a flame into contact with the liquid."[39] The court fashioned its definition on the model of the American Heritage dictionary and incorrectly spoke of contact with the liquid rather than the vapor of the liquid, since it is the vapor not the liquid which burns.

The Michigan situation with respect to whether poured gasoline can be an explosive is unique. In two connected cases arising out of the destruction by a gasoline accelerated fire of the Soul Expression Bar in Detroit in 1969, two panels of the same Michigan Court of Appeals have come to diametrically opposed conclusions on the matter. In People v. Kelley,[40] a prosecution for burning the bar with gasoline under a statute[41] proscribing the use of "gun powder or any other explosive substance" was upheld even though another statute[42] prohibited the use of incendiary or flammable substances to cause property damage or personal injury. Another alleged participant in the fire at the Soul Expression Bar, who was separately tried and convicted under the same statute charged in People v. Kelley, managed to obtain a reversal of his conviction however. A different panel of judges of the Michigan appeals court, after hearing the same argument as in People v. Kelley, conceded that gasoline is capable of causing an explosion but held that gasoline, not being commonly used for that purpose, was not an explosive substance.[43]

Both destructive devices as well as explosives are separately regulated in some states but the terms are not mutually exclusive.[44] The situation parallels that in the Federal statutes. Maryland, in one all encompassing phrasing, prohibits the employment of "destructive explo-

---

36. 39 A.D.2d 631, 331 N.Y.S.2d 298 (1972).

37. N.Y.—McKinney's Penal Law § 265.05. Explosive devices are covered by § 265.05(7).

38. Matthews v. State, 276 A.2d 265, 267 (Del.1971).

39. Saunders v. State, 275 A.2d 564, 566 (Del.1971).

40. 32 Mich.App. 126, 188 N.W.2d 654 (1971).

41. Mich.Comp.Laws Ann. § 750.207.

42. Mich.Comp.Laws Ann. § 750.77.

43. People v. Robinson, 37 Mich.App. 15, 194 N.W.2d 436 (1971), remanded 387 Mich. 758, 195 N.W.2d 278 (1972).

44. See, e.g., West's Ann.Cal.Penal Code § 12301, West's Ann.Cal.Health and Safety Code § 12000.

sive devices." [45] In a New York decision,[46] the statutory terms "incendiary", "bomb" and "explosive substance" were said to be "susceptible of reasonable application in accordance with the common understanding of men." As a consequence, the unassembled watches with holes drilled in their crystals, with wires soldered to their backs which were, in turn, connected to batteries and then to flashbulbs were, in the presence of potassium chlorate and sugar, held to be an incendiary bomb containing an explosive substance beyond a reasonable doubt. At least one state distinguishes an explosive or incendiary device from an explosive or incendiary part.[47] In People v. Lovato,[48] the court, in reversing the trial judge's ruling to the contrary, concluded that four blasting caps are so intrinsically harmful, apart from any association with other items, that they are explosive devices and not merely explosive parts.

In spite of the confused medley of statutes and decisions among the states, it is plain that the existence of a bomb, explosive or incendiary device, however denominated, may be satisfactorily proved without evidence of its ability to detonate[49] or the fact that it has ignited.[50]

The state statutes and decisions manifest considerable jurisdiction by jurisdiction individuality and terminological muddling in the statutory control of explosive, incendiary and destructive devices. No consistent pattern of definitions has been found. The trial attorney, therefore, for both prosecution and defense, will be hard pressed to find compelling persuasive authority for any definitional position from any other state but his own.

§ 7.16   Qualifying the Expert

1. IN GENERAL

In general, an expert is a person qualified on a particular subject by either actual experience or careful study. Such an expert is entitled to express an opinion on a matter within the scope of his expertise where persons having no particular training or special study are incapable of forming accurate opinions or of deducing correct conclusions on the subject. There is no precise requirement as to the mode in which an expert's skill or experience shall have been acquired, and thus either practical experience or academic study may qualify an expert. Whether a witness is competent to testify as an expert is a preliminary question that rests within the sound discretion of the trial judge, only disturbed upon a showing of abuse of discretion.

Arson experts are relied on to testify as to the signs and to the fact of an incendiary fire. They are generally of two types: arson investiga-

---

45. Md. Code, 1957, Art. 27, § 139B.

46. People v. Cruz, 34 N.Y.2d 362, 357 N.Y.S.2d 709, 714, 314 N.E.2d 39, 44 (1974).

47. West's Colo.Rev.Stat.Ann. § 18–12–109 (1973).

48. 630 P.2d 597 (Colo.1981).

49. United States v. Evans, 526 F.2d 701 (5th Cir.1976); State v. Van Arsdale, 20 Ariz.App. 253, 511 P.2d 697 (1973).

50. People v. Westoby, 63 Cal.App.3d 790, 134 Cal.Rptr. 97 (1976).

tors who are skilled in investigating the causes of fires and firefighters who may or may not know more than the best methods to prevent or to extinguish a fire. Qualifying witnesses as arson experts is troublesome since standards by which their qualifications can be judged are in short supply.

Many arson experts have had some experience fighting fires and afterwards have been assigned to the arson squad, but have had little formal training in arson investigation, other than a short course or two.

Very few persons are qualified as arson experts on the basis of firefighting experience alone,[1] although a firefighter with as little as four and a half years experience coupled with the investigation of two dozen fires has been qualified to give an opinion on the cause of a fire.[2]

The decisions indicate that arson experts usually have practical experience approaching a minimum of ten years with at least some formal study. In State v. Wilbur,[3] the arson expert who qualified had worked seven years as a firefighter, received several months of extensive training for the inspector's position including mandatory attendance at formal seminars, and three years as a fire inspector with a division that investigated about 10 fires a day. The arson expert in Commonwealth v. Stickle[4] had been a fire marshal for six years assigned to over 2000 fires in addition to previously working as a fire officer for three years and a firefighter for eight years. He had attended a number of outside seminars. A one year employee of the state marshal's office who had ten years of previous experience on the state police force and who had attended and taught classes on the investigation of fires was held to be a duly qualified expert on the causation of fires in Parris v. State.[5]

Witnesses who have less experience and more academic background may also be qualified as arson experts, particularly when all of their experience is in arson investigation. In Commonwealth v. Rhoades[6] the

§ 7.16

1. See, Audubon Ins. Co. v. State Farm Mut. Ins. Co., 425 So.2d 907 (La.App.1983) where a firefighter with six years experience was not qualified as an expert since he had no formal courses in fire origins; Burrell v. Kirkpatrick, 410 So.2d 1255 (La.App. 1982) where a fireman with twenty-seven years experience was held not to be a qualified expert on the causes of fires; State v. Williams, 654 S.W.2d 292 (Mo.App.1983) where a twenty year veteran firefighter was concededly an expert fireman but not an expert on the causes of fires.

2. Billings v. State, 503 S.W.2d 57 (Mo. App.1973). See also, Fox v. State, 179 Ind. App. 267, 384 N.E.2d 1159 (1979). A firefighter has been qualified to testify on electrical arcing; Fortson v. Cotton States Mutual Ins. Co., 168 Ga.App. 155, 308 S.E.2d 382 (1983), and on electrical short circuits, Jaklitsch v. Finnerty, 96 A.D.2d 690, 466 N.Y.S.2d 774 (1983). See, United States v.

Stillwell, 690 F.Supp. 641 (N.D.Ill.1988), (Arson of private residence that receives natural gas from other states constitutes arson of building used in activity affecting interstates commerce with in meaning of title 18 sec. 844(i)).

3. 115 R.I. 7, 339 A.2d 730 (1975).

4. 484 Pa. 89, 398 A.2d 957 (1979). The expert had also previously testified to the cause of fires in over 300 trials.

5. 270 Ark. 269, 604 S.W.2d 582 (1980).

6. 379 Mass. 810, 401 N.E.2d 342 (1980). And see, Godwin v. Farmers Insur. Co. of Am., 129 Ariz. 416, 631 P.2d 571 (1981) where the court concluded that a witness with two years of fire investigation experience combined with study at a community college and attendance at a week long seminar was an expert in fire reconstruction. A variety of educational attainments qualified the expert in Connecticut

expert witness, who was in charge of the local fire prevention bureau, had investigated the causes of fifty fires but buttressed this experience with an associate degree in fire science and attendance at two arson schools and several seminars.

Generally, witnesses with many years experience and schooling in the skills and techniques of fire fighting and arson investigations are presumptively qualified to express an opinion as an arson expert. In State v. Lakes [7] the arson expert had served two years as a fire investigator, been a fireman for twenty-one years, graduated as an arson investigator, and taught arson investigation for the U.S. Navy. The court in State v. Barnett,[8] however, held that a fire chief with eighteen years firefighting experience, formal training from the Air Force, city fire department and fire academy, and a state marshal's office, as well as fire investigation experience in the Air Force, as a consultant, and as a member of fire departments of several large corporations was not qualified as an expert on the causes of fires. The court emphasized that the witness himself said he was not qualified to pinpoint the causes of all fires. But such an admission by a witness of a lack of qualifications is not necessarily controlling, since the ultimate decision as to an expert's qualifications is that of the court, not the expert.

The qualifications of a fire expert should be keyed to the particular fire in issue. Where it is claimed that the fire was accidentally caused by the explosion of a heating stove, an expert should be proficient in the operation of stoves and the like. In State v. Wardwell,[9] a state fire inspector was held properly qualified to state his opinion that neither of two stoves he inspected on the burned premises has exploded causing the fire where the witness had been schooled in fire prevention, arson investigation, including the functioning of electricity, heating units, stoves and furnaces and had examined more than 300 stoves in his career.

Sometimes persons have been permitted to testify on subjects which, on their face, are beyond their competence. A forensic chemist has been permitted to answer questions on the use of toluene in the spalling of concrete.[10] A fire marshal with general training in the use of explosives has been allowed to testify that dynamite was the cause of an explosion.[11]

2. VERIFYING THE EXPERT'S CREDENTIALS

That the prosecution has a constitutional obligation to verify the

---

Fire Ins. Co. v. Gusman, 259 Iowa 271, 144 N.W.2d 333 (1966).

7. 120 Ohio App. 213, 201 N.E.2d 809 (1964). See also, Commonwealth v. Perry, 385 Mass. 639, 433 N.E.2d 446 (1982); State v. Garrett, 682 S.W.2d 153 (Mo.App. 1984); State v. Turnbough, 388 S.W.2d 781 (Mo.App.1965).

8. 480 A.2d 791 (Me.1984).

9. 158 Me. 307, 183 A.2d 896 (1962).

10. State v. Miller, 61 N.C.App. 1, 300 S.E.2d 431 (1983).

11. Stoner v. State, 418 So.2d 171 (Ala. App.1982).

credentials of its expert witnesses was held in People v. Cornille.[12]   Amil Cornille had been convicted of arson and sentenced to five years imprisonment.   The evidence introduced at trial was sharply conflicting and expert testimony from the prosecution's expert, Dennis Michaelson, a self styled "consultant in fire investigations," was extremely significant since he had asserted that his patented gas chromatographic technique had enabled him to discover the presence of accelerants in samples from the area of the fire.   However, the Illinois state crime laboratory had been unable to detect any accelerants.   And Cornille had made out a compelling case for faulty electrical wires having ignited the fire.

Two years after Cornille's conviction, Michaelson admitted in a newspaper interview that he had lied about his credentials as an arson investigating expert when appearing for the prosecution at Cornille's trial.   Michaelson had testified that he had investigated over 1300 fires in fourteen years as a fire investigator, earned both an associate's degree from Wright College and a bachelor of science degree from the Illinois School of Technology and received twenty-five postgraduate credits in subjects related to fire investigation.   In fact, Michaelson had no academic degree of any kind.   As a consequence of the newspaper accounts, Michaelson was charged with perjury.

Cornille filed a motion under Illinois' post conviction hearing act for a new trial based on Michaelson's perjury.   The lower Illinois courts held that Michaelson's conviction demonstrated no constitutional defect since only the state's knowing use of false testimony violated due process guarantees.   The Illinois Supreme Court disagreed, holding that the prosecutor's lack of diligence in verifying Michaelson's supposed qualifications was equivalent to a knowing use of false testimony.   The court stated that both the defense and the state had a duty to verify its experts' credentials especially when, as in Cornille's case, the verifying information was readily available.

The Cornille case could be considered to be limited to the prosecution's duties when employing private, as opposed to government supported, experts.   Such a narrow reading would be unwarranted, however.   The Illinois high court delineated no such distinction in express terms, nor would the obligations of due process seem to insulate the prosecutor from being accountable for the perjurious testimony of its government experts.   Certainly if the prosecutor and its government witnesses are deemed to be involved in a team effort, then the sins of the government expert should be chargeable to the prosecutor.

However, the Cornille case's imposition of a prosecutorial duty has been rejected when the bogus expert's testimony was not material to the conviction and the other evidence overwhelmingly indicated the defen-

12. 95 Ill.2d 497, 69 Ill.Dec. 945, 448   N.E.2d 1114 (1981). In People v. Hanna, N.E.2d 857 (1983). See also, People v. Alfa-   120 Ill.App.3d 602, 75 Ill.Dec. 793, 457 no, 95 Ill.App.3d 1026, 51 Ill.Dec. 556, 420

dant's guilt.[13]

§ 7.17　Arson Indicators

In an arson case, testimony as to sensory perceptions, such as smell or sight, which indicate arson, is relevant and often dispositive on the issue of whether an incendiary fire occurred. There are many such indicators, some noticed as the fire burned, such as the color of the smoke, and others upon later investigation, such as trailers, alligatoring and spalling. Courts generally accept such evidence even without establishing a foundation as to what different indicators can demonstrate,[1] or after adopting definitions of them which vary from jurisdiction to jurisdiction.[2] The courts are sensitive to the cumulative effect resulting from the existence of numerous arson indicators and seem less likely to question the admissibility of a particular indicator when evidence is available as to many of them.[3]

In State v. DuBose,[4] two fire investigators, who had conducted separate investigations, each testified that multiple fires, inverted cone patterns, and alligatoring, all indicating arson, existed at the burned premises and the appellate court accepted this evidence as establishing the incendiary nature of the fire without inquiring, for example, as to what an "inverted cone pattern" was.

Many of the arson indicators which are commonplace assertions in arson prosecutions are deficient for want of any established scientific validity. In many instances the dearth of published material in the scientific literature substantiating the validity of certain arson indicators should be sufficient grounds to mount a challenge to the general scienti-

---

N.E.2d 1352 (1983) the same duty was extended to a defense attorney.

13. Stevenson v. State, 299 Md. 297, 473 A.2d 450 (1984)—which also challenged Michaelson's testimony.

Michaelson is one of a number of charlatans who are exposed in Starrs, "Mountebanks among Forensic Scientists" in Saferstein, *Forensic Science Handbook II,* Chapter 1 (Prentice Hall 1988).

§ 7.17

1. See, e.g., United States v. Gere, 662 F.2d 1291 (9th Cir.1981); United States v. Gargotto, 476 F.2d 1009 (6th Cir.1973).

2. Compare People v. Green, 146 Cal. App.3d 369, 194 Cal.Rptr. 128 (1983) (burn patterns indicate the cause of fire) with In re Beverly Hills Fire Litigation, 695 F.2d 207 (6th Cir.1982) (burn patterns are marks indicating the path taken by the fire which enable an expert to pinpoint the location of the origin of the fire).

3. See, Zaitchick v. American Motorists Ins. Co., 554 F.Supp. 209 (S.D.N.Y.1982) (evidence introduced as to burn patterns, odor, black smoke, spalling of concrete);

T.D.S., Inc. v. Shelby Mut. Ins. Co., 760 F.2d 1520 (11th Cir.1985) (observations made of multiple separate fires, pour pattern, burn patterns spalling of concrete). In People v. Lippert, 125 Ill.App.3d 489, 80 Ill.Dec. 824, 466 N.E.2d 276 (1984) expert testimony was presented for both the defense and the prosecution as to the cause of the fire. The prosecution offered several arson indicators as evidence of the defendant's guilt, but could not suggest a reasonable motive. The defense presented expert testimony that a furnace was the accidental cause of the fire and the defendant had no motive for murdering his wife.

The court considered the cumulative effects of several arson indicators offered by the prosecution's experts: doors were shown to have melted at the bottom: there was evidence of a trail left by accelerants: the fire was said to be uncommonly hot; there was evidence of flashbacks; and a forensic chemist was able to determine that a T-shirt found on the premises had forty points of similarity with gasoline. This evidence gave the prosecutor the edge.

4. 617 S.W.2d 509 (Mo.App.1981).

fic acceptability of such indicators.[5] It is clear, from the cases, however that arson indicators are given a talismanic quality which they have not earned in the crucible of scientific validation.

1. ODOR

Testimony to the nature of a particular odor must be carefully circumscribed. No evidence of the identification of a smell as having derived from a specific flammable liquid or from an explosive compound should be received unless there is a preliminary demonstration that the witness is familiar with the distinctive odor which is claimed to have been identified.[6]

In Wilcutt v. State,[7] a fire marshal was said to possess a demonstrated recognition of the smell of exploded dynamite to such an extent as to enable him to testify that the odor he detected was that of dynamite. And in Commonwealth v. Theberge, a policeman assigned to the fire marshal's staff who had investigated six hundred fires was deemed adequately experienced to distinguish the smell of a burning ordinary oil lamp from that of range oil.[8]

Moreover, where the odor is commonly recognizable by lay persons, the court may permit such identifying testimony. In State v. Brooks,[9] police officers as knowledgeable lay persons, were permitted to testify that the odor of kerosene or heating oil was on the defendant's jacket despite a finding by an expert witness that the jacket contained no traces of accelerants when analyzed. The court upheld the testimony of the police officers since the expert stated that all traces of the accelerant could have evaporated through the plastic evidence bag before the testing was performed.

And the testimony of an expert has been allowed where he gave evidence that the odor he detected was that of a flammable liquid, without specifying the particular kind.[10]

2. BURN PATTERNS

Unusual burn patterns indicative of arson noticed during the fire by a firefighter or after the fire by an arson or fire investigator have been accepted into evidence by the courts, without close analysis, as having a

---

5. See, for example Frye v. United States, 293 F. 1013 (D.C.Cir.1923), and discussion in Chapter 1 at § 1.03, supra.

6. Pinnington v. State, 24 Ala.App. 227, 133 So. 311 (1931); Watson v. State, 23 Ala.App. 73, 120 So. 917 (1929); Anderson v. State, 20 Ala.App. 505, 103 So. 305 (1925).

7. 41 Ala.App. 25, 123 So.2d 193 (1960), cert. denied 271 Ala. 315, 123 So.2d 203 (1960).

8. 330 Mass. 520, 115 N.E.2d 719 (1953).

9. 126 N.H. 618, 495 A.2d 1258 (1985).

10. Stumbaugh v. State, 599 P.2d 166 (Alaska 1979); Zaitchick v. American Motorist Ins. Co., op. cit. supra note 3, "odor of petroleum,"

variety of meanings, such as suggesting that an accelerant was used,[11] indicating areas of flame intensity,[12] or revealing that the rapid spread of the fire was distinguishable from that of an accidental fire.[13] This general judicial use of the term burn patterns is supplemented by judicial recognition of specific types of burn patterns.

A. DEPTH OF CHAR; ALLIGATORING

To the courts, depth of char is a burn pattern which may indicate the duration of the fire,[14] its point of origin,[15] and whether the fire was ignited by an accelerant.[16] In Schneider v. Rowell's, Inc.[17] the expert pinpointed the duration of the fire as being from one to one and a half hours as represented by the depth of char. When finger-like projections of an accelerant are observed radiating from the point of initial impact where the deepest charring exists, the depth of char has been accepted as indicating both point of origin and the use of an accelerant.[18] One court has classified depth of char as light (¼ inch or less), medium (¼ inch to ½ inch), or heavy (¾ inch plus or minus).[19]

Alligatoring is a burn pattern often confused with depth of char[20] or defined as being equivalent to low burn,[21] even when experts are relied upon to propound a definition.[22] The significance attributed to alligatoring varies between jurisdictions, and even within the same jurisdiction courts have held that alligatoring indicates a rapid spreading of fire,[23] the use of an accelerant,[24] or both.[25]

B. FLASHBACK

The incendiary origin of a fire is indicated, so the cases say, when firefighters observe at the scene of the fire that a flashback occurs when the fire reflares after appearing to be extinguished. Testimony on a flashback has been admitted as signifying a pattern inconsistent with an

---

11. E.g. Commonwealth v. Wisneski, 214 Pa.Super. 397, 257 A.2d 624 (1969).

12. E.g. In re James H. Metcalf, 530 F.Supp. 446 (S.D.Tex.1981).

13. E.g. The Travelers Indemnity Co. v. Hunter, 585 F.Supp. 613 (E.D.La.1984).

14. Connecticut Fire Ins. Co. v. Gusman, 259 Iowa 271, 144 N.W.2d 333 (1966).

15. State v. Spearin, 463 A.2d 727 (Me. 1983).

16. Hughes v. State, 6 Md.App. 389, 251 A.2d 373 (1969).

17. 5 Wash.App. 165, 487 P.2d 253 (1971).

18. People v. Smith, 44 Ill.App.3d 237, 2 Ill.Dec. 877, 357 N.E.2d 1320 (1976).

19. In re J.E. Brenneman Co., 157 F.Supp. 295 (E.D.Pa.1957). The court didn't address the problem of how to determine where the measuring point begins when condensed or flaking burned material is involved.

20. E.g. People v. Cornille, 95 Ill.2d 497, 69 Ill.Dec. 945, 448 N.E.2d 857 (1983).

21. E.g. Kaminski v. Employers Mut. Casualty Co., 338 Pa.Super. 400, 487 A.2d 1340 (1985).

22. See, e.g., State v. Paglino, 319 S.W.2d 613 (Mo.1958) where an expert, in explaining a burn pattern, suggested that alligatoring was considered synonymous with depth of char.

23. People v. Lippert, 125 Ill.App.3d 489, 80 Ill.Dec. 824, 466 N.E.2d 276 (1984).

24. People v. Smith, op. cit. supra note 17.

25. Op. cit. supra note 19 (1983). People v. Cornille, op. cit. supra note 20.

accidental fire without any explanatory statements relating why only intentionally set fires flashback.[26]

C. MULTIPLE FIRES

When two or more simultaneous but non-communicating fires are observed, experts often testify that they would have had to be ignited independently of one another, indicating arson.[27] The existence of numerous unrelated fires, without additional arson indicators, is a sufficient basis in some courts for a conclusion that the fire was incendiary in origin [28] even when an exhaustive search reveals no evidence of accelerants or trailers.[29] Multiple fires in different locations on the same premises which are connected by trailers are strongly indicative of arson.

D. TRAILERS

Trailers are often observed along with multiple fires, either connecting the fires or spreading the fires to other parts of the structure. Courts have defined a trailer as "a combustible material that is used to spread and direct a fire in a particular pattern." [30] Expert testimony has been accepted that trailers are sign posts that an accelerant has been used.[31] In other cases, an expert has been allowed to state that gasoline or kerosene "had been poured in trailer fashion around the base of all the walls." [32] The trailer may itself be an accelerant, for example where firemen and investigators determined that the fire had been set "with the use of trailers of photocopier fluid and fluid-soaked material." [33]

E. POUR PATTERNS

Pour patterns from the liquid accelerant used will often be described and relied upon by experts in determining whether the fire was incendiary. The burn patterns are said to indicate "the area upon which and the direction in which a flammable liquid has been poured." [34] Pour patterns may signify that an accelerant was used [35] or what type of

26. See, Stumbaugh v. State, op. cit. supra note 10; The Travelers Indemnity Co. v. Hunter, op. cit. supra note 13. In State v. Berndt, 392 N.W.2d 876 (Minn. 1986), the accused claimed the fire deaths resulted from an accidentally ignited fire and an *accidental* flashback. The convictions were reversed for insufficient evidence of guilt.

27. See, e.g., State v. Jacobson, 326 N.W.2d 663 (Minn.1982); United States v. Gargotto, op. cit. supra note 1.

28. E.g., State v. Harris, 639 S.W.2d 122 (Mo.App.1982).

29. Commonwealth v. Harris, 1 Mass. App.Ct. 265, 295 N.E.2d 687 (1973).

30. United States v. Lorence, 706 F.2d 512, 514 (5th Cir.1983).

31. O'Keefe v. State, 687 S.W.2d 345 (Tex.Cr.App.1985).

32. People v. Tyler, 14 A.D.2d 609, 221 N.Y.S.2d 804 (1961).

33. United States v. Gere, op. cit. supra note 1.

34. State v. Nelson, 674 S.W.2d 220 (Mo.App.1984).

35. E.g. Hutt v. Lumbermens Mut. Casualty Co., 95 A.D.2d 255, 466 N.Y.S.2d 28 (1983).

flammable liquid was poured.[36]

F.   V (INVERTED CONE) PATTERN, INVERTED V PATTERN

While pour patterns are found on the floor, V patterns are found on the wall or items of furniture and allow investigators to determine the point of origin of the fire as well as, from the shape of the V, whether an accelerant was used.[37]   If the V pattern indicates that the fire was burning freely upward and outward then an accidental fire is suggested.[38]   If instead of a V pattern or inverted cone, an inverted V pattern exists, an incendiary fire caused by the use of a flammable liquid placed at a low level is said to be indicated.[39]   When an investigator observes an inverted V pattern with a "burn through" this has been held to be convincing evidence that a flammable substance was applied to the area and that the fire burned downward in response to the accelerant.[40]

G.   LOW BURN

A low burn is a pattern which courts have said indicates that the ignition source was near the floor[41] or points to the fire's origin.[42] When an investigator finds evidence of low burning coupled with trailers, the observations are said to signify the use of an accelerant.[43] Evidence of low burning without other arson indicators is rarely sufficient to establish the incendiary nature of a fire.

H.   SPALLING

In the few decisions that have addressed the subject of the spalling of concrete, the courts have generally credited the explanations of the experts on the appearance, the cause and the meaning of spalling. Consequently, spalling has been generally, but erroneously, considered as highly probative of the incendiary origin of a fire.[44]   In State v. Danskin,[45] spalling was described as "a condition of exfoliation" of concrete whereas in Zaitchick v. American Motorists Insurance Co.,[46] a "powdering" of the concrete was said to be the effect of spalling.

36.   E.g. Powell et al. v. State, 171 Ga. App. 876, 321 S.E.2d 745 (1984).

37.   E.g., Demyan's Hofbrau, Inc. v. INA Underwriters Ins. Co., 542 F.Supp. 1385 (S.D.N.Y.1982).

38.   Levy–Zentner Co. v. Southern Pacific Transp. Co., 74 Cal.App.3d 762, 142 Cal. Rptr. 1 (1977).

39.   See, e.g., State v. Belt, 6 Kan.App.2d 585, 631 P.2d 674 (1981); State v. Nelson, op. cit. supra note 33.

40.   State v. Cornille, op. cit. supra note 20.

41.   Landry v. Nusloch, 297 So.2d 759 (La.App.1974).

42.   The Aetna Casualty and Surety Co. v. General Elec. Co., 581 F.Supp. 889 (E.D.Mo.1984).

43.   O'Keefe v. Texas, op. cit. supra note 29.

44.   Baugh v. State, 776 S.W.2d 583 (Tex.Cr.App.1989). An expert erroneously testified that "spaulding" (sic) occurs when accelerant penetrates the pores of the concrete which is ignited by fire blowing away the top layer leaving open concrete below.

45.   122 N.H. 817, 451 A.2d 396 (1982).

46.   554 F.Supp. 209 (S.D.N.Y.1982).

Another court [47] has viewed the appearance of concrete after spalling as presenting a "scalped-out" look.

Most courts have accepted at face value the unproved assumption of fire investigators that spalling results from the effect of intense heat on moisture locked within the concrete.[48] As the expert was quoted as saying in Security Insurance Company of Hartford v. Dudds,[49] spalling occurs when intense heat causes "the moisture part or particles within the concrete to explode."

Even though spalling is taken, in most instances to be but one of many circumstantial signs of arson,[50] still there is an occasional decision which gives much too much weight to spalling as the sole basis for an opinion that a fire was of incendiary origin.[51] Then again the majority of courts seem to be taken in by the experts' assertions that the existence of spalling means that an accelerant was used.[52] However, an infrequent decision does pause to reflect that spalling can be accidentally induced and, therefore, explained as resulting from a non-criminal cause.[53]

When experts appear for both prosecution and defense concerning the significance of fire indicators, the courts tend to view these indicators more conservatively and to avoid giving undue weight to any one of them. In People v. Lippert,[54] the defendant was convicted of murdering his wife through asphyxia from smoke inhalation resulting from his setting fire to their marital residence. Even after careful analysis of the crime scene and laboratory testing no accelerant could be "definitely identified."[55] In addition, no clear cut motive for such a crime was advanced by the prosecution. In the absence of such evidence, signs of arson at the fire scene had overriding importance.

The trial was substantially devoted to the testimony of experts for both sides, the defense seeking to demonstrate that a malfunctioning furnace caused the conflagration. The prosecution sought to aggregate all the fire indicators, and other evidence, to prove its arson theory. Doors were shown to have melted at the bottom; "crescent shaped" pour patterns were discerned; a trail left by accelerants was said to be in evidence; the fire was said to be uncommonly hot and notably subject to flashbacks.

The spalling of concrete in the Lippert's basement also emerged in the prosecution's direct case as some proof of the use of an accelerant to spread the fire. But the defense countered with two experts of its own.

47. McClain v. General Agents Insurance Company of America, Inc., 438 So.2d 599 (La.App.1983).

48. Id.; Security Insurance Company of Hartford v. Dudds, Inc., 648 F.2d 273 (5th Cir.1981).

49. Id.

50. Reed v. Allstate Insurance Company, 376 So.2d 1303 (La.App.1979).

51. Northwestern National Casualty Co. v. Global Moving & Storage, Inc., 533 F.2d 320, 325 (6th Cir.1976).

52. Op. cit. supra note 45; Bufkin v. Texas Farm Bureau Mutual Insurance Company, 658 S.W.2d 317 (Tex.App.1983).

53. Op. cit. supra note 3.

54. Op. cit. supra note 23.

55. Id. at 466 N.E.2d 281.

One, referring to an unnamed "learned treatise," declared that spalling was frequently but incorrectly used as a sign of the presence of an accelerant. Another expert, described by the court as a "concrete expert," stated his opinion that other heat sources, such as wood or metal, were as likely to cause spalling as would an accelerant. After restating this conflicting testimony, the Illinois appellate court affirmed the murder conviction, but prudently did not mention the matter of spalling as corroborative of its decision. Similarly, the uncertainties in the cause and occurrence of spalling should lead other courts to accord it little or no probative value in establishing a case of arson.

§ 7.18   Testimonial Conditions

1.   IN GENERAL

A defense allegation of governmental misconduct in the intentional destruction of potentially exculpatory fire or explosives evidence is not well-taken unless the defense can demonstrate "the significant possibility"[1] that the destroyed evidence would have been exculpatory. In addition, even the intentional destruction of three hundred and fifty pounds of dynamite will not be challengeable where the government acted in good faith based on its lack of storage of facilities and public safety concerns.[2] But such a good faith destruction may call for an instruction to the jury that they may infer, from the destruction, that the true facts were against the government's interests.[3] Similarly, the inadvertent loss of evidence by the government's conduct goes to the weight of the evidence, not its admissibility.[4]

In most states, the defense retains the right to inspect, examine, and test physical evidence of alleged arson that is in the custody of the state. In Georgia the state's failure to comply with such discovery requests amounts to a denial of due process. Thus, in Pervis v. State, evidence of arson had been recovered from the fire-destroyed building and turned over to a private investigator employed by an insurance company for the accused. Despite timely attempts by the defense to compel discovery, the evidence remained in the possession of the private investigator until the time of trial. The State's Attorney had known of the existence of the evidence for six months. The appellate court held that denial of the defense's motion to inspect and examine the physical evidence at the trial deprived the defendant of his due process rights.

Where the state is in possession of exculpatory information, a failure to disclose it to the defense constitutes a denial of due process so long as prejudice arises from the prosecutor's non-disclosure. In State v. Swen-

---

§ 7.18

1. Lahrman v. State, 465 N.E.2d 1162 (Ind.App.1984), where a state fire marshal hosed down floor of burned building after collecting debris.

2. United States v. Loud Hawk, 628 F.2d 1139 (9th Cir.1979)—seven cases con-

taining fifty pounds each of DuPont Gelex 2 70% dynamite.

3. State v. Willits, 96 Ariz. 184, 393 P.2d 274 (1964).

4. Gedicks v. State, 62 Wis.2d 74, 214 N.W.2d 569 (1974).

son [5] a crime lab report which reported a failure to detect the presence of any liquid accelerant in fire debris was not disclosed to the defense, apparently since the prosecutor was unaware of its existence. This prosecutorial omission was deemed insufficient to warrant reversing an arson conviction since the evidence overwhelmingly indicated that the accused had suffered no prejudice from the omission and may, indeed, have waived his due process claim.

A gas chromatogram of a test on fire debris has been claimed to be the best evidence of the results of such testing, with an expert's testimony on it contingent upon the introduction into evidence of the chromatogram.[6] Although the point was said to have merit, the defense's failure to raise the issue in a timely fashion caused the error, if any, to be waived. Certainly the government would be well advised to preserve the chromatogram or the computer printout from the mass spectrometer on the possibility that the defense can prove it to be material.[7]

The results of a gas chromatographic test of wood, carpeting and vinyl tile from the scene of a fire where four members of one family died were found to be insufficient without more, to warrant the murder convictions in State v. Berndt.[8] The gas chromatographic test was interpreted by an expert to indicate the presence of an accelerant which was said to be gasoline. Other witnesses asserted that five gallons of gasoline would have been needed to fuel the fire that consumed the Berndt residence. In spite of these findings, the state did not offer any evidence of the smell of or traces of gasoline on or about the accused, which would have been expected since, with a blood alcohol level as high as .13 percent at the time of the fire, he could hardly have avoided splashing himself with gasoline if the state's theory was correct. In spite of the incriminating gas chromatographic results, the conviction was set aside for lack of proof of a motive for the killings or any "nexus" connecting the accused to the gasoline. The evidence was wholly consistent with a reasonable hypothesis of the innocence of the accused.

Although there is some considerable doubt that scientific methods of comparison are adequate in all cases to connect crime scene evidence to its source, the courts have not been chary of receiving such evidence. In Rogers v. State,[9] a chemist was permitted to testify that a black substance on a brace and bit found on burned premises with holes in floors and roof and a substance from the roof near the holes in it "were similar in all respects and probably originated from the same source." And in State v. Pisano,[10] gas and oil from a fire scene were said to the same as that from the defendant's outboard motor.

5. 396 N.W.2d 855 (Minn.App.1986).

6. State v. Burtchett, 165 Mont. 280, 530 P.2d 471 (1974).

7. Fitzpatrick v. Procunier, 750 F.2d 473 (5th Cir.1985) (drug prosecution).

8. 392 N.W.2d 876 (Minn.1986).

9. 161 Tex.Crim.R. 536, 279 S.W.2d 97, 99 (1955).

10. 33 N.J.Super. 559, 111 A.2d 279 (1955), cert. denied 19 N.J. 385, 117 A.2d 324 (1955).

In prosecutions for arson, the usual rules of evidence pertain. Thus an expert's opinion that a fire was set is inadmissible as based upon hearsay where it was founded on an extra-judicial conversation with a fire chief.[11]

2. ELECTRICAL FIRES

The discovery of evidence of beading, arcing, or fusing at a fire scene is sometimes considered evidence of the actions of an electrical fire. In Jaklitsch v. Finnerty [12] an expert reinforced his conclusion that the cause of the fire was electrical by his observation that the wiring had beaded. Testimony that electrical arcing was seen near the point of origin of the fire is often admitted into evidence as indicating that the cause of fire was electrical in nature.[13] Without any signs of beading or fusing experts have testified that an electrical short was not the cause of a fire.[14]

Some studies point out, however, that arcing is a natural consequence of a fire as well as possibly being a cause, suggesting the limited utility of arcing as an indicator.[15] In Fortson v. Cotton States Mut. Ins. Co.[16] an expert testified that although a great deal of electrical arcing had occurred, it was impossible to determine whether the arcing had caused the fire or if it was fire initiated. Moreover, one study [17] has concluded that beading may form either when the ends of wires are melted by fire or when arcing severs wires, perhaps eliminating the usefulness of beading as an indicator of an electrical fire. Fusing of wires is the result of an electrical short circuit, but a short circuit, as indicated above, is often the result and not the cause of a fire.

Identifying electrical ignition is further complicated since fire damage often precludes a conclusive analysis of the physical evidence. The electrical origin of a fire should not be assumed when no other logical method of ignition can be ascertained.[18] Some courts have taken this warning quite seriously and in arson trials have refused to admit expert testimony on electrical wiring as a cause of fire without a preliminary showing of a possibility that defective wiring was the cause.[19]

---

11. Commonwealth v. Rucker, 358 Mass. 298, 264 N.E.2d 656 (1970).

12. 96 A.D.2d 690, 466 N.Y.S.2d 774 (1983).

13. Foster v. Bi–State Development Agency, 668 S.W.2d 94 (Mo.App.1984) where observations of arcing were made before the fire, indicating defective wiring.

14. Dycus v. State, 440 So.2d 246 (Miss. 1983).

15. See, Beland, "Some Thoughts on Fire Investigation," 33, The Fire and Arson Investigator, 23, 26 (June 1983). The fire will destroy the insulation resulting in the wires touching and electrical arcing. When arcing is observed before the fire, see supra note 1, section 7.09, there is no controversy that the arcing does not suggest an electrical fire.

16. 168 Ga.App. 155, 308 S.E.2d 382 (1983).

17. Ettling, "Arc Marks and Gouges in Wires and Heating at Gouges," The Fire and Arson Investigator, June 1983.

18. For a summary of the difficulty of proving that a fire was electrical in origin see, Electrical Origin of Fire, 5 POF 135.

19. E.g., State v. Teitle, 117 Vt. 190, 90 A.2d 562 (1952).

The investigator must establish that sufficient electrical energy was present to cause ignition of the surrounding materials. In People v. Trippoda [20] a fireman stated his opinion that a lamp could not have been the cause of the fire in question since the arcing and sparking necessary to start a fire would have caused the fuse controlling that circuit to blow and there was no evidence of a blown fuse.[21] Defendant's arson conviction was affirmed since his defense that the fire was caused by an electrical malfunction was inconsistent with the competent expert evidence.

Courts generally consider an electrical fire to be synonymous with a fire of accidental origin,[22] although an electrical fire could also be incendiary in nature.

§ 7.19 The Search Warrant Requirement

Investigations at the scene of a fire or an explosion can have two quite disparate objectives. On the one hand, the investigation may serve the purpose of bringing the fire or the after-effects of the explosion under control. An investigation of this kind is premised on the need to remove the dangers, both public and private, inherent upon the occurrence of a fire or an explosion and to discover the origin and the cause of the incident. Ancillary to these objectives is the effort to preserve evidence helpful in accomplishing these goals. In the language of the United States Supreme Court, such an investigation constitutes an investigative search.[1]

The health and safety concerns of such an investigative search are of a different order from those which support an investigation which is designed to marshall physical evidence to buttress a criminal charge. Searches at the fire or explosion scene which are motivated by police and prosecutorial needs bring into obvious focus the requirements of a search warrant under the Fourth Amendment to the United States Constitution.

In two decisions [2] both involving fire scene investigations, the United States Supreme Court has sought to outline the circumstances under which fire investigators must secure a search warrant prior to their entry upon premises in which a citizen has a reasonable expectation of privacy protectible by the search warrant requirements of the Fourth Amendment. Bomb site investigations, having constitutional concerns and factual patterns analogous to fire scene investigations, are construed

---

20. 40 A.D.2d 388, 341 N.Y.S.2d 66 (1973).

21. The fireman was incorrect. Fuses are designed to protect branch circuitry up to the point where an appliance, such as a lamp, plugs in. While a fuse or circuit breaker might do an adequate job of protecting a 12 or 14 gauge wire, it is generally not expected that the fuse will protect an 18 or 20 gauge lamp cord as in *Trippoda*.

22. See, e.g., op. cit. supra note 12.

§ 7.19

1. Michigan v. Tyler, 436 U.S. 499, 507 (1978).

2. Id. and Michigan v. Clifford, 464 U.S. 287 (1984). A workmanlike analysis of Tyler and Clifford and their potentialities appears in Comment, "Firemen and the Fourth Amendment: What are the Requirements of a Post–Fire Search?", 10 *No.Ky. L.Rev.* 153–180 (1986).

for the purposes of this section as within the ambit of the holdings in *Tyler* and *Clifford*.[3]

These two Supreme Court decisions are alike in that they both recognize that a fire scene, or the like, is not exempt from the search warrant mandate of the Fourth Amendment, even though an investigation in such an event may be devoid of any criminal law enforcement motivation. These opinions recognize that no search warrant need precede an official's entry into premises or places where a fire is then underway, since a search warrant is inapposite where emergency conditions prevail.

Furthermore, the Supreme Court has adopted, for fire investigations, the search warrant pronouncements of its earlier decisions in *Camara*[4] and *See*[5] which cases arose out of inspections for housing and similar administrative and non-criminal purposes. *Camara* and *See* had settled that even searches for administrative, rather than criminal law, purposes are bound by the Fourth Amendment's warrant requirements, and, a fortiori, that an administrative warrant can issue without probable cause to believe that a crime has been committed. Those decisions, as a consequence, gave rise to a vast body of Fourth Amendment law distinguishing administrative warrants for investigative purposes from traditional search warrants with criminal law enforcement in mind.

By the application of its prior decisions in *Camara* and *See* to fire scene investigations, the Supreme Court has created a situation where some fire scene investigations will not require the prior issuance of any warrant at all. Others will necessitate the issuance of an administrative warrant and still another category of cases will not pass muster without a showing that a search warrant, in the usual form, authorized the search. To understand the method by which the rules governing these different occasions work in practice, it is necessary to be familiar with the Supreme Court's holdings in *Tyler* and *Clifford*.

In *Tyler,* the two defendants were convicted of conspiracy to burn real property upon evidence secured without the defendants' consent and without a search warrant on three separate occasions at the scene of a fire in a furniture store which had been leased to one of the defendants. Two plastic containers of flammable liquid were removed from the burned-out remains of the store by the local Fire Chief who arrived at the scene while the fire department was "watering down smoldering embers" in closing out its firefighting chores. Some four hours later, fire officials and a police detective returned to the store and retrieved evidence on a stairway and a carpet indicative of a fuse trail used to initiate a fire. Three and a half weeks later more evidence was uncovered upon a further search of the premises and the photographing of it.

---

3. The lower court decisions are in accord with this appraisal. United States v. Urban, 710 F.2d 276 (6th Cir.1983) and United States v. Callabrass, 607 F.2d 559 (2d Cir.1979), cert. denied 446 U.S. 940 (1980).

4. Camara v. Municipal Court, 387 U.S. 523 (1967).

5. See v. Seattle, 387 U.S. 541 (1967).

All of this evidence was admitted, over Fourth Amendment objections, at the defendants' joint trial in a Michigan state court.

The United States Supreme Court, in a separate consideration of the legitimacy of each of these three entries into the defendants' furniture store, upheld the admission of evidence derived from the first two searches but agreed with the Michigan Supreme Court's reversal of the convictions for the violation of the defendants' Fourth Amendment rights in the warrantless search three and a half weeks after the fire had been extinguished. Justice Stewart, writing for the majority, first held that the Fourth Amendment is not to be narrowly limited to "the paradigmatic entry into a private dwelling by a law enforcement officer in search of the fruits or instrumentalities of crime." [6] Commercial buildings not open to the public which are subjected to intrusions by firefighters and others on non-criminal law missions are within the sweep of the Fourth Amendment so long as privacy interests are jeopardized by the entry. "Searches for administrative purposes," the court declared, "like searches for evidence of crime, are encompassed by the Fourth Amendment." [7]

The court went on to affirm that both innocent and guilty fire victims may have protectible expectations of privacy in the remains of their property. No presumption of the abandonment of such rights is to be read into either a fire innocently set or one resulting from arson. As a general proposition, therefore, the Fourth Amendment's requirement for a warrant is a prerequisite to an official entry onto premises to investigate the cause or origin of a fire.

But there are certain well-rooted exceptions to this warrant requirement. The most relevant to a fire investigation is the catch-all exception which permits a warrantless entry in an emergency. Self-evidently, an emergency is at hand when a fire is burning out of control. But the emergency nature of the situation was not defined so narrowly by the Supreme Court as to cease "with the dousing of the last flame." [8] To do so was correctly conceived to be a misapprehension of a firefighter's task, which is not only to extinguish a fire but to prevent its rekindling and to do all that is reasonably necessary to find its cause. As a consequence, no warrant need be obtained authorizing fire investigators to remain in a building for a reasonable time after the fire has been extinguished in order to probe its cause.

The high court saw the entry of the firefighters in *Tyler* to combat the blaze as justified due to the emergency at hand. The warrantless return of a fire investigator four hours after the firefighters had exited was also permissible as "no more than an actual continuation of the first" [9] entry. But no exigent circumstances were revealed to justify the warrantless search three and half weeks later.

6. Op. cit. supra note 1 at p. 504.

7. Id.

8. Id. at p. 510.

9. Id. at p. 511.

In sum, the Supreme Court in *Tyler* established the following rules to control the admissibility of evidence obtained by a fire investigator during a warrantless search at the scene of fire:

Evidence is admissible when obtained during:

a.   an entry to fight a fire then in progress, or

b.   an investigation of the cause of the fire by officials who remain on the premises for a reasonable time after the fire has been quenched, or

c.   an "actual continuation" of an investigation to determine a fire's cause which had been commenced, but interrupted, during the effort to bring the blaze under control.

In addition, the court enunciated rules to govern the occasions when administrative, as distinct from true search, warrants must be obtained. The essential distinction stressed by the court related to the object of the fire investigator's search. If the search is premised on a desire to determine a fire's cause, an administrative warrant will suffice. But if the search is designed to secure evidence of the commission of a crime, then a full probable cause type search warrant is required.

The court also took note, unfortunately merely in a footnote reference,[10] of the factual variability of fire investigations. In recognition of this innate factual diversity from investigation to investigation, the strictures of *Tyler* must be applied on a case by case basis according to the divergent circumstances presented in each fire investigation. Such a frame of reference was bound to create confusion among fire investigators and the courts in applying the mandate of Michigan v. Tyler.

Thus, the Supreme Court's warrant prescriptions in *Tyler* were by no means a litmus-paper test sufficient to resolve the need for a warrant in any and all future fire investigations. The most hotly disputed issue elicited in the post-*Tyler* cases has concerned whether a warrantless fire scene search had been conducted within a reasonable time of the fire being extinguished. There is no clear consensus among these cases, even in those where the search could in no sense be said to be a continuation of a prior search initiated before the fire was put out.[11] This discord among the cases may be attributed to the *Tyler* court's defining a flexible warrant standard which gives considerable heed to the facts and circumstances presented in each case.

Other post-*Tyler* issues have been resolved with a similar lack of unanimity among the courts. The limits of the fire scene have been debated. A search of outbuildings detached from the main building in which the fire was confined has been, in dictum, upheld.[12] A Wisconsin

---

10. Id. at p. 510 footnote 6.

11. Anno., Admissibility, in criminal case, of evidence discovered by warrantless search in connection with fire investiga-tion—post-Tyler cases, 31 A.L.R.4th 166, 199.

12. Patri v. Percy, 530 F.Supp. 591 (E.D.Wis.1982).

court [13] has observed, quite sensibly, that a fire investigation can not practically be limited only to the area damaged by the fire since to remove the entire building from the reach of fire investigators would unreasonably encumber the investigation.

The decisions are in harmony in interpreting *Tyler* not to require that exactly the same persons re-enter the fire damaged premises to gather evidence subsequent to the extinguishment of the fire as were on the premises initially to fight the fire.[14] Any other holding would be a most untenable constricting of the scope of *Tyler*. Further, the cases have established that the evidence-gathering activities of fire investigators may include the seizure of any incriminating evidence, for example as to illegal drug possession, even though that evidence had no relationship to the fire, so long as the objectives of the warrantless search were not overstepped.[15]

A sizeable number of post-*Tyler* courts have been troubled by the legitimacy of warrantless fire investigations where the subjective motive of the official conducting the inspection demonstrated an effort to ferret out evidence of criminal behavior rather than to explain the cause or origin of the fire. The cases have split on the question of the admissibility of evidence located during such searches [16] with the better reasoned and well-founded excluding the evidence.[17]

Not unexpectedly, the post-*Tyler* decisions have struggled to elucidate when a re-entry is only an "actual continuation" of an earlier permissible entry. In a Delaware case,[18] evidence seized beginning twenty-four hours after an initial inspection of a fire scene by fire marshalls was deemed to be clearly detached from the original entry and not a product of an actual continuation of that entry.

Other puzzling questions remained during the years following *Tyler*. What were the differences in the evidentiary proof necessary for an administrative warrant as opposed to a search warrant? On what occasions might an individual's right to privacy in fire damaged properties be terminated so that no warrant of any kind would be a required

13. State v. Monosso, 103 Wis.2d 368, 308 N.W.2d 891 (App.1981), cert. denied 456 U.S. 931 (1982).

14. Shaffer v. State, 640 P.2d 88, 31 A.L.R.4th 166 (Wyo.1982); Schultz v. State, 593 P.2d 640 (Alaska 1979); State v. Jorgensen, 333 N.W.2d 725 (S.D.1983).

15. State v. Olsen, 282 N.W.2d 528 (Minn.1979). See also, State v. Bell, 108 Wash.2d 193, 737 P.2d 254 (1987) where the court upheld the warrantless seizure of nearly 90 marijuana plants inadvertently discovered in the defendant's attic after a blaze. Firefighters sent to the attic to make sure there were no smoldering embers discovered the contraband in plain view. The court held that the subsequent warrantless seizure of the plants by a deputy sheriff acting to secure evidence of criminality was justified where the firefighters had lawfully discovered the evidence of criminal activity in plain view.

16. Compare Cleaver v. Superior Court of Alameda County, 24 Cal.3d 297, 155 Cal. Rptr. 559, 594 P.2d 984 (1979) which upheld the seizure of evidence relating to a shoot-out with the police with United States v. Hoffman, 607 F.2d 280 (9th Cir. 1979) which reversed a firearm possession conviction for the illegal seizure of the sawed-off shotgun possessed by the accused.

17. People v. Calhoun, 49 N.Y.2d 398, 426 N.Y.S.2d 243, 402 N.E.2d 1145 (1980).

18. Passerin v. State, 419 A.2d 916 (Del. 1980), affirmed 449 A.2d 192 (Del.1982).

prelude to an investigator's entry? The *Clifford* decision, in 1984, sought to clarify a number of these unresolved perplexities.

The defendants, in *Clifford,* were Michigan homeowners who were charged with arson in connection with a fire at their home which occurred while they were out of town. As in *Tyler* the firefighters performed their tasks and left the scene. Some six hours later, an arson investigator arrived at the Cliffords' partially damaged residence only to find that the premises were being boarded up on the instructions of the Cliffords who had been notified of the fire. Without the authority either of the Cliffords or a warrant, the investigator proceeded to survey the premises.

A Coleman fuel can which the firefighters had placed in the driveway was confiscated and the search then moved to the interior of the house. In the basement, two more Coleman fuel cans were located in close proximity to a crock pot which was connected to an electrical timer which was plugged into an outlet. Following this highly incriminating discovery, the investigator then carried out a more thorough-going search of the remainder of the house, making observations and taking photographs to support the later filing of criminal charges. All of this evidence was admitted against the Cliffords, over their Fourth Amendment protests, at their Michigan arson trial at which convictions were returned against them.

In the United States Supreme Court, the state did not seek to justify these searches as founded on a fire emergency. Rather the high court was asked either to overrule *Tyler* or to modify it. The court, speaking through Justice Powell in a plurality opinion of four justices, refused to heed the state's promptings, but it did add some flesh to the bare bones of the *Tyler* opinion.

After reiterating its *Tyler* position that an administrative warrant will suffice for an investigation into the origin and cause of a fire, the court detailed the differences in the proof that fire officials must amass to authorize the issuance of an administrative warrant in contrast with that necessary for a stereotypical search warrant. A two-prong test was formulated under which fire investigators need only show that:

　　1. a fire of undetermined origin has occurred on the premises and that

　　2. the conduct of the search is reasonable, which is to be decided by the extent of the intrusion into the fire victim's privacy. Specifying a reasonable and convenient time for the execution of the search will demonstrate the sincerity of the interest in recognizing the fire victim's privacy interests.

In contrast, whenever the thrust of the search is for criminal law purposes, then a search warrant is necessary upon proof that there is probable cause to believe that a crime has occurred on the premises. Such a search warrant is mandated even when a valid investigative search is in progress, if during the conduct of that search, evidence pointing with reasonable assurance to criminal behavior is forthcoming. When such criminal evidence is uncovered, the investigative search is at an end since the cause of the fire is now known. Any continuation would entail a search, not of an investigative nature, but to collect evidence of criminal wrongdoing, which would require a search warrant.

Further, the state, in *Clifford,* conceded that no *Tyler*-type continuation of an earlier search had occurred when the arson investigator entered the basement of the Cliffords' residence six hours after the fire had been put out. Mr. Justice Powell found this concession appropriate since the search in *Tyler* was distinguishable from that in *Clifford* in two ways. *Clifford* involved an entry into a private dwelling, not a commercial building. Prior decisions of the Supreme Court have made it evident that privacy interests in a private residence are entitled to much more protection than those interests in other places. Moreover, the Cliffords had taken affirmative steps to protect their privacy interests in their home by having it boarded up, once the firefighters' tasks were accomplished.

The Supreme Court, in *Clifford,* seems to be saying that a reasonable continuation of a prior search argument under *Tyler* will be rejected when it is demonstrated that the legitimate privacy interests of the owners of a private residence are likely to be compromised. This would be a significant limitation upon the searches of fire investigators authorized under *Tyler*.

In applying the foregoing precepts to the facts in *Clifford,* the Supreme Court viewed the fire official's search of the Cliffords' home as a two-step process. The basement search, being without any emergency foundation and predicated on a need to determine the cause and origin of the fire should have been preceded by an administrative warrant. The remainder of the house search, being a search for further evidence of criminal activity, should have been authorized by a search warrant upon a showing of probable cause that a crime had been committed. The evidentiary fruits of both searches were, consequently, improperly admitted at the Cliffords' state trial. Only the Coleman fuel can found in the driveway survived challenge since it had been seen in plain view of the firefighters during their legitimate entry to fight the blaze.

What then is the constitutional status of searches by fire and kindred personnel following *Clifford?* It seems plain that the only warrantless search that is certain to be upheld is that of firefighters who discover evidence in plain view in the course of fighting the fire or, without departing the premises, in its immediate aftermath.[19] Other searches will generally be permissible only after either an administrative

---

19. The ruling in *Clifford* was interpreted by a Georgia court to allow firefighters to remain at the scene up to eight hours after the fire was controlled based on testimony that a fire could rekindle within that time. During the eight hours that the firefighters remained on duty investigators entered the premises without a search warrant and obtained evidence which was later used to convict the homeowner of arson. The Georgia appellate court concluded that the *Clifford* standards had been satisfied and the warrantless search was justified. Waters v. State, 174 Ga.App. 916, 331 S.E.2d 893 (1985).

warrant, where the cause and origin of the fire are undetermined, or a search warrant, where criminal activity is reasonably suspected, has been issued. In assessing whether a warrant is critical, it is important to appraise the remaining privacy interests of the owners of the fire damaged structure. Commercial buildings and private dwellings are distinguishable in this regard, at least so long as the premises are not totally destroyed, after which, it would appear, that only negligible privacy interests, if any, would survive.[20]

Among the major uncertainties remaining in the wake of *Clifford* is the extent to which its being only a plurality opinion will affect its longevity. The opinion of Justice Powell for the court stated the position of only four Justices while Justice Rehnquist, in dissent, spoke the views of four others. The swing person, who gave Justice Powell a majority, was Justice Stevens. Yet Justice Stevens disagreed with the Justice Powell faction that an administrative warrant should have preceded the entry into the Clifford's basement. To him, advance warning of the impending search to the home owners or a reasonable effort to do so would have sufficed. In general, Justice Stevens' position, although unrealistic since certainly an open invitation to the home owner arsonist to destroy the evidence of his perfidy, has a strong likelihood of future acceptance since Justice Stevens' opinion is replete with praise for the views of Justice Rehnquist's dissent.

The state decisions since *Clifford* have emphasized two aspects of that opinion. The first is the need to demonstrate that the lack of a warrant prejudiced the legitimate privacy interests of the accused. In State v. Snider,[21] for example, the defendant lived with his mother in the house which was burned but his privacy expectations, according to the Louisiana court, were limited to his bedroom and no other area of the premises. A second factual feature of *Clifford* has also bulked large in later cases. The lack of efforts by a property owner to secure and protect the situs of the fire before the entry of fire investigators has induced a number of courts to countenance a warrantless entry for an investigation into the cause and origin of the fire.[22]

Clearly *Clifford* has left the courts, both state and federal, with new guidelines and with additional cause for further clarification of the need for warrants, whether administrative or search.

20. The Pennsylvania Supreme Court in Commonwealth v. Smith, 511 Pa. 36, 511 A.2d 796 (1986), in a four to three vote upheld a *Tyler*-type search occurring the morning after a blaze. The majority held the warrantless search constitutional since its purpose was to discover the origin of the fire. The court pointed out that darkness and the still hot building precluded an investigation the night the fire was put out.

21. 449 So.2d 749 (La.App.1984). No privacy interest exists where the fire totally consumes or makes rubble of the place in which an accused claims to have Fourth Amendment rights. Pervis v. State, 181 Ga.App. 613, 353 S.E.2d 200 (1987) (House destroyed, only brick chimney left); United States v. Metzger, 778 F.2d 1195 (6th Cir. 1985) (Automobile reduced to "little more than scrap metal" by explosion).

22. State v. Burge, 449 So.2d 196 (La. App.1984); Commonwealth v. Smith, 331 Pa.Super. 66, 479 A.2d 1081 (1984).

§ 7.20 Experimental Evidence

Evidence of experiments conducted to determine the flammability, rapidity of burning, flash point, or explosiveness of various substances and materials is admissible in criminal prosecutions, at the court's discretion, as long as the conditions surrounding the experiment are not too dissimilar to those surrounding the event in question.[1]

The trial court's ruling on the admissibility of experimental evidence will not be reversed absent an abuse of discretion. In People v. Skinner[2] the trial court was held not to have abused its discretion in allowing the expert to testify as to the results of an experiment and in refusing to admit other experimental evidence in an arson trial.[3] Experiments were conducted on, among other things, the flammability of monks' cloth and the rapidity of burning of paint thinner. The testimony on the monks' cloth experiment was inadmissible since the cloth used in the experiment could not be shown to be similar in age and weave to the cloth that was ignited at the scene of the fire. The testimony on the paint thinner experiment was admissible, in rebuttal to a fire inspector's testimony, since the conditions of the experiment were similar. The appellate court concluded that there would be no abuse of judicial discretion unless no logical reason existed for the court's action.

The experiment and actual event must be similar but the degree of similarity required may vary according to the facts. In Erickson's Dairy Products Co. v. Northwest Baker Ice Machine Co.,[4] the court held that there was no hard and fast rule as to the degree of similarity required, and that the dissimilarity affected the probative value of the evidence, which was a matter for the jury. The plaintiff contended that a fire in his plant had been started when some welding had been done by defendant's employee too close to a wall. At trial the plaintiff objected when an expert testified as to a welding experiment, claiming that the test was not made under the same conditions inasmuch as no twelve inch wall was involved as in the actual circumstances. The trial court held the experiment was similar and the ruling was affirmed on appeal. And an expert's courtroom demonstration of one of many possible methods by which a bomb might have been triggered during the absence

---

§ 7.20

1. Anno., "Admissibility of experimental evidence to determine chemical or physical qualities or character of material or substance," 76 ALR2d 354. But if the experiment is illustrative only, similarity of conditions is not required. People v. Freeman, 107 Cal.App.2d 44, 236 P.2d 396, 401–402 (1951), where prosecutor, in his summation, threw lighted matches to show that they would continue to burn.

2. 123 Cal.App.2d 741, 267 P.2d 875 (1954). See also, Standard Oil Co. v. Reagan, 15 Ga.App. 571, 84 S.E. 69 (1915) where the experimental evidence was material and relevant in determining the identi-

ty of a liquid used in kindling a fire and thus there was no abuse of discretion in admitting the evidence even though the experiment did not exactly duplicate the conditions of the event.

3. When expert testimony as to an experiment is held inadmissible, the attorney may instead ask a hypothetical question. E.g., Schwartz v. Peoples Gas Light and Coke Co., 35 Ill.App.2d 25, 181 N.E.2d 826 (1962).

4. 165 Or. 553, 109 P.2d 53 (1941). See also, State v. Molitor, 205 Or. 698, 289 P.2d 1090 (1955); State v. Moore, 262 N.C. 431, 137 S.E.2d 812 (1964).

of the bomber has been allowed even though the export disclaimed an intention to demonstrate the actual triggering mechanism that had been used in causing the explosion.[5]

Experimental evidence is not limited to expert testimony. In People v. Freeman[6] motion pictures of an experiment were shown at trial. If the experiment is simple and easily understandable then a non-expert may conduct the experiment and testify to it, although the degree of knowledge necessary to perform the test will be a matter of argument to the jury.[7]

Some courts have held that experiments may be conducted in the courtroom in front of the jury, although it is unusual for the conditions of the experiment to be sufficiently similar to the actual event.[8] Demonstrative evidence may not be presented to the jury when it is merely a spectacular exhibition.[9]

When an arson investigator is permitted to express an opinion based, in part, on controlled experiments conducted by the expert, a defense attorney would be well advised to examine the nature and circumstances of the experiment with careful questioning on cross-examination. Questions should be considered probing the type of object upon which the experiment was carried out. If wood, for example, inquiry should be made of the expert as to the kind and size of the wood which was tested. Variations in the type and size of wood can have a direct effect upon the comparability of the experiment to the actual fire situation. Red oak, for example, is rated at the top of the burning scale since it possesses a uniform burning character.

The humidity, the temperature and the wind conditions, as well as the method of extinguishing the blaze, might also be matters upon which the validity of the experiment could be contested. Also, small scale laboratory experiments are most often unsuited to the duplication of the circumstances of an actual fire scene. The fire evidence cannot be properly evaluated without a full understanding of the intricate chemical and physical mechanisms at work in a fire. Such a comprehension can be gleaned only from full scale experiments. Laboratory experiments on a smaller order can usually generate only approximations concerning the totality of a fire.

An experiment may also be employed to disprove an allegation as to

5. People v. McDaniel, 16 Cal.3d 156, 127 Cal.Rptr. 467, 478–479, 545 P.2d 843 (1976).

6. 107 Cal.App.2d 44, 236 P.2d 396 (1951).

7. See, e.g. Standard Oil v. Reagan, 15 Ga.App. 571, 84 S.E. 69 (1915). See Anno, Admissibility of Experimental Evidence to Determine Chemical or Physical Qualities of Character of Material or Substance, 76 A.L.R.2d 354 (1994).

8. See, e.g., Moses v. J.H. Bowman & Son, 65 Dauph. 143 (Pa.1953); People v. Black, 45 Cal.App.2d 87, 113 P.2d 746 (1941).

9. Faulkner v. State, 43 Tex.Crim.R. 311, 65 S.W. 1093 (1901). But see, op. cit.

the cause of a fire. Beland [10] has presented a situation where all the evidence pointed to an electrical fire since the signs of arcing and the typical beaded electrical wire were present. Further, an extension cord plugged into a wall receptacle was demonstrated to have been overloaded. The facts predominated in favor of an electrical cause for the fire. Yet, Beland himself ignited the fire after pouring a flammable fluid accelerant on the carpet adjoining the receptacle. The experiment proved that the electrical malfunctions were the consequences, not the causes, of the conflagration. To distinguish between the cause and the consequence of a fire is one of the trickiest assessments by the arson expert.

An unsuccessful attempt through an experiment by the government to detonate a dynamite bomb has been held not to warrant the dismissal of Federal criminal charges. In United States v. Evans,[11] the court was not convinced that nondetonation was fatal to a charge under the Federal destructive devices statute,[12] since the capacity for detonation did not seem to be a required element of the crime. On that reasoning, the failure of the government to inform the defense of its inability to detonate the bomb did not result in the withholding of evidence favorable to the accused in violation of his due process rights.[13]

§ 7.21 Expert Testimony

1. CAUSE AND SITUS OF ORIGIN OF FIRE OR EXPLOSION

In arson prosecutions, two types of expert evidence are particularly relevant, although not always admissible. In most jurisdictions an expert can give an opinion on the cause of a fire [1] and the point of its origination whenever the jury is either unable adequately to understand the facts or draw inferences from them without expert assistance. The majority view is in accord with the Federal Rules of Evidence which allow the opinion testimony of experts if it assists the trier of fact in understanding the evidence or in determining a fact in issue.[2]

Expert testimony as to the cause of a fire or the location of its origin, as with expert evidence on any other matter, must be based on evidentiary facts.[3] In arson and explosives prosecutions, experts testify-

---

supra note 6 where no exact replication of a bomb was required.

10. Beland, "Comments on Fire Investigation Procedures," 29 *J.For.Sci.* 190, 196 (1984).

11. 526 F.2d 701, 707 (5th Cir.1976).

12. 26 U.S.C.A. § 5845(f)(3).

13. Brady v. Maryland, 373 U.S. 83 (1963).

§ 7.21

1. Anno., "Expert and Opinion Evidence as to Cause or Origin of Fire," 88 A.L.R.2d 230.

2. Fed.R.Evid. 702.

3. Traditionally, facts observed by the witness or testified to by other witnesses constitute a proper basis for expert testimony. See, e.g., People v. Lockhart, 200 Cal. App.2d 862, 19 Cal.Rptr. 719 (1962); State v. Smith, 34 N.C.App. 671, 239 S.E.2d 610 (1977); Commonwealth v. Colon, 264 Pa.Super. 314, 399 A.2d 1068 (1979).

In addition, the federal rules now permit inadmissible facts or data presented to the expert before trial in the formulation of his opinion suffice as a proper basis for testimony if such is the general practice.

ing from facts revealed through their own investigation and investigations under their direction satisfy this foundational requirement.[4] Even where there is a proper factual basis for the testimony, most jurisdictions limit the admissibility of expert opinion evidence on the cause or point of origin of a fire to cases where the opinion was a conclusion drawn from facts which cannot be accurately described without the witness stating an opinion.[5] The courts reason that if common knowledge enables the jury to competently reach a conclusion from the facts, then opinion evidence should be excluded.

The cause of fires is generally held to be beyond the scope of ordinary training and knowledge [6] and thus expert testimony is admissible. In Commonwealth v. Nasuti [7] the court, in affirming defendant's conviction of intentionally setting fire to his restaurant, sustained the admission of expert testimony by fire captains that the fire was incendiary in origin. Although no trace of flammable liquids was found on the premises, the experts testified to other indications of the incendiary origin of the fire. The court held that supplementation by expert opinion was clearly needed, although in some arson cases such supplementation may not be necessary. "Certainly laymen could hardly be expected to have knowledge in regard to various types of fires and the difference in the nature, violence, and intensity of flames resulting from the burning of inflammable liquids or other materials as contrasted with the burning of a wooden counter or chair upholstery." [8]

In a few cases jurors have been deemed qualified by personal knowledge and experience to determine the issues relating to the cause of fire without the aid of expert testimony.[9] In Superior Ice and Coal Co. v. Belger Cartage Service, Inc.[10] expert testimony on the cause of the fire was held inadmissible. The fire began after workers had been cutting pipe with a blow torch near combustible materials which were doused periodically with water during the cutting. The evidence was detailed and the court concluded that it was "a matter of common knowledge that a fire may be started in combustible materials that are compressed or moist and that it will smolder for as long as several hours and then burst into a flame." [11]

Fed.R.Evidence 703. See, Frazier v. Continental Oil Co., 568 F.2d 378 (5th Cir.1978), where an expert, testifying on the cause of a flash fire, was permitted to refer to petroleum industry standards, not admitted into evidence, which he had reviewed before trial.

4. Commonwealth v. Rigler, 488 Pa. 441, 412 A.2d 846 (1980), cert. denied 451 U.S. 1016 (1981); State v. Hallam, 175 Mont. 492, 575 P.2d 55 (1978).

5. See, e.g., Nationwide Mut. Ins. Co. v. Security Bldg. Co., 42 N.C.App. 21, 255 S.E.2d 590 (1979).

6. See, e.g., George v. Bekins Van & Storage Co., 33 Cal.2d 834, 205 P.2d 1037 (1949); State v. Gore, 152 Kan. 551, 106 P.2d 704 (1940); Harris v. Commonwealth, 342 S.W.2d 535 (Ky.1960).

7. 385 Pa. 436, 123 A.2d 435 (1956).

8. Id. at 438.

9. Miller v. Great Am. Ins. Co., 61 S.W.2d 205 (Mo.App.1933); People v. Vincek, 75 A.D.2d 412, 429 N.Y.S.2d 928 (1980); Sperow v. Carter, 8 Pa.D. & C.2d 635 (1957).

10. 337 S.W.2d 897 (Mo.1960).

11. Id. at 906.

In arson cases, expert evidence on causation of fires focuses on whether an accelerant was used and whether the fire was incendiary in nature. These two categories of testimony should be distinguished although the case law does not do so. When an expert testifies that kerosene or other flammable materials were involved in a fire he is indicating that an accelerant was present but is not necessarily stating that the fire was of incendiary origin, meaning that the accelerants were intentionally used to set a fire. In addition, to say that a fire was deliberately set is not to say that its spread to unintended places was incendiary in nature.

A minority of jurisdictions, such as Virginia, Alabama and New York,[12] maintain the position that expert witnesses cannot express an opinion that a fire was intentionally set, some on the view that such testimony invades the domain of the jury since it addresses the ultimate fact.[13] Most courts agree that the cause of fire is an ultimate issue in an arson case, although a few jurisdictions, like Pennsylvania, have held that the only ultimate issue is whether the defendant was guilty of the perpetration of the crime.[14] It is the minority view, however, that the incendiary origin of the fire cannot be the subject of expert testimony [15] and that the admission of such evidence invades the province of the jury.[16]

Expert testimony on the location of the origin of a fire is admissible [17] unless the type of observations made by the expert render the jury equally capable to determine the point of origin. When a duly qualified expert testified only that "I can definitely say that [the fire] did not start in the rear, but what part of the front it started in I cannot say, but it had to start in the front because it destroyed it," [18] the court concluded the expert had gone farther than he ought. The jury were thought to be capable of determining the point of origin of the fire without the expert's testimony, simply by relying on the facts already in evidence. In Nationwide Mut. Ins. Co. v. Security Bldg. Co.[19] expert evidence as to point of origin of the fire was held to be inadmissible. The witness had observed the areas where charred wood was found at the fire scene, the perimeter of the charring, and the points of severest charring. However,

12. See, e.g., Colvin v. State, 247 Ala. 55, 22 So.2d 548 (1945). Moreland v. State, 373 So.2d 1259 (Ala.App.1979). See also, Hughes v. State, 412 So.2d 296 (Ala.App. 1982); Ramsey v. Commonwealth, 200 Va. 245, 105 S.E.2d 155 (1958) and see, People v. Vincek, op. cit. supra note 9.

13. The Federal Rules of Evidence specifically abolish the ultimate issue rule. Fed.R.Evid. 704. An expert may testify that a fire was not chemically, mechanically, electrically, or naturally occurring, thus allowing the jury to infer by the process of elimination that the cause of the fire was arson. See, People v. Maxell, 116 A.D.2d 667, 497 N.Y.S.2d 735 (1986).

14. Commonwealth v. Nasuti, 385 Pa. 436, 123 A.2d 435 (1956).

15. Moreland v. State, op. cit. supra note 279. See also, Hughes v. State, op. cit. supra note 12.

16. Ramsey v. Commonwealth, op. cit. supra note 12.

17. See, Galloway v. State, 416 So.2d 1103 (Ala.Cr.App.1982); State v. Garrett, 682 S.W.2d 153 (Mo.App.1984).

18. Wimpling v. State, 171 Md. 362, 189 A. 248, 255 (1937).

19. 42 N.C.App. 21, 255 S.E.2d 590 (1979) where, in addition, the witness was not properly qualified as an expert.

these facts could be clearly related to and interpreted by the jury without the witness stating an opinion on where the fire originated.

Of course, an expert must state an opinion based on something more certain than speculation. In Schwartz v. Peoples Gas Light and Coke Co.,[20] for example, an expert was improperly allowed to guess at the ignition point of the vapor in question and to state that the fire might have spread downward rather than upward.

Expert testimony on the explosive potential of natural gas is necessary since the subject is beyond the understanding of lay jurors. Without such evidence a conviction for reckless endangerment for closing all windows, turning on a gas jet and setting a burning candle in a second story bedroom while leaving the victim bound and gagged on the premises must be reversed.[21]

§ 7.22　Explosive Traces From the Person

Most of the decisions evaluating the legitimacy of obtaining trace evidence of explosive residues, generally through the swabbing of a suspect's hands, have been concerned less with the scientific accuracy and reliability of the technique used than with the constitutional protection to which the suspect is entitled when incriminating trace evidence is obtained or tested.[1]

Recently, however, the English judicial system has been criticized for its use of trace evidence of explosive residue in a case in which six family members and one neighbor were convicted of illegally possessing an explosive, namely nitroglycerine (NG).[2] The so-called "Maguire Seven" were arrested in 1974 when police were under intense pressure to solve a rash of IRA bombings. The seven, including two children, were convicted after lab tests reportedly found traces of the explosive under their fingernails.[3] The case was reopened after all seven had served their terms in jail when it was determined that the informant naming the Maguire Seven had not been reliable due to police coercion.[4]

The Maguire case was reviewed upon the House of Commons appointment of John May, an independent appeals court judge. The May Report is harshly critical of the government's scientific evidence.[5] The essence of the prosecution's case at trial was that after swabbing the defendants' hands and scraping their fingernails and then testing with

---

20. 35 Ill.App.2d 25, 181 N.E.2d 826 (1962). But to couch an opinion in terms of probabilities rather than possibilities has been accepted. Gichner v. Antonio Troiano Tile and Marble Co., 133 App.D.C. 250, 410 F.2d 238 (1969).

21. People v. Grossman, 124 A.D.2d 974, 508 N.Y.S.2d 815 (4th Dept.1986).

§ 7.22

1. Although no longer considered an efficient option, at one time taggants were thought to be of great assistance in the identification and detection of traces.

2. The Rt. Hon. Sir John May, "Return to an Address of the Honorable House of Commons Dated 12 July 1990 for the Inquiry into the Circumstances Surrounding the Convictions Arising out of the Bomb Attacks Guildford and Woolwrich in 1974," London HMSO, July 12, 1990.

3. Id. p. 31.

4. R. v. Richardson (Crim.App.1989) *The Times*, Oct. 10, 1989.

5. Supra note 1.

one thin layer chromatography (TLC) system using toluene as the solvent there was evidence of NG residue on the hands of six of the defendants and on gloves used by the other. The problem with this conclusion was that the TLC test is not specific for NG. The case was based on the premise that the TLC tests had conclusively found NG. Government scientists working on the case knew that the TLC test using toluene could also detect pentaerythritol tetranitrate (PETN) and without further tests a positive result could be either NG or PETN.[6] This fact was only brought to the court's attention at the last moment and was down-played in jury instructions.[7] The May Inquiry also determined that it was possible that the tests were positive as a result of "innocent contamination" even to the extent of becoming lodged under the Maguires' fingernails.[8] For example, if there was a bath towel in the house with NG residue on it and all used it, later TLC tests could detect NG on the hands of those who used the towel. This issue was never fully explored at trial.[9] The May Report recommended that the case should be reviewed by the Court of Appeal.[10] Upon such review the convictions were set aside.

In the United States issues of scientific accuracy and reliability have been less thoroughly questioned, whereas the issues of the constitutional protections receive regular scrutiny.

In United States v. Sizemore,[11] an analysis of the hand swabs from defendant Frank Sizemore were negative for nitroglycerine but those used on co-defendant Elzie Sizemore's hands tested positive for nitroglycerine. The government's chemist testified that the test results proved that Elzie had handled "something" containing nitroglycerine. This and other circumstantial evidence of an incriminating nature were held to be sufficient to support Elzie's conviction but Frank's was reversed for a lack of similar, convincing evidence. The state's chemist in State v. Thoe [12] did not couch his opinion in such prudent terms as did the expert in the Sizemore case. In Thoe, dynamite residues were found under the fingernails of the accused. That determination, and apparently nothing more, led the expert to conclude that "Thoe had handled commercial dynamite on or about the date of the explosion" [13] some days before the testing. In spite of this evidence, however, the totality of the

---

6. Id. at p. 50, para. 14.4.

7. Id. at p. 51, para. 14.6.

8. Id. p. 29, para. 9.5.

9. It was shown that one of the principal scientists for the Crown, a Mr. Higgs, had co-authored a report published in a scientific journal in 1982. The article concluded that under-fingernail traces of NG can migrate there without a person kneading or handling explosives containing NG.

10. Id. p. 52, para. 14.11.

11. 632 F.2d 8 (6th Cir.1980).

12. 565 S.W.2d 818 (Mo.App.1978).

13. Id. at p. 821. See also, State v. Parsons, 513 S.W.2d 430, 435 (Mo.1974) where the expert stated his finding nitroglycerine on the hand swabs meant dynamite had been handled within a day or two of the blast and that the handler would have had to open the dynamite or have touched dynamite which was split in order to contaminate his hands. No reputable scientist should state that NG traces indicate the handling of explosives. The government, in United States v. King, 461 F.2d 53, 57 (8th Cir.1972) proposed to introduce evidence from swabs taken nine days after the explosion at issue. A new trial was awarded on other errors.

circumstantial evidence was too insubstantial to convince the appellate court to affirm the conviction.

Aside from the rulings on the sufficiency of the evidence in the Thoe and Sizemore cases, most other cases according judicial review to the obtaining of explosive traces from the person have involved claims of a constitutional dimension. In United States v. Love,[14] for example, the defendant's assertion of a constitutional right to the presence of his attorney at the swabbing of his hands for nitrates was rejected since the arrest was lawful and the evidence was so evanescent [15] that "merely rubbing the hands would have destroyed the nitrate oils." [16] But the appeals court was concerned lest a due process violation ensue if a defense expert were not permitted to participate in the actual conduct of the laboratory tests of the contents of the swabs, particularly since the testing would consume the evidence. No error was discerned in the failure to follow such a procedure in this case, but "in future cases participation should be allowed." [17]

Even recognizing that a right to counsel at the hand swabbing does not pertain, still must the swabbing be preceded by the issuance of a search warrant? By implication, U.S. v. Love rejects such a notion. State v. Parsons [18] does so explicitly, once again on the logic of the evidence being evanescent in nature. Yet where evidence of dynamite traces was held to be illegally seized from the accused's clothing, it was still permissible to subject the accused to questioning on that highly incriminating matter during his cross-examination at trial.[19] If the swabbing is preceded by the giving of the Miranda warnings, then the accused's silence in the face of inquiries about whether he had handled explosives cannot constitutionally be the basis for comment or discussion at his trial.[20]

§ 7.23   The Pathologist's Testimony

Forensic pathologists have been permitted to testify on a variety of issues concerning burns and fires. It has been deemed within their expertise to express an opinion that burn patterns on the body of a child abuse victim were not consonant with a claim of accidental scalding with hot water.[1] And in Commonwealth v. Stickle,[2] a forensic pathologist's testimony that a fire victim, who survived almost one month from the

14. 482 F.2d 213 (5th Cir.1973). Accord: People v. McDaniel, 16 Cal.3d 156, 127 Cal.Rptr. 467, 545 P.2d 843 (1976), cert. denied McDaniel v. California, 429 U.S. 847 (1976).

15. Pursuant to Cupp v. Murphy, 412 U.S. 291 (1973).

16. United States v. Love, 482 F.2d 213, 214 (5th Cir.1973).

17. Id. at p. 220.

18. Op. cit. supra note 13. No case has required a search warrant for the taking of GSR swabs, which is done far more frequently than swabbing for explosive traces.

19. United States v. Tweed, 503 F.2d 1127 (7th Cir.1974).

20. United States v. Bridges, 499 F.2d 179 (7th Cir.1974).

§ 7.23

1. Marshall v. State, 646 P.2d 795 (Wyo. 1982); Williams v. State, 680 S.W.2d 570 (Tex.App.1984); State v. Cummings, 607 S.W.2d 685 (Mo.1980).

2. Op. cit. supra note 1, section 7.13.

date of the fire, died as a result of extensive thermal burns was accepted. Of course, a pathologist may always give a well-buttressed opinion that death was due to asphyxia from smoke inhalation [3] or that death by strangulation, not fire, was the cause of death.[4]

In Green v. United States,[5] the defendant was charged with murder in setting fire to the deceased's residence. The Coroner testified that death resulted from pulmonary edema from inhaling the hot, irritating gases of the fire. The defense, however, sought to prove that the deceased's pre-existing heart disease had been the immediate cause of her death. The Coroner responded that the victim's blood contained a 14 percent carbon monoxide level, which, taken with the pulmonary edema, was further assurance that the fire was the cause of her death. The reviewing court found no error in this testimony.

In State v. Domer [6] an Ohio appeals court put too much faith in the pathologists' failure to find any evidence of carbon monoxide in the blood of the deceased. As a result Domer's conviction for murder was reversed for the insufficiency of the evidence to prove that his victim, one Riddle, was incinerated in Domer's car which Domer conceded having deliberately ignited, using gasoline. Further there was evidence to support Domer's theory that the victim, having a grave, pre-existing heart condition, might have died of natural causes.

According to Domer, he incinerated the already dead body of Riddle to fake his own death in order for his beneficiary to collect his life insurance. The pathologists for the defense had stated their "positive conclusion" that the absence of carbon monoxide in the blood of the fire victim was "positive proof that the body that was burned in defendant's automobile was dead when the fire was started." [7] In spite of the state's witnesses having stated their correct belief that fire could cause death even without any evidence of carbon monoxide in the blood of the victim, the Ohio court found the evidence of Domer's guilt confused and deficient.

VI. TRIAL AIDS

§ 7.24 Locating and Engaging the Expert

The prosecution has little problem in obtaining expert testimony from the arson and bomb squads of the police departments, fire investigators and fire fighters of the fire departments, and other specialists

---

3. Op. cit. supra note 23, section 7.17.

4. In State v. Wardwell, op. cit. supra note 2, section 7.13, strangulation was stated to be the cause of death based on an autopsy which disclosed fracture of the thyroid and cricoid cartilages, hemorrhaging in the adjoining tissues, no soot or smoke in the throat and only 10% carboxyhemoglobin in the blood. The fire was apparently a cover-up.

5. Op. cit. supra note 1, section 7.13.

6. 1 Ohio App.2d 155, 204 N.E.2d 69 (1964).

7. Id. at 204 N.E.2d at 77.

attached to city, state, or federal agencies which service the office of public prosecutors. When the prosecution retains a forensic chemist to testify on laboratory test results, the chemist will often be permitted to answer questions as to the nature of bombs and explosives, flash points, ignition temperatures, and burning rates, giving the prosecution another source of expert testimony.[1]

A defense attorney in an arson or explosives prosecution is not the beneficiary of so many avenues of access to experts. However, the fact that arson may be relevant in a civil law context, such as in the processing of insurance claims, as well as in criminal prosecutions has given rise to a large cadre of highly qualified arson experts. As experts in arson, such persons will of necessity have a considerable knowledge of explosives and their operations as well.

An excellent starting point in the defense attorney's quest for an expert is the International Association of Arson Investigators.[2] The IAAI has over 7500 members in the United States, Canada and 25 foreign countries, many of whom have qualified as experts. Upon phoning the IAAI, a list of experts in the particular jurisdiction in question may be obtained. The National Fire Protection Association[3] has a published list available of fire protection professionals, which should be useful in the search for an expert. By contacting the National Fire Academy[4] an attorney may secure a listing of active members in the arson and explosives field, some of whom may qualify as forensic experts. The Forensic Services Directory, available both in print, on Westlaw through the National General Databases and on Nexis, accessed by "REF SRV" library and the "EXPERT" file, supplies a listing of a few hundred experts in the arson and explosives field, who are unscreened subscribers to the Directory. In the explosives field, the International Association of Bomb Technicians and Investigators,[5] which publishes a quarterly journal entitled The Detonator, should be consulted. The American Academy of Forensic Sciences,[6] in the membership of its engineering or criminalistics sections, should be of assistance. The Lawyers Desk Reference,[7] in its March 1985 supplement lists 1500 fire

§ 7.24

1. State v. Miller, 61 N.C.App. 1, 300 S.E.2d 431 (1983) chemist testifies on spalling of concrete.

2. Whose address is:

5616 Bardstown Rd.
P.O. Box 91119
Louisville, KY 40921

3. Which can be reached at:

1 Batterymarch Park
P.O. Box 9101
Quincy, MA 02269

The list, on a state by state basis, appears in the 1984 Fire Almanac 85–99 (N.F.P.A.).

4. Which is an agency in the United States Fire Administration at:

16825 South Seton Avenue
Emmitsburg, MD 21727
(301) 447–6771

5. Whose address is:

1270 Friendship Lane West
Colorado Springs, Colorado 80904

6. Whose address is:

410 North 21st St., Suite # 203
Colorado Springs, CO 80904–2798
719–636–1100

7. I Philo, *Lawyers Desk Reference* 1:16 (6th Ed.1979).

and explosion experts, but they are listed alphabetically without designation of the particulars of their expertise.

The trial attorney should be aware that the American Society for Testing and Materials [8] publishes standards for fire tests of building construction materials, the combustibility of them and recommends practices for fire test standards. ASTM has also recently adopted test methods for fire debris analysis.

————

VII. MISCELLANEOUS

§ 7.25 Bibliography of Additional References

Note: Books and articles cited in the footnotes are not repeated in this section.

Extensive and up to date bibliographies on arson and explosives are available from Charles Midkiff, Jr., A.T.F. National Laboratory, 1401 Research Blvd., Rockville, MD 20850.

1. EXPLOSIVES

Amas & Yallop, "The Identification of Industrial Blasting Explosives of the Gelignite Type," 6 *J.Forens.Sci.Soc.* 185 (1966).

—"The Detection of Dinitro and Trinitro Aromatic Bodies in Industrial Blasting Explosives," 91 *The Analyst* 336 (1966).

Basch and Kraus, "Analysis and Characterization of Military–Grade Trinitrotoluene by Gas Chromatography," 24 *J.For.Sci.* 870 (1979).

Beveridge, Payton, Audette, Lambertus & Shaddick, "Systematic Analysis of Explosive Residues," 20 *J.For.Sci.* 431 (1975).

Blasters Handbook, 175th Anniv. Ed.

"Bomb Scene Investigations and the FBI Laboratory," *FBI Law Enforcement Bull.* 30 (Mar.1972).

Bratin et al., "Determination of Nitroaromatic, Nitramine, and Nitrate Ester Explosive Compounds in Explosive Mixtures and GSR by Liquid Chromatography and Reductive Electrochemical Detection," 130 *Anal.Chim.Acta* 295 (1981).

Brauer, *Handbook of Pyrotechnics* (1974).

Brodie, *Bombs and Bombings* (1980).

—*Bombs and Bombings: A Handbook to Detection, Disposal & Investigation for Police and Fire Departments* (1980).

Buechele & Reutter, "Determination of Ethylenediamine in Aqueous Solutions by Ion Chromatography," 54 *Anal.Chem.* 2113 (1982).

————

8. 1916 Race Street, Philadelphia, PA 19103.

—Techniques in Collecting Explosive and Gunshot Residue (ATF P. 7500.1 1976).

Chasan & Norwitz, "Quantitative Analysis of Primers, Tracers, Igniters, Incendiaries, Boosters, and Delay Compositions on a Microscale by Use of Infrared Spectroscopy," 17 *Microchemical J.* 31 (1972).

Chrostowski, Holmes & Rehn, "The Collection and Determination of Ethylene Glycol Dinitrate, Nitroglycerine, and Trinitrotoluene Explosive Vapors," 21 *J.For.Sci* 611 (1976).

Cook, *The Science of High Explosives* (1958).

Crippin, "Chemical Analysis of Selected Explosive Compounds," 4 *Midwestern Assoc. of For. Scientists* 10 (Oct. 1984).

Dahl & Lott, "The Differentiation of Black and Smokeless Gunpowders," 57 *Anal.Chem.* 446A (1985).

Davis, *The Chemistry of Powder and Explosives* (1943).

DeHaan, *Rick's Fire Investigation* (3rd Ed., 1990).

Elie–Calmet & Forestier, "Characterization of Explosives' Traces After an Explosion," 326 *Inter.Crim.Pol.Rev.* 62 (1979).

—"Characterization of Explosives' Traces After an Explosion," Part III, 325 *Inter.Crim.Pol.Rev.* 38 (1979).

Ellern, *Military and Civilian Pyrotechnics* (1968).

Encyclopedia of Explosives and Related Items, 10 volumes, alphabetically arranged (Picatinny Arsenal, Dover, N.J.).

Finnie & Yallop, "The Application of Diphenylamine and Related Compounds to Spot–Tests for Nitrate and Nitramine Explosives," 82 *The Analyst* 653 (1967).

Fisco, "A Portable Explosives Identification Kit for Field Use," 20 *J.For.Sci.* 141 (1975).

Forestier, "Characterization of Explosives Traces After an Explosion," 277 *Inter.Crim.Pol.Rev.* 99 (1974).

Grasselli, "Ion Chromatography in Bombing Investigations," 55 *Anal. Chem.* 1468A (1983).

Hayes, "A Systematic Procedure for the Identification of Post–Explosion Samples of Commercial Blasting Explosives," 21 *J.Forens.Sci.Soc.* 307 (1981).

Higgs & Hayes, "Post–Detonation Traces of Nitroglycerin on Polymeric Materials: Recovery and Persistence," 22 *J.For.Sci.Soc.* 343 (1982).

Kaplan & Zitrin, "Identification of Post–Explosion Residues," 60 *J.A.O.A.C.* 619 (1977).

Kempe & Tannert, "Detection of Dynamite Residues on the Hands of Bombing Suspects," 17 *J.For.Sci.* 323 (1972).

Krull & Camp, "Analysis of Explosives by HPLC," *Am.Lab.* 63 (1980).

Laposata, "Collection of Trace Evidence from Bombing Victims at Autopsy," 30 *J.For.Sci.* 789 (1985).

Lenz, *Explosives & Bomb Disposal Guide* (1976).

Lloyd, "Detection of Microgram Amounts of Nitroglycerin and Related Compounds," 7 *J.Forens.Sci.Soc.* 198 (1967).

Lyter, "A High Performance Liquid Chromatographic (HPLC) Study of Seven Common Explosive Materials," 28 *J.For.Sci.* 446 (1983).

McLain, *Pyrotechnics* (1980).

McLuckey, Glish & Carter, "The Analysis of Explosives by Tandem Mass Spectrometry," 30 *J.For.Sci.* 773 (1985).

Meyer, *Explosives* (1987).

Midkiff & Washington, "Systematic Approach to the Detection of Explosive Residues. III. Commercial Dynamite," 57 *J.A.O.A.C.* 1092 (1974).

—"Systematic Approach to the Detection of Explosive Residues. IV. Military Explosives," 59 *J.A.O.A.C.* 1357 (1976).

Mitchell & Tippett, "Explosive Damage to the Head," 9 *J.For.Sci.Soc.* 26 (1969).

Newlon and Booker, "The Identification of Smokeless Powders and Their Residues by Pyrolysis Gas Chromatography," 24 *J.For.Sci.* 87 (1979).

Olsen & Greene, *Laboratory Manual of Explosive Chemistry* (1943).

Parker, "Analysis of Explosives and Explosive Residues—Monomethylamine Nitrate," 20 *J.For.Sci.* 257 (1975).

Parker, et al., "Analysis of Explosives and Explosive Residues—Thin Layer Chromatography," 20 *J.For.Sci.* 254 (1975).

Parker, et al., "Analysis of Explosives by Liquid Chromatography— Negative Ion Chemical Ionization Mass Spectrometry," 27 *J.Forens.Sci.* 495 (1982).

Pate & Mach, "Analysis of Explosives Using Chemical Ionization Mass Spectroscopy," 26 *Inter.J.Mass.Spec. & Ion Physics* 267 (1978).

Peimer, Washington & Snow, "On the Examination of the Military Explosive, C–4," 25 *J.For.Sci.* 398 (1980).

Saferstein, Chao, Manura, "Isobutane Chemical Ionization Mass Spectrographic Examination of Explosives," 58 *J.A.O.A.C.* 734 (1975).

Sanger, "The Detection of Chlorates in the Presence of Sugar," 13 *J.Forens.Sci.Soc.* 177 (1973).

Stoffel, *Explosives and Homemade Bombs* (1977).

Styles, "The Car Bomb," 15 *J.Forens.Sci.Soc.* 93 (1975).

Tardif et al., "Explosively Produced Fractures and Fragments in Forensic Investigations," 12 *J.For.Sci.* 247 (1967).

Townshend, "Identification of Electric Blasting Caps by Manufacturer," 18 *J.For.Sci.* 405 (1973).

Twibell et al., "Assessment of Solvents for the Recovery of Nitroglycerine from Hands Using Cotton Swabs," 27 *J.For.Sci.* 792 (1982).

—"The Efficient Extraction of Some Common Organic Explosives from Hand Swabs for Analysis by Gas Liquid and Thin–Layer Chromatography," 29 *J.For.Sci.* 277 (1984).

Vouros, Peterson, Colwell & Karger, "Analysis of Explosives by High Performance Liquid Chromatography and Chemical Ionization Mass Spectrometry," 49 *Anal.Chem.* 1039 (1977).

Washington, Kopec & Midkiff, "Systematic Approach to the Detection of Explosive Residues. V. Black Powders" 60 *J.A.O.A.C.* 1331 (1977).

Washington & Midkiff, "Explosives" in Imwinkelried, ed., *Scientific and Expert Evidence* (2nd. Ed.1981).

—"Systematic Approach to the Detection of Explosives Residues, I. Basic Techniques," 55 *J.A.O.A.C.* 811 (1972).

—"Forensic Applications of Diamond Cell–Infrared Spectroscopy. 1: Identification of Blasting Cap Leg Wire Manufacturers," 21 *J.For. Sci.* 862 (1976).

—"Systematic Approach to the Detection of Explosive Residues. II. Trace Vapor Analysis" 56 *J.A.O.A.C.* 1239 (1973).

Washington, Midkiff & Snow, "Dynamite Contamination of Blasting Cap Leg Wire Insulation," 22 *J.For.Sci.* 329 (1977).

Yallop, *Explosion Investigation* (1980).

—"The Staining of Cast High Explosives for Observation of the Crystallizing Structure, 85 *The Analyst* 300 (1960).

—"Breaking Offenses with Explosives—The Techniques of the Criminal and the Scientist," 14 *J.Forens.Sci.Soc.* 99 (1974).

Yinon, "Analysis of Explosives by Negative Ion Chemical Ionization Mass Spectrometry," 25 *J.For.Sci.* 401 (1980).

—"Mass Spectrometry of Explosives: Nitro Compounds, Nitrate Esters, and Nitramines," 1 *Mass Spectrometry Rev.* 257 (1982).

Yinon, *Toxicity & Metabolism of Explosives* (1990).

Yinon, Harvan & Hass, "Mass Spectral Fragmentation Pathways in RDX and HMX. A Mass Analyzed Ion Kinetic Energy Spectrometric/Collisional Induced Dissociation Study," 17 *Organic Mass Spectrometry* 321 (1982).

Yinon & Zitrin, *The Analysis of Explosives* (1981). A comprehensive bibliography appears on pages 267 to 293 but the titles to articles listed are not included, minimizing the value of the compendium.

—"Processing and Interpreting Mass Spectral Data in Forensic Identification of Drugs and Explosives," 22 *J.For.Sci.* 742 (1977).

Yip, "A Sensitive Gas Chromatographic Method for Analysis of Explosive Vapours," 15 *Can.Soc.Forens.Sci.J.* 87 (1982).

2. ARSON

Adams, "The Extraction and Identification of Small Amounts of Accelerants from Arson Evidence," 8 *J.For.Sci.* 593 (1963).

Adelson, *The Pathology of Homicide* (1974).

—"Role of the Pathologist in Arson Investigation," 45 *J.Crim.L., Criminol. & P.S.* 760 (1955).

Aldridge, "A Thin Layer Chromatographic Clean–Up for Arson Distillates," 5 *Arson Analysis Newsletter* 39 (1981).

Andrasko, "The Collection and Detection of Accelerant Vapors Using Porous Polymers and Curie Point Pyrolysis Wires Coated With Active Carbon," 28 *J.For.Sci.* 330 (1983).

Beland, "Electricity: The Main Fire Cause," 32 *The Fire and Arson Investigator* 18 (Jan.1982).

—"Electrical Damages—Cause or Consequence?," 29 *J.For.Sci.* 747 (1984).

Bennett, "Physical Evidence with Arson Cases," 44 *J.Crim.L., Criminol. & P.S.* 652 (1953–54).

—"The Arson Investigation and Technicalities," 49 *J.Crim.L., Criminol. & P.S.* 172 (1958–59).

Bennett and Hess, *Investigating Arson* (1984).

Benz, "Thermal Deaths," in Curran, McGarry and Petty, *Modern Legal Medicine, Psychiatry, and Forensic Science* 269 (1980).

Bland, "Petrol, Paraffin and Arson," 19 *J.For.Sci.Soc.* 81 (Apr.1979).

Brackett, "Separation of Flammable Material of Petroleum Origin From Evidence Submitted in Cases Involving Fires and Suspected Arson," 46 *J.Crim.L., Criminol. & P.S.* 554 (1955).

Brannigan, Bright and Jason, *Fire Investigation Handbook,* NBS Handbook 134, Natl.Bur. Of Stds, Wash.D.C., Aug. 1980.

Brunelle, Garner & Wineman, "A Quality Assurance Program for the Laboratory Examination of Arson and Explosives Cases," 27 *J.For. Sci.* 774 (1982).

Byron, "Arson Analysis for the Non–Scientist," 35 *Fire Arson Inv.* 6 (1984).

Cain, "Comparison of Kerosenes Using Capillary Column Gas Liquid Chromatography," 15 *J.Forens.Sci.Soc.* 301 (1975).

Camp, "Analytical Techniques in Arson Investigations," 52 *Anal.Chem.* 422A (1980).

Carter, *Arson Investigation,* (1978).

Chao, "Laboratory Aspects of Arson: Accelerants, Devices, and Targets," 2 *Arson Analysis Newsletter* 1 (Aug. 1978).

Chisum & Elzerman, "Identification of Arson Acclerants by Gas Chromatographic Patterns Produced by a Digital Log Electrometer," 17 *J.For.Sci.* 280 (1972).

Clodfelter, "A Comparison of Decomposition Products from Selected Burned Materials with Common Arson Accelerants," 22 *J.For.Sci.* 116 (1977).

Covey, "Application of Energy Dispersive X–Ray Spectroscopy in Fire Investigation," 22 *J.For.Sci.* 325 (1977).

Davis, "Automobile Arson Investigation," 37 *J.Crim.L., Criminol. & P.S.* 73 (1946–47).

DeHaan, "Laboratory Aspects of Arson," 2 *Arson Analysis Newsletter* No. 2 (April 1978).

Doud & Hilton, "The Document Examiner Aids the Arson Investigation," 46 *J.Crim.L., Criminol. & P.S.* 404 (1955–56).

Driscoll & Krull, "Improved GC Separations with Chemically Bonded Supports," *American Lab* 42 (May 1983).

Ettling, "Determination of Hydrocarbons in Fire Remains," 8 *J.For.Sci.* 261 (1963).

—"Consumption of an Animal Carcass in a Fire," 60 *J.Crim.L., Criminol. & P.S.* 131 (1969).

Finney, "Investigation of Arson," 27 *J.Crim.L., Criminol. & P.S.* 421 (1936–37).

Goldman, "Update on Arson Analysis Using Microprocessor Controlled Gas Chromatography and Basic Programming," 5 *Arson Analysis Newsletter* 29 (1981).

Graves, Hunter & Stewart, "Accelerant Analysis: Gasoline," 1 *Arson Analysis Newsletter* 4 (1977).

Hrynchuk, Cameron & Rodgers, "Vacuum Distillation for the Recovery of Fire Accelerants from Charred Debris," 10 *Can.Soc.Forens.Sci.J.* 41 (1977).

Kirwan, "The Value of Medicolegal Autopsy to the Arson and Criminal Investigator," 43 *J.Crim.L., Criminol. & P.S.* 396 (1952).

Kolb, "Application of an Automated Head–Space Procedure for Trace Analysis by Gas Chromatography," 122 *J.Chroma.* 553 (1976).

Kubler, Given & Stackhouse, "Gas Purge and Trap Isolation of Accelerants from Fire Debris," 5 *Arson Analysis Newsletter* 82 (Nov. 1981).

Kubler, Greene, Stackhouse & Stoudemeyer, "The Isolation of Accelerants by Head–Space Sampling and by Steam Distillation," 5 *Arson Analysis Newsletter* 64 (Sept. 1981).

Kubler & Stackhouse, "Relative Hydrocarbon Detectibility by Flame Ionization Detection for Various Isolation Methods," 4 *Arson Analysis Newsletter* 73 (July 1982).

Kurz, Jakacki & McCaskey, "Effects of Container Size and Volatility on Relative Detectability of Accelerants by Purge and Trap Versus Heated Head–Space Method," 8 *Arson Analysis Newsletter* 1 (1984).

Kuvshinoff, *Fire Sciences Dictionary* (1977).

Lockwood, "Arson and Sabotage," 45 *J.Crim.L., Criminol. & P.S.* 340 (1954–55).

Lloyd, "Capillary Column Gas Chromatography in the Examination of High Relative Molecular Mass Petroleum Products," 22 *J.Foren.Sci.Soc.* 283 (1982).

Lomonte, "Use of Dedicated Mini–Computers in Arson Investigation," 1 *Arson Analysis Newsletter* 1 (1977).

Loscalzo, DeForest and Chao, "A Study to Determine the Limit of Detectability of Gasoline Vapor from Simulated Arson Residues," 25 *J.For.Sci.* 162 (1980).

Lowry, et al., *Scientific Assistance in Arson Investigation: A Review of the State of the Art and a Bibliography,* (LEAA 1977).

Lucas, "The Identification of Accelerants in Fire Residues by Capillary Column Gas Chromatography," 5 *J.For.Sci.* 662 (Apr.1960).

Mach, "Gas Chromatography—Mass Spectrometry of Simulated Gasoline Residues from Suspected Arson Cases," *Aerospace Report No. ATR–76* (9472)–2, May 1976.

McKinnon & Tower, editors, *Fire Protection Handbook.* (Natl. Fire Protection Assoc.), (1986).

Malik, "Histochemical Changes as Evidence of the Antemortem Origin of Skin Burns," 15 *J.For.Sci.* 489 (1970).

Martin, "Application of Legal Authority in Arson Investigations," 42 *J.Crim.L., Criminol. & P.S.* 468 (1951–52).

Midkiff, "New Weapons Against Arson," 22 *The Fire and Arson Investigator* 12 (1971).

—"Identification of Accelerants," 125 *Fire Engineer* 28 (1972).

Midkiff & Washington, "Gas Chromatographic Determination of Traces of Accelerants in Physical Evidence," 55 *J.A.O.A.C.* 840 (1972).

Morgan, "Preventive Arson," 44 *J.Crim.L., Criminol. & P.S.* 258 (1953–51).

Muehlberger, "The Handling of Explosives and Suspected Bombs," 38 *J.Crim.L., Criminol. & P.S.* 100 (1947–48).

Nicol & Overley, "Combustibility of Automobiles: Results of Total Burning," 54 *J.Crim.L., Criminol. & P.S.* 366 (1963).

Nowicki, "Control Samples in Arson Analysis," 5 *Arson Analysis Newsletter* 1 (Jan. 1981).

Nowicki & Strock, "Comparison of Fire Debris Analysis Techniques," 7 *Arson Analysis Newsletter* 98 (1983).

Presley, "Evaluation of a Portable Gas Chromatograph for Arson Analysis: Column Selection," 3 *Arson Analysis Newsletter* 18 (1979).

Rehling, "Legal Requirements of Preserving and Processing Evidence in Arson and Other Criminal Investigations," 48 *J.Crim.L., Criminol. & P.S.* 339 (1957–58).

Roblee, and McKechnie, *The Investigation of Fires* (1981).

Russell, "The Concentration and Analysis of Volatile Hydrocarbons in Fire Debris Using Tenax–GC," 21 *J.Forens.Sci.Soc.* 317 (1981).

Sadler, "The Crime of Arson," 41 *J.Crim.L., Criminol. & P.S.* 290 (1950–51).

Saferstein & Park, "Application of Dynamic Headspace Analysis to Laboratory and Field Arson Investigations," 27 *J.For.Sci.* 484 (1982).

Saterfield, "Criteria for Detection and Control of Arsonists," 44 *J.Crim. L., Criminol. & P.S.* 417 (1953–54).

Savage, "Investigative Techniques Applied to Arson Investigation," 48 *J.Crim.L., Criminol. & P.S.* 213 (1957–58).

Shifflett, "Investigating Automobile Fire Causes," 49 *J.Crim.L., Criminol. & P.S.* 276 (1958–59).

Smith, "Arson Analysis by Mass Chromatography," 54 *Anal.Chem.* 1399A (1982).

—"Mass Chromatographic Analysis of Arson Accelerants," 28 *J.For.Sci.* 318 (1983).

Stone & Lomonte, "False Positives in Analysis of Fire Debris," 34 *The Fire and Arson Investigator* 36 (1984).

Stone, Lomonte, Fletcher & Lowry, "Accelerant Detection in Fire Residues," 23 *J.For.Sci.* 78 (Jan. 1978).

Straeter, "Insurance Motive Fires," 46 *J.Crim.L., Criminol. & P.S.* 277 (1955–56).

Thornton & Fukayama, "The Implications of Refining Operations to the Characterization and Analysis of Arson Accelerants," 5 *Arson Analysis Newsletter* 1 (1979).

Tontarski & Strobel, "Automated Sampling and Computer–Assisted Identification of Hydrocarbon Accelerants," 27 *J.For.Sci.* 710 (1982).

Twibell, Home & Smalldon, "A Comparison of the Relative Sensitivities of the Adsorption Wire and Other Methods for the Detection of Accelerant Residues in Fire Debris," 22 *J.Foren.Sci.Soc.* 155 (1982).

Tyrrell, "The Decipherment of Charred Documents," 30 *J.Crim.L., Criminol. & P.S.* 236 (1939).

Ury, "Automated Gas Chromatographic Analysis of Gasolines for Hydrocarbon Types," 53 *Anal.Chem.* 481 (1981).

—"Rural Arson Problems," 45 *J.Crim.L., Criminol. & P.S.* 613 (1954–55).

Wetherell, "The Occurrence of Cyanide in the Blood of Fire Victims," 11 *J.For.Sci.* 167 (1966).

Willis, "Method of Identifying Fuels After a Fire or Explosion," 3 *J.Occupational Accidents* 217 (1981).

Willson, "A Unified Scheme for the Analysis of Light Petroleum Products Used as Fire Accelerants," 10 *For.Sci.* 243 (1977).

Woycheshin and DeHaan, "An Evaluation of Some Arson Distillation Techniques," 2 *Arson Analysis Newsletter* 1 (Sept.1978).

Yallop, *Fire Investigation* (1984).

Yates & Stafford, Fire Investigation Part I: Scene Investigation, 13 *Crime Lab Dig.* 70 (July 1986).

Yip & Clair, "A Rapid Analysis of Accelerants in Fire Debris," 9 *Can.Soc.Fores.Sci.J.* 75 (1976).

Chapter 8

FINGERPRINT IDENTIFICATION

I. INTRODUCTION

I. INTRODUCTION

§ 8.01 Scope of the Chapter

The attorney who is going to practice criminal law will almost certainly have frequent contact with the subject of fingerprint identification. The prosecutor who is unfamiliar with the subject may fail to elicit from his expert the positive identification evidence which would convince the fact finder. The defense attorney who relegates omnipotence to the state's fingerprint expert often does his client a disservice. On the other hand, in order to effectively cross-examine the expert, the attorney must understand the subject matter itself.

Attorneys practicing civil law will also have occasion to utilize a fingerprint examiner or to cross-examine such an expert. Will contests, insurance fraud, wrongful death, personal injury and medical malpractice actions are an example of just a few of the civil actions in which the services of a fingerprint expert may be required.

In order to present the subject clearly and concisely, the chapter will be divided into the classification and recordation of types of fingerprint patterns, the method of detecting fingerprints, and the theory and practice of identifying fingerprints for use at trial. The problem of finding a fingerprint expert will be examined from both the prosecution and defense standpoint.

The attorney who familiarizes himself with the basics of fingerprint identification will find that his inquiry of the expert will be more incisive. The defense cross-examiner may bring to bear material which will aid in demonstrating to the jury that though facts do not lie, they are often susceptible to more than one interpretation.

§ 8.02 The Origin of Fingerprinting

Fingerprints have been used as seals or in lieu of signatures since antiquity. Modern usage as a means of establishing the identity of individuals, however, is less than a century old. In the late 1850s, a British colonial civil servant in Bengal, India, started some limited use of handprints and fingerprints on contracts to prevent impersonation among natives. Independently, a Scottish doctor working in Japan became interested in the subject and eventually postulated, in the first published writing on establishing identity by fingerprints in 1881, that the skin designs found at crime scenes could be used to identify criminals.[1] The first textbook on the subject was authored by Sir Francis Galton in England in 1892.[2] Some limited experimental use was made of fingerprints between that time and its official adoption at Scotland Yard right after the turn of the century.

Meanwhile, the French policeman Alphonse Bertillon had developed a system of personal identification by bodily measurements which gained swift popularity in Europe and in the United States during the 1880s. The system was called *anthropometry,* but it became known as the Bertillon system, just as the early identification officers came to be referred to as "Bertillon officers." This name lingered on even after the unreliability of anthropometry had been exposed and the superiority of fingerprinting established. So deeply ingrained became the use of the term "Bertillon officers" for identification technicians that to this date some policemen, lawyers and laymen alike still refer to Bertillon as the "inventor" of fingerprinting, although he had nothing to do with its development as a means of identification. In fact, he opposed, throughout his life, its introduction in France, except as an adjunct to his anthropometry system.

Fingerprinting came into widespread use in this country from about 1910 on, after some isolated experiments on a local level, beginning in 1902. Today, most law enforcement agencies have fingerprint identification bureaus; some are independent units, others are part of a crime laboratory. Most states also have statewide identification agencies, often part of the Department of Public Safety or the Attorney General's office. The largest collection of fingerprints in the world is housed in the Federal Bureau of Investigation in Washington, D.C.[3]

§ 8.03 Definitions of Terms

Accidental: A subclass of the whorl-type patterns which consists of a combination of two pattern types or a pattern which conforms to none of the pattern types, and which has two or more deltas.

A.F.I.S.: Automated Fingerprint Identification System. A computer system which electronically compares unknown latent prints to known prints in a data base. The computer produces a candidate list of those prints which meet identifying criteria. A latent print examiner then determines whether a match can be made between the unknown and one of the candidates.

§ 8.02

1. Faulds, "On the Skin–Furrows of the Hand," 22 *Nature* 605 (1880).

2. Galton, *Finger Prints,* 1892. Long out of print, this book was reprinted in 1965 by Da Capo Press (New York) with a new foreword by the late Dr. Harold Cummins of Tulane University.

3. The F.B.I. presently houses in excess of 202 million ten print cards. Identification Division Statistical Report, Fingerprint Card Statistics, September 1993.

The F.B.I. Criminal Justice Information Services Division (CJIS) will be moving to a new facility in Clarksburg, West Virginia in 1995. For further details on the history of fingerprinting, see, Moenssens, *Fingerprint Techniques* (1971) 1–26.

Anthropometry: System of identification of individuals by measurements of parts of the body, invented by Alphonse Bertillon, but discredited because of its unreliability.

Arch: A pattern type in which the ridges flow from left to right with a slight rise or hill in the center of the pattern.

Bifurcation: A forking or dividing of one line into two or more branches.

Blocking Out: A procedure preliminary to determining the classification of a set of recorded fingerprints.

Central Pocket Loop: A subclassification of the whorl which has two deltas and at least one ridge making a complete circuit that may be spiral, oval, circular or variant of a circle, and a second ridge recurve either connected to or independent of the first recurve.

Chance Impression: See Latent Print.

Classification: A numerical formula derived from a study of all of the patterns in a set of fingerprints, which serves as a guide for filing and searching. It consists of a number of subclassifications.

Core: The approximate innermost center of the finger impression.

Cyanoacrylate ester: Substance commonly known as "Super Glue" which has become a very popular method for developing latent fingerprints by exposing objects suspected of bearing prints to its fumes.

Dactyloscopy: A term used in European and South American countries for the science of identification by the study and comparison of fingerprint patterns.

Delta: A point on a ridge at or in front of and nearest the center of the divergence of the type lines; may be a bifurcation, an abrupt ending ridge, a dot, a short ridge, or a meeting of two ridges.

Dermis: Inner skin which holds the dermal papillae, that serve as the mold for the development of friction ridges upon the epidermis through a process of differential growth.

Divergence: A spreading apart of two lines which have been running parallel or nearly parallel.

Double Loop: A subclass of the whorl group with two separate loop formations containing separate sets of shoulders and two deltas.

Enclosure: A ridge characteristic comprised of a single ridge which bifurcates and shortly thereafter again reunites to continue as a single ridge.

Epidermis: The outermost layer of skin composed of stratum corneum, cornified dead cells that constantly slough off as scales.

Flexion Creases: The folds in the skin of the palm, at the junction of the digits and at the joints of the phalanges.

Friction Skin: The ridged skin on the inner surface of the palms, fingers and feet; characterized by absence of hair and by sweat exuding glands.

Henry Classification: The system of classification developed by Sir Edward Henry around the turn of the century which still serves as the basis for the extended manual system of classification in the United States and in all English speaking countries.

Laser Development: Among the new methods for developing latent fingerprints, one makes use of the argon-ion (or other type) laser instrument to excite the inherent luminescence of some components in human perspiration.

Latent Print: Unintentional fingerprints left at a crime scene; frequently invisible to the unaided eye.

Loop: A type of fingerprint pattern in which one or more of the ridges enter on either side of the impression, recurve, touch or pass an imaginary line drawn from the delta to the core, and terminate or tend to terminate on or toward the same side of the impression from whence such ridge or ridges entered.

Pattern Area: The part of a loop or whorl utilized in classifying the print in which appear the cores, deltas, and ridges needed for pattern interpretation.

Plain Arch: A pattern in which the ridges enter on one side of the impression and flow out the other with a rise or wave in the center.

Poroscopy: The science of identification which studies the sweat pore configuration of the fingerprint impression. Although seldom used today, it could be employed when only a fragment of a latent print is found. Pore structure is often difficult to discern in prints.

Pressure Distortion: The distortion of a pattern caused by imprinting a finger upon a surface with unusual pressure and force.

Radial Loop: A loop in which the flow of the ridges is in the direction of the radius bone of the forearm (toward the thumb).

Ridge Characteristics: Minute ridge endings, bifurcations, enclosures, and other ridge details which must match in two prints in order to establish their identical nature. Also called, Galton Details.

Ridge Count: The number of ridges intervening between the delta and the core. It is used to subdivide loop patterns.

Ridge Pattern: The contour patterns formed by the flowing ridges of the friction skin appearing on the inside terminal bulbs of the fingers and thumb.

Ridge Trace: A process for subdividing whorl-type patterns into Inner, Meeting, or Outer whorls by considering the flow of the ridges from the left to the right delta.

Super Glue: See Cyanoacrylate ester.

Tented Arch: A pattern in which most of the ridges enter upon one side of the impression and flow out the other side with the exception of the ridges at the center which form an upthrust or an angle.

Type Lines: The two innermost ridges which start parallel, diverge and surround the pattern area of loops and whorls.

Ulnar Loop: A loop which flows in the direction of the ulna bone of the forearm (toward the little finger).

Whorl: A pattern having at least two deltas with a complete recurve in front of each. A plain whorl has two deltas and at least one ridge making a complete circuit which may be spiral, oval, circular or any variant of a circle.

II.   CLASSIFICATION AND USES OF FINGERPRINTS

§ 8.04   Physiology of the Fingerprints

A fingerprint is an impression of the intricate design of friction skin ridges found on the palmar side of a person's finger or thumb. The same type of friction skin, with tiny ridge configurations, can also be found on the whole palmar surface of the hands and on the plantar surfaces (soles) of the feet in humans and higher primates. There is no physical, physiological, or biological difference between the friction skin on the fingers and that on the palms of the hands and the soles of the feet.

The friction skin ridges bear rows of sweat pores, through which perspiration is exuded which flows over the ridges; the perspiration acts as a lubricant, and insures a firmness of grip. Because of this perspiration, and the incidental coating of the skin with other bodily oils, an impression of the ridge pattern of the finger is left whenever that finger touches a relatively smooth surface. Since individuals vary in the amount of perspiration exuded, some are less likely than others to leave identifiable fingerprint impressions. The impression that is accidentally left on a surface is called a latent print.

Latent prints may be of three varieties:

(1) Plastic print—a visible, long-lasting chance fingerprint impression made in candle wax, tar, clay, oil film, grease, or putty;

(2) Visible print—a visible, easily destroyed chance fingerprint impression made in dust, soot, blood, or powder, as well as any other impression resulting from the fingers being covered with foreign matter;

(3) Invisible print—an invisible, easily destroyed chance fingerprint impression resulting from the grease-sweat-dirt coating on the ridges of the friction skin as contact is made with a relatively smooth surface.

Even though latent prints are ordinarily of the invisible type, they can be made to appear quite distinct through the proper use of fingerprint powders, vapors and chemicals, and other developing methods.

Inked prints are those made on special fingerprint record cards. Inked prints may be used either for comparison with latent prints for the purpose of identification, or to impeach a defendant or other witness by proof of a prior conviction of a serious nature, or at the penalty stage of the bifurcated trial as part of the state's proof concerning the defendant's prior criminal record. While the very durable inked finger impressions, recorded by the police, are certainly "visible" impressions, they do not come within the second group of "latent" prints because they were intentionally recorded, rather than accidentally deposited.

Figure 1 shows inked prints, and in Figure 2 developed latent prints are illustrated.

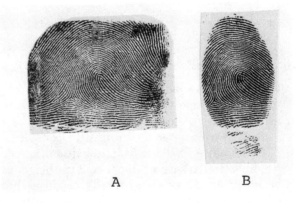

A   B

Fig. I. Example of a print obtained by rolling the digit from nail to nail (Print A), and of a plain impression made by pressing the finger down on a surface without a rolling motion (Print B).

Fig. 2. Latent impressions developed on the handle of a hammer with special magnetic powder. *Courtesy: MacDonell Associates, Corning, N. Y.*

§ 8.05   Fundamental Premises of Fingerprint Individuality

The practical uses in law enforcement of a system of fingerprint identification derive from three well established premises: (1) the friction ridge patterns that begin to develop during fetal life remain unchanged during life, and even after death, until decomposition destroys the ridged skin; (2) the patterns differ from individual to individual, and even from digit to digit, and are never duplicated in their minute details; and, (3) although all patterns are distinct in their ridge characteristics, their overall pattern appearances have similarities which permit a systematic classification of the impressions.

From childhood to maturity, the friction skin patterns grow and expand in size. As an adult grows old, the finger patterns may shrink in size, but the characteristic points used to determine their individuality do not undergo any natural change in relation to one another. Rare cases of mutilation, or the occurrence of some skin disease, such as leprosy, may partially or totally destroy the epidermal ridges. If the destruction is only partial, it will not affect the value of the impressions for identification purposes, since complete patterns are not needed.

The friction skin patterns are formed through a process of differential growth in the dermis layer of the skin. If the finger is superficially hurt or mutilated to a depth of not more than approximately one millimeter, the injury will reflect itself in the pattern as a temporary scar. Upon healing of the scarred area, however, the pattern will return exactly to its same image as before the injury. If the injury inflicted is more serious and reaches into the dermis layer of the skin to damage the ridge molding "dermal papillae," a permanent scar will remain after the healing process is completed. Such permanent scars do not affect identification, as long as sufficient undamaged skin remains. (See Figure 3)

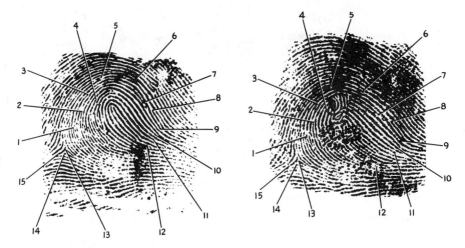

Fig. 3. This is an exhibit of the type fingerprint experts often use in court to illustrate their testimony. The print at the right shows extensive scar tissue resulting from intentionally inflicted pattern mutilation. Yet, this does not prevent identification of the print on the basis of a pre-scarification impression of the same digit.

When a person is arrested by the police, his fingerprints are recorded on standard 8 × 8–inch fingerprint cards. This is done by rolling the fingers, one by one, over an inked slab, then onto the card. In addition to rolled impression, the card also has spaces for plain impressions, made by pressing down the fingers and thumbs without a rolling motion. (See Figure 4)

One of the problems with traditional fingerprinting is that dirt, contamination by other materials, or uneven pressure may result in distorted, blurred or smudged inked prints thus rendering them useless for identification purposes. New technologies have been developed to eliminate problems of illegible prints. An electronic scanning system creates a fingerprint image when a person places his finger on a glass plate and highly sensitive optical equipment photographs the finger. The F.B.I. has been testing such systems. The F.B.I. has also been testing a mobile scanning unit which will allow officers on the street to transmit a suspect's fingerprints directly to a central location to see if the individual has any outstanding warrants.

If the department maintains a 10–finger filing system that is manually operated, the fingerprint card is then given a classification formula based upon a study of the general types of patterns and their subdivisions so that it can be filed, and subsequently located. When the subject is again fingerprinted at a later date, a new set of prints will be recorded and classified, and in the process of filing this new card according to its formula, the existence of a prior record of fingerprints may be determined.

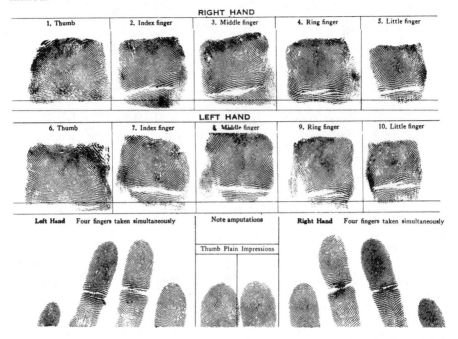

Fig. 4. The rolled and plain impressions recorded on a typical 8″ x 8″ fingerprint card, slightly reduced here. The spaces on the card provided for information about the subject have been cropped off.

In a department that no longer uses manual searching and filing methods, the card will be processed for optical scanning of the individual ridge characteristics that are then retained in a computer storage system, and the actual fingerprint card, after such processing, may be filed in a criminal history folder on its subject, rather than in a centralized fingerprint collection.

If an individual attempts to deceive the police by the use of an alias or by a changed appearance, the fingerprint file serves to establish his former identity. Latent impressions found at the scene of the crime may be rendered visible and they, too, may be compared with the impressions on file. Thus, by means of fingerprints, the police may be able to discover the identity of the person who has left his latent fingerprints at an incriminating location.

An important fact for lawyers to remember is that *classification* and *identification* are two distinct concepts which have very little in common, except that they both deal with fingerprints. The classification of a set of fingerprints is traditionally derived by a mathematical formula based upon the types of patterns occurring on the ten fingers of an individual and the various subclassifications and divisions given to these patterns upon the basis of the location, within the patterns, of fixed reference points such as deltas and cores. Identification, on the other hand, is concerned largely with a comparison of the individual ridge characteristics such as bifurcations, ridge endings, enclosures, ridge dots, etc. Before it can be said that two fingerprint impressions were produced by the same finger, the patterns must of course be of the same pattern type. That, however, is largely insufficient and meaningless since all fingerprints can be brought within three general classes of patterns: arches, loops and whorls. To establish identity, it must be shown that a sufficient number of ridge characteristics are found in the same position and relative frequency, quantitatively and qualitatively, in the same area examined in both finger impressions. The five principal ridge characteristics are illustrated in Figure 5.

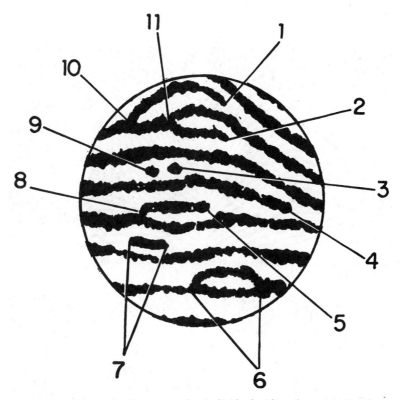

Fig. 5. In this fingerprint fragment, the individual ridge characteristics have been marked. Points 1, 2, 4 and 5 are ridge endings. Points 8, 10 and 11 are bifurcations. Point 7 is a short ridge. Points 3 and 9 are ridge dots or islands. Point 6 is an enclosure.

§ 8.06   Fingerprint Classification

1.   PATTERN INTERPRETATION

The traditional classification formula of a set of fingerprints, as used until the advent of computerized fingerprint storage and retrieval systems, is assigned on the basis of the preliminary process known as pattern interpretation and blocking out of the set of prints. All finger-prints can be brought within one of three main pattern type groups: arches, loops and whorls. Arches account for approximately 5% of all fingerprints, loops approximately 60% and whorls 35%.

Arches are subdivided into plain arches and tented arches (see Figure 6). Loops are initially subdivided into ulnar and radial loops, depending upon the slant of the loops and the hand on which they appear (see Figure 7); they are further subdivided by a process known as ridge counting. Whorl-type patterns are divided into four subgroups: plain whorls, central pocket loops, double loops and accidental whorls (see Figure 8); and they may be further subdivided by a process known as ridge tracing.

Fig. 6. The pattern on the left is typical of the plain arch; the one on the right of the tented arch type.

Fig. 7. Two loop-type patterns with the core and delta locations marked.

Fig. 8. The four different whorl-type patterns: upper left, a plain whorl; upper right, a central pocket loop; lower left, a double loop; lower right, an accidental whorl.

Within all loop and whorl patterns there are also fixed reference points known as deltas. Loops have one delta each. Plain whorls, central pocket loops and double loops have two deltas, while accidental whorls have at least two deltas but can have more. Another fixed reference point in loops is the core. There are arbitrary rules, set up by the early fingerprint pioneers who devised the classification schemes, which the technician follows to determine the exact location, within a pattern, of the core and delta.

Ridge counting in loops is a process of counting all the ridges which cross an imaginary line drawn between the core and the delta, not counting these two reference points themselves. Ridge tracing in whorls is a process whereby the line of friction skin detail which constitutes the left delta is traced toward the right delta. If the traced ridge flows above or to the inside of the right delta by three or more ridges the whorl is called "inner" (symbol I); if the traced ridge meets the right delta or passes either over or under it with not more than two intervening ridges, the whorl is called "meeting" (symbol M); if the ridge traced from the left delta flows under or to the outside of the right delta by three or more ridges, the pattern is "outer" (symbol O).

2. CLASSIFICATION FORMULA

The classification formula of a set of prints that is to be filed in or searched for in the traditional, manually services fingerprint collections, can be derived after all the patterns that make up the set have been interpreted and appropriate symbols marked below and above the pattern blocks on the card. The formula is written in the form of a fraction in the modified Henry system of classification with FBI Extensions that has long been generally used in this country. It is composed of a primary classification, secondary classification, subsecondary; major division; final classification; and key. Within the formula, the symbols that represent these various divisions are not written in the same order. A typical classification formula with its separate components identified, follows here:

Key	Major	Primary	Secondary	Subsecondary	Final
7	I	6	U	IOO	12
	O	18	Ur	OOM	

For an expansive discussion of the manner in which fingerprint classification formulae are obtained, the reader is referred to the various fingerprint identification textbooks listed in the Bibliography at the end of this chapter. The traditional system of filing fingerprint cards by a classification formula, while used for many decades, is falling more and more into disuse as a way of filing and retrieving sets of fingerprints because of the advances made in the computerized automated fingerprint filing and retrieval systems (AFIS) which are now widely used.

3. AUTOMATED FINGERPRINT IDENTIFICATION SYSTEMS (A.F.I.S.)

As a natural outgrowth of the somewhat limited efforts of the 1950s to store fingerprint information on punch cards which could then be mechanically searched, in the early 1970s, research on optical scanning of fingerprints for the purpose of creating computerized fingerprint storage systems began to show increasing promise. This research culminated in the eventual deployment at the Federal Bureau of Investigation and at a few other large fingerprint repositories of computer systems that stored fingerprint information in their memories and that, by and large, dispensed with the need for the traditional filing cabinets wherein millions of sets of fingerprints were stored by the classification formula described in § 8.06.

Automated fingerprint identification systems are fast becoming standard tools for investigation in police departments nationwide. At present 38 states and the District of Columbia have AFIS systems in place, statewide or in large metropolitan areas. There are seven operational automated fingerprint identification systems: Cogent, DeLaRue Printrak, Inc., F.B.I., Logica, Ltd., Morpho Systems, Identification and

Security Systems, Inc., and NEC Information Systems, Inc.   These systems replace the labor intensive method of hand sorting and matching latent prints.   Instead of taking days or weeks to do a "cold search," an A.F.I.S. computer can scan thousands of prints in minutes.

Fingerprint data are no longer classified by means of the traditional fingerprint formula.   Rather, the computer scans the fingerprint and detects the minutiae consisting of ridge endings and bifurcations.   Once detected, the minutiae's relative positions and orientations are recorded.

Most AFIS systems can process a full set of ten prints.   However, most law enforcement agencies enter only one finger or thumb from each hand into the file as file conversion is time consuming and expensive.   It took the F.B.I. three years to complete the conversion of 14 million criminal fingerprint cards.[1]   The F.B.I. enters all prints except those from pinky fingers.   The one or two finger approach has been accurate/successful particularly because thumb prints are the most common latents found at the scene of a crime.[2]

When an AFIS computer scans and digitizes a person's fingerprints it creates a spatial map of the ridge pattern.   The computer then translates the spatial relationships of these patterns into a binary code so the computer can then employ a searching algorithm.   This allows the computer to compare the unknown print with prints already in the data bank.   The computer then identifies the most likely matches between those in the data bank and the unknown latent print and produces a list of candidates which meet the identifying criteria.   Most AFIS computers assign the candidates a score based on how well they meet the criteria and then rank the candidates by their score with the highest score first.[3]

Upon receiving the print-out, a technician can retrieve, by means of the references contained on the print-out sheet, the original fingerprints that most closely match the prints being searched, wherever the actual fingerprint card may be kept, and then visually compare the prints just received against the new prints which are to be filed.   It is to be noted that while the storing of new fingerprint information and the searching of existing fingerprint files is done with the use of computers, the final determination that a set of prints received is identical to one already on file will be done by a fingerprint expert, who will compare the actual fingerprints, in the method later described in Section 8.08.

§ 8.07   Detection and Development of Latent Fingerprints

There are many methods for developing latent fingerprints on

§ 8.06

1.   Moore, "Automatic Fingerprint Identification Systems," *Advances in Fingerprint Technology,* Lee and Gaensslen, eds., at 173 (1991).

2.   Informal survey conducted by F.B.I. Latent Fingerprint Section, August 20, 1969 based on 2000 latent fingerprint identifications.

3.   The highest ranked candidate may not always be the match.   One candidate could have the highest score due to an operator error when entering data or there could have been a problem with the clarity of the print.

porous and non-porous surfaces. These include the use of powders,[1] crystal violet,[2] Sudan Black B,[3] iodine fuming,[4] lasers,[5] physical developer,[6] small particle reagent,[7] cyanoacrylate esters (super glue fuming)[8] and even bacteriological techniques.[9]

The oldest and most common method of developing a latent sweat print on a hard, smooth object is by use of a fine powder applied to its surface with a fingerprint brush. The powder adheres to the sweat outlines of the ridges. A modern variant on this method involves spraying of the print area with magnetized powder and removal of the excess by a magnet. The color of the fingerprint powder will be varied by the technician according to the background surface to provide contrast. Gray and black powders are common but other colors are available. It is possible for the powder used to develop the prints to spread between the ridges and cause an apparent distortion in the print. Powder may also cause the ridges to appear wider than an inked impression. The powdered print is fragile enough to be obliterated by a stroke of the brush.[10] Dust may obliterate sweat prints; sunlight and/or heat also affect their usefulness.

If the developed visible print is photographed using a fixed-focus fingerprint camera, the photographic negative of a fingerprint impression will be a correct one-to-one representation of the ridges of the fingerprint. After photographing the developed print, it can then be "lifted" to provide a permanent record. A transparent lift is a cellophane-like tape with an adhesive surface which is placed over the print, smoothed down and removed, carrying the print with it. The transfer of a latent to the lift may be adversely affected by cold, dirt, moisture or non-receptive surfaces. The upside of a transparent lift contains the

§ 8.07

1. James, Pounds, & Wilshire, "Magnetic Flake Powders for Fingerprint Development," 38 *J.For.Sci.* 391 (March 1993).

2. Menzel, "The Development of Fingerprints," *Scientific and Expert Evidence* 619, 627 (2d ed. 1981).

3. Mitsui, "Development of Latent Fingerprints Using a Sudan Black B Solution," 30 *Identification Newsletter* 9 (1980); Mitsui, Kaltro and Shionade, "Development of Latent Prints Using a Sudan Black B Solution," 41 *Fingerprint Whorld* 84 (1981).

4. Haque, Westland and Kerr, "An Improved Non-destructive Method for Detection of Latent Fingerprints on Documents with Iodine-7,8-benzoflavone," 21 *Forensic Sci.Int.* 79 (1983).

5. Menzel, *Fingerprint Detection with Lasers* (1980).

6. Haque, "Physical Developer—After 13 years," 5 *The Identification Specialist* 1 (1987).

7. Haque, et al., "A Small Particle (Iron Oxide) Suspension for Detection of Latent Fingerprints on Smooth Surfaces," 41 *Forensic Sci.Int'l.* 73 (1989).

8. Howorka & Kretschmer, "Experimental Study of Using Cyanoacrylate Ester Vapour for Developing Latent Fingerprints," 46 *For.Sci.Int'l.* 31 (1990).

9. Harper, et al., "A Bacteriological Technique for the Development of Latent Fingerprints," 33 *For.Sci.Int'l.* 209 (1987). In this method microorganisms which grow on the compounds present in sebum are placed on surfaces suspected to contain latent prints. When the microorganisms grow, the prints develop.

10. See, e.g., James, J. et al., "Obliteration of Latent Fingerprints," 36 *J.For.Sci.* 1376 (1991), in which a study concluded that sebum rich prints tended to smear more readily than ordinary prints; that smearing decreased with increasing print age; that the number of brush strokes used and type of brush used affected the clarity of the print; and that prints may be obscured by using excess powder or excessive brush passes over the print.

positive position of the print. Conversely, when viewed from the side containing the glue, the reverse position of the print appears. Therefore, if it is photographed from the lift, the negative is printed from the upside of the lift to depict the correct position of the print. Ordinarily this is no problem as the transparent strip is mounted for photographing onto a transfer card with the adherent side toward the mounting medium.

A non-transparent lift may also be used, consisting of a sticky surfaced rubber pad that is placed over the dusted print. It contains a negative impression of the print. Because of the opaqueness of rubber, the non-transparent lift must be photographed from the front side. Hence, it yields a reverse impression requiring that the photographic negative be tone-reversed in printing.

The small particle reagent technique is similar to the powder technique. Iron oxide black or molybderium disulfide powder are suspended in a solution of various chemicals and distilled water. Items for developing are then immersed in a tray containing the suspension. The receptacle is gently agitated for 20–60 seconds, until the fingerprints are developed. This method can be used on objects where the powder technique cannot be applied. Results have been obtained on dry, wet, and frost-covered non-porous surfaces.[11]

A latent sweat print on paper, cardboard or unpainted wood may also be detected and developed by the use of iodine fumes from heated iodine crystals. The fat and oils in the sweat physically absorb the iodine, although there is no chemical reaction. Once the iodine fuming ceases, the prints begin to fade. Thus they must be immediately photographed. The surface and texture of the paper are variable, influencing the quality of the development.

With the advent of the 1980s, a new fuming method gained widespread acceptance. Some fingerprint technicians had discovered that the ingredients contained in the popular "Super–Glue" product gave off fumes which developed latent fingerprints. From this crude beginning sprang a new developing method, now called the cyanoacrylate fuming process. The cyanoacrylate ester compound reacts, like the chemical ninhydrin, to the amino acids residue in perspiration that is left in the form of latent impressions. By means of various improvements, such as the application of heat sources and accelerators, or even laser enhancement, the "Super Glue" method is now an integral part of the arsenal of developing techniques available to the latent print searcher.

The latest development in the cyanoacrylate technology was achieved after 5 years of research by the Alaska Department of Public Safety Scientific Crime Detection Laboratory and 3M. The crime lab developed a vapor wand which heats rechargeable cartridges of cyano-

---

11. Onstewedder, J. and Gamboe, T., "Small Particle Reagent: Developing Latent Prints on Water–Soaked Firearms and Effect on Firearms Analysis," 34 *J.For.Sci.* 321 (March 1989) (study results revealed small particle reagent analysis yielded better latent impressions than cyanoacrylate ester fuming followed by black powder).

acrylate and emits a stream of vapor. It can be used in fume hoods, normal fuming chambers or in outside environments. The lab also developed a crime scene vapor pump which can be used to process entire residences. 3M developed sublimating thermal dye which co-polymerizes with the cyanoacrylate on the fingerprint and results in fluorescent cyanoacrylate. Thus, when the vapor wand is operated with the 3M sublimation dye in the cartridge it yields fluorescent fingerprints in one step.[12] Six colors are presently available and two emit exceptional luminescence with short wave ultra violet excitation.

In addition to powders and vapors, latent prints may be developed by spraying with or immersion in chemical solutions. One such method is the silver nitrate technique, depending for its probity upon the presence of salt (sodium chloride) in the sweat. Silver nitrate reacts in the presence of sodium chloride to form silver chloride which is reduced to silver on exposure to ultraviolet light with a resultant brown image which must be photographed or fixed before it is blackened out by the excess silver nitrate. Another technique for detecting aged prints on paper which has been kept dry utilizes a reagent called ninhydrin. The reagent reacts with the amino acids in the sweat to form a visible print which can be photographed. Other reagents have been developed for the visualization of latent fingerprints on porous surfaces.[13] Also laser aided detection or enhancement of latent fingerprints has been used.

The late 1970s also saw the development of an entirely novel method of developing latent fingerprints by the use of laser illumination. Spectroscopists had, for some time, noted that perspiration impressions of fingerprints tend to fluoresce when exposed to laser lighting, and from these early observations, a Canadian forensic scientist, B.E. Dalrymple, published a paper advocating the use of the argon-ion laser to illuminate and make visible the compounds contained in palmar sweat that are present in perspiration prints in too small a quantity to become visible with ordinary lighting techniques. This beginning sparked extensive research and experimentation in the use of various laser techniques to make visible latent prints that might not be developed by other means. Now the use of lasers and filtered light sources is widespread. Even if other methods might yield adequate results, the detection of latent fingerprints by their luminescence as revealed in laser lighting is a preferred approach in cases where the staining that is a necessary consequence of most fuming and chemical methods needs to be avoided.[14]

12. Weaver and Clary, "A One–Step Fluorescent Cyanoacrylate Fingerprint Development Technology," 43 *J.For.Ident.* 481 (1993).

13. See, Almog, J. et al., "5-Methylthio Ninhydrin and Related Compounds—A Novel Class of Fluorogenic Fingerprint Reagents," 37 *J.For.Sci.* at 688 (1992).

14. See, Dalrymple et al., "Inherent Fingerprint Luminescence—Detection by Laser," 22 *J.For.Sci.* 106 (1977). See also,

Menzel, "Comparison of Argon–Ion, Copper–Vapor, and Frequency–Doubled Neodymium: Yttrium Aluminum Garnet (ND:YAG) Lasers for Latent Fingerprint Development," 30 *J.For.Sci.* 383 (1985); Burt & Menzel, "Laser Detection of Latent Fingerprints: Difficult Surfaces," 30 *J.For. Sci.* 364 (1985).

Current research and advances in laser development are summarized and contained in Moenssens, op. cit. at note 3 in section 8.02.

Argon-ion lasers, filtered mercury vapor, metal halide or xenon arc lamps produce fluorescence from residues in latent prints. Today fluorescent stains or reagents are also used to develop or enhance the prints.[15]

The detection of latent fingerprints on human skin has been the subject of research over the last 25 years. Fingerprint transfer techniques onto glass, polyethylene terephthalate (PET) and photographic paper have shown limited success. Cyanoacrylate fuming followed by luminescent staining generally produces good results. Research in this area of latent print detection is continuing.[16]

Fingerprint evidence developed through these various techniques has been held admissible.[17]

Fingerprints in blood present special concerns regarding their detection, development and enhancement.[18] Also of concern is the order in which other forensic tests must be done on such evidence.

§ 8.08　Fingerprint Identification

To compare an unknown latent impression with an inked impression of known origin with the aim of determining whether both were made by the same finger, the technician looks for four different elements: the likeness of the general pattern type, (or, if the type cannot be determined because the questioned pattern is incomplete, for a general similarity in flow of the ridges); the qualitative likeness of the friction

15. See, Pounds, Grigg & Mongkolaussavaratana, "The Use of 1,8-Diazafluoren-9-One (DFO) for the Fluorescent Detection of Latent Fingerprints on Paper. A Preliminary Evaluation," 35 *J.For.Sci.* 169 (1990); Menzel, "Pretreatment of Latent Prints for Laser Development," 1 *For.Sci.Rev.* 43 (1989); Menzel, "Detection of Latent Fingerprints by Laser–Excited Luminescence," 61 *Analytical Chemistry* 557A (1989); Almog & Hirshfeld, "5-Methoxyninhydrin: A Reagent for the Chemical Development of Latent Fingerprints that is Compatible with the Copper–Vapor Laser," 33 *J.For.Sci.* 1027 (1988).

16. Hebrard & Donche, Fingerprint Detection Methods on Skin: Experimental Study on 16 Live Subjects and 23 Cadavers, I.A.F.S. Poster Presentation, Dusseldorf, Germany, August 23, 1993; Guo & Xing, "Visualization Method for Fingerprints on Skin by Impression on a Polyethylene Terephthalate (PET) Semirigid Sheet," 37 *J.For.Sci.* 604 (1992); Bettencourt, "A Compilation of Techniques for Processing Deceased Human Skin for Latent Prints," 4 *J.For.Ident.* 111 (1991).

17. See, e.g., People v. Webb, 6 Cal.4th 494, 24 Cal.Rptr.2d 779, 862 P.2d 779 (1993) (Fingerprint evidence developed

through chemical and laser processes admissible); Johnson v. State, 620 So.2d 679 (Ala.Cr.App.1992), reversed on other grounds 620 So.2d 709 (Ala.1993) (Ninhydrin process for developing latent prints is reliable evidence obtained through the process is admissible); People v. Eyler, 133 Ill.2d 173, 139 Ill.Dec. 756, 549 N.E.2d 268 (1989), cert. denied 498 U.S. 881 (1990), rehearing denied 498 U.S. 993 (1990). (Expert testimony regarding superglue fuming process admissible); Cavazos v. State, 779 P.2d 987 (Okl.Cr.1989) (Court held the trial court properly admitted a fingerprint in blood made on the victim's unclothed back which was detected after spraying the body with a chemical mixture. The evidence was ruled admissible notwithstanding the state's failure to prove the method's accuracy and acceptance by the scientific community. The court noted the procedure used was different from dusting for prints only in the substance utilized to reveal the existing print.)

18. See, Midkiff, "Prints in Blood, A Scientific Sleuthing Review Bibliography" (July 27, 1992) for a list of articles discussing the various techniques for the detection of fingerprints and footwear impressions in blood.

ridge characteristics; the quantitative likeness of the friction ridge characteristics; and the likeness of location of the characteristics.

Many latent impressions developed at crime scenes are badly blurred or smudged, or consist of partially superimposed impressions of different fingers. As long as a sufficiently large area of friction skin is available which is not blurred, smudged, or rendered useless through superimposition, identity can be established. (See Figure 10.) The size of area required varies according to the number of individual ridge characteristics discovered and the frequency of their appearance in a given area. This relates to the element of quantitative likeness in that it requires that a sufficient number of characteristics be found to match in both prints, without unexplained dissimilarities. By tradition, though not by empirical studies, latent print examiners in the United States have required a matching of at least six to eight characteristics in both prints for identity, though most experts prefer at least 10–12 concordances. In England, 14 to 16 matches are required for court testimony. The qualitative comparison of the friction ridge characteristics refers to whether or not the characteristics (bifurcations, ridge endings, enclosures, ridge dots, etc.) are the same in both prints. The likeness of location of the friction ridge characteristics refers to the relationship with one another within the contours of the pattern. In other words, identity can be established if the ridge characteristics are in the same relative position to one another in both prints, with the same number of intervening ridges in both.

Because of criticism that had been leveled against the fingerprint examiners for failing to agree on a rule setting the minimum number of ridge characteristics that must establish a match between two prints before they can be said to be from the same digit, the International Association for Identification, a professional body composed primarily of fingerprint identification specialists, created in 1970 a Standardization Committee. The Committee consisted of 11 members whose aggregate experience in the identification field amounted to roughly 250 years.[1]

§ 7.08

1. The senior co-author of this text (Moenssens) was one of the Committee members.

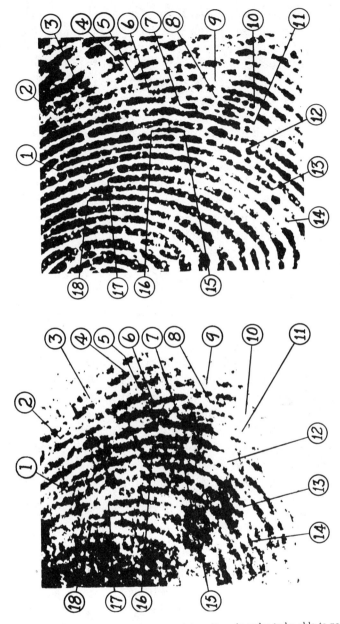

Fig. 10. It is not necessary to have a complete pattern in order to be able to positively identify fingerprints. Eighteen identical characteristics have been charted in these latent and inked impressions. It is the exhibit used in the famous 1941 Texas case of Grice v. State, referred to infra in § 8.09(1), at footnote 7.

The group was charged with several mandates, one of which was to recommend adoption of a minimum standard for matching characteristics, if feasible. After a concentrated study of nearly three years' duration, the committee concluded that there exists no valid basis, at this time, for requiring a predetermined minimum number of friction ridge characteristics in two impressions in order to establish positive identification. The decision on whether two prints under examination are made by the same digit is one that must be made, the committee concluded, on the basis of the expert's experience and background, taking into account, along with the number of matching characteristics, other factors such as clarity of the impressions, types of characteristics found, location of the characteristics in relation to the core or delta, etc. The committee's formal report was unanimously approved by the association's general membership at the 58th annual conference of the IAI in 1973.

In extensive testing and research with tens of thousands of "similar," though not identical prints, experts have been unable to find more than four *clearly defined* characteristics that are quantitatively and qualitatively the same in two prints known to be from different fingers. By adhering to the old-time tradition in the profession that at least eight matching characteristics be found in both the known and the unknown print before identity is established, a degree of certainty of identification is introduced which accounts for the fact that there is very seldom a "battle of opposing experts" in fingerprint cases. Yet, in a great number of criminal cases an expert or consultant on fingerprints for the defense has been instrumental in seriously undermining the state's case by demonstrating faulty procedures used by the state's witnesses or by simply showing human errors in the use of fingerprint evidence.

In comparing latent prints with inked impressions, a number of apparent dissimilarities may be noted. If these dissimilarities are explainable as having been brought about through ordinary pressure distortion (very common), partial blurring or filling up of ridges with developing powder, etc., they have no effect on the process of establishing identity. Should an unexplained dissimilarity occur, as for example the appearance of a clearly defined ridge characteristic in a latent print which does not exist in the inked impression, the conclusion is inescapable that the prints were not made by the same finger.

In attempting to improve the quality of latent impressions and in an effort to identify marginally clear-blurred prints, research has been conducted in the application of space age technology to fingerprint identification by use of computer assisted digital image processing. This is the same methodology which was used to improve rather blurred pictures sent by our space probes to the Moon and to Mars into clear photographs.

Jet Propulsion Laboratory of Pasadena, California, was charged with examining whether it was possible to restore with digital image processing a palmprint in blood on a textured cotton fabric bed sheet. The palmprint was only marginally visible prior to enhancement; it appeared much clearer after enhancement. Many problems still remain, however. Since the enhancement is done by eliminating "image noise," those details contributed to the overall picture by background, dirt, and many other factors, there is a danger that certain identifiable ridge details, or parts of ridges, are mistaken for unwanted detail by the computer processing, which would tend to damage the quality of the initial image present. Conversely, it is possible that "noise" might be mistaken by the computer for real ridge detail and "enhanced" so as to create ridge detail where none were present before.

The digital enhancement technique, using Fourier transform methods, could conceivably be used more speedily and more reliably to separate superimposed latent impressions. It is not uncommon to discover, upon processing of a crime scene for the presence of latent prints, that friction skin patterns from different skin areas or different digits have been superimposed. Latent print experts tend to discard these impressions as worthless for identification purposes because it may be impossible to determine which ridge detail belongs with what print. Digital processing of the image might be used to eliminate the unwanted ("noise") pattern so that only one of them remains clearly visible. Extensive experimentation of a rigidly controlled nature is still ongoing.[2] Digital image processing has been admitted in a few cases.

III. FINGERPRINTS AS EVIDENCE

§ 8.09   Admissibility in Evidence of Fingerprint Comparisons

1. PROOF OF DEFENDANT'S IDENTITY

The first American appellate decision involving fingerprint evidence was rendered in 1911 in Illinois, in People v. Jennings.[1] The defendant

2. Kaymaz & Mitra, "A Novel Approach to Fourier Spectral Enhancement of Laser–Luminescent Fingerprint Images," 38 *J.For.Sci.* 530 (May 1993); Krile and Walkup, "Enhancement of Fingerprints Using Digital and Optical Techniques," *Image Analysis Applications,* Ch. 10, Kastori & Trivedi, eds. (1990).

Blackwell & Crisci, "Digital Image Processing Technology and Its Application in Forensic Sciences," 20 *J.For.Sci.* 288 (1975). Blackwell also investigated the possibility of using the same method to classify and identify firearms evidence, as well as processing images from photographic surveillance systems in banks, motion picture frames, and television. Tiller & Tiller, "The Power of Physical Evidence: A Capitol Murder Case Study," *J.For.Ident.* 79 (1992) (describes digital image enhancement of a fingerprint in blood used in a sexual assault and murder case in Henrico County, Virginia in 1991.)

§ 8.09

1. 252 Ill. 534, 96 N.E. 1077 (1911).

argued that fingerprint evidence was not of a class of testimony admissible under common law rules of evidence and, since there was no Illinois statute authorizing it, the trial court should have refused to permit its introduction. In a well reasoned opinion, the court held that expert testimony was not limited to classed and specified professions but would be admissible where the witness had peculiar knowledge or experience not common to the world, and which knowledge and experience might aid the court and jury in determining the issues.

The *Jennings* case further held that persons experienced in the matter of fingerprint identification may give their opinions as to whether or not the fingerprints found at the scene of a crime corresponded with those of the accused. The conclusions in the *Jennings* case were based upon a comparison of the photograph of the crime scene prints with inked impressions made by the accused.

A few years later, a New Jersey court had occasion to deal with the same matter in State v. Cerciello.[2] In that case, bloody fingerprints were found on a hatchet at the scene of a murder. The defendant was arrested and at the identification bureau he was asked to sign his name on a sheet of paper. In the process of handling the paper he unknowingly left latent fingerprints which were developed and found to match those on the hatchet. The court held that fingerprint testimony, presented by a qualified fingerprint expert, was admissible:

> "The admission of fingerprints as legal evidence is based upon the theory that the evolution in practical affairs of life, whereby the progressive and scientific tendencies of the age are manifest in every other department of human endeavor, cannot be ignored in legal procedure, ... the law, in its efforts to enforce justice by demonstrating a fact in issue, will allow evidence of those scientific processes which are the work of educated and skilful men in their various departments...."[3]

Since these early cases many others have held that fingerprint evidence, when competent, relevant, and material, and when presented by qualified experts, is admissible for the purpose of establishing the identity of an individual defendant.[4] The reliability of fingerprint evidence as a means of identification, and the fact that the practice of taking and classifying fingerprints rests on a substantial scientific basis, have been so universally admitted in this country and abroad that many

---

2. 86 N.J.L. 309, 90 A. 1112 (1914).

3. Id. at 312, 90 A. at 1114.

4. See, e.g.: Moon v. State, 22 Ariz. 418, 198 P. 288 (1921); People v. Van Cleave, 208 Cal. 295, 280 P. 983 (1929); State v. Chin Lung, 106 Conn. 701, 139 A. 91 (1927); Murphy v. State, 184 Md. 70, 40 A.2d 239 (1944); People v. Roach, 215 N.Y. 592, 109 N.E. 618 (1915); State v. Caddell, 287 N.C. 266, 215 S.E.2d 348 (1975); State v. Viola, 148 Ohio St. 712, 76 N.E.2d 715 (1947), cert. denied 334 U.S. 816 (1948); United States v. Magee, 261 F.2d 609 (7th Cir.1958).

courts have taken judicial notice of the fact that fingerprints do offer a means of positive identification,[5] and have upheld the admissibility of fingerprint testimony in words amounting to judicial recognition.[6] In 1941, the Texas Court of Criminal Appeals held that since it is so well established that no two fingerprints are alike, henceforth the prosecution would be relieved of the burden of proving this contention, and that the burden of proof to the contrary rests on the accused.[7]

In light of the U.S. Supreme Court's decision in Daubert v. Merrell Dow Pharmaceuticals,[8] in which the court held that the *Frye* test is "absent from and incompatible with the Federal Rules of Evidence"[9] generally accepted techniques like fingerprint identification are now vulnerable to challenge. In *Daubert,* the Court construed FRE 702 to require the trial court to make a two-fold inquiry: whether the expert testimony will assist the trier of fact and whether it amounts to scientific knowledge. Therefore the court needs to focus on how the conclusions or opinions were reached. The Court identified factors judges should consider in applying their definition of scientific knowledge. The Court stated the list is not a definitive checklist, but are pertinent considerations.[10] These considerations include: whether the proposition is testable and has been tested; whether the proposition has been subjected to peer view and publication; whether the methodology or technique has a known error rate; whether these are standards for using the methodology; and whether the methodology is generally accepted. The Court recognized that general acceptance of the methodology could be persuasive circumstantial evidence that the methodology is sound.

While the Supreme Court based its analysis on the statutory construction of the language of the Federal Rules of Evidence, the decision has implications beyond federal practice. By 1993, 35 states had adopted evidence codes patterned after the federal rules.[11] Therefore *Daubert* will be persuasive authority in those jurisdictions.[12]

---

5. See, e.g.: People v. Jennings, supra note 1; Lamble v. State, 96 N.J.L. 231, 114 Atl. 346 (1921); State v. Rogers, 233 N.C. 390, 64 S.E.2d 572 (1951); State v. Bolen, 142 Wash. 653, 254 P. 445 (1927); Piquett v. United States, 81 F.2d 75 (7th Cir.1936), cert. denied 298 U.S. 664 (1936).

6. People v. Adamson, 27 Cal.2d 478, 165 P.2d 3 (1946), affirmed 332 U.S. 46 (1947), rehearing denied 332 U.S. 784 (1947): fingerprints are the strongest evidence of identity of a person; Anderson v. State, 120 Ga.App. 147, 169 S.E.2d 629 (1969): fingerprints serve as the most scientifically accurate method of identifying an individual yet devised; McLain v. State, 198 Miss. 831, 24 So.2d 15 (1945): fingerprints have been declared unforgeable signatures and we desire to declare here our confidence in them; Bingle v. State, 144 Tex. Crim.R. 180, 161 S.W.2d 76 (1942): fingerprints are the strongest evidence of a per-

son's identity; United States v. Magee, 261 F.2d 609 (7th Cir.1958): there can be no more reliable evidence of identity than one's own fingerprints.

In Avent v. Commonwealth, 209 Va. 474, 164 S.E.2d 655 (1968), the court recognized that fingerprinting is actually an "unforgeable signature."

7. Grice v. State, 142 Tex.Crim.R. 4, 151 S.W.2d 211 (1941).

8. 113 S.Ct. 2786 (1993). Discussed in Chapter 1 at § 1.03.

9. Id.

10. Id. at 2796.

11. Imwinkelreid "The Daubert Decision: Frye is Dead, Long Live the Federal Rules of Evidence," 29 *TRIAL,* September 1993, at 60, 63.

12. Id. at 64.

When fingerprint evidence is admitted at the trial, it is to be considered along with all other evidence; the weight and value to be given to it was up to the finder of fact.[13]

Many evidentiary aspects of the use of fingerprint expert testimony, to prove that a defendant has been at a crime scene so as to provide an incriminating link with the overall theory of the prosecution's case, involve issues dealing with sufficiency of evidence, witness qualifications, validity of the underlying premises upon which the evidence relies. These issues are discussed later in this chapter.[14]

2. PROOF OF VICTIM'S IDENTITY

In most instances fingerprint evidence is proffered for the purpose of identifying a defendant and connecting him with the scene of a crime, but such evidence is also admissible to prove the identity of a victim. Thus, a victim in a homicide trial was identified through fingerprints after an autopsy surgeon demonstrated that a torso found in one place and a head and arms found elsewhere belonged to the same body.[15] In a similar vein, the identity of a headless corpse as being the victim was established by a comparison of fingerprints taken from the body with those which were in the FBI files by virtue of the victim's former employment in the Post Office Department, Washington, D.C.[16]

Decomposed bodies, fire victims and mummified bodies present special difficulties in identification. In seeking to identify unknown corpses by means of fingerprints, it is often necessary to use "skinslip" or to amputate fingers in order to obtain legible impressions, particularly when the body has become mummified or has been watersoaked for some time.[17] The California Supreme Court held that, in such a case, the testimonial evidence of a fingerprint expert would be sufficient to establish identity, but that in this case it was improper and erroneous for the trial court to admit in evidence the three fingers of the victim which had been cut off by the pathologist who performed the autopsy. The court said that the introduction into evidence of the fingers served no useful purpose and may have been prejudicial in effect.[18]

---

13. See, e.g.: Anthony v. State, 85 Ga. App. 119, 68 S.E.2d 150 (1951); State v. Combs, 200 N.C. 671, 158 S.E. 252 (1931); Commonwealth v. Walker, 178 Pa.Super. 522, 116 A.2d 230 (1955); Stoppelli v. United States, 183 F.2d 391 (9th Cir.1950), cert. denied 340 U.S. 864 (1950), rehearing denied 340 U.S. 898 (1950).

14. See, infra, at § 8.16.

15. People v. Ditson, 57 Cal.2d 415, 20 Cal.Rptr. 165, 369 P.2d 714 (1962), cert. denied 371 U.S. 852 (1962), vacated 371 U.S. 541 (1963), cert. dismissed 372 U.S. 933 (1963).

16. Newberry v. Commonwealth, 191 Va. 445, 61 S.E.2d 318 (1950). The sister of the victim also identified the body by a scar.

17. See, Haglund, W., "A Technique to Enhance Fingerprinting of Mummified Fingers," 33 J.For.Sci., at 1244 (Sept. 1988).

18. People v. Cavanaugh, 44 Cal.2d 252, 282 P.2d 53 (1955), cert. denied 350 U.S. 950 (1956).

3. PROOF OF INNOCENCE

It is well settled that a defendant may introduce evidence in his own behalf, tending to show that certain fingerprints are *not* his.

For instance, in Commonwealth v. Loomis,[19] a murder case, it was the theory of the prosecution that the deceased had been murdered in the perpetration of a robbery. An alleged accomplice of the defendant, who tried to put all the blame for the murder on the defendant by pretending to have been an innocent bystander, told how the defendant had held a tin box when he forcibly opened it. There were several marks on the box, including a fingerprint located at the point where the box allegedly had been held by the defendant. Fingerprint experts identified the print as one of the defendant's. Even though the house was ransacked and even though, according to the testimony, it appeared that defendant had touched just about everything in the house, the only latent print that was offered in evidence was the one on the tin box. Following conviction, an appeal resulted in a new trial on grounds not related to the fingerprint evidence.

At the second trial, the prosecution offered no evidence with regard to the tin box and admitted that the latent mark was not made by the defendant, but the trial judge refused to permit the defendant to introduce evidence on that point. On appeal, the court reversed again and held that the defendant should have been permitted to introduce fingerprint testimony on his own behalf to prove the mark was not made by his finger.[20]

In Willoughby v. State,[21] the defendant had allegedly handled bottles of liquor during a holdup to revive one of the victims who had fainted. Two bottles were turned over to a detective agency and fingerprints were developed on them. The trial judge refused, however, to permit the defendant to introduce evidence, by the testimony of the chief of the New Orleans police identification bureau, that the prints were not those of the defendant. It appeared that there were other undeveloped finger smudges on the bottles. On appeal, this fact was held to justify the trial judge's exclusion of fingerprint evidence for the defense.

Some courts state that a defendant may not introduce evidence that there were fingerprints other than his own left at the crime scene,[22] after the prosecution has shown evidence of the presence of the defendant's

19. 267 Pa. 438, 110 A. 257 (1920).

20. Commonwealth v. Loomis, 270 Pa. 254, 113 A. 428 (1921). See also, Corley v. State, 335 So.2d 849, 850 (Fla.App.1976): "[W]e reverse ... because of the trial court's erroneous exclusion of proffered testimony that the only identifiable fingerprints on a vodka bottle found on a couch near the victim's body were those of an unidentified third person and had been made neither by decedent nor the defendant."

21. 154 Miss. 653, 122 So. 757 (1929).

22. In State v. Olsen, 135 Wash. 240, 237 P. 502 (1925), the defendant was permitted, apparently without objection, to introduce evidence by a fingerprint expert showing the absence of any prints on the crime weapon. In Watts v. State, 354 So.2d 145 (Fla.App.1978), the court held it was error not to permit evidence that fingerprints found in a truck did not match those of the defendant or the victim truck owner.

fingerprints there.[23]   Yet, this fact would appear to be, at times, extremely significant and relevant.   Where the defense has been allowed to show the absence of defendant's fingerprints at the scene of an offense, the prosecution has also been allowed to introduce evidence which tends to explain why defendant's prints could not have been left there.   Thus, in Draper v. State,[24] testimony that the accused had put on gloves before going into the room where the killing took place was held to authorize a closing argument to show why accused's fingerprints were not found in the room.   In State v. Kleier,[25] the prosecution was allowed to show gloves found in an auto used in a burglary to explain the absence of fingerprints in the car, a fact brought out by the defendant's own evidence.

The defense may be permitted to comment on the failure to present fingerprint evidence, at least where there is an unexplained silence concerning a routine and reliable method of identification.   In Eley v. State,[26] defendant was supposed to have stolen an automobile as a getaway vehicle in an assault with intent to murder.   Defense counsel sought to argue that the prosecutor had not produced any evidence of fingerprints taken from the escape car, but was prevented from doing so by the trial judge, who ruled that such argument would be an improper comment as mentioning facts not in evidence.   In reversing, the court said that such comment was proper, especially in a case where the identification of the defendant as the perpetrator of the offense was subject to some question.[27]

4.   SUFFICIENCY OF THE EVIDENCE

To support a conviction based solely or primarily on fingerprint evidence, it must be shown that the defendant's fingerprints were found under such circumstances as to exclude any reasonable possibility of consistency with innocence.   If fingerprints corresponding to those of the accused are found at the place where a crime has been committed and in such a manner as to exclude every reasonably hypothesis save that the fingerprints were impressed at the time the crime was committed, then a conviction on the sole evidence of such fingerprints may be sustained.[28]

23. United States v. Farley, 292 F.2d 789 (2d Cir.1961). In People v. Peter, 55 Ill.2d 443, 303 N.E.2d 398 (1973), the book "Valley of the Dolls" was seized from defendant's car and was found to contain a fingerprint of a murdered young girl. The fact that prints of other individuals might also be found in the book was held only to affect the weight of the evidence.

See also, Commonwealth v. LaCorte, 373 Mass. 700, 369 N.E.2d 1006 (1977).

24. 192 Ark. 675, 94 S.W.2d 119 (1936).

25. 69 Idaho 278, 206 P.2d 513 (1949). See also, Commonwealth v. Wallace, 326 Mass. 393, 94 N.E.2d 767 (1950).

26. 288 Md. 548, 419 A.2d 384 (1980).

27. See also, State v. Caldwell, 322 N.W.2d 574 (Minn.1982), and the discussion at notes 31 and 32, section 8.19, infra.

28. People v. Rodis, 145 Cal.App.2d 44, 301 P.2d 886 (1956); People v. Daly, 168 Cal.App.2d 169, 335 P.2d 503 (1959); Anthony v. State, 85 Ga.App. 119, 68 S.E.2d 150 (1951); State v. Helms, 218 N.C. 592, 12 S.E.2d 243 (1940); Lawless v. State, 3 Md.App. 652, 241 A.2d 155 (1968); Fladung v. State, 4 Md.App. 664, 244 A.2d 909 (1968); Grice v. State, 142 Tex.Crim.R. 4, 151 S.W.2d 211 (1941).

The argument that the presence of fingerprints at a crime scene only showed that defendant was at that place at one time or another, but not necessarily at the time the crime was committed, and that therefore the state had the burden to prove beyond a reasonable doubt that the print was left there at the time of the crime, was rejected in Lawless v. State.[29] The defendant's argument that, since he had a constitutional right not to testify, the burden of explaining the innocent presence of his finger-prints at the scene should not fall upon him, was rejected by the court:

> "A latent fingerprint found at the scene of the crime, shown to be that of an accused, tends to show that he was at the scene of the crime. The attendant circumstances with respect to the print may show that he was at the scene of the crime at the time it was committed. If they do show, it is a rational inference, consistent with the rule of law both as to fingerprints and circumstantial evidence, that the accused was the criminal agent. While a defen-dant does not have the obligation to testify himself or to offer testimony to explain the presence of his prints, a court cannot supply evidence that is lacking." [30]

In amplifying the concept that all the state must do is present evidence of the prints in such surrounding circumstances that exclude the hypothesis of innocence, the court continued:

> "We also feel that the rule ... does not compel the State to negative every conceivable possibility that an accused, shown to be at the scene of crime by his fingerprints, was present other than at the time of the commission of the crime. The fingerprint evidence, as we construe it, need be coupled only with evidence of other circumstances *tending* to *reasonably* exclude the hypothesis that the print was impressed at a time other than that of the crime. The rule does not require under all circumstances in every case that the State affirmatively and conclusively prove that the defendant could *not* have been there other than a time when the crime was commit-ted." [31]

The simple concept that the finding of a person's fingerprints at a crime scene is not proof of his guilt beyond a reasonable doubt unless circumstances are such that the fingerprints could only have been impressed there at the time when the crime was committed,[32] has led to some extreme judicial misunderstandings, as is illustrated by the follow-ing series of Texas cases.

---

29. Supra note 28.

30. Id. at 160.

31. Id. See also, Curry v. State, 440 N.E.2d 687 (Ind.App.2d Dist.1982) where the expert testimony provided a credible inference that a print in a place accessible to the public was made at the time of the breaking and entering offense with which defendant was charged.

32. Borum v. United States, 127 U.S.App.D.C. 48, 380 F.2d 595 (1967). See

In McGarry v. State,[33] the defendant's fingerprints were discovered on the window of a burglarized depot, a place where he was known to have had lawful access. His burglary conviction was reversed on the theory that while the fingerprint evidence was admissible, it was insufficient to support a conviction. Some time later, in Graves v. State,[34] the same court again reversed a burglary conviction because the defendant had been a prior employee of the victimized firm and the fingerprint identification was not inconsistent with innocence. A third conviction was reversed, a year later, under similar circumstances when the court decided Weathered v. State.[35]

These three decisions were interpreted, in Davis v. State,[36] as establishing the rule that fingerprints, while admissible in evidence, are not conclusive as to the identity of an individual, and the same rule was applied in Conners v. State,[37] which only cites the *Davis* case. It was not until the 1941 decision in Grice v. State,[38] that the Texas courts observed the faulty reasoning and recognized that the chain of cases starting with *McGarry* held only that fingerprint evidence alone was insufficient to convict if the fingerprints could have been left at the crime scene while the person was on the premises on another occasion, and evidence of such other occasions had been produced.

It is apparent, of course, that when the defendant can be shown to have had access to the scene of a crime at some time other than when the offense was committed, the state might have to prove the precise time when the latent prints were deposited, a challenge not easily met. It is very difficult, if not impossible, to determine precisely the age of latent prints,[39] but proof of other circumstances may sometimes supple-

---

also, State v. Minton, 228 N.C. 518, 46 S.E.2d 296 (1948).

33. 82 Tex.Crim.R. 597, 200 S.W. 527 (1918).

34. 119 Tex.Crim.R. 68, 43 S.W.2d 953 (1931).

35. 119 Tex.Crim.R. 90, 46 S.W.2d 701 (1932).

36. 125 Tex.Crim.R. 6, 66 S.W.2d 343 (1933).

37. 134 Tex.Crim.R. 278, 115 S.W.2d 681 (1938).

38. Supra note 28. See also, Mason v. Commonwealth, 357 S.W.2d 667 (Ky.1962).

39. Moenssens, *Fingerprint Techniques,* 1971, at pp. 130–133 ("Latent Print Age and Duration"). In cases where the time of placing the latents was important because defendants were shown to have had lawful access to the objects or premises, experts have testified, without a scientific basis for their opinions, that a fingerprint found on a bottle had been left not more than 18 hours prior to the date the print was developed: McNeil v. State, 227 Md. 298, 176 A.2d 338 (1961); that the print had been placed on

an envelope containing heroin not earlier than four weeks previously: Stoppelli v. United States, 183 F.2d 391 (9th Cir.1950), cert. denied 340 U.S. 864 (1950), rehearing denied 340 U.S. 898 (1950); that the prints were "relatively fresh," in State v. Hulbert, 621 S.W.2d 310 (Mo.App.1981); that the print was dark and clear and "fresh," in State v. Nash, 621 S.W.2d 319 (Mo.App. 1981); or, more appropriately, that fingerprints could have been on jars containing coins for several years: Stevenson v. United States, 127 U.S.App.D.C. 43, 380 F.2d 590 (1967), cert. denied 389 U.S. 962 (1967), and Borum v. United States, 127 U.S.App. D.C. 48, 380 F.2d 595 (1967).

In Graves v. State, supra note 34, an expert testified that latents would stay on a metal filing cabinet about three days, but admitted on cross-examination that they might also last as long as two weeks to a month.

Fingerprint evidence on a front door of a city store, readily accessible to the public, does not establish guilt of burglary, unless the prosecution can fix the time when the prints alleged to be defendant's were placed

ment the lack of available scientific proof. It would be nearly impossible to prove that a defendant, shown to have been in and around a cocktail lounge during the day when it was open for business, had left a particular latent impression, discovered the following day, while he supposedly burglarized the lounge at night. Yet, a conviction based on such evidence was sustained, because the owner of the bar testified that the evening before the crime, and after the defendant had left, he had cleaned and washed the countertop where the print was found.[40]

That the courts sometimes go overboard in holding that the presence of fingerprints at a crime scene is consistent with innocence is dramatically demonstrated in Borum v. United States.[41] Here, a housebreaking conviction was reversed because the prosecution failed to establish that the objects in the burglarized home which revealed defendant's fingerprints had been generally inaccessible to defendant. His fingerprints had been found on one of two empty jars which had contained a valuable coin collection. Because one of the government's experts testified that fingerprints could remain on such jars "indefinitely," the court held that the prosecution should have accounted for the custody of location of the jars "during that period." In a scathing dissent, Circuit Judge (now a retired Chief Justice of the United States Supreme Court) Burger stated that the majority had set a new record of usurpation of the jury's fact finding function. He suggested that what the majority did was to hold that the prosecution must not only prove a case beyond a reasonable doubt, but must also remove *all* possible doubt. He further intimated that, according to the majority opinion, the burden rests on the victim of crime to prove exclusive possession of an object, even if the object in question had been kept in an upstairs bedroom of a private home to which the defendant had no lawful access.[42] There is, of course, no such rule of law.[43]

on the glass: Wilkerson v. State, 232 So.2d 217 (Fla.App.1970).

See, Midkiff, "Lifetime of a Latent Print: How Long? Can You Tell?," 43 *J.For. Ident.* 386 (1993) (The article surveys studies done on aging prints and concludes that development of a print at a crime scene is not guarantee of it being placed recently and that speculation or court testimony concerning the time a print was placed is fraught with danger).

40. Hack v. Commonwealth, 433 S.W.2d 877 (Ky.1968).

41. Supra note 39.

42. Maybe the majority in *Borum* was not too worried about freeing a burglar who had been convicted of three similar crimes, all committed within a relatively short period of time, because on the same day it reversed *Borum* it also affirmed another conviction for housebreaking of Borum and his brother-in-law committed one month af-

ter the first one: Stevenson and Borum v. United States, 127 U.S.App.D.C. 48, 380 F.2d 595 (1967). The only difference between these two cases was that in the latter the government had introduced evidence indicating that the objects upon which defendants' fingerprints were discovered were generally inaccessible to the defendants and that therefore the objects were probably touched during the commission of the crime.

43. A more correct approach seems to be that taken in Fladung v. State, 4 Md. App. 664, 244 A.2d 909 (1968), where the court stated, at 912:

"While there was no evidence as to how long appellant's fingerprints had been on the window, the evidence did show that his was the only print lifted therefrom, and that his print was so positioned on the inside of the window as to make it reasonably inferable that the person who entered the building through the window

Other courts require the presentation of some evidence to allow the factfinder to determine when the prints were left, in order for the evidence to be sufficient to sustain a conviction. In State v. Dukes,[44] the court held that the evidence of the defendant's fingerprints on an acetone can and a mason jar, standing alone, was insufficient to sustain a conviction for attempted manufacture of methamphetamine. No other evidence was introduced by the prosecution to preclude the possibility that the prints were placed on the items at another time. The prosecutor has to show there was no other opportunity for the defendant to touch the items other than during the course of the criminal activity.

In Mikes v. Borg,[45] the federal circuit court held there was insufficient evidence for murder when the only evidence was the defendant's fingerprints on the murder weapon, a turnstile post found in the basement of the decedent's fix-it shop. The officers lifted forty-six fingerprints from the crime scene, sixteen of which were identifiable. Of those sixteen, ten did not belong to the defendant. The court stated there must be some evidence presented to allow the factfinder to determine when the prints were left, in order for the evidence to be sufficient to sustain a conviction. As the court pointed out,

> Under the evidence presented, the fingerprints in question could have been placed on the posts by a person who disassembled the turnstile, a person who sold the turnstile to Hansen, or any person who considered buying the turnstile prior to Hansen's acquisition. It is also possible, though less likely, that the fingerprints could have been impressed on the posts on the last occasion on which the turnstile was in general use, either in the hardware store or elsewhere.[46]

The court stated that the custody, location and function of the evidentiary objects involved must be examined in order to establish that the fingerprints could only be placed on the item at a certain time. The case contains an excellent survey of the case law in the federal circuits regarding fingerprint evidence.

In Turner v. Commonwealth,[47] the only evidence linking the defendant to the crime was a latent print discovered at the scene of a brutal murder. The print was found on a flashlight and was made in blood. No other fingerprints of his were discovered and there were no occurrence witnesses. On his appeal from a conviction he contended that a single fingerprint on a readily movable object such as a flashlight, which is in common use, is insufficient when found at a crime scene, without more, to prove the criminal agency of the defendant beyond a reasonable doubt. In affirming the conviction, the Virginia Supreme Court said

was the same person who left the print thereon. . . .

"[W]hile it may be true that appellant may have had many opportunities to have impressed his print on the window at a time other than the commission of the crime, such speculation does not take the place of evidence in the case and . . . the court cannot supply evidence that is lacking."

44. 609 So.2d 1144 (La.App.1992).

45. 947 F.2d 353 (9th Cir.1991).

46. Id. at 359.

47. 218 Va. 141, 235 S.E.2d 357 (1977).

that fingerprints found at a crime scene establish that the defendant was there at some time, even though they do not establish criminal agency unless coupled with evidence of other circumstances tending to reasonably exclude the hypothesis that the print was impressed there at a time other than when the crime was committed. These other circumstances, however, said the court, need not be independent from the fingerprints themselves. Since the murder was very brutal, the fact that the fingerprint was impressed in blood on the flashlight found near the bed was itself a circumstance from which it might be rationally concluded that the prints were left there at the time the crime charged was committed.[48]

The finding of latent fingerprints at a place of forced entry, usually inaccessible to others, leads to a reasonable inference that the prints were made at the time of the commission of the offense.[49] A single print on or near some unusual means of access has been held sufficient to support a burglary conviction,[50] and where it is shown that a window through which access had been gained was more than nine feet from the ground and that the defendant's latent prints were discovered on the outside of the window, the evidence was held sufficient to sustain a conviction, especially if the window is also protected on the outside by a screen,[51] even though there may be other unidentified impressions near the area.[52]

Where, however, a thumbprint was found on a rearview mirror of a stolen car, which print was later identified as being the defendant's, a conviction of larceny of an automobile was reversed on the theory that while the fingerprint evidence clearly established that the defendant had been in the car, it did not show, in the absence of other evidence, defendant's guilt of the offense with which he was charged, since he might have deposited the prints in the commission of a trespass.[53]

---

48. For another case involving a fingerprint impressed in blood, found on a movable object, see, State v. Phillips, 15 N.C.App. 74, 189 S.E.2d 602 (1972), cert. denied 281 N.C. 762, 191 S.E.2d 359 (1972).

In Barnett v. State, 153 Ga.App. 430, 265 S.E.2d 348 (1980), a defendant's conviction for entering thirteen automobiles without authority and stealing the spare tires from them was reversed. The evidence of guilt was found to be insufficient to exclude every reasonable hypothesis except his guilt. The prosecution relied exclusively on fingerprints, and a defense witness showed he had driven the cars on several occasions and that defendant had accompanied him.

49. People v. Ramirez, 113 Cal.App. 204, 298 P. 60 (1931).

50. People v. Corral, 224 Cal.App.2d 300, 36 Cal.Rptr. 591 (1964); barefoot latent print on the top of an automatic washer immediately under a back porch window through which entrance was gained.

In Bowen v. State, 460 S.W.2d 421 (Tex. Cr.App.1970), the court said that fingerprints alone may be sufficient to convict, but the failure of the prosecution to show that the defendant had ever been in the State of Texas made the evidence insufficient.

51. People v. Rodis, 145 Cal.App.2d 44, 301 P.2d 886 (1956). In Solis v. People, 175 Colo. 127, 485 P.2d 903 (1971), a burglary conviction could not be sustained by fingerprint evidence taken from broken glass in front of the building, where there was no showing that the fingerprints were on the inside or outside of the glass. For a similar holding, see, Rogers v. State, 7 Md. App. 155, 254 A.2d 214 (1969).

52. People v. Taylor, 32 Ill.2d 165, 204 N.E.2d 734 (1965).

53. McLain v. State, 198 Miss. 831, 24 So.2d 15 (1945). See also, People v. Flores, 58 Cal.App.2d 764, 137 P.2d 767 (1943); Barnett v. State, 153 Ga.App. 430, 265 S.E.2d 348 (1980).

Fingerprint evidence may sometimes serve to corroborate other evidence. Thus, a court stated that the presence of defendant's fingerprints on a jar found in a burglarized building tended to corroborate an accomplice's testimony.[54]

§ 8.10 Admissibility of Palmprints and Soleprints in Criminal Cases

The papillary ridges which make up finger impressions extend over the whole palm of the hand and, indeed, over the soles of the feet. Originally, research conducted on the individuality of papillary ridge characteristics was not confined to an examination of the finger skin; it extended to the skin on the palmar surfaces of the hands and the plantar surfaces of the feet. At the beginning of this century, however, when identification by friction ridge designs gained widespread use in this country, the convenience in using fingerprints and their more frequent appearance at crime scenes caused law enforcement specialists to concentrate on the impressions of the fingers.

1.   PALMPRINT EVIDENCE

The first case where palmprint evidence was in issue is the case of State v. Kuhl,[1] decided by the Nevada Supreme Court in 1918. Part of the extensive opinion of the court, in the words of Justice McCarran, reads:

> "We have gone at length into the subject of palm print and finger print identification, largely for evolving the indisputable conclusion that there is but one physiological basis by which identity is thus established; that the phenomenon by which identity is thus established exists, not only on the bulbs of the finger tips, but is continuous and coexisting on all parts and in all sections and subdivisions of the palmar surface of the human hand."[2]

The same position has been taken repeatedly by all of the courts which have been faced with palmprint evidence. They have upheld the admissibility of evidence of identity based on a comparison of palmprint ridge characteristics.[3] One court specifically stated that palmprint evidence has force and conclusiveness equal to fingerprint evidence, and, as such, is ordinarily sufficient in itself to identify the defendant as the guilty party when the palmprint is placed under such circumstances as

54. Braham v. State, 376 P.2d 714 (Alaska 1962). See also, Rushing v. State, 88 Okl.Cr. 82, 199 P.2d 614 (1948).

§ 8.10

1. 42 Nev. 185, 175 P. 190 (1918).

2. Id. at 190, 175 P. at 194.

3. People v. Buckowski, 37 Cal.2d 629, 233 P.2d 912 (1951), cert. denied 342 U.S. 928 (1952); People v. Parella, 158 Cal. App.2d 140, 322 P.2d 83 (1958); State v.

Reding, 52 Idaho 260, 13 P.2d 253 (1932); State v. Dunn, 161 La. 532, 109 So. 56 (1926), error dismissed 273 U.S. 656 (1927); Jones v. State, 242 Md. 95, 218 A.2d 7 (1966); People v. Les, 267 Mich. 648, 255 N.W. 407 (1934); Sharp v. State, 115 Neb. 737, 214 N.W. 643 (1927); Xanthull v. State, 403 S.W.2d 807 (Tex.Cr.App.1966); State v. Lapan, 101 Vt. 124, 141 A. 686 (1928).

to exclude innocence.[4]

2. SOLEPRINT EVIDENCE

Barefoot traces, while rarely occurring in the United States, can be identified in the same manner as fingerprints and palmprints.[5] In a Texas case involving palmprint evidence, the defendant-appellant alleged that the court erred in permitting a fingerprint expert to testify about palmprint comparisons. The court concluded that inasmuch as the witness was shown to be qualified as a fingerprint expert, and inasmuch as he had testified that palmprints were akin to fingerprints and were a series of friction ridges biologically the same as fingerprints, it was permissible for the witness to testify as an expert on palmprints.[6] The profession itself has strongly emphasized that there is no difference between fingerprints, palmprints, and soleprints when considered as evidence of identity, and that a fingerprint expert is fully competent to identify individuals by the ridge characteristics of all of these bodily surfaces bearing friction skin.[7]

As yet there have been no reported appellate cases in the United States involving evidence of toeprint comparisons only. If the time comes when such a case is brought to the attention of our reviewing courts and the issue of admissibility of toeprint evidence is presented, the evidence will be properly ruled admissible, if offered by a competent expert. The basic principles involving friction skin identification of toeprints are exactly the same as those underlying finger, palm, and sole identifications.[8] Toeprint evidence has been admitted in a number of trial courts.

§ 8.11 Expert Qualifications

Fingerprint identification testimony must be presented by an expert witness; lay testimony is not allowed.[1] The trial judge determines, in his discretion, whether a witness is qualified to testify as an expert and such a determination will not be reversed on appeal unless a clear abuse of discretion is shown.[2] In the absence of an attack on the witness's

---

4. People v. Atwood, 223 Cal.App.2d 316, 35 Cal.Rptr. 831 (1963). See also, State v. Banks, 295 N.C. 399, 245 S.E.2d 743 (1978).

5. Evans v. State, 39 Ala.App. 404, 103 So.2d 40 (1958), cert. denied 267 Ala. 695, 103 So.2d 44 (1958); People v. Corral, 224 Cal.App.2d 300, 36 Cal.Rptr. 591 (1964); Mincey v. State, 82 Ga.App. 5, 60 S.E.2d 389 (1950); Commonwealth v. Bartolini, 299 Mass. 503, 13 N.E.2d 382 (1938), cert. denied 304 U.S. 565 (1938); State v. Rogers, 233 N.C. 390, 64 S.E.2d 572 (1951).

6. Xanthull v. State, supra note 3.

7. See, Moenssens, *Fingerprints and the Law*, 1969, at pp. 137–138. For a more modern treatment of the issue, see the au-thor's 1986 text, *Fingerprint Identification: Techniques and Law.*

8. For an account of a famous case involving a partial impression of a big toe, tried before the High Court of Justiciary in Glasgow, Scotland, see, Moenssens, op. cit. note 7, at p. 138.

§ 8.11

1. McGarry v. State, 82 Tex.Crim.R. 597, 200 S.W. 527 (1918).

2. Davis v. State, 33 Ala.App. 68, 29 So.2d 877 (1947); People v. Flynn, 166 Cal. App.2d 501, 333 P.2d 37 (1958); Green v. Commonwealth, 268 Ky. 475, 105 S.W.2d 585 (1937); People v. Speck, 41 Ill.2d 177,

qualifications, the issue is foreclosed on appeal.[3]

The qualifications as an expert must be established prior to the admission of his testimony on the disputed issues of a case. It is not sufficient to show that a witness belongs to a group of people to which the subject matter of the inquiry relates; testimony must be presented that the expert witness possesses special knowledge on the very subject on which he proposes to express an opinion.[4] Since the field of fingerprinting encompasses a variety of different tasks, persons may be expert in one area of fingerprinting and yet have only a rudimentary knowledge of other phases of the work.[5] For some the skill may be confined to the recording of the fingerprints of arrestees; others may possess nothing more than the special skill required for the development of latent traces at crime scenes; still others might be experts only with regard to the classification of fingerprints. None of these skills, by themselves, will qualify a witness as an expert to determine identity or non-identity by fingerprints on the basis of a comparison of latent and inked prints. It must be established, therefore, that the witness has had extensive training and experience in the comparison of latent traces with inked impressions.

The overwhelming majority of fingerprint experts have acquired their knowledge and experience "on the job." There are few courses of formal study at universities or colleges leading to a degree in fingerprint identification or for preparing one to become a fingerprint expert. But there is voluminous literature on the subject, and there are also various training courses organized by law enforcement agencies on state and federal levels, as well as a private correspondence school which prepares law enforcement officers in the fundamentals of fingerprint identification.[6] None of these courses, however, purport to prepare its students for the job of being a fingerprint expert; they aim only to teach the rudimentary skill which will permit one to work in an identification bureau. According to the standards evolved by the profession, to become sufficiently proficient in the comparison of latent and inked impressions requires long experience and work under the supervision of a competent

242 N.E.2d 208 (1968); State v. Tyler, 349 Mo. 167, 159 S.W.2d 777 (1942).

3. People v. Speck and State v. Tyler, supra note 2.

4. State v. Robinson, 223 La. 595, 66 So.2d 515 (1953).

5. See, Moenssens, *Fingerprint Techniques*, 1971, at pp. 252–255 ("Functions in the Identification Bureau").

6. The Institute of Applied Science, founded in 1916, in Chicago, Ill., became highly reputed for its quality basic instruction in fingerprint identification. In the late 1960s the school was sold to a national home study conglomerate which went into bankruptcy in 1977 and in 1978 became again independent as the American Institute of Applied Science and then was absorbed again by another company. The Institute of Applied Science also published the only journal in the world devoted primarily to fingerprint science, titled *Fingerprint and Identification Magazine*, and did so continuously from 1919 to 1977. Literally hundreds of identification personnel around the country received their initial instruction in fingerprinting from this institution.

examiner, coupled with a thorough study of the literature.[7] Experience is a necessary adjunct.

In the early 1970s, the American Academy of Forensic Sciences began a concerted effort to increase professionalization among the practitioners of the forensic sciences. Largely as a result of this impetus, the International Association for Identification,[8] in 1977, set up a certification board for latent print examiners. In order to be eligible to take the examination for board certification, the applicant must meet certain technical training and experience criteria.[9] Certification is determined after testing in three areas: a written test covering the technical aspects and the historical development of the "science" of fingerprint identification; the classification of inked fingerprints and comparison of latent and inked prints; and either oral board testing and/or presentation of a case for review if the applicant has not yet qualified as an expert in court. The procedure recognized temporary waivers for qualified fingerprint specialists with demonstrated experience, who could receive board certification upon less demanding requirements. The certification is valid for three years, after which time it is necessary to undergo re-credentialing and certification.

Today, no one ought to be permitted to testify as a witness who has not been board certified or can show that, for some special reason, he is qualified but chose to forego certification. The sponsors intended the certification program to be a very serious one, and contemplated that some persons previously presenting testimony in court would be unable to qualify for certification.

It may be expected that in the future courts having to decide whether fingerprint witnesses are qualified to give opinion evidence as experts will require board certification by the witness' peers as routinely as they require a license to practice medicine for experts on medical issues. Conversely, it may be expected that if a witness has been board certified as a latent print examiner, courts may dispense with a further need for showing expert qualifications. Such a result, however, is not

---

7. The International Association for Identification, composed mainly of law enforcement fingerprint specialists, at one time debated whether it ought to impose minimum requirements for entry in the profession, but abandoned that effort, leaving it up to each agency to decide its own criteria. Indirectly, it relegated that responsibility to the new certification board it sponsored. See discussion in text, infra.

8. The association's 1995 secretary-treasurer and address is: Ashley R. Crooker, Jr., P.O. Box 2423, Alameda, CA 94501–2423

The association's more than 3800 members also belong to state or regional divisions throughout the United States. The IAI publishes bimonthly the *Journal of Forensic Identification* whose 1995 editor is David

L. Grieve, P.O. Box 2226, Carbondale, IL, 62902–2226

9. An applicant for certification must possess certain educational qualifications or their equivalent. A Bachelor's Degree plus three years basic experience in classification and identification; or an Associate Degree plus three years basic experience in classification and identification plus four years full-time experience as a latent print examiner; or three years basic experience in classification and identification plus eight years full-time experience as a latent print examiner.

The current (1995) executive secretary of the Latent Print Certification Board of the IAI is Kenneth O. Smith, 8117 Walters Dr., Norfolk, VA 23518–2345

necessarily desirable. First, by virtue of the "grandfather clause," the bulk of the certified examiners consists of those who were already in the field when certification began. These experts were never truly tested for competence by a peer group; they have had their recertifications granted every three years in a rather routine fashion, based solely upon continued activity in the field and the absence of any known "mistakes." Since the express intention of the originators of the certification concept was to weed out incompetents, and since they felt some of the current people in the field who were testifying in court would be unable to pass the test, it follows that some who are now certified and testifying, may not be competent.[10]

Second, if persons are routinely disqualified by courts from testifying if they are not board certified, this will prevent some highly qualified individuals who have great expertise in fingerprinting but who have voluntarily refrained from participating in the certification process [11] from lending their assistance to the courts in the fact finding process.

It should be noted, therefore, that board certification does not guarantee competence, nor does an absence of certification mean the individual is incompetent. But until the courts have had an opportunity to deal with the peer certification system in determining expert witness qualifications, we are left with a consideration of those court decisions handed down prior to the start of peer competency testing. Many of the older cases deal with issues that involve witness qualifications.

An appellate court has held that where the defendant presented a witness as a fingerprint expert, who had completed college courses in criminology to the extent of three semester hours of college credit but who had never worked in criminology, and had no practical experience with fingerprints in actual law enforcement work after leaving school, the trial court did not abuse its discretion in its determination that the defendant's witness was not qualified as an expert.[12]

The training required to qualify as an expert may be acquired by study at recognized fingerprint schools,[13] in the armed forces,[14] at the

---

10. Some certified examiners who had misidentified fingerprints and were caught have had their certifications withdrawn. See, infra, text at note 31, section 8.19. See also, Smith, "Latent Print Certification Board Annual Report," 43 *J.Forensic Ident.* 646 (1993). [Applicants since inception of program: 1685; applicants tested: 762; applicants passing the test 366 or 48.03%; Total certified examiners: 803.]

11. A few do so because they do not believe in peer review, which they see as a usurpation of judicial prerogatives or an attempt to create a police dominated monopoly; a few object to joining the ranks of certified members because they believe that a number of currently certified experts are incompetent; and others may have different reasons.

12. People v. Eaton, 171 Cal.App.2d 120, 339 P.2d 951 (1959); bachelor's degree in science with major in criminology; had taken "several courses" in fingerprinting.

13. Weir v. State, 139 Tex.Crim.R. 33, 138 S.W.2d 805 (1940); McLain v. State, 198 Miss. 831, 24 So.2d 15 (1945). In People v. Speck, 41 Ill.2d 177, 242 N.E.2d 208 (1968), both experts were graduates of the Institute of Applied Science, referred to in note 6, supra.

14. State v. Combs, 200 N.C. 671, 158 S.E. 252 (1931).

Federal Bureau of Investigation,[15] or simply by being taught by recognized fingerprint experts.[16] In some cases the courts have simply assumed training from the work experience shown.[17] In most instances, of course, experts testifying in court had gained their training by a combination of several of these educational opportunities.[18]

§ 8.12　Courtroom Experiments

It has been held that an expert may demonstrate, by experiments in court, that every finger bears distinctive marks. Such demonstrations are within the discretion of the trial judge. In Moon v. State,[1] each juror was permitted to place his fingers upon separate sheets of white paper, while the fingerprint expert was absent from the courtroom. Upon his return, he developed the latent prints on the sheets with black powder and then secured inked comparison prints of the fingers of the jurors. He then correctly paired off the latent prints with the inked ones to illustrate to the jury that latents can be identified when made on an apparently clean sheet of paper.

In the United States v. Dressler,[2] the prosecution let the members of the jury compare alleged fingerprints of the defendant with genuine fingerprints, after the expert had compared them in the presence of the jury and had testified that they corresponded. This experimentation was held proper, as being within the sound discretion of the trial judge.

In People v. Speck,[3] the refusal of the defendant's request that the jury be permitted to examine the fingerprint evidence, under a magnifying glass, to determine the weight to be given to the testimony of the expert witnesses, was upheld as within the trial court's discretion. Any

---

15. State v. Viola, 148 Ohio St. 712, 76 N.E.2d 715 (1947), cert. denied 334 U.S. 816 (1948).

16. State v. Huffman, 209 N.C. 10, 182 S.E. 705 (1935); State v. Cage, 224 La. 65, 68 So.2d 759 (1953); Todd v. State, 170 Tex.Crim.R. 552, 342 S.W.2d 575 (1961).

17. Lamble v. State, 96 N.J.L. 231, 114 A. 346 (1921): 15 to 20 years of experience, having examined about 15,000 subjects; Leonard v. State, 18 Ala.App. 427, 93 So. 56 (1922): superintendent of police identification bureau with 5 years fingerprint experience; Stacy v. State, 49 Okl.Cr. 154, 292 P. 885 (1930): jailer and identification officer engaged in fingerprint work for about 21 years.

18. In People v. Speck, supra, note 13, one expert testified he started the study of fingerprints 18 years prior to trial, had taken a course at the Institute of Applied Science, had studied under officers skilled in the subject, had read numerous books and publications, and had made thousands of fingerprint comparisons. The other witness had studied fingerprinting in Belgium, had written a fingerprint course, graduated

from the Institute of Applied Science where he later became head instructor, had written articles and books on the subject, was associate editor of a fingerprint magazine, and had lectured on fingerprinting.

In Collins v. State, 87 Nev. 436, 488 P.2d 544 (1971), the witness had studied fingerprints for five years, had taken a home study course four years earlier, had two years in-service training under supervisory personnel in his department, and had made over 1,000 fingerprint comparisons.

§ 8.12

1. 22 Ariz. 418, 198 P. 288 (1921). Similar experiments have been permitted in a number of other jurisdictions, e.g.: Evans v. State, 39 Ala.App. 404, 103 So.2d 40 (1958), cert. denied 267 Ala. 695, 103 So.2d 44 (1958); Hopkins v. State, 174 Ark. 391, 295 S.W. 361 (1927); People v. Chimovitz, 237 Mich. 247, 211 N.W. 650 (1927); Stacy v. State, 49 Okl.Cr. 154, 292 P. 885 (1930).

2. 112 F.2d 972 (7th Cir.1940).

3. 41 Ill.2d 177, 242 N.E.2d 208 (1968).

such individual juror examination is unwarranted, of course, for the obvious reasons of basic inability to obtain proper focus, or even to know adequately what is the objective of the viewing process.

Since the identification of individuals by means of fingerprints is now so generally recognized, there is today little or no reason for courtroom experimentation before the jury, and all such exhibitions should probably be banned as irrelevant, except where the qualifications of the expert are disputed, or where it may be doubted that a latent print could be successfully obtained from a particular surface or object, or could have been placed there in a manner consistent with the prosecution's theory.[4]

§ 8.13 Admissibility of Photographs and Fingerprint Records

1. PHOTOGRAPHS

The admissibility of real evidence—objects bearing latent prints discovered at crime scenes—requires no further elaboration, and if photographs of such latent fingerprints are properly authenticated, they too are generally admissible.[1]

In Lamble v. State,[2] photographic enlargements of fingerprints found on the door of a stolen automobile were held admissible without the production of the car door. In another case, under similar circumstances, it was held proper to show, by a photograph, the fingerprints found upon the columns or balcony post of a house without the column being produced in court.[3]

2. FINGERPRINT RECORDS

Fingerprint record cards as proof of identity may be introduced in evidence when they are properly authenticated. Even if the cards taken from identification bureau files contain notations of the criminal record of the accused, it is not error to produce the card after the criminal record has been covered up so it cannot be seen by the jury.[4] In United

4. It was deemed improper to ask a defendant to participate in a contrived experiment designed to show that he could not possibly have left a latent print innocently at the particular location where it was found. The court said: "There is no difference between this requested demonstration and the prosecution attempting to call the defendant to the witness stand and explain how he would have gotten his fingerprint on the stove where it was found while standing on the floor. This kind of evidence is prohibited ..." Serratore v. People, 178 Colo. 341, 497 P.2d 1018, 1022 (1972).

§ 8.13
1. An extensive listing of case citations may be found at n. 118 on p. 236 of Moenssens, Fingerprints and the Law, 1969.

2. 96 N.J.L. 231, 114 A. 346 (1921).

3. State v. Connors, 87 N.J.L. 419, 94 A. 812 (1915); Duree v. United States, 297 Fed. 70 (8th Cir.1924). Failure to produce the object on which latents appear, if objectionable at all, goes only to the weight and not to the competency of the exhibits or photographs of the original: State v. Witzel, 175 Wash. 146, 26 P.2d 1049 (1933).

4. Moon v. State, supra note 1, section 8.10.

States v. Dressler,[5] however, a conviction was reversed because the jury had been permitted to examine and compare, and take with them to the jury room, the questioned prints and standard specimens of defendant's fingerprints as they appeared on police fingerprint cards. The court held that the information on defendant's prior record, on the back of the fingerprint card, might have had a prejudicial effect and should not have been permitted to reach the jury. The proper way for utilizing such standards would be to record a new set of inked impressions of the defendant containing no other information than the defendant's name and the date on which the prints were taken.

Duly authenticated fingerprint records may be used to prove a prior conviction for the purpose of providing enhanced punishment,[6] or to impeach a defendant testifying as a witness in his own behalf.[7] Decisions indicate, however, that duly authenticated fingerprint cards with a record of prior convictions noted on them are not sufficient proof of the prior convictions without introduction of either the original or certified copies of the conviction record.[8] The mere fact that one has established a fingerprint record in the name of a defendant is not proof that he is a criminal or has been previously convicted.[9] The authentication requirement must extend, therefore, not only to the fingerprints, but also to the criminal record contained on the card.[10]

IV. FINGERPRINTS IN NON-CRIMINAL CASES

§ 8.14 Use of Fingerprints for Non-criminal Purposes

As a technique for establishing the identity of an individual, fingerprinting is obviously of as great a value in non-criminal cases as it is for the identification of criminal offenders. Yet, few court decisions have been found where the admissibility of fingerprint evidence in civil cases was at issue.

5. 112 F.2d 972 (7th Cir.1940). Also, Serratore v. People, supra note 4, section 8.12.

6. E.g., People v. McKinley, 2 Cal.2d 133, 39 P.2d 411 (1934); People v. Reese, 258 N.Y. 89, 179 N.E. 305 (1932); State v. Clark, 360 S.W.2d 666 (Mo.1962); State v. Lawson, 125 W.Va. 1, 22 S.E.2d 643 (1942). See also, State v. Emrick, 129 Vt. 475, 282 A.2d 821 (1971).

7. People v. D'A Philippo, 220 Cal. 620, 32 P.2d 962 (1934).

8. People v. Fine, 140 Misc. 592, 251 N.Y.S. 187 (1931). Some statutes provide that copies of fingerprints, duly certified to be true copies, shall be admissible in court in the same manner as the original might be: e.g., 11 Del.Code § 8516; Utah Code Ann.1953, 77–59–26.

9. Bundren v. State, 152 Tex.Crim.R. 45, 211 S.W.2d 197 (1948). "In this age ... it is a matter of common knowledge that fingerprinting is used in numerous branches of civil service and is not in itself a badge of crime.... Whenever a fingerprint card is introduced as evidence, however, an implication of criminal history potentially arises which, of course, should be dispelled. Certainly, the better practice is to cover every questionable element of the card, including dates and other printed matter....": State v. Ralls, 167 Conn. 408, 356 A.2d 147 (1974).

10. People v. Darling, 120 Cal.App. 453, 7 P.2d 1094 (1932).

In the educational field, there are many opportunities for the use of fingerprinting. For instance, fingerprinting candidates for examinations in schools, colleges and universities prior to admitting them to the examination rooms, and then comparing them—if a question of identity is raised—with the fingerprint records taken at the time of registration, prevents false impersonations.

§ 8.15 Constitutional Issues

Better known, however, is the use of fingerprints for employment applications. Many industries and companies now require a fingerprint check of their new employees.

All companies engaged in the performance of contracts for the national defense establishment are required, as a condition for obtaining the contract, to submit the fingerprints of their employees, or at least of those who will be directly called upon to fulfill duties in the defense project. Compelling an applicant to submit to fingerprinting for the purpose of ascertaining if he has been convicted of crimes has been held not to be an unwarranted invasion of privacy. In Young v. Chicago Housing Authority,[1] the court said that no stigma is attached to fingerprinting, because it is a widely accepted and widely used method of determining employee fitness.

Ordinances requiring secondhand dealers to take and furnish to the police department the thumbprint of persons from whom property has been received and purchased, have been held reasonable and valid.[2] Some city ordinances require that pawnbrokers' reports of transactions contain fingerprints of customers.[3] The rule of a commissioner of licenses requiring submission of fingerprints as a condition to granting original and renewal licenses to deal in secondhand articles also has been held reasonable and valid.[4]

A city ordinance in Las Vegas requiring fingerprinting and photographing of persons seeking employment in liquor stores and bars was held not to violate the Nevada constitutional guarantees of life, liberty, and the pursuit of happiness.[5] However, an ordinance which infringes on First Amendment rights may be found to be unconstitutional. In New Jersey Citizen Action v. Edison Township[6] the U.S. Court of Appeals held that provisions of the municipal ordinances which required the fingerprinting of canvassers and solicitors as a condition for obtaining a license violated the First Amendment when the municipalities

§ 8.15

1. 350 Ill.App. 287, 112 N.E.2d 719 (1953) (complaint to enjoin such fingerprinting held properly dismissed for want of equity).

2. See, e.g., Wichita v. Wolkow, 110 Kan. 127, 202 P. 632 (1921); Medias v. Indianapolis, 216 Ind. 155, 23 N.E.2d 590 (1939).

3. See, Miller v. Murphy, 143 Cal. App.3d 337, 191 Cal.Rptr. 740 (1983) 1st Dist.Ct. of App. which held the requirement in San Francisco Municipal Police Code Art. 28 § 2815 did not violate pawnbrokers' rights to contract or to engage in an occupation or their customers' right to privacy.

4. M. Itzkowitz & Sons v. Geraghty, 139 Misc. 163, 247 N.Y.S. 703 (1931).

5. Norman v. City of Las Vegas, 64 Nev. 38, 177 P.2d 442 (1947).

6. 797 F.2d 1250 (3d Cir.1986).

failed to demonstrate the canvassers and solicitors had a significant history of criminal behavior and the requirements effectively prevented canvassers from espousing their causes to the city residents.

§ 8.16 Use of Fingerprints in Civil Cases

The admissibility of fingerprint evidence in civil cases should be unquestioned, provided the evidence is relevant to the issues. It is the best evidence of identity available. "The fingerprints of an individual are personal to him, without duplication in the prints of any other person." [1]

In an action on a burglary insurance policy, it was held that the trial court did not err in admitting into evidence photographs of fingerprints of unknown origin, found on the burglarized premises, and shown not to be those of members of the family having access to the building. [2]

1. FINGERPRINTS IN LIEU OF SIGNATURES

A few cases have been discovered in the probate area where fingerprints have been used as a substitute for, or in conjunction with, the signatures of testators. An early case in the Philippines held that a law requiring that a will be signed by the testator may be complied with not only by the customary, written signature, but also by the testator's thumbprint, in the presence of the proper number of attesting witnesses required by statute. [3]

So convinced was another Philippine court of the value of fingerprints as a substitute for a signature that it allowed itself to be carried too far. A will was signed by the testator, who had allegedly also placed his thumbprint on it. The print was made with ordinary ink, and understandably, quite blurred. It was compared with a thumbprint on a bill of sale, which was conceded to have been placed there by the testator. A qualified fingerprint expert was called to testify. His conclusion was that the prints were either not identical or too blurred to allow for proper identification. In substituting its own conclusion for that of the expert, the court, after examining the fingerprints, concluded that they were identical. [4]

Evidence has been admitted in England to the effect that a testator who was unable to write had put his thumbprint on a will in the presence of an attesting witness. [5]

In a New York case, a will that had a fingerprint as a signature was denied probate. The denial was affirmed on appeal. When it later

§ 8.16

1. Cowdrick v. Pennsylvania R. Co., 132 N.J.L. 131, 39 A.2d 98 (1944), cert. denied 323 U.S. 799 (1945) (a suit to recover under the Federal Employer's Liability Act—45 U.S.C.A. Ch. 2, § 51 et seq.).

2. New Amsterdam Casualty Co. v. James, 122 Fla. 710, 166 So. 813 (1935).

3. De Gala v. Gonzalez, 53 P.I. 104 (1929).

4. Dolar v. Diancin, 55 P.I. 479 (1930).

5. Finn's Estate, 52 Times L. 153 (Engl. 1935).

appeared that a comparison with police records proved that the finger-print was that of the testator, this was, in view of other evidence, held insufficient to grant a new trial since the fact that testator's fingerprint appeared on the will was not contradicted at the trial.[6]

Shortly thereafter, another case came up in New York where an illiterate alien had placed his fingerprints upon a will in lieu of his signature. The placing of the prints was attested to by two subscribing witnesses. This witnessing was held sufficient proof that the finger-prints were those of the testator, without an expert comparison.[7] In that case, a fingerprint expert did testify. He stated that he had compared, and found identical, the post mortem prints of the testator with the prints on the will. While this testimony was held commendable by the court, it was deemed unnecessary. The court commented on the fact that the execution of the will be placing fingerprints in lieu of a signature showed more than ordinary intelligence on the part of the testator, since fingerprints are much better than an ordinary cross mark.

A few years later, a typewritten will was admitted to probate, bearing two red finger impressions on the line reserved for the testatrix' signature. Beneath the impressions was written, "Anna Arcowsky, her name and her mark by two impressions of her right thumb." In admitting the will to probate, the court commented:

> "... As a strict matter of fact, it is obvious that a subscription by fingerprints is much more individual and reliable than one by a mere cross mark which has uniformly been sustained."[8]

If and when other cases arise where fingerprints are used in lieu of signatures, there should be no problem with such evidence, when offered by a qualified expert witness.

In addition to the foregoing usages, fingerprints might be used on contracts, deeds, or any other type of document which requires the signature or mark of the maker.

2. FINGERPRINTS FOR GENERAL IDENTIFICATION PURPOSES

Very early in this century, advocates of fingerprinting, most of whom were already in the law enforcement field, advocated footprinting babies upon birth, right in the delivery rooms of hospitals, along with a fingerprint of the mother, so that should there ever be a question as to the identity of a baby, its identity could be positively established. Hospitals find this method of identification much more certain than the practice of attaching identification bands to the wrists or ankles or babies, since these bands might be removed and then lost or misplaced. The reason footprints rather than fingerprints are recorded is that the ridge detail of fingers of newly born children is so small and delicate that

6. Re Meltzer's Will, 248 App.Div. 645, 287 N.Y.S. 931 (1936).

7. Re Romaniw's Will, 163 Misc. 481, 296 N.Y.S. 925 (1937).

8. Re Arcowsky's Will, 171 Misc. 41, 42, 11 N.Y.S.2d 853, 854 (1939).

it is extremely difficult to record legible prints. The ridges on the feet, on the other hand, are somewhat coarser and larger. In theory at least, footprints would be much easier to obtain.[9]

Most hospitals recording footprints consider it no more than a formality, with little effort being made to instruct nurses in the proper techniques required for obtaining identifiable impressions, even though, in a great number of instances, hospitals have avoided costly law suits by being able to prove that they did send the right baby home with the mother. In rare cases, an error made at the hospital has been subsequently corrected by a comparison of the footprints.

The media have largely acquainted the American public with the many beneficial uses of fingerprints in establishing the identity of victims of train, sea or air disasters. Often, victims of a plane crash or of an explosion are mutilated beyond recognition and cannot be identified by their clothing or physical appearance. Dental identification may serve the purpose, but in most instances only fingerprints can provide positive proof of identity. The FBI has a special disaster squad, which is immediately flown to any scene of a disaster where their services may be needed for identification purposes. Even though only one portion of the skin of one finger remains to identify the victim, the FBI has had tremendous success in this gruesome task.[10] Apart from its criminal files, that bureau maintains a gigantic civilian identification file that, in all aspects, rivals the collection of criminal records.[11]

3. FINGERPRINT LEGISLATION

The utility of civilian fingerprinting has been recognized by the legislatures, however. A number of states provide for the maintenance of civilian identification files and allow for voluntary contributions of identification data for that purpose. Typically, statutes dealing with such data require that the civilian files be maintained apart from the criminal files, even though law enforcement is usually charged with providing the technical assistance needed for effecting civilian registration.

A Delaware statute directs officers of the identification bureau to record the fingerprints of residents of the state who voluntarily appear

---

9. In practice, footprinting has not worked out as well, because the taking of the prints is a job often given to nurses who have not received any special training in recording legible prints. As a result, most baby footprints taken at hospitals where such conditions prevail resemble nothing more than indistinct ink blobs, showing no identifiable ridge detail. Professor Moenssens has been called upon to examine babies' footprints on a number of occasions. In only one case was a footprint found to be identifiable. Special finger and footprint supplies are manufactured for hospitals which do away with the necessity of smearing ink on the baby's feet—an unsanitary process frowned upon by infection-conscious medical personnel.

10. As of October 1993 the FBI team has assisted in 181 major disasters and identified 58% of the victims through fingerprints.

11. In 1993, the FBI's collection of civilian fingerprints exceeded 86 million sets of prints.

before them and request an impression of their fingerprints. The officers must record the prints in duplicate, sending one copy to the FBI and one to the State Bureau of Identification, together with any personal identification data obtainable. The state bureau must accept and file such fingerprints and personal identification data submitted voluntarily in a separate filing system, "for the purpose of securing a more certain and easy identification in case of death, injury, loss of memory or change of appearance." [12]

A Louisiana statute provides that the State Bureau of Identification "shall accept and file the names, fingerprints, photographs, and other personal identification data voluntarily submitted by individuals or by parents on behalf of their children for the purpose of securing a more certain and easy identification in case of death, injury, loss of memory, or change of appearance. Upon the application of a person identified under the provisions of this section, all data received under this section with relation to him shall be surrendered to him." [13]

Civilian identification statutes also exist in Hawaii [14] and Michigan. [15] They provide for the maintenance of a filing system separate from that of the collections of criminal fingerprints.

That fingerprints are useful to establish identity of victims of crime was recognized in State v. Mares. [16] In that case the court held that fingerprints taken from a badly decomposed body found in a canal, and forwarded to the Federal Bureau of Investigation in Washington, D.C. for identification, established the identity of the body as that of the suspected victim by usual fingerprint comparison.

California requires each coroner to furnish to the State Bureau of Criminal Identification and Investigation the fingerprints, along with other data, of all deceased persons whose deaths are in classifications requiring inquiry by the coroner. The statute also states that "[w]hen it is not physically possible to furnish prints of the 10 fingers, prints or partial prints of any fingers, with other identifying data, shall be forwarded by the coroner to the department." [17]

Similar statutes exist in Oklahoma, [18] and New Mexico, [19] but in these states the coroner is simply given the authority to record the prints, although not the duty.

For many non-criminal purposes, fingerprinting has been made mandatory. In this area, we must distinguish a category of cases where the fingerprinting is purely for civilian purposes and another category where the fingerprinting is required prior to obtaining a license. In the

12. Del.Code tit. 11, § 8510 (1987).

13. La.—LSA–Rev.Stats. § 15:582 (West 1992).

14. Hawaii Rev.Stat. §§ 846–28, 846–30 (Supp.1992).

15. Mich.Comp.Laws Ann. § 28.271 (West Supp.1993).

16. 113 Utah 225, 192 P.2d 861 (1948).

17. Cal.Penal Code § 11113 (Deering 1992).

18. Okl.Stat.Ann. tit. 63, § 941 (West 1984).

19. N.M.Stat.Ann., § 24–11–7 (Michie 1991).

latter case, the fingerprints thus furnished are searched through the criminal fingerprint files. If it is found that a criminal record of convictions exists, the license may, in most instances, be denied.

In the former category, a Pennsylvania statute provides that the trustees, directors, managers, proprietors, or other person or persons in charge of any state, county, city, or other municipal or privately owned hospital, or of other places where maternity cases are handled and where infants are born other than in private residences, must establish and maintain a system for the identification of all infants born there. The statute provides that the superintendent or person in charge of such hospitals or places where maternity cases are handled must, immediately after the birth of any infant, have suitable footprints of such infant and suitable fingerprints of the infant's mother taken and recorded for the purposes of identification. Such records must be chronologically filed and indexed in the name of the parents of the child. Violation of this statute is punishable by fine and deemed a misdemeanor.[20]

In the area of licensing for businesses or professions, the statutory provisions requiring a fingerprint check, or, at least, the submission of a set of fingerprints are so numerous that they defy enumeration. New York, for instance, has about twenty different code sections dealing with fingerprinting for the purpose of obtaining licenses or employment.

Subject to a fingerprint check by specific statutory mention are, school bus drivers,[21] applicants for a private detective license or employees of private detective agencies,[22] labor union business agents,[23] wholesale cigarette dealers,[24] real estate appraisers,[25] bail bondsmen or bail runners,[26] applicants for manufacturing, distributing, selling of alcoholic beverages,[27] and applicants for a license to direct day care centers and be employed by day care centers[28] to name but a few. Some states require the fingerprinting of applicants for admission to the bar by statute[29] or by Supreme Court rule.[30] Minnesota requires all employees of the state lottery to be fingerprinted.[31]

In Arizona, as in many other states, it is provided that when a plaintiff files a complaint for support, she may include in or attach to her complaint any information which may help in locating or identifying the

---

20. Pa.Stat. tit. 35, §§ 351–353 (1993).

21. N.J.Stat.Ann. 18A:39–17 to 18A:39–18 (West 1989).

22. See, e.g., N.J.Stat.Ann. 45:19–16 (West 1978); Official Code Ga.Ann. §§ 43–38–6, 43–38–7, 43–38–7.1, 43–38–9 (1991).

23. West's Fla.Stat.Ann. §§ 447.04, 447.16 (1993).

24. West's Fla.Stat.Ann. § 210.15 (1993).

25. Md.Code, Business Occupations & Professions, § 15.5–303 (Supp.1993).

26. West's Fla.Stat.Ann. §§ 648.34, 648.37 (1993); N.C.Gen.Stat. § 58–71–50 (1993).

27. Official Code Ga.Ann. § 3–3–2 (1990).

28. Official Code Ga.Ann. §§ 49–5–64, 49–5–65, 49–5–68 (1990).

29. Official Code Ga.Ann. § 15–2–8 (1990).

30. West's Fla.S.A. Admission to Bar, Art. IV § 5.a.(2).

31. Minn.Stat.Ann. § 349A.02 Subd. 6 (West 1990).

defendant, including his fingerprints.[32] In New York a court has held
that a husband could be compelled to submit handwriting examples and
palmprints to the administrator in actions for wrongful death and
equitable distribution, when the administrator alleged that the husband
was responsible for the death of his wife.[33]

Nearly all states require fingerprinting and a records check prior to
the issuance of a license to carry a firearm. A typical statute of this
nature provides that no permit to carry any pistol or revolver shall be
issued unless the applicant submits to fingerprinting and to an investigation concerning his suitability to carry any such weapon.[34] Some states
require the submission of a fingerprint on an application for a driver's
license.[35] In Perkey v. Department of Motor Vehicles[36] the plaintiff
sought to compel the Department of Motor Vehicles to renew her
driver's license without her fingerprint. Her application for renewal was
denied. The Supreme Court of California held that the fingerprinting
requirement was rationally related to highway safety and fingerprinting
did not infringe upon an individual's right to privacy. The court also
held that the fingerprint information was personal and not subject to
public disclosure.

IV. TRIAL PRACTICE

§ 8.17 Locating the Expert

Prosecutors generally have no difficulty in obtaining the services of
highly qualified fingerprint experts, since they can draw upon the
manpower available in local, state, and federal police identification
services. Since there is very little need for such experts outside law
enforcement, the defense attorney is frequently at a loss to obtain the
assistance of a qualified expert when he wishes to examine the correctness of the state's expert's conclusions or obtain the service of a
fingerprint consultant in the preparation of his defense. Yet, there are a
number of highly qualified individuals who have retired after a long
career in law enforcement identification, as well as a few individuals are
highly respected as authorities in fingerprinting because of their research in identification, even though they were never employed in a law
enforcement capacity. Among the sources to be contacted when in need
of expert testimony are: the International Association for Identification,
a group primarily, though not exclusively, composed of law enforcement

---

32. Ariz.Rev.Stat. § 12–1660 (1982).
See also, West's Fla.Stat.Ann. § 88.111
(1993);   Miss.Code, § 93–11–21 (Supp.
1993); N.J.Stat.Ann. § 2A:4–30.35 (West
1987); Me.Rev.Stat.Ann. tit. 19, § 394
(West 1981).

33. Estate of Schwartz, 135 Misc.2d
125, 514 N.Y.S.2d 875 (Sur.Ct.1987).

34. Conn.Gen.Stats.Ann. § 29–29 (West
1993).

35. West's   Ann.Cal.Vehicle   Code
§ 12800(c) (Deering Supp.1994).

36. 42 Cal.3d 185, 228 Cal.Rptr. 169,
721 P.2d 50 (1986).

connected fingerprint experts (address of secretary-treasurer: P.O. Box 2423, Alameda, CA 94501–2423 [1995]; the Latent Print Certification Board of the IAI which has a number of certified latent print examiners who act as private consultants (address of secretary: 8117 Walters Drive, Norfolk, VA 23518–2345 [1995]); and the heads of identification bureaus in important police departments, who usually know the competent individuals available for defense work.

§ 8.18 The Prosecutor's Approach

Fingerprint evidence does not differ from other types of circumstantial evidence; a proper foundation must be laid for the introduction of this type of evidence and for the opinion of the expert.

Basically, the prosecutor must establish: the qualifications of the witness; the competency of the techniques utilized by the witness; the chain of evidence and its integrity; and the examination process conducted by the witness. He must also have the expert present his opinion.

Since the prosecutor's prime objective is to convince the jury that he is prosecuting the perpetrator of a crime, he must make the evidence clear and understandable to them. That is the aim of using a step-by-step approach to the presentation of fingerprint evidence.

A pre-trial conference with the fingerprint expert will acquaint the prosecutor with the type and quantity of evidence that is available. It will also permit him to evaluate the probative effect of that evidence and whether or not it needs to be supplemented by additional information. It will also settle the question of the expert's need of photographic exhibits of the testimony, and if required, how many. The decision to use photographic enlargements must ultimately be made by the prosecutor alone, based upon his experience in presenting evidence to the jury and his knowledge of the rules of evidence. The expert witness, however, is in an excellent position to assist the prosecutor in making that decision, because he has already evaluated the available evidence and is better able to judge whether photographic exhibits will accomplish the purpose for which they are intended, namely, to illustrate his testimony so that the results of the examination and the expert's findings may be clarified.

§ 8.19 The Defense Approach

It is widely stated that fingerprint evidence, by itself, is of unimpeachable value in proving identity. Yet, the defense attorney in a criminal case in which such evidence is introduced is by no means condemned to stand mute. Fingerprint evidence, as with all other forms of scientific proof, is handled, recorded, interpreted, and compared by human beings. As human beings the technicians are subject to committing errors. Members of the identification profession, especially those who work in large city crime laboratories, are, as a rule, very competent technicians who are conscientious in their work. They are less likely, therefore, to commit glaring errors. Nevertheless, defense counsel performs a duty to his client in assuring himself that only competent, reliable testimony is presented to the jury. In planning his defense, an attorney must consider a number of possible lines of approach.

1. UNLAWFUL ACQUISITION OF THE EVIDENCE

The most effective means of countering fingerprint evidence is to have it excluded. The United States Supreme Court held, in Davis v. Mississippi,[1] that fingerprints of a defendant, recorded incident to an unlawful arrest, are inadmissible in a criminal trial. The Court said that fingerprint evidence is subject to the same proscription as any other illegally seized evidence. Whether the suppression greatly furthers the defense's case remains to be seen, since in most instances it is possible to use a different set of prints, not related to the unlawful arrest or detention.[2] In that connection, the argument might be advanced in some cases that the use of a different set of known prints should also be prohibited on a theory somewhat related to the primary taint doctrine or derivative evidence concept elaborated in a series of confession cases.[3] The theory underlying this approach is that the use of the fingerprints not connected with the unlawful arrest should be prohibited since the whole identification was tainted by the earlier unlawful acts and is therefore the "fruits of the poisonous tree."[4] So far, the United States Supreme Court has not ruled on this point. It remains an open question, therefore, and a point that should be raised if applicable.

The Supreme Court has held that the Fifth Amendment privilege against self-incrimination is not violated by the compulsory taking of fingerprints of a defendant.[5] Again, by way of *dictum*, the Court has also decided that a defendant does not have a right to counsel, or the right to confer with counsel during, or prior to, the taking of his fingerprints.[6]

§ 8.19

1. 394 U.S. 721 (1969). This decision was reaffirmed in Hayes v. Florida, 470 U.S. 811 (1985). The *Hayes* Court reiterated the dictum first announced in *Davis* that it might approve of a judicial method of compelling a suspect to come to the police station for fingerprinting on less than probable cause. The *Hayes* court also added the new suggestion that fingerprints might be recorded on the street without a need for probable cause if the process can be carried out on the spot.

2. See, e.g., Bynum v. United States, 104 U.S.App.D.C. 368, 262 F.2d 465 (1958); on retrial, conviction affirmed: 107 U.S.App.D.C. 109, 274 F.2d 767 (1960).

3. "The essence of a provision forbidding the acquisition of evidence in a certain way is not merely evidence so acquired shall not be used before the Court but that it shall not be used at all.": Silverthorne Lumber Co. v. United States, 251 U.S. 385, 392 (1919). See also, Wong Sun v. United States, 371 U.S. 471 (1963).

4. The phrase "fruits of the poisonous tree" was coined by Justice Frankfurter in Nardone v. United States, 308 U.S. 338, 341 (1939).

5. Schmerber v. California, 384 U.S. 757 (1966). This applies also to the taking of palmprints: Early v. People, 178 Colo. 167, 496 P.2d 1021 (1972). Palmprints, like fingerprints, can be taken after a lawful arrest, there being no Fifth Amendment strictures against self-incrimination. Anderson v. State, 241 So.2d 390 (Fla.1970).

6. United States v. Wade, 388 U.S. 218 (1967). Admitting fingerprints does not involve Fifth Amendment protections even

2. LACK OF PROBATIVE VALUE

In a 1967 decision of the Court of Appeals for the District of Columbia Circuit, it was held that where the prosecution, in presenting fingerprint evidence, did not show that the objects upon which the prints were discovered were generally inaccessible to him, the evidence should have been excluded.[7] That holding is consistent with the view that fingerprints lack probative value, and *should therefore be excluded as irrelevant or immaterial,* if they appear at the crime scene in a location consistent with innocence. On the other hand, a number of cases cited in § 7.09(4) seem to indicate that such evidence is admissible, the infirmity going to the weight of the evidence and not to admissibility.

One of the limiting factors in fingerprint identification is that from a study of a latent fingerprint alone it cannot be determined at what time or date the impression was made. Nevertheless, in some cases convictions have been reversed for failure, by the prosecution, to prove the age of a fingerprint. When the possibility exists, therefore, that the defendant could have had innocent access to a location or object where his fingerprint appears, failure to prove *when* the fingerprint was impressed may be reversible error.[8] If a person never had legitimate access to the premises where the print was discovered, an inference may be drawn that the print was deposited at the time the crime was committed. But if the print is just as consistent with innocence, then the probative value is too weak. Considering the fact that juries tend to be overawed by the bad implications (for the defendant) of the presence of his fingerprint at the scene, the probative value probably is outweighed by prejudicial impact.[9]

Even if the evidence cannot be excluded, the most effective defense against fingerprint evidence is a showing by the defendant that he could have impressed his fingers innocently at the scene of a crime. If the defense can show that the accused had access to the crime scene at some time reasonably close to the time of the commission of the offense, at which occasion he might have impressed his fingers there, the evidence of identity would be lacking in probative value, unless the prosecution can show that the particular latents were impressed at the moment of the crime. This is generally very difficult to do, since, from a technical standpoint, the fingerprint expert is seldom able to pinpoint the precise time at which latent impressions were made, or how old latent prints are.

though no "Miranda" warnings were given: Paschall .v. State, 152 Ind.App. 408, 283 N.E.2d 801 (1972).

7. Borum v. United States, 127 U.S.App.D.C. 48, 380 F.2d 595 (1967). Review here the text accompanying note 41, section 8.09, supra.

8. See, People v. Ware, 82 Ill.App.3d 297, 37 Ill.Dec. 760, 402 N.E.2d 762 (1980);

but see, People v. Van Zant, 84 Ill.App.3d 355, 39 Ill.Dec. 902, 405 N.E.2d 881 (1980), where appellate court's reversal of conviction was in turn reversed and conviction reinstated in 85 Ill.2d 241, 52 Ill.Dec. 603, 422 N.E.2d 605 (1981).

9. Not all courts agree: See, e.g., Commonwealth v. Hunter, 234 Pa.Super. 267, 338 A.2d 623 (1975).

Wide variations exist in the ability of a latent print to survive, even under harsh conditions. "Additionally, studies suggest no reliable indication of a print's freshness can be obtained from its rate of development or appearance after it is developed." [10]

If, then, the defense can show that the accused had innocent access to the location at some time reasonably close to the time of the commission of the crime, the fingerprint evidence is largely useless. This is obviously the case when latent prints are discovered in a company office where the accused had been employed prior to a theft,[11] or on the window of a train depot.[12]

3. CHAIN OF EVIDENCE

Occasionally, a lack of proper proof of integrity of the evidence may be fatal to the prosecution's case. In People v. Rice,[13] for instance, a break in the chain of evidence was held to constitute reversible error. The defendant had been convicted of burglary and the evidence against him was dependent wholly upon latent fingerprints found at the crime scene and identified as having been made by him. The latent prints were photographed and the developed negative was introduced as Exhibit B in the case. A little more than ten months had elapsed between the time of the offense and the recording of defendant's fingerprints. This comparison record card was shown at trial as Exhibit C. The fingerprint witness used an enlarged photograph of the inked print, shown as Exhibit F which was said to be an enlargement of two of defendant's fingers as appearing on Exhibit C, the comparison inked prints. It appeared that, in making the photographic enlargements of the two fingers of defendant, the witness had used another recorded fingerprint card of the defendant, *not* the one introduced as Exhibit C. This difference, and other slight discrepancies, made it clear to the court that even though no allegation was made that the fingerprint on Exhibit F was not that of defendant, nevertheless Exhibit F was not an enlargement of Exhibit C as it had been described. The conviction was reversed.

4. TESTING THE WITNESS' QUALIFICATIONS

As a rule, fingerprint experts called upon to testify for the state have had many years of experience and training in the identification of individuals by friction skin characteristics. An attack on their qualifications will usually not be productive. Nevertheless, the defense must assure itself of the competency of the expert witness. He can do so by making sure that the prosecutor adequately covers the witness' experi-

10. Midkiff, "Lifetime of a Latent Print: How Long? Can You Tell?" 43 *J.For. Ident.* 386, 391 (1993).

11. Graves v. State, 119 Tex.Crim.R. 68, 43 S.W.2d 953 (1931).

12. McGarry v. State, 82 Tex.Crim.R. 597, 200 S.W. 527 (1918).

13. 306 Mich. 352, 10 N.W.2d 912 (1943).

ence in identifying fingerprints. In many departments, not all persons connected with the identification bureau receive actual field experience in examining and comparing latent and inked impressions. Their duties may be confined largely to classifying and interpreting inked sets of prints. Since the competency of an expert depends largely upon the extent of his experience in dealing with latent rather than inked impressions, a distinction between the two fields of experience must be made. That it sometimes pays off to examine the qualifications of a fingerprint expert, when there is some doubt as to his background, is revealed in a series of cases from Kentucky, all predating World War II.[14]

As fingerprint experts begin to seek board certification as a result of the 1977 organization of such a credentialing body, and the courts are made aware of this new development, it is foreseen that no law enforcement person will be permitted to give opinion testimony on the comparison of latent and inked impressions unless he is properly certified.[15] It will, however, take some time for the accrediting body to process the many applications of those currently in the field. It should also be understood that the board certification process is designed to screen only those who testify to the comparison between latent and known prints and who have arrived at an opinion as to their identity. The credentialing process is not designed to test the qualifications of persons who work in other fingerprint functions in an identification bureau, such as the fingerprint classifiers, or latent print technicians who search crime scenes and process them to discover chance impressions, or persons who record fingerprints.

5. INCORRECT PROCEDURES

The textbooks have recommended certain standard practices in some cases. Fingerprint technicians occasionally do not follow the recommended procedures and seek to save time by omitting certain steps. They may be cross-examined by the use of learned treatises in the field which recommend the procedures which were omitted. Nevertheless, a technician may knowingly discard the recommended procedure because it does not apply to the special case he faces; that, however, is a rather rare occurrence.

If a case requires an item of evidence to be subjected to more than one forensic analysis, it is important for counsel to determine the order of the analyses as well as the protocol used. For example, if a piece of paper must be examined for indented writing as well as for latent print examination, the electrostatic detection apparatus must be used first to

---

14. Ingram v. Commonwealth, 265 Ky. 323, 96 S.W.2d 1017 (1936); Green v. Commonwealth, 268 Ky. 475, 105 S.W.2d 585 (1937); Shelton v. Commonwealth, 280 Ky. 733, 134 S.W.2d 653 (1939). The sequence of these interrelated cases is particularly worth exploring.

15. See discussion on the process, supra at § 8.11.

detect the indentations.[16] If the paper is treated with ninhydrin first, to detect fingerprints, it can effectively destroy any indentations. Likewise, in cases in which requests are made to document the presence of trace amounts of drugs as well as possession by the accused (through latent print examination) it is necessary to establish the order of the analysis and the potential for one examination to interfere with the other.[17]

6. VALIDITY OF THE IDENTIFICATION

While ordinarily two equally competent fingerprint experts will not come to opposite conclusions on identity, in some cases of marginal ridge detail a difference of opinion can arise on whether the evidence is conclusive. From the defense point of view, there are a number of circumstances which may interfere with the correctness of an identification, if they are not properly explained or accounted for:

(1) A ridge count between two characteristics may be erroneous if dirt or dust has caused a ridge to appear as one or two islands;

(2) Variation in pressure may cause discrepancies between prints such as a bifurcation being registered in another print as an ending ridge;

(3) Excess pressure in an inked print may squeeze several ridges together so that they appear as one ridge;

(4) Flexion creases, mottling, or even furrows might be erroneously interpreted as ridges;

(5) Powder used to develop prints may stick between ridges, indicating the presence of a ridge characteristic where there is none;

(6) Scars may interfere with comparison of pre-scarred record impressions.

Certainly, the best possible scenario, from the defense perspective, is to be able to show, through unassailable expert testimony of his or her own, that the prosecution's expert, for whatever reasons, misidentified the crime scene latent as made by the defendant. This would be the fastest way to have the charges dropped, assuming no other seriously incriminating evidence existed. Unfortunately for the defendants, such errors are rare. Identification persons assert the rarity springs from the fact they do not make mistakes in identifying individuals accused of crimes. Skeptics assert the mistakes are seldom caught. There are instances, nevertheless, where such mistakes occurred and were not

---

16. Moore, "The Electrostatic Detection Apparatus (ESDA) and Its Effect on Latent Prints on Paper," 33 *J.For.Sci.* 357 (1988).

17. One study has suggested the following protocols for items processed for drug residue and latent prints: Non-porous surfaces: super glue fuming, followed by recovery of drug residues, followed by visualization of the latent prints allows for optimum recovery of evidence; porous surfaces: collection of drug residue by swabbing should be done before processing the evidence with ninhydrin. Nielson, J. and Katz, A., "A Processing Protocol for Drug Residue and Latent Print Evidence," 33 *J.For.Sci.* 1463 (1988).

ascertained *until after conviction*.　One might assume that when such a case is found, it will have involved a new, relatively inexperienced young "expert" who was overeager in seeking to make an "ident."　This, however, may not be the explanation.

As mentioned in chapter one with respect to the expert witness malpractice cause of action, even with well-accepted scientific techniques, negligence occurs.　In North Carolina, officials had to reconsider 159 criminal cases because local authorities discovered questionable fingerprint identifications.[18]　The fingerprint misidentification resulted in two murder charges being dropped by the district attorney's office.[19] In June 1985 Bruce Basden was arrested and indicted for the murders of Remus and Blanche Adams in Fayetteville, North Carolina on the basis of a fingerprint found in the decedents' home.[20]　Basden's attorney requested funds to have the fingerprint evidence reappraised and filed a motion to discover the physical evidence in the possession of the state.[21] "At this point the state's fingerprint expert made enlargements of the prints from which he had made an identification of Basden as the intruder. . . .　[The state's expert] admitted that he found unexplained dissimilarities along with similarities in the prints."[22]　These discrepancies caused him to change his mind.　The state subsequently dismissed all charges against Basden, who had been incarcerated in the local jail for thirteen months.[23]

The fingerprint examiner's explanation for his mistake was that he did not make photographic enlargements of Basden's prints and the latent print from the crime scene until the public defender's discovery motion.[24]　In the regular course of fingerprint comparison, enlargements are the rule rather than the exception.[25]　The enlargements detailed the differences rather than the similarities in the prints.[26]

The F.B.I. and North Carolina authorities were then summoned to reevaluate the fingerprint work done by the State's fingerprint examiners.[27]　The F.B.I. reappraised fifty-one identifications made in 1986.[28] The North Carolina State Bureau of Investigation examined 118 fingerprint identifications made in 1987.[29]　The F.B.I. review revealed that "three fingerprints did not belong to three defendants in three separate cases."[30]

18.　Bowden & Barrett, "Fingerprint Errors Raise Questions on Local Convictions," *Fayetteville Times*, Jan. 15, 1988, at 1A.

19.　Id.

20.　Starrs, More Saltimbancos on the Loose?—Fingerprint Experts Caught in a Whorl of Error, *Sci. Sleuthing Newsl.* (Forensic Sci.Dep't of Geo.Wash.U., Washington, D.C.), Spring 1988, at 1 [hereinafter Fingerprint Experts].　Identifications that had convicted Morris Gaining of burglary have already resulted in the award of a new trial.　Id. at 5.

21.　Id. at 5.

22.　Id.

23.　Id.

24.　Id.

25.　See generally, Gianelli & Imwinkelried, *Scientific Evidence* (1993); Moenssens et al., *Scientific Evidence in Criminal Cases* (3d ed. 1986).

26.　Fingerprint Experts, supra note 20, at 5.

27.　Id.

28.　Id.

29.　Id.

30.　Id.

In another well documented misidentification case, a long-time and experienced fingerprint expert working for a state identification agency, who was also a board certified latent print examiner, misidentified a fingerprint, which resulted in a conviction. To compound the error, another board certified latent print examiner, who was a former identification bureau head with extensive experience in testifying, was retained by the defense as a consultant, and he confirmed the identification! A non-law enforcement, uncertified, fingerprint expert, thereafter, assisted by others of the law enforcement profession whose help was enlisted, established the error, and the conviction was reversed.[31] (It should be noted that the two "experts" had their certifications revoked by the Board.)

7. FORGERY OF FINGERPRINT EVIDENCE

While the use of "planted" or forged fingerprints is theoretically within the realm of possibilities, in practice few such actual cases have been discovered. Many reasons make it unlikely that such an occurrence may happen, unless the complicity of a fingerprint expert is assumed. Nevertheless, the detection of fingerprint forgeries would call for a thorough expert examination of the kind in which only the most competent would engage.

For many years, it was asserted by some identification officers that it was impossible to transfer an undeveloped perspiration impression of a finger, located on one place, to another place. Careful research has proved this premise false. There are some ways in which latent fingerprints can be made to appear in a place where they were not initially deposited. To achieve that end with any hope to escape detection, considerable sophistication in fingerprint techniques is required. The few cases which have been discovered where such a latent print transfer occurred all involved dishonest identification personnel.[32] Unfortunate-

31. The case is State v. Caldwell, 322 N.W.2d 574 (Minn.1982). For a discussion of this and similar instances, see, Starrs, "To Err is Human, Infallibility is Divine," *Scientific Sleuthing Newsletter*, Jan. 1983, p. 1 (Part I); Oct. 1983, p. 10 (Part II). See also, Starrs, "A Miscue in Fingerprint Identification: Causes and Concerns," 12 *J.Pol. Sci. & Admin.* 287 (1984).

32. See, e.g.; "Fingerprint Identification Rocked to the Core: Seeing is Not Observing," 17 *Scientific Sleuthing Review* Summer 1993, at 7. In 1991 David Harding, a New York State police lieutenant applied to the Central Intelligence Agency for a position as a covert operative. During a lie detector test, he boasted of having faked fingerprint evidence in criminal investigations in New York. He claimed to have lifted prints from crime scenes where in fact they had come from other sources. He pled guilty to perjury in four cases.

Harding's partner pled guilty to having manufactured fingerprint evidence in 21 cases. He was sentenced to a six to eighteen year term. In September 1993 the head of the same identification unit was sentenced to two and a half to seven and a half years, the maximum term permissible for the three perjury cases to which he pled guilty. New York Times, Sept. 9, 1993 at B8. A continuing investigation has uncovered other troopers' wrongdoing. See, "Trooper's Wrongdoing Taints Cases," A.B.A.J., March 1994, at 22. Dunleavy, "Fabricated Identification Detected," *Fingerprint Whorld*, 8:104 (1983); "Falsified Latent Prints," *Identification News*, Sept. 1981, p. 10; Bonebreak [Sic], "Fabricating Fingerprint Evidence," *Identification News*, Oct. 1976, p. 3: Mr. Bonebrake, then the supervisor of the Latent Fingerprint Section of the FBI Identification Division, related in this article 15 cases of fabricated

ly, such transfers (inaccurately called "forgeries"), are difficult to detect unless one makes a determined effort to look for precisely such an eventuality—something few identification personnel would have reason to suspect. Furthermore the detection of fraudulent transfers requires skills in microscopy or in chemical analysis which most fingerprint examiners do not possess.

§ 8.20 Defense Right to Inspection

In Chapter 1, we dealt with the general subject of Discovery. From the older view that no discovery in criminal cases was permitted, the law has moved toward recognizing broad discovery rights to the defense regarding all types of scientific evidence.

Trial courts and motion judges are no longer reluctant to sign orders compelling the police to permit defense inspection of fingerprint evidence or to furnish photograph copies of such evidence, even where no statutory authority or court rule exists. The refusal to permit such an inspection today would routinely be found to be reversible error.

§ 8.21 Bibliography

1. BOOKS

Alexander, *Classifying Palmprints: A Complete System of Coding, Filing and Searching Palmprints* (1973).

Bridges, *Practical Fingerprinting* (2d ed. 1964).

Cummins & Midlo, *Finger Prints, Palms and Soles* (2d ed. 1964).

Federal Bureau of Investigation, *The Science of Fingerprints* (1984).

Galton, *Finger Prints* (2d ed. 1965).

Illsley, U.S. Dep't of Justice, *Juries, Fingerprints and the Expert Fingerprint Witness* (1987).

fingerprint evidence that came to the FBI over a 30–year period. Mr. Bonebrake, upon his retirement, became the Executive Secretary of the Latent Print Certification Bureau of the International Association for Identification, and has been very instrumental in upgrading the education and professional competence of fingerprint experts as well as in detecting and exposing incompetency and erroneous identifications.

One of the cases that was primarily responsible for the widespread concern about integrity of the identification expert was the DePalma case, publicized in the *Readers Digest,* where a police department identification officer identified a latent print which had purportedly come from the counter of a bank that was robbed as having been made by DePalma. The defendant was convicted despite a strong alibi defense. It was later established that the "latent" was not a latent print at all, but a xerox print of an inked impression of the defendant's print, and that the faking was done to frame the defendant. Because several FBI experts had been unable, initially, to detect the fabrication, the chairman of the professional association's Science and Practice Committee, Mr. Brunelle, was led to state: "... in certain cases it may be very difficult to distinguish between authentic and fabricated prints and ... laboratory techniques such as a scanning electron microscope may be necessary to verify an authentic print." See, Brunelle, "Science and Practice Committee Report (1976)," II. Fingerprint Fabrication, *Identification News,* Aug. 1976, p. 7.

Kolb, *H.I.T.—A Manual for the Classification, Filing, and Retrieval of Palmprints* (1979).

Lee & Gaensslen, *Advances in Fingerprint Technology* (1991).

Moenssens, *Fingerprints and the Law* (1969).

Moenssens, *Fingerprint Techniques* (1971).

Scott, *Fingerprint Mechanics* (2d ed. by Olsen 1977).

Sharp, *Palm Prints: Their Classification and Identification* (1937).

Tarantino, *Strategic Uses of Scientific Evidence* § 2 (1988 & 1990 Cum.Supp.)

2. ARTICLES

"Fingerprints," 5 Am.Jur. Proof of Facts 77.

"Fingerprints," 1 Am.Jur. Trials 672.

"AFIS: Whorl'd of Difference in Fingerprint Identification," Vol. 4. No. 22 *BNA Criminal Practice Manual* 505 (October 31, 1990).

Anno., "Fingerprints, Palm Prints or Bare Footprints," 28 A.L.R.2d 1115 (1953).

Anno., "Footprints as Evidence," 35 A.L.R.2d 856 (1954).

Almog & Gabay, "Chemical Reagents for the Development of Latent Fingerprints, III: Visualization of Latent Fingerprints by Fluorescent Reagents in the Vapor Phase," 25 *J.For.Sci.* 408 (1980).

Almog & Gabay, "A Modified Super Glue Technique—The Use of Polycyanoacrylate for Fingerprint Development," 31 *J.For.Sci.* 250 (1986).

Almog, et al., "Reagents for the Chemical Development of Latent Fingerprints: Synthesis and Properties of Some Ninhydrin Analogues," 27 *J.For.Sci.* 912 (1982).

Bramble & Jackson, "Operational Experience of Fingermark Enhancement by Frequency Domain Filtering," 39 *J.For.Sci.* 920 (1994).

Burt & Menzel, "Laser Detection of Latent Fingerprints: Difficult Surfaces," 30 *J.For.Sci.* 364 (1985).

Dalrymple, et al., "Inherent Fingerprint Luminescence—Detection by Laser," 16 *J.For.Sci.* 106 (1976).

Duff & Menzel, "Laser–Assisted Thin–Layer Chromatography and Luminescence of Fingerprints: An Approach to Fingerprint Age Determination," 23 *J.For.Sci.* 129 (1978).

Garner, et al., "Visualization of Fingerprints in the Scanning Electron Microscope," 15 *J.For.Sci. Society* 281 (1975).

German, "Analog/Digital Image Processing," *Identification News,* Nov. 1983, p. 8.

Hebrard & Douche, "Fingerprint Detection Methods on Skin: Experimental Study on 16 Live Subjects and 23 Cadavers," 44 *J.Forensic Ident.* 623 (1994).

Herod & Menzel, "Laser Detection of Latent Fingerprints: Ninhydrin Followed by Zinc Chloride," 27 *J.For.Sci.* 513 (1982).

Lee & Gaensslen, "Cyanoacrylate Fuming," *Identification News,* June 1984, p. 4.

Melton, et al., "Final Report on Investigation of Improved and New Methods for the Detection and Characterization of Latent Fingerprints to Federal Bureau of Investigation," Sep. 1979.

Menzel, et al., "Laser Detection of Latent Fingerprints: Treatment with Glue Containing Cyanoacrylate Ester," 28 *J.For.Sci.* 307 (1983).

Menzel & Almog, "Latent Fingerprint Development by Frequency–Doubled Neodymium: Yttrium Aluminum Garnet (Nd:YAG) Laser: Benzo(f)ninhydrin," 30 *J.For.Sci.* 371 (1985).

Menzel, "A Guide to Laser Fingerprint Development Procedures," *Identification News,* Sept. 1983, p. 7.

Misner, Wilkinson & Watkin, "Thenyl Europium Chelate: A New Fluorescent Dye with a Narrow Emission Band to Detect Cyanoacrylate Developed Fingerprints on Non-porous Substrates and Cadavers," 43 *J.Forensic Ident.* 154 (1993); see also Letters to the Editor regarding this article at 43 *J.Forensic Ident.* 339 (1993).

Moenssens, "Poroscopy—Identification by Pore Structure," *Fingerprint & Ident. Mag.,* Jul. 1970, p. 3.

Moenssens, "Testifying As A Fingerprint Witness," *Fingerprint & Ident. Mag.,* Dec. 1972, p. 3. See also the sequel in April, 1973.

Moenssens, "The Fingerprint Witness in Court," *Fingerprint & Ident. Mag.,* Apr. 1973, p. 3.

Osterburg, "An Inquiry Into the Nature of Proof," 9 *J.For.Sci.* 413 (1964).

Reichardt, et al., "A Conventional Method for Lifting Latent Fingerprints from Human Skin," 23 *J.For.Sci.* 135 (1978).

Shin & Argue, "Identification of Fingerprints Left on Human Skin," 9 *Canadian Soc.For.Sci.J.* 81 (1976).

Smith, "Developing Latent Prints on Heroin Papers," *Fingerprint & Ident. Mag.,* May 1976, p. 3.

Smith, "A Practical Method for the Recovery of Latent Impressions On Adhesive Surfaces," *Ident.News,* Oct. 1977, p. 3.

Spjut, "An Alternative Method of Photographing Cyanoacrylate Developed Latent Prints on Clear Plastic Material," 44 *J.Forensic Ident.* 187 (1994).

Thornton, "Modification of Fingerprint Powder with Coumarin 6 Laser Dye," 23 *J.For.Sci.* 536 (1978).

Tuthill, "Ninhydrin," *Identification Newsletter* (Canada), Apr. 1982, p. 3.

Vickery, "California's Automated Latent Print System," *FBI Law Enforcement Bulletin,* Aug. 1981, p. 2.

Watling, "Using the FFT In Forensic Digital Image Enhancement," 43 *J.Forensic Ident.* 573 (1993).

Weaver, et al., "Large Scale Cyanoacrylate Fuming," 43 *J.Forensic Ident.* 135 (1993).

Wertheim, "Detection of Forged and Fabricated Latent Prints," 44 *J.Forensic Ident.* 652 (1994).

Wickett & Bowen, "Effects of New Fingerprinting Techniques on Bloodstains," *Ident.News,* Dec. 1985, p. 13.

Wilkinson & Watkin, "A Comparison of the Forensic Light Sources: Polilight, Luma-Lite, and Spectrum 9000," 44 *J.Forensic Ident.* 632 (1994).

Wilson and Woodard, *Automated Fingerprint Identification Systems: Technology and Policy Issues,* U.S. Dept. of Justice (1987).

Yamashita, "Use of a Benchtop Dessicator for Vacuum Cyanoacrylate Treatment of Latent Prints," 44 *J.Forensic Ident.* 149 (1994).

Chapter 9

TRACE EVIDENCE—THE SOURCE IDENTIFI-
CATION AND COMPARISON OF SMALL
OBJECTS AND PARTICLES

555

I.   INTRODUCTION

§ 9.01   Scope of the Chapter

The term "trace evidence" is a catch-all term that might well be applied to all types of physical evidence that may be circumstantial evidence in the trial of a case. We have already discussed certain types of "trace evidence" in earlier chapters [1] and will do so in subsequent chapters as well.[2] In these other parts of the book, however, the special types of "trace evidence" there discussed are typically examined by a specialist dealing only or principally with the one particular type of evidence which defines the expert's job status. Thus, biological evidence is examined by serologists, toxicologists, or DNA specialists; paper and ink evidence is the special province of questioned document examiners; bullets and anything pertaining to weapons is typically the province of the firearms examiner. In this chapter, by contrast, we deal with a

---

§ 9.01

1. See, e.g.: evidence of papers, in Chapter 5 on Questioned Document Examination; bullets, cartridge cases, wadding, gunshot residues, metal residues in toolmarks, etc. in Chapter 6 on Firearms and Toolmark Examinations; evidence of explosives and accelerants described in Chapter 7 on Arson and Explosives; and fingerprint traces discussed in Chapter 8 on Fingerprint Identification.

2. E.g.: Biological evidence discussed in Chapters 12 (Pathology), 13 (Toxicology), and 15 (DNA); evidence of drugs dealt with in Chapter 14.

variety of types of trace evidence analyzed by experts who are sometimes identified as "microanalysts," sometimes as "trace evidence examiners," or as "criminalists," or indeed by several different specialists. Indeed, there is no one profession or job classification which claims all trace evidence analyses as its own. In some laboratories, for example, hairs and fiber analyses are done by serologists, because these types of traces are frequently found along with biological evidence such as blood, semen, perspiration, saliva, and vomitus.[3] Recognizing that the examiner of trace evidence may be designated by a variety of job titles, we will use the term "microanalyst" for the sake of simplicity.

While evidence of the type discussed in this chapter is presented more frequently in criminal cases, some aspects have particular application to civil litigation as well. Evidence of glass particles, for example, can be extremely important in tort litigation stemming from automobile accidents. Thus, the identification and comparison of minute particles and objects plays an important role in litigation.

Not only is it often crucial to determine the nature of small items of trace evidence, it is also frequently desirable to be able to compare it with known materials for the purpose of determining the origin of the trace evidence.

Because of the minute size of the particles involved, and the necessity to examine microscopic characteristics of the evidence, the science of analyzing, identifying, and comparing evidence of that type with items of known nature has been called the science of microanalysis. The word *micro* in microanalysis, then, does not refer to the microscope as a tool in conducting this investigation, but rather to the microscopic size of the particles involved.

It is true that many of the examinations are conducted by the use of a microscope, but the various optical instruments known by that name are by no means the only tools of the microanalyst, who also utilizes instrumentation of a far more complex nature, particularly adapted for special inquiries. Some of these instrumental techniques will be referred to here. There is a considerable overlap in instrumentation and methodology used in the various disciplines and a good understanding of the material covered in this chapter would also require basic familiarity with the subject matter covered elsewhere in this book. But in the context of this chapter, the items of trace evidence discussed consist mainly of hair, fibers, wood, paint chips, glass, and the like. These are the particles with which the typical trace evidence analyst is mainly concerned.

§ 9.02 Definitions of Common Terms

(See also the definitions of laboratory instrumentation and techniques shared by the serologist, chemist, or drug analyst, given in Chapter 13.)

---

3. E.g., in the Virginia Forensic Science Division.

Atom: The smallest particle of any element capable of existing independently, yet retaining the qualities that mark it as a specific element.

Atomic Number: The number of protons in the nucleus of an atom. The number of protons in the nucleus is generally equal to the number of electrons revolving around the nucleus.

Atomic Weight: The relative average weight of an atom of the element, compared to a value of exactly 12 for the principal stable isotope of carbon (carbon–12).

Chromatography: A process of separation of compound materials by percolation through a selectively absorbing medium (paper, liquid, gas-liquid, gas-solid, etc.).

Cortex: (in this chapter) The interior portion of a hair.

Cuticule: (in this chapter) The layer of scales covering a hair, or the thickened scale or plate at the free end of some epithelial cells.

Decay: The spontaneous change of a radioactive (unstable) nucleus to a stable atomic nucleus. In different kinds of decay, the process is accompanied by the emission of energetic beta particles, x-ray photons, or gamma-ray photons.

Density: The mass per unit volume of a substance, usually expressed in grams per cubic centimeter, under special or standard conditions of pressure and temperature. The density can be determined by ascertaining the volume of the substance whose mass is known by weighing.

Electron: Particle possessing a negative charge equal to the positive charge of the proton.

Electron Microprobe Analysis: A research instrument for analyzing any element heavier than sodium in the periodic table.

Elements, Difference Between: The difference between any two elements lies in the number of protons in the nucleus of each atom. This number is expressed as the atomic number.

Gamma Rays: High energy, very penetrating electromagnetic radiation emitted in the decay of many radioisotopes. Gamma rays, emitted by specific radioisotopes, have characteristic energy levels which can be measured to identify the source elements.

Half Life: The half life of a radioisotope is the time it takes for one half of the radioactive atoms in a given sample to decay.

Isotope: A form of an element having the same number of protons in its nucleus but a different number of neutrons. The stable form of an isotope does not decay.

Mass Number: The total number of neutrons plus protons in the nucleus of a stable or radioactive isotope. Shown as a superscript to the left of the chemical symbol (e.g., the carbon isotope of mass number 12 is shown as ^{12}C).

Medulla: (in this chapter) The core or axial structure of a hair.

Melanin: A dark pigment found in the hair, skin, and retina.

Neutron: Subatomic particle, found in the nucleus of an atom, which possesses no electrical charge and has the same approximate mass as a proton.

Nucleus of Atom: The center of an atom around which electrons revolve at tremendous speed. The nucleus is composed of protons and neutrons.

Pigment: A substance of matter used as a coloring; in paints, an insoluble powder to be mixed with oil, water, or another base to produce paints, varnishes, and similar products.

Polymer: Any of a number of natural and synthetic compounds composed of usually high molecular weight consisting of up to millions of repeated linked units, each of a relatively simple and light molecule.

Pyrolysis: The process of inducing chemical changes by heat or burning.

Refractive Index: The ratio of the speed of light in a vacuum to the speed of light through a transparent medium (in this chapter glass).

Specific Gravity: The ratio of the density of a substance to that of water.

Spectrograph: A spectroscope equipped to photograph the spectra of substances being examined.

Spectrometer: A spectroscope equipped with scales for measuring the positions of spectral lines, or to determine wavelengths and intensities of the various radiations of substances being examined.

Spectrophotometer: An instrument for measuring the relative amounts of radiant energy or radiant flux in a spectrum of luminous radiation.

Spectroscope: Any one of a series of instruments designed to resolve and observe the visible spectrum.

Synthetic: Man-made substance produced by synthesis usually from non-natural materials.

II. INSTRUMENTATION AND METHODS OF ANALYSIS

§ 9.03 The Purposes of Microanalytic Methods

An expert microscopic analysis of small objects and particles can serve two primary functions: (1) in criminal cases it may be an investigative aid in the apprehension of an offender or the elimination of an innocent suspect; (2) in both civil and criminal litigation, it may permit us to associate a small piece of physical evidence with a particular location, or establish the common origin of several items of trace evidence. In order to establish these connections, it becomes important that evidentiary principles be observed. Thus, care must be taken in the collection of evidence that it not be contaminated or altered; it must be properly marked and identified; the chain of possession must be carefully noted; and the proper investigative techniques must be followed by the expert analyst. All of these will be explored in the section dealing with the evidentiary aspects of trace evidence.

§ 9.04   Qualifications of the Microanalyst

In the examination of physical evidence, the microanalyst must, of necessity, be an expert in microscopy. The use of proper optics, illuminators, filters, and the correct preparation of specimens for examination are essential if the desired results are to be obtained. In addition, the microanalyst should possess a thorough working knowledge of photomacrography and photomicrography, both in color and in black and white, and be skilled in the collection of standards, such as hairs, fibers, paints, safe insulation, glass, etc., and retain these standards in the laboratory reference file for identification and comparison purposes. In addition, the microanalyst must be trained in the manipulation of the smallest of specimens without damaging, altering, or losing the specimens. It becomes quite obvious, then, that the microanalyst is a specialist who needs not only a solid formal education, at least at the baccalaureate level, in one or more of the basic sciences, but also requires specialized training and experience in the legal applications of these sciences.

As in all the forensic sciences, there is currently a strong trend toward licensing or board certification of criminalistics practitioners.

§ 9.05   Tools of the Microanalyst

Perhaps the most basic instrument in the examination of physical evidence is the microscope. There is a great variety of different types of microscopes. Among them are: compound microscopes, stereo-binocular microscopes, phase and dark field microscopes, polarizing microscopes, and comparison microscopes. Of these, the stereo-binocular microscope (Figure 1) is probably the most frequently used. In the hands of the trained microanalyst, this instrument affords a magnified image of the object exactly as it appears in nature, the three dimensions of length, breadth, and depth being visible. It is employed in the examination of bulk items such as clothing and weapons, and also minute items such as glass, hairs, fibers, paint, soil and other trace materials. One of the best uses of the instrument is to extract and isolate minute particles that may be present on a larger item and to separate debris into separate constituents.

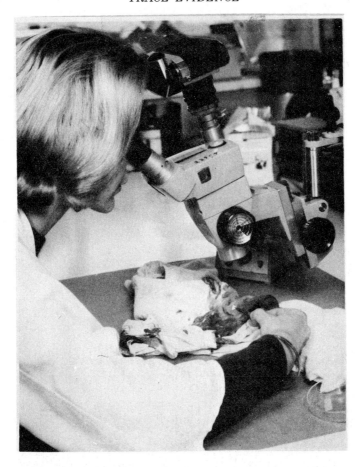

Fig. I. A technician is using the stereo-binocular microscope equipped with a 35 mm. camera to locate, photograph, and remove paint particles embedded in a garment. *Courtesy: Chicago Police Department, Criminalistics Division.*

A second important instrument at the disposal of the trained microanalyst is the polarizing (petrographic) microscope. The unit allows for the study of specimens in very exact detail with respect to their physical and chemical properties. The assignment of mathematical values to the results of these examinations and tests makes this instrument extremely valuable. It is used to identify and compare hair, fibers, glass, paint, soil, dust, safe insulation, etc.

The comparison microscope is another widely used and valuable instrument. This microscope actually consists of two microscopes with identical optical systems, matched objectives and eyepieces and identical light sources of equal intensity. The two microscopes are connected by an optical bridge. One specimen is placed on the stage of one microscope, and a second specimen placed on the other microscope stage. When these specimens are observed through the optical bridge they appear side by side as if both specimens were in one field (one specimen appearing as a continuation of the other, as was illustrated earlier in the examination of bullet markings in Chapter 6). This instrument is used mainly in the comparison of morphological characteristics. To the microanalyst, it is extremely valuable in the comparison of hairs and fibers.

The phase contrast, interference, and dark field microscopes are also available to the microanalyst. These instruments, through the use of special objectives, condensers, and illuminators, diffract certain rays of light coming through the objective, improving the resolving power of the microscope and thereby exhibiting greater detail of the object being examined. The use of these instruments is usually resorted to in the examination of certain types of specimens or to search for characteristics that will not be revealed in great detail by the ordinary bright field microscope.

Of equal importance to the microanalyst is the use of such instrumentation as emission spectrography, infrared and ultraviolet spectrophotometry, scanning electron microscope (SEM)[1], atomic absorption spectrophotometry[2], electron microprobe x-ray analysis[3], x-ray diffraction, and gas chromatography. These instruments, used in conjunction with microscopic examinations of physical evidence, provide the analyst with the necessary equipment for the examination of physical evidence.

The microanalyst is a scientist, working in the laboratory. In most law enforcement agencies, he never visits scenes of crimes. He is dependant, therefore, upon the field investigator, or, in civil cases, upon

§ 9.05

1. Korda, MacDonell & Williams, "Forensic Applications of the Scanning Electron Microscope," 61 *J.Crim.L., C. & P.S.* 453 (1970).

In their article, Peterson, et al., "The Capabilities, Uses, and Effects of the Nation's Criminalistics Laboratories," 30 *J.For.Sci.* 10 (1985), the authors report on their survey of criminalistics laboratories in the United States, noted the rapid increase in laboratories during the 1970s, the continued rise in the number of scientific personnel, and that the laboratories are relatively successful in updating and acquiring new instrumentations. The authors also point out that only minimal original research and writing comes out of the crime laboratories.

On the growing pains of such laboratories, see, Moenssens, "Admissibility of Scientific Evidence—An Alternative to the *Frye* rule," 25 *Wm. & Mary L.Rev.* 545, at 549–551 (1984). See also, Chapter 1, supra, at footnote 10 for a description of proficiency testing of crime laboratory personnel which caused a forensic scientist to say, "the crime labs flunk analysis."

2. The test is one used to examine gunshot residues (see, supra § 4.12, generally). In Chatom v. State, 348 So.2d 838 (Ala. 1977), the Alabama Supreme Court, in a plurality opinion (with four Justices dissenting), held that the result of an atomic absorption test was not inadmissible as a matter of law. A dissenting justice felt that scientific tests which, according to the state's own expert witness, are only 75% to 80% accurate "are so unreliable as to raise serious due process questions." (Id. at 842.) Upon remand to the appellate court, that tribunal affirmed the conviction expressing "doubt as to the sufficiency of the evidence without the results of the atomic absorption test" but feeling compelled to let the jury verdict stand since a fact question was created after the scientific test became "admissible by default" as a result of the lack of diligence in properly objecting by defense counsel at trial. Chatom v. State, 348 So.2d 843, 844 (Ala.App.1977).

See also, State v. Shapiro, 431 So.2d 372 (La.1982), where conviction of murder was reversed, though evidence of atomic absorption spectroscopy test for gunshot residues was positive and other circumstantial evidence was introduced, by prosecutor. A battle of experts (pathologists) caused the court to find that the traditional heavy burden of proof was not sustained in this case.

3. Whitney & MacDonell, "Forensic Applications of the Electron Microprobe," 9 *J.For.Sci.* 511 (1964).

the litigants' attorneys, not only for the collection and preservation of trace evidence, but also for the relevant information that is needed to conduct a scientific examination. It is important, therefore, that the field investigator be adequately trained in the collection and preservation of evidence. This becomes particularly important if the evidence is to be used in court, because of the judicial requirement of proper identification of the evidentiary items and proof of the chain of custody. Trace evidence should be submitted to the laboratory, therefore, in clean containers, usually pill boxes, vials, bottles, test tubes, envelopes, boxes, plastic bags, etc. These containers should be carefully tagged or labeled with the following information: (1) contents; (2) owner or possessor, if known; (3) location where evidence was discovered; (4) date and time of recovery; (5) type of case; (6) name of parties involved, if any; (7) case number, if assigned; (8) signature or initials of the person who found and recovered the evidence.

To prevent loss, alteration and/or contamination of physical evidence, the field investigator should also avoid having the evidence specimens handled by any persons not necessary to the inquiry. It is also important that each sample of evidence be placed in separate containers, and the investigator should not attempt to separate evidence, for example, fibers and hairs found tangled together.

Evidence must be properly handled and expeditiously submitted to the laboratory, if the microanalyst is to perform his duties in such a manner that evidence may be admissible in a trial.

§ 9.06 Neutron Activation Analysis

Some years ago, scientists in specialized laboratories developed a method for the analysis of small particles which utilizes nuclear age instrumentation and techniques. The method is called "neutron activation analysis" and is commonly referred to as NAA. It is a nuclear, as opposed to a chemical or spectrographic, method of quantitatively analyzing samples for the elements they contain.

Neutron Activation Analysis (NAA) is a method of determining the qualitative and quantitative elemental composition of a sample by bombarding that sample, for a controlled period of time, with an intense stream of nuclear particles, usually neutrons, produced by a research-type nuclear reactor. This bombardment ("neutron activation") produces radioactive species (radionuclides) of almost all of the elements that are present in the sample.

The radioactive isotopes tend to return to a stable (non-radioactive) form. This process is called the decay, and the disintegration of the radioactive elements is accompanied with the emission of high-energy electromagnetic radiations called gamma rays. The gamma rays emitted by an activated sample are then detected and measured by a gamma-ray spectrometer, which indicates the energy and number of a given energy of each of the various gamma rays being emitted. By comparison of the data then obtained with theoretical equations and experimental parameters, or by comparison with the data obtained from activating pure samples of the elements, the quantity of each element present in the substance can be determined.[1]

When a radioactive element decays with the emission of gamma rays, the energy level generated differs depending upon the binding energy of the nucleus. Each isotope has one or more distinct binding energies, and therefore a characteristic gamma ray energy level. The energy of the gamma ray is designated in Mev, for "Million electron volts." The ability of a nucleus of an atom to capture bombarding neutrons also varies for each element. The probability that a stable nucleus will capture thermal neutrons is measured by its "cross section" and is expressed in "barns." Some elements have low "barn" values, meaning that they capture thermal neutrons very reluctantly. An example of that is oxygen, whose ^{18}O isotope has a cross section of only 0.0002 barn, which makes it virtually unusable for NAA. Cross sections of stable isotopes range from about 10^{-5} barns all the way up to 10^{5} barns. The higher the barn value, the more sensitively the element can be detected. These three values, half life, decay energy in Mev, and capture rate in barns, form the basis of NAA.[2]

The device used in NAA to provide a high flux of thermal (slow) neutrons is a research-type nuclear reactor. The reactor is fueled with a core of enriched uranium–235, which is the source of the neutrons used to bombard a suspect sample. The central core of the reactor is immersed in high-purity water. The water serves three purposes: (1) it slows down fast-moving neutrons which are released when the nucleus of a uranium–235 atom splits ("fissions"); (2) it removes heat created by the "chain reaction" as one after another of the uranium–235 atoms fission; and (3) it acts as a shield to protect personnel from the harmful effects of neutrons and gamma rays. The intensity of the chain reaction within the reactor can be controlled by instrumentation.

NAA techniques employ a high thermal-neutron flux produced in a research-type nuclear reactor. High-flux NAA provides much greater sensitivity than the much lower thermal-neutron fluxes available with smaller neutron generators.

While, at one time, NAA was perceived as the panacea for all trace evidence analysis, practical experience did not satisfy these expectations. NAA analysis was extremely costly and required a research nuclear reactor not readily available for ordinary cases. Moreover, as the years passed, highly sophisticated instrumentation that was affordable for most laboratories was adapted for forensic purposes and gave results that were deemed to be as accurate as NAA had promised to provide. For all practical purposes, therefore, NAA was no longer needed and is, today, not used on a regular basis for routine trace evidence analysis in

§ 9.06

1. Guinn, "Neutron Activation Analysis and its Forensic Applications," *Proc. 1st Int'l Conf. on Forensic Activation Analysis,* 1966.

2. Ruch, et al., "Neutron Activation Analysis in Scientific Crime Detection— Some Recent Developments," 9 *J.For.Sci.* 119 (1964).

crime laboratories, though it is still used to a limited extent by the FBI and also in civil litigation.[3]

III. EXAMINATION OF HAIR

§ 9.07 Glossary of Terms

As a result of meetings in 1983 and 1984, at the FBI's Forensic Science Research and Training Center, Quantico, Va., of the Ad Hoc Committee on Forensic Hair Comparison, one purpose of which was to standardize the terminology of hair comparisons, the following definitions were agreed upon by the participants:

Central Region: In a transverse plane, the area of the hair shaft toward the core area of the shaft.

Characteristic: Any feature of the hair which may be useful for identification and/or comparison purposes.

Characterize: The process of examining and describing features of hair.

Class: A category of hair (e.g., scalp hair, dog hair).

Comparison: The process of examining two or more hairs for the purpose of either identifying them as having come from the same class of hairs or attempting to associate them with or dissociate them from a given individual.

Dimensions: Metric measurements are used without exception. The usual units used are millimeters and micrometers. Hair length is usually also given parenthetically in inches.

Distal End: In a longitudinal plane, the end of the hair shaft distant from the root.

Exclusion: The questioned hairs are unlike the known hairs; therefore, they could not have originated from the same source as the known sample.

Identification: The process of determining that a given hair belongs to or came from a defined class of hairs.

Inconclusive: When compared, the questioned and known hair samples exhibit both similarities and dissimilarities such that no meaningful conclusion can be drawn.

Individualization: The process of determining that a given hair came from one particular (individual) source to the exclusion of all other similar sources. (This is presently an unachieved goal of forensic hair comparison.)

---

3. Capannesi & Sedda, "Bullet Identification: A Case of a Fatal Hunting Accident Resolved by Comparison of Lead Shot Using Instrumental Neutron Activation Analysis," 37 *J.For.Sci.* 657 (1992).

Known: A sample taken as representative of a particular body area of a specific person or animal.

Limited Range: The range of values exhibited by an incomplete or inadequate sample of the hair of one individual with regard to a specific characteristic.

Magnification Ranges: 1. Unaided eye observation;

   2. Low-power magnification, e.g., 1–50X;

   3. Microscopic: observable only under the compound microscope at higher magnification, e.g., 25–1000X.

Medial Region: The portion of the hair shaft, in longitudinal plane, intermediate between the proximal and distal ends.

Peripheral Region: In a transverse plane, the portion of the hair shaft toward the outermost areas of the hair, including the cuticle and the outer areas of the cortex, distant from the medullary region.

Proximal End: In a longitudinal place, the end of the hair shaft nearest the root.

Questioned: A sample collected for the purpose of identification and/or comparison with a known sample.

Range: The complete range of values exhibited by the hair of one individual with regard to a specific characteristic.

Reference Sample: One of a collection of samples which are used for further hair study.

Regions of the Hair Shaft: 1. In longitudinal plane, see: Proximal End; Medial Region; and Distal End.

   2. In transverse plane, see: Peripheral Region; and Central Region.

Sample: One or more hairs used for identification, comparison or reference.

Similar: The combination of microscopic characteristics of the questioned hair is exhibited by the known hair sample.

Spectrum: The range of values exhibited collectively by all individuals with regard to a specific characteristic.

Type I Error: Incorrect exclusion.

Type II Error: Incorrect inclusion.

Value: The qualitative or quantitative assessment of a particular characteristic based on a single observation.

   No further terminology was agreed upon at the FBI sponsored event. The other definitions of parts of the hair, such as the surface cuticle, cortex of shaft, medulla, etc., can be found in § 8.08.

§ 9.08   The Structure of Hair

Hair is indigenous to the mammalian species. Untrained observers may, however, easily confuse hair with certain plant fibers such as silk, cotton, and hemp. Hair grows from the hair follicle located in the skin. The root or bulb of the hair is embedded in the follicle. As the hair cells harden, they are extruded from the follicle with the results that the hair grows outward from the root end. The growth rate of human hair is about one-half inch every thirty days, although considerable variation may be noted. Hardening of the hair cells results from the influx of the inert protein keratin. Hair structure resembles somewhat the scales of fish, with overlapping scales giving it the appearance of a spiral.

External mammalian hair consists of three layers: (1) the surface cuticle composed of transparent pigment-free overlapping scales pointing toward the tip end of the hair; (2) the cortex or cornified shaft surrounding the medulla and containing some color pigment granules of melanin; and (3) the medulla or core which contains cellular debris and some pigments. A cross-section of hair at 500–magnification is shown in Figure 2. In the absence of melanin granules, hair is white or gray. The color and distribution of these granules are important for identification purposes. There are two principal types of mammalian hair, namely short, fine fuzz, and long stiff strands which are commonly known as down and guard hairs, respectively.

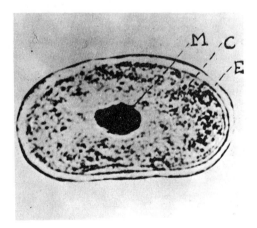

Fig. 2. Cross-section of hair (500X). *M* indicates the medulla; *C* is the cortex; and *E* the cuticle.

An important feature of hair is that it retains its structural characteristics for extremely long periods. It resists putrefaction remarkably well, which makes it of great potential importance in the identification of mutilated corpses and disaster victims (other than burned corpses). Professor J. Glaister of the University of Glasgow examined hair from embalmed subjects classified as belonging to the 11th, 12th and 20th Dynasties. He stated that the microscopical features could be clearly observed even in transverse section.[1]

A mistaken popular notion holds that hair continues to grow for a short period after death. This is not so. The skin, however, by dehydration shrinks or pulls together, so that the hair, especially the beard, has the appearance of having grown somewhat.

§ 9.09 Importance of Hair Examinations

Although there is no known way yet of positively identifying hair as having come from a particular individual, except in a few rare instances, an ascertainment of similarity in color, structure, pigmentation and other characteristics can be of considerable probative value when considered along with other evidence against a person. Among the uses in civil and criminal cases, we can note:

1. An intruder may be attacked by a dog and hairs from the animal may be deposited on clothing of the burglar. Identification and comparison of these hairs may contribute to placing a suspect on whose body or clothing dog hairs are found at the crime scene. Of course, it must be remembered that this circumstantial proof may lose much of its probative value if the suspect has a dog himself, or can prove contact with another dog, since not as much can be learned from studying animal hairs as can from human hair.

2. In sexual assaults and rape cases including civil suits that flow from sexual attacks,[1] pubic hairs from the victim on the suspect's body or clothing, or those of the suspect on the victim, may tend to substantiate the fact that an assault occurred. Head hairs present on the clothing or body of the victim may establish the color of the suspect's hair, and thus furnish a valuable investigative aid.

3. Damaged hair from the victim of a crime may furnish a clue as to the type of weapon used. Fragments of the weapon, or paint from it, may also be present on the hair.

4. Hair recovered from a suspect's vehicle and compared with hair from the victim of a hit-and-run accident may establish that the vehicle was involved in the incident.

Much more can be learned from hair examination, as will be further explored. It must be reemphasized, however, that it is presently impossible to definitely state that a hair belongs to a given individual. The most that can be stated is that a questioned hair matches a hair sample of known origin in all microscopic characteristics.[2]

---

§ 9.08

1. Glaister, "Contact Traces," 7 *J.For. Med.* 44 (1960).

§ 9.09

1. E.g., in custody proceedings flowing from parental abuse accusations or in in-cest; also in damage actions against child care providers.

2. When a hair root is present, DNA analysis may permit a near positive identification. See, infra Chapter 15.

§ 9.10　Collection of Proper Known Standards

One of the popular mystery stories has been provocatively titled, "Caught by A Hair," suggesting to the reader that a single hair may solve the mystery and be responsible for the arrest and conviction of the culprit. Moreover, the modern day Sherlock Holmes is often portrayed as comparing the one crime scene hair that is discovered, with a single hair of the primary suspect. Nothing could be further from reality. Regardless of how many or how few crime scene hairs were retrieved and submitted to the laboratory, an ample amount of known standards is needed to be able to competently conduct hair comparisons. Yet, even crime laboratory technicians have been heard to say they will compare a single questioned hair against a single known standard!

It is illuminating, therefore, to read the preliminary report of the Committee on Forensic Hair Comparison, issued in 1984 by the Federal Bureau of Investigation's Forensic Science Research and Training Center (hereinafter referred to as FBI Hair Comparison Report). It sets out a number of recommendations to be followed in collecting known specimens. Here are its provisions in that regard:

> Because of the variation in microscopic characteristics among different hairs from the same body region of one person, it is important to obtain a sufficient number of hairs in order to adequately represent the ranges of all characteristics present. If the ranges of characteristics are large, it becomes necessary to obtain a large number of hairs. Because they differ in their characteristics, it is important to obtain hairs from different areas of the scalp. Full-length hairs with roots should be obtained for the examiner to adequately examine and compare the variations along the length of a single hair and to determine its growth phase. Since the vast majority of pulled hairs will be in an active growing stage, a combing procedure is also desirable to obtain hairs in the telogen or dead stage.

It is recommended that a known head hair sample consist of at least 20 hairs from each of 5 different areas of the scalp (center, front, back, and both sides) and that these hairs be obtained by both pulling and combing. The recommended procedure for obtaining combed hairs is to use either a comb packed with cotton or a multibristle brush. The various areas of the scalp should be repeatedly combed over a large sheet of clean paper in a direction opposite to that in which the person usually combs the hair.

From these 100 hairs, a number of hairs (usually 6 to 20, depending on the homogeneity of the sample) should be selected by the examiner as representative of the entire known sample. The selection should be based primarily on gross characteristics such as length, coarseness and color as observed by macroscopic and stereomicroscopic examination. These hairs should be used for comparison. The remaining hairs are then available for future use if subsequent examinations reveal that, whereas a questioned hair has characteristics close to those of the known sample, a good match to any of the 6 to 20 hairs originally selected cannot be found.

A known pubic hair sample should consist of at least 30 hairs obtained by both pulling and combing from different areas of the pubic region.

For exclusionary purposes, known samples should be requested from all persons who might reasonably be considered a source of a questioned hair. If such samples are obtained and excluded, the significance of any ensuing association is increased.

Some examiners believe that a known sample does not require a large number of hairs and that hairs cut close to the scalp, being easier to obtain, should be used for the comparison process. The committee members, in formulating the recommendation of 100 pulled and combed hairs, believe that 100 pulled and combed hairs are required to guarantee full-length hairs, and that the number chosen should help minimize type I errors. Since an individual loses an average of 100 scalp hairs a day as part of the normal hair cycle, the collection of 100 hairs is not unreasonable. While hairs cut close to the skin line can, if necessary, be used for comparison purposes, the root and root end are important parts of the hair and should be obtained whenever possible. It is recommended that research be conducted as to the content and methods of collection of known hair samples.

§ 9.11 Aims of Hair Examinations

Among the most important issues that the examination of suspect particles seeks to resolve are:

1. Is the questioned particle hair?
2. If so, is it of human or animal origin?
3. If animal, to what family of animals does it belong?
4. If human, from what part of the body did it come?
5. What is the racial origin and sex of the person from whom the hair came?

1. IS IT HAIR?

To determine if a specimen is mammalian hair or vegetable fiber, the microanalyst may want to examine the specimen microscopically. Hair is recognized by the presence of a root (when present) embedded in the hair follicle, and a shaft. It contains three layers, as previously described. Synthetic hairs or other fibers do not possess these three elements. They are constructed in an entirely different way.

2. HUMAN OR ANIMAL ORIGIN

Human hair has certain microscopically observable characteristics which permit differentiation from hair of other mammals. The examiner will usually have a large group of reflective comparison samples from different mammalian species to aid in determining species origin.

The medullary layer of the hair in cross section is narrower in man and a few other mammals (such as the horse and the monkey) than in other mammals. It is usually fragmented but may even be absent in some human hair. A medullary index is used to identify species origin from medullary diameter. It measures the relation between the diameter of the medulla and the whole hair. Figure 3 illustrates three different types of medullas. A low index is indicative of human origin.

Fig. 3. Three types of medullas are illustrated. On the left, the medulla is frag-mental; in the center, it is interrupted; on the right, the medulla is continuous.

The cortex layer of the human hair contains most of the pigment granules while in other mammals pigmentation is found primarily in the medulla. Examination of the pattern of cuticle scale is useful in determining species origin. In the human, the scales overlap smoothly, while in other mammalian species they protrude in a rough serrated form. A squared-off end from cutting may also be a factor suggesting human origin. Most importantly, however, human hair tapers gradually to a point; animal hair comes to a point abruptly.

Animal hair comparisons are usually not as determinative and conclusive as human hair comparisons. The variations found in the hair from a single animal can be very great. It is also difficult to differentiate between breed of a same animal family by hair comparison. Sometimes this is true even between animals of different species. Hairs of dogs and cats, for example, look very similar under the microscope. Some deer hair resembles that of rabbits.

3. DETERMINATION OF BODY PART OF ORIGIN

It must be noted that the diversity in appearance of human hair is very great. This is true even among a group of hairs from different body parts of one individual. Human hair may originate from any part of the body: the head, eyelashes, beard, chest, arms, legs, or genital area. The determination of the region of the body from which a hair came can sometimes be accomplished as well.

Head (scalp) hair is ordinarily more uniform in diameter size and has a more even pigment distribution than hair from other body parts. Hairs from the eyebrows or eyelids, by contrast, are short and stubby and they have wider medullas. In general shape, they taper to a finer point than do scalp hairs. Nose or ear hairs share these same characteristics, whereas beard hair is curved and coarse; it appears triangular in cross section in most instances.[1]

Hairs from the chest or back appear immature. They vary in thickness along the shaft, having fine and gradual tip ends. In other respects they are somewhat like scalp hairs, although they may look like immature pubic hairs as well. Hairs from the legs and arms are shorter, less course, and contain less pigment as a rule.

Pubic hairs are wiry and have more constrictions and twists than other hairs. They ordinarily have unevenly distributed pigments and continuously broad medullas. They also may vary in diameter along the shaft. A cross-section of hair may also reveal the body part of origin; for instance, beard hair is triangular in cross-section.

4. RACE AND SEX DETERMINATION

From the hair of an individual, it may usually be established whether he is Caucasian, Negroid, Mongoloid or of mixed race. This is done primarily by a study of pigment distribution, and other physical characteristics.

Pigment distribution is more even in Caucasians, from very fine to coarse. In Negroids, the pigment is heavy and distributed unevenly. Mongoloids (which includes American Indians, Eskimos, and Orientals) have very dense pigment distributed more evenly than in Negroids.

In a cross-section of the hair, that of Caucasians is oval to round, in members of the Negroid race flat to oval in shape, and round to oval in Mongoloids. Negroid hair is usually tightly curled and has marked variations in the hair diameter along the shaft. Mongolian hair is coarse and straight and varies little in diameter along the shaft. Caucasian hair is ordinarily straight or wavy but not as curled as in Negroids; the diameter along the shaft varies less markedly also.

§ 9.11

1. The identification of chin hair was a matter of expert testimony, the court said in Watson v. State, 64 Wis.2d 264, 219 N.W.2d 398 (1974). While the expert, in his conclusions, may be impeached by other experts who come to opposing conclusions or by treatises, his testimony may be believed, the court said, despite scientific evidence to the contrary. (at 403).

Determining the sex of a person from an examination of hair may be attempted by staining the follicular cells from the hair root sequentially for the Y and the X chromosomes. Following staining, the fluorescence of the Y and X chromosomes is observed by epifluorescence. By a chromosome count, a Y–X score is determined, which has permitted a rather precise, though not absolutely positive, determination of the hair donor's sex.[2] There are other observable characteristic differences between hair of males and of females, but because of the great variations encountered, they are less significant. Among these differences is the fact that male hair may generally be larger in diameter than female hair. There are also significant differences between male and female cosmetic preparations, dyes and laquers, which can often be identified.

§ 9.12   Examination Procedures

When a hair has been found, it is first observed by the traditional microscopic method. This affords an opportunity to look for the presence of foreign matter, such as blood, dyes, fibers, etc. If the contaminants are of sufficient quantity, they too should be identified. Dyed hair, under the microscope, has a duller appearance than natural hair; the inner margin of the cuticle is obscured and the pigment granules will be less prominent than those of natural hairs.[1] The growth of hair after dyeing will be clearly observable, and considering that we know at what rate hair grows (see § 8.07), it is possible to estimate the approximate time of the dyeing. Microscopic examination will also afford an opportunity to observe whether the hair has a natural or an artificial curl.

The 1984 FBI Hair Comparison Report (to which we referred in § 8.10) sets out a number of recommendations to be followed by criminalists who engage in hair comparisons. Since attorneys will prefer to be able to consult what will undoubtedly become the "Bible" in the field, and since the report is still not widely circulated or known outside criminalistics laboratories, here is its recommendation concerning the process of microscopical human hair comparison. (All italicized emphasis is by the authors of this book.)

> *Hair comparisons, as generally conducted by forensic scientists, are somewhat subjective.* Only a few important characteristics of a human hair can be described quantitatively. Accordingly, it is vital that both the procedures and thought processes involved in a hair comparison be selected by the examiner to minimize type II errors. Many factors must become a part of the examiner's thought processes, both before and during a hair examination, regardless of the

2. Mudd, "The Determination of Sex from Forcibly Removed Hairs," 29 *J.For. Sci.* 1072 (1984); Nagamori, "Sex Determination from Plucked Human Hairs Without Epithelial Root Sheath," 12 *For.Sci.International* 167 (1978); King & Wigmore, "Sexing of Hair Sheath Cells Using Y–Chromosome Fluorescence," 20 *J.For.Sci. Soc.* 263 (1980); Amador, et al., "Sex De-termination of Human Hair by Cortical Cell Nuclei Sex Chromatin Staining," 17 *Can. Soc.For.Sci.* 22 (1984).

§ 9.12

1. Bleached hair has a very rough appearance; its pigment content which is considerably less than in natural hair, is dependent on the degree of bleaching.

technique utilized for the comparison. Consideration of these factors forces the hair examiner into a certain protocol for conducting comparisons. This subcommittee report presents a recommended process for the comparison of human hairs based primarily on their microscopic characteristics. Emphasis is on the procedural aspects of the comparison process and the explanation and justification of the steps used.

Most often, only hairs from the scalp and pubic regions of the body are involved in comparisons made by crime laboratories. There is considerably more variability in the characteristics of scalp or pubic hairs among different people than in the hairs from other body regions (of the two hair types, scalp hairs usually show more interpersonal variation, resulting in stronger associations). Hairs from other body areas can be compared, but these comparisons are usually less significant and less frequently encountered. Accordingly, this report mainly reflects the considerations of human scalp hair comparison. To a lesser extent, human pubic hair comparison was also considered. With some modifications, however, these recommendations could apply to any type of macroscopic and microscopic hair comparison.

GENERAL CONSIDERATIONS

Hair evidence differs in many respects from other types of physical evidence commonly encountered in a crime laboratory. *One major difference lies in the variety of characteristics that exist among the hairs from a single body region of any one person and the range of values for a particular characteristic over that region.* This range is, nevertheless, only an extremely small part of the spectrum of values exhibited by the entire population, i.e., intrapersonal variation is much less than interpersonal variation. Further, a portion of a single hair always contains only a limited range of values with respect to each type of characteristic present in a representative known sample of hair.

The hair growth cycle is at least partially responsible for the range that exists with regard to a single characteristic. Hairs in different growth phases from the same person will exhibit obvious differences in some microscopic characteristics. *It is important, therefore, that the hairs be compared in the same growth phase.* This usually requires the presence of the root, and demonstrates the need for obtaining complete hairs in the known sample.

The value of a particular characteristic is usually not constant along successive portions of a single hair from root to tip. In some hairs only slight changes are seen; in others great changes occur. The variation in any one type of characteristic for any single hair is dependent on numerous factors, including the hair length and the health, lifestyle, environment, and grooming habits of the person. Because of such variation within one type of characteristic along a single hair, the value of a characteristic at any one position along the length of a hair should be compared with the value of that type of characteristic at corresponding points along the hairs being compared. Variations such as these, which are not present in most other types of evidence, usually force the hair examiner to use full-length hairs in the comparison process.

Microscopic characteristics exhibited within a human hair can be grouped into two categories—general and individual. Both categories are important in the actual comparison process. The following subcategories describe general characteristics:

1. Color
    a. hue
    b. pigmentation
    c. variation
2. Structure
    a. form
    b. diameter
    c. cross-sectional shape
    d. cortex
    e. medullation
    f. shaft aberration
3. Cuticular traits
    a. scales
    b. thickness
    c. margins
    d. sequence
    e. weathering
4. Acquired characteristics
    a. proximal ends (roots)
    b. distal ends (tips)
5. Length

At a given position along a hair many characteristics can be assessed. Most values, individually, would not be considered unusual or uncommon. There are, however, numerous ways in which all of the values of each of these subcategories can occur, and this gives a hair some uniqueness.

Individual characteristics differ from general characteristics in that they occur infrequently. Individual characteristics include:

1. Artificial coloration;

2. Abnormalities;

3. Uncommon structural conditions;

4. An unusual value for a particular general characteristic;

5. Artifacts.

In a hair match, the presence of an individual characteristic adds considerable strength to the association, because the chance of finding the same characteristic in a hair taken from someone at random would be very small. Individual characteristics are readily recognized and are easier to describe than a particular value of a general characteristic. *The determination of which characteristics are unusual (and, therefore, uncommon) is an important part of the hair examiner's job. Considerable experience is necessary to develop a foundation upon which to make this determination.*

Through the proper use of various microscopes and their accessories, the hair is studied for all its distinguishing features outlined in the preceding paragraphs. Cuticular scale type is determined while the hair is either mounted dry or in a transparent cast; the examination is made by placing a drop of tinted varnish or collodion on a microscope slide to form a film on which the hair is placed. After the film is dry, the hair can be lifted off and a cast of the cuticular scale outlines will remain. The medulla and cortex are examined either in a mounting medium, oil or balsam. If the hair is densely pigmented, it may have to be bleached to render the characteristics visible.

Age of the subject cannot be accurately determined by a study of the hair. But it can be ascertained whether the hair was cut recently. Since hair tapers to a fine point, due to brushing, combing, or even naturally, a square appearance will be noted after it has been recently cut. If the root end is present, it can be determined whether the hair has fallen out naturally, or was pulled out. The naturally fallen hair has a clean bulb formation at the root end (see Figure 4); if it was pulled forcibly it will usually have a portion of the sheath clinging to the bulb, which may also appear mutilated. Hairs which have been bleached or artificially waved will frequently show splitting at the tip ends and damaged cuticle scales.[1]

Fig. 4. The bulb formation is the root end of a hair (160X), and indicates by its presence and form that it has fallen out naturally.

A few decades ago, neutron activation analysis (NAA), was touted as a panacea for hair examinations, and it was even suggested that NAA might be able to individualize human hairs. That prediction has not materialized.

§ 9.12

1. See also, Andrasko & Stocklassa, "Shampoo Residue Profiles in Human Head Hair," 35 *J.For.Sci.* 569 (1990). Rodriguez–Calvo, et al., "Isoelectric Focusing of Human Hair Keratins: Patterns and Effect of Cosmetic Treatments," 37 *J.For.Sci.* 425 (1992).

Hairs can also be used to determine the presence of drugs used by the source. See, e.g., Baumgartner, Hill & Blahd, "Hair Analysis for Drugs of Abuse," 34 *J.For.Sci.* 1433 (1989); Nakahara, et al., "Hair Analysis for Drug Abuse," 36 *J.For.Sci.* 70 (1991); Offidiani, et al., "Drugs in Hair: A New Extraction Procedure," 41 *For.Sci. Int'l* 35 (1989).

In NAA, hair is bombarded with neutrons, making it radioactive. By measuring emission spectra and decay, the radiation reveals the tiniest micro-quantities of trace elements that are present. Hair is individualized by one's genetic structure as much as by what one eats or even the air one breathes. Through NAA it can be shown to several decimal points how much gold there is in one person's hair as compared to that of another. It is very unlikely that two people would have exactly the same amount, but some twenty different elements may at times be discovered in human hair. A coincidence of that many elements between hairs from different individuals is said to be astronomical. One research project shows different trace element patterns depending on color of hair, for male and female, for people working in certain industries, or who have different dietary intakes. It reportedly can distinguish between drinkers (more zinc) and non-drinkers; smokers (less mercury) and non-smokers.[2]

Because of the advent of less costly methods that are more readily available to crime laboratory examiners than the research nuclear reactor required for NAA, the latter technique has fallen into disuse even before it became widely known. It is no longer considered a standard tool for the examination of hairs.

§ 9.13 Probabilities, Statistics, and Hair Comparisons

There are various other, more sophisticated, methods for examining hair,[1] but the details of the techniques are less significant than are the evidential implications that the results portend in the courtroom. While there is no technique known today that can positively identify a crime scene hair as having come from a specific individual, experts testifying to hair comparisons are likely to make a probabilistic assessment as to the likelihood of this occurrence. They will couch their opinion in the form of a statistical likelihood that is so high as to suggest, to the scientifically illiterate juror, judge, and/or lawyer, that the possibility of error is

2. Petrasco, et al., "The Morphology and Evidential Significance of Human Hair Roots," 33 *J.For.Sci.* 68 (1988).

§ 9.13

1. See, e.g., the studies reported in the following literature: Brenner, et al., "A Measurement of Human Hair Oxidation by Fourier Transform Infrared Spectroscopy," 39 *J.For.Sci.* 420 (1985); Choudhry, et al., "Individual Characteristics of Chemically Modified Human Hairs Revealed by Scanning Electron Microscopy," 28 *J.For.Sci.* 293 (1983); Riggott & Wyatt, "Mensuration of Scanning Micrographs—A Possible Means of Hair Identification," 23 *J.For.Sci. Soc.* 155 (1983); Toribara, et al., "Nondestructive X–Ray Fluorescence Spectrometry for Determination of Trace Elements Along A Single Strand of Hair," 54 *Anal.Chem.* 1844 (1982); Bagliano, "A Rapid and Simple Method for the Determination of Trace Metals in Hair Samples by Atomic Absorption Spectrometry," 123 *Anal.Chim.Acta* 45 (1981).

It is also possible to determine a person's blood factor in several blood grouping systems from his hair. See, e.g., Sutton, et al., "Polymorphic Enzyme Systems in Human Hair," 22 *J.For.Sci.Soc.* 199 (1982); Yoshida, et al., "Studies on the Frequencies of PGM_1, PGM_3 and Es–D Types from Hair Roots in Japanese Subjects and the Determination of these Types from Old Hair Roots," 14 *For.Sci.International* 1 (1979); Lawton & Kerr, "Phosphoglucomutase Types in Blood and Hair Roots Taken from Post–Transfusion Subjects," 29 *J.For.Sci.* 445 (1984).

statistically insignificant.   The problem with such estimates is to determine their meaningfulness in the context of a criminal prosecution.

If a certain number of measured and observed factors are shared by a crime scene hair and the known standard specimens, they are reported as "matching in all microscopic detail."   It is rare that experts are thereafter asked to explain the significance of that finding.   Yet, to *know* the significance of this "matching," the expert must know the frequency of occurrence of the measured characteristics in the general population. If all of the observed details in combination can only be found in one individual, then the examination has resulted in a *positive identification*. If, on the other hand, the observed characteristics occurs in a significant segment of the population, then their concurrence is meaningless and, in the context of criminal evidence, not very probative of guilt.   If the evidence only shows that the crime scene hair *could* have come from the defendant, it remains to be assessed how likely this fact might be.

Since the crime laboratory examiner who testifies to a hair comparison will not have done any original statistical research, the examiner must of necessity rely on published statistical data compiled by other forensic scientists.   This immediately creates tremendous credibility gaps, since the examiner is typically in no position to assess the validity of the data, or the conclusions drawn therefrom, yet, will be sorely tempted to use the statistics because they will make it much easier for a fact finder to believe the conclusions to which he is prepared to testify. There are Canadian studies by Gaudette that have been published, which have been interpreted to mean that a number of characteristics in hair can make the hair specimens of people significantly different.[2] These studies have induced experts in hair comparisons to make estimates that are extremely impressive to the non-scientist, estimates of 1 in 4,500 for scalp hair and 1 in 800 for pubic hair that the same characteristics would be found to match in hairs of different individuals. The problem with using these statistics is that, while they appear to tell the jury that the likelihood is great that we are dealing with a near positive match between the crime scene hair and the hairs known to have come from the defendant, that is not at all what they mean.[3]   What

---

2.   The leading studies were described in the following sequence of articles: Gaudette & Keeping, "An Attempt at Determining Probabilities in Human Scalp Hair Comparison," 19 *J.For.Sci.* 499 (1974); Gaudette, "Probabilities and Human Pubic Hair Comparisons," 21 *J.For.Sci.* 514 (1976); Gaudette, "Some Further Thoughts on Probabilities and Human Hair Comparisons," 23 *J.For.Sci.* 758 (1978).   Criticized in Barnett & Ogle, "Probabilities and Human Hair Comparison," 27 *J.For.Sci.* 272 (1982); response by original researcher in, Gaudette, "A Supplementary Discussion of Probabilities and Human Hair Comparisons," 27 *J.For.Sci.* 279 (1982).   Hoffman, "Statistical Evaluation of the Evidential Value of

Human Hairs Possibly Coming from Multiple Sources," 36 *J.For.Sci.* 1053 (1991).

Gaudette chaired, in June, 1983, the First Symposium of the Committee on Forensic Hair Comparison at the FBI Forensic Science Research and Training Center in Quantico, Virginia, which issued the FBI Hair Comparison Report.

3.   Yet, that is exactly how the lawyers, judge, and jury will interpret the expert's opinion.   See, State v. Asherman, 193 Conn. 695, 478 A.2d 227 (1984).   One of the authors of this book, took testimony from a transcript where a microanalyst had quoted these statistics, and asked ten randomly selected trial lawyers and twenty non-law-

would be the most useful to know in a criminal case is: Assuming a hair comparison has shown that a crime scene hair matches a representative known sample, what is the probability that the unknown and the known came from the same person? This calls for a determination of the probability of positive identification, which cannot be calculated, unless the size of the population from which the suspect could have come is known. The Gaudette statistics do *not* provide the answer to that question.

The next most useful information for the fact finder would be the probability of misidentification. Assuming a hair comparison has shown that a crime scene hair matches a representative known sample, what is the probability that the crime scene hair came from a different person than the one who supplied the known sample? Gaudette's statistics do *not* answer that either.

What the Gaudette statistics attempt to do, is to calculate yet another probability: Assuming a single hair sample and another representative hair sample are known to have come from two different persons, how probable is it that the single hair will match the representative sample? This is the converse of the misidentification probability! It is because of these, and other factors, that Gaudette's statistics were said to be "grossly in error because of experimental bias and improper statistical treatment of the data." In referring to the improper use of such statistics, forensic scientists Barnett and Cole have stated:

> "The hair studies described ... [listed in footnote 12 of this text] represent an attempt to provide an objective basis for opinions regarding the confidence level of hair individualization. Unfortunately, the bias in the experimental design and the failure to relate probabilities to the questions posed generated probability estimates that were irrelevant to hair individualization. Furthermore, the errors in the derivation introduced a problem to the administration of justice greater than that which the experiments attempted to solve ..."[4]

Small wonder that some of the courts have been reluctant in permitting expert witnesses to talk in terms of mathematical probabilities of error.[5]

yers, representative of jurors, to interpret the testimony. Of the 30 people, one (a layman) expressed his inability to do so because, as he said, statistics were meaningless. But the other 29 (which included all ten trial lawyers) said the witness had positively identified the hair as having come from the defendant, with the chance of error being so remote that it could be safely ignored.

Vigorously challenging the evidential use of statistical estimates in litigation, see, Jaffee, "Of Probativity and Probability: Statistics, Scientific Evidence, and the Calculus of Chance at Trial," 46 U.Pittsburgh L.Rev.

925 (1985). Prof. Jaffee's extensive essay concludes that probability evidence is irrelevant and incompetent and distorts the fact finding process.

See also, Callen, "A Brief Word On the Statistical Evidence Debate," 66 *Tul.L.Rev.* 1405 (1992), referring to several other recent sources.

4. Barnett & Ogle, op. cit. note 2 at 273.

5. See, infra, § 9.15. It should also be remembered that hair identifications faired poorly in the crime laboratory proficiency testing. The rate of error was in excess of 50%. See sources cited in Chapter 1, supra, at footnote 5, section 1.05.

§ 9.14   Evidence of Hair Comparisons

While it is not possible to definitely determine that questioned hair came from one particular individual, courts have been willing to admit evidence of a close similarity as a circumstance to be considered along with other evidence. Comparisons of the defendant's hair with hair found at the crime scene were used to connect him with that particular location in State v. Baldwin,[1] where hair found on a comb near the deceased was unlike the hair of the victim but similar to that of the accused. In State v. Andrews,[2] pubic hairs found in the bed where a rape occurred were identified as having the same source as pubic hairs removed from the body of the defendant. Similarly, hair found in the rape bed in State v. Barber,[3] was reported to match the defendant's hair in all microscopic details. However, a 1981 capital conviction was reversed on habeas corpus because the hair comparison used to obtain the conviction was based on limb hair.[4]

Arguments that microscopic hair comparisons lack sufficient scientific acceptability to be admissible in evidence are now routinely rejected by the courts.[5] However, in United States v. Brown,[6] the court held that the ion microprobic analysis had not yet been established as a reliable and accurate means of identifying hair specimens. The experiments had involved only 150 samples and had not been replicated through the use

---

§ 9.14

1. 47 N.J. 379, 221 A.2d 199 (1966), petition for certif. to App.Div. denied 52 N.J. 502, 246 A.2d 459 (1968), cert. denied 385 U.S. 980 (1966).

2. 86 R.I. 341, 134 A.2d 425 (1957), cert. denied 355 U.S. 898 (1957).

3. 278 N.C. 268, 179 S.E.2d 404 (1971). In United States v. Holleman, et al., 575 F.2d 139 (7th Cir.1978), the court upheld a district court ruling admitting the testimony of a FBI microanalyst who testified that the hair in a mask and hat discarded at the scene of a robbery matched "in every one of 20 microscopic, identifiable characteristics" the hair of one of the three robbers. The court stated that "even though the identification possible through hair sample comparison is not as positive and absolute as identification by fingerprints the expert testified that in thousands of similar examinations, he had never found hair that matched in all microscopic characteristics that did not come from the same person."

In United States v. Oaxaca, 569 F.2d 518 (9th Cir.1978), the court held testimony of hair comparisons admissible even though the expert noted that some 2,000,000 people had similar hair to the defendant's. The expert conceded his identification was not and could not be positive. They held these

factors to go to the weight and credibility of the evidence only, and not to admissibility. Objections to expert testimony in People v. Watkins, 78 Mich.App. 89, 259 N.W.2d 381 (1977) to the effect that defendant's hair sample matched in fifteen points of comparison that found upon the pants of the victim were also held to go to weight and not to admissibility.

4. Nelson v. Zant, 261 Ga. 358, 405 S.E.2d 250, 252 (1991), the FBI expert who testified at the habeas proceeding stated that limb hairs "lack sufficient individual microscopic characteristics to be used for significant comparison purposes, and are so fine and small that they are unsuitable either to include or to exclude a particular individual as the source of the hair."

5. United States v. Brady, 595 F.2d 359 (6th Cir.1979), cert. denied 444 U.S. 862 (1979); State v. Kersting, 50 Or.App. 461, 623 P.2d 1095 (1981); People v. Schultz, 99 Ill.App.3d 762, 55 Ill.Dec. 94, 425 N.E.2d 1267 (1981); State v. Clayton, 646 P.2d 723 (Utah 1982); State v. Carlson, 267 N.W.2d 170 (Minn.1978); People v. Columbo, 118 Ill.App.3d 882, 74 Ill.Dec. 304, 455 N.E.2d 733 (1983); People v. Pride, 3 Cal.4th 195, 10 Cal.Rptr.2d 636, 833 P.2d 643 (1992).

6. 557 F.2d 541 (6th Cir.1977).

of a statistically valid test group.[7]

The presence of the victim's hair on or about the person of the accused has also been deemed to provide incriminating evidence. The shirt of the defendant in the *Andrews* case,[8] for example, was found to bear hairs similar to those from the head of the victim. Hair of the victim was compared with hair found in the defendant's automobile in Padilla v. People.[9]

Presence of the victim's hair can also be used to demonstrate that an object or weapon is an instrumentality of the crime, or that the offense was committed in a particular place. The former situation was present in State v. Wilson,[10] where hair taken from a bloody stick was found to be similar to the hair of the deceased. The latter situation occurred in State v. Harris,[11] a case in which hair found in a gravel pit was determined to have belonged to the murder victim.

The trained microanalyst will also be permitted to offer his expert opinion that a hair sample he has examined originated from a subject of a particular race.[12] The defense objected to testimony of this type in People v. Kirkwood,[13] in disputing the reliability of race determination through the microscopic examination of hair. The court held, however, that any difference in expert opinion affected the weight of the evidence, but not its admissibility.

There are very few reported cases where microanalysts testified on the comparison of animal hairs. In Claud v. Commonwealth,[14] a certifi-

7. The ion microprobic analysis method is described in the court's opinion at 555.

8. State v. Andrews, supra note 2.

9. 156 Colo. 186, 397 P.2d 741 (1964).

10. 217 La. 470, 46 So.2d 738 (1950), affirmed 341 U.S. 901 (1951), rehearing denied 341 U.S. 934 (1951). The fact that positive identification could not be made went to the weight of the evidence.

11. 241 Or. 224, 405 P.2d 492 (1965). In State v. Bauman, 77 Wash.2d 938, 468 P.2d 684 (1970), a positive identification of the hair on a floor was not possible, but this went to the weight of the evidence. In Delaware v. Fensterer, 474 U.S. 15 (1985) per curiam, the Court held that the Confrontation Clause of the Sixth Amendment was not violated by the admission of a prosecution expert witness' opinion on hair comparisons, when the expert was unable to recall the basis for his conclusions that the victim's hair was similar to hairs found on defendant's cat leash, and that one of the hairs had been forcibly removed.

12. Hair was identified as being of Negro origin in: State v. Barber, supra note 1; State v. Ray, 274 N.C. 556, 164 S.E.2d 457 (1968); State v. Wilson, supra note 10; and in Parks v. State, 203 Ga. 302, 46 S.E.2d

504 (1948), rehearing denial affirmed 206 Ga. 675, 58 S.E.2d 142 (1950). Hair was identified as being of Caucasian origin in People v. Kirkwood, 17 Ill.2d 23, 160 N.E.2d 766 (1959), cert. denied 363 U.S. 847 (1960).

On whether an expert should be permitted to testify to a conclusion, the basis for which he does not recall, see, supra Chapter 1, at footnote 7, section 1.22, for a discussion of Delaware v. Fensterer, 474 U.S. 15 (1985).

13. People v. Kirkwood, supra note 12.

14. 217 Va. 794, 232 S.E.2d 790 (1977). The court recognized that the certificate did not intend to prove that the hog bristles found in the truck were of the hogs stolen, but only that the specimens came from hogs.

Dog hairs also featured in the Wayne Williams "Atlanta murders" case, which is discussed in the next section because of its extensive use of fiber evidence. The prosecution argued that dog hairs were consistent with those of a German Shepherd such as Williams owned, but according to recent efforts to obtain a new trial, police are alleged to have withheld information from the defense that a veterinarian had con-

cate of analysis from the crime laboratory showing that specimen hairs retrieved from the vehicle of a suspect charged with grand larceny of hogs were in fact hog bristles was deemed to be competent evidence.

§ 9.15 Evidence of Probabilistic Estimates

As might be expected, the courts have been divided on whether evidence of probabilistic estimates ought to be admissible. Some courts have held that the jury is perfectly capable to deal with such evidence and give it its due weight—a conclusion that is subject to some doubt in light of the unscientific poll described earlier in this chapter (supra, footnote 3, section 9.14)—while others held that such evidence ought not to be admitted.

In State v. Clayton,[1] the defendant's conviction was based entirely on circumstantial evidence: a yellow baseball cap found at the crime scene was shown to have been seen on the defendant earlier on the day of the homicide; a hair from the hat was compared with known hair samples from the defendant. While there was some other evidence, the hair comparison testimony was undoubtedly essential to a conviction. On appeal, the defendant's challenges included a claim of error based on the fact that the probability of hair matches was too speculative for a jury to handle justly and knowledgeably. The Utah high court rejected this argument, and then, but only in a footnote, it also rejected the philosophy of other cases, cited later in this section, which took too low an opinion of the jury's ability "to weight the credibility of such figures." The exact nature of the statistical testimony of the hair expert, to which exception was taken, was not given in the opinion.

Similarly, in People v. DiGiacomo,[2] the defendant was convicted of various crimes, including rape and deviate sexual assault which occurred in the back seat of the victim's car. A criminalist took hair samples from the car and compared them with the defendant's hair. At trial, the expert was allowed to testify that the samples were identical[3] and that there was only a 1 in 4500 chance that the hair from the victim's car did not belong to defendant. The exact basis for this opinion was not referred to in the decision, but it is obvious that the expert witness used the Gaudette statistics.[4] On appeal, the defendant challenged the admission of the statistical testimony. The court upheld the expert's testimony, citing the broad discretion as to admissibility of such evi-

---

cluded the dog hairs on the victims could only have come from a Siberian husky or an Alaskan malamute. See, Curriden, "New Questions in Atlanta Murders," *ABA Journal,* May 1992, at 36.

§ 9.15

1. 646 P.2d 723 (Utah 1982).

2. 71 Ill.App.3d 56, 27 Ill.Dec. 232, 388 N.E.2d 1281 (1979). For further case history, see also, footnote 5. Accord: People v. Rainge, 112 Ill.App.3d 396, 68 Ill.Dec. 87, 445 N.E.2d 535 (1983).

3. If the expert meant the two samples came from the defendant, he testified to a fact which his discipline agrees is impossible to determine. (See the FBI definition of "Individualization" in Glossary of Terms, supra in § 9.07.) If he meant only that they *could* have had the same source, he was understood differently by the court and jury—a confirmation of the "poll" described in footnote 3, section 9.13, supra.

4. See, supra, § 9.13. Gaudette's statistics do not support the expert's conclusion as reported in the court's opinion.

dence. The court also stated simply that "a foundation was laid" for the testimony and that the mathematical odds were "immaterial," though properly considered by the jury.

The Seventh Circuit Court of Appeals has upheld the admission of the Gaudette statistics by the Illinois courts, even though the jury had apparently been confused by the probability evidence. During the deliberations, the jury had submitted a note to the judge asking if the hair sample conclusively established that defendant was present in the victim's car. The trial judge refused to answer the question, and a conviction followed.[5] A clearer picture of how juries perceive the "scientific" evidence of hair comparisons in a light totally different from that which the expert purports to shed cannot be found.

Small wonder that other courts have not been so kind to probabilistic evidence. The leading case rejecting the admissibility of statistical testimony in hair comparisons is State v. Carlson.[6] In *Carlson*, an analyst from the Minnesota state crime laboratory testified that defendant's pubic hairs matched two pubic hairs found stuck to the victim in all 15 categories of microscopic comparison. The expert reported the same results from comparisons between foreign head hairs found on the victim and the defendant's head hairs, and between head hairs found on a shoe polish rag discovered in the defendant's bedroom and the victim's hair.

The state also called Gaudette himself, an expert on comparative microscopy from the Royal Canadian Mounted Police (RCMP), who had tested the same sets of hair samples using 26 categories of comparison. He found the hairs to be similar in all 26 categories and stated that, based on his own studies,[7] there was a 1 in 800 chance that the pubic hairs found stuck to the victim were not the defendant's, and a 1 in 4,500 chance that the foreign head hairs were not the defendant's. The defense objected without success to both experts' testimony. On appeal the defendant argued, in part, that it is improper to allow evidence in a criminal trial to be expressed statistically, and the Minnesota Supreme Court agreed. Though it found that the expert testimony had been properly founded on valid scientific studies, the court stated that "Testimony expressing opinions or conclusions in terms of statistical probabilities can make the uncertain seem all but proven, and suggest, by quantification, satisfaction of the requirement that guilt be established 'beyond a reasonable doubt.' " The statistical testimony was therefore improperly received.[8]

The 8th Circuit Court of Appeals, in United States v. Massey,[9] has also rejected statistical probabilities testimony and reversed a bank

---

5. United States ex rel. DiGiacomo v. Franzen, 680 F.2d 515 (7th Cir.1982), per curiam.

6. 267 N.W.2d 170 (Minn.1978).

7. The studies cited in footnote 2, section 9.13, supra.

8. However, since the state's own expert's testimony—who had not been asked to give statistical estimates—was properly admitted, the court found Gaudette's expert testimony to be "cumulative and thus nonprejudicial on the facts of this case."

9. 594 F.2d 676 (8th Cir.1979).

robbery conviction because of its improper admission. In addition to testimony that the defendant cased the bank two days before the robbery, the evidence against the defendant included pictures of the two men robbing the bank, jackets similar to those worn by the bank robbers, and a blue ski mask similar to that worn by one of the robbers. Of the five hairs found in the ski mask, three were found by an expert in microscopic analysis to be similar "in all areas of microscopic comparison" with the defendant's hair. In response to questions posed by the trial court, the expert stated that in his own experience he had examined approximately 2,000 cases and in only one or two instances "was he ever unable to make identification." In addition, the witness referred to the Gaudette study which concluded that there is a one in 4,500 chance of mismatching hair samples when matched in the manner used by this expert.

The reviewing court concluded that an insufficient foundation was laid for the expert's testimony regarding the Gaudette study in that the expert stated "that he did not know the nature and extent of the studies from which the statistics were gathered." It also stated that the trial court's conversation with the expert "concerning mathematical probabilities was speculative and confusing." Moreover, prejudicial error was held to have occurred in the prosecutor's closing argument "which exacerbated the trial judge's misunderstanding of the evidence." In summation the prosecutor claimed that the expert had stated that out of 2,000 or 2,500 examinations only in 3 to 5 instances was he "unable to distinguish the hair from two different people." Reference to probabilities as determined by the Gaudette study were also made. The prosecutor also made the following statement: "A handful—3 to 5 out of 2,000—that's better than 99.44 percent; it's better than Ivory soap, if you remember the commercial. It's very convincing." He then went on to claim that the hair sample alone would constitute proof beyond a reasonable doubt that the defendant was guilty.

In reversing the defendant's conviction and ordering a new trial, the *Massey* court stated that the prosecutor had used "misleading mathematical odds" and had "infused in the minds of the jury the confusion in identifying the hair with identifying the perpetrator of the crime."

Other courts also have held that probability estimates based upon studies done by researchers others than the witness, on the significance of hair comparisons, should not be admitted because the opinion relied upon hearsay.[10]

In light of the general lack of understanding of mathematical probability theories, how they affect a given case, and the general scientific ignorance of judges, lawyers and jurors, and also the persistent misinterpretations given to statistical evidence by the fact finders despite

---

10. E.g., State v. Scarlett, 121 N.H. 37, 426 A.2d 25 (1981); State v. Bridges, 107 N.C.App. 668, 421 S.E.2d 806 (1992). In both cases the courts held, however, that the admission was harmless error.

For an exhaustive legal study on the evidentiary implications of probabilistic evidence, highly critical of the cases admitting such testimony, see, Jaffee, op. cit. supra note 3, section 9.13.

cautionary instructions, it would seem that courts ought to be extremely reluctant in admitting statistical evidence of any type in the area of hair comparisons.

IV. FIBERS

§ 9.16 Fibers in Criminal Investigations

When, in early 1982, Wayne Williams went to trial for the killing of two of twenty eight blacks murdered in Atlanta, Georgia, nationwide attention was drawn on the art/science of fiber comparison. No less than 62 fiber comparisons were made, linking the defendant to the two murders for which he was indicted and to ten other crimes. Animal hairs were also examined and found to be consistent with the hairs of defendant's dog.[1] Probabilistic estimates were given by the microanalyst who testified for the state that it was "virtually impossible" for the fibers obtained from the bodies of eleven of the twelve bodies to have originated anywhere other than from the Williams environment. Despite this mass of scientific evidence, the Georgia Supreme Court's opinion affirming the conviction is singularly uninformative on the scientific evidence, treating it with a broad brush, in a few brief generalities.[2]

Fibers, as evidence, are much like hair. They are usually found in the same places where hairs are discovered. They may adhere to objects or be imbedded in them. Their presence at a given location may be accidental through normal shedding or they may have been pulled out in a struggle. They may simply have been transferred from one surface to another through ordinary, non-violent physical contact.

Fibers of value to the microanalyst may be found in a victim's hands, under his fingernails, and in or on other parts of the body or clothing. They may also be found in or on motor vehicles (for example, the trunk of a car in a kidnapping or murder case, or underneath a hit-and-run vehicle); on weapons such as knives, clubs, firearms, or on fired bullets that have penetrated clothing. They may also be located embedded in blood, tissue, semen, or other body substances.

---

§ 9.16

1. But see, Curriden, "New Questions in Atlanta Murders—Did Prosecutors withhold evidence of Klan involvement in children's deaths?," *ABA Journal,* May 1992, at 36: "Among the other evidence presented in the hearings that was not disclosed by prosecutors before Williams' trial: * * * A police report by a University of Georgia veterinarian concluded that dog hairs found on victims' bodies could only have come from a Siberian husky or an Alaskan malamute. Sanders [Klan member who was another suspect not revealed to the defense] owned a Siberian husky while Williams owned a German Shepherd. At Williams' trial, prosecutors told jurors that the dog hairs were consistent with those of a German shepherd."

2. Williams v. State, 251 Ga. 749, 312 S.E.2d 40 (1983). The case is further discussed in § 9.19.

Following is a listing of the reasons why investigators should look for and carefully preserve fiber materials:

1.   Fibers present on a weapon may help to establish that the weapon was the one used on a particular occasion.

2.   On a fired bullet, they may establish that the bullet penetrated a certain garment or garments.

3.   Fibers present on a vehicle may establish that the particular vehicle was involved in a hit-and-run or other incident.

4.   The presence of trace materials on fibers may tend to indicate the offender's environment or occupation and lead to his apprehension.

5.   Fibers present on the body, or clothing of the victim of an assault, rape, or homicide, may help identify the assailant.

6.   The interchange of fibers between two individuals may tend to establish physical contact between the two.

7.   The presence of fibers at a location may tend to indicate the color of the clothing of the person(s) present, which may be an important investigative aid.

8.   Deposits of blood or semen may be present on fibers, which may result in determining the blood group or the isolation of spermatozoa.

9.   The condition of damaged fibers may reveal information as to the type of instrument that caused the damage to the fiber as a wound was inflicted.

10.   Fibers from stolen furs may be present in or on the clothing of a suspect and thereby tend to establish his connection with the incident.

11.   The absence of fibers in a close contact situation is not necessarily proof of no contact; some fibers, especially synthetic ones, have very few loose fibers.

Just as in these instances, fiber evidence can be used by the plaintiff in a civil case or the prosecution in an effort to convict, so can it frequently be useful to the defense.   The presence of fibers not matching a criminal defendant or the victim's clothing, and which cannot be otherwise accounted for, can be profitably used to establish a reasonable doubt about the guilt of the defendant.   It should be proper to show, even, that the *absence* of any fibers on clothing allegedly worn by a defendant when he purportedly committed a crime is so unusual as to cause some doubt about his presence, though examiners opine that the absence of fibers in a close contact situation is not necessarily important, because some fibers, especially synthetics, do not shed easily.   Even where fibers are discovered which tend to incriminate it still deserves pointing out that it is not always possible to definitely state that a given fiber came from one, and only one, source.   At most, conclusions generally are couched in the form of establishing a possible common origin.

§ 9.17 The Nature of Fibers

Generally speaking, fibers fall into four broad categories: animal, vegetable, mineral, and synthetics or man-made. In the first class are wool, silk, camel's hair, and furs. Vegetable fibers include cotton, linen, hemp, sisal, jute. Mineral fibers can be, among others, asbestos, glass wool, or fiber glass, materials commonly used in safe insulation.

Among the man-made fibers, there is a large class of materials. Glass fibers are among them. In a second group of man-made fibers, we classify those known as regenerated fibers, such as rayon ("Fortisan") and acetates ("Arnel"). The third group of man-made fibers is that of the synthetics. Synthetics may be nylon ("Antron"), polyesters ("Dacron" and "Fortrel"), acrylics ("Acrilian," "Creslan," "Orlon"), modacrylics ("Dynel", used for wigs), etc.

All of these possess certain characteristics which the trained microanalyst can recognize.

§ 9.18 Examination of Fibers

In an examination of most fibers, the first step would be to distinguish natural from man-made fibers, and, among the man-made ones, those characteristics that are sought to be determined by the criminalist include color, surface appearance, cross-sectional shape and diameter, fluorescence, and type. For many of the fiber examinations, the mainstay of the forensic laboratory is the microscope. A variety of them are usually necessary to a competent fiber comparison.[1]

A stereobinocular microscope, which can magnify a single fiber about 70X, is used to visually compare fibers. Compound microscopes, with magnification of 400X to 500X, are also used to visually examine fibers. Comparison microscopes, which can magnify two fibers side by side, are used to compare the microscopic and optical properties of the two fibers.[2]

A microspectrophotometer (MSP) is an instrument designed to measure the color of microscopic materials such as fibers. The material to be examined is first placed on a microscope slide and placed under the lens; light is then passed through the material, on through the microscope, and into a spectrophotometer which is perched on top of the microscope. Once inside the spectrophotometer, the light passes into a monochrometer, an instrument which basically splits the light into its component parts or wavelengths. That information is then amplified, sent through a microprocessor, and recorded on a graph, which consists of a series of curves representing the color of the material.[3]

§ 9.18

1. See, Grieve, "The Role of Fibers in Forensic Science Examinations," 28 *J.For. Sci.* 877 (1983).

2. Williams v. State, supra note 2, section 9.16, at 52.

3. Id. at 50. Macrae, et al., in "The Characterization of Dyestuffs on Wool Fibers with Special Reference to Microspectrophotometry," 24 *J.For.Sci.* 117 (1979) indicates that no significant procedure has been described for testing the spectra of differences.

Other instruments used include a polarizing microscope, which is used to examine the optical properties of fibers in a more discriminating fashion than that provided by a comparison microscope; a fluorescence microscope to determine the type of light a fiber emits after it has been illuminated with a certain light; and the scanning electron microscope may be occasionally utilized.[4]

1. NATURAL FIBERS

Most textile fibers rarely present any problems of identification, particularly cotton and wool. They are examined microscopically and chemically, and their characteristics compared with those of known standards.

The most common fiber material is probably cotton. It is easily recognizable microscopically because its soft and short fibers resemble a flat, spirally twisted, or corkscrew appearing band. Linen fibers resemble those of cotton, but are smoother; they also show numerous cross bands. Linen fibers can be either bleached or unbleached. Jute fibers are coarse and stiff and, when viewed microscopically, display marked differences from, for example, linen. Hemp, another vegetable fiber, resembles somewhat unbleached linen, but is even lighter in appearance. Other vegetable fibers, too, exhibit quite characteristic differences when viewed under magnifications of over 300X. Even at lower magnifications, differences are noticeable, as can be observed in the nine photomicrographs in Figure 7.

---

4. Williams v. State, supra note 2, section 9.16, at 52. Also, Paplauskas, "The Scanning Electron Microscope: A New Way to Examine Holes in Fabric," 1 *J.Pol.Sci. &* *Admin.* 362 (1973).

Fig. 7. Photomicrographs of various types of natural fibers. All photographs are longitudinal views. Top row, left to right, the specimens are wool, silk, and cotton. Second row, they are mohair, camel hair, and Tussah silk. Bottom row, they are flax, jute, and kapok.

The difference between vegetable and animal fibers is easily established, since animal fibers used in the textile industry have medullas and show cuticular cells. (See, supra, § 9.08 on the structure of hairs.) Natural silk fibers are composed, chemically, of two proteins and are ordinarily spun from 5 cocoon threads, although some fibers are spun from as few as 3 or as many as 8.

There is another way to distinguish animal and vegetable fibers, but one which can only be attempted when a considerable quantity of fibers is available. The burning test reveals a marked difference in the behavior of animal and vegetable fibers. When animal fibers are withdrawn from a flame, they will continue to burn for a short time only, while emitting an odor that is characteristic of sulphur. The fibers will also have a swollen appearance at the ends. Vegetable fibers, on the other hand, will continue to burn quite easily after they are withdrawn from the flame. The smell emitted will resemble that of burned wood; also, the burned ends of the fibers will appear sharp. The flame test cannot be utilized when only one or a few fibers are available, since it results in at least a partial destruction of the evidence. Chemical tests of great variety also result, to a certain extent, in a degradation of the evidence.

The dyestuffs used for coloration of fibers can be analyzed for comparison purposes. For example, the complex protein structure of wool can accept a wide range of dyestuffs. Thin-layer chromatography and visible absorption spectroscopy are among the tools used to examine dye solutions.[5]

2. MAN–MADE FIBERS

Because of the tremendous increase in the use of man-made fibers since 1935, when rayon, the first man-made regenerative fiber was produced, the modern methods of fiber identification have largely centered on man-made, and particularly synthetic, fibers. Various tests have been developed to supplement microscopy; the greatest strides in analytic techniques have come not from the criminalists and microanalysts, but largely from research scientists and chemists working in the textile industry.

Among the standard tests in this area are examinations for solubility, appearance of cross-section, reactions to different dye stains, burning tests, and examination of physical properties (refractive index, density, and melting point). For example, the melting point is measured by the use of a special microscope to which an attachment known as a hot stage is fitted.[6] The fabric is then heated and the temperature at which the fiber melted is noted. The significance of this is that different substances have different melting points.

Other techniques used in the examination of man-made fibers include the application of pyrolysis and programmed temperature gas chromatography, measuring of infrared spectra of fibers by the infrared spectrophotometer,[7] micro fusion methods, optical crystallography, small-angle light scattering,[8] dispersion staining, etc.[9]

---

5. See, Shaw, "Micro-sale Thin Layer Chromatographic Method for the Comparison of Dyes Stripped from Wool Fibres," 105 *Analyst* 729 (1980); Macrae & Smalldon, "The Extraction of Dyestuffs from Single Wool Fibers," 24 *J.For.Sci.* 109 (1979).

6. Petraco et al., "A New Approach to the Microscopical Examination and Comparison of Synthetic Fibers Encountered in Forensic Science Cases," 25 *J.For.Sci.* 571 (1980).

7. Grieve, "Preparing Samples for the Recording of Infrared Spectra from Synthetic Fibers," 21 *J.For.Sci.* 307 (1976); Garger, "An Improved Technique for Preparing Solvent Cast Films from Acrylic Fibers for the Recording of Infrared Spectra,"

28 *J.For.Sci.* 632 (1983); Tungol, Bartick & Montaser, "Analysis of Single Polymer Fibers by Fourier Transform Infrared Microscopy: The Result of Case Studies, 36 *J.For. Sci.* 1027 (1991).

8. Bresee & Crews, "Using Small–Angle Light Scattering to Discriminate Among Single Fibers Subjected to Consumer–Like Uses," 26 *J.For.Sci.* 51 (1981), follow-up in 26 *J.For.Sci.* 184 (1981).

9. See also, Grieve & Kotowski, "The Identification of Polyester Fibers in Forensic Science," 22 *J.For.Sci.* 390 (1977); Saferstein & Manura, "Pyrolysis Mass Spectrometry—A New Forensic Science Technique," 22 *J.For.Sci.* 748 (1977); Martinelli et al., "Thermomechanical Examination of

Glass fibers, also man-made, are formed from glass marbles which are melted in a furnace which has tiny holes in its base. Ceramic fibers are formed from aluminum silicate in a manner similar to that of (staple form) glass fibers.

There are many synthetic fiber manufacturers. To date, no satisfactory method has been discovered to differentiate between products of various manufacturers. Fibers of questioned and known origin can be shown to be made of the same polymer, but that would not establish that they were made by the same manufacturer. In fact, similar polymers made by different manufacturers cannot be distinguished.

§ 9.19   Evidence of Fiber Comparisons

Fiber comparison is most frequently but not exclusively used in connection with threads and bits of cloth. Thus, fabric recovered from a stolen auto was compared with the jacket and shirt of the defendant and was found to be identical in color, weave, and fiber content.[1] In another case, blue fibers found under the murder victim's fingernails were determined to be identical in appearance to threads taken from the overalls of the defendant.[2] In Nixon v. State,[3] the murder weapon (a waxer handle) was identified by the presence of fibers from the victim's shirt.

Traces of clothing left on automobiles can be of importance in vehicular homicides and assaults such as in Hunter v. State,[4] where the blouse of the prosecutrix was matched with a swatch of cloth snagged on the defendant's car. And in another case, a piece of torn sheet discovered in the defendant's automobile was positively compared with the sheet used to cover the victim's body.[5]

In Williams v. State,[6] a prosecution for two of twenty-eight killings of blacks in Atlanta, Georgia, the court upheld the conviction with one judge dissenting. Lacking a confession or eye witness to the murders, the prosecution's case rested upon three main legs: laboratory analysis of fibers and hairs; a police stake-out that led to the pre-dawn questioning of Williams near the Chattahoochee River in May of 1981; and a pattern of possibly perverse behavior sketched by eye witnesses. The crux of the case against Williams, however, was the fiber evidence—thus prompting some public concern over the almost exclusive reliance on

Fabric Composed of Synthetic Polymers," 24 *J.For.Sci.* 130 (1979).

§ 9.19

1. Tomolillo v. State, 4 Md.App. 711, 245 A.2d 94 (1968); identification was made in spite of burnt condition of the fabric.

2. State v. Johnson, 37 N.M. 280, 21 P.2d 813 (1933).

3. 204 Md. 475, 105 A.2d 243 (1954). Wax deposited by the handle was found on the victim's shirt.

4. 468 S.W.2d 96 (Tex.Cr.App.1971). See also, Parks v. State, supra note 1, section 9.14, where cloth found clinging to a barbed wire fence through which the blood trail of the deceased was followed matched the fabric of the victim's clothes.

5. Padilla v. People, supra note 3, section 9.13. See also, Cordes v. State, 54 Tex.Crim.R. 204, 112 S.W. 943 (1908), for a case where a blanket found wrapped around a dead baby was similar to a blanket found in defendant's home.

6. 251 Ga. 749, 312 S.E.2d 40 (1983).

forensic fiber evidence. Is it enough to convict? Clearly, in Atlanta, Georgia, in the spring of 1981, it was.

Although Williams, a 23–year–old black photographer, was charged with only two of the 28 murders which terrorized Atlanta for two years, the prosecution successfully linked Williams to ten other killings through the use of evidence of microscopic examinations of 62 fibers retrieved from twelve victims' bodies, their clothing, or on items used in the recovery of their bodies, which were compared with and linked to fibers coming from the defendant's environment: from his body, his home and the cars he had used, and his German shepherd dog. Defendant objected to the admissibility of the comparisons on the ground that the state had failed to adequately demonstrate the scientific reliability of fiber methodology which was employed by its experts. The Supreme Court, in a terse one-sentence statement, disposed of this issue by stating that it was for the trial court to determine whether a given scientific principle or technique is competent evidence, and finding no error in that regard. The reliability of fiber analysis methods was never discussed by the court, and in a case where the fiber evidence was both so voluminous and critical to the prosecution, one might have expected a more enlightening discussion on the subject, especially since the dissenting judge found that the fiber evidence could only be characterized as "weak," purely circumstantial, and of "questionable reliability and probative worth."[7] The only discussion on the technique in question was in the dissent, which noted that the cases cited at trial to support admissibility were not in point, and that the trial judge never was asked to make a specific finding that the fiber comparison methodology used by the state had reached a "scientific stage of verifiable certainty."[8]

In addressing the issue whether fiber analysis has reached a scientific stage of verifiable certainty—which was the legal standard for admissibility of novel scientific evidence in Georgia—the dissent found not a single case that had made that determination. For that reason, the trial court could not possibly have made that determination, the dissent argued, concluding that the present transcript of evidence did not permit such a conclusion either. The court's majority, which presumably had determined the evidence was sufficiently reliable to support a conviction even where proof of guilt was almost exclusively dependent upon fiber evidence, did jurisprudence a disservice by not squarely addressing that issue and elaborating on the reasons for its conclusion.

While there really are no cases that have considered, in some detail, the scientific principles underlying laboratory examination of fibers, evidence has been admitted and considered, to a limited extent, in other court decisions. In State v. Hall,[9] the crime evidence of blue fiber was said to be similar to the fibers of the pants the defendant was wearing

---

7. Id. (Dissenting opinion at 92.)

8. Id. (Dissenting opinion at 96.) The dissenting judge cited the failure to properly object as a reason why he would hold that the defendant was deprived of due process of law due to incompetency of counsel.

9. 297 N.W.2d 80 (Iowa 1980).

and he argued that such evidence ought to be excluded because thousands of pairs of jeans had been made from the same cloth. The court held that the evidence was nevertheless admissible.

Microscopy has been used to compare pieces of string and twine and a large variety of other fibrous materials. In Commonwealth v. Bartolini,[10] testimony was introduced to the effect that twine found in the home of the accused was similar to that used to wrap the body of the deceased. A burglary suspect was connected with the crime scene in People v. Smith[11] by microscopic examination of fibers taken from his shirt and from the rug of the burglarized premises.

In Maxwell v. State,[12] an FBI specialist testified that in his experience, when clothing comes in contact with other clothing or objects, there is an interchange of fibers. His testimony that red cotton fibers from the rape prosecutrix's pajamas were found on the accused's T-shirt, suitcoat, and trench coat was held properly admitted. In People v. Wallage,[13] a hit-and-run driver was properly identified by the dent of a button and an imprint of cloth fiber corresponding to the clothing of the deceased on the fender of the defendant's car.

The troublesome issue of the use of probabilities and statistical evidence, ever present in forensic sciences,[14] to support fiber comparison opinions, has seldom been dealt with in cases. One of the recent decisions is, again, the Atlanta *Williams* case.[15] The majority opinion of the Georgia Supreme Court, in the terse manner already alluded to earlier, rejected defendant's contention that it was error to permit the state's expert to discuss mathematical probabilities concerning the fiber evidence and in permitting the prosecutor to argue these probabilities to the jury. "Neither of these contentions has merit," said the court, "as experts are permitted to give their opinions, based upon their knowledge, including mathematical computations. Counsel are given wide latitude in closing argument and are not prohibited from suggesting to the jury inferences which might be drawn from the evidence. Such suggestions may include those based on mathematical probabilities."[16]

Nowhere in the court's opinion is there any information given on what the statistical evidence was or how the prosecutor used the statistics in closing argument. We must go to the dissent, again, to find these additional pieces of information. There we find that the state's microanalyst had "attempted to use the calculus of compound probabilities to perform a series of calculations to establish the rarity of that type of carpet [found in the Williams home] in the Atlanta metropolitan area.

10. 299 Mass. 503, 13 N.E.2d 382 (1938), cert. denied 304 U.S. 565 (1938). See also, Bester v. State, 222 Miss. 706, 77 So.2d 270 (1955), where a stolen sack of tung nuts was identified through the specially treated string used to tie it.

11. 142 Cal.App.2d 287, 298 P.2d 540 (1956).

12. 236 Ark. 694, 370 S.W.2d 113 (1963).

13. 353 Ill. 95, 186 N.E. 540 (1933).

14. See discussions on mathematical probabilities evidence, supra, in §§ 9.13 & 9.15, dealing with hair comparisons.

15. Williams v. State, 251 Ga. 749, 312 S.E.2d 40 (1983).

16. Id. at 72–73.

He finally concluded that there was a one in 7792 chance of randomly selecting a home in the Atlanta area and finding a room containing carpet similar to the Williams bedroom carpet." [17]   The prosecutor, embellishing on the probative worth of the bedroom carpet and the Williams car rug, argued to the jury that the approximate figure of probability was actually "one in one hundred fifty million." [18]   In fact, the FBI fiber expert who testified at the trial would later write: "To convey the unusual nature of the Williams residential carpet, an attempt was made to develop a numerical probability—**something never before done in connection with textile materials used as evidence in criminal trials.** [Emphasis Supplied.]" [19]   It clearly appears the court was all too willing to accept the expert's testimony without a critical analysis as to whether there was a scientific basis for the statistical computations that had survived peer review in the scientific community![20]

In the absence of any indication in the court's opinion that the dissent misconstrued the evidence, or that other evidence was in fact introduced which casts an entirely different light on the probative worth of the evidence, the dissent's reasons for concluding the evidence was legally insufficient make sense, stand unrebutted, and create a clear impression that the Georgia Supreme Court's majority inadequately considered the merits or demerits of the scientific evidence of fiber comparisons.   It is veritably incomprehensible that in an appellate opinion affirming a conviction that hinged so materially on fiber evidence, the court's thirty + -page opinion disposes of the admissibility of fiber evidence and of the probabilistic estimates issues in a mere 19 lines! [21]

We will need to await a later decision to establish a more credible legal precedent for the type of scientific recognition the courts are willing to accord fiber comparisons and probabilities evidence.[22]

----

17.   Id. at 98 (dissenting opinion).

18.   Ibid.

19.   Deadman, "Fiber Evidence and the Wayne Williams Trial," *FBI Law Enforcement Bull.*, May 1984, at 13.

20.   For comments on probabilistic evidence of doubtful reliability, see, Moenssens, "Novel Scientific Evidence in Criminal Cases: Some Words of Caution," 84 *J.Crim.L. & Criminology*, 1, at 18 (1993).

21.   On the issue of the scientific reliability of fiber comparisons, the court writes 12 lines, including 2 lines of a case citation; on the probabilities issue, both relating to the expert testimony and the prosecutor's summation, the court writes another 12 lines, again including 3 lines devoted to two

case citations.   The court spends far more time on describing the various microscopes the fiber expert uses, but not in connection with any issue of admissibility or reliability!

See the recent study, not yet evaluated by the forensic science community at the time of publication, by Fong & Inami, "Results of a Study to Determine the Probability of Chance Match Occurrences Between Fibers Known to be from Different Sources," 31 *J.For.Sci.* 65 (1986).

22.   There are, of course, ample cases dealing with probabilities used by experts in other disciplines. See, e.g., § 9.15 on statistical evidence on hair comparisons.   See also Chapters 13 & 15 dealing with statistics in connection with evidence of biological fluids and DNA.

V. PAINT

§ 9.20 Paint as Evidence in Criminal Cases

Paint as evidence is usually associated with burglaries, automobile accidents, hit-and-run crimes, and other cases involving the use of vehicles.

Paint is either removed from an object or transferred onto an object or both removed from and transferred to the object. Paint evidence is recovered in the form of chips or smears. Usually, oil base paint is recovered in the form of smears and automobile paint in the form of chips. A person may have paint on his clothing from a given location, as where paint is deposited on the clothing as a result of using force or a tool or other implement to enter an automobile or a home, or to open a safe or cabinet. If the tool or implement has a painted surface, paint from the tool or implement may be found superimposed on a painted object at the scene or embedded in the wood or metal of the object with which the tool came in contact. Where an assault occurs, and a painted object is used as the weapon, paint particles may be present on the clothing of the victim, on his body, or embedded in his wounds.

In the investigation of automobile accidents and hit-and-run cases the scene is ordinarily thoroughly searched for paint particles that may have been left there as a result of the impact between the pedestrian and auto, or between two or more cars. In addition, the clothing of the pedestrian-victim, if any, is ordinarily submitted to the microanalyst so that the garments can be examined for the presence of paint particles that might be embedded in the clothing and compared with paint samples from the suspect vehicle. Evidence thus collected by law enforcement may later become valuable in civil litigation that ensues.

In cases where there is no suspect vehicle, an examination and analysis of the paint particles left at the scene can sometimes lead to the manufacturer, and information developed as to what type of cars were coated in a particular year with that particular type of paint. In cases where a truck was used to remove merchandise from a warehouse, paint from the truck may have been deposited on the loading dock.

In cases involving forcible entry, tools in the possession of the suspect are submitted to the microanalyst to be examined for paint that may be similar to the paint present on objects at the scene of the incident.

In the recovery of paint particles or stains, as with all physical trace evidence, the investigators must exercise care so as not to destroy other evidence. Paint is chipped loose with a toothpick and should be placed in a clean pillbox, envelope, or vial and suitably marked. Investigators are advised to use wooden applicators such as toothpicks to chip loose the paint rather than a metal object such as a knife or razor blade. If they use the latter type of implements, minute fragments of the metal may become embedded in the paint and can affect the instrumental analysis of the paint, a point which should certainly be explored on cross-examination of the person who gathered the evidence. Paint chips can also be removed through the use of transparent pressure sensitive tape.

Whenever possible, all weapons with painted surfaces are also submitted to the microanalyst. Field investigators are advised not to remove any paint that may be present on such objects. Correct field practices—not always followed—require that the weapon be placed in a plastic bag or other suitable container and sealed so that any paint that may fall off the object will remain in the container and can be recovered. Field investigators should also make no effort to remove paint embedded in or superimposed on garments, but should place each garment to be examined in a clean plastic bag or other suitable container, sealed and properly marked, and submitted to the microanalyst.

In recovering paint from an automobile, the inside of the fender or door is tapped lightly and the paint chips from the outer surface may, if they are loose, fall and may be collected on a clean piece of paper and then placed in a suitable container. Or they may be removed through the use of transparent pressure sensitive tape. The same method—pressure sensitive tape—is used to retrieve paint particles from wounds of victims of assault or homicide cases.

Paint may also be embedded in or attached to fired bullets. This may establish that the victim was struck by a bullet that ricocheted off a wall or other painted surface before striking the victim, as for example when a warning shot has been fired.

When more than one paint sample is recovered from a source, investigators are required to put each in a separate container, suitably marked with the exact location from where it was recovered.

The importance of paint analysis is such that it may establish that a particular person was at a particular scene, a certain automobile struck a certain individual or another automobile or stationary object, a weapon was responsible for inflicting an injury, or a specific tool or instrument was used to effect a forcible entry.

§ 9.21 The Nature of Paint

The purpose of paint is to provide a covering over another surface. To achieve that result, a liquid or semi-liquid substance, such as an oil, in which color pigments have been suspended, is used. When confronted with paint in criminal investigations, however, the examiner usually deals with paint in hardened (dried) solid form. Both the substance and the pigment possess characteristics that can be detected and isolated.[1]

In the manufacture of paints, the pigment is suspended in a medium (drying oil, or water). To this may be added certain fillers to give lustre or dullness, a thinner or volatile solvent (turpentine, benzene, gasoline,

---

§ 9.21

1. The terminology of paint chemistry is described by Thornton in his chapter titled "Forensic Paint Examination," in *Forensic Science Handbook* (Saferstein, ed.) 1982, 529, at p. 531.

etc.) or a drier to hasten the hardening of the drying oil, such as manganese borate, red lead, cobalt, or any one of a long list of other substances. Water based paints need the addition of other products to enhance adhesiveness and film forming, such as natural resins, synthetic resins, latex, nitrocellulose, etc. Varnishes resemble paints containing thinner, a medium that evaporates and leaves the resins or ester as an adherent film.

Classifying paints by color requires a consideration of the pigments used. White pigments are calcium carbonate (the least expensive), zinc oxide, lead basic carbonate, lead basic sulfate, titanium dioxide, silica, barium sulfate, and zinc sulfide mixed with barium sulfate. Black pigments usually are either amorphous carbon (lamp black), bone black, ivory black (one of the most expensive), graphite, or asphalt. The most common pigments for other colors are:

Yellow: hydrated ferric oxide with clay (ochres), lead monoxide, lead chromate, zinc chromate, arsenic trisulfide, cadmium sulfide, cadmium lithopones, and gamboge.

Brown: hydrated ferric oxide and manganese dioxide with clay minerals (the yellow-brown forms are called siennas, the red-brown ones umbers), or Vandyke brown.

Red: ferric oxide, trilead tetroxide, and antimony trisulfide.

Green: chromic oxide, copper basic carbonate, copper basic arsenite, or copper acetoarsenite.

Blue: iron ferroferricyanide, sodium aluminosilicosulfide (ultramarine), cobalt aluminate, or copper basic carbonate (azurite).

Considering paints from the viewpoint of their suspension medium, they fall basically into three groups: (1) drying oil types; (2) solvent types; and (3) synthetic emulsion types.

Among the drying oil types of paint are most enamels and exterior building paints. They harden after application by means of autocatalytic polymerization of unsaturated fatty acids in drying oils such as linseed, tung, and other vegetable oils. In the solvent or spirit types (spirit varnishes and lacquers), drying is achieved by evaporation of an organic solvent. The synthetic emulsion types contain a polyvinyl acetate, with or without additives, emulsified in water.

Most vehicles for paint are organic based (oil, resins, nitrocellulose, etc.). The variety of additional matters of organic nature which have been added in the past twenty years make the paint vehicle of an almost greater value for identification purposes than an analysis of the pigments, because a practically limitless number of possible combinations of ingredients now exists. In automobile paints, about 90% are very similar in their inorganic compounds but very different in their vehicle; in house paints, on the other hand, entirely different proportions occur.

§ 9.22 Paint Examination Methods

Because of the tremendous variety of different paints, there are many different methods for the identification and comparison of paint samples. They can be roughly classified into physical and microscopic examinations, chemical solubility tests, and instrumental analysis.

In many cases where the paint particles to be compared contain a number of layers of paint, the microscopic determination that the pigment, pigment distribution, number of layers and sequence of layers are the same in both samples may be sufficient to effect an identification. In situations where there is only one layer of paint, chemical solubility tests may determine the type of paint and spectrographic analysis can disclose the chemical elements present. In addition, infrared spectrophotometric examinations of the paint can reveal information as to the organic components of the paint. The paint may also be decomposed by heat (pyrolysis) and the gaseous products analyzed by a gas chromatograph. Among the other instrumental methods used in paint examinations are laser spark emission spectrography, x-ray diffractometry, energy dispersive x-ray analysis, as well as electron microscopy.[2]

Paint evidence is rather inconclusive, because it is very seldom unique. Even when the paint chips are multilayered and an analysis of two different paints is possible, the probative value is not that much stronger since it is not possible to positively link a suspected paint sample to a given source. The only type of comparison where a positive link between an evidence paint chip and a source is by precise fracture matching along the lines where the paint chip separated from its source, but only if the breaking point is of a sufficient size and displays uneven edges so that a credible match can be made.

§ 9.23 Evidence of Paint Comparisons

The microanalyst may be called upon to testify regarding the identification of automobile paint traces left on damaged vehicles,[1] or removed

2. See generally, Thornton, op. cit. n. 69. Also, Boudreau & Cortner, "Application of Differential Interference Contrast Microscopy to the Examination of Paints," 24 *J.For.Sci.* 148 (1979); Thornton et al., "Solubility Characterization of Automotive Paints," 28 *J.For.Sci.* 1004 (1983); Ward & Carlson, "Paint Analysis Using the Scanning Electron Microscope," *Crime Lab.Dig.* 2 (Feb. 1983); Petraco & Gale, "A Rapid Method for Cross–Sectioning of Multilayered Paint Chips," 29 *J.For.Sci.* 597 (1984); Jain, Fontan & Kirk, "Identification of Paints by Pyrolysis–Gas Chromatography," 5 *J.For.Sci.Soc.* 102, 103 (1965); Manura & Saferstein, "Examination of Automobile Paints by Laser Beam Emission Spectroscopy," 56 *J.Assoc.Off.Analytical Chem.* 1227 (1973); Whitney & MacDonell, "Forensic

Applications of the Electron Microprobe," 9 *J.For.Sci.* 511 (1964); Gothard, "Evaluation of Automobile Paint Flakes as Evidence," 21 *J.For.Sci.* 636 (1976); Reeve & Keener, "Programmed Energy Dispersive X–Ray Analysis of Top Coats of Automotive Paint," 21 *J.For.Sci.* 883 (1976); Krishnan, "Examination of Paints by Trace Element Analysis," 21 *J.For.Sci.* 908 (1976).

§ 9.23

1. State v. Andrews, 86 R.I. 341, 134 A.2d 425 (1957), cert. denied 355 U.S. 898 (1957). Here the charge was assault with intent to kill. The paint on the assailant's vehicle was matched with a smear left on a parked car which was sideswiped during the crime.

from the clothes of vehicular homicide, assault, or accident victims.[2] Motor vehicles involved in accidents or the commission of various other offenses have also left paint samples for identification and comparison. In the cattle theft trial of State v. Hansen,[3] for example, paint smears and chips deposited on a cattle chute were matched to the paint on the tailgate of defendant's trailer.

The repainting of a stolen vehicle called for the testimony of a microscopist in United States v. Longfellow.[4] The coat of paint examined was found to possess characteristics similar to the paint seized from the defendant pursuant to a search warrant. In Pearson v. United States,[5] a hijacking prosecution, the fresh paint on the stolen vehicle was matched to paint smears on gloves found in a car the defendant had used.

As with other trace materials, microscopic bits of paint may be carried away from the scene of a crime on the clothes,[6] shoes, or tools of a criminal offender. Such was the situation in State v. Orricer,[7] where the paint from a burglarized safe was identified with paint on a pair of gloves found in the car of the accused and on a hammer. Similar facts appear in State v. Walker,[8] where the paint on a ransacked safe was of the same type and color as that found on tools taken from the suspect's car.

The most striking example of the connection with a crime scene that can be demonstrated by microanalysis of paint traces is found in State v. Menard.[9] The paint chips taken from the defendant's clothes were composed of distinctly colored layers, and were examined to determine texture, color, gloss, and thickness. One group of chips were black, over yellow, over grey, and were identified as having a common origin with paint from a truck parked outside the burglarized premises. A second group of chips were olive green, over pastel green, over white and were identified as having come from an inside door of the crime scene.

VI. GLASS

§ 9.24 Glass as Evidence in Criminal Cases

In some instances the breaking of glass may be the result of an intentional act; in others, the result of an accidental occurrence. An

2. McCray v. State, 365 S.W.2d 9 (Tex. Cr.App.1963). The evidence here was admitted erroneously because of a lapse in the chain of custody.

3. 199 Kan. 17, 427 P.2d 627 (1967).

4. 406 F.2d 415 (4th Cir.1969), cert. denied 394 U.S. 998 (1969).

5. 192 F.2d 681 (6th Cir.1951).

6. State v. Campos, 61 N.M. 392, 301 P.2d 329 (1956). Paint traces matched with paint of a burglarized safe.

7. 80 S.D. 126, 120 N.W.2d 528 (1963). The suspect was further implicated through analysis of soap used to fill the cracks in the safe and soap traces found on the gloves.

8. State v. Walker, 6 N.C.App. 447, 170 S.E.2d 627 (1969).

9. 331 S.W.2d 521 (Mo.1960).

illustration of the former is the breaking of the window of an automobile or a building to steal something within it. An accidental breaking of a glass object such as a lamp may occur in the course of a struggle between an offender and his victim. In either situation, glass fragments may become embedded in the offender's clothing or deposited in his pocket or trouser cuffs. Fragments may even become lodged in the implement used in an intentional breaking.

Broken headlight glass at the scene of automobile collisions and hit-and-run accidents frequently affords an opportunity to identify the involved vehicles.

The physical and chemical properties of glass fragments may be compared with those of broken glass at the scene of a crime and a determination thereby made as to whether the fragments came from that source.

The retrieval, transporting, and preserving of glass fragments of evidentiary value proceeds pretty much in the same fashion as that discussed earlier for hairs, fibers, and paints. Extreme care must be used in marking the containers in which trace evidence is collected to preserve and avoid contamination of the evidence.

§ 9.25   The Nature of Glass

Glass has been defined as a rigid liquid, which includes naturally occurring rock glasses (such as obsidianite) as well as industrially formed metallurgical slags. They are all made by cooling a previously molten mass in such a speedy manner that there is not enough time during the cooling process for crystallization to occur. Because the viscosity that characterizes liquids is not present, the material is rigid and appears solid.

Common window glass contains mostly silica sand, with soda ash, lime and soda. Plate glass, on the other hand, contains, in addition to silica sand, soda ash, salt cake, limestone, and a small quantity of charcoal. The composition of glass may be altered considerably to produce special types and colors of glass.

The constituent elements are heated in a furnace until the whole mass is fused. After the gases have been allowed to escape, the liquid is withdrawn and worked while still in a heated form, by blowing, molding, or rolling.[1]

§ 9.26   Glass Examination Techniques

The first type of examination of glass involves the fitting together of broken glass. A careful study of impact fracture evidence permits the examiner to place broken pieces together, much like a jigsaw puzzle, and determine the point of impact as well as whether the impact came from

§ 9.25

1. On the nature of glass and its variability, see the Chapter by Miller titled "Forensic Glass Comparisons," in *Forensic Science Handbook* (Saferstein, ed.), 1982, p. 139.

"inside" or "outside," assuming it is possible to make this determination in a particular case, which also assumes that enough pieces of the glass were recovered to permit the reconstruction of the pane of glass. The skilled examiner will have no difficulty distinguishing fractures caused by impact, by heat, by projectiles, or by glass cutters.

In the event sufficient pieces of evidence glass can be recovered so that it is possible to determine whether they can be fitted to a known source by a mechanical fit, the examiner can make a positive identification. In such a case the examiner can conclude with near absolute certainty that the two or more pieces once were part of the same pane of glass.

Other comparisons of glass fragments can be made to determine whether they have a common source. Some use microscopy, others rely upon instrumental analysis to determine the physical and chemical properties of the glass.

The refractive index of the glass fragments is first determined microscopically. Refractive index is based on the fact that light travels through air at a greater velocity than through glass. When the light enters the glass at an angle, some of the light waves enter the glass ahead of others, causing a bending of the beam. The amount of bending of the light wave entering the glass is dependent upon the ratio between the speed of light in air and its speed in the glass. If both glass fragments bend the light entering them to the same degree, they are considered to have the same refractive index.

Another physical property of the glass is measured microscopically through the use of a technique known as dispersion staining. By preparation of the glass in an oil of known refractive index and a refractive index near to that of the glass, and introducing white light and observing through a special microscope objective, the interface at the edges between the glass and liquid will appear colored. The color will be that for which the refractive indices of the glass and liquid are the same. If further modifications are made in the microscope objective, the complementary colors may also be studied. This method determines whether two glass fragments disperse white light similarly.

A third method used in comparing glass fragments is to determine their densities. Liquids of different densities are placed in a glass tube which is closed at one end. The heavier liquids are at the bottom of the tube and the lighter liquids toward the top of the tube. The two glass particles are introduced into the tube and if they both come to rest, or float, at the same point in the tube they are said to have equal densities.

A fourth method of testing glass is to determine the chemical components of the glass through spectrographic analysis. The glass is burned at a very high temperature and each chemical element produces characteristic wavelengths of light when burned. These wavelengths are recorded on film from which the chemical composition of the glass can be determined.

New methods are constantly being devised and tested. Much research continues in the industrial as well as forensic laboratories that may ultimately translate itself in investigative or test conclusions on which testimony is offered.[1]

On the basis of one or several of these examination techniques, the scientist can extract much valuable information from glass. In Figure 8, for example, is illustrated a glass fragment found at the scene of a hit-and-run accident. An examination of the fragment revealed that it was of a borosilicate composition with a density of 2.34 grams per cubic centimeter. Visual examination further disclosed three letters and two figures, "M" and "N" and another "N," as well as the number "3" and a portion of the figure "0." On the basis of these factors alone, and through a comparison with a large library of known specimens, the expert was able to conclude that the glass fragment was once a portion of an upper sealed beam headlamp lens of model # 4001, with a diameter of 5¾", manufactured by the General Electric Company as original equipment for use on Ford Motor Company cars after 1961.

When the expert was later shown a glass fragment taken from a 1963 Ford automobile belonging to the suspected hit-and-run driver, he was able to state that the fragment of unknown origin, found at the accident scene, was in all its characteristics identical to the fragment of known origin, and that the unknown sample could therefore have come from the known vehicle.

It must be remembered that the expert in glass comparisons can render a positive opinion that two or more pieces of glass had a common origin only where a mechanical fit (jigsaw puzzle) has been made. The examiner might also be able to state, positively, that the pieces could *not* have had a common origin. Beyond these two possible opinions, the expert can frame an opinion only in terms of possibilities and probabilities. They are bound to use three different standards: (1) most probably came from a common source; (2) could have come from a common source; and (3) are consistent with a common source. There is no information available at this time which permits a quantifying of an opinion, and it is therefore less likely that statistical evidence will be

§ 9.26

1. See, e.g., Underhill, "Multiple Refractive Index in Float Glass," 20 *J.For.Sci.Soc.* 169 (1980); Beveridge & Semen, "Glass Density Method Using A Calculating Digital Density Meter," 12 *J.Can.Soc.For.Sci.* 113 (1979); Thornton & Cashman, "Reconstruction of Fractured Glass by Laser Beam Interferometry," 24 *J.For.Sci.* 101 (1979); Thornton et al., "Correlation of Glass Density and Refractive Index—Implications to Density Gradient Construction," 29 *J.For. Sci.* 711 (1984); Zetlein, "Glass Classification by Elemental Composition: Numerical Evaluation," 13 *For.Sci.International* 55 (1979); Haney, "Comparison of Window Glasses by Isotope Dilution Spark Source Mass Spectrometry," 22 *J.For.Sci.* 534 (1977); Reeve, et al., "Elemental Analysis by Energy Dispersive X-Ray: A Significant Factor in the Forensic Analysis of Glass," 21 *J.For.Sci.* 291 (1976); Powell, "Interpretation of Vehicle Globe Failures: The Unlit Condition," 22 *J.For.Sci.* 628 (1977); Hickman, "Glass Types Identified by Chemical Analysis," 33 *For.Sci.Int'l* 23 (1987); Fong & Slater, "Density, Refractive Index, and Dispersion in the Examination of Glass: Their Relative Worth as Proof," 27 *J.For. Sci.* 474 (1982); Mires, "Magnetic Identification of Headlight Glass," 31 *J.For.Sci.* 913 (1986); Lentini, "Behavior of Glass at Elevated Temperatures," 37 *J.For.Sci.* 1358 (1992).

offered by experts, as has been done in the case of hairs and fiber comparisons.

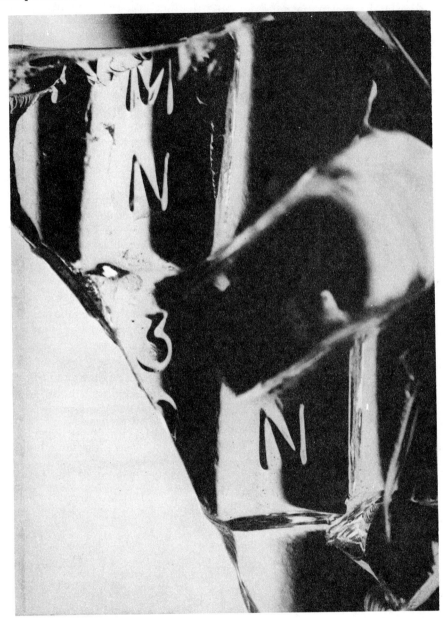

Fig. 8. *Courtesy: Herbert L. MacDonell, Corning, N. Y.*

§ 9.27   Evidence of Glass Examinations

Burglaries and crimes involving motor vehicles as well as automobile accident scenes are the situations which most frequently call for microanalysis of glass particles. Testimony that the glass fragments recovered from a location resembled pieces removed from the defendant's shoes was received in Moreno v. People.[1] The defendant's clothes produced the incriminating fragments in the case of State v. Menard.[2]

As with any type of trace evidence, a proper foundation must be laid for the admission of glass comparison evidence, by showing a "reasonable assurance that the exhibits at trial are the same and in the same condition as when they were first obtained,"[3] although in a civil case questions as to the chain of custody were held to go only to weight, and not to admissibility.[4] It must also be shown that the expert possesses the proper qualifications. In light of the low threshold of competency that the courts require for opinion testimony,[5] the decision of a trial court in permitting expert opinion testimony is given great deference.[6]

At times, the opinion must be qualified. For example, in cases that involved testimony based on the refractive index of glass and density comparisons, experts qualified their opinions by stating that it was "impossible to exclude other sources,"[7] or that "six windows [out of one hundred] could have the same properties."[8] In another case, the expert could only state that four out of one hundred [glass] samples could have the same physical properties.[9]

The case of Rolls v. State[10] illustrates the value of glass analysis with regard to a vehicular collision. Here the microanalyst presented evidence that the glass collected at the scene of the accident and the glass removed from the damaged headlight of the suspect's automobile were of the same origin. Significant evidence regarding glass identification was also presented in the murder prosecution in Wheeler v. State.[11] In that case the soles of the assailant's shoes bore a glass splinter which was matched with the broken lens of the deceased's eyeglasses.

As new techniques permit forensic scientists to match glass with greater levels of confidence, evidence of glass becomes a more helpful

§ 9.27

1. 156 Colo. 503, 400 P.2d 899 (1965).

2. 331 S.W.2d 521 (Mo.1960); the witness was also allowed to testify as to the mathematical probability that the similarities he described could have occurred at random. See also, State v. Spring, 48 Wis.2d 333, 179 N.W.2d 841 (1970), where glass particles found on the defendant's boots were compared to glass present near footprints at the crime scene.

See also, State v. Allen, 111 Ariz. 546, 535 P.2d 3 (1975)—glass density; cf. State v. Brierly, 109 Ariz. 310, 509 P.2d 203 (1973).

3. Horsley v. Commonwealth, 2 Va.App. 335, 343 S.E.2d 389, 390 (1986).

4. Evans v. Olinde, 609 So.2d 299 (La. App.1992)—headlight glass to determine whether a car had its lights on at the time of the impact.

5. Federal Rule of Evidence 702 permits a person to give opinion testimony if the witness is qualified as an expert "by knowledge, skill, experience, training, or education."

6. People v. Williams, 790 P.2d 796 (Colo.1990).

7. People v. Frisby, 160 Ill.App.3d 19, 111 Ill.Dec. 700, 512 N.E.2d 1337, 1349 (1987). The prosecutor's comment in closing that the glass samples "matched" was not held to be reversible error.

8. Hicks v. State, 544 N.E.2d 500, 504 (Ind.1989).

9. Johnson v. State, 612 So.2d 1288, 1301 (Ala.Cr.App.1992).

10. 35 Ala.App. 283, 46 So.2d 8 (1950).

11. 255 Ind. 395, 264 N.E.2d 600 (1970).

and common tool, especially in civil and criminal litigation involving motor vehicle collisions.

VII.   MISCELLANEOUS PARTICLES

§ 9.28   Soil and Dust

1.   IMPORTANCE OF TRACES OF SOIL AND ANALYTICAL METHODS

Soil is present at every crime scene in one form or another and is usually recovered as a heterogeneous mixture which may include clay, sand, rocks, black dirt, coal, plant material, and other debris. Soil is usually associated with cases involving outdoor crime scenes, but it may also feature in indoor scenes.

In many instances, soil is either deposited at or carried away from a crime scene. It may be transported on the shoes, clothing, or body of an individual from a specific location. It may be recovered at the scene of an automobile accident or hit-and-run incident where, due to the impact of the car with a pedestrian, another automobile, or a stationary object, soil present on the undercarriage of the vehicle may have been jarred loose and deposited on the street or sidewalk. It may also be present on the clothing of a hit-and-run victim. Soil may also be removed from a particular location by a vehicle, usually embedded in the tire grooves or attached to the undercarriage of the vehicle.

Weapons and tools used to commit crimes may have been set down momentarily at the scene of the crime and soil may have become embedded in them. If such instruments are found in the possession of a suspect, an analysis of the soil could be an important factor in placing the suspect at the crime scene.

In some situations where the clothing of an unknown deceased is submitted for examination, and there are no cleaning, laundry or other marks for examination, an analysis of the soil present on the shoes or clothing of the victim may give some indication as to his occupation or environment, e.g., a gardener, a construction worker, etc.

The accurate, scientific analysis and comparison of soil is very difficult because of the presence of extremely small particles not capable of accurate analysis. Among the methods used are microscopy and other laboratory instrumental techniques. Initially, the heterogeneous mixture is studied through the stereo-binocular microscope and the larger, easier identifiable components are removed. Using the polarizing microscope and crystallographic studies, the particles may be identified. The sample is then passed through a series of sieves to determine particle size and distribution. The use of a density gradient, described under glass examination techniques in the previous section, serves to furnish information as to particle density and as a comparison tool. In addition, the soil may be subjected to spectrographic analysis, or even neutron activation analysis, to determine the chemical elements present in the sample. X-ray diffraction and differential thermal analysis may also be employed, as well as several other sophisticated analytical methods.[1]

It should be noted that, because of the wide variety of trace evidence of soil and dust, as well as the limitless scientific analytical approaches that might be selected, it is impossible to suggest the degree of certainty with which an opinion of a soil comparison might be expressed. There are undoubtedly cases where two soil samples might be positively identified as having come from a common source, but those cases would be rather rare. In most instances, the opinion would be couched in terms of probable, possible, or consistent with.

2. EVIDENCE OF SOIL COMPARISONS

The courts have recognized that the microscopic analysis of soil can also lead to the admission of significant expert testimony. The evidence developed by the scientific examination of particles of this type is usually utilized to connect an individual or an object with a particular place. Such was the situation in State v. Baldwin,[2] where similar soil was found at the crime scene and in the defendant's car. The incriminating evidence was found on the accused's boots in State v. Spring,[3] and in State v. Atkinson[4] the dirt removed from a shovel in the defendant's home was compared with the dirt found at the victim's burial scene.

Both positive and negative test results were introduced in the Hawaiian case of Territory v. Young.[5] In this instance a soil smear on the suspect's trousers was found to be identical to the soil present at the scene of a rape. The defendant claimed that the smear was picked up in a field some distance away from the crime scene, but an analysis of the soil found at the accused's alibi field showed it to be different from the smear on his pants, thus disproving his story.

The testimony of a microscopist with regard to dust particles has

§ 9.28

1. See the chapter by Murray, titled "Forensic Examination of Soil," in *Forensic Science Handbook* (Saferstein, ed.), 1982, p. 653. See also, e.g., Siegel & Precord, "The Analysis of Soil Samples by Reverse Phase–High Performance Liquid Chromatography Using Wavelength Ratioing," 30 *J.For.Sci.* 511 (1985); Wamogho et al., "A Statistical Method for Assessing Soil Comparisons," 30 *J.For.Sci.* 864 (1985); Van Gricken & Van't Dack, "Soil Analysis by the Thin–Film Energy Dispersive X–Ray Fluorescence," 108 *Anal.Chim.Acta* 93 (1979); Dudley, "The Use of Density Gradient Columns in the Forensic Comparison of Soils," 19 *Med.Sci.Law* 39 (1979); McCrone, "Soil Comparison and Identification of Constitu-

ents," 30 *Microscope* 17 (1982); Graves, "A Mineralogical Soil Classification Technique for the Forensic Scientist," 24 *J.For.Sci.* 323 (1979); Antoci & Petraco, "A Technique for Comparing Soil Colors in the Forensic Laboratory," 38 *J.For.Sci.* 437 (1993).

2. 47 N.J. 379, 221 A.2d 199 (1966), petition for certification to App.Div. denied 52 N.J. 502, 246 A.2d 459 (1968), cert. denied 385 U.S. 980 (1966).

3. Supra note 1, section 9.18.

4. 275 N.C. 288, 167 S.E.2d 241 (1969), remanded for resentencing 279 N.C. 386, 183 S.E.2d 106 (1971).

5. 32 Hawaii 628 (1933).

been of significance in numerous criminal cases. In State v. Coolidge,[6] for example, particulate matter removed from the clothes of the victim was found to be similar to matter removed from the suspect's automobile.

Dust can be deposited on the criminal offender's person during a struggle, or while making an illegal entry. In Aaron v. State,[7] dust from a wallboard broken during a rape was matched with the dust on the clothes of the defendant. In People v. Smith,[8] on the other hand, a particular type of plaster dust implicated a burglary defendant, while in State v. Washington[9] mortar particles on the accused's clothes matched those found in a burglary access hole. Results of analysis of dirt retrieved from fingernail scrapings have also been held to be admissible when relevant to the triable issues in a case.[10]

Dust bearing tools have been examined by microanalysis and resulted in testimony that the dust was similar to that present at the crime scene.[11]

§ 9.29 Cosmetics Evidence

The most frequently encountered traces of cosmetics at crime scenes are lipstick marks. While identification and detailed analysis appears difficult when dealing with trace amounts, greater possibilities of success exist when enough of a stain is available. Even though there are a great variety of makes of lipstick, there are probably not more than 90–110 different tint shades. Traditional methods of analysis, producing largely unsatisfactory results, consist of visual comparison under different light sources (a process which may not necessarily be determinative since different shades of lipstick may show up identical under white or ultraviolet light), and color reactions to strong acids.

More satisfactory methods of analysis are those by visible absorption spectrophotometry and by paper chromatography. A combination of both methods allows for greater differentiation than can be obtained through either visual comparison or color reactions.[1]

---

6. 109 N.H. 403, 260 A.2d 547 (1969), reversed on other grounds 403 U.S. 443 (1971). Forty sets of particles were matched microscopically with regard to color, hue, and texture. Instrumentation found at least 27 sets to be indistinguishable in all tests.

See also, State v. Nevallez, 10 Ariz.App. 135, 457 P.2d 297 (1969); State v. Guerrero, 58 Ariz. 421, 120 P.2d 798 (1942).

7. 271 Ala. 70, 122 So.2d 360 (1960), petition for writ of error denied 275 Ala. 377, 155 So.2d 334 (1963).

8. 142 Cal.App.2d 287, 298 P.2d 540 (1956).

9. 335 S.W.2d 23 (Mo.1960).

10. State v. Ford, 108 Ariz. 404, 499 P.2d 699 (1972).

11. People v. Conley, 220 Cal.App.2d 296, 33 Cal.Rptr. 866 (1963): white plaster-like dust found on a hammer and a crowbar was similar to the dust at the crime scene; People v. Jenkins, 68 Ill.App.2d 215, 215 N.E.2d 302 (1966): red brick dust similar to that found at scene was removed from a sledge hammer.

§ 9.29

1. Keagy, "Examinations of Cosmetic Smudges Including Transesterification and Gas Chromatographic/Mass Spectrometric Analysis," 28 *J.For.Sci.* 623 (1983); Lucas & Eijgelaar, "An Evaluation of a Technique for the Examination of Lipstick Stains," 6 *J.For.Sci.* 354 (1961).

Face powder, another trace element sometimes encountered, consists of several materials such as talc, kaolin, wheat or rice starch, titanium dioxide, zinc oxide, or magnesium stearate. Added to it are certain perfumes as well as organic and inorganic pigments. These constituents can ordinarily be identified quite readily through microscopy.

The testimony of microscopists has been admitted in cases involving the identification of cosmetic traces. Microscopic bits of lipstick found under the fingernails of the suspect in State v. Johnson [2] were matched with a tube of lipstick found in the bedroom of the deceased's mother. The results of this examination were admitted in evidence at the trial.

Lipstick traces also figured in People v. Ervine.[3] Here, similarities were found between a smear discovered on the accused's hand and the lipstick worn by the robbery victim. In Bennett v. State,[4] a burglary prosecution, the examination of fingernail polish found on coins in the suspect's possession showed it to be the same as that found on coins in the burglarized premises.

§ 9.30 Wood Evidence

Wood identification by matching a cut piece of timber to another piece, has been briefly discussed earlier in Chapter 6. It may involve a physical matching of cut forms, a matching of wood grain patterns (see Figure 9), or a determination that a piece of wood was tooled or sawed with a given tool. This type of wood identification might be handled by the comparative micrographist. We enter the area of trace evidence, however, when we consider the identification of wood flour, sawdust, or wood splinters, the types of materials frequently collected from the clothing of a suspect or victim of crime, primarily in trouser cuffs and pockets. As with other items of trace evidence, identification or comparison of wood particles may assist in placing a person at a given location.

2. 37 N.M. 280, 21 P.2d 813 (1933).   **4.** 450 S.W.2d 652 (Tex.Cr.App.1969).

3. 64 Ill.App.2d 82, 212 N.E.2d 346 (1965).

Fig. 9. This photograph, taken with oblique lighting, illustrates a physical matching of wood grain patterns of two ends of lumber, to demonstrate that they were once in one piece. The board on the left has been stained after it was cut from the one on the right.

The identification of the particular species of wood from which the dust or splinters came may at times present serious difficulties, considering that they may come from any of 2,000 genera and approximately 99,000 species of wood or woody plants.[1] The examination is one that calls for skills and experience not ordinarily possessed by the microanalyst, but found at times among forest products technologists of the Forest Service of the United States Department of Agriculture. Yet, it has been discovered that it is almost always possible to identify the wood as to its genus, and sometimes to the exact species. Among the techniques used to examine trace evidence of wood are microscopy of the specimen or the ash picture after burning, x-ray microscopy, and microradiography.

§ 9.31 Identification Methods Based on Trace Evidence

Elsewhere in this volume, various identification methods have been explored that are dependent upon trace evidence. Thus, for example, we discussed the identification for individuals by latent impressions in the

§ 9.30

1. Kukachka, "Wood Identification: Limitations and Potentialities," 6 *J.For.Sci.* 98 (1961). See also, "Wood as Evidence," *FBI Law Enf.Bull.*, Oct. 1975, p. 5; Fralick, "Matches Match," *Ident.News*, Apr. 1975, p. 3; Richardson, "Wood and the Law," *Med.Sci.Law*, July, 1974, p. 200.

For cases involving the discovery and comparison of wood, see: Commonwealth v. Fugmann, 330 Pa. 4, 198 A. 99 (1938); and Smith v. State, 215 Ind. 629, 21 N.E.2d 709 (1939). See also the excellent article, Koehler, "Technique Used in Tracking the Lindbergh Kidnapping Ladder," 27 *J.Crim.L., C. & P.S.* 712 (1937).

previous chapter.[1]   Later in this tome, we will explore the possibilities of identifying an individual by biological evidence on the basis of DNA analysis,[2] or by bitemarks.[3]   In this section, we discuss some other methods of personal identification which either have not proved to be sufficiently reliable, or wherein practitioners have not as yet developed a distinct discipline of professionals engaged in that type of analysis.

1. IDENTIFICATION BY LIP IMPRESSIONS

Related to our earlier discussion of the examination of trace evidence of cosmetics, is the identification of individuals by their lip impressions left at a location, usually in lipstick or by an impression upon glass.   It has been suggested that the various wrinkles and crevices that make up the fleshy parts of the lips may be unique to each individual, similar to fingerprints, and could be a useful identifying technique.[4]   Such an area of observation and analysis is known as "celioscopy."[5]   In the late 1960s, researchers began exploring the possibility of identifying human beings by their lip impressions left with lipstick.   Various experimenters reported that the lines and fissures on upper and lower lips show great variations from person to person.[6]

The premise on which lip identification is based is the immense variety of lip patterns and their individuality—a premise which has not been established—and an identification of six basic types of lips that have been recognized.[7]   These classifications include:

Type I: VERTICAL GROOVES ACROSS THE LIP: These grooves generally run in a straight line from the top of the upper lip down to the bottom of the lip, or from the bottom of the lower lip upwards to the top of it.   This type may also include PARTIAL LENGTH GROOVES which run vertically but do not fully stretch from either the top to the bottom or the bottom to the top of the lip.

Type II: BRANCHED GROOVES: These types of grooves will usually start in a single line from either the top of the upper lip or bottom of the lower lip but will branch out into two or more grooves.

Type III: INTERSECTED GROOVES: These grooves will start at the top of the upper lip or bottom of the lower lip and will

§ 9.31

1. See Chapter 8, supra.

2. See Chapter 15, infra.

3. See Chapter 16, infra.

4. Suzuki & Tsuchihashi, "A New Attempt for Personal Identification by Means of Lip Prints," 17 *J.For.Med.* 52 (1970).

5. Rogers, *The Personal Identification of Living Individuals* (1987).

6. Suzuki & Tsuchihashi, "A New Attempt For Personal Identification by Means of Lip Prints," *Int. Microform J.Leg.Med.* 4

(1969).   By the same authors, see contributions with the same title in 42 *J. Indian Dent.Assoc.* 8 (1970);   17 *U.For.Med.* 52 (1970);   4 *Can.Soc.For.Sci.J.* 154 (1971); Burns, "A 'Kiss' for the Prosecution," *Ident. News,* July, 1981 at 3; Williams, "Lip Prints—Another Means of Identification," 41 *J.For.Ident.* 190 (1991).

7. Tsuchihashi, "Studies on Personal Identification By Means of Lip Prints," 3 *J.For.Sci.* 233 (1974).

intersect or "criss-cross" with other similarly running grooves.

Type IV:　RETICULAR GROOVES: These grooves will usually appear to be a combination of branched and intersected grooves as there will be a number of lines in the lip running and intersecting at various locations.

Type V:　OTHER PATTERNS: These will include any other pattern not associated with the other types of classified grooves.

Recording a lip impression is accomplished by employing a four quadrant chart, similar to what dentists use when recording teeth. The chart has two upper quadrants, which symbolize the right and left halves of the upper lip, and two lower quadrants which represent the same corresponding halves of the lower lip. Thus, an investigator would supposedly study a set of lips and then make notations in each of the quadrants depicting the various types of grooves (identified by the Roman Numerals above) found on that section of the lip. A charting of such an examination may look similar to this:

I	III	II	II	I	I	I	IV
I	II	III	II	I	III	V	

In the early 1970s Tsuchihashi conducted a study on 1364 Japanese subjects which showed that there were no identical lip patterns of these individuals. However, follow up studies showed noticeable changes in the patterns of these individual's lip patterns.[8] A similar study of identical twins indicated that groove patterns were quite alike, indicating that the various patterns on the lips may be inherited from the parents.

Currently, however, lip prints are not a viable means by which an investigator may identify an individual. While there are considerable variances of lip grooves between individuals, no clear study has shown them to be sufficiently distinct and unique, and unchanging in their detail during a person's lifetime, so that lip prints of unknown origin can be determined to have been made by a set of lip prints of known origin. Complicating further study in this area is the lack of any useful or comprehensive data bank from which to compare impressions and conduct further research.

Lip impressions may be compared in their status as an identification technique to a similar attempt at developing a new means of identification by studying the surface pattern of the palatal grooves and ridges known as rugae. This method has been dubbed rugoscopy. Although the use of human palatal rugae was suggested as a method of identification by Harrison Allen in 1889,[9] it has not been widely credited or used for identification purposes. The relative dimension, morphology and

8. Id.　　　　　　　　　　　　**9.** Sognnaes, "Forensic Stormatology," 29 *N.E.J.Med.* 79 (1977).

number of rugae are the criteria supposedly used for the identification.[10] Several studies of palatal rugae have been done, but until recently, few concluded that legal identification could be made solely on palatal rugae. Recent studies have concluded that the rugae patterns are sufficiently unique to discriminate between individuals and base identification upon their comparison.[11] There has, however, been no serious peer review to show that either identification by lip impression or by palatal rugae with any degree of confidence is a possibility.

2. IDENTIFICATION BY EAR IMPRESSIONS

The analysis of the form and detail of ears for identification purposes, known as otoscopy, is another means by which some law enforcement investigators have suggested humans can be identified. Anthropologists and researchers have suggested that the ears, and their various characteristics, can be used to identify individuals.[12] A close look at the external part of the ear shows that it contains numerous complicated details which may be arrayed in particular combinations possibly unique to each person. It is these particular combinations that a few technicians in other fields have attempted to study in an attempt to use ear impressions as a means of identification of humans.

Iannarelli's system of ear identification [13] suggests that the ear be photographed and then enlarged. While completing the enlargement a piece of glass, with a pattern of four black lines that intersect and create a radiating pattern of eight triangular segments, is placed over the enlarging pattern. Prior to enlarging the picture, the point of intersection of the lines on the glass plate is carefully located on the crus of the helix,[14] in order to insure that each set of pictures of each ear will be measured in the same fashion. When the picture of the ear is enlarged the lines on the glass plate are superimposed onto the enlarged picture of the ear and can now be used to make various measurements.

The expert will then make "marks" at numerous points on the photograph where the superimposed guidelines intersect certain details or structures of the ear. Measurements are taken and distances between the "marks" on the photograph are noted. In addition, various other physical characteristics of the ear are noted. These include, the degree of protrusion from the head, and the general shape of the ear: oval, triangular, rectangular and round. Additionally, notes can be made as to whether the lobe of the ear is full and pendulous, or fully attached with no dependent position. This data is recorded and is said to be useful for later identification purposes.

10. Id.

11. English, Summitt, Oestesle, Brannon & Barland, "Individuality of Human Palatal Rugae," 33 *J.For.Sci.* 718 (1988).

12. Martin & Saller 1961: 2069–2080 (ears may be used to show racial characteristics); Iannarelli 1964; 1989 (classification of ears for purposes of identification).

13. Iannarelli, *The Iannarelli System of Ear Identification,* 1964, 1989.

14. The crus of the helix is the small appendage in the front area of the ear that we usually will push inward in an attempt to "close our ears."

Although persons can potentially be recognized, as opposed to positively identified, on the basis of the shape and characteristics of their ears, no empirical research apart from Iannarelli's purported research has verified the uniqueness of persons' ears, or their invariability during lifetime.　A similar system of bodily measurement for identification purposes, was developed in the late 1800's in France by Alphonse Bertillon, who called his system anthropometry.　It was later discarded in favor of fingerprint identification when the Bertillon method proved unreliable and unworkable.

While ear identification by a process of measuring one's ears has not been proved scientifically respectable, some technicians in other disciplines have sought to extend Iannarelli's premises to apply to ear "impressions" left, for instance, on a pillow case or against a wall, which impressions are "developed" (made visible and permanent) much like latent fingerprints are developed.　On the basis of these latent ear impressions, a few occasional literature pieces have suggested identifications were made or could be made.　There is, however, no published empirical research establishing the uniqueness of ears, let alone a technique of comparing two-dimensional ear impressions discovered in a location against photographs of ears of known origin.　The occasional "comparisons" which have been attempted do not qualify as "research" or as "identifications."　Forensic anthropologists recognize the possible individuality of an individual's ears, but not as a means of identification via ear impressions.

There is a significant difference between comparing actual ears and photographs of ears, and the comparing of earprints to each other.　The ear is a three dimensional object that is very malleable.　There are no friction ridges as in fingerprints.　Different pressures may cause different results with the same ear, and may cause the impressions of different ears to look similar.

Thus, earprint identification is not currently a field, discipline, task, function, or technique which has been proved reliable in the forensic science community.　There is no published system which sets forth standards for the identification of individuals by earprints that has been proved reliable and replicable;　there have been no professional conferences devoted to the dissemination of information on an earprint identification technique or to discuss findings and conclusions of researchers, such as is common in other recognized forensic science fields.　In fact, the underlying premise upon which earprint identification techniques must necessarily rest—that the configuration of individuals' ears are unique, invariable, and possessing of characteristics that are reliably discernible and classifiable—has never been proved empirically in the forensic science literature.　Since there is no established discipline of earprint identification, there are also no qualified earprint identification specialists.　Professional criminalists and trace evidence examiners do not claim proficiency in this "technique."　At best, earprint identification has not passed from the stage of experimentation and uncertainty to that of reasonable demonstrability.　There are also no court decisions on the appellate level recognizing such a discipline and admitting evidence based upon its comparisons.

3. SHOEWEAR AND FOOTPRINT COMPARISONS

Traces of shoes, sometimes inaccurately referred to as "footprints," are found at scenes of crimes with great regularity. For that reason, they have long been studied by police and crime laboratory personnel. There is no doubt that a comparison of a shoe trace found at a crime scene with footwear obtained from a defendant can be a valuable link associating the defendant with a crime. The question that is more difficult to answer is whether a particular shoe trace can be positively identified as having been made by a specific item of footwear. Even though there is no recognized "science" of footwear comparisons, it has been widely accepted by law enforcement as well as by the courts that such identifications can be made "in the proper case," meaning when adequate evidence is available.

Shoe prints may be found as either prints or impressions. Prints are two-dimensional, made by depositing or removing material from a hard surface. Impressions are three-dimensional and made in a pliable material. Both class and individual characteristics are present in each of the two types of trace evidence and are identifiable. A shoe print is unique due to its many variables: length of wear, random marks and scratches and the design on a particular sole. For prints, photography is the major technique, and is combined with casting for impressions.[15]

Few specialists in footwear identification exist although the Federal Bureau of Investigation has established a Footwear and Tire Tread Identification Unit. The examination and comparison of impressions or prints of footwear seems to be done mostly by identification technicians, though, in recent years, the physical anthropologists have paid much attention to the subject of foot and shoe prints, as will again be seen in our discussions in § 17.11(5)(B), infra. At times, fingerprint experts, firearms and toolmark examiners, document examiners, and even serologists, are seen to present evidence in court on the identification of footwear. However, some courts have held it reversible error for an expert not qualified as a shoe pattern analyst to give testimony regarding the identification of injuries caused by a suspect shoe.[16]

The United States Supreme court has held that distinctive shoeprints establish probable cause for an investigative stop of suspected smugglers of illegal aliens. In United States v. Cortez,[17] the Court

15. Segura, "Footprints and Tire Marks Recordings and Preserving Them for Evidence," *For.Sci.Digest* No. 7, p. 1 (1981); Bodziak, "Shoe and Tire Impression Evidence," *FBI Law Enf.Bull.*, Jul. 1984 & *Ident.News*, Dec. 1984, p. 3; Nayar & Gupta, "Personal Identification Based on Footprints Found on Footwear," 326 *Int.Crim. Pol.Rev.* 83 (1979); Wojcik & Sahs, "Reproducing Footwear Evidence Impressions," *Ident.News.* Jul. 1984, p. 6; Sahs, "An In-

teresting Case Involving Automotive Pedal Control/Shoe Imprinting," 20 J.For.Ident. 43 (1993). See also, Chapter 2, supra, on the use of casts.

16. See, *Gilliam v. State,* 514 So.2d 1098 (Fla.1987) (medical examiner was not expert in shoe pattern analysis therefore, it was error to allow her to testify that defendant's sneaker left marks on decedent).

17. 449 U.S. 411 (1981).

affirmed the convictions of persons charged with transporting illegal aliens in the vicinity of the Mexican border where it was alleged that the defendants had been stopped in violation of their rights under the Fourth Amendment. The border patrol agents who had effected the stop of the vehicle in which six illegal aliens had been hiding did so, in part, because of distinctive (described as "chevron-like") shoeprint pattern that they had observed criss-crossing the border between Mexico and the United States. In following the trail of this shoeprint the agents had engaged in what counsel for the government in oral argument characterized as "brilliant border-patrol work." Without agreeing with this characterization, the Supreme Court approved the stop as predicted upon a "reasonable surmise" that a violation of the immigration laws was in the offing.

Courts have also held that an officer who observes and photographs shoe tracks in the front yard, front porch and driveway of accused's residence and the residence of the accused's parent is not conducting a search in violation of the Fourth Amendment.[18] Courts have also held that shoe print evidence standing alone may be sufficient to sustain a conviction.[19]

Perhaps because no recognized discipline of footwear specialists exists, courts have admitted opinion testimony on identifications of shoe impressions by laymen. Thus, in State v. Curry,[20] the defendant's conviction for first degree burglary was obtained in part on the testimony of an investigating officer that he had detected similarities in the tread design between footprints found at the scene of the break-in and the shoes worn by defendant when he was apprehended immediately after the occurrence of the burglary was reported. The court held that lay opinion testimony is admissible, in the discretion of the trial court, because the witness's testimony was founded on "his own personal knowledge" which he had gained "soon after the crime by examination and observation of the footprints and shoes at the scene of the burglary."

In State v. Jells,[21] a police officer was allowed to testify as a lay witness and express his opinion that the footprint lifted from the

---

18. People v. Edelbacher, 47 Cal.3d 983, 254 Cal.Rptr. 586, 766 P.2d 1 (1989) (court also held that the probative value of the evidence that the shoe tracks at the defendant's residence and those leading to the vehicle last driven by him were consistent with those found at the murder scene outweighed any prejudice).

19. People v. Campbell, 146 Ill.2d 363, 166 Ill.Dec. 932, 586 N.E.2d 1261 (1992) (Shoeprint evidence with evidence of opportunity and evidence of flight sufficient to sustain conviction for burglary.) See also, Hutt v. State, 70 Md.App. 711, 523 A.2d 643 (1987) (Convictions for housebreaking and theft supported by officer's testimony that shoeprints at both crime scenes

matched those of defendant and defendant's admission of participation in crimes).

20. 103 Idaho 332, 647 P.2d 788 (1982). The conviction was reversed on other, unrelated grounds.

21. 53 Ohio St.3d 22, 559 N.E.2d 464 (1990). Other courts have also held that testimony on footprints can be given by lay witnesses. State v. Johnson, 120 N.J. 263, 576 A.2d 834 (1990); State v. Hairston, 60 Ohio App.2d 220, 396 N.E.2d 773 (1977); Hutt v. State, 70 Md.App. 711, 523 A.2d 643 (1987) (expert testimony unnecessary, trier of fact as capable as any witness to examine the evidence and note any similarities or dissimilarities between the shoe

windshield of the defendant's van matched that of the murder victim. He was also allowed to testify that a footprint taken from a piece of cardboard found near the victim's body matched that of the defendant's shoe. According to the court, even though this was the first time the officer had examined a shoe print taken from a windshield, his past experience in firearms identification was similar to comparing the grooves left by tennis shoe patterns and therefore he could render a lay opinion.

In Hamilton v. State [22] the court upheld the trial court's admission of testimony by the State's expert regarding why fingerprint evidence was "better" than shoeprint evidence. The court stated such testimony was relevant and admissible in the prosecution for burglaries and trespass to explain why the state did not attempt to compare the defendant's shoe print with a shoe found near the scene of the crime.

The newest arena in footwear examinations is not directed toward identifying the shoe that made a crime scene impression, but rather determining the foot that wore a found shoe. This process has been termed "Cinderella analysis" by courts as well as technicians.

In People v. Daniels,[23] the expert witness was a criminalist (who is misidentified as a "criminologist" throughout the opinion) who had done both a vaginal swab analysis for sperm, and a footprint comparison. The same criminalist who did the blood work on the vaginal swab also testified that there was a "good probability" that the accused man had worn the tennis shoe which the police found in the path of flight taken by the victim's attacker. The expert's conclusion was based on a comparison of the insole of the tennis shoe, an inner sole from a shoe worn by the accused after his arrest, an inked impression of the accused's bare foot and a cast of the upper portion of his foot. Using a grid system, the expert found "no inconsistencies" between the recovered tennis shoe and the identified samples. The appellate court, with some measure of hesitancy, found that the footprint comparison testimony was "properly admitted." This was so in spite of the court's recognition that this was the first time the state's expert had performed this type of comparison and that "such comparisons were not widely performed." Further, the court did not find support in the record for

print photographs and casts found at the scenes of three break-ins and the workboots worn by the defendant when he was arrested and the tennis shoe recovered from his home. Officers testified as lay witnesses to their observations); State v. Edmondson, 70 N.C.App. 426, 320 S.E.2d 315 (1984) affirmed 316 N.C. 187, 340 S.E.2d 110 (1986); State v. Plowden, 65 N.C.App. 408, 308 S.E.2d 918 (1983); White v. State, 375 So.2d 622 (Fla.App.1979); D'Antignac v. State, 238 Ga. 437, 233 S.E.2d 206 (1977); People v. Lomas, 92 Ill.App.3d 957, 48 Ill. Dec. 377, 416 N.E.2d 408 (1981); State v. Haarala, 398 So.2d 1093 (La.1981); State v. Walker, 319 N.W.2d 414 (Minn.1982);

State v. Cullen, 591 S.W.2d 49 (Mo.App. 1979). In a Minnesota cattle theft case, the court upheld the admission of a deputy sheriff's opinion that defendant's books made the footprints at the crime scene: State v. Walker, 319 N.W.2d 414 (Minn. 1982). See also, Johnson v. State, 177 Ind. App. 501, 380 N.E.2d 566 (1978) (harmless error to allow police officer to testify "that the footprints . . . were the same as defendant's shoe soles").

22. 205 Ga.App. 422, 422 S.E.2d 263 (1992).

23. 172 Cal.Rptr. 353 (Cal.App.1981).

the conclusion that foot impressions have a unique individuality like fingerprints. But the court said that all of this went to the weight and not to admissibility of the evidence. In view of the United States Supreme Court's insistence that trial judges are the "gatekeepers" charged with keeping out expert opinion evidence which has not proved to be reliable,[24] it is to be doubted whether the Daniels court's characterization of the issue as one of credibility is defensible.

Another reported appellate court opinion finding the testimony of an expert admissible to identify the feet which made the impressions in a pair of shoes, is People v. Puluti.[25] The scientific analysis in this case by a physical anthropologist on the faculty of the University of North Carolina was designated as "Cinderella analysis" because it was founded on an evaluation of the marks and measurements found on the interior of a pair of shoes, the ownership of which was in question.

The defendant in *Puluti* was accused of murdering his wife of just two months in a bedroom of their home in California and disposing of her body, wrapped in a sleeping bag, along with "two bloodied king size pillows, a washrag and a pink blanket, a piece of folded clear plastic, a woman's white purse, a pair of men's shoes with tied laces, and a pair of rolled socks stuffed inside the toe of the shoes" in a "gravesite" in a remote camping and hunting area in Northern California. The body was not discovered until nearly two years after the unexplained disappearance of the defendant's wife. The testimony of various pathologists who studied and examined the remains left the cause of death uncertain, but the identity of the remains was established through examination of the dental work on the body.

The state, in trying the defendant for the murder of his wife, introduced a variety of circumstantial evidence pointing to his complicity in her death. The Cinderella analysis which was challenged on the defendant's appeal from his conviction resulted from the finding of the shoes at the wife's gravesite and a comparison with a number of shoes seized under a search warrant from the accused's apartment. In addition, the defendant was required to give inked foot impressions. These items, of known and unknown origin, were used by Dr. Louise Robbins, the expert, in making her assessment that "the same person who wore defendant's shoes wore the gravesite shoes," and that "the probability of another person being in that location at that time, and the person having those particular combination of features in the boot, would be of an astronomical order."

The expert explained her methodology as using a "grid system consisting of points of measurements devised to analyze the pressure points of the feet." This enabled her to examine 68 "points of shape" within 13 major categories of the toe, ball of foot, heel and arch, and to take 46 points of measurement and "7 rations" of measurement (ex-

---

24. Daubert v. Merrell Dow Pharmaceuticals, 113 S.Ct. 2786 (1993).

25. 174 Cal.Rptr. 597 (Cal.App.1981). The expert explained her methods in a book. See, Robbins, *Footprints*, (1985). Since the testimony was furnished by a physical anthropologist, the case is also discussed extensively at § 17.11(5)(B), infra.

plained as length-to-width). The defendant objected to this testimony as based on a novel scientific theory of an unfounded nature. He also introduced the testimony of his own expert, a podiatrist, to refute it.

The appellate court upheld the admission of the testimony of the state's physical anthropologist but did not seem persuaded of one overriding rationale. After finding no new experimental techniques involved since the analysis was predicted on "accepted techniques, observations, simple measurements and deductive reasoning," the court stated that even if it were a new technique, it fulfilled the requirements of reliability of the methodology, accuracy of the procedures, and competence of the expert. But, said the court, even if the trial court had improperly admitted the evidence, the error in doing so had not prejudiced the defendant who had been linked to the murder by other formidable circumstantial evidence.

The *Puluti* case is not the only one in which Dr. Robbins displayed her prowess. For a while she was a very popular witness with prosecutors, since she was able to assist them with opinion evidence obtainable from few others.[26] Since the *Puluti* case, "Cinderella analysis" has been both embraced and roundly criticized.

Dr. Robbins' prowess brought one of her cases before the United States Supreme Court. In Buckley v. Fitzsimmons,[27] the key piece of evidence in this abduction-murder case was a bootprint found on the front door of the victim's house. Buckley, after police contact, brought his boots to the police for analysis. Three separate studies of the bootprint and Buckley's boots were made by state and county crime labs. Neither could conclude there was a connection between the bootprint and Buckley's foot. The prosecution then went "expert shopping" and obtained a "positive identification" from Dr. Louise Robbins. Buckley and two others were indicted, arrested and tried in 1985. The two codefendants were found guilty and sentenced to death. There was a hung jury as to Buckley and a retrial was scheduled. Further investigation on another case uncovered evidence that another person killed the victim Buckley had been accused of murdering. Dr. Robbins then died and since no one else was found who could testify definitively that the bootprint was Buckley's, the charges against him were dismissed. Since Buckley had been unable to raise the $3 million bail imposed at his arrest, he had spent three years in prison before the charges were dismissed and Buckley brought a suit for malicious prosecution. The

26. Among the other cases in which Dr. Robbins testified are: People v. Knights, 166 Cal.App.3d 46, 212 Cal.Rptr. 307 (1985); State v. Bullard, 312 N.C. 129, 322 S.E.2d 370 (1984); State v. Maccia, 311 N.C. 222, 316 S.E.2d 241 (1984); United States v. Ferri, 778 F.2d 985 (3d Cir.1985). In Bird v. State, 594 So.2d 644 (Ala.Cr.App. 1990), reversed on other grounds 594 So.2d 676 (Ala.1991), the state had originally sent the evidence to Dr. Robbins, but she died before she could complete her examination.

By contrast, the conviction was overturned in People v. Ferguson, 172 Ill. App.3d 1, 122 Ill.Dec. 266, 526 N.E.2d 525 (1988), the court finding that Dr. Robbins' theories were not generally accepted by the scientific community in which she practiced.

27. 113 S.Ct. 2606 (1993).

Seventh Circuit held that the prosecutor had complete immunity.[28] After an interlude wherein the Supreme Court ordered the 7th Circuit to reconsider its decision,[29] the Supreme Court focused on the following series of events:

1. The commission of the crime on February 25, 1983;

2. The initial investigation by both the police and prosecutors, which involved expert-witness shopping and which turned up insufficient evidence to indict anyone;

3. The convening of a special grand jury devoted solely to investigating the murder for eight months. The jury heard the testimony of over one hundred witnesses, including the bootprint experts;

4. A public statement by State's Attorney Fitzsimmons on January 27, 1984, admitting that there was insufficient evidence to indict anyone for the murder and rape of Jeanine Nicarico;

5. Not until an indictment was returned in March, 1984, was additional evidence presented to the special investigatory grand jury, at which time Fitzsimmons held a defamatory press conference practically on the eve of his electoral contest with Ryan;

6. Ryan defeated Fitzsimmons in a Republican primary race on March 21, 1984, and became his successor in December, 1984.

The Court held that prosecutors have only qualified immunity for their participation in pretrial or precharge police investigative work or in collateral law enforcement administration.[30] It does not pay for prosecutors to shop for the expert witness who professes to be able to identify a perpetrator on the basis of a fairly novel and only partly recognized theory, when the state's own crime laboratories profess their inability to accomplish this feat!

With the exception of the so-called Cinderella analysis, courts readily admit evidence that footprints found in certain relevant locations were made by the defendant's footwear.[31]

---

28. Buckley v. Fitzsimmons, 919 F.2d 1230 (7th Cir.1990).

29. The Seventh Circuit was directed to reconsider the case in the light of Burns v. Reed, 500 U.S. 478 (1991) which held that a prosecutor had only limited immunity when it came to giving advice to the police in the investigative phase of a criminal prosecution, but the 7th Circuit affirmed its prior ruling and the Supreme Court grant Buckley's second certiorari petition.

30. Buckley v. Fitzsimmons, 113 S.Ct. 2606, 2617 (1993).

31. State v. Boobar, 637 A.2d 1162 (Me. 1994)—detective's testimony that the crime scene footprints "could have been made by defendant's sneakers" was admissible; State v. Ingold, 450 N.W.2d 344 (Minn.App. 1990)—expert testimony that burglary suspect made shoe print on back door of restaurant properly admitted; State v. Rhodes, 552 So.2d 585 (La.App.1989)—plaster cast of shoeprint said to be made with tennis shoes defendant was wearing when arrested; People v. Campbell, 146 Ill.2d 363, 166 Ill.Dec. 932, 586 N.E.2d 1261 (1992): in the proper case shoeprint evidence alone is sufficient to convict. But in McDonnell v. United States, 455 F.2d 91 (8th Cir.1972), the court said that shoeprint will be admitted only when it is established that the shoeprints and shoes are distinctive enough to afford reliable comparison.

A final issue related to footwear identification is the determination of the shoe size and height of a person on the basis of a shoe impression. While there have been reported studies that purport to be able to calculate the concordance between footwear size and the height of the person who left the imprint,[32] in State v. Harvey [33] the methods of Dr. Claude Lovejoy for determining the height of a person from his shoe print were deemed not to be scientifically reliable, where the state did not provide evidence that anyone in the scientific community other than the expert vouched for his methods.

VIII.   TRIAL AIDS

§ 9.32   Expert Qualifications and Testimony

As with other scientific evidence, the microanalyst may use pictures or project microscope slides to demonstrate his findings to the jury.[1] The production of such aids, however, is not required. Neither is it mandatory that the expert testimony be accorded scientific certainty in order to be admitted.[2] Where the witness stated that material found on the sweater "was consistent with" material found at a crime scene, his testimony was held properly admitted and deemed sufficient to convict a defendant of murder.[3] Testimony that fibers from defendant's shirt were similar "in every microscopic detail" with fibers found on deceased's clothes at the time of her death was also held properly admitted.[4]

Normal chain of custody requirements must be observed, and failure to do so will result in suppression of the physical evidence as well as any expert testimony accompanying it.[5] Also, the condition of the physical

---

32. E.g., Giles & Vallandigham, "Height Estimation from Foot and Shoeprint Length," 36 *J.For.Sci.* 1134 (1991)—this article chronicles all of the research on the topic since the 1800's. It is also critical of Dr. Robbins' book *Footprints: Collection, Analysis, and Interpretations,* 1985.

33. 121 N.J. 407, 581 A.2d 483 (1990), cert. denied 499 U.S. 931 (1991).

§ 9.32

1. E.g., State v. Menard, 331 S.W.2d 521 (Mo.1960). See also, Chapter 2, infra, on photographic evidence.

2. E.g., United States v. Longfellow, 406 F.2d 415 (4th Cir.1969), cert. denied 394 U.S. 998 (1969), and many other cases cited in the sections on hairs and fiber examinations.

3. Commonwealth v. Perez, 357 Mass. 290, 258 N.E.2d 1 (1970).

4. Mattox v. State, 240 Miss. 544, 128 So.2d 368 (1961). "Microscopically identical," when referring to comparison of defendant's pubic hair and that found on the victim was permissible testimony in State v. Golladay, 78 Wash.2d 121, 470 P.2d 191 (1970). Testimony that the refractive index of glass specimens was "similar" and that putty had "similar" chemical properties was properly submitted to the jury as corroborative of the commission of armed robbery in People v. Nelson, 127 Ill.App.2d 238, 262 N.E.2d 225 (1970).

5. E.g. State v. Wilroy, 150 Mont. 255, 434 P.2d 138 (1967). But see, Nixon v. State, 204 Md. 475, 105 A.2d 243 (1954), where the chain of custody was broken but the evidence was admissible due to the remote chance of contamination.

evidence prior to scientific examination and analysis must not be significantly altered.[6]

Unlike the expert in comparative micrography, who can frequently testify that two articles were once joined together, the microanalyst can frequently testify only to the fact that items he has examined have a common source. For example, a microanalyst could testify that a certain fiber and a shirt he had examined had a common origin; perhaps they came from the same batch of material, but he was unable to specifically state that the particular fiber under examination came definitely from the shirt.[7]

The witness also must be shown to be a competent expert.[8] A police officer's testimony that pieces of cloth or fabric and a jacket were of the same material was held inadmissible because the officer had not been shown to be competent to give opinion testimony as an expert.[9]

The competency of crime laboratory examiners is difficult to assess. Without a doubt, the nation's crime laboratories possess some fine researchers and extremely competent expert witness. It is also true that there are a great number of examiners and workers who are not very skilled in the tasks they are asked to undertake.[10] Some are trained to operate sophisticated instrumentation, the inner workings of which they do not understand. They are basically "readers" who note the results shown on their instrumentation and compare the data collected to reference data compiled by others.[11]

6. E.g. Cordes v. State, 54 Tex.Crim.R. 204, 112 S.W. 943 (1908); blanket permitted to undergo fiber analysis although it had been washed of blood.

7. Tomolillo v. State, 4 Md.App. 711, 245 A.2d 94 (1968). In the general area of expert testimony, see, People v. Conley, supra note 2, section 9.19, where an expert was allowed to testify although he did not perform all available tests.

8. A witness who had attended various universities, had studied and later lectured on forensic microanalysis, including the identification of paint and glass, and who had made over two thousand prior analyses similar to the one involved in the trial, was deemed competent as an expert in forensic microanalysis: People v. Green, 28 Ill.2d 286, 192 N.E.2d 398 (1963).

Similarly, an employee of the FBI for nine years, having received B.S. and M.S. degrees, trained at the FBI for one year, and thereafter having conducted over 1,000 examinations of hairs and fibers, was properly qualified as an expert in State v. Wallace, 181 Conn. 237, 435 A.2d 20 (1980).

9. People v. Patno, 13 A.D.2d 870, 215 N.Y.S.2d 309 (1961).

10. Consider, for example, the results of proficiency testing in crime laboratories for very common functions, which were so appallingly in error that one crime laboratory director was moved to state: "Crime laboratories flunk analysis." Supra, Chapter 1, at footnote 5, section 1.03.

11. They have, of course, no knowledge of how the reference data were collected. In regard to such overreliance on instrumentation, one noted criminalist remarked: "I have observed that when an overabundance of sophisticated expensive instrumentation is available they are used because they are there. This tends to produce limited and dependent workers having a narrow understanding of the proof value of their results. These are relatively ineffective workers seeking to use esoteric devices to dazzle the less scientifically oriented users of their services, and to cover up their inability to cope with simpler methods requiring understanding as well as observational skill and deducted power." Wilkaan Fong in a letter to the editor, 29 *J.For.Sci.* 958 (1984). The author hastened to add that "a worker is not to be identified as an ineffective worker simply because he or she uses or advocates usage of instrumentation."

Mr. Fong himself qualified as an expert witness in the use of one of the most so-

Because of the great diversity of backgrounds from which forensic scientists are drawn, it is difficult to define precise educational backgrounds which are required for competency in a given area. A bachelor's of science degree in the appropriate academic area that supports the forensic examinations an examiner is asked to perform, plus a year of actual forensic in-house training and case work experience, would be the minimum qualifications for the criminalist. Many would have master of science degrees as well. It is regrettable that there are not more Ph.D. degree holders in the crime laboratories. Graduate and post graduate degrees are a must when one is asked to engage in meaningful original research and the development of novel scientific applications.

In the absence of any clear peer review and comprehensive certification programs in criminalistics, courts continue to do the best they can in determining the qualifications of witnesses said to be experts in the various fields of physical evidence or particle analysis. They should not be too hasty, though, as they are apt to be in the average case, to recognize as expert witnesses all those who perform certain analysis functions in a crime laboratory. Not all who are employed there are truly experts in the field(s) in which they are asked to labor.

§ 9.33 Locating and Engaging the Expert

Crime laboratories across the country, whether municipally, state, or federally supported and maintained, employ competent microanalysts to examine evidence and offer testimony in court on behalf of the prosecution, although occasionally the services of highly reputed scientists outside law enforcement are sought in support of the prosecution's case.

Civil litigators and criminal defense lawyers however, are by no means helpless and can draw upon a very large core of technicians and scientists for the purpose of verifying prosecution findings and, if necessary, offer expert testimony in court. Many of these are employed in private research laboratories or by manufacturers. Microanalytic techniques and other instrumental methods of detection are standard and not specifically devised for law enforcement. The textile industry, the paint industry, and the glass manufacturers employ many specialists who are as competent to analyze fibers, paints, and glass respectively as the men working for the crime laboratories. The cosmetics industry is no exception. Anthropologists and scientists working in the hair products or wig manufacturing industries are experienced at studying and comparing hairs.

Sometimes, even crime laboratories are forced to seek expert advice outside. There are probably very few, if any, truly competent experts in wood identification in law enforcement agencies. The Forest Products Laboratory of the Forest Service, U.S. Department of Agriculture, main-

---

phisticated of instruments: the Scanning Electron Microscope (SEM) for the interpretation of gunshot residues (GSR), even though he testified the case was the first in which he used the SEM for GSR analysis: People v. Palmer, 80 Cal.App.3d 239, 145 Cal.Rptr. 466 (1978).

tained at Madison, Wis., has perhaps the most outstanding experts. They have testified both for the prosecution and defense.

A great number of these experts, both state or independent, belong to professional organizations. One such group is the American Academy of Forensic Sciences,[1] which numbers many qualified experts in the microanalytic fields among its members of the Criminalistics and the Toxicology sections.

When seeking to engage an expert, it must be remembered that not only should he have an adequate formal education, but he should also have practical experience in the analysis and examination of the particular types of trace evidence which he is asked to examine.

IX. MISCELLANEOUS

§ 9.34 Bibliography of Additional References

Note: Books or articles cited in the footnotes are not repeated herein.

1. GENERAL ANALYTICAL PROCEDURES

De Forest, "Foundations of Forensic Microscopy," Ch. 9 in *Forensic Science Handbook* (Saferstein, ed.), 1982, p. 416.

Saferstein, "Forensic Applications of Mass Spectrometry," Ch. 3 in *Forensic Science Handbook* (Saferstein, ed.), 1982, p. 92.

Smith, "Forensic Applications of High–Performance Liquid Chromatography," Ch. 2 in *Forensic Science Handbook* (Saferstein, ed.) 1982, p. 28.

Whitney & MacDonnell, "Forensic Applications of the Electron Microprobe," 9 *J.For.Sci.* 511 (1964).

Wilmott, "Pyrolysis–Gas Chromatography of Polyolefins," 7 *J.Chromatographic Sci.* 101 (1969).

2. NEUTRON ACTIVATION ANALYSIS

Chan, "Identification of Single–Stranded Copper Wire by Nondestructive Neutron Activation Analysis," 17 *J.For.Sci.* 93 (1972).

Forslev, "Nondestructive Neutron Activation Analysis of Hair," 11 *J.For.Sci.* 217 (1966).

Guinn, "Recent Significant U.S. Court Cases Involving Forensic Activation Analysis," 15 *J.Radioanal.Chem.* 389 (1973).

§ 9.33

1. The address of the Academy is: 225 So. Academy Blvd., Colorado Springs, Colo. 80910.

There are also a great number of regional associations of forensic scientists.

Guinn, "Applications of Nuclear Science in Crime Investigation," 24 *Annual Rev. of Nuclear Sci.* 561 (1974).

Karjala, "The Evidentiary Uses of Neutron Activation Analysis," 59 *Calif.L.Rev.* 997 (1971).

Kilty, "Activity after Shooting and Its Effect on the Retention of Primer Residue," 20 *J.For.Sci.* 219 (1975).

Krishnan, et al., "Rapid Detection of Firearm Discharge Residues by Atomic Absorption and Neutron Activation Analysis," 16 *J.For.Sci.* 144 (1971).

Krishnan, "Detection of Gunshot Residue on the Hands by Neutron Activation and Atomic Absorption Analysis," 19 *J.For.Sci.* 789 (1974).

Krishnan, "Examination of Paints by Trace Element Analysis," 21 *J.For.Sci.* 908 (1976).

Lukens et al., "Forensic Neutron Activation Analysis of Paper," U.S. AEC Report GA–10113 (1970), 50 pages.

Renshaw, "The Distribution of Trace Elements in Human Hair and its Possible Effect on Reported Elementa; Concentration Levels," 16 *Med.Sci.Law* 37 (1976).

Ruch et al., "Detection of Gunpowder Residues by Neutron Activation Analysis," 20 *Nuclear Sci. & Engin.* 381 (1964).

Rudzitis & Wahlgren, "Firearm Residue Detection by Instrumental Neutron Activation Analysis," 20 *J.For.Sci.* 119 (1975).

Schlesinger, et al., "Special Report on Gunshot Residues Measured by Neutron Activation Analysis," U.S. AEC Report GA–9829 (1970), 144 pages.

Schlesinger, et al., "Forensic Neutron Activation Analysis of Paint," U.S. AEC Report GA–10142 (1970), 261 pages.

Schmitt & Smith, "Identification of Glass by Neutron Activation Analysis," 15 *J.For.Sci.* 252 (1970).

Smith, "The Interpretation of the Arsenic Content of Human Hair," 4 *J.For.Sci.Soc.* 192 (1964).

Smith, "Interpretation of Results Obtained by Activation Analysis," 9 *J.For.Sci.Soc.* 205 (1969).

3. HAIRS

Anno., "Admissibility and Weight, In Criminal Case, of Expert or Scientific Evidence Respecting Characteristics and Identification of Human Hair," 23 *A.L.R.4th* 1199 (1983).

Baumgartner et al., "Detection of Phencyclidine in Hair," 26 *J.For.Sci.* 576 (1981).

Bisbing & Wolner, "Microscopical Discrimination of Twins' Head Hair," 29 *J.For.Sci.* 780 (1984).

Bisbing, "The Forensic Identification and Association of Human Hair," Ch. 5 in *Forensic Science Handbook* (Saferstein, ed.) 1982, p. 184.

Comment, "Splitting Hairs in Criminal Trials: Admissibility of Hair Comparison Probability Estimates," 1984 *Ariz.St.L.J.* 521.

Cox, "Analysis of Hair Traces Drug Use; New Wave in Narcotics Testing," 27 *Nat'l L.J.* 3 (1987).

Gaudette, "Probabilities and Human Pubic Hair Comparisons," 21 *J.For.Sci.* 514 (1976).

Gislason, et al., "The Variation of Trace Element Concentrations in Single Human Head Hairs," 17 *J.For.Sci.* 426 (1972).

Imwinkelried, "Forensic Hair Analysis: The Case Against The Underemployment of Scientific Evidence," 39 *Wash. & Lee L.Rev.* 41 (1982).

Ishiyama et al., "Detection of Basic Drugs (Methamphetamine, Antidepressants, and Nicotine) from Human Hair," 28 *J.For.Sci.* 380 (1983).

Johri & Jatar, "Young's Modulus in Identification of Human Scalp Hair," 22 *Med.Sci. & Law* 63 (1982).

Kidwell, "Analysis of Phencyclidine and Cocaine in Human Hair by Tandem Mass Spectrometry," 38 *J.For.Sci.* 272 (1993).

Kind, "Metrical Characters in the Identification of Animal Hairs," 5 *J.For.Sci.Soc.* 110 (1965).

Kirk, "Human Hair Studies I—General Considerations of Hair Individualization and Its Forensic Importance," 31 *J.Crim.L. & Criminology* 486 (1940).

Kirk & Gamble, "Human Hair Studies II—Scale Counts," 31 *J.Cr.L. & Criminology* 627 (1941).

Kirk, et al., "Human Hair Studies III—Refractive Index of Crown Hair," 31 *J.Cr.L. & Criminology* 746 (1941).

Longia, "Increase in Medullary Index of Human Hair with Passage of Time," 57 *J.Cr.L., C. & P.S.* 221 (1966).

Mackintosh & Pate, "The Absorption of Mercuric Ion in Single Head Hairs," 27 *J.For.Sci.* 572 (1982).

Michaldimitrakis, "Detection of Cocaine in Rats from Analysis of Hair," 27 *Med.Sci. & Law* 13 (1987).

Miller, "Procedural Bias in Forensic Science Examinations of Human Hair," 11 *Law & Hum.Beh.* 157 (1987).

Niyogi, "Abnormality of Hair Shaft Due to Disease," 15 *J.For.Med.* 148 (1968).

Petraco, "A Modified Technique for the Cross Sectioning of Hairs and Fibers," 9 *J.Pol.Sci. & Admin.* 498 (1981).

Pushel, et al., "Opiate Levels in Hair," 21 *For.Sci.International* 181 (1983).

Renshaw, et al., "Determination of Lead and Copper in Hair by Non–Flame Atomic Absorption Spectrophotometry," 18 *J.For.Sci.* 143 (1973).

Rosen & Kerley, "An Epoxy Method of Embedding Hair for Histologic Sectioning," 16 *J.For.Sci.* 236 (1971).

Rosen, "Identification of Primate Hair," 19 *J.For.Sci.* 109 (1974).

Shaffer, "A Protocol for the Examination of Hair Evidence," 30 *Microscope* 151 (1982).

Stone, "Hair and Its Probative Value as Evidence," 45 *Tex.B.J.* 275 (1982).

Tarantino, *Strategic Use of Scientific Evidence,* 1988.

Verhoeven, "The Advantages of the Scanning Electron Microscope in the Investigative Studies of Hair," 63 *J.Crim.L., C. & P.S.* 125 (1972).

Viala et al., "Determination of Chloroquine and Monodesethylchloroquine in Hair," 28 *J.For.Sci.* 922 (1983).

Wickenheiser & Hepworth, "Further Evaluation of Probabilities in Human Scalp Hair Comparisons," 35 *J.For.Sci.* 1323 (1990).

Yuracek, et al., "Analysis of Human Hair by Spark Source Mass Spectrometry," 41 *Analytical Chem.* 1666 (1969).

4. FIBERS

Beattie et al., "The Extraction and Classification of Dyes from Cellulose Acetate Fibers," 21 *J.For.Sci.Soc.* 233 (1981).

Bortniak, et al., "Differentiation of Microgram Quantities of Acrylic and Modacrylic Fibers Using Pyrolysis Gas–Liquid Chromatography," 16 *J.For.Sci.* 380 (1971).

Bresee, "Density Gradient Analysis of Single Polyester Fibers," 25 *J.For.Sci.* 564 (1980).

Bresee & McCullough, "Discrimination Among Acrylic Fiber Types by Small–Angle Light Scattering of Single Fibers," 26 *J.For.Sci.* 184 (1981).

Brewster et al., "The Retention of Glass Particles on Woven Fabrics," 30 *J.For.Sci.* 798 (1985).

Catling & Grayson, *Identification of Vegetable Fibers,* 1982.

Fong, "Rapid Microscopic Identification of Synthetic Fibers in a Single Liquid Mount," 27 *J.For.Sci.* 257 (1982).

Fong, "Fiber Evidence: Laboratory Methods and Observations From Casework," 29 *J.For.Sci.* 55 (1984).

Forlini & McCrone, "Dispersion Staining of Fibers," 19 *Microscope* 243 (1971).

Grieve & Kotowski, "The Identification of Polyester Fibers in Forensic Science," 22 *J.For.Sci.* 390 (1977).

Grieve, "The Role of Fibers in Forensic Science Examinations," 28 *J.For.Sci.* 877 (1983).

Janiak & Damereau, "The Application of Pyrolysis and Programmed Temperature Gas Chromatography to the Identification of Textile Fibers," 59 *J.Crim.L., C. & P.S.* 434 (1968).

Philip, "The Use of Differential Scanning Calorimetry in the Identification of Synthetic Fibers," 17 *J.For.Sci.* 132 (1972).

Resua, "A Semi–Micro Technique for the Extraction and Comparison of Dyes in Textile Fibers," 25 *J.For.Sci.* 168 (1980).

Smalldon, "The Identification of Acrylic Fibers by Polymer Composition as Determined by Infrared Spectroscopy and Physical Characteristics," 18 *J.For.Sci.* 69 (1973).

5. PAINT, GLASS, AND OTHER PHYSICAL EVIDENCE

Andrasko & Maehly, "The Discrimination Between Samples of Window Glass by Combining Physical and Technical Techniques," 23 *J.For. Sci.* 250 (1978).

Audette & Percy, "A Rapid, Systematic, and Comprehensive Classification System for the Identification and Comparison of Motor Vehicle Paint Samples. I. The Nature and Scope of the Classification System," 24 *J.For.Sci.* 790 (1979).

Beam & Willis, "Analysis Protocol for Discrimination of Automotive Paints by SEM–EDXA Using Beam Alignment by Current Centering," 35 *J.For.Sci.* 1055 (1990).

Calloway & Jones, "Enhanced Discrimination of Glass Samples by Phosphorescence Analysis," 23 *J.For.Sci.* 263 (1978).

Crocket & Taylor, "Physical Properties of Safety Glass," 9 *J.For.Sci.Soc.* 119 (1969).

Choudhry, "Comparison of Minute Smears of Lipstick by Microspectrophotometry and Scanning Electron Microscopy/Energy–Dispersive Spectroscopy," 36 *J.For.Sci.* 366 (1991).

Dabbs & Pearson, "Some Physical Properties of a Large Number of Window Glass Specimens," 17 *J.For.Sci.* 70 (1972).

Fish, "The Identification of Wood Fragments," 6 *J.For.Sci.Soc.* 67 (1966).

Guinn, "The Identification of Hair, Paper and Paint Specimens by Means of Neutron Activation Analysis," *Identification News,* Mar. 1966, p. 4.

Gupta & Cerar, "The Application of Soft X–Rays in Criminalistics— Identification of Wood Chips," 9 *J.For.Sci.* 140 (1964).

Haer, *An Introduction to Chromatography on Impregnated Glass Fiber,* 1969.

Hagstrom & Soder, "Light Filament of Incandescent Lamps Studied by Auger Electron Spectroscopy," 25 *J.For.Sci.* 103 (1980).

Hartley & Inglis, "The Determination of Metals in Wool by Atomic Absorption Spectrophotometry," 93 *The Analyst* 394 (1968).

Hickman, "Glass Types Identified by Chemical Analysis," 33 *For.Sci. Int'l* 23 (1987).

Hoffman, et al., "Forensic Comparison of Soils by Neutron Activation and Atomic Absorption Analysis," 60 *J.Crim.L., C. & P.S.* 395 (1969).

Jain, et al., "Identification of Paints by Pyrolysis–Gas Chromatography," 5 *J.For.Sci.Soc.* 102 (1965).

Kehl, *The Principles of Metallographic Laboratory Practice,* 1949.

Kretschmer & Helbig, "Chemical Analysis of Macromelocular Particles Using Two–Dimensional High–Performance Liquid Chromatography (HPLC), Illustrated by Polymeric Automobile Direction Indicator Lenses (DILs)," 36 *J.For.Sci.* 1010 (1991).

Laux, "Identification of a Rope by Means of Physical Match Between the Cut Ends," 29 *J.For.Sci.* 1246 (1984).

Lichtenstein, "Active Paint Reference Collection," *Ident.News,* May 1976, p. 5.

Liva, "Refractive Index–Wavelength and Temperature Dependence," 29 *Microscope* 93 (1981).

Lloyd, "A Simple Density Gradient Technique for the Comparison of Glass Fragments," 9 *J.For.Sci.Soc.* 115 (1969).

McMinn et al., "Pyrolysis Capillary Gas Chromatography/Mass Spectrometry for Analysis of Automotive Paints," 30 *J.For.Sci.* 1064 (1985).

Paul, et al., "Reflection Spectra of Small Paint Samples: A Potential Solution," 16 *J.For.Sci.* 241 (1971).

Percy & Audette, "Automotive Repaints: Just a New Look?", 25 *J.For. Sci.* 189 (1980).

Pitts & Kratochvil, "Statistical Discrimination of Flat Glass Fragments by Instrumental Neutron Activation Analysis Methods," 36 *J.For. Sci.* 122 (1991).

Ryland & Kopec, "The Evidential Value of Automobile Paint Chips," 24 *J.For.Sci.* 140 (1979).

Schmitt & Smith, "Identification of Glass by Neutron Activation Analysis," 15 *J.For.Sci.* 252 (1970).

Siegel, et al., "Fluorescence of Petroleum Products," 30 *J.For.Sci.* 741 (1984).

Smalldon, "The Identification of Paint Resins and Other Polymeric Materials from the Infrared Spectra of Their Pyrolysis Products," 9 *J.For.Sci.Soc.* 135 (1969).

Smith, "A Quantitative Evaluation of Pigment Dispersions," 16 *Microscope* 123 (1968).

Tippett, et al., "The Evidential Value of the Comparison of Paint Flakes from Sources Other Than Vehicles," 8 *J.For.Sci.Soc.* 61 (1969).

VanHoven & Fraysier, "The Matching of Automotive Paint Chips by Surface Striation Alignment," 28 *J.For.Sci.* 463 (1983).

von Bremen & Blunt, "Physical Comparison of Plastic Garbage Bags and Sandwich Bags," 28 *J.For.Sci.* 644 (1983).

Wingard, "Video System for Glass Refractive Index Measurement," 21 *J.For.Sci.Soc.* 363 (1981).

Zeichner, Levin & Landau, "A Study of Paint Coat Characteristics Produced by Spray Paints from Shaken and Nonshaken Spray Cans," 37 *J.For.Sci.* 542 (1992).

Chapter 10

SPECTROGRAPHIC VOICE RECOGNITION

I. INTRODUCTION

I. INTRODUCTION

§ 10.01 Scope of the Chapter

Evidence of the identification of individuals by other individuals, based upon the sound of their voices, has long been accepted by the courts,[1] but in many cases the reliability of such identification may be seriously questioned. Some research has indicated that voice sound identification is even considerably less reliable than eye witness identifi-

---

§ 10.01

1. Generally, testimony by a witness that he recognized the accused by the sound of his voice is admissible, provided the witness has some basis for comparing the accused's voice with the voice identified by the witness as that of the accused: Pilcher v. United States, 113 Fed. 248 (5th Cir. 1902); People v. Smith, 36 Cal.2d 444, 224 P.2d 719 (1950); Ogden v. People, 134 Ill. 599, 25 N.E. 755 (1890); Commonwealth v. Williams, 105 Mass. 62 (1870); People v. Ward, 3 N.Y.Crim.R. 483 (1885); People v.

Strollo, 191 N.Y. 42, 83 N.E. 573 (1908). Uncertainty on the part of the witness affects only the weight of the testimony and not its admissibility. See, e.g., People v. Sica, 112 Cal.App.2d 574, 247 P.2d 72 (1952); Deal v. State, 140 Ind. 354, 39 N.E. 930 (1895).

On the admissibility of taped sound recordings, see: Anno., 58 A.L.R.2d 1024 (1958). See also, Conrad, "Magnetic Recordings in the Courts," 40 *Va.L.Rev.* 23 (1954); "Tape Recordings as Evidence," 17 Am.Jur.Proof of Facts 1.

cations. Within the last few decades, however, a scientific technique of voice recognition using the sound spectrograph was developed by Lawrence G. Kersta, formerly with the acoustics and speech research laboratory of the Bell Telephone Laboratories at Murray Hill, N.J.[2]

Spectrographic voice identification requires (1) a recording of the questioned voice, (2) a recording of known origin for comparison, and (3) a sound spectrograph instrument adapted for "voiceprint" studies.

A means of positively identifying individuals by their voices, relying on scientific instrumentation rather than on the frailty and untrustworthiness of human senses, would certainly be a most potent evidentiary tool in both civil and criminal cases. Public agencies, including rescue squads, fire stations, police departments, and medical facilities such as hospitals, routinely record most incoming calls. It may later become necessary to establish the identity of a particular caller whose voice has been recorded. In kidnapping cases, police frequently are able to obtain tape recordings of ransom demands and extortion threats. Thus, a scientific means to identify individuals by their voices could help tremendously in solving legal issues.

§ 10.02   Sound and Speech

Sound, like heat, can be defined as a vibration of air molecules or described as energy in the form of waves or pulses, caused by vibrations. In the speech process, the initial wave producing vibrations originate in the vocal cords. Each vibration causes a compression and corresponding rarefications of the air, which in turn form the aforementioned wave or pulse. The time interval between each pulse is called the frequency of sound; it is expressed generally in hertz, abbreviated *hz.*, or sometimes in cycles-per-second, abbreviated *cps*. It is this frequency which determines the pitch of the sound. The higher the frequency, the higher the pitch, and vice versa.

Intensity is another characteristic of sound. In speech, intensity is the characteristic of loudness. Intensity is a function of the amount of energy in the sound wave or pulse. To perceive the difference between frequency and intensity, two activities of air molecules in an atmosphere must be considered. The speed at which an individual vibrating molecule bounces back and forth between the other air molecules surrounding it is the frequency. Intensity, on the other hand, may be measured by the number of air molecules that are being caused to vibrate at a given frequency. We can understand the difference between frequency and intensity even easier by imagining a gong that is being struck with a hammer. The force with which the gong is struck determines intensity: the loudness of the sound produced. The harder the strike, the louder the sound. Frequency, on the other hand, consists of the speed with which the sound vibrates; it determines the pitch of the sound. The pitch will remain the same no matter how hard the gong is struck.

---

2. For a history of "voiceprint" recognition, written by a current practitioner and researcher, see, Truby, "Voiceprint Identification: Speechpattern Matching and Differentiation," *Identification News*, Apr. 1985, p. 3.

The human voice, unlike the gong, is capable of a very wide range of pitches and intensities. But that is not the only thing that makes it different from the gong. The human voice is incapable of producing one pitch (or frequency) at a time. Instead, all speech is composed of several frequencies produced simultaneously. The lowest pitch or frequency is called the fundamental and is accompanied by several overtones, each having frequencies which are even multiples of the fundamental. It is these overtones that give the voice its tonal quality.

The frequency at which air particles vibrate (the frequency of the sound source) is also the frequency of the sound wave. If that frequency falls roughly between 60 cps and 16,000 cps, the air vibration can be perceived by the human ear as "sound." There exist sound waves at much higher frequencies, but our human hearing mechanism is not equipped to perceive them.

Not all creatures hear within the same frequency ranges as do human beings. Everyone is familiar, for example, with the "silent" dog whistles. The whistle emits a sound of a frequency that human ears cannot perceive, yet the hearing mechanism of the dog is equipped to receive it. Bats use high frequency sound waves to locate their prey, much as we "perceive," by the use of radar, targets on a screen that may be invisible because hidden by fog.

If a sound wave strikes another medium, the energy from the sound wave causes this new medium to vibrate. An example of this might be the passing of a heavy truck in front of a house which causes the windows to vibrate. This is the same principle upon which the human ear functions. The sound waves in the air cause the eardrum to vibrate. The vibrating motion of the eardrum is then converted into nerve impulses which are sent to the brain where the impulses are "perceived" as sounds which we hear. Just as the brain can record sound, as sound, in our memory, so can we devise instruments that record sound waves as visual patterns. By looking at the "output" of these machines, much as we might consult our memory, we can "see" sound, or at least observe a pictorial representation of sound. The sound spectrograph is such an instrument.

§ 10.03 The Sound Spectrograph

The sound spectrograph is an electromagnetic instrument which produces a graphic display of speech in the parameters of time, frequency and intensity. The display is called a sound spectrogram. The sound spectrograph made its appearance in 1941, as a result of communications research in the Bell Telephone Laboratories. It was devised as a tool for basic studies of speech and signals as they relate to communications services, and has come to be widely used in many laboratories for research studies of sound, music, and speech.

To operate the instrument, a speech sample is recorded onto a magnetic tape loop which can be played back continuously. The sound spectrograph "reads" the various frequencies of the sound as a variable filter changes settings and an electric stylus simultaneously records the output onto electrically sensitive paper which is affixed to a rotating drum.[1]

For two sounds to be absolutely identical, they must be composed of the same sound wave frequencies and the same intensities. A sound once made, however, can never be duplicated in all of its characteristics. But duplication of all characteristics is not required. Variance in intensity, for instance, does not affect frequency (pitch) and is therefore not a particular hindrance to comparison of the frequency ranges of two samples of sound.

While working for the Bell System, Lawrence G. Kersta adapted the sound spectrograph to the process of identifying individuals by their speech, creating what he called the "voiceprint" identification method. Kersta started his research from the unproven hypothesis that each person's voice is as unique as his fingerprints when the voice is subjected to spectrographic analysis.

The term "voiceprint identification" was coined by Kersta and became a company trademark. Because of its popular appeal and its similarity to "fingerprint identification" the term caught on readily, so that, to date, the entire field of spectrographic voice recognition is (erroneously) being referred to by its proponents and opponents, in the literature, and by the courts, as the field of "voiceprint identification." Indeed, Kersta frequently compared voice spectrograms to fingerprints, a comparison which is most unfortunate and entirely improper but which appeared to give "voiceprints" a face value which it had not earned. Fingerprints have a degree of permanency and unchangeability that voice spectrograms lack. Identification of fingerprints, assuming competent comparison and an adequate latent print, is positive and practically infallible; voice spectrogram identification, on the other hand, has been proven wrong in an uncomfortable number of cases and the chances of error are, as of now, unacceptably high when the criminal conviction of an individual is based solely on it. Fingerprint identification is generally accepted as an accurate means of personal identification, whereas the acceptability of identifying individuals by sound spectrograms is still very much in issue. It would, therefore, be far more accurate to abandon the term "voiceprint identification" to describe the technique itself and use spectrographic voice recognition as an alternative.[2]

§ 10.03

1. The technique of making sound spectrograms is explained in some detail in People v. King, 266 Cal.App.2d 437, 72 Cal. Rptr. 478 (1968), and in Cornett v. State, 450 N.E.2d 498 (Ind.1983), both of which held the test results inadmissible. See also, Truby, op. cit., supra note 2, section 10.01.

2. Dr. Henry M. Truby, a "voiceprint" proponent, concedes that use of the term "voiceprint" is inaccurate, albeit more popularly remembered. See, Truby, op. cit., supra note 2, section 10.01, at 4. Courts have recognized the inappropriateness of comparing voice comparisons with fingerprint identifications. See, e.g., United States v. Baller, 519 F.2d 463 (4th Cir. 1975), cert. denied 423 U.S. 1019 (1975). In footnote 1, the Court admitted that "The use of the term 'voiceprint,' with its overtones of 'fingerprint,' gives voice spectrographic identification an aura of absolute certainty and accuracy which is neither justified by the facts nor claimed by experts in the field."

II. THE SPECTROGRAPHIC VOICE RECOGNITION PROCESS

§ 10.04   Theory of Voice Uniqueness

The claimed uniqueness of speech results from the process by which human speech is produced physiologically and from the process whereby one learns to speak. Kersta contended that voice individuality is founded in the mechanism of speech. The parts of the vocal tract which determine voice uniqueness are the vocal cavities and the articulators. The vocal cavities are resonators which, much like organ pipes, cause energy to be reinforced in specific sound spectrum areas dependent upon their sizes. The major cavities affecting speech are the throat, nose, and two oral cavities formed in the mouth by positioning of the tongue. The contribution of the vocal cavities to voice uniqueness lies in their size and in the manner in which they are coupled, with the likelihood being remote that two persons will have all vocal cavities of the same size and identically coupled.

A still greater factor in determining voice uniqueness, according to Kersta, is the way in which the articulators are manipulated during speech. The articulators include the lips, teeth, tongue, soft palate, and jaw muscles, whose controlled dynamic interplay result in intelligible speech, something that is not a spontaneous process but a studied process of imitation and trial and error.

Kersta contended that the chance that two individuals would have the same dynamic use patterns for their articulators would also be remote, and his overall claim to voice pattern uniqueness when submitted to the sound spectrograph rests on the improbability that two speakers would have vocal cavities dimensions and articulator use patterns identical enough to confound "voiceprint" identification methods.[1]

The underlying premise of voice uniqueness upon which spectrographic voice recognition is based has never been empirically established. Further, the invariability of speech patterns of an individual when attempts are made to alter, muffle, mimick, or disguise the voice, has been explored only tentatively and not in any large-scale scientific research effort. There is also no authoritative data on the effect of voice spectrograms of use of dentures, the effects of background noise, emotional state, puberty, and the like. Since translation of speech into unique voice spectrograms depends, as Kersta explained, on the size of the vocal cavities and their "dynamic interplay" with articulator use

---

§ 10.04

1. See, e.g., the articles authored by Kersta listed in § 10.09 (Bibliography) at the end of this chapter. It was noted in People v. King, 266 Cal.App.2d 437, 72 Cal. Rptr. 478 (1968) that Kersta, who made these claims in his early publications as well as when testifying as an expert witness, had no formal training in the field of physiology, acoustical sciences, audiology, or anatomy which would permit him to justify these claims from his own educational background. The King court found him not qualified as an expert in these fields, pointing to Kersta's background in electrical or electronics engineering.

patterns, little research has been done on the effect upon speech recognition of changes in the size of the vocal cavities because of teeth extraction, dental abscesses, nasal congestion, holding one's nose, speaking while eating, etc.

While research in related commercial applications of voice identification systems based on computer-driven speech-recognition programs seems to assume the premise of voice uniqueness,[2] it at the same time recognizes the fallibility of the systems that have been developed by illustrating speech spectrograms of the sentences "It's hard to recognize speech," and "It's hard to wreck a nice beach," that appear indistinguishable.[3] Despite these limitations, speech recognition programs are destined to become a major factor in the way mail-order business is going to be run in the near future. At some U.S. Postal Service branches, zip codes are read off labels on large sacks and spoken into microphones; calling-card frauds will be reduced by storing a "voiceprint" of each customer; telephone company computers are taught to recognize "yes" or "no" when a customer is being asked to accept a collect call; voice-activated dialing is already available on some cellular telephones; voice-recognition computers of direct marketers will accept calls from their dealers.

§ 10.05   "Voiceprint" Methodology

To apply these principles, Kersta initially used two different kinds of voice spectrograms: bar spectrograms, showing the resonance bars of the voice with dimensions of time, frequency and loudness, and contour spectrograms, measuring levels of loudness, time and frequency in a shape much like a topographical map. The two different types of voice spectrograms are illustrated in Figure 1. After considerable experimentation, Kersta determined that bar spectrograms afforded much better results in matching known and unknown speech samples. Contour spectrograms, on the other hand, are deemed more useful for computerized spectrographic voice classification.

2. Schwartz & Hammond, "A Computer That Recognizes Its Master's Voice?," *Business Week*, June 3, 1991 at 130, states, in describing speech-recognition hardware and software now being developed for powerful but inexpensive desktop computers that means billions of dollars of income to hi-tech companies: "Since a voice is as unique as a fingerprint, phone cheats would be foiled."

3. If lack of expertise is supposed to account for an inability to distinguish differences, refer to § 10.05, infra, wherein Kersta sought to validate his method by using non-expert high school children. The *Business Week* article describes limited-application programs that are said to work adequately. Thus, a computer program designed to accept hotel reservations "would understand a customer who says, 'I want to check in.' But, if it were programmed to take fast food orders, it might understand the sentence as 'I want two chicken.' " Id. at 131.

 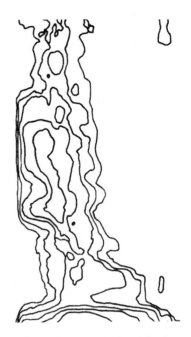

Fig. 1. The illustration on the left is a bar voiceprint; the one on the right is a contour voiceprint. In today's voiceprint instruments, bar prints are used almost exclusively. *Courtesy: Lawrence C. Kersta, Somerville, N. J.*

To arrive at a conclusion of identity, or lack of it, it is required that a recording of questioned speech and a recording of known speech be available.

Initially, to compare both for the purpose of determining whether the questioned speech was produced by the suspect, the spectrographic impressions of ten commonly used English cue words found in the questioned speech were visually compared with the spectrographic impressions of these same cue words in the known speech sample. The cue words used by Kersta were: *the, to, and, me, on, is, you, I, it* and *a.* If the spectrographic impressions of these words matched to a sufficient degree in both samples, Kersta concluded that both speech samples were uttered by the same individual. Of course, the method is not restricted in its use to cases where the so-called cue words are present or when the speech is in the English language only. The "voiceprint" technique theoretically can be used for speech in any language; in fact, it has been suggested that identifications can be made when a person speaks one language in the unknown sample of speech and different language in the known sample, as long as similar *sounds* be present in both samples.

After a number of years of work with the technique, technicians have concluded that the use of cue words as suggested by Kersta is wholly inadequate and unreliable. The technique now used compares the unknown speech sample with sound spectrograms of known speech samples containing precisely the same language.

As early as 1962, Kersta claimed that in over 50,000 tests he obtained a percentage of accuracy greater than 99%.[1] Such a percentage of accuracy in his findings has never been claimed by any other researcher in the field. Indeed, as will be evident in the following sections, it is greatly at odds with findings in controlled research.

Kersta also conducted a study to demonstrate that there are certain individual traits in the quality of the voices of individuals even when speech producing mechanisms may be expected to be similar and when environmental effects are alike, as in the case of identical twins. In promotional literature of Voiceprint Laboratories distributed by Kersta in 1969, he asserted that the individuality of these traits could be detected even by the untrained. His panel of testers consisted of two seventeen-year old high school girls, who prior to the experiment had no knowledge of "voiceprint" techniques and whose scientific background consisted of standard high school science courses. Their only instruction in the technique was that they were to look for a pattern that looked most similar to another pattern in comparing spectrograms.

The voice samples used in the study were those of fifteen pairs of fraternal male twins, and fifteen pairs of fraternal female twins. Fraternal twin voices were selected to enable the panelists to gain familiarity with the technique and note familial likenesses. A second group of voice samples came from thirty identical twins. All twins, fraternal and identical, were under twelve years of age so that uniqueness of the voice at pre-puberty would at the same time be demonstrated.

The high school testers had an overall identification success score of 87%, according to Kersta, with an 84% score on female voices and a 90% score on male voices. Kersta then repeated the experiment using a female tester who had, at that time, eight months of experience in spectrographic voice identification and who was employed in his office, but who never studied voices of identical twins. Kersta reported in the same promotional literature that this technician identified sixty identical twins with only one error. Later experiments by others did not yield comparable successes; the Kersta methodology also would come under severe criticism in subsequent research.

In describing the process of comparing sound spectrograms in a recent article, Dr. Truby states that "the significant essence of Voiceprint Identification is found in the **speechsound patterns** ... their similarities and resemblances, their dissimilarities and differences. Voiceprint Identification is primarily Speechpattern **Matching** ... and to a much lesser degree Speechpattern **Differentiation,** since the

---

§ 10.05

1. In one of Kersta's earliest articles, appearing in *Finger Print and Identification Magazine* of July, 1963, the claim of accuracy was stated as "greater than 90%." The editors of that journal acknowledged this to be a proofreading error and affirmed, in a private communication, that Kersta's manuscript did in fact state the figure 99% rather than 90%.

sources of pattern **differences** are—however predictably—manifold and complex." [2]

In completing a comparison, the examiner will make one of five decisions:

"(a) high level of confidence that the unknown and known voices belong to the same person,

(b) probability that the unknown and known voices belong to the same person,

(c) high level of confidence that the unknown and known voices belong to different persons,

(d) probability that the unknown and known voices belong to different persons, and

(e) no opinion one way or the other." [3]

III. EVIDENCE OF VOICE COMPARISONS BY SPECTROGRAMS

§ 10.06 Evaluation of Reliability

When Kersta first published a report on his voice spectrogram experiments, no one was in a position to challenge his claim of voice uniqueness with empirical data. For some time thereafter, it was also difficult to test the accuracy of his findings, since he did not initially make public the techniques he was using in his comparison. Very soon after the announcement of his system of "voiceprint" identification, a great number of other authorities attacked both his claims of voice uniqueness and the obtainable accuracy results. In fact, it might well be stated that the scientific community was united in denouncing spectrographic voice identification as of unproved worth. It was denounced from the witness stand in court as well as from the podium at professional meetings, though it needs noting that quite a few of these denouncers never had experience with the sound spectrograph and most of them admitted knowing little or nothing about Kersta's techniques.

Gradually, others commenced doing research in the same field. At the 80th meeting of the Acoustical Society of America in Houston, Texas, in November, 1970, Dr. Oscar Tosi of the audiology department at Michigan State University reported on his experiments with voice identification by visual inspection of spectrograms, based upon research conducted under a research grant obtained in 1968. He concluded that the

---

2. Truby, "Voiceprint Identification: Speechpattern Matching and Differentiation," *Identification News,* Apr. 1985, p. 3 at 4. (The quote is verbatim from the source, including the bold typeface and the ellipses which do *not,* in this quote, indicate deletions of text.)

3. Tosi, "Methods of Voice Identification for Law Enforcement Agencies," *Identification News,* Apr. 1981, at 6.

reliability of speaker identification varied according to the particular conditions included in the trial tests with a range of errors from .9% to 29.1%. He used as testers college students without extensive "voice-print" identification experience.

Tosi's findings did not produce a rate of accuracy approaching that which was claimed by Kersta. His tests were based on samples of speakers who did not attempt to disguise their voices. Dr. Tosi also concluded that the range of test errors had a tendency to discard the guilty rather than to accuse the innocent, but he suggested that extensive further testing would be necessary since the various persons participating in voice identification tests could not consistently approach the degree of accuracy claimed by Kersta.[1]

Since these early experiments, considerable additional research has been conducted. In the early 1970s, the work of Tosi and his collaborators in support of voice identification appeared to be swaying some of the earlier critics toward acceptance of the underlying principles. Later research, however, did not provide the solid confirmation that had been expected.[2]

The most significant study was one conducted by the National Academy of Sciences (NAS), at the request of the Federal Bureau of Investigation. The study group, composed of a number of eminent scientists and chaired by Dr. Richard H. Bolt, was asked to evaluate the accuracy of the "voiceprint" technique. In its report, *On the Theory and Practice of Voice Identification,* published in 1979, the Academy carefully refused to make a recommendation as to admissibility or inadmissibility of test results, believing this to be a legal decision not in its purview and competence. On the very important issues of technique reliability, and the basic underlying premise of voice uniqueness upon which the discipline rests, the report states that the assumption of the "voiceprint"

§ 10.06

1. Tosi, Oyer, Pedrey, Lashbrook & Nicol, "An Experiment on Voice Identification By Visual Inspection of Spectrograms," report delivered at 80th Meeting of the Acoustical Society of America at Houston, Nov. 1970. The report was the result of a two-year project conducted in the Department of Audiology and Speech Sciences, Michigan State University, and supported by a U.S. Dept. of Justice grant to the Michigan State Police. Later published reports on this and subsequent studies include: *Voice Identification Research*, (U.S. Dept. of Justice publication PR 72–1) Feb. 1972.

Tosi seemed to concede, in the reports, a 6% minimum rate of error. His findings do not appear highly probative of the theory of voice uniqueness in that the sampling of test students was from such a geographic diversity that voices were highly discernible. Might it not be expected that the rate of error would increase were the sampling of voice to originate from a homogeneous population group?

2. Indeed, in the first edition of our text, published in 1973, it was stated at p. 517, "It appears that at the current stage of development most of the earlier critics of the method are beginning to extend scientific acceptance to spectrographic voice identification." By 1978, however, when the second edition of this book appeared, the foregoing statement definitely did not represent the attitude in the professional fields of speech, audiology, phonetics, and acoustics—the fields involving studies of the voice by means of sound spectrographs. Cases, also, had become critical of the technique and we concluded in the 2d edition, on p. 583, that "it does not appear, at this time, that there is a sufficient basis for accepting either the principle of voice uniqueness or the reliability of the art of comparing speech spectrograms."

proponents, "that intraspeaker variability is less than ... interspeaker variability ... is not adequately supported by scientific data." The study group found a lack of agreement among speech scientists that the accuracy claims of the proponents would be representative of voice identifications made "under forensic conditions," and also stated that there has been, to date, insufficient data to let us conclude that sound spectrography can positively identify a speaker by a voice spectrogram.

The principal conclusion, as far as bearing on reliability of the technique and replicability of results obtained by any one examiner was stated thusly:

> "The degree of accuracy, and the corresponding error rates, of aural-visual voice identification vary widely from case to case, depending upon several conditions including the properties of the voices involved, the conditions under which the voice samples were made, the characteristics of the equipment used, the skill of the examiner making the judgments, and the examiner's knowledge about the case. Estimates of error rates now available pertain to only a few of the many combinations of conditions encountered in real-life situations. These estimates do not constitute a generally adequate basis for a judicial or legislative body to use in making judgments concerning the reliability and acceptability of aural-visual voice identification in forensic applications." [3]

Even though many courts had already extended recognition to the point of admitting test results in evidence, they were probably hasty in doing so. The initial belief of these courts that spectrographic voice recognition was generally accepted in the scientific community was an assumption that proved unfounded in fact. Whatever "general acceptance" existed, it was only among those few workers who had staked a career on practicing "voiceprint" identification. There certainly was no general acceptance of the identification technique as sufficiently accurate and reliable by the researchers in speech, audiology, phonetics, and acoustics. Yet, other than "voiceprint" identifiers, these are the scientists and professionals who are primarily occupied with studies of the voice and sound, and who use sound spectrographs in their research.

§ 10.07 Admissibility of Sound Spectrographic Test Results

To properly assess the value, as precedent, of prior cases dealing with "voiceprint" comparisons, the court decisions might be usefully divided into three time periods: (1) the early cases that were decided prior to the first critical look, in 1976, by the courts, at the "voiceprint" identification discipline; (2) the cases that followed this analysis of a community of experts who had staked their careers on advocating "voiceprint" reliability, but which preceded the National Academy of Sciences study group; (3) and the cases decided since the Academy's report was published.

---

3. From the previously discussed book,   *Identification* (1979), p. 60.
Bolt, *On the Theory and Practice of Voice*

1. EARLY CASES THROUGH 1976

The very first police application of spectrographic voice identification established a suspect's innocence. Spectrograms showed that he was not the depraved caller who had made violent death threats to a Connecticut family, even though the victims, upon hearing the suspect's voice, believed him to have been the caller. Subsequently, the true offender was found and he pleaded guilty.[1]

Kersta has testified on voice identification for the prosecution in a number of trials, beginning in 1966. The appellate courts, however, initially were far from enthusiastic on the issue of admissibility. The first state reviewing court to be confronted with the issue was the New Jersey Supreme Court in State v. Cary.[2] On an interlocutory appeal from an order compelling the defendant to submit to a sampling of his voice for "voiceprint" analysis, it was held that since a person's voice is a physical characteristic, such as fingerprints, and is not testimonial in character, it is not protected from compulsory disclosure by statutory or constitutional prohibitions against self-incrimination.[3] However, since an intrusion into one's privacy is an authorized search and seizure only when the product of the search has the capacity of being admitted in evidence in court, the tribunal remanded the case for a hearing to determine admissibility of "voiceprint" data.[4]

After reviewing the history of the sound spectrograph as well as the principles underlying "voiceprint" identification and the testimony of four experts who testified concerning the test, the court on remand held that the technique had not, of that date, attained such degree of scientific acceptance and reliability as to be acceptable in evidence.[5]

In an earlier appellate test involving the conviction of a young airman for making obscene telephone calls to two women working at an airbase hospital, the admission of voice spectrogram testimony at an Air

---

§ 10.07

1. Kersta, "Speaker Recognition and Identification by Voiceprints," 40 *Conn. Bar.J.* 586, 593 (1966).

2. 49 N.J. 343, 230 A.2d 384 (1967), on remand 99 N.J.Super. 323, 239 A.2d 680 (1968), cause remanded 53 N.J. 256, 250 A.2d 15 (1969), affirmed 56 N.J. 16, 264 A.2d 209 (1970), supplemented 56 N.J. 16, 264 A.2d 209 (1970).

3. The distinction between testimonial and non-testimonial evidence as affecting the applicability of the self-incrimination privilege springs from Schmerber v. California, 384 U.S. 757 (1966). In United States v. Wade, 388 U.S. 218 (1967) and Gilbert v. California, 388 U.S. 263 (1967), the United States Supreme Court held that to compel one to appear in a line-up, give an exemplar of his handwriting for handwriting comparison, or speak for voice identification purposes, was not within the prohibitions against compulsory self-incrimination of the Constitution.

4. The underlying reason given was one of fundamental fairness, the concept elaborated by the Supreme Court in Rochin v. California, 342 U.S. 165 (1952), which held that stomach pumping of a defendant constituted a fundamentally unfair means of obtaining evidence from an individual.

5. State v. Cary, supra note 2. See also, State v. Cary, 53 N.J. 256, 250 A.2d 15 (1969), supplemented 56 N.J. 16, 264 A.2d 209 (1970). In its third consideration of the admissibility of voiceprints, the New Jersey Supreme Court held the evidence inadmissible: State v. Cary, 56 N.J. 16, 264 A.2d 209 (1970).

Force Court Martial was held proper by the Air Force Board of Review.[6]

The most extensive early consideration given the spectrographic voice recognition technique by a reviewing court occurred in People v. King,[7] a prosecution arising as a consequence of the Watts area riots in Los Angeles of 1965.

On a nationwide CBS television program entitled "Watts, Riot or Revolt," there appeared an unidentifiable young black male who admitted participating in the riots and in burning a building. At some later date, the defendant in the *King* case was arrested on a narcotics charge. When he was booked, some information found on his person indicated he might have had contact with the CBS cameraman and the producer of the Watts program. Kersta identified King's voice, from a speech sample recorded during questioning in the county jail, as being the individual who participated in the CBS broadcast and had admitted participating in the burning of the building. Largely on the basis of this voice identification, King was convicted of arson.[8]

In an exhaustive analysis of the status of "voiceprint" identification, the California Court of Appeal reversed the conviction, holding that Kersta's claims for accuracy of the method were founded on theories and conclusions which were not yet substantiated by accepted methods of scientific verification.[9]

In late 1971 the first non-military appellate court to take a contrary position was the Minnesota Supreme Court. In State ex rel. Trimble v. Hedman,[10] that court upheld the use of voice spectrograms in criminal prosecutions as an aid in voice identification, at least insofar as the expert's opinion corroborates identification by means of the ear alone. Cognizant that two other state courts had declared the test results to be inadmissible, the Minnesota high court pointed out that since the date of these decisions much additional testing and research had occurred and that the technique now appeared "extremely reliable." [11] The court was apparently quite impressed by the fact that Dr. Tosi, who had appeared as a defense witness in the *Cary* case,[12] had switched sides and now had testified as a prosecution witness in the Minnesota trial.[13]

Thereafter, the courts remained divided on admissibility. Some decisions, interpreting *Trimble* to be broader than the opinion warranted, or minimizing the opposition, decided that sufficient progress had been made in voice spectrogram identification to warrant admission of

6. United States v. Wright, 17 U.S.C.M.A. 183, 37 C.M.R. 447 (1967). Judge Ferguson wrote a vigorous dissent.

7. 266 Cal.App.2d 437, 72 Cal.Rptr. 478 (1968).

8. Id.

9. Id.

10. 291 Minn. 442, 192 N.W.2d 432 (1971).

11. Id.

12. State v. Cary, supra note 2.

13. Other former critics have followed Tosi's example. On Feb. 1, 1972, Dr. Ladefoged, who was one of the most vocal early opponents of voiceprint identification and the defense expert witness in the *King* and *Trimble* cases, testified for the prosecution in United States v. Raymond, 337 F.Supp. 641 (D.D.C.1972). He has since also testified for the prosecution and defense in other cases as well.

test results.[14] Others held that the *Frye* test of general acceptance had not yet been met and refused to admit the test results in evidence.[15]

A significant decision was Commonwealth v. Lykus,[16] handed down in 1976, wherein the Massachusetts Supreme Judicial Court held that voice spectrographic identification evidence was admissible. In commenting on the relatively few experts who supported the technique, the Court said, "Limited in number though the experts may be, the requirement of the *Frye* rule of general acceptance is satisfied, in our opinion, if the principle is generally accepted by those who would be expected to be familiar with its use." [17] In support of that proposition, the court quoted from the *Williams* [18] decision involving Nalline test admissibility. The analogy was not entirely appropriate, since the Nalline test discussed in *Williams* was developed by doctors who worked in the narrow field of detecting drug addiction in individuals. Few medical doctors were so occupied, and for that reason the *Williams* court had held that not all medical doctors would be expected to be familiar with the test and to have generally accepted its validity.[19]

2. THE 1976–1979 PERIOD

The slow trend toward recognizing the admissibility of voice identification tests which had started with the *Trimble* case came to an abrupt halt when, in 1976 also, the California Supreme Court decided People v. Kelly.[20]

In *Kelly,* the court carefully examined the technique, the backgrounds of the proponents as well as opponents of the technique, and the extensive case law. It then squarely faced the issue of whether spectrographic voice identification had met the *Frye* test of general acceptance.

14. Worley v. State, 263 So.2d 613 (Fla. App.1972); Alea v. State, 265 So.2d 96 (Fla. App.1972); Hodo v. Superior Court, 30 Cal. App.3d 778, 106 Cal.Rptr. 547 (1973) overruled in People v. Kelly, infra note 20; United States v. Baller, 519 F.2d 463 (4th Cir.1975), cert. denied, 423 U.S. 1019 (1975); United States v. Franks, 511 F.2d 25 (6th Cir.1975); State v. Olderman, 44 Ohio App.2d 130, 336 N.E.2d 442, 73 O.O.2d 129 (1975); United States v. Williams, 443 F.Supp. 269 (S.D.N.Y.1977).

15. United States v. Addison, 162 U.S.App.D.C. 199, 498 F.2d 741 (1974); United States v. McDaniel, 176 U.S.App. D.C. 60, 538 F.2d 408 (1976); People v. Law, 40 Cal.App.3d 69, 114 Cal.Rptr. 708 (1974).

16. 367 Mass. 191, 327 N.E.2d 671 (1975).

17. Id. at 677.

18. People v. Williams, 164 Cal.App.2d Supp. 858, 331 P.2d 251 (1958), extensively discussed supra in Chapter 1, § 1.03.

19. The court was cognizant of the controversies which still existed in the field and indicated that "voiceprint" evidence would be subject to the closest judicial scrutiny, especially where it is the sole evidence of identity. Justice Quirico, in a concurring opinion, was "persuaded that the testimony of properly qualified expert witnesses as to the results of spectrographic analysis is, in the careful discretion of the trial judge, properly admissible in evidence," (327 N.E.2d at 679), though he said he was not entirely free from doubt. Justice Kaplan, in a separate opinion, was not persuaded of scientific validity at all, and made the suggestion that, in cases of this nature, "the law might preferably proceed by a 'commission' procedure to handle questions of validating new methods of scientific measurement or demonstration intended for use in a court room." (327 N.E.2d at 683.)

20. 17 Cal.3d 24, 130 Cal.Rptr. 144, 549 P.2d 1240 (1976).

In its unanimous decision, the court held that it had not been shown that the test had received general acceptance in the scientific community, but only among that limited group of individuals, most of whom were connected with a law enforcement agency, whose professional careers depended entirely upon acceptance of the reliability of the technique. Most of these persons, the court recognized, had impressive credentials, but they were those of technicians and law enforcement officers, not scientists. Recognizing that ongoing research might, some time in the future, cause the court to change its stance on the issue, the court decided that the proponents of the technique could not "fairly and impartially assess the position of the scientific community," [21] and held that spectrographic voice identification testimony was not admissible in California courts.

The *Kelly* court was not alone in suggesting that the testimony of persons whose career is staked on advocating the reliability of a technique might be insufficient to establish general scientific acceptance. The Pennsylvania Supreme Court, in Commonwealth v. Topa,[22] also held that the testimony of one expert witness who was a law enforcement officer and had made a career of testifying around the country on "voiceprint" issues was insufficient. "(H)is opinion, alone, will not suffice to permit the introduction of such scientific evidence into a court of law. Admissibility of the evidence depends upon the *general* acceptance of its validity by those scientists active in the field to which the evidence belongs." [23]

Agreeing with the Pennsylvania Court that the field in which spectrographic voice recognition belongs is that of the acoustical sciences, the Michigan Supreme Court, in 1977, sided with the California and Pennsylvania courts in holding that the technique had not been proven to be sufficiently reliable so as to be accepted within the scientific community. In People v. Tobey,[24] the Michigan court said that "general scientific recognition may not be established without the testimony of 'disinterested and impartial experts,' 'disinterested scientists whose livelihood was not intimately connected with' the new technique." [25] The two experts who had testified in this case, as in nearly every other case in the country, were Dr. Tosi and his close collaborator, Lt. Ernest Nash of the Michigan State Police. Nash was a pupil of Kersta and Tosi's assistant in the validation studies. The court concluded that, "Neither Nash nor Tosi, whose reputations and careers have been built on their voiceprint work, can be said to be impartial or disinterested." [26]

Following the *Kelly, Topa,* and *Tobey* cases, other courts began to look at voice recognition by means of the sound spectrograph in a more critical fashion than many older cases had done. As a result, a renewed

21. Id. at 38, 130 Cal.Rptr. at 153, 549 P.2d at 1249.

22. 471 Pa. 223, 369 A.2d 1277 (1977).

23. Id. at 1281.

24. 401 Mich. 141, 257 N.W.2d 537 (1977).

25. Id. at 539.

26. Ibid.

trend denying admissibility began to be noted,[27] though some courts continued to be satisfied that the results were admissible.[28]

3. POST–1979 NATIONAL ACADEMY OF SCIENCES STUDY

In the wake of the National Academy of Sciences study, concluding that the premises upon which "voiceprint" recognition and comparison was supposed to rest had not been empirically validated, and that the professed low error rates claimed by proponents of "voiceprint" recognition could not be substantiated in forensic practice,[29] it might have been expected that most courts would hold that "voiceprint" testimony was no longer admissible to prove the identity of a speaker. Furthermore, the Federal Bureau of Investigation had decided that, in the light of the National Academy of Sciences study it had commissioned and whose conclusions it had accepted, it would not offer any court testimony on speaker identity through spectrographic voice comparisons.[30] The "voiceprint" might thus have descended from its exalted level of court-admissible evidence to that of a valuable investigative tool designed to screen potential suspects, as has long been the status accorded the polygraph technique.

Nevertheless, this is not what happened. The earlier court trends, some going away from admissibility, others going toward it, continued. Courts, in assessing the merits or demerits of "voiceprint" comparisons, continued to "count noses" by adding up the cases for and the cases against, even though quite obviously most of the earlier decisions determining the technique was "reliable" were based on expert testimony from the "voiceprint" community only, without the benefit of dispassionate studies such as were conducted by the National Academy of Sciences.

In *Cornett v. State*,[31] and in *State v. Gortarez*,[32] state supreme courts held, in 1983 and 1984, that voice spectrography had not gained the degree of scientific respectability and reliability which ought to be required of court evidence of identity in a criminal case. The *Gortarez* court held that the relevant scientific community which must validate the technique ought not to be made up only of those individuals who use voice spectrograms for identification purposes, but ought to include disinterested and impartial scientists in many fields, possibly including acoustical engineering, acoustics, communications electronics, linguistics,

---

27. E.g., voice identification testimony based on spectrographic analysis inadmissible because the technique has not yet gained general scientific acceptance in the community of relevant experts: Reed v. State, 283 Md. 374, 391 A.2d 364 (1978).

28. E.g., speech spectrography or "voiceprint" evidence sufficiently reliable to qualify as "relevant" under state evidence code patterned after Federal Rules of Evidence: State v. Williams, 388 A.2d 500 (Me. 1978).

29. See § 10.06, supra, on an evaluation of the credibility of the technique.

30. See, Koenig, "Speaker Identification (Part 1)," *FBI Law Enf. Bull.*, Jan. 1980, p. 1. At p. 4, the author concludes by saying: "The FBI conducts voice identification examinations for Federal, State, and local law enforcement authorities for investigative purposes only and will not provide expert testimony."

31. 450 N.E.2d 498 (Ind.1983).

32. 141 Ariz. 254, 686 P.2d 1224 (1984).

phonetics, physics, and speech communications. In referring to the obvious bias of the proponents of the technique, whose livelihood depends on continued acceptance of the test results, the *Cornett* court recognized that only a small number of the same people "testify again and again in order to get this evidence admitted." [33] Referring to the failure of that group to convince their peers to join them in the "crusade," the opinion stated: "If the experts themselves cannot agree about the reliability of a scientific technique the courts should restrain its introduction because of potential harm and prejudice to the parties involved." [34] The two cases also noted that since the NAS study, no new data has been published to indicate its findings are now obsolete.

Another recent case, however, has taken a different approach. In State v. Wheeler,[35] the Rhode Island Supreme Court held that voice identification testimony by means of spectrographic analysis was properly admitted in the trial of two police officers accused of making false statements in connection with an investigation. The court said that such evidence may be admitted if (1) the trial court decides the evidence is relevant; (2) that the jury will be aided by hearing it; and (3) the witness is qualified as an expert.

The difference between the *Cornett* and *Gortarez* cases on the one hand, and the *Wheeler* case on the other, appears to hinge on whether the court uses, as the test for the admission of novel scientific evidence, the "general acceptance in the scientific community" test of Frye v. United States,[36] or whether the court rejects *Frye* in favor of a more relaxed, general relevancy test of admissibility. Yet, it is difficult to see how a test that identifies a defendant by a technique that is based on unproven premises, practiced according to protocols that are not scientifically respectable, by "experts" who are not scientists, can furnish evidence that is *relevant,* even when relevancy is rather loosely defined. The *Frye* rule had been severely criticized by many scholars and courts, yet, a select group of lawyers and scientists, brought together in a workshop sponsored by the National Conference of Lawyers and Scientists, unanimously rejected the idea that *Frye* was to be replaced with a broad and open relevancy concept such as Rule 401 of the Federal Rules of Evidence is said to be. This group strongly advocated that whatever the test selected by a court, it should be one wherein there is a

33. Cornett v. State, supra note 31, at 503.

34. Id. But the court found admission of the evidence to have been harmless error in light of other evidence. See also, Windmere, Inc. v. International Insurance Co., 105 N.J. 373, 522 A.2d 405 (1987), where the court found admission of voiceprints into evidence improper but not prejudicial error. Accord, State v. Free, 493 So.2d 781 (La.App.1986).

35. 496 A.2d 1382 (R.I.1985). See also, United States v. Baynes, 687 F.2d 659 (3d

Cir.1982), and State v. Williams, 4 Ohio St.3d 53, 446 N.E.2d 444 (1983) (citing A. Moenssens, et al., Scientific Evidence in Criminal Cases (1st ed. 1973)).

36. 293 Fed. 1013 (D.C.App.1923). For an extensive discussion of this issue, see Chapter 1, supra, § 1.03.

Suggesting that neither the *Frye* test nor the general relevancy test appropriately solves all legitimate concerns, see, Moenssens, "Admissibility of Scientific Evidence—An Alternative to *Frye,*" 25 *Wm. & Mary L. Rev.* 545 (1984).

requirement of a meaningful screening of novel scientific evidence by the court, for reliability and replicability.[37]

The NAS study, discussed earlier, represents about as clear a consensus by a body of respectable, well-credentialed, and impartial scientists as one can gather, that the "voiceprint" technique is to be approached "with great caution," and does not provide an adequate basis for believing it is reliable. It was widely viewed as "setting back" for years the field of voice analysis as an important new technique in police investigation.[38] Douglas Hogan, Director of the National Research Council of the NAS that conducted the study, said in an interview … that he did not want to dismiss "voiceprint" examinations as a bunch of nonsense, but asserted that the spectrographic voice recognition community might accomplish something "if they get their act together," and added, "in fact, you do have to get your act together!" In reviewing the voice identification study of NAS, Paul P. Rothstein, who served as a legal consultant, concluded that the report must be viewed as "a setback for the admissibility of voicegram evidence, at least until further studies are done."[39]

Rothstein also addressed some other concerns not dealt with in the report. He cited as a great deficiency the lack of adequate access of both the defense and prosecution to qualified experts. He also noted that the study points out how little is known about the accuracy of present methods of voice identification "in the real world outside the laboratory."[40]

Spectrographic voice recognition offers hope of becoming, possibly, a reliable means of establishing identity, but only if the claims of the originators of the "voiceprint" technique can be substantiated by reliable, unbiased research of the type that is still lacking, research that explores the many as yet unanswered questions referred to earlier. If intensive testing and experimentation in the matter continues, the substantiation may well come at some future date. But if admissibility is to hinge on whether the technique meets the new "reliability" standard for novel scientific methods, it is clear that, at this time, there is neither a sufficient basis for accepting the principle of voice uniqueness, nor the art of comparing voice spectrograms for the purpose of determining identity.[41]

37. See "Symposium on Science and the Rules of Evidence," 99 F.R.D. 187 (1983); also its follow-up symposium at 101 F.R.D. 599 (1983). The reports are discussed in Chapter 1 under § 1.03.

The Supreme Court ultimately rejected *Frye* as well in Daubert v. Merrell Dow Pharmaceuticals, 113 S.Ct. 2786 (1993), replacing it with a test which focuses on proof of "reliability" of the test results. Substituting proof of "reliability" as a condition for admissibility may place greater obstacles to admissibility than "general acceptance" required.

38. Moskowitz, "The Feds Voice Doubts About Voice Analysis," *Police Mag.,* Sept. 1979, p. 63.

39. Rothstein, "Voiceprint Report Will Change Law," *N.Y. Law Journal,* Apr. 20, 1979, at 26, col. 1.

40. Id.

41. In People v. King, supra note 7, Kersta was quoted as stating that voiceprint identification is an art and that his opinion as an expert is entirely subjective. This statement has been echoed by all examiners of the Kersta–Tosi school.

A further development must be noted that will have an impact of the credibility of voice spectrogram comparisons. There has been a considerable movement toward "enhancing" voice samples so as to make them more appropriate for examination purposes. The term "enhancement" by some will no doubt translate, for others, as "evidence tampering." Tosi has also reported the creation of a computer method of voice identification "that allows the use of different text for the unknown voices to perform a voice identification analysis." [42] The true impact on accuracy and reliability of this and other related studies, if any, remains to be determined.

§ 10.08   Expert Qualifications

When one looks at the experts who testified in favor of spectrographic voice identification in the early cases, at the time when admissibility was still a novel issue, we discover that just two or three individuals' names keep recurring in nearly all of the decisions: Kersta, the originator of the "voiceprint" technique, Ernest Nash, then with the Michigan State Police, a pupil of Kersta, and Dr. Oscar Tosi of Michigan State University, who collaborated with Nash on the LEAA-financed validation study mentioned earlier in this chapter.[1]

Dr. Tosi testified against the reliability of the technique in a few of the earliest cases,[2] before he had conducted his research project, but then began to testify for the prosecution, most frequently in conjunction with Nash, asserting that the "voiceprint" technique had been generally accepted.[3] It should be noted, however, that the "general acceptance" was conferred, not by disinterested scientists, but by Nash, Tosi, and Kersta, who established in 1972 the International Association of Voice Identification (IAVI). Both Nash and Tosi held the highest offices in this association, whose only purpose was to certify experts in "voiceprint identification."[4] Except for Tosi, no scientists were among its early members; the majority of them were, and still are, police officers who have been trained by either Kersta or Tosi to become "voiceprint" technicians. In 1980, the IAVI members voted to disband the organization and to apply for membership, on an individual basis, in the International Association for Identification (IAI), an organization composed

---

42. Tosi, "Methods of Voice Identification for Law Enforcement Agencies," *Identification News,* Apr. 1981, p. 6. See also, Lundgren, "Voice Prints," *Identification News,* Jan. 1978, p. 3, at p. 9, describing his work on a computer system called Semiautomatic Speaker Identification System (SASIS), which was dropped for a variety of reasons; and Bunge, "Forensic Voice Identification by Computers," *Inter. Crim. Pol. Rev.,* 254 (1979).

§ 10.08

1. For a detailed discussion of "the limited breadth of [Tosi's and Kersta's] experience and their potential bias," see, *Windmere* supra note 34, section 10.07, at 409.

2. E.g., State v. Cary, supra note 5, section 10.07.

3. The fact that Tosi had changed sides impressed the court greatly in State ex rel. Trimble v. Hedman, 291 Minn. 442, 192 N.W.2d 432 (1971), and caused it to conclude that the technique had gained general scientific acceptance. It probably had the same effect on other courts.

4. Lundgren, "Voice Prints," *Identification News,* Jan. 1978, p. 3, at 7. For the first three years of IAVI's existence, Nash was its president and Tosi its vice-president.

mainly of law enforcement officers in various disciplines, though primarily in fingerprint identification. After a sufficient number of the former IAVI members had applied for membership, the IAI created a subcommittee on voice identification of its Science and Practice Committee. Following in the wake of the IAI's certification program for fingerprint experts, the organization also instituted a Voice Identification and Acoustic Analysis Section certification program, modeled after the one IAVI had been conferring on its members before joining with IAI, which was given full faith and credit by IAI.[5]

As some of the courts have recognized, most of the IAVI members are law enforcement officers who have taken the courses which the organization sponsors and have been certified as "voiceprint" experts; they are not scientists. Since the certification program also certifies schools for training, and since only the schools or programs founded by the originators are on the approved list, it would appear that graduate or doctoral studies at accredited universities in speech, audiology, phonetics, or related sciences, coupled with a background of published research in respectable scientific journals on the use of the sound spectrograph, will not qualify for certification by IAVI/IAI.[6]

The underlying premise of the "voiceprint" identification program is that one cannot be certified in voice identification and acoustic analysis unless one believes in the premises that underlie the "voiceprint" technique. If one disagrees with IAVI advocacy on the as yet unverified principle of voice uniqueness, and if one does not believe that persons can be positively identified by their voices, one simply cannot be an expert.[7] Such an attitude of some key members reflects poorly on the other members who are concerned with professionalism and who favor an approach to spectrographic voice recognition research that is more scientifically respectable.[8]

---

5. See, "Voice Identification and Acoustic Analysis Section Certification Program," *Identification News*, Dec. 1982, p. 5. At that time, Tosi and Kersta were also among the 5 individuals sitting as the certification board. This source also indicates that the only approved schools are: one founded by Kersta, Tosi's institute at Michigan State University, and the Michigan State Police Voice Identification workshops. The latter is a newcomer, and prior to joining IAI, IAVI recognized only the Kersta and Tosi schools. See Lundgren, op. cit. note 4.

6. Officers of IAVI expressed an intention to write letters to defense attorneys seeking to employ such graduate audiologists or speech researchers, stating that they do not consider others qualified to testify in a court of law on the identification of voices. Lundgren, op. cit. note 4, stated that "This is the sort of thing we will do if it becomes necessary." Some IAVI members and/or supporters sought to block admission to membership of a respected scien-

tist attached to a major American university research institute, *to a different national professional organization,* by writing letters (in possession of co-author Moenssens) impugning the scientist's ethics by referring to the fact that he had testified against the validity of "voiceprint identification" in court as a defense expert!

7. Dr. Tosi, unhappy about the parochialism and proprietary appearance of IAVI, resigned in 1974 as director of the board and vice president, but rejoined again later, and became a member of the IAI voice identification board.

8. Small wonder that the Michigan Supreme Court, closest to the nerve center of IAVI at a time when that organization had sixteen "voiceprint" examiners, said in People v. Tobey, 401 Mich. 141, 257 N.W.2d 537, 539 (1977), that general scientific recognition "may not be established without the testimony of ... disinterested scientists whose livelihood was not intimately con-

The competence of some of the main proponents has been questioned by other proponents. In the Marin County, California, case of People v. Chapman, expert witness Nash, in 1973, matched the letter "E" in one voice spectrogram with the word "eight" in another and declared them to be from the same speaker. Tosi thereafter took the stand, stating that no such comparison was possible. When informed that an expert had matched them, but probably unaware that Nash had preceded him on the witness stand, Tosi stated, "Obviously the man is incompetent."[9] Tosi was also unable to make an identification on the basis of voice spectrograms used by Nash in the 1974 Michigan case of People v. Chaisson when the court asked him to do so. He stated the spectrograms were not usable "to attempt any kind of examination,"[10] although he did express the opinion of a "possible match" on the basis of new voice samples taken at the request of the court.[11] In Brown v. United States,[12] Tosi also testified that Nash had made an identification under circumstances one should never have been attempted.

The possibility of erroneous identifications cannot be ruled out, even when the technique is used by its own developer. There is at least one case where Kersta, himself, has been reported to have made an erroneous identification on the basis of which the subject of the test was discharged from his position as a deputy inspector of police. The official's voice had been identified by the voiceprint technique as being that of the individual who had made telephone calls to a known gambler. Later, another man is reported to have confessed to having made the call and his confession was corroborated by the "voiceprint" technique![13]

---

nected with the new technique," and that "(N)either Nash nor Tosi, whose reputations and careers have been built on their voiceprint work, can be said to be impartial or disinterested."

9. *Pacific Sun,* San Rafael, California, July 26, 1973, p. 5. Tosi, in his chapter titled "The Problem of Speaker Identification and Elimination," in Singh, ed., *Measurement Procedures in Speech, Hearing and Language,* 1975, at 428, reports only that "the Court ruled that Nash had produced several errors in the evidence he presented."

On previous occasions, Tosi had testified that there was only a "negligible" probability that Nash would make a mistaken identification: United States v. Raymond, 337 F.Supp. at 644; People v. Law, 40 Cal. App.3d at 78; Commonwealth v. Lykus, 327 N.E.2d at 677. See also, People v. Law, 40

Cal.App.3d 69, 80, 114 Cal.Rptr. 708, 715 (1974), where various experts discussed each other's rates of error.

10. Tosi, op. cit. note 9, at 428. Lundgren, op. cit. note 4, at 9, seems to suggest that Nash's experience was far superior to that of the primary investigator and scientific researcher in the field. He states, about this incident, "Dr. Tosi did not do the spectrograms as Nash did; he did not spend the time on the case, and he has not done that many criminal cases. Dr. Tosi is a scientist, a researcher; he is a professor."

11. At the request of the prosecution, the case was dismissed.

12. 384 A.2d 647 (D.C.App.1978).

13. "Use of Voiceprint in Court Proceedings Creates Legal Debate," *The Wall Street Journal,* Mar. 13, 1972, p. 1.

IV. MISCELLANEOUS

§ 10.09 Bibliography of Additional References

Articles cited in the footnotes are not repeated here.

Baldwin, "Phonetics and Speaker Identification," 19 *Med.Sci.Law* 231 (1979).

Boren, "Voiceprint—Staging a Comeback," 3 *U.San Fernando Valley L.Rev.* 1 (1974).

Bolt, et al., "Speaker Identification by Speech Spectrograms: A Scientist's View of its Reliability for Legal Purposes," 47 *J. Acoustical Soc. of Am.* 597 (1970).

Bolt, et al., "Speaker Identification by Speech Spectrograms: Some Further Observations," 54 *J. Acoustical Soc. of Am.* 531 (1973).

Cederbaums, "Voiceprint Identification: A Scientific and Legal Dilemma," 5 *Crim.L.Bull.* 323 (1969).

Comment, "The Evidentiary Value of Spectrographic Voice Identification," 63 *J.Crim.L., C. & P.S.* 343 (1972). An excellent analysis.

Heckler, et al., "Manifestations of Task–Induced Stress in the Acoustic Speech Signal," 44 *J. Acoustical Soc.Am.* 993 (1968).

Hennessy & Romig, "A Review of the Experiments Involving Voiceprint Identification," 16 *J.For.Sci.* 183 (1971).

Hollien & McGlone, "The Effect of Disguise on 'Voiceprint' Identification," 2 *J.Crim.Defense* 117 (1976).

Hollien, "Peculiar case of 'voiceprints'," 56 *J. Acoustical Soc. of Am.* 210 (1974).

Kersta, "Voiceprint Identification," 19 *Nature* 1253 (Dec. 29, 1962).

Manning, "Understanding Speaker Identification Techniques," *Trial Mag.,* Oct. 1981, p. 61.

Nash, "Voice Identification By the Voiceprint Technique," *Identification News,* Nov. 1971, p. 13.

Presti, "High–Speed Sound Spectrograph," 40 *J. Acoustical Soc. of Am.* 628 (1966).

Tosi, *Voice Identification Theory and Legal Implications,* 1979.

Williams & Stevens, "Emotion and Speech: Some Acoustical Correlates," 52 *J. Acoustical Soc.Am.* 1238 (1972).

CHAPTER 11

ACCIDENT RECONSTRUCTION

I. INTRODUCTION

I. INTRODUCTION

§ 11.01 Scope of the Chapter

The use of accident reconstruction technology in civil and criminal litigation involving vehicle accidents has dramatically increased in the past fifteen years.

In some motor vehicle accident cases, it is only through the use of an accident reconstructionist that a judge or jury can even begin to understand how and why the accident occurred. An accident reconstructionist may be able to determine the speed of the vehicles, who was driving, which vehicle was left of center, and may even be able to testify regarding human factors (including reaction and perception). These reconstruction techniques gain great importance when there are no eyewitnesses to the occurrence and when the only witnesses testifying are the opposing parties in the case. Where fatal accidents occurred, the ability of the deceased's counsel to present "his client's" side of the story is very tenuous and difficult. It is precisely in these cases that accident reconstruction can supply expert opinion evidence relevant to the issues available. It is this need for expert testimony in an accident case that has spawned the specialized field of accident reconstruction.

Accident reconstruction deals with various accepted and established laws of motion, mechanics, mathematics, algebra, geometry, physics, and other physical sciences. Basically, an accident reconstructionist examines the surroundings in which the motor vehicles were being operated, the physical makeup of the vehicles, the physical characteristics of the roadway upon which those vehicles were being operated and any outside influences that may have affected both the roadway and/or the motor vehicles.

Thus, the accident investigation expert will attempt to reconstruct the behavior of the vehicles both prior to and during the accident. This is done by means of deductions, inductions and inferences concerning the physical facts found at the scene of the occurrence. These physical facts are primarily, but not limited to, skidmarks, tire imprints, yaw marks, and of course the vehicle itself. By properly piecing together these bits of evidence, and correctly interpreting them, the accident reconstructionist can create for the court an accurate post-accident picture of how and why the accident occurred.[1]

§ 11.02 Background Information to Be Collected

In order for an accident reconstruction expert to formulate an accurate picture of how the accident occurred, it is necessary to gather as much background information as possible. This background information includes, but is not limited to, the types of vehicles involved, the environment in which the vehicles were being operated, and the human factors of both drivers prior to the accident.

In gathering information on the vehicles involved in an accident, the reconstructionist will want to have information on the type of vehicles involved (model and year), the various design characteristics of each (weight and dimensions), the speed at which the vehicles were travelling,

---

§ 11.01

1. This concept is by no means a novel one. After the discovery of the planet Uranus, Leverrier, the French mathematician, and others as well, calculated that the motion of the planet was slightly irregular. Leverrier sought to discover what was causing the irregularities in an unknown world which was nearly three billion miles away, and postulated that it was caused by the gravitational effect of another planet. This led to the discovery of another planet, Neptune, in 1846. All of his deductions were based on the accepted laws of motion and mechanics. The similarly accepted laws of motion and mechanics led to the development of missiles with which certain modern military jet aircraft are equipped. Such missiles can identify, track, and launch separate missiles simultaneously at six different attacking aircraft while the enemy force is still fifty miles or more away.

On the subject of accident reconstruction generally, see: Badger, "Reconstruction of Traffic Accidents," 9 *Am.Jur.3d Proof of Facts* 115 (1990); Van Kirk, "A Scientific Approach to Documenting Evidence for Accident Reconstruction," 29 *J.For.Sci.* 806 (1984); Whitnall & Playter, "The Nitty 'Griddy' of Accident Reconstruction," *Law Enf. Technology,* Jan. 1985, at 20; Chi & Vossoughi, "Engineering Aspect of Automobile Accident Reconstruction Using Computer Simulation," 30 *J.For.Sci.* 814 (1985); Lacy, *Scientific Automobile Accident Construction* (1966).

and the direction of travel of the vehicles. Other important information may include the point of first impact of the vehicles, locations where each came to rest, any modifications to any of the vehicles involved, any repairs that have been done, or needed to be done, and any mechanical problems associated with the vehicles.

The environment in which the vehicles were being operated at the time of the accident also provides important information. Weather conditions (rain, fog, snow), the physical surroundings of the accident scene, and the actual roadway conditions will all help the reconstruction expert in arriving at expert deductions. The reconstruction expert may also want to know if there had been any accidents at that scene prior to this accident. A recurring pattern of accidents at a particular point may very well depict a roadway design problem and not driver related negligence.

Human factors, or the conditions of both drivers, are also significant in accident reconstruction. Whether the drivers were intoxicated or under the influence of some substance, or impaired in any other way, or whether one of them fell asleep behind the wheel, may all be factors in determining how the accident occurred. The drivers' driving experience, emotional status, physical deficiencies and familiarity with the vehicle, road and surroundings also need to be evaluated.

II. THE INVESTIGATION OF ACCIDENTS

§ 11.03 Skidmarks

Skidmarks are marks left on the road surface by tires sliding over it. These marks are created by the abrasive action between the sliding tire (when the wheels are locked) and the road surface. Rubber particles are torn off the tire and the tire's temperature may increase anywhere from 200 degrees to one thousand degrees Fahrenheit depending on the composition of the tire. Natural rubber stays the coolest while synthetic rubber increases the most in temperature during skids. If the temperature becomes sufficiently high from friction, the tire literally melts. Skidmarks of tires may show, among other things, the speed, course and position of the vehicle and braking coordination between wheels.

Certain factors unrelated to the accident may affect skidmarks. After an accident has occurred, drivers of oncoming cars may not see the scene of the accident until they are very close. This may force them to apply their brakes, creating road surface marks which may obliterate those made by the vehicle or vehicles involved in the accident. All skidmarks and other road surface marks will eventually be worn away by traffic passing over them. Also, weather conditions such as rain, snow and wind wash off or blow away tire marks under varying conditions. Some road surface marks are visible because they contain particles with moisture in them. When the sun dries up these particles, the marks start to disappear. Other factors such as road repair work right after the accident or sweeping the area to remove broken glass and debris will affect the road surface marks.

When commencing an inspection of the locale, one may encounter difficulties in determining where skidmarks begin. Since accurate measurements are needed to arrive at a meaningful conclusion, it is important that the measuring practices be carefully explored. Skidmarks are measured from the terminal point backward. The marks created by the front wheels must be distinguished from those created by the rear wheels. Also, each tire mark must be measured separately as all four wheels may not lock at the same time; the length of the skidmark is the average length of the marks of all four wheels. Usually the rear wheels are slightly misaligned from those of the front wheels, but if there is a perfect overlap, the wheelbase of the vehicle is used to determine front and rear wheel marks.

Some skidmarks appear curved. This may be caused by unequal braking pressure on the wheel, as well as by a driver attempting to compensate for skidding by turning the steering wheel, or by the slope of the road, or even by variations in the pavement drag resistance.

What appears to be a curved skidmark may, in fact, be a yaw mark.[1] A tire creates a yaw mark as it tries to rotate in one direction while sliding in another.[2] The striations or force lines in skidmarks are parallel with the mark. The striations in a yaw mark are oblique to the mark.

Skips in skid marks must be distinguished from gaps between successive skidmarks. Skips are created when the skidding vehicle hits a bump or hole in the road and starts bouncing. The initial skid in such a case is sometimes more than a yard long. Skips are included in the measurement of a skidmark because the tires incur increased resistance when they jump up and come back down, which compensates for the lack of friction while they are in the air. Gaps in skidmarks are longer than skips. Gaps usually result from releasing or pumping the brakes. They should be measured and the marks treated separately.

Since skidmarks are important in calculating the speed of the automobile, as well as being an elementary step in reconstructing the accident, one other problem facing the accident reconstructionist is the advent of anti-lock braking systems (ABS) installed into many of today's automobiles. Unlike older braking systems in which the brakes would "lock up" the wheels during a sudden, hard braking situation, anti-lock brakes are designed to prevent such locking up. Instead of closing and locking, the braking calipers around the brake disc—the cause for the brakes locking and the vehicle skidding—anti-locking braking calipers pulsate many times per second to avoid locking up and skidding. These new braking systems prevent locking up and allow maneuverability in

§ 11.03

1. Badger, "Reconstruction of Traffic Accidents," 9 *Proof of Facts 3d 115*, 136 (1990). Yaw marks are sometimes called scrubs, scuffs or sideslip marks.

2. Id.

difficult braking conditions. While an important safety feature for drivers, since the anti-lock brakes prevent a car from skidding, they deny the reconstructionist information regarding the initial point at which the driver applied his brakes.

§ 11.04   Tire Imprints

Tire imprints are marks left on the road surface by tires that are rolling over it. These imprints may be made by depositing matters previously picked up, by wiping aside wet or viscous substances on the paved highway surface, or by making an impression in soft materials such as wet clay, gravel, mud, sand, or snow. They show, among other things, the course and position of a vehicle (whether on the wrong side of the road), whether the vehicle failed to stop at an intersection, or signal that the brakes on the wheel were not being applied or not holding.

Tire imprints, which may appear to be skidmarks under some conditions, are distinguished from skidmarks in several ways: (1) tire imprints show the tire tread, whereas skidmarks appear slick and smooth; (2) tire imprints are uniform in intensity and in degree, whereas skidmarks are likely to be darker or more prominent at their beginnings and ends; (3) the appearance of "stipples" is highly characteristic of tire imprints; such stipples are made when a tire, rolling through a viscous substance such as oil or slime, pulls up little points of the sticky material as it passes through; (4) splatters of bits or mud on each side of the tire are also characteristic of tire imprints because a rolling tire creates these marks by squirting wet substances from its treads as they press down on the roadbed, whereas sliding tires do not squirt the substance out but splash it to each side.

Tire imprints are not as affected by driver actions, as are skid marks. While skid marks will only occur once the driver applies the brakes, and the car's wheels lock up, tire imprints are left simply by the mere physical characteristics of the tire and the road surface. A tire imprint will be the same under varying conditions because they are nothing more than a picture of the tire tread and its physical characteristics.

§ 11.05   Scuff Marks

Scuff marks are marks left on the surface by tires that are both sliding and rolling over it, or that are rolling and slipping sideways at the same time. In other words, they are a combination of tire imprints and skidmarks. They may show the speed of a vehicle in a curve, whether a vehicle had a blowout or a flat tire, how far and in which direction a vehicle was knocked sideways in a collision, etc. Side scuffs occur when the rolling wheel is sliding to one side. Critical-speed scuff marks are side scuffs left when a vehicle is taking a curve at a critical speed, which is the sharpest turn it can make at that speed without skidding off the road. Scuff marks are usually made only by the outside edges of the outside front and rear tires and show a pattern similar to the milled edge of a coin.

§ 11.06 Scratches, Gouges, and Holes

Scratches are made by damaged solid parts of the vehicle other than the tires when they cut into, press into, or slide along the paved surface. They indicate the course of movement of the vehicle, ordinarily after impact; they also may indicate the position of the vehicle when the impact occurred. Scratches may also indicate that a vehicle overturned, because vehicles sliding along on their side or top leave distinctive scratches made by their trim, bumpers, door handles, and other protruding parts: they often contain minuscule samples of paint of the vehicle which can be compared with paint samples of known origin; and they may show the force and direction of impact. Scratches made before a collision, indicating that a part or parts of the vehicle broke down, may show the cause of the accident. Wheel rim scratches occurring before the collision point may show that a flat tire or blow-out caused the accident.

Gouges are like scratches, but are deeper and wider. Rather than merely tearing or separating road surface materials, gouges chip chunks out of it. They often appear at the collision point in a head-on accident, where the colliding vehicles dug in with great force in meeting. Groove gouges are made by bolts or other similar elongated vehicle parts which dig into the surface and scoop parts of it out. If the groove curves or appears in a wavy line, it may indicate the vehicle was starting to spin at the time. Chop gouges are made when broad sharp edges of parts such as cross frame members or transmission housing hit the pavement while moving. The chop gouge is usually followed by a broad rubber scratch running in the direction of vehicle movement.

When vehicle wheels roll in snow, mud, moist soil, or clay, ruts are made. Furrows are similar to ruts, but differ in that furrows are made by sliding wheels or other vehicle parts. They often are a continuation of skidmarks after the vehicle left the paving. Holes, which may be found at the end of ruts, furrows, skidmarks, or scuffs, are made when vehicle wheels or parts move sideways and scoop out broad pits in the earth. They are usually a foot or so in depth and one or two feet wide. They tend to show a pivotal point on which a vehicle started to spin or began to roll over.

Debris left by the accident, and rust, paint, or small vehicle parts, vehicle fluids, solid or liquid cargo, blood, etc., may indicate a number of things to the trained investigator other than the path of the vehicle as it moved along.

§ 11.07 Speed Estimation From Skidmarks and Yaw Marks

The speed of a vehicle on a level surface may be determined from both skidmarks and yaw marks. Speed determination from a yaw mark is generally more accurate than one from a skidmark.[1] Many factors need be considered in making speed determinations such as the weight of the vehicle, tire pressure, wind velocity, tire tread pattern, pavement

---

§ 11.07

1. Badger, supra § 11.03, note 1 at 137.

temperature, etc. The attorney who needs detailed information about this technique is advised to consult the sources referred to in the bibliography which follows this section. There is an established science/art of estimating the speed of vehicles and reconstructing what happened at accidents of collisions by the evidence left at the scene. The Traffic Institute at Northwestern University, in Evanston, Illinois, has long been a pioneer in research and education on accident reconstruction and has trained many excellent specialists. The Institute of Police Technology and Management (IPTM) at the University of North Florida in Jacksonville, Florida, also provides management and traffic training to approximately 12,000 municipal, county, state and federal law enforcement officers per year. Many of IPTM's courses and publications deal with the field of accident reconstruction. Both institutes can be contacted for advice in appropriate circumstances.

III. LEGAL STATUS OF ACCIDENT RECONSTRUCTION

§ 11.08 Admissibility of Accident Reconstruction Evidence

Most jurisdictions today allow the testimony of accident reconstruction experts, albeit with some restrictions and exceptions. Most jurisdictions leave admission up to the sound discretion of the trial judge.[1] The rules of evidence allow for the introduction of evidence that is relevant to the matter in controversy, as long as the expert is qualified, the testimony assists the trier of fact or meets the applicable test for the admission of scientific evidence, and the probative value of the expert's testimony is not outweighed by prejudice.

A lay witness usually may only testify to his or her sensory perceptions. A lay witness may testify under certain circumstances in the form of an opinion. The Federal Rules of Evidence and the evidence codes of most states permit opinion testimony by lay witnesses when the witness cannot readily communicate what he has perceived without resorting to opinion, or if the witness won't mislead the finder of fact, or if the witness doesn't possess special knowledge, skill, experience or training. Even lay opinions must meet certain predicates before they are admitted. For example, in Lawlor v. State,[2] a manslaughter case, the lay witness resided approximately 100 feet from the highway where a collision occurred. He testified he was inside his house and heard a car pass at a very high speed. He stated the car was travelling so fast that he did not hear it approach. Approximately two seconds after it passed he heard the impact of the collision. The Court found that the testimony was improperly admitted because there was no sufficient predicate laid for

§ 11.08

1. Reed v. United States, 584 A.2d 585 (D.C.App.1990) (decision whether to allow expert testimony concerning causes of injury in vehicle accident within the discretion of the trial court and will only be overturned if the ruling was manifestly erroneous); Dixon v. International Harvester Co., 754 F.2d 573 (5th Cir.1985) (The court has discretion in determining whether an expert is qualified to testify).

2. 538 So.2d 86 (Fla.App.1989).

his testimony. The court stated that an opinion as to the speed of the vehicle should be predicated on certain identifying factors such as the weight of the respective vehicles involved, road conditions, and the coefficient of friction.[3]

In Wicks v. Commonwealth of Pennsylvania, Department of Transportation,[4] appellant argued that the court erroneously permitted a lay witness to estimate the speed of the motorcycle at the time of the accident. Citing to Radogna v. Hester,[5] the court held that a lay witness' testimony as to speed depends on the overall opportunity for adequate observation and the witness' experience with moving vehicles. The lay witness was passed approximately 250–300 feet before the accident and had been driving that piece of road for 25 years to and from work. The court held that the lay witness was in an excellent position to observe the accident, thus he was properly allowed to testify.

Fieser v. Snyder [6] arose out of a collision between defendant's Jeep and plaintiff's three-wheeled all-terrain-vehicle. At trial the investigating police officer testified as to the scene of the accident and the presence of skidmarks. Plaintiff sought to exclude the officer from testifying because he was not qualified as an expert. The Missouri Court of Appeals upheld the trial court's decision to allow the officer to testify. The Court held that the officer did not testify where the accident occurred; rather he testified as to the presence and existence of skid marks which tend to designate the location of the vehicles on the road. The Court of Appeals held that a lay witness may testify about perceptible facts that may tend to describe where an accident happened. Therefore, the officer did not need to be qualified as an expert in order to give his testimony.

The testimony of an accident reconstruction expert is properly admissible even if there is eyewitness testimony where it is necessary to rely on the expert's knowledge and the application of principles of physics, engineering and other sciences beyond the ken of the average juror.[7]

In Rios v. Navistar International Transportation Corp.,[8] the operator of a tractor brought an action against the manufacturer of the

---

3. 538 So.2d at 88, citing Brown v. State, 477 So.2d 609 (Fla.App.1985).

4. 139 Pa.Cmwlth. 336, 590 A.2d 832 (1991).

5. 255 Pa.Super. 517, 388 A.2d 1087 (1978).

6. 797 S.W.2d 752 (Mo.App.1990).

7. Palmer v. Craig, 246 Ill.App.3d 323, 186 Ill.Dec. 237, 615 N.E.2d 1294 (1993); See also, People v. Rushton, 254 Ill.App.3d 156, 193 Ill.Dec. 827, 626 N.E.2d 1378 (1993), appeal denied (1994).

8. 200 Ill.App.3d 526, 146 Ill.Dec. 289, 558 N.E.2d 252 (1990). (The court also held that the trial court did not abuse its discretion in admitting a videotape of an experiment designed to test whether the tractor operator's striking range lever could engage transmission without use of the clutch when the tractor was in first or second gear, even though the experiment took place nine years after the plaintiff's accident, at which time the tractor had been "reconditioned." The court upheld the admissibility of the experiment since it duplicated "essential conditions" of the accident and the tractor manufacturer's witness established that repairs to the tractor did not involve the transmission. "Essential conditions" need not involve exact duplication of accident conditions, although, if

tractor for injuries sustained when the tractor rolled over his leg. The appellate court affirmed the trial court's holding for the manufacturer stating that the trial court did not abuse its discretion in admitting accident reconstruction testimony. The court stated that such testimony would not be allowed in products liability actions where available physical evidence or eyewitness testimony is sufficient for the jury to draw its own conclusion. However, it may be allowed in addition to eyewitness testimony when matters in the case involve scientific principles beyond the understanding of the jury and the expert testimony will assist the jury in understanding those principles. The court reiterated the holding in Augenstein v. Pulley,[9] in which the court stated that the availability of eyewitness testimony should be considered as merely one factor in determining whether the expert's testimony will aid the fact finder in arriving at a just result. The court believed that the expert's testimony was valuable in assisting the jury and understanding the defendant's theory of the case and was therefore admissible.

In DeFries v. Post,[10] the plaintiff contended on appeal that the trial court erred by allowing the investigating police officer, who was called in to investigate the day after the accident, to give expert testimony as to plaintiff's speed before the accident. The court upheld the trial court ruling that the officer was an expert and was indeed qualified to give such testimony. The court relied upon State v. Stringer[11] in which the Supreme Court of Oregon held that certain expert accident reconstruction evidence was admissible and the admissibility of such evidence is not dependent on the expert having witnessed the accident or on there being no other eyewitnesses. In the *Stringer* case the court held that to restrict the use of experts who did not witness the accident to instances in which no eyewitnesses are available is a distinction which unnecessarily clutters the law of evidence. If the expert testimony has probative value it should be admitted. Therefore, the trial court did not err by admitting the testimony.

In Hubbard v. Commonwealth,[12] the appellant, who was convicted of involuntary manslaughter, contended on appeal that the trial court erred in admitting reconstruction opinion evidence of her speed. The investigating officer was received by the court as an expert in accident investigation. The officer observed and measured a 90 foot long yaw mark caused by the front tire of the Hubbard car. A second expert conducted experiments. He estimated that the defendant's vehicle was traveling at 89 miles per hour when it began its final fatal swerve.

The defense called two practicing professional engineers. However, neither they nor anyone else could offer any evidence to contradict the

---

the test is presented to be a reenactment of occurrence at issue, it would be necessary to show that the test was performed under conditions that duplicated, as closely as possible, the conditions at the time of the occurrence.

9. 191 Ill.App.3d 664, 138 Ill.Dec. 724, 547 N.E.2d 1345 (1989).

10. 108 Or.App. 298, 815 P.2d 224 (1991).

11. 292 Or. 388, 639 P.2d 1264 (1982).

12. 12 Va.App. 250, 403 S.E.2d 708 (1991).

measurement or the resulting calculation by the state's experts. They disputed the prosecution expert's determination of the coefficient of friction and concluded that the speed of the defendant's car at the beginning of the final swerve was 65–70 miles per hour.

The court stated that the fact that an expert's measurements, methods and determinations are challenged or contradicted by other experts does not render inadmissible expert opinion based on those measurements and computations. Those challenges go to the weight of the evidence not to its admissibility and are factual questions to be determined by the jury. The court stated that the measurements and calculations by the experts were matters not within the realm of ordinary observations and depended upon particular and specialized scientific training and experience. Therefore, the judgment of the trial court was affirmed.

In Sledge v. Meyers,[13] the critical dispute was which vehicle crossed over into the other lane of travel. At trial the plaintiff called a state trooper to testify to her investigation of the accident. The trooper had nine years of experience as a police officer. In her five years as a state trooper she investigated more than 100 accidents each year and had successfully completed a course in accident investigation. Without making a clear ruling on the matter, the trial judge refused to allow the trooper to testify to her opinion as to the vehicle's point of impact.

On appeal the Supreme Court of Arkansas reversed the trial court's ruling. The Supreme Court stated that prior to 1983 a police officer was not allowed to give opinion evidence about the point of impact or location of vehicles based on skid marks or debris. However, the Supreme Court changed its view in Smith v. Davis,[14] which held that an officer may give an opinion of point of impact based on skid marks, debris, and other observations. This view was re-affirmed in Ferrell v. Southern Farm Bureau Cas. Ins. Co.,[15] where the Supreme Court held that a trooper could testify as to who crossed over the center line. In light of the court's holdings since 1983 the court ruled that the trial court's refusal to allow the plaintiff's trooper to testify constituted reversible error.

In State Farm Mut. Auto. Ins. Co. v. Smith,[16] appellee had obtained an order from the trial court excluding State Farm's accident reconstruction expert based on the expert's failure to make himself available for deposition at a reasonable time before trial. The appellate court held that the exclusion of the witness was well within the trial court's discretion.

State Farm raised the seat belt defense.[17] Smith moved *in limine* to exclude the seat belt defense, arguing that the defense was unavailable

---

13. 304 Ark. 301, 801 S.W.2d 650 (1991).

14. 281 Ark. 122, 663 S.W.2d 165 (1983).

15. 291 Ark. 322, 724 S.W.2d 465 (1987).

16. 565 So.2d 751 (Fla.App.1990), review dismissed 570 So.2d 1306 (Fla.1990).

17. The Supreme Court of Florida established the seat belt defense in Insurance Company of North America v. Pasakarnis, 451 So.2d 447 (Fla.1984). The Pasakarnis

in the absence of expert testimony and that her failure to wear her seat belt contributed to the herniated disc. State Farm contended that expert testimony was not required to establish the seat belt defense. The court stated that it was obvious that the specific dynamics of the seat belt in automobile collisions is not a matter within the common understanding of juries, or for that matter, judges. However, there is case law in Florida [18] that implies that the jury's common sense may be enough where the evidence establishes that the injury complained of is an impact injury.

Defendant attempted to proffer an accident reconstruction expert. Plaintiff's counsel argued that this testimony would be incompetent because the accident reconstructionist had no medical training and thus could not testify concerning the cause of herniated disc. The court concluded that the defense did not provide competent evidence in the present case. Competent evidence is a standard requiring the defendant to introduce evidence of the causal relationship between the injury and the failure to use a seat belt that is not speculative or conjectural.

In Felton v. White,[19] the investigating police officer was called to testify as an expert. He had 15 years of experience as a police officer investigating traffic accidents and had investigated between 1000 and 1500 accidents. His opinion was based on his observation of the physical evidence found at the scene, the position of the vehicles, and the truck driver's statement. Plaintiff sought to exclude the officer's opinion because it was based on hearsay from the truck driver. The trial judge disagreed and allowed it. The jury's verdict found both plaintiff and defendant equally at fault and plaintiff appealed.

The Court of Appeals upheld the trial court's ruling stating that when an expert's opinion is based on hearsay, the lack of personal knowledge by the expert does not mandate exclusion of the opinion. Lack of personal knowledge by the expert presents a jury question regarding the weight which should be given to the opinion.

Marshall v. Osborn [20] involved a wrongful death action brought on behalf of decedent's estate after he was struck by an automobile and killed. At trial, plaintiffs called an expert to testify to the speed of defendant's car. The expert had 35 years of experience in body and fender work and was familiar with defendant's type of car. He had no formal education in physics or engineering and was not a high school graduate. The trial court did, however, qualify him as an expert but limited his testimony to the extent of his answers on the interrogatory.

case requires the defense to introduce competent evidence on the issue. In some cases the defendant will not need an expert to sustain his burden of proving the causal relationship between the injury sustained and the plaintiff's seat belt. But other cases may require an expert's opinion as to causation.

18. Burns v. Smith, 476 So.2d 278 (Fla. App.1985).

19. 197 Ga.App. 367, 398 S.E.2d 425 (1990).

20. 213 Ill.App.3d 134, 156 Ill.Dec. 708, 571 N.E.2d 492 (1991).

In his interrogatory, plaintiff's expert said that defendant's car was traveling at a speed much greater than 10–15 mph. At trial plaintiff sought to admit testimony from the expert that defendant's car was traveling between 40–45 mph. The trial court did not allow this testimony at trial because it went beyond the scope of the facts known or opinions disclosed during the discovery proceedings. The Appellate Court agreed with the trial court's ruling holding that the plaintiff's expert's testimony went beyond the fair scope of facts known during discovery because the later testimony was decidedly more specific and its implications were profoundly different than the general opinion expressed in the interrogatory.

Another issue regarding the scope of the admissibility of scientific evidence is the ultimate issue doctrine. It is a general rule that an expert who testifies as to cause and effect from his analysis must state his conclusion in the form of an opinion rather than as an absolute fact. A line of cases extended this rule and concluded that testimony from an expert witness in the form of an opinion or inference which embraces the ultimate issue is inadmissible. The rationale for the rule is that the expert should not be permitted to invade the province of the jury. Rule 704, Federal Rules of Evidence, has rejected the ultimate issue rule: "Testimony in the form of opinion or inference otherwise admissible is not objectionable because it embraces an ultimate issue to be decided by the trier of fact." A majority of states have abandoned the ultimate issue doctrine. Most jurisdictions now allow experts to testify to ultimate issues, such as negligence, leaving it to the jury to decide how much weight to give the ultimate opinion. A minority of states still follow the ultimate issue doctrine.

In Marks v. Gaskill,[21] the Supreme Court of Indiana held that the police officer's testimony that the truck driver was "at fault" in causing the accident was inadmissible. Permitting the police officer to testify in his opinion to this ultimate issue was held to be reversible error. The decision of the trial court was reversed and the case was remanded. Therefore, in Indiana, permitting an expert to give an opinion regarding which of the drivers were at fault is reversible error.

In Shields v. South Carolina Department of Highways and Public Transportation,[22] a wrongful death action was brought after plaintiff's son died when his car fell into a 40 foot wide, 15 foot deep washout on a secondary road. The road hazard was marked only by a sign reading "road closed." During trial plaintiff called an accident reconstruction expert to testify. Among other things, the expert stated that the lack of warning signs and other devices near the washout bordered on "criminal negligence." Defendant argued on appeal that this statement was inadmissable because the expert was incompetent to make a conclusion of law. The South Carolina Court of Appeals disagreed and upheld the trial court's ruling. The Court held that the expert's statement was not

21. 563 N.E.2d 1284 (Ind.1990).   **22.** 303 S.C. 439, 401 S.E.2d 185 (App. 1991), cert. denied (1991).

an express opinion of law, but rather the expert was merely making an opinion as to an issue of fact—the adequacy of the warning sign. Therefore, the trial court did not err in allowing the expert's statement.

Jones v. Garnes [23] involved evidence at trial of the investigating officer who was said to be qualified as an expert because of his experience as a police officer since 1980, his training at West Virginia State Police Academy, and his previous investigation of several hundred to one thousand accidents. However, the trial judge refused to allow him to testify that the defendant failed to yield the right of way because it embraced the ultimate issue of fact. On appeal the court held that what is otherwise admissible is not objectionable solely because it goes to the ultimate issue of fact. The court continued stating that since the investigating officer was qualified as an expert he was allowed to give an opinion. Since his opinion was otherwise admissible it could not be excluded only because it embraced the ultimate issue of fact. Therefore, since the trial court qualified the investigating officer as an expert it was error to prohibit his opinion that the defendant failed to yield to the right of way.

In Lopez v. Dobson,[24] the Supreme Court of Virginia held that the accident reconstruction expert's opinion testimony as to point of impact based on the location of debris and other physical evidence was not admissible. Citing Hill v. Lee,[25] the Supreme Court stated that opinion evidence is not admissible when it deals with matters of common knowledge of the jury because the jury is as equally competent to form an intelligent and accurate opinion as the expert. Citing an earlier case, Richardson v. Lovvorn,[26] the Supreme Court reiterated the view that inferences or opinions drawn from skid marks are solely for the jury. The court held there was no difference between an opinion that was based on skid marks and one that was based on the location of debris. Since the defendant's expert based his opinion on location of debris it was inadmissible under the *Richardson* and *Hill* decisions.

The court also held that since the issue of point of impact was such a critical issue in this case the trial court's error in admitting the opinion testimony was reversible error.

§ 11.09 Qualifications of the Accident Reconstruction Expert

An expert witness is permitted to testify not only to facts but also to his opinions and conclusions drawn from his analysis of the facts. As a predicate to the expert's opinion testimony, it must be demonstrated to the court that the expert is qualified to render an opinion based upon his knowledge, skill, experience, training, or education or any combination thereof. The expert qualifications are usually probed during a hearing before the court, in a procedure known as the voir dire of the expert. The court will then determine the witness's competency to testify as an

---

23. 183 W.Va. 304, 395 S.E.2d 548 (1990).

24. 240 Va. 421, 397 S.E.2d 863 (1990).

25. 209 Va. 569, 166 S.E.2d 274 (1969).

26. 199 Va. 688, 101 S.E.2d 511 (1958).

expert. The court has broad discretion as to whether or not to find a person qualified as an expert. The court's ruling will only be overturned on appeal if it was an abuse of discretion. The court may consider the following with respect to an expert's qualifications: degrees and licenses, awards, publications, membership in professional associations, teaching, and the number of times the expert has conducted examinations.

In Laffman v. Sherrod,[1] the appellate court reversed the trial court's ruling permitting a police officer, who was not an eyewitness, to testify on the basis of field examination that the head lamp on a moped involved in a collision was not on at the time of the accident. In fact, the officer arrived on the scene several minutes after the collision. Since the officer was not qualified as an expert, he was not competent to opine that the head lamp was not on at the time of the accident. The court also held that an expert in accident reconstruction and metallurgy was not qualified to render an opinion based on an examination of orthopedic x-rays as to the cause of appellant's injuries.

In Commonwealth v. Bowser,[2] State trooper was properly found qualified to testify as an expert in accident reconstruction where she had received advanced training in the field, was a member of the traffic unit, performed six reconstructions and was a member of the National Association of Professional Accident Reconstruction Specialists.

In Mathieu v. Schnitzer,[3] at trial Mathieu attempted to have an accident investigator declared an expert in accident reconstruction. The trial court recognized the witness only as an expert in accident investigation, and concluded that her qualifications were inadequate for her to testify as an accident reconstructionist. The appellate court, while conceding that a trial court's decision on the qualifications of an expert is ordinarily conclusive and entitled to great weight on appeal, ruled the trial court applied erroneous legal principles in arriving at its decision. The appellate court concluded that the witness' years of experience in investigating the causes of accidents were sufficient to qualify her as an expert in accident reconstruction. Thus, although a trial court's decision on the qualifications of an expert witness ordinarily will not be overturned on appeal unless it is determined the trial court abused its discretion, such an abuse of discretion may be found when the court excludes a proffered expert whose specialized training or experience established a *prima facie* case of their expertise.

In Bales v. Shelton,[4] the court held that the lower court's finding that a doctor with a specialty in orthopedic surgery was qualified to give an expert opinion on whether or not the plaintiff's injuries could have been reduced through the use of a seat belt and shoulder harness, even though the doctor had not been qualified as an expert in accident reconstruction. Previous case law in Georgia has held that one may

§ 11.09

1. 565 So.2d 760 (Fla.App.1990).

2. 425 Pa.Super. 24, 624 A.2d 125 (1993).

3. 559 So.2d 1244 (Fla.App.1990), review dismissed 570 So.2d 1306 (Fla.1990).

4. 197 Ga.App. 522, 399 S.E.2d 78 (1990).

qualify as an expert by special knowledge derived from experience as well as study. The doctor's familiarity with seat belts and shoulder harnesses and their usage as well as his unquestioned orthopedic expertise and his thorough knowledge of the plaintiff's physical condition, following the failure of the use of the harness, amounted to such special knowledge.

In an attempt to prove a defect in the seat lock mechanism, the plaintiffs in Armstrong v. Lorino[5] offered the testimony of a safety expert from Louisiana State University. The expert had forty years' experience in the field of safety and was the safety director at LSU for eleven years. He admitted he wasn't a mechanical engineer and had no experience in designing automobile seats. He also testified he did not consider himself an accident reconstruction expert nor an expert in the field of biomechanics. He testified he had no experience with automobile crash tests. The trial court, considering the witness's experience and expertise, limited his testimony to the field of safety and refused to permit him to express his opinion as to whether the design of the seat was proper. Upon cross-examination the witness advised the court that his opinion was partially based on a misreading of the National Highway Traffic Safety Administration Department of Transportation Standard. However, when he was presented with a correct reading of the standard, coupled with mathematical calculations in the standard for determining the striking force the seat must withstand, he conceded that the seat was exposed to force well in excess of that required by the standard. In this instance, the trial court did not abuse its discretion in limiting the expert's testimony.

The trial court also excluded a photograph of a seat locking mechanism by General Motors since it was mislabeled with the name of another General Motors matter with which the General Motors expert was involved. The General Motors counsel argued in favor of excluding the photograph on the basis of relevance maintaining similar to Federal Rule of Evidence 403, that its probative value is outweighed by its prejudicial effect, since maintaining the picture would merely confuse the jury. This decision was upheld on appeal since the trial judge has great discretion to exclude even relevant evidence whenever it may confuse the issue. The appellate court held that it was no abuse of the trial court's discretion. The General Motors expert refuted allegations that the locking mechanism was defective. The expert has a bachelor's and a master's degree in mechanical engineering with a thesis concentration in biomechanics. She testified as to her certainty that the seat locked during the accident and in fact did not cause the Armstrong injuries. Therefore, the appellate court concluded that the trial judge did not err in directing a verdict in favor of General Motors.

In Harrington v. Velinsky,[6] the court held that the fact that an expert witness is a party to the suit by itself is not sufficient to exclude his testimony.

---

5.   580 So.2d 528 (La.App.1991).   6.   567 So.2d 148 (La.App.1990).

In State v. Honeyman,[7] the investigating officer was qualified as an expert on the basis of his credentials. He had completed course work in accident reconstruction at Louisiana State University as well as a seminar in advanced accident reconstruction offered by the Institute for Police Traffic Management [sic] in Jacksonville, Florida. He also attended a DUI vehicular homicide conference and other seminars sponsored by the Institute for Police Traffic Management [sic]. The fact that the accident occurred on an old bridge and the witness had no knowledge of bridge dynamics or construction did not preclude the officer from giving his expert opinion.

Leibovich v. Antonellis[8] involved the issue of whether an expert is admitted as an expert if the court never expressly rules on the expert's qualifications. During trial the plaintiff called the investigating officer to testify. The officer was questioned extensively about his qualifications in the area of accident reconstruction but the trial judge never expressly ruled on his qualifications. The trial judge allowed the officer to give his expert opinion regarding the speed of defendant's truck at the time of the collision. Furthermore, the trial judge instructed the jury to evaluate the officer's qualifications in their deliberations.

On appeal the defendant argued that the trial judge's jury instruction and the lack of an express ruling as to expert qualifications was an improper delegation of judicial function to the jury and required reversal of the trial court ruling. The appellate court held that since the officer's qualifications had been laid out and he was allowed to testify as an expert implied that the trial judge qualified him as such, even though an express ruling was not made. The Court also held that it was not a delegation of judicial authority to instruct the jury to evaluate the officer's qualifications during their deliberations. An impermissible delegation of judicial authority would only arise if the trial judge expressly left the matter of expert qualification to the jury.

In In re William R.,[9] a juvenile was adjudged delinquent of four charges arising out of a single car accident involving a stolen car in which one passenger was killed and two others were seriously injured. One of the issues on appeal was whether the trial judge erred in refusing to qualify the officer as an expert in accident reconstruction. The officer had been qualified at the probable cause hearing and no objection was made as to his qualifications at that hearing. The Supreme Court held that they would only review a trial court's decision regarding qualifications for an abuse of discretion. Even though the officer was qualified as an expert at a probable cause hearing, he was not automatically qualified to testify at trial because the rules of evidence are more stringently applied at trial. Furthermore, no objection was made to the officer's qualifications at the prior hearing. Thus, the trial court did not

---

7. 565 So.2d 961 (La.App.1990).

8. 410 Mass. 568, 574 N.E.2d 978 (1991).

9. 586 A.2d 540 (R.I.1991).

abuse its discretion in refusing to qualify the officer as an expert in accident reconstruction.

In Cobe v. Hersey,[10] the Rhode Island Supreme Court held that the investigating officer's experience as a police officer for more than two years, his training in accident investigation at both the city and municipal police academies, training that involved determining point of impact of accident vehicles, and his one and one half hours of investigation at the accident scene qualified him to form an opinion. The court further held that the trial judge's refusal to allow the officer to give his opinion because he could not connect the debris to the vehicles with absolute certainty was not a valid reason. The court held that the officer's opinion was necessary because his opinion was the only unbiased and impartial one available since both the plaintiff's and defendant's accident reconstructionists' opinions were conflicting.

In Trailways, Inc. v. Clark,[11] the officer investigating a bus accident was allowed to testify as an expert witness as to the cause of the accident. The officer was a supervisor with the Mexican Federal Police. His education consisted of junior high school, one and one-half years of vocational school, and courses with the Mexican Federal Police in traffic accidents investigation. He had also taken several recent courses covering traffic accidents and a 12–day engineering course that related engineering to traffic accidents. Throughout his training he was taught to determine a vehicle's speed by the length of skid marks, taking into account the type of vehicle, the road conditions, and the driver.

The Court of Appeals of Texas in Corpus Christi held that even if some of the more technical aspects of accident reconstruction are generally beyond the competence of most police officers, an investigative officer may testify as to the speed of a vehicle once the officer is shown to be qualified.

In Fox v. Dannenberg,[12] appellant argued that the trial court committed reversible error by not allowing his experts to testify as to who was driving at the time of the accident. The trial court refused to qualify the engineers as experts because they did not have any medical training. The trial court did, however, allow defendant's expert to testify that it was not possible that defendant was driving.

The Court of Appeals held that a witness may be qualified as an expert if he possesses sufficient knowledge gained from practical experience, regardless of the lack of academic qualification in the particular field. The two witnesses offered as experts by the plaintiff had academic backgrounds in engineering as well as accident investigation. One had a bachelor's degree and had investigated over 1,000 accidents. The other was the Associate Dean of the School of Engineering at University of Kansas specializing in transportation engineering. The Court of Appeals held that the District Court's finding was an abuse of discretion. The

---

10. 576 A.2d 1226 (R.I.1990).   **12.** 906 F.2d 1253 (8th Cir.1990).

11. 794 S.W.2d 479 (Tex.App.1990).

court stated that the question of who was driving was primarily a question of physical science rather than medical science. Since both engineers have significant background in physical science they should have been allowed to testify. The shortcomings in the engineers' backgrounds with regard to medical science did not render them incompetent to testify.

In Rosado v. Deters,[13] the appellate court affirmed the trial court's decision to exclude accident reconstruction testimony. The proffered witness had last qualified as an accident reconstructionist almost thirty years before, had taken no refresher courses and admitted he could not independently establish the physical and mathematical basis for his opinion.

§ 11.10   Bases of Expert Opinion

Federal Rule of Evidence 703 states that:

The facts or data in the particular case upon which an expert bases an opinion or inference may be those perceived by or made known to the expert at or before the hearing. If of a type reasonably relied upon by experts in the particular field in forming opinions or inferences upon the subject, the facts or data need not be admissible in evidence.

The facts or data upon which expert opinions are based derive from three sources:

(1) First hand observation of the witness;

(2) Presentation at trial;

(3) Presentation of data outside of court and outside the expert's perception; yet relied upon by other experts in his field.

A court may properly restrict an accident reconstruction expert's testimony to the circumstances of the accident and exclude testimony unrelated to the expert's knowledge of accident reconstruction.[1] If an expert's opinion is based on neither personal knowledge nor observation, there is no factual basis and therefore an improper foundation for his opinion.[2]

A trial court may properly exclude a proffered accident reconstruction expert if he failed to account for differences between the accident and his simulation of the accident, coupled with his inability to verify the impact of the vehicles and the engagement of the brakes.[3] Thus there is

13. 5 F.3d 119 (5th Cir.1993).

§ 11.10

1. Crawford v. Koloniaris, 199 A.D.2d 235, 605 N.Y.S.2d 718 (1993) (No foundation laid for testimony regarding standard procedures for police on pulling speeding motorist off highways. It was also within the ability and experience of the jury to determine if the state trooper was negligent in pulling motorist over.)

2. Wallach v. Board of Education of Prince George's County, 99 Md.App. 386, 637 A.2d 859 (1994).

3. Kirk v. Union Pacific Railroad, 514 N.W.2d 734 (Iowa App.1994).

an inadequate foundation for his opinion and it would not assist the trier of fact.

It has been held there was an insufficient foundation for admission of testimony of an accident reconstruction expert when the expert failed to inspect the intersection where accident occurred until three years after the accident and did not use other sources to become familiar with the condition of the intersection at the time of the accident.[4]

Reed v. United States[5] involved an involuntary manslaughter conviction. The defendant's car had crossed the median and collided with another car traveling in the opposite direction. The driver of the other car was killed instantly. The defendant was found in his car with the back of his seat in a horizontal position. A subsequent blood test revealed that defendant's alcohol level was .152.

During the trial the defense was that he looked over his shoulder and the seat back fell backwards and he lost control of his car. As part of this defense an accident reconstruction expert was called to testify. This expert concluded that defendant's seat mechanism had broken before the accident. The expert's opinion was based on his own observation and a report by General Motors to the National Highway Traffic Safety Administrator (NHTSA). The NHTSA report included letters from customers and data from General Motors pertaining to instances of seat back mechanism failure. The trial judge allowed the defense expert's testimony on the failure of the seat mechanism but did not allow any testimony on the contents of the NHTSA report on the basis that the report itself was inadmissible.

The court of appeals upheld the trial court's evidentiary ruling citing Federal Rule of Evidence 703. This rule permits an expert to rely upon facts or data that are reasonably relied upon by experts in the particular field, even if such facts and data are not otherwise admissible in evidence. The appeals court went on to hold that even if the underlying facts or data of the expert's opinion were admissible in evidence, they could still be subject to exclusion in instances where the probative value of the data is substantially outweighed by the danger of unfair prejudice. The court held that this decision is within the discretion of the trial court and would not be overturned unless the ruling was "manifestly erroneous."

McDowell v. Kawasaki Motors Corporation USA[6] arose out of a collision between a truck and a motorcycle. Plaintiff brought this products liability suit to recover damages sustained when a metal bracket supporting the windscreen deflected into his leg causing injury. At trial the jury found for the plaintiff. The defendant appealed, claiming, among other things, that the trial court should have stricken the plaintiff's expert's testimony because it was based on mistaken facts. Plaintiff's expert testified that the only mechanism present that could

---

4. Dulin v. Maher, 200 A.D.2d 707, 607 N.Y.S.2d 67 (1994).

5. 584 A.2d 585 (D.C.App.1990).

6. 799 S.W.2d 854 (Mo.App.1990).

have caused plaintiff's injury was the metal faring bracket. Defendant argued that plaintiff's expert's opinion was based on the mistaken assumption there was a left turn lane at the accident scene.

The Court of Appeals held that the mistakes were not relevant to the expert's opinion. In its holding the court stated that the facts that the expert was mistaken about were not necessary for the expert to reach a valid opinion. The court held that factual underpinnings of expert opinion go to the weight and credibility of the testimony not to its admissibility. Furthermore, the expert's opinion was primarily based on analysis of the damage caused to the vehicles at impact. Any mistake by the expert regarding the left turn lane or the speed of the vehicles did not affect the expert's final conclusion about the accident.

In Morrison v. Flintosh,[7] the defendants had moved for summary judgment to dismiss the complaint. The plaintiff made a motion to renew, which was granted, and, upon renewal, the New York Supreme Court adhered to its prior decision, dismissing the appeal by the plaintiff.

In support of her renewal motion, the plaintiff came forward with photographs of the accident and two separate affidavits of "a purported expert" it hired as an accident reconstructionist. The court concluded the affidavits did not satisfy the plaintiff's burden of coming forward with evidence sufficient to create a factual issue. The court noted that the expert was not licensed as a professional engineer, although he did have a master's degree in civil engineering and taught civil engineering technology at a community college. The court also noted that the witness offered no foundational facts to support his opinion. The witness stated the accident occurred in an intersection. However, it was undisputed that the accident did not occur in an intersection. The court also found that the witness did not state the type of sight distance he investigated and offered no detail as to running speed, roadway conditions, reaction time or braking time, nor did he give an indication of applicable industry standards or practices. Without a foundation based upon facts of the records or personal knowledge, the opinion of an expert is purely speculative and thus lacks sufficient probative force to constitute *prima facie* evidence of negligence. The court affirmed the previous ruling for summary judgment dismissing the complaint.

In Wicks v. Commonwealth of Pennsylvania, Dept. of Transportation,[8] the plaintiff argued on appeal that the trial court allowed defendant's expert to impermissibly testify beyond the scope of his expertise. Defendant's expert was Vice–President of the Institute for Safety Analysis and had published articles in various trade journals. The trial court qualified him as a motorcycle expert. Plaintiff argued that it was beyond the scope of the expert's qualifications to testify to what happened to the motorcycle when it went out of control and what speed plaintiff could have safely negotiated the embankment. The court held that the expert's testimony was within the realm of handling and

7. 163 A.D.2d 646, 558 N.Y.S.2d 690 (1990).   **8.** 139 Pa.Commw. 336, 590 A.2d 832 (1991).

movement aspects of motorcycles. The expert also gave an opinion as to the cause of the accident. The court held this was permissible because plaintiff "opened the door" on cross examination.

§ 11.11 Use of Demonstrative Evidence

Even though demonstrative evidence was addressed in general in Chapter Two, this section discusses case law addressing the use of demonstrative evidence in accident reconstruction cases.

In Foskey v. Williams Brothers Trucking Co.,[1] the court held the defendant's expert could use and testify concerning a diagram and, even if the expert's testimony concerning the diagram did not comply with particular interrogatories as to the production of diagrams, the driver was not harmed by the expert's testimony at trial.

The diagram in question showed the lay of the highway and the expert's depiction of the accident. The court found that the use of the exhibit was proper because the defendant provided the expert's name more than one year before the trial and stated that his testimony would be based on "laws of physics and computations of speed and distance"; plaintiffs made no inquiry of the expert as to his expected testimony; the diagram was identical to another which was introduced; the exhibit was not sent out with the jury; and the plaintiffs had a complete opportunity to cross-examine the experts.

As for the appellants' complaint that it was error to let the expert testify as to relative "fault", the court noted it was well settled that the expert could give his opinions as to calculations of speed and distance and when he does so, he is not testifying as to "fault":

> Testimony by an expert as to what one party or the other should have done or could have done in the factual or hypothetical circumstances is arguably within the realm of his expertise and is not per se inadmissible as being testimony upon the ultimate jury question of actual fault and liability.... Admissibility of evidence rests in the trial court's sound discretion, and wherever the evidence is of doubtful relevance or competence, it should be admitted and its weight left to the jury.[2]

Crispin v. Volkswagenwerk AG,[3] involved a products liability suit brought to recover damages resulting from a multi-car accident. Plaintiff's car was struck in the rear as he entered a highway. The impact of the collision caused the seat back at Plaintiff's 1971 Volkswagen Beetle to collapse. Plaintiff was rendered quadriplegic as a result of the accident.

On appeal the defendant argued that the trial court erred in not admitting videotapes of Volkswagen Beetle crash tests. They were offered to rebut plaintiff's explanation for why the pictures and videotape of the ODI crash vehicles showed much less damage than the pictures of the actual accident vehicles. The trial court excluded the defendant's videotapes because the tests shown were conducted under different circumstances than the ODI tests. The ODI test showed straight on front to rear-end collisions while the defendant's test showed test crashes at a fifteen degree angle. There were also other differences, but the court did not elaborate on them. The court of appeals thus held that given these differences it was within the trial court's discretion to admit or exclude defendant's videotapes and the trial court did not abuse its discretion.

In Mancuso v. Compucolor, Inc.,[4] the court held that the exclusion of a diagram of the accident scene contained in the police report was proper. Such a non-witness police report diagram purporting to show the location of the vehicles immediately after an accident is admissible when it is shown that the vehicles were not moved before the reported diagram was made. It also may be admissible when the skidmarks or measurements have been taken by an officer who is an expert in traffic reconstruction.

In Vogel v. Wells,[5] a wrongful death action, defendant at trial sought to admit a videotaped reconstruction of the driver's view on the approach to the stop sign. This video was made by an expert in accident reconstruction. The expert testified that the video camera was mounted at eye level immediately beside the driver defendant's head in a car similar to the one involved in the accident. The expert, with the defendant driving, videotaped the approach to the stop sign. The expert testified that the conditions depicted on the videotape were substantially similar to those on the day of the accident because he had adjusted camera lens aperture setting, camera angle, and lighting conditions. The trial court allowed the videotape to be admitted. The trial court ruled in favor of decedent's survivors.

On appeal the court held that evidence of experiments can be admitted or rejected within the trial court's sound discretion. The appellate court also held that since the expert was cross-examined regarding his credibility, the jury should have the opportunity to see the videotape and weigh it against the other evidence presented.

In Tritt v. Judd's Moving & Storage, Inc.,[6] plaintiffs argued that they were unfairly surprised by defendant's expert's testimony regarding the distance taillights could have been seen. During his deposition, defendant's expert testified primarily as to the speed of the plaintiff's car and did not indicate he would testify regarding the taillights. Defendant's expert conducted his illumination experiment after the trial had begun. The Ohio Court of Appeals held that there was simply no

---

4. 172 A.D.2d 153, 567 N.Y.S.2d 694 (1991).

5. 57 Ohio St.3d 91, 566 N.E.2d 154 (1991).

6. 62 Ohio App.3d 206, 574 N.E.2d 1178 (1990).

justification for the defendant to wait until after the commencement of trial to conduct the experiment.

Plaintiff's second point of contention was the defense expert's experiment itself. The expert went to the accident in June one-half hour before sunrise to perform the test. The accident occurred in February one half hour before sunrise. The expert used a new, clean taillight, while the one on the vehicle involved in the accident was dirty. The court referred to other dissimilarities and held that the experiment was not substantially similar to the actual accident and therefore, the experiment was not admissible.

The plaintiffs also argued that the trial court erred in not allowing their expert to use a scale model. The model consisted of a rectangular gray board with a black stripe across the center depicting the road. This model was supposed to depict vision in low light. The trial court would not admit the model. The Court of Appeals agreed with the trial court's ruling of inadmissibility of plaintiff's expert's model. However, the court did state that the trial court, in allowing defendant's expert's experiment to be admitted, should have been consistent in its discretion and admitted plaintiff's expert's model.

In Whitehead v. American Motors Sales Corporation,[7] a products liability suit was brought when plaintiff's Jeep Commando rolled over causing serious injury. At trial the plaintiff was allowed to show crash test films to demonstrate the jeep's crashworthiness. These films depicted the jeep CJ–5 and not the Commando that was involved in the accident in question. The trial court allowed the films over defendant's objection because the vehicle and crash test circumstances were "substantially similar." Defendant was not allowed to show films. The trial court found for plaintiff and defendant appealed arguing, among other things, that it should have been able to show films of jeep Commandos to rebut plaintiff's film and that their cross-examination of plaintiff's expert was too limited.

The Supreme Court of Utah held that the admissibility of crash test films is established when the data is relevant, the test conditions are substantially similar to those of the actual accident, and the presentation does not take undue amounts of time, confuse the issues, or mislead the jury. In the court's explanation of the criteria, they stated that the requirement of "substantially similar" does not mean absolute identity. It must, however, be so nearly the same in substantial particulars in order to give a fair comparison with the respect to the issue to which it is directed. Plaintiff's expert witness testified as to the handling similarities between the Commando that was involved in the actual accident and the CJ–5 in the films. This testimony was enough for the trial court, in its discretion, to allow the plaintiff's film.

Due to discovery violations by the defendant, it was precluded from admitting crash test films of the Jeep Commando. However, the discov-

7. 801 P.2d 920 (Utah 1990).

ery sanctions against the defense only prohibited it from showing films about the Commando. They sought to introduce a film showing the CJ–5 but the trial court refused to allow it. The Utah Supreme Court held that since there were no discovery sanctions prohibiting the CJ–5 films and the substantially similar test had already been met by plaintiff's film, the defendant's CJ–5 film should have been allowed.

Kudlacek v. Fiat S.p.A.,[8] involved a products liability action against the automobile manufacturer, which arose out of an automobile accident. The court ruled that videotapes depicting tests run on other automobiles were admissible as was the passenger's expert's testimony regarding a computer simulation of the path of the automobile on the roadway.[9] But in Dyer v. R.E. Christiansen Trucking, Inc.,[10] the court upheld the trial court's exclusion of a videotape demonstration of the phenomena of "trailer sweep" as conditions depicted in the videotape were so dissimilar to conditions in the instant case as to render the videotape irrelevant.

§ 11.12   Sufficiency of Evidence and Other Legal Issues

In this section we address cases which concern accident reconstruction yet do not fit in any particular niche previously described. For example, some of these cases address sufficiency of evidence, the legality of searches, attorneys' ethics and expert fees.

In Mack v. Transport Ins. Co.,[1] the Court of Appeals decided several issues. One of importance was the issue pertaining to expert witness fees. During trial an accident reconstructionist and a consulting engineer both testified as experts as to the distance that the defendant could have seen the garbage truck in front of him. The accident reconstructionist further testified to how long it would have taken defendant's truck to stop. The trial court's award granted the consulting engineer and the accident reconstructionist $1,759.52 and $1,365.00 in fees respectively.

In deciding the issue of fees the Court of Appeals held that the factors the trial judge is to consider in determining expert witness fees include: time spent testifying, time spent in preparation for trial, time spent away from regular duties while waiting to testify, extent and nature of work performed, and knowledge, attainments and skill of expert. Also to be considered are the helpfulness of the expert's testimony, the amount in controversy, the complexity of the problem addressed, and awards to experts in similar cases. Given these guidelines and considering the evidence on record by the engineer and accident reconstructionist the Court of Appeals reduced the fee award to $500.00 each. The court reasoned that minimal evidence as to time and value spent in preparation by the respective experts warranted the reduction in fees.

8.   244 Neb. 822, 509 N.W.2d 603 (1994).

9.   See § 2.19 in Chapter Two for additional case law regarding computer animation and simulation evidence.

10.   318 Or. 391, 868 P.2d 1325 (1994).

§ 11.12

1.   577 So.2d 112 (La.App.1991).

In Commonwealth v. Mamacos,[2] the defendant had been charged with two counts of homicide by negligent operation of a motor vehicle. After two mistrials the defendant filed a motion to suppress the results of tests done to a vehicle and all items removed from the vehicle on the ground that the evidence was obtained without a search warrant. A police officer was called to the scene of the motor vehicle accident at which two teenagers on a scooter had been killed. His duties included investigation and reconstruction of accidents. When he arrived at the scene, he saw the scooter lying under the front bumper and frame of the defendant's pickup truck. The Police Department then towed the truck to a fenced security area. The officer conducted an external examination of the truck's braking system and also recreated the scene of the accident. The officer and a mechanic dismantled the brake system. He then obtained a search warrant to retain the pieces of the braking system that he had dismantled.

The court had to decide whether the officer's actions had intruded on the defendant's reasonable expectation of privacy. Therefore the court had to ask whether the defendant had subjective privacy in his truck brakes, and if he did, was that one that society was prepared to recognize as reasonable. The burden of proving that he had a subjective and objective reasonable expectation of privacy rests on the defendant. The court held that the police were in rightful possession of the defendant's truck after the accident. The court set forth state statutes to illustrate the legislators' intent that society places great importance on learning all the circumstances of a motor vehicle accident resulting in death and expects that during the investigation the police may find it necessary to conduct the kind of test that the officer here conducted on the braking mechanism of a vehicle in its lawful possession. The court also pointed out that motor vehicles are subject to extensive regulation and inspection and such requirements tend to reduce the vehicle owner's reasonable expectation of privacy with respect to safety equipment on his vehicle even without an accident occurring. After an accident resulting in death occurs there could be no reasonable expectation of privacy in the safety features of an involved vehicle in the rightful possession of the police.

In In re Attorney Fees of Klevorn; People v. Kosciecha,[3] the appeal arose out of trial court's refusal to pay court appointed counsel fees for an accident reconstructionist during a criminal trial. Under Michigan law, court appointed counsel is entitled to receive all reasonable compensation for services performed. At trial, defendant's appointed counsel requested an accident reconstruction expert to rebut the prosecution expert. The trial judge refused the request but defendant's counsel retained an expert nonetheless. After trial counsel requested payment of fees for the expert amounting to $2,605.89. The trial judge denied the request.

2. 409 Mass. 635, 568 N.E.2d 1139 (1991).

3. 185 Mich.App. 672, 463 N.W.2d 175 (1990).

On appeal the Court of Appeals of Michigan held that the accident reconstruction expert was necessary for an adequate defense at trial to rebut the prosecution's experts and therefore defense counsel was entitled to the expert witness fees.

Appointed counsel must demonstrate that the expense for experts is reasonable. In State v. Gage,[4] the court appointed counsel sought fees for an accident reconstruction expert. The fee request was denied and defendant appealed. Oregon law provides that a defendant with appointed counsel is entitled to reasonable expenses for expert witness fees. In this case defendant's counsel requested a minimum of $1,000 for fees. The services to be rendered by the expert were four hours of investigation at a rate of $60 per hour. The Court of Appeals held the trial court did not abuse its discretion in denying defendant's request. Four hours of work at $60 per hour only amounts to $240. The Court of Appeals, therefore, held that a request of a minimum of $1,000 was not a reasonable expense as a matter of law.

In State v. Aamold,[5] the defendant was convicted of second-degree felony murder, vehicular homicide and fourth degree assault. At trial his court-appointed counsel requested an accident reconstruction expert to aid in defendant's defense. The expert would allegedly testify that had the defendant's brakes not failed he would not have crashed into the house killing an infant asleep in its crib. The trial judge denied this request and defendant appealed.

The Court of Appeals in Washington held that a defendant with court appointed counsel is entitled to expert witness expenses when they are necessary for an adequate defense. At the hearing on defendant's request for an expert, the prosecution offered the report of an investigation by a private consultant which stated that only one of the four brakes were "legal" at the time of the accident. According to the prosecutor the consultant was available and willing to testify. Defense counsel refused to use the consultant for an unspecified reason and gave no offer of proof pertaining to the necessity of another expert. Therefore, the trial court did not err in ruling that an additional expert was not necessary.

IV. MISCELLANEOUS

§ 11.13 Bibliography of Selected References

1. JOURNALS

Accident Investigation Quarterly and *Accident Reconstruction J.* (Bimonthly journal) (both edited by Victor Craig (301) 843–1371).

4. 106 Or.App. 153, 806 P.2d 1159 (1991).   **5.** 60 Wash.App. 175, 803 P.2d 20 (1991).

2. BOOKS AND ARTICLES

Badger, "Reconstruction of Traffic Accidents," 9 Am.Jur.3d Proof of Facts 115 (1990).

Baxter, *Motorcycle Accident Investigation,* 1991.

Chieco & Kwasnoski, *Establishing Liability in Vehicular Accidents,* 1989.

Coben, "Investigating Automotive Accidents," *Trial* March 1994, at 22.

Daily, *Fundamentals of Traffic Accident Reconstruction,* 1991.

Garcia & Trocino, *Traffic Accident Reconstruction: Legal Issues in the 1990's,* 1991.

Kuhlman, *Killer Roads: From Crash to Verdict,* 1986.

Kwasnoski, "Constructing Hypotheticals in Motor Vehicle Homicide Cases," *The Champion* November 1992, at 6.

Limpert, *Motor Vehicle Accident Reconstruction and Cause Analysis,* 3d ed. 1989.

Lofgren, *Handbook for the Accident Reconstructionist,* 3d ed. 1990.

McDonald, *Tire Imprint Evidence,* 1989.

Rivers, *Traffic Accident Investigation,* 1988.

Schwartz, *Engineering Evidence,* 2d ed. 1987.

Stephens, *Formula Workbook for Traffic Accident Investigation and Reconstruction,* 1989.

Tarantino, "How the Accident Reconstruction Expert Can Contribute to DUI Defense," 6 *D.W.I.J.* 6 (April 1989).

Tarantino, *Strategic Use of Scientific Evidence,* (Chapter 14) 1988.

Van Kirk, "A Scientific Approach to Documenting Evidence for Accident Reconstruction," 29 *J.For.Sci.* 806 (1984).

Williams, *Legal Aspects of Skidmarks in Traffic Case,* 5th ed. 1982.

Zurmuhlen, "Automobile Accident Reconstruction" 18 *Trial Law Q.* 49 (Winter 1987).

PART III

EXPERT TESTIMONY IN THE BIOLOGICAL AND LIFE SCIENCES

In Part III, the authors focus on the biological and life sciences and their part in the justice system. Experts in this area are medical doctors, doctors of philosophy with specialties in the biological and life sciences, as well as other trained and skilled researchers and technicians in disciplines as varied as pathology, serology, hematology, toxicology, pharmacology, biochemistry, dentistry, and anthropology.

To introduce this section of the book, we begin with an exploration of the forensic pathologist/medical examiner/coroner and that professional's participation in the justice system in both civil and criminal cases. Next comes the forensic toxicologist who examines biological fluids and tissues and is a necessary adjunct to the pathologist in the proper determination of the cause, manner, and time of death. We also discuss drug chemistry and the related issues of compelled drug testing. The relatively novel area of so-called "DNA fingerprinting" is explored in great detail in a new chapter dealing with the identification of individuals by their deoxyribonucleic acid in violent offenses, and in civil cases where paternity is an issue.

Part III concludes with two other chapters that have seen great changes since the last edition of the book. Chapter 16 deals with forensic dentistry (odontology) and its still sometimes controversial personal identification method by bite mark impressions. The final chapter in Part III is also a new chapter which has gained great prominence in courts throughout the world since the last decade: it is that of physical anthropology.

Chapter 12

FORENSIC PATHOLOGY *

I. INTRODUCTION

  * The authors specially acknowledge the valuable comments and assistance given by several forensic pathologists who assisted in this or the earlier versions of this chapter.

I. INTRODUCTION

§ 12.01 Scope of the Chapter

This chapter focuses on the basic legal and scientific factors relevant to a forensic pathologist's testimony as to proof of the cause of death, separating death due to disease from death due to external causes, identity of the deceased, time of death, the nature and consequences of wounds, or the type of wound inflicting instrument.

Forensic medicine has been utilized in criminal prosecutions for many years. One of the most famous early cases was undoubtedly the indictment of the Earl and Countess of Somerset for the mercury poisoning of Sir Thomas Overbury. The Countess had previously poisoned the Earl of Essex and, according to historians, was well on her way toward eliminating a significant segment of British nobility. As one of the reverse bounces of the law, it is worth noting that the Somersets were pardoned while the Countess' apothecary and a few others who had assisted in preparing the drugs were executed.

Pathology was formerly the study of the structural changes caused by disease, but the field has been widened to include the studies of disease insofar as it may be investigated by laboratory methods. This has brought within the scope of pathology the bacteriology of pathogenic organisms, and the functional alterations induced by disease as revealed by chemical investigation. Pathology is most commonly divided into two principal subdivisions: anatomic pathology, which continues to deal with the gross and microscopic structural alterations caused by disease and clinical pathology, which deals with the laboratory examination of samples removed from the body, including blood, serum, spinal fluid, etc. Further specializations include neuropathology, hematology, clinical chemistry, or forensic pathology.[1]

In order to qualify as a pathologist one must undergo a minimum of four additional years of specialized training after graduation from an approved medical school and licensing by the state in which he is to practice as a Doctor of Medicine. To be eligible for examination to

---

§ 12.01

1. Forensic Pathology, one of the recognized subspecialties of pathology, utilizes the tools of the anatomic pathologists to study the structural alterations arising out of unnatural disease, the relationship of such entities to natural disease processes, and the interrelationship of both with information of an investigatory nature arising from exploration of those circumstances surrounding the death. Subsequently all of this information is related to the solution of legal issues.

obtain certification in the specific field of forensic pathology from the American Board of Pathology, a candidate must spend a year in additional training in the special field of anatomic pathology or anatomic and clinical pathology.[2] Should a candidate desire to combine from the beginning of his training the two fields of anatomic and forensic pathology he is expected to spend at least two years of training in each of these two fields prior to the examination for certification in both forensic and anatomic pathology.

Such training allows a forensic pathologist to answer, at a minimum, a number of cause and effect questions in both civil and criminal cases. Among the functions of the pathologist are:

(1) To establish a diagnosis of apparent cause of death, either as due to natural causes or violence;

(2) To estimate the time of death;

(3) To infer the type of weapon used to inflict wounds;

(4) To distinguish suicide from homicide and accident;

(5) To establish the identity of the deceased; and

(6) To determine the additive effect of trauma and natural disease.

This chapter will discuss the basic criteria used by the forensic pathologist in determining these issues. The more common types of violent death, with the symptomatology typically accompanying them, will be considered. Throughout the discussion reference will be made to statutory and case law involving the use of the pathologist's expertise. Brief suggestions concerning the appropriate use and source of pathologists as defense witnesses will also be offered.

§ 12.02 Medical Examiner System

The introduction of the medical examiner system in the United States was in Massachusetts in 1877. A few states have central offices with state-wide jurisdiction, although local deputy examiners may function under the direction of the state medical examiner. Approximately half of the states have adopted a limited form of the medical examiner system.

Medical examiners are frequently vested with a quasi-judicial function in that they may conduct inquests as to causes of death as well as administer oaths to persons testifying at such inquests. Their customary role, however, is to perform autopsies and microscopic tissue exami-

---

2. The best reference delineating the current methods and standards for certification by the American Board of Pathology or any other specialty board, and also those who are currently so certified, is the book entitled *Directory of Medical Specialties* published by the Marquis' "Who's Who" in Chicago. This book, at the beginning of the listing of each group of specialists by their specialty breakdown, lists the current requirements for certification by that particular specialty board. There are other roundabout ways of obtaining this information, but the volume referred to is considered the most satisfactory.

See also §§ 12.14 and 12.15, infra.

nations, recording all remarkable findings in detail and ordering any appropriate chemical, toxicological, serological or bacteriological analyses. Their job is to tie together all of the above information with the investigational data concerning the circumstances surrounding the death. Medical examiners are usually forensic pathologists with sufficient medico-legal training to insure reasonable adroitness in translating medical findings into answers to legal issues. They are usually free from overt political pressures.

The defense attorney ordinarily enters the criminal case after the autopsy has been completed and the body has been materially altered for burial or perhaps even after burial. To determine the findings of the medical examiner, the defense, therefore, must be prepared to initially use the available informal and formal pretrial discovery procedures discussed in Chapter 1.

The results of a complete or partial autopsy conducted by a medical examiner, including the name of the deceased, and the diagnosis of cause and manner of death, are in some states, considered to be privileged medical documents, not to be disseminated to the general public.[1] It is only under very unusual circumstances that the defendant's attorney is aware of his involvement in the case prior to the performance of the autopsy. Therefore, only rarely does he have the opportunity to nominate a medical expert to be present at the time of the autopsy. Perhaps more frequently, the defendant's attorney is involved in the initiation of exhumation so that a body previously unautopsied can be examined. In rare instances a second and sometimes even a third autopsy may be required at the behest of the defendant's counsel.

Typically, a report of the investigation by the medical examiner is made. The purpose of this report is to furnish a permanent legal record and source of relevant information of those deaths requiring investigation in the public interest.

§ 12.03　Coroner System

In many states, jurisdiction over violent, unnatural or sudden deaths in which the manner of death is in doubt lies with the coroner. In most of these states the coroner is an elected official and, in certain jurisdictions, he need not be a medical doctor, although in most states today the candidates for the office have in fact had medical training. Some states have provisions which provide counties with an option of adopting the medical examiner system or retaining the coroner system. Using the State of Texas as an example of a state with such provisions, any county can adopt a medical examiner's system in lieu of the justice of the peace being designated as the coroner. According to a recent modification of the law, contiguous counties may join together to provide for a common

§ 12.02

1. See, Anno., Official Death Certificate as Evidence of Cause of Death in Civil or Criminal Action, 21 A.L.R.3d 418 (1968).

medical examiner system. This renders economically feasible the appointment of a person well-trained in the field of pathology and forensic pathology who will have the responsibility of investigation of the deaths in the interest of the public. The justice of the peace can still call and swear witnesses in conjunction with an inquest to determine cause of death (conducted with or without jurors). He may also order chemical, serological, toxicological and histological tests. The results of the inquest, including the detailed findings of the autopsy as well as the time, date and place where the body was found, are then certified to the clerk of the district court. There is usually no specific provision in the statutes designating the proceedings of justice of the peace's inquest as public records.

It has been suggested that the coroner may be seen as a poorly paid, undertrained and unskilled individual, popularly elected to a somewhat obscure office for a short term, with a staff of mediocre ability. Since it is frequently difficult for the trained forensic pathologist to distinguish the cause of death, that task is obviously much more difficult when the physician is not a trained forensic pathologist, or perhaps not even a pathologist.

In rural communities, local physicians and surgeons who are available to the coroner to perform autopsies may lack the necessary experience and training in pathology to make meaningful diagnoses. If a capable pathologist from another jurisdiction is not called in to do the autopsy, serious errors in postmortem diagnosis are likely. When matters proceed to criminal trial, an untrained physician who is offered as an expert to prove cause and effect issues may be effectively impeached by a well prepared cross-examiner.

With the advent of an increasingly technological society, there is increased feeling that the medical examiner system should be universally adopted, on a state level to service all communities.

Medical examiners and their staff are generally conceded to have immunity from tort liability for their negligent acts in the performance of their duties. An aggrieved citizen may also be deprived of an actionable claim on other grounds.

In Koeller v. Cook County [1], a sister sued the Chicago deputy medical examiner for his negligent misidentification of her brother, a fire disaster victim, which misidentification caused emotional distress to the sister when she learned that her brother's body had been cremated. Whereas the trial court dismissed the claim on the basis of the M.E.'s immunity from suit, the appellate court affirmed finding that, no matter what the negligence, the plaintiff's emotional distress was not compensable.

§ **12.03**

1.   180 Ill.App.3d 425, 129 Ill.Dec. 353, 535 N.E.2d 1118 (1989).   See, Starrs, "Forensic Pathologists on Trial," 13 *Sci.Sleuth. Rev.* 1 (Spr.1989).

Even where the medical examiner is sued not for damages but for injunctive relief to prevent the performance of an autopsy, the courts have been reluctant to interfere with a medical examiner's statutory authority. In Robison v. Maynard [2], an Oklahoma death row inmate sought to prevent his post-execution autopsy. The trial court granted the petition but the Oklahoma appeals court overturned that order. The statutes of Oklahoma, as in most states, required an autopsy when bodies are to be cremated (the plaintiff wanted to be cremated) and when inmates die in a place of penal incarceration. In light of such a statute, the M.E. was within his rights in conducting an autopsy of this death row inmate.

II. POSTMORTEM DETERMINATIONS

§ 12.04 Autopsy

The purpose of an autopsy is to observe and record as soon as possible the minute and gross anatomical peculiarities of the recently discovered dead body as they are observed by the forensic pathologist. Exhumation of a body for postmortem examination is generally allowed only when imperatively demanded by the circumstances and necessary for the due cause of justice.[1] The autopsy and its results furnish the real evidence upon which the pathologist will predicate his medico-legal opinions. Examination is typically done in an autopsy room of a local hospital or at the county morgue, although in many rural sections of the country, these continue to be performed in funeral parlors or undertakers' establishments.

As the pathologist proceeds with the autopsy, he may dictate the description of his findings. This is then later reduced to writing. On the other hand, he may make notes at the time of autopsy and sketch and diagram the various pertinent features and later dictate his findings which are then reduced to writing. An important part of his autopsy undertaking is to search the body and the clothing for physical evidence of significance. In many instances photographs are taken of the noteworthy portions of the body. For a discussion of photographs and their admissibility see Chapter 2.

A typical autopsy report will include a general description of the deceased (sex, age, color, race, frame, deformities, stature, nutrition, musculature, scars, tattoos, hair distribution, moles); the signs of death (rigor mortis, lividity, heat loss, and decomposition); an external examination of the head, trunk, extremities and genitalia; an examination of external wounds; a charting of the internal course of such wounds; an

2. 857 P.2d 817 (Okl.App.1992).   Cases, 63 A.L.R.3d 1294 (1975).

§ 12.04
1. Anno., Disinterment in Criminal

internal examination of the organ systems, the heart, the major vessels, the stomach and its contents, the small intestines, the rectum, the genitalia, the neck, the head and the spinal cord. A complete sample autopsy report in a homicide case is found in § 12.14, infra. Thin slices of various tissues may be removed for histological study under a microscope.

Pathologists should insure that an x-ray examination is made in every instance of death due to firearms injuries. Even in those cases where the bullet has exited, fragments useful for comparison purposes may be located by means of an x-ray examination. Further, x-ray examination can aid in establishing direction of fire and to recognize bullet embolism (enters one part of body and travels within the bloodstream). X-ray examination can be helpful in investigation of deaths caused by stab-wounds to establish if there remain any broken weapon parts and to demonstrate break-pattern of the weapon. The exclusion of foul play can be determined by x-ray examination of decomposed bodies. In autopsy examination of child deaths, x-ray can be utilized to demonstrate signs of child abuse by the evaluation of bone fractures of different ages of origin.

The forensic pathologist generally considers the anatomic lesion directly or indirectly responsible for death to be the "cause of death." In some instances there may be no anatomic counterpart of the "cause of death." In such instances the forensic pathologist may depend to a greater or lesser extent upon investigations as to the circumstances surrounding the death.

In addition to the physical autopsy, a psychological autopsy has been developed and continues to evolve today to aid pathologists in determining the manner of death, generally whether it was homicide or suicide. In some cases, a physical autopsy may be inconclusive by itself. For example, a multiple gunshot wound death is usually homicide but can be suicide in rare cases.[2] The psychological autopsy is performed by collecting data from interviews with people who knew the deceased. The pathologist uses this information to evaluate the decedent's intention at the time of death. This data assists the pathologist in piecing together the circumstances surrounding the death. The details gathered include life history, psychiatric-psychological data, communication information, and pertinent non-psychiatric information.[3]

The results of a psychological autopsy have been "less readily admitted in criminal cases"[4] than in civil actions, such as workers' compensation claims, will contests and life insurance claims. The only criminal case in which a psychological autopsy has thus far been admit-

---

2. Thomas Marsh et. al., "Six-shot Suicides in Close Geographic and Temporal Proximity," 34 *J.For.Sci.* 491 (March 1989).

3. Theodore J. Curphey, "The Psychological Autopsy: The Role of the Forensic Pathologist in the Multi-disciplinary Approach to Death," *Bull. Suicidology* 44 (July 1968).

4. Ogloff & Otto, "Psychological Autopsy: Clinical and Legal Perspectives," 37 *St. Louis Univ.L.J.* 607, 644 (1993).

ted is the bizarre Florida prosecution [5] of a mother for causing the suicide of her daughter by forcing her to engage in strip dancing.

Prosecutors should be prepared to prove that care was taken to protect the body from any additional wounds or fractures inflicted while it was transported from the crime scene to the autopsy area. Otherwise, the defense may have the opportunity to discredit the autopsy findings. Also, if a body has been embalmed with artificial preservatives prior to autopsy, a meaningful postmortem examination, and particularly a toxicological study may be thwarted. With the advent of highly sophisticated toxicological examination systems such as atomic absorption spectrophotometry, it may now be possible to derive meaningful information from the toxicologic examination of specimens removed from embalmed bodies. Atomic absorption may be able to determine metals like mercury and lead in brain tissue. The reaction of embalming fluid with other substances must be taken into account.

The autopsy rate in the United States had declined at a dramatic rate since World War II. This cutback in autopsies is due to several factors. First, pathologists have many duties to perform. Some of these responsibilities assist the living and take precedence over autopsies. Second, autopsy is one of the most expensive and time-intensive procedures in the practice of medicine. Third, as a result of greater reliance upon improved diagnostic technologies and fear of malpractice claims, clinicians are requesting fewer autopsies. Fourth, obtaining consent to perform an autopsy, even when no consent is required by law, can be a controversial matter. In some states, like California, for instance, consent can be withheld based upon a religious objection and an autopsy can by undertaken over such an objection only under certain rigid statutory exceptions.[6] Additionally, family members may be too emotionally affected by the person's death to permit or request an autopsy. In such cases, the relative may not understand the importance of an autopsy.[7] Fifth, the minimum autopsy rate necessary for accreditation of a hospital has been reduced while consideration of the autopsy in the medical school curriculum has decreased.[8] The result is that clinicians, pathologists, and non-medical persons who recognize the benefits of the autopsy are calling for increased use of the procedure.

§ 12.05　Cause, Manner and Mechanism of Death

The cause of death is the trauma, disease or combination of them which brought about the termination of life. When reporting on the cause of death, pathologists determine the immediate cause and any additional causes of death. The immediate cause of death is the factor contributing to the death which is most proximate to it. Other causes of

---

5.　Jackson v. State, 553 So.2d 719 (Fla. App.1989).

6.　West's Ann.Cal.Gov.Code § 27491.43 (Supp.1985). See also, Pathology, 10 *Sci. Sleuth.Rev.* 1 (Summer 1986).

7.　Stephen J. McPhee & Kent Bottles, Autopsy: Moribund Art or Vital Science?, 78 *Am.J.Med.* 107 (Jan. 1985).

8.　Maarten Boers, "The Prospects of the Autopsy: Mortui Vivos Docuerunt? ('Have the Dead Taught the Living?')", 86 *Am.J. of Med.* 322 (March 1989).

death are the traumas or diseases that remotely contributed to the series of pathogenic factors leading to the person's death. For example, an automobile driver suffers a myocardial infarction, loses control of his car and dies from injuries sustained in the accident. The injuries are the immediate cause of death while the "heart attack" is a contributing cause of death. Where the initial injury or disease kills so quickly that there is no chance for complications to develop, that injury or disease is both the immediate and contributing cause of death.[1]

The mechanism of death is the "physiologic derangement or bio-chemical disturbance incompatible with life."[2]

The responsibility for determining the manner of death is often lodged by statute in the medical examiner. Under the coroner system, on the other hand, a pathologist usually furnishes the coroner with a finding establishing the cause of death, and the coroner, by inquest or other means, puts this information together with investigative findings to arrive at a decision as to the manner of death. Both systems employ the same possible alternatives for the manner of death: natural, homicidal, accidental, suicidal, and undetermined.

When the cause of death is solely disease, the manner of death is natural, unless the disease was initiated by a third person. If the death is caused solely by injury, an injury which aggravates a pre-existing condition, an injury that leads to a natural condition which proves fatal, or an injury which precedes or follows a natural condition which the person might have otherwise survived, the manner of death is violent or unnatural. A violent death will be labeled homicide, suicide, accidental or of undetermined origin.[3]

The manner of death is homicide if someone other than the decedent was the source of the cause of death. For example, "X" intentionally puts rat poison into a cup of coffee and gives the coffee to "Y" to drink. The manner of death is still homicide if "Z" drinks the coffee instead of the planned victim. However, if "A" intentionally puts the rat poison in his own cup of coffee and drinks it, his deliberate act to end his own life is classified as suicide. When a person causes a death without intending to do harm, the resulting manner of death is accidental. Using the poison example, if "A" mistakenly, but without negligence or reckless-ness, confuses the box of rat poison with the box of sugar next to it and places rat poison instead of sugar in his and his friend's coffee, the resulting manner of death for both would be accidental. Common examples of accidental deaths include electrocution by lightning and most traffic fatalities.

The forensic pathologist identifies the manner of death as undeter-mined whenever the circumstances leading to death cannot be ascer-tained. One type of death of undetermined origin occurs when the

§ 12.05

1. Adelson, *The Pathology of Homicide* 15 (1974).

2. Id. at 16.

3. Wecht, ed., *Forensic Science,* § 26.-06[c], pp. 16–32 (1994).

mechanism of death is known. For example, if the mechanism is the result of poisoning but the pathologist cannot establish how the decedent came to ingest the lethal substance, the manner of death would likely be labeled undetermined. The pathologist would need more information than the cause and mechanism of death to determine whether the decedent intentionally poisoned himself, accidentally was poisoned, or was intentionally given the poison by another person.

A second type of death of undetermined origin occurs when the forensic pathologist cannot identify the mechanism of death. One of the most perplexing examples of this phenomenon is the sudden infant death syndrome (SIDS). SIDS is also known as crib death, or cot death. By 1989, fatalities from SIDS still occurred at the rate of 2–3 infant deaths per 1000 live births.[4] The number of total infant deaths per live births in 1988 was 10.0 and was 9.8 in 1989.[5] Breakthroughs about the causation of SIDS continually prove to be false. For example, one of the more recent beliefs was that SIDS is only a proper diagnosis when the infant dies in the prone sleeping position. However, this hypothesis has led only to a decrease in SIDS diagnoses while infant deaths attributed to other specific and nonspecific causes increased where the infant was found in a non-prone sleeping position.[6] Only identification of the underlying pathologic mechanisms that create SIDS will lead to strategies which will prevent this leading cause of post-neonatal death.

The following is an example of how the mechanism, cause and manner of death might be reported. A person contracts fatal pneumonia. The infection generates a condition where the alveoli sacs of the lungs become edematous and can no longer transport oxygen. This is the mechanism of death. The inability to transport oxygen results in hypoxia (although it can have other effects, too). The contributing cause of death is the pneumonia. The immediate cause of death is hypoxia. Since the cause of death is solely disease related without the intervention of any third person, the manner of death is natural.

§ 12.06 Causes of Death

In a criminal prosecution, the burden is on the state to prove that the death was the result of a criminal act. In a civil action, the burden is on the proponent, plaintiff or defendant, to establish the cause of the deceased's death. Until this is done, it is presumed that death was due to natural causes.[1] In the absence of eyewitness testimony or an admissible dying declaration or other circumstantial evidence[2] relevant

---

4. Adelson, "Forensic Pathology Then and Now: Retrospect and Reflections." 10 *Am.J.For.Med. & Path.*, 258 (1989).

5. "The Institute of Medicine Report," 267 J.A.M.A. 1182(2) (March 4, 1992).

6. Hanzlick et al., Ltr. to Ed., 270 J.A.M.A. 2684(2) (December 8, 1993).

§ 12.06

1. The state must establish, as part of the corpus delicti of homicide, that death occurred by a criminal agency: 41 C.J.S. Homicide § 312(d)(1).

2. Dying declarations of a homicide victim are admissible in evidence when they refer to the perpetrator of the crime and circumstances surrounding the crime as an exception to the Hearsay Rule.

to the cause of death, the testimony of the expert may be the sole evidence which the state can produce concerning the issue.[3]

At the autopsy the pathologist examines the body of the deceased externally and internally for signs of mechanical or dynamic injury. A search is also made for the presence of naturally occurring diseases, i.e., heart disease, lung disease, etc., in the circulatory, respiratory, nervous and alimentary systems. Disease may be caused by the presence of hereditary, congenital, infectious, cancerous, metabolic or toxic abnormalities rather than trauma. Thus, the pathologist must be able to distinguish between structural changes produced by trauma and those produced by the disease process.

The identification of the victim, or indeed, any deceased individual may depend upon the proper examination by a pathologist who may in turn employ other scientists to aid him in establishing identification or to help establish or explain other facts that may assist in determining the cause of death. For example, a pathologist may employ a toxicologist for the purpose of poison analysis. Anthropologists are sometimes utilized to determine trauma to skeletal remains.[4]

The cause of death may also be proved without the aid of expert testimony where the circumstances are such that a layman could reasonably ascertain what act caused death. In determining whether or not the layman may give an opinion as to the cause of death, the court considers such factors as the nature and position of wounds, the time between infliction of trauma and death, prior health of the deceased, etc. Laymen such as undertakers,[5] constables and justices of the peace have been allowed to testify as to cause of death.[6] Peace officers have even been held qualified to render an opinion distinguishing an entrance wound from an exit wound,[7] and a mortician has been held competent to testify as to the type of instrument used to inflict the fatal wound.[8]

A forensic pathologist can provide scientific contributions of useful data concerning each of the medico-legal issues surrounding a suspicious death. It is not surprising, therefore, that the parties in modern trials, particularly the prosecutor in criminal trials, use this particular expert to prove cause of death. Such testimony becomes even more convincing when emphasized by the use of plastic skeletal parts as demonstrative aids in the explanation of wounds.

3. Anno., "Necessity and Effect, in Homicide Prosecution, of Expert Medical Testimony As to Cause of Death," 65 A.L.R.3d 283 (1975).

4. For a discussion of toxicological methods, see Chapter 13. The subject of physical anthropology is dealt with in Chapter 17.

5. Anno., Admissibility of Testimony of Coroner or Mortician as to Cause of Death in Homicide Prosecution, 71 A.L.R.3d 1265 (1976).

6. Smith v. State, 282 Ala. 268, 210 So.2d 826 (1968)—Coroner/undertaker with 27 years experience did not qualify to express opinion as to cause of death. Stout v. State, 460 S.W.2d 911 (Tex.Cr.App.1970)—Justice of the Peace acting as coroner.

7. E.g., Fisher v. State, 100 Tex.Crim.R. 205, 272 S.W. 465 (App.1925).

8. Sims v. State, 258 Ark. 940, 530 S.W.2d 182 (1975) wound produced by shotgun.

Consider the following causes of death and the medicolegal findings which typically accompany them.

1. ANOXIA (ASPHYXIA)

The common denominator in all of these types of deaths is the insufficient amount of oxygen reaching the brain and other essential tissues or organs of the body. There are many ways in which this can be accomplished: (a) by a decrease in the capability of the tissues to utilize oxygen such as in cyanide poisoning; (b) by a reduced capability of the blood to carry oxygen to the tissues, such as in carbon monoxide poisoning or in instances of acute decrease in the amount of blood, such as with massive hemorrhage; (c) in instances where the blood does not circulate rapidly enough to keep up with the demands of the brain and other tissues, such as in shock; (d) from breathing air which contains an insufficient amount of oxygen to sustain life; (e) from a mechanical interference with the passage of air into the respiratory tract such as in smothering or drowning and in some instances manual strangulation and hanging; and (f) by cutting off the circulation to or from the brain by pressure, as in manual or ligature strangulation and in most instances of hanging.

Some body changes or signs of death resulting from acute anoxia have been described as follows:

(1) Cyanosis, occurring in the form of a blue discoloration of the lips and fingertips, due to the reduction in oxygen carrying hemoglobin in the blood of the veins and capillaries.

(2) Petechial hemorrhages, occurring as small, pin-point, dark red spots directly beneath the skin surface, especially of the face and conjunctiva of the eye as well as within the lungs and the pericardium membrane surrounding the heart. These spots are caused by the rupture of small blood vessels called capillaries which bleed into the tissues; they may be confused by some observers with Tardieu spots, which are postmortem phenomena resulting from the rupture of tiny capillaries on the skin.

(3) There may be dilatation of the right side (ventricular) chamber of the heart, along with pulmonary congestion.

A histological examination of the temporal bone for hemorrhages and congestion in the mastoid air cells and inner ear can help the pathologist diagnose the cause of asphyxia.[9]

Death from asphyxia may occur as the result of certain natural disease conditions such as emphysema, asthma, pulmonary embolism, tumor of the larynx, edema of the larynx, etc. There are three common types of traumatic death by asphyxia, any one of which may involve criminal conduct.

---

9. See, Yohko Ito and Hiroshi Kimura, "Histological Examination of the Temporal Bone in Medicolegal Cases of Asphyxia," 44 *For.Sci.Internat'l.* 135 (1990).

A.   STRANGULATION [10]

Strangulation may be homicidal, suicidal or accidental.   Homicidal strangulation may be manual or by ligature.   Death from strangulation by compression of air passages is typical of hangings, most of which are suicides.   Intense congestion, venous engorgement and cyanosis are present above the rope or ligature.   In this type of hanging, the vertebral column is not dislocated and the vital nerves of the spinal cord are intact.   The victim dies of strangulation as a result of noose pressure on the neck exerted by body weight.   (see Figures 1–A and 1–B).   Accidental strangulation by hanging is often associated with sexual asphyxia, mostly involving male victims.[11]

10. For a helpful explanation of the physics of asphyxial deaths by strangulation and the anatomic structures of the neck see, Taff and Boglioli, "Strangulation: A Conceptual Approach for Courtroom Presentation," 10(3) *Am.J.For.Med. & Path.* 216 (1989).

11. McDowell, Death Investigation: Sexual Asphyxia, 4 *For.Sci.Digest* 162 (1978).

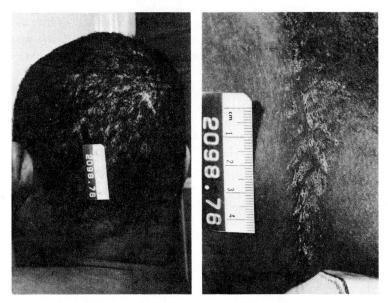

Fig. 1–A. Anoxia—hanging by suspension. Note mark made by noose on left side and back of neck, tenting upward toward the point of suspension.
Fig. 1–B. Same case as Fig. 1–A. Mark made by the braided cloth which comprised the noose. The braided pattern is apparent.

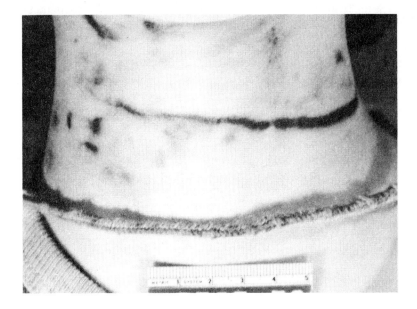

Fig. 2. Asphyxia-ligature and manual strangulation. The mark made by the garrote is evident, and the cord used is shown immediately below it. Fingernail marks, most apparent on the right side of the neck, resulted from the assailant's hand exerting a strong constricting pressure.

In addition to strangulation by hanging and accidental strangulation, in rare and unusual circumstances strangulation may be manual. Strangulation by constriction is accomplished by the use of a ligature which is twisted around the neck and tightened by some means other than body weight (see Figure 2).   Since the pressure on the neck depends on a voluntary action which is discontinued when the power of decision is obliterated with the loss of consciousness, many believe that manual self-strangulation is impossible and that manual strangulation is always homicidal.   A recent British study, however, casts doubt on this common sense theory.   It discusses three uncommon cases in which individuals committed suicide by manual self-strangulation using a ligature.   All three decedents managed to exert and maintain sufficient pressure long enough to result in death.[12]

A knowledgeable pathologist can differentiate between strangulation by hanging and strangulation by ligature by looking at the grooved imprint in the neck.   Although anatomic findings in hanging deaths are relatively scarce, subtle differences in these findings can indicate how death occurred.   Ligature furrows are consistently present in all types of hanging deaths.   Hemorrhage of the soft tissues or strap muscle of the neck is frequently found in victims who were completely suspended.[13] Thyroid trauma and hyoid fractures occur independently of age in complete suspension hangings, while such fractures become increasingly age-dependent with increased body support.   Conjunctival and facial petechiae are also related to body position, and, in fact, there is a direct correlation between conjunctival petechiae and increased body support. This results from reduced ligature pressure to the neck with increased body support which raises intravascular pressure, thus causing petechiae.

Bruising of the underlying soft tissues of the neck and sometimes a fracture of the hyoid bone or cartilage of the trachea or larynx is a sign of death by manual strangulation.[14]   The marks of fingernails or thumbs on the neck are a sign of manual strangulation and defensive wounds are frequently found such as nail marks and bruises at an attempt to remove constriction, just as the furrow impressions of a rope or cord are indicative of strangulation by ligature or hanging.   In the latter cases, the examiner must exercise caution not to mistake fat furrows for strangulation marks.   The tongue may be protruded if pressure was placed low on the neck.   If pressure was exerted on the upper neck, the tongue will be back in the mouth.[15]   Strangulation may be quickened by the struggling of the victim, the inhalation of vomitus or by shock

12. Claydon, "Suicidal Strangulation by Ligature: Three Case Reports," 30 *Med. Sci.Law* 221 (1990).

13. On the importance of hemorrhage at the fracture site of the hyoid bone when making a diagnosis of manual strangulation, see, O'Halloran & Lundy, "Age and Ossification of the Hyoid Bone: Forensic Implications," 32 *J.For.Sci.* 1655 (1987). The article also suggests that a detailed examination of the hyoid bone may aid in gender and age determinations.

14. Luke, "Correlation of Circumstances with Pathological Findings in As-

phyxial Deaths by Hanging: A Prospective Study of 61 Cases for Seattle WA", 30 *J.For.Sci.* 3 (1985). See also, Rao and Wetli, The Forensic Significance of Conjunctival Petechiae, 9 *Am.J.For.Med. & Path.*, 32 (1988).

15. The importance of careful examination of the tongue in strangulation cases is discussed in Sperry, "An Unusual, Deep Lingual Hemorrhage as a Consequence of Ligature Strangulation," 33 *J.For.Sci.* 806 (1988).

triggering a vagal nerve mechanism. The testimony of a medical doctor that the cause of death of the deceased was by anoxia due to strangulation has been held competent.[16]

B. DROWNING

Drowning results from submersion or partial submersion in a fluid medium. A classic drowning has five stages. The first stage is the surprise stage where the person is stunned and may involuntarily inhale some water. The second stage occurs when the person attempts to hold his breath while struggling to reach air. In the third stage, the person inhales deeply and white or pinkish foam is expelled from his mouth and nose. Often, the person's mouth and eyes are open as he ceases to struggle. A stage of respiratory arrest follows in which there is no thoracic movement and the pupils dilate. The final stage involves three to four quick respiratory movements.

The inhalation of water or other liquid into the air passages as the result of submersion causes choking which in turn results in the formation of mucus in the throat and windpipe. This foamy mucus passes into the lungs and disrupts the air passages. Thus, drowning is a form of choking in that death results from an obstructing agency within the throat. The postmortem signs of drowning are pale color of the body, swelling or edema of the lungs due to water passing in them, foam in and about the mouth and nostrils and aspirated marine life and considerable quantities of water in the stomach. Not all of these signs are necessarily present in any single drowning victim. There are many reasons other than drowning for edema of the lungs causing a "foam cone" about the mouth and nostrils. A drug overdose is one possible cause.

On occasion (approximately 20% of the cases of drowning), a victim will die of asphyxia due to submersion in water without inhaling a significant amount beyond the larynx. The inhalation of a small amount of water or other liquid into the air passage as a result of submersion or aspiration while drinking may result in spasm of the larynx and immediate obstruction of the passage of air into the lungs. Under these conditions, the more classical alterations within the body, associated with regurgitation and swallowing of large quantities of water, may not occur. Hence, the expression "dry drowning" in which the lungs are relatively dry and the stomach free of fluid, in contrast with the more frequently encountered "wet drowning" wherein there is evidence of fluid inhalation and swallowing with intense edema of the lungs, foam in the mouth and, on occasion, aspirated marine life.

There are no specific pathologic findings or diagnostic tests for drowning. The determination is based upon evaluation of the results of

---

16. Commonwealth v. Lanoue, 392 Mass. 583, 467 N.E.2d 159 (1984); McKinstry v. State, 264 Ind. 29, 338 N.E.2d 636 (1975); Commonwealth v. Pettie, 363 Mass. 836, 298 N.E.2d 836 (1973).

the investigation, autopsy, chemical studies and toxicological examinations, as well as the exclusion of other possible causes of death.

Several external signs are often found in drownings. Injuries on the body of a person found in water may not be causally related to that person's death. The action of fish eating the flesh or boat propellers or other factors may cause apparent lacerations or severing of the trunk or appendages which are artifacts unrelated to the cause of death. See Figure 3. Severely wrinkled skin called "washerwoman's skin," cold pale skin, and gooseflesh can occur in a body that has been exposed to water for a period of time. This not only occurs in drownings but is also found in cases where the person died before the body entered the water. Discharge of urine, semen and feces can also be found in both drownings and unrelated deaths.[17] The external sign most indicative of drowning is the presence of foam near the mouth and nose. The foam, a mixture of air, mucus and water, is produced during violent respiratory movements. It is thick and does not readily dissolve in water. This, too, occurs in other types of death such as strangulation, electric shock, and drug overdoses. The hands of the body should be checked for material that might have been clutched during cadaveric spasms. Aquatic organic material can help prove where the death took place as well as that the person drowned.

An internal examination is necessary before a pathologist should diagnose drowning as the cause of death unless the presence of gunshot wounds or the like are dispositive on the question. In an internal examination in a classic drowning, the lungs will be distended and contain water fluid, a condition called "emphysema aquosum." [18]

The body should be checked for trauma to rule out other non-drowning causes. The temporal bone should be removed and checked for hemorrhages in the middle ear.[19] While blood in the mastoid air cells occurs in other types of deaths, it can be used to help confirm a drowning. The pathologist next can perform a series of diagnostic tests. Although none of these tests reliably certifies drowning as the cause of death to the exclusion of all other causes, they help determine the more likely cause of death.

Diatom (unicellular algae) analysis[20] can be helpful evidence of death due to drowning. This method only works when a significant number of diatoms are present in the water in which the person allegedly drowned. When a person inhales the water, the diatoms in that water can enter the circulatory system and reach the organs. During such testing, the diatoms are recovered from the organs, identified by species, and compared with the types present in the water where

17. Tedeschi, Eckert, Tedeschi (eds.), *Forensic Medicine—A Study in Trauma and Environmental Hazards* 132 (1977).

18. See, Spitz, *Medico–Legal Investigation of Death* 435 (1993).

19. Fatteh, "The Diagnosis of Drowning," *The Handbook of Forensic Pathology* 159 (1973).

20. Pachar & Cameron, "Diagnosis of Drowning by Quantitative and Qualitative Diatom Analysis," 33 *Med.Sci.L.*, 219 (1993).

the body was found. When there are few to no diatoms in the water or the person is a victim of dry lung drowning, diatoms will not be present in the body tissues. Additionally, diatoms can be found in non-drowned individuals due to their presence in air and food. While many critics oppose the use of diatom analysis,[21] the method provides some of the strongest evidence of drowning when diatoms are found in the decedent's body and carefully correlated with those present in the water.

Another test used to determine the likelihood that death was due to drowning is chloride concentration testing.[22] The chloride concentrations in blood in the left and right ventricles of the heart are compared. Differences in concentration greater than 25% indicate the person drowned rather than died before his body entered the water. Whether the left side contains a higher or lower chloride concentration depends on whether the person drowned in salt (hemoconcentration) or fresh water (hemodilution), respectively. The problem with this test is that 2 to 24 hours after death the chloride shift is gone. Only when the blood samples are taken quickly enough does chloride concentration analysis provide evidence that can be used to confirm a diagnosis of death by drowning.

The chloride content determination is especially fallible if artificial respiration and cardiac massage have been employed as resuscitative measures, thus mixing the blood from both sides of the heart.

The newest test, which is still being developed, looks at blood levels of atrial natriuretic peptide (ANP). ANP is a recently discovered hormone that is connected to blood volume and electrolyte balance. The results of a study using rabbits indicates there is a significant increase in the blood levels of ANP in drowned bodies. The conclusion is that ANP may be a potential marker to differentiate between victims of drowning and victims of post-mortem immersion.[23]

Chemical analysis to estimate the postmortem interval has proved useful, particularly in light of the varying decomposition rates between summer and winter drownings. Specifically, chloride levels of the vitreous humor begin to decline after the first postmortem day and continue to fall for ten days. Potassium levels, on the other hand, rise over the first seven days postmortem. A formula utilizing both levels balances the effects of dilution on chloride and potassium concentration in the vitreous humor, and is quite accurate in estimating the duration of cold water submersion. The formula cannot be applied to summer cases because of the effects of temperature.[24]

21. Foged, "Diatoms and Drowning— Once More," 21 *For.Sci.Internat'l*. 153 (1983).

22. Camps (ed.), *Recent Advances in Forensic Pathology* 72 n. 6 (1969) and Schwar, "Drowning: Its Chemical Diagnosis. A Review," Wecht, ed. 1 *Forensic Science* 411 (1972).

23. See, Lorente et al., "Plasmatic Levels of Atrial Natriuretic Peptide (ANP) in Drowning. A Pilot Study," 44 *For.Sci.Internat'l*. 69 (1990).

24. Bray, "Chemical Estimation of Fresh Water Immersion Intervals," 6 *Am. J.For.Med. & Path*. 2 (1985).

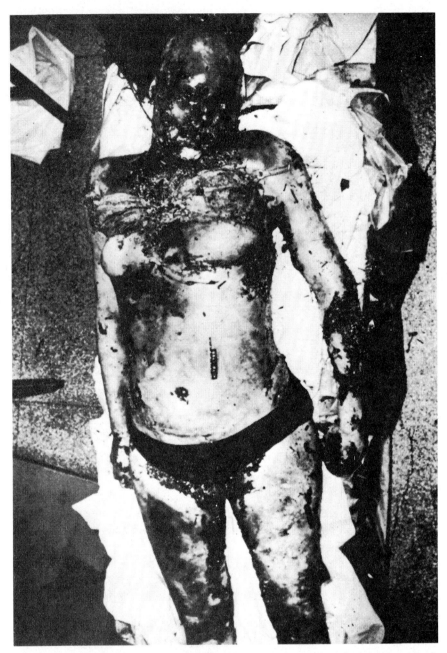

Fig. 3. The injuries caused to the face and body of this drowning victim were caused by having been submerged in a river; they are not the result of violence by a criminal attack.   Courtesy: *Allegheny County Coroner, Pittsburgh, Pa.*

A body submerged in water for a considerable period of time, depending upon the temperature of the water, will rise due to the formation of bacteria-producing gas during the decomposition process. Cold water retards the bacterial gas production. This buoyant body is called a "floater." After a few days submerged or floating in the water, the outer shell of skin on the hands and feet begins to slough off. This process is called maceration. Six to eight weeks of submersion sometimes results in the transformation of superficial fat tissue into a yellowish-white, waxy substance called adipocere. This process, when it occurs, acts to preserve the body.

C. Smothering

The external openings of the air passages, the nostrils and the mouth, are closed by an obstructing object with resulting suffocation. Postmortem examination may reveal a general discoloration associated with the accumulation of fluid or edema. There may be small or faintly discernible contusions or lacerations on the inner aspects of the lips. Petechial hemorrhages may be seen. If a soft object has been used to obstruct the external orifices of the air passages, the body itself may disclose no visible signs of trauma.

In fatalities where general signs of hypoxia are present but there is a lack of evident injury, histological examinations of the lungs have proved valuable in establishing homicide as the manner of death. Electron microscopy can aid in the examination if the period of autolysis is less than twenty-four hours.[25]

2. WOUNDS

Typical issues which may be put to the examining pathologist concerning wounds are:

Q: Could the wound have been self-inflicted or inflicted by another in self-defense?

Q: What was the nature of the instrument which inflicted the wound, and could it have been inflicted with the suspect weapon?

Q: What was the range at which a firearm wound was inflicted?

Q: Was the wound inflicted before or after death?[26]

Q: What is the period from incurring fatal injury to the time of death?[27]

25. Brinkmann, "Identification of Mechanical Asphyxiation Cases of Attempted Masking of the Homicide," 26 *For.Sci.Internat'l.* 32 (1984).

26. Experimentation was undertaken to determine ante or postmortem character of skin wounds in general by the presence of enzyme reactions in vital ante mortem wounds distinguished from an absence of such reactions in postmortem wounds: Fatteh, "Histochemical Distinction Between Antemortem and Postmortem Skin Wounds," 11 *J.For.Sci.* 17 (1966); Raekallio, "Histochemical Distinction Between Ante Mortem and Postmortem Wounds," 9 *J.For.Sci.* 107 (1964).

27. Estimating post-injury survival time is important for purposes of scene reconstruction and court testimony. For a study on estimating survival time see, Levy and Rao, "Survival Time in Gunshot and Stab Wound Victims," 9 *Am.J.For.Med. & Path.* 215 (1988).

Testimony concerning the pathologist's observation of a wound is suspect if the wound had previously been subject to material change such as being washed, sewn up, enlarged by the insertion of probes, enlarged by operative procedures, etc.[28] Many alterations of wounds may occur as a result of therapeutic actions on the part of the treating physician. Incisions may be made through the wounds, drainage tubes may be inserted through the wounds, the wounds may be debrided to such an extent that their original appearance is completely lost. Recovery of debrided tissues from the surgical pathology department of the hospital where the victim is treated may be of great importance in the ultimate reconstruction of the wound, and to the testimony of the pathologist.

A. GUNSHOTS AND WOUND BALLISTICS

The pathologist studies the gunshot wound to determine the nature of the weapon and projectile used, the number of gunshot wounds and their location, the instantaneousness of death, the distance (range) and direction of fire and, in the case of suspected foul play, the relative position of the victim and his assailant, although extreme care must be exercised in stating opinions on this latter issue.

Care must be exercised in recovering foreign objects from the body. Forceps and probes wielded by a hospital surgeon can mutilate striations on a bullet which a firearms examiner otherwise might have linked to a suspect weapon. The examining pathologist will usually determine the extent and course of the wound, whether or not it was mortal, whether or not it could have been self-inflicted and whether or not it was inflicted before or after death.

Bullets removed from bodies and crime scenes need to be carefully examined before being cleaned or otherwise handled or else valuable information may be lost. The use of SEM–EDXA (Scanning Electron Microscopy and Energy Dispersive X–Ray Analysis) provides a nondestructive method for examining and identifying foreign material on bullets, and can have rather dramatic results. In two suspected homicides, SEM–EDXA of bullets provided the necessary information to make the final determination as to how death occurred, resulting in clearing the names of the alleged perpetrators.[29]

The greater the energy of the missile at the moment of impact, the greater the tissue destruction. According to the laws of physics, the striking energy of a projectile is the product of its mass or weight multiplied by the square of its velocity, as expressed by the formula MV_2.

---

28. Testimony from an expert as to the entry and exit wounds of a gunshot victim may be excluded if such an alteration of the body occurs as to distort the examination, i.e., where cotton was stuffed in to the wounds prior to expert's examination: Roberts v. State, 70 Tex.Crim.R. 297, 156 S.W. 651 (1913).

29. DiMaio, "Use of Scanning Electron Microscopy and Energy Dispersive X–Ray Analysis (SEM–EDXA) in Identification of Foreign Material on Bullets," 32 *J.For.Sci.* 38 (1987).

Velocity, because it is squared, is the most important factor in the transmitted effect of the projectile. Handgun discharges are usually not so damaging as those of high powered rifles because of the much lower velocity of the projectiles. Shotgun discharges, because of the immediate scatter of shot upon entering the body, may be much more damaging than the external wound would make it appear.

Several types of handgun rounds are designed to provide greater stopping power than conventional ammunition or to meet specialized needs (i.e. exploding, fragmentation or, perforating ammunition, and expansion bullets). Because of their unique design, these projectiles expend their energy in the target faster than conventional ammunition and can cause much greater wound damage.[30]

A pathologist testifying as an expert in a homicide case involving gunshot wounds must be knowledgeable concerning the rudiments of firearm identification and the science of ballistics, which involves the law of physics. If he lacks such knowledge, the well-prepared cross-examiner can cast doubt on his opinion.

The pathologist must also be familiar with the various characteristics of improvised firearms revealed on the bodies of firearms victims. Homemade firearms are made from a variety of materials and in a wide range of calibers. Their barrels, which are frequently short, and their use of loose fitting ammunition create pressure normally below that of equivalent commercial firearms, and powder may be observed in firings from up to three meters, and the partially burned grains will be larger than normal. In the firing of improvised shotguns, the pellet pattern may resemble that of a conventional firearm at greater range. A combination of wide shot pattern spread and a strong powder pattern may indicate the use of an improvised firearm.[31]

To answer the questions that will be put to him, a pathologist must be aware of variables which could influence his opinion, such as the position and movement of the body, the clothing, and blood traces. For example, a single layer of clothing[32] may completely remove the secondary effects of a very short range gunshot wound such as tattooing or soot deposit. Thus, if the clothes were ripped off of the victim and discarded, the appearance of the bullet wound may mislead the pathologist. Speculation as to the range of the shot then becomes pure conjecture.

B. BULLET WOUNDS

The entrance wound will vary according to the type of weapon, the ammunition, the area of the body affected and the distance of the weapon from the body of the victim. Location of the entrance and exit

---

30. Gern, "Wounding Effects of Unconventional Ammunition," 10 *For.Sci.Dig.* 13 (1984).

31. Modi, "Improvised Firearms Versus Regular Firearms," 26 *For.Sci.Internat'l.* 199 (1984).

32. See, Anno., "Admissibility in homicide prosecution, of deceased's clothing worn at time of killing," 68 A.L.R.2d 903 (1959).

wounds are of material importance in cases involving the issue of self-defense. The bullet, as it strikes the skin, is moving forward at high speed and is also rotating on its axis as a result of the spin imparted to it by the rifling of lands and grooves in the barrel. At the point of entry the bullet pushes the skin in and perforates it while it is in a state of stretch and indentation. Because of this, the entrance defect (in all but contact wounds) most often is smaller in diameter than the bullet which caused it.

The size of the entrance wound may correspond roughly to the caliber of the bullet but not to such an extent so as to enable an expert in wound ballistics to consider the wound diameter as an index to bullet size. After the bullet has passed through the skin, the hole it leaves in the skin may become smaller in diameter than when the bullet was passing through. This principle does not apply to contact wounds where the explosive action of powder gases may result in a large gaping wound.

Position of a bullet hole in a powder tattooed area, taken in conjunction with the course of the bullet through the body and the position of the body, tends to establish the position in which the weapon was held. The course of the bullet cannot be determined from external examination. Because of variation in the resistance of different tissues to the passage of the bullet, the bullet may not travel in a straight line internally. Indeed, there may be internal ricochet which may materially alter the course of the bullet in the body. Precision requires that the pathologist examine the internal course of the bullet. The exit wound may at times be larger than the entrance wound as shown in Figure 4.

A contact entrance wound may result from the placement of the muzzle of the firearm on the skin of the victim at the time it was fired. A close (intermediate) bullet wound is considered as one in which the muzzle was held from one inch to approximately twenty inches from the point of entry at the time of discharge.

Depending on the variable types of firearms and ammunition used, the science of wound ballistics recognized general characteristics which may appear in contact and/or close entrance wounds on bare skin. These peculiarities aid the pathologist in determining the distance and direction of fire:

a. A scorching of hairs and skin results from flame discharge and hot powder gases in very close shots. The degree of scorching varies according to the surface of the target, the type of powder, the pressure of the gases as well as distance.

b. A blackening called smudging or fouling of the skin results from powder smoke or dirty powder gases. (Figure 5 and Figure 10). Smudging or fouling is found internally if a muzzle is in direct contact with skin and externally in the case of a close shot. External smudges usually may be wiped away with a damp cloth. If this is done, the wound may mislead the pathologist who speculates as to the range of the shot.

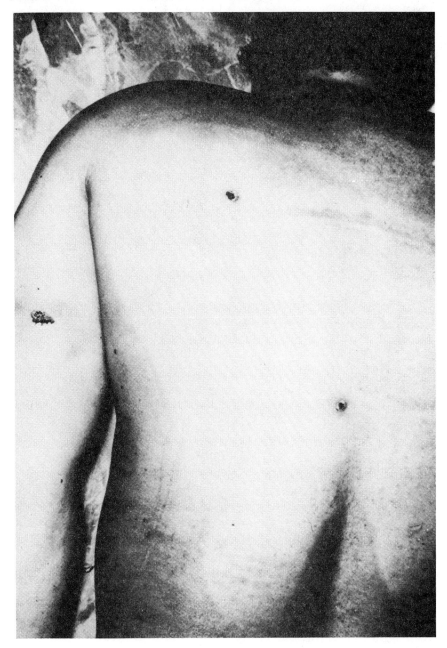

Fig. 4.　The difference between exit and entrance wounds is clearly visible here. Two typical small caliber distant gunshot wounds of entrance can be seen in the back of the victim.　Note the symmetrical skin defects circumscribed by a uniform margin of blanched abrasion consistent with clothing contact.

The posterior side of the arms shows a typical gunshot wound of exit.　Note the irregular skin defect with slight extrusion of underlying fat circumscribed by irregular swelling and superficial black and blue discoloration or bruising of the skin. *Courtesy: Utah Office of the Medical Examiner, Salt Lake City, Utah.*

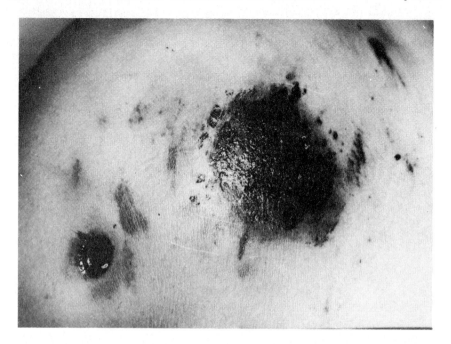

Fig. 5. Two gunshot wounds near the shoulder. The wound nearer the center of the body is surrounded by much black soot deposit from the powder gases. This indicates a very short range, perhaps 1 to 3 inches. There is an absence of such soot deposit about the other wound of entry. This was either inflicted at several or more feet of range, or clothing may have covered the area preventing the deposit of firearms residues. The former was true in this instance.

    c. A contusion ring (abrasion collar) of stretched skin around the perforation formed by the rotation of the bullet against the skin immediately prior to penetration, sometimes indicates bullet angle. When it is symmetrically round, a square-on shot is indicated. When it is oval, an angular shot is suggested. The contusion ring is wider in the direction from which the bullet entered. In a contact wound it is poorly defined.

    d. A tattooing or stippling of the epidermal layer of skin with embedded grains of burned or partially burned powder may occur in close wounds but not in contact wounds (Figure 11). Unburned, smokeless powder tattoos embed themselves in the skin. Unburned, black powder only smudges the skin. Partially burned grains of either type of powder burn themselves into the skin. Powder tattoos cannot be rubbed off. Scanning Electron Microscopy (SEM) of the dermal surface of tattooing from powder burns may reveal that these particles remain trapped in the basement membrane despite mechanical separation of the epidermis and a thorough washing of the area. This suggests that GSR particles may be identified even on skin in an advanced state of decomposition.[33] The proportion of unburned powder depends on the barrel

33. Torre, "New Observation on Cuta-   & *Path.* 3 (1986).
neous Firearm Wounds," 7 *Am.J.For.Med.*

length, type of powder and gas pressure.

In recent years the increasing use of ball powder (a type of smokeless powder that is manufactured in small spheres or balls) has led to greater variation in powder tattooing than previously was encountered. Therefore, it is essential that the type of powder be known by the pathologist if he is to properly interpret the wound and make any estimate as to the range of fire. Different types of ammunition, even though fired from the same gun, may give different powder patterns because of variance in powder type, concentration, load and dampness. The shorter the barrel, the more substantial the pattern of tattooing when distance is constant. Note that the exact identification of powder particles is for the explosives chemist. Figures 6 and 7 illustrate revolver powder tattoo patterns.

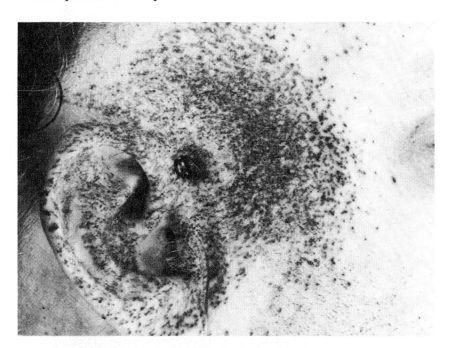

Fig. 6. A gunshot wound of entry inflicted with the firearm held at a "medium" range, in this instance perhaps 4 to 12 inches. The cartridge was loaded with ball powder. Each of the tattoo marks is the result of an unburned grain of powder being blown into the skin. The dense tattooing pattern is characteristic of ball powder. (Compare with Figure 11A, the tattoo pattern made with flake powder).

e. A gray ring around the entrance perforation, sometimes obliterating the contusion ring may be caused by bullet grime being wiped off onto the skin upon entry of the bullet. Absence of the gray ring may result when a clean jacketed bullet causes the wound or when a lubricated bullet has passed through another object such as firm clothing before entering the body.

f. A gaping wound may be caused by the explosive force of gases tearing and blowing back the skin, especially when there is bone backing the skin, i.e., flat bones of the skull. The bone behaves like a hard surface and, collaterally, there may be a back-splash of blood onto the hand holding the gun.

g. A muzzle imprint in contact wound. (Figure 8.)

The entrance of a contact wound is usually larger than the bullet due to the force of the powder gases in the cartridge load which enlarge and stretch the surrounding skin. Inasmuch as a normal person cannot fire a shot at himself at a distance greater than arm's length (roughly twenty inches) the presence of a contact entry wound and sometimes a close entry wound is compatible with suicide.[34] Gunshot suicides usually display contact wounds.[35] Perhaps out of a desire to be sure of the shot, the suicide commonly places the muzzle of the gun directly against the skin of such favored places as the temple, the center brow, the roof of the mouth or over the heart.

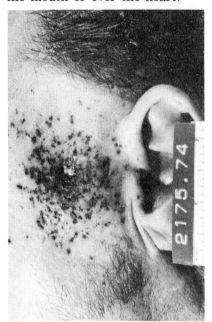 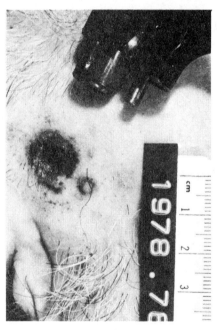

Fig. 7. (Left) Medium range inshoot wound. In this instance flake powder was used in the cartridge. Range was 2 to 4 inches. (Compare with ball powder tattooing as shown in Figure 10).

Fig. 8. Inshoot contact wound made with the muzzle of the auto-loading pistol held firmly against the head at the moment of discharge. Note the barrel and recoil spring pin imprints as compared with the weapon used.

34. For more information on suicide versus homicide determinations see, Suwanjutha, "Direction, Site and the Muzzle Target Distance of Bullet in the Head and Neck at Close Range as an Indication of Suicide or Homicide," 37 *For.Sci.Internat'l.* 223 (1988).

35. For an analysis of entrance wound sites in gunshot suicides see, Eisele, Reay and Cook, "Sites of Suicidal Gunshot Wounds," 26 *J.For.Sci.* 480 (July 1981).

Many suicide victims who shoot themselves in the trunk of the body bare their skin.

The on-the-scene investigator or pathologist should also look for the presence of a hammer spur impression on the victim's fingers as further evidence that death was caused by a self-inflicted gunshot wound.[36]

Every experienced pathologist will concede that there are cases of multiple bullet-wound suicides. The medical examiner of Hennepin County, Minnesota, reported a case where an 80–year old woman was found dead in her home with a .22 caliber revolver lying alongside her right knee. All of the chambers of the nine-shot revolver contained expended shells and the deceased had nine wounds of entry in the left anterior thorax. See Figure 9. A thorough examination of all of the circumstances lead to a medical conclusion that the wounds were self-inflicted. While unusual, this case is not unique.[37]

36. Johnson, "Hammer Spur Impressions: Physical Evidence in Suicides," *FBI L.Enf.Bull.* 11 (Sept. 1988).

37. See, e.g., Hirsch & Adelson, "A Suicidal Gunshot Wound of the Back," 21 *J.For.Sci.* 659 (1976). Timperman & Cnops, "Tandem Bullet in the Head in a Case of Suicide," 15 *Med., Sci. & L.* 280 (1975), reports a suicide in which two fired cartridges were found and the victim showed only one entrance wound. Tandem bullets were removed from the head. Such misfirings reportedly due to faulty ammunition are considered most exceptional.

In Bartram v. State, 33 Md.App. 115, 364 A.2d 1119 (1976) affirmed 280 Md. 616, 374 A.2d 1144 (1977), the defendant claimed decedent committed suicide. The case has an interesting factual issue involving proof of murder by sequential shots which made it necessary, as a practical matter, for the defendant to take the stand after the pathologist testified that the third shot could not have been fired by the victim.

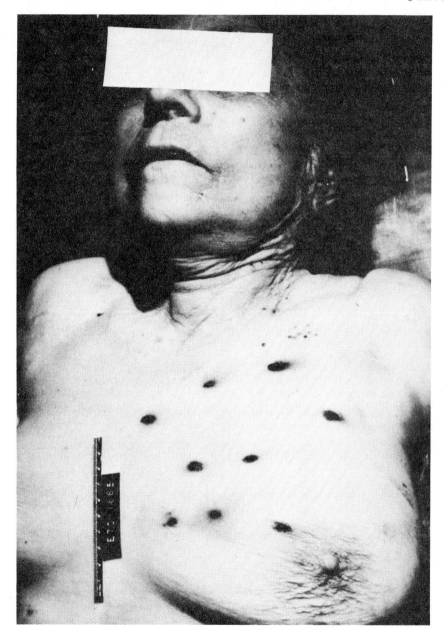

Fig. 9. The deceased's nine gunshot wounds were determined to have been self-inflicted with a .22 caliber revolver. *Courtesy: Hennepin County Medical Examiner, Minneapolis, Minn.*

A homicide prosecution based on circumstantial evidence may turn then, on whether the deceased expired from self-inflicted gunshot wounds or as the result of the criminal act of the accused. In cases involving multiple shots, the medical examiner may determine the sequence of the shots [38] to further determine the degree of incapacity that results from each shot.[39] It is important, therefore, that the typical signs of a suicidal gunshot wound be noted by the attorney who wants to raise such an issue in behalf of the accused.

The exit or outshoot of a contact or close wound will not display a gray ring or powder burns or a marginal abrasion collar. (Figures 10 and 11.) The exiting projectile has a conical dispersal of force. Size of a wound does not depend only on the gun type, ammunition and type of bullet. The path of the bullet can have an effect on the entrance and exit wound. The bullet may continue to spin on its axis or it may keyhole end over end or wobble in a yaw-like fashion. Also, it may strike bone and fragment. Size of a wound can vary according to whether or not the bullet's velocity is diminished. A sidewise yaw spin will cause more tearing than an axis spin. Bone splinters will cause laceration tears and stellate exit appearance; low velocity will cause the bullet to burst free with a lacerating effect. Thus, if the bullet encounters resistance within the body, its form will be altered, with a consequent enlargement of the exit wound into a stellate or jagged form. If it passes on its axis through the soft body tissues unobstructed by bone, the exit wound may be small with the edges of the skin surrounding it turned out. If the bullet has fragmented, there may be multiple exit wounds. If the skin is supported in the area where the bullet exits, the wound may very closely resemble a wound of entrance. It may occur when the area of exit is in contact with an unyielding surface such as a floor or wall, or when the area is covered by tight fitting clothing such as a belt or bra strap. This type of supported wound is sometimes termed a "shored exit wound." [40]

A distant bullet wound is deemed to result when the muzzle of the discharging firearm is far enough from the point of entry so that no powder tattooing or other indication of powder residue can be seen.[41] This distance, depending somewhat upon the nature of the powder, cartridge, and weapon is usually three or four feet. Pistol killings usually occur with no more than 60 yards between the parties. High velocity rifles can accurately kill from distances up to 200 yards. Since rifled firearms are ordinarily used to fire single missiles there is no "scatter" as with ordinary shotgun loads. Unburned powder and per-

---

38. In cases of multiple injuries to the skull, it is difficult but not impossible to determine the order in which the traumas occurred. See, Madea and Staak, "Determination of the Sequence of Gunshot Wounds of the Skull," 28 *For.Sci.Soc.J.* 321 (1988).

39. For a study of nine cases of multiple bullet-wound suicides see, Introna & Smialek, "Suicide from Multiple Gunshot Wounds," 10 *Am.J. of For.Med. & Path.,* 275 (1989). Also see, Habbe et al., "Nine-Gunshot Suicide," 10 *Am.J.For.Med. & Path.,* 335 (1989).

40. Dixon, Characteristics of Shored Exit Wounds, 26 *J.For.Sci.* 691 (1981).

41. In State v. Massey, 242 Kan. 252, 747 P.2d 802 (1987), there were no powder burns at the entrance wound on the decedent's head. No lab tests were performed on the bedspread which covered the decedent and contained what appeared to be bullet holes in it. Without such evidence, the absence of powder burns could be explained as either a distant bullet wound (which supported the defendant's accidental discharge defense) or a bullet wound inflicted with the bedspread between the gun and the decedent's head.

haps lead fragments and the products of combustion are apparent only within a few feet of the muzzle. A wound ballistics expert is unable to give a precise opinion as to the distance at which a shot was fired by examination of a distant bullet wound. Such a wound displays the same basic characteristics anywhere within this range. A gray ring may appear; an abrasion collar will be present. There is an absence of tattooing and scorching of the area surrounding the entrance wound. Distant bullet wounds are smaller than contact entrance wounds and may appear smaller than the bullet diameter because of the elastic tendency of the skin to close. There may be a similarity in the size of entrance and exit wounds if the path of the bullet was uninterrupted by hard tissue such as bone. The exit wound is similar in characteristics to that of the contact wound, although the entrance would usually be more regular and smaller than the exit wound. Wounds of the hands and forearms may be seen when the victim has attempted to defend himself. These wounds are properly termed "defense" wounds.

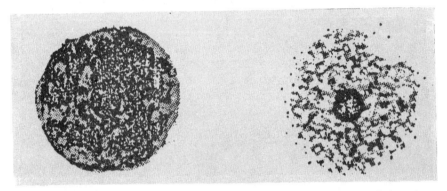

Fig. 10. Close-range gunshot entrance with smoke or soot around hole.

Fig. 11. Close-range gunshot entrance with powder "tattooing" or "stippling" on the skin.

A typical gunshot wound [42] created by tumbling bullets can present interpretation problems to the forensic pathologist. These wounds are produced by bullets in unstable non-axial flight usually due to some type of deflection from an intermediate target or ricocheting bullets. One type of wound found is a non-penetrating gunshot wound called a "slap" wound. Another wound is the atypical gunshot entrance wound which shows spatially separated abrasions. When both wounds are produced by one bullet, they are described as "an atypical gunshot wound with tumbling abrasion." The forensic pathologist must be careful not to misinterpret a tumbling abrasion as blunt force trauma. The features of an atypical gunshot wound with tumbling abrasions include an elliptical, oblique entrance wound, a collar of contusion around the entrance wound, linear patterned abrasions in the line of fire or ricochet, possible

42. Hawley et al., "Tumbling Abrasions: *J.For.Med. & Path.* 229 (1987).
Injuries from Ricocheting Bullets," 8 *Am.*

gunpowder stippling with "shadowing" by the intermediate target, the possible presence of particles from the intermediate target in the wound and possible satellite wounds produced by particles from the intermediate target.

C. SHOTGUN WOUNDS

A shotgun held within one or two feet from the skin surface will make a large single hole. (Fig. 12.) As it is moved farther away, its progressively expanding pattern of shot will result in multiple pellet wounds. (Figs. 13 & 14.) Within a distance of four or five yards, wadding pads or plastic sleeve collars used to contain the shot may be propelled into the wound. At somewhat longer ranges the individual wads may not penetrate the skin but may leave rather typical appearing "wad marks" on the skin. (Fig. 15.) The presence of wads or sleeves combined with a charting of the uniform cone-like shot patterns by test firing the suspect weapon or a facsimile under similar conditions as prevailed at the time of the homicide provides a good index of shotgun distance.[43]

In case of burned or ravaged bodies, it is tempting to use X-rays of the shot retained in the body to determine the diameter of the shot dispersion pattern within the body. However, even at close range the shot graphically disperses when it comes into contact with the body,

---

43. In Miller v. State, 250 Ind. 656, 236 N.E.2d 585 (1968), a shot range experiment did not meet evidentiary standard of exactitude.

See also, Williams v. State, 147 Tex. Crim.R. 178, 179 S.W.2d 297 (1944), holding that where it was shown that an expert used standard recognized experiments with defendant's shotgun to determine the pattern made by similar cartridges using similar loads to the ones found in defendant's shotgun, the results of such tests were admissible to show range.

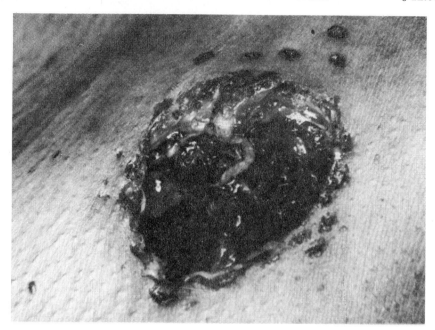

Fig. 12. A shotgun wound of entrance. This was inflicted with the weapon at a range sufficient to permit the shot to begin to break away from the main mass of shot and wads. Note the irregular edge and the satellite wounds caused by individual shot. The range of fire depends on many variable factors and in this instance is at least 6 or so feet.

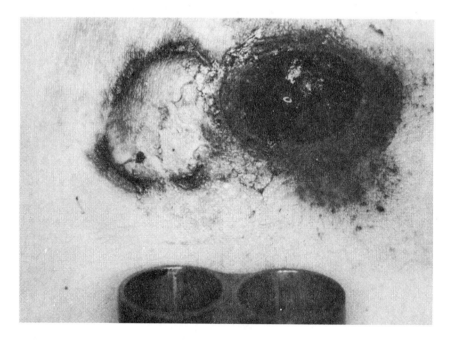

Fig. 13. Imprint made by a double-barreled shotgun fired in contact with the upper abdomen. Note the relatively smooth edge of the defect made when the shot and wads entered in one mass (compare with Figure 12).

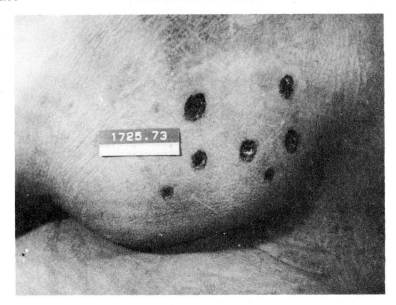

Fig. 14. Buckshot wounds of buttock. Nine 00 buckshot were loaded into one 12 gauge shotgun shell. All nine shot struck the buttock. Note that two of the wounds are "doubles"; defects made by two shots striking very close to one another.

Fig. 15. Long range shotgun wound. One of the felt-type wads has separated from the separating shot and has made an imprint. A wad of the type employed is shown next to the imprint. Wads frequently penetrate into the body at ranges up to 20 feet.

yielding an exaggerated X-ray result. Care should also be taken not to mistake foreign objects for shot pellets in the case of a firing through glass. Estimation of range of fire is less accurate as the distance between the gun muzzle and the target increases, especially if only some rather than all of the pellets strike the victim.

There can be wide variability with shotgun injuries. Careful examination and investigation are necessary to avoid misinterpretation of shotgun wounds. In two rather extreme cases, a contact wound to the temple resulted in the injection of large amounts of gas into the skull. This caused a gas blowout wound between the eyes. Such blowouts can be mistaken for entry wounds if the pathologist is not aware of this unusual shotgun injury.[44] In another case, what was initially thought to be two shotgun charges from different ranges was actually the result of an unusual intermediate target. A "dust cover" consisting of a shotgun casing had been inserted into the muzzle of the shotgun. This intermediate target actually became part of the projectile and produced the unusual defects.[45]

The significant factors in evaluating shotgun wounds to determine whether or not death resulted from suicide, homicide or accident are the gauge and choke of the weapon, the size and number of shots within the shell fired and the proximity of the muzzle to the victim.

D. Incised Cuts, Stab and Chop Wounds

As in the other types of wounds, the key issue for the pathologist's determination in cases of cutting and stabbing is whether or not the wound is the result of homicide or suicide. A pathologist is often asked whether or not the deceased could have produced the injuries which caused death and whether or not there were any body signs of a struggle. In cases of suicide by sharp instrument, "hesitation marks" point to suicide. Hesitation marks are superficial cuts inflicted by the suicide in the general area of the fatal wound as a test of the weapon prior to gaining the courage to make the fatal slash or plunge. (Fig. 16.) Reportedly, it is extremely rare for suicidal slash wounds to be inflicted in the absence of hesitation marks.[46] The direction of the cut and whether or not the victim was right or left handed are factors that enter into an expert's opinion as to whether or not death was by the victim's own hand. It should be further noted that cuts in suicide are usually found on areas such as the wrists, thighs, or throat. These cuts are typically regular and parallel.[47]

44. Johnson, "Unusual Shotgun Injury—Gas Blowout of Anterior Head Region," 6 *Am.J.For.Med. & Path.* 3 (1985).

45. Challener, "An Unusual Shotgun Injury Pattern Produced by an Intermediate Target," 7 *Am.J.For.Med. & Path.* 3 (1986).

46. For examples of suicidal stab cases where there were no hesitation marks see,

West, "Single Suicidal Stab Wounds" A Study of Three Cases," 21 *Med.Sci. & Law* 198 (1981).

47. See, Karlsson et al., "Patterns in Sharp Force Fatalities—A Comprehensive Forensic Medical Study. Part 2. Suicidal Sharp Force Injury in the Stockholm Area 1972–1984," 33 *J.For.Sci.* 448 (March 1988).

The incised cut wound is linear, that is, its length is greater than its depth. The edges are typically clean-cut, sharp and even. A pathologist may misinterpret a bullet wound which grazes the skin but does not enter as a slash wound. The nature of an incised cut wound varies with the instrument used,[48] the manner of use, the type, length, and sharpness of the blade as well as the area in which the wound is inflicted. What appears to be a clean-cut wound in an area of skin backed by bone such as the skull, elbow or knee may actually be the result of a dull edge or even a blunt instrument which usually produces lacerations or tears. In determining whether or not an incised wound was inflicted before or after death it may be indicative that an ante mortem wound gapes and bleeds profusely whereas a postmortem wound generally does not. On the other hand, it must be noted that postmortem wounds which occur fairly soon after death to areas of the body where there is a rich blood supply, particularly the scalp, may bleed quite profusely for an extended period of time, if this portion of the body is in a dependent location.

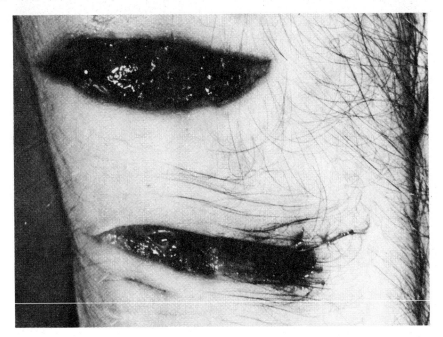

Fig. 16. "Hesitation" marks about a self inflicted wound (the lower of the two on the forearm). Such so-called hesitation marks nearly always indicate suicidal intent on the part of the victim. Note that there are no such marks near the upper of the two incised wounds. "Hesitation" marks are not always indicative, however, of self-inflicted wounds; they can be caused by an assailant, though it rarely occurs.

The mechanism of death in cases of stabbing usually results from internal hemorrhage of a vital vessel or the perforation of a vital organ.

48. Stab-cut dimensions in clothing do not accurately disclose knife blade widths. Costello and Lawton, "Do Stab–Cuts Reflect the Weapon Which Made Them?," 30 *J.For.Sci.Soc.* 89 (1990).

Homicidal stab wounds are usually found in different areas of the dead body if any struggle was involved. Examination of the corners of the stab wound will often assist in determining the nature of the instrument. With only one edge of the blade sharpened, this extremity is sharply incised. (See Figures 17–A and 17–B.) It is possible to distinguish a weapon of which both edges are sharpened, such as stiletto, wherein both extremities of the stab wound will be sharply incised. Similarly, a weapon which is sharpened on one side only will usually leave a wound with this extremity sharply incised while the other may be bluntly torn and even undetermined. Whether or not the wound gapes or closes will depend somewhat on whether or not the stab wound was cut at right angles to the elastic fibers of the dermal skin or whether it was cut along the line of the fibers. The edges of the stab wound are clean-cut in comparison with the blunt instrument wound.

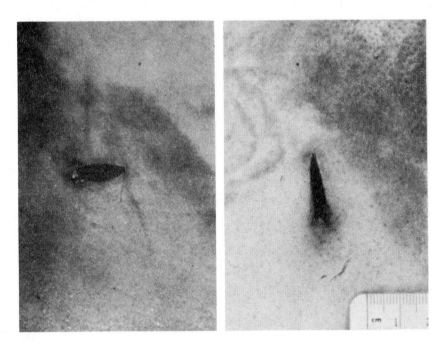

Figs. 17–A–B. These are stab wounds made by a knife with a single cutting edge. The dull side of the blade leaves a squared-off, torn, or two tailed appearance. The sharp edge of the blade leaves an acute angle.

The nature of the stab wound varies with the instrument used, the manner in which it was used, and the length and sharpness of the blade. (Fig. 18.)[49] The victim of a homicidal stabbing or cutting will often have defense wounds on the palms of the hands, fingers, or forearms where thrusts were parried. (Fig. 19) The lack of defense wounds can be of importance on a claim of self-defense.

49. In Fisher v. State, 361 So.2d 203 (Fla.App.1978), a conviction was reversed where the state's pathologist testified that the knife wounds on the deceased were characteristic of those produced by a woman.

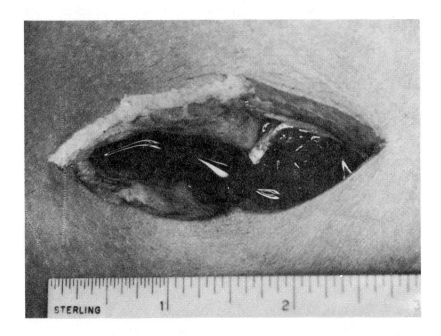

Fig. 18. A compound stab wound. Three strokes of the knife are necessary to cause this. The serrated border clearly indicates three strokes.

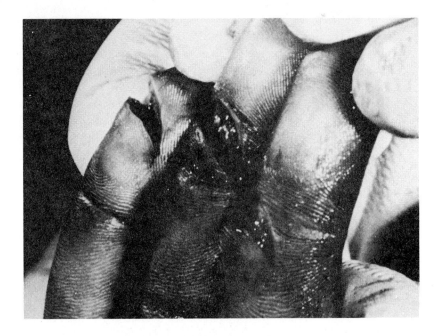

Fig. 19. "Defense" wounds of the hand. The victim seized the blade of the knife in a vain attempt to prevent his death.

In cases of stab wounds a pathologist may be queried on the depth of the wounds to prove or disprove their consistency with the suspect weapon. Depth cannot be determined merely by an observation of the size of the wound or the amount of bleeding. The nature of the soft tissues in the thorax and abdomen, their degree of stretching and displacement, and the degree of compression accompanying stabbing makes it difficult, if not impossible, to accurately determine the length of a weapon by measurement of the track of the wound at autopsy, except in extreme circumstances. The possibility of suicide in circumstantial evidence cases may be raised by the defense when the facts show possible hesitation stab wounds, especially if associated with the area of the major wound.

Chop wounds, typically inflicted by an axe, cleaver, hatchet, or machete, are rarely suicidal and are governed by the above considerations regarding cut and stab wounds.

E.   BLUNT FORCE

Blunt force wounds can jar, crush (as with a hammer) or tear the body. They may result from clubbing, kicking, being struck by an automobile or any other blunt force. They may result in contusions, abrasions, lacerations, fractures or rupture of vital organs. Fatal blunt instrument wounds are often delivered to the head, spine, neck, chest or abdomen. A grazing bullet may produce a wound that looks like a laceration. Red-blue contusions (bruises) result when blood extravasates into subcutaneous tissues as a result of compression produced by blunt force. It is important to note that existing bruises are greatly magnified by the embalming process due to the increased pressure exerted on the ruptured vessels by the embalming fluid and its tendency to pale surrounding skin. Obese individuals bruise easier than do lean persons. These considerations may be particularly important when photographs of an allegedly bruised but previously embalmed body are relied on by the state.

It is virtually impossible for a pathologist or examining physician to venture an opinion as to whether a bruise was delivered as part of an ante or postmortem attack if it occurred within a few minutes after death. In the case of scrapes or abrasions inflicted during life there will be an exudation of amber serum from the blood. These signs will be absent when the abrasion is inflicted after death because circulation has ceased. Differentiation can be made of a bruise from early rigor mortis since pressure will not dispel a bruise. Although it is common knowledge that the color of a bruise changes from purple to green to yellow as healing occurs, the rate of this change is so variable from one person to another as to make it virtually impossible to determine by inspection alone the length of time a bruise has been present.

Fatal injuries involving blunt force violence to the head frequently occur. Contusions to the cerebral tissue have patterns that are of great importance in cases of alleged homicide. If the moving head strikes a fixed object, as with a fall, then the cerebral contusions resulting from this trauma will be more severe on the point of the brain that is opposite from the site of impact (contrecoup). If the fixed head is struck by a moving object, as with a blow from a weapon, the cerebral damage will be more severe beneath the area of impact (coup). The identification of coup and contrecoup contusions can be used for reconstructing the direction of the impacting force, for estimating its relative magnitude and for determining whether the head was struck by an object or whether it struck an object in a fall or fall-like motion.

Fatal blunt force injuries to the head involving intracranial hemorrhage are of four types: (a) extradural; (b) subdural; (c) subarachnoid; and (d) within the brain (intracerebral).

Extradural bleeding involves a tearing or rupture of an artery, traversing between the layers of the thick dura mater membrane firmly adherent to the inner surface of the skull cap. Laceration is invariably a consequence of displacement of one of the margins of a fractured skull. Death results rapidly from compression of the brain by the blood clot so formed.

Subdural hemorrhage, the most common form of traumatic blunt force injury causing death, involves bleeding usually from a ruptured vein leading from the dura mater membrane to the underlying brain. Death from a subdural hematoma (blood clot) formed from a torn bridging vessel may occur several days or even weeks after the traumatic event. Venous bleeding is slow, hence, formation of the blood clot in the cranial cavity may occur over a matter of days and attendant brain compression may be delayed. In such cases death may occur several days after the infliction of trauma.

Due to the fact that extradural bleeding, because of its arterial origin, occurs more briskly than subdural hemorrhage, the duration of life following the infliction of the injury will also vary considerably. The lucid interval refers to the interval between the infliction of the injury and the onset of definite symptoms due to the bleeding in both extradural and subdural hemorrhages. The lucid interval is much longer in a subdural hemorrhage than in the extradural hemorrhage.

Subarachnoid hemorrhage is bleeding beneath the thin, transparent outer covering of the brain itself, into an artificial space which does not exist until so created by the bleeding.

Deep brain hemorrhage occurs within the substance of the brain and is not usually the result of trauma. It may be difficult and sometimes impossible for the pathologist to determine the amount of internal damage by simply examining the outer surface of the body. (Fig. 20.) Also, resuscitative measures may cause injuries that cannot be differentiated from those that antedated the collapse that made necessary the resuscitative efforts. (Fig. 21.)

3.   RAPE—MURDER

The pathologist does not usually come into contact with the rape victim unless she has been killed, though in some jurisdictions the pathologist is the physician who makes the examination of the living rape victim. Whether the victim is living or dead, the pathologist's examination for signs of intercourse is most important. He examines the genitals for tearing, scratching or bruising of the vulva, lacerations of the labia, tears in vaginal wall and of the hymen, if any. The collection of specimens from the rectum and mouth for examination for semen must not be neglected. The existence of previous venereal disease and/or pregnancy will also be determined. Suspected foreign pubic hair, blood stains and seminal stains are collected from the victim and her clothes for further analysis by the crime laboratory. See Chapters 9 and 13. In cases where the assailant ejaculated, DNA typing can be used to identify the person who deposited the sperm.[50] The pathologist may microscopically examine the specimen obtained as a result of vaginal, anal and oral swabs for the presence of motile or inactive spermatozoa. Motile sperm may be found in rapes resulting in

---

50. For more on DNA profiling and its courtroom use, see DNA chapter 15, infra.

death within four to six hours after death immediately subsequent to intercourse, although in some cases they have been found after a longer time. If the body is appropriately preserved in a cool, damp environment, non-motile sperm may be found for weeks following death, assuming decomposition has not occurred, since the decomposition process tends to destroy the spermatozoa.[51]

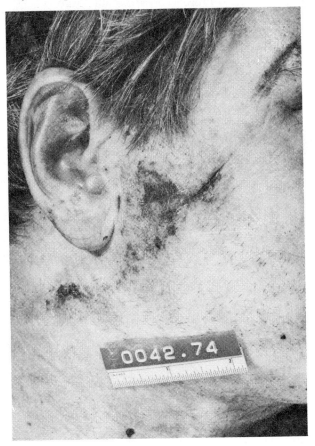

Fig. 20. The external appearance of the body may not really indicate the extent of the underlying injury. This man during a fight was struck by a hard object just under the ear. He died as a result of a fracture of one of the vertebra in the neck with a tear of one of the major arteries leading to the brain, and massive hemorrhage beneath the soft coverings of the brain (subarachnoid hemorrhage).

If a pathologist finds sperm, he should mount the specimen and preserve it as real evidence. It is advisable for attorneys to keep in mind that the average amount of ejaculate is from 2.5 to 5 cc and that each cc in a fertile male contains over 100,000,000 spermatozoa. This statistic

51. Three of the victims of London mass murderer John Christie were found on autopsy with "fresh" sperm up to nine weeks after they were murdered. Camps, F.S., *Medical and Scientific Investigations in the Christie Case,* 43–45, Medical Publications Ltd., London, 1953.

may make the discovery of one sperm cell seem quite insignificant. Certainly, if the sperm specimen has not been preserved, the knowledgeable defense attorney looking for a will of the wisp argument might be quick to bring to the jury's attention that motile protozoans such as trichomonas, a one-celled flagellate, could be mistaken for a sperm cell. This organism may inhabit the vagina causing the disease vaginitis. Its presence is in no way connected with recent intercourse. But it can be transmitted by intercourse, which might be a valuable investigative lead.[52]

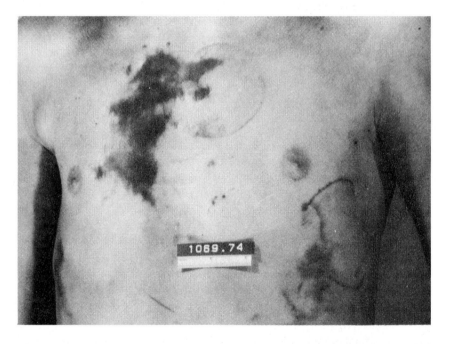

Fig. 21. The external appearance of injury may be due in whole or in part to resuscitative efforts. The "paddle" marks of the defibrillator are clearly shown here (note the circular marks on the chest). But are the bruises also due to attempted resuscitation (external cardiac massage)? Good liaison with the emergency medical technicians is necessary to determine whether or not the bruises antedated the resuscitative measures!

When 24 hours or more have elapsed after death and the body is in an environment wherein postmortem decomposition commences, the vagina may become enlarged and capacious, draining blood stained fluid which may be erroneously construed as evidence of violent rape. These changes are normally and correctly attributable to the relaxation of the perineal musculature and postmortem seepage of blood or escape of gas. Similar observations may be noted about the anus and rectum and similar misinterpretations rendered.

---

52. See, People v. Scott, 21 Cal.3d 284, 145 Cal.Rptr. 876, 578 P.2d 123 (1978) where a defendant's being forced to provide a semen sample for testing for the presence of trichomonias resulted in the reversal of an incest conviction.

4. POISONS AND BURNS

As mentioned before, observations such as the cherry-red or carmine lividity of a body, most noticeable on the cheeks and lower limbs even up to eight weeks postmortem, may lead a pathologist to suspect death by carbon monoxide poisoning.[53] In such a case a toxicological examination of the victim's blood would be necessary to determine if it contains a lethal quantity of carbon monoxide. Poisoning by sodium or potassium cyanide also produces a bright red or brick color of livor in the body. However, such a death may display additional signs in the form of a slight cyanosis of the face, froth of the lips, and the smell of burned almonds emanating from the body and its organs. However, the odor of burned almonds may attend the body of one dead of nitrobenzene poisoning. Corrosion of the skin around the mouth may indicate death by drinking acid or alkali. Brown coffee-ground-like vomitus is also characteristic of acid of alkali poisoning. Certainty of diagnosis requires toxicological confirmation. Since overlapping symptoms can lead to misinterpretation of cause of death, it is integral to pretrial preparation that the attorneys for each side consult a medical text describing poison symptomatology.

Other triggering signs beyond the scope of this text may cause a pathologist to retain the stomach contents, the kidney, the bile, the lungs or the fluid from the eyeballs for toxicological examination. Samples of the blood and liver will be taken. Metallic poison such as arsenic given in repeated small doses accumulates in the bone and horny material such as skin, hair and fingernails. Hence, samples of these structures may be retained for toxicological or nuclear activation analysis. The detection of poisons is principally a job of the toxicologist whose functions are described in Chapter 13. However, the pathologist should become versed in the fundamentals of toxicological analysis and the interpretation of analytical results so as to become an expert if allied specialists are unavailable.

Burns may be caused by heat, a chemical, or electricity.[54] Fire victims are usually found in a "pugilistic" position with clenched fists or bent arms, similar to the pose of a boxer. This phenomenon is caused by the heating of protein in muscle cells which causes contraction. Pathologists may uncover a homicide in which an attempt was made to simulate accidental death by burning the body.[55] Smoke contains carbon monoxide. Therefore, if carbon monoxide is lacking from the victim's lungs, death probably occurred prior to the fire. Minor (sub-

---

53. For an excellent description, see, Dutra, "Physiological Principle of Carbon Monoxide Poisoning," 54 *J.Crim.L., C. & P.S.* 513 (1963).

54. Massello, "Lightning Deaths," 37 *Med–Leg.Bull.* 1 (Jan.–Feb. 1988).

55. An interesting example is reported where the defendant picked up a drifter and killed him in a petroleum fire. The defendant intended to use the charred body as a substitute for his own in order to make it appear that he, the defendant, died in an "accidental" fire. Brown & Tullett, *The Scalpel of Scotland Yard: The Life of Sir Bernard Spilsbury,* 339–357 1952.

lethal) concentrations of cyanide as well as carbon monoxide may be found in the blood of burn victims. The cyanide is the product of combustion of plastics and certain synthetic fabrics. Therefore, the mere presence of cyanide in the blood of a burn victim exposed to burning plastics and synthetics does not indicate that he was poisoned with cyanide prior to the beginning of the fire.[56]

§ 12.07 The Forensic Pathologist in Civil Cases

The forensic pathologist's report regarding cause and manner of death is not only used in criminal proceedings, but the pathologist is also often called to testify as an expert witness in civil proceedings as well. In cases of an adversarial bent, two or more pathologists may testify as to cause and manner of death, each stating their opposing views. One pathologist will be the medical examiner or coroner who performed the original autopsy. Attorneys whose clients are adversely affected by the original diagnosis will employ pathologists for second opinions in order to provide alternate theories to the original diagnosis of cause or manner of death.

Although many civil causes require the testimony of a pathologist, three categories are featured here, viz: environmental injuries and diseases, accidental traffic injuries and medical malpractice.[1]

1. ENVIRONMENTAL INJURIES AND DISORDERS

Environmental pathology is one of the newest areas of study in medicine. Since the autopsy is an effective tool for recognizing new disorders due to occupational or environmental influences, forensic pathologists have stepped into subject areas like public health, industrial safety, environmental hazards and occupational disease.[2] State medical examiners and coroners diagnose many natural deaths each year due to trauma and diseases associated with the environment. Although the bulk of evidence linking specific environmental factors to effects on organs is circumstantial and contentious[3], environmental factors must be identified and considered whenever possible.

Pneumoconiosis is an environmental pathology caused by inhaling minute airborne particulates. When the solid matter is inhaled, it produces reactions in the body which result in various debilitating conditions. The most common historical pneumoconiosis affects coal miners. The resultant condition coal miners suffer from is called Black Lung Disease and is prevalent enough that Congress enacted the Black Lung Benefits Act.[4]

---

56. See, Noguchi et al., "Significance of Cyanide in Medicolegal Investigations Involving Fires," 9 *Am.J.For.Med. & Path.* 304 (1988).

§ 12.07

1. Disputed life insurance claims on behalf of a decedent whose death might have been a suicide constitute another category.

2. Wecht, ed., *Forensic Science,* pp. 23–28, § 23.02.

3. Geller, "Autopsy," 248 *Sci.Am.* 124 (Mar. 1983).

Another common pneumoconiosis is caused by asbestos. Asbestos was widely used for years as a fireproofing agent and an insulator. It is found in many buildings including schools and hospitals. Since exposure to asbestos dust only occurs once the particles are freed into the air, many local governments have decided it is safer not to remove asbestos from public buildings unless there is structural damage that exposes the asbestos to the air.

Mesothelioma is a type of tumor that has been found almost exclusively in people who have been exposed to asbestos. It has a distinct histological appearance that is readily identified today. The tumor may occur thirty or more years after the exposure which explains why asbestos dust was believed to be harmless for so long.[5] In 1990, nine thousand cancer deaths were estimated to be due to asbestos exposure.[6] Asbestos-related litigation is increasing as our ability to gather forensic evidence is enhanced through improved clinical assessment techniques such as "computerized tomographic scanning which may provide a more sensitive indicator of asbestos-induced pleural and parenchymal change."[7]

Lead poisoning is another prominent environmental pathology. Lead poisoning is defined as "a concentration of lead in whole blood exceeding 50/Micro/g/dL."[8] Exposure to lead most often occurs from lead-based paint. Until 1980, lead-based paint was widely used in homes, public buildings, and as a coating for steel structures. Today, lead poisoning usually occurs as a result of low-level exposure over a period of time. Chronic lead poisoning leads to an accumulation of lead concentrations in the body which result in brain damage and death.[9] The less common acute poisoning mostly occurs in children who ingest large quantities of lead-based paint chips.

Lead poisoning is no longer a major cause of death because the public has an increased awareness of the danger of exposure and affected industries have begun to take safety precautions. However, lead levels are still a public health problem. Studies indicate that children with lead levels exceeding 10/mu/g per deciliter of blood score lower on intelligence tests than children with levels under 10. It has been estimated that if children had levels between 10 and 25/mu/g/dL (which

---

4. Black Lung Benefits Act, 30 U.S.C.A. § 901. See, Amax Coal Company v. Director, Department of Labor, 993 F.2d 600 (7th Cir.1993). A battle of pathologists occurred as to whether the decedent had suffered from Black Lung Disease so that the court could determine whether his widow was entitled to disability benefits.

5. Wecht, op. cit. supra note 2 at pp. 23–29, § 23.02(a)(1).

6. McGinnis and Foege, "Actual Causes of Death in the United States," 270 J.A.M.A. 2207 (Nov. 10, 1993).

7. Frank, "Occupational and Environmental Medicine (Trends)," 268 J.A.M.A. 385 (July 15, 1992).

8. Center for Disease Control, "Request for Assistance in Preventing Lead Poisoning in Construction Workers," 267 J.A.M.A. 2012 (April 15, 1992).

9. Wecht, op. cit. supra note 2 at pp. 23–31, § 23.02(b).

is considered a safe level by current standards) there would be no children with superior intelligence and 12% with inferior intelligence.[10] Far-reaching reproductive effects from industrial exposure have also been documented. For women the effects include higher occurrences of infertility, spontaneous abortions, stillbirths, prenatal deaths, and neurological and psychological impairments in offspring. The effects on lead-exposed men include impotence, sterility, decreased fertility, Wilm's tumors in offspring, and increased rates of stillbirths, miscarriages, and spontaneous abortions suffered by their wives.[11] In deaths where lead poisoning is implicated the pathologist seeks to determine if the cause of death was chronic or acute lead poisoning. In cases of acute poisoning the pathologist will often find renal damage, arteriolar degeneration and areas of renal-sclerosis and lead lines in the bones.[12] This information can then be used in litigation to be connected to the most probable source of the lead poisoning.

A third environmental pathology is reflected in diseases arising from chemical fumes. This is a relatively new area that has expanded with the increased demand for synthetic products. Many organic solvents, ketones and halogenated hydrocarbons used in industry have been shown to produce liver necrosis, bone marrow changes and peripheral nerve damage.[13] Tumor pathologists have linked certain types of cancer to exposure to certain chemicals and drugs. The potential role for the pathologist as someone to monitor the effects of chemicals on the body is great in this area.

A fourth area of environmental pathology involves radiation injuries. All persons are exposed to natural and man-made sources of radiation. Natural sources include radiation from outer space, like solar radiation, and radiation from the earth, such as radon gas,[14] and naturally-occurring radioactive minerals like uranium. Man-made radiation includes x-rays, nuclear power plant produced radioactive substances, other industrial radiation sources and above ground electric lines. Pathologists can help determine if lesions and increased density or eburnation of the bone is linked to radiation.[15] This case-related information can be used to encourage the reduction of radiation hazards and is helpful in litigation where an injured party seeks compensation for radiation-induced trauma or disease.

10. Skolnick, "Tenth Annual AMA Science Reporters Conference Focuses on a Variety of Public Health Issues," 266 J.A.M.A. 2336 (Nov. 6, 1991). See also, Fulginiti, "Control of Lead Exposure in Children: Are We Doing It Correctly?," *Am.J.Dis.Chil.* 1275 (Nov.1992).

11. Sor, "Fertility or Unemployment: Should You Have to Choose?," 1 *J.L. & Health* 141 (1986).

12. Wecht, op. cit. supra note 2 at pp. 23–31, § 23.02(b).

13. Ehrenreich and Selikoff, "Medicolegal Aspects of Occupational and Environ-mental Disease," *For.Med.: A Study in Trauma and Environmental Hazards* 1271 (1977).

14. Radon is a radioactive gas that seeps up from the earth and can be released through concrete, tile or brick. It has been blamed for 5,000 to 20,000 lung cancer deaths per year. See Baker & Sherman, Saving Your Lungs and Your Life, 28 *Health* 63 (June 1991).

15. Wecht, op. cit. supra note 2 at pp. 23–33, § 23.02(d).

2.   TRAFFIC FATALITIES [16]

The pathologist's role is well-nigh essential sorting out the ambiguities in traffic fatalities. The forensic pathologist may be asked to tell
from the injuries sustained whether the decedent was the driver, a
passenger, a pedestrian, or a person who suffered a non-vehicular death
on the side of the road. Additionally, she may be called on to estimate
the speed of the vehicle, the position of a person in the car or, in the case
of a pedestrian, the position of the person relative to the car, and
sometimes the type of car. The repetitive nature of car crash injuries
has led to an expertise among forensic pathologists that can be vital in
litigation. To reach accurate conclusions, however, the pathologist must
be given data about the road, weather conditions and the like to enable
her to identify the instrumentality that produced the injuries which have
been observed.

Certain injuries can point to the decedent as driving at the time of
impact. The most obvious evidence is a circular impression on the skin
of the chest which is caused by the steering wheel. Such impact often
causes fracturing of the sternum and ribs with compression of the chest
and lacerations of the lungs. It may also cause injury to the liver,
pancreas, and surrounding vessels.[17] The driver may also sustain a skull
fracture when striking the headliner, roof, or windshield. One or both
feet on the brake may indicate the drive anticipated the accident
whereas a foot on the accelerator may suggest the crash was unexpected
or intentional. The driver and other front seat occupants will sustain
fractures of the ankles different from the leg fractures suffered by a
pedestrian.

In contrast, a passenger in the right front seat (unless protected by
an airbag) will sustain face, chest, abdomen, and knee injuries due to
being thrust against any combination of the following: windshield, roof,
dashboard, glove compartment, and floorboard. Horizontal bruising of
the lower abdomen indicates the use of a seat belt and is important to
note in the autopsy report for insurance purposes.

Motorcycle injuries differ from automobile injuries largely in degree
of injury. While there are no steering wheel impact injuries, more
massive fractures of the skull (where no crash helmet is worn) and
extremities may be present. If the driver anticipates the crash and
decides to take it "lying down," he will suffer massive abrasions from
the sliding stop on the pavement. The pathologist must examine and
retain the helmet in all motorcycle deaths since there will likely be
future litigation regarding whether the individual was wearing a helmet

---

16. Information on accidental traffic injuries from Wecht, op. cit. note 2 at pp. 23–
34—23–48, § 23.03.

17. Weisz, et al., "Injury to the Driver,"
14 *J. Trauma* 212 (1974). Also note that a

driver will sustain fewer injuries and will
likely survive an accident if the car is
equipped with an automatic airbag which is
triggered upon impact.

and whether the headgear measured up to protective standards for impact resistance.

Pedestrians killed in roadway accidents fall into three distinct categories. The first is the person walking along the side of the road in the same direction as the flow of traffic. Such a person will sustain bumper fractures when struck by a car. A bumper fracture is a fracture found in the lower third of the pedestrian's legs which is due to the force of the bumper of the automobile. If lower on the legs than the height of the bumper, the motorist can be said to have been braking at the moment of impact. The pedestrian can also be yanked out of his shoes. When hit, he will cartwheel up and back which will cause him to severely arch his spine and to strike his head on the hood, windshield, or roof of the car. How the pedestrian hits the car depends on a number of variables including the speed and design of the car. The arching can result in fracture-dislocations of the thoracic and/or lumbar spine while the impact of the head can produce a skull fracture.

The second category of pedestrian is the person walking along the side of the road facing on-coming traffic. Such a person will sustain similar injuries to the above discussed pedestrian. However, since this pedestrian may react to the oncoming collision, his bumper fractures may be replaced with evidence of high speed impact higher up on the body and more extensive fractures in his extremities from attempting to jump up or out of the way.

The third type of pedestrian is the person struck while attempting to cross the street. This pedestrian may also sustain injuries but, since the impact will probably be from the side, there is less likely to be extensive skull injuries or other effects from the cartwheel motion experienced by the other two types of pedestrians. This pedestrian is less likely to be thrown up and back, but more likely to be run-over by the wheels of the vehicle. Run-over injuries are compressed injuries that are readily distinguished from other impact pattern injuries. In such cases, a tire pattern is often found on the skin or clothing and the pathologist should carefully measure and photograph it for later comparison and testimony.

In addition to the injuries themselves, pathologists can gather other evidence that could have great importance in future litigation. Whether the deceased is a driver, passenger, or pedestrian, the pathologist should do a toxicological study for blood alcohol, carbon monoxide, and drug levels. These findings could evidence the circumstances leading to the accident and, in some jurisdictions, may support a contributory negligence defense. A search of the dents or cracked windshield of a suspect car may turn up evidence of embedded hair that can link the car to the accident victim. A post-mortem x-ray of the decedent's body may reveal the presence of parts of the accident-causing car which can later be matched and used to identify the vehicle. Also, the victim's clothing may contain fragments of paint, metal, soil and vegetation that can be used to identify the automobile involved in the accident. Paint analysis, for example, can identify the make, model, and year of some cars.

It is standard practice for pathologists to gather information and make comparative studies to help them better analyze traffic accidents. This collection of data can be instrumental in aiding automobile manufactures to make their vehicles safer. Improvements that have resulted from such studies include different designs in seat belts, airbags, impact absorbing steering wheels and use of tempered glass. Recognition of wheel design, tire manufacture and location of gasoline tanks and their relationship to injuries has resulted in many successful civil suits.[18] Finally, it must be mentioned that some fatalities behind the wheel arise from natural causes. Individuals sometimes have heart attacks, strokes, or other sudden crippling conditions while driving. Forensic pathologists must look beyond the traffic injuries and often must examine in detail the internal organs to determine whether contributory disease states are present. Generally, though, forensic pathologists will label a death at the wheel following a non-fatal pathological reaction as accidental because in the absence of the traffic accident, the person might have received treatment permitting him to survive the attack. Also, it is not necessarily clear whether the pre-existing condition caused the accident or the accident aggravated the pre-existing condition. The outcome of future litigation can hinge on whether the forensic pathologist classifies the death as natural or accidental.

3. MEDICAL MALPRACTICE

Forensic pathologists are often used to diagnose iatrogenic causes of death (sometimes called medical misadventures). An iatrogenic medical disorder is defined as one caused by the diagnosis, manner, or treatment of a physician on medical facility. When a patient dies in a hospital, the hospital pathologist may perform an autopsy with the permission of the decedent's family. In some jurisdictions, the local medical examiner or some other independent pathologist will review the matter instead of the hospital pathologist. This is often done to avoid a possible conflict of interests. The patient's medical record, the medication that was prescribed, and any surgical procedures that were performed will be reviewed. The purpose of this retrospective is to find out what went wrong so that it can be prevented in the future. This information will also be used in any litigation that is generated by the death.

Sometimes a course of treatment or therapy is used which results in more injury than what would have occurred without the treatment. Any death resulting from a procedure or medication prescribed by a doctor must be investigated to determine if the doctor is possibly guilty of medical neglect. The testimony of a pathologist as to whether the death

---

18. Whenever an attorney is basing his case on a defective vehicle issue, he needs to have testimony from an automotive engineer or mechanic who investigated the defect. A pathologist is not an automotive expert upon whom an attorney should base a case without additional expert testimony from an engineer.

is due to a pre-existing condition or the medical treatment itself will be key evidence in a potential medical malpractice action and in any hearing by the state medical licensing board.

In some cases, the forensic pathologist may have to review the record to make sure that the minimum care was offered. If treatment of a patient was refused or not followed up, a physician may be guilty of medical negligence. The forensic pathologist's findings are fundamental in determining whether the doctor acted according to the standards prescribed for the customary practice of the profession or was negligent in his care of the decedent.

§ 12.08 Time of Death

A pathologist's opinion as to time of death based on his postmortem examination of the deceased is always an estimate of an interval during which death might have occurred. It cannot be exact. Since exact specificity is virtually impossible, attorneys should be alerted by any pathologist who postulates an exact time of death. If the pathologist is so dogmatic as to state an exact time of death, it is entirely possible that he will be most vulnerable to competent, knowledgeable cross examination both in regard to the time of death as well as with respect to other matters.

In reaching an opinion on the time of death a pathologist will rely upon a number of assumptions drawn from sequential relationships involving known or postulated acts by the deceased and secondary observations at postmortem examination. All standard death certificates require a statement as to time of death, although the determination is of most significance in cases of suspected homicide.

The major factors involved in a determination of postmortem interval by examination of the body alone can be categorized as follows:

(1) Early postmortem interval, principally including

    a. Livor mortis: the pinking of death;

    b. Rigor mortis: the stiffening of death;

    c. Algor mortis: the cooling of death; and

    d. Other factors: corneal clouding, potassium level in the vitreous humor, gastric emptying.

(2) Late postmortem interval.

It should be borne in mind that embalming prior to a postmortem examination can affect external and internal observations giving rise to artifactual wounds and purging and contamination of organs and tissues. Consequently embalming should follow and never precede a postmortem examination.

Each of the above factors in time of death determinations will be discussed in more detail to reveal its contributions and drawbacks in establishing the time of death.

1.　EARLY POSTMORTEM INTERVAL

The early postmortem interval includes the period of time up to 48 hours after death. Livor, rigor, and algor mortis all occur during this time interval. Other factors present in the first 48 hours can also be used to determine the approximate time of death.

A.　Livor Mortis: The Pinking of Death

Livor mortis is also known as vibice, suggillation, and hypostasis. When blood is not circulating, it has a tendency to sink due to the force of gravity. Quite naturally, it sinks to the lowest (dependent) portions of the body in relation to the earth's surface. As the term lividity indicates, the lower surfaces of the body consequently assume a discoloration ranging from standard purplish-red to cherry-red (in deaths from carbon monoxide poisoning, hypothermia, acute cyanide poisoning, and iatrogenic administration of 100 percent oxygen prior to death) to sometimes a purplish-blue (in asphyxial deaths) to dark blue. This discoloration occurs as the finer subcutaneous capillary vessels become engorged with blood. The upper portions of the body pale as they are drained of blood. The livor of the down side of a body may be disrupted by blanched areas. These pale patches of skin are caused by the failure of blood to flow into those areas of the down side of the body where the vessels were compressed by the weight of the body on its reclining surface. Blanched areas sometimes show a patterned livor distribution which may mimic a ligature impression and the surface where the body lay when livor mortis began may leave its imprint. An impression from a surface may be used to determine if the body was moved after death.

The onset of livor mortis becomes noticeable one-half to three hours after death. The livor becomes fixed when the pressure exerted on the capillary walls cause them to rupture so that the blood is no longer in the vessels. According to expert estimates, this occurs from 6 to 24 hours after death. Subsequently, but before the onset of putrefaction, the lividity undergoes a color change to greenish and then a brownish hue as the blood diffuses from the vessels into the tissues. The time of onset of lividity is subject to a number of variables. For example, an anemic person would characteristically develop livor more slowly than a normal person. The degree of lividity will decrease in instances of substantial blood loss from trauma.

Livor mortis can be difficult to distinguish from contusions to skin. In recently deceased persons, the pathologist can tell the difference by several factors. First, livor tends to be of a uniform color while a bruise may take on varying shades. Second, livor usually has a linear margin while contusions occur in all shapes. Third, when a contusion occurs less than four hours before death, it will not have an inflammatory reaction around it like livor has.[1] Livor also can be distinguished from a bruise by its tendency to blanch from the skin when pressure is applied. A bruise does not do so. However, once the livor becomes fixed, its color cannot be blanched by finger pressure. The distinction is further complicated once decomposition begins because the blood from ruptured vessels tends to form pools where blood has settled previously.

Postmortem movement of a body from one place or position to another may also become an issue in a suspected homicide. If livor has not become fixed when the body is moved, the blood will again flow with gravity, and new areas of livor will appear on the body surfaces then closest to the earth. The subsequent livor may be inconsistent with the initial livor. Pathologists use this observation in deciding whether or not a corpse has been moved from the original crime scene to the place where it is found. Lividity may also be helpful in suggesting a cause of death, as in carbon monoxide or cyanide poisoning where livor is of a telltale cherry-red color. Large splotches or discolorations on the face, anterior neck and chest wall that are inconsistent with the expected livor do not necessarily indicate the body was moved. Such splotches are often not true livor and are evidence of death involving congestion. Because livor will not appear as clearly in a very heavily pigmented individual, its value in the estimation of time of death in such persons is negligible.

B. RIGOR MORTIS: THE STIFFENING OF DEATH

Concerning rigor mortis, it is most important that attorneys recognize that the order and speed of rigor mortis are by no means regular. Immediately after death, most bodies are limp and relaxed. At the expiration of approximately two to six hours after death, detectable stiffening of the involuntary and voluntary muscles begins with consequent stiffening of the body at the joints. This postmortem stiffening of the body musculature is known as rigor mortis. Rigor, as it is usually termed, typically becomes fully established between twelve to twenty-four hours after death. Rigor mortis is believed to disappear in order of appearance between 36 to 72 hours postmortem. The extreme onset range of rigor mortis is from immediately following death to several days depending on a number of variables which may hasten or delay its appearance. The appearance of rigor stiffening at the joints is first noticeable in the facial and upper body areas and thence downward to the toes. This is due to the fact that the small muscles and their joints become noticeably involved first.[2] During the period of rigor mortis, the

---

§ 12.08

1. Wecht, ed., *Forensic Science*, § 25.-03[c], pp. 24–25.

2. It has been said that rigor mortis does not follow the generally accepted anatomical sequence. It is hypothesized that rigor as a physiochemical process most likely develops simultaneously in all muscles.

Fixed rigor occurs more rapidly in smaller muscle groups. Therefore, the progression of rigor is determined by the variations in joint size and muscle mass. Gordon, Shapiro & Berson, *Forensic Medicine: A Guide to Principles* 30 (3rd ed., Churchill Livingstone 1988).

forcible "breaking" of a stiff joint will result in tearing of the surrounding musculature and flaccidity of the joint.

Heat hastens the onset of rigor mortis and causes it to be pronounced. Cold has the effect of delaying the onset of rigor. Rigor mortis may also appear quicker in situations of violence where the victim has exerted muscular activity immediately prior to death, i.e., electrocution, carbon monoxide poisoning, fights and struggles. Environmental heat or physical exertion before death accelerate the depletion of adenosine triphosphate (ATP) and glycogen. Anaerobic glycogenolysis produces pyruvic and lactic acid. The muscle protoplasm hardens or congeals when it becomes acid. This results in a quickened onset of rigor stiffening which is known as acid rigor for its association with low pH. If the person was exhausted or starved before death, the glycogen stores will be minimal, pyruvic and lactic acid will not be formed, and the muscle will remain alkaline (alkaline rigor).[3] Other variables which indirectly affect the time range of rigor mortis are the state of the deceased's nutrition, preexisting disease or debilitation, high fever at the time of death, movement of atmospheric air, amount of clothing worn, and age. For example, rigor is often of short duration in infants and sickly adults.

Estimating time of death from the degree of rigor is an uncertain science.[4] Using rigor to determine the position of a body at the time of death is equally uncertain. When rigor mortis is fully developed, the joints of the body become fixed dependent upon the position of the body at the onset of stiffening. If the body is moved prior to the onset of rigor mortis, the fixed extension of the joints will not indicate the original position at the time of death. However, if stiffening began prior to moving a body, examination of the rigor will indicate the change in position unless the rigor mortis was broken down by force. In such a case, the stiffening of the joint will not recur and the muscle will be torn.

A phenomenon known as cadaveric spasm or instantaneous rigor adds another note of uncertainty to the variable onset of rigor mortis. It is characterized by instantaneous rigidity of the whole body or an appendage such as the hand gripping a weapon or a clump of the assailant's hair or clothing. Instant rigor may suggest the manner and cause of death. For example, certain poisons like strychnine may cause instant rigor. A cadaveric spasm during which the decedent grabbed a piece of soap in the bathtub or some vegetation in a lake indicate the person was alive when submerged and likely drowned. Natural death

---

3. The rate of the loss of ATP in the muscles is directly related to the onset of rigor. Therefore the period of delay between death and the onset of rigor is dependent upon the reserves of glycogen stored in the muscle. Normally, a gradual loss of ATP occurs after death. To maintain chemical equilibrium, the body produces ATP through glycogenolysis. After all the glycogen is chemically converted, ATP levels fall and rigor begins. Gordon, Shapiro, and Berson, id. at 23.

4. While many forensic pathologists disagree as to whether the degree of rigor mortis is a reliable indicator of the time of death, courts allow expert testimony as to the approximate time of death upon rigor observations. [See, United States v. Kennedy, 890 F.2d 1056 (9th Cir.1989)].

involving sudden, intense pain may also cause instant rigor.[5] Experts believe instantaneous rigor is linked to emotion and violent muscular exertion since the essential physiochemical changes are the same as found in ordinary rigor mortis but at a greatly accelerated pace and exaggerated degree.

C. Algor Mortis: The Cooling of Death

Normal body temperature is 98.6°F. There is no hard and fast rule as to the exact progression of heat loss that bodies will display. Generally, the clothed adult will reach environmental temperature in an average room temperature environment in approximately 20 to 30 hours. One rough approximation is that the body suffers 1°C of heat loss per hour after death. Another rule of thumb is that the body loses from 2°F to 2½ °F for the first three hours after death and thereafter loses 1°F to 1½°F until reaching environmental atmospheric temperature. The following formula has also been used to measure heat loss:

$$\frac{\text{98.6°F less Rectal Temperature}}{\text{1.5°F per hour}} = \begin{array}{l}\text{Postmortem interval} \\ \text{(in hours)}\end{array}$$

Generally, it is agreed that there is no such thing as a regular fall of body heat after death since this is greatly dependent on the variables of the ambient atmosphere. If there are only a few degrees difference between the environmental and body temperature, heat loss is meaningless in determining time of death. While not precise, heat loss from the standard body temperature is a useful tool in estimating time of death in cases where death occurred within eight to twelve hours prior to examination. The investigator should take the body's temperature by insertion of a thermometer in the rectum, brain or upper abdomen beneath the liver.

Cooling depends on the temperature of the environs surrounding the body and on the clothing, ventilation, degree of body fat, size and age of the deceased. The head and hands of a clothed body cool first. Clothing causes heat retention as does obesity and size. Disease which causes an increase of body temperature (fever), will, for readily understandable reasons, influence the rate of cooling. The body begins cooling quicker from a higher temperature than a normal one. Deaths that occur with the body having been in convulsions or seizures prior to death will also have a higher initial body temperature than normal. Examples of such diseases and types of death are numerous and include cholera, typhoid fever, strychnine poisoning, cerebral strokes, strangulation, brain injury and heat stroke. The activity of maggots after death will also artificially raise the body temperature.

There have been recent studies using a mathematical formula to represent the body's postmortem cooling curve. This double exponential

5. Polson, Gee and Knight, *The Essentials of Forensic Medicine* 18 (4th ed., Pergamon Press 1985).

cooling model enables the time of death to be calculated using data readily available on examination of a corpse. This technique estimates time since death without the need for prior knowledge of ambiguous constants or allowances for body size or clothing.[6]

The use of tracheal temperature to estimate time since death also does not require allowances for body size, clothing and environmental temperature. However, since tracheal temperature can fluctuate during life, the assumed temperature at the time of death must be carefully assessed. Possible delay in postmortem cooling may also be necessary to consider for a more accurate determination when using tracheal temperature.[7]

D. OTHER FACTORS

The most common signs of death, such as stoppage of the heart and respiration and pallor of the skin, are not useful to pathologists in fixing the postmortem interval. Hair growth after death is a well-entrenched myth. Hair only appears to grow due to factors like dehydration of the skin.

The external surface of the eyeball begins to show a film as soon as ten minutes after death. Cloudiness of the cornea appears in 12 to 24 hours postmortem, depending on variables such as humidity, temperature and position of the eyelids. Its onset is much quicker when the eyelids are open. The cornea is completely opaque by 48 to 72 hours.

There is a linear relationship between the level of potassium in the fluid (vitreous humor) of the eye and the postmortem interval (PMI). Potassium levels have been shown to begin increasing shortly after death. The levels may continue to rise for several days after death. The possibilities of error in tests that utilize potassium levels to estimate time of death increase the longer the PMI. The factor which most influences the final result is the environmental temperature during the PMI. Other factors which influence the outcome include sampling techniques, age of the individual, duration of the terminal episode and the presence or absence of nitrogen retention.[8] A second chemical method for determining PMI measures the level of metabolite 3–methoxytyramine (3–MT) in the putamen of the brain. While levels of 3–MT can be affected by certain causes of death and specific classes of drugs, its results are at least as accurate as potassium accumulation in the vitreous humor. When both methods are properly performed with

6. Brown, "Determination of Time Since Death Using the Double Exponential Cooling Model," 25 *Med., Sci. & L.* 223 (1985).

7. Nokes, "The Use of Trachea Temperature as a Means of Determining the Postmortem Period," 26 *Med., Sci. & L.* 199 (1986).

For a survey of additional techniques that estimate time of death using body temperature see, Bernard Knight, "The Evolution of Methods for Estimating the Time of Death From Body Temperature," 36 *For.Sci.Internat'l* 12 (1988).

8. John I. Coe, "Vitreous Potassium as a Measure of the Postmortem Interval: An Historical Review and Critical Evaluation," 42 *For.Sci.Internat'l* 201, 209 (1989).

controls accounting for cause of death and temperature factors, the PMI can be estimated up to ± 8.0 hours.[9]

Four other methods show potential for determining PMI. One method analyzes cardiac blood pH. In controlled studies using rats and a pilot study in eleven human subjects, a strong negative linear correlation was found between PMI and cardiac blood pH.[10] The second recent promising development in the determination of the postmortem interval uses ultrasound. The velocity of ultrasound in the calf muscle of cadavers was measured at various postmortem intervals and the effects of variations in temperature were eliminated. It was found that the time of death can be predicted within one hour in most cases.[11] A third method, examination of the electrical excitability of skeletal muscle, is a simple and quick procedure that can be performed when the body is found. If used with the cooling of the body (algor mortis) method, the time of death can be estimated with some precision.[12] The fourth method involves the ageing of wounds. Microscopic examination of the tissue aids the pathologist in determining the age of the wound and whether it occurred before or after death. This method may help to determine the PMI.[13]

The inspection of stomach contents is part of every postmortem examination since it may provide information as to the cause of death as well as the time of death. The stomach usually empties from two to four hours following the last meal, and the intestine usually does so from ten to twelve hours after the last meal was eaten. This guide is only general and may not be correct if the individual was sick or under great stress for a period of several hours following the eating of the last meal. A variety of factors can affect gastric emptying so that time of death estimates based on it are of corroborative value only and must be stated with extreme caution.[14] Digestion also continues during the in mortuo period as putrefaction takes its course. Therefore, the best use of stomach contents for time purposes is to support or negate a time of death which a suspect may claim for the purposes of exoneration.[15] The

9. Sparks et al., "Comparison of Chemical Methods for Determining Postmortem Interval," 34 *J.For.Sci.* 197 (Jan. 1989).

10. Sawyer et al., "Cardiac Blood pH as a Possible Indicator of Postmortem Interval," 33 *J.For.Sci.* 1439 (Nov. 1988).

11. Webb et al., "A Method for Time of Death Determination Using Ultrasound—A Preliminary Report," 26 *J.For.Sci.Soc.* 393 (1986).

12. Madea and Henssge, "Electrical Excitability of Skeletal Muscle Postmortem in Casework," 47 *For.Sci.Internat'l* 207 (1990).

13. Maeno et al., "A Study on the Vital Reaction in Wounded Skin: Simultaneous Determination of Histamine and Polyamines in Injured Rat Skin by High Performance Liquid Chromatography," 46 *For.Sci.Internat'l* 255 (1990) and Thornton and Jolly, "The Objective Interpretation of Histopathological Data: An Application to the Ageing of Ovine Bruises," 31 *For.Sci.Internat'l* 225 (1986).

14. Horowitz, "Gastric Emptying—Forensic Implications of Current Concepts," 25 *Med., Sci. & L.* 3 (1985).

While the use of stomach contents in fixing time of death is highly questionable, the courts still allow such testimony. For example, see, State v. Origer, 418 N.W.2d 368 (Iowa App.1987), where the court admitted into evidence testimony as to time of death based upon stomach contents.

15. Jaffe, "Stomach Contents and Time of Death: Reexamination of a Persistent Question," 10 *Am.J. of For.Med. & Path.* 37

Crimmins murders in New York are a celebrated illustration of the ability of stomach contents to prove that a prime suspect recited errone-ously and exculpatory information to investigators.[16]

5. LATE POSTMORTEM INTERVAL
A. Putrefaction

Putrefaction by decomposition of a body exposed to the air in mild weather begins soon after death and is apparent in some corpses 24 to 72 hours after death. Its onset is characterized by a greenish discoloration of the skin of the flanks and abdomen. Anaerobic bacteria, micro-organisms from the intestinal tract and wounds enter the blood vessels and tissues through the walls of the intestines and from the air. It is the gas formed by the bacteria which gives the body a bloated aspect beginning with a swelling of the abdominal area. In drownings these gases will often cause the body to rise and float. The action of putrefy-ing bacteria is largely dependent on access to free oxygen. Thus, a body submerged in water or buried in soil will putrefy more slowly than one exposed directly to the air since air contains higher levels of free oxygen. The generally accepted approximation for degree of decomposition is that one week in air is equivalent to two weeks in water and eight weeks in soil. Blisters filled with fluid or gases may form on the skin surfaces as a sign of decomposition. The body skin color of Caucasians turns progressively darker.

The higher the temperature, the faster the rate of decomposition. In hot, humid climates it may be apparent as early as two or three hours after death. Conversely, cold weather retards decomposition.[17] Other variables such as the action of predatory animals or birds, the amount of clothing, and insect activity can also affect the rate of decomposition. The presence of certain chemicals may also alter the rate. For example, arsenic in the tissues and kerosene-soaked skin both delay decomposi-tion.

Although many homicide victims are disposed of by burial, there is little information regarding estimation of time since death of a buried body. It has been determined, however, that the decomposition of buried bodies occurs at a much slower rate because of decreased or absent insect activity, cooler below ground temperatures, and less oxy-gen. In fact, there is a direct correlation between the decay rate and the depth of burial—the deeper the burial, the slower the rate of decomposi-

(1989) and Suzuki, "Experimental Food Studies on the Presumption of the Time After Food Intake From Stomach Con-tents," 35 *For.Sci.Internat'l* 83 (1987).

  16. Jaffe id. at 40; Halpern, *Autopsy—The Memoirs of Milton Halpern* (1977).

  17. For more information on how temp-erature affects decomposition, see the con-trolled study by Micozzi, "Experimental Study of Postmortem Change Under Field Conditions: Effects of Freezing, Thawing, and Mechanical Injury," 31 *J.For.Sci.* 953 (July 1986) and see generally, Galloway et al., "Decay Rates of Human Remains in an Arid Environment," 34 *J.For.Sci.* 607 (1989).

tion.[18]

Decomposition of the body in water or wet soil may result in the formation of a waxy, yellowish-white substance from decomposed fat beneath the skin. This is called adipocere. This will aid an expert in estimating the approximate length of time a body had been in water.

B.   INSECT ACTIVITY

When an estimate of time of death is required on a body discovered more than several days postmortem, entomological data is invaluable. Insects such as flies may lay eggs in the mucous membranes of eyes, mouth and nose, or in wounds within a matter of several hours after death. The activity of the insect infestation may be of value in determining the earliest possible postmortem interval, assuming that a competent entomologist is allowed to view the body.[19] The entomological opinion concerning minimum time of death is based on a knowledge of the length of gestation of the larval and pupal stages of insect development when compared to those found in the body. It is generally believed that maggots can completely destroy the soft tissues in four to six weeks during the summer. In very warm and dry climates where bacteria and insect life are sparse, the body may dehydrate and become mummified. For mummification to occur there must be sufficient air currents to facilitate water loss. Worms and ants feed off bodies embedded in the soil. Birds, cats, pigs, foxes, rats, dogs and moles may eat the extremities of bodies exposed to the air. As decomposition ensues over a period of days, a pathologist's estimation of time of death will become less precise.

A major problem in accurate estimation of time of death from entomological data is that insect larval development is greatly affected by temperature. Two computer programs have been developed which are capable of modeling development of the insect species present in a local area. In tests of the model, the estimates generated have agreed well with those made based on other information.[20] A recent study using the green bottlefly (Lucilia sericata) compared their growth cycle in the field versus the laboratory under artificial conditions set to mimic the field. The results showed no difference in the lifecycles of both groups. This means that if the microclimatic conditions in which the larvae developed on a corpse is known, those conditions can be recreated in a lab to determine a reliable time of death index.[21] This may extend to other species of larvae. Furthermore, the presence of specific species

18. Rodriguez, "Decomposition of Buried Bodies and Methods That May Aid Their Location," 30 *J.For.Sci.* 3 (1985).

19. Information and assistance in locating such an expert can be obtained from the Entomological Society of America, 9301 Annapolis Road, Lanham, MD 20706–3115. Phone (301) 731–4535.

20. Williams, "A Model for the Aging of Fly Larvae in Forensic Entomology," 25 *For.Sci.Internat'l* 91 (1984).

21. Introna et al., "Time Since Death Definition by Experimental Reproduction of Lucilia Sericata Cycles in Growth Cabinet," 34 *J.For.Sci.* 478 (March 1989).

or their remains on a skeleton may indicate the season of death.[22] Sometimes the presence of non-indigenous insects may indicate the body was moved from another locale and dumped.

Where a cadaver has been exposed for more than a year, roots and stems of perennial plants may be an important source of information for estimating time of death. To be of use, the roots or stems must penetrate the body, clothing, or other personal effects. If the plant indicates growth changes associated with decomposition of the body or soil disturbance, the plant still can be used to estimate the time of death. The time of death is estimated by the number of growth rings in the perennial plant. Since the cadaver may have been deposited years before the plants grew, the estimate is of a minimum time of death.[23]

§ 12.09   Identity of Deceased

In the case of a body which is badly decomposed, charred or dismembered, a forensic pathologist may be able to formulate a general description of the victim as a result of the postmortem examination. The examination furnishes the predicate for an inferential identification of the deceased. When the condition of a body is such that identification by a death witness is impossible, this, naturally, becomes an important step in establishing the corpus delicti in a homicide prosecution. Specific identification from fingerprints, dental work, etc. can be complimented by general postmortem examination. The condition of the joints, the presence of arthritic disease, the teeth, and the degree of ossification in bone endings and the cranial sutures are guide signs in determining approximate age. Amyloid deposits can be used to corroborate age determinations.[1] A physical anthropologist may be utilized as a consultant and expert witness to determine sex, age, and race from human skeletal remains, among other possible uses for this expert's skills.[2] This is especially true when the examining pathologist has not become an expert in this allied field through study.

An odontologist (dentist) can be helpful in identifying dental work or dental plates. The forensic dentist uses dental x-rays, models, records, and smiling photographs in antemortem/postmortem comparisons to identify the individual. Today, the FBI and many states operate computerized dental identification systems through which pathologists can identify bodies and human bite marks.[3] A similar but often forgotten

---

22. For example, the sole presence of empty puparia of Phormia terraenovae, a type of blowfly, on a corpse indicates that death occurred in winter or early spring. Pekka Nuorteva, "Empty Puparia of Phormia Terraenovae R.–D. (Diptera, Calliphoridae) as Forensic Indicators," 53 *Ann.Entomol.Fennici* 53 (1987).

23. Willey and Heilman, "Estimating Time Since Death Using Plant Roots and Stems," 32 *J.For.Sci.* 1264 (Sept. 1987).

§ 12.09

1. Eriksson and Westermark, "Amyloid Inclusions in Choroid Plexus Epithelial Cells: A Simple Autopsy Method to Rapidly Obtain Information on the Age of an Unknown Dead Person," 48 *For.Sci.Internat'l* 97 (1990).

2. Refer further to physical anthropology, in Chapter 17, infra.

3. Sperber, "Identification of Children and Adults Through Federal and State Dental Identification Systems: Recognition of

technique for establishing identification is the comparison of antemortem and postmortem x-rays. Using radiographs to establish personal identity is the least time consuming and most technically exacting procedure available to today's pathologist. In cases of severe burning or mutilation, radiograph comparison of the skull and other anatomical features may be the only way to establish the victim's identity.[4] When identification must be done from skeletal remains, the pathologist can use skull superimposition as an aid, but only an aid, to identification once he has determined the skeleton's sex, age, race and height from other clues.

The basic sex indicators are the configuration of the pelvic bones (more widely spaced in the female to allow for childbirth), the skull, the long bones and the vestiges of the uterus or prostrate gland. Both the uterus and the prostrate gland are strongly decomposition resistant soft tissue. Cellular analysis of chromosomes also provides a method for determining sex. Measurement of the trunk and long bones provides an estimate of height. Microscopic examination of the hair, skin and eyes is sometimes valuable in determining race or coloring. If soft tissue remains, this may be subjected to serologic examination and blood type information of great value in establishing identification may result.

III. PATHOLOGICAL FINDINGS AS EVIDENCE

§ 12.10 Pathologist as an Expert Witness

The field of pathology, as a specialty of medicine, is most definitely one in which expert testimony is entirely appropriate, since the jury cannot be expected to have any familiarity with its procedures and the meaning of its findings. The courts generally do not impose a requirement of specialization or board certification in pathology as a prerequisite to a witness' testifying as an expert on pathological findings. This is probably due to the fact that specialists other than pathologists often qualify as expert witnesses in regard to studies made on human body tissues or fluids as a result of autopsies.[1]

Many courts have held that a properly qualified physician may express an opinion on the cause of death,[2] and the general view appears to be that all that is required to qualify as an expert is that the medical

Human Bite Marks," 30 *For.Sci.Internat'l* 187 (1986).

4. Jablonski and Shum, "Identification of Unknown Human Remains by Comparison of Antemortem and Postmortem Radiographs," 42 *For.Sci.Internat'l* 221 (1989).

§ 12.10

1. Consider, for example, the expertise of toxicologists, serologists, hematologists,

and chemists, discussed in Chapter 13, infra.

2. Barber v. State, 628 S.W.2d 104 (Tex. App.—San Antonio 1981, pet. ref'd), cert. denied Barber v. Texas, 459 U.S. 874 (1982); State v. Carter, 217 La. 547, 46 So.2d 897 (1950); Commonwealth v. Juvenile (No. 1), 365 Mass. 421, 313 N.E.2d 120 (1974).

witness be a licensed member of his profession.[3] This view is obviously quite unrealistic in this age of specialization.[4] In view of the tremendous advances in analytical techniques which have come about in the past decades, the minimum requirement to qualify as an expert witness on pathological findings should be nothing less than board certification as a pathologist when these findings are strictly within the pathologist's—as opposed to another medical specialist's—field.[5] In dealing with cases where correlation of investigatory information and pathologic data is required it may be of great value to obtain the services of a forensic pathologist.

While it might be argued that only board certified pathologists should be allowed to give expert testimony as to cause of death, the courts are more lenient. Not only do most courts allow any licensed medical doctor to testify as to cause of death, many courts are expanding the scope of medical testimony. In addition to cause of death, medical experts have been permitted to testify as to manner of death,[6] time of death, ballistics,[7] the muzzle to target distance, victim's position, the assailant's position,[8] time when victim clutched grass,[9] the relation between injuries and speed of the vehicle at time of ejection,[10] whether the injuries show intent,[11] and even the number of attackers and their strength.[12] Most courts also admit into evidence autopsy reports in lieu of live medical examiner testimony as to cause of death. The court need only find the report reliable to admit it as an exception to the hearsay rule and reliability is often assumed due to the special responsibility assigned by the law to the medical examiner.[13]

3. Cases show that testimony need not be given by a physician. Funeral directors and non-physician coroners have been permitted to testify as to the cause of death: State v. Howard, 274 N.C. 186, 162 S.E.2d 495 (1968); Jackson v. State, 412 So.2d 302 (Ala.Cr.App.1982); Neal v. State, 386 So.2d 718 (Miss.1980).

See also, Cobb v. State, 50 Ala.App. 707, 282 So.2d 327 (1973), allowing a doctor who was not licensed to practice medicine to testify as to cause of death.

4. In Smith, "Scientific Proof and Relations of Law and Medicine," 23 *B.U.L.Rev.* 143, 147 (1943), the doctor-author stated: "Courts have plodded along, quite willing to recognize any holder of an M.D. degree as a universal expert on science. This naivete is surprising, for the same judge who rules a general practicioner [sic.] competent on his qualifying or voir dire examination will take the train for the Mayo Clinic if he stands in personal need of specialized surgery."

5. On qualifying a pathologist, see, 9 Am.Jur. Proof of Facts, Physicians and Surgeons, 291.

State v. Melvin, 390 A.2d 1024 (Me.1978). Failure to be certified by a Board of Forensic Pathologists would bear on the weight, not the admissibility, of evidence.

6. State v. Langley, 354 N.W.2d 389 (Minn.1984) and Fridovich v. State, 489 So.2d 143 (Fla.App.1986).

7. State v. Spears, 70 N.C.App. 747, 321 S.E.2d 13 (1984).

8. People v. Britz, 128 Ill.App.3d 29, 83 Ill.Dec. 639, 470 N.E.2d 1059 (1984).

9. State v. Pridgen, 313 N.C. 80, 326 S.E.2d 618 (1985).

10. Stiegele v. State, 714 P.2d 356 (Alaska App.1986).

11. Harris v. State, 489 So.2d 688 (Ala. Cr.App.1986); State v. Knowles, 598 So.2d 430 (La.App.1992).

12. Endress v. State, 462 So.2d 872 (Fla.App.1985).

13. Manocchio v. Moran, 919 F.2d 770 (1st Cir.1990); Montgomery v. Fogg, 479 F.Supp. 363 (S.D.N.Y.1979); Mancusi v. Stubbs, 408 U.S. 204 (1972).

§ 12.11 Use of Demonstrative Evidence

In testifying, a pathologist may use demonstrative evidence to assist the jury in better understanding his expert findings. The admissibility of demonstrative evidence is ordinarily within the sound discretion of the trial judge, whose determination will ordinarily be reversed only when an abuse of discretion is shown.[1] Such aids may include photographs,[2] color slides,[3] infrared photographs,[4] x-rays,[5] charts, maps, and even skeletons,[6] and videotapes of the autopsy.

The admissibility of gruesome photographs in homicide cases[7] is a highly charged subject of frequent occurrence among the cases. The trial judge must determine whether the probative value of such photographs outweighs any prejudicial effect, and that determination will not be overturned on appeal absent an abuse of a rather vast and undefined discretion accorded the trial judge. Generally, the courts tend to approve the admission of photographic evidence, and a photograph will not be deemed inadmissible merely because it is gruesome.

Most photographs of the victim as found at the crime scene are admitted because they show the condition, position, and location of the body, as well as the surrounding circumstances of the death. A videotape of the recovery of a corpse from a river was held to be admissible to show the condition and location of the body in Thompson v. State.[8] In State v. Harris,[9] a photograph of the victim lying in a pool of blood was held to have evidentiary value to show surprise on the victim's face consistent with a sneak attack. In Griffin v. State,[10] crime scene photographs of two bodies were admitted to identify the scene and the victims even though the defendant was on trial for only one of the killings. Because the bodies were together and had been killed within minutes of each other by the same weapon, the court reasoned that the crimes were so connected as to constitute a single event.

Autopsy photographs are often admitted because they demonstrate the nature, extent and location of injuries, and the cause of death.

§ 12.11

1. 32 C.J.S. Evidence § 709.

2. Admissibility of colored photographs: Brumbley v. State, 453 So.2d 381 (Fla. 1984): color photographs of homicide victim's skeletal remains admissible; State v. Stephens, 672 S.W.2d 714 (Mo.App.1984). See further, Chapter 2, dealing with photographs, motion pictures, and videotape.

3. Chandler v. State, 275 Ind. 624, 419 N.E.2d 142 (1981).

4. E.g., State v. Cunningham, 173 Or. 25, 144 P.2d 303 (1943).

5. State v. Torres, 60 Hawaii 271, 589 P.2d 83 (1978): X-ray photography used by forensic pathologist to determine the caliber of bullet lodged in victim.

6. Anno., 83 A.L.R.2d 1097, on the propriety, in the trial of criminal cases, of using skeletons and models of the human body or parts thereof. See also two articles dealing with civil cases primarily: Averbach, "Medical Demonstrative Evidence," 58 Ky.L.J. 423 (1970); Bolen "The Blackboard Jungle of Demonstrative Evidence: View of a Defense Attorney," 48 Va.L.Rev. 913 (1962).

7. See generally, Anno., admissibility of photograph of corpse in prosecution for homicide or civil action causing death, 73 ALR 2d 769 (1960); 11 Sci.Sleuth.Rev. 12 (Summer '87); and 12 Sci.Sleuth.Rev. 8. (Fall '88)

8. 724 P.2d 780 (Okl.Cr.1986).

9. 106 Wash.2d 784, 725 P.2d 975 (1986).

10. 504 So.2d 186 (Miss.1987).

Thus, a videotape of a badly decomposed body was admitted to show blunt trauma to the skull,[11] and a photograph of a victim's cut throat was permitted to show premeditation.[12] However, photographs of a victim's scalp surgically pulled away from her skull and her surgically opened vaginal cavity were found to be inadmissible [13] along with photographs taken during evisceration.[14] Such gruesome sights are construed to have no purpose other than to inflame the jury.

Photographs of the victim before death can also be admitted into evidence, if found relevant to the proceeding. Photographs of the victim undergoing treatment in the emergency room have been admitted to show multiple bruises as evidence of malice, as well as the extent of head and facial trauma.[15] Even a photograph of a victim and his wife can be admitted if needed to identify the victim.[16]

Although the courts normally limit the number of gruesome photographs admitted in order to avoid prejudice through proliferation and repetition,[17] one court admitted 60 photographs of the murder victim's nude and battered body. The court stated that the defendant would not be allowed to erase the ugly parts of the crime by substituting words in place of the pictures.[18]

The question occasionally arises as to whether it is permissible to display, in court, severed parts of the body of a murder victim. Generally, courts tend to look with disfavor on such demonstrative aids,[19] although occasionally the courts have upheld the admissibility over objections based on goriness and gruesomeness.[20] In such cases, of course, particular care would be needed to preserve the chain of evidence and properly identify the dismembered part.

It would appear that the display of dismembered body parts has a natural effect of unduly influencing the jury. The better rule would seem to be that if a showing of the separated parts of the body is

11. Kealohapauole v. Shimoda, 800 F.2d 1463 (9th Cir.1986).

12. State v. Giffing, 45 Wash.App. 369, 725 P.2d 445 (1986).

13. State v. Middleton, 288 S.C. 21, 339 S.E.2d 692 (1986).

14. Sipsas v. State, 102 Nev. 119, 716 P.2d 231 (1986).

15. Wetz v. State, 503 So.2d 803 (Miss. 1987).

16. Clay v. State, 256 Ga. 797, 353 S.E.2d 517 (1987).

17. Berry v. State, 290 Ark. 223, 718 S.W.2d 447 (1986).

18. Todd v. Commonwealth, 716 S.W.2d 242 (Ky.1986).

19. Harper v. Bolton, 239 S.C. 541, 124 S.E.2d 54 (1962), a personal injury case wherein the trial judge was held to have committed error in admitting a glass vial containing the removed and preserved eye of the plaintiff which she had lost in the injury.

20. E.g.: State v. Boozer, 80 Ariz. 8, 291 P.2d 786 (1955), showing the fetus, placenta and blood clots passed by a woman aborted by the defendant; Wallace v. State, 204 Ga. 676, 51 S.E.2d 395 (1949), ashes of the decedent, allegedly killed by defendant. In Washburn v. State, 167 Tex.Crim.R. 125, 318 S.W.2d 627 (1958), cert. denied 359 U.S. 965 (1959), the judge refused to admit a jar containing flesh and skin of decedent. On appeal, it was held error to permit the jar to remain in view of the jury where it was not used in evidence. In State v. Spodnick, 292 S.C. 68, 354 S.E.2d 904 (1987), a two to three inch segment of human bone was admitted even though the defendant was willing to stipulate to anything the prosecutor wanted in order to keep the evidence from the jury. The bone was never proved to be from the victim.

material and relevant to issues in dispute, that the display be made by the production of a color photograph rather than by the part itself. The pathologist must exercise great care in making certain that the background to be shown in the photograph is free of blood, instruments, and other objectionable objects. Their presence in the background may well render the photographs inadmissible to the court.

§ 12.12   Evidence of Expert Findings

Expert testimony is proper when the subject matter of the inquiry is of such character that only persons of special skill or experience can judge the applicable facts. If a jury is competent to determine and understand the facts, then expert testimony is not proper and should not be admitted. For example, one court found that a jury is capable of determining whether the defendant could have accidentally rolled over in her sleep and suffocated her child.[1]

The conclusions of pathologists and other medical experts may vary among a broad range of subject matters, from the diagnosis of the apparent cause of death as due to either natural causes or violence, to the inference of the type of weapon used to inflict wounds and the position of the assailant.[2] An expert witness may be permitted to state the degree of confidence that he has in his opinion, and that, where an autopsy had been conducted, it would still more positively have confirmed his finding.[3]

When causation is the exact point to be decided by the jury, the expression of opinions by a medical expert as to cause of death does not invade the province of the jury.[4]

The medical expert need not testify as to cause of death beyond a reasonable doubt.[5] He may state the basis for his opinion, as well as the degree of certainty, as "probable," "likely," or "could have caused." He may also state the basis for his opinion, as well as the degree of certainty such as "possible," "probable," "likely," or "could have caused." Qualifications of this nature do not render the evidence too uncertain for court purposes.[6]

§ 12.12

1. People v. Perry, 147 Ill.App.3d 272, 101 Ill.Dec. 659, 498 N.E.2d 1167 (1986).

2. People v. Britz, 128 Ill.App.3d 29, 83 Ill.Dec. 639, 470 N.E.2d 1059 (1984); pathologist gave opinion that wound was consistent with a scenario in which deceased was kneeling and the assailant was standing.

3. Evidence of postmortem examination of the body of the deceased to show cause of death is generally admissible; State v. Zweifel, 570 S.W.2d 792 (Mo.App.1978), on rehearing State v. Zweifel, 615 S.W.2d 470 (Mo.App.1981); People v. Jackson, 64 Ill. App.3d 1014, 20 Ill.Dec. 764, 380 N.E.2d 973 (1978).

4. Bell v. State, 435 So.2d 772 (Ala.Cr. App.1983); People v. Goolsby, 45 Ill.App.3d 441, 4 Ill.Dec. 38, 359 N.E.2d 871 (1977), later app. People v. Goolsby, 70 Ill.App.3d 832, 26 Ill.Dec. 893, 388 N.E.2d 894 (1979), cert. denied Goolsby v. Illinois, 445 U.S. 952 (1980).

5. Commonwealth v. Floyd, 499 Pa. 316, 453 A.2d 326 (1982).

6. McMillian v. State, 570 So.2d 1285 (Ala.Cr.App.1990) (probable), remanded on other grounds 594 So.2d 1288 (1992); People v. Davis, 7 Cal.4th 797, 30 Cal.Rptr.2d 50, 872 P.2d 591 (1994) (probably); Hollingsworth v. State, 549 So.2d 110 (Ala.Cr. App.1988) (possible); State v. Webb, 309 N.W.2d 404 (Iowa 1981); Reed v. State, 180

There is controversy over whether "consistent with" testimony is admissible. One court found testimony stating that the injuries were consistent with a pedestrian-vehicular accident was proper.[7] Another court found testimony that bruises were consistent with bitemarks inadmissible.[8]

Establishing the cause of death when non-criminal causative factors also are present is a much litigated area in which a defendant will challenge a homicide conviction claiming that intervening factors, rather than his wrongdoing, actually caused the victim's death. However, courts routinely uphold homicide convictions as long as the defendant's criminal conduct can be shown to have set in motion the sequence of events which culminated in the victim's death.[9]

When an assailant inflicts wounds which are themselves life-threatening, the fact that other factors may have contributed to the victim's death will not relieve the assailant of responsibility for that death. In State v. Smith,[10] for example, the court upheld a murder conviction where the assailant stabbed the victim in the chest and inadequate medical care contributed to the death. In another case, a court upheld a murder conviction when death resulted from the victim being hit on the head with a metal pipe and arteriosclerosis was a contributing factor.[11] While at common law the victim must die within a year and a day of the criminal act for the actor to be culpable, the passage of time is not a sufficient intervening factor in homicide prosecutions where the evidence establishes that the victim's death resulted from the defendant's conduct.[12]

Ind.App. 5, 387 N.E.2d 82 (1979): mere suspicion of possibility not sufficient to support conviction. 66 A.L.R.2d 1082 (1959): Admissibility of opinion evidence as to cause of death, disease, or injury.

In Drury v. Burr, 13 Ariz.App. 164, 474 P.2d 1016 (1970), "probable cause" of murder was not established when the doctor's testimony was couched in terms of "possibility" rather than "probability" on cause of death by criminal agency, vacated 107 Ariz. 124, 483 P.2d 539 (1971).

On the issue, generally, see, McNeal, "The Medical Expert Witness—Positive, Negative, Maybe," 2 *J.For.Sci.* 135 (1957); Rheingold, "The Basis of Medical Testimony," 14 *Vand.L.Rev.* 473 (1962).

7. Thomas v. State, 455 So.2d 278 (Ala. Cr.App.1984). Accord: State v. Hebert, 480 A.2d 742 (Me.1984).

8. State v. Adams, 481 A.2d 718 (R.I. 1984).

9. For example, courts have upheld murder convictions where the fright and shock of a robbery lead to the victim's death. In Stewart v. State, 65 Md.App. 372, 500 A.2d 676 (1985), an unarmed robber was convicted of felony murder when the victim died from cardiac arrest two hours after the holdup.

Courts have even upheld murder and manslaughter convictions when the victim died from a heart attack suffered several days after the robbery or assault. See, State v. Allen, 710 S.W.2d 912 (Mo.App. 1986) (the elderly victim died of a heart attack two days after the assault which left her battered, cold and immobile) and Matter of Anthony M., 63 N.Y.2d 270, 481 N.Y.S.2d 675, 471 N.E.2d 447 (1984) (death occurred two and a half days after the attack).

See also, Kohler v. State, 713 S.W.2d 141 (Tex.App.1986), where an infant died from malnutrition and the parents were convicted of murder for failing to provide food and medical care during the child's three months of life.

10. 496 So.2d 195 (Fla.App.1986).

11. People v. Tackett, 150 Ill.App.3d 406, 103 Ill.Dec. 574, 501 N.E.2d 891 (1986).

12. People v. Kennedy, 150 Ill.App.3d 319, 103 Ill.Dec. 687, 501 N.E.2d 1004 (1986).

In the area of gunshot wounds, medical experts' testimony may be directed toward a broad variety of conclusions, such as the nature of the weapon used, the number of wounds inflicted, their location, the trajectory of the bullets through the body, the distance and direction of the fire, as well as the nature and extent of the wound.[13] In Tolston v. State,[14] medical witness testimony as to the nature of the projectile used was held proper. In Ward v. State,[15] testimony regarding the location of gunshot wounds met with approval. On the other hand, the pathologist or other medical witness should not be permitted to testify concerning the caliber of the bullet unless he is shown to be qualified as a firearms expert.[16]

This, however, should not prevent the pathologist from making a general statement as to the approximate caliber of the bullet. There appears to be a great deal of variation among the courts as to whether or not the pathologist should be permitted to testify as to the range of fire based on his examination of the clothing that he removed from the body. This involves comparison of firearms residues on that clothing with residues obtained by firing test shots with the alleged murder weapon. In People v. Calhoun,[17] a murder conviction was reversed because the Illinois Appellate Court believed that the state pathologist's testimony on the trajectory of a bullet inside deceased's body and, the state's firearms expert testimony on bullet deformations actually supported the theory of the defense that death had been accidental.

Expert medical testimony is also admissible to show that death occurred by poisoning,[18] strangulation,[19] drowning,[20] or by asphyxiation.[21]

Previously, the opinion of one expert based upon that of another expert, not received into evidence at the trial, was deemed inadmissible by the courts in view of the witness's having relied upon what would be hearsay. With the coming of Federal Rule of Evidence 703 in 1974 [22]

13. State v. Clark, 171 W.Va. 74, 297 S.E.2d 849 (1982).

14. 93 Tex.Crim.R. 493, 248 S.W. 50 (App.1923).

15. 427 S.W.2d 876 (Tex.Cr.App.1968). See also, Bryant v. State, 539 S.W.2d 816 (Tenn.Cr.App.1976).

16. Lee v. State, 661 P.2d 1345 (Okl.Cr. 1983).

17. 4 Ill.App.3d 683, 281 N.E.2d 363 (1972).

18. State v. Buck, 88 Kan. 114, 127 P. 631 (1912); Byrd v. State, 243 Ind. 452, 185 N.E.2d 422 (1962); Hand v. State, 77 Tex. Crim.R. 623, 179 S.W. 1155 (App.1915).

19. People v. Lowe, 184 Colo. 182, 519 P.2d 344 (1974); Commonwealth v. Tallon, 478 Pa. 468, 387 A.2d 77 (1978).

20. People v. Barker, 60 Mich. 277, 27 N.W. 539 (1886). A justice of the peace was

permitted to estimate the length of time a body had been in the water in West v. State, 116 Tex.Crim.R. 468, 34 S.W.2d 253 (1930).

21. State v. Mondaine, 655 S.W.2d 540 (Mo.App.1983); Schultz v. State, 82 Wis.2d 737, 264 N.W.2d 245 (1978). See, Anno., 66 A.L.R.2d 1082 (1959).

22. Rule 703 reads: "The facts or data in the particular case upon which an expert bases an opinion or inference may be those perceived by or made known to him at or before the hearing. If of a type reasonably relied upon by experts in the particular field in forming opinions or inferences upon the subject, the facts or data need not be admissible in evidence."

See also, Pattendon, "Expert Opinion Evidence Based on Hearsay," *The Crim.L.Rev.* 85 (1982); Pratt, "A Judicial Perspective

this situation has changed in the federal courts and in those numerous jurisdictions which have adopted the Federal Rules. Rule 703 allows a pathologist to give his opinion on the cause of death even though it was predicated in part on a toxicological report which had been made by another expert and which had not been put into evidence.[23] But Rule 703 and its state counterparts cannot be used to bypass the necessity to establish the trustworthiness of the expert's underlying data.

However, other jurisdictions have continued to require that an expert's opinion be based either on facts within the personal knowledge of the witness or upon facts shown by other evidence in the case.[24] It may be that these states have adhered to the older view because of a concern lest an accused's constitutional right of confrontation be infringed by the liberalized approach under Federal Rule 703 and its offspring in the states.

The majority of jurisdictions permit the cross-examination of an expert from any book or periodical recognized as an authority in the expert's field, in order to establish the existence of a contrary opinion, even if the expert has not specifically stated his reliance upon that particular book or periodical.[25] The authoritativeness of the text may be established by judicial notice or by a witness expert in the subject.[26]

IV. TRIAL AIDS

§ 12.13 Government–Employed Experts

The prosecution seldom has to concern itself with locating a pathologist to perform a postmortem examination. If the state or county of jurisdiction functions under a medical examiner system, the medical examiner or one of his deputies perform the complete postmortem. If the jurisdiction has a coroner or a justice of the peace serving as coroner, he may have to employ a pathologist for autopsy purposes. In the latter situation, the prosecuting attorney should satisfy himself of the autopsy surgeon's medicolegal qualifications. He should also indicate, as a matter of practice, that a complete autopsy should be performed in every case with possible criminal overtones. Minimum standards of qualifica-

---

on Opinion Evidence under the Federal Rules," 29 *Wash. & Lee L.Rev.* 313 (1982).

23. Typically, a treating physician in a clinical environment can rely on a third party's test results in giving testimony while a forensic expert (other than the medical examiner) called in only for trial purposes cannot rely on another's tests. A medical examiner is characterized as a treating physician so he may rely on toxicological reports completed by another expert. State v. Dame, 488 A.2d 418 (R.I.1985).

24. Ohio Evid.Rule 703. Simpson v. Commonwealth, 227 Va. 557, 318 S.E.2d

386 (1984): pathologist opinion from medical records not in evidence restricted.

On this issue, review modern legal developments discussed in some detail in Chapter 1, supra.

25. Darling v. Charleston Community Memorial Hospital, 33 Ill.2d 326, 211 N.E.2d 253 (1965), cert. denied 383 U.S. 946 (1966).

26. Id. See also, supra, Chapter 1 on Expert Witness.

tion should require that the autopsy surgeon be certified as an anatomic pathologist by the American Board of Pathology.

§ 12.14   Experts in the Private Sector

Attorneys may have occasion to employ a pathologist at one of three stages.

1. If the client is charged with a crime and counsel has been retained before a medicolegal autopsy is performed on the deceased, permission for a defense-employed pathologist to observe the autopsy may be sought. This request should be addressed to the court, to the local prosecutor's office, and to the office of the medical examiner, coroner, or justice of the peace. The justification for such a request would be founded on the transient nature of the body and the impossibility of duplication of the examination, coupled with the statutory privilege of pretrial discovery.

2. If the state autopsy has been completed, an attorney may wish to have a employed pathologist examine the organs and tissues privately or simply review the work product of the medical examiner.[1]

The microscope slides of these organs, tissues, etc., can usually be obtained from the autopsy surgeon. In addition, it may be that the pathologist will have preserved entire organs such as the heart, or brain; such may be preserved for long periods of time and are excellent specimens to be re-examined. Photographs not made a part of the autopsy report may also be on file with the pathologist who conducted the original autopsy.

3. If all real evidence has been destroyed or the subject cremated, the attorney should seek discovery of the autopsy report, autopsy photographs and the pathologist's notes, sketches, and diagrams pertaining to the postmortem examination. All such items may not have been filed with the pathologist's final report and may have to be sought separately.

While there are relatively few board certified forensic pathologists in the United States, the task of finding expert assistance is not hopeless. The most immediate source of information concerning local pathologists can be obtained from the local medical society. Local hospitals and medical schools invariably have pathologists attached to their staffs, although most of these potential experts are certified only as anatomic and/or clinical pathologists. Many medical schools, however, have specialists in forensic pathology on their faculties. Biographical information can be obtained from a number of excellent sources available in

§ 12.14

1. Williams v. Martin, 618 F.2d 1021 (4th Cir.1980): Failure to provide forensic pathologist deprived criminal defendant of effective assistance of counsel and due process of law in violation of the Sixth and Fourteenth amendments. Contra: McKinley v. Smith, 838 F.2d 1524 (11th Cir.1988).

In McKinley v. Smith, 838 F.2d 1524 (11th Cir.1988), the court held that due process does not require a state trial court to provide an indigent defendant with funds to retain an independent pathologist. The medical examiner and his superior are available to explain the autopsy report to defense counsel.

most county medical society libraries.[2] Professional organizations of pathologists on the local and national level are a source of aid in securing an expert.[3] A number of national scientific societies include forensic pathologists in their membership.[4]

V. MISCELLANEOUS

§ 12.15 Example of a Typical Autopsy Report

The following is a report such as one might encounter in homicide cases and illustrates the type of information that will be contained in a report of a complete and competently performed autopsy.

GLOSSARY OF TERMS USED IN AUTOPSY REPORTS

SUPERIOR OR CRANIAL: toward the head end of body; upper

INFERIOR OR CAUSAL: away from the head; lower

ANTERIOR OR VENTRAL: front

POSTERIOR OR DORSAL: back

MEDIAL OR MESIAL: toward the midline of body

LATERAL: away from the midline of body

PROXIMAL: toward or nearest the trunk or the point of origin of a part

DISTAL: away from or farthest from the trunk or the point of origin of a part

SAGITTAL: a lengthwise plane running from front to back; divides the body or any of its parts into right and left

WOUNDS:

    Penetrating: one which enters but does not exit the body or an organ or other bodily part.

    Perforating: one which passes completely through the body or an organ or other bodily part.

---

2. The most thorough listing and biographical data on pathologists, certified or not, is in the *Directory of Medical Specialists,* 1991–1992, 3. vols. 25th ed. published by Marquis Who's Who, 121 Chanlon Road, New Providence, NJ 07974, 1–800–521–8110.

3. On the National Level, contact: College of American Pathologists, 325 Waukegan Road, Northfield, IL 60093–2750; (708) 446–8800.

American Society of Clinical Pathologists, 2100 W. Harrison, Chicago, IL 60612; (312) 738–1336.

American College of Legal Medicine, 611 E. Wells Street, Milwaukee, WI 53202; (414) 276–1881.

American Board of Pathology, Lincoln Center, 5401 W. Kennedy Blvd., P.O. Box 25015, Tampa, FL 33622; (813) 286–2444.

National Assoc. of Med.Exam., 1402 S. Grand Blvd., St. Louis, MO 63014.

4. American Academy of Forensic Sciences, 410 N. 21st, Suite 203, Colorado Springs, CO 80904–2798. Phone (719) 636–1100.

DEPARTMENT OF HEALTH
OFFICE OF THE CHIEF MEDICAL EXAMINER

Autopsy No. _____
Date ____ _____
Time _____

REPORT OF AUTOPSY

DECEDENT _____
           First   Middle   Last

Autopsy Authorized by: _____

Body Identified by:

Persons Present at Autopsy:

Rigor: complete ___X___ jaw _____ neck _____ arms _____ legs _____
Livor: color ___reddish___ distribution: posterior
Age _50_ Race _W_ Sex _M_ Length _69½"_ Weight _est.175_ Eyes _Hazel_ Pupils: R _rre_ L _rre_
Hair _Black_ Mustache _____ Beard _____ Circumcised _no_ Body Heat _cool_

Clothing, Personal Effects; External wounds, scars, tattoos, other identifying features: See attached sheet.

PATHOLOGICAL DIAGNOSIS:

CARDIOVASCULAR SYSTEM: Heart, no evidence of hypertrophy, valvular, or congenital abnormalities. Coronary arteries, normal origin and distribution; right coronary artery predominance; no significant alteration all segments. Myocardium, no evidence of trauma, fibrosis, or inflammation. Aorta, moderate arteriosclerosis.
RESPIRATORY SYSTEM: Larynx, trachea, and bronchi, no evidence of trauma or obstruction. Lungs, pulmonary congestion and edema; upper lobes, apical chronic obstructive pulmonary disease with pleural scarring; No evidence of inflammation or pulmonary artery emboli.
LIVER: No evidence of trauma or inflammation.
SPLEEN: No evidence of trauma.
PANCREAS AND ADRENAL GLANDS: No significant alterations.
THYROID GLAND: Lymphocytic thyroiditis.
G.I. TRACT: No evidence of trauma, hemorrhage, or ulceration.
GENITOURINARY TRACT: Kidneys, no evidence of trauma or inflammation. Urinary bladder, trabeculation; prostate, nodular hyperplasia.
HEAD: Perforating gunshot wound with entrance on right side of head and wound track extending backward and to the left and exit from left side of head.

Cause of Death:

PERFORATING GUNSHOT WOUND OF THE HEAD.

The facts stated herein are true and correct to the best of my knowledge and belief.

_____   _____   _____
  Date Signed   Place of Autopsy   Signature of Pathologist

[D7649]

GROSS DESCRIPTION

PLEURA, PERITONEUM, & PERICARDIUM:	Intact, smooth, and glistening.
HEART:	415 gm. No valvular or congenital abnormalities. Coronary arteries, normal origin and distribution; right coronary artery predominance; no significant sclerosis all segments. Right ventricle 3 mm.; left 15 mm. Myocardium is intact but no gross evidence of trauma, fibrosis, or inflammation. Aorta, moderate arteriosclerosis.
LUNGS:	Right 640 gm.; left 490 gm. Larynx, trachea, and bronchi intact and free of trauma or obstruction. Lungs are intact and exhibit pulmonary congestion and edema and at the apex of the upper lobes there is evidence of pleural scarring and underlying chronic obstructive pulmonary disease. No signs of trauma, inflammation, or pulmonary artery emboli.
LIVER:	1840 gm. Capsule intact and smooth and on section there is congestion but no evidence of trauma, fibrosis, or nodularity.
GALLBLADDER:	No significant alberatation.
SPLEEN:	140 gm. Capsule intact.
PANCREAS AND ADRENAL GLANDS:	No significant alteration.
THYROID GLAND:	Both lobes are enlarged, firm, and very pale in color.
G.I. TRACT:	Stomach empty. No evidence of trauma, hemorrhage, or ulceration.
KIDNEYS:	175 gm. each. Capsules strip with ease to reveal an intact, pale smooth surface.
URINARY BLADDER:	Trabeculation.
GENITALIA:	Nodular hyperplasia of prostate.
BRAIN:	1575 gm. Perforating gunshot wound – entrance in right side of head superior to right external ear, oval wound 5/8 inch by 1/2 inch with rim of powder debris and powder debris also present in soft tissues and on outer table of skull. The wound track extends backward and to the left. Entrance in the skull near the medial end of the lesser wing of the right sphenoid bone with passage through the temporal lobe of the right cerebral hemisphere, across the midline, and passage through the parietal lobe of the left cerebral hemisphere and exit through the left parietal bone and scalp. There is extensive tissue damage along the wound track and there is also multiple fracture lines passing from the skull entrance site to the skull exit site.
MICROSCOPIC:	Sections taken through the wound track in the brain reveals extensive tissue disruption and hemorrhage. Sections of the entrance wound are positive for powder debris. Sections of thyroid gland reveals distortion of architecture with prominent large lymphoid follicles. No other significant alterations.

[D7650]

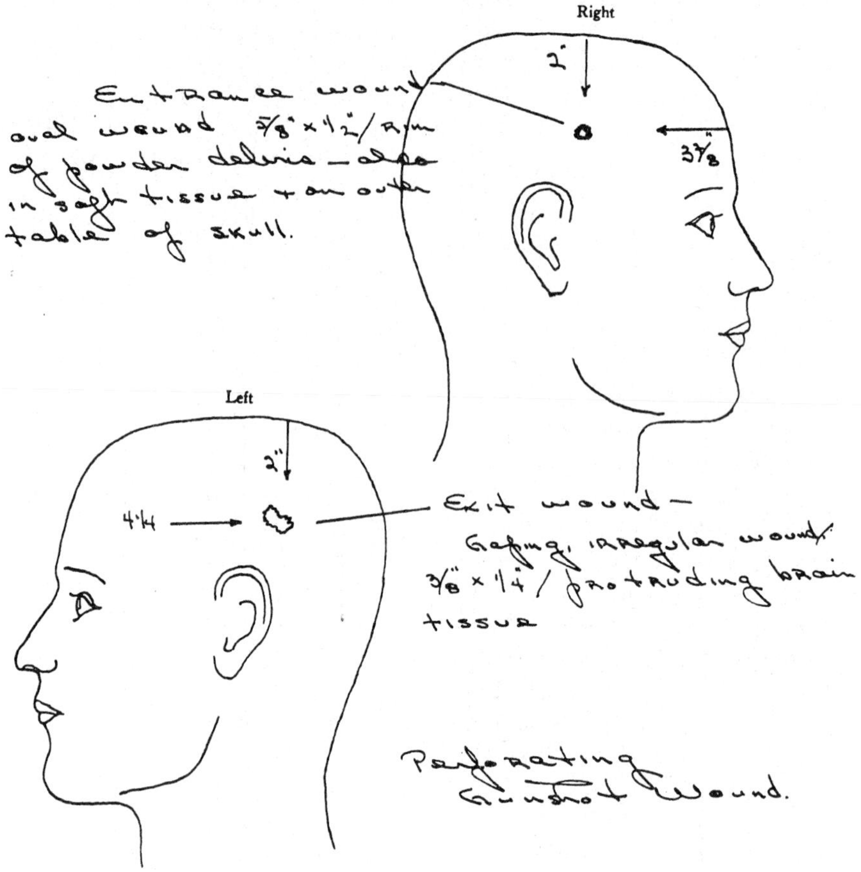

Right

2″

3⅞″

Entrance wound
oval wound ⅜″ × 1½″ / rim
of powder debris — also
in soft tissue + on outer
table of skull.

Left

2″

4¼

Exit wound —
Gaping, irregular wound
⅜″ × 1¼″ / protruding brain
tissue

Perforating
Gunshot Wound.

Decedent's Name _____

Examined

By _ _____ Date _____

[D7651]

BODY DIAGRAM

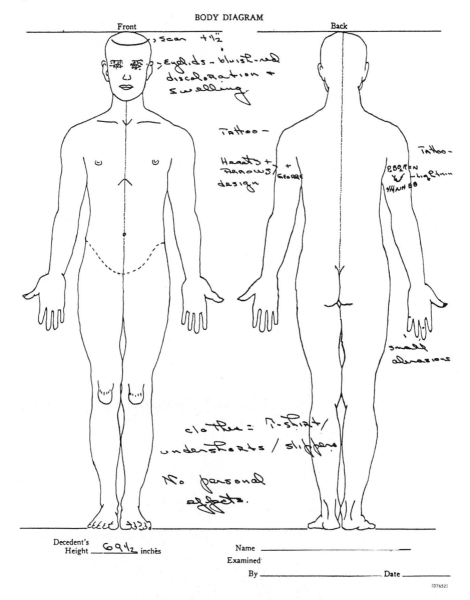

Front   Back

> Scar + 1/2"

> Eyelids – bluish-red discoloration + swelling.

Tattoo –

Hearts + Arrows/ + George design

Tattoo –

Robert & –lightnin' Yvonne 68

small abrasions

clothes = T-shirt/ undershorts / slippers

No personal effects.

Decedent's Height ____69 1/2___ inches

Name _____

Examined
By _____ Date _____

[D7652]

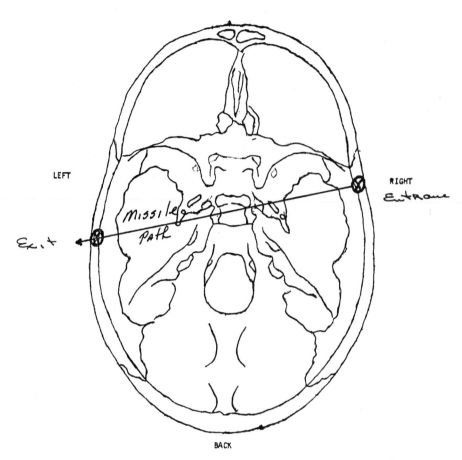

§ 12.16 Bibliography of Additional References

Adelson, *The Pathology of Homicide,* 1974.

Anderson, *Synopsis of Pathology,* (8th ed.) 1972.

Arena, *Poisoning,* (4th ed.) 1979.

Cameron & Rae, *Atlas of the Battered Child Syndrome,* 1975.

Curry, *Poison Detection in Human Organs,* (3rd ed.) 1976.

DiMaio & DiMaio, *Forensic Pathology,* 1989.

DiMaio, *Gunshot Wounds: Practical Aspects of Firearms, Ballistics and Forensic Techniques,* 1985.

DiMaio, *Symposium on Forensic Pathology,* 1983.

Eckert, *Introduction to Forensic Sciences,* 1980.

Fatteh, *Medicolegal Investigation of Gunshot Wounds,* 1976.

Fisher & Petty, *A Handbook of Forensic Pathology for Non–Forensic Pathologists,* 1977.

Goodman & Gilman, *The Pharmacological Basis of Therapeutics,* (6th ed.) 1980.

Gordon, *Forensic Medicine: A Guide to Principles,* 1982.

Gradwohl, *Legal Medicine,* (3rd ed.) 1976.

Gray & Gordy, *Attorney's Textbook of Medicine,* (3rd ed.) 1985.

Gustafson, *Forensic Odontology,* 1966.

Harvey, *Dental Identification and Forensic Odontology,* 1976.

Hendrix, *Investigation of Violent and Sudden Death: A Manual for Medical Examiners,* 1972.

Jaffe, *A Guide to Pathological Evidence for Lawyers and Police Officers,* 1983.

Knight, *Forensic Pathology,* 1991.

Krogman, *The Human Skeleton in Forensic Medicine,* 1986.

Leestma, *Forensic Neuropathology,* 1988.

Mason, *The Pathology of Trauma,* (2nd Ed.) 1993.

Mason, *Butterworth's Medico–Legal Encyclopedia,* 1987.

Mason, *Forensic Medicine, An Illustrated Reference,* 1993.

Moritz, & Morris, *Handbook of Legal Medicine,* (5th ed.) 1979.

O'Hara, *Fundamentals of Criminal Investigation,* (5th ed.) 1979.

Phillips, *Forensic Science and the Expert Witness,* 1985.

Plueckhahn, *Ethics, Legal Medicine, and Forensic Pathology,* (4th ed.) 1985.

Polson, Gee & Knight, *The Essentials of Forensic Medicine,* (4th ed.) 1985.

Reichs, *Forensic Osteology: Advances in the Identification of Human Remains,* 1986.

Rezek & Millard, *Autopsy Pathology: A Guide for Pathologists and Clinicians,* 1963.

Romenesko, *Death Log,* 1982.

Schmidt, *Attorneys' Dictionary of Medicine and Word Finder,* 4 vols., 1986.

Simpson, *Forensic Medicine,* (10th ed.) 1991.

Snyder, *Homicide Investigation,* (3rd ed.) 1977.

Sopher, *Forensic Dentistry,* 1986.

Spitz, ed., *Medicolegal Investigation of Death,* (1993).

Taylor, *Principles and Practice of Medical Jurisprudence* (Mant Ed. 1984).

Walkory, *Science and Medicine of Autopsy: Subject Analysis and Research Index with Bibliography,* 1985.

Waltz & Inbau, *Medical Jurisprudence,* 1971.

Watanabe, *Atlas of Legal Medicine,* (3rd ed.) 1975.

Wecht, *Forensic Sciences,* 3 vols., 1981 (with annual supplements).

Wecht, *Microscopic Diagnosis in Forensic Pathology,* 1980.

Woodburne, *Essentials of Human Anatomy,* (8th ed.) 1988.

Chapter 13

SEROLOGY AND TOXICOLOGY
OF BODY FLUIDS *

I. INTRODUCTION

* This chapter is an extensively rewritten and updated version of part of old Chapter 6 in the Third Edition of the text by Charles R. Midkiff, Jr., National Laboratory Center, BATF. The contents of this chap- ter reflects the views of its primary author and the co-authors of the text, and may not necessarily reflect the views of the Bureau of Alcohol, Tobacco and Firearms.

V. EVIDENTIAL STATUS OF TEST RESULTS

I. INTRODUCTION

§ 13.01 Scope of the Chapter

In the resolution of factual disputes, chemistry, serology and toxicology often play significant roles. Experts in these specialities frequently appear for the prosecution and to a lesser extent in criminal cases, for the defense. In civil litigation, expert chemical or biochemical testimony is often essential in establishing the claims of the plaintiff. In toxic tort cases or environmental actions, results of scientific tests may be the only effective approach to countering evidence proffered by an opposing party. This chapter will provide an overview of, and guidance in using or challenging, the results of chemical, toxicological or serological examinations.

1. TOXICOLOGY AND CHEMISTRY

Although discussion of the scientific principles underlying chemical or toxicological examinations is beyond the scope of this book, an attempt will be made to highlight areas where the chemist-toxicologist can contribute information and opinions of value in the preparation and litigation of a criminal or civil case.

Toxicology is essentially a specialty area within the broader field of Analytical Chemistry and a clear distinction between them is not readily made. The analytical chemist conducts examinations on a variety of materials and for purposes ranging from product quality control or detection of contaminants in the environment to identification of traces of a flammable liquid in debris from a fire scene. The focus of the toxicologist is the detection and identification of foreign chemicals in the body or in materials originating from living organisms. Particular emphasis is placed on substances considered toxic or potentially hazardous to living organisms. These are normally present only at very low levels and the toxicologist routinely makes use of the sensitive analytical instruments available to the chemist. Because of similarities in function and analytical techniques, for the purpose of this chapter, analytical chemists and toxicologists will be considered as one. Subsequently, information to assist the attorney in locating and using the services of a chemist-toxicologist will be provided.

2. EXAMINATION OF BLOOD

In criminal investigations, especially in homicides, assaults, sex offenses and other violent crimes, blood is common as physical evidence. Determination of the type and characterization of blood is primarily the realm of the biochemist or serologist while detection of toxins in blood is the province of the chemist-toxicologist. Examination of blood can provide information about the victim or offender or to link a suspect to the crime; information useful in the investigative phase or for presentation at trial. In civil cases, blood testing may provide information in paternity or malpractice actions, show that an illness was the result of exposure to toxic materials in the environment or workplace or that an accident is attributable to such exposure. Results from an examination of the victim's blood may also provide evidence that a death was natural, accidental or suicide.

A portion of this chapter will describe some of the tests conducted on blood for identification or to aid in the reconstruction of the facts in a criminal or civil case. An attempt will be made to describe, in terms understandable by the non-expert, terminology used by the serologist or toxicologist. Familiarity with the limitations, as well as the advantages, of the methodology used in serological and toxicological testing is essential to the attorney in preparing for trial and in ensuring that the trier of fact has an accurate portrayal of the value of expert medico-legal testimony offered in the case.

3. OTHER BIOLOGICAL MATERIAL

In sex offenses, the principal biological material of interest is seminal fluid and/or sperm cells ejaculated by the male perpetrator. When rape is alleged, detection of seminal fluid is often essential in demonstrating that the assault occurred, particularly when the primary evidence of the crime is the uncorroborated testimony of the victim. Information from characterization of the biological nature of the seminal fluid may tend to incriminate or exonerate a suspect and methodology used for examination of seminal fluid will be described.

In the examination of samples collected at the scene or from the body of the victim, a number of factors affect the ability of the laboratory to detect and/or characterize seminal fluid or to locate intact sperm cells. These factors limit the data available and the conclusions drawn from laboratory results. A knowledge of these limitations is required to comprehend, effectively present or counter expert testimony regarding conduct and results of serological examinations.

Evidence collected in sexual assault cases may also include bodily fluids such as saliva, fecal matter or urine. Identification of seminal fluid in the former two can support claims of oral or anal intercourse or of homosexual rape. In view of the potential value of adequate sample collection and examination in sexual assault cases, the defense should be alert to any failure by the prosecution to properly collect, preserve and examine relevant body fluids from the victim's body, clothing or from the scene of the alleged crime.

In other situations, bodily fluids such as vomitus or perspiration may be encountered and their examination be essential to a reconstruction of the facts in the case. For the detection of toxic materials in the body, stomach contents, tissue or body organs frequently are optimum samples for toxicological examination. With a body in an advanced stage of decomposition, suitable body fluids or tissue samples may be unavailable and durable materials such as hair or fingernails should be collected. Such samples have been used effectively to demonstrate the presence of common drugs or poisons, heavy metals or pesticides and which could have been either a primary or contributing cause of death. In deaths where litigation is potentially forthcoming, reliable information for determination of the cause is essential. To ensure effective representation of his party, the attorney in either criminal or civil cases, must be aware of the types of information available from body fluids or other biological material.

II. TOXICOLOGY AND CHEMISTRY—IN GENERAL

§ 13.02 Terminology Commonly Used in Toxicological or Chemical Laboratory Reports and Testimony

These terms and others may be further described elsewhere in this chapter.

Absorption: One material taken up by another and held within the absorbing material. It differs from adsorption which occurs when a liquid or gas is taken up by a solid but held only on the surface of the solid material.

Alcohol: Commonly used in reference to ethyl or grain alcohol. Alcohols are actually a class of organic compounds which includes methyl, propyl, isopropyl, butyl and others.

Aldehydes: A class of compounds produced from oxidation of alcohols. Certain aldehydes may interfere in the determination of alcohol in chemical tests for intoxication. Examples of aldehydes include formaldehyde and acetaldehyde.

Alkaloids: A group of complex nitrogen-containing compounds of vegetable origin. Many are toxic to humans and most are colorless, crystalline solids with a bitter taste.

Atomic Absorption Spectrometry: An analytical technique primarily used to measure metals in a sample. The sample in solution is vaporized and compounds in the sample decomposed into free atoms. These atoms absorb light at wavelengths characteristic of a particular element. From the amount of light absorbed at a selected wavelength, the concentration of the element in the sample is determined.

Boiling Point: The temperature at which the vapor pressure of a liquid is equal to the pressure of the surroundings.

Chromatography: A category of analytical techniques for the separation of mixtures, usually involving the retention of components of a mixture on a fixed material phase. Chemical compounds differ in their retention on the non-moving phase and some are held to a greater extent than others. Weakly retained compounds move quickly through the system while those more strongly held move more slowly and complete their passage through the system later. Because of differences in this retention time, effective separation of a mixture's components can be made. Types of chromatography used in the analytical laboratory include: paper, thin-layer, gas-liquid and liquid chromatography.

Column Chromatography: A technique for the separation of mixtures in which a solution is passed through a column containing a solid adsorbent. Certain materials in the solution are retained by the solid while others pass through with the solvent. The ability of the technique to effect efficient separation can be enhanced by careful solvent selection or by changing the composition of the solvent added to the column. This technique is often referred to as liquid chromatography.

Compound: A molecule composed of two or more atoms representing different elements combined to produce a unique material. Water (H_2O) is a compound, consisting of two atoms of hydrogen and one of oxygen whereas a chlorine (Cl_2) molecule contains only two atoms of chlorine and is not a compound.

Concentration: The quantity of a given material in a mixture or solution. It may be expressed as percent by volume or weight, parts-per million or in chemical terms such as molarity.

Cubic Centimeter: Equivalent to 0.0610 cubic inch in volume or approximately one thousandth of a liter (milliliter).

Density: Mass per unit volume, usually expressed as grams per cubic centimeter or pounds per cubic foot.

Derivative: A substance extracted or produced from another. One natural derivative is morphine from opium. In chemical analysis, derivatives of a compound are often chemically prepared to obtain another compound more easily detected by the analytical technique used.

Detection: In chemistry, indication of the presence of a substance in the material being examined. Detection, however does not prove that the material has been uniquely identified.

Detection Limit: The minimum concentration of a material capable of reliable detection with the analytical system used. It is usually determined from the ratio of the analytical signal to the background noise in the system, often a minimum of 3:1. Detection limits expressed for pure solutions of the analyte will not represent the results obtained during the examination of actual samples.

Gas Chromatography: A technique for separation of components of a mixture in the vapor state. The sample to be examined is vaporized and carried through a small diameter column by a flowing gas stream. Components of the mixture dissolve in a viscous liquid inside the column and are retained to varying degrees to effect a separation. As a component of the mixture completes its passage through the column, it enters a detector which produces an electrical signal indicating its arrival and quantity. The signals from the detector are recorded on a moving chart to produce a chromatogram. The chart pattern is compared with those of known materials for identification. Because the non-moving phase in the column is a liquid, the technique may be called gas-liquid chromatography. A very small diameter, or capillary, column improves component separation and for materials which move slowly through the column, increasing the temperature reduces analysis time and is known as programmed temperature gas chromatography.

Grain: Equivalent to 0.00648 gram in weight.

Gram: Equivalent to 15.43 grains. About 454 grams are one pound.

Identification: In chemistry, identification of a substance means that its chemical structure has been determined.

Isomers: Two or more chemical compounds containing the same number and kinds of elements but arranged differently within the molecule's structure. The result may be totally different chemical compounds such as ethyl alcohol or dimethyl ether, both having the elemental composition of C_2H_6O. Another type of isomer may contain the same basic structure but certain elements or groups of elements in different positions. For example, in a particular drug an atom such as chlorine can occupy any of several positions. While the basic composition of the molecule is the same, physiological properties may differ markedly from one isomer to another.

Ketones: A class of compounds formed by oxidation of alcohols which can interfere with intoxication testing. Volatile ketones are common components of paint removers or industrial solvents and toxic at high levels.

Kilogram: One thousand grams or 2.205 pounds.

Mass Spectrometry: An analytical method to identify materials based upon production and detection of characteristic molecular fragments. The molecule is vaporized and fragmented in a high energy field. The fragments are separated by velocity or behavior in a magnetic field, detected and their mass determined. Because the fragments produced under controlled conditions are reproducible, they can be related to the original structure of the molecule. Combining the separating power of gas or liquid chromatography with the ability of the mass spectrometer to identify a compound provides a powerful tool for the identification of individual components in a mixture and is widely used to confirm preliminary identification of a suspected drug or toxin.

Melting Point: The temperature at which liquid and solid forms of a material are in equilibrium. Generally, the temperature at which a solid begins to change to a liquid.

Molecular Structure: The exact sequence and arrangement of the atoms within the molecule of a chemical compound.

Molecule: The smallest unit of a substance which exhibits the properties of that substance. Further reduction of the molecule of a substance will produce a new substance or atoms comprising the original composition of the substance. For example, reduction of a water molecule will produce hydrogen and oxygen, neither of which exhibits the properties of water.

Nicotine: A highly toxic alkaloid derived from plants of the tobacco genus. It has limited use as an insecticide and for making alcohol unfit for beverage purposes.

Organophosphates: A group of organic compounds containing phosphorus, many of which are highly toxic. Originally produced as chemical warfare agents, some are now used as potent insecticides and occasionally encountered in poisonings.

Ounce: 28.35 grams or 437.5 grains in weight.

Paper Chromatography: A technique for separation of mixtures by differential migration on paper. A mixture is placed as a spot on a strip of filter paper and the end of the paper allowed to dip into a reservoir of solvent. As the solvent, wick-like, moves up the paper, it dissolves the components of the spot and carries them up the paper strip. Depending on the extent to which they are retained by the paper, the components separate into spots higher on the paper. After the solvent has moved a pre-determined distance, the paper is removed and dried. The distance each spot has moved is used to tentatively identify the material in a particular spot.

Qualitative Analysis: A chemical analysis to determine the composition of a sample, i.e. what materials are present.

Quantitative Analysis: A chemical analysis to determine the relative concentrations of one or more components of a sample.

Selectivity: The ability of an analytical technique to discriminate between similar materials in the sample. Selectivity is essential to
avoid "false positives" and obtain reliable analytical results.

Sensitivity: The minimum amount of a component capable of reliably
being detected by the analytical system. It is affected by other
components in the sample and values attained with pure solutions
often do not represent the sensitivity attained with more complex
samples. When the working sensitivity of the method is below that
assumed by the analyst, "false negatives" may be obtained, i.e. the
analyte is present above a threshold level but undetected in the
analysis.

Specific Gravity: The ratio of the weight of a substance to an equal
volume of water. Because weight and volume vary with temperature, the temperature of the substance and water must be specified.
Water at 4° C, its maximum density, is normally used as a standard
and assigned a value of 1.

Spectrophotometry: A category of analytical techniques for identification
of a chemical compound. Most types involve the measurement of
light or other radiation absorbed by or emitted from a sample. The
specific wavelengths of radiation absorbed/emitted are related to the
chemical structure of the molecule. Measurement of the radiation's
frequency or wavelength and/or the amount absorbed/emitted is
used to identify a particular chemical species or determine the
quantity present. Most types are named for the radiation used such
as visible, infrared or ultraviolet light or X-ray.

Strychnine: White crystalline powder, a toxic alkaloid sometimes used as
a hallucinogen but more often encountered as a poison.

Thin–Layer Chromatography: Analytical separation method superior to
paper chromatography. A glass plate with a thin coating of silica
gel, cellulose or alumina is the stationary phase on which the sample
is spotted. The plate is placed in a tank containing a small amount
of solvent and developed as described for paper. The method is
simple, inexpensive and sensitive to extremely low levels of a material in the sample. Spraying of the dried plate with a specific
chemical reagent develops a color to aid in identifying the material
in a particular spot.

§ 13.03 Toxicological Examinations in Criminal and Civil Cases

The forensic toxicologist is concerned with the detection and characterization of poisons or toxins exhibiting adverse physiological effects. A
toxin is considered as any material which when introduced, directly or
indirectly, into a living system exerts an effect which may ultimately be
life threatening to the organism. This intentionally broad definition
covers not only classic poisons, detection of which is often considered the
principal task of the toxicologist, but a number of other less well known,
but equally hazardous materials. Among these are toxic gases such as
carbon monoxide and hydrogen cyanide, industrial solvents and refriger-

ants, heavy metals, pesticides, and a wide range of environmental pollutants. Toxic materials may be ingested, inhaled or absorbed through the skin. Poisons may enter the body in a single massive dose, acute poisoning, or gradually, accumulating in the body and causing illness or death. A series of sub-lethal exposures over time results in chronic poisoning and may go undetected in the absence of suspicion that the victim's illness or death is not the result of disease or natural causes. Although the largest numbers of toxicological examinations are conducted in alcohol or drug related incidents, toxicology plays an important role in other cases for determination of cause and manner of death or injury. With prescription drugs or over-the-counter medications, questions may arise involving adverse reactions to medicinal drugs, improper prescription by the physician, suspected error by the pharmacist or excessive use by the patient.

While blood is the most commonly examined body fluid for detection of toxins, others such as urine, stomach contents,[1] and vitreous humor, the fluid from the eye, etc. are also useful. Tissue from body organs such as the brain or liver[2] offers advantages in certain situations[3] and, in bodies in an advanced stage of decomposition, hair or nail samples may provide otherwise unobtainable information. Because suitable samples may be difficult to obtain after an autopsy or extensive medical treatment, these should be collected during treatment or autopsy. Another reason for obtaining samples as soon as possible is to avoid potential loss of evidential value with time or as a result of chemical interaction; as for example, destruction of cyanide traces in the body by embalming fluid containing formaldehyde. In fatalities, blood should always be obtained, preferably two samples, one from the heart and another from a major vein. For toxicological examination, the collected samples are often preserved with sodium fluoride to prevent deterioration by microorganisms. The presence of a preservative, however, may cause difficulties if the sample is to be used for certain other types of examinations.

As a toxicological sample, urine offers some advantages over blood but levels of a toxin or its metabolites in urine are difficult to relate to earlier levels in the body. Stomach contents provide a rapid route to detection of ingested toxins and are often available from pumping or lavage in suspected poisoning cases. In postmortem sample collection, particularly when the postmortem interval is greater than several days,

§ 13.03

1. Stevens, "The Detection of Some Non-drug Poisons in Simulated Stomach Contents by Diffusion into Various Colour Reagents," 26 *J.Forensic Sci.Soc.* 137 (1986).

2. Stevens, "The Stability of Some Drugs and Poisons in Putrefying Human Liver Tissues", ibid. 24 *J.Forensic Sci.* 577 (1984).

3. The highly toxic protein ricin, extracted from the castor bean, has a history of use for medicinal and criminal purposes and is determinable at extremely low levels in tissue extracts. Leith, Griffiths and Green, "Quantitation of Ricin Toxin Using a Highly Sensitive Avidin/Biotin Enzyme-Linked Immunosorbent Assay," 28 *J.Forensic Sci.Soc.* 227 (1988); Griffiths, Neweman and Gee, "Identification and Quantification of Ricin Toxin in Animal Tissues Using ELISA", ibid. 26 *J.Forensic Sci.* 349 (1986).

vitreous humor is an excellent sample medium, being more resistant to putrefaction than blood.

Based on their chemical composition, toxins are classifiable as organic or inorganic. Inorganic poisons may be placed into sub-classes such as metallic poisons (lead, mercury, barium or thallium), non-metallic poisons (cyanide or iodine) and corrosives (acids, alkalis, bleach). Organic poisons include: volatile organic poisons (alcohol, acetone, benzene), alkaloids (many drugs, nicotine, strychnine) and non-alkaloidal poisons (rodenticides, and carbamate, halogenated, or organophosphate insecticides). Gaseous poisons may be organic or inorganic (phosgene, carbon monoxide, carbon dioxide, chlorine, hydrogen sulfide). Metallic poisons do not disappear with decomposition and may be detected in remains long after death. Arsenic, for example, has been detected in hair and nails of aged remains such as the hair of the Emperor Napoleon.[4] An acute dose of arsenic may be detected in tissue samples; however, chronic arsenic poisoning may best be detected in the shaft of the hair. By examining sections taken along the length of the hair, chronic ingestion of sub-lethal doses over a period of time can be demonstrated.[5] Similarly, heavy metals such as mercury present in the environment may be detectable in hair or in the bodies of insect larvae feeding on the body.[6] Lead poisoning is not uncommon, particularly in inner city children. The lead may arise from lead-based paints in old buildings, drinking water or other environmental sources. Lead is readily determined in blood using atomic absorption analysis. If drinking water is considered as a potential source of heavy metal poisoning, analysis of the water can provide valuable information for civil litigation.[7]

Carbon monoxide (CO), when inhaled, combines with the hemoglobin in the blood to form a stable compound and deprive the body of oxygen. When carbon monoxide poisoning is suspected, as for example, from a cherry red color of the body, analysis of a blood sample readily detects it and permits an estimate of its concentration. Although homicides from CO have occurred, most such fatalities are results of accident or suicide. The best known source of CO is automotive ex-

4. Using Neutron Activation Analysis (NAA), arsenic was detected in samples of hair collected from Napoleon after his death. Forshfvud, Smith and Wassen, "Arsenic Content of Napoleon I's Hair Probably Taken Immediately After His Death" 192 *Nature* 103 (1961).

5. NAA of sections of hair from several individuals suspected of having been poisoned demonstrated murder by prolonged chronic exposure to arsenic. Guinn and Demiralp, "Arsenic in Hair by NAA—A Major Recent Murder Case" 168 *J.Radioanal.Nucl.Chem.* 249 (1993). Flameless atomic absorption spectrometry also offers sufficient sensitivity for the sectional analysis of hair to determine levels and times of exposure to arsenic. Koons and Peters, "Axial Distribution of Arsenic in Individual Human Hairs by Solid Sampling Graphite Furnace AAS" 18 *J.Anal.Toxicol.* 36 (1994).

6. Nuorteva, P., "Sarcosaprophagous Insects as Forensic Indicators" in: *Forensic Medicine* Vol. II, Physical Trauma Tedeschi, Eckert and Tedeschi—Eds. Philadelphia, PA, W.B. Saunders Co. 1072 (1977).

7. Schmelzel, Karpova and Dulude, "Simultaneous Determination of Copper and Lead in Drinking Waters by Graphite Furnace Atomic Absorption Spectrometry" 2 *Spectroscopist* 12 (1993).

haust, but poorly vented stoves or banked fires are also potential causes of CO poisoning.

A wide range of readily available materials have the potential to be toxic at sufficiently high levels. In the workplace, exposure to elevated levels of potentially toxic materials including petroleum products, industrial solvents, paint thinners, degreasers, pesticides, toxic gases and other materials can result in death or, with prolonged low level exposure, illness and disability. Most volatile poisons, pesticides and gases can be detected in the blood by gas chromatographic analysis.[8] Exposure to organophosphate pesticides can be demonstrated by measurement of the cholinesterase level in blood.[9] Similarly, suicide by ingestion of a carbamate pesticide was demonstrated through measurement of the blood cholinesterase activity and the pesticide identified in blood and gastric contents by thin-layer chromatography.[10] Household products including drain cleaners, mothballs, detergents, weed killers, paint removers, etc. have been involved in suicidal or accidental death or injury.[11] Over-the-counter and prescription drugs, pepper,[12] tear gas and surgical anesthetics or muscle relaxants [13] have also been involved in deaths by accident, suicide or homicide. Another source of potentially hazardous materials is environmental contamination. Contamination of the soil or groundwater by improper waste disposal or runoff of toxic chemicals poses a problem which may not be identified for years. Among better known examples are: pesticide waste contamination of the Love Canal area near Buffalo, N.Y. and Kepone contamination of the Shenandoah River and Times Beach, Missouri. In each of these, con-

8. Logan, "Analysis of Alcohol and Other Volatiles" in *Gas Chromatography in Forensic Science* New York, NY, Ellis Horwood 87 (1992); Streete et al., "Detection and Identification of Volatile Substances by Headspace Gas Chromatography to Aid the Diagnosis of Acute Poisoning" 117 *Analyst* 1111 (1992); Fitzgerald, Fishel and Bush, "Fatality Due to Recreational Use of Chlorodifluoromethane and Chloropentafluoroethane" 38 *J.Forensic Sci.* 476 (1993).

9. The organophosphate pesticides are structurally similar to modern chemical warfare agents and depress cholinesterase activity. The extent of depression can be measured in the blood as an indicator of exposure. Klette et al., "Cholinesterase Activity in Postmortem Blood As a Screening Test for Organophosphate/Chemical Weapon Exposure" 38 *J.Forensic Sci.* 950 (1993).

10. Ferlew, Hagardorn and McCormick, "Poisoning from Oral Ingestion of Carbofuran (Furadan 4F), a Cholinesterase–Inhibiting Carbamate Insecticide, and its Effects on Cholinesterase Activity in Various Biological Fluids" 37 *J.Forensic Sci.* 337 (1992).

11. Sperry and Pfalzgraf, "Fatal Ethanol Intoxication from Household Products Not Intended for Ingestion" 35 *J.Forensic*

Sci. 1138 (1990). In an action against a hospital, chemical analysis of residue in a cup inadvertently left on the patient's meal tray identified it as bleach. Lewis v. St. Frances Cabrini Hosp., 566 So.2d 970 (La. App. 3 Cir.1990).

12. Adelson, "Homicide by Pepper" 9 *J.Forensic Sci.* 391 (1964); Cohle, "Homicidal Asphyxia by Pepper Aspiration" 31 *J.Forensic Sci.* 1475 (1986).

13. The muscle relaxant succinylcholine chloride was identified as the cause of death in the landmark *Coppolino* case; Coppolino v. State, 223 So.2d 68 (Fla.App.1968). Similarly, curare, or its active ingredient d-tubocurarine, was suspected in the alleged murders of surgical patients in a New Jersey hospital. Hall and Hirsch, "Detection of Curare in the Jascalevich Murder Trial" 51 *Anal. Chem.* 812A (1979). In 1981, twelve patients in the Intensive Care Unit of a California hospital suffered seizures and died. Tissue analyses showed high levels of lidocaine and a male nurse was convicted of the homicides. People v. Diaz, 3 Cal.4th 495, 11 Cal.Rptr.2d 353, 834 P.2d 1171 (1992).

tamination from pesticide production resulted in numerous instances of illness and disability and protracted litigation. Similarly, hazards posed by improper disposal of polychlorinated biphenyls (PCBs) used as insulators in electrical transformers has given rise to extensive litigation. Major concerns are now being raised about potential health hazards from residual coal tar residues at abandoned sites of lighting gas plants and soil and groundwater contamination from explosives disposal at military munitions plants and decommissioned military installations worldwide.[14] Environmental contamination cases may involve soil contamination, release of solvents or waste streams containing potentially toxic compounds into the water supply or discharge of hazardous materials into the atmosphere. Examples include solvents from chemical or paint production, cyanide containing waste from ore processing or electroplating, metals such as lead or selenium from smelting operations and mercury released from chemical plants.

Toxins in foods are another potential source of illness or death from environmental causes. In addition to toxins from improper packaging or spoilage of food such as botulism, an unusual source of toxins is contaminated shellfish. These natural toxins are produced from intake by shellfish such as mussels of certain diatoms. Consumption of contaminated shellfish can result in severe and long-lasting neurological effects.[15] Although several states have programs to monitor these toxins in commercial shellfish, the effects of shellfish poisoning could result in civil litigation.

Product tampering, such as the much publicized cyanide in Tylenol cases, can also lead to involvement of the chemist-toxicologist in both civil and criminal cases.[16]

When effects on individuals or animals are alleged, chemical-toxicological examination results are essential for both plaintiff and defendant. With the wide variety of materials having the potential for serious injury or death, the challenge facing the toxicologist is formidable. He or she must be skilled in use of the most modern analytical techniques for detection and identification of any of thousands of materials capable of causing death or illness, whether through accident or design.

§ 13.04 Laboratory Methods Used in Chemical/Toxicological Analyses

A wide range of laboratory methods are used by the chemist or toxicologist to answer medico-legal questions. The questions posed

---

14. Le Brun, Rethwell and Matteson, "Determination of Explosives in Surface and Groundwater" 5 *Environmental Lab* 12 (1993).

15. Shellfish poisoning causes and physiological effects of the toxins are discussed by Quilliam and Wright, "The Amnesic Shellfish Poisoning Mystery" 61 *Anal. Chem.* 1053 (1989). A state monitoring program to prevent toxic shellfish distribution is described by Langlois et al., "Toxins on the Half Shell: Shellfish Monitoring Along the California Coast" 9 *LC–GC* 838 (1991).

16. An overview of chemical tampering is illustrated by several significant cases. Logan, "Product Tampering Crime: A Review" 38 *J.Forensic Sci.* 918 (1993); Logan, Howard and Kiesel, "Poisonings Associated with Cyanide in Over the Counter Cold Medication in Washington State" 38 *J.Forensic Sci.* 472 (1993).

include not only detection of a toxic material and/or determination of the quantity present but also questions as to whether or not the materials identified could arise as a result of environmental exposure or represent intentional administration. Laboratory methods for toxin detection may be broadly classified as follows:

(1) Physical Tests: These include differentiation of materials based on determination of boiling point, melting point, density, refractive index or other physical properties.

(2) Crystal Tests: These involve treatment of a suspect material with a specific chemical reagent to produce crystals of characteristic color or shape. The crystals are examined under a microscope using either ordinary or polarized light. Crystal tests are simple and rapid to perform and require only small samples but it must be recognized that a single such test does not uniquely identify the material. Crystal tests are normally used as a preliminary indication of identity and the results confirmed by another unrelated method.

(3) Chemical Spot Tests: Similar to crystal tests are chemical spot tests in which a reagent or series of reagents is added to a small amount of the suspect material. The reactions observed may be development of a particular color with a single reagent or observation of a series of colors or other changes occurring as different reagents are added. Spot tests are used primarily as screening or presumptive tests. For definitive identification, a series of chemical tests is used or the identity of the material is confirmed by other methods.

(4) Spectrophotometric Tests: Some of these provide definitive identification of a material by measurement of the absorption or emission of light or another form of radiation. For a particular chemical element or compound, absorption or emission of radiation occurs at specific wavelengths depending on the structure of the molecule. For example, using infrared (IR) spectroscopy, the recorded pattern of absorption of infrared light (IR spectrum) of an alkaloid such as strychnine definitively identifies the compound if it is pure. IR spectra are less useful for identification of components in a mixture but may be used to determine the concentration of one component. By measuring the absorption at a wavelength characteristic of one material, such as alcohol, in the mixture, its concentration can be determined. Ultraviolet spectra are regularly used for quantitation of components, such as one drug in a formulation containing several compounds. Other spectrometric methods include atomic absorption spectrophotometry, useful for the determination of species, principally metals, present at levels of only a few parts per million in a sample. X-ray diffraction (XRD) is a technique for the identification of compounds based upon the characteristic scattering of X-rays by the crystal structure of the compound. XRD is useful for the identification of compounds in an unknown mixture. Other spectrometric methods involve use of microwaves or gamma rays for detection and identification of elements or compounds. Gamma ray spectrometry is used in Neutron Activation Analysis to determine a variety of elements

at levels of parts-per-million levels or below. For definitive identification of compounds, such as drugs, mass spectrometry is both sensitive and specific and widely used in toxicological examinations.

(5) Chromatographic Tests: Chromatography is primarily a technique to separate the individual components of a complex mixture. For volatile materials such as petroleum products or solvents, comparison of the gas chromatographic (GC) pattern (chromatogram) of an unknown with those from known materials, e.g. gasoline or kerosene, is valuable for identification of product type. In most instances, however, GC is not reliable for determination of brand or intended end use, e.g. whether the product is a paint thinner, dry cleaning solvent or charcoal starter. Other types of chromatography include liquid and thin-layer. Thin-layer chromatography (TLC) is simple and sensitive for the detection of drugs and poisons. Because multiple samples can be done on a single plate, it is widely used for screening in the toxicology laboratory. When combined with other techniques such as chemical color tests directly on the TLC plate, specific detectors or spectrophotometric analysis, identification of the separated material can be made.

III. THE INVESTIGATION OF BLOOD

§ 13.05 Definition of Blood Analysis Terms

Absorption–Elution: A method for the classification of dried blood stains.

Absorption–Inhibition: An indirect method for the determination of blood type of dried blood stains.

Agglutination: The clumping and precipitation that may occur when blood from persons with different blood types is mixed. It is the principal reaction used in the determination of blood type.

Agglutin: An antibody in the plasma portion of blood which causes the red blood cells to clump or agglutinate.

Agglutinogen: A substance in red blood cells which acts as an antigen (defined below) and stimulates the production of agglutinin.

Antibodies: A type of protein in the plasma of blood which react with foreign materials to protect the body from infection.

Antigen: A protein on the surface of the red blood cells which reacts with antibodies.

Benzidine: A very sensitive test for the presence of traces of blood. Because benzidine is a carcinogen, it is no longer used; however, it has been partially replaced by tetramethybenzidine which does not appear to be carcinogenic.

Electrophoresis: A technique for the separation of molecules, primarily by weight, based upon the distance moved in a stationary phase. The most common type of electrophoresis uses a flat gel as the stationary phase and the molecules move under the influence of an electric field. A newer type of electrophoresis uses a capillary tube for the stationary phase.

Enzyme: A protein that initiates or facilitates a biochemical reaction. Although the enzyme participates, on completion of the reaction, it remains unchanged.

Grouping: Classification of blood by type depending on the agglutination of red cells in the presence of anti-sera. Blood groups A, B, AB and H (formerly known as O) are named by the presence of their antigens which react with the anti-sera. The ABH grouping system is only one of several systems for classification of blood and is discussed in more detail in Sec. 13.11.

Hemoglobin: An iron containing protein in the red cells which carries oxygen through the body.

Immuno–Electrophoresis: A test to determine the species of blood. The blood is separated into fractions by electrophoresis and the separated fractions react with an immune serum.

Leuco Malachite Green: A chemical reagent used to detect the presence of traces of blood.

Luminol: A sensitive spray reagent used to detect traces of blood. In a darkened area, light (luminescence) is produced indicating blood.

Phenolphthalein: A reagent used with peroxide to produce a color in the presence of blood. Although not specific, the pink color is highly indicative of blood.

Plasma: The colorless, liquid portion of the blood remaining after the red and white cells are removed. Plasma is principally water and represents about 55 percent of the blood.

Precipitin Test: A sensitive test to determine if a protein or blood sample is human or animal and if animal, the species.

Serum: The portion of the blood plasma remaining after the fibrin is removed. It is the fluid that remains after blood clots.

Takayama Test: A crystal test for hemoglobin to show that a sample is blood.

Teichmann (hemin crystal) Test: A test to produce crystals with heme and show that a material is blood.

Wagenhaar Test: A crystal test for blood.

§ 13.06   Nature of Blood

In addition to its use for toxicological examinations, blood is commonly used as a source of proof in crimes of violence. Blood may be found on the surface of the body, on clothing, under the fingernails and in the surroundings on floors, rugs, furniture, weapons, sink or bathtub, waste containers or in an automobile. It is a slightly alkaline fluid which circulates through the vascular system carrying nourishment and oxygen to all parts of the body and transporting waste products to be excreted.

The fluid portion of the blood is called plasma. Red and white corpuscles are suspended in the blood. The red cells (erythrocytes) are yellowish, bi-concave, circular disks with thick edges. They contain hemoglobin, the red pigment which carries oxygen. The white cells (leukocytes and lymphocytes) are white, round, amoebic masses of protoplasm. Platelets, oval, circular disks, are also present in the plasma. The ratio of red to white cells is typically about 500 to 1. Detection and identification of blood is normally the result of reactions of the hemoglobin in the blood with the test reagent. Clotting of blood, the clumping of the solid corpuscles and separation from the fluid serum usually begins several minutes after exposure to air and may serve to indicate the freshness of a blood sample or spot.

§ 13.07 Evidentiary Limits of Blood Analysis

Blood can be useful evidence in a criminal investigation to aid in demonstrating that a crime occurred, or to provide characterizing information about the perpetrator or victim. It can link a suspect to either the victim or the crime scene or link victim and crime scene. The value of blood evidence depends on its recognition, collection and proper preservation when initial evidence processing occurs. Liquid blood is readily putrefied and much of its evidentiary value lost whereas dried bloodstains have generally good stability. When liquid blood is recovered, it should be preserved or refrigerated. Alternatively, blood can be left on the object on which it was located, dried in air and packaged in a porous container for shipment to the laboratory. It should be recognized that some blood grouping systems suitable for fresh blood are less effective with dried bloodstains.

Analysis of a blood sample does not permit the analyst to state without qualification that the blood originated from a particular individual. Analysis by the serologist is primarily aimed at answers to the following questions:

(1) Is the sample under examination blood?

(2) If blood, is it human or another animal species?

(3) If animal, from what species did it originate?

(4) If the blood is human, what is its type?

(5) Can the sex of the source of the blood be determined?

(6) With a bloodstain, what is its approximate age?

In numerous instances, the courts have permitted lay or scientific witnesses to testify that a substance was blood although no tests to identify it were conducted. Because of the potential for error in visual identification involving paint, rust, ink and other stains, there is an increasing tendency to require serological testing prior to the statement that the questioned material was blood.[1]

After extensive testing of a sample using multiple blood grouping tests, perhaps encompassing testing of enzymes and proteins and antibody profiling, the analyst can only report or testify that the questioned sample could have originated from a particular individual. Based on data for the occurrence of various blood factors in the general population, or preferably, in a segment thereof, the probability of a sample being included in a group having the same combination of blood types can be calculated. In addition, the size of this group relative to the general population can be estimated.[2] For example, a given combination of blood types may occur in only one individual in 100,000. An individual with this combination, when the same as that in an evidential sample, would then appear to be unlikely to have been selected by chance.

Probability estimates of a "chance match" are frequently used in blood testimony. Because variations in type and sub-type frequency are observed between racial and ethnic groups and there is minor variance in frequency of blood types from one section of the country to another, estimates of "non-chance match" are subject to challenge.[3] In a case involving murder and rape, testimony was introduced that the defendant had Type A blood and that semen from the victim was from a male of that blood type. It was held that in view of the large proportion of the population having this blood type, this testimony should not have been admitted.[4] In some situations, blood from both victim and suspect may be of the same type, e.g. Type H. Unless information from other grouping systems is available, the only statement that can be made is that the suspect can neither be included nor excluded.

Despite the inability of the serologist to definitively link blood to an individual, exclusion may be made with confidence. If the individual's

§ 13.07

1. Problems with confusion over the unconfirmed identification of blood were exemplified in Miller v. Pate, 386 U.S. 1 (1967) where the Supreme Court found that the prosecutor had misrepresented paint on a pair of shorts introduced at trial as blood. Subsequently, the Illinois Supreme Court constituted a special commission to determine if the prosecutor, who had subsequently entered private practice, should be disbarred. After an extensive nine month inquiry, the commission concluded in its report dated May 14, 1968 that the shorts had contained both blood and paint. They found that the Supreme Court had no basis for its finding that the prosecutor had misrepresented the evidence at trial. "The Vindication of a Prosecutor" 59 *J.Crim.L., Crim. and Pol.Sci.* 335 (1969).

2. Rare variants in both the PGM and EAP systems were identified in blood of an

attempted murder victim and in bloodstains on the suspect's shoes. This combination, together with results from the ABH, Gm and Hp systems provided a level of individualization comparable to those using DNA. Thompson and Higaki, "A Double Variant Encountered During Routine Casework" 26 *Can.Soc.Forensic Sci.J.* 111 (1993).

3. Gaensslen, "When Blood is Their Argument: Use and Interpretation of Population Genetic Marker Frequency Data in Forensic Serology" 12 *Crime Lab.Dig.* 75 (1985); Buckleton et al., "A Stratified Approach to the Compilation of Blood Group Frequency Surveys" 27 *J.Forensic Sci.Soc.* 103 (1987); Walsh and Buckleton, "A Discussion of the Law of Mutual Independence and its Application to Blood Group Frequency Data" ibid. 28 *J.Forensic Sci. Soc.* 95 (1988).

4. People v. Macedonio, 42 N.Y.2d 944, 397 N.Y.S.2d 1002, 366 N.E.2d 1355 (1977).

blood differs in any of several successfully typed grouping systems, he or she cannot be the source of the questioned blood or bloodstain.

§ 13.08 Identification of Stains as Blood

Frequently, blood encountered in a criminal investigation is present in the form of dried stains. When properly examined, dried bloodstains have the potential for providing considerable information about their source. In instances where mere traces of blood are detected, they may show that a location could have been the scene of a violent crime or that a bloody body was moved through the area. Patterns of bloodstains can provide information regarding the motion of the source or victim, direction of attack, etc.

When a stain alleged to be blood is submitted for examination, it must first be identified. Among materials visually resembling blood are paint, rust, ketchup, shoe polish, dye, and ink. Several tests, none of which are specific for blood, are used to presumptively identify a stain as blood. If conducted with care, crystal tests made under the microscope are sensitive and good indicators of blood. Rust or other contaminants in the sample may interfere with crystal tests for blood and these are less sensitive than color tests. Three of the most widely used crystal tests are:

(1) Teichmann (hemin crystal) test: A portion of the stain is treated with saline to release the hemoglobin, dried and glacial acetic acid added. On evaporation, in the presence of hemoglobin, brownish-red, rhombic crystals of hemin are formed singly, in rosettes or clusters. The hemin crystals are distinguished from salt, from the saline, by their color.

(2) Takayama test: In the presence of hemoglobin, characteristic crystals of hemochromogen are formed.

(3) Wagenhaar test: Acetone reacts with hemoglobin to form small, dark crystals of acetone-hemin.

Color reaction tests are a second method for the identification of blood. They are based on the activity of hemoglobin as a catalyst to promote peroxide oxidation of compounds in the reagent, producing a characteristic color. Although none of these tests are specific, when conducted in combination by an experienced analyst, they provide reasonable confidence that the material tested is blood.

Several color tests are:

(1) Tetramethylbenzidine (TMB) test: This reagent has replaced the carcinogenic benzidine for use in blood identification. Solutions of TMB are more difficult to prepare than those of benzidine and somewhat less sensitive to traces of blood but generally exhibit the same behavior as benzidine.[1] Treatment of the suspected blood with TMB yields a blue

---

§ 13.08

1. Garner et al., "An Evaluation of Tetramethylbenzidine as a Presumptive Test for Blood" 21 *J.Forensic Sci.* 816 (1976).

or green color indicative of blood. The color is produced as a result of the peroxidase activity of blood. A variety of materials including horseradish, some vegetables and citrus juices interfere with the test so it must be considered non-specific. Experienced analysts contend that most common interferants produce the color at a different hue or rate than blood or that the sequence of color development differs. As a result, many interferences are readily distinguished from blood. For definitive identification, however, the TMB test should be supplemented by other tests.

(2) Phenolphthalein test: The test is sensitive, producing in 15 to 20 seconds, a pink to deep rose color in the presence of blood. Interference can be caused by alkalis, copper, nickel, potassium ferrocyanide and sodium cobaltinitrate.

(3) Leuco Malachite Green test: This test is less sensitive than phenolphthalein, producing a green color in 15 to 20 seconds in the presence of blood. False positives may be caused by rust, lead oxide, potato juice and permanganates.

(4) Luminol test: Although having relatively low sensitivity, this test suffers from false positives, i.e. it is more specific.

Other color tests such as the quaiacum test have been used but most have low sensitivity and suffer from a number of interferences. For adequate assurance that a substance is blood, the principal tests in combination should be used. A positive reaction with each test reduces the potential for errors attributable to false positives. Spectrophotometric measurement of wavelengths at which blood characteristically absorbs light may also be used for identification. More specific is immunoassay for blood.

§ 13.09 Identification of Species Origin of Blood

To confirm that a presumptively identified stain is human blood, the precipitin test is used. Of the techniques proposed for conducting this test, the simplest is to layer an extract of the stain above anti-human serum in a small tube. If the sample is of human origin, it will react with antibodies in the antiserum and form a cloudy ring at the interface of the two liquids.

Anti-human serum and antisera for a number of other animal species are commercially available but until relatively recent years many laboratories prepared their own. The serum was produced by injecting laboratory animals, primarily rabbits, with human blood, or that from another animal for whom antiserum was required. The rabbit's system reacts to the foreign blood and produces antibodies highly specific to it. Blood samples are collected from the rabbit and the serum portion isolated. The species specific antibodies remain in the serum and it is used in the precipitin test. (See Fig. 1.)

Fig. 1. An illustration of the precipitin test. The sample on the right is positive for human blood, as can be observed by the appearance of a ring, indicated by the arrow. *Courtesy: Louis R. Vitullo.*

Although antibodies are highly specific in their reactions, there is some cross-reactivity with blood from animals in closely related genera. An example is the reaction of anti-human serum to the blood of the gorilla or chimpanzee. Cross-reactions are not uncommon with blood from animals within a single genus, e.g. dog or wolf, members of the cat family, etc.

The gel diffusion technique is another approach to verification of the species of a blood or protein sample. In this technique, an extract of the blood sample is placed in a well on an agar gel covered plate. In another well, antiserum to the suspected species is placed. Antigens from the test sample and antibodies from the antisera diffuse or move through the gel. At the interface of the two, a line of precipitate is formed if the test sample represents the species to which the antibodies were produced. Although simple, this test must be repeated a number of times if the species origin of a questioned blood is to be determined rather than merely verified.

The Agar Double Diffusion method allows a number of species to be discriminated in a single test. In this approach, the sample to be tested is placed in a well in the center of an agar gel coated glass plate about 3 by 3 inches. Antisera to several animal species are placed in wells surrounding the test sample. Antigens from the test sample diffuse outward through the gel as do antibodies from each of the sera. A reaction to a particular antiserum is indicated by the formation of a line of precipitate between the two wells. Because the reaction of antibodies and antigens is essentially species specific, the line formed between the test sample and a particular antiserum indicates the species of the unknown sample. No reaction indicates that the blood is not that of the animal for which the antiserum was prepared. If no reaction to any of the antisera is obtained, it may indicate that the blood is decomposed or has undergone a severe chemical change. Blood subjected to acids, alkalis, heat, soap, detergents or peroxide may react poorly or not at all.

By applying an electrical potential to the plate, the sera and antibodies can be made to move and react more rapidly. This approach is known as the electrophoretic method or electrophoresis. The precipitin test is highly sensitive and works with extremely dilute blood or protein samples and even on very old samples. Proteins from 4000 to 5000 year old mummies have given reactions in the test.[1]

When results from the precipitin test are used in court, the analyst should be questioned regarding control tests conducted with known samples to verify the quality of any commercial antisera used. If the analyst prepares his own antisera, he or she should be questioned on the method of preparation, storage and testing to ensure the reliability and freedom from contamination of the antisera used. If the analyst is unable to concisely describe his preparation, test, and quality control procedures, doubt may be cast on the reliability of the identification. Similarly, when commercial antisera are used, inquiry should be made concerning their age and tests conducted to verify their reliability.

§ 13.10 Identification of Human Blood Types

After determining the species of the blood sample, if human, the blood is further classified as to blood group. Blood characterization and type determination is based primarily on antigen-antibody reactions with the most widely used antigen systems being ABH, MN, mn, Rh and Gm. Enzyme grouping systems, protein polymorphisms and, in some instances, identification of antibodies to specific diseases or environmental contaminants provide additional information for individualization of a blood sample or stain.

Although infrequently used, identification of non-genetically dictated antibodies to diseases or contaminants provides information unob-

§ 13.09

1. Crainie et al., "ABO Tissue Antigens of Egyptian Mummies" 43 Forensic Sci.Int. 113 (1989).

tainable from conventional blood grouping to aid in confirming identity of an individual. Examples of antibodies to common diseases include those to tuberculosis (TB), or smallpox. Environmental contaminants responsible for allergies include ragweed pollen, a common North American weed but rare in Europe; cat or dog "scales" and pigeon droppings, observed in a pigeon breeder.[1] Antibodies to these can be identified in blood or bloodstains.

It is beyond the scope of this chapter to explain in detail each and every system used for the characterization of blood. By way of example, the basic and oldest blood grouping method—the ABH system is described as representative of antigen systems.

Blood grouping into A, B, AB and H (formerly known as O) may be used as positive or negative evidence in a criminal case or where erroneous blood transfusions could have been a cause of injury. Blood groups are named for the antigen on the surface of the red cell and the cells will agglutinate in the presence of antibodies to that antigen. For example, type A blood contains an A antigen and is clumped by anti-A antibodies present in type B and H blood. Similarly, type B blood contains the B antigen and agglutinates in the presence of anti-B antibodies from type A and H blood. Type AB blood contains both A and B antigens and is agglutinated by either anti-A or anti-B antibodies. Blood type H was originally known as type O (or zero) because it contained neither A nor B antigens and did not react to either anti-A nor anti-B. As previously indicated, the frequency of occurrence of blood groups varies by race, ethnicity and region but, for the United States, distribution of the major groups in the ABH system is roughly: H—43%, A—42%, B—12% and AB—3%. Figures 2 and 3 show agglutinated and unagglutinated blood cells, respectively.

§ 13.10

1. Antibody profiling to provide identification information was developed at the U.K. Home Office Central Research Establishment in the mid 1970s. Werrett et al., "The Detection of Allergen–Associated Antibodies in Bloodstains" 16 *J.Forensic Sci. Soc.* 121 (1976); King et al., "Antibody Profiling of Bloodstains" 8 *Forensic Science* 151 (1976); Werrett and King, "Application of Allergy Diagnosis in Forensic Science" 22 *J.Forensic Sci.* 763 (1977).

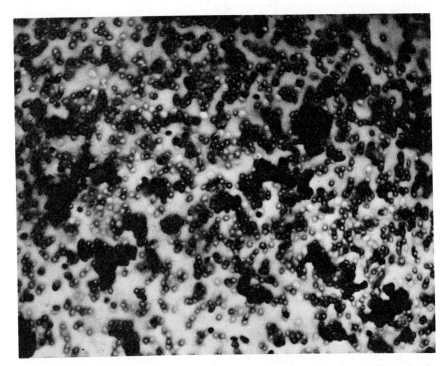

Fig. 2. Agglutinated blood cells, enlarged approx. 300X. *Courtesy: Louis R. Vitullo.*

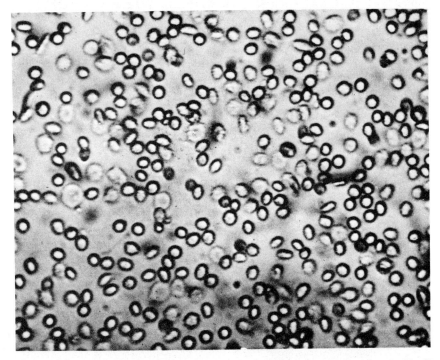

Fig. 3. Unagglutinated blood cells, enlarged approx. 430X. *Courtesy: Louis R. Vitullo.*

With fresh liquid blood, only anti-A and anti-B sera are required to determine the ABH blood type. Failure to observe any reaction with either anti-A or anti-B suggests type H but may result from other factors. A more definitive test involving a serum which clumps type H blood is desirable. It was observed that extracts of certain plant materials known as lectins clump type H blood. One of these is available from an extract of the seeds of Ulex europaeus and is known as anti-H serum. Other lectins have also been identified which react with subgroups of type A and with other blood grouping systems.[2] For example, the A group actually contains two major subgroups, A_1 and A_2 and are distinguished by testing with a specific lectin. With two subgroups of type A, type AB thus also has two subgroups, A_1B and A_2B.

Further characterization of the blood is made using other blood grouping systems. Among the most useful are Rh, which has a number of subgroups, and MNSs which is also quite complex. The significance of subgroup identification is that it places the questioned sample in a smaller group within the larger system, e.g. A_1 rather than just A, in the ABH system. Subgrouping rapidly decreases the size of the population group into which blood from an individual falls, lessening the prospect of a "chance match."

Other approaches to the individualization of blood are typing of proteins and enzymes. Both enzymes and proteins are polymorphic, that is, they exist in several forms or variants and the variants are identifiable by electrophoresis. Enzyme names typically have the suffix "ase". Among those commonly used in forensic serology are:

PGM	(phosphoglucomutase)
EAP	(erythrocyte acid phosphatase)
EsD	(esterase D)
AK	(adenyl kinase)
ADA	(adenosine deaminase)
GPT	(glutamic pyruvate transaminase)
6–PGD	(6-phosphogluconate dehydrogenase)
G–6–PD	(glucose–6–phosphate dehydrogenase)

Hemoglobin also exhibits variants and can be typed to distinguish the blood of an adult from a child[3] or identify variants such as the sickle cell trait Hb_s.

While grouping of fresh blood is relatively straightforward, bloodstains pose special problems. During the drying and aging process, a number of genetic markers deteriorate and some typing systems usable

---

2. Lectins are widely used for identification of subgroups in blood grouping and their applications extensively reviewed: Tumosa, "The Use of Lectins in Forensic Science" 1 *Forensic Sci.Rev.* 67 (1989).

3. Wraxall, "The Identification of Foetal Haemoglobin in Bloodstains" 12 *J.Forensic*

Sci.Soc. 457 (1972); King and Whitehead, "The Differentiation of an Adult's Bloodstain from that of a Child Using an Indirect Fluorescent Antibody Technique" 6 *Forensic Sci.* 197 (1975).

with fresh blood are less effective.[4] On drying, blood cells are destroyed so direct observation of agglutination is not possible. The antigens on the cell surfaces of non-putrefied blood, however, remain. To identify these, either of two indirect methods are used, absorption-elution or absorption-inhibition. Of these, absorption-elution, a four step process, is more common in forensic laboratories: (1) a portion of the bloodstain is treated with antiserum and allowed to react with their specific antigen; (2) excess antibodies are removed by washing; (3) the antigen-antibody is heated to 56° C to break the complex and elute the antibodies; and (4) blood cells of known type are added and the presence of agglutination observed. From the observed reactions, the ABH type of blood in the original stain is determined. This technique is highly sensitive and very small stains can be typed. It is also usable with aged stains and ones more than 10 years old have been typed.

In addition to the ABH grouping of stains, enzyme typing of bloodstains can also be performed. PGM (see above) has three major polymorphs or iso-enzymes: PGM 1, PGM 2–1 and PGM 2 and these vary in the population. PGM 1 is present in about 58% of the population while PGM 2–1 occurs in 36% and PGM 2 is found only at about 6%.

Using more refined electrophoretic techniques, additional subgroups of the PGM system can be identified and ten subgroups are now known. Even when only the three major PGM subgroups are used, they rapidly limit the population to which the bloodstain could belong. For example, if a stain is type A (42% of the population) and PGM 2–1 (36%), this combination occurs in only about 15% of the population (.42 × .36 = .15). Typing of all 10 PGM subgroups makes the population group even smaller because several of the subgroups occur in only a few percent of the population. Although the number of grouping systems usable with dried stains is smaller than with fresh blood, the more typing systems used, the more definitive the characterization of a bloodstain becomes. As a result, forensic scientists continue to search for grouping systems usable with dried stains and to refine techniques for identifying subgroups within these systems.

§ 13.11 Blood Stains

1. TYPES AND COLLECTION

Blood is usually recovered as (1) fresh blood, (2) clotted blood, (3) spatters, (4) smears or (5) blood flakes. The entire bloodstained item should be preserved for laboratory examination if possible. Preservation of the entire item is particularly important when weapons containing blood or bloodstained clothing are recovered.

In an instance where clothing containing wet blood is recovered, if sufficient blood is present, it is removed and placed in a vial or small

---

4. Denault et al., "Detectability of Selected Genetic Markers in Dried Blood on Aging" 25 *J. Forensic Sci.* 479 (1980).

bottle and refrigerated. The garment is then allowed to air dry, placed in a paper, not plastic, bag for submission to the laboratory. In most instances, with clothing, the best approach is to air dry the garment and package it in a porous container to avoid spoilage of the sample prior to serological analysis. With multiple items of clothing, each should be separately packaged and labeled.

To recover a specimen of fluid blood, a clean medicine dropper may be used to remove the blood from the surface. The blood is then placed in a small vial or tube and the vial sealed to prevent loss or contamination. Alternatively, the evacuated tubes used by hospitals for blood sample collection may be useful for obtaining a liquid sample at a crime scene. If the entire surface on which dried bloodstains are present cannot be submitted to the laboratory, stains are recovered by scraping from the surface onto a clean piece of paper using a clean knife, scalpel, spatula or tongue depressor. The paper and fragments are placed in a pill box or similar small container, sealed and labeled with information on source, date, case number and name of individual collecting the sample. Whenever blood samples are collected, wet or dry, they should be protected from strong light, moisture and heat. Because liquid blood decomposes rapidly without addition of a preservative, samples should be delivered to the laboratory promptly.

2. BLOOD SPATTERS

Prior to removing spots of blood from an object or location, the droplets should be photographed as they appear, with a suitable scale included in the photograph. From the shape of individual blood spots or a pattern of spots, considerable information may be available. For example, the size of spots may indicate the height from which they fell, as shown in Figure 4. The shape of a spot may indicate motion by the source and its direction. It must be recognized that the appearance of a blood spot is strongly affected by the surface onto which the blood falls. This effect is shown in Figure 5 which is taken from *Flight Characteristics and Stain Patterns of Human Blood* by H.L. MacDonell. All show the appearance of a single drop of human blood after falling 42 inches, but striking different surfaces. In the upper left photograph, the drop struck a plastic tile; upper right, a newspaper; lower left, an asbestos floor tile; and in the lower right, a heavy irregularly textured wallpaper.[1]

§ 13.11

1. White, "Bloodstain Patterns on Fabrics: The Effect of Drop Volume, Dropping Height and Impact Angle" 19 *Can.Soc.Forensic Sci.J.* 3 (1986).

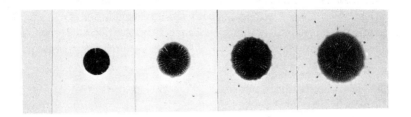

a   b   c   d

Fig. 4. Size of blood drops from different heights: (a) 1 inch; (b) 6 inches; (c) 24 inches; and (d) 72 inches.

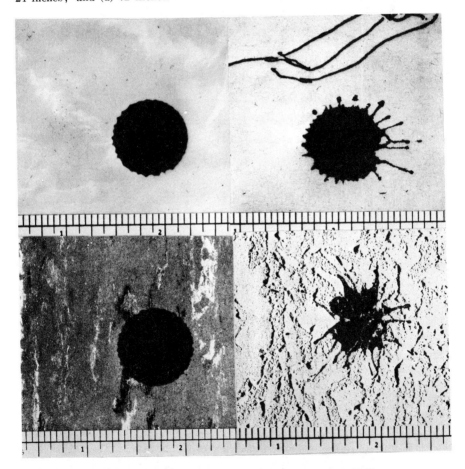

Fig. 5. *Courtesy: Herbert L. MacDonell, Corning, N. Y.*

When multiple blood spots are observed, they may form a spatter pattern which, upon analysis, can provide information useful in reconstruction of the sequence of events. The shape and relative positions of the spots may indicate direction of impact, motion of the victim, droplet velocity, etc.[2] When numerous spots are observed, the pattern can be enhanced and additional spots visualized by spraying the area a blood visualization reagent such as luminol and photography using an infrared reflection technique.[3]

Although bloodstain pattern analysis can provide useful information in the investigation of an accidental death, as for example, a pedestrian struck by an automobile or in a criminal assault, variables inherent in the interpretation of bloodstain patterns should not be overlooked. As a result, caution should be exercised in evaluating reports and testimony of the expert in this area.

3. SEX OF A BLOODSTAIN

Determination of the sex of a bloodstain may be important evidence in criminal cases. Two approaches to sex identification which have been used are determination of testosterone, progesterone and estradiol levels[4] and detection of the fluorescent Y-chromosomes present only in males.[5] A similar hormone approach can also be used to show pregnancy from analysis of bloodstains.[6]

4. AGE OF BLOODSTAINS

A variety of factors affect the rate at which blood dries and thus limit the reliability of estimation of the age of a bloodstain. A major factor in drying rate is the surface type; on hard, non-porous surfaces, such as floor tile, the blood may form a surface film on the drop and then dry slowly. By contrast, on a porous surface, such as paper, the liquid portion will be absorbed and the droplet dries quickly. Other factors influencing drying rate include temperature and humidity. As it ages, the color of a bloodstain changes from scarlet to dull brown with breakdown of the hemoglobin to hemin. Approximate age of fresh stains can be estimated if it can be shown that the hemoglobin has not yet

---

2. Sweet, "Bloodstain Pattern Analysis" 16 *Ident. Canada* 7 (1993); Sweet, "Velocity Measurements of Projected Bloodstains from a Medium Impact Source" 26 *Can.Soc.Forensic Sci.J.* 103 (1993); Anno., "Admissibility, in Criminal Prosecution, of Expert Opinion Evidence as to 'Blood Splatter' Interpretation" 9 A.L.R. 5th 369 (1993).

3. Raymond and Hall, "An Interesting Application of Infra-Red Reflection Photography to Blood Splash Pattern Interpretation" 31 *Forensic Sci.Int.* 189 (1986).

4. Brown, "The Determination of the Sex of an Individual from a Dried Bloodstain Using Radioimmunoassay of Testosterone, Progesterone and Estradiol–17b" 26 *J. Forensic Sci.* 766 (1981).

5. Thomsen and Buchhave, "The Effects of Various Fixatives on Y–chromosome Detection in Leucocytes" 29 *Forensic Sci. Int.* 21 (1985).

6. Osuna et al., "Diagnosis of Pregnancy in Bloodstains. Study of Progesterone and Leuteniaing Hormone Levels" 42 *Forensic Sci.Int.* 61 (1989); Brown et al., "Pregnancy Protein–SP₁: Identification Tool in Forensic Bloodstains" 26 *Can.Soc.Forensic Sci.J.* 69 (1993); Vergote et al., "Forensic Determination of Pregnancy Hormones in Human Bloodstains" 31 *J.Forensic Sci.Soc.* 409 (1991).

turned to hemin crystals. The degree of clotting may also be used in estimation of stain age.

One test used to estimate the age of an older stain, weeks or months old, is known as the "silver method," a color reaction test using silver nitrate. Exact determination of the age of a bloodstain is currently impossible.

§ 13.12   Blood Testing in Paternity Cases

Blood testing to establish paternity, or more rigorously, non-paternity, i.e. that the alleged father could not have been the biological parent of the child, dates to the 1920s. Initial testing focused on the use of ABH groupings of the trio: mother, child and alleged father. Probably the most publicized of early paternity cases involved Charlie Chaplin. ABH testing conclusively excluded him as the biological father; however, the blood group evidence was excluded and he was required to pay child support.[1] Subsequently, a precedent was established to permit use of blood test results excluding the alleged father.[2]

Use of blood testing in paternity disputes was accepted by the American Medical Association and many states have adopted the Uniform Act on Blood Tests to facilitate paternity actions. Development of the Human Leukocyte Antigen (HLA) test in the 1960s provided a method sufficiently specific alone to exclude about 90% of falsely accused men. When combined with red cell antigen studies or electrophoretic methods, exclusion can rise above 98%.[3] A recent study of the effectiveness of HLA phenotyping in excluding the alleged father in known false trios gave an exclusion of 81.7%. Use of other systems including ABO, Rh, MNSs, Kell, Duffy, and Kidd raised exclusion to 90.3% in an extremely diverse racial and ethnic population.[4] Paternity testing has been applied in: (1) divorce proceedings where adultery is alleged, (2) annulment proceedings, (3) affiliation of children with their biological parents and (4) situations involving surrogate parentage. Although superseded in part by DNA testing, blood grouping tests continue to play a significant role in civil cases involving disputed paternity.

§ 13.12

1. Berry v. Chaplin, 74 Cal.App.2d 652, 169 P.2d 442 (1946).

2. Cortese v. Cortese, 10 N.J.Super. 152, 76 A.2d 717 (1950).

3. For an extensive discussion of blood testing in paternity cases describing history, legal developments, genetic basis, blood grouping systems used and future developments, see: Melvin et al. in: *Forensic Science Handbook* Volume II Saferstein—Ed. Englewood, NJ Prentice–Hall 273; Boon-layangoor, "True Paternity or Exclusion: Analysis in the Case of a Deceased Party" 34 *J.Forensic Sci.* 703 (1989); Anno., "Admissibility and Weight of Blood–Grouping Tests in Disputed Paternity Cases" 43 A.L.R.4th 579 (1988).

4. Salaru, "Evaluation of HLA in Detection of Non–Parentage Among False Trios" 38 *J.Forensic Sci.* 1478 (1993); Salaru, "Paternity Investigation Among Known False Trios: ABO, Rh, MNSs, Kell, Duffy, Kidd, and HLA" ibid. 1482.

IV. THE INVESTIGATION OF OTHER BIOLOGICAL MATTER

§ 13.13 Other Biological Matter in Civil and Criminal Cases

Among the biological materials examined in civil and criminal cases, in addition to blood are semen, seminal stains, fecal matter, vomitus, saliva and tissue. Of these, the most commonly encountered in criminal cases are semen and seminal stains. These are frequent in sexual assault cases but may also be recovered from the body or clothing of victims in homicides. They may also be important evidence in the investigation of accidental autoerotic deaths and have even been found at the scenes of arson or burglaries.

In the investigation of alleged rape, particularly when the principal evidence of the crime is the uncorroborated testimony of the victim, detection of semen is nearly essential for proof of the crime. The crime of rape, homosexual or heterosexual, differs from other crimes of violence in two respects: (1) it rarely takes place in the presence of witnesses other than the victim and the perpetrator; (2) although it characteristically involves a man and a woman or female child, either as strangers or acquaintances, male homosexual rapes are not uncommon, particularly in child abuse cases. In cases of rape involving a stranger, a persistent problem involves identification of the assailant. Where the alleged rape is by an acquaintance, an essential element is showing that sexual intercourse occurred. In acquaintance (or date) rape, a frequent issue is that of consent, one which, in the absence of other evidence, identification and characterization of the seminal fluid is unable to resolve. In instances of sexual abuse of a child or a mental retardate, the issue of consent is not relevant and characterization of the seminal fluid or stain provides powerful evidence of the crime.

The microbiological analysis of a specimen believed to contain sperm or seminal fluid can answer the following medico-legal questions:

(1) Did the victim engage in sexual intercourse within the recent past?

(2) Are spermatozoa found in connection with the alleged incident of human origin?

(3) Are the spermatozoa or seminal fluid found in connection with the incident of a type that tends to exclude the suspect as their donor?

Microbiological or microanalytical testimony from laboratory analysis is principally concerned with the microscopic examination of seminal stains and smears of spermatozoa rather than with the traumatic indicia of rape.

§ 13.14 Detection and Identification of Seminal Fluid and Sperm Cells

1. TRADITIONAL METHODS

Seminal fluid is a mixture of secretions of the glands along the genital tract, the prostatic fluid secreted by the prostate gland and the sperm from the testes. The fluid consists of a highly proteinaceous

serum rich in choline and seminal acid phosphatase. The head of the
ʅperm cell is pear shaped and the flagellate tail is 10 to 12 times the
length of the head. (See Figure 6). During sexual intercourse, the
sexually mature male ejaculates seminal fluid containing the sperm cells.
The first portion of the ejaculate is reported to consist primarily of the
excretion of the bulbo-urethral glands and prostatic fluid, with relatively
few sperm cells. The mid portion of the ejaculate contains the mass of
the sperm cells and the final portion is primarily seminal vesicle secretion with relatively few sperm cells.

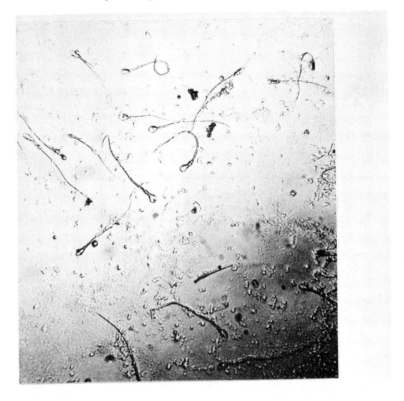

Fig. 6. Human spermatozoa, showing the characteristic head and tail.

The normal sperm count runs between 70,000,000 to 150,000,000
per milliliter, comprising roughly 10% of the total volume of the ejaculate. Some males exhibit naturally low sperm counts and less than
50,000,000 per milliliter is considered indicative of male infertility. In
males with successful vasectomies, sperm count will be essentially zero
so spermatozoa will be undetectable in samples from the victim of an
assault by a vasectomized individual; however, presumptive identification of seminal fluid will still be possible. If a condom ʅs used during the
assault, seminal fluid will be undetectable.

In rape cases, urethral and cervical smears are made by the examining doctor or pathologist from swabs of the vaginal pool or cervix of the

victim. In appropriate instances, rectal swabs may also be taken; however, these pose problems in examination [1] and are not reliable indicators of anal sodomy in heterosexual rapes.[2] Many rape examination protocols now call for the collection of oral swabs of saliva even though no oral intercourse is indicated by the victim.[3] Victims often are reticent about reporting "an unnatural sex act" so collection of these samples as part of the sampling protocol avoids further embarrassment.

Sperm cells and/or seminal stains may also be found on the victim or assailant's clothing or at the scene of the attack. Microbiological smears may also be taken from the suspect. The presence of intact sperm cells is the best indicator of recent intercourse although determination of zinc levels in vaginal fluid may also be a useful indicator.[4] Sperm cells may remain motile (active) for six to seven hours after coitus, except in unusual circumstances and thereafter become nonmotile. Nonmotile sperm may be detected for periods up to fourteen hours but normally are totally dissolved or excreted by a living victim within a day or so.[5] In a deceased victim, they have been found after a considerably longer time. Detection of seminal stains on the clothing of a suspect has relatively limited value because studies have shown them not to be uncommon.

The minuscule size of the sperm cells ($\frac{1}{6000}$th inch) requires examination of the specimen in slide form under a microscope. The microscopic examination is made by a microbiologist, serologist or trained specialist. With a dried sperm cell, the analyst must be careful to avoid detachment of the brittle tail from the body of the sperm cell; otherwise in the absence of the complete organism (head, connecting piece and tail) positive identification becomes difficult and may require use of specialized microscopic techniques. When dry, the sperm cell is resistant to decomposition and may be identifiable from 5 to 12 months after deposition.

Three different approaches may be used for the microscopic identification of sperm cells: (1) Interference–Phase microscopy; (2) stained slides; and (3) Phase–Contrast microscopy. Use of xylene in the latter facilitates screening of a smear for spermatozoa.[6]

§ 13.14

1. Green and Sayce, "Problems Associated with the Typing of Semen on Anal Swabs" 25 *J.Forensic Sci.Soc.* 55 (1985).

2. In a study of 72 cases where the complainant indicated that no anal intercourse occurred, spermatozoa were identified on 42% of anal and 35% of the rectal swabs. The results may be due to vaginal drainage, a struggle during the assault or other factors. Hageman et al., "Identification of Semen on Anal and Rectal Swabs in Cases not Involving an Alleged Anal Intercourse Assault" 26 *Can.Soc.Forensic Sci.J.* 129 (1993).

3. Willott and Crosse, "The Detection of Spermatozoa in the Mouth" 26 *J.Forensic Sci.Soc.* 125 (1986).

4. Rogers et al., "Vaginal Fluid Zinc Concentration as a Marker for Intercourse" 33 *J.Forensic Sci.* 77 (1988).

5. Randall, "Persistence of Vaginal Spermatozoa as Assessed by Routine Cervicovaginal (Pap) Smears" 32 *J.Forensic Sci.* 678 (1987).

6. Fraysier, "A Rapid Screening Technique for the Detection of Spermatozoa" 32 *J.Forensic Sci.* 527 (1987). The enzyme Protinease K dissolves all cellular material except spermatozoa and facilitates their identification. Chapman, Brown and Keating, "The Isolation of Spermatozoa from Sexual Assault Swabs using Protinease K" 29 *J.Forensic Sci.Soc.* 207 (1989); Iwasaki et al., "A Demonstration of Spermatozoa on

Microscopic examination of extracts of a seminal stain may not reveal the presence of spermatozoa. This may be the result of conditions known as ogliospermia or azoospermia where the semen contains few or no sperm cells; the sperm cells may have been destroyed by bacterial action or the assailant may have been vasectomized. It may still be possible to show that intercourse has occurred by detection of seminal acid phosphatase (SAP), an enzyme of the seminal fluid of humans or higher primates. Acid phosphatase (AP) is the name applied to enzymes capable of hydrolyzing certain acid phosphates in a mildly acid medium. One form, SAP, is secreted by the prostate gland located just above the urethra. Its concentration in semen is about 400 times that in any other bodily fluid. The SAP test is of no value if the prostate gland has been surgically removed.

The acid phosphatase test results in a color reaction when AP in seminal fluid is treated with any of several reagents. One of the most widely used is an acidic solution of sodium alphanaphthylphosphate and Fast Blue Dye which produces a purple color in the presence of semen. Other reagents may produce different color reactions. As time passes, the ability of a stain or deposit to react with the test reagent generally decreases, although with specimens stored at room temperature, positive tests have been obtained up to 6–8 months.

As a general rule, a negative reaction on a relatively fresh specimen indicates the absence of semen. Some of the test reagents used in the AP test are unstable and decompose in the presence of light, heat or alkalinity. If the reagent is contaminated with alpha-naphthol, a false positive may be obtained. Detergents used in cleaning laboratory apparatus may inhibit the AP reaction. In court, the expert should be queried about the control tests run along with the suspect sample.

A number of organisms and biological fluids contain acid phosphatase including bacteria; human milk, liver, urine and kidney; red blood cells; snake toxins; rice bran; sweet almonds; cauliflower; brussels sprouts; clover; bindweed; turnips; raisins; mango; ginger; figs and dates. Some stains such as those from figs and dates even look like semen stains in dry form. In tests, the relatively high percentage of acid phosphatase in seminal fluid causes a rapid and permanent development of color. Based upon this difference, experienced analysts claim to be able to differentiate between the enzymatic vegetable or fruit stains and seminal stains because most of the former react rather slowly. A reaction time of less than 30 seconds is normally considered as indicative of semen. Some substances such as cauliflower; however, are reported to produce a color reaction as vivid as that from semen. Another form of acid phosphatase is also found in vaginal secretions, vaginal acid phosphatase, but can be discriminated from seminal AP by a form of

Vaginal Swabs after Completed Destruction   *Sci.* 659 (1989).
of the Vaginal Cell Deposits" 34 *J.Forensic*

electrophoresis known as isoelectric focusing.[7]

Several other tests for semen have the potential for identification of seminal fluid in the absence of spermatozoa. One of these is for a protein designated p30 found in semen and in no other bodily fluids. When p30 is isolated and injected into a rabbit, antibodies (anti-p30) are produced. Using this antisera and electrophoresis, detection of p30 can provide a definitive identification of semen representing a significant improvement over the presumptive test for prostatic acid phosphatase.[8] Another approach is the detection of prostaglandins as specific markers for semen.[9] Immunoassay,[10] monoclonal antibodies[11] and a sperm specific isoenzyme[12] have also been evaluated for specific identification of seminal stains.

In addition to the Fast Blue test, three tests are widely used for presumptive identification of seminal stains by detection of choline and spermine, both present in high levels in seminal fluid. Choline has also been detected with an enzymatic method.[13] None of these, however, is absolute and a negative test with any of them does not preclude the presence of seminal stains.

(1) Florence test: a microcrystalline test for choline. The suspected seminal stain is put into solution; a drop put onto a glass slide and allowed to dry. A drop of Florence's solution (potassium iodide and iodine in water) is added and the slide viewed under the microscope.

7. Ablett, "The Identification of the Precise Conditions for Seminal Acid Phosphatase (SAP) and Vaginal Acid Phosphatase (VAP) Separation by Isoelectric Focusing" 23 *J.Forensic Sci.Soc.* 255 (1983). For a general discussion of Isoelectric Focusing see: Murch and Budowle, "Applications of Isoelectric Focusing in Forensic Serology" 31 *J.Forensic Sci.* 869 (1986).

8. Masibay and Lappas, "The Detection of Protein p30 in Seminal Stains by Means of Thin–Layer Immunoassay" 29 *J.Forensic Sci.* 1173 (1984); Stubbings and Newall, "An Evaluation of Gamma–Glutamyl Transpeptidase (GGT) and p30 Determinations for the Identification of Semen on Postcoital Vaginal Swabs" 30 *J.Forensic Sci.* 604 (1985); Poyntz and Martin, "Comparison of p30 and Acid Phosphatase Levels in Postcoital Vaginal Swabs from Donor and Casework Studies" 24 *Forensic Sci.Int.* 17 (1984); Kamenev, Leclercq and Francois–Gerard, "Detection of p30 Antigen in Sexual Assault Case Material" 30 *J.Forensic Sci. Soc.* 193 (1990). In this study p30 exhibited superior sensitivity to AP and no false positives were obtained.; Kamenev, Leclercq and Francois–Gerard "An Enzyme Immunoassay for Prostate-Specific p30 Antigen Detection in the Postcoital Vaginal Tract" ibid. 29 *J.Forensic Sci.* 233 (1989);

Johnson and Kotowski, "Detection of Prostate Specific Antigen by ELISA" 38 *J.Forensic Sci.* 250 (1993).

9. Sutton et al., "Evaluation of the 19–OH Analogs of Prostaglandins E_1, E_2, F_{1a} and F_{2a} as Specific Markers for the Identification of Human Semen in Body Fluid Mixtures" 33 *Forensic Sci.Int.* 103 (1987). Note: this group subsequently published additional articles on this work in the same journal.

10. Itoh and Matsuzawa, "Electronic Data Processing Latex Immunoassay for the Identification of Human Seminal Stains" 37 *Forensic Sci.Int.* 91 (1988).

11. Herr and Woodward, "An Enzyme Linked Immunosorbent Assay (ELISA) for Human Semen Identification Based on a Biotinylated Monoclonal Antibody to a Seminal Vesicle–Specific Antigen" 32 *J.Forensic Sci.* 346 (1987).

12. Powlowski and Brinkmann, "Evaluation of Sperm–Specific Lactate Dehydrogenase Isoenzyme C4 (LDH C4) Application to Semen Detection in Stains" 4 *Advances in Forensic Haemogenetics* 420 (1992).

13. Noppinger et al., "An Evaluation of an Enzymatic Choline Determination for the Identification of Semen in Casework Samples" 32 *J.Forensic Sci.* 1069 (1987).

Seminal fluid, if present, will form hemin-like brown rhombic crystals of needle and lance shapes, singly, in clusters and in rosettes. Although not specific for semen, a negative test strongly indicates that the stain is not of seminal origin.

(2) Barbario's test: A microcrystalline test for spermine. Treatment of a solution from the suspected stain with picric acid will produce yellow, needle-shaped crystals if semen is present. The test is not specific.

(3) Examination of the stain with ultraviolet (UV) light. Choline in a seminal stain will fluoresce white or blue-white under UV light. While the fluorescence is not specific for semen because a number of other materials also fluoresce under UV, a negative test indicates that the stain does not contain semen. UV light examination is most useful in screening of large surfaces such as a bedsheet for seminal stains but because many commercial laundry detergents now contain fluorescent brighteners which strongly fluoresce under UV light, the test is less useful for screening than formerly. Other light sources such as lasers and high intensity quartz lamps have also been evaluated for the detection of body secretions such as semen, saliva and perspiration.[14]

2. INDIVIDUALIZATION OF SEMINAL STAINS

The blood type of a sperm donor, A, B, AB or H, can often be determined by analysis of a seminal fluid sample in the same manner as for blood but stability is a problem for some grouping systems.[15] See: § 13.10. Approximately 80% of the population, called secretors, secrete their blood group factors into body fluids such as semen, saliva, tears, perspiration, vaginal fluid and nasal mucus. The major limitation in the identification of the blood group of the assailant is that it must differ from that of the victim. For example, with a victim of blood group A and the suspect also type A, if the only blood type detected in a vaginal swab sample from the victim is type A, then no conclusion regarding the suspect can be drawn. If the blood group of the suspect is type B, then detection of this group in the sample from the victim has some probative value, but limited because of the large number of individuals with this blood type.

For individualization of the semen donor, in addition to ABH grouping, Lewis groups and human leucocyte antigen (HLA) can be determined.[16] Highly polymorphic enzymes such as PGM, Esterase D,

14. Auvdel, "Comparison of Laser and Ultraviolet Techniques Used in the Detection of Body Secretions" 32 *J.Forensic Sci.* 326 (1987); Auvdel, "Comparison of Laser and High Intensity Quartz Arc Tubes in the Detection of Body Secretions" ibid. 33 *J.Forensic Sci.* 929 (1988).

15. Davis, "The ABH Reactions of Seminal Stains" 37 *Forensic Sci.Int.* 105 (1988); Baechtel, "Secreted Blood Group Sub-

stances: Distributions in Semen and Stabilities in Dried Semen Stains" 30 *J.Forensic Sci.* 1119 (1985); Sheikh and Chander, "Effect of Ageing on ABO–Agglutinogens in Seminal Stains" 21 *J.Indian Acad.Forensic Sci.* 14 (1982).

16. Bassler, "Determination of the Lewis Blood Group Substances in Stains of Forensically Relevant Body Fluids" 30 *Forensic Sci.Int.* 29 (1986); Regueiro and Arnaiz–

PepA (pepsidase A) and alpha-L-fucosidase [17] are also typable in semen. As with blood, recent efforts in individualization of semen have focused on the use of DNA, discussed in Chapter 15.

3. RELIABILITY AND COURTROOM USE

A properly conducted microscopic examination of a sample from the victim resulting in the identification of intact spermatozoa is the most reliable indicator of recent intercourse. Although some laboratories consider detection of both SAP and p30 adequate for identification of seminal fluid, many forensic laboratories will not testify to its identification without observation of intact sperm cells.

Reports and testimony will be limited to terms such as "highly indicative" of semen. Failure to observe spermatozoa in a sample should not be considered as evidence that no sexual assault occurred. A variety of factors may lead to failure to observe sperm cells or identify seminal fluid. In addition to those previously mentioned is the not infrequent occurrence of sexual dysfunction during an assault, i.e. no ejaculation occurred.

In a case illustrative of the difficulties in interpreting the results of seminal blood group testing results, a woman was raped but no ejaculation occurred. Vaginal swabs collected six hours later contained intact sperm cells, however, the victim denied any sexual contact for a month prior to the rape. Testing of the crotch area of the victim's underpants detected seminal fluid but PGM typing distinguished it from that of the suspect. Because the suspect confessed to the crime, the laboratory results were considered not relevant and no expert testimony was given to explain the anomalous results.[18]

Blood grouping tests on seminal fluid are, in general, somewhat less reliable than those in blood. Studies have shown that in some instances, grouping of seminal stains gives inconclusive results although good results were obtained in grouping tests of blood from the same individual.[19]

§ 13.15 Other Biological Matter

1. SALIVA

The identification of saliva or saliva stains may be important in the investigation of criminal incidents and could have utility in civil cases as well. For example, a cigarette butt, chewing gum or handkerchief left at

Villena, "HLA Typing of Dried Sperm" 29 *J.Forensic Sci.* 430 (1984).

17. Garlo, "Phosphoglucomutase and Esterase D Activity in Postcoital Vaginal Swabs" 25 *J.Forensic Sci.Soc.* 301 (1985); Garg and Koblinsky, "Seminal Alpha–L–Fucosidase Polymorphism in New York City" 25 *Can.Soc.Forensic Sci.J.* 71 (1992).

18. Brauner, "The Evidence Notwithstanding—A Case Report on a Rape" 37 *J.Forensic Sci.* 345 (1992).

19. Fowler and Scott, "Examination of the Correlation of Groupings in Blood and Semen" 30 *J.Forensic Sci.* 103 (1985).

a crime scene may have saliva stains present. If the individual responsible for these stains is a "secretor" (see § 13.14), his/her blood group may be identifiable.[1] Saliva has been collected by swabbing the area of bite marks in simple or sexual assault cases for use in the identification of the assailant. Saliva stains can be of value in civil litigation, as for example, blood grouping of saliva stains on postage stamps or the glued flap portion of an envelope could be used to demonstrate that an individual may have stamped and sealed an envelope at issue. Conversely, identification of a different blood group in the saliva tends to show noninvolvement. Similarly, blood grouping of saliva in a cigarette butt could demonstrate the presence of an individual at the location of a crime or where a civil fraud was alleged to have occurred.

As indicated previously, saliva may be a fruitful sample for the detection of seminal fluid when oral copulation may have occurred. Some problems have been observed in apparent differences between the blood group determined in saliva as compared to that of the individual.[2] As a result, it is desirable to perform other typing for individualization. One of these is typing of certain polymorphic proteins and enzymes common in saliva.[3]

2. FECAL MATTER

Fecal deposits on clothing occur in incidents involving male homosexuality or homosexual rapes and may be observed in heterosexual rapes involving anal intercourse. Fecal matter may also result from nervous tension of either the victim or assailant or from an abnormal mental aberration of the perpetrator. Although blood groups may be typable in fecal material, only limited success has been reported. In some instances, a false positive test for acid phosphatase is obtained with fecal matter and identification of spermatozoa in this material is extremely difficult. Characterizing information from fecal material may be available through identification of incompletely digested food from a recent meal or the detection of intestinal parasites.

3. VOMITUS

Vomitus on a garment at a particular location or on a suspect's clothing may corroborate the story of the victim of a deviate sexual

§ 13.15

1. Harrington et al., "Detection of Hemagglutins in Dried Saliva Stains and their Potential Use in Blood Typing" 33 *J.Forensic Sci.* 628 (1988); Takatori and Tsutsubuchi, "An ELISA Using Avidin–Biotin Complex for the Determination of ABH Group from Saliva" 31 *Forensic Sci.Int.* 61 (1986); Ogata et al., "Detection of Le [a] Substance in Saliva Stains by Enzyme–Linked immunosorbent Assay (ELISA) Using Anti–Gum Arabic Serum" 32 *J.Forensic Sci.* 1551

(1987). The latter technique is suitable for small or old stains.

2. Fiori et al., "The ABO(H) Paradoxical and Aberrant Secretion in Human Saliva" 17 *Forensic Sci.Int.* 13 (1981).

3. Tsuchida and Ikemoto, "Genetic Polymorphisms of Human Parotid Saliva and their Application to Forensic Science" 5 *Forensic Sci.Rev.* 15 (1993); Auvdel, "Amylase Levels in Semen and Saliva" 31 *J.Forensic Sci.* 426 (1986).

assault. Detection may be based on identification of gastric fluids by an enzyme assay [4] and blood grouping may also be possible. More generally useful is examination of vomitus to show the presence of alcohol, drugs or ingestion of a toxic or emetic mixture, spoiled food, etc.; determinations which may be relevant in civil as well as criminal cases.

4. PERSPIRATION

If an individual is a secretor, his/her blood groups are also identifiable in perspiration stains. Suitable items for testing include handkerchiefs, bandannas or headbands or a shirt or blouse stained under the arms or around the collar. The inside band of a hat or cap, the waist band of undershorts, undershirts, Teeshirts or "tank tops" are also potentially attractive for testing if these are discarded or inadvertently left behind at the crime scene.

5. URINE

Like other body fluids, the detection of urine stains at a scene may be supportive of statements or reconstruction of the sequence of events. Although a stain may appear to be urine, without confirmatory testing, it has little value. Among the approaches applied to the identification of urine stains are: radioimmunoassay for urinary proteins, radial gel diffusion for urea and immunological techniques.[5] To identify the urine stain as human, detection of human uromucoid by immunosorbent assay is used.[6] Blood typing in both the ABH and Lewis systems has been reported and provides limited characterization of the stain.[7] Blood grouping of liquid urine samples has been beneficial in drug testing programs when a claim is made that a sample testing positive is not that of a particular individual.[8] A showing that the blood group in the questioned urine differs from that of the named individual supports a claim of sample labeling error.

4. Lee et al., "Enzyme Assays for the Identification of Gastric Fluid" 30 *J.Forensic Sci.* 97 (1985).

5. Taylor and Hunt, "Forensic Identification of Human Urine by Radioimmunoassay for Tamm–Horsfall Urinary Glycoprotein" 23 *J.Forensic Sci.Soc.* 67 (1988); Bedrosian et al., "Development of a Radial Gel Diffusion Technique for the Identification of Urea in Urine Stains" 29 *J.Forensic Sci.* 601 (1984); Poon, "Identification of Human Urine by Immunological Techniques" 17 *Can.Soc.Forensic Sci.J.* 81 (1984).

6. Tsutsumi et al., "Identification of Human Urinary Stains by Enzyme–Linked Immunosorbent Assay for Human Uromu-

coid" 33 *J.Forensic Sci.* 237 (1988). Although this technique discriminates human urine from most other animals, it does not distinguish urine of humans from that of chimpanzees and certain old world monkeys.

7. Chase, "ABO typing on Liquid Urines" 31 *J.Forensic Sci.* 881 (1986); Kotowski, "Typing of Urine in the ABO and Lewis Systems" 32 *J.Forensic Sci.* 1065 (1987).

8. Holland et al. "Application of Serological and DNA Methods for the Identification of Urine Specimen Donors" 5 *Forensic Sci.Rev.* 1 (1993).

6. TEETH, TISSUE, HAIR AND OTHER BIOLOGICAL MATERIAL

Blood grouping of tissue and other body organs may eliminate a sample as having originated from a particular individual when this issue is in question or for identification of recovered body parts.[9] In criminal cases, recovered tissue, as for example, skin from under the fingernails of an assault victim, can be compared to the blood group of the suspect. Similarly, skin from the nails of the suspect can be compared to that of the victim.   In the investigation of the strangulation death of his estranged wife, blood and fingernail scrapings were taken involuntarily at the police station from Daniel Murphy, who was neither under arrest nor detained at the time.   Each sample was typed as the blood group of the victim and their admission, over objection, at trial was upheld by the Supreme Court as arising from exigent circumstances.[10]

Teeth are durable and survive accidents and decomposition. When recovered, the dental pulp inside the tooth may be typed for both blood group and enzymes.[11] Hair is another material which may be encountered at a crime scene and it too, can be typed if the root portion is available.[12] Sex can also be determined in hair based upon the levels of the fluorescent Y-chromosomes present. Reliability is good even with old hairs. The major limitation of the technique is that hair from a small number of males with naturally low Y-chromosome levels may be misidentified as female. This limitation is easily overcome by analysis of hair or blood from the suspect to determine if his Y-chromosome count is also low. Bone is also capable of being typed in the ABH system.[13]

In decomposed or badly mutilated bodies, two other body fluids containing blood group factors are the vitreous humor,[14] the fluid from the eye, and the fluid from the inner ear.[15] These are potentially attractive for collection and study because they are not readily affected by putrefaction.

V. EVIDENTIAL STATUS OF TEST RESULTS

§ 13.16 Introduction

The breadth of the subject matter covered in the preceding sections requires a different approach in discussing the legal aspects of the various issues. Expert qualifications will be dealt with first, followed by

9. Reisner et al., "Tests of Genetic Markers on Aborted Fetal Material" 33 *J.Forensic Sci.* 1262 (1988).

10. *Cupp v. Murphy,* 412 U.S. 291 (1973).

11. Turowska and Trela, "Studies on the Isoenzymes PCM, ADA and AK in Human Teeth" 9 *Forensic Sci.* 45 (1977).

12. Yuasa et al., "Esterase D Phenotyping of Bloodstains and Hair Roots by Low Voltage Isoelectric Focusing" 28 *Forensic Sci.Int.* 63 (1985); Tahir and Welch, "Simultaneous Typing of Erythrocyte Acid Phosphatase, Adenyl Kinase and Adenosine Desaminase in Human Hair Root Sheaths" 26 *J.Forensic Sci.Soc.* 335 (1986).

13. Lee et al. "Genetic Markers in Human Bone: II. Studies on ABO (and IGH) Grouping" 36 *J.Forensic Sci.* 639 (1991).

14. Dimo–Simonin et al., "Gm(1, 2, 4, 10, 21) and Km(1) Factors in Vitreous Humor" 30 *Forensic Sci.Int.* 23 (1986).

15. Trela and Turowska, "ABO(H) Group Substances in Human Inner Ear Fluid" 6 *Forensic Sci.* 5 (1975); Turowska and Trela, "Gm(1) Factor in Human Inner Ear Fluid" ibid. 89.

consideration of specific issues relating to toxicological and serological testing and results.

§ 13.17 Expert Qualifications

The determination of whether a witness is qualified to give opinion testimony will be left to the "sound discretion" of the trial court.[1] This determination will not be overturned absent a showing of abuse of this discretion.[2] While either formal study or sufficient practical experience ordinarily suffices to qualify one as an expert in a particular subject area, in the areas of chemistry-toxicology or serology, some formal education in a related science should be required. Relevant fields of study could include: chemistry, biochemistry, toxicology, serology, hematology, pharmacology, etc. depending upon the material at issue. This formal study should be supplemented by practical experience in the specialty area. It should be recognized that, in some instances, these requirements may tend to exclude as experts college teachers or professors who, though familiar with the field through study, lack practical experience.

Courts have held that formal study in the field alone may qualify one as an expert even though the individual lacks experience in the field.[3] A second "gray area" in qualification as an expert is the skilled technician, who although lacking extensive formal study, has combined experience and training in the subject matter.[4] Emerging areas of technology, where few formal educational programs exist, also pose problems but this is less severe in chemistry-toxicology or serology than in other areas of scientific investigation.

In certain circumstances, a lay witness may be permitted to express an opinion that normally requires expert testimony. For example, a witness may be permitted to state that material at the scene appeared to be blood although no testing was conducted to verify its identification. Similarly, police officers have long been allowed to express an opinion that material was a controlled substance based on experience and limited

---

§ 13.17

1. Redi Roast Products, Inc. v. Burnham, 531 So.2d 664 (Ala.Civ.App.1988); Cody v. Louisville & Nashville R. Co., 535 So.2d 82 (Ala.1988); Mathis v. Glover, 714 S.W.2d 222 (Mo.App.1986).

2. Mathews v. Chrysler Realty Corp., 627 S.W.2d 314 (Mo.App.1982). In Stuart v. Director of Revenue, 761 S.W.2d 234 (Mo.App.1988), the trial court was found to have abused its discretion in rejecting the testimony of a police officer trained in the operation of the breathalyzer.

3. Riggle v. State, 585 P.2d 1382 (Okl. Crim.1978), a recent graduate of a school of osteopathic medicine, not yet licensed as a

medical doctor, was permitted to testify to cause of death despite lack of practical experience. In Darling v. Reid, 534 So.2d 255 (Ala.1988), objection to Professor of medicine who had never practiced and was not board certified went only to weight of testimony and was not grounds for disqualification as expert. Accord: Lavespere v. Niagara Machine & Tool Works, Inc., 910 F.2d 167 (5th Cir.1990).

4. A public health investigator without medical training or science degree but with 8 years of experience involving sexually transmitted diseases could testify as expert to probability of transmission of gonorrhea from rape victim to defendant. Davis v. United States, 865 F.2d 164 (8th Cir.1988).

training in drug recognition.[5] Chemists have been permitted to testify to the identification of material as marihuana (cannabis) based solely on chemical test results and without formal training in botany.[6]

Ordinarily the requirement for formal education is not a problem with chemists, toxicologists or serologists because the requisite education and specialized training are requirements for employment and the expert will usually have sufficient experience to satisfy the court that he/she is qualified to give expert testimony. Nevertheless, in some instances, the court is unaware of the specialized training and experience needed to conduct a particular type of test and properly interpret the results. Even one well qualified as a chemist may be permitted to testify to the results of examinations beyond his area of expertise.[7] In addition, in the interpretation of data from a test where statistics are involved, the expert may be challenged on his knowledge of statistical processes and calculations.[8]

It is desirable for the attorney planning to use or facing testimony in a narrow speciality area to contact practitioners in the specialty and inquire as to the specialized knowledge and training required to function effectively in the area.

In today's medico-legal departments, specialization is commonplace. Provided an individual possesses the necessary basic education in a scientific discipline, his specialized work experience may permit him to stray into areas normally considered as requiring different formal training (Ph.D. in toxicology versus an M.D. or pharmacology degree, for example). There is normally no evidentiary barrier to a B.S. degree chemist or biochemist testifying to the results of a chemical analysis conducted in accord with standard and established techniques, provided he or she has sufficient practical experience in conducting such tests.

As noted, although the field of toxicology is essentially a subspecialty within analytical chemistry, the proposed expert should have acquired, through experience and specialized training, a working familiarity with relevant aspects of biology, pharmacology and physiology.

---

5. Cory v. State, 543 P.2d 565 (Okl. Crim.1975); State v. Detlefson, 335 So.2d 371 (Fla.App.1976) or State v. Clark, 30 N.C.App. 253, 226 S.E.2d 398 (1976) contra: People v. Park, 72 Ill.2d 203, 20 Ill.Dec. 586, 380 N.E.2d 795 (1978).

6. An experienced toxicologist is qualified to testify, from chemical analysis and a "gastromatographic (sic) analysis," that a substance is marihuana. His lack of qualifications as a botanist, if relevant, goes to the weight of the testimony rather than its admissibility. State v. Cochrane, 114 R.I. 710, 339 A.2d 256 (1975).

7. Ward v. State, 427 S.W.2d 876 (Tex. Cr.App.1968). Chemist testified to the results of a neutron activation analysis (NAA) of hair despite lack of practical experience.

He referred to it as a "nuclear activator test" and contended he understood the test and could do it. His testimony, however, made it apparent that he lacked understanding of the complexity or instrumentation of NAA and the factors involved in the interpretation of the results.

8. Analytical methods such as Neutron Activation Analysis involve measurement of radioactivity, emission of which is a statistical phenomenon. Other types of analytical determinations involve statistical mathematical techniques in calculation of the results or interpretation of the data to reach a conclusion. Questioning of the expert on his/her training in, and knowledge of, statistics can be a fruitful area. Karjala, "The Evidentiary Uses of Neutron Activation Analysis" 59 *Calif.L.Rev.* 997 (1971).

Similarly, the serologist should be familiar with significant concepts in biochemistry and physiology. To interpret blood grouping results and calculate population size, a working knowledge of genetics is also required.

Analytical chemistry methodology is the basis for the work of the toxicologist whether in environmental, medical or physical evidence examinations. In each instance, the toxic compounds being sought may be present in biological material so the analyst must have a knowledge of biological phenomena. Many of the compounds detected are drugs so training, even if informal, in pharmacology is essential as is a familiarity with the relevant pharmaceutical and toxicological literature. To interpret the effects of toxins on biological systems, the toxicologist should also have some training in physiology.

To ensure the qualifications of practicing forensic toxicologists, a certification program has been established by the American Board of Forensic Toxicology. For certification an individual must possess a Ph.D. or D.Sc. degree in one of the natural sciences (e.g. Chemistry or Toxicology) from an accredited institution of higher learning whose program is also accredited.[9] The applicant must also possess an adequate undergraduate and graduate education in biology, chemistry, pharmacology or toxicology.

Certification by the board is also dependent on meeting the requirements for relevant experience in forensic toxicology. If all requirements are met, the expert holding a certification may use the designation "Diplomate of the American Board of Forensic Toxicology" (DABFT). Certification is valid for three years and must be renewed.

In both crime laboratories and those performing a range of analytical testing, it must be recognized that there may be no clear distinction between job title and job function. In one laboratory, certain types of tests may be conducted by a chemist while in others, similar examinations may be performed by a toxicologist or criminalist. As a result, certification of the analyst may be through another certifying organization. One such organization is the American Board of Criminalists (ABC). This organization has begun a certification program for those employed in crime laboratories.

The ABC certification program requires verification of an undergraduate education in a physical or biological science [10] and a general test covering a variety of areas of forensic science for initial certification. Meeting these requirements permits an individual to be certified as a

---

9. Toxicologists lacking the doctorate or other graduate degree but with six or more years of experience in forensic toxicology were allowed by a "grandfather clause" to qualify for certification if they applied prior to December 31, 1977.

10. One of the most significant aspects of the ABC Certification process is a requirement for documentary verification of claimed education. Examples of experts claiming formal degrees never earned are numerous. See: Starrs, "Mountebanks Among Forensic Scientists" in: *Forensic Science Handbook* Volume II Saferstein— Ed. Englewood Cliffs, NJ Prentice–Hall 1. When using or confronted by an expert, an attempt should always be made to determine if his/her credentials are as represented.

"Diplomate of the ABC". Tests in specialty areas including Drug Analysis and Forensic Biology, which includes modules on serology and DNA testing, have been developed and others are planned. Having completed the basic certification requirements, an individual may sit for an examination in the speciality area. Successful completion of one or more of the specialty examinations and meeting of other requirements including proficiency testing and continuing education qualifies an individual as a "Fellow of the ABC".

Although certification or licensing [11] is not a legal requirement for court qualification as an expert, practitioners in the forensic sciences recognize the need for programs to ensure that those purporting to be experts in a particular speciality possess the requisite skills and education of the specialty. One facet of assurance of the quality of forensic laboratory work is the necessity for proficiency testing in specialty areas. A regular proficiency testing program is a requirement for laboratories certified by the American Society of Crime Laboratory Directors (ASCLD) and for individuals certified in specialty areas by the ABC. Currently, only a limited number of forensic laboratories have elected voluntary certification and certification of a laboratory by ASCLD does not carry with it certification of individual laboratory staff members. It may be desirable to inquire if a proffered expert is certified in the specialty in which the testimony will be presented but inquiry should always be made to determine if he/she regularly participates in proficiency testing in the specialty area. While such inquiries may not result in disqualification of the expert, they could affect the weight given to his/her testimony by the trier of fact. In a contest involving experts for both parties, the use of a certified expert, particularly one with an advanced degree and publications in the specialty, may offer considerable advantage.

When the type of test or the opinion offered is in a field for which there are no formal education programs and only limited specialized training, a person can qualify as an expert witness only when he/she is shown to have conducted sufficient experimentation to lend credence to her findings. One example is in the interpretation of evidence from blood spatter patterns (See, infra § 13.19). In this instance, a showing that the individual has personally conducted numerous tests and has accumulated reference patterns on which to base his opinion should be required. The individual should demonstrate familiarity with relevant literature in the field. Because seminars or training sessions on blood spatter pattern interpretation are now available, the expert should have attended one or more of these.

§ 13.18   General Toxicology Results

Traditionally, the general guidelines for admissibility of scientific

---

11. Jones v. Jones, 117 Idaho 621, 790 P.2d 914 (1990).

test results were similar to those laid down in *Frye* [1] requiring that the test be considered reliable and accurate by scientists in the field in which it belongs. Some jurisdictions never explicitly accepted the *Frye* rule and have modified these guidelines to better define the relevant field or to permit wider acceptance of the test results. Examples include *Williams* [2] and *Coppolino*. [3] Others have held to the rule that the testimony of the expert should not be allowed to invade the province of the jury, i.e. to address the ultimate issue, [4] but this view is no longer widely held.

In many situations, the expert is permitted to express a conclusion, in the form of an opinion or otherwise, even though this may tend to usurp the role of the trier of fact. [5] It is generally conceded that the jury is capable of recognizing that the opinion of the expert is not binding on their findings. The recent *Daubert* [6] case has brought the requirement for admissibility more in line with Federal Rule 702 but it is reasonable

§ 13.18

1. Frye v. United States, 293 Fed. 1013 (App.D.C.1923). Although it set the standard for admissibility of scientific evidence and is oft quoted, the facts of *Frye* are frequently misstated. The issue before the D.C. Circuit involved a "systolic blood pressure measurement" to detect prevarication. Blood pressure measurement is but one aspect of a true polygraph examination. Nevertheless, *Frye* is often referred to as involving the admissibility of the polygraph, which it did not. At the time, the polygraph *per se* did not exist.

2. People v. Williams, 164 Cal.App.2d Supp. 858, 331 P.2d 251 (1958). This landmark case involved the Nalline test for opiate addiction, widely used among those involved in drug abuse treatment programs but probably not well known in the broader medical community. The California court determined that the technique was "generally accepted" within the community expected to be familiar with it and thus admissible. The effect was to narrow the *Frye* community in which a technique required "general acceptance."

3. *Coppolino*, note 7 infra was another landmark case in determining admissibility of scientific evidence. Although Florida had never specifically adopted *Frye,* the effect was to further liberalize the *Frye* guidelines. In this instance, tests were specially developed to detect succinyl choline in tissue adjacent to several needle tracks on the victim's exhumed body. Although newly developed for the purpose, the tests were based on accepted medical technology and performed by qualified scientists. Thus, their novelty alone did not prohibit admissibility.

4. Expert testimony on causation is still held in some states to embrace the ultimate issue and is impermissible. Virginia, for example, has long held that the testimony of a fire investigator, even though qualified as an expert, that a fire was intentionally set is inadmissible. As recently as 1984, in Bond v. Commonwealth, 226 Va. 534, 311 S.E.2d 769, the Virginia Supreme Court reiterated its opposition to expert testimony to resolve conflicting inferences. They emphasized the imbalance between the resources of the state which could hire, at public expense, a bevy of experts whereas similar resources were unavailable to an indigent defendant. Civil cases not allowing ultimate issue testimony include: Fogarty v. Parichy Roofing Co., 175 Ill.App.3d 530, 124 Ill.Dec. 938, 529 N.E.2d 1055 (Ill. App. 1 Dist.1988) and Harris v. Pacific Floor Mach. Mfg. Co., 856 F.2d 64 (8th Cir.1988). In State v. Oliver, 108 Ga.App. 47, 372 S.E.2d 256 (1988) an opinion on an ultimate issue of fact was found permissible only where the inference to be drawn was beyond the ken of the jurors.

5. In the Federal courts and those states which have adopted the Federal Rules of Evidence, Rule 704 provides that otherwise admissible testimony in the form of opinion or inference is not objectionable merely because it embraces an ultimate issue to be decided in the case.

6. Daubert, et ux., et al. v. Merrell Dow Pharmaceuticals, Inc., 113 S.Ct. 2786 (1993). For discussions of the effects of *Daubert* on the admissibility of expert testimony see: Ego, "Supreme Court Knocks Out Frye Admissibility Test for Scientific Evidence in Federal Arena" 20 *FBI L.Enf. Bull* 41 (1993); Giannelli, "*Frye, Daubert,*

that a showing of reliability and a sound scientific basis for the tests conducted will still be required for their admission.

Toxicologists and chemists are frequently allowed to testify to the effects of particular substances on the body even though they are not pharmacologists or medical doctors.[7] Similarly, a medical examiner, qualified as an expert, was permitted to testify to the results of a toxicology report even though he did not personally perform the tests.[8] Physicians are generally considered qualified to testify to physiological effects, even in the absence of personal experience and relying solely on published information.[9] Hearsay rules are frequently relaxed when an expert's opinion is based in part on laboratory or medical records produced by other experts but these must be considered reliable.[10] A chemist, under whose supervision tests were conducted by another chemist in the laboratory, was permitted to testify from the laboratory records to the results of the tests.[11] Although this practice is regularly followed in some laboratories where tests are performed primarily by technicians, both in civil and criminal cases, it raises serious confrontational questions.[12]

Statutory provisions in some states permit laboratory reports to be admissible as exceptions to the hearsay rule. The objective of such statutes is to reduce demands of court testimony on medical and laboratory personnel. These statutes affect a variety of laboratory reports but their impact is primarily in trials involving analyses of drugs and blood or breath alcohol. The constitutionality of one such statute was upheld by the Virginia Supreme Court in Robertson v. Commonwealth.[13] This

and the Federal Rules" 29 *Crim.L.Bull.* 428 (1993).

7. Ph.D. microbiologist and professor in a university medical school who had done research on Toxic Shock Syndrome permitted to testify to diagnosis and cause even though not a medical doctor. Baroldy v. Ortho Pharmaceutical Corp. Corp., 157 Ariz. 574, 760 P.2d 574 (1988). Biochemist, professor of biochemistry and immunology can testify regarding causal connection between flu vaccine and recipient's disease. Wyeth Laboratories v. Fortenberry, 530 So.2d 688 (Miss.1988). Ph.D. biochemist qualified as expert in pulmonary biochemistry and could testify to physiological effects of phosgene gas even though some of his testimony comprised medical opinion. Walls v. Olin Corp., Inc., 533 So.2d 1375 (La.App. 3 Cir.1988). Similar, testimony of toxicologist to effects of dibromochloropropane. Loudermill v. Dow Chemical, 863 F.2d 566 (8th Cir.1988); Toxicologist to intoxication in automobile accident. May v. Strecker, 453 N.W.2d 549 (Minn.App.1990); Biochemist to link of PCB exposure with colon cancer. Rubanick v. Witco Chemical Corp., 242 N.J.Super. 36, 576 A.2d 4 (App. Div.1990), remanded to reconsider in light

of new standard, 125 N.J. 421, 593 A.2d 733 (1991).

8. Commonwealth v. Gilliard, 300 Pa.Super. 469, 446 A.2d 951 (1982).

9. Hext v. State, 100 Tex.Crim.R. 24, 271 S.W. 81 (App.1925).

10. Kanvick v. Reilly, 233 Mont. 324, 760 P.2d 743 (1988); McMunn v. Tatum, 237 Va. 558, 379 S.E.2d 908 (1989) but see: Missouri Farmers Ass'n v. McBee, 787 S.W.2d 756 (Mo.App.1990) where a Ph.D. in soil chemistry was not allowed to testify to the results of a laboratory report identifying the chemical applied to soil.

11. Preston v. State, 450 S.W.2d 643 (Tex.Cr.App.1970); State v. Clapp, 335 A.2d 897 (Me.1975); Reardon v. Manson, 644 F.2d 122 (2d Cir.1981).

12. State v. Henderson, 554 S.W.2d 117 (Tenn.1977).

13. 211 Va. 62, 175 S.E.2d 260 (1970). Accord: State v. Christianson, 404 A.2d 999 (Me.1979)—analyst's report on PCP analysis; State v. Smith, 312 N.C. 361, 323 S.E.2d 316 (1984)—blood alcohol content. Contra: State v. Matulewicz, 198 N.J.Super. 474, 487 A.2d 772 (1985) but see af-

case involved the admission of a laboratory report regarding a vaginal swab test for semen, admitted pursuant to a statute which had as its purpose the avoidance of summoning as witnesses physicians and technicians who make pathological, bacteriological and toxicological examinations in the Chief Medical Examiner's Office.

Because they are prepared in the normal course of business, laboratory reports may be admitted as business records, a recognized exception to the hearsay rule but in this instance, are usually accompanied by the testimony of the analyst. In some jurisdictions, while the report is admissible by statute without the necessity for testimony of the analyst, the defense is permitted, with advance notice, to call the analyst to testify to the conduct of the tests made and conclusions drawn.

In laboratories where the principal conduct of the tests is by technicians who do not testify, a serious threat to confrontational rights would result from a statute insulating laboratory technicians from defense subpoenas. Currently, most laboratory reports contain only findings and conclusions and do not describe the tests conducted. Because the probative value of the conclusions depends largely on the type of testing performed, they can range from highly significant to extremely low. Without the testimony of the examiner, the report can be misconstrued and given weight well beyond or well below that merited.

Studies demonstrate that the quality of laboratory testing, conclusions drawn and reports prepared are highly variable. Many laboratories do not participate in regular proficiency testing and many of those who do, fail to test in all areas of laboratory work. Such testing is the only mechanism available to verify the quality of the work performed and the scientific validity of the conclusions drawn. Reports prepared by laboratories without documented quality assurance programs including proficiency testing and internal review of reports should be viewed with suspicion.

§ 13.19 Evidence of Blood Analysis

1. EVIDENCE OF BLOOD, GENERALLY

Verdicts in many homicides and sexual assaults have been based in large part on testimony of experts that a stain was identified as blood and on the typing of that blood. Blood stained articles discovered at a crime scene are generally admissible in evidence if they aid in providing information about the crime to the jury. Although in some instances, bloodstained items have been admitted at trial without verification that the stain was blood or with only a statement that the stain appeared to

---

firmed as modified and remanded 101 N.J. 27, 499 A.2d 1363 (1985). No Federal statute specifically authorizes admission of a laboratory report in lieu of the chemist's testimony. An attempt to construe the Federal Rules of Evidence's hearsay rules to cover such admissibility was rejected in United States v. Oates, 560 F.2d 45 (2d Cir.1977), on remand United States v. Oates, 445 F.Supp. 351 (E.D.N.Y.1978); affirmed without opinion United States v. Oates, 591 F.2d 1332 (2d Cir.1978).

be blood as in Miller v. Pate,[1] this is fraught with danger and expert testing should be required to verify the composition of a stain. When an apparently bloodstained item is introduced, the defense should introduce expert testimony to show that it is not blood or is not the blood type of the victim or otherwise explain away the contrary evidence.

2. BLOOD GROUP EVIDENCE

Evidence of blood grouping test results is now generally accepted in the United States. There has been some reluctance to accept results of newer test procedures such as Multi–System grouping of polymorphic enzymes. Currently, absent a showing of improper test conduct, a wide range of grouping systems are acceptable and objections go primarily to the weight of the evidence and not to admissibility. The use of electrophoresis techniques was controversial until relatively recently but now even its principal protagonists have conceded its reliability.

Use of blood grouping tests for exclusion of an individual is generally not controversial unless it can be shown that factors such as contamination of the sample have made the testing unreliable.

Still at issue are the statistics upon which inclusion group size is calculated. Frequencies of blood type vary within racial and ethnic groups and to some degree, from one section of the country to another. As a result, objections are often raised to the estimated size of the group into which an individual with particular blood groups may fall. When probabilistic calculations are proffered, the court may decline to accept such testimony. When such testimony is adduced, the opposing party should introduce opposing testimony to alert the trier of fact that probabilistic calculations involve certain assumptions, any one of which, if inappropriate for the case at hand, would lead to inaccurate conclusions regarding inclusion of the defendant in the relevant group. When only a single system such as ABH is used, introduction of the testimony has limited probative value because even with a less common group such as type B, about 15% of the population will have this blood type. As a result, such testimony may be inadmissible in the absence of significant other evidence tending to include the defendant.

3. BLOOD SPATTER EVIDENCE

Evidence of interpretation of geometric patterns of spattered blood has had limited exposure in the courts but is receiving increasing attention. In addition to the work of the principal proponent of such evidence, see Sect 13.11 infra, others are now actively studying the information derivable from blood droplets and interpretation of the pattern of spatters at a crime scene. Regular courses in blood spatter pattern interpretation are now available in both the U.S. and Canada and the number of investigators familiar with the technique is increasing.

§ 13.19
1.   386 U.S. 1 (1967).

Testimony to the interpretation of blood spatter patterns may be offered by pathologists or medical personnel to show the angle or distance from which a shot was fired, the angle of impact of a blunt instrument or the position of the victim. Many of these individuals have little or no formal training in interpretation of spatter patterns and have conducted few, if any, experiments on the subject.[2] When such testimony is offered, it should be determined if the expert has adequate training and has conducted controlled experiments to support his/her conclusions. In the limited number of cases where blood spatter patterns were contested before the reviewing courts, they have been generally found to be based on accepted principles in geometry and physics and objection to their admission has been held to go only to the weight and not the admissibility of the evidence.[3]

4. OTHER EVIDENTIAL ISSUES

Blood evidence examinations frequently involve small amounts of material; stains on clothing, droplets on a weapon, smears on a wall or floor, etc. Significant opportunities exist for contamination of the sample with materials such as dirt, grease, various chemicals, etc. Exposure to contaminants can destroy blood or severely restrict the validity of conclusions drawn from its examination. Putrefaction of blood poses special problems in identification and characterization and may give rise to inconclusive results, even to identification of the sample as blood or determination if it is human or animal.

The amount of the sample available may limit the extent to which testing is performed; however, with current technology, even tiny spots can be subjected to considerable testing. If destructive testing is conducted, consumption of the entire sample leaves none available for testing by the opposing party and this issue should be raised. Even if unsuccessful as a challenge to the admissibility of the evidence,[4] the trier of fact will be made aware that the defense had no opportunity to independently assess the validity of the results of the prosecution's tests. With the small samples common with blood evidence, chain-of-custody becomes an important issue. Counsel should extensively scrutinize the

---

2. A pathologist who had conducted only one experiment on blood spatter patterns, and that on the morning of trial, was permitted to testify to the position of the victim when she was shot. State v. Satterfield, 3 Kan.App.2d 212, 592 P.2d 135 (1979). By contrast, a proffered defense witness with extensive crime scene and autopsy investigative experience and specific training in blood spatter pattern interpretation but who had not previously testified as an expert on the subject was not accepted as an expert by the trial court. On appeal, the trial court was found to have too rigorously applied the criteria for expert qualification. Refusal to accept the expert denied

the defendants an opportunity to present a complete defense and constituted reversible error. State v. Myers, 301 S.C. 251, 391 S.E.2d 551 (1990).

3. State v. Hall, 297 N.W.2d 80 (Iowa 1980); People v. Carter, 48 Cal.2d 737, 312 P.2d 665 (1957); Farris v. State, 670 P.2d 995 (Okl.Cr.1983); Pedersen v. State, 420 P.2d 327 (Alaska 1966); People v. Goldfaden, 52 A.D.2d 790, 383 N.Y.S.2d 37 (1976); State v. Willis, 109 N.C.App. 184, 426 S.E.2d 471 (1993).

4. Arizona v. Youngblood, 488 U.S. 51 (1988).

collection, preservation and handling of blood evidence to ensure that no possibility of contamination or sample misidentification exists.

§ 13.20   Other Biological Matter as Evidence

Evidence of seminal stains on the clothing or bedding of the victim of a homicide or sexual assault is generally admitted to show opportunity. Although similar stains on the clothing of a defendant have been admitted, stains on the underwear or trousers of a male suspect have little probative value. Studies in the U.K. have shown that such stains are not uncommon so, absent unusual circumstances, objection should be raised to admission of these items. The finding of seminal fluid or preferably, intact sperm cells, in samples from the victim's vagina is the most persuasive evidence of penetration in alleged rape cases. In some instances, a qualified medical doctor has been allowed to testify to the recency of intercourse and if it occurred more than once.[1] Such testimony must be considered dubious in view of the widely varying lengths of time which spermatozoa have been reported to persist in the vagina[2] and the variation in concentration of spermatozoa in the ejaculate. In another instance, medical testimony was presented in an alleged rape even though the examination of the prosecutrix was made five days after the incident.[3] It should be recognized that failure to detect intact spermatozoa or even seminal fluid in a vaginal sample does not preclude penetration. Sexual dysfunction by the rapist, use of a condom, or post-incident cleanup by the victim may make detection of seminal fluid impossible. A vasectomy can reduce spermatozoa levels to undetectable levels although presumptive detection of seminal fluid is still made.

Detection of fecal matter from the suspect's penis area was admitted in a prosecution for sodomy.[4] Similarly, smears from the defendant's penis showing the presence of epithelial cells found only in the rectum, mouth and vagina were properly admitted[5] as were scrapings of the defendant's penis showing menstrual blood of the victim's type.[6]

With secretors, determination of the blood type can also be made in semen. It can be argued that, as with blood, introduction of the ABH type alone may have limited probative value in demonstrating the involvement of the defendant in a sexual assault. If, however, the blood type of a defendant differs from that identified in a seminal sample, this evidence tends to exclude the defendant.[7]

§ 13.20

1. Rogers v. State, 124 Tex.Crim.R. 430, 63 S.W.2d 384 (App.1933).

2. Note 3, section 13.12, infra.

3. Gonzales v. State, 32 Tex.Crim.R. 611, 25 S.W. 781 (1894).

4. People v. Morgan, 146 Cal.App.2d 722, 304 P.2d 138 (1956).

5. Myhand v. State, 259 Ala. 415, 66 So.2d 544 (1953).

6. Brent v. White, 398 F.2d 503 (5th Cir.1968). Over a claim that the penis scraping which revealed menstrual blood of the victim's type violated Fourth Amendment rights, the court found this to be a permissible search of the person incident to a lawful arrest and that no intrusion of the body surface was involved. They also noted that there was threat of imminent destruction of the menstrual blood, i.e. exigency in collection of the sample.

7. In Grubbs v. Hannigan, 982 F.2d 1483 (10th Cir.1993), PGM typing of seminal stains in the panties of a child victim differed from that of the suspect. Only one

VI. TRIAL AIDS

§ 13.21 Locating and Engaging the Expert Witness

In criminal cases, chemists, toxicologists, serologists and related specialists are readily available to the prosecution as federal, state or local crime laboratory personnel. In addition, such specialists are also available in governmental agencies such as the coroner or medical examiner's office, government run medical facilities, public health service, etc. For the defense in a criminal case or the attorney in a civil action, unlike many other specialty areas of forensic science, expert assistance in these areas is widely available. Hospitals, clinics or private clinical laboratories are potential sources of assistance for either toxicological or serological examinations and private analytical laboratories can provide chemical analyses. These may also be able to provide expert testimony if required.

In requesting assistance from a private laboratory, the major obstacle is assessing their familiarity with, and proficiency in, testing the material of interest. For blood, urine and, to a lesser extent, other body fluids, certified clinical laboratories must meet standards set by a regulatory organization. These include use of proper analytical protocols and participation in regular proficiency testing programs. For non-routine or specialized testing, these laboratories may be less satisfactory. Where feasible, known as well as evidentiary samples should be submitted for testing or samples can be examined by more than one laboratory.

When an unusual test or chemical analysis is required, it is far more difficult to ensure that the laboratory is capable of providing authoritative results and conclusions. Private, for-profit laboratories, when asked if they can conduct a particular test generally similar to those they perform may respond in the affirmative. Unless they perform such analyses on a regular basis, however, they may lack sufficient familiarity with the material being examined and not be fully aware of limitations and potential problem areas. As a result, the reported results may be of limited validity.

Rather than randomly contact a laboratory and ask if they can conduct a particular test, it may be more productive to select laboratories specializing in the service desired. This information can be gleaned from perusal of advertisements in the journals and newsletters of national or regional societies. These advertisements will indicate the specialty areas of the laboratory and the types of analyses conducted. Many of the advertisements will also indicate the length of time the laboratory has been in business, not an infallible indicator of competence but a good suggestion of experience. Examples would include advertisements in *Chemical and Engineering News* or *Analytical Chemistry,* both published

test was conducted by the state serologist who testified at trial to the variance. Other evidence against the suspect, however, was compelling. On appeal, the conviction was upheld despite results from a retest affirming the state's initial results.

by the American Chemical Society or newsletters of regional chemical societies such as *The Capital Chemist,* published by the ACS affiliate The Chemical Society of Washington. After tentative selection of a candidate laboratory, its promotional materials should be requested. These are examined to determine if the organization indicates its capability to conduct the examination desired. If not, it is prudent to look further to ensure that an qualified laboratory is used.

Colleges and universities, particularly those offering a program in forensic science or a closely related specialty area are other sources of expert analysis and testimony. When court testimony may be required, it should be determined if the personnel conducting the analysis or providing technical assistance have experience in expert testimony. Although not essential, actual courtroom experience has obvious benefits. University chemistry or biochemistry departments or medical schools are also potential sources of expert assistance but here again, inquiry regarding specific experience in the examination of the material of interest and court testimony should be made.

Other potential sources of expert assistance include national or regional societies in forensic science or the particular scientific discipline required. The American Academy of Forensic Sciences has sections in Criminalistics and Toxicology with many recognized authorities in chemistry, toxicology and serology experienced in expert testimony and who perform private work. Regional forensic societies such as the Mid–Atlantic, Northwest, Southern or Midwest Associations of Forensic Science and the California Association of Criminalists may suggest sources of expert assistance.

Subject area societies such as the Society of Forensic Toxicologists (SOFT) can provide guidance to potential experts. Several private organizations also publish directories and/or advertisements of experts, frequently in very narrow specialty areas, offering their services for hire. Unfortunately, it may be difficult to determine the qualifications and experience of these "professional witnesses." Most are undoubtedly capable and well qualified but others are suspect. Requirements for inclusion in such listings are highly variable and no verification of qualifications may be required. When employing a private expert regardless of field and apparent reputation, the attorney should attempt to verify the expert's claimed credentials and problems with prior testimony. In a trial relying heavily on expert testimony, few events can be more devastating to the offering party than to have it revealed on the stand that the expert offered is either a charlatan or has been discredited in prior testimony in the same subject area.

In considering employment of a private expert, initial contacts should include discussion of the precise work and reports expected, fees for the work, expenses and court testimony, if required. Agreement on the method of payment and party responsible, the client or retaining attorney, should be reached prior to formal employment of an expert. In a civil case, in no instance should the expert be retained on a contingency basis. Contingency payment, if brought out at trial, raises questions of bias potentially compromising the expert and is generally considered a serious violation of ethics.[1]

VII. MISCELLANEOUS

§ 13.23 Bibliography of Additional References

1. GENERAL TOXICOLOGY AND CHEMISTRY

Briglia et al., "Attempted Murder with Pancuronium" 35 *J.Forensic Sci.* 1468–1476 (1990).

Cousins et al., "Microspectrophotometry as an Aid for the Identification of Rodenticides and Other Pesticide Preparations" *J.Forensic Sci. Soc.* 1987, 27(4) 247–252.

de Zeeuw, "Laboratory Guidelines for Analytical Toxicology: How to Approach Qualitative Analysis" 37 *J.Forensic Sci.* 1992, 37(6) 1437–1442.

Dulude and Karpova, "Simultaneous Determination of Arsenic and Antimony by Hydride Generation AAS" 1 *The Spectroscopist* 1992, 18–21.

Ember, "Need for Better Tests for Lead in Blood is Urgent" *Chemical and Engineering News* 1993, 71(43) 7.

Hidalgo, "Simultaneous Determination of Antimony, Arsenic, and Selenium in Water and Wastewaters by Hydride Generation Inductively Coupled Plasma Atomic Emission Spectrometry" 2 *The Spectroscopist* 19–22 (1993).

Levine, "Forensic Toxicology" 65 *Analytical Chemistry* 272A–276A (1993).

Moore and Tebbett, "Gas Chromatographic Applications in Forensic Toxicology" in: *Gas Chromatography in Forensic Science,* 1992 pp. 55–85.

Picotte et al., "Interpretation des Concentrations Sanguines Post–Mortem de Digoxine" 24 *Can.Soc.Forensic Sci.J.* 97–101 (1991).

Riley and Koves, "HPLC Identification and Quantitation of Warfarin in Postmortem Blood" 25 *Can.Soc.Forensic Sci.J.* 191–199 (1992).

Rule, McLaughlin and Henion, "A Quest for Oleandrin in Decayed Human Tissue" 65 *Analytical Chemistry* 857A–863A (1993).

Saferstein, *Criminalistics* (4th ed.) 1990.

§ 13.21

1. Feder, *Succeeding as an Expert Witness: Increasing Your Impact and Income* 1991.

Schrier and Manahan, "An Overview of Xenobiotic Analysis. The Determination of Cd, Hg, and Pb in Human Matrices by Atomic Absorption Spectroscopy" *Spectroscopy* 1994, 9(2) 24–29.

Stafford, "Forensic Gas Chromatography" in: *Gas Chromatography in Forensic Science* Tebbett—Ed. New York Ellis–Horwood 1992 pp. 1–26.

Steentoft and Worm, "Cases of Fatal Triazolam Poisoning" 33 *J.Forensic Sci.Soc.* 45–48 (1993).

2. BLOOD GROUPING AND BLOOD ANALYSIS

Anno., "Admissibility, in Criminal Cases, of Evidence of Electrophoresis of Dried Evidentiary Bloodstains" 66 A.L.R.4th 588 (1988).

Anno., "Admissibility, Weight and Sufficiency of Blood–Grouping Tests in Criminal Cases" 2 A.L.R.4th 500 (1980).

Baxter and White, "A Method for the Identification and Typing of the Subtypes of the Gc1 Allele from Dried Bloodstains" 24 *J.Forensic Sci.Soc.* 483–488 (1984).

Cecka, "Direct Blood Group Typing of Forensic Samples Using a Simple Monoclonal Antibody Assay" 34 *Forensic Science International* 205–216 (1987).

Gaensslen, Bell and Lee, "Distributions of Genetic Markers in United States Populations: I. Blood Group and Secretor Systems" 32 *J.Forensic Sci.* 1016–1058 (1987).

". . . . II. Isoenzyme Systems" ibid. 32(5) 1348–1381.

". . . . III. Serum Group Systems and Hemoglobin Variants" ibid. 32(6) 1754–1774.

Gaensslen et al., "Studies on ABH Antigen Grouping of Ammoniacal Extracts of Bloodstains by Absorption–Elution" *Forensic Science International* 1986, 31(3) 145–157.

Gaensslen et al., "Evaluation of Antisera for Bloodstain Grouping I. ABH, MN and Rh" *Journal of Forensic Sciences* 1985, 30(3) 632–654.

". . . . II. Ss, Kell, Duffy, Kidd and Gm/Km" ibid. 30(3) 655–676.

Grunbaum, "Potential and Limitations of Chemical Analysis of Physiological Evidence" in: *Analytical Methods in Forensic Chemistry,* Ho—Ed. Ellis Horwood New York 1990 pp. 417–431.

Horscroft and Westwood, "Group–Specific Component Content in Bloodstains. An Ageing and Distribution Study" *Journal of Forensic Science Society* 1986, 26(4) 275–280.

Koblinsky and Sheehan, "Human Blood Typing: A Forensic Science Approach Part I. Background" *Journal of Chemical Education* 1988, 65(6) 531–533.

". . . . Part II. Experiments" ibid. 65(7) 624–626.

Lee, "Identification and Grouping of Bloodstains" in: *Forensic Science Handbook,* Saferstein—Ed. Englewood Cliffs, NJ Prentice–Hall 1982 pp. 267–337.

Lee and Gaensslen, "Interpretation of Serological Test Results" *Crime Laboratory Digest* 1987, 14(3) 86–94.

Lenth, "On Identification by Probability" *Journal of the Forensic Science Society* 1986, 26(3) 197–213.

Monroe, "Enzyme Immunoassay" *Analytical Chemistry* 1984, 56(8) 920A–931A.

Pawlowski et al.; "Usefulness of Two Methods of Isoelectric Focusing for the Erythrocyte Acid Phosphatase Phenotypes Determination in Human Bloodstains" *Forensic Science International.* 1990, 41 51–54.

Rao and Kashyap, "A Simple Dipstick Immunoassay for Detection of A and B Antigens" *Journal of Immunoassay* 1992, 13(1) 15–30.

Samples, Shenouda and de Castro, "A Simplified Method for Typing Haemoglobin Using Ultrathin-layer Isoelectric Focusing" *Journal of the Forensic Science Society* 1993, 33(3) 165–167.

Sensabaugh, "Biochemical Markers of Individuality" in: *Forensic Science Handbook,* Saferstein—Ed. Prentice–Hall New York 1982 pp. 338–415.

Sharma and Chattopadhyay, "Blood Groups and Enzyme Types from Human Teeth" *Journal of the Forensic Science Society* 1993, 33(1) 39–44.

Walsh and Buckleton, "Calculating the Frequency of Occurrence of a Blood Type for a 'Random Man'" *Journal of the Forensic Science Society* 1991, 31(1) 49–58.

Whitehead, "A Historical Review of the Characterization of Blood and Secretion Stains in the Forensic Science Laboratory Part One: Bloodstains." *Forensic Science Review* 1993, 5(1) 35–51.

Winchester, "ABO, Phosphoglucomutase and Erythrocyte Acid Phosphatase of Blood Samples Containing Added Fluoride" *Journal of the Forensic Science Society* 1993, 33(3) 159–164.

3. OTHER BIOLOGICAL SUBSTANCES

Anno. "Admissibility, in Prosecution for Sex–Related Offense, of Results of Tests on Semen or Seminal Fluids" 75 A.L.R.4th 897 (1990).

Baechtel, "The Identification and Individualization of Semen Stains" in: *Forensic Science Handbook* Volume II Saferstein—Ed. Englewood Cliffs, NJ Prentice–Hall 1988 pp. 347–392.

Bryson, Garlo and Piner, "Vaginal Swabs: Endogenous and Postcoital Components" *Journal of the Forensic Science Society* 1989, 29(3) 157–171.

Garlo, "Phosphoglucomutase and Esterase D Activity in Post-coital Vaginal Swabs" *Journal of the Forensic Science Society* 1985, 25(4) 301–311.

Harada et al. "Orosomucoid 1 Phenotyping from Human Urine by Isoelectric Focusing" *Journal of Forensic Sciences* 1990, 35(5) 1191–1195.

Keating, "The Laboratory's Approach to Sexual Assault Cases. Part 1: Sources of Information and Acts of Intercourse" *Journal of the Forensic Science Society* 1988, 28(1) 35–47; "Part 2: Demonstration of the Possible Offender" ibid. 28(2) 99–110.

Koblinsky and Harrington, "Detection and Use of Salivary Hemaglutins for Forensic Blood Grouping" *Journal of Forensic Sciences* 1988, 33(2) 396–403.

Marshali, "Sex Origin Determination of Body Fluid and Stain" *Forensic Science Review* 1993, 5(2) 130–138.

Mukoyama and Seta, "The Determination of Blood Groups in Tissue Samples" in: *Forensic Science Progress* 1 Maehly and Williams—Eds. Springer–Verlag New York 1986 pp. 37–90.

Roy, "Concentration of Urine Samples by Three Different Procedures: ABO Typing from Concentrated Urine Samples" *Journal of Forensic Sciences* 1990, 35(5) 1133–1137.

Saneshinge and Woodfield, "Detection of Isoagglutinins in Saliva Using Toluene" *Journal of the Forensic Science Society* 1984, 24(5) 489–493.

Uchimura *et al.*, "Purification of Blood–Group Substances in Human Hepatic Bile (HHB) and Immunological Characterization of Anti-HHB Serum" *Forensic Science International* 1993, 61 7–20.

Zhou et al., "The Rapid Determination of the ABO Group from Body Fluids (or Stains) by Dot Enzyme–Linked Immunosorbent Assay (Dot–ELISA) using Enzyme–Labeled Monoclonal Antibodies" *Journal of Forensic Sciences* 1990, 35(5) 1125–1132.

Chapter 14

DRUGS AND THEIR CONTROL

I. INTRODUCTION

II. DRUGS

III. STATUTORY CONTROL OF DRUGS

IV. EVIDENTIAL STATUS OF TEST RESULTS

V. SPECIAL DEFENSES

I.   INTRODUCTION

§ 14.01   Scope of the Chapter

Prosecutors are making increasing use of expert witnesses to bolster their prosecutions of drug offenses.   Toxicologists and chemists are the main reliance of prosecutors in this regard.   As yet, however, defense attorneys have not demonstrated a determined inclination to use the chemical sciences for exculpatory evidence.   This chapter contains facts that may spur the defense to action.

The forensic chemist-toxicologist must be a master not only of the test tube but also of the myriad mechanical apparatuses that comprise the analytical tools of modern laboratory investigation.   This section and, indeed, all of the other sections of Chapter 14, considers the chemist and the toxicologist as one.   We do this as a matter of practicality since the forensic chemist in criminal matters is frequently engaged primarily in detecting and quantifying poisons.   A later section of this chapter provides the attorney with a frame of reference for locating an expert chemist-toxicologist.

---

§ 14.02   Glossary of Drug Terminology

Ace: marijuana cigarettes.

Acid: LSD or other hallucinogenic drug.

Acid head: LSD user.

Angel dust: phencyclidine on parsley.

Bambita: desoxyn, amphetamine derivative.

Bennies: amphetamine sulphate (benzedrine).

Bernice: cocaine; also sometimes referred to as Bernies flake.

Bhang: Marijuana.

Big O: opium.

Black beauties: amphetamines.

Black stuff: opium.

Blue birds: Amobarital sodium (amytal); also called Blue devils.

Blue velvet: an antihistamine known as pyribenzamine.

Bobo bush: marijuana.

Bombida: amphetamine that can be injected.

Boomer: mixture of cocaine and heroin.

Boy: heroin.

Brick: compressed block of marijuana.

Browns: capsules of various colors containing long acting amphetamine sulfate.

Burned: cheated on drug transaction.

Burn transaction: selling substance as a drug when it really is something else.

Businessman's trip: dimethyltryptamine (DMT).

"C": cocaine.

California sunshine: LSD.

Candy: barbiturates.

Candy man: pusher.

Carmanis: marijuana.

Carrie: cocaine.

Cartwheels: round, white, double-scored tablets of amphetamine sulfate.

Cecil: cocaine.

Cholley: cocaine.

Co-pilots: amphetamines.

Coast to coasts: capsules, in many colors, of long acting amphetamine sulfate.

Coke: cocaine.

Cooker: bottle cap for heating heroin and water.

Corinne: cocaine.

Crack: smokable cocaine.

Crank: methamphetamine; also Crink, Cris, and Cristina.

Crystal: methamphetamine in smokable form.

Cube (The): LSD.

"D": LSD.

Dead on arrival: phencyclidine base.

Designer drugs: non-controlled substances produced privately from common chemicals.

Dexies: orange-colored, heart-shaped tablet of Dexedrine (dextroamphetamine).

Domes: LSD tablets.

Double trouble: Tuinal, amobarbital sodium and secobarbital sodium.

Dream: cocaine.

Dujie: heroin.

Dust: heroin; cocaine.

Dust of angels: phencyclidine base.

Dynamite: heroin and cocaine taken together.

Ecstacy: MDMA, a drug analogue of the family of amphetamines.

Emsel: morphine.

Eye openers: amphetamines.

Flake: cocaine.

Flats: LSD tablets.

Foolish powder: heroin.

Footballs: oval-shaped tablets of amphetamine sulfate.

Freeze: cocaine.

Fu: marijuana.

Gee head: paregoric user.

Girl: cocaine.

Glass: crystal methamphetamine; see Ice.

Gold dust: cocaine.

Goof balls: barbiturates.

Grape parfait: LSD.

Grass: marijuana.

Greenies: green and clear capsules of amphetamine sulfate.

Griefo: marijuana.

"H": heroin.

Hairy: heroin.

Happy dust: cocaine.

Hard stuff: morphine.

Harry: heroin.

Hawaiian Sunshine: LSD.

Hearts: pink-colored, heart-shaped tablet of dexedrine (dextroamphetamine).

Hemp: marijuana.

Hocus: morphine.

Hop: opium.

Horse: heroin.

Hot sticks: marijuana cigarettes.

Hype: one who injects with hypodermic needle.

Ice: methamphetamine in smokable form.

Indian bay: marijuana; also sometimes Indian hay.

Jive: marijuana; jive sticks are marijuana cigarettes.

Joy powder: cocaine.

Killer weed: phencyclidine on marijuana or parsley.

K9: Dilaudid, also called "D".

L.A. turnabouts: capsules in many colors containing long acting amphetamine sulfate.

Lady: cocaine.

Lid poppers: amphetamines.

Loco weed: marijuana; also, Love weed.

Ludes: qualudes (methaqualone).

"M": morphine.

Mary Jane: marijuana; also Mary Warner.

Mexican horse: brown heroin from Mexico.

Mezz: marijuana.

Mickey: chloral hydrate.

Micro dots: LSD.

Mini-bennies: small white double-scored tablets supposedly containing amphetamines.

Miss Emma: morphine.

Morph: morphine, also morphie, or morpho.

Muggles: marijuana.

Nimby (Nimbies): Nembutal (pentobarbital sodium).

Noise: heroin.

Nose candy: cocaine.

Orange wedges: LSD.

Owsley's acid: LSD.

P.G.: paregoric, also P.O.

PCPA: p-Chlorophenylalanine.

Peace pill: phencyclidine HCLI.

Peace tablet: LSD tablets.

Peaches: rose-colored, heart-shaped amphetamine sulfate, benzedrine.

Peanuts: barbiturates.

Pep pills: amphetamines.

Peter: chloral hydrate.

Pinks: secobarbital sodium, seconal.

Pin Yen: opium.

Pod: marijuana, also pot.

Purple barrels: LSD, also purple haze and purple ozoline.

Rainbows: amobarbital sodium and secobarbital sodium, Tuinal.

Reds and Blues: same as "Rainbows."

Red Birds: secobarbital sodium, seconal, also Red devils, or Reds.

Reefer: marijuana cigarette.

Roaches: butts of marijuana cigarettes.

Rock: cocaine in smokable form; crack.

Roses: rose-colored, heart-shaped amphetamine sulfate (Benzedrine).

Sativa: marijuana.

Scag: heroin.

Schmeck: heroin.

Skee: opium.

Sleeping pills: barbiturates.

Smack: heroin.

Smears: LSD.

Snow: cocaine.

Speed: methamphetamine; sometimes used for any stimulant.

Speedball: heroin and cocaine mixture; also some other mixtures.

Splash: amphetamine powder; also Splivins.

Squirrels: LSD.

Star Dust: cocaine.

Stepped on: substance that has been diluted or cut.

Stoppers: barbiturates.

Strawberry field: LSD.

Sweet Lucy: marijuana.

Tar: gum opium.

Texas tea: marijuana.

TNT: heroin.

Truck drivers: amphetamines.

Unkie: morphine.

Uppers: stimulants.

Viper's weed: marijuana.

Wedges: LSD tablets.

Weed: marijuana.

Wen-shee: gum opium.

White junk: heroin.

White lightning: LSD.

White merchandise: morphine; also white stuff.

Whites: amphetamine sulfate tablets; also white crosses.

Whiz bang: mixture of cocaine and morphine mostly.

XTC: same as ecstasy.

Yellow dimples: LSD.

Yellow jackets: pentobarbital sodium, Nembutal, also Yellows.

II. DRUGS

§ 14.03 Opiates

All drugs such as opium, morphine, codeine and heroin, that are derived from the opium poppy are termed opiates; in fact all opiates are of natural vegetable origin. Each of the opiates is highly addictive, creating both a psychological and physical dependence on the drug in the user. Each is also a depressant to the central nervous system.

All opiates are considered as narcotic drugs. Medically, the true narcotic drugs (opiates and their derivatives) are truly addictive. The dosage required to maintain euphoria must be gradually stepped up as a tolerance or comparative immunity is built up. Physical dependence on the drug as an escape from reality also develops. One danger involved in the use of opiates is the risk of impurities added to a substance in order to stretch out the substance and create more sales. A shipment of imported opiates generally reaches primary dealers in the United States in very pure form. Each dealer down the line "steps on" the batch (adds cutting agents) to increase the supply, and thus, increase the value of the shipment. Since the illicit market is entirely unregulated, users do not know what chemicals they may be ingesting along with the active ingredient.

A further danger for the opiate user occurs when a user, whose body is accustomed to a low purity percentage, obtains a batch which has a higher purity than he is accustomed to. If the user is not aware of the higher concentration of the opiate, he or she risks using a higher level of the opiate than the body can tolerate. This could cause an overdose fatality.

It is withdrawal, however, which inflicts the most serious bodily damage upon an addict. If use of a true narcotic drug is withdrawn, the addict becomes very sick. The confirmed narcotics addict becomes a danger to his fellowmen when he turns to crime, principally petty theft, forgery, burglary and prostitution, to raise money to supply an ever-increasing habit.

Contrary to the belief harbored by a large segment of the general public, the true narcotics (opiates) do not accelerate the sex drive. The reverse is true. They reduce the sex drive by inducing a somnolent (sleep-like) state. Sex crimes are less likely from a narcotics addict than a non-user.

Narcotic addiction is recognized as a disease which should be treated. There are two federal addiction research centers, one at the Baltimore City Hospital[1] and the other at Lexington, Kentucky.[2]

a. Opium is the coagulated juice derived from the oriental opium poppy, a plant which grows to some four feet in height with flowers approximately four inches wide. Raw opium is harvested by slitting the capsule of the flower and collecting the milky latex exudate. In the moist state this residue is dark brown; however, on exposure to air, it hardens and lightens in color when dried and ground to powdered form. Man's first discovery of the analgesic effects of opium is not recorded in history.

Turkey, China, India, and Mexico are major producers of opium. In these countries the raw product may be smoked, eaten or drunk with coffee. Mexican opium may be distinguished from opium of eastern origin by absorption spectrophotometry,[3] gas chromatography, or high pressure liquid chromatography.[4]

Opium per se no longer constitutes an addiction problem in the United States, although early abuse was facilitated by old-fashioned patent medicines which were liberally spiced with opium and large quantities of opium were imported by Chinese laborers in the 1860's. Westerners and particularly those involved in law enforcement and criminal law practice, are more familiar with the unlawful use of the alkaloid[5] derivatives of opium—morphine, codeine and heroin—which are produced by pharmaceutical treatment of raw opium.

b. Morphine, a natural alkaloid contained in opium with a molecular weight of 285.33, is the active ingredient of opium. Morphine was discovered about 1805, and with the development of the hypodermic syringe, became widely introduced in the Civil War period. Raw opium contains about 10 percent morphine. Morphine is legally used for prescribed medical purposes, but it is also illegally used by addicts. Medically, morphine is invaluable because of its pain relieving effect. Pain may be present, but the drug allays the hurt and the anxiety or

§ 14.03

1. Baltimore City Hospital, 4940 Eastern Ave., Baltimore, Md. 21224.

2. Lexington Addiction Research Center, P.O. Box 12390, Lexington, Ky. 40593.

3. Grlic, "A Simple and Rapid Method for Distinguishing Opium of Mexican Origin from Other Types of Opium," 52 *J.Crim.L., C. & P.S.* 229 (1961).

4. Stein, Laessig & Indriksons, "An Evaluation of Drug Testing Procedures Used by Forensic Laboratories and the Qualifications of Their Analysts," 433 in Imwinkelried, ed., *Scientific and Expert Evidence* (2d Ed.1981).

5. An alkaloid is an organic base of a chemical makeup which allows it to unite with acids to form salts; its basic molecular structural constituent is the pyridine ring of 5 carbon atoms and one nitrogen atom; basic nitrogen is present in synthetic or plant alkaloids.

anticipation of pain.   Physically, morphine is a white crystalline powder with a bitter taste.   As the drug takes effect, the subject becomes drowsy ("on the nod") and experiences a euphoric feeling.   Paregoric contains a small amount of morphine in an alcohol solution.

   c.   Codeine (methylmorphine), a natural alkaloid contained in opium with a molecular weight of 299.36, is prepared by methylation of morphine.   It is a mild analgesic and a common ingredient of many cough medicines such as elixir of terpinhydrate, which are legally available to consumers.   In large doses, codeine may be used as a substitute for morphine.   Physically, it is a crystalline powder of long, slender, white crystals.

   d.   Heroin (diacetylmorphine), a synthetic alkaloid of opium with a molecular weight of 369.40, is prepared by treating raw opium chemically with acetic anhydride.   In most cases heroin will be treated with hydrochloric acid to yield heroin hydrochloride.   This latter compound is soluble in water, a necessary quality for users who inject the substance into their vascular system.   Untreated, heroin is insoluble in water and cannot be hypodermically injected.

   Heroin was first produced in Germany in 1898.   It is at least three to four times more potent in effect than morphine, and it has the same addictive properties and action as morphine.   Physically, it is an odorless, brownish-white to white powder, with a bitter taste.   On the illicit market pure heroin is "cut" or diluted so that the user receives a sample ("paper" or "deck") containing only 3 to 5 percent heroin.   Various substances are used as diluting agents, of which milk sugar is the most common.   As common sense would suggest, the greater the degree of dilution, the less residual dependence effect.

   Apart from medical research, no legal use of heroin exists;   its manufacture, sale, distribution, and possession is presently strictly prohibited.

   e.   Synthetic narcotics such as Demerol (meperidine) and methadone (Dolophine) are made by chemical processes, but they have the same addictive potential as the opiates produced from plant opium.

§ 14.04   Marijuana

   Although marijuana is considered scientifically as an hallucinogen, it is discussed here because the criminal drug abuse laws of many states, and the federal government treat it as a Schedule I drug.[1]   Marijuana is an hallucinogenic plant substance comprising the flower tops, seeds, hulls, twigs, and leaves of the cannabis (hemp) plant.   Hashish is the purified extract of the marijuana plant, cannabis sativa.   Bhang refers to the dried flowering tops of uncultivated female cannabis sativa plants. Charas or Indian hemp refers to the pure resin of the plant.

§ 14.04

1.   21 U.S.C.A. § 812 (1994); West's Fla. Stat.Ann. § 893.03(1)(c)4 (1994).   It has been held that inclusion of marihuana in the statutory definition of narcotics together with physically addictive drugs is not unreasonable or arbitrary in the sense that if offends due process or equal protection: Reyna v. State, 434 S.W.2d 362 (Tex.Cr. App.1968).

The hemp plant (cannabis sativa) is a hardy weed growing to a height of five feet. It is sticky to the touch and has a distinctive odor. The main stalk varies from ½ to 2 inches in diameter. It has fluted leaf stalks and narrow, compound palmate leaves containing variable numbers of leaflets up to seven in number. The leaves are lance-shaped with serrated edges and they may be up to five inches long. (See Figure 1.) The upper surface of the pointed leaves is of a darker green than the lime-colored under leaf. The leaves are covered with one-celled, curved hair-like fibers. The flower is greenish-yellow in color.

Marijuana seeds are composed of a greenish-yellow hull which browns as it ripens and a core of brown or greenish-yellow moss that whitens as it ripens. The plant, especially the flowering tops of the female plant, contains a resinous substance (tetrahydrocannabinol) which creates mild hallucinogenic effects and acts as a depressant to the central nervous system.

Fig. 1. The characteristic leaf shape of a marijuana (Cannabis sativa) plant. *Courtesy: Chicago Police Department Criminalistics Division.*

There did exist a controversy in scientific circles as to the exact classification of genus of marijuana plants. Some botanists and taxonomists contend that the plant cannabis is polytypic and that there are three varieties of cannabis plants, namely *Cannabis sativa L., Cannabis indica L.,* and *Cannabis ruderalis.*[2] In states which defined and made it a crime to possess marijuana cannabis sativa L., it was argued that a conviction would be impossible unless the prosecution were able to prove that the marijuana was in fact cannabis sativa L., and not another variety of cannabis. This became known as the "species defense."

2. Hauber, "Summary of Distinguishing Features of the Three Proposed Species of Cannabis," 13 *Midwest Assoc.For.Scientists Newsletter* 33 (Oct. 1984) in which it is concluded that a lack of "reproductive isolation" proves marijuana is monotypic.

Other botanists and most crime laboratory drug chemists (who are not botanists or taxonomists) hold to the view that cannabis is monotypic and that the three varieties, if indeed such varieties exist, are all covered by the statute prohibiting the possession and sale of Cannabis. While the scientific controversy may not be said to be conclusively resolved, the "species defense" itself is as good as dead since a great number of courts have sided with the position that marijuana is monotypic [3] or have gone to the legislative history of the statutes to show that the legislature meant to ban the transfer of all forms of marijuana.[4] Most legislatures have foreclosed the issue by amending their statutes [5] so that possession of any form of cannabis is explicitly prohibited.[6]

Although marijuana is sometimes mixed with liquids, or eaten, it usually is smoked as a cigar, a cigarette ("joint," "stick" or "reefer"), or in a pipe. The smoke is taken in slow, deep inhalations. The smoker becomes mildly intoxicated and experiences a distortion of time and space. Vision and muscular control are temporarily impaired. Tolerance and physical dependence on the drug do not develop, although there is evidence of psychological dependence. Some authorities indicate that it is easier to give up marijuana smoking than to stop smoking tobacco. Thus, in the sense that there are mild withdrawal symptoms or physical changes resulting from discontinued use, marijuana is not considered medically addictive. Perhaps this is because the marijuana mixture in reefers is only one-tenth as strong as the hashish used in certain foreign countries. Also, marijuana, when smoked, is diluted with air. No comparable dilution is found when it is drunk or eaten. At any rate, the studies that have been done suggest that the effects of moderate doses of marijuana and alcohol are similar,[7] except that alcohol abuse can result in psychosis and frequently promotes aggressive behavior.

Marijuana is almost non-toxic. No human deaths have been attributed directly to the toxic effects of smoking or other method of using

---

3. A defense viewpoint is given by Shellow, "The Expert Witness in Narcotics Cases," *Crim.Defense,* Dec.1973, p. 4, who argues that cannabis is polytypic on the authority of Dr. Richard Schultes, Professor of Biology and Director and Curator of Economic Botany at Harvard University, and Dr. William Klein of the Missouri Botanical Gardens. Listing some of the prosecution arguments is a Letter to the Editor in 21 *J.For.Sci.* 453 (1976). See also articles cited at note 9, infra.

4. See, Schwartz v. State, 177 Ind.App. 258, 379 N.E.2d 480 (1978).

5. Winters v. State, 646 P.2d 867 (Alaska App.1982).

6. In Craig v. United States, 490 A.2d 1173 (D.C.App.1985), it was held that the new statutory definition of marijuana in the District of Columbia encompasses all species of marijuana, obviating the need to prove the existence of THC.

7. See, Blum, et al., "Mind Altering Drugs and Dangerous Behavior: Dangerous Drugs," in President's Commission on Law Enforcement and Administration of Justice, Task Force Report: Narcotics and Drug Abuse 22 (1967), indicating that marijuana is not overly dangerous.

In a report presented to Congress and President Nixon on March 22, 1972, the National Commission on Marijuana and Drug Abuse recommended that all criminal penalties for private use and possession of marijuana be dropped. The conclusion was based on its findings that marijuana is not addictive, is not shown to be physically harmful, and does not appear to lead to the use of hard drugs or to crime.

marijuana.[8] That marijuana use can impair the motor and cognitive skills necessary for safe driving has been recognized but the exact nature and degree of the decrements in performance are as yet unknown.[9]

The subjective effects are dependent on variable factors such as the dosage, the means of administration, the personality of the user, and the circumstances in which it is used.

An average marijuana cigarette contains between .5 and 1% delta 9–tetrahydrocannabinol. THC doses in this range have shown to produce effects on mood, memory, motor coordination, cognitive ability, time and self-perception. A euphoric effect, followed by a feeling of relaxation and lethargy are commonly exhibited by individuals using marijuana. Behavior is impulsive but infrequently aggressive.[10]

Marijuana has an approved medical use as a treatment for the severe nausea and vomiting that often accompany cancer chemotherapy as well as for the pain caused by disabling spasticity associated with being a quadriplegic,[11] as well as to relieve the intra-ocular pressure that glaucoma sufferers experience.

The defense of medical necessity has been raised in marijuana possession prosecutions.[12] The basic premise of the necessity defense is that a person who is compelled to commit an illegal act in order to prevent a greater harm should not be punished for that act.[13] Persons arguing for acquittal under this defense claim that the marijuana in their possession was being used for medicinal purposes. In State v. Hastings,[14] several marijuana plants were found in the defendant's home. Hastings, the defendant, claimed that the marijuana was used to control pain and muscle spasms caused by her rheumatoid arthritis. The trial court refused to instruct the jury on medical necessity. The Idaho Supreme Court upheld the trial court ruling, but remanded to allow Hastings to present evidence of the common law defense of necessity. Other states have at first recognized the necessity defense, but later rejected it,[15] and most states reject it out right.[16]

---

8. The Interim Report of the Canadian Government's Le Dain Commission 76 (1976).

9. U.S. Department of Transportation, "Marijuana, Other Drugs, and Their Relationship to Highway Safety: A Report to Congress," (Washington, D.C.1979).

10. Mason and McBay, "Cannabis: Pharmacology and Interpretation of Effects," 30 *J.For.Sci.* 615, 624 (1985); Winek, "Forensic Toxicology," in Wecht, ed. 2 *Forensic Sciences* 31–5 (1981); Goodman & Gilman, *The Pharmacological Basics of Therapeutics,* 3d. ed., 1965; Murphy, "The Cannabis Habit: A Review of Recent Psychiatric Literature," 16 U.N.Bull. on Narcotics No. 1 at 19 (1963); McBay, "Marihuana: Current Assessment," 22 *J.For.Sci.* 493 (1977).

11. A THC pill, marinol, was approved in 1985 by the F.D.A. as having an accepted medical use.

12. See generally, Anno., Defense of Necessity, Duress, or Coercion in Prosecution for Violation of State Narcotics Laws, 1 A.L.R.5th 938 (1993).

13. See generally, 1 A.L.R.5th 1207 (1993).

14. 118 Idaho 854, 801 P.2d 563 (1990).

15. See, e.g., State v. Tate, 194 N.J.Super. 622, 477 A.2d 462 (1984), necessity defense statutory in this state, thus reversed and remanded 102 N.J. 64, 505 A.2d 941 (1986).

16. See, e.g., State v. Hanson, 468 N.W.2d 77 (Minn.App.1991).

No federal court has yet recognized the medical necessity defense to a drug prosecution.[17] For example, in United States v. Belknap,[18] fifty-four marijuana plants were found growing in the defendant's house. The defendant claimed that he used marijuana to relieve pain and to help overcome a previous drug and alcohol addition. The district court refused to instruct the jury on medical necessity. This ruling was upheld by the Federal court of appeals.

§ 14.05 Cocaine

Cocaine, the principal alkaloid found in coca leaves with a molecular weight of 303.35, is a powerful stimulant which has the effect of releasing the normal inhibitions of the user. The coca plant is a shrub native to South America. The native peoples of Bolivia and Peru chew the leaves of the coca plant to relieve hunger pangs and fatigue. Cocaine is a white, crystalline powder. Tolerance does not develop; rather, the drug's effects are magnified with increased use. Ingestion is by absorption through the nasal mucous membrane as a result of sniffing the powder or by injection directly into the vascular system. The effect produced by cocaine use is fleeting. Dosage must be repeated to recapture it. Users sometimes mix the drug with heroin to form a "bam." The depressant effect of heroin acts to stabilize the exhilarant effect of the cocaine. Abuse may result in toxic effects such as hallucinations, delusions and, in the case of "sniffers," deterioration of the nasal septum.

Cocaine may be smoked, rather than "snorted," but only after its melting point has been reduced by the freebasing of cocaine hydrochloride. Freebasing releases the hydrochloride either through the highly dangerous use of flammable substances like ether or alcohol or through a less risky process using baking soda. The byproduct has come to be known as "crack." Unlike street cocaine, (cocaine hydrochloride) crack is not water-soluble. Consequently, it cannot be snorted or injected but is always smoked in order to obtain the quickest and most intense reaction.

§ 14.06 Barbiturates

Barbiturates are classified as hypnotic anesthetic or sedative drugs. There are manifold types of barbiturates, and some are synthetic. Some of the commonly encountered capsules are nembutal (sodium pentobarbital—"yellow jackets"), seconal (sodium secobarbital—"red birds"), Tuinal (a 50/50 mixture of sodium secobarbital and sodium amobarbital—"Christmas trees") and amytal (sodium amobarbital—"blue birds"). They depress the higher cerebral nerve centers, removing control over learned behavior and inhibitions governing instinctive behavior.

Barbiturate intoxication is markedly similar in effect to alcohol intoxication. Symptoms which are displayed by the person intoxicated

---

17. See, e.g., United States v. Burton, 894 F.2d 188, 191 (6th Cir.1990), cert. denied 498 U.S. 857 (1990).

18. 985 F.2d 554 (4th Cir.1993).

on such drugs are a staggering gait, slurred speech, lack of coordination, confusion, disorientation, delusions, aggressive behavior, and physical incapacity.

Barbiturates are often medically prescribed for sedation or as nerve tranquilizers. Taken in prescribed therapeutic doses, barbiturates do not appear to produce physical dependence or toxic results. Significant physical dependence is reported when the daily misuse of the drug is in excess of five therapeutic doses per day. In such cases abstinence may result in withdrawal symptoms such as delirium tremens, convulsions, and vomiting.

§ 14.07   Amphetamines

Amphetamines are central nervous system stimulants which act to increase physical activity and euphoric spirit and to heighten wakefulness. They have proved medically effective as a stimulant in the treatment of narcolepsy and in improving the performance of children whose learning has been impaired by an inability to concentrate. Well-known amphetamines are benzedrine (amphetamine sulphate), dexedrine (dextroamphetamine sulphate) and methedrine (methamphetamine hydrochloride). Dexedrine is twice as powerful as benzedrine, and methedrine is far more powerful than dexedrine. Amphetamines may be in spansule form. A spansule contains delayed action capsules of the particular amphetamine to prolong the effect. Amphetamines are contained in the so-called "diet pill" used by obese people to lose weight and in pills taken by truck drivers to increase work capacity and as "pep pills" to keep students wakeful during their studies. They are contained as part of the survival packs of military special forces to increase alertness.

Large doses and prolonged use of amphetamines can result in depression and fatigue, as in the case of cocaine use. The ease of obtaining chemical precursors for amphetamines has seen the emergence of clandestine speed laboratories, some even as primitive as "bath-tub" laboratories.

§ 14.08   Hallucinogens

Hallucinogenic drugs include marijuana, mescaline, LSD, and PCP. Mescaline is a natural alkaloid which induces visual hallucinatory effects, particularly emphasizing vividness of color. It is the active ingredient of the peyote cactus. Continued dosage of mescaline can build up a physical tolerance, but there is no evidence of physical dependence or withdrawal symptoms resulting from abstinence. On the illicit market, LSD is sold as a mescaline which can be dissolved in water or placed in gelatin capsules. Often the capsule is swallowed. Some users dissolve it in hot orange juice or cocoa. It takes a dose of approximately 500 milligrams (7.5 grains) of mescaline to induce full clinical effects in an average 150 pound person.

Peyote is the term used to describe the green mescal button of the peyote cactus found in the southwestern United States. It contains mescaline in its raw form. The mushroom-like button of this small cup-shaped spineless plant is baked, chopped up and ingested as a solid or in a brew. Because of its gritty bitter taste, peyote is normally taken in combination with a liquid chaser.

Peyote is best known in connection with religious rites of certain Indians of northern New Mexico. It is found in arid regions of Texas and Mexico and has been used sacramentally since the days of the Aztecs. Peyote rites existed among the Mescalero Apaches, the Comanches and the Kiowas, who attributed religious significance to its results. The services of the Native American Church, which numbers a quarter of a million members, still include peyote ingestion.[1]

A number of hallucinogens can be synthetically produced. LSD, mescaline, psilocybin and phencyclidine (PCP) are of this type.

LSD (lysergic acid diethylamide), with a molecular weight of 323.42, causes visual and auditory hallucinations, mental aberrations and impaired judgment even at very low dosage levels.[2] It is a very potent synthetic chemical, some 400 times more hallucinogenically powerful than mescaline. It is taken orally on a sugar cube or as a small white pill. Twenty five micrograms of LSD is sufficient to induce full clinical effects in an average 150 pound person.

Although it has been used in psychotherapy, research indicates LSD may promote chromosomal damage to the blood cells of the user as well as transmutation of chromosomes in the body cells of offspring. LSD tolerance occurs rapidly but symptoms of withdrawal have not been reported. The effects of LSD use are relatively long lasting, up to seven hours or more. LSD may precipitate a psychotic reaction among those who are bordering on psychoses.

Phencyclidine (PCP) was at first commercially manufactured as an anesthetic, used to tranquilize animals in veterinary practice, and was marketed under the trade name Sernyl. PCP has no known legitimate use in humans because of the severe hallucinogenic reactions it produces resulting in mental and muscular disorientation and even death.[3] PCP has been customarily synthesized in clandestine drug laboratories. It is

---

§ 14.08

1. In People v. Woody, 61 Cal.2d 716, 40 Cal.Rptr. 69, 394 P.2d 813 (1964), the California Supreme Court held that the state statute prohibiting possession of peyote was unconstitutional as applied to bona fide religious ceremonies of the Native American Church. But see, State v. Bullard, 267 N.C. 599, 148 S.E.2d 565 (1966), cert. denied 386 U.S. 917 (1967).

In Employment Div., Department of Human Resources v. Smith, 494 U.S. 872 (1990), the Supreme Court declared that the First Amendment does not protect the members of the Native American Church when they use peyote in their religious ceremonies. Congress has restored the right which the Supreme Court abrogated temporarily. See, Religious Freedom Restoration Act, 42 U.S.C.A. 2000bb (1993).

2. Fink, "Prolonged Adverse Reactions to LSD," 15 *Arch. Gen. Psychiat.* 450 (1966); Brecher, *Licit and Illicit Drugs* 337 (1972).

3. Nakamura and Noguchi, "PCP: A Drug of Violence and Death," 7 *J.Pol.Sci. & Admin.* 459 (1980).

often ingested with marijuana or parsley. When so administered, PCP is known as "killer weed" or "wobble weed." PCP can be sold to the unknowing under the misrepresentation that it is LSD or mescaline or even unadulterated marijuana.

PCP is controlled under Federal Schedule II as are its salts, isomers and salts of its isomers. Two of the precursors of PCP are also controlled by statute since the clandestine manufacture of PCP would be an easy matter if these chemicals were legitimately available over the counter.

§ 14.09   Anabolic Steroids

Public awareness of anabolic steroids has increased in the past several years through revelations of its use by prominent athletes, such as Canadian sprinter Ben Johnson and N.F.L. linebacker Lyle Alzado. However, the fact is that athletes have been using steroids for years to better their performance.[1] Professional athletes participating in sports in which steroid use is common may see its use as necessary for their performance.[2] Steroid use is especially common in weightlifting, bodybuilding, football and track and field events.[3]

Anabolic steroids are merely the most publicized form of steroids. Another type of steroids, the cortico steroids, are used for many legitimate medical purposes, generally to relieve inflammation in tissues caused by arthritis or injuries. Unlike cortico steroids, anabolic steroids are used to promote muscle growth, resulting in their proliferation among athletes. Anabolic steroids are many and varied, one estimate finding "eighty anabolic/androgenic steroids marketed worldwide."[4]

Anabolic steroids are synthetic analogues of testosterone, the male sex hormone (thus described as androgenic). Since one of their characteristics is the stimulation and synthesis of cellular proteins which help in the growth and repair of bodily tissues, athletes use anabolic steroids to increase muscle mass and strength as well as for increased workout stamina. Some athletes also believe that steroids increase aggressiveness, which some believe enhances training and performance.[5]

In the past, experts did not recognize steroids as providing the benefits athletes claimed steroids gave them. In 1977, the American College of Sports Medicine published its official position on anabolic steroid use in sports. The conclusion reached was that medically-approved steroid dosages do not often cause significant improvements in

§ 14.09

1. Boje, "Doping," *Bull. of the Org. League Nations* 439 (1939).

2. See, Johnson, "Special Reports: Steroids, A Problem of Huge Dimensions," *Sports Illustrated,* May 13, 1985, at 38–61.

3. See, e.g., Lamb, *Anabolic Steroids in Ergogenic Aids in Sport* 32 (M. Williams ed. 1983).

4. Colman et al., "Anabolic Steroids—Analysis of Dosage Forms from Selected Case Studies from the L.A. County Sheriff's Scientific Services Bureau," 36 *J. For. Sci.* 1079 (1991).

5. Thurston, "Chemical Warfare: Battling Steroids in Athletics," 1 *Marq. Sports L.J.* 93, 99 (1990).

strength, aerobic endurance, lean body mass, or body weight.[6] This discrepancy between athlete self-reports and scientific evidence could be attributable to the fact that athletes typically exceed medically recommended dosages. Recently, however, several studies have shown that steroid use, in combination with heavy weight training and a specific diet, will in fact cause substantial increases in the size and strength of muscle mass.[7]

Testing for steroids in urine relies upon a determination of the ratio of testosterone to epitestosterone. The ratio in healthy young men is said to be less than 1:2. A higher ratio indicates steroid usage.[8] Blood testing for testosterone levels is said to be unreliable due to poor characterization.[9]

Athletes have gone to great lengths to beat steroid urine testing. One method was to inject a combination of testosterone and epitestosterone so that the ratio of acceptable limits will not be altered significantly. Another method is based on the knowledge that steroids, when taken orally, can be detected for weeks. As a result, athletes have relied upon injectable testosterone.

§ 14.10 Drug Analogues—"Designer Drugs"

Designer drugs are substances which mimic the effects of already federally controlled substances, but whose molecular composition has been altered. The development of substances within this category began as an effort to market substances with the same or similar effects as the mimicked drug without the potential of criminal prosecution, since the newly designed drugs were not controlled substances within the federal schedule. Substances considered designer drugs include MDMA (Ecstasy, XTC), crack (freebased cocaine), designer narcotics made to simulate the effects of opiates (alpha-methyl fentanyl, 3–methyl fentanyl and meperidine, among others), as well as PCP (angel dust), and crystal methamphetamine (ice). Nexus, a psychoactive substance which can cause fearsome hallucinations, is the latest designer drug. Under its chemical name of 4–bromo–2,5–dimethoxyphenethylamine, it has been temporarily placed in Schedule I by the Drug Enforcement Administration as an emergency measure for the public welfare.

MDMA/Ecstasy—3,4 methylenedioxymethylamphetamine (also XTC, ADAM, MDM)

MDMA was originally developed for use as an appetite suppressant, but it was never manufactured for that purpose because of unpleasant

---

6. American College of Sports Medicine Position Statement on the Use and Abuse of Anabolic–Androgenic Steroids in Sports, 9 *Med. & Sci. Sports & Exercise* xi (1977).

7. See, e.g., Pope & Katz, "Affective and Psychotic Symptoms Associated with Anabolic Steroid Use," 145 *Am. J. Psychiatry* 488 (1988); Hapty & Rovere, "Anabolic Steroids: A Review of the Literature," 12 *Am. J. Sports Med.* 474 (1984); Plymate & Freidl, Anabolic Steroids and Muscle Strength, 116 *Ann. Intern. Med.* (3) 270 (1992).

8. Karch, *The Pathology of Drug Abuse* 359 (1993).

9. Id. at 369.

side effects.[1] Users claim that its benefits are therapeutic, however, despite the long list of potential side effects.[2] Prior to federal scheduling of MDMA as an illicit substance, a prestigious group of researchers, psychologists, psychiatrists, and lawyers demanded that MDMA be included as a Schedule III drug, as opposed to the more restrictive Schedule I. The debate continues over whether the DEA prematurely scheduled a drug that was said to have great therapeutic value, but whose potential could only be discovered through continued research.[3]

Adverse effects from what has become a widespread use of MDMA are reported to be rare.[4] The fatalities that have been described occurred in England where use of MDMA was followed by frenzied dancing in over-heated clubs.[5]

Crack

Crack, a free base (alkaline) form of cocaine, was first noticed in the middle 1980s.[6] It became popular because the high from cocaine use would reach peak levels much sooner through inhalation than through the snorting of cocaine. The freebasing of cocaine was necessary to reduce the melting point of cocaine (195°C) to a level where it could be smoked without scorching the air passages. Freebase cocaine has a melting point of 98°C. The chemical formula for freebase is $C(17)H(21)NO(4)$, whereas cocaine is $C(17)H(22)CLNO(4)$.

Crack cocaine results from freebasing cocaine using a less dangerous process (baking soda) rather than the traditional freebasing process (which uses highly volatile chemicals). Crack cocaine is made by mixing cocaine hydrochloride with an equal weight of water in which bicarbonate has been dissolved. The precipitate that remains in pellet form is the crack cocaine. Although many users believe that this crystalline form of cocaine is purer than the powdered version, many synthetic and naturally occurring substances used to cut the cocaine are based through along with the cocaine.[7]

§ 14.10

1. Unpleasant side effects include muscle tightness, involuntary teeth-clenching and biting inside of cheek, nausea/vomiting, dehydration, muscle aches and pains which may persist for six weeks, restlessness, tremors. Karch, *The Pathology of Drug Abuse* 88 (1992).

2. Users and manufacturers of MDMA list the potential benefits of MDMA use as enhanced alertness and mental clarity; more positive mood, feelings, and attitudes toward self and others; increased ability to effectively work on problems and conflicts in lives and relationships; increased emotional warmth, love and empathy. Id. at 88.

3. Grobetal, The MDMA–Neurotoxicity Controversy Implications for Clinical Research with Novel Psychoactive Drugs, 180 *J.Nerv.Ment.Dis.* 355 (1992).

4. Karch, *The Pathology of Drug Abuse* 212 (1992).

5. Henry, Toxicity and Deaths from 3, 4 Methylenedioxymethamphetamine (Ecstasy), 340 *Lancet* 384 (1992).

6. Washton, Gold, and Pohash, 'Crack': Early Report in a New Drug Epidemic, *Postgrad. Med.* 52 (1989).

7. The purity myth was most likely developed in popular culture because of the faster and more intense rush achieved by smoking crack as opposed to snorting cocaine. The reason for the increased intensity is that freebased cocaine is smoked and therefore will cross the blood-brain barrier.

The greyish rock which is the product of the freebasing is usually smoked in a glass pipe. The "rock" is placed in the bowl of the pipe and heated with a torch. Crack was given its name because the rock gives off a crackling sound when heated thoroughly. The high is experienced within seconds after smoking, and lasts for five to ten minutes. The euphoria it brings is promptly followed by an equally intense comedown and craving to duplicate the high.[8]

Dopamine, one of the neurotransmittors in the brain, is thought to be responsible for euphoria and pleasure. Cells in the brain discharge dopamine into nerve synapses. The dopamine then attaches to receptors and a signal to stop transmission is conveyed. The dopamine is then immediately reabsorbed for future use. Smoking freebased cocaine (as well as snorting or shooting) blocks the reabsorption of the dopamine. This causes prolonged activity in the synapses, manifesting itself in a feeling of exhilaration, mental superiority, confidence, power, and excitement. When crack is smoked frequently or during a "binge," the available dopamine supply is depleted. As the acute effects wear off, the user craves more. This craving has been directly linked to the shortage of dopamine.[9] When a person smokes crack often, the body's natural supply of dopamine is depleted. The dopamine is metabolized and excreted before the body can reabsorb it and replenish its limited supply. The user's ability to experience pleasure is altered.[10] This is because the body's natural chemical mechanism for making the person feel good has been damaged. While some researchers believe that chronic use of crack may cause a permanent depletion of dopamine and other neurotransmittors, it is apparent that continued research must be conducted in order to ascertain whether or not the body can naturally regenerate neurotransmittors such as dopamine. Giving the user supplementary vitamins that would supply the basic precursors needed by the body to synthesize new neurotransmittors has been discussed but not yet researched.[11] Other adverse effects of crack on the body include various pulmonary pathologies.[12]

Both freebase cocaine (crack) and cocaine hydrochloride are absorbed by the skin. The amount absorbed is usually insufficient to produce the symptoms of cocaine use but it can cause positive urine tests for the presence of cocaine. Freebase cocaine is more lipophilic than cocaine hydrochloride and is thus more readily absorbed through the skin.[13]

---

8. This effect is observed equally in individuals with nonaddictive histories and personalities as with individuals having a propensity toward chemical dependence.

9. It has been noted that when the artificial promoter of dopamine activity is prescribed (such as bromocriptine), the user's craving temporarily subsides because such drugs bind to the same sites in the brain that cocaine binds to and block its action. Kirsch, supra, note 1, at pp. 63–65.

10. For example, users have reported that ordinary pleasures like music, a breath of fresh air, an afternoon nap, and the touch of a friend seem strangely devoid of joy for them. Id. at p. 67.

11. Kirsch, supra, note 1 at p. 68.

12. Id. at pp. 61–62.

13. Baselt, Chang & Yoshikawa, "On the Dermal Absorption of Cocaine," 14(6) *J. Anal. Toxicol.* 383 (1990).

Cocaine rapidly metabolizes in the body. Its half-life in humans is about 40 minutes. The principal breakdown products of cocaine are benzoylecgonine (BEG) and ecgonine methyl ester (EME). A toxic byproduct, cocaethylene, will be produced when alcohol is taken with cocaine.[14] Its toxic effects upon the organs (heart, lungs, kidneys) are firmly documented.[15]

Crystal Methamphetamine (Ice)

Ice, or Glass, made its appearance on the illicit market in the mid–1980s. It is a concentrated form of methamphetamine resulting when a solvent is used as a crystallizing agent. Law enforcement chemists believe it is freebased smokable crystal methamphetamine. Those operating in the black market, as well as doctors who see the effects on users, say it is merely a new way of making crystal methamphetamine and warn it is very toxic because of the cutting agents which contaminate it, such as belladonna.[16]

Methamphetamine produces a feeling of euphoria, suppresses appetite, and reduces the need for sleep. The effects on the central nervous system and cardiovascular system are very similar to cocaine. When it is used, it provides a sense of well-being and mental clarity.[17]

Opiate Look–Alikes: Fentanyl

Fentanyl was first introduced in the early 1960s as an intravenous analgesic-anesthetic under the trade name Sublimaze. It is, like most of the other opiate look-alikes, many times more potent than morphine. By rearranging, adding, or taking off groups of atoms from the morphine molecule, underground chemists created a new drug that was initially legal, that provided the same type of rush as heroin, and would not have the hazards of withdrawals.

Alpha-methyl fentanyl (200 times more potent than morphine) was the first of ten fentanyl designer opiates to appear on the black market. Later, 3–methyl fentanyl appeared (approximately 6000 times more potent than morphine),[18] and several other molecularly similar analogs. The look-alikes are often sold to the unsuspecting buyer as the "real" thing—heroin.

Fentanyl is marketed as "China White," "Mexican Brown," and "Persian White," among other names. White fentanyls are sold as Persian White, light tan as China White or synthetic heroin and fentanyl. Light brown is sold as Mexican Brown by carmelizing the lactose in the substance or using dye.

Although some of the synthetics have been on the market since the late 1960s, the use of synthetics was not nearly as widespread as it is

14. Karsh, supra, note 4 at 33.

15. Id. at 68–95.

16. Ice cut with belladonna can produce excessively rapid heartbeat and breathing, dizziness, fever, hallucinations, agitation, flushed face, and possible convulsions. Kirsch, supra note 1, at 168.

17. Id., at 166.

18. Id. at 3.

now. The marked increase in the number of deaths due to "overdoses" of opiate look-alikes [19] indicates a rise in sales and usage of the synthetics. The demand for heroin created a unique marketing opportunity for individuals with some knowledge of chemistry. Black market chemists and sellers seized the opportunity and began selling designer opiates as heroin to addicts, with the bonus of the (initially) legal status of their products.

The fentanyls are generally introduced into the body intravenously. But they can be snorted as well. Since the fentanyls are lipophilic, it can be readily absorbed through the skin. Patches for this purpose obtained from U.S. hospitals have been diverted for street use.

The fentanyls act primarily on the central nervous system and the gastro-intestinal tract, like opiates. They produce analgesia (relief from pain), euphoria, and drowsiness. They can also produce respiratory depression, constipation, and muscle rigidity. Many deaths have been attributed to the use of these designer opiates. However, the exact cause of death in fentanyl-related overdoses has not been agreed upon. Some experts believe it is the potency of the drug. Three indicators that this may be true are (1) the physical symptoms of the deaths (especially the massive pulmonary edema) and the sudden manner in which the user dies (the needle is found still in place at the injection site), (2) several times deaths occurred in groups in the same areas at the same time, which indicates that users (both novices and addicts who can tolerate extremely high doses) have taken the same batch of opiate look-alike, (3) the size or quantity of the dose—since doses are in microgram amounts, an extra grain or two can triple potency.[20] This can have disastrous results for a buyer who thinks he or she has purchased real heroin and measures an amount in accordance with that belief. The synthetics are so much more potent than the real thing that it generally takes a much smaller amount of synthetic heroin to give the same effects of even the purest real opiate. An injection of a synthetic substance in a dosage amount appropriate only for real heroin seems to pose a worse health risk than heroin itself.

Urine testing for the metabolites of fentanyl can be done within 72 hours of its administration.[21]

§ 14.11 Qualitative Analysis of Drug Samples in General

The chemist-toxicologist frequently deals with substances whose identity is unknown and which may be present in a questioned sample in quantities bordering on the threshold of analytical recognition. In most instances the chemical tests are made directly on a suspect sample which is thought to be contraband. On occasion, drug identification may be

19. Henderson,   "Fentanyl–Related Deaths: Demographics, Circumstances, and Toxicology of 112 Cases," 36 *J.For.Sci.* 422 (1991).

20. Id. at p. 34. A single dose of 3–methyl–fentanyl contains five to ten micrograms (equivalent to about one-quarter to one-half of one grain of salt).

21. *Fentanyl Analogues, Information Manual on Designer Drugs*, World Health Org., 1990.

conducted in conjunction with a suspicious death or a traffic violation. In D.U.I.D. cases, chemical tests allow for the detection of opiates and barbiturates in the driver's blood or urine.

Seven general classes of qualitative tests are used in determining the identity of a suspect drug sample (see § 13.04):

(1) Physical tests

(2) Crystalline precipitate tests

(3) Chemical color change tests

(4) Spectrophotometric analyses

(5) Chromatographic tests

(6) Biological tests (such as the identification of morphine by observing the peculiar S-shaped curve appearing in the tail of the laboratory mouse injected with the substance).

§ 14.12 Analysis of Opiates

Some of the crystalline and reagent color test results for the principal alkaloids derived from opium and coca leaves are detailed in this section, but reference is made only to the most commonly employed tests. The reader will note that many reactions are not exclusive to a particular drug. Chemists use a number of crystalline and color tests to winnow out false positives that may occur when only one test is used.

1. HEROIN HYDROCHLORIDE

Heroin hydrochloride melts at 243–244° C. and is soluble in alcohol, chloroform, ether and water. It forms spherical clusters of golden-yellow, needle-like crystals on treatment with platinum chloride. Concerning the qualitative color tests, heroin gives the following colors on treatment with the corresponding reagent: Marquis' reagent [1]—purple; Froehde's reagent [2]—purple changing to green; Mecke's reagent—green; Mandelin's reagent—light brown; concentrated nitric acid—yellow changing to green; ferric chloride [3]—no color reaction. The lack of specificity accompanying the running of only one color test is illustrated by the fact that morphine, metopon, and heroin hydrochloride give the same color result with Marquis' reagent.[4] An infrared spectrophotometer may be used as a clinching test. In this latter event, the chemist will have a graphic chart which may be compared with a known chart as demonstrative proof before a jury. For percentage quantification, some laboratories use the ultraviolet spectrophotometer, preceded by extrac-

§ 14.12

1. Marquis' reagent consists of 1 drop of 40% formaldehyde solution in 1 ml of concentrated sulfuric acid.

2. Froehde's solution consists of an ammonium molyodate in concentrated sulfuric acid.

3. Ferric chloride is used in a 10% aqueous solution.

4. See, Gonzalez, *Legal Medicine, Pathology and Toxicology* (1954), p. 1298, for a flow chart of analytic test reactions of many compounds. This is invaluable in cross-examination.

tion or some other means of purification. This test also charts a graphic result. If the sample is minute, thin layer or gas-liquid chromatography may be used in quantification.[5]

2. MORPHINE

Morphine alkaloid melts at about 230° C. It is soluble in water, alcohol, chloroform and ether, and is slightly soluble in benzene. Precipitated with Wagner's reagent,[6] it forms red, overlapping plate-like crystals; with Marme's reagent,[7] colorless, medium-sized needles are quickly formed singly and in sheaves; with sodium carbonate, small, sharply-defined rods in rosettes form. Concerning the color tests, morphine treated with Marquis' reagent gives a purple color; concentrated nitric acid produces an orange-red color fading to yellow. In neutral aqueous solution, morphine gives a deep blue-green color with ferric chloride. With Froehde's reagent, morphine yields a deep purple color fading to a slate color; with Mandelin's reagent [8] morphine gives a yellow color changing to violet-brown and then to slate. Physically, morphine in a pasty, sugar solution turns violet to green to yellow when treated with concentrated sulfuric acid.[9]

3. CODEINE

Codeine alkaloid has a melting point of 154–156° C. It is soluble in ether, chloroform, alcohol, water and benzene but insoluble in petroleum ether. The crystalline precipitate formed with Marme's reagent is composed of dark rosettes of small rods; with Wagner's reagent, large, yellow, branched plate-like crystals; with potassium iodide, long needle-like crystals. Marquis' reagent produces a reddish-violet changing to blue-violet on application to codeine; nitric acid produces orange changing to yellow; Mecke's reagent produces an instant green changing to blue-green; Froehde's reagent produces a green changing to red-brown. Note the necessity for several different color tests, as the Marquis' result for codeine is also common to dilaudid, a morphine derivative.

---

5. On the subject of narcotic identification tests generally, see, Shellow, "The Expert Witness in Narcotics Cases," *Criminal Defense*, Dec. 1973, p. 4. See also, Stein et al., op.cit. supra note 4, section 14.03.

6. Wagner's reagent is an aqueous solution of iodine and potassium iodide.

7. Marme's reagent is an aqueous solution of cadmium oxide and potassium iodide.

8. Mandelin's reagent consists of ammonium vanadate in concentrated sulfuric acid.

9. For a sampling of a few of the other tests used, see: Sullivan, et al., "Detection and Identification of Ibogaine and Heroin," 59 *J.Crim.L., C. & P.S.* 277 (1967); Goldbaum & Williams, "The Identification and Determination of Micrograms of Morphine in Biological Samples," 13 *J.For.Sci.* 253 (1968); Miller, "The Determination of Excipient Sugar Diluents in Illicit Preparations Containing Heroin by Gas Chromatography," 17 *J.For.Sci.* 150 (1972); Wilkinson, et al., "Identification of Drugs and Their Derivatives," 21 *J.For.Sci.* 564 (1976); Clark, "A Study of Procedures for the Identification of Heroin," 22 *J.For.Sci.* 418 (1977).

4. OPIUM

Opium itself is the dried latex from the unripe seed capsule of the opium poppy.   Opium in the natural state consists of a number of alkaloids which themselves constitute the narcotic portion of opium. Two of the most important alkaloids naturally occurring in opium are morphine, which comprises about 10 percent of the raw opium and codeine, which comprises about .3 percent.   A number of other narcotic drugs also occur as constituents of the opium.   Opium itself is really a combination of naturally occurring alkaloids.   Since the narcotics traffic consists of opium refined to morphine, codeine, or heroin, no discussion will be made concerning tests for raw opium other than notation of the following color reactions of raw opium: blue-violet with Froehde's reagent; red-violet with Marquis' reagent; red-orange with nitric acid; and blue-green with ferric chloride.

5. COCAINE

Cocaine has a melting point of approximately 98° C. and is soluble in ether, water, alcohol and chloroform.   Treatment with platinum chloride produces feathery, pale-yellow crystals; gold chloride produces long, rod-like crystals with short arms extending at right angles.   Colorwise, cobalt thiocynate produces a blue, flaky precipitate.   There is no reaction to the Marquis' reagent, Froehde's reagent or Mecke's reagent.

§ 14.13 Analysis of Hallucinogens

1. MARIJUANA

Marijuana is identified by microscopic and chemical tests.   Microscopically, the leaves, seed hulls, small twigs and flowering tops display a warty appearance as a result of single-celled hair-like fibers, some of which resemble bear claws.   The base of each fiber contains crystallized calcium carbonate.   A negative test can be performed by adding a drop of dilute hydrochloric acid to the base of the fiber on the slide and noting the presence or absence of effervescence (bubbling).   Lack of bubbling indicates the substance is not marijuana.   Bubbling indicates it could be marijuana.

Chemically, the Duquenois–Levine test is the principal test for tetrahydrocannabinol, the hallucinogenic constituent of marijuana.   The test procedure involves the application of Duquenois' reagent [1] to an extract of the sample, or directly to the sample.   Concentrated hydrochloric acid is added.   At this juncture a color will develop in the solution.   The solution is drawn off and placed in a test tube with chloroform.   If marijuana is present, a violet color is transferred from the solution to the layer of chloroform which settles to the bottom because of its weight.   This reaction occurs because tetrahydrocannabi-

----

§ 14.13

1. This reagent is composed of acetaldehyde and vanillin in alcohol solution.

nol is soluble in chloroform. The test is not wholly uniform, however, as samples of marijuana from different soil and weather regions will vary in tetrahydrocannabinol concentration and display varying shades of the final color shades. There are compounds other than marijuana which may display similar color changes when treated by Duquenois' reagent. However, if the treated reagent is placed with chloroform and the purple coloration is absorbed into the chloroform, most chemists will state that marijuana is present.[2] Well-equipped laboratories may utilize gas chromatography or other instrumentation.[3]

For many years, marijuana seeds were a major ingredient of birdseed. If an unknown, suspected sample consists of marijuana seeds alone, identification can only be determined by planting the seeds and observing them after germination.

To determine if a person is under the influence of marijuana a new device known as the ADMIT[4] system (Alcohol Drug Motorsensory Impairment Test) may be utilized. ADMIT determines whether or not a person is impaired by electronically reading wave patterns identifiable to different drugs' effect upon the brain. Another technology, EMIT (enzyme multiplied immunoassay technique), indicates from detectable traces in bodily fluids that a person has used marijuana.

2. LSD

LSD may be negatively identified by a color test using p-dimethylaminobenzaldehyde. Formation of a blue color on treatment indicates that the substance is one of the lysergic acid derivatives. Absence of a color reaction demonstrates that the substance is not LSD. Chromatography is also used to identify LSD. As is true with marihuana, no test has yet been devised to determine if a subject is under the influence of LSD.

3. PCP

When tested with the Marquis reagent (formaldehyde/sulfuric acid), PCP will undergo a color change ranging from colorless to faint pink.

2. False positives have been reported in testing some coffee brands and some chemicals. See, Fochman & Winek, "A Note on the Duquenois–Levine Test for Marijuana," 4 Clinical Toxicology 287 (1971).

3. See, e.g.: Backer, et al., "A Simple Method for the Infrared Identification of Cannabinoids of Marihuana Resolved by Gas Chromatography," 15 J.For.Sci. 287 (1970); Bellman, et al., "Spectrometric Forensic Chemistry of Hallucinogenic Drugs," 15 J.For.Sci. 261 (1970); Carew, "Microscopic, Microchemical, and Thin–Layer Chromatographic Study of Marihuana Grown or Confiscated in Iowa," 16 J.For. Sci. 87 (1971); de Faubert Maunder, "The

Forensic Significance of the Age and Origin of Cannabis," 16 Med.Sci.Law 78 (1976).

On the dispute whether cannabis is monotypic or polytypic, see, Small, "The Forensic Taxonomic Debate on Cannabis: Semantic Hokum," 21 J.For.Sci. 239 (1976); Kurzman & Fullerton, "Winning Strategies for Defense of Marijuana Cases: Chemical and Botanical Issues," 1 J.Crim.Defense 487 (1975). Review the text at § 14.04, supra.

4. ADMIT is manufactured by Pharmometrics Corporation, 783 Jersey Avenue, New Brunswick, N.J. 08901.

Of the microcrystalline tests, PCP is distinctive in the presence of potassium iodide which causes it to display crystals first in the form of needles, shortly changing to blades which are colorless under plain light but gray under polarized light.[5] PCP can be qualitatively identified through the normal separation processes of the various chromatographic techniques. Quantitative tests also exist [6] as do more costly procedures, like nuclear magnetic resonance.[7]

§ 14.14　Analysis of Barbiturates

There are more than one hundred different barbiturates, all of which are barbituric acid derivatives. Identification of barbiturates singularly and as a class is done by one of the following types of tests:

(1) Color reaction—particularly the Dille–Koppanyi test—in which the appearance of a red-violet color on treatment of the sample with cobalt acetate and isopropylamine indicates a barbituric acid derivative, but this test is not specific for any single barbiturate;

(2) Microscopic crystalline examination of the precipitate of the treated sample; [1]

(3) Melting point examination;

(4) Mass spectrometry, which measures molecular weights;

(5) Thin layer chromatography and infrared spectrophotometer.

These methods and those dealing with the detection of barbiturates or opiates in the urine of a D.U.I.D. suspect can only be adequately explained by an expert chemist and no effort will be made to detail the methodology involved in testing for the different barbiturates.

Consider the basic properties of the following most commonly abused barbiturates:

(1) Nembutal (Yellow jackets)—sodium pentobarbital molecular weight 248.26; melting point 126–130° C.; soluble in water and alcohol; insoluble in ether; blade-like crystals formed on treatment with Wagenaar's reagent;

(2) Seconal (red birds)—sodium secobarbital molecular weight 260.27; melting point 100° C.; soluble in water and alcohol; insoluble in ether; rosettes of five needles form on treatment with Wagenaar's reagent;

5. Ruybal, "Microcrystalline Tests for Narcotics and Dangerous Drugs," *Crime Lab.Digest* 6 (Dec.1980).

6. Rockley, et al., "Determination of Phencyclidine and Phenobarbital in Complex Mixtures by Fourier–Transformed Infrared Photoacoustic Spectroscopy," 55 *Anal.Chem.* 32 (1983).

7. Bailey & Legault, "Identification of Cyclohexamine, Phencyclidine and Simple Analogues by Carbon–13 Nuclear Magnetic Resonance Spectroscopy," 113 *Analytica Chimica Acta* 375 (1980).

§ 14.14

1. For a pictorial illustration of the various crystalline tests used to identify specific barbiturates, see, David, "Barbiturate Differentiation by Chemical Microscopy," 52 *J.Crim.L., Criminol. & P.S.* 459 (1961).

(3) Amytal (Blue birds)—sodium amobarbital molecular weight 226.27; melting point 156–158° C.; soluble in water, alcohol, ether and benzene; insoluble in petroleum ether; large light-blue crystalline needles form in clusters on treatment with Wagenaar's reagent; acetic acid produces long, branching needle-like crystals and some hexagonal plates;

(4) Tuinal (Christmas trees)—a 50/50 mixture of sodium secobarbital and sodium amobarbital; small rectangular crystalline prisms precipitate with Wagenaar's reagent.

§ 14.15   Analysis of Amphetamines

Chemists use a number of approaches to detect amphetamines, singularly and as a class. They include:

(1) Microscopic examination of the crystalline structure of the treated sample;

(2) Chemical odor and color tests such as the phenylisocyanide odor test for identity of amphetamine as a class;

(3) Melting point of the extracted derivative;

(4) Infrared and ultraviolet spectrophotometric examination of light waves emitted from the sample; and

(5) Paper chromatography, where a drop of the questioned material is placed on filter paper, treated with a solvent and dried; amphetamine present can be identified as a class through the color staining.[1]

Consider the following characteristics of the three amphetamines most commonly involved in criminal drug prosecution.

(1) Dextroamphetamine sulfate (dexedrine)—molecular weight 368.49; melting point above 300° C.; soluble in water and alcohol; insoluble in ether and chloroform; long, yellow crystalline rods and blades with gold chloride treatment; platinic chloride in phosphoric acid create long, rectangular blade-like crystals; picric acid forms small, yellow five-sided crystals in clusters; Marquis' reagent treatment yields an orange-red or orange-brown color; Mandelin's reagent yields dark-green changing to emerald then to reddish brown.

(2) Racemic amphetamine sulfate (benzedrine)—molecular weight 368.49; melting point above 300° C.; soluble in water and alcohol; insoluble in ether and chloroform; gold chloride yields plate-like or square crystals with blade-like arms; platinic chloride in phosphoric acid yields blades, needles and plates; treatment with gold bromide displays plate-like crystals; picric acid forms long, yellow needle-like crystals;

§ 14.15

1. See also, Nix & Hume, "A Spectrophotofluorometric Method for the Determination of Amphetamine," 15 *J.For.Sci.* 595 (1970); Canfield et al., "Gas Chromatographic Analysis of Amphetamine Derivatives and Morpholine–Related Drugs," 22 *J.For.Sci.* 429 (1977); Lomonte et al., "Contaminants in Illicit Amphetamine Preparations," 21 *J.For.Sci.* 575 (1976).

Marquis' and Mandelin's reagent have the same result as with dexedrine.

(3) Methamphetamine hydrochloride (methefrine)—molecular weight 185.69; melting point 170–175° C.; soluble in water, alcohol and chloroform; insoluble in ether; platinic chloride forms plates and fernlike crystals; picric acid forms broad, yellow crystalline blades.[2]

§ 14.16　Drug Testing in Employment and Other Civil Areas

Drug tests analyze a body specimen for the presence of drugs or metabolites, the by-products found in the body. These metabolites are excreted by the body in urine, and can also be found in blood, as well as in hair shafts.

To be scientifically valid, drug testing should follow a two-part process. The first is a screening test which eliminates samples where the results are negative, indicating an exclusion. Samples with positive results indicate substance levels at or above the designated threshold level. Such positive specimens should then be subjected to a confirmatory test.

There are three types of initial screening tests: color or spot tests, thin layer chromatography, and immunoassays. The most common tests are the immunoassays, of which there are three types: enzyme, radio, and fluorescence.[1]

The most frequently used immunoassay of bodily fluids is the enzyme multiplied immunoassay technique (EMIT).[2] The EMIT detects substances through an antigen-antibody reaction. When antibodies are added, they will bind to the tested-for substances. For instance, to check for heroin in a sample, heroin antibodies are added to the sample. Heroin or its metabolites in the sample will combine with the antibodies. An enzyme-labeled heroin drug is then combined with the sample. Any heroin antibodies which did not combine with the heroin in the sample will combine with the enzyme-labeled drug. Finally, the amount of enzyme-labeled drug which did not combine is measured. This figure is an indicator of the quantity of heroin which was originally present in the sample.

There are several advantages to EMIT: it tests for a wide spectrum of substances and their metabolites; it produces quick results; it is a relatively inexpensive test to conduct; and it can be administered by personnel who lack specialized technological training. In addition, it is a highly sensitive test, detecting low levels of drugs or their metabolites.

2. See also, Dugar and Catalano, "Spectrophotometric Determination of Methamphetamine in Contraband Seizures," 4 *J.Pol.Sci. & Admin.* 298 (1976).

§ 14.16

1. Other screening technologies are available, but only these three will be addressed because they are the most frequently used tests.

2. The newest technique is called EMIT II and is discussed extensively in Armbruster et. al., Method Comparison of EMIT II and OnLine with RIA for Drug Screening, 38 *J.For.Sci.* 1326 (1993).

Radioimmunoassay (RIA) also tests for a wide spectrum of substances, but it can measure only one substance at a time. RIA is also more expensive to run than EMIT. Studies have indicated disparate results when EMIT and RIA are used on the same samples for the same drugs.[3] The fluorescence polarization immunoassay (FPIA) is a relatively new technique and is not widely used yet.

The screening test techniques are very sensitive in order to minimize false negatives,[4] but because they are only presumptive evidence, they must be followed-up with a confirmatory test for scientific specificity. Professionals recommend that screening test results be confirmed through the use of gas chromatography/mass spectrometry or other confirmatory tests in situations in which positive test results have an impact on the life, liberty, property, reputation, or employment of the person being tested.[5]

The most commonly used confirmatory test is gas chromatography/mass spectrometry (GC/MS). To run this test, the specimen is pretreated to extract drugs from it. The sample is then converted to a gaseous form and transported through a long glass column of helium gas. The column is then subjected to varying temperatures which result in any drugs separating according to their individual properties (e.g. molecular weight and retention time). These properties are then analyzed by the mass spectrometer to determine what substances are present in the sample. GC/MS requires expensive equipment and highly trained technicians to prepare the specimens and interpret the results of the test. It is also a very time-consuming process because only one sample and one drug per sample may be tested at a time.

a.   The Accuracy and Reliability of Urinalysis

Urinalysis drug tests detect metabolites of the substances rather than the substances themselves. As a result, screening tests like EMIT sometimes incorrectly identify metabolites created by legal substances or human enzymes, such as lysozyme and malate dehydrogenase, as the metabolite of an illicit substance.[6] For example, aspirin, amphetamines, methaqualone, and ibuprofen are said to produce false positives for marijuana.[7]

3. Frederick & Green, "Comparison of Six Cannabinoid Metabolite Assays," 9 *J.Anal.Tox.* 116 (1985).

4. A false negative is a test result which indicates that no drugs or metabolites were found, even though the drugs or metabolites are actually present in the biological sample.

5. See, Rosen, "The Fourth Amendment Implications of Urine Testing for Evidence of Drug Use in Probation," 55 *Brook.L.Rev.* 1159 (1990) at fn. 30.

6. Rothstein, "Drug Testing in the Workplace: The Challenge to Employment Relations and Employment Law," 63 *Chi.-Kent L.Rev.* 683 (1987); Council of Scientific Affairs, Scientific Issues in Drug Testing, 257 J.A.M.A. 3110 (1987).

7. Zeese, "Marijuana Urinalysis Tests," 1 *Drug L.Rep.* 25 (May–June 1983); Greenblatt, The Admissibility of Positive EMIT Results as Scientific Evidence, 19 *Journal of Clinical Psychopharmacology* 114 (1985). See generally, K. Zeese, *Drug Testing Legal Manual*, s 2.02[4]–[6]; Council on Scientific Affairs, supra note 6 at 3113–3114.

The problem of false positives for opiates due to the ingestion of foods containing poppy seeds is by now well-known and scientifically documented.[8] The detection of 6–MAM, a metabolite of heroin, but not of morphine, has been suggested as a means to differentiate heroin users from poppy seed ingestors. Yet even that is recognized as unsatisfactory since 6–MAM has a short half-life in urine and it has been suggested that there may be a transacetylation of aspirin and the morphine in poppy seeds creating in the one case the possibility of a false negative and in the other a false positive.[9]

Sometimes a positive result is obtained when neither the tested-for substance or a cross-reactant is present.[10] Also, in the case of cannabinoids and cocaine, passive inhalation of the smoke from some other person's use can result in the presence of the THC metabolite or the cocaine metabolite, benzoylecgonine in an exposed individual's urine specimen.[11] No biochemical urinalysis test can differentiate between active and passive inhalation.[12] False positives for marijuana in EMIT testing are claimed to have considerable variability, ranging from very high rates, to relatively low rates.[13]

The proper interpretation of the results of urinalysis testing requires expertise which is not widely available presently.[14] The Center for Disease Control reported in 1985 that lab accuracy ranges from 37% to 69%.[15] The interpreter must have proper qualifications and experience in analytical toxicology, including drug testing, as well as an understanding of the physiology and clinical chemistry of biological specimens, knowledge of the pharmacology and pharmacokinetics of illicit drugs, and an adequate working knowledge of the relevant forensic

---

8. ElSohly, Hala N., Standord, Don F. et al., "Gas Chromatographic/Mass Spectrometric Analysis of Morphine and Codeine in Human Urine of Poppy Seed Eaters," 33 *J.For.Sci.* 347 (March 1988); Salerno, Charles, Wisniewski, M.D., Ph.D., Rudelli, Raoul D., M.D., "Effect of Poppy Seed Ingestion on the TDx Opiates Assay," 12:2 *Therapeutic Drug Monitoring* 210 (1990). One New York appellate court upheld a trial court's refusal to dismiss a complaint brought by a plaintiff claiming a positive result for morphine was caused by eating poppy seeds. Doe v. Roe, 160 A.D.2d 255, 553 N.Y.S.2d 364 (1990). A bibliography of 69 references is available from *Sci.Sleuth. Rev.*, c/o Charles R. Midkiff, Jr., A.T.F. Nat'l Lab., 1401 Research Blvd., Rockville, MD 20850.

9. Midkiff, "Countering the Poppy Seed Defense: No Piece of Cake," 14 *Sci.Sleuth. Rev.* 4, at 13–14 (Spring 1990) and "Food for Thought: Poppy Seed Comments," 14 *Sci.Sleuth.Rev.* 6 (Summer 1990).

10. Altunkaya, Diane and Smith, R.N., "Aberrant Radioimmunoassay Results for Cannabinoids in Urine," 47 *For.Sci.Int'l.* 195 (1990).

11. Perez–Reyes, DiGuiseppi & Davis, "Passive Inhalation of Marijuana Smoke and Urinary Excretion of Cannabinoids," 249 *J.A.M.A.* 475 (1983); Baselt, et al., "Passive Inhalation of Cocaine," 37 *Clin. Chem.* 2160 (1991).

12. Affidavit of Dr. McBay, Plaintiff's Exhibit 1 at 1, *Brooks v. Marsh,* No. 83–39–CIV–3 (E.D.N.C. filed July 27, 1983). However, the THC metabolite's level of concentration is substantially lower in an individual who was exposed only to passive inhalation. Biochemical urinalysis test may more easily distinguish active from passive inhalation if urine specimens are tested for higher levels of THC metabolite concentration. *Perez–Reyes,* supra note 11.

13. O'Donnell, Michael R., Note: "Employee Drug Testing—Balancing the Interests in the Workplace: A Reasonable Suspicion Standard," 74 *Va.L.Rev.* 969 (Aug. 1988).

14. Dubowski, Kurt M., "Drug-Use Testing: Scientific Perspectives," 11 *Nova L.Rev.* 415, 497 (1987).

15. 253 *J.A.M.A.* 2382 (26 April 1985).

science and legal implications.[16] Most forensic toxicologists certified by the American Board of Forensic Toxicology would qualify, as well as most certified in Toxicological Chemistry by the American Board of Clinical Chemistry. Beyond these few hundred persons, emphasizes Kurt Dubowski,[17] the only other qualified interpreters would be either qualified biomedical personnel or physicians whose basic knowledge and experience in their primary field has been supplemented by training and experience in the areas discussed above.

The occurrence of false positives demonstrates the necessity for confirmatory testing. Experts warn that screening tests are not intended to be definitive. They are only to be used to determine which samples may be eliminated from those which require further testing.[18] Unfortunately, a confirmatory test is often bypassed due to cost considerations resulting in a growing number of Americans experiencing the detrimental effects that a positive drug screening test result can have on the ability to find or keep a job. In 1984, Major Robert Mirelson, an Army spokesman at the Pentagon, said that "probably the majority" of 9,099 persons discharged in 1982 and 1983 for drug and alcohol abuse were implicated by dubious evidence.[19] As of 1984, the Army was reported to have mishandled fifty-two thousand urine samples.[20]

b. Measurement of Use, Not Impairment

A positive result on a drug test does not indicate a person's impairment. Drug testing cannot determine the level of impairment of a user because they only measure the metabolites, not the psychoactive ingredient in the substance.[21] Drug metabolites in the urine are inert, inactive by-products of drugs and cannot be used to determine impairment.[22] The time that a drug was used cannot be established from urine concentrations because most drugs can be found in urine for one day to one week after use.[23] Marijuana metabolites may be found in urine three to eighteen days after light use (one or less use weekly).[24] As the

---

16. Id.

17. Dubowski, supra, note 14.

18. Warner, Mary, "Jumping to Conclusions," 59 *Anal.Chem.* 521, 522 (April 1, 1987).

19. Harris, Scott, " 'Dubious' Drug Tests May Have Forced Thousands From Service," *Los Angeles Times,* San Diego County section, September 9, 1984 at 1. The same article also reports that in June of 1984 Army officials announced they would try to locate between 60,000 and 70,000 soldiers to notify them of their rights to appeal disciplinary action because of problems in documentation of evidence reviewed at five labs. Air Force Col. William W. Manders, former chief of quality control for the drug testing program at the Armed Forces Institute of Pathology, has become one of its leading critics. He pro-

vided expert testimony for the defense in more than 100 disciplinary actions.

20. BNA, *Alcohol and Drugs in the Workplace* 19 (1986).

21. Norton & Garriot, "Detection of Marijuana Use by GC/MS Analysis of Mouth Swabs," 4 *Am.J.Forensic Med. & Path.* 185 (1983).

22. Rothstein, supra, note 6.

23. Affidavit of Dr. McBay, supra, note 12. See, K. Zeese, supra, note 7 at sec. 3.02.

24. This time is extended to one month or more with daily uses. Ellis, Mann, Judson, Schramm and Tashchian, "Excretion Patterns of Cannibinoid Metabolites after Last Use in a Group of Chronic Users," 38 *Clinical Pharmacology and Therapeutics* 572 (1985).

following table [25] indicates, drug metabolites can be detected in urine from one day to several weeks following exposure.

Substances	Approximate Duration of Detectability
Amphetamines	2 days
Barbiturates	1–7 days
Benzodiazepines	3 days
Cocaine metabolites	2–3 days
Methadone	3 days
Codeine	2 days
PCP	8 days
Cannibinoids, single use	3 days
moderate use (4 times/week)	5 days
heavy smoker (daily)	10 days
chronic heavy smoker	21 days

Although the actual effects of most drugs last for a few hours, they are detectable for much longer, as the above table indicates. Any correlations between a positive test and impairment are impossible.[26] In addition, it cannot be determined through urinalysis whether a particular subject is a chronic or occasional user.[27] For that purpose, multiple urinalyses must be conducted within days of each other.

c. Drug Testing of Hair

As hair grows it absorbs drugs and their metabolites into the hair shaft while the hair is being formed in the follicle. As the hair shaft grows, it forms a longitudinal record of the compounds it has absorbed, including illicit substances. The drug metabolites appear in detectable levels about a week after ingestion. Hairs are collected by pulling or cutting. Positive results can be obtained through the use of a single strand of hair, but a larger sample (between 40 and 50 hairs) is preferred.[28] Scalp hair is most commonly used, but any body hair can be used.[29] After collection of the hair sample, the sample is washed in order to remove any possible external contaminants.[30] An initial screening test is then performed using the radioimmunoassay technique. If positive results are obtained, a confirmatory test using gas chromatography/mass spectometry is conducted.

Several features which distinguish hair testing from bodily fluid testing make hair testing an attractive option for employers and law

25. Rothstein, supra, note 6.

26. Id.

27. Dubowski, supra note 14 at 527–528.

28. Smith and Pomposini, "Detection of Phenobarbitol in Bloodstains, Semen, Seminal Stains, Saliva, Saliva Stains, Perspiration, and Hair," 26 *J.For.Sci.* 582, 583 (1981) (positive test results from analysis of a single strand); Baumgartner, "Hair Analysis for Drugs of Abuse: Solving the Problems of Urinalysis," testimony before Subcommittee on Human Resources, House Comm. on Post Office and Civil Service, U.S. House of Representatives (May 20, 1987).

29. Rob, "Drug Detection By Hair Analysis," 1991–*Jan Army Law.* 10 (Jan. 1991).

30. See, Martz, "Identification of Cocaine in Hair by GC/MS and MS/MS," *Crime Lab. Dig.*, 67 (Jul. 1988).

enforcement officials. It provides a longer time window within which substances can be detected. Short periods of non-use will not significantly alter the results. This factor makes retesting a fruitful option. The test itself is less intrusive than bodily fluid testing. It simply requires the snipping of a small section of hair from the scalp, whereas the taking of blood requires an invasive procedure and those giving urine specimens are often subject to close observation to prevent adulteration of the sample. Intentional alteration of the sample is much less likely in hair testing. It is not possible to wash the drugs or metabolites out of the hair, even with very strong compounds.[31] Additionally, hair samples are not as labile as urine samples. They are more chemically and physically stable than urine specimens.[32] This makes the samples less subject to destruction during collection, storage and shipment of the samples to and from testing sites.

There is a significant amount of scientific writing on the subject of RIA hair analysis which point toward its reliability and acceptance in the field of forensic toxicology for the identification of drug use,[33] and it may even be more effective than urinalysis.[34] The RIA hair test appears to be an effective testing method for cocaine, amphetamines, barbiturates, opiates, and other drugs including PCP and anti-depressants.[35] However, there are some few drawbacks to the use of hair testing. A significant number of forensic scientists have questioned the technique's ability to quantify drug use.[36] The ability to detect chronic drug use requires that hair be allowed to grow. Scalp hair which is kept very short will not reveal a long history of drug use.[37] The rate of growth of hair has often been said to be 1 cm./month or 0.5 inches/month. But this fails to take into account a number of recognized variables, such as

31. Baumgartner, Werner A., Hill, Virginia A., and Blahd, William H., Hair Analysis for Drugs of Abuse, 34(6) *J.For.Sci.* 1433, 1436 (1989). The study examined effects of cosmetic treatment on the drug content of hair (shampooing, perming, relaxing, and dyeing). Repeated shampooing was found to have no significant effect, but levels were found to be affected under some conditions by some of the other treatments. The extent of this depends on type of hair (fine, coarse, or ethnic origin), severity, type of treatment, and type of drug. However, none of the treatments reduced the detectable drug level to a point at which a user would have escaped detection.

32. Baumgartner, Jones and Black, "Detection of Phencyclidine in Hair," 26 *J.For.Sci.* 576 at 580 (1981).

33. See, e.g., Arnold, "Radioimmunological Hair Analysis for Narcotics and Substitutes," 25 *J.Clin.Chem. & Clin.Biochem.* 753 (1987); Balabanova, Brunner & Nowak, "Radioimmunological Determination of Cocaine in Human Hair," 98 *Z Rechtsmed* 229 (1987); Baumgartner, Baer,

Hill & Blahd, "Hair Analysis for Drugs of Abuse," 34 *J.For.Sci.* 1433 (1989); Graham, Koren, Klein, Schneiderman, & Greenwald, "Determination of Gestational Cocaine Exposure by Hair Analysis," 262 *J.A.M.A.* 3328 (1989); Midkiff, "Detecting Drugs in Hair: Targets and Techniques," 13 *Sci.Sleuth.Rev.* 1 at 14 (Winter 1989).

34. Baumgartner, Baer, "Hair Analysis for Drugs of Abuse in Parole/Probation Populations," *N.I.J.Prog.Rep.* (Oct. 86–Mar. 88) (study compared results of RIA hair analysis with urinalysis and determined that hair analysis provided more accurate detection rates).

35. Midkiff, supra, note 33.

36. See, Bailey, "Drug Screening in an Unconventional Matrix," 262 *J.A.M.A.* 3331 (1989); Harkey and Henderson, "Hair Analysis for Drugs of Abuse," 2 *Advances in Analytical Toxicology* 298, 326 (R.Baselt ed. 1989).

37. Isikoff, "Splitting Hairs to Find the Roots of Drug Use," *Wash. Post*, Mar. 14, 1990, at A15, col. 1.

hair type and anatomical location among other factors, and is thus an oversimplification.[38]

d. Admissibility of Drug Test Results

Blood and urine drug testing has been deemed a reliable and accurate measure of drug use by a majority of courts. EMIT results are often accepted by courts as evidence of drug use in parole and probation cases, without discussion of reliability, even when a confirmatory test has not been conducted.[39] Other courts have accepted EMIT results if they are confirmed by a second EMIT test.[40]

The testing of hair is a relatively new procedure which has had very limited attention at the appellate court level. In United States v. Foote,[41] the Eighth Federal Circuit expressed its skepticism of hair testing by RIA. In *Foote,* a detective, acting undercover, allegedly purchased cocaine from the defendant. Without explanation or elaboration, the Eighth Circuit upheld the magistrate's refusal to require the detective to undergo drug testing (that the defendant had requested) because of "the intrusive and unreliable nature of the experimental radioimmunoassay of hair." [42] Even though there is a paucity of cases dealing with the admissibility of radioimmunoassay of hair, it has been ruled admissible into evidence,[43] and even deemed generally accepted by the scientific community, under the Frye standard.[44] Judge Weinstein's dissent in United States v. Riley [45] acknowledged that hair may be analyzed to indicate use of narcotics,[46] indicating that acceptance of the method may be on the rise.

Unlike the judiciary, the scientific community has been subjecting hair analysis for drugs of abuse to considerable attention lately.[47] This intense scrutiny has revealed that much about hair analysis for drugs of abuse is more conjecture than proven scientific fact. For example, drugs are regularly asserted to enter hair via the blood stream. Studies have revealed that the route of entry is much more diverse and variable.[48] It is quite likely that drugs are transferred to hair through sweat, sebaceous and apocrine gland secretions as well as from the external environ-

---

38. Harkey, "Anatomy and Physiology of Hair," 63 *For.Sci.Int'l* 9, 15 (1993).

39. See, e.g., Song v. Smith, 952 F.2d 407 (9th Cir.1992) (court deemed EMIT results to be "sufficient evidence to meet the 'some evidence' standard required in disciplinary hearings"); Jones v. United States, 548 A.2d 35 (D.C.App.1988).

40. See, Acuna v. Lewis, 937 F.2d 611 (9th Cir.1991).

41. 898 F.2d 659 (8th Cir.1990).

42. Id. at 665. The court gave no citations or references to any legal or scientific sources to support this statement.

43. United States v. Medina, 749 F.Supp. 59 (E.D.N.Y.1990).

44. In the Matter of Baby Boy L., 157 Misc.2d 353, 596 N.Y.S.2d 997 (1993) (holding RIA hair testing a reliable and accurate method of ascertaining and measuring cocaine use when used in conjunction with GC/MS).

45. 906 F.2d 841 (2d Cir.1990).

46. Id, at 853–854.

47. See the 314–page special issue of 63 *For.Sci.Internat'l* (1993) which compiles the papers from the 1st International Meeting on Hair Analysis as a Diagnostic Tool for Drugs of Abuse Investigational held at Genoa, Italy, 10–11 Dec. 1992.

48. Henderson, "Mechanisms of Drug Incorporation into Hair," 63 *For.Sci.Internat'l* 19, 24–27 (1993).

ment through the skin, at least as to those drugs that are lipophilic in addition to or in conjunction with its transfer from the bloodstream.

The mechanism of drug transfer to hair is "of more than academic interest." [49]   If the transfer occurs via glandular secretions, then hair may not be useful as a longitudinal record of drug use by chronic or only occasional abusers.   Clearly more studies in depth on this subject are required before hair analysis for drug abuse will measure up to a scientific standard of acceptability.

Further, although Baumgartner and Hill [50] have intimated that external contamination of hair is unlikely, still if contaminants can be transferred to sweat and sweat is a source of drugs in hair, then external contamination is a problem of large proportions.[51]   In any event, at this time, it cannot be said that hair analysis for drugs of abuse will not engender false positives and, in light of this probability, that hair analysis for drugs of abuse has reached an acceptable level of scientific certainty.

III. STATUTORY CONTROL OF DRUGS

§ 14.17   In the Federal System

In response to the increasing amount of drug abuse in the United States, Congress in 1970 approved legislation which provided for increased efforts in prevention of drug abuse and rehabilitation of drug users, more effective law enforcement for drug abuse prevention and control, and an overall balanced system of criminal penalties for offenses involving drugs.   Under its authority to regulate interstate commerce,[1] Congress passed the Comprehensive Drug Abuse Prevention and Control Act, that part which regulates the possession and use of drugs is known as the Controlled Substances Act.   The Act exempts tobacco and alcohol from the definition of controlled substances.   Nutmeg and jimson weed, two naturally produced hallucinogens, are not within the act.   Street

---

49. Id. at 28.

50. Baumgartner and Hill, "Hair Analysis for Drugs of Abuse: Decontamination Issues," in *Recent Developments in Therapeutic Drug Monitoring and Clinical Toxicology,* 1992, pp. 577–597.

51. Blank and Kidwell, "External Contamination of Hair by Cocaine: An Issue in Forensic Interpretation," 63 *For.Sci.Internat'l* 145, 155 (1993). Baumgartner and Hill replied that their procedure will discriminate between exogenous and endogenous drugs in hair. Comments on the Paper by David L. Blank and David A. Kidwell: "External Contamination of Hair by Cocaine: An Issue in Forensic Interpretation," 63 *For.Sci.Internat'l* 157 (1993).

The dispute is so vigorous and so unresolved that the courts would be ill-advised to take sides at this juncture.

§ 14.17

1. Congressional findings make it clear that it would be contrary to the statute's enforcement objectives to differentiate between drugs which move across state lines and those which only move intrastate, since both types will ultimately affect interstate commerce.   21 U.S.C.A. § 801 (1981). Compare the Harrison Narcotic Act of 1914 which was repealed by the 1970 Act.   The prior act was based on the congressional taxing power and was part of the Internal Revenue Code.

drugs and prescription drugs are included. The Act established five schedules for controlled substances based on the substance's potential for abuse or addiction, the current medical uses for the substance, the available scientific knowledge of the effects of the substance on the human body, and the scope of current and past abuse of the substance.

The Controlled Substances Act sets out the prison terms and fines for violations of each schedule. For all violations, repeat offenders of the Act are subject to double penalties. Double penalties are also placed on first offenders over 18 who distribute controlled substances to a person under 21.[2] The most serious penalties were enacted for a "continuing criminal enterprise."[3]

Under the Controlled Substances Act, authority has been delegated to the Drug Enforcement Administration to schedule, deschedule, or reschedule substances.[4] In order to effectively combat drug abuse and illicit activity, schedule updating must be timely and accurate.

The actions of the D.E.A. under the Act must, however, give notice and an opportunity to be heard to all concerned persons. Notifications of this type appear in the Federal Register. The recent emergency scheduling of the new designer drug "Nexus" was announced in the Federal Register.[5] Such authority for temporary emergency scheduling is authorized by the Comprehensive Crime Control Act of 1984.[6]

FEDERAL CONTROLLED SUBSTANCES ACT AT A GLANCE

Scheduling Criteria	Examples of Drugs Included	Maximum Trafficking Penalties: First Offense, Small Quantities
Schedule I High potential for abuse, no accepted medical use.	Heroin—narcotic * mescaline, psilocybin, LSD—nonnarcotic Marijuana; Hashish	Up to 15 years imprisonment and/or a $125,000 fine. Up to 5 years imprisonment and/or a $50,000 fine.
Schedule II High potential for abuse, accepted medical use, abuse may lead to severe psychic or physical dependence.	Methadone, morphine, oxycodone cocaine—Narcotic Amphetamine, methaqualone, PCP, phenmetrazine, methamphetamine—nonnarcotic	15 years and/or a $125,000 fine.

2. 21 U.S.C.A. § 845 (1981). Triple penalties may also be imposed for a repeated violation of this section.

3. 21 U.S.C.A. § 848 (1981). The elements of this offense are: (1) a violation of the Act which is punishable as a felony and which is (2) part of a continuing series of violations in which a person supervised 5 or more people who acted in concert with him and (3) from which such person obtains substantial income or revenue.

4. Executive Order 11727, July 6, 1973, 38 Fed.Reg. 18357. Originally Congress delegated authority to the Attorney General. The delegation of legislative authority was made in order to ensure current updating by a less cumbersome procedure and a more informed body.

5. 58 Fed.Reg. 58819 (11/4/93), 59 Fed. Reg. 671 (1/6/94).

6. Pub.L. 98–473.

* Narcotic is defined as opium, coca leaves, and opiates or any derivative, preparation, compound, manufacture, or salt thereof or any chemically identical substance. 21 U.S.C.A. § 802(16).

Scheduling Criteria	Examples of Drugs Included	Maximum Trafficking Penalties: First Offense, Small Quantities
Schedule III		
Less potential for abuse than I or II, accepted medical use, abuse may lead to moderate dependence	Codeine—narcotic; methyprylon, glutethimide (Doriden)—non-narcotic; anabolic steroids	5 years and/or a $50,000 fine.
Schedule IV		
Low potential for abuse, may lead to limited dependence relative to III.	Barbital, meprobamate (equinol, milzown) phenobarbital, benzodiazepines; (librium, valium)	3 years and/or a $25,000 fine.
Schedule V		
Low potential for abuse relative to IV, accepted medical use, abuse may lead to limited dependence relative to IV.	Cough syrups containing codeine (Cheracol)—narcotic; Restricted over the counter drugs—non-narcotic	1 year and/or a $10,000 fine.

§ 14.18 The Regulation of Anabolic Steroids

To meet what one U.S. Senator called "one of America's most serious drug problems", Congress enacted the Anabolic Steroids Control Act of 1990 [1] which classifies anabolic steroids as a Schedule III controlled substance under the Controlled Substances Act.[2] The Act also criminalizes physician prescription of anabolic steroids for any use other than for the treatment of a disease or other recognized condition. This section has been criticized as not rationally related to the legitimate legislative purpose articulated by Congress.[3] However, the Food and Drug Administration has approved other non-disease uses and prescriptions for steroids, such as for allergies, premature growth stoppage in childhood, and the maintenance of muscle mass in geriatric patients.[4] Regardless of this allowance, the section is said to have the potential of forcing more athletes to seek steroids on the black market, rather than through physicians. The self-administration of steroids without supervision or training, as well as the risks implicit in obtaining a drug through an unregulated source, create even more dangers in steroid use.[5]

States have approached the use of steroids in several different ways. California classifies steroids as a controlled substance, but also requires posting of notices designed to educate the public on the dangers of steroid use.[6] Steroids are also statutorily classified as a controlled substance in Texas,[7] with specific language directed to physicians that administering steroids for the enhancement of athletic performance is not a legitimate medical purpose.[8] As of 1991, there were reported to be twenty-two states classifying anabolic steroids as controlled substances.[9]

§ 14.18

1. 21 U.S.C.A. § 801 (1990).

2. 21 U.S.C.A. § 812(c) (1990).

3. Black, "The Anabolic Steroids Control Act of 1990: A Need for Change," 97 *Dickinson L.Rev.* 131, 138 (1992).

4. Id., at 140.

5. Thurston, "Chemical Warfare: Battling Steroids in Athletics," 1 *Marq.Sports L.J.* 93, 107 (1990).

6. West's Ann.Cal.Civ.Code § 1812.-97(a) (Supp.1993).

7. Vernon's Ann.Tex.Civ.St. art. 4476-15 (Supp.1993).

8. V.Tex.C.A., Education Code § 21.928 (Supp.1993).

9. Reddig, Anabolic Steroids: The Price of Pumping Up!, 37 *Wayne L.Rev.* 1647, note 38 at 1663 (1991); Shapiro, Symposium, The Technology of Perfection: Performance Enhancement and Control Attributes, 65 *Cal.L.Rev.* 11, 22 (1991).

Scientific studies have indicated that steroid use can cause violent mood swings.[10] The media has recently given some attention to crimes in which a "roid rage" might be involved.[11] Defendants have argued that they were without the specific intent required for certain crimes because of a "roid rage." For example, in State v. Knowles,[12] the defendant was charged with murder. The defendant argued that his steroid use caused the behavior that led to the murder of the victim.[13] A government witness, a pathologist play-acting as a psychiatrist, testified that the placement of wounds close to the heart, and not all over the body, indicated that the killing was not the product of a "wild rage." [14] The jury found the defendant guilty, and the court of appeals upheld the verdict.[15] The number of "roid rage" defenses raised will undoubtedly increase when knowledge of steroids' effects on mood and behavior becomes more widely disseminated.

§ 14.19 Controlled Substance Analogue Enforcement Act of 1986

This Federal act makes illegal all analogues of controlled substances and drugs created to act as stimulants, depressants, or hallucinogens.[1] In order to fall under the Act, the substance must meet either one of two criteria. It must have a stimulant, depressant, or hallucinogenic effect on the central nervous system which is similar to or greater in effect than a Schedule I or II controlled substance, or it must be represented by the seller to have the above attributes.[2] The Act was drafted to encompass new drug analogues which were not technically illegal under the Controlled Substances Act of 1970.[3]

Objections have been lodged to the Act on constitutional grounds. In United States v. Desurra,[4] it was argued that the Controlled Substance Analogue Act was impermissibly vague. The court, however, decided that the MDMA in the defendant's possession was a prohibited drug analogue within the meaning of the Act.[5]

The states have also passed statutes governing designer drugs. These have been subject to many constitutional challenges.[6] Due pro-

---

10. See, Hannan & Friedl, et al., "Psychological and Serum Homovanillic Acid Changes in Men Administered Androgenic Steroids," 16 *Psychoneuroendocrinology* 35 (1991) and Su & Pagliaro, Neuropsychiatric Effects of Anabolic Steroids in Male Normal Volunteers, 269 *J.A.M.A.* 2760 (1993).

11. See, e.g., After Bodybuilder is Accused of Murder, Many Point Finger at Steroid Use, The New York Times, § 1 at 45 (July 3, 1993); 'Frisco Bodybuilder May Face Murder Charges in Death of His Girlfriend, *Jet* at 18 (July 12, 1993); Bodybuilder Slain, Boyfriend to be Charged—He's Tied to Steroid Scheme, *The San Francisco Chronicle* at A1 (June 24, 1993).

12. 598 So.2d 430 (La.App.1992).

13. Id., at 433.

Moenssens et al. Scientific Evid. 4th Ed. FP—20

14. Id., at 434.

15. Id., at 430.

§ 14.19

1. 21 U.S.C.A. 813 (1986).

2. DalCason, Characterization of MDA Analogs, 34 *J.For.Sci.* 928, 929 (1989).

3. 21 U.S.C.A. §§ 810 et seq.

4. 865 F.2d 651 (5th Cir.1989).

5. Id.

6. See, P. Carter, Validity, Construction, and Effect of State Statutes Regulating Sale of Counterfeit or Imitation Controlled Substances, 84 A.L.R.4th 936.

cess challenges have been raised against state designer drug laws which penalize trafficking in drug analogues more severely than non-analogue controlled substances. In Thompson v. State,[7] the court upheld the penalty provision of the Georgia designer drug statute,[8] refusing to substitute its judicial judgment for the legislature's reasoning. In People v. Upton,[9] an Illinois court, applying the rational basis test, upheld the constitutionality of the penalty provision of the Illinois designer drug statute, despite harsher penalties for drug analogues.

State statutes have also been said to be vague. Such challenges have generally been unsuccessful.[10] For example, in People v. Moore,[11] the trial court held the state designer drug statute unconstitutionally vague. The Colorado Supreme Court reversed and held the state law constitutional. The petitioner's objection was to the statute's language about a reasonable person's believing the designer drug to be a controlled substance. The Court held that this language was not impermissibly vague.[12]

§ 14.20   The Structure in the States

The need to solve the "drug problem" has been a recurrent theme of political and social commentary in the United States since the 1960's. The Federal Controlled Substances Act served as a model for the drafting of a uniform state law which has now been adopted in 48 states and the District of Columbia.[1] The Uniform Controlled Substances Act has the same objectives and scheduling scheme as its Federal counterpart. In each state a state board or agency is delegated the authority to administer the Act and add, delete, or reschedule substances.

Unlike the Federal Act, the Uniform Act does not include the offense of "continuing criminal enterprise." None of the offenses correspond to exact penalties as in the Federal Act, the specifics being left to the state legislatures, but the Uniform Act was written with the idea that the penalties would mirror those of Federal law. The Uniform Act contains different provisions for the distribution of controlled substances to minors, requiring that there be a 3 year age difference between the purchaser and the seller.[2] In a divergence from the Federal Act, the Uniform Act excludes not for profit distribution of marijuana as well as

---

7.   254 Ga. 393, 330 S.E.2d 348 (1985).

8.   Id.

9.   114 Ill.2d 362, 102 Ill.Dec. 842, 500 N.E.2d 943 (Ill.1986).

10.   See, e.g., Morrow v. State, 704 P.2d 226 (Alaska App.1985) and People v. Moore, 674 P.2d 354 (Colo.1984).

11.   Id.

12.   Id.

§ 14.20

1.   New Hampshire and Vermont have not adopted the Uniform Controlled Substances Act. N.H. retains its own Con-

trolled Drug Act enacted in 1969 and Vt. its Possession and Control of Regulated Drugs Act of 1967. See, N.H.Rev.Stat.Ann. 318–B (1955) and Vt.Stat.Ann. tit. 18 § 4201 et seq. (1947).

2.   9 Uniform Controlled Substances Act (U.L.A.) § 406 (1979). A double penalty is imposed on anyone 18 or over who distributes to anyone who is at least 3 years his junior and under 21.

possession for personal use, adopting the recommendations of the National Commission on Marijuana and Drug Abuse.[3]

Both Federal and Uniform Acts prohibit the delivery of imitation or counterfeit substances.[4] A major problem facing law enforcement today is that substances consisting of non-controlled substances are being either manufactured to closely resemble or promoted in the same manner as well-known, highly abused controlled substances.[5] In prosecutions of "burn" transactions,[6] where the seller offers to sell a controlled substance and instead delivers a substitute non-controlled substance, there is no need to prove the intent to sell a counterfeit substance. The requisite "knowing" mental state is implied.[7]

§ 14.21   Constitutional Challenges

A variety of constitutional challenges has been mounted against both the Federal Act and the Uniform Controlled Substances Act. Of these claims, the assertions of a denial of equal protection of the laws or of a due process infraction have bulked largest. A subsidiary, but often mooted, charge is that the scheduling technique for controlled substances impermissibly delegates an exclusively legislative function to an administrative agency.

The scheduling of both cocaine and marijuana has been vigorously opposed. The decisions from the Federal courts are unanimous in upholding the Federal statute's classification of cocaine as a Schedule II drug.[1] Defendants have argued that the classification violates the equal protection guarantee. The courts have responded that since there is no constitutional right to possess, use, or sell cocaine, the legislation must

---

3. 9 Uniform Controlled Substances Act (U.L.A.) § 409 (1979). The Uniform Act provides more liberal treatment of small scale marijuana offenses than the Federal Act. § 409 provides that (1) possession for personal use is not unlawful, (2) distribution of small amounts of marijuana for no profit is not unlawful, (3) possession of less than one ounce of marijuana is presumed to be for personal use, (4) knowingly or intentionally smoking, ingesting or distributing marijuana in public is prohibited and punishable by fine. The states have taken various approaches toward the punishment of small scale marijuana offenses and not all have adopted § 409, although most states have retained marijuana as a Schedule I substance. Some states have made marijuana an unscheduled substance carrying its own code sections and penalties. See, Va.Code 1950, §§ 18.2–248.1, 18.2–250.1.

4. 9 Uniform Controlled Substances Act 9 (U.L.A.) § 401 (1979). In Federal jurisdictions a defendant must be charged with attempt when the substances involved are counterfeit since the Federal Controlled Substances Act does not include the prohibition of counterfeit substances. See, Unit-

ed States v. Oviedo, 525 F.2d 881 (5th Cir. 1976).

5. Counterfeit substances are within the Uniform Controlled Substances Act § 401 (9 U.L.A. (1979)) and within the Federal Controlled Substance Act, 21 U.S.C.A. §§ 352(i)(2), 802 and 841. See, State v. Castleman, 116 N.M. 467, 863 P.2d 1088 (App.1993) upholding the validity of the statute. In general, see, Anno., Validity, Construction, and Effect of State Statutes Regulating Sale of Counterfeit or Imitation Controlled Substances, 84 A.L.R. 4th 936 (1993).

6. For a good summary of "burns" see, Uelman and Haddox, *Drug Abuse and the Law Sourcebook*, § 7.6 (1984).

7. See, e.g., People v. Moore, 674 P.2d 354 (Colo.1984). State v. Castleman, supra note 5.

§ 14.21

1. See, United States v. Vila, 599 F.2d 21 (2d Cir.1979); United States v. Solow, 574 F.2d 1318 (5th Cir.1978); and United States v. Stieren, 608 F.2d 1135 (8th Cir. 1979).

simply bear a rational relationship to a legitimate state interest. The decisions further conclude that the criteria for classification are rationally related to the legitimate legislative interest in mitigating drug abuse. Most state courts have rejected a similar contention of unconstitutionality.[2]

Several unsuccessful objections to the scheduling of marijuana in the Federal statute have been made by the National Organization for the Reform of Marijuana Laws (NORML)[3] and other groups.[4] In Louisiana Affiliate of NORML v. Guste, it was held that the Federal law does not unconstitutionally infringe upon rights of privacy or equal protection or transgress the prohibition against cruel and unusual punishment by including marijuana in Schedule I. In general, both federal and state courts hold that the scheduling of marijuana does not violate constitutional protections.[5] It is noted that since there is no constitutional right to smoke marijuana and that since there is scientific evidence of possible detrimental effects of the use of marijuana, the classification of it meets the test of reasonableness.[6] Although the legislative classification may, arguably, be unwise, no unconstitutionality pertains to it and the administrative process, not judicial action, is said to be the proper forum for the contest to decriminalize the possession of marijuana.[7]

The delegation of scheduling authority to an administrative agency within the executive branch of government has also been the subject of constitutional challenge as an unconstitutional delegation of legislative power. Such an objection has been uniformly unsuccessful at the federal level,[8] but a few state courts have balked at this delegation of authority.[9]

2. Cardwell v. State, 264 Ark. 862, 575 S.W.2d 682 (1979); People v. Stout, 116 Mich.App. 726, 323 N.W.2d 532 (1982); State v. Dudley, 104 Idaho 849, 664 P.2d 277 (1983); State v. Harris, 637 S.W.2d 896 (Tenn.Cr.App.1982); State v. McMinn, 197 N.J.Super. 621, 485 A.2d 1072 (1984).

3. 380 F.Supp. 404 (E.D.La.1974), affirmed 511 F.2d 1400 (5th Cir.1975), cert. denied 423 U.S. 867 (1975). Accord: NORML v. Bell, 488 F.Supp. 123 (D.D.C. 1980).

4. Alliance for Cannabis Therapeutics v. D.E.A., 15 F.3d 1131 (D.C.Cir.1994). Alliance for Cannabis Therapeutics v. D.E.A., 930 F.2d 936 (D.C.Cir.1991). In both cases, a rescheduling to Schedule II was unsuccessfully litigated to enable doctors to prescribe marijuana for therapeutic purposes.

5. State v. Mitchell, 563 S.W.2d 18 (Mo. 1978); People v. Schmidt, 86 Mich.App. 574, 272 N.W.2d 732 (1978); State v. Stallman, 673 S.W.2d 857 (Mo.App.1984). The arguments for the scheduling of marijuana by the Federal government are stated in 44 Fed.Reg. 36,123 (1979). A vast array of constitutional arguments against the prohi-

bition of marijuana use including a freedom of expression claim were rejected in People v. Renfro, 56 Hawaii 501, 542 P.2d 366 (1975).

6. For a comprehensive summary of the competing arguments concerning the classification of marijuana, see, Soler, "Of Cannabis and the Courts: A Critical Examination of Constitutional Challenges to Statutory Marihuana Prohibitions," 6 *Conn. L.Rev.* 601 (1974).

7. NORML v. Bell, op. cit. supra note 3.

8. See, in general, Anno., "Validity of Delegation to Drug Enforcement Administration of Authority to Schedule or Reschedule Drugs Subject to Controlled Substances Act," 47 A.L.R.Fed. 869 (1980).

9. In Utah, South Dakota, Michigan, and Georgia, the delegation of legislative power has been held unconstitutional. State v. Gallion, 572 P.2d 683 (Utah 1977); State v. Johnson, 84 S.D. 556, 173 N.W.2d 894 (1970); People v. Turmon, 117 Mich. App. 345, 323 N.W.2d 698 (1982), reversed 417 Mich. 638, 340 N.W.2d 620 (1983); Sundberg v. State, 234 Ga. 482, 216 S.E.2d 332 (1975). In Mississippi, Louisiana and

In United States v. Pastor,[10] the Federal court held that the extensive legislative history and congressional intent evident in the statute indicated that the scheduling authority was delegated to provide flexibility and speed in scheduling of substances. This valid purpose, combined with procedural safeguards and the availability of judicial review, was held to be sufficient protection against arbitrary action. The majority of state courts have adopted a like reasoning.[11]

The Federal Sentencing Guidelines [12] have been contested under the due process and equal protection clauses of the Fourteenth Amendment for imposing a higher sentence for an offense involving crack than for an offense involving cocaine hydrochloride. These challenges assert that the aggravated penalties discriminate against African–Americans [13] who use crack whereas whites use cocaine hydrochloride. Such attacks have been rejected by the Federal appeals court as frequently as they have been made.[14] The Second Circuit [15] has held that higher sentences for crack could be imposed even where the cocaine seized was not in base form, but was only destined to be converted to the base form of cocaine (crack).

Drug testing procedures necessarily require the scientific examination of a person's urine, blood, or hair. Since the results of such testing may be used against a person as incriminating evidence, a number of constitutional protections are impacted.[16] The argument has been made that admitting any test results into evidence violates the Fifth Amendment privilege against self-incrimination. Drug testing does not infringe the Fifth Amendment because the privilege has long been construed to protect persons from state compulsion to reveal testimonial or communicative evidence only.[17]

The search and seizure provisions of the Fourth Amendment present a more realistic opportunity to challenge mandatory drug testing. A search or seizure implicates the Fourth Amendment when there is a legitimate expectation of privacy which has been invaded unreasonably.

Washington the state's delegation of scheduling authority to a federal administrative agency has been voided. Howell v. State, 300 So.2d 774 (Miss.1974); State v. Rodriguez, 379 So.2d 1084 (La.1980); and State v. Dougall, 89 Wash.2d 118, 570 P.2d 135 (1977). Contra, State v. Ciccarelli, 55 Md. App. 150, 461 A.2d 550 (1983).

10.   557 F.2d 930 (2d Cir.1977).

11.   State v. Reed, 14 Ohio App.3d 63, 470 N.E.2d 150 (1983).

12.   18 U.S.C.A. § 3551 (1993).

13.   According to information from the Sentencing Commission, 92.6% of crack defendants are black, 4.7% are white, while 29.7% of powder cocaine defendants are black and 45.2% are white. United States v. D'Anjou, 16 F.3d 604, 612 at note 3 (4th Cir.1994).

14.   A sampling of such rejections would include: United States v. D'Anjou, 16 F.3d 604 (4th Cir.1994); United States v. Parris, 17 F.3d 227 (8th Cir.1994); United States v. Herrera, 16 F.3d 418 (10th Cir.1994); United States v. Tinker, 985 F.2d 241 (6th Cir.1992), cert. denied 113 S.Ct. 1872 (1993). Contra: State v. Russell, 477 N.W.2d 886 (Minn.1991).

15.   United States v. Palacio, 4 F.3d 150 (2d Cir.1993).

16.   Anno., "Validity, Under Federal Constitution, of Regulations, Rules, or Statutes Requiring Random or Mass Drug Testing of Public Employees or Persons Whose Employment is Regulated by State, Local, or Federal Government," 86 A.L.R.Fed. 420.

17.   Schmerber v. California, 384 U.S. 757, 761, 764 (1966).

In Skinner v. Railway Labor Executives Assn.,[18] the Supreme Court held that urine testing for drug metabolites is a Fourth Amendment search. Matters of a most intimate and personal nature would be invaded in the collection of the urine. Indeed, urinalysis can reveal a great deal of private medical facts about a person (for example, the presence of dilantin would reveal that a person is under treatment for the affliction of epilepsy).[19]

Although certain testing schemes have failed constitutional challenges,[20] drug testing of public employees has not been held to be unconstitutional. In *Skinner*,[21] decided the same day as *Von Raab*,[22] the United States Supreme Court held that federal regulations requiring employees of private railroads to produce urine samples for testing implicate the Fourth Amendment, as those tests invade a person's reasonable expectations of privacy. However, the testing was upheld as constitutional under the rationale of *Von Raab*.[23] The Supreme Court in *Von Raab* had held that the validity of a drug testing scheme was to be determined by balancing the public employer's interest in limiting the use of illicit drugs in the workplace against the employee's privacy expectations.[24] It would seem that the logic of this balancing test would limit its application to employees in sensitive areas with some responsibility which would affect the public interest. Private employers, not cloaked with a similar public nexus, would appear to be outside the permissible limits of employee drug testing under the Fourth Amendment as articulated by the U.S. Supreme Court.

IV.　EVIDENTIAL STATUS OF TEST RESULTS

§ 14.22　Expert Qualifications

The determination of whether a witness is qualified to give opinion evidence as an expert is ordinarily within the discretion of the trial court. Its determination will not be reversed unless a clear abuse of discretion is shown. While ordinarily either formal study or practical experience may qualify one as an expert, it would appear that in the area of toxicological-chemical investigations formal education in some related branch of science (chemistry, serology, pharmacology, biochemistry, he-

---

18. Skinner v. Railway Labor Executives Assn., 489 U.S. 602 (1989).

19. Id. at 1413.

20. Numerous courts have held that certain random drug-testing programs involving an element of state action violate the fourth amendment's prohibition against unreasonable search and seizure and that testing must be based on a reasonable suspicion standard. But see, In the Matter of Seelig v. Koehler, 151 A.D.2d 53, 546 N.Y.S.2d 828 (1989); Burka v. New York City Trans. Auth., 680 F.Supp. 590 (S.D.N.Y.1988); and In the Matter of Dozier v. New York City, 130 A.D.2d 135, 519 N.Y.S.2d 135 (1987).

21. Op. cit. supra note 18.

22. National Treasury Employees Union v. Von Raab, 489 U.S. 656 (1989).

23. Id.

24. Id.

matology, etc.) should definitely be required in addition to practical experience in the field in which the witness seeks to qualify as an expert.

It is of course true that, under proper circumstances, even a layman may contribute proper opinion testimony on issues which ordinarily call for expert testimony. Thus, a finance company manager who was the victim of a robbery has been permitted to testify that the accused robber was under the influence of drugs at the time of the robbery, basing his opinion on his experience in observing the physical condition of drug addicts while in the Air Force,[1] but his conclusion was based upon *physical* outward observations.

In some cases, the courts have relaxed the requirement of formal education. In one such case, the court held that a police officer who was not a college graduate might nevertheless testify as an expert in narcotic drug analysis on the basis of other technical training and pretrial experience.[2] Ordinarily, however, higher qualifications should be required.

Formal education *and* practical experience are usually necessary to qualify as an expert in toxicology-chemistry. In Scott v. State,[3] for instance, it was held that a witness was qualified as an expert on the effects of poisons on the human system and competent to testify that death was caused by morphine in the stomach, where it was shown that the witness was a chemist and professor in chemistry who had been for ten years a state chemist and toxicologist, even though he was neither a druggist nor a pathologist. Similarly, a witness who had a Ph.D. in organic chemistry with a specialization in biochemistry, and worked continuously in the field of toxicology for sixteen years was held qualified to testify as to how long it might take for a victim to become asphyxiated and die from carbon-monoxide poisoning.[4]

In today's medico-legal departments, the distinctions between various branches and specialties are becoming easier to make since there is a higher degree of specialization. Provided the suitable educational background is present, the work experience of a scientist often permits him to validly stray into a field which traditionally has been thought of as requiring a different formal training (Ph.D.s vs. M.D. degree holders, for instance). There should be no evidential barriers, therefore, to permitting a witness with a B.S. degree in chemistry to testify as to the results of chemical analyses run according to standard and proven techniques, provided he has had sufficient practical experience in conducting such tests, along with a sound educational background.

§ 14.22

1. Pointer v. State, 467 S.W.2d 426 (Tex.Cr.App.1971). In Howard v. State, 496 P.2d 657 (Alaska 1972), the court held that the addict who used drugs may testify to the narcotic quality of the substance. Similarly, in State v. Johnson, 54 Wis.2d 561, 196 N.W.2d 717 (1972), the court held that a LSD user was qualified to give an opinion that a substance was LSD.

2. White v. People, 175 Colo. 119, 486 P.2d 4 (1971).

3. 141 Ala. 1, 37 So. 357 (1904). See also, Hand v. State, 77 Tex.Crim.R. 623, 179 S.W. 1155 (1915); State v. Carvelle, 290 A.2d 190 (Me.1972), testimony on Duquenois test to identify Cannabis.

4. People v. Richards, 120 Ill.App.2d 313, 256 N.E.2d 475 (1970).

It must be remembered that the field of forensic toxicology is one that borrows from many scientific areas. It requires specialized on-the-job training which is tailored to the type of tasks the toxicologist will be performing in his job. The educational background should be a mixture of analytical chemistry, biology, pharmacology and physiology.

Analytical chemistry is important for its methodology is used in identifying and quantitating organic compounds. Since the toxic compounds encountered in the field of criminal investigation are usually present in biological material, a knowledge of biological phenomena is also required. Most of the compounds dealt with are drugs, so that the expert should also have some basic training in pharmacology. Because a knowledge of body functions is essential to interpret analytical results, some training in physiology is also desirable or even necessary.

In the mid-seventies, a momentum developed in the American Academy of Forensic Sciences to create or co-sponsor credentialing or certification bodies within the various scientific disciplines to which its members belong. As a result of this impetus, there was created and chartered the American Board of Forensic Toxicology, to act as a certifying and recertifying body of professionals in its discipline.

The educational qualifications set by the Board require that an applicant possess an earned Ph.D. or D.Sc. degree in one of the natural sciences from an accredited institution of higher learning whose pertinent educational programs (e.g., chemistry) were also accredited.[5] The applicants must also have had an adequate undergraduate and graduate education in biology, chemistry, and pharmacology or toxicology.

Certification is also dependent upon meeting the professional experience requirements in forensic toxicology. If all requirements are met, a person holding a certificate of qualification—which is valid for three years—may use the designation "Diplomate of the American Board of Forensic Toxicology" (abbreviated "DABFT").

It must be noted that in crime laboratories generally there may not be a clear distinction between job titles and job functions. Examinations of certain types of evidence may be handled in one laboratory by a toxicologist, in another by a chemist or serologist, and in yet another by a criminalist. Therefore, some specialists may be subject to certification from other designated scientific disciplines. Also, certification is not a legal necessity to qualify as an expert, although there is a considerable movement under way among experts themselves to establish their own in-house certification programs.

§ 14.23 General Toxicology Test Results

The general rule for the admissibility of scientific test results is either that the test must be considered reliable and accurate by scientists in the field to which it belongs or that the test results are relevant

---

5. A "grandfather" clause permitted toxicologists who lack the doctorate or other graduate degree but have at least six full years of experience in forensic toxicology to qualify for certification if they applied before December 31, 1977.

to a matter in controversy. Toxicologists, therefore, are frequently permitted to state the effects of certain substances on the human body even though they do not have medical degrees.[1] Physicians are also generally deemed qualified to testify on these matters, even though they may lack practical experience and draw their knowledge solely from books.[2]

When conclusions to be drawn from novel tests properly belong in a broad general field of science, but scientists generally are not yet familiar with it, opinion testimony on the test results is nevertheless admissible upon a showing that those within the field who might be expected to be familiar with it have accepted the test as reliable.[3]

In Coppolino v. State,[4] it was held that the judge did not abuse his discretion in holding admissible expert testimony relating to the death of defendant's wife by a toxic amount of succinylcholine chloride, even though the expert opinion was arrived at by tests which had been developed specially for this case, and which were totally unknown in the specialized field, and on which there was neither literature nor case law. All that was required was a showing that the experts were generally qualified in their field (pathologists) and used recognized toxicological procedures in devising their novel tests.

Hearsay rules are frequently relaxed when an expert's opinion is based in part on laboratory or hospital reports prepared by other experts. Thus, a chemist under whose supervision laboratory analysis of certain specimens was made by another chemist in the laboratory was permitted to testify from the records of the laboratory as to the results of the tests.[5] Some states have statutory provisions making such laboratory reports admissible as exceptions to the hearsay rule. The constitutionality of one such a statute was upheld by the Virginia Supreme Court in Robertson v. Commonwealth.[6] The case dealt with the admission of

§ 14.23

1. Wilson v. State, 243 Ala. 1, 8 So.2d 422 (1942)—mercury; People v. Richards, supra note 9, section 14.21—carbon monoxide; Davis v. State, 116 Neb. 90, 215 N.W. 785 (1927)—strychnine; State v. Crivelli, 89 N.J.L. 259, 98 A. 250 (1916)—chemist's testimony on what portion of morphine and opium would likely be absorbed through system; Hand v. State, 77 Tex.Crim.R. 623, 179 S.W. 1155 (1915)—chemist allowed to testify on effects of strychnine on human body.

2. Hext v. State, 100 Tex.Crim.R. 24, 271 S.W. 81 (1925).

3. People v. Williams, 164 Cal.App.2d Supp. 858, 331 P.2d 251 (1958)—Nalline test. A chemist is also permitted to analyze a small amount of a substance and then give an opinion as to the substance as a whole: People v. Yosell, 53 Ill.App.3d 289, 11 Ill.Dec. 184, 368 N.E.2d 289 (1977). See, infra sec. 14.25.

4. 223 So.2d 68 (Fla.App.1968), appeal dismissed 234 So.2d 120 (Fla.1969), cert. denied 399 U.S. 927 (1970).

5. Preston v. State, 450 S.W.2d 643 (Tex.Cr.App.1970); State v. Clapp, 335 A.2d 897 (Me.1975). Accord: Reardon v. Manson, 806 F.2d 39 (2d Cir.1986).

Contra: State v. Henderson, 554 S.W.2d 117 (Tenn.1977) holding supervising chemist cannot introduce laboratory report of analyst without violating accused's confrontation right.

6. 211 Va. 62, 175 S.E.2d 260 (1970).

Accord: State v. Christianson, 404 A.2d 999 (Me.1979) as to chemist's report on PCP analysis; State v. Smith, 312 N.C. 361, 323 S.E.2d 316 (1984), as to an analyst's report of blood alcohol content. There is no Federal statute specifically authorizing the admission of a laboratory report in lieu of a chemist's testimony. An attempt to

laboratory reports regarding a vaginal swab test for semen, admitted pursuant to a statute which had as its purpose the avoidance of the necessity of summoning as witnesses physicians and technicians who are required to make various pathological, bacteriological, and toxicological investigations in the Chief Medical Examiner's office.

A serious issue of the constitutional right to confrontation would arise if a law sought to insulate the crime laboratory technicians from defense subpoenas. Most reports of crime laboratories (including FBI reports) only state conclusions; they do not state the types of tests conducted. The probative worth of the conclusion depends highly on the type of test conducted and may range from very high to insignificant. Without the testimony of the examiner-witness, the report may easily be given far more significance in court than it rightfully deserves.

Moreover, it must be noted that not all crime laboratories maintain high standards in their examinations. An LEAA funded study in proficiency testing of crime laboratories, conducted by The Forensic Science Foundation, showed in 1977 that many laboratories "flunked" the proficiency test and made erroneous determinations on known test samples submitted to them.

If the report does not qualify as an official record, it may at times qualify for admission under the "business records" exception to the hearsay rule. However, in Wing v. State,[7] the court held that it was error to admit a penitentiary inmate's record containing his blood type in the absence of a statute which requires the keeping of inmates' blood types. In this case the prison hospital administrator testified he did not know who made the actual blood type test or who recorded it on the hospital record.

§ 14.24 Drug Analysis as Evidence

The nature of narcotic substances can be proved by competent expert testimony. Thus, it has been held that where a qualified expert stated he knew the tests which were used to determine whether a substance was morphine, and that he conducted the proper tests, his identification testimony was admissible even though on cross-examination he could not state the names or number of the tests he used.[1]

construe the Federal Rules of Evidence's hearsay rules to make a laboratory report admissible was rejected in United States v. Oates, 560 F.2d 45 (2d Cir.1977), on remand United States v. Oates, 445 F.Supp. 351 (E.D.N.Y.1978), affirmed without opinion United States v. Oates, 591 F.2d 1332 (2d Cir.1978).

7. 490 P.2d 1376 (Okl.Cr.1971); the court held it was harmless error. But in Wesley v. State, 225 Ga. 22, 165 S.E.2d 719 (1969), it was held reversible error to allow in evidence a laboratory report that examination of a specimen contained sperm when there was no showing that person preparing

report was qualified and another doctor relied upon hearsay evidence of report to express his opinion that the victim had had sexual intercourse.

See also, United States v. Oates, 560 F.2d 45 (2d Cir.1977), holding that a chemist's report and worksheet were improperly admitted into evidence, not satisfying Fed. Rule Evid. 803(8).

§ 14.24

1. State v. Baca, 81 N.M. 686, 472 P.2d 651 (1970), cert. denied 81 N.M. 721, 472 P.2d 984 (1970). The narcotic quality of a substance may be shown by testimony of

Although the United States Supreme Court has held unconstitutional a state statute making the status of drug addiction a crime in itself,[2] scientific proof of the drug identity, and even of the status of being under the influence of drugs, can still be used effectively as circumstantial evidence of various miscellaneous drug offenses.

Tests showing that a person is currently under the influence of narcotics have also received judicial approval. In People v. Williams,[3] the California court held that evidence of the Nalline test to indicate recent use of narcotics was properly admitted where it was shown that the test was accepted as a reliable means of detecting the presence of an opiate in a person's system. Even though the test had not yet gained general acceptance in the medical field—because most doctors were as yet ignorant of its existence and use—the court felt that all that is required is a showing that the segment of the medical profession which could be expected to be familiar with it had accepted its results as reliable. In State v. Smith,[4] the court held that testimony regarding the presence of "track marks" found on defendant's arms, one described to be 24 hours old, one between 24 and 72 hours old, and others which were older but without recent scar tissue, was proper proof of guilty knowledge in a prosecution for possession of heroin.

V. SPECIAL DEFENSES

§ 14.25 Quantitative Considerations

1. SAMPLING METHODS

The government may seek to establish through expert testimony that, even though only a fraction of a larger amount of a seized substance was analyzed for the presence of a controlled substance, the entire quantity confiscated can be inferred to be of the same quality as the sample which has been tested. Such an inference from the testing of a sample generally appears in prosecutions where a statutory minimum

the addict-user: Howard v. State, 496 P.2d 657 (Alaska 1972).

See, in general, anno., "Competency of Drug Addict or User to Identify Suspect Material as Narcotic or Controlled Substance," 95 A.L.R.3d 978 (1979). Expert shown to be trained to use standard chemical test to identify Cannabis (Duquenois test) was properly permitted to testify, there being no evidence the test was not a valid one to identify Cannabis or that the witness improperly used the test: State v. Carvelle, 290 A.2d 190 (Me.1972).

On the admission of estimates of quantities of drugs possessed by arrestees for sale, see, United States v. Pugliese, 712 F.2d 1574 (2d Cir.1983) where a DEA agent was permitted to give his expert opinion as to the quantity of a typical heroin purchase

for an addict's own use. Cf: State v. Ogg, 243 N.W.2d 620 (Iowa 1976), holding that police testimony that the amount of LSD "far exceeds what one might possess for personal use" (46 tablets) was improperly admitted as an outright opinion as to defendant's guilt on one of the essential elements of the crime.

2. Robinson v. California, 370 U.S. 660 (1962), rehearing denied 371 U.S. 905 (1962).

3. 164 Cal.App.2d Supp. 858, 331 P.2d 251 (1958). See also, People v. Hightower, 189 Cal.App.2d 309, 11 Cal.Rptr. 198 (1961).

4. 257 La. 896, 244 So.2d 824 (1971).

quantity must be established to sustain the validity of the prosecution [1] or where a certain quantity is alleged in order to prove an intent to sell the controlled substance [2] or to disprove its possession for personal use.[3]

The common theme running through the cases which discuss the propriety of crime laboratory sampling techniques is that the sample tested must be representative of the whole lot [4] and that the selection of the sample must be random in nature.

The sample size and the randomness of its selection can, according to statistical principles, be the linchpin upon which conclusions concerning the nature of the entire lot can properly turn.[5] Sample size selection tables are available [6] as are the rules for random sampling [7] but the courts have not generally given voice to these rules of probability theory as governing legal precepts. In Morrison v. State,[8] for example, the police took a pinch from each bale of green plant material totalling 467 pounds in all. The sum total of the pinches amounted to 18.1 grams, which upon testing proved to be marijuana. The court found the inference strong and persuasive that the untested material was the same as that tested, in spite of the fact that a random "pinch" does not comport with a table of random numbers, a more statistically fine-tuned approach to randomness.[9]

2. THE USABLE OR MEASURABLE QUANTITY RULE

Some state courts [10] and some state legislatures [11] have adopted a rule requiring the prosecution to prove that the defendant possessed a

§ 14.25

1. People v. Yosell, 53 Ill.App.3d 289, 11 Ill.Dec. 184, 368 N.E.2d 735 (1977).

2. State v. Riera, 276 N.C. 361, 172 S.E.2d 535 (1970).

3. In Dutton v. Commonwealth, 220 Va. 762, 263 S.E.2d 52 (1980) 90 grams of marijuana in plastic bags, packaged as if for distribution, found in defendant's car were insufficient to disprove possession for personal use. But in State v. Vaughn, 577 S.W.2d 131 (Mo.App.1979), one bottle out of 180 bottles was tested for and found to contain codeine. The remainder was assumed also to contain codeine, which was beyond that needed for personal use.

4. State v. Absher, 34 N.C.App. 197, 237 S.E.2d 749 (1977). A chemist's visual examination of the entire lot of marijuana and PCP tablets was sufficient to prove the commonality of the whole. In State v. Riera, op. cit. supra note 2, that all tablets had the same manufacturer's markings adequately linked the sample to the whole. See also, Vaughn v. State, op. cit. supra note 3. Some courts have held that a failure to test the entire batch goes to the weight rather than the admissibility of the

expert's testimony. People v. Kline, 41 Ill. App.3d 261, 354 N.E.2d 46 (1976), People v. McCord, 63 Ill.App.3d 542, 20 Ill.Dec. 257, 379 N.E.2d 1325 (1978).

5. See, Ostle and Mensing, *Statistics in Research* 50 (1975); Stuart, *Basic Ideas of Scientific Sampling* (1962).

6. Yamane, *Elementary Sampling Theory* 398–399 (1967).

7. Natrella, *Experimental Statistics* 1–4 (1963).

8. 455 So.2d 240 (Ala.Cr.App.1984). The haphazard, "grab a handful" approach to random sampling is not adequate as a random sampling technique. Cochran, Mosletter and Tukey, "Principles of Sampling," 47 *J.Am.Statis.Assoc.* 13, 23 (1954).

9. *A Million Random Digits with 100,-000 Normal Deviates,* The Rand Corporation (1955).

10. Edelin v. United States, 227 A.2d 395 (D.C.App.1967); Anno, "Minimum Quantity of Drug Required to Support Claim that Defendant is Guilty of Criminal 'Possession' of Drug Under State Law," 4 A.L.R.5th 1.

11. See note 11 on page 861.

usable quantity of a controlled substance. The reasoning underlying this rule is either that the courts interpret the legislative intent in proscribing drug use to be to sanction the possession of more than a mere trace of a controlled substance, even though the amount suffices for qualitative analysis in the crime laboratory, or that the prosecution has conclusively failed to prove a knowing possession of a controlled substance when a usable quantity has not been demonstrated.[12]

No agreement exists among the cases as to the exact amount necessary to constitute a usable quantity. In Cooper v. State,[13] less than two ounces of a loose leafy substance which tested as marijuana was inadequate as a usable quantity, but in People v. Stark,[14] .16 grams of cocaine scraped from a crusher and a screen was considered to be more than a mere trace.

The majority of courts which have rejected the usable quantity rule have adopted a measurable quantity standard which requires only that the amount in question be large enough to be analyzed.[15] To the chemist, the usable quantity rule mandates the quantification of a suspect sample as well as a determination of its nature. A measurable quantity criterion might have the same outcome as a usable quantity rule where the identification of a substance by testing will not be adequate to prove it to be measurable.[16]

3. PURE OR AGGREGATE QUANTITY

Under the Uniform Controlled Substances Act,[17] offenses are punishable based on the amount of the drug possessed by the accused, the higher the amount, the greater the penalty. The Federal Controlled Substances Act [18] as well as the Federal Sentencing Guidelines [19] also graduate punishments based on the weight of the controlled substance in question.

The courts in most Uniform Act states have permitted convictions to stand upon proof of the possession of the proscribed quantity regardless of whether the substance also contains a mix of other, non-prohibited or

---

11. Tx. Health & Safety Code 481.121; Me.Rev.Stat.Ann. tit. 22, sec. 2383—possession of a usable amount of marihuana is a civil violation, not criminal.

12. Cooper v. State, 648 S.W.2d 315 (Tex.Cr.App.1983). It has also been suggested that the government's consumption of the traces of a substance in testing which deprives the accused of an opportunity to retest justifies the existence of the usable quantity rule. Uelman and Haddox, *Drug Abuse and the Law Sourcebook* 6–41 (1984).

13. 648 S.W.2d 315 (Tex.Cr.App.1983).

14. Op.Cit. supra note 10.

15. United States v. Jeffers, 524 F.2d 253 (7th Cir.1975); State v. Kuhrts, 571 S.W.2d 709 (Mo.App.1978); Frasher v.

State, 8 Md.App. 439, 260 A.2d 656 (1970); Partain v. State, 139 Ga.App. 325, 228 S.E.2d 292 (1976). An identifiable quantity rule is statutorily prescribed in Nevada. Nev.Rev.Stat. 453.570 (1975). The Federal statutes require a "detectable amount." 21 U.S.C.A. 802, 841 (1993).

16. United States v. Martinez, 514 F.2d 334 (9th Cir.1975).

17. 9 Uniform Laws Annotated 406 (1979).

18. 21 U.S.C.A. 841 (1993).

19. 18 U.S.C.A. App. X.

prohibited, substances.[20]   A few states, however, take the view that the requisite quantity can be proved only by separating out non-prohibited contaminants or cutting agents and proving that the pure amount which remains is of the quantity required by the statute under which the charge has been drawn.[21]

The pure weight argument has been given more credence in those cases where the statute specifically exempts certain substances from legislative control.   Thus, the exclusion of sterile marijuana seeds from Ohio's marijuana prohibition resulted in the reversal of a marijuana possession conviction where the weight of the sterile seeds had not been subtracted from the total amount which the accused was charged with possessing.[22]

Not infrequently persons charged with drug offenses based on the aggregate quantity of the drug possessed have interposed a constitutional challenge to the charges grounded on a claimed denial of equal protection of the laws.[23]   The defense theory is that it constitutes an arbitrary and unreasonable legislative classification to punish possessors of aggregate quantities equally with the possessors of pure quantities. In People v. Campbell, for example,[24] it was noted that, under the Michigan statutory scheme, one who possesses more than 50 grams of cocaine in the aggregate is punished more severely than one who possesses less than that amount in the pure form.   As a consequence, a person convicted of possessing 51 grams of a mixture containing but 15% of pure cocaine would be more heavily punished than a person convicted of possessing pure cocaine in an amount of 49.9 grams.   Like the Michigan reviewing court in Campbell, other courts have been unpersuaded by the defense's arguments.[25]   The courts have not perceived evidence of unconstitutional legislative irrationality in punishing street dealers in drugs, who tend to cut their product before sale, more heavily than major drug traffickers, who tend to sell the drug in its pure form.

The practice of determining sentence lengths based on the weight of a carrier medium added to the weight of the substance itself has also been challenged.

In Chapman v. United States,[26] the petitioner argued that the blotter paper used as a carrier medium for LSD should not be tacked on to the total weight for sentencing purposes.   Since such an aggregation

20.   People v. Stahl, 110 Mich.App. 757, 313 N.W.2d 103 (1981); People v. Campbell, 115 Mich.App. 369, 320 N.W.2d 381 (1982); People v. Bradi, 107 Ill.App.3d 594, 63 Ill.Dec. 363, 437 N.E.2d 1285 (1982).

21.   State v. Yanowitz, 67 Ohio App.2d 141, 426 N.E.2d 190 (1980); Sims v. State, 402 So.2d 459 (Fla.App. 4th Dist.1981). In Hall v. State, 273 Ind. 425, 403 N.E.2d 1382 (1980), the state's failure to prove the pure weight of the cocaine resulted in a reversal of the conviction. See also, Jones v. State, 435 N.E.2d 616 (Ind.App. 1st Dist.1982)

and Hill v. Commonwealth, ___ Va.App. ___, 438 S.E.2d 296 (1993).

22.   State v. Yanowitz, op. cit. supra note 21.

23.   People v. Stahl, op. cit. supra note 20; People v. Bradi, op. cit. supra note 20; People v. Campbell, op. cit. supra note 20.

24.   People v. Campbell, op. cit. supra note 153.

25.   People v. Bradi, op. cit. supra note 20.

26.   500 U.S. 453 (1991).

would violate the equal protection and the due process clauses of the Fourteenth Amendment.[27] The Supreme Court decided that the Sentencing Guidelines are not arbitrary in defining the weight of a mixture to include the carrier medium. In addition, the Federal statute [28] plainly refers to a "mixture or substance containing a detectable amount." Thus, although the petitioner's pure LSD weighed only 50 milligrams, the entire "mixture" weighed in at 5.7 grams, subjecting the petitioner to the mandatory minimum sentence of five years.

If a statute uses ounces as the measure of the prohibited quantity, whether aggregate or pure, it may become necessary to decide whether the legislature intended the avoirdupois ounce (28.35 grams) or the apothecaries (troy) ounce (31.10 grams). On the general theory that statutory ambiguities are to be resolved in favor of the accused, the court in Horton v. State,[29] reversed a conviction for possessing more than one ounce of marijuana since the weight of the substance totalled only 29.8 grams, short of the weight of the apothecaries ounce.

§ 14.26   The Cocaine Isomer Defense

The cocaine isomer defense had its roots, like the marijuana species defense, in the language of the legislative proscription on cocaine's use, possession or sale. The Federal statute, until 1984,[1] had declared criminal the abuse of "coca leaves and any salt, compound, derivative, or preparation of coca leaves, and any salt, compound, derivative or preparation thereof which is chemically equivalent or identical with any of these substances." The Uniform Controlled Substances Act has an identical phrasing of the cocaine prohibition,[2] both of which statutes were immediately notable in their failure to use the popular word "cocaine."

The statutes, therefore, punished the abuse of derivatives of coca leaves as well as other substances which were chemically equivalent to these derivatives. With this statutory framework in mind, at least one chemist appearing for the defense in cocaine prosecutions asserted,[3] quite correctly, that the only naturally produced derivative of coca leaves was l-cocaine. Therefore, it was maintained that the prosecution bore the burden of proving that the substance involved in a particular cocaine prosecution was not only cocaine but the type known as l-cocaine, to the exclusion of all synthetically produced varieties.

---

27. Id.

28. The section calls for a five-year mandatory minimum sentence for the offense of distributing more than one gram of a "mixture or substance containing a detectable amount" of LSD. 21 U.S.C.A. § 841(b)(1)(B).

29. 408 So.2d 1197 (Miss.1982). Accord: People v. Gutierrez, 132 Cal.App.3d 281, 183 Cal.Rptr. 31 (1982).

§ 14.26

1. 21 U.S.C.A. § 812(c) Sched. II(a)(4) but effective October 12, 1984 the Federal statute was amended to include "cocaine and ecgonine and their salts, isomers, derivatives, and salts of isomers and derivatives."

2. 9 Uniform Laws Annotated sec. 206(b)(4) (1979).

3. Shapiro, "An Introduction to Chemistry for Lawyers," 4 *J.Crim.Def.* 13 (1977).

The death-knell for the cocaine isomer defense came through statutory revisions of the definition of the prohibition of cocaine. In the Federal System, the statutory language was amended to include every conceivable version of cocaine, natural, synthetic or otherwise in terms like "cocaine, its salts, optical and geometric isomers, and salts of isomers"[4] or as cocaine and "all salts, isomers, and all salts of isomers."[5] The states too have reacted to the cocaine isomer defense by amending their statutes, but without using a uniform phraseology. The Texas statute includes cocaine's "salts, isomers (whether optical, position, or geometric) and salts of such isomers."[6] Other states have simply added the word isomer to the cocaine statute.[7] Either way, the cocaine isomer defense has been dispatched to the pages of ancient history in drug control litigation.

§ 14.27 Chain of Custody

The requirement that the integrity of evidence be proved by an accounting of all of the successive steps in the handling of a specimen, from the time of collection by law enforcement authorities to the time of trial, is met, at the trial, by proper "foundation" testimony. Some aspects of "laying a foundation" have been discussed earlier in this chapter in connection with specific types of samples or tests. Some frequently encountered problems in satisfying foundation requirements deserve special emphasis, however.

Blood samples, for instance, must be handled carefully prior to trial and an accounting offered for all changes of possession. In People v. Lyall,[1] the Michigan Supreme Court held that to sustain a conviction for driving while intoxicated on the basis of a blood alcohol test, testimony was required from all the "persons with personal knowledge of each step in the passage of the specimen." The lack of such testimony from the toxicologist who analyzed the blood sample was held to be fatal error. Some courts take a little more relaxed attitude. Thus, in People v. Pack,[2] the court stated that the presumption that a deputy on duty at a crime laboratory had the vial of defendant's blood placed in a refriger-

---

4. 21 U.S.C.A. §§ 802(D), 812(4), 960 (1993).

5. 18 U.S.C.A. App. X, § 201.1 (1993).

6. Vernon's Ann.Tex.Stat. 85–4476–15, § 4.02(b)(3)(D).

7. Ill.—S.H.A. 720 ILCS 570/206, 570/206(b)(4), also 720 ILCS 570/102.

§ 14.27

1. 372 Mich. 607, 622, 127 N.W.2d 345, 352 (1964). The court recognized that a more relaxed burden of proof exists in civil cases. A similarly stringent standard of proof of custody was required in People on Information of Buckhout v. Sansalone, 208 Misc. 491, 146 N.Y.S.2d 359 (Co.Ct.1955); and in People v. Pfendler, 29 Misc.2d 339,

212 N.Y.S.2d 927 (Co.Ct.1961). See also, People v. Anthony, 28 Ill.2d 65, 190 N.E.2d 837 (1963)—narcotics; Rogers v. Commonwealth, 197 Va. 527, 90 S.E.2d 257 (1955)—blood vials.

2. 199 Cal.App.2d 857, 19 Cal.Rptr. 186 (1962). For similar holdings, see: Patterson v. State, 224 Ga. 197, 160 S.E.2d 815 (1968); People v. Wyatt, 62 Ill.App.2d 434, 210 N.E.2d 824 (1965), cert. denied 384 U.S. 992 (1966); Ritter v. State, 3 Tenn.Cr. App. 372, 462 S.W.2d 247 (1970). But where a police officer kept a blood sample overnight in his home refrigerator, which was open to a number of persons, the chain of custody was inadequate. People on Information of Buckout v. Sansalone, 208 Misc. 491, 146 N.Y.S.2d 359 (1955).

ator from which the forensic chemist removed it, was sufficient. The chain of evidence of the vial was held adequately established where no evidence was shown to rebut the presumption of regularity.[3]

The requirement of proper proof of custody finds its origin in the opportunities for tampering, contamination, and error, which arise when possession of a specimen cannot be accounted for at all times. But in some cases courts have found the custody requirement satisfied even though it was shown that blood specimens might have been accessible to persons not called as witnesses at the trial. This is typically the case when the U.S. mail has been used to ship a specimen from one place to another and when it is unknown which postal employees handled the specimen during shipment. In People v. Goedkoop,[4] the custody of the specimen was traced from the time the sample was withdrawn until it was placed in a sealed container and sent, by registered mail, to the laboratory. Testimony then revealed that it was received at the laboratory in the same condition. The court held that there was reasonable ground for a belief that the evidence had not been tampered with in the interval.

And in State v. Lunsford,[5] circumstantial evidence of the improbability that ten pounds of marijuana had been tampered with sufficed in the absence of the direct testimony of one of its custodians. Although marijuana and other drug samples are not uniquely identifiable without some marking, still the chain of custody requirement is satisfied by proof of the reasonable likelihood, not the certainty, that the evidence was not tampered with.

The initial ingredient of foundation testimony should be proof that the specimen or item taken can be definitely identified as having come from the accused.[6] This requires adequate marking or initialing of the specimen or its container. In Easley v. State,[7] for instance, the court held that the custodial chain was broken where it was shown that the police officer did not place any identifying marks on cigarettes seized from defendant, nor did he properly mark the container in which the cigarettes were mailed.

---

3. The subject of blood alcohol intoxication is dealt with in Chapter 3, supra. On the preservation of chemical test evidence and similar chain of custody problems as discussed herein, see the discussion on People v. Hitch, 12 Cal.3d 641, 117 Cal. Rptr. 9, 527 P.2d 361 (1974) in § 3.13, supra.

4. 26 Misc.2d 785, 202 N.Y.S.2d 498 (Co.Ct.1960). See also, Ray v. State, 170 Tex.Crim.R. 640, 343 S.W.2d 259 (App. 1961). But in Tonnan v. State, 171 Tex. Cr.R. 570, 352 S.W.2d 272 (1961), the court held a blood sample inadmissible in a drunken driving prosecution where the sub-

mission form that accompanied the vial showed the date of the offense but not the date the test was taken and the container itself bore an illegible postmark.

5. 204 N.W.2d 613 (Iowa 1973).

6. State v. Foster, 198 Kan. 52, 422 P.2d 964 (1967).

7. 472 S.W.2d 128 (Tex.Cr.App.1971). See also, State v. Reese, 56 Ohio App.2d 278, 382 N.E.2d 1193 (1978) where a drug conviction was reversed when the arresting officer did not mark the envelope in which he placed the pills he seized nor were the circumstances of transport to the laboratory detailed.

However, in Ingle v. State,[8] a laboratory technician inadvertently placed the wrong case number on the package containing the marijuana said to be seized from the defendant. The admission of the evidence was upheld since the exhibit's location at all pertinent times was shown by very specific testimony. Similarly, where the inventory numbers on a bag of heroin admitted into evidence differed from the numbers recorded as placed on the contraband seized from the accused, the court was willing to surmise that the incorrect numbers probably resulted from a typographical or transcription error, not amounting to reversible error.[9]

The judicial penchant for characterizing a break in the chain of custody as only a harmless mistake reached new heights in State v. Nieves[10] when discrepancies between a police officer's record of the contents of an evidence packet and the records of the contents from laboratory personnel diverged markedly. The reviewing court speculated that these differences sprung from a mistake in inventorying the evidence by the police or the laboratory as well as from the sample's changing from a powder to a resinous form during the transmittal from the police to the laboratory.

Marking a container may not be sufficient proof of lack of tampering where an unsealed container is open to the intermeddling of third persons. In State v. Serl,[11] an undercover agent bought a foil packet said to contain PCP, then placed the evidence in his wallet and adjourned to a party where drugs were consumed. The agent spent two nights at this location sleeping in a dormitory-like area where his trousers were accessible to other persons while he slept. The unique facts of this case and the nature of PCP as not bearing any singularly identifiable characteristics induced the court to find the PCP inadmissible for lack of a proper chain of custody.

When the substance is tested in a crime laboratory and then is altered or destroyed between the time of testing and the time of entry into evidence, it has been held that there is no basis for a chain of custody objection. The integrity essential to the chain of custody is necessary only until the testing. Inadvertent, purely accidental and non-negligent alterations in the evidence after testing are not a chain of custody concern.[12] But the failure to insure the integrity of the evidence up to the trial may prevent the government from introducing the item into evidence or otherwise making a tangible display of it to the jury.

The loss of evidence may also give rise to constitutional claims of the government's failure to preserve material evidence which the defense

8. 176 Ind.App. 695, 377 N.E.2d 885 (1978).

9. People v. Perine, 82 Ill.App.3d 610, 37 Ill.Dec. 845, 402 N.E.2d 847 (1980).

10. 186 Conn. 26, 438 A.2d 1183 (1982).

11. 269 N.W.2d 785 (S.D.1978). Contrast People v. Mascarenas, 666 P.2d 101 (Colo.1983) where the fact that unsealed bottles of drugs were in the possession of the pharmacist victim of the armed robbery for one day prior to trial was deemed an insubstantial break in the chain of custody.

12. Riggins v. State, 437 So.2d 631 (Ala. Cr.App.1983) where mice had eaten into the marijuana during its storage after testing.

might seek to retest for its own uses.[13]

VI. TRIAL AIDS

§ 14.28 Locating and Engaging the Expert Witness

The prosecution has little problem in obtaining expert testimony and services from toxicologists, chemists, and other specialists attached to crime laboratories of city, state, or federal law enforcement agencies. It can likewise draw upon the manpower resources of coroner's offices or medical examiner laboratories, public health departments, and county or state hospitals.

The defense is not much hampered in its search for experts. There are many independent, commercial laboratories with highly qualified chemists and toxicologists, who are equipped to conduct analyses of evidentiary samples or verify the prosecution's findings. Experts in the various disciplines can also be found on the faculties of the medical schools and undergraduate chemistry, biology, biochemistry and pharmacology departments.

Local hospitals, independent analytical or clinical laboratories, research laboratories of important industries, can supplement the list of sources of experts. If local sources prove unproductive, further assistance can be sought from national societies.[1]

§ 14.29 Bibliography of Additional Materials on Drugs and Their Control

Achari & Jacob, "A Study of the Retention Behavior of Some Basic Drug Substances by Ion–Pair H.P.L.C.," 3 *J.Liq.Chroma.* 81 (1980).

Alcohol and Drugs in the Workplace: Costs, Controls, and Controversies, Bureau of National Affairs Special Report (1986).

---

13. But the test results on physical evidence which was only inadvertently lost or destroyed was held not to be erroneously admitted in Schwartz v. State, 177 Ind.App. 258, 379 N.E.2d 480 (1978). But if the defense has a right to conduct an independent test of the evidence, its loss would compromise this right. As to the defense right to an independent test, see the guidelines announced in State v. Faraone, 425 A.2d 523 (R.I.1981). Compare to Commonwealth v. Dorsey, 266 Pa.Super. 442, 405 A.2d 516 (1979).

§ 14.28

1. One such society is the American Academy of Forensic Sciences, which counts among its members in the Toxicology and Criminalistics sections a great number of qualified specialists in the various fields dealt with in this chapter. It is located at 410 North 21st, Suite 203, Colorado Springs, Colo. 80904–0669. Two professional associations of toxicologists may be of value. See: The Society of Forensic Toxicologists, c/o Alphonse Poklis, Ph.D., Box 597, MCV Station, Medical College of Virginia, Richmond, VA 23298. Phone 804–786–0272. A listing of Diplomates in Toxicology appears in I Houts, Courtroom Toxicology 5–33 (1981).

Bernheim, *Defense of Narcotics Cases* (2 vols.) (1982 rev.).

Bonnie & Whitehead, *The Marijuana Conviction: A History of Marijuana Prohibition in the United States* (1974).

Bost, "3,4–Methylenedioxymethamphetamine (MDMA) & Other Amphetamine Derivatives," 33 *J.For.Sci.* 576 (1988).

Bowen, et al., "Determination of Heroin by Circular Dichroism," 54 *Analytical Chem.* 66 (1982).

Bowen, et al., "Identification of Cocaine and Phencyclidine by Solute–Induced Circular Dichroism," 53 *Analytical Chem.* 2239 (1981).

Bowen, et al., "Circular Dichroism: An Alternative Method for Drug Analysis," 26 *J.For.Sci.* 664 (1981).

Brotherton & Yost, "Determination of Drugs in Blood Serum by Mass Spectrometry," 55 *Analytical Chem.* 549 (1983).

Budgett, et al., "Comparison of Abbott Fluorescence Polarization Immunoassay (FPIA) and Roche Radioimmunoassay for the Analyses of Cannabinoids in Urine Specimens," 37 *J.For.Sci* 632 (1992).

Canaff & De Zan, "Determination of LSD in Illicit Preparations by Fluorescence Spectroscopy," 3 *Microgram* 194 (1980).

Clanton, *Amphetamines & Other Stimulants,* (1993).

Clark & Miller, "High Pressure Liquid Chromatographic Separation of Dyes Encountered in Illicit Heroin Samples," 23 *J.For.Sci.* 21 (1978).

Clarke's *Isolation and Identification of Drugs* (2d ed. 1986).

de Silva & D'Arconte, "The Use of Spectrophofluorometry in the Analysis of Drugs in Biological Materials," 4 *J.For.Sci.* 184 (1969).

Doyle and Levine, "Review of Column Partition Chromatography of Drugs," 61 *J.Assoc.Off.Anal.Chem.* 172 (1978).

Eldridge, *Narcotics and the Law* (2d ed. 1967).

Fales, et al., "Identification of Barbiturates by Chemical Ionization Mass Spectrometry," 42 *Analytical Chemistry* 1430 (1970).

Finkle & Closkey, "The Forensic Toxicology of Cocaine (1971–1976)," 23 *J.For.Sci.* 173 (1978).

Fulton, *Modern Microcrystal Tests for Drugs* (1969).

Harbin and Lott, "The Identification of Drugs of Abuse in Urine Using Reverse Phase High Pressure Liquid Chromatography," 3 *J.Liq.Chroma.* 243 (1980).

Henderson & Hsia, "The Specificity of the Duquenois Color Test for Marihuana and Hashish," 17 *J.For.Sci.* 693 (1972).

Henderson, "Designer Drugs: Past History & Future Prospects," 33 *J.For.Sci.* 569 (1988).

Hughes & Warner, "A Study of False Positives on the Chemical Identification of Marijuana," 23 *J.For.Sci.* 304 (1978).

Kempe et al., "Application of Thin Layer Chromatography to the Identification of Charred Marijuana," 63 *J.Crim.L., Criminol. & P.S.* 593 (1972).

Krivanek, *Drug Problems, People Problems: Causes, Treatment, & Prevention* (1982).

Laposata & Mayo, "A Review of Pulmonary Pathology & Mechanisms Associated with Inhalation of Freebase Cocaine ('Crack')," 14(1) *Am.J.For.Med. & Path.* 1–9 (1993).

Lawrence and Macneil, "Identification of Amphetamine and Related Illicit Drugs by Second Derivative Ultraviolet Spectrometry," 54 *Anal.Chem.* 2385 (1982).

Manno, et al., "Analysis and Interpretation of the Cannabinolic Content of Confiscated Marijuana Samples," 19 *J.For.Sci.* 884 (1974).

Manura, et al., "The Forensic Identification of Heroin," 23 *J.For.Sci.* 44 (1978).

McLinden and Stenhouse, "A Chromatography System for Drug Identification," 13 *For.Sci.Inter.* 71 (1979).

Miller, *Drugs & the Law: Detection, Recognition & Investigation* (1992).

Nahas, et al., *Marijuana in Science & Medicine* (1984).

Nakamura & Thornton, "The Forensic Identification of Marijuana: Some Questions and Answers," 1 *Jl.Pol.Sci. & Admin.* 102 (1973).

Nielsen, *Handbook of Federal Drug Law* (1986).

N.I.J., *Topical Bibliography: Drug Law Enforcement* (1987).

Randall, *Marijuana & AIDS: Pot, Politics, & PWAS in America* (1992).

Redda, Walker, Barnett, *Cocaine, Marijuana, Designer Drugs: Chemistry, Pharmacology, & Behavior* (1989).

Rothstein, *Drug Testing in the Workplace.* 63 Chi–Kent L.Rev. 683 (1987).

Saferstein, et al., "Drug Detection in Urine by Chemical Ionization Mass Spectrometry," 23 *J.For.Sci.* 29 (1978).

Shirley, "An Approach to Automated Drug Identification," 16 *J.For.Sci.* 359 (1971).

Sloan, *Alcohol & Drug Abuse & the Law* (1980).

Stead et al., "Standardized Thin–Layer Chromatographic Systems for the Identification of Drugs and Poisons," 107 *Analyst* 1106 (1982).

Uelman & Haddox, *Drug Abuse & the Law Sourcebook,* 2 vols. (1983).

U.S. Congress House Committee on Ways & Means, Subcommittee on Trade, *International Drug Enforcement Act: Hearing Before the Subcommittee on Trade of the Committee on Ways and Means,* House of Rep., 99th Congress, 2d. Sess. on H.R. 5310, Aug. 5, 1986 (1987).

Chapter 15

DETERMINING INDIVIDUALITY BY DNA

By
Kenneth E. Melson *

I. INTRODUCTION

* Kenneth E. Melson is a federal prosecutor in Alexandria, Virginia, and an adjunct faculty member of the National Law Center and the Department of Forensic Sciences, The George Washington University, Washington, D.C. The contents of this chapter are the views of its primary author and this text's co-authors, and may not necessarily reflect the views of the United States Department of Justice.

The authors wish to thank Mark D. Stolorow, Director of Operations, Cellmark Diagnostics, Germantown, Maryland, for his review of this chapter and for his insightful comments and suggestions.

I. INTRODUCTION

§ 15.01   Scope of the Chapter

Not since the widespread use of dermatoglyphic fingerprint comparisons began in this country in the 1920's, has the potential for near absolute human identification come so close to reality. First characterized as DNA "fingerprinting" by the pioneers in forensic DNA research, this relatively recent adaptation of a medical research tool to the forensic sciences already rivals traditional fingerprint comparison for virtual certainty in identification.

The characteristics of the deoxyribonucleic acid (DNA) molecule make it perfect for the investigation of violent and sex related crimes. It is highly stable in stains, such as those resulting from a deposit of blood, semen or saliva, and is found in almost all human cells.[1] See Figure 1. Because the DNA molecule is extremely polymorphic, that is, it has slight differences in its characteristics from one individual to another, DNA typing can be almost statistically conclusive in establishing the identity of the contributor of biological fluids or substances.[2]

§ 15.01

1. Waye & Fourney, "Forensic DNA Typing of Highly Polymorphic VNTR Loci," Ch. 7 in Vol. III, *Forensic Science Handbook* (Saferstein, ed.) 1993, p. 359.

2. Kobilinsky, "Deoxyribonucleic Acid Structure and Function—A Review," Ch. 6 in Vol. III, *Forensic Science Handbook* (Saferstein, ed.) 1993, p. 335.

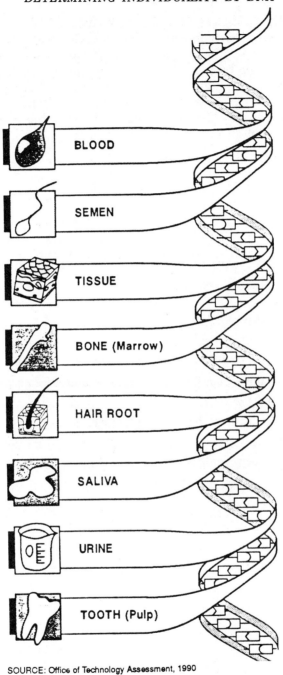

BLOOD

SEMEN

TISSUE

BONE (Marrow)

HAIR ROOT

SALIVA

URINE

TOOTH (Pulp)

SOURCE: Office of Technology Assessment, 1990

Fig. 1.   Sources of DNA. *Courtesy: Office of Technology Assessment.*

In the civil context, DNA typing has also become the dominant method by which determinations of parentage and identity are made. From paternity cases to proof of identity in life insurance claim cases, DNA typing may bring a degree of certainty to identity issues seldom before encountered.

Just as DNA typing can be such a powerful identification tool, it can also be a very dangerous implement of injustice if misused, abused, or, in some cases, unused. Consequently, the collaborative scrutiny being given to DNA typing by the judicial and legislative branches of government, by attorneys for both the government and the defense, and by the very scientists who utilize the process, is imperative, and recognizes the paramount role this invaluable technique will play in the evolution of the forensic sciences and the administration of justice.

This chapter will begin its review of DNA typing by examining the DNA molecule itself and the techniques employed for typing it, including the newly evolving PCR process, the standards for declaring a match and its significance in statistical terms, as well as the vulnerabilities of the typing process. The legal landscape over which DNA typing has travelled will also be explored, along with those issues on the legislative horizon relating to DNA data banking and statutory admissibility. A glossary of useful terms and a bibliography for further research are also provided for the reader's convenience.

§ 15.02 Definitions of Terms [1]

A: Single letter designation of the purine base adenine. Used in diagrams to represent a nucleotide containing adenine.

Adenine: One of the four nitrogen containing molecules present in DNA. Designated by the letter A.

Agarose: Support medium for electrophoresis.

Allele: One of a series of alternative forms of a gene (or VNTR) at a specific locus in a genome.

Amplification: Increasing the number of copies of a desired DNA molecule.

Autoradiograph: The resultant X-ray film after exposure to a radioactive source.

Autosome: Any of the chromosomes other than the sex chromosomes, X and Y.

Band: The visual image representing a particular DNA fragment on an autoradiogram.

Band shifting: The phenomenon where DNA fragments in one lane of an electrophoresis gel migrate through the gel at a different rate of speed than identical fragments in a second lane.

---

§ 15.02

1. The glossary of terms has been compiled from the following sources: Kirby, *DNA Fingerprinting: An Introduction* (1990), pp. 325–342; Committee on DNA Technology in Forensic Science, Board on Biology, Commission on Life Sciences, National Research Council, *DNA Technology in Forensic Science* (1992), pp. 167–172; *Forensic DNA Technology* (Farley & Harrington, eds. 1991), pp. 237–240; and Lovell & Mifflin, "A Glossary for Molecular Biology," 35 *Clinical Chem.* 1816–1818 (1989).

Base pairs (bp): Two complementary nucleotides held together by hydrogen bonds. Base pairing occurs between A and T and between G and C.

Base sequence: Order of bases in a DNA molecule.

Bayes' theorem: A statistical procedure to assess the relative probability of two alternative possibilities.

C: Single letter designation of the pyrimidine base cytosine.

Chromosome: Structure of DNA and associated proteins that contains the hereditary material within the cell. Genes are organized in a linear arrangement in the chromosome.

Controls: Tests performed in parallel with experimental samples and designed to demonstrate that a procedure worked correctly.

Cytosine: One of the four nitrogen-containing molecules in DNA; designated by the letter C.

Denaturation: The process of unfolding of the complementary double strands of DNA to single strands by use of heat or high pH.

Deoxyribonucleic acid: See DNA.

Digested DNA: DNA cleaved by the action of restriction enzymes.

Dot-blot: A DNA analysis system where sample DNA is directly pipetted onto a membrane, as opposed to the Southern blot procedure of enzymatic digestion, electrophoresis, and Southern transfer.

DNA: Deoxyribonucleic acid, the stable double-stranded helical molecule that makes up chromosomes.

Electrophoresis: The process of separating charged molecules, for example, negatively charged DNA fragments, in a porous medium such as agarose, by the application of an electric field. DNA separates according to size with the small fragments moving most rapidly.

Ethidium bromide: An organic molecule that binds to DNA and fluoresces under ultraviolet light and is used to identify DNA.

Exponential increase: An increase at a rate defined by raising a number to a power, for example, 10, 10^2, 10^3.

G: Single letter designation of the purine base guanine.

Gel: Gels, such as agarose or polyacrylamide, used in electrophoresis.

Gene: Unit of heredity. A region of DNA containing the blueprint for specific RNA formation or regulation of the formation.

Genome: Entire set of heredity factors of an organism, contained in the chromosomes.

Genotype: The specific genes that are present in an individual.

Guanine: One of the four nitrogen-containing molecules present in DNA. Designated by the letter G.

Haploid: The nuclear state in which only one member of each homologous chromosome pair is present, for example, human gametes (egg or sperm).

Hardy–Weinberg Law: In a large random intrabreeding population, not subjected to excessive selection or mutation, the gene and genotype frequencies will remain constant over time.

Heterozygote: A diploid organism that carries different alleles at one or more genetic loci on its homologous chromosomes.

Heterozygous: The presence of different alleles at corresponding homologous chromosome loci.

HLA (human leukocyte antigen): Antigens located on the surface of most cells, excluding red blood cells and sperm, that differ among individuals. The locus HLA DQ*a* is used for forensic analysis with PCR.

Homologous: Refers to the chromosome pairs found in diploid organisms. The human has 22 homologous pairs of autosomes (non-sex chromosomes) plus two sex chromosomes per nucleus. The members of each pair have an identical sequence of genes; however, the alleles at corresponding loci may be identical (homozygous) or different (heterozygous).

Homozygote: A diploid organism that carries identical alleles at one or more genetic loci on its homologous chromosomes.

Hybridization: Process of complementary base pairing between two single strands of DNA.

Hypervariable region: A segment of a chromosome characterized by considerable variation in the number of tandem repeats at one or more loci.

In vitro: Means "in glass" and refers to a biological process carried out in the laboratory separate from an organism.

In vivo: Refers to a biological process within a living organism.

Insertion: Addition of one or more nucleotides into a DNA strand. This may result in a gene mutation.

Linkage disequilibrium: The phenomenon of a specific allele of one locus being associated or linked to a specific allele or marker of another locus, on the same chromosome, with a greater frequency than expected by chance.

Linkage: A measure of association between loci. Loci on different chromosomes are nonlinked. Those close together on the same chromosome are closely linked and are usually inherited together.

Locus (pl. loci): A specific position on a chromosome.

Meiosis: The process whereby a sex cell nucleus, after chromosomal replication, divides twice to form four nuclei, each with one-half the original chromosome number.

Minisatellites: Regions of tandem repeat sequence DNA scattered throughout animal (and probably plant) genomes.

Monomorphic bands: DNA fragments of specific sizes found in most individuals. Each different size monomorphic fragment is detected by cleaving genomic DNA with a specific restriction enzyme and hybridizing with a specific monomorphic probe. These fragments have been used as markers for use in quality control, especially as related to band shifts.

Multi-locus: Refers to a number of different loci or positions in the genome. A Multi–Locus Probe is a DNA probe that detects genetic variation at multiple sites.

Nucleotide: Combination of a base with a sugar and phosphate group.

Oligonucleotide: A polymer composed of a few, usually less than 100, nucleotides; usually synthesized by automated machinery and used as primers in the PCR and as probes.

Palindrome: A DNA site where the base order in one strand is the reverse of that in the complementary strand, for example, 5'GAATTC3',3'CTTAAG5'.

PCR: Polymerase Chain Reaction.

Phenotype: Physical make-up of an individual as defined by genetic and nongenetic factors.

Polymerase Chain Reaction: An *in vitro* process whereby specific regions of double-stranded DNA can be amplified more than a million fold using thermal stable Taq 1 polymerase. Oligonucleotide primers must be annealed to the target DNA sequence 5' flanking regions. The PCR may be likened to a molecular xeroxing machine.

Polymorphism: More than one form. See RFLP.

Probe: A fragment or sequence of DNA that hybridizes to a complementary sequence of nucleotides in another single-strand nucleic acid (target).

Putative father: A man accused but not proven to be the biological father of an offspring.

Restriction endonucleases: See Restriction enzymes.

Restriction enzymes: Enzymes (molecular scissors) that cleave double stranded DNA at specific base recognition sites. The sequences at restriction sites are usually different for each enzyme.

Restriction fragment length polymorphism: Variation among different individuals in a population in the size of DNA fragments produced by restriction enzyme digestion of a genomic DNA.

RFLP: See Restriction fragment length polymorphism.

Size Marker: DNA fragment of known size used to calibrate an electrophoretic gel.

Single locus probe: A DNA probe that detects genetic variation at only one site in the genome.

Southern blotting (Southern transfer): Procedure for transferring denatured DNA fragments from an agarose gel to a nylon membrane where it can be hybridized with a complementary DNA probe.

Star activity: Relaxation of the strict canonical recognition sequence of a restriction enzyme specifically resulting in the production of additional cleavages within DNA.

Stringency: Conditions of hybridization that increase the specificity of binding between two single-strand portions of DNA, usually the probe and an immobilized fragment. Increasing the temperature or decreasing the ionic strength results in increased stringency.

T: Single letter designation of the pyrimidine base thymine.

Taq polymerase: A DNA polymerase isolated from the bacterium *Thermus aquaticus* that lives in hot springs. This enzyme is capable of withstanding high temperatures and is, therefore, very useful in the polymerase chain reaction (PCR).

Tandem repeat. The end-to-end duplication of a series or core of identical or almost identical stretches of DNA. See VNTR.

Thymine: One of the four nitrogen-containing molecules present in DNA. Designated by the letter T.

Variable number of tandem repeats (VNTR): The variable number of repeat core base pair sequences at specific loci in the genome. See Tandem repeat. The variation in the length of alleles formed from the repeats provides the basis for unique individual identification.

X-chromosome: A chromosome responsible for sex determination. Two copies are present in the genome of the homogametic sex (female) and one copy in the heterogametic sex (male). The human female has two X-chromosomes and the male one X-chromosome.

Y-chromosome: A chromosome responsible for sex determination in the heterogametic sex (male).

§ 15.03   The Origin of DNA Typing

DNA identity testing is the result of modern biological research which began in the early nineteenth century when the development of both powerful light microscopes and techniques for fixing and staining living tissues first allowed scientists to see into the cell, the basic unit of living material. With this ability, it became possible to begin the process of learning how life reproduces itself and to see the relationship between the content of the individual cell and the characteristics of the species and the individual living organism. It was discovered that every cell results from the growth and splitting of a parental cell into two daughter cells and that every cell has within it a nucleus. By the 1860s, chromosomes had been identified as rod-like bodies within the nucleus. The individual chromosomes within a cell can be distinguished by their size and shape, and for most species the number of chromosomes per cell is constant and is an even number. In 1865, the Austrian monk Gregor Mendel crossed peas, proving that traits like color and shape are controlled by hereditary factors, now called genes, and describing the phenomenon of genetic inheritance. By 1901, science had established that chromosomes are the carriers of all hereditary characteristics.

In 1869, a Swiss scientist discovered a substance known as deoxyribonucleic acid (DNA), which was recognized to be a major constituent of the nucleus. In the 1920s it was learned that DNA was found exclusively on the chromosomes within the nucleus, and by 1944 it became generally accepted that DNA was, indeed, the basic genetic material. Meanwhile, physical chemists and x-ray crystallographers in the United States and Europe were studying the size and shape of the DNA molecule and the spatial relationship of the atoms within it. After much study and experimentation on the part of many scientists, in the spring of 1953, the American scientist James Watson and the British scientist Francis Crick, working together at Cambridge University, England, announced their discovery that DNA is a double Helix in which two chains of nucleotides (the building blocks of nucleic acid) running in opposite directions, are held together by hydrogen bonds between pairs of centrally located bases. The discovery of the DNA structure by Watson and Crick has been recognized as one of the major scientific events of this century and it has caused an explosion in biochemistry that has transformed the science. Its application to forensic identification is merely one aspect of its vast biological implications.

Scientists thereafter proceeded to develop ways to reveal the exact nucleotide sequences and thus to decipher the genetic codes. In 1970, the first enzyme was isolated that cuts DNA molecules at specific sites, a restriction enzyme. Other restriction enzymes were thereafter identified and put to use in segmentation of strands of DNA. These enzymes, together with other developments in DNA technology, led to powerful methods for the sequencing of DNA, enabling specific portions of the separated DNA strands to be examined.

Before forensic scientists focused on DNA, serologists examined variations in blood groups, physiological fluids and tissues in attempts to distinguish biological evidence. The emphasis was on variations in those products which were under genetic control. Now, technology has shifted the emphasis so that the variations or polymorphisms can be studied directly in the actual genetic material, the DNA molecule.[1]

§ 15.04 Introduction to the DNA Molecule

Cells are the foundation of life in plant and animal. Humans have

§ 15.03

1. Committee on DNA Technology in Forensic Science, Board on Biology, Commission on Life Sciences, National Research Council, *DNA Technology in Forensic Science* (1992), p. 32 [hereinafter cited as *DNA Technology in Forensic Science*]; 3 Wecht, *Forensic Sciences* (1992), p. 37C–5; Kobilinsky, "Deoxyribonucleic Acid Structure and Function—A Review," Ch. 6 in Vol. III, *Forensic Science Handbook* (Saferstein, ed.) 1993, p. 288.

approximately 100 trillion cells in their bodies.[1] Each cell is its own manufacturing unit, processing amino acids, simple carbohydrates, lipids and trace elements into proteins, complex lipids, carbohydrates, and nucleic acid, and disposing of the by-products.[2]

Within the cell are chromosomes, which are structures of DNA and proteins carrying hereditary material. Every human nucleated cell has 22 matched pairs of nonsex chromosomes, called autosomes, and two sex chromosomes.[3] One autosome in each pair of chromosomes, plus one sex chromosome, are derived from each parent at the time of conception, for a total of 23 pairs of chromosomes.[4] Along the rod-like chromosomes in the cell's nucleus are genes, which are the basic carriers of inherited traits. Genes, comprised of a coding sequence of DNA nucleotides, are located at particular sites, or loci, on the chromosome. Various versions of genes are called alleles. The autosomal genes are inherited in pairs, and signals the body's cells to make proteins that determine the inherited characteristics of a person.[5] A complete set of chromosomes, with all its genes, is called the genome, and encompasses the total genetic make-up of an individual.[6]

§ 15.04

1. Saferstein, *Criminalistics* (4th ed. 1990), p. 334; Kirby, *DNA Fingerprinting: An Introduction* (1990), p. 8; Kahn, "An Introduction to DNA Structure and Genome Organization," *Forensic DNA Technology* (Farley & Harrington, eds. 1991) [hereinafter cited as Kahn], p. 26.

2. Kirby, *DNA Fingerprinting: An Introduction* (1990), p. 8.

3. The exceptions are the sperm cell and the unfertilized egg, which have 23 unpaired chromosomes each. Baechtel, "A Primer on the Methods Used in the Typing of DNA," 15 *Crime Lab. Dig.*, Supp. 1, 3 (1988) [hereinafter cited as Baechtel].

4. Kirby, *DNA Fingerprinting: An Introduction* (1990), p. 8. The number of chromosomes varies in animals, although the same genetic principles apply.

5. Baechtel, op. cit. note 3, section 15.03. See, *DNA Technology in Forensic Science*, op. cit. note 1, section 15.04, at p. 3.

6. *DNA Technology in Forensic Science*, op. cit. note 1, section 15.03 at p. 34; 3 Wecht, *Forensic Sciences* (1992), p. 37C–7.

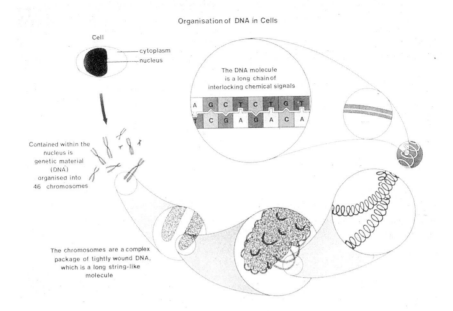

Fig. 2. Organization of DNA in cells. *Courtesy: Cellmark Diagnostics*

Each of the 46 chromosomes has a DNA molecule constructed as a double helix, which together form a combined length of six to nine feet.[7] See Figure 2. The total length of all the DNA molecules in the 100 trillion cells of the human body is 93 billion miles![8] The DNA molecule is found in all cells which have a nucleus, such as white blood cells, sperm, cells found in saliva, cells surrounding hair roots, and bone tissue. Mature red blood cells do not contain the DNA molecule.[9] The entire genetic code is written in its entirety in each cell nucleus, and each set of chromosomes of a single individual is identical,[10] and absent a rearrangement or somatic mutation, they remain constant over a lifetime. DNA molecules are also unique to each person, except in the case of identical twins.[11]

Each single strand of the double helix DNA molecule consists of alternating sugar groups (deoxyribose) and phosphate groups. Linked to the sugar group is a nitrogen-containing molecule called a base. These nitrogenous organic bases, which are covalently linked to the sugar

7. 3 Wecht, *Forensic Sciences* (1992), p. 37C–6; Kahn, op. cit. note 1 at p. 26.

8. Kahn, op. cit. note 1 at p. 26.

9. Giannelli & Imwinkelreid, *Scientific Evidence* (2nd ed. 1993), p. 2; *DNA Technology in Forensic Science* op. cit. Note 4 at p. 33.

10. While DNA in all nucleated cells of the body are identical, the stability of DNA

in forensic evidence might differ significantly from one tissue to another. Lee, et al., "Genetic Markers in Human Bone: 1. Deoxyribonucleic Acid (DNA) Analysis," 36 *J.For.Sci.* 320, 321 (1991).

11. Identical twins are conceived by the union of a single sperm with a single egg, so they will share identical DNA molecules.

group, are of four types, designated as adenine (A), cytosine (C), guanine (G), and thymine (T). They are referred to by the first letter of their name.

A phosphate group, linked to a sugar group with its connected base is called a nucleotide. See Figure 3. The nucleotide is the smallest unit of organization of genetic material, while the largest is the chromosome.

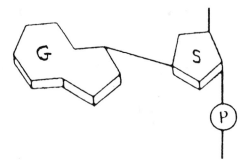

Fig. 3. A single nucleotide is represented. S designates the sugar component, P designates the phosphate group, and G is one of the four bases. *Courtesy: Saferstein, Criminalistics (4th Ed., 1990), Prentice–Hall.*

These nucleotide units repeat themselves as they form one strand of the double helix. See Figure 4. Consequently, the DNA molecule is characterized as a polymer, that is a large molecule made by linking together a series of repeating units, in this case the nucleotides depicted in Figure 4.[12]

12. Saferstein, *Criminalistics* (4th ed. 1990), p. 344; *DNA Technology in Forensic Science*, op. cit. note 1, section 15.03, at p. 33; 3 Wecht, *Forensic Sciences* (1992), p. 37C–5.

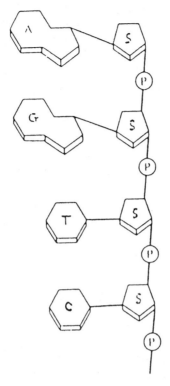

Fig. 4. Repeating nucleotides form one strand of the double helix. The sugar and phosphate groups join together to form one strand of the double helix. *Courtesy: Saferstein, Criminalistics (4th Ed., 1990), Prentice–Hall.*

A single strand of the double helix DNA molecule defines how the other strand in the same helix will look. This is because the strands are complementary in nature.[13] The two single strands of the helix bond together by the linkage of the bases by hydrogen bonds in a predetermined manner. This is called base pairing. Adenine (A) always bonds to thymine (T), and guanine (G) always bonds to cytosine (C). Base pairing results in a double helix DNA molecule having the appearance of a twisted ladder or spiral staircase, where the rungs or steps are the base pairs (A–T, G–C, T–A or C–G) and the side supports are the sugar and phosphate groups. See Figure 5.

13. 3 Wecht, *Forensic Sciences* (1992), p. 37C–6.

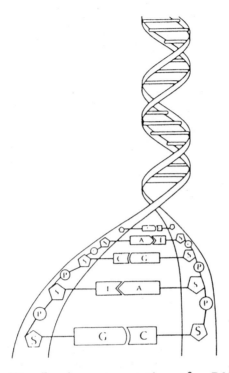

Fig. 5. A representation of a DNA double helix. Notice how the bases G and C pair with one another, as do the bases A and T. This is the only arrangement in which the two DNA strands can align with one another in a double helix configuration. *Courtesy: Saferstein, Criminalistics (4th Ed., 1990), Prentice–Hall.*

While the bases bond to each other in specifically determined pairs, the individual bases attach to the sugar groups in any order, creating a tremendous potential for variations in the sequencing of bases. An example of this potential is a strand of DNA molecule only 10 nucleotides (base pairs) long (i.e. a sequence of ten sugar groups, each to which a phosphate group and one of the four bases are linked) which has 4^{10} or 1,048,580 different possible sequences.[14]

14. Budowle, Deadman, Murch and Baechtel, "An Introduction to the Methods of DNA Analysis Under Investigation in the FBI Laboratory," 15 *Crime Lab. Dig.* 8, 9 (1988); 3 Wecht, *Forensic Sciences* (1992), p. 37C–5. When measuring a strand of DNA, its length is normally described by the number of base pairs (bp). In the example given, the unit measurement of the strand would be 10 bp. Strands reaching into the thousands of base pairs would be measured in kilobases (kb). 3 Wecht, *Forensic Sciences* (1992), p. 37C–6. The length of an average human chromosome is 100,000 kb. There are about three billion base pairs collectively in all the human chromosomes. Saferstein, *Criminalistics* (4th ed. 1990), p. 346.

A sequence of two complementary strands of a double helix DNA molecule's base pairs might look like Figure 6.

– A – C – G – T – A – A – A – A – G – T – T – C – C –

– T – G – C – A – T – T – T – T – C – A – A – G – G –

Fig. 6.[15]

The order, or sequence, of these base pairs is the genetic code and determines the role and function of the DNA molecule.[16] Certain protein producing sequences of DNA nucleotides, which are the genes, result in visible traits in the individual, such as eye and hair color. Many of these base pair sequences are common to everyone, since they account for the common or class characteristics of all human beings.

In the haploid human genome (one set of the 23 pairs of chromosomes), there may be up to an estimated 100,000 genes, or protein coding sequences, with an approximate length of 5–10 kb. Most of these genes are only present as a single copy.[17]

In addition, there are other sequences such as signal sequences and spacer DNA, which, along with the protein coding DNA (genes), account for approximately 70 to 80 percent of the total human genome. Repetitive copies of primarily non-coding sequences make up the remaining 20 to 30 percent of the genome. These remaining sequences of base pairs have no or an uncertain function, but are the primary focus of DNA typing, because of their interindividual genetic variation.[18]

§ 15.05   The Foundation of DNA Typing

1.   VARIABLE NUMBER OF TANDEM REPEAT POLYMORPHISMS (VNTRs)

The DNA molecule is ideally suited to forensic typing because it is polymorphic in nature. Polymorphism refers to different forms (variations) of the same structure, the DNA molecule in this case, or more specifically, the alleles (particular variations of base pair sequences) within the DNA molecule.[1] For forensic science purposes, it is the variation between individuals which makes discrimination and, therefore, individualization possible. Consequently, when examining the DNA molecule, it is the variations, or polymorphisms, within it which are important.

The variations in DNA base pair sequencing result from several types of mutations: point mutation, and insertion/deletion mutation of

15. Baechtel, op. cit. note 3, section 15.-04.

16. Saferstein, *Criminalistics* (4th ed. 1990), p. 346; Giannelli & Imwinkelreid, *Scientific Evidence* (2nd ed. 1993), p. 2.

17. Fowler, Burgoyne, Scott, Harding, "Repetitive Deoxyribonucleic Acid (DNA) and Human Genome Variation—A Concise Review Relevant to Forensic Biology," 33 *J.For.Sci.* 1111, 1112 (1988).

18. Id. at 1112–1113.

§ 15.05

1. Kirby, *DNA Fingerprinting: An Introduction* (1990), p. 24. The terms "variation" and "polymorphism" are used interchangeably in DNA typing.

the type appearing as a point mutation, both of which affect only a *single* base pair, and neither of which are particularly helpful in DNA typing.[2] Of greater use in DNA typing, is the polymorphism created by a second form of insertion/deletion mutation, which is more variable in character than the single nucleotide mutations.[3] This type of polymorphism results from variations in DNA duplication which create short, repetitive units of DNA material arranged in tandem. These repeating sequences of base pairs, usually 10 to 50 bp in length, are referred to as variable number of tandem repeat (VNTR) polymorphisms.[4]

VNTRs are non-coding DNA nucleotide sequences. While the number of base pairs involved in a repeated sequence might be relatively small, the number of repeats of a specific sequence can be large, resulting in variations in the length (number of base pairs) of the VNTRs. The number of repeats may also vary considerably in number between individuals. These variations form the basis of VNTR polymorphisms,[5] and are significantly responsible for allowing forensic scientists to distinguish one individual from another through DNA typing. The numerous possibilities for the sequence of base pairs, the number of base pairs within a repeating unit, and the number of times a unit can repeat itself within a DNA molecule are staggering, and give an idea of the potential for identifying differences among individuals.

Another factor allows for very discrete discrimination between individuals. Each cell carries an homologous pair of chromosomes, referring to the chromosome pairs found in a diploid organism, in which one chromosome of each pair is inherited from each parent.[6]

Although each chromosome in a pair has identical sequences of genes, there may be different alleles in the form of VNTRs at corresponding loci on each chromosome. An individual showing differences of that kind between two chromosomes at a particular locus is called a heterozygote, and is considered to be heterozygous, having different alleles for that locus. On the other hand, an individual who shows no difference between two homologous chromosomes at corresponding loci is a homozygote, or homozygous, having two identical alleles.[7] Heterozygosity is a measure of genetic variability.

2. 3 Wecht, *Forensic Sciences* (1992), p. 37C–9—37C–10. They are sometimes referred to as single-nucleotide differences. *DNA Technology in Forensic Science,* op. cit. note 1, section 15.03, at p. 35.

3. There are many mutations in an individual's genome. The great majority of these mutations do not produce disease, because the changes do not involve the critical DNA sequences which code for proteins. Witkowski, "Milestones in the Development of DNA Technology," *Forensic DNA Technology* (Farley & Harrington, eds. 1991), p. 13.

4. 3 Wecht, *Forensic Sciences* (1992), p. 37C–9; Waye & Fourney, "Forensic DNA Typing of Highly Polymorphic VNTR Loci," Ch. 7 in Vol. III, *Forensic Science Handbook* (Saferstein, ed.) 1993, p. 361; *DNA Technology in Forensic Science,* op. cit. note 1, section 15.03, at pp. 34–35. VNTR polymorphisms are also referred to as "minisatellite" polymorphisms. Fowler, et al., op. cit. note 17, Section 15.04 at 1116.

5. 3 Wecht, *Forensic Sciences* (1992), p. 37C–14.

6. 3 Wecht, *Forensic Sciences* (1992), p. 37C–9.

7. 3 Wecht, *Forensic Sciences* (1992), p. 37C–9.

The statistical significance of more than one VNTR is affected by a phenomenon called linkage disequilibrium. One of Mendel's two laws is the law of independent assortment. According to that principle, different pairs of alleles, if located on separate chromosomes, or far apart on the same homologous chromosome pair, sort independently into a reproductive cell.[8] Thus, when two polymorphic sites are examined, the inheritance at one site is independent of that at the other site. In other words, which allele is inherited at site one bears no relationship to which allele is inherited at a second site elsewhere on the same or a different chromosome.

Two sites on the same chromosome may be transmitted independently, if they are distant enough from each other. However, when they are too close together, there may be a deviation from independent inheritance as described above. Instead, the alleles at the two sites could tend to be transmitted together, causing a phenomenon called linkage disequilibrium.[9] Consequently, when using more than one VNTR for comparison purposes, this phenomenon must be considered in determining the statistical significance of their appearance.

2.   RESTRICTION ENZYMES

VNTR polymorphisms are useful for DNA typing only if they can be detected and isolated. This can be done by identifying specific sequences (alleles) and cutting the double helix both before and after each such sequence (but not in the middle of the key sequence), resulting in a fragmentation of the DNA molecule. The mechanism for such an operation is the use of restriction enzymes, also known as restriction endonucleases. The restriction enzymes are naturally occurring protein molecules of bacterial origin, and can be thought of as specialized scissors which cut (cleave) the double helix DNA molecule at only each locus where it recognizes a specific sequence of bases.[10]

The points at which the restriction enzymes cut the DNA molecule are called restriction or recognition sites, and appear on both sides of a repeated sequence. These recognition sites are specific base sequences usually 4 to 6 bp long and are palindromic, that is, the order of the bases in the recognition site on one DNA strand is the exact reverse of that in the complementary strand.[11] Thus, the restriction enzyme Taq 1, for example, cleaves the DNA wherever it recognizes the sequence TCGA.

8. Kirby, *DNA Fingerprinting: An Introduction* (1990), p. 7.

9. *DNA Technology in Forensic Science,* op. cit. supra note 1, section 15.03.

10. Baechtel, "A Primer on the Methods Used in the Typing of DNA," 15 *Crime Lab.Dig.,* Supp. 1, 3, 4 (1988); Budowle, Waye, Shutler and Baechtel, "HAE III—A Suitable Restriction Endonuclease for Restriction Fragment Length Polymorphism Analysis of Biological Evidence Samples," 35 *J.For.Sci.* 530 (1990); Saferstein, *Criminalistics* (4th ed. 1990), p. 351; 3 Wecht, *Forensic Sciences* (1992), p. 37C–10.

11. Kirby, *DNA Fingerprinting: An Introduction* (1990), p. 23.

Its complementary sequence contains the same bases, but in reverse order, and would be AGCT.[12] See Figure 7.

VNTR POLYMORPHISM

–**T**–**C**–**G**–**A**–G–T–C–A–G–T–C–A–G–T–C–A–G–T–C–A–**T**–**C**–**G**–**A**–

–**A**–**G**–**C**–**T**–C–A–G–T–C–A–G–T–C–A–G–T–C–A–G–T–**A**–**G**–**C**–**T**–

| RECOGNITION | RECOGNITION |
| SITES | SITES |

Fig. 7.

3. RESTRICTION FRAGMENT LENGTH POLYMORPHISMS (RFLP)

The cleavage of the DNA molecule at these recognition sites by the restriction enzymes, results in the digestion (segmentation) of the molecule into fragments of different lengths. The length of each fragment depends on the number of base pairs between recognition sites. These digested fragments (individualized VNTRs) are called restriction fragment length polymorphisms (RFLPs).[13] Variations in the number and length of these restriction fragments occur among individuals when their DNA sequences differ between the recognitions sites cut by the restriction enzyme.

Although there may be differences in the number of base pairs between the RFLPs at similar areas of the genome among two individuals, the sequences of the base pairs are likely to be similar.[14] The differences among base pair sequences, in this instance those composing VNTRs, between individuals allow for a useful comparison of RFLPs. RFLPs are also very common and exist throughout the genome. In addition, they are easy to analyze using standard techniques utilized in molecular biology laboratories.[15] In 1985, Alec Jeffreys identified VNTR loci which were highly polymorphic. By 1987, at least 77 VNTR loci had been identified in the human genome, and more are constantly being discovered.[16] These hypervariable polymorphisms are extremely useful in identifying individuals because of the remote possibility that two individuals other than identical twins would by chance have the same

---

12. 3 Wecht, *Forensic Sciences* (1992), p. 37C–11. Another restriction enzyme is Hae III, which has been selected by the FBI as the restriction enzyme of choice for RFLP typing, and which is described in Budowle, et al., op. cit. note 10, section 15.05, at 530. The preferable attributes of a restriction enzyme for forensic applications are described by the authors.

13. 3 Wecht, *Forensic Sciences* (1992), p. 37C–10.

14. 3 Wecht, *Forensic Sciences* (1992), p. 37C–11.

15. Witkowski, "Milestones in the Development of DNA Technology," *Forensic DNA Technology* (Farley & Harrington, eds. 1991), p. 14.

16. 3 Wecht, *Forensic Sciences* (1992), p. 37C–15.

RFLPs.[17]

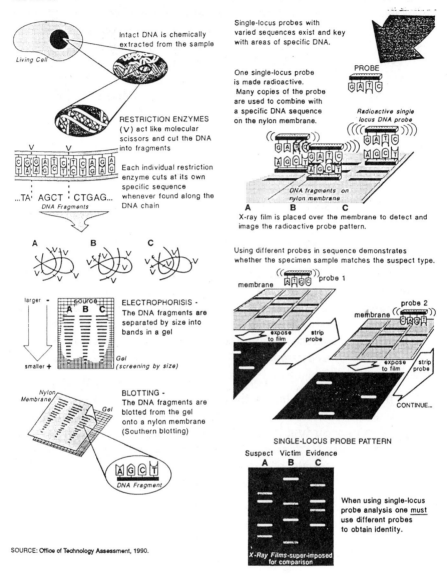

SOURCE: Office of Technology Assessment, 1990.

Fig. 8.   Diagram of RFLP Process.

4.   THE DETECTION OF RFLPs

The basic technique for the detection of restriction fragment length polymorphisms in a forensic laboratory setting for purposes of identifying the donor of biological fluid, stains, tissue or other substances, has been drawn from molecular biology laboratories involved in medical and

17.   Witkowski, *supra* note 15.

genetic research. While discussing the transfer to, and use of this technology in the forensic setting, the differences between the pristine samples in a medical laboratory [18] and the often times contaminated and mixed crime scene samples in a forensic laboratory must be kept in mind. Some observers contend that forensic samples create a host of problems which potentially have an impact on the reliability of the typing process, some of which will be discussed later in this chapter.

II. THE DNA TYPING PROCESSES

§ 15.06   RFLP–Based Typing Process

1.   EXTRACTION OF DNA SAMPLES

The typing procedure in the forensic laboratory begins with the isolation of the DNA from the questioned biological samples and the known samples of the victim and any suspects submitted for analysis. The quality of the testing results depends, as with any biological test, on the quality of the specimen submitted for analysis. The samples must be handled and stored properly to avoid unnecessary degradation or contamination.[1]

The procedure for isolating the genomic DNA from forensic specimens has been described as "relatively simple," and, while variation in procedure occurs according to sample type, the basic process is the same for all sample types.[2] The objective of the extraction procedure is to recover the greatest yield of high molecular-weight DNA, from which restriction enzyme inhibitors, such as protein, are absent.[3]

The cellular material in the forensic sample is suspended in a buffered solution and lysed. Cellular debris is then removed by an extraction technique and the remaining genomic DNA is precipitated.[4] The procedures for extraction can be performed either by automated or

---

18. Exception has been taken to the statement that forensic samples, which often have degraded or modified DNA, small amounts of DNA see Figure 8, or mixtures of DNA from several sources, are inherently different from clinical samples. Blake, Mihalovich, Higuchi, Walsh, Erlich, "Polymerase Chain Reaction (PCR) Amplification and Human Leukocyte Antigen (HLA)–DQ*a* Oligonucleotide Typing on Biological Evidence Samples: Casework Experience," 37 *J.For.Sci.* 700, 721–722 (1992).

§ 15.06

1. Kirby, *DNA Fingerprinting: An Introduction* (1990), pp. 52–55.

2. Waye & Fourney, "Forensic DNA Typing of Highly Polymorphic VNTR Loci," Ch. 7 in Vol. III, *Forensic Science Handbook* (Saferstein, ed.) 1993, p. 363.

3. Kirby, *DNA Fingerprinting: An Introduction* (1990), p. 55.

4. Waye & Fourney, supra note 2 at p. 365. Methods for the recovery of DNA from liquid bloods, dried stains, and vaginal swabs are discussed in Baechtel, "Recovery

manual systems.[5]

A differential extraction system is used in sexual assault cases where specimens examined may be a mixture of DNA donated by a male and female. Sperm and female epithelial cells, for example, may be present in the postcoital vaginal swabs of an assault victim. The same may be true of oral swabs obtained from a female victim of oral sodomy. To avoid a mixture of male and female DNA resulting from the general extraction method, a process is utilized to isolate the intact sperm heads from other cellular material found on the swabs.[6] This process may not always result in an absolute separation of the male and female fractions, and some cross-contamination may still remain. Sex-typing tests can provide a good indication of the success of the separation. Despite cross-contamination, the interpretation of a mixed sample VNTR pattern is considered to be relatively simple and highly probative.

The success of RFLP typing depends in great measure on the amount and quality of the DNA present. A greater quantity of DNA is needed for the RFLP method than for the PCR method of typing. It is also difficult to detect high molecular-weight alleles from highly degraded samples.[7]

A "yield gel" is prepared to determine the quantity and quality of the DNA extracted from a specimen. A small portion of the unknown and undigested DNA sample is subjected to agarose gel electrophoresis. Control samples of DNA of known concentration, and size markers, are also included.[8] Staining with ethidium bromide allows the DNA to be visualized by ultraviolet light fluorescence. A discrete high molecular-weight band, greater than 20 kb, normally indicates intact DNA of suitable molecular weight for RFLP typing.[9] Partially degraded DNA forms a long smear of large to small fragments on the gel. Highly degraded DNA has a singular presentation as a diffuse spot near the dye migration position.

2. DIGESTION OF DNA WITH RESTRICTION ENZYMES

Once DNA of sufficient quantity and quality is extracted from the questioned and known samples, it is digested by exposure to restriction enzymes, as explained earlier in this chapter. Several hundred restric-

of DNA from Human Biological Specimens," 15 *Crime Lab.Dig.* 95 (1988).

5. See generally: Kirby, *DNA Fingerprinting: An Introduction* (1990), pp. 51, 55–68; Waye & Fourney, supra note 2; Kahn, "An Introduction to DNA Structure and Genome Organization," *Forensic DNA Technology* (Farley & Harrington, eds. 1991), p. 39.

6. See generally: Kirby, *DNA Fingerprinting: An Introduction* (1990), p. 63; Waye & Fourney, supra note 2 at p. 365; Baird, "Analysis of Forensic DNA Samples

by Single Locus VNTR Probes," *Forensic DNA Technology* (Farley & Harrington, eds. 1991), p. 39.

7. Waye & Fourney, supra note 2 at p. 368.

8. The yield gel cannot distinguish between human DNA and nonhuman DNA. "Slot blot" quantification can quantify the amount of human DNA. Waye & Fourney, supra note 2 at p. 369.

9. Waye & Fourney, supra note 2 at p. 369.

tion enzymes have been discovered.[10]   When choosing a restriction enzyme for RFLP typing, it is important to choose an enzyme which has recognition sites flanking the VNTRs.   Cleavage within a repeat sequence, that is, within the VNTR itself, must be avoided, because it will obviously affect the size of the resulting RFLPs by breaking the RFLP fragment of interest into many smaller fragments.[11]

If chosen properly, and implemented correctly,[12] a restriction enzyme should cleave an individual's DNA in the same location every time, producing the same length restriction fragments.   Since different individuals have varying numbers of repeating base pairs comprising the VNTRs between recognition sites, the fragment lengths or RFLPs will differ among individuals.[13]

3.   ELECTROPHORESIS OF THE RESTRICTION FRAGMENTS

After the DNA molecule is segmented into fragments by the restriction enzymes, they must be sorted by size to assist in the analysis.   The sorting is accomplished by using agarose gel electrophoresis.   Samples of the digested DNA are placed in wells at the negative electrode end of a slab of 1% agarose gel, which acts like a molecular sieve.   An electrical current is applied to the gel and the negatively charged DNA fragments migrate through the gel toward the positive electrode.   The smaller fragments (measured in base pairs) migrate further toward the positive end of the gel.   The larger the fragments are, the less they migrate. The result is a continuum of fragment sizes from largest to smallest, increasing in distance from the negative electrode, where the sample was originally placed.[14]   See Figure 9.   The distance which the DNA fragments migrate on the gel is inversely proportional to the length, measured in base pairs, of the fragments.

NEGATIVE ELECTRODE

–A–C–A–T–C–A–T–C–A–T–C–A–T–C–A–T–C–A–T–
–T–G–T–A–G–T–A–G–T–A–G–T–A–G–T–A–G–T–A–

–A–C–A–T–C–A–T–C–A–T–
–T–G–T–A–G–T–A–G–T–A–

POSITIVE ELECTRODE

Fig. 9.[15]

Along with samples of the DNA from the victim, suspect, and questioned specimens, control DNA and size markers are also included.

10.   Two examples of popular restriction enzymes are Hae III, which recognizes the sequence 5′–GGCC–3′, and Pst I, which recognizes 5′–CTGCAG–3′. Waye & Fourney, supra note 2 at p. 369; Baird, supra note 6 at p. 41.

11.   Kirby, *DNA Fingerprinting: An Introduction* (1990), pp. 94, 143.

12.   Digestion of DNA is a routine procedure involving the incubation of DNA and the restriction enzyme pursuant to conditions prescribed by the supplier of the restriction enzyme.

13.   Giannelli & Imwinkelreid, *Scientific Evidence* (2nd ed. 1993), p. 6.

14.   Waye & Fourney, supra note 2 at p. 96.

15.   Modified from Baechtel, "A Primer on the Methods Used in the Typing of

The size markers, also known as sizing ladders, are placed in every four to five lanes to assist in correcting for electrophoretic variations.[16] These markers are commercially prepared solutions containing DNA fragments of known, predetermined length. On the final autoradiograph, these size markers appear as an array of bands relatively evenly distributed (usually 100 bp apart) along the length of the gel. The size of the DNA bands in the sample lanes can be determined by comparison to the size markers of known length which are nearest in location to each sample DNA band.[17]

Ethidium bromide is used to stain the gel, which allows for visualization under ultraviolet irradiation. Photographs of the electrophoretic results are then taken.

The arrays of DNA fragments appearing on the agarose gel as a result of electrophoresis must be immobilized before further steps can be taken in DNA typing. Immobilization is accomplished by transferring the DNA to a thin nylon membrane so as to create a display of the DNA identical to that on the agarose gel. This transfer is referred to as Southern transfer or Southern blotting.

The first step in Southern blotting is to denature the DNA by soaking the gel in an alkali solution, or exposing it to specific temperatures.[18] Denaturing unfolds and separates the complementary double stranded DNA helix into two single strands. The thin nylon or nitrocellulose membrane is then placed on the surface of the gel. Capillary action, direct vacuum, or vertically applied electrical current, draws a transfer solution through the gel and the membrane, causing the single-stranded DNA fragments to transfer from the gel to the membrane.[19] Finally, the transferred DNA fragments are covalently bonded to the membrane by baking or exposure to ultraviolet irradiation.[20] To confirm the success of the transfer, the agarose gel can be stained with ethidium bromide and examined under ultraviolet light. An incomplete

DNA," 15 *Crime Lab.Dig.*, Supp. 1, 3, 5 (1988). (The base pairing of the smaller fragment as shown in the *Digest* appears to be incorrect.)

16. Kirby, *DNA Fingerprinting: An Introduction* (1990), p. 96; Baird, op. cit. note 6 at p. 43. These authors, in their respective texts also suggest an appropriate arrangement of lanes.

17. Springfield v. State, 860 P.2d 435, 445 (Wyo.1993); United States v. Yee, 134 F.R.D. 161, 172 (N.D.Ohio 1991), affirmed 12 F.3d 540 (6th Cir.1993).

18. Budowle, Deadman, Murch and Baechtel, "An Introduction to the Methods of DNA Analysis Under Investigation in the FBI Laboratory," 15 *Crime Lab.Dig.* 8, 9 (1988).

19. Waye & Fourney, "Forensic DNA Typing of Highly Polymorphic VNTR Loci," Ch. 7 in Vol. III, *Forensic Science Handbook* (Saferstein, ed.) 1993, pp. 373–374; 3 Wecht, *Forensic Sciences* (1992), p. 37C–17.

20. 3 Wecht, *Forensic Sciences* (1992), p. 37C–17.

transfer, however, cannot be corrected because of the removal of the membrane from the gel.[21]

4. HYBRIDIZATION WITH PROBES

The nylon membrane now contains the unwound, single-stranded fragments resulting from the denaturation. Only certain fragments are of interest for comparison and identification purposes. These restriction fragments must be located and visualized. To accomplish that, DNA probes are introduced to bond with the single-stranded restriction fragments of interest. A probe is itself a short, single-stranded segment of DNA which embodies a specific sequence of base pairs, which will bond to its complementary sequence.[22] The probes act as templates for the sequences which are subjects of the search. When the probe and their complementary, membrane-bound fragments find each other and bond, a process called hybridization takes place. The strength of the bond between the probe and the DNA fragment depends on the degree to which they are homologous. Identical sequences complementary to the probe bond (hybridize) very strongly. Those that are not as identical do not have as strong a bond.[23] See Figure 10.

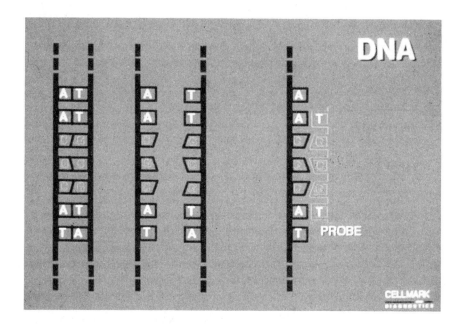

Fig. 10. Denatured DNA fragments hybridize with probes. *Courtesy: Cellmark Diagnostics*

21. Waye & Fourney, supra note 19, page 374.

22. A description of the development of a DNA probe can be found in Budowle et al., supra note 18 at p. 11.

23. 3 Wecht, *Forensic Sciences* (1992), p. 37C–17; Waye & Fourney, supra note 19 at p. 374.

In order to locate the hybridized sequences and later visualize them, one or more reporter molecules are incorporated into the probe's sequence. The reporter molecule is a single nucleotide within the sequence which carries a radioisotope of phosphorous in its phosphate group.[24] Probes used in forensic science contain many reporter molecules in order to maximize the sensitivity of the DNA analysis.

The probes and the DNA fragments on the membrane are allowed to hybridize in a hybridization solution. Strands of the probe which do not hybridize are washed off, leaving on the membrane the digested (non-hybridized) and the newly hybridized DNA from the samples originally subjected to the agarose gel electrophoresis.

Stringency conditions of the wash, including the salt concentration and temperature, affect the sensitivity and specificity of the hybridization. High stringency washes, usually used for single locus probes, remove all strands of the probe which are not tightly bound to fragments carrying sequences identical to itself. Low stringency washes leave probe fragments hybridized to the membrane-bound DNA fragments with identical or very similar sequences, and are of particular value for multi-locus probes.[25]

After washing off the non-hybridized probe with a wash of appropriate stringency to the typing process being used, the membrane is exposed to a photographic film. This exposure creates a visual image of the hybridized DNA because of the radioactive isotopic reporter molecule in the probe. The non-hybridized DNA fragments do not show up on the resulting autoradiograph, leaving a useful visual image of the targeted restriction fragments. The image is in the form of bands appearing at various locations on the autoradiographs, according to the size of the hybridized restriction fragment.[26] Single locus probes will result in one or two bands, depending on whether the person is a homozygote or a heterozygote.[27] On the other hand, multi-locus probes may have many bands of varied intensity, with 20 or more bands being interpretable.[28]

---

24. 3 Wecht, *Forensic Sciences* (1992), pp. 37C–17—37C–18. Non-isotopic labelling techniques are now being considered. These new reporter molecules are chemically altered nucleotides which are detected by adding reactive reagents which result in colored bands in the membrane. Also see, Committee on DNA Technology in Forensic Science, Board on Biology, Commission on Life Sciences, National Research Council, *DNA Technology in Forensic Science* (1992), p. 38.

25. 3 Wecht, *Forensic Sciences* (1992), pp. 37C–18—37C–19; Kirby, *DNA Fingerprinting: An Introduction* (1990), pp. 135–139.

26. 3 Wecht, *Forensic Sciences* (1992), p. 37C–18; Giannelli & Imwinkelreid, *Scientific Evidence* (2nd ed. 1993), p. 9; Kirby, *DNA Fingerprinting: An Introduction* (1990), pp. 135–139.

27. *DNA Technology in Forensic Science*, op. cit. note 24 at pp. 38–40.

28. Baechtel, "A Primer on the Methods Used in the Typing of DNA," 15 *Crime Lab.Dig.*, Supp. 1, 3 (1988). After producing the autoradiographs, the radioactive probes can be stripped from the membrane, allowing other probes that detect different restriction fragments to be introduced for hybridization. Waye & Fourney, supra note 19 at p. 375.

5. MULTI–LOCUS AND SINGLE LOCUS PROBES

Multi-locus probes hybridize simultaneously to one or more polymorphic loci throughout the human genome and on many pairs of chromosomes. As discussed above, low stringency washes are used on the membranes, allowing sequences which are not just identical, but also similar, to the probe to remain hybridized. A relatively larger sample of DNA is needed for use of the multi-locus probe than for use of the single locus probe. Many bands of varying intensities appear on the autoradiograph, creating a more complex pattern, and therefore a more challenging interpretation.[29]

The multi-locus probe is very informative, because it recognizes multiple sites simultaneously. The chances, therefore, of two individuals randomly matching at all band positions is extremely low. A single multi-locus probe alone could individualize a body fluid.[30]

Single locus probes, used by Lifecodes Corporation of Valhalla, New York,[31] as well as Cellmark Diagnostics and the FBI, detect repetitive sequences that occur at a single location in the DNA from one pair of chromosomes. The use of a single locus probe results in one or two bands on the autoradiograph, which allows for more simplified interpretations than with multi-locus probes.[32] Unlike the multi-locus probe, however, the single locus probe is not as probative by itself, simply because of the fewer bands revealed on the autoradiograph. This deficiency is overcome by using several single locus probes, each searching for a different locus on a different pair of chromosomes.[33] Increased probability estimates can thereby be achieved.[34]

Cellmark Diagnostics employs its single locus probes in a "cocktail" format. That is, several different single locus probes are mixed together, producing an autoradiograph exhibiting that complete mixture. After employing a single locus probe "cocktail," five single locus probings are performed sequentially, one at a time. See Figure 11.

---

29. It is not uncommon to have 20 or more fragment bands appear on the autoradiograph. Baechtel, op. cit. note 28, *DNA Technology in Forensic Science,* op. cit. note 24 at p. 40.

30. Baechtel, op. cit. note 28.

31. 90% of the laboratories conducting DNA typing use single locus probes, according to a review of the laboratories, in Giannelli & Imwinkelreid, *Scientific Evidence* (2nd ed. 1993), p. 10.

32. The use of single locus probes is favored by the NRC. See, *DNA Technology in Forensic Science,* op. cit. note 24, at p. 40.

33. The potential affect of linkage disequilibrium is diminished since each probe tests a different chromosome. Giannelli & Imwinkelreid, *Scientific Evidence* (2nd ed. 1993), p. 10.

34. Baechtel, supra note 30 at 6.

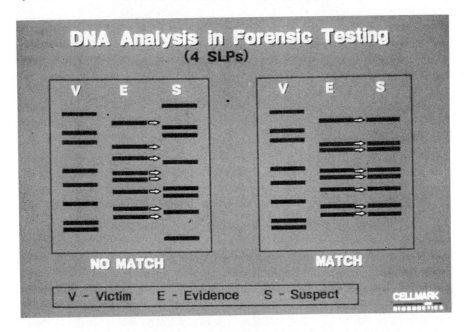

Fig. 11. Examples of autorads using single locus probe cocktail.
Courtesy: Cellmark Diagnostics

The FBI, on the other hand, uses only a single locus probe, resulting in one autoradiograph at a time. This process is then repeated several times with different probes. It has been reported that the FBI follows this procedure because, even with the cocktail method, the technician must still run each probe individually to determine which bands are associated with which probe.[35] According to Cellmark Diagnostics, however, the single locus probe cocktail is run first in order to maximize the possibility of demonstrating the existence of a non-matching pattern, if it exists, in the specific case being tested. When insufficient DNA is extracted from an evidence stain to guarantee interpretable results with four or five sequential, separate single locus probings, there is always the chance that the first probing or two will match by coincidence with too little DNA left on the membrane for the remaining probings, which could have shown an exclusion. Thus, to assure the suspect the maximum safeguards scientifically available, Cellmark elects to begin with the single locus probe cocktail.[36]

§ 15.07 Factors Affecting the Validity and Reliability of RFLP–Based Typing

The potential effect that a positive match between a questioned biological fluid or tissue found at a crime scene with that of a defendant

---

35. People v. Mehlberg, 249 Ill.App.3d 499, 188 Ill.Dec. 598, 618 N.E.2d 1168 (1993).

36. Personal communication with Mark D. Stolorow, Cellmark Diagnostics, February 14, 1994.

in a criminal case may have in a judicial proceeding requires that DNA typing possess a high degree of reliability and validity. Experts express a certainty of individual identification with such a high degree of confidence that the convincing effect of such evidence on the fact finder tends to be overwhelming. The validity of DNA typing—that is the ability to achieve correct results—is, therefore, paramount. Reliability—which is the ability to reproduce correct test results by applying a protocol—is of equal importance.

The Office of Technology Assessment, in its report to Congress on DNA typing, concluded that the "forensic uses of DNA tests are both reliable and valid when properly performed and analyzed by skilled personnel." [1] Many factors that affect the validity and reliability of DNA typing are discussed below.[2] The proficiency of the analyst in applying the proper protocol is discussed later.

Regardless of the matching criteria used, the declaration of a match or an exclusion, or the conclusion that the test is inconclusive, may each be affected by factors which might alter band appearance on the autorad. These factors, whether resulting from potential aberrations in the process itself, or from the test sample's quality, may, according to some experts, either produce extra bands, inhibit the appearance of bands or shift the location of the bands upward or downward in their lanes relative to bands in other lanes.

1. ARTIFACT OR GENETIC FACT?

When the bands in two lanes appear to match in all respects, but for the presence of an extra band in one lane, the analyst must decide whether the additional band is an artifact created by an aberration in the process, or a genetic fact requiring a conclusion that the DNA in the two lanes do not match. A close examination of the autorad often will not by itself disclose the reason for the extra band. Assuming the band is not caused by a true genetic difference, that is, the samples originated from two different individuals, it is important to determine the reason for the appearance of the extra band. Among the possible causes of additional bands are:

1. Sample cross-contamination;

2. Mixed stains;

3. Partial digestion;

4. Star activity;

5. Biological and non-biological contamination;

6. Washes of reduced stringency; and

---

§ 15.07

1. U.S. Congress, Office of Technology Assessment, *Genetic Witness: Forensic Uses of DNA Tests,* (1990) pp. 7–8.

2. A general trouble shooting guide for testing problems in RFLP typing, and causes and solutions to the problems can be found in Kirby, *DNA Fingerprinting: An Introduction* (1990), pp. 121–126.

7. Incomplete membrane stripping before reprobing.

A. Sample Cross-Contamination

The cross-contamination of samples may occur at the time of collection or in the laboratory during the typing procedure. Such contamination might result in extra bands appearing in one lane, creating the possibility of misinterpretation.[3]

Cross-contamination can also occur by the lateral movement of DNA from one lane to another in the gel. This can be prevented by leaving an empty lane between samples. If such lateral movement does occur, it is sometimes apparent because of streaks on the autorad from one lane to another.[4]

B. Mixed Stains

Mixed stains are different from cross-contaminated samples, in that DNA from separate sources have already been mixed at the time the sample is obtained. An example is a postcoital vaginal swab containing semen and epithelial cells from the female. Earlier in this chapter, a process to fractionate the male and female DNA was described. Reference was made to the possibility that the separation may not be complete. In those instances, the male and female lanes on the autorad may show extra bands belonging to the other sex. These extra bands can be accounted for by running known samples from the individuals thought to be contributors to the mixed samples.[5]

---

3. Thompson & Ford, "The Meaning of a Match: Sources of Ambiguity in the Interpretation of DNA Prints," *Forensic DNA Technology* (Farley & Harrington, eds. 1991), p. 111.

4. Id. at 111–116.

5. Thompson & Ford, op. cit. note 3 at pp. 116–120.

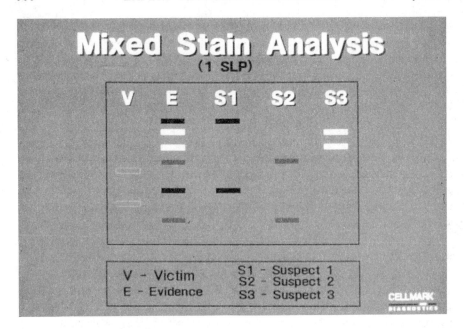

Fig. 12. A mixed stain analysis. *Courtesy: Cellmark Diagnostics*

Mixed blood samples cannot be separated, as can a mix of semen and epithelial cells. The autorad of such a mix will show a superimposition of DNA banding over one another. However, the intensity of the bands belonging to each contributor should vary according to the amount of DNA in the mix from each contributor. An excess number of bands, along with variation in intensity, is a reliable indication of mixed stains. Running known samples of the suspected contributors should account for all the bands.[6] See Figure 12.

A study of mixed samples other than vaginal samples, including blood, urine, saliva and semen, to determine whether accurate profiles from the various contributors could be obtained has been undertaken. It indicated that DNA analysis by the RFLP procedure using single locus probes gives a reliable characterization of mixed body fluid stains. It was determined that profiles could be obtained from each donor of the mixed body fluid samples, which compared favorably to those of the controls, except for urine. No false-positive or false-negative results were produced.[7]

Another type of mixed sample which might occur, is that containing human blood and animal blood. Although mixtures of the two bloods were not tested in a study completed by the FBI, dried blood stains from

---

6. Id.

7. Adams, Presley, Baumstark, Hensley, Hill, Anoe, Campbell, Giusti, Smerick, Baechtel, "Deoxyribonucleic Acid (DNA) Analysis by Restriction Fragment Polymorphisms of Blood and Other Body Fluid Stains Subjected to Contamination and Environmental Insults," 36 *J.For.Sci.* 1284, 1287, 1292–95, 1298 (1991).

primates, and domestic and wild game animals were subjected to RFLP analysis using FBI single locus probes. Some of the primates produced RFLP patterns when hybridized with probes used by the FBI. DNA from the blood of the domestic and wild game animals did not produce RFLP patterns, except with respect to one probe, which did produce results as to the bird species and the domestic cat, but only after long autoradiography exposures.[8]

C. PARTIAL DIGESTION

As explained earlier, restriction enzymes cleave the DNA molecule at restriction sites producing restriction fragments, which are eventually hybridized with probes and visualized on autorads. When digestion is incomplete, in that the molecule is not cut at each restriction site, partial digestion occurs. The result is longer fragments having higher molecular weight than those properly cleaved. Extra bands typically appear at the upper region of the gel, since they will not migrate as far because of their size. Their appearance is obvious and easily diagnosed. Factors which might inhibit the restriction enzyme from properly cutting the DNA molecule originate from both technical and human problems.[9]

D. STAR ACTIVITY

Star activity is the other side of partial digestion. With star activity, a restriction enzyme cleaves at too many restriction sites, thus creating the possibility of an extra band appearing for reasons other than genetic differences. Which restriction enzymes are more susceptible to star activity is still unsettled, but it is clear that restriction enzymes with a high degree of specificity should be chosen for the digestion process. As with partial digestion, the analyst must not mistake the extra band as a genetic difference or a mixed sample. Star activity, like the appearance of other artifacts, is usually obvious and self-evident, but infrequently may not necessarily be apparent from the autorad, increasing the importance of carefully controlling the restriction digestion procedure.[10]

E. CONTAMINATION

(i) Biological Contaminants

Bacterial contamination of crime scene samples containing biological substances from which DNA is extracted can occur because of the nature of many crimes and crime scenes. Several biological substances may have been mixed, other organic materials may have invaded the biological fluids and tissues, and environmental factors may have affected the

8. Adams, et al, op. cit. note 7, at pp. 1284, 1288, 1295.

9. Thompson & Ford, op. cit. note 3 at pp. 120–124.

10. Id.

samples. If as a result, there is bacterial contamination of the DNA, some have argued that extra bands may appear on the autorad reflecting the bacteria's presence. Several laboratories claim that their systems are immune from artifacts created by bacterial contamination. It has also been asserted that some polymorphic probes which are currently in use do not hybridize with bacterial DNA.[11]

One study has examined the effect of five microbial contaminants on RFLP analysis of DNA from blood and semen.[12] Blood and semen mixed with the contaminants produced RFLP profiles consistent with those of uncontaminated blood and semen samples. DNA isolated from the purified cultures of the biological contaminant controls did not hybridize with the single locus probe used in the study and used in forensic casework. In one phase of the study of biological contaminants, *Escherichia coli* did hybridize with a size marker probe, creating a series of seven fragments. These fragments, however, would not be mistaken for a human DNA profile. In addition, they showed up repeatedly in the same positions during subsequent hybridizations with each single locus probe, thus alerting the examiner.

Another study, also involving microbial contaminants, mimicked the gross contamination of samples from crime scenes by exposing single locus probes to bacterial, yeast and fungal contaminants similar to those found on samples submitted to forensic laboratories. No DNA sequences of nonhuman origin were observed on autoradiographs or lumigraphs following hybridization to radioactively labeled and nonisotopically labeled single locus probes. Moreover, no DNA profiles were produced that could have lead an examiner to make a false-positive or false-negative conclusion.[13]

(ii) Nonbiological Contaminants

It is not uncommon that nonbiological contaminants are mixed with forensic samples submitted for examination. Frequently, the contaminants are already on the material, or substrate, when the human fluid is deposited. A study involving nonbiological contaminants including unleaded gasoline, motor oil, detergent, chlorine bleach, salt, base and acid was conducted to determine their influence on single locus probes during a DNA analysis of bloodstains using the RFLP method. High molecular-weight DNA was recovered from all contaminated bloodstains and result-

---

11. Thompson & Ford, op. cit. note 3 at pp. 128–130. Cellmark Diagnostics claims that it would not be possible for its probes to attach to bacterial DNA under its testing conditions, and, as of February 1994, such a phenomenon had not happened at Cellmark. Personal communication with Mark D. Stolorow, Cellmark Diagnostics. Also see, People v. Mehlberg, 249 Ill.App.3d 499, 188 Ill.Dec. 598, 610, 618 N.E.2d 1168, 1180 (1993).

12. The five microbial contaminants were *Staphylococcus epidermidis, Candida valida, Escherichia coli, bacillus subtilis* and *Candida albicans*. See, Adams et al., op. cit. note 7.

13. Webb, Williams, Sutton, "Microbial DNA Challenge Studies of Variable Number Tandem Repeat (VNTR) Probes Used for DNA Profiling Analysis," 38 *J.For.Sci.* 1172 (1993).

ed in profiles consistent with those of the uncontaminated bloodstains from the same origin.[14]

F. Washes of Reduced Stringency

At the conclusion of the hybridization process, the membrane is washed in order to remove strands of the probe that did not hybridize to their complementary DNA sequences. The stringency of the wash will affect the specificity of the hybridization. The higher the stringency, the higher the complementarity must be for the probe to resist the wash. On the other hand, when the stringency of the wash is reduced, probes will remain hybridized not only to identical sequences, but also to those which are nearly identical to the probe. These more distantly related targets produce secondary bands on the autorad which are fainter than the bands resulting from the more strongly bonded fragments.

Consequently, the analyst must be cognizant of this source of extra bands and be able to distinguish them from the true targets of the probe. At the same time, the analyst must not confuse the lighter bands with the possibility of the presence of cross-contamination or mixed stains.[15]

G. Incomplete Stripping Before Reprobing

Frequently, multiple probes are used in the DNA typing process. Particularly when using single locus probes, several probes are used which search for different loci on different chromosomes. After the autorad is produced, the membrane is stripped of the probe, allowing another probe to be introduced. If the stripping process is not completely successful, the remaining segments of the first probe may produce extra bands on the autorad created from the residual radioactivity of the first probe, as well as that of the second probe.[16] A geiger counter can be used to determine the efficiency of the stripping process when radioisotopic probes are used. The geiger counter detects radioactivity caused by residual probe remaining on the membrane.

Another method to determine the efficiency of the stripping procedure is to expose the stripped membrane to X-ray film, or in other words to create a test autorad. If no reporter molecules remain bound to the membrane, the autorad will be blank.[17]

2. ALLELIC DROPOUT OR GENETIC EXCLUSION?

There may be occasions when the DNA band pattern from the same individual may appear differently from one autorad to another because of a missing band. The phenomena of band loss, or allelic dropout, may

---

14. Adams et al., op. cit. note 7 at pp. 1286–87, 1290.

15. Thompson & Ford, op. cit. note 3 at pp. 130–131.

16. Id.

17. Waye & Fourney, "Forensic DNA Typing of Highly Polymorphic VNTR Loci," Ch. 7 in Vol. III, *Forensic Science Handbook* (Saferstein, ed.) 1993, p. 375; Thompson & Ford, op. cit. note 3 at p. 131.

be caused by one of several factors. The analyst must be aware of these factors in order to differentiate an apparent difference in band patterns because of allelic dropout from those which are actual genetic differences. Allelic dropout, which can be caused by insufficient DNA, can also be caused by degraded DNA and aberrations in the typing process.

A. DEGRADATION OF DNA

When a DNA sample degrades, the high molecular-weight DNA molecules are the first to be lost. Consequently, the larger fragments which would appear at the top of the gel in the absence of degradation may not appear, except in the form of "background" which cannot be interpreted. An example of when this type of allelic dropout may affect the interpretation of an autorad is the use of single locus probes. When there is an apparent match between two samples thought to be from homozygotes, only one band will appear in each lane. In reality, one lane may contain heterozygous DNA, but have lost the larger second band because of allelic dropout caused by degradation of the DNA sample, resulting in a false positive.[18]

A "yield gel" can be used to measure the quality of the DNA in the sample at the conclusion of the extraction process. It has been suggested that another, and perhaps better, approach is to utilize a monomorphic probe of high molecular weight. Such a procedure would result in a band on the autorad high on the gel where you would expect to see bands from larger fragments. If the expected band is missing, then that fact might suggest that the DNA has degraded beyond the point of appropriate testing.[19] Even the use of a monomorphic probe, however, is not fail safe, since there may be other reasons that a large DNA fragment is missed.

B. ABERRATIONS IN THE TYPING PROCESS

It has been suggested that bands in the middle and lower portions of the autorad may be missing because of aberrations during the typing process. The causes for allelic dropout of this nature may be from:[20]

    1. Problems occurring during Southern transfer where DNA transfer to the membrane is incomplete.

    2. A loss of DNA during stripping of probes before a second or subsequent hybridization.

    3. Problems with the hybridization process, such as the presence of bubbles, causing a failure of the DNA to adhere to some portion of the membrane.

    4. Selective protein binding during electrophoresis causing the retardation of some bands, resulting in a smear at the top of the gel.

---

18. Thompson & Ford, op. cit. note 3 at pp. 132, 134.

19. Id.

20. Ibid. at p. 135.

3.   MISALIGNMENT OR MISMATCH?

A phenomenon may occur which causes DNA fragments in one lane to migrate more rapidly than identical fragments in another lane during the electrophoretic process. The affected lane ends up with bands which appear to have shifted downward relative to the other lane containing identical DNA or to standard markers. The causes of band shifting, according to some experts, are not completely understood, and the conditions under which it occurs not reliably replicated. One explanation for band shifting is the overloading of gel tracks with too much DNA. Forensic laboratories often quantify DNA in each sample before electrophoresis to monitor the amount of DNA loaded in each lane, although the accuracy of such measurements is open to question.[21]

Contaminants such as clothing dyes, soil or foreign proteins may survive the extraction and purification process and cause band shifting. Other contaminants may be introduced during the extraction process and not completely removed thereafter. These contaminants may alter the conditions in an agarose gel lane, changing the migration rate of the DNA fragments, or may inappropriately bind to the DNA in a particular lane, affecting the size and therefore the migration of the fragments.[22]

Changes in mobility of DNA in a lane during electrophoresis, resulting in a band shifting, may occur because proteins that bind with DNA escaped extraction during enzymatic digestion stages prior to electrophoresis. The effect is to retard the mobility of the DNA during electrophoresis.[23] Ethidium bromide is also thought to cause band shifting to a degree associated with the amount of DNA loaded in the gel lane. In these instances, variations in the intensity of the bands from lane to lane also occur in relation to variations in the amount of DNA per lane.[24]

Dyes other than ethidium bromide may also be related to band shifting, although sufficient analysis of this premise has not been undertaken. A tendency for clothing dye to cause band shifting has also been reported by Cellmark.[25] Soil may also contaminate DNA so as to cause band shifting because of the presence of humic acid. The structure and properties of humic acid closely resemble DNA, and thus may have a tendency to copurify with it, although this has never been demonstrated. There are no stages currently in use to extract humic acid from samples contaminated with soil. While some theories suggest why humic acid may cause band shifting, the reasons are not yet known.[26] Other affects of soil contamination are discussed later in this chapter.

21. Thompson & Ford, "The Meaning of a Match: Sources of Ambiguity in the Interpretation of DNA Prints," *Forensic DNA Technology* (Farley & Harrington, eds. 1991), at pp. 100, 102, 104.

22. Id. at pp. 102–103.

23. Ibid.

24. Thompson & Ford, "The Meaning of a Match: Sources of Ambiguity in the Interpretation of DNA Prints," *Forensic DNA Technology* (Farley & Harrington, eds. 1991), p. 104.

25. Id.

26. Ibid.

Band shifting obviously creates an ambiguity in the interpretation of the autorad, and requires the laboratory to implement methods to identify band shifting. One method for determining the presence of band shifting is the use of a monomorphic probe. Such a probe produces a band of known length, and the examiner knows where to expect its appearance on the autoradiograph. An appearance at some other position, indicates band shifting may have occurred and that bands of similar length found at similar positions may also have shifted. The amount of shift can be determined by establishing the degree to which the known monomorphic probe has shifted. Although it is maintained by some that monomorphic probes are not accepted in the scientific community, it is suggested by others that it is an effective way to discern band shifting.[27]

A monomorphic probe creates a band at specifically known positions and therefore should be constant on every autorad, resulting in an objective measure of its accuracy. A determination could be made between the estimated size of the monomorphic probe fragment as measured on the lane and the known size of the fragment. The band created by the monomorphic probe would be used as a benchmark to determine whether band shifting occurs and if so, in which direction.[28] It is argued that a monomorphic probe creates more problems than it solves because the percentage of shift varies from one end of the gel to the other. A single monomorphic band is diagnostic only in the molecular weight region near where it occurs.

Another suggested approach propounded by some critics is the use of mixed samples, where a 50:50 mixture of the sample is run in a lane to be compared with the mixture's components displayed in separate lanes. Theoretically, there would be absolute alignment in the mixed lane, since lane-to-lane variation would not be a factor. There are, however, several fallacies in the mixed sample approach which has discouraged its use.[29]

If it can be determined that band shifting has occurred, and the result is an apparent difference in phenotype between two samples from the same donor, the band shifting can be taken into account in declaring a match. The real concern, although very theoretical, is that the bands from two lanes containing DNA from separate donors will shift in such a way that truly different phenotypes will appear identical. While it may be more likely with only one single locus probe, the possibility of a false positive being created using four or five single locus probes is remote.[30]

27. State v. Futch, 123 Or.App. 176, 860 P.2d 264, 272 (1993). Lifecodes uses a monomorphic probe, or "constant band." The court, at 272, rejected the defendant's claim that the use of a monomorphic probe to detect band shifting is unreliable. Cellmark Diagnostics takes the position that monomorphic probes are not generally accepted in the scientific community. Instead, they like to use a conservative match criteria. Results which fall outside those criteria cannot be called a match. Personal communication with Mark Stolorow, Cellmark Diagnostics, 1993.

28. Waye & Fourney, "Forensic DNA Typing of Highly Polymorphic VNTR Loci," Ch. 7 in Vol. III, *Forensic Science Handbook* (Saferstein, ed.) 1993, pp. 383–386.

29. Thompson & Ford, op. cit. note 24 at p. 105; Waye & Fourney, op. cit. note 28 at p. 383.

30. Waye & Fourney, op. cit. note 28 at p. 386; Thompson & Ford, op. cit. note 24 at p. 105.

4. ENVIRONMENTAL INSULTS AND VALIDITY OF RFLP TYPING PROCEDURES

In the transfer of technology from research to forensic laboratories, serious consideration has to be given to the quality of the forensic sample. Unlike the pristine samples often used in the research laboratory, crime scene samples encountered in forensic laboratories are often subjected to extreme environmental conditions which might affect the quality of the extracted DNA and, therefore, the validity of the test results.

The FBI Laboratory has conducted studies on the effect of environmental insults on the RFLP typing procedures.[31] The categories of environmental insults, relevant here, include exposure to sunlight, to time, temperature and substrate, and long-term exposure to warm temperatures. It was discovered that DNA is not stable indefinitely and that it is affected adversely by sunlight. DNA in bloodstains exposed to sunlight filtered through greenhouse glass for either 12 days or 8 weeks was degraded to such a degree that no RFLP banding patterns appeared on the autoradiograph. Bloodstains exposed directly to sunlight, instead of through greenhouse glass, for up to 10 days, did, however, produce DNA profiles consistent with the control stains.[32]

In the time, temperature, and substrate testing, bloodstains were created on cotton, nylon, denim, glass, wood, and aluminum and exposed to various temperatures and analyzed from two days to five months after initiating the experiment.[33] Stains from all of the substrates mentioned above produced RFLP profile results, even after five months, which were consistent with the controls. Results did vary, however, depending on the temperature and substrate involved. For example, a more intense DNA profile was obtained from stains maintained at room temperature and from nonporous substrates.[34] It was more difficult, on the other hand, to achieve easy recoveries of DNA from bloodstains on cotton and blue denim maintained at higher temperatures, resulting, in some cases, in no profiles.

When bloodstains were exposed to 37 degree temperatures for four years, only low molecular-weight DNA could be detected, and no RFLP

---

31. Budowle, Baechtel & Adams, "Validation with Regard to Environmental Insults of the RFLP Procedure for Forensic Purposes," *Forensic DNA Technology* (Farley & Harrington, eds. 1991), pp. 83–91.

32. Adams, Presley, Baumstark, Hensley, Hill, Anoe, Campbell, Giusti, Smerick, Baechtel, "Deoxyribonucleic Acid (DNA) Analysis by Restriction Fragment Polymorphisms of Blood and Other Body Fluid Stains Subjected to Contamination and Environmental Insults," 36 *J.For.Sci.* 1284, 1285–89 (1991).

33. Id.

34. Another study has examined the effects of substrates on the quality of DNA isolated from evidentiary stains. This study analyzed scrapings, plastic bags, synthetics, denim, and carpet. The results exhibited that sufficiently high quality and high molecular-weight DNA can be reliably recovered from bloodstains dried on a variety of substrates and exposed to unknown environmental conditions. McNally, Shaler, Baird, Balazs, Kobilinsky, and De Forest, "The Effects of Environment and Substrata on Deoxyribonucleic Acid (DNA): The Use of Casework Samples from New York City," 34 *J.For.Sci.* 1070 (1989).

results were obtained.[35] When incubated at the same temperature for only five days, however, there was no adverse affect on the ability to obtain consistent RFLP patterns.[36]

Time, temperature, and substrate are also operative factors for determining the identity of human remains. Postmortem analyses of DNA from 24 bodies exposed to varying temperatures, humidity, and light, were conducted to determine if high molecular-weight DNA could be extracted from tissue samples even after postmortem delay. Successful extraction occurred from samples taken up to 85 days after death. The tissue of choice for examination after a three week postmortem period is the brain cortex.[37]

The effect of soil on DNA typing has also been studied. A possible causal connection between band shifting and soil contamination has been discussed earlier under Misalignment or Mismatch in § 15.07(3). It appears that in samples of blood mixed with soil high molecular-weight DNA is difficult to recover, and no RFLP results were obtained when testing soil-contaminated bloodstains. It is believed that this result was achieved because components of the soil physically inhibited DNA extraction.[38]

§ 15.08 Determining Match Criteria for RFLP–Based Typing

Many of the variables just discussed may affect the appearance and placement of bands on the autorad. To avoid interpretive errors, the examiner must be cognizant of these aberrations. Once they have been considered, the examiner must make a determination whether there is a match, no match, or whether the test is inconclusive. Limited resolving capabilities often add a final dimension to the interpretations of the autorad by causing the bands from samples from the same individual to have slightly different measurements. Match criteria have to be developed to determine how much of a difference in band measurements will result in an inconclusive or nonmatch conclusion.[1]

---

35. Adams et al., op. cit. note 32 at p. 1289.

36. McNally et al., op. cit. note 34 at pp. 1061–62. The same study indicates that humidity does not influence the ability to obtain consistent band patterns.

37. Ludes, Pfitzinger, and Mangin, "DNA Fingerprinting from Tissues After Variable Postmortem Periods." 38 *J.For. Sci.* 686 (1993).

38. Adams et al., op. cit. note 32 at p. 1290. An earlier study has indicated that soiled substrates may adversely affect the quality of DNA. McNally, Shaler, Baird, Balazs, Kobilinsky, and De Forest, op. cit. note 34 at p. 1074. McNally, Shaler, Baird,

Balazs, De Forest, and Kobilinski, "Evaluation of Deoxyribonucleic Acid (DNA) Isolated from Human Bloodstains Exposed to Ultraviolet Light, Heat, Humidity, and Soil Contamination," 34 *J.For. Sci.* 1059, 1066 (1989), wherein the lack of RFLP patterns from soil-contaminated samples indicated that sufficient intact human DNA was not present to give a hybridization signal.

§ 15.08

1. Committee on DNA Technology in Forensic Science, Board on Biology, Commission on Life Sciences, National Research Council, *DNA Technology in Forensic Science* (1992), p. 61.

Figure 13—The Polymerase Chain Reaction

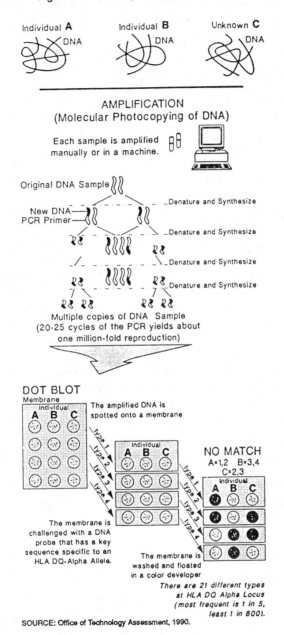

SOURCE: Office of Technology Assessment, 1990.

Fig. 13. The PCR (polymerase chain reaction). *Courtesy: Office of Technology Assessment.*

Unaided visual comparison of the autorads has been criticized as being too subjective and interpretive. Through the use of computer imaging software, an objective and quantitative rule for declaring a match will meet this criticism and heighten the confidence of autorad interpretations. A "match window", which is the percentage difference in measurement within which two fragment lengths must fall before they will be considered to match each other, has been defined to achieve that objectivity.[2]

Lifecodes's match window is ± 1.8% of the average of the two fragment sizes (mean size); the FBI uses a window of ± 2.5% of the mean size to determine a match. In addition to using that matching criterion, the FBI also uses a computerized digitizing system to make their match declaration more objective.[3] Cellmark Diagnostics will not call a match unless the bands fall within plus or minus one millimeter of each other. They use computer imaging software to apply Cellmark's match criterion, which was chosen because one millimeter is the measurement of the gel's ability to resolve one band from another within the gel.[4]

§ 15.09   PCR–Based Typing

The single locus and multi-locus RFLP methods of typing DNA are just two of the technologies available. Another group of methods is associated with a DNA amplification technology called polymerase chain reaction (PCR). See Figure 13. PCR is a relatively new technology, having been first described in 1985,[1] and refined in recent years.[2] It has advantages over RFLP technology and is gaining widespread acceptance in the forensic science community. The Cetus Corporation in Emeryville, California, developed the patent for PCR, which was later purchased by Hoffman LaRoche, and is also known as *in vitro* cloning, gene amplification and allele specific probe analysis.[3]

Polymerase chain reaction selectively amplifies, or duplicates, short segments of DNA, increasing the amount of the sample DNA available for typing.[4] The primary advantage of the PCR amplification is that smaller samples of biological material can be analyzed. At least 10 to 50 ng (nanograms) of good, high molecular-weight DNA are required for analysis of evidentiary samples with several polymorphic VNTR probes.[5] Using PCR, a significantly smaller amount is necessary for analysis, as

---

2. Waye & Fourney, op. cit. note 28, section 15.07, at p. 387.

3. Giannelli & Imwinkelreid, *Scientific Evidence* (2nd ed. 1993), p. 19.

4. People v. Mehlberg, 249 Ill.App.3d 499, 188 Ill.Dec. 598, 613, 618 N.E.2d 1168, 1183 (1993).

§ 15.09

1. Sensabaugh & Von Beroldingen, "The Polymerase Chain Reaction: Application to the Analysis of Biological Evidence," *Forensic DNA Technology* (Farley & Harrington, eds. 1991), p. 63.

2. Lee, Pagliaro, Berka, Folk, Anderson, Ruano, Keith, Phipps, Herrin, Garner, and Gaensslen, "Genetic Markers in Human Bone: 1. Deoxyribonucleic Acid (DNA) Analysis," 36 *J.For.Sci.* 320, 321 (1991).

3. Sensabaugh & Blake, "DNA Analysis in Biological Evidence: Applications of the Polymerase Chain Reaction," Ch. 8 in Vol. III, *Forensic Science Handbook* (Saferstein, ed.) 1993, p. 417.

4. Blake, Mihalovich, Higuchi, Walsh, Erlich, "Polymerase Chain Reaction (PCR) Amplification and Human Leukocyte Antigen (HLA)–DQα Oligonucleotide Typing on Biological Evidence Samples: Casework Experience," 37 *J.For.Sci.* 700, 701 (1992); Sensabaugh & Blake, op. cit. note 3 at p. 147; Kirby, *DNA Fingerprinting: An Introduction* (1990), p. 75.

5. Comey and Budowle, "Validation Studies on the Analysis of the HLA DQα Locus Using the Polymerase Chain Reaction," 36 *J.For.Sci.* 1633 (1991).

small, theoretically, as a single nucleated cell.[6] Analysis of single shed hairs and saliva from cigarette butts is possible using PCR, for example, thus increasing the array of biological samples from crime scenes subject to analysis.[7] In addition, PCR can be used to determine ABO blood groups from body fluids, irrespective of the contributor's secretor status, thereby allowing investigators to screen suspects by determining their blood group type from easily accessible records.[8] The sex of the contributor can also be determined by amplification of the X and Y sequences.[9]

The need for only minute amounts of DNA for PCR analysis makes it useful for degraded samples, where a significant proportion of the DNA is broken down, leaving only very small fragments for analysis. Small sample size requirements for PCR testing may also ensure that some residual DNA from the original sample is available for retesting by other laboratories.

Other advantages of using PCR include the relative simplicity of the operation and the speed with which it can be accomplished. Results can be routinely achieved within several days, as opposed to several weeks in the case of RFLP typing. In addition, because PCR amplification results in an exponential increase (a million fold or more) of DNA, typing detection techniques can rely on nonisotopic methods.[10]

The PCR process is similar to cellular replication of DNA, achieved through a three-stage procedure. The DNA is first denatured to obtain unwound, single strands of complementary DNA, similar to the denaturing process in RFLP typing. Primers, which are small molecules of known nucleotide sequences (also known as oligonucleotides: a polymer, usually composed of less than 100 nucleotides), are added to the denatured DNA to hybridize with complementary sequences. One primer hybridizes to the end preceding each DNA target sequence strand in such a way that they flank the sequence region of interest. A DNA polymerase then facilitates the extension of each primer across the target sequence.[11] The target sequence acts as a template for the primer and results in a replicated complementary sequence. This newly synthe-

---

6. Akane, Shiono, Matsubara, Nakamura, Hasegawa and Kagawa, "Purification of Forensic Specimens for the Polymerase Chain Reaction (PCR) Analysis," 38 *J.For. Sci.* 691 (1993); Committee on DNA Technology in Forensic Science, Board on Biology, Commission on Life Sciences, National Research Council, *DNA Technology in Forensic Science* (1992), p. 40.

7. Sensabaugh & Blake, op. cit. note 3.

8. Lee and Chang, "ABO Genotyping by Polymerase Chain Reaction," 37 *J.For.Sci.* 1269, 1272 (1992).

9. Gaensslen, Berka, Grosso, Ruano, Phil, Pagliaro, Messina and Lee, "A Polymerase Chain Reaction (PCR) Method for Sex and Species Determination with Novel Controls for Deoxyribonucleic Acid (DNA) Template Length," 37 *J.For.Sci.* 6 (1992).

10. Blake et al., op. cit. note 4, pp. 700–701; Comey and Budowle, supra note 5 at p. 1634. See generally, Sensabaugh & Blake, op. cit. note 121; *DNA Technology in Forensic Science,* op. cit. note 1, section 15.08, at p. 40.

11. A highly thermal stable DNA polymerase called Taq polymerase, isolated from the bacterium *Thermus aquaticus* or similar commercially produced polymerases, simplifies the procedure by allowing PCR to be automated in a thermocycler at relatively high temperatures and for the desired number of cycles. The higher temperature increases the specificity and yield of the reaction. Sensabaugh & Von Beroldingen, op. cit. note 1 at pp. 65–66; Sensabaugh & Blake, op. cit. note 3 at pp. 419–420.

sized complimentary sequence is then denatured to provide twice the number of templates for the next cycle.[12] The result is replication of the DNA exponentially. Twenty PCR cycles should produce about one million copies of the original template.[13]

A number of detection techniques are available for PCR-based DNA typing. Table One lists several techniques available.

PCR–BASED DETECTION SYSTEMS

Sequence-based detection systems

Allele-specific oligonucleotide (ASO), also known as Sequence-specific oligonucleotide (SSO)

Length variation systems

AMP–FLPS (Amplified Fragment Length Polymorphisms)

STRs (Short Tandem Repeats)

Analysis of nucleotide sequences

Mitochondrial DNA sequencing

Table 1. Techniques available for detection of variations using PCR.

The most generalized approach to identifying alleles with varying sequences is the method called sequence specific oligonucleotide (SSO), known also as allele-specific oligonucleotide (ASO). This method involves the introduction of a sequence specific probe, that is, a short oligonucleotide 15 to 30 nucleotides in length, with a sequence identical to the target allele. The sequence (allele)-specific probe will hybridize only with identical complementary sequences.[14] A "dot blotting" procedure, analogous to Southern blotting, or alternatively, "reverse dot blotting" also known as "blot dotting" is utilized to identify the hybridized sequences.[15] See Figure 14. The probes might be tagged with the enzyme horseradish peroxidase which causes a display of color when the

---

12. The primers become part of the amplification products. See, *DNA Technology in Forensic Science*, op. cit. note 1, section 15.08, at p. 42.

13. Sensabaugh & Blake, op. cit. note 3; Kirby, *DNA Fingerprinting: An Introduction* (1990), p. 76. The efficiency of the amplification is not 100%. The actual effective amplification at 30 cycles is generally 10^6 to 10^7 copies of the template. More than 30 cycles is usually not productive because the polymerase becomes limiting and the amount of replication levels off. Sensabaugh & Von Beroldingen, op. cit. note 1 at p. 66; *DNA Technology in Forensic Science*, op. cit. note 6 at p. 40.

14. The human leukocyte antigen HLA–DQ*a* locus was the first polymorphic locus analyzed using this oligonucleotide approach. Blake et al., op. cit. note 4 at p. 701. See, PCR Typing Using DQ*a* Locus, infra.

15. The detection principle for these two typing methods are the same. Both are based on the sequence specific hybridization reaction between the PCR product and an oligonucleotide probe of defined sequence. The reverse dot-blot method may be preferred, because in the non-isotopic format it has been shown to be two to four times more sensitive than dot-blot, and not subject to some handling errors that can be incurred using the dot-blot method. Blake et al., op. cit. note 4 at p. 704.

probe bonds with a DNA strand in the presence of certain reactive chemical dyes.[16]

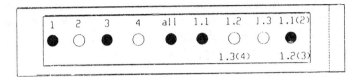

Fig. 14. Schematic for Immobilized ASO Probe method of DQ–alpha typing. The filter has 9 probes affixed to it in a horizontal array. The first four probes are for alleles 1–4. The next probe, "all", hybridizes if any DQ–alpha DNA amplifies at all. The next four probes detect one or more alleles and are used for subtyping for allele 1. Two of the probes, as indicated in the schematic, detect more than one allele, but by analyzing the pattern of hybridized dots the allele 1 subtype can be determined. The pattern shown is for the genotype 1, 3, with the allele 1 subtype 1.1. *Courtesy: Cellmark Diagnostics.*

Another method for the detection of genetic variation for PCR based systems is the identification of VNTR polymorphisms. This method offers great promise. The identification of VNTR polymorphisms offers convenience and good discrimination potential. The immediate drawback to this method is two fold. First, some of the most polymorphic VNTR loci have sequences greater than 5 kb, which is the upper base pair limit for PCR technology. Second, the efficiency of the amplification process decreases as the target sequence increases in size. Consequently, only some VNTR polymorphisms can successfully be identified and analyzed.[17]

However, a group of VNTR loci with very short core sequence repeat units have been identified. These are called SRTs (short tandem repeats) with core sequences from only three to seven base pairs in length. These promise to be readily amplifiable and statistically highly discriminating within the human population. Cellmark Diagnostics is now offering a line of STRs for forensic case analysis.

1. PCR TYPING USING DQa LOCUS

The success of the PCR system depends in great measure on determining basic DNA sequence information about a particular locus,

16. *DNA Technology in Forensic Science,* op. cit. note 6 at p. 42; Sensabaugh & Von Beroldingen, op. cit. note 1 at pp. 66–67.

17. Sensabaugh & Von Berolding, op. cit. note 1 at p. 69.

on being able to characterize the nature and extent of the variation at that particular locus, and developing a suitable method of detecting those variations. Several methods for detecting variations have been developed and discussed above. The sequencing of loci, on the other hand, has been more of a hurdle for PCR. One locus which has been the target of a major sequencing effort is the locus DQ*a*.[18]

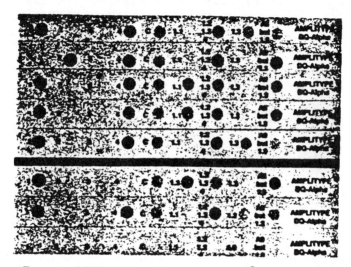

Example of DQA typing using the Amplitype®reverse dot blot system. DQA typing in a rape case is illustrated.Types are determined by the pattern of PCR product binding to the immobilized SSO probes; the C probe is an internal standard for PCR product binding. The samples and their types are as follows:

Sample	1	Suspect #1	DQA 1.3,4
	2	Suspect #2	2,4
	3	Victim	1.1,4
	4	Swab epithelial cell	1.1,4
	5	Swab sperm	1.3,4
	6	Typing control	1.1,1.2
	7	Typing control	1.3,4
	8	Blank	—

The evidence includes suspect #1 and excludes suspect #2 as the source of the sperm on the vaginal swab from the victim.

Fig. 15.   Example of DQa Typing Results. AmpliType is a registered trademark of Roche Molecular Systems, Inc. *Reprinted with permission of the Perkin–Emer Corporation.*

18. The DQ*a* locus is also currently known as DQA1. Blake et al., op. cit. note 4 at p. 702; Sensabaugh & Von Beroldingen, op. cit. note 1 at p. 70.

The use of specific primers and sequence (allele)-specific oligonucleotide probes described above, to detect the alleles at the DQ*a* locus, is the best developed PCR procedure applicable to forensic identification thus far.[19] Six alleles are typed at that locus.[20] The DQ*a* typing system has been subjected to extensive validation testing, and because of the discriminatory power of the test and the simplicity of its use, it is now widely used in forensic case work.[21] See Figures 14 and 15.

2.   PCR TYPING USING DIRECT SEQUENCING

Direct sequencing of DNA is a method which utilizes PCR as a starting point.[22] A requirement for direct sequencing is highly variable sequence regions. Such regions occur in mitochondrial DNA (mtDNA), found in mitochondria, the energy producing centers of the cells. The mitochondrial genome is 16,569 base pairs in length, is circular, and consists of coding regions and a noncoding hypervariable control region.[23] Three characteristics make the control region of mtDNA useful for forensic identification. First, two of the hypervariable segments have been studied and exhibit a rapid evolution five to 10 times faster than in the nuclear genome. These areas of relatively high mutability assist in the discrimination among individuals. Among Caucasians, it has been estimated that there is an average of one nucleotide difference every 100 bases, or 1%, in the most variable regions of mtDNA, while among African–Americans, the average is higher, being estimated at 2.3%.[24]

The second useful characteristic of mtDNA is that it is passed from mother to child, making everyone haploid with only one mtDNA type. Thus, the mtDNA is identical for siblings and all their maternal rela-

---

19. Lee et al., op. cit. note 2 at 321.

20. The six alleles are typed as DQA1.1, DQA1.2, DQA1.3, DQA2, DQA3, and DQA4. From these six alleles, 21 genotypes are possible. Comey, "The Use of DNA Amplification in the Analysis of Forensic Evidence," 15 *Crime Lab. Dig.* 99 (1988); see also, Blake et al., op. cit. note 4, at p. 702. None of the 21 genotypes is more frequent than about 11% in the caucasian population. The chance that two individuals chosen at random would share the same DQ*a* type is about 7%. Sensabaugh & Von Beroldingen, op. cit. note 1 at pp. 70–72. The major allele DQA4 has also been subdivided into subtypes DQA4.1, DQA4.2 and DQA4.3. The Cetus Corporation's commercial test kit does not provide for the detection of those subtypes. Sensabaugh & Blake, op. cit. note 3 at p. 426.

21. In one study, samples from 96 cases, previously analyzed by RFLP typing, were typed using PCR DQ*a*. All PCR interpretations were compatible with interpretations using the RFLP method. Comey, Budowle,

Adams, Baumstark, Lindsey and Presley, "PCR Amplification and Typing of the HLA DQ*a* Gene in Forensic Samples," 38 *J.For. Sci.* 239 (1993). Other validation studies include: Comey and Budowle, "Validation Studies on the Analysis of the HLA DQ*a* Locus Using the Polymerase Chain Reaction," 36 *J.For.Sci.* 1633 (1991) and Blake et al., op. cit. note 4.

22. Sensabaugh & Von Beroldingen, op. cit. note 1 at p. 69; Sensabaugh & Blake, op. cit., note 3 at p. 430.

23. Holland, Fisher, Mitchell, Rodriquez, Canik, Merril and Weedn, "Mitochondrial DNA Sequence Analysis of Human Skeletal Remains: Identification of Remains from The Vietnam War," 38 *J.For. Sci.* 542 (1993).

24. Wilson, Stoneking, Holland, DiZino and Budowle, "Guidelines for the Use of Mitochondrial DNA Sequencing in Forensic Science," 20 *Crime Lab. Dig.* 68 (1993); Holland et al., supra note 23.

tives, barring any mutation. Consequently, maternal relatives can provide reference samples for direct comparison to a questioned mtDNA type, a helpful advantage in forensic cases.[25]

Finally, human cells contain hundreds to thousands of copies of the mtDNA genome, while there are only two copies of the nuclear genome in each cell. Thus, when the evidentiary sample contains only limited quantities of DNA or degraded DNA, as in such tissues as bone, teeth, and hair, there is a greater chance of recovering mtDNA than nuclear DNA.[26]

While limitations currently exist on the application of direct sequencing, many believe that it will be the ultimate test used for individual identification.[27] For example, there appears to be a possibility that the ethnic background of a donor of a DNA sample may be determined by the mtDNA sequence found in the sample, because some mtDNA sequences seem to be found in some ethnic groups and not in others. As with other procedures for DNA typing, guidelines must be implemented for the use of mtDNA sequencing. Contamination, for example, is an important source of error in mtDNA sequencing, more so than in the typing process for nuclear DNA. In late 1993, the FBI established just such a set of guidelines for mtDNA sequencing in forensic cases.[28]

§ 15.10 Factors Affecting Validity and Reliability of PCR–Based Typing

Many of the factors affecting RFLP typing also affect the typing process utilizing PCR-based methods, because a number of the same technical procedures used in RFLP typing are applicable both before and after the amplification of the DNA using PCR. However, there are additional considerations pertaining to the PCR amplification process which must be recognized when assessing its validity and reliability. The following discussion of those factors is not exhaustive. Rather, it is an overview of some of the problems which can arise.[1]

Aberrations in the amplification process which affect the PCR products raise questions of fidelity, that is the degree to which those end products represent, in both qualitative and quantitative aspects, the underlying DNA in the sample. The impact of amplification inhibitors and environmental/contamination factors on the amplification process

25. Id.

26. Holland et al. supra note 23 at p. 543. The article describes the use of mtDNA sequencing to confirm the identity of skeletal remains of a Vietnam War serviceman thought to be dead for 24 years. See also, Wilson, Stoneking, Holland, DiZino and Budowle, "Guidelines for the Use of Mitochondrial DNA Sequencing in Forensic Science," 20 *Crime Lab. Dig.* 68 (1993).

27. Sensabaugh & Blake, op. cit., note 20 at pp. 430–431; Sensabaugh & Von Ber-

oldingen, op. cit., note 17 at pp. 69–70; Committee on DNA Technology in Forensic Science, Board on Biology, Commission on Life Sciences, National Research Council, *DNA Technology in Forensic Science* (1992), p. 44.

28. Wilson et al., supra note 24.

§ 15.10

1. Kirby, *DNA Fingerprinting: An Introduction* (1990), p. 78.

are also issues affecting the reliability and validity of PCR-based DNA typing.

1. QUALITATIVE FIDELITY

The specificity of the amplification process is important to the degree of fidelity the amplified product has to the original sample DNA. If there is low specificity during the primer hybridization process, then unintended products may result, which may in turn be used as templates for further amplification. Factors which affect hybridization specificity include the length and sequence of the primers and the temperature of the annealing process.[2]

Nucleotide misincorporation may occur during amplification, but these aberrations should not result in a change of genetic type.[3] The level of misincorporation is low, estimated at a rate of less than one per 10,000 nucleotides per cycle.[4] Given the low misincorporation rate and its random nature, misincorporation errors will not be amplified appreciably, and, therefore, not be detected or have any effect on the typing outcome.[5] For the genotype to change, the misincorporation would have to be at a specific site in the DNA sequence and be present in a significant proportion.[6]

Alignment errors can also affect the qualitative fidelity of amplification. DNA sequences containing tandem repeat sequences cause problems when the primer misaligns on the template strand, resulting in a heterogeneous collection of fragments, making interpretation more difficult.[7]

2. QUANTITATIVE FIDELITY

The efficiency of the amplification process determines how faithful the amplified product will be quantitatively to the DNA in the original sample. The overshadowing of one allelic product over another may lead to a misinterpretation of the results. Thus, it is important to determine why some alleles amplify more efficiently than others. Efficiency of

2. Sensabaugh & Blake, "DNA Analysis in Biological Evidence: Applications of the Polymerase Chain Reaction," Ch. 8 in Vol. III, *Forensic Science Handbook* (Saferstein, ed.) 1993, pp. 420–421.

3. Sensabaugh & Von Beroldingen, "The Polymerase Chain Reaction: Application to the Analysis of Biological Evidence," *Forensic DNA Technology* (Farley & Harrington, eds. 1991), p. 73.

4. Committee on DNA Technology in Forensic Science, Board on Biology, Commission on Life Sciences, National Research Council, *DNA Technology in Forensic Science* (1992), p. 64.

5. Id. Even where an attempt to create a typing error due to misincorporation was

made, none could be produced. Sensabaugh & Von Beroldingen, op. cit. note 3 at p. 74.

6. Sensabaugh & Blake, op. cit., note 2 at p. 422. The proportion of the amplification product representing a specific misincorporation depends on the number of copies of the template DNA and the PCR cycle at which the misincorporation occurs. Sensabaugh & Von Beroldingen, op. cit. note 3 at p. 73.

7. *DNA Technology in Forensic Science*, supra note 27, section 15.09, at p. 64; Sensabaugh & Blake, op. cit. note 2 at pp. 423–424.

amplification is affected by the length of the targeted sequence. Shorter sequences amplify more efficiently resulting in a preference for shorter sequences when amplifying sequences in the range of 100 to 2000 bp in length. Differential amplification can occur when allelic sequences of varying lengths are being amplified.[8]

Differential amplification may also be caused by amplification of sequences that differ significantly in GC content. Sequences containing high GC contents require higher temperatures during denaturing for strand dissociation. If the temperature is not high enough, strands with high GC contents may clamp together causing a problem during coamplification with strands exhibiting lower GC contents. Measures to achieve full strand dissociation, such as optimized denaturation duration and temperature, should ameliorate this problem.[9]

Base pair mismatch can affect amplification in several ways. If the mismatch is near the end of the primer from which the primer is extended during amplification (the 3′ end), then amplification may be inhibited. On the other hand, if the mismatch is in the interior of the primer binding region, the efficiency of the primer annealing is reduced, and accordingly affects the amplification efficiency.[10]

Replication problems can also result from a stochastic effect, when starting samples of DNA contain a low number of templates either because of small cell numbers or degradation, which has reduced the viable DNA molecules susceptible to testing. In such cases, a "founder" effect occurs during which one allele of a pair begins to amplify before the other. When the first allele begins to multiply ahead of the other, and does so exponentially, the second allele is overshadowed and becomes indiscernible. As the number of starting templates increases, the statistical probability of the "founder" effect occurring diminishes.[11]

3. MIXED SAMPLES

The problem of mixed samples can be approached during PCR analysis much like it is using the RFLP approach. In sexual assault cases the male and female fractions can be separated, as described earlier in this chapter. Other mixtures, however, cannot be separated, such as mixed blood stains or postcoital samples involving more than one assailant. Interpretations based on quantity in mixed sample situations must be approached with caution. A mixed stain must first be identified as such, and then interpreted appropriately to identify the different genotypes present.

---

8. Sensabaugh & Blake, op. cit. note 2 at p. 421; *DNA Technology in Forensic Science,* supra note 4 at p. 64.

9. Sensabaugh & Blake, op. cit. note 2 at p. 422; *DNA Technology in Forensic Science,* supra note 27, section 15.09, at p. 64; Sensabaugh & Von Beroldingen, supra note 3 at pp. 74–75.

10. Sensabaugh & Von Beroldingen, supra note 3 at p. 74.

11. Sensabaugh & Blake, supra note 2 at p. 424; Sensabaugh & Von Beroldingen, supra note 3 at p. 75.

One individual can have at most two alleles of a given gene. When more than two are present, it is an indication of an admixture of substances. If only two alleles are present, the dot intensities for each allele may be different when there is an uneven mixture of DNA from each contributor. It appears, however, that the ratio of the contaminated DNA to the majority DNA in the stain is important to the relative intensities of the dots. When the ratio is low, variations in dot intensity may not be such as to signal the presence of mixed stains. Therefore, if both of the contributors to the stain are homozygotes, or one is a heterozygote and the other a homozygote who shares his or her allele with the heterozygote, the existence of a mixed stain might not be discernable, even if the DNA is present in unequal amounts.[12] When an equal amount of DNA from each contributor is present, and each contributor is a homozygote, then the dot intensities will be the same, and the typing pattern will be indistinguishable from a heterozygous sample.[13]

The same type of analysis is done to interpret the different genotypes present in a mixed sample. The contributions by each contributor can sometimes be interpreted based on relative dot intensities. Dots corresponding to the component comprising the smallest amount of DNA will be lighter than the dots corresponding to the largest amount of DNA contributed. This analysis has been validated in studies of experimental mixtures of different DNA samples of known proportion.[14] However, it appears that such interpretations, based on dot intensities, may be hazardous, unless there are clear indications that the system used achieved quantitative fidelity, as described above.[15]

4. CONTAMINATION

There are several generally recognized sources of potential contamination of DNA samples, in addition to mixed stains, which are important to recognize, because of PCR's sensitivity to very small amounts of DNA and to very small amounts of some contaminants. These sources include contamination from laboratory handling, carry-over of PCR products from one analysis to another, and biological and nonbiological substances. While some contaminants may suppress PCR amplification or otherwise affect the reaction, for the most part they do not prevent the success of PCR typing.[16]

---

12. Comey and Budowle, "Validation Studies on the Analysis of the HLA DQα Locus Using the Polymerase Chain Reaction," 36 *J.For.Sci.* 1633, 1642 (1991); Blake, Mihalovich, Higuchi, Walsh, Erlich, "Polymerase Chain Reaction (PCR) Amplification and Human Leukocyte Antigen (HLA)–DQα Oligonucleotide Typing on Biological Evidence Samples: Casework Experience," 37 *J.For.Sci.* 700, 706 (1992).

13. Blake et al., supra note 12 at p. 706.

14. Blake et al., supra note 12 at p. 706.

15. *DNA Technology in Forensic Science,* op. cit. note 4 at pp. 65–66; Sensabaugh & Von Beroldingen, op. cit. note 3 at p. 77.

16. Akane, Shiono, Matsubara, Nakamura, Hasegawa and Kagawa, "Purification of Forensic Specimens for the Polymerase Chain Reaction (PCR) Analysis," 38 *J.For. Sci.* 691 (1993).

One preventable source of contamination is the improper handling of the sample in the laboratory itself. Contamination of the subject sample may come from a transfer from other samples or from the laboratory technician doing the work. "Handling" contaminants from the laboratory technician might be dandruff, sloughed skin or hair from the examiner. As a practical matter, however, these contaminants will not affect the end result for two reasons. First, sloughed skin cells and other dermal cells are not nucleated. Second, the amplification product is in proportion to the starting proportions of the mixture. Therefore, except with samples containing very small amounts of DNA, PCR products from the handling contaminants will not be observed.[17]

The FBI has conducted a study to determine the affect of "handling" contamination on typing results when PCR-based typing is used. The results indicate that no DNA contamination is introduced from extensive handling of a sample, coughing on a sample, shed scalp skin, scissors previously used to cut other bloodstains, or clothing subjected to heavy perspiration. One finding, thought to be significant, concerns the drying of two wet stains while in contact with one another. In the study, one stain was blood and the other was an equal amount of saliva. DQa alleles from both sources were observed, with the saliva type being significantly stronger. When two stains were again dried in contact with each other, this time with 10 times more blood than saliva, studies showed alleles from both sources in approximately equal amounts. The importance of this to the crime scene technician and the forensic laboratory is that the presence of saliva or other body fluids may be undetectable or unknown to the technician when the evidence is being packaged.[18]

The National Research Counsel recommends the routine use of appropriate positive-control and blank-control amplifications to assure recognition of contamination problems.[19] Of course, good laboratory practices will reduce this type of contamination.

Carry-over contamination may be the most serious of all contaminations. The source of this contamination is from the PCR products of other amplification reactions, and might contain millions of target sequences which would overwhelm the correct signal from the evidence sample.[20] Carry-over contamination might be discerned by using a blank or negative control, by observing a single type appearing in many samples or by observing a sample with what appears to be excessive

17. Sensabaugh & Blake, "DNA Analysis in Biological Evidence: Applications of the Polymerase Chain Reaction," Ch. 8 in Vol. III, *Forensic Science Handbook* (Saferstein, ed.) 1993, p. 441; Sensabaugh & Von Beroldingen, "The Polymerase Chain Reaction: Application to the Analysis of Biological Evidence," *Forensic DNA Technology* (Farley & Harrington, eds. 1991), p. 77.

18. Comey and Budowle, op. cit. note 12 at pp. 1642, 1646.

19. Committee on DNA Technology in Forensic Science, Board on Biology, Commission on Life Sciences, National Research Council, *DNA Technology in Forensic Science* (1992), p. 66.

20. *DNA Technology in Forensic Science,* supra note 19 at p. 66; Sensabaugh & Blake, supra note 17 at p. 441.

types.[21] Precautions similar to those used in infectious disease laboratories have been suggested to minimize the potential for carry-over contamination.

Biological contaminants have also been studied in relation to PCR-based typing. These contaminants included bacteria and yeast. DNA extracted from all the bloodstains contaminated with these substances typed correctly, while the microorganism stains failed to amplify or type.[22] Likewise, the effects of chemical contaminants have been studied. Specifically, gasoline, motor oil, acid, base, bleach, salt, soap, and soil were mixed with bloodstains. All contaminated samples typed correctly, except for soil. DNA from soil-contaminated blood failed to amplify. This could have been caused by elements of the soil binding to the DNA, thereby defeating the extraction process, by degradation of the DNA, or by the presence of inhibitors of DNA amplification.[23]

5.   ENVIRONMENTAL FACTORS

As with RFLP typing, environmental insults to the sample specimen may affect the success of PCR-based typing. The extraction process may produce small amounts of DNA, the polymerase may be inhibited and the DNA itself may be damaged, all due to environmental conditions affecting the sample. As a consequence, the analysis that can be accomplished may be limited, and the quality of that which is done may be affected.[24]

A study conducted by the FBI indicates that DNA from stains exposed to light through greenhouse glass for up to six weeks can be amplified and correctly typed. DNA extracted from stains placed outdoors for three weeks amplified and typed correctly, giving the same approximate results as the typing of the greenhouse stains after a six week exposure. Substrates were also studied, including 30 different fabrics and material such as drywall, linoleum, metal, paper, wood, and leaves, using four different extraction methods. No DNA was detected in any of the extracts from bloodstains on leaves. Denim fabric and cotton upholstery appeared to contain an inhibitor of PCR not removed by any of the extraction procedures, and, therefore, the DNA from those substrates did not amplify. All the remaining substrates yielded DNA from at least one of the extraction methods of sufficient quality and quantity to typed.[25]

21. Blake, Mihalovich, Higuchi, Walsh, Erlich, supra note 12 at p. 723; *DNA Technology in Forensic Science,* supra note 19 at p. 67; Sensabaugh & Von Beroldingen, supra note 17 at p. 78.

22. The bacteria *Escherichia coli, Bacillus subtilis,* and *Staphylococcus epidermidis* and the yeast *Candida albicans* were used. Comey and Budowle, supra note 12 at pp. 1636, 1641.

23. Comey and Budowle, supra note 18 at p. 1641.

24. Sensabaugh & Von Beroldingen, op. cit. note 17 at pp. 75–77. Specific forms of DNA damage may be linked to environmental insults and are outlined in Sensabaugh & Blake, op. cit. note 17 at p. 439.

25. Comey and Budowle, "Validation Studies on the Analysis of the HLA DQ*a* Locus Using the Polymerase Chain Reaction," 36 *J.For.Sci.* 1633, 1640 (1991).

§ 15.11 Other Scientific and Medical Procedures Affecting RFLP and PCR–Based Typing

Evidentiary samples submitted to crime laboratories are often analyzed for several purposes. An envelope, for example, could be examined for indented writing, latent fingerprints, and the presence of biological fluids (i.e. saliva), which may have been left when the perpetrator sealed the flap or secured a stamp to the envelope. Consideration must be given to the order of such examinations, or at least to the effect of one examination on subsequent examinations.

PCR-based DNA analysis using the HLA DQα region is not affected by the previous application of the Electrostatic Detection Apparatus (ESDA), when used to identify indented writing.[1] Nor does it appear that laser or alternate light sources, used to detect latent fingerprints and biological stains, affect RFLP profiles obtained from bloodstains on white cloth material.[2]

The visualization of latent fingerprints can be accomplished several ways. A popular method is by cyanoacrylate (super glue) fuming. Tests on the effect of such fuming on bloodstains indicated no adverse effects as to quantity of DNA extracted or the susceptibility of the DNA to digestion. Expected RFLP profiles were observed following hybridization with a polymorphic probe.[3]

Other processes are also used to raise latent fingerprints, several of which have also been examined to determine their effect on PCR-based typing. DFO, a fluorescent chemical process, ninhydrin, which contains a variety of chemical solvents, and a physical developer, consisting of numerous chemicals in a liquid solution, were examined. Analysis of those samples treated with ninhydrin or DFO yielded quantities of DNA consistent with samples not subjected to those processes and were of sufficient quality for PCR-based typing. However, no detectable DNA was recovered from the samples treated with the physical developer, either because the chemicals in the developer degraded the DNA, or the process diluted the DNA to the point where none was recovered.[4]

Even where examinations unrelated to biological fluids are not necessary, presumptive tests are still routinely performed on material suspected to contain biological substances. Suspecting that some presumptive tests might have an adverse effect on conventional genetic marker analysis, a study was conducted to determine their effect on RFLP typing, with mixed results. Some presumptive tests performed on bloodstains, semen stains, and vaginal swabs showed no observable

§ 15.11

1. Presley, Baumstark and Dixon, "The Effects of Specific Latent Fingerprint and Questioned Document Examinations on the Amplification and Typing of the HLA DQ Alpha Gene Region in Forensic Casework," 38 *J.For.Sci.* 1028, 1030 (1993).

2. Shipp, Roelofs, Togneri, Wright, Atkinson, and Henry, "Effects of Argon Laser Light, Alternate Source Light, and Cyanoacrylate Fuming on DNA Typing of Human Bloodstains," 38 *J.For.Sci.* 184, 187 (1993).

3. Id. at p. 187.

4. Presley, Baumstark and Dixon, supra note 1 at pp. 1030–1032.

effects on RFLP patterns from those stains. However, several reagents used for presumptive testing of bloodstains did have a negative effect on the ability to produce RFLP patterns or to extract a sufficient amount of high molecular-weight DNA.[5]

Medical interventions in rape and sexual assault cases may raise questions concerning how they influence later DNA analysis. One such area involves the effect of the active ingredient of most spermicides, nonoxinol–9. Several studies have indicated that the use of nonoxinol–9 inhibits a number of sexually transmitted infectious agents and may inactivate HIV *in vivo*. One study has shown that nonoxinol–9 affects neither the quality or quantity of DNA recovered, nor the reliability of RFLP or PCR-based DNA analysis.[6]

III. THE EVALUATION OF DNA TYPING METHODS

§ 15.12 Statistical Evaluation of a Match

In medical laboratories the frequency with which an allele appears in the population is not of great significance. That is not true in the forensic laboratory, where DNA is being used to match a questioned sample, often of limited size and quality, to a single individual in the population, and to few or no others. In the latter case, the frequency with which the matching alleles appear in the population is the life blood of DNA typing. "To say that two patterns match, without providing any scientifically valid estimate (or, at least, an upper bound) of the frequency with which such matches might occur by chance, is meaningless," reported the NRC.[1] The more infrequent the random match, the better.

From a lay person's point of view, some frequency calculations exclude for all practical purposes the possibility that nearly anyone but the defendant was the contributor of the forensic sample. In one of the first murder and rape cases to go to trial in which DNA evidence was admitted, the expert testified that the defendant's DNA characteristics would be present in only one out of every 135 million African–American individuals. There were only about 10 million African–American males

---

5. Hochmeister, Budowle and Baechtel, "Effects of Presumptive Reagents on the Ability to Obtain Restriction Fragment Length Polymorphism (RFLP) Patterns from Human Blood and Semen Stains," 36 *J.For.Sci.* 656 (1991).

6. Hochmeister, Budowle, Borer and Dirnhofer, "Effects of Nonoxinol–9 on the Ability to Obtain DNA Profiles from Post-coital Vaginal Swabs," 38 *J.For.Sci.* 442 (1993).

§ 15.12

1. Committee on DNA Technology in Forensic Science, Board on Biology, Com-

mission on Life Sciences, National Research Council, *DNA Technology in Forensic Science* (1992), p. 74.

This perspective is characterized as a "source probability error." Frequency calculations do not show the probability (or improbability) that someone else is the source of the questioned DNA. Rather, they show the probability that a randomly selected person, if tested, would have the same DNA profile as the questioned DNA. State v. Bloom, 516 N.W.2d 159, 161–63 (Minn.1994). But see, United States v. Martinez, 3 F.3d 1191, 1194 (8th Cir.1993); Commonwealth v. Crews, 536 Pa. 508, 640 A.2d 395, 401 (1994).

in America at the time.[2] The importance of the statistical evaluation of the DNA match cannot, therefore, be overstated.

Although there are proponents of the use of Bayes' Theorem to determine frequency calculations, the most generally used statistical basis for interpretation is the multiplication or product rule.[3] Using that rule, the expert multiplies the frequencies of each genotype together to arrive at the probability of a random match. The validity of the product rule depends upon the application of two principles found in the discipline of population genetics, the Hardy–Weinberg law and the principle of linkage equilibrium.

1. HARDY–WEINBERG LAW

To utilize the product rule, frequencies must be assigned to the alleles. The determination of these frequencies does not require a large sample of the population. The American Association of Blood Banks maintains that a 200–individual data base is sufficient to generate valid statistical frequencies for that group.[4] The NRC, on the other hand, suggests that it is quite adequate to collect 100 randomly chosen people, which would provide a sample of 200 alleles.[5] The FBI, on the other hand, started with a Caucasian database of approximately 225 individuals.[6]

To determine the frequency of an allele in these random population samples, one can count the number of times it appears in the sample. The population frequency can then be determined from that calculation. Since it is impossible or impractical to obtain a sufficiently large population sample to empirically test the calculated frequencies for a particular DNA profile much below 1 in 1,000,[7] validity of population frequency calculations is instead based on theoretical models, which rely, in part, on the principle that the matches at each allele are statistically independent.

The fact that each allele is independently randomly selected from a common gene pool in a population assumes that there are no subpopulations or substructures for which the allele has a different frequency. Such subpopulations might be Hispanics in Miami, Florida, who are mostly Cuban and those in Houston, Texas, who are mostly Mexican. It is argued by some that mating may not be random in these subgroups,

---

2. Melson, "Legal and Ethical Considerations," in Kirby, *DNA Fingerprinting: An Introduction* (1990), p. 191. In State v. Futch, 123 Or.App. 176, 860 P.2d 264, 272 (1993), one expert testified that the odds were on in 66 *billion*, with his most conservative estimate being one in 6.3 billion.

3. *DNA Technology in Forensic Science,* supra note 1 at p. 85. No forensic laboratory in the United States was found by the NRC to use the Bayesian approach. Giannelli & Imwinkelreid, *Scientific Evidence* (2d ed. 1993), p. 20.

4. Giannelli & Imwinkelreid, *Scientific Evidence* (2d ed. 1993), p. 20.

5. *DNA Technology in Forensic Science,* supra note 1 at p. 84.

6. United States v. Jakobetz, 747 F.Supp. 250, 253 (D.Vt.1990), affirmed 955 F.2d 786 (2d Cir.1992), cert. denied 113 S.Ct. 104 (1992).

7. *DNA Technology in Forensic Science,* supra note 1 at p. 77.

resulting in Hardy–Weinberg disequilibrium.[8] As a result, the frequencies in the subpopulation may be different from the frequencies calculated in the general ethnic or racial population.

Some commentators have argued that Hardy–Weinberg equilibrium cannot be assumed, but must be demonstrated before the product rule can have a sound basis. The practice of endogamy, that is, marrying within one's own group, detracts from the principle of random mating underlying the Hardy–Weinberg law, according to those commentators.[9] Consequently, it is submitted by some population geneticists that North American Caucasians, African–Americans, Hispanics, Asians and Native Americans are admixtures of subgroups containing varying allele frequencies, and not homogeneous in nature. The absence of this subpopulation variation cannot be predicted, they maintain, but rather must be proven empirically, which to date has not been done satisfactorily, according to some critics.[10] If these arguments are accepted, the result of using the product rule when significant subpopulations exhibiting varying allelic frequencies exist, is to underestimate the frequencies of DNA profiles within a subgroup.[11]

Although the debate over the existence of subpopulations and varying allele frequencies continues to rage, the actual effect of these substructural variants on the estimated frequencies of a DNA match has not been resolved. As mentioned previously, there are those who contend that the impact of subpopulations on frequencies has not yet been demonstrated.[12] Others have suggested that the effect on genotype frequency estimates is minimal.[13] Several recent empirical studies with respect to specific polymorphic loci, indicate that multiplication of gene

8. Herrin, "A Comparison of Models Used for Calculation of RFLP Pattern Frequencies," 37 *J.For.Sci.* 1640, 1641 (1992). Hardy–Weinberg principle states that in a large random intrabreeding population, which lacks excessive natural selection or mutation, the gene and genotype frequencies will remain constant over time. Several studies have examined population samples to determine the frequencies of DQa genotypes. The observed distribution of genotypes did not deviate significantly from the expected distribution based on Hardy–Weinberg equilibrium assumptions. Comey and Budowle, "Validation Studies on the Analysis of the HLA DQa Locus Using the Polymerase Chain Reaction," 36 *J.For.Sci.* 1633, 1642 (1991); Blake, Mihalovich, Higuchi, Walsh, Erlich, "Polymerase Chain Reaction (PCR) Amplification and Human Leukocyte Antigen (HLA)–DQa Oligonucleotide Typing on Biological Evidence Samples: Casework Experience," 37 *J.For.Sci.* 700, 703 (1992).

9. Lewontin and Hartl, "Population Genetics in Forensic DNA Typing," 254 *Science* 1745 (1991).

10. *DNA Technology in Forensic Science,* supra note 1 at pp. 79–80.

11. Waye & Fourney, "Forensic DNA Typing of Highly Polymorphic VNTR Loci," Ch. 7 in Vol. III, *Forensic Science Handbook* (Saferstein, ed.) 1993, p. 391.

12. There is a lack of data demonstrating the presence of population subgrouping within the Caucasian and African–American populations which would significantly change the final calculated frequencies. Herrin, op. cit. note 8 at p. 1647. Waye & Fourney, op. cit. note 11 at p. 391.

13. *DNA Technology in Forensic Science,* supra note 1 at p. 80; See, Chakraborty, and Kidd, "The Utility of DNA Typing in Forensic Work," 254 Science 1735 (1991); Budowle, Monson, Giusti, and Brown, "The Assessment of Frequency Estimates of Hae III–Generated VNTR Profiles in Various Reference Databases," 39 *J.For.Sci.* 319 (1994); Budowle, Monson, Giusti, and Brown, "Evaluation of Hinf I–Generated VNTR Profile Frequences Determined Using Various Ethnic Databases," 39 *J.For.Sci.* 988 (1994).

frequencies across loci does not lead to major inaccuracies in estimates of DNA profile frequencies.[14]

One way to compensate for potential errors resulting from subpopulation allele frequency variations is to calculate conservatively allele frequencies using the "fixed bin" procedure adopted and promoted by the FBI.[15] Using this procedure, the gamut of fragment lengths are divided into bins, defined as an arbitrary range of base pairs, which must be wider than the measurement error of the analytical system employed.[16] An example of a bin used by the FBI is one having boundaries of 872 and 963 base pairs. Any allele having a number of base pairs within that range is placed within the bin. The alleles from a targeted population are sorted according to the established bins. If an allele falls on the boundary of two bins, it is categorized as belonging to the bin with the higher frequency.[17] As an additional standard statistical safety measure, the FBI also requires at least five bands in a bin. If there are fewer than five, then the bin is "collapsed" into an adjacent bin, resulting in a larger bin, until there are at least five bands in the bin.[18]

The frequency of the alleles falling within their respective bins is then calculated for each probe by dividing the number of DNA fragments falling into each bin by the total number of fragments measured in a sample population for that probe.[19] Once the bin frequencies for a targeted population are determined using a specific probe, then the frequency of bands from the forensic samples falling into those bins can also be determined.

The fixed bin process results in frequencies for alleles within a bin averaging at least two times greater than the actual frequencies in the sample population for those alleles.[20] The frequencies resulting from

14. *DNA Technology in Forensic Science,* supra note 1.

15. This method of determining genotype frequency is currently used by most crime laboratories in North America performing RFLP analysis. See, Herrin, op. cit. note 8 at p. 1642. See also, Monson and Budowle, "A Comparison of the Fixed Bin Method with the Floating Bin and Direct Count Methods: Effect of VNTR Profile Frequency Estimation and Reference Population," 38 *J.For.Sci* 1037, 1038 (1993).

16. The FBI fixed bin system has an observed measurement error of ± 2.5% of the estimated base pair size of a DNA fragment, for a total of 5%. Monson and Budowle, op. cit. note 15 at p. 1038.

17. Monson and Budowle, op. cit. note 15; United States v. Jakobetz, 747 F.Supp. 250, 253 (D.Vt.1990), affirmed 955 F.2d 786 (2d Cir.1992), cert. denied 113 S.Ct. 104 (1992).

18. Springfield v. State, 860 P.2d 435, 445 (Wyo.1993); United States v. Yee, 134 F.R.D. 161, 172 (N.D.Ohio 1991), affirmed 12 F.3d 540 (6th Cir.1993). In *Springfield,* supra, at 446, the American Indian population was one of the relevant populations. The American Indian population data base was composed of four tribes. To add an additional degree of conservatism to the statistics, the FBI binned each tribe, then compared the bin frequencies side-by-side. The bin with the highest frequency was then chosen for the statistical calculation.

19. Monson and Budowle, op. cit. note 15 at p. 1038; United States v. Jakobetz, 747 F.Supp. 250, 253 (D.Vt.1990), affirmed 955 F.2d 786 (2d Cir.1992), cert. denied 113 S.Ct. 104 (1992).

20. United States v. Jakobetz, 955 F.2d 786 (2d Cir.1992), cert. denied 113 S.Ct. 104 (1992).

this method are conservative and are said to be much more likely to be biased in favor of an accused individual.[21]

The NRC approached the subpopulation issue differently. It resolved for itself the subpopulation controversy by assuming that population substructure does exist, and, therefore, devised a method for estimating population frequencies which accounts for it.[22] Termed the "ceiling principle", it is based upon the premise that estimates will be appropriately conservative, even for subpopulations, when the allele frequencies used in the product rule exceed the allele frequencies in any of the subpopulation groups. Thus a "ceiling frequency" must first be determined for each allele at each locus. This frequency must be an upper bound for the allele frequency, independent of the ethnic background of the suspect. To accomplish this, 100 random samples should be taken from each of 15–20 populations that represent a group relatively homogeneous genetically. The largest frequency obtained in any of these populations for the allele in question is the ceiling frequency. If the frequency is less than 5%, then 5% becomes the ceiling frequency.[23] The goal of establishing a ceiling frequency is to define the likely range of allele frequency variation.[24]

After determining the allele ceiling frequencies, the product rule is invoked, using the ceiling frequencies for the calculation. The ceiling principle eliminates the need to calculate the allele frequency for a particular suspect's population, since the process is designed to give an upper bound to the frequency obtained from the suspect's group. Whatever power of individualization is lost by the use of a more conservative approach can be reestablished by testing additional loci, according to the NRC report.[25]

Both the NRC report and its ceiling principle are coming under increased criticism. Some critics argue that the ceiling principle is built on erroneous assumptions about population genetics and is unnecessarily conservative.[26] Others view the report's conclusions as seriously flawed

21. Waye & Fourney, op. cit. note 11 at p. 392.

22. Committee on DNA Technology in Forensic Science, Board on Biology, Commission on Life Sciences, National Research Council, *DNA Technology in Forensic Science* (1992), p. 80. The NRC also appears to assume in using the ceiling principle that the loci are in Hardy–Weinberg equilibrium. Herrin, "A Comparison of Models Used for Calculation of RFLP Pattern Frequencies," 37 *J.For.Sci.* 1640, 1648 (1992).

23. 5% was chosen because the NRC concluded that this frequency was a reliable predictor for unsampled subgroups. During the interim period while the reference samples are being collected from the 15–20 populations, however, the NRC recommends that 10% should be used temporarily instead of 5%. *DNA Technology in Forensic Science,* supra note 22 at pp. 84, 95.

24. *DNA Technology in Forensic Science,* supra note 22 at pp. 82–85.

25. The FBI's approach to calculating frequencies using the ceiling approach is described in Budowle and Monson, "The Approach Used by the FBI for Calculating Ceiling Frequencies," 19 *Crime Lab.Dig.* 84 (1992). The establishment of methods to calculate ceiling frequencies by the FBI is specifically disclaimed by them as an endorsement of the ceiling approach.

26. See, Delvin, Neil and Roeder, "Comments on the Statistical Aspects of the NRC's Report on DNA Typing," 39 *J.For. Sci.* 28 (1994); Budowle, Monson, Giusti, and Brown, "The Assessment of Frequency Estimates of Hae III–Generated VNTR Profiles in Various Reference Databases," 39 *J.For.Sci.* 319 (1994); Budowle, Monson, Giusti, and Brown, "Evaluation of Hinf I-

because the NRC panel lacked the necessary expertise in population genetics.[27] The degree to which the ceiling principle is accepted by population geneticists and other experts is unknown at this time.

2. LINKAGE EQUILIBRIUM

Earlier in this chapter, the concept of linkage equilibrium was discussed. The principle involves Mendel's law of independent assortment. The product rule will be valid only if the alleles, the frequencies of which are multiplied by each other, are independent, or said differently, if their inheritance is not linked together. If they tend to be transmitted together, linkage disequilibrium results. By using loci on different chromosomes, independent assortment is more likely, and conversely, the likelihood of linkage is diminished. The fixed bin and floating bin (discussed below) methods of determining frequencies assume an independence among loci, which is consistent with the lack of data demonstrating linkage between VNTR loci. The ceiling principle, proposed by the NRC, although assuming that population subgroups exist, also assumes that loci are in linkage equilibrium.[28]

3. A COMPARISON OF METHODS

There are two approaches to calculating the frequency of a particular pattern using RFLP analysis. One approach is the phenotype method, in which the banding pattern from a specific locus is treated in its entirety. The pattern frequency is determined using the observed number of occurrences of that particular pattern within the database, by counting the number of occurrences of a particular RFLP banding pattern at each locus within the data base and dividing the number of occurrences by the number of samples in the data base. The phenotype method, particularly when only one or two bands appear, is analogous to the method used for determining the frequency of blood groups, from which only phenotypes can be determined. This method avoids some assumptions made by the Hardy–Weinberg principle, and assumes linkage equilibrium and a lack of population subgroups.[29]

The second approach is the genotype method in which each band from a specific locus is treated as an independent allele. Genotype calculations can be accomplished by several approaches—the fixed bin, the floating bin, and the NRC method.[30]

Generated VNTR Profile Frequences Determined Using Various Ethnic Databases," 39 *J.For.Sci.* 988 (1994).

27. See, Aldhous, "Geneticists Attack NRC Report as Scientifically Flawed," 259 *Science* 755 (1993).

28. Herrin, op. cit. note 22.

29. Id. at pp. 1641, 1647.

30. Fixed bins are based on a series of DNA fragments of defined length which are included within each analysis. Floating bins are based on the calculated size of the fragment in question and a match criterion empirically determined within the laboratory. On the subject, generally, see Herrin, op. cit. note 22, from which the material in this subsection is derived primarily. See also, Monson and Budowle, op. cit. note 15.

Five variations of the above calculation methodologies were compared to determine how consistent the results might be. The five methods tested were: fixed bin genotype, floating bin genotype, floating bin phenotype, the NRC method using fixed bin, and the NRC method using floating bins. The results indicate that all five methods produce frequencies which are very similar in practical terms. A ranking of the methods from most conservative to least conservative put the NRC ceiling method, using 5% as the lowest ceiling frequency, on top. The fixed bin genotype and floating bin phenotype were about the same, and the floating bin genotype appeared to be the least conservative.[31] Another study confirms that the fixed bin method is more conservative than the floating bin, by one to four orders of magnitude.[32] The recent study on VNTR frequency estimations examined the forensic consequences of using a general reference data base to calculate frequencies when it is the inappropriate data base for the circumstances of a particular case. Samples were examined from 2,046 unrelated individuals identified as African–Americans, Caucasians, or Hispanics. The Hispanics were divided into a group from Florida and a group from Texas and California.

The resulting data from the study indicates that, although the bin frequencies are different among the four populations tested, they all exhibit high gene diversity for all loci. All VNTR profiles in the sample populations were found to be rare. It was concluded that profile frequency estimates from different reference populations do not deviate significantly, for purposes of forensic science applications.[33]

§ 15.13 From Theory to Practice: Assurances of Quality

The power to identify contributors of forensic samples through DNA typing imposes a heavy responsibility on those employing the procedure and interpreting the results to ensure that the laboratory process utilizes appropriate standards and controls to achieve valid and reliable test results. As the technology becomes more sophisticated and the results more precise, laboratories must be able to ensure for themselves, and thereby be able to assure their users, the courts, and the public, that they maintain the highest standards. In its report on DNA technology, the NRC reported a consensus among both critics and supporters of forensic DNA typing that standardization of practices and uniformly accepted methods for quality assurance had heretofore been lacking.[1]

In Part V of this chapter, the legal perspective on DNA typing will be discussed, and it will be seen that the courts have exhibited a

31. Herrin, op. cit. note 22 at pp. 1645–48.

32. Monson and Budowle, supra note 15 at 1049.

33. Id.

§ 15.13

1. Committee on DNA Technology in Forensic Science, Board on Biology, Commission on Life Sciences, National Research Council, *DNA Technology in Forensic Science* (1992), p. 97. An earlier report to Congress concerning the forensic uses of DNA encouraged the early development of technical, operational, and quality assurance standards. U.S. Congress, Office of Technology assessment, *Genetic Witness: Forensic Uses of DNA Tests*, (1990) pp. 59–88.

particular concern with issues of quality assurance when dealing with DNA typing. They often want to determine, prior to admitting results of DNA testing, that proper procedures were followed, that appropriate quality controls were employed and that a quality assurance program was in place to ensure that the defined standards of quality were indeed met.

The Technical Working Group on DNA Analysis Methods (TWGDAM) has developed guidelines for a quality assurance program for RFLP and PCR-based DNA typing.[2] TWGDAM is a group of scientists working in DNA typing who represent many federal, state and local forensic laboratories in both the United States and Canada. The group's purpose is to assemble active practitioners in the field to discuss methodology, compare their accomplishments, share protocols and establish guidelines. The FBI has been instrumental in the work of the group, as has been the California Association of Criminalists Ad Hoc Committee on DNA Quality Assurance. The recommendations for quality assurance contained in the guidelines have been endorsed by the American Society of Crime Laboratory Directors (ASCLD).[3] They are a model for laboratory managers to set up appropriate quality assurance programs.

The goal of the TWGDAM guidelines is to ensure the quality, integrity and reliability of the DNA typing data, accomplished by the use of quality control standards, proficiency tests and routine audits. Besides establishing the parameters of a quality assurance program within a laboratory, the guidelines establish qualifying standards for technical personnel, required documentation to provide historical data for post-test quality assurance audits, and developmental validation of the DNA analysis procedures. The guidelines also suggest appropriate maintenance, operation and handling of laboratory equipment, materials and facilities, as well as procedures for the correct handling, processing and storage of evidence. Analytical procedures are also suggested for each stage of the typing process to ensure an efficient and effective product, free of aberrant activity. Moreover, the guidelines provide a framework of checks and balances to ensure the reliability and completeness of documentation, data analysis reports and review process.

Significantly, TWGDAM promotes proficiency testing in their guidelines, in the form of both open and blind case evidence.[4] The open

2. "Guidelines for a Quality Assurance Program for DNA Restriction Fragment Length Polymorphism Analysis," 16 *Crime Lab. Dig.* 40–59 (1989); "Guidelines for a Proficiency Testing Program for DNA Restriction Fragment Length Polymorphism Analysis," 17 *Crime Lab. Dig.* 59–64 (1990); "Guidelines for a Quality Assurance Program for DNA Analysis," 18 *Crime Lab. Dig.* 44–75 (1991).

3. Bashinski, "Managing the Implementation and Use of DNA Typing in the Crime Laboratory," *Forensic DNA Technology* (Farley & Harrington, eds. 1991), p. 209.

4. Several blind trials using DQa typing on a total of 299 simulated evidentiary samples have been conducted. The California Association of Crime Laboratory Directors (CACLD) directed two studies, one in 1987 (one sample out of 50 was incorrectly typed) and the second in 1989 (all 50 samples were correctly typed). In 1990 Cetus conducted a blind trial involving 5 forensic science laboratories using the AmpliType (trade-

testing, which is recommended twice a year, is used to establish the reliability of a laboratory's analytical methods and the interpretive skills of the examiner. The blind proficiency test is more representative, but is recommended only once a year. This test evaluates all aspects of the laboratory procedure from evidence handling to report writing.

Missing from the guidelines are recommendations as to retention periods for the results of the proficiency tests, other than according to established laboratory policy. Nor is guidance given concerning the availability of the test results to litigants or other third parties.[5] The NRC report, however, does speak to these issues, calling for public disclosure of error rates and test results of laboratory proficiency tests.

The NRC report indicates that the TWGDAM guidelines are a good start, but do not go far enough to meet some of the committee's concerns on technical considerations and statistical interpretation.[6] The NRC also feels that the principles of quality assurance must be enforced by an appropriate combination of carrots and sticks, such as certification of individuals, accreditation of laboratories and incentive funding for compliance.[7]

Associated with quality control and quality assurance is the development of standard reference materials to be used in DNA typing. Reference material in the form of standards and controls have been assembled by the United States Department of Commerce, National Institute of Standards and Technology (NIST) and referred to as Standard Reference Material (SRM) 2390. The intended use of SRM 2390 is for paternity and forensic laboratory quality assurance programs which use RFLP testing involving the HaeIII restriction enzyme.

The development of standards and standardized practices for DNA typing has become a fact of life for the forensic laboratories. Pragmatically, such standardization is necessary to achieve the full potential of DNA typing. The establishment of national data banks, for example,

---

mark) HLA–DQ*a* kit. Of the 178 samples with results, all were correctly typed. Two California trial courts also organized blind trials in two cases. Out of a total of 17 samples with results, all were correctly typed. Blake, Mihalovich, Higuchi, Walsh, Erlich, "Polymerase Chain Reaction (PCR) Amplification and Human Leukocyte Antigen (HLA)–DQ*a* Oligonucleotide Typing on Biological Evidence Samples: Casework Experience," 37 *J.For.Sci.* 700, 704–705 (1992). See also, Walsh, Fildes, Louie and Higuchi, "Report of the Blind Trial of the Cetus Amplitype HLA DQ*a* Forensic Deoxyribonucleic Acid (DNA) Amplification and Typing Kit," 36 *J.For.Sci.* 1551 (1991). In the *Mehlberg* case, an FBI expert testified that the FBI had never been subjected to a proficiency test by an outside agency. All proficiency testing of personnel is conducted internally by the FBI's Forensic Science Research and Training Center. People v.

Mehlberg, 249 Ill.App.3d 499, 188 Ill.Dec. 598, 618, 618 N.E.2d 1168, 1188 (1993).

5. "Guidelines for a Quality Assurance Program for DNA Analysis," 18 *Crime Lab. Dig.* 46, 65–69 (1991).

6. *DNA Technology in Forensic Science,* supra note 1 at p. 99.

7. *DNA Technology in Forensic Science,* op. cit. note 1 at pp. 99–101. For the FBI's response to the NRC's recommendation on ensuring high standards, see: "The FBI's Responses to Recommendations by the NRC's Committee on DNA Technology in Forensic Science," 19 *Crime Lab. Dig.* 49 (1992). The "DNA Identification Act of 1994" (Section 210301 et seq. of the Violent Crime Control Act of 1994) makes federal funds available to state and local governments to acquire laboratory equipment to improve the quality and accessibility of DNA analysis.

will require that participating laboratories utilize the same practices to achieve results on a particular sample which are as nearly identical as possible. Standardization is also necessary to interlaboratory collaboration such as that which resulted in NIST's SRM 2390, and to the training effort and technology transfer which is now on going among forensic laboratories.[8]

IV. PARENTAGE AND IDENTITY

§ 15.14 Parentage and Identity Determinations

As in criminal cases involving violent crime, issues of identity are also paramount in cases where parentage or other blood relationships must be determined. These issues arise in paternity cases to establish the obligation of child support, in government entitlement cases to determine the right to receive benefits such as social security,[1] in immigration cases to determine if children are the true offspring of legal aliens,[2] and in proof-of-death, mass disaster, Missing in Action (MIA), and missing persons cases to establish the true identity of the deceased.[3] While traditional serological tests and other forensic examinations, such as dental and skeletal radiographic comparisons, and fingerprint comparisons contribute significantly to resolving identity issues in these cases, in many situations DNA typing can be more specific, or, at least, provide a meaningful alternative to traditional means of identification, when they are unavailable, insufficient or render inconclusive results.[4]

---

8. Bashinski, op. cit. note 3 at pp. 201, 208. The author describes the negative aspects of standardization.

§ 15.14

1. Odelberg, Demers, Westin, and Hossaini, "Establishing Paternity Using Minisatellite DNA Probes When the Putative Father is Unavailable for Testing," 33 *J.For.Sci.* 921 (1988). The case described by the authors entailed the determination of social security benefits for an alleged surviving child.

2. Kelly, Rankin and Wink, "Method and Application of DNA Fingerprinting: A Guide for the Non-Scientist,"—*Crim.L.Rep.* 105 (1987).

3. Holland, Fisher, Mitchell, Rodriquez, Canik, Merril and Weedn, "Mitochondrial DNA Sequence Analysis of Human Skeletal Remains: Identification of Remains from The Vietnam War," 38 *J.For.Sci.* 542 (1993). Very small amounts of mtDNA have been recovered from bone specimens 5500 years of age and older. Mitochondrial DNA was also analyzed in a case of a missing child, as reported in Blake et al., op. cit. note 4, section 15.13, at pp. 709–10. The determination of parentage may also be

helpful in cases of crimes against the person, such as infanticide, and incest and rape when impregnation of the victim occurs.

4. Tonelli, Markowicz, Anderson, Green, Herrin, Cotton, Dykes, Garner, "Use of Deoxyribonucleic Acid (DNA) Fingerprints for Identity Determination: Comparison with Traditional Paternity Testing Methods— Part I," 35 *J.For.Sci.* 1265, 1268 (1990). The first reported case where DNA typing was used in a parentage context to establish identity of unidentified, decomposed human remains is found in Haglund, Reay and Tepper, "Identification of Decomposed Human Remains by Deoxyribonucleic Acid (DNA) Profiling," 35 *J.For.Sci.* 724 (1990). Also see, Holland et al., op. cit. note 3, in which the identification of a serviceman, thought to be dead for 24 years, was made using mitochondrial DNA. DNA from bone tissue is also suitable for both RFLP and PCR analysis. In addition, dental pulp has also yielded high molecular-weight DNA. Lee, Pagliaro, Berka, Folk, Anderson, Ruano, Keith, Phipps, Herrin, Garner, and Gaensslen, "Genetic Markers in Human Bone: 1. Deoxyribonucleic Acid (DNA) Analysis," 36 *J.For.Sci.* 320, 321 (1991). Also see, Hochmeister, Budowle, Borer, Eggmann, Comey and Dirnhofer, "Typing

The same well-known genetic principle discussed earlier form the basis for establishing paternity. (Likewise, the same principle applies to establishing maternity, and hereinafter, reference will be made to parentage, rather than paternity alone.) The principle referred to states that a child will possess the composite genetic traits of the parents. Half of a child's chromosomes are inherited from the mother and half from the father. Thus, blood samples from the child, known parent and putative parent are compared to determine whether the genetic markers detectable in the child could have been inherited from the putative parent.

Traditional tests for determining parentage have involved genetic marker systems, including red cell antigens, red cell enzymes, serum proteins, and the Human Leukocyte Antigen (HLA), in conjunction with statistical analyses. HLA, for example, entails an analysis of the antigens found in an individual's white blood cells, and is a commonly accepted test with extremely discriminating results.[5] This and other commonly used tests can only conclusively exclude the putative parent. If the alleged parent is not excluded, a calculation can be made to estimate the likelihood of the individual being a parent, called the Paternity Index.[6] The polymorphic markers used in these blood tests have established frequencies of occurrence in the population, which form the basis for calculating the chance the putative parent has of passing to the child all the necessary markers, as opposed to a randomly selected male or female. When using the available range of polymorphic markers, the probability of parentage, in cases where no exclusion is determined, can reach 99 percent in most cases and over 99.75 percent in a majority of cases.[7]

Even with those statistically significant probabilities, DNA typing is useful, and has distinct advantages over traditional methods of determining parentage in some cases. DNA typing can conclusively establish that an individual is or is not the biological parent of a child.[8] Using multilocus probes, for example, half of the DNA fragments appearing on the child's lane of the autoradiograph will match the mother's and the other half the father's. If this occurs, the putative parent's relationship to the child is established, because all but the biological parent will be excluded. See Figure 16.

of Deoxyribonucleic Acid (DNA) Extracted from Compact Bone from Human Remains," 36 *J.For.Sci.* 1649 (1991); Smith, Fisher, Weedn, Warnock and Holland, "A Systematic Approach to the Sampling of Dental DNA," 38 *J.For.Sci.* 1194 (1993), and Schwartz, Schwartz, Mieszerski, McNally and Kobilinsky, "Characterization of Deoxyribonucleic Acid (DNA) Obtained from Teeth Subjected to Various Environmental Conditions," 36 *J.For.Sci.* 979 (1991).

5. Articles describing this and other tests can be found in Comment, "DNA Fin-

gerprinting and Paternity Testing," 22 *U.C.D. L.Rev.* 609, 614, fn. 15 (1989).

6. Tonelli et al., op. cit. note 4 at pp. 1265–66.

7. 3 Wecht, *Forensic Sciences* (1992), pp. 37C–21—37C–22.

8. Tonelli, Markowicz, Anderson, Green, Herrin, Cotton, Dykes, Garner, "Use of Deoxyribonucleic Acid (DNA) Fingerprints for Identity Determination: Comparison with Traditional Paternity Testing Methods—Part II," 35 *J.For.Sci.* 1265 (1990) and "Part II," 35 *J.For.Sci.* 1270 (1990).

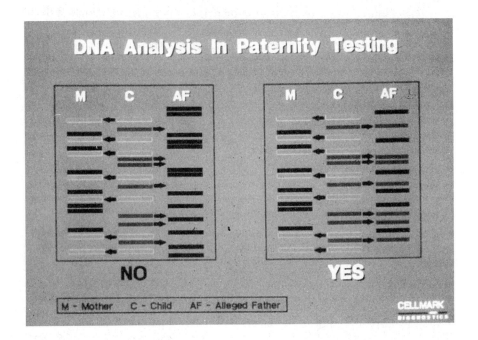

Fig. 16. DNA analysis used in paternity testing. *Courtesy: Cellmark Diagnostics*

Existing blood tests require a series of tests to establish a significant probability of parentage. DNA typing, on the other hand, requires only a single test when using multi-locus probes, and a limited repetition of the same test, or the use of a "cocktail", when using several different single-locus probes. Moreover, the determination of parentage can be made while the child is under six months of age using DNA typing. Current blood testing methodology suggests that the child be at least six months old to obtain meaningful results,[9] since the blood antigens for genetic markers analyzed by these tests do not develop in sufficient quantity until the child is three to six months old. In fact, the DNA make-up of a newborn, as well as a fetus, can be ascertained, giving DNA typing greater flexibility in parentage determinations.

DNA analysis may also be more definitive than traditional serological tests, because of the limitations of those tests. For example, it has been reported that traditional tests may result in an indirect exclusion when a child does not inherit a genetic marker that should have been received from a parent who is believed to be homozygous for that marker. An indirect exclusion often occurs because that parent has a rare allele that is not observed and is only detected by a specialized reagent. The significant possibility of error in this regard causes many laboratories to require that an exclusion in at least two different genetic

9. Ludes, Mangin, Malicier, Chalumeau, and Chaumont, "Parentage Determination on Aborted Fetal Material Through Deoxy-ribonucleic Acid (DNA) Profiling," 36 *J.For. Sci.* 1219 (1991).

marker systems must be found before parentage is excluded. In a comparison of paternity determinations between DNA and traditional methods, DNA analysis was able to definitely exclude parentage when indirect exclusions occurred in traditional testing.[10]

Unlike traditional testing, DNA typing can be accomplished not only with a variety of biological fluids and tissues, but also with much smaller samples, such as a simple heel stick from a newborn, than can be tested by traditional serological methods. Moreover, the DNA molecule is much more stable than other genetic markers.[11]

The importance of these advantages of DNA typing may not be readily apparent in routine testing where, for example, paternity is an issue in a civil cause of action for child support. However, cases do arise where alternative types of biological fluid or tissue other than blood, of necessity, must be used. One example may be the identity determination of the remains of a deceased individual, which might be in such condition so as to preclude traditional means of identification, leaving it to DNA typing to determine identity or parentage.[12]

Another example might arise where the putative parent might not be alive or available to give a sample of blood for testing. This situation could result in two possible scenarios. The first is where the child, whose parent is in dispute, has siblings. In that case, the siblings can be used to establish common parentage among all of them. Where the father of one child is in dispute, for example, the autoradiographs of all the siblings will exhibit bands, half of which are in common with the known mother. The remaining bands will be in common among all the siblings, if there is a common father among them. When such similarity is present, the known, but absent, father of the child's siblings is established as the father of the child also.

A situation may also occur where the child, whose parent is in dispute, has no siblings, and the alleged parent, for example, the father, is dead or otherwise absent. In such a case, the putative father's parents and their siblings can be used for testing, and DNA analysis can give nearly conclusive evidence that the putative father is the biological father of the child.[13]

However, DNA analysis for parentage determination is not without its limitations. There appear to be several conditions which might in

---

10. Tonelli et al., op. cit. note 4 at pp. 1267–68 (1990).

11. Markowicz et al., op. cit. note 8 at p. 1274.

12. Several fragments of tissue were recovered from 64 tons of silage, after a 2 year old girl was reported missing. She was last seen in a corn field being harvested by a tractor pulling a corn chopper. The tissue was analyzed using PCR DQa and RFLP DNA typing and compared to the couple who reported the child missing. The relative chance of the couple being the bio-logical parents exceeded 99.99%. Mulhare, McQuillen, Collins, Heintz, and Howard, "An Unusual Case Using DNA Polymorphisms to Determine Parentage of Human Remains," 12 *Am.J.For.Med. & Path.* 157 (1991).

13. Odelberg, Demers, Westin, and Hossaini, "Establishing Paternity Using Minisatellite DNA Probes When the Putative Father is Unavailable for Testing," 33 *J.For.Sci.* 921 (1988).

some cases, although very rarely, cause a false exclusion in those cases. The first is the occurrence of a meiotic cross-over, which takes place at a restriction enzyme cleavage site. As a result, the child could inherit a slightly different DNA sequence from the parents than would be inherited had no crossover taken place. If that occurs, DNA analysis of the child results in a banding pattern different than one expected from an examination of the parent's DNA.[14]

Another possibility for a false exclusion could arise from a mutation in a spermatogonial cell. This mutation might affect the DNA analysis only if the mutation occurs at a restriction enzyme cleavage site. While the incidence of this mutation has not yet been established, it is believed that it is so low that the mutation rate should be expressed in terms of evolutionary time frames.

A third possibility, relevant particularly to paternity determinations, is called uniparental disomy, caused by meiotic nondisjunction. In that case, a child carries two copies of a maternal chromosome and lacks a chromosome derived from the father. This situation has been estimated to occur in 1/30,000 conceptions, and a verified case, although not involving disputed paternity, has been documented.[15]

A final concern raised by the same commentators regarding false parentage exclusion involves meiotic recombinations when VNTRs are the genetic markers used in parentage testing. When this type of mutation occurs, new fragment lengths may result, causing a false exclusion, if they are inherited. Guidelines have been proposed to determine the mutation rate for the VNTR loci, and to discourage the use of loci for paternity testing which exhibit high rates of mutation.

Although emphasis has been placed on determinations of paternity, frequently maternity must be established. These cases might involve the discovery of aborted fetuses, abandoned babies, abduction of newborns, and the intentional or unintentional switching of babies in a hospital. In maternity testing, the analysis of mitochondrial DNA (mtDNA) can be very useful.[16] Mitochondrial DNA is inherited solely from the mother, because spermatozoa do not transfer mitochondria to the egg during fertilization. Profiles of mitochondrial DNA are exclusively maternal in inheritance. It has been shown that profiling mito-

---

14. Kobilinsky and Levine, "Recent Application of DNA to Issues of Paternity (Letters to the Editor)," 33 *J.For.Sci.* 1107 (1988). This possibility, as well as others described, infra, are deemed by others to be unlikely and extremely rare events, and that error could more likely be caused through laboratory mistakes than through the processes described in the article. These scenarios could also occur in conventional serological testing. See, Waye, "Discussion of 'Recent Applications of DNA Analysis to Issues of Paternity' (Letters to the Editor)," 35 *J.For.Sci.* 5 (1990) and Pignatti and Marigo, "Discussion of 'Recent

Applications of DNA Analysis to Issues of Paternity' (Letters to the Editor)," 35 *J.For.Sci.* 517 (1990).

15. Kobilinsky and Levine, supra note 14 at pp. 1107–08 (1988); Waye, "Discussion of 'Recent Applications of DNA Analysis to Issues of Paternity' (Letters to the Editor)," 35 *J.For.Sci.* 5 (1990).

16. Mitochondrial DNA has also been used to identify the remains of individuals exposed to extreme environmental conditions for many years. See, Holland et al., op. cit. note 3.

chondrial DNA from a child, her mother and unrelated females can clearly resolve cases of disputed maternity.[17]

1. SINGLE LOCUS PROBES

The same advantages and disadvantages of using a single locus probe, versus a multi-locus probe, apply in parentage testing, as they do in crime scene sample analysis. If a single-locus probe is used, heterozygous parents will each display two bands. One band from each parent will be inherited by their child. Virtually every wrongly named putative parent will be excluded using this test. When several or more probes are used on the same sample, near absolute probability of parentage can be obtained.[18]

2. MULTI–LOCUS PROBES

Using a multi-locus probe system, a number of bands will appear on the autoradiograph. Still, half of the child's bands will be identical to the mother and half to the father. Although there has been some reservation about the use of multi-locus probes, its use in distinguishing first-degree relatives and in determining paternity in incest cases can be effective.[19]

3. QUALITY ASSURANCE

In true paternity cases, the samples from the child, the known parent and the putative parent should be in virtually pristine condition. They are not subject to the environmental insults, mixing and contamination to which crime scene samples are exposed. Nevertheless, quality assurance in the laboratory is still important. The American Association of Blood Banks (AABB) has developed a laboratory certification for clinical DNA testing laboratories. It is also exploring with the College of American Pathologists a cooperative effort to develop proficiency testing for specialty laboratories.[20]

---

17. Kobilinsky and Levine, "Author's Response (Letters to the Editor)," 35 *J.For. Sci.* 518, 519 (1990); Orrego, Wilson and King, "Identification of Maternally Related Individuals by Amplification and Direct Sequencing of a Highly Polymorphic, Noncoding Region of Mitochondrial DNA," 43 *Am. J.Hum.Gen.* A219 (1988).

18. Odelberg, Demers, Westin, and Hossaini, "Establishing Paternity Using Minisatellite DNA Probes When the Putative Father is Unavailable for Testing," 33 *J.For.Sci.* 921, 926–27 (1988); 3 Wecht, *Forensic Sciences* (1992), pp. 37C–23—37C–27. The possibility of distinguishing between possible fathers who are brothers is still difficult to do.

19. 3 Wecht, *Forensic Sciences* (1992), pp. 37C–27—37C–30. Wecht reports that in some quarters, multi-locus probes are deemed not as desirable because of the less clearly defined statistics available. In addition, the mutation rates for multi-locus systems are higher and there is insufficient information about linkage equilibrium in the use of multi-locus probes.

20. Committee on DNA Technology in Forensic Science, Board on Biology, Commission on Life Sciences, National Research

V. EVIDENTIAL AND PRACTICAL ASPECTS OF DNA TYPING

§ 15.15 DNA Typing in the Courts

When DNA typing began to appear on the forensic and legal horizons, many individuals predicted that it would have a major impact in criminal cases, and to a lesser, but still significant degree, in civil cases. High expectations were rampant. A co-author of this book proclaimed that "DNA analysis will be to the end of the 20th Century what fingerprinting was to the 19th."[1] A state trial judge wrote an opinion pronouncing DNA typing as the "... single greatest advance in the 'search for truth,' and the goal of convicting the guilty and acquitting the innocent, since the advent of cross-examination."[2] Even the corporate trademark of "DNA fingerprinting" reflected the confidence of its promoters that DNA typing would undoubtedly gain widespread confidence, utility, and acceptance by forensic scientists, criminal justice professionals, judges and the public.

As early as 1989, several state legislatures leapt onto the DNA bandwagon by recognizing the potential of DNA typing. The Maryland General Assembly mandated the admissibility of DNA typing in any criminal proceeding on the issue of identity, after having proclaimed that DNA identification had been refined to a level of scientific accuracy that approaches an infinitesimal margin of error.[3] The Washington State legislature, while enacting a data banking statute, determined the accuracy of DNA identification to be superior to that of any presently existing technique.[4] In addition, scientists, legal commentators, and attorneys all recognized the reliability and validity of the theory and technique underlying the process of DNA typing. Reviewing courts were also equally unanimous about the fundamental reliability and admissibility of DNA typing.[5]

Indeed, the fundamental utility and widespread use of DNA typing in criminal and civil cases has been demonstrated beyond reasonable rebuttal. The FBI, only one of many laboratories analyzing DNA in criminal cases, is doing so in 1500 to 2000 cases per year,[6] and the reported cases are replete with examples of the use of DNA typing to identify the perpetrator of a crime by analysis of biological evidence left at a crime scene or on an implement used by the criminal. Hair, blood,

---

Council, *DNA Technology in Forensic Science* (1992), p. 102.

§ 15.15

1. Comment, "DNA Fingerprinting and Paternity Testing," 22 *U.C.D. L.Rev.* 609, 635 n. 98 (1989), quoting Professor James E. Starrs.

2. People v. Wesley, 140 Misc.2d 306, 533 N.Y.S.2d 643 (Co.Ct.1988).

3. See Preamble to Md.Code, Cts. & Jud. Proc., § 10–915 (Supp.1993) found in 1989 Laws of Md., ch. 430.

4. See legislative finding (1989 C.350) accompanying West's Wash.Rev.Code Ann. § 43.43.752 (Supp.1992).

5. Moenssens, "DNA Evidence and Its Critics—How Valid are the Challenges?" 31 *Jurimetrics J.* 87, 93 (1990).

6. Springfield v. State, 860 P.2d 435, 444 (Wyo.1993).

semen, saliva, skin and bone are only examples of the trace evidence collected by crime scene investigators which are eventually linked to a defendant through DNA analysis.

But evidence linking a victim to the suspect or suspect's belongings is also important. One of the better known cases in which such evidence was available is People v. Castro.[7] Joseph Castro was accused of stabbing to death a 20–year–old pregnant mother and her 2–year–old daughter. When arrested, he was wearing a wristwatch, which the police confiscated because it appeared to contain bloodstains. Hoping to prove that the bloodstains were from the deceased mother, rather than from Castro, the prosecution sought to introduce DNA identification tests conducted by Lifecodes, a commercial laboratory. In one of the first extended legal battles over the admissibility of DNA evidence, the trial court excluded the evidence for reasons to be discussed later in this chapter. The case became a bench mark for many courts grappling with this new and highly technical area of forensic science.

Another use of forensic DNA typing in criminal cases involves the determination of parentage. Aborted fetuses, conceived as a result of rapes, have been shown through DNA typing to be the off-spring of defendants.[8] And in Oklahoma the police were able to link a mother to a newborn baby found in a garbage can.[9]

Investigators have also utilized DNA typing to identify murder victims when other means of identification were not possible, and to associate body parts in cases of dismemberment. Human tissue found on the grille of an automobile, for example, was identified as having come from a possible victim by comparing the sample with the DNA of the victim's parents.[10] Badly decomposed bodies and skeletal remains of victims of foul play have also been frequently identified through DNA technology.

DNA analysis can also be helpful in identifying serial crimes where a common perpetrator is involved, or to disassociate cases thought to be related, but in actuality committed by a "copycat" criminal. Just as important, is the capability of excluding a suspect by DNA analysis, allowing the police to expand or re-focus their investigation. Such was a 1986 case, made famous by Joseph Wambaugh's "The Blooding", where a suspect was charged in England with murder and rape. He was eventually exonerated by DNA technology, after thousands of men living near the victim's home voluntarily submitted blood samples for DNA testing. The real perpetrator was eventually suspected of the crime when the authorities learned that he had sent a friend to give blood

---

7. 144 Misc.2d 956, 545 N.Y.S.2d 985 (1989).

8. United States v. Young, 754 F.Supp. 739 (D.S.D.1990) and People v. Bailey, 140 Misc.2d 306, 533 N.Y.S.2d 643 (Co.Ct.1988); People v. Atoigue, 1992 WL 245628 (D.Guam App.Div.1992).

9. Comment, "DNA Fingerprinting and Paternity Testing," 22 *U.C.D. L.Rev.* 609, 640 (1989).

10. Comment, "DNA Identification Tests and the Courts," 63 *Wash.L.Rev.* 903, 905 n. 2 (1988).

under his name. He was convicted in early 1988, after being linked to the crime by DNA analysis.[11]

The use of DNA evidence is not limited to the investigative and trial stages of a criminal investigation. Post-conviction relief has been granted in a number of cases, including capital cases, where evidence has been re-examined using new DNA analytical methods.

Glen Woodall was convicted of multiple felonies, including two counts of sexual assault and sentenced to a prison term of 203 to 335 years. At his trial, a West Virginia state trooper, who was also in charge of the state police crime laboratory's serology section, testified falsely that serological examinations he conducted determined that the "assailant's blood types" were identical to Woodall's, and that his blood traits would statistically occur in only 6 of 10,000 males in West Virginia.[12] Woodall's convictions were affirmed on appeal.[13] In a subsequent habeas corpus proceeding, the West Virginia Supreme Court of Appeals ordered DNA testing of the evidence. The laboratory, using RFLP-based DNA typing, reported "insufficient high molecular weight DNA" for testing. PCR testing, using the DQa locus, was then successfully performed, conclusively establishing that Woodall could not have been the perpetrator.[14]

After a civil suit brought by Woodall was settled for one million dollars, the Superintendent of the Division of Public Safety was ordered to conduct an internal audit of the trooper's work in the serology department. The audit, conducted by the American Society of Crime Laboratory Directors (ASCLD), revealed a long and shocking history of falsifying evidence in criminal prosecutions by the trooper.[15] It was determined that the trooper had made positive identifications of either the suspect or the victim in 133 cases. A post-conviction habeas corpus form, designed to identify those individuals who desired to seek habeas relief on the issue of the trooper's improprieties was distributed to the defendants in those cases. As a condition for obtaining such relief, the convicts were required to consent to a DNA test, if there was any serological evidence available. A special report to the West Virginia Supreme Court of Appeals recommended that "[i]f such testing conclu-

---

11. Also see a discussion of *California v. Quintinilla* in Blake, Mihalovich, Higuchi, Walsh and Erlich, "Polymerase Chain Reaction (PCR) Amplification and Human Leukocyte Antigen (HLA)–DQa Oligonucleotide Typing on Biological Evidence Samples: Casework Experience," 37 *J.For.Sci.* 700, 710 (1992), where DNA evidence cleared an initial suspect and helped convict another.

12. In the Matter of an Investigation of the West Virginia State Police Crime Laboratory, Serology Division, 190 W.Va. 321, 438 S.E.2d 501 (1993).

13. State v. Woodall, 182 W.Va. 15, 385 S.E.2d 253 (1989).

14. Blake, Mihalovich, Higuchi, Walsh and Erlich, "Polymerase Chain Reaction

(PCR) Amplification and Human Leukocyte Antigen (HLA)–DQa Oligonucleotide Typing on Biological Evidence Samples: Casework Experience," 37 *J.For.Sci.* 700, 718 (1992).

15. The trooper's misconduct ranged from overstating the strength of results to reporting scientifically impossible or improbable results. In the Matter of an Investigation of the West Virginia State Police Crime Laboratory, Serology Division, 190 W.Va. 321, 438 S.E.2d 501 (1993). For comments on this case, and additional cases involving retesting, by DNA, of previously convicted inmates, see, Moenssens, "Novel Scientific Evidence in Criminal Cases: Some Words of Caution," 84 *J.Crim.L. & Criminology* 1, 13–16 (1993).

sively establishes the innocence of the petitioner, then an order granting his or her release should *ordinarily* be entered" (emphasis added).[16]

Post-conviction DNA tests which eliminate the convicted person as the source of the biological fluid being examined, however, do not always mean exoneration. After being convicted of a rape occurring four years earlier, Gary Yorke filed a motion for a new trial based on newly discovered evidence. The laboratory report, which was submitted as new evidence, concluded that Yorke's DNA pattern did not match the pattern from the male fraction of the vaginal washings obtained from the 15–year–old victim at the time of the offense. The laboratory could not ascertain the origin of the questioned evidence at all. Despite the new evidence, Yorke's motion for a new trial was denied. A Maryland appellate court agreed with the trial court that the new evidence would not have affected the outcome of the case. Although the absence of Yorke's DNA excluded him as the source of that particular semen, the evidence did not eliminate him as a possible perpetrator, since the victim did not know if the rapist ejaculated.[17]

The application of DNA technology in civil cases is well documented also. Parentage and identity determination cases abound with references to the utilization of DNA identification technology.[18]

It is readily apparent, then, that there is a current and expansive use of DNA analysis in criminal and civil cases and the early prognostications of the ultimate success of this new forensic adaptation of a traditional medical research technique have been prophetic, to say the least. However, DNA's ride over the scientific and legal landscape, from its beginning as a novel scientific technique to a forensic methodology worthy of judicial notice, has not been without incident and has yet to be completed.

§ 15.16 DNA Typing as a "Novel Scientific Technique"

If the introduction of DNA analysis has done nothing else, it has fanned the flames of the debate over the proper test for admitting novel

---

16. In the Matter of an Investigation of the West Virginia State Police Crime Laboratory, Serology Division, 190 W.Va. 321, 438 S.E.2d 501 (1993). Also see the discussion of the Gary Dotson case, where post-conviction relief was granted. Blake, Mihalovich, Higuchi, Walsh and Erlich, "Polymerase Chain Reaction (PCR) Amplification and Human Leukocyte Antigen (HLA)–DQα Oligonucleotide Typing on Biological Evidence Samples: Casework Experience," 37 *J.For.Sci.* 700, 716 (1992).

17. Yorke v. Maryland, 315 Md. 578, 556 A.2d 230 (1989). These and other examples and applications of forensic DNA analysis are described in Kirby, *DNA Fingerprinting: An Introduction* (1990), pp. 189–192, 217–259.

18. See examples in § 15.14, supra. In Department of Social Services ex rel. Wolf v. McCarty, 506 N.W.2d 144 (S.D.1993), a former DEA agent contended he was not the father of a child conceived by a woman who was not his wife. Despite two DNA tests which determined a probability of paternity from 99.5 to 99.89%, he maintained that he should have been allowed to present evidence of his sterility. He denied any sexual encounter, claimed he was tortured by drug dealers by application of electrodes to his genitals, rendering him sterile, asserted he was unable to have any children with his wife since the torture, and produced evidence of fertility tests conducted prior to trial which indicated he was, in fact, sterile. The South Dakota Supreme Court ruled that the trial court erred when it excluded that evidence.

scientific evidence.   The primary tug-of-war has been between the *Frye* test,[1] applied by the majority of jurisdictions,[2] and the relevancy test,[3] a more liberal test of admissibility, or variations of each of those evidentiary themes.   Many legal commentators have debated which test should apply to DNA technology in particular.[4] Regardless of the particular test applied, however, courts have universally agreed that the underlying theory and technique used for DNA typing is valid and reliable.[5] No court has rejected RFLP-based DNA typing on the basis that it is not generally accepted by the scientific community.[6] PCR-based DNA typing has also been adjudicated admissible evidence.[7] Even those courts that ultimately rejected DNA evidence, recognized the general acceptance of the underlying theory and technique.[8]

One of the early and most influential cases on the issue of admissibility is People v. Castro, 144 Misc.2d 956, 545 N.Y.S.2d 985 (1989). Although New York is a *Frye* jurisdiction, the Castro court took a more conservative approach to DNA, creating a standard of admissibility even more stringent than *Frye*.   In addition to requiring general acceptance of the theory and technique in the scientific community, the Castro court added a requirement that a determination be made that the laboratory properly applied the technique on each particular occasion.   Thus, *Castro* broke from tradition, along with other courts which later adopted *Castro*'s reasoning,[9] by making the proper application of the generally

§ 15.16

1. Frye v. United States, 293 F. 1013 (App.D.C.1923). The court ruled that the new scientific technique must be sufficiently established to have gained general acceptance in the particular field to which it belongs. The *Frye* test is extensively discussed in Chapter 1 of this text.

2. United States v. Martinez, 3 F.3d 1191, 1195 (8th Cir.1993), cert. denied 114 S.Ct. 734 (1994).

3. The relevancy test is embodied in Rules 401, 402, and 403 of the Federal Rules of Evidence and various state court evidence codes modeled after the Federal Rules. See also, Daubert v. Merrell Dow Pharmaceuticals, Inc., 113 S.Ct. 2786 (1993), which did away with the *Frye* test in federal civil and criminal trials. Andrews v. State, 533 So.2d 841 (Fla.App. 5 Dist. 1988) [extensively quoting the 3rd edition of this text] was the first appellate court to rule DNA evidence admissible under the relevancy test. Also see, United States v. Jakobetz, 955 F.2d 786 (2d Cir.1992), cert. denied 113 S.Ct. 104 (1992); United States v. Bonds, 12 F.3d 540 (6th Cir.1993); and United States v. Martinez, 3 F.3d 1191, 1195 (8th Cir.1993), cert. denied 114 S.Ct. 734 (1994).

4. See generally, Giannelli, "The Admissibility of Novel Scientific Evidence: Frye v. United States, a Half–Century Later", 80 Colum.L.Rev. 1197 (1980); Moenssens, "Admissibility of Scientific Evidence— Should the Frye Rule Be Maintained?," 25 *Wm. & Mary L.Rev.* 545 (1984). "Rules for the Admissibility of Scientific Evidence," 115 FRD 79 (1978); Starrs, " 'A Still–Life Watercolor': Frye v. United States," 27 *J.For.Sci.* 684 (1982).

5. Springfield v. State, 860 P.2d 435, 442 and n. 1 (Wyo.1993); United States v. Martinez, 3 F.3d 1191, 1194 (8th Cir.1993), cert. denied 114 S.Ct. 734 (1994); Harmon, "General Admissibility Considerations for DNA Typing Evidence: Let's Learn From the Past and Let the Scientists Decide This Time Around," *Forensic DNA Technology* (Farley & Harrington, eds. 1991), p. 168.

6. State v. Cauthron, 120 Wash.2d 879, 846 P.2d 502, 511 (1993).

7. State v. Lyons, 124 Or.App. 598, 863 P.2d 1303 (1993).

8. Commonwealth v. Curnin, 409 Mass. 218, 565 N.E.2d 440 (1991); State v. Schwartz, 447 N.W.2d 422 (Minn.1989); State v. Woodall, 182 W.Va. 15, 385 S.W.2d 253 (1989); People v. Castro, 144 Misc.2d 956, 545 N.Y.S.2d 985 (1989).

9. See, for example, United States v. Two Bulls. 918 F.2d 56 (8th Cir.1990), vacated and dismissed as moot 925 F.2d 1127 (8th Cir.1991); State v. Schwartz, 447

accepted technique a condition of admissibility. The court observed that "a scientist may have no trouble accepting the general proposition that DNA typing can become reliable, yet still have doubts about the reliability of the test performed by a particular laboratory." 545 N.Y.S.2d at 995. The trial court found that the defense successfully demonstrated a failure by the laboratory to perform the accepted scientific techniques and experiments in several major respects. As a result, and even though the court found the theory and technique to be generally accepted, the evidence of a match, and the frequency estimate of 1 in 1 billion were ruled inadmissible.[10]

Other courts, however, while recognizing the general proposition that proper application of the accepted techniques may be an issue in many cases, have held to the more traditional view that the degree to which proper protocols were followed during the administration of the tests goes to the weight of the evidence rather than its admissibility.[11] In those jurisdictions, once the general test of admissibility has been met, the courts may thereafter take judicial notice of the reliability and validity of the theory and technique underlying DNA typing, and discard the requirement of further admissibility hearings.[12] In fact, the NRC recommends that courts take judicial notice of three scientific underpinnings of DNA typing. They are:

1. The study of DNA polymorphisms can, in principle, provide a reliable method for comparing samples.

2. Each person's DNA is unique (with the exception of identical twins), although the actual discriminatory power of any particular DNA test will depend on the sites of DNA variation examined.

N.W.2d 422 (Minn.1989). The NRC report recommends that the adequacy of the method used to acquire and analyze samples in a given case should bear on the admissibility of the evidence and be adjudicated on a case by case basis. Committee on DNA Technology in Forensic Science, Board on Biology, Commission on Life Sciences, National Research Council, *DNA Technology in Forensic Science* (1992), p. 149. Cf. United States v. Martinez, 3 F.3d 1191, 1198 (8th Cir.1993), cert. denied 114 S.Ct. 734 (1994) (even under *Daubert,* supra, the court should make an initial inquiry into the proper application of the technique, and only if error negates the basis for the reliability of the principle itself will there be a reason for exclusion).

10. As a result of the Castro case, Lifecodes, the examining laboratory, changed some of its methods, such as standards for declaring matches and for calculating frequency estimates. See, People v. Golub, 196 A.D.2d 637, 601 N.Y.S.2d 502 (1993).

11. See generally, Fishback v. People, 851 P.2d 884, 893 (Colo.1993); State v.

Cauthron, 120 Wash.2d 879, 846 P.2d 502, 512 (1993); Springfield v. State, 860 P.2d 435, 444 (Wyo.1993).

12. See, Fishback v. People, supra note 11; State v. Bible, 175 Ariz. 549, 858 P.2d 1152 (1993); State v. Davis, 860 S.W.2d 369 (Mo.App.1993); Nichols v. State, 210 Ga. App. 134, 435 S.E.2d 502 (1993); United States v. Jakobetz, 955 F.2d 786, 799 (2d Cir.1992), cert. denied 113 S.Ct. 104 (1992); and United States v. Martinez, 3 F.3d 1191, 1197 (8th Cir.1993), cert. denied 114 S.Ct. 734 (1994) (in the future, courts can take judicial notice, unless new techniques are offered, and then the court must hold an *in limine* hearing under *Daubert*). In Minnesota, a *Frye* hearing is still required. However, the hearing need only focus on the laboratory's compliance with appropriate standards and controls, not on whether they are the correct standards or on the basic DNA RFLP testing procedures themselves, since the latter two subject areas affect only the weight of the evidence. State v. Johnson, 498 N.W.2d 10, 14 (Minn. 1993).

3. The current laboratory procedure for detecting DNA variation (specifically, single locus probes analyzed on Southern blots without evidence of band shifting) is fundamentally sound, although the validity of any particular implementation of the basic procedure will depend on proper characterization of the reproducibility of the system (e.g., measurement variations) and the inclusion of all necessary scientific controls.[13]

The proper foundation for the evidence, such as the expert's qualifications, proper application of testing techniques and accurate recording of test results, still must be presented. That evidence may be elicited in front of the jury, or alternatively, outside of the jury's presence.[14]

Despite the initial success enjoyed by proponents of DNA typing in convincing courts of the general acceptance of the theory and technique underlying the process, a debate erupted in late 1991 over the statistical calculation process, which raised doubts over the general acceptance of frequency computations.[15] As a result, the courts began to focus on probability calculations which accompany a declared match of DNA banding patterns. Numerous courts considering the question have found the statistical frequencies to lack general acceptance in the relevant scientific communities.[16] Some courts have not only disallowed evidence of the statistical probability of a random match, but, in the

13. The NRC report also suggests that the proper implementation of the technology in a given case bears on the admissibility of the evidence and should be examined on a case by case basis. Committee on DNA Technology in Forensic Science, Board on Biology, Commission on Life Sciences, National Research Council, *DNA Technology in Forensic Science* (1992), p. 149.

14. State v. Bible, 175 Ariz. 549, 858 P.2d 1152, 1184 (1993); United States v. Jakobetz, 955 F.2d 786, 799–800 (2d Cir. 1992), cert. denied 113 S.Ct. 104 (1992). In State v. Schwartz, 447 N.W.2d 422 (Minn. 1989), the court felt that cross-examination and limiting instructions were inadequate protection for the defendant from the undue weight and credence likely to be given to statistical evidence by the jury. 447 N.W.2d at 428–429. The opposite view is taken by the court in State v. Futch, 123 Or.App. 176, 860 P.2d 264, 270 (1993).

15. State v. Bible, 175 Ariz. 549, 858 P.2d 1152, 1187 (1993). A discussion of the positions taken by the leading antagonists of the debate over frequency calculations can be found in People v. Barney, 8 Cal. App.4th 798, 10 Cal.Rptr.2d 731 (1992).

16. Fishback v. People, 851 P.2d 884, 894 (Colo.1993). Also see, People v. Barney, 8 Cal.App.4th 798, 10 Cal.Rptr.2d 731

(1992); United States v. Porter, 618 A.2d 629 (D.C.App.1992); People v. Atoigue, 1992 WL 245628 (D.Guam App.Div.1992); Commonwealth v. Lanigan, 413 Mass. 154, 596 N.E.2d 311 (1992) (see, Bowers, "DNA Evidence and Massachusetts: An Analysis of Commonwealth v. Lanigan," 19 *Crime Lab. Dig.* 73 (1993) which concludes that the court misinterpreted the findings and conclusions of the NRC report and fails to understand the conservative nature of the FBI's fixed-bin method. As a result, the article continues, it is unlikely that the court's reasoning in the Lanigan case will be followed by those who are well-informed about the processes of DNA–RFLP profiling and the related admissibility issues); State v. Vandebogart, 136 N.H. 365, 616 A.2d 483 (1992); State v. Anderson, 115 N.M. 433, 853 P.2d 135 (App.1992), reversed 881 P.2d 29 (N.M.1994) (controversy over statistical calculations only goes to weight and not to admissibility of DNA evidence); State v. Cauthron, 120 Wash.2d 879, 846 P.2d 502, 516 (1993); People v. Watson, 257 Ill. App.3d 915, 196 Ill.Dec. 89, 629 N.E.2d 634 (1994); Vargas v. State, 640 So.2d 1139 (Fla.App.1994); Commonwealth v. Crews, 536 Pa. 508, 640 A.2d 395 (1994); State v. Bible, 175 Ariz. 549, 858 P.2d 1152 (1993) (admission of probability calculations harmless error). Cf. State v. Clark, ___ Ariz. ___, ___ P.2d ___, 1994 WL 178569 (Ariz.

absence of a statistical interpretation of the significance of a declared match, have held that evidence of the match itself is also inadmissible.[17] Consequently, these courts have excluded all evidence of DNA analysis because of the concerns over the reliability of the probability calculations.

Another approach was initially taken by a Minnesota court. In remanding the case to the trial court after a pretrial appeal of an evidentiary order, the Court of Appeals in State v. Alt [18] directed the lower court to allow only the statistical frequencies of individual loci into evidence, if calculated by the NRC's modified ceiling principle.[19] The Court of Appeals declined to authorize the admission of evidence of the combined statistical analysis resulting from the multiplication of each of the individual frequencies according to the product rule. The court also rejected the state's request to allow the expert to testify that his conclusion that the banding patterns matched was "to a reasonable degree of scientific certainty." However, the expert could give nonstatistical opinion testimony that the test results were consistent with the defendant being the source of the forensic sample, as well as opine that those results did not exclude the defendant.[20]

Those courts which continue to allow questions concerning the proper application of the technique to go to the weight of the evidence, hold that issues concerning the proper size of the data base and the effect of Hardy–Weinberg equilibrium do not affect admissibility of the evidence, but are properly left for the jury to consider.[21] Since the substructure argument involves a dispute over the accuracy of the

App.Div. 1, 1994) (admission of probability calculations not harmless error).

17. Commonwealth v. Daggett, 416 Mass. 347, 622 N.E.2d 272, 275 (1993) (the fact that the Commonwealth presented the evidence in nonnumerical terms does not alter the result); Nelson v. State, 628 A.2d 69 (Del.1993). Since two unrelated individuals may have identical DNA patterns from fragments examined in a particular analysis, the potential exists for a match to be mistakenly found. Therefore, statistical interpretations regarding the probability of a coincidental match or the likelihood that two unrelated individuals have the same DNA type is necessary. *Nelson,* supra; People v. Watson, supra note 16 (probability assessment is essential in order to give meaning to a "match," and in the absence of such an assessment, the fact of a match, standing alone, is inadmissible); State v. Hummert, ___ Ariz. ___, ___ P.2d ___, 1994 WL 384979 (App.Div. 1, 1994) (testimony that from a comparison of three probes, the possibility of a random match was "rare" and that a match meant that "[e]ither you're brothers, identical twinsm ir that would be a very unique experience," was

not harmless error); but see, Commonwealth v. Crews, supra note 16 (despite inadmissibility of statistical evidence, expert properly testified that finding matching profiles at three loci "extremely strongly associated [the crime scene DNA] with the DNA from the defendant").

18. 504 N.W.2d 38 (Minn.App.1993), cert. granted in part & remanded 505 N.W.2d 72 (Minn.1993).

19. The Minnesota Supreme Court granted the petition for further review for the purpose of emphasizing that the only DNA frequency evidence to be admitted at trial "is the population frequency evidence of the individual bands". State v. Alt, 505 N.W.2d 72 (Minn.1993).

20. State v. Alt, 504 N.W.2d 38, 52–53 (Minn.App.1993), cert. granted in part & remanded 505 N.W.2d 72 (Minn.1993); State v. Bloom, 516 N.W.2d 159 (Minn. 1994) (expert may also give verbal, qualitative, non-statistical opinion based upon underlying statistical evidence).

21. Springfield v. State, 860 P.2d 435, 447 (Wyo.1993).

probability statistics and, as such is an application question, it is for the jury to assess.[22]

Several courts have expressed some optimism that the ceiling principle, propounded by the NRC, will be the talisman for judicial as well as scientific acceptance of statistical probability calculations. In the opinion of one court, the adoption of the ceiling principle by the NRC "... indicates that sufficient acceptance within the scientific community has been achieved to satisfy Frye in appropriate circumstances."[23] But, as mentioned in the section in this chapter on Statistical Evaluation of a Match,[24] the NRC's ceiling principle is coming under increased attack as being flawed in concept and overly conservative in practice. It is all together possible that in the not too distant future, judicial affection for the ceiling principle may begin to wane.

A collateral issue that has been raised by the belated appearance of the debate over calculating allele frequencies is what state of knowledge should be used by a reviewing court to determine the propriety of admitting frequency calculations—that which existed at the time of the admissibility hearing, or that existing at the time of the appellate review. One school of thought suggests that under *Frye,* the proponent of novel scientific evidence does not have to prove absolute validity of the technique, only that it is generally accepted at the time it is offered.[25]

A contrary view holds that the appellate court should not ignore vital scientific evolution. Rather than look at a snapshot of the technology taken at the trial, appellate courts should view the motion picture of technological advancement. Thus, scientific literature published well after the trial, and for which the party adverse to the literature's point of view will have no opportunity to cross-examine or rebut, should nevertheless be considered by the court.[26] One appellate court has ruled it will apply a "limited de novo review" to the threshold question of whether the method of calculating frequencies is generally accepted in

---

22. United States v. Bonds, 12 F.3d 540 (6th Cir.1993).

23. State v. Cauthron, 120 Wash.2d 879, 846 P.2d 502, 517 (1993). Also see, Fishback v. People, 851 P.2d 884, 895 (Colo. 1993) (issue rendered moot if alternative methods for calculating allele frequencies are determined to be generally accepted, referencing the NRC report); People v. Barney, 8 Cal.App.4th 798, 10 Cal.Rptr.2d 731, 745 (1992) (it appears likely that method of calculating frequencies proposed by the NRC report will be generally accepted by population geneticists); United States v. Porter, 618 A.2d 629, 642–644 (D.C.App. 1992) (noting scientific consensus satisfying *Frye* appears to exist on NRC approach, but remanding to trial court); State v. Vandebogart, 136 N.H. 365, 616 A.2d 483, 494–495 (1992) (remanding issue of Frye consensus on NRC approach); State v. Bloom, supra note 20 (NRC's interim ceiling method justifies creation of DNA exception to general rule against admission of statistical probability evidence); People v. Watson, supra note 16; Vargas v. State, supra 16.

24. Supra, § 15.12.

25. Fishback v. People, 851 P.2d 884, 891 (Colo.1993); United States v. Bonds, 12 F.3d 540 (6th Cir.1993); People v. Mehlberg, 249 Ill.App.3d 499, 188 Ill.Dec. 598, 620, 618 N.E.2d 1168, 1190 (1993) (court struck portions of the defendant's appendix containing secondary-source articles not considered by the trial court and never subjected to cross-examination).

26. State v. Bible, 175 Ariz. 549, 858 P.2d 1152, 1189 (1993). Also see, State v. Anderson, 115 N.M. 433, 853 P.2d 135 (App.1992) (considering NRC report issued while case on appeal); State v. Vandebogart, 136 N.H. 365, 616 A.2d 483 (1992) (using NRC report to conclude that probability methods are not generally accepted); People v. Barney, 8 Cal.App.4th 798, 10 Cal.Rptr.2d 731, 741 (1992) (court solicited comment on the NRC report which postdated the briefing papers for the appeal); State v. Cauthron, 120 Wash.2d 879, 846 P.2d 502, 504 (1993) (court requested additional briefing on NRC report after oral argument).

the scientific community. Thus, courts may look outside the record to case law and relevant scientific literature to determine general acceptance.[27] In that connection, it is important to note that an article published in late-1994, in the prestigious journal *Nature,* co-authored by a leading opponent and a proponent of DNA, declared that the DNA war was over, and that the scientific controversies over the methods of forensic DNA testing and calculation of probabilities have been resolved.[28] Courts that previously expressed reservations about or were critical of DNA evidence may, in light of this recent message, reassess their position in the future.

§ 15.17 Procedural Considerations

Several courts, concerned with establishing that the procedure for DNA typing was properly applied in a particular case prior to it being exposed to the jury, have suggested a number of safeguards, to assure not only the defense, but also the scientific community, access to information. In *Castro,* supra, the following pretrial procedures were recommended: [1]

1. Notice of intent to offer DNA evidence should be served as soon as possible.

2. The proponent, whether defense or prosecution, must give discovery to the adversary, which must include: (1) copies of autorads, with the opportunity to examine the originals; (2) copies of laboratory books; (3) copies of quality control tests run on material utilized; (4) copies of reports by the testing laboratory issued to proponent; (5) a written report by the testing laboratory setting forth the method used to declare a match or nonmatch, with actual size measurements, and mean or average size measurements, if applicable, together with standard deviation used; (6) a statement by the testing lab, setting forth the method used to calculate the allele frequency in the relevant population; (7) a copy of the data pool for each of the loci examined; (8) a certification by the testing lab that the same rule used to declare a match was used to determine the allele frequency in the population; (9) a statement setting forth observed contaminants, the reasons therefor, and tests performed to determine the origin and the results thereof; (10) if the sample is degraded, a statement setting forth the tests performed and the results thereof; (11) a statement setting forth any other observed defects or laboratory errors, the reasons therefor and the results thereof; and (12) chain of custody documents.

3. The proponent shall have the burden of going forward to establish that the tests and calculations were properly conducted.

27. E.g. People v. Atoigue, 1992 WL 245628 (D.Guam App.Div.1992).

28. Lander & Budowle, "DNA fingerprinting dispute laid to rest," 371 *Nature* 735 (Oct. 27, 1994). A subtitle to the authors' lengthy commentary declared that "Two principals in the once-raging debate over forensic DNA typing conclude that the scientific issues have all been resolved."

§ 15.17

1. On the issue of discovery, see, United States v. Yee, 129 F.R.D. 629 (N.D.Ohio

1990) (extensive discovery request granted to allow defense to prepare for admissibility hearing); Moody v. State, 210 Ga.App. 431, 436 S.E.2d 545 (1993) (abuse of discretion not to grant defendant a continuance when laboratory report was not disclosed within statutory time before trial; when laboratory report is in possession of the FBI laboratory, it is tantamount to being in the possession of the district attorney).

Once this burden is met, the ultimate burden of proof shifts to the *adversary* to prove, by a preponderance of the evidence, that the tests and calculations should be suppressed or modified (citations omitted). *Castro,* supra, at 999.

At least one court has gone so far as to deny admission of DNA test results when data relied upon by the laboratory in the performance of the tests are not available for review and cross-examination.[2] Liberal access to the data, methodology and actual test results is the best way to assure the defense has an adequate opportunity for an independent review, according to the Minnesota Supreme Court. Another reason for full access to a laboratory's protocol is to assure its availability for peer review. Accessibility of testing data and results is one of the linchpins of admissibility for that court.

In a recent decision, the Virginia Court of Appeals decided that "[d]efense counsel must have access to adequate expert assistance, even when the admissibility of the results on analytical techniques is not in question," and that due process was violated when the trial court failed to appoint an expert in DNA to assist the defense in the preparation of its case.[3]

In those jurisdictions, such as New York, where the admissibility determination includes an assessment of the application of the process in each particular case, the proponent of the DNA testimony has the burden of going forward with the evidence, whereupon the defendant must present proof by a preponderance of the evidence that the tests and calculations should be suppressed or modified.[4] The defendant must present evidence at the pretrial hearing. Once the determination has been made that the evidence is admissible, attacks on the process made at trial merely affect the weight of the evidence.

§ 15.18   Prosecution and Police Strategy

The greatest obstacle to the prosecution's use of DNA evidence is with regard to the admissibility of probability evidence. As noted earlier in this chapter, a debate is on-going over the method of computing the statistical probability that another, unrelated individual, chosen at random would match the DNA band patterns exhibited by the defendant and the questioned evidence. While the ceiling principle may indeed result in unnecessarily conservative frequencies, they are often still significant enough to be very helpful to the prosecution's case. Consequently, in light of the current case law, prosecutors and experts should be encouraged to come to court armed with statistics calculated by the

---

2. State v. Schwartz, 447 N.W.2d 422 (Minn.1989). Also see, People v. Davis, 196 A.D.2d 597, 601 N.Y.S.2d 174 (1993), in which the court reversed the defendant's multiple convictions because no evidence was adduced regarding the population data base or the statistical standards employed by Lifecodes Laboratories used as a basis for testimony concerning probability calculations.

3. Husske v. Commonwealth, ___ Va. App. ___, 448 S.E.2d 331, 340 *, applying

Ake v. Oklahoma, 470 U.S. 68, 105 S.Ct. 1087, 84 L.Ed.2d 53 (1985).

4. People v. Castro, 144 Misc.2d 956, 545 N.Y.S.2d 985 (1989). On the other hand, the burden of proof of general scientific acceptance, to be met by the proponent of novel scientific evidence, is proof by a preponderance of the evidence. United States v. Yee, 134 F.R.D. 161, 165 (N.D.Ohio 1991), affirmed 12 F.3d 540 (6th Cir.1993); People v. Atoigue, 1992 WL 245628 (D.Guam App.Div.1992).

laboratory's own method, as well as by the ceiling principle propounded by the NRC. As one court put it, the persistence of the debate over the calculation of probability statistics threatens the admissibility of this extremely important forensic tool. "This is no time for purist insistence that DNA evidence should be admitted on one's own terms or not at all." [1]

DNA typing is a complicated laboratory process involving technicians who perform the tests and qualified scientists who interpret the results. The prosecutor must decide who to call to the stand to lay the proper foundation for the evidence.[2] It appears that the government does not have to call the technicians to testify to the proper application of the technique in a given case or to lay the foundation for the scientist's interpretation of the results of the analysis. Courts allow experts to testify concerning the results of tests performed by nontestifying technicians who were under the expert's supervision when conducting the tests.[3] It is considered generally accepted within the scientific community that a scientist may view an autoradiograph, prepared by another, determine its quality, and whether there are any matching bands.[4] These same experts can testify to the laboratory's protocol and procedures for producing the autoradiographs admitted into evidence.[5] When experts testify, it will generally aid the jury in understanding the underpinnings of DNA typing and, therefore, the expert's testimony, if visual aids are used.

The police may try to use, as part of an investigative strategy, a ploy to deceive a suspect into believing there is overwhelming evidence of his guilt, and thereby inducing him to make incriminating admissions about his participation in the crime under investigation. In a Wyoming case, Division of Criminal Investigation agents told a defendant during a post-arrest interrogation that the police had "... a towel with blood on it, DNA residue and gun oil," when in fact the evidence did not exist. During the interrogation, the defendant confessed to the murder which was the subject of the investigation. The Wyoming Supreme Court rejected the defendant's due process claims, finding there was no significance to confronting the defendant with non-existent physical evidence,

---

§ 15.18

1. State v. Alt, 504 N.W.2d 38, 51 n. 21 (Minn.App.1993), cert. granted in part and remanded 505 N.W.2d 72 (Minn.1993). But see the recent article by Lander and Budowle, declaring that the scientific dispute has been laid to rest, supra Sec. 15.16 at footnote 28.

2. The chain of custody must also be established before the admission of DNA typing evidence. See, Pena v. State, 864 S.W.2d 147 (Tex.App.—Waco 1993) (minor theoretical breaches in the chain of custody will not affect admissibility in the absence of affirmative evidence of tampering).

3. People v. Mehlberg, 249 Ill.App.3d 499, 188 Ill.Dec. 598, 618, 618 N.E.2d 1168, 1188 (1993); Moody v. State, 210 Ga.App. 431, 436 S.E.2d 545, 547 (1993); State v. Futrell, 112 N.C.App. 651, 436 S.E.2d 884, 892 (1993) (defendant's Sixth Amendment right to confront witnesses against him was not violated by admission into evidence of DNA test results based on autorads prepared by a technician who did not testify at trial).

4. People v. Mehlberg, 249 Ill.App.3d 499, 188 Ill.Dec. 598, 614, 618 N.E.2d 1168, 1184 (1993).

5. People v. Mehlberg, 249 Ill.App.3d 499, 188 Ill.Dec. 598, 625, 618 N.E.2d 1168, 1195 (1993).

particularly in light of the fact that it was not suggested that the false representations influenced the defendant in any way.[6]

The opposite conclusion was reached in a Florida case where the police, with the knowledge of the prosecutor, fabricated two scientific reports and used them as ploys to question a suspect in a sexual assault and murder case.[7] The false scientific reports were prepared on official stationary of the police department and the examining laboratory, and purported to establish that the semen stains on the victim's underwear came from the suspect. The suspect confessed. The appellate court affirmed that trial court's suppression of that part of the defendant's statement given subsequent to the use of the fabricated documents, although a clear majority of federal and state courts agree that police deception does not render a confession involuntary per se. What is determined to be outrageous government misconduct, however, may bar the government from invoking judicial process to convict the defendant.

The distinction in the Florida case, in that court's mind, was the qualitative difference between verbal artifices and falsely contrived scientific documents, the latter impressing one as being inherently more permanent and outwardly reliable. The court was further concerned that the false documents might be kept and filed away in police records, eventually making their way to the courtroom or to the press. In the end, the use of such documents erodes the public's confidence in law enforcement generally.[8]

§ 15.19 Defense Strategy

When faced with the ominous task of refuting a positive DNA "match," the defense attorney must carefully choose the battlefield upon which to challenge the DNA evidence. Where courts have not reached the stage of widespread taking of judicial notice of DNA typing, a defense attorney will want to pursue a pre-trial hearing to determine the admissibility of the evidence. Failure to do so may prevent the defense from attacking the admissibility issue on appeal.

In People v. Moore,[1] Cellmark Diagnostics performed an analysis on the questioned blood samples, resulting in the presentation of six bands on the autorad. An analysis of the defendant's blood showed six matching bands, and an additional seventh band.[2] The defendant presented experts at trial challenging Cellmark's methods. The appellate court would not allow the defendant's evidence to affect the trial court's pretrial ruling that the DNA evidence was admissible, since the defense

---

6. Roderick v. State, 858 P.2d 538 (Wyo. 1993).

7. State v. Cayward, 552 So.2d 971 (Fla. App. 2d Dist.1989).

8. Id.

§ 15.19

1. 194 A.D.2d 32, 604 N.Y.S.2d 976 (1993).

2. It was explained that the seventh band, shorter than 2 kilobases, was outside the "window" that Cellmark looks at when making a comparison of banding patterns and is, therefore, not counted.

experts testified at trial and not the admissibility hearing. Therefore, their testimony affected only the weight of the evidence.

If admissibility questions have been largely resolved by the courts of a particular jurisdiction, a better use of resources might be to attack the evidence by discrediting the application of the DNA typing technique used in the particular case or the method by which statistical calculations were determined. In the past, the latter type of challenge has had the most promise, though, as indicated at the conclusion of § 15.16, a recent publication suggests the scientific controversy has been resolved.

A defense attorney may also desire to have the forensic sample re-tested by a defense expert. Such opportunities, however, are dependent on whether there is a sufficient sample remaining for re-testing. RFLP-based DNA testing uses a larger amount of DNA than PCR-based typing. The NRC report recommends that whenever possible, DNA samples should be preserved for re-analysis by the defense.[3] Sanctions imposed for the destruction of evidence through scientific testing will unlikely be imposed, however.[4] At least one court has recognized that saving a portion of the forensic sample for the defense to have analyzed is impractical, since the samples are often so small that the entire sample is used in testing.[5]

When the prosecution has not submitted the evidence for DNA analysis, the defense might want to consider doing so.[6] As one court has noted, DNA testing may be of potential benefit to the prosecution or the defense. If the testing fails to yield a match, it would likely exonerate the defendant, even though there is other evidence linking the defendant to the crime.[7]

Another impediment to the re-testing of evidence by the defense, and to the initial defense testing, is the availability of funds. Defense attorneys should look to the law of their jurisdiction to determine under what circumstances testing, re-testing or expert witnesses for the defense will be paid for by the court.

Experts for the defense may be useful even if the evidence is not to be re-tested. Countervailing expert testimony at trial may cast doubt on prosecution expert testimony that a match exists, or the significance of the match by an attack on the statistical computations. Dubose v.

---

3. Committee on DNA Technology in Forensic Science, Board on Biology, Commission on Life Sciences, National Research Council, *DNA Technology in Forensic Science* (1992), pp. 147, 150.

4. See, Arizona v. Youngblood, 488 U.S. 51 (1988).

5. State v. Schwartz, 447 N.W.2d 422, 427 (Minn.1989).

6. Hymer, "DNA Testing in Criminal Cases: A Defense Perspective," *Forensic DNA Technology* (Farley & Harrington, eds. 1991), p. 182.

7. State v. Johnson, 498 N.W.2d 10, 13 (Minn.1993). But see, State v. Hammond, 221 Conn. 264, 604 A.2d 793 (1992), where the defendant was convicted by a jury of kidnapping and sexual assault despite DNA typing evidence, presented by an FBI expert in the defendant's case, that neither the defendant nor the victim's boyfriend could have been the source of the semen stains. The Supreme Court remanded the case to the trial court to reconsider the defendant's motion to set aside the verdict.

State,[8] contains an extended discussion of the indigent defendant's right to funds for expert assistance. The case also is illustrative of the strategies and approaches which might be used to lay a firm foundation for the request for expert witness fees.

Defense counsel also know all too well that their choice of a specific trial strategy might well preclude certain arguments on appeal. Other strategies may result in claims of ineffective assistance of counsel, regardless of the well founded reasons for counsel's choice of strategy.[9] But some strategies may be better than others. In People v. Mehlberg,[10] the defense had to change strategy early in the case when forensic samples examined by Cellmark Diagnostics, at defense counsel's request, revealed a match between the questioned sperm and the defendant's DNA. Upon learning of the laboratory's conclusion, defense counsel told Cellmark not to do any further testing, except upon the advice of the State's Attorney's office. The State's Attorney, of course, requested that a frequency calculation be computed by Cellmark. The FBI was also requested by the State's Attorney to analyze the evidence, which it did, with results similar to Cellmark's.

At trial, the Cellmark and FBI experts testified as government witnesses only to the fact of a match. They did not offer an opinion as to the likelihood of a random match. However, on cross-examination, defense counsel asked both witnesses whether a statistical analysis was done. Both answered in the affirmative. The Cellmark expert concluded that the appropriate frequency was one in 12,000. The FBI expert responded that the likelihood of another, unrelated individual chosen at random having the same DNA profile as the defendant was one in 1.7 million, and in fact, since the population data base is not broken down by gender and only males can produce sperm, the probability increases algebraically by a factor of two.[11]

In other cases, defense counsel have also wavered at different stages of the proceeding on the question of the admissibility of probability evidence. When the trial court in United States v. Martinez,[12] decided to admit evidence of the DNA analysis, it invited counsel to comment on the propriety of admitting statistical evidence concerning the probability

---

8. ___ So.2d ___, 1993 WL 381482 (Ala. Cr.App.1993). In Husske v. Commonwealth, ___ Va.App. ___, 448 S.E.2d 331 (Va.App.), the court held that because of the complexities of DNA evidence and its still challenged procedure, a defendant was entitled to the assistance of a DNA expert under the 6th Amendment right-to-counsel provision.

9. See, for example, State v. Cromwell, 253 Kan. 495, 856 P.2d 1299, 1308 (1993) (failure of counsel to cross-examine DNA expert at trial did not constitute ineffective assistance of counsel, since such examination might have accomplished nothing more than confirming direct examination, and, therefore, may have been a sound tactical

decision); State v. Hayes, 1993 WL 333650 (Ohio App. 2d Dist.) (failure to retain services of a DNA expert did not constitute ineffective assistance of counsel).

10. 249 Ill.App.3d 499, 618 N.E.2d 1168 (1993).

11. When an identification is done by more than one laboratory on the same sample using differing probes, the finding of matching bands by both laboratories becomes even more conclusive. *Mehlberg*, supra, at 1185.

12. 3 F.3d 1191 (8th Cir.1993), cert. denied 114 S.Ct. 734 (1994).

of a match. Defense counsel argued for the exclusion of probability evidence, citing authority for the proposition that only evidence of a match should go to the jury. The trial court adopted that position and barred the expert from testifying that one Native American in 2600 could have provided DNA that matched the samples found on the victim.

On appeal, however, the defense counsel switched positions and argued that it was error to exclude the probability evidence. Without that evidence, he argued, the jury could only have been left with the impression that the defendant was the sole person who could have been the source of the semen. The Court of Appeals held, on the basis of the doctrine of invited error, that having specifically requested that the district court exclude the statistical evidence, the defendant may not complain about its exclusion on appeal.

Finally, if random match probability statistics are to be allowed, defense counsel should consider requesting that cautionary instructions be given to the jury. After making a DNA exception to the general rule excluding statistical probability evidence in criminal prosecutions, the Supreme Court of Minnesota, in State v. Bloom,[13] reminded the trial court judges of their responsibility to craft cautionary instructions to prevent the jury from being misled by the DNA evidence. In a concurring opinion, one justice, believing that specific direction should be given to the trial courts, suggested that the jury be told:

1. A given DNA profile may be shared by two or more people;

2. The random match probability statistic is not the equivalent of a statistic that tells the jury the likelihood of whether the defendant committed the crime;

3. The random match probability statistic is the likelihood that a random person in the population would match the characteristics that were found in the crime scene evidence and also in defendant's DNA;

4. Where the known DNA sample from the defendant matches the unknown sample obtained from the crime scene, it does not necessarily mean the defendant is the source of the sample found at the crime scene; and

5. That jurors alone have the final responsibility to decide the weight to be given to DNA random match probability statistics.

§ 15.20 Legislation Affecting the Admissibility of DNA Typing Evidence

Seven legislatures have delivered preemptive strikes to the debate over the admissibility of DNA evidence and corollary statistical probability calculations, by legislatively determining that the results of DNA typing are relevant and admissible evidence.[1] These statutes vary from

---

13.   516 N.W.2d 159 (Minn.1994).

§ 15.20

1.   West's Ann.Ind.Code 35–37–4–13 (Supp.1992); La.Stat.Ann.—R.S. 15:441.1

state to state in the scope, antecedent procedural requirements, and protections they afford. Judicial acceptance and recognition of the statutes have also been mixed.[2]

The statutory schemes accomplish legislatively what the courts often do when taking judicial notice of a fact; they recognize the reliability of DNA typing. That recognition is sometimes done explicitly, as in Virginia. Others do so implicitly, by eliminating the need for expert testimony that DNA analysis is trustworthy and reliable as a condition precedent to its admission into evidence, as do the statutes in Indiana, Minnesota and Tennessee.

On the other hand, Maryland's statute simply makes such evidence admissible if certain procedural requirements are met, and Nevada's statute states that DNA evidence "may be received in evidence." On the other end of the spectrum is Louisiana, whose statute merely makes evidence of DNA profiles "relevant as proof in conformity with the Louisiana Code of Evidence."

All of the statutes apply to criminal cases, and the Minnesota, Nevada and Tennessee statutes pertain to civil cases as well. Three statutes contain no explicit language regarding the purposes for which DNA evidence can be received, while Virginia and Maryland specifically allow the use of DNA evidence to prove or disprove the identity of *any person*. Nevada does the same, but extends the permissible scope to parentage determinations and identification of corpses.

Louisiana, on the other hand limits the scope of its statute by providing statutory admissibility only to "establish the *identity* of the *offender*" (emphasis added). The language of that statute seems unfortunately narrow, since DNA evidence is frequently used to identify biological substances from victims, and to identify the remains of murder victims, neither of whom are "offenders." One should certainly be allowed to argue, however, that if the defendant can be associated with such biological evidence, or if the identification of a murder victim proves the defendant to be an offender, then by implication such identification would also establish the identification of the offender, and thus fall within the statute's purview.

Both the Minnesota and Tennessee statutes condition the admissibility of DNA evidence on the showing that the testimony concerning the evidence "meets the standards for admissibility set forth" in their own rules of evidence. Two other statutes require compliance with notice and discovery provisions. In Virginia, the proponent of the evidence

(West 1992); Md.Code Ann., Courts & Judicial Proceedings, § 10–915 (Supp.1993); Minn.Stat.Ann. § 634.25–634.26 (West Supp.1994); Nev.Rev.Stat.Ann. § 56.020 (Michie Supp.1993); Tenn.Code Ann. § 24-7–117 (Supp.1993); Va.Code Ann. § 19.2–270.5 (Michie 1990).

2. Department of Social Services ex rel. Wolf v. McCarty, 506 N.W.2d 144, 147 (S.D.

1993) (unnecessary to have a hearing on admissibility of DNA when statute provides for its admission); State v. Alt, 504 N.W.2d 38, 41 n. 2 (Minn.App.1993), cert. granted in part and remanded 505 N.W.2d 72 (Minn.1993) (Supreme Court has questioned the legislature's authority to create an exception for DNA evidence to Supreme Court decision).

must give notice 21 days in advance of the proceeding in which the evidence will be offered and at least make available copies of the profiles and report or statement to be introduced. Failure to comply with those provisions authorizes the court to grant a continuance to the opposing party or, in appropriate cases, bar the introduction of the evidence.

The Maryland statute requires 45 days notice and provides substantially more discovery than does the Virginia statute, and mandates its delivery to the opposing party 30 days prior to the criminal proceeding. If requested in writing, the following discovery is required:

(i) Duplicates of actual autoradiographs generated;

(ii) The laboratory protocols and procedures;

(iii) The identification of each probe utilized;

(iv) A statement describing the methodology of measuring fragment size and match criteria; and

(v) a statement setting forth the allele frequency and genotype data for the appropriate data base utilized.

Certain trial and privacy protections are also provided by two states. Tennessee makes it clear that nothing in its statute can be construed as limiting the right to rebut the proposition that DNA provides a trustworthy and reliable method for identifying characteristics in an individual's genetic material. Nor does the statute prohibit cross-examination of the proponent's expert on the issue of the reliability and trustworthiness of the analysis.

The Virginia statute's trial protections for the opponent of the evidence are broader in scope. The statute provides that there is no limitation on the introduction of any relevant evidence bearing upon any question at issue before the court. More specifically, it does not limit any relevant evidence of the identity of the accused as shall be admissible in evidence, regardless of the outcome of the DNA analysis. In addition, the Virginia statute provides further protections. No evidence submitted to the laboratory for purposes of introduction under its admissibility statute can be included in the DNA data bank or otherwise used in any way with identifying information on the person whose sample was submitted.

As to frequency calculations, three states provide explicitly for their admissibility, and one does so implicitly. Nevada allows the opinion of an expert concerning the results of DNA typing to be "weighted" in accordance with evidence of statistical probabilities. Both Minnesota and Tennessee have identical provisions providing that statistical population frequency testimony is admissible in evidence to demonstrate the fraction of the population that would have the same combination of genetic markers as was found in a specific biological specimen. The Minnesota Supreme Court has taken a contrary view, however, and has determined that statistical evidence is inadmissible.[3]

---

3. State v. Schwartz, 447 N.W.2d 422 (Minn.1989). The Minnesota Supreme Court has called into question the legislature's authority to create an exception for

Maryland does not specifically mention the admissibility of statistical computations. However, in the list of discoverable information, required by statute to be provided by the proponent of the evidence, are the allele frequency and genotype data for the appropriate data base utilized, which seem to envision a calculation of the probability of a random match by an unrelated individual.

Several methods of DNA analysis are now being used. Only one statute limits admissibility to a single technology. Maryland's statute applies only to RFLP-based DNA typing. While all the other statutes will encompass PCR-based DNA typing and other methods which may evolve, Maryland's statute may become outdated as technology advances.

While only the Nevada statute refers specifically to parentage determination, other statutes allow for DNA analysis in civil cases where paternity or maternity are in issue. The Uniform Parentage Act, adopted in 17 states, is broad enough to encompass DNA testing. The same is probably also true in those states which have legislation requiring court-ordered blood or tissue testing in parentage cases.[4]

§ 15.21 DNA Data Banking Statutes

In addition to passing legislation pertaining to the admissibility of DNA typing evidence, legislatures have wasted little time in recognizing the efficacy of DNA typing as an investigative tool, and its potential as a deterrent to crime. As of the end of 1993, a total of twenty-three states had passed DNA data banking statutes.[1] Generally, the concept of the

DNA evidence to the court created limitations on the use of statistical probability evidence in criminal trials. See, State v. Nielsen, 467 N.W.2d 615 (Minn.1991). The legislature, not to be misunderstood, passed in 1992 a statute which takes away from the supreme court the power to promulgate rules of evidence which conflict, modify, or supersede the statute relating to the admissibility of statistical probability evidence based on genetic or blood test results. 1993 Minn.Laws ch. 326, art. 7 § 12, amending Minn.Stat.Ann. § 480.0591, subd. 6. State v. Alt, 504 N.W.2d 38, 41 n. 2 (Minn.App. 1993), cert. granted in part and remanded 505 N.W.2d 72 (Minn.1993).

4. Starrs, *Twists and Turns in DNA's Legislative Ladder*, 2 Benchmark 1 (Fall 1989) (Benchmark is a publication of Cellmark Diagnostics). The New York Family Court Act directs the court to order the parties in a parentage case to submit to one or more genetic marker tests and authorizes the results of the blood genetic marker tests to be received in evidence. For purposes of that act, the DNA probe is considered a blood genetic marker test. In re the Adoption of "Baby Girl S," 140 Misc.2d 299, 532 N.Y.S.2d 634 (Sur.Ct.1988). In

South Dakota, upon appropriate motion, the court shall order "an examination of blood and tissue specimens for the purpose of testing any genetic systems that are generally accepted within the scientific community for the conclusive determination of paternity probability." S.D. Codified Laws 25–8–7.1 (1992).

§ 15.21

1. Ariz.Rev.Stat. § 31–281 (West Supp. 1993); West's Ann.Cal.Penal Code § 290.2 (Supp.1994); West's Colo.Rev.Stat.Ann. § 17–2–201 (Supp.1993); West's Fla.Stat. Ann. § 943.325 (1993); Official Code Georgia Ann. §§ 24–4–60 to 24–4–65 (Supp. 1993); Haw.Rev.Stat. § 706–603 (Supp. 1993); 730 ILCS 5/5–4–3 (1993); Ind.Code Ann. §§ 20–12–34.5–1 to 20–12–34.5–6 (Burns 1991); Iowa Code Ann. § 13.10 (West 1989); Kan.Stat.Ann. 21–2511 (Supp. 1992); Ky.Rev.Stat.Ann. §§ 17.170, 17.175 (Michie 1992); La.—LSA–Rev.Stat. § 15:578 (West 1992); Mich.Comp.Laws. Ann. § 750.520m (West 1991); Minn.Stat. Ann. §§ 299C.155, 609.3461 (West 1991 & Supp.1994); Vernon's Ann.Mo.Stat. § 650.-050 (Supp.1993); Nev.Rev.Stat.Ann. § 176.111 (Michie 1992); Okl.Stat.Ann.Tit. 57, § 584 (West 1993–94); Or.Rev.Stat.

DNA data bank is to catalog the individual DNA of felons falling within certain classes of convicts for comparison with future crime scene samples. In addition, such statutes are expected to act as a deterrent to recidivism.[2]

Similar to the Automated Fingerprint Identification System (AFIS), the data bank will give law enforcement officials the ability to make a computerized search for a presumptive match between a crime scene DNA pattern and a convicted felon's pattern. See Figure 17. The increased use and availability of PCR-based typing and the potential of automating the process will make this system an extremely valuable tool in the fight against violent crime.

137.076, 181.085 (Supp.1992); S.D.Codified Laws 23–5–14 to 23–5–18 (Supp.1993); Tenn.Code Ann. § 38–6–113 (1991); Va. Code Ann. §§ 19.2–310.2 to 19.2–310.7 (Michie 1990); West's Rev.Code Wash.Ann. 43.43.752 to 43.43.759 (Supp.1993–94).

2. Jones v. Murray, 763 F.Supp. 842, 846 (W.D.Va.1991), affirmed in part and reversed in part by Jones v. Murray, 962 F.2d 302 (4th Cir.1992), cert. denied 113 S.Ct. 472 (1992); Iowa Code Ann. § 13.10 (1990).

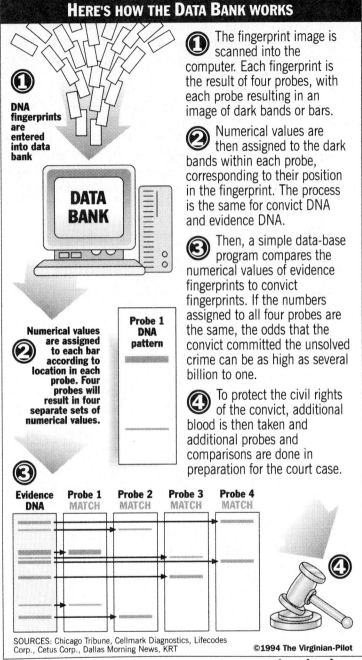

Fig. 17. The inner workings of a DNA data bank.
Courtesy: The Virginian Pilot.

The "DNA Identification Act of 1994"[3] provides forty million dollars in funding for states to develop or improve a DNA analysis capabili-

---

3. See, Section 210301 et seq. of the Violent Crime Control and Law Enforcement Act of 1994.

ty in their forensic laboratories. As a condition of the funding, the state laboratories will have to meet or exceed certain quality assurance standards, employ external proficiency testing, and restrict access to the DNA typing results performed by the laboratory in the ordinary course of its business.

The act also appropriates twenty-five million dollars to the FBI and provides for an index to facilitate the exchange of DNA identification information among law enforcement agencies. The FBI would be authorized to establish a national identification index of (1) DNA identification records of persons convicted of crimes; (2) analyses of DNA samples recovered from crime scenes; and (3) analyses of DNA samples recovered from unidentified human remains.

The advantages of this identification index to effective criminal law enforcement are obvious. Significantly, the law would create a uniform system, with appropriate quality control and assurance guidelines, so that the index can become truly national in scope. Most of the state DNA data banking statutes do not require that the analyses be done in such a way as to create results which can be compared to results generated in other states. The Kentucky, Missouri and Washington statutes do, however, require that the state system be compatible with the FBI system or the National DNA Identification Index.

As one would expect, the state statutes vary in their application, scope and procedures.[4] Generally, most of the statutes are triggered by the conviction of the individual, although South Dakota's statute becomes applicable when an individual is "taken into custody" for a sex offense. While most statutes encompass only individuals convicted of sex or sex related offenses, some include those convicted of violent crimes also. Virginia's statute applies to every person convicted of a felony. While many statutes limit the applicable convictions to felonies, others describe classes of offenses which may, under state law, include misdemeanors. The Iowa statute specifically refers to "felonies and indictable misdemeanors." Minnesota and Tennessee have statutes which reach those children who juvenile courts adjudicate delinquent in relation to the commission of sex offenses. Oklahoma, and in part California, define the applicable class of individuals included within their statute as those required to be registered as sex offenders under the state sex offender statute.

All but a few of the statutes specifically seek blood samples, although about a third of the statutes also require saliva samples to determine the convict's secretor status. Minnesota and Tennessee are more flexible, by requiring more generally a "biological specimen."

---

4. With one exception, all the statutes envision that the blood or other biological sample taken from the convicted person will be used for comparison purposes at a later date. Indiana's statute is the one exception. It appears that the sole purpose of that statute is to provide a population database to determine allele frequencies and demographics based upon the analysis of the specimens. Population statistics derived from the information will then be given to any person who pays the required fee.

Arizona, on the other hand, requires that the convict submit to DNA testing for identification purposes, without mentioning anything about the nature of the substance to be analyzed.

Almost half of the statutes provide some procedural guidance or place certain limitations on use or access to the analysis results. Most frequently, the reason for gathering the samples is specifically limited to law enforcement purposes, and access to the information is restricted.[5] Some legislatures explicitly direct that blood samples be drawn in a medically accepted manner, and if done in that way, several statutes (Kentucky, Kansas and Oregon) also grant immunity from civil or criminal liability for those performing the medical procedure. Kentucky and Oregon also provide procedures for the expungement of all identifiable information in the data bank pertaining to a person whose felony conviction, which formed the basis for obtaining the biological sample, was reversed and dismissed, as well as for the destruction of all the samples taken from the person.

Despite the narrow focus of these statutes, the procedural safeguards imposed by them, and their relationship to legitimate governmental objectives, many legal commentators saw them as causing serious constitutional violations, threatening the privacy and security of the individual, and leading to "genetic redlining." Two appellate courts have now reviewed these concerns and dismissed, in most part, any constitutional bases for overturning the statutes.[6] The challenges in those cases included:

(1) Violations of the prohibition against unreasonable searches and seizures. The Fourth Circuit Court of Appeals in responding to that argument in *Jones v. Murray,* a suit brought by prisoners pursuant to 42 U.S.C.A. § 1983, recognized that taking the blood sample required for the DNA analysis, with respect to free persons, constituted a search within the scope of the Fourth Amendment. However, with respect to convicted felons lawfully confined, the same protections do not apply. Consequently, the court held that the Fourth Amendment did not require an additional finding of individualized suspicion or probable cause before blood can be taken from an incarcerated felon for purposes of later identifying them.[7]

As to the reasonableness of the search, if indeed it is a search with respect to lawfully confined prisoners, the court weighed the minor intrusion caused by the extraction of blood against the state interest in preserving a permanent identification record of convicted felons for resolving past and future crimes. In light of the potentially greater

---

5. The California, Kentucky and Virginia statutes make it a misdemeanor for the unauthorized use or dissemination of information in the database. Kentucky makes it a felony for any person to tamper with any sample of blood or the container collected pursuant to the statute.

6. Jones v. Murray, 962 F.2d 302 (4th Cir.1992), cert. denied 113 S.Ct. 472 (1992); State v. Olivas, 122 Wash.2d 73, 856 P.2d 1076 (1993).

7. *Jones,* supra, 962 F.2d at 306–307. In fact, since the purpose of the statute is for use in prospective crimes, no such individualization or probable cause could exist.

precision of DNA sampling and matching methods that this dramatic new law enforcement tool offers, the court found the state's interest to outweigh the felon's interest.[8]

The United States District Court in Virginia, which was the lower court in the *Jones v. Murray* case, and the Washington Supreme Court, both agree with the Fourth Circuit that the statutes do not violate the Fourth Amendment. Those courts differed with the Fourth Circuit, however, as to the reasons. Instead of analyzing the limited privacy rights of convicted prisoners, the Washington Supreme Court found a better and more reasoned approach to be the "special needs" analysis, which was the approach taken by the District Court in Jones v. Murray.[9] Under that approach, the court balanced the general right of persons to be free from unjustified governmental intrusion against the "special needs beyond normal law enforcement" of the government, which justify departures from the usual warrant and probable cause requirements. The courts found that the DNA testing procedures bore a close and substantial relationship to the state's goal of identifying suspects and deterring recidivism by convicted felons.

A third analytical approach, explained in both the *Jones* and *Olivas* concurring opinions, applied "traditional principles" of Fourth Amendment law, and was adopted by an Illinois appellate court to uphold the constitutionality of the Illinois DNA data banking statute.[10] Resorting to traditional principles, the court balanced: (1) the state's interest in obtaining the sample (conducting the search); (2) the degree to which that interest is advanced by the search; and (3) the gravity of the intrusion upon personal privacy to determine the reasonableness of the search. Where the intrusion is minimal, as it was in that case, and the state's interest significant, as it also undoubtedly was, the requirement of probable cause or individualized suspicion can be relaxed. In addition, the court reasoned that the statute's narrow scope and objective, its non-discretionary nature, and regular and uniform application, adequately addressed the concerns underlying the warrant requirement of the Fourth Amendment.

(2) Constitutional right of privacy. The District Court in *Jones v. Murray*, found that the convicted prisoners do not enjoy a legitimate expectation of privacy where the analysis reveals identification characteristics only. One's genetic history is not accessible by law enforcement agents through the data bank. To the contrary, only identification characteristics are available, and then only to a law enforcement officer, if the sample provided by the officer matches a sample in the data base. No random searches can be made, and normally only one sample has to be taken from the felon and kept on file. Since the felon has a lower

---

8. *Jones,* supra, 962 F.2d at 307. The state argued that DNA will be left at up to 30% of violent crime scenes. 962 F.2d at 304.

9. 763 F.Supp. 842, 850 (W.D.Va.1991), affirmed in part and reversed in part by

Jones v. Murray, 962 F.2d 302 (4th Cir. 1992), cert. denied 113 S.Ct. 472 (1992).

10. People v. Wealer, ___ Ill.App.2d ___, 201 Ill.Dec. 697, 636 N.E.2d 1129 (1994).

privacy interest than the general population, and only limited use can be put to the DNA analysis, no right of privacy is encroached upon either under the Fourth Amendment or any general constitutional right of privacy.

(3) *Ex post facto*. The Virginia federal courts were faced with an argument that the Virginia statute violated the *ex post facto* provisions of the Constitution because the enforcement provisions of Virginia's DNA blood testing requirement retroactively authorizes detaining prisoners who fail to comply with the statute past their discretionary parole date, and in some cases past mandatory parole dates.[11] Finding that the statute is not penal in nature, the Court of Appeals concluded that it was not *ex post facto*, even though there would be some punishment, within the terms of the prisoner's original sentence, for a violation of the requirement to submit to the DNA testing. Only in those cases where the mandatory parole, inherent in the original sentence given him was denied, would the *ex post facto* laws be violated.[12]

(4) Other arguments. The Washington Supreme Court also rejected claims that the procedure for taking blood violated due process because it shocks the conscience of the court or offended its sense of justice. An equal protection argument was also rejected by the court.[13]

Thus, the statutes stand as formidable tools of law enforcement, providing either a deterrent to future crime, or failing to do that, a tool for identifying and convicting the recidivist. The latter usage yielded results by the end of 1993. Four "cold hits," resulting in arrests were made by matching crime scene samples with a DNA data bank profiles.

Virginia's first "cold hit" came in late 1993 and solved an 8 month old rape of a 63 year old woman. The suspect in that case broke into the victim's home, raped and beat her and attempted to engage in sodomy.

Having been released from prison four and a half months earlier, the suspect clearly wanted to avoid being returned to the prison cell where he had spent the last fifteen years of his life for a rape he committed as a juvenile. Consequently, after raping his most recent victim, the suspect dragged her into a bathtub and attempted to wash away the evidence from areas of the house, trying to make good on a statement to the victim that he would leave no clues behind to tie him to the crime. He almost succeeded.

11. The Virginia statute, effective July 1, 1990, provides, in part, that all felons convicted prior to July 1, 1990 and incarcerated on July 1, 1990, shall be covered by the statute. The state maintained that the blood test requirement is not a requirement of parole eligibility. The prisoner is not detained because he is being punished for a past crime. Rather, he is held because he refused to provide a blood sample, which is an administrative sanction. Jones v. Murray, 763 F.Supp. 842, 850 (W.D.Va.1991), affirmed in part and reversed in part by Jones v. Murray, 962 F.2d 302 (4th Cir. 1992), cert. denied 113 S.Ct. 472 (1992).

12. Jones v. Murray, 962 F.2d 302, 310 (4th Cir.1992), cert. denied 113 S.Ct. 472 (1992).

13. Another argument furthered by the defendants, and also rejected by the court, was that the pleas of guilty were not knowingly, intelligently and voluntarily made because they were not informed of the required DNA testing before they entered their pleas. State v. Olivas, 122 Wash.2d 73, 856 P.2d 1076, 1087 (1993).

The victim could give no physical description of her assailant, because he had tied a torn curtain over her eyes. Forensic scientists examined 23 separate items of evidence which revealed no identifying information about the perpetrator, except for a small seminal fluid stain found on the victim's clothing.

That discovery was the suspect's Achilles's heel, for it allowed forensic scientists to compare the DNA type of the contributor of the stain to the types catalogued in Virginia's three-year-old DNA data bank. The computer search of 1350 profiles in the data bank resulted in a match of the crime scene evidence to the DNA type of a single individual, leading to the arrest of the suspect.[14]

That case reaffirms the maxim that wherever anyone goes, whatever anyone does, he leaves something behind or takes something with him. All the police and forensic scientists have to do is find the trace evidence and analyze it. With the use of DNA technology and the convicted felon data banks, even those who make a concerted effort not to leave trace evidence behind can be identified, arrested and brought to justice. It is no longer prognostication to say that DNA typing technology has, in fact, revolutionized the criminal justice system.

---

14. DNA Databank Makes Its First 'Cold–Hit,' " *The Forensic Examiner*, Vol. 3, No. 1, published by the Virginia Division of Forensic Science; Carlos Sanchez, "Woman, 64, Describes Rape," *Washington Post,* December 15, 1993, at D4. Also see, State v. Bloom, 516 N.W.2d 159 (Minn.1994), a case in which the DNA profile of the semen samples taken from the victim were compared by computer against the state's sex-offender DNA data base. The court's opinion details the process used by the examiner to discover potential suspects and confirm the contributor of the semen.

Chapter 16

FORENSIC ODONTOLOGY

I. INTRODUCTION

I. INTRODUCTION

§ 16.01 Scope of Dental Identification

In recent years, forensic odontology, or forensic dentistry, has gained considerable importance in civil and criminal cases. In many instances, bodies are recovered that cannot be identified by such traditional means of recognition as (1) physical characteristics, marks or deformities, (2) fingerprints, or (3) clothing and personal effects. This often occurs in disaster cases, whether they be the result of car, train, or airplane crashes, shipwrecks, tornadoes, storms, or fires. It also occurs in an important number of criminal cases where the identity of the victim cannot be established.

In some cases, a person may be identified by his bite impression left in food products, or even in the skin of victims of crimes. Bite marks are often observed on victims of battery, rape, child abuse and homicide. They are found on all areas of the body with more than one bite occurring in 40% of incidents.[1]

§ 16.01

1. Vale & Noguchi, "Anatomical Distribution of Human Bite Marks in a Series of 67 Cases," 28 *J.For.Sci.* 61 (1983).

Forensic dentistry has four major areas of application: identification of human remains by dental techniques; bite mark comparison as an identification and detection method; medico-legal assessment of trauma to the oral tissues; and dental malpractice and negligence.[2]

§ 16.02   Glossary of Common Terms

Amalgam: The most commonly used filling material for posterior teeth consisting of silver or some of its alloys combined with mercury to make a plastic mass that can be fitted into a tooth cavity and will harden in a short time.

Antemortem Record: Dental records taken prior to the individual's death consisting of charts, X-rays and dental casts.

Anterior Teeth: Teeth readily visible in the center of the mouth, including the central and lateral incisors and the cuspids.

Bicuspid: Also called premolars; tooth adjacent to the cuspid. An adult has eight bicuspids.

Buccal: One of the five surfaces of a tooth, the surface of the posterior teeth on the side toward the cheek.

Caries: Decay of the teeth, produced by acid dissolution of the calcium salts which make up most of the teeth.

Crown: The portion of the tooth that is visible above the gum.

Cuspid: Also called canine. Tooth adjacent to the incisors and primarily used for cutting and tearing. An adult has four cuspids; they are at the corner of the mouth, the third tooth from the midline on both sides. The shape is frequently pointed and peglike.

Deciduous Dentition: Baby or "milk" teeth which begin to erupt from the gums when a child reaches the age of seven months. Deciduous dentition consists of 20 teeth only, 10 in each jaw, 5 in each of the right and left quadrants. In each quadrant there are 2 incisors, 1 cuspid, and 2 molars.

Dentition: A set of teeth of an individual. Humans acquire two sets of teeth during their lifetime, the first acquired during childhood (deciduous or primary dentition), the second set which replaces the first set one by one as the jaw grows (the permanent or secondary dentition). There are four different types of teeth: incisors, cuspids (canines), bicuspids (premolars) and molars. An adult dentition comprises 32 teeth. Each tooth has five surfaces: occlusal, mesial, distal, buccal, and lingual.

Denture: Upper and lower false teeth. See prosthesis.

Distal: (abbrev. "D") Tooth surface in direct contact with the adjacent tooth on the side away from the midline of the jaw. (Opposite side of the tooth is Mesial surface.)

---

2. Sopher, *Forensic Dentistry* (1976), at 3–4.

Enamel: The outer surface of a tooth and the most resistant and hardest substance of the body.

Filling Materials: Materials used to fill cavities in teeth. The most commonly used are amalgam, silver, cast-gold, gold foil, silicate, acrylic; others are baked porcelain, silicous cement, etc.

Gold Foil: Restorative material of superior quality though expensive and very time consuming to insert.

Incisor: Tooth primarily used for biting and cutting and placed in the center of the mouth. An adult has 8 incisors, 2 in each quadrant of the mouth. The upper central incisor is the largest tooth, the lateral incisors are a little smaller. The lower incisors are smaller than either the upper central or lateral incisors.

Lingual: (abbrev. "L") The surface of a tooth facing toward the inside of the mouth.

Mandible: Lower jaw, which is movable.

Maxilla: Upper jaw, which is stationary.

Mesial: (abbrev. "M") Tooth surface which is in direct contact with an adjacent tooth on the side facing the midline of the jaw. (Opposite side of tooth is Distal surface.)

Molar: The teeth farthest back in the mouth. An adult has three molars in each quadrant of the mouth, or a total of 12. Their primary use is to grind and smash food.

Occlusal: (abbrev. "O") Tooth surface which contacts the opposing tooth when the jaws are closed (in occlusion).

Palate: The roof of the mouth, consisting of a hard bony forward part (the hard palate) and a soft fleshy back part (the soft palate).

Perikymata: Wavelike features found in the surface enamel of teeth. They result from the incremental deposits of enamel during tooth crown development. They undergo changes due to age, location of tooth in mouth and oral habits.

Posterior Teeth: The teeth in the back of the mouth, all bicuspids and molars.

Postmortem Record: Dental record obtaining by charting the dentition, extractions and restorations of a dead body.

Pulp: Material occupying a cavity located inside the teeth comprised of nerves, lymph, blood vessels and fibrous tissue.

Prosthesis: Artificial teeth which may either be fixed or removable. Fixed prosthesis could be a bridge consisting of a device used to span a gap in the dentition. A removable prosthesis is either a complete or a partial set of false teeth. The partial denture would attach to remaining teeth by clasps and hooks.

Root Canal (endodontia): The procedure of removing the pulp from a tooth and filling the space with some substance. Since this work is then covered by a restoration, it can only be discovered through X-rays.

Rugae: Ridges or folds as those on the palate.

Tooth: Hard white structure in mouth used primarily for mastication of food; a tooth is comprised of a crown (the functional part that is visible above the gum) and one or more roots (the unseen portion that attaches the tooth to the jaw).

§ 16.03   Early Identification Attempts

Identification by the teeth is not a modern concept. During the Revolutionary War, Dr. Joseph Warren, who was a prominent physician and a general in Washington's army, had a young Boston dentist construct a silver-ivory bridge for him. Later, he made use of the dentist's services for a totally different task. He sent him around the countryside to warn the people of the impending approach of the British, for the young dentist was none other than Paul Revere. Warren was killed in the Battle of Bunker Hill and buried in an unmarked grave along with many other casualties. After the war, the bodies were exhumed and Revere identified Warren through the bridgework he had constructed for him earlier.

The earliest recorded court case in which dental evidence was used to prove the corpus delicti was Commonwealth v. Webster,[1] a Massachusetts case in which Dr. John White Webster, a professor at the Harvard Medical School, was convicted of the 1849 murder of Dr. George Parkman, a wealthy benefactor of various Boston charities. In this case, the dismembered remains of the victim were identified by his dentist, a Dr. Nathan Keep. On the witness stand, Dr. Keep, on being shown the charred teeth and pieces of porcelain denture that had been removed from a furnace next to where the body had been discovered, identified them as the dentures he had constructed for Dr. Parkman 3 years before, in 1846. On the basis of that evidence, the remains were identified as those of Dr. Parkman.

Dental identification also played an important role in the identification of the bodies of Adolf Hitler and Eva Braun, after the fall of Berlin toward the end of World War II and in the identification, after exhumation, of the body of Lee Harvey Oswald, accused assassin of President John F. Kennedy.[2]

There have been other dramatic events in which many individuals had to be identified through an examination of their teeth or dentures; for instance, the 1944 Barnum and Bailey circus fire in Connecticut, the 1949 Noronic steamship fire in Toronto, Canada, and more recently the

§ 16.03

1. 59 Mass. (5 Cush.) 295 (1850).

2. Norton et al., "The Exhumation and Identification of Lee Harvey Oswald," 29 *J.For.Sci.* 19 (1984).

bombing at the World Trade Center in New York City and the Branch Davidien siege in Texas as well as many airplane crashes.

II. DENTAL IDENTIFICATION TECHNIQUES

§ 16.04 Principles of Identification by Dental Characteristics

Teeth, dentures and dental restorations are some of the most durable structures in the body. They are highly resistant to destruction, decomposition and mutilation.[1] Therefore, it is frequently possible to discover both the teeth and fillings of a victim among his bodily remains, even when the rest of the body has been totally destroyed.

Each human has five surfaces on as many as 32 teeth for a total of 160 surfaces. The number of conceivable combinations of features notable by clinical examination and by radiograph is astronomical.[2] Teeth also have individual characteristics caused by wear patterns, spacing, fillings and restorations, among other things, thus rendering each person's dentition unique. Therefore, dentists have concluded that given sufficient data, no two mouths will have identical characteristics.[3] Even identical twins have been shown to have different dentition.[4]

While the premise of individuality of human dentition has been long accepted in the forensic dentistry profession, it is only recently that some actual studies have been made to attempt to establish it in a scientific fashion.[5] By comparing the antemortem (before death) data of suspected victims with the postmortem (after death) data from an unknown body, its identity may sometimes be established. The antemortem data important for identification include written dental records, casts and radiographs. There exists a wide variety of dental records. There are more than 150 different types of records in regular use in the United States alone.[6]

The comparison of the characteristics of dental fillings is usually accomplished by examining both the x-rays preserved in dentists' offices with the characteristics shown in the teeth of an unidentified body. If the data match to a sufficient degree, it may be possible to establish

---

§ 16.04

1. Fire, one of the most destructive elements, does not always destroy dental evidence. Teeth can withstand temperatures of up to 2000 degrees fahrenheit and still remain recognizable.

Methods are being developed to stabilize teeth in incinerated remains. See, Mincer, Berryman, Murray & Dickens, "Methods for Physical Stabilization of Ashed Teeth in Incinerated Remains," 35 *J.Forensic Sci.*, 971 (1990).

2. Mertz, "Dental Identification," 21 *Dental Clinics of North America* 47 (1977).

3. Id.

4. Sognnaes, Rawson, Gratt & Nguyen, "Computer Comparison of Bitemark Patterns in Identical Twins," 105 *J.Am.Dental Ass'n.* 449 (1982).

5. Rawson et al., "Statistical Evidence for the Individuality of the Human Dentition," 29 *J.For.Sci.* 245 (1984).

6. Fischman, "Role of the General Practitioner in Data Collection and Cross Matching," 37 *Int'l Dental J.* 201 (1987).

definitely that an unknown body is that of a suspected victim whose dental charts have been obtained, just as it may be possible to establish that the body is definitely *not* that of the suspected individual.

Postmortem tooth loss may complicate the identification process. However, methods are being developed to reconstruct the root morphology of missing teeth in skeletonized human remains for the purpose of radiographic comparison and identification.[7] When a victim has no natural teeth, but has a denture, identity nevertheless can frequently be established by a study of the denture itself. It often contains the markings of the manufacturer, just as the individual teeth that make up the denture may have specific mold numbers corresponding to their shape and color shade numbers. Most dentists maintain accurate records of these identifying details and when a body is suspected to be that of a particular individual, his dentist may be able to establish the truth or falsity of the assumption to a considerable degree of certainty.[8]

The identity of an offender might be established by teeth impressions left in foodstuffs, or even in skin—the so-called bite marks. There have been instances of hungry burglars leaving teeth impressions in cheese from which they have been identified.[9] Criminal investigations have also involved bite marks left in apples, chewing gum, leather, filter tip cigarettes, soft wood, car hoods, empty beer cans and even soap.[10]

An illustration of how teeth identifications are made may be seen by studying Figures 1 and 2. It should be noted there are a number of

7. Smith, "Reconstruction of Root Morphology in Skeletonized Remains with Postmortem Dental Loss," 37 *J.Forensic Sci.* 176 (1992) (Describes a technique in which the socket walls are sealed with a coat of cyanoacrylate cement and injected with a radiopaque mixture. Then it is x-rayed which highlights the morphology of the roots. The impression material can be removed without altering the evidence.).

8. It remains within the realm of possibility, of course, that the denture was found or stolen by the victim in whose mouth it was discovered.

Bodies without natural teeth are called "edentulous" bodies. Postmortem identification of the endentulous deceased has not been as successful as dentate identification, but some identifications have been made

through the use of a maxillary denture prosthesis. *See*, Jacob & Shallya, "Postmortem Identification of the Edentulous Deceased: Denture Tissue Surface Anatomy," 32 *J.Forensic Sci.* 698 (1987).

9. For one such case, see, Doyle v. State, 159 Tex.Crim.R. 310, 263 S.W.2d 779 (1954). The subject is discussed more fully in section 16.05.

10. State v. Ortiz, 198 Conn. 220, 502 A.2d 400 (1985) (bite mark left in apple); Vale, "Bite Mark Evidence in the Investigation of Crime," 14 *Cal.Dental Ass'n.J.* 36 (March 1986); Weigler, Note, "Bite Mark Evidence: Forensic Odontology and the Law," 2 *Health Matrix* 303 (1992); Corbett & Spence, "A Forensic Investigation of Teeth Marks in Soap," 157 *Br.Dent.J.* 270 (1984).

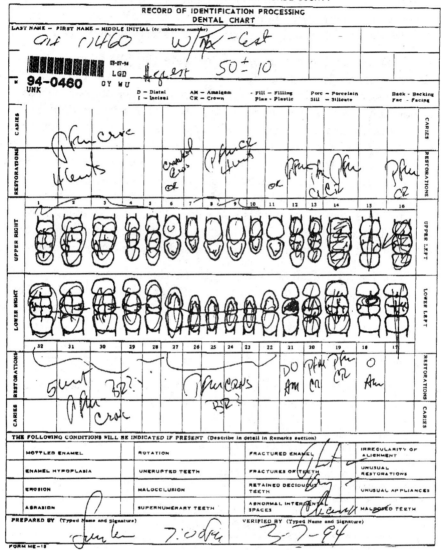

Fig. 1.   *Courtesy: Richard R. Souviron, D.D.S.*

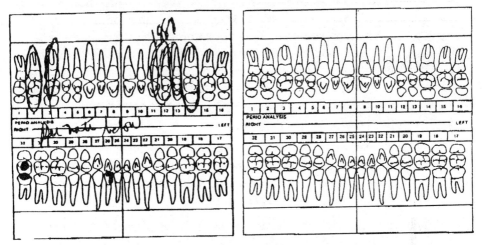

Fig. 2. *Courtesy: Richard R. Souviron, D.D.S.*

different tooth numbering systems in the world. For example the most widely used system in the United States is the universal numbering system which employs a system of numbering the teeth consecutively from 1 to 32 beginning with the upper right third molar.[11] Figure 1 represents a postmortem chart. Figure 2 is an antemortem dental chart of an individual. By comparing the antemortem chart with the chart illustrated in Figure 1, even the uninitiated examiner can notice the resemblance in the postmortem chart. In evaluating such dental charts it must be remembered that natural teeth which are missing on the antemortem chart—and designated by a horizontal line—must of necessity be missing on the postmortem chart. On the other hand, of course, teeth that are missing postmortem may still show up on the antemortem chart; and the older the antemortem chart, the more often intervening changes will occur. Fillings noted on antemortem charts will also be present on postmortem charts, but they may have been replaced, of course, by larger fillings, a crown, or an extraction.

Problems are sometimes encountered in obtaining *suitable* postmortem X-rays for comparison with antemortem records. It may be necessary to take a number of X-rays of varying densities. If the dentist is confronted with a skeleton, he may have to separate the skull from the cervical vertebral column to be able to take the proper X-rays. Intact but decomposed bodies are dealt with differently and at times it has been recommended that the dental apparatus be removed from the body.

11. Mertz, "Dental Identification," 21 *Dental Clinics of North America* 47 (1977) (describes the Universal System, the Palm-er Notation System and the Federal Dentaire International System).

It has been suggested that to identify positively or exclude an individual by a comparison of antemortem and postmortem records, the following criteria are examined: "(1) matching the locations and shapes of fillings, (2) concordance of extracted and remaining teeth, (3) structure of individual teeth including the configuration of their roots, (4) relationship of adjacent teeth, (5) orientation of twisted or tilted teeth ..., and (6) correspondence of pathological findings or anatomical peculiarities in the teeth and jaws." [12]

Dental development can be used to estimate the age of a deceased.[13] Younger ages can be assessed with greater accuracy because more teeth are undergoing formation and the intervals between developmental stages are shorter and therefore, more precise.[14]

The Gustafson method which uses six features of dental microstructure is still considered by most forensic science textbooks to be the reference method for determining age at death in adults.[15] Improvements to the original technique have been suggested [16] and disadvantages to the method have been noted, such as the requirement of a well-trained dental histologist to make the longitudinal thin sections of tooth required for microscopic examination and the fact that such examination destroys the tooth, making reexamination by other methods impossible.[17] New methods are being investigated, such as the Lamendin method which determines age from rooted teeth based upon a formula based upon the measurement of periodontosis (gingival regression) and transparency of the root.[18] Another recent study by the Research Committee of the American Board of Forensic Odontology evaluated the accuracy of estimating age from the development of third molars viewed radiographically.[19]

---

12. Adelson, et al., "Medicine, Dentistry and Law—A Partnership for Criminal Justice," Paper, The Law–Medicine Center, Case Western Reserve U., 1977.

13. Gustafson, "Age Determination on Teeth," 41 J.A.D.A. 45 (1950).

14. Smith, "Standards of Human Tooth Formation and Dental Age Assessment," *Advances in Dental Anthropology,* Kelley & Larsen eds. 1991, at 143–168.

15. Spitz & Fisher, *Medicolegal Investigation of Death,* 1980 at 71.

16. Some experts have reported that Gustafson's techniques are difficult to repeat with consistent results and are best done by specially trained odontological coroners. See, Maples & Rice, "Some Difficulties in the Gustafson Dental Age Estima-

tion," 24 *J.For.Sci.* 168 (1979). Other studies have concluded that Gustafson's cited features do not help predict age. Miller, Dave and Cottone, "Failure of Use of Cemental Annulations in Teeth to Determine the Age of Humans," 33 *J.For.Sci.* 137 (1988) (concluded determining chronologic age in humans from cemental annulations is not possible).

17. Lamendin, Baccino, Humbert, Tavernier, Nossintchouk & Zerilli, "A Simple Technique for Age Estimation in Adult Corpses: The Two Criteria Dental Method," 37 *J.For.Sci.* 1373 (1992).

18. Id.

19. Mincer, Harris & Berryman, "The A.B.F.O., Study of Third Molar Development and Its Use As An Estimator of Chronological Age," 38 *J.For.Sci.* 379 (1993).

Some states now require that forensic odontologists be consulted in the identification of dead or missing individuals.[20]

A computer-assisted postmortem identification (CAPMI) system was developed at the U.S. Army Institute of Dental Research in 1983.[21] It has been used to aid in the identification of missing in action personnel from the Vietnam War.[22] With the CAPMI system dental information obtained from an unknown set of remains is rapidly compared against the antemortem dental data base, for example, the U.S. Army Central Identification Laboratory's dental data base which consists of the antemortem dental records of the Vietnam War MIAs. Such computer systems will prove useful in the identification of remains at mass disasters. Various identification systems using data encoded microchips placed in teeth or under amalgam restorations have also been introduced and evaluated for identification.[23]

From a profession that, in the early 1960s was practically unknown and had but few practitioners who "did their own thing" unhampered by professional guidelines and standards other than those applying to dentists generally, forensic odontology has grown in a mere thirty years to a discipline that has set clearly defined standards for the forensic examination of evidence of dentition, competency standards for certification in the subspecialty field of forensic odontology, and developed a methodology for the examination and identification of bite marks.[24]

20. West's Ann.Cal.Health & Safety Code § 10254 (1993); Official Code Ga. Ann. § 45–16–25 (1993); La.—LSA–Rev. Stat. § 33:1563(H) (1992); Mass.Gen.Ann. Laws c. 22A, § 5 (Law.Co-op.1993); Mich. Comp.Laws Ann. § 333.2844a (1992); Vernon's Ann.Mo.Stat. § 43.410 (1992); Mont. Code Ann. 44–2–402 (1993); N.H.Rev.Stat. Ann. 611:15–a (1993); N.Y.—McKinney's Exec.Law § 838 (Consol.1993); West's Rev. Code Wash. 68.50.330 (1992).

21. Lorton, Rethman and Friedman, "The Computer–Assisted Postmortem Identification (CAPMI) System: A Computer–Based Identification Program," 33 *J.For. Sci.* 977 (1988).

22. Dailey, "Computer–Assisted Identification of Vietnam War Dental Remains," 152 *Military Medicine* 179 (1987).

23. Muhlemann, Steiner & Brandestini, "Identification of Mass Disaster Victims: The Swiss Identification System," 24 *J.Forensic Sci.* 173 (1979); Wilson & Kolbinson,

"The Heat Resistance of a Data–Encoded Ceramic Microchip Identification System," 4 *Am.J.Forensic Med. & Path.* 209 (Sept. 1983).

24. During the early 1970s, ten dentists engaged in forensic work joined together to create a forensic odontology section within the prestigious American Academy of Forensic Sciences. In 1994 the forensic odontology section had 337 members. In 1976, that body sponsored and incorporated the American Board of Forensic Odontology. By 1994 the board had certified 94 diplomates.

The American Society of Forensic Odontology was founded in 1970. At present it is the largest organization of forensic dentists with 411 members. The American Dental Association (ADA) has not recognized Forensic Odontology as one of its ten specialties. The ADA does provide reference packages on forensic dentistry to dentists. (1–800–621–8099)

§ 16.05 Bite Marks and Their Identification

When some of the newly organized forensic odontologists first professed to be able to identify the makers of bite marks left in human skin, forensic dentistry became divided in a way that threatened the life of the young professional discipline. Many of the early founding members of the odontology section of the American Academy of Forensic Sciences had doubts whether such an identification was possible in the routine bite mark case. Most would have agreed that, in exceptional circumstances, when a bite mark is deep, pronounced, clearly visible, and well preserved, and contains unusual characteristics of the teeth that made the impression, an identification would be possible.[1] All would also have agreed that a careful investigation and examination of bite marks could offer a valuable investigative lead to either suggest the possibility or impossibility of a particular individual having made questioned impressions. But all forensic odontologists would certainly not have agreed that it was possible to determine the exact individual in a significant number of cases. Furthermore, there existed no agreed upon procedure, either for the collection or preservation of such evidence, nor for the actual comparison with known standards. No generally accepted examination protocol existed.

Despite these difficulties and, at times, limitations upon the ability to make a bite mark identification, the forensic odontology profession now is in agreement that bite marks can be vital evidence in connecting an accused to a victim, alive or deceased. But proper procedures must be followed in detecting the existence of the bite mark, in photographing it at intervals over a set period of days, as well as in obtaining impressions of the bite mark. The odontology profession has worked together to develop procedures and protocols.

Bite marks which may be discovered may have changed their shape and size considerably from the time they were inflicted. Skin tissue is very elastic. Some bite marks disappear altogether after a short time while some remain for days. Most become significantly altered as time goes by. Bite marks inflicted when a subject was alive may change, in addition to the natural elasticity of the skin, due to tearing of the tissue, subsequent bleeding, swellings, and discolorations of the skin, whether or not the skin was punctured by the teeth. The change in shape is sometimes drastic; the change in size may be caused by shrinkage as well as, though more rarely, enlargement.

If the bite mark was left upon a dead body, or immediately prior to death, the skin alteration will be entirely different. It has been said that the turgor of the skin may last for several hours after death, during which time the marks remain quite visible, but after the turgor leaves the bite marks may become indistinguishable except under ultraviolet

---

§ 16.05

1. See, e.g., Vale et al., "Unusual Three–Dimensional Bite Mark Evidence in a Homicide Case," 21 *J.For.Sci.* 642 (1976).

light. In evaluating the results of experiments in the profession, one researcher found:

> "Studies have shown that the duration of a bite mark on human skin varies considerably, depending upon the force applied and the extent of damage to the underlying tissue. Bite marks that do not break the epithelial layer last from 3 min. to 24 h. In cutting bites, which break the epithelial layers, the edges last from one to three days, depending on the thickness of the area bitten, with the thinner area retaining a sharp edge the longest. Other studies have determined that bites on the face disappear more rapidly than those on the arms. It is interesting that the bites in women were found to be visible longer than those in men. The studies mentioned all agree that the most insignificant bite marks are those that are made without breaking the continuity of the epithelial covering." [2]

Bite marks also show changes and become distorted when the posture of the victim changes. They may shrink in one dimension and become elongated in another. If, as some odontologists have said, there is no mouth which is identical to another, bite marks made by different persons may certainly appear identical because the great variety in characteristics that may be found in the teeth themselves is not visible in an impression of the teeth.[3]

The American Society of Forensic Odontology has produced the useful Manual of Forensic Odontology [4] which details body identification guidelines, guidelines for bite mark analysis, and computer use in forensic dentistry, among other things.

In 1980 the Odontology Section of the American Academy of Forensic Sciences appointed a committee to develop bite mark standards. In 1981, the American Board of Forensic Odontology voted to undertake a similar activity. Both groups formed a joint committee to develop the guidelines. After a 1984 workshop on bite mark analysis at the American Academy of Forensic Sciences meeting in Anaheim, California, the guidelines were adopted.[5] The ABFO guidelines separate the bite mark analysis into the description of the bite mark, collection of the evidence from the victim, collection of the evidence from the suspect, and an analysis of the evidence.[6] The guidelines are considered dynamic and will be modified as significant developments evolve. A workshop on bite mark analysis was conducted at the 1994 annual meeting of the American Academy of Forensic Sciences in San Antonio, Texas. New guidelines addressing terminology, methodology, peer review, and other areas will be forthcoming in 1995 as a result of that workshop. The ABFO has

2. Dinkel, "The Use of Bite Mark Evidence as an Investigative Aid," 19 *J.For. Sci.* 535 (1973–74). See also, De Vore, "Bitemarks for Identification?—A Preliminary Report," 11 *Med.Sci. & Law* 144 (Jul. 1971).

3. Gustafson, *Forensic Odontology*, 140 (1966).

4. *Manual of Forensic Odontology*, Averill, ed. (1991).

5. "Guidelines for Bite Mark Analysis," 112 *J.Am.Dental Ass'n.* 383 (1986).

6. Id. at 384.

also developed a standard reference scale for use in bite mark photography.[7]

The theory behind bite mark analysis is that "teeth, like tools can leave recognizable marks."[8] While there is no one method of bite mark analysis,[9] there is general consensus in the odontological community that the standard comparison technique is to match a photograph or model of the bite mark to a template of the suspect's dentition through an overlay technique at the same scale.[10] Analysis may also be done by direct comparison of photographs[11] or comparison of photographs with models.[12] New techniques for analysis include CAT scanning,[13] ultraviolet forensic imaging,[14] scanning election microscopy,[15] and computerized bite analysis.[16]

The difficulties in examining bite marks and evaluating their worth for identification purposes are many and varied. It is critical that a pathologist performing an autopsy or a physician examining a victim correctly recognize injuries resulting from human bites. Other pattern injuries, abrasions and insect bites have been misidentified as bite marks by forensic pathologists and odontologists.[17]

A bite mark is not an accurate representation of the teeth that caused its impression. To understand this, one must consider the bite dynamics and its effects on the impression made by the teeth. The lower jaw (mandible) is movable and delivers the bite force against the upper jaw (maxilla) which is stationary. The upper teeth hold the substance which is being bitten as the lower teeth approach for the purpose of cutting the substance. When referring to bitemarks in skin, this would mean that the skin is curved between the upper and lower teeth but as the lower jaw moves up to cut the tissue, the skin is stretched away from its normal curvature between the teeth. It will be considerably out of shape when the force is actually inflicted that causes the skin to be pinched between the upper and lower teeth. In this whole

---

7. Hyzer & Krauss, "The Bite Mark Standard Reference Scale—ABFO No. 2," 33 *J.For.Sci.* 498 (1988); See also, Letters to the Editor 33 *J.For.Sci.* 301 (1988) (discussing the scale and previously cited article).

8. Johnson, "Bite Mark Evidence: Recognition, Analysis and Court Room Presentation," 55 *N.Y.S.Dental J.* 153 (1990).

9. See, *Manual of Forensic Odontology* (Averill, ed. 1991).

10. Id.

11. Sperber, "Forensic Odontology," *Scientific and Expert Evidence* 721, 744–47 (Imwinkelreid, ed. 1981).

12. Id.

13. Farrell, et al., "Computerized Axial Tomography as an Aid in Bite Mark Analysis: A Case Report," 32 *J.For.Sci.* 266 (1987).

14. West & Barsley, "Ultraviolet Forensic Imaging," *F.B.I. Law Enforcement Bull.* 14 (May 1992).

15. David, "Adjunctive Use of Scanning Election Microscopy in Bite Mark Analysis: A Three Dimensional Study," 31 *J.For.Sci.* 1126 (1986).

16. Sognnaes, Rawson, Gratt & Nguyen, "Computer Comparison of Bitemark Patterns in Identical Twins," 105 *J.Am.Dental Ass'n* 449 (1982).

17. See, e.g., Sperry & Campbell, "An Elliptical Incised Wound of the Breast Misinterpreted as a Bite Injury," 35 *J.Forensic Sci.* 1226 (1990); "Odontologist Misses the Mark—Post–Mortem Abrasions Mistaken for Bitemarks," 16 *Sci.Sleuthing Rev.* 5 (Spring 1992) (discussing *Czapleski v. Woodward*, C–90–0847 MHP (N.D.Cal. 1991).

process, the skin itself has not been stationary, because it tends to slip along the upper teeth until they catch hold when the bite occurs. (For illustrations of bite marks in skin, see Figs. 3 and 4.)

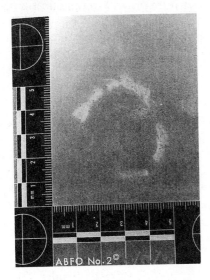 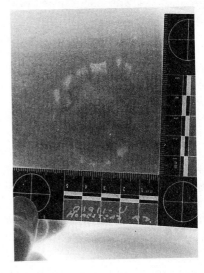

Fig. 3   Fig. 4

Figures 3 and 4 illustra, bite marks left by the so called "biting bandit," a serial robber who, during a crime spree in South Dade County, Florida in the fall and winter of 1989, would jump his victims from behind and clamp his teeth on their flesh until they would surrender their wallets. *Photos courtesy of Richard R. Souviron, D.D.S.*

Marks by teeth left in foodstuffs will also change in size and shape, depending upon the hardness or consistency of the material in which the impression is left. Extremely soft substances are totally useless for identification purposes. This would include all bread products, pies, baked goods, soft or overripe fruits, etc. By contrast, relatively good impressions may be found in hard cheese, apples, and hard candy. The changes in size and shape which occur here are not as drastic as those of bite marks in human skin. It is also possible to preserve and "fix" foodstuffs so that no change will occur.[18] If improperly handled during the evidence collection stages, however, bite marks in foodstuffs, which are fragile, can be easily damaged. Sometimes the damage done by improper handling may not be readily noticeable and the expert thus considers as bite marks impressions which were in some fashion partially altered inadvertently by improper evidence collection procedures.

---

18. Several types of impression and casting materials have been tested with foodstuffs. See, Kogan et al., "Selection of the Appropriate Impression and Casting Materials for Reproduction of Bitemarks from Foodstuffs for Forensic Dental Investigations," 23 *Can.Soc.Forensic Sci.J.* 147 (1990).

If a cast is made of a bite impression left at a crime scene, there is a good chance that it does not accurately represent the true shape of the dental apparatus of the suspect who made the impression. The forensic odontologist who has a possible suspect in mind will take impressions of the teeth of that individual for comparison purposes, but considering the changes that may have occurred in the questioned bite mark before casting, the chances of making a reliable and accurate identification are highly dependent upon the quality and extent of the crime scene bitemark as well as the presence of certain easily recognizable remarkable characteristics.[19]

Photography of teeth impressions is also recommended as a matter of course, but it, too, has serious limitations. A photograph is a two-dimensional pictorial representation that depends for its validity and easy examination primarily on its three-dimensional features. Also, photography renders a representation in a flat plane whereas the impressions may occur on a curved surface, such as a human arm or leg.[20] Also useful in the individualization of bite marks is the analysis of the bacterial pattern in the saliva of the attacker,[21] the analysis of the attacker's genetic markers, if the person is a secretor,[22] or DNA analysis of the saliva.[23]

III. EVIDENCE OF DENTAL IDENTIFICATIONS

§ 16.06 Evidence of Dental Comparisons

As early as 1931, the Illinois Supreme Court was confronted with testimony concerning dental identification in the case of People v. Greenspawn.[1] There, the defendant was prosecuted for passing a forged

19. A review of the ample (and recent) technical literature will reveal different methods of obtaining known standards.

20. The technique of photographic superimposition of antemortem photographs over postmortem skulls to establish personal identification has gained increasing credibility in recent years. McKenna, Jablonski, and Fearnhead, "A Method of Matching Skulls with Photographic Portraits Using Landmarks and Measurements of the Dentition," 29 *J.For.Sci.* 787 (1984); McKenna, "Studies of the Method of Matching Skulls with Photographic Portraits Using Landmarks and Measurements of the Dentition," 3 *J. of Forensic Odonto–Stomatology* 1 (1985); Bastiaan, Dalitz, and Woodward, "Video Superimposition of Skulls and Photographic Portraits—a New Aid to Identification," 31 *J.For.Sci.* 1373 (1986); Thomas, Nortje, and van Ieperen, "A Case of Skull Identification by Means of Photographic Superimposition," 4 *J. of Forensic Odonto–Stomatology* 61 (1986).

21. Elliot, et al., "Analytical Pyrolysis of Streptococcus Salivarius as an Aid to Identification in Bitemark Investigation," 26 *For.Sci.Int.* 131 (1984); Brown, et al., "The Survival of Oral Streptococci on Human Skin and Its Implication in Bitemark Investigation," 26 *For.Sci.Int.* 193 (1984).

22. Seventy–Five to Eighty percent of the population secrete genetic markers into their saliva or other body fluids. Saferstein, *Criminalistics An Introduction to Forensic Science* (1987) at 326.

23. See Chapter 15 on DNA analysis.

§ 16.06

1. 346 Ill. 484, 179 N.E. 98 (1931). The court held that although the dentist's records were not of themselves competent evidence of the facts stated in them, they were of such a character that the doctor might make use of them to refresh his recollection; and that the X-rays themselves should have been received in evidence.

paper. He attempted to prove his alibi through the testimony of an X-ray technician that X-rays of his teeth were taken by the technician at the precise time the crime was supposed to have been committed and that thereafter the defendant had taken these X-rays to his dentist who proceeded to extract three teeth. The X-rays were offered in evidence, along with the testimony of the dentist who offered to identify them as being of the defendant's teeth. The trial court excluded much of the testimony but the Illinois Supreme Court reversed the conviction, holding that the dental identification evidence should have been admitted. Other courts also recognized the value of dental identification. For example, in Fields v. State,[2] a murder prosecution in a case in which the victim was burned beyond recognition, dental identification was admitted. In Wooley v. People,[3] the court admitted testimony by a dentist, apparently without objection, who had compared the dental records of a patient with the teeth of a corpse and had positively identified the corpse as his former patient. The Illinois Appellate Court, in People v. Mattox,[4] recognized that dental structure constitutes a valid means of identifying a deceased person who is otherwise unrecognizable when there is a dental record of that person with which the structure may be compared.

In all of the cases to which we have referred, testimony was given by dentists. Presumably the courts will hold to the view that any licensed dentist is competent to give opinion evidence as an expert on the subject of dental identification, just as the courts have generally permitted all medical doctors to qualify as experts on nearly any and all medical issues. It must be noted, however, that there is a definite class of forensic odontologists who specialize in dental identification and who have associated in a professional society.[5] Nevertheless, it is suggested that a dental technician who is not a doctor or a licensed dentist would also qualify as an expert witness, provided it is shown that he has had sufficient practical experience in the field of dental identification, specifically obtained while assisting a properly qualified dentist in that type of work.

§ 16.07 Evidence of Bite Mark Identifications

In dealing with the admissibility of bite mark evidence, the courts have been remarkably unanimous in upholding testimony of dentists to the effect that a bite mark found on a victim of a crime had been produced by the defendant's teeth.

2. 322 P.2d 431 (Okl.Cr.1958).

3. 148 Colo. 392, 367 P.2d 903 (1961).

4. 96 Ill.App.2d 148, 237 N.E.2d 845 (1968).

For additional cases, see, Lindsay v. People, 63 N.Y. 143 (1875); and Commonwealth v. Webster, 59 Mass. (5 Cush.) 295, 52 Am.Dec. 711 (1850); for two early cases recognizing the admissibility of testimony of a dentist on the question of personal identification. Later cases include, Haw-kins v. State, 60 Neb. 380, 83 N.W. 198 (1900); People v. Westlake, 106 Cal.App. 247, 289 P. 212 (1930); and State v. Johnston, 62 Idaho 601, 113 P.2d 809 (1941).

5. An extensive list of reference sources in forensic dentistry, including address list of active scientific workers in the field, appeared in "The Role of Dentistry in The Forensic Sciences," *INFORM* (Bulletin), Vol. 5, April 1973 at p. 7. See also, infra, § 16.08 on qualifications of the forensic odontologist.

By 1993 bite mark evidence had been admitted in more than thirty jurisdictions.[1]

Bite mark evidence has been admitted as prior bad acts evidence pursuant to Federal Rule of Evidence 404(b).[2] Bite marks have also been introduced to show aggravating circumstances for death penalty purposes.[3] They have also been admitted to show a defendant's state of mind,[4] and as evidence of unfitness of a parent in a child custody

§ 16.07

1.

Alabama: Handley v. State, 515 So.2d 121 (Ala.Cr.App.1987); Ex parte Dolvin, 391 So.2d 677 (Ala.1980);

Alaska: Chase v. State, 678 P.2d 1347 (Alaska App.1984);

Arkansas: Davasher v. State, 308 Ark. 154, 823 S.W.2d 863 (1992) (admitting dog bite evidence);

Arizona: State v. Richards, 166 Ariz. 576, 804 P.2d 109 (App.1990);

California: People v. Marx, 54 Cal.App.3d 100, 126 Cal.Rptr. 350 (1975);

Colorado: People v. Vigil, 718 P.2d 496 (Colo.1986);

Connecticut: State v. Asherman, 193 Conn. 695, 478 A.2d 227 (1984);

Florida: Bundy v. State, 455 So.2d 330 (Fla.1984), cert. denied 476 U.S. 1109 (1986); Bradford v. State, 460 So.2d 926 (Fla.App.1984);

Georgia: Smith v. State, 253 Ga. 536, 322 S.E.2d 492 (1984);

Illinois: People v. Johnson, 8 Ill.App.3d 457, 289 N.E.2d 722 (1972); People v. Milone, 43 Ill.App.3d 385, 2 Ill.Dec. 63, 356 N.E.2d 1350 (1976);

Indiana: Wade v. State, 490 N.E.2d 1097 (Ind.1986); Niehaus v. State, 265 Ind. 655, 359 N.E.2d 513 (1977), cert. denied 434 U.S. 902 (1977);

Kansas: State v. Peoples, 227 Kan. 127, 605 P.2d 135 (1980);

Louisiana: State v. Stokes, 433 So.2d 96 (La.1983);

Maine: State v. Joubert, 603 A.2d 861 (Me. 1992);

Massachusetts: Commonwealth v. Cifizzari, 397 Mass. 560, 492 N.E.2d 357 (1986);

Michigan: People v. Marsh, 177 Mich.App. 161, 441 N.W.2d 33 (1989);

Missouri: State v. Sager, 600 S.W.2d 541 (Mo.App.1980), cert. denied 450 U.S. 910 (1981);

Nevada: Bludsworth v. State, 98 Nev. 289, 646 P.2d 558 (1982);

New York: People v. Middleton, 54 N.Y.2d 42, 444 N.Y.S.2d 581, 429 N.E.2d 100 (1981);

N. Carolina: State v. Green, 305 N.C. 463, 290 S.E.2d 625 (1982); State v. Temple, 302 N.C. 1, 273 S.E.2d 273 (1981);

Ohio: State v. Sapsford, 22 Ohio App.3d 1, 488 N.E.2d 218 (1983);

Oklahoma: Kennedy v. State, 640 P.2d 971 (Okl.Cr.1982);

Oregon: State v. Routh, 30 Or.App. 901, 568 P.2d 704 (1977);

Pennsylvania: Commonwealth v. Henry, 524 Pa. 135, 569 A.2d 929 (1990); Commonwealth v. Edwards, 521 Pa. 134, 555 A.2d 818 (1989);

Rhode Island: State v. Correia, 600 A.2d 279 (R.I.1991);

S. Carolina: State v. Jones, 273 S.C. 723, 259 S.E.2d 120 (1979);

Tennessee: State v. Gardner, 1990 WL 160967 (Tenn.Cr.App.1990);

Texas: Doyle v. State, 159 Tex.Crim.R. 310, 263 S.W.2d 779 (1954); Patterson v. State, 509 S.W.2d 857 (Tex.Cr.App.1974); Spence v. Texas, 795 S.W.2d 743 (Tex.Cr. App.1990);

Vermont: State v. Howe, 136 Vt. 53, 386 A.2d 1125 (1978);

Virginia: Harward v. Commonwealth, 5 Va. App. 468, 364 S.E.2d 511 (1988);

Washington: State v. Bingham, 105 Wash.2d 820, 719 P.2d 109 (1986);

West Virginia: State v. Armstrong, 179 W.Va. 435, 369 S.E.2d 870 (1988);

Wisconsin: State v. Stinson, 134 Wis.2d 224, 397 N.W.2d 136 (App.1986);

Military Cts: United States v. Martin, 13 M.J. 66 (C.M.A.1982).

2. See, United States v. Dia, 826 F.Supp. 1237 (D.Ariz.1993).

3. Commonwealth v. Edwards, 521 Pa. 134, 555 A.2d 818 (1989).

4. People v. Stanciel, 225 Ill.App.3d 1082, 168 Ill.Dec. 157, 589 N.E.2d 557 (1991) (that he intended to do great bodily harm to a three year old decedent when he bit her).

matter.[5]

Bite mark evidence is so routinely accepted that some courts are taking judicial notice of its general reliability.[6] One court has even held that bite mark evidence need not meet the *Frye* standard since it is in the nature of a physical comparison rather than a scientific test.[7]

Yet, at the time of the earliest decisions, the profession of forensic odontology, then in its infancy, at least insofar as bitemarks were concerned, had not reached any agreement on whether bitemarks could be used for identification purposes and had not developed any criteria or protocols by which such comparisons were to be made. Indeed, one of the first two appellate decisions was soundly criticized by prominent odontologists.

The first case was People v. Marx,[8] involving an extremely unusual three-dimensional bite mark, made by a suspect who had distinctive teeth characteristics. One of the three prosecution experts stated that the bitemarks in this case were exceptionally well defined. He made the point that he has, in many bite mark cases, refused to testify or give definite opinions as to their identity with a known individual, but he termed the bite impressions in this case the clearest he had ever seen personally or in the published literature.

Since the evidence clearly revealed to the California Appellate Court that, at the time, there was no accepted methodology in identifying bite marks and that there was indeed "no established science of identifying persons from bite marks as distinguished from, say, dental records and X-rays," [9] and since there also was no evidence of any systematic, orderly experimentation in the area, the court would have been hard pressed in finding that the forensic odontology of bite mark identification had gained the "general acceptance" of the field in which it belongs.[10] It clearly had received no such acceptance.

The court resolved this problem by holding that "we do not believe that under all the circumstances of this case the standard of 'general acceptance in the field,' is determinative of admissibility." [11] The appellate court made this determination despite the fact that its own supreme court has repeatedly held "general acceptance" to be the standard for the admission of novel scientific evidence.[12] Apart from whether the

5. In re Rimer v. Rimer, 395 N.W.2d 390 (Minn.App.1986).

6. State v. Armstrong, 179 W.Va. 435, 369 S.E.2d 870 (1988).

7. Ex parte Dolvin, 391 So.2d 677 (Ala. 1980) (Expert compared teeth in human skull with inter vivos photographs of decedent to make an identification.)

8. 54 Cal.App.3d 100, 126 Cal.Rptr. 350 (1975).

9. Id. at 353.

10. The "general acceptance" test finds its origin in Frye v. United States, 54 App.

D.C. 46, 293 Fed. 1013 (1923). It is discussed extensively in Chapter 1 of this book, at § 1.03, supra.

11. People v. Marx, 54 Cal.App.3d 100, 110, 126 Cal.Rptr. 350, 355 (1975).

12. See, e.g., Huntingdon v. Crowley, 64 Cal.2d 647, 51 Cal.Rptr. 254, 414 P.2d 382 (1966). In People v. Leahy, 34 Cal.Rptr.2d 663, 882 P.2d 321 (Cal.1994), the California Supreme Court reaffirmed its adherence to the Kelly-Frye test and held inadmissible, as not having met such test, evidence of horizontal gaze nystagmus field sobriety

appellate court correctly followed state law, the outcome of the case was likely to be correct in view of the highly unusual nature of the evidence and the striking characteristics of the suspect's dentition.[13]

In People v. Milone,[14] the Illinois Appellate Court was also faced with the issue of bite mark evidence. Unlike *Marx*, the claim that the *Milone* bite marks were in any way unique or unusual was disputed. What appears clearly is that there was a sharp conflict in the testimony as well as a battle of experts. One of the prosecution experts was a major proponent of the utility and value of bite mark identifications. One of the defense's forensic odontologists maintained that bite marks could only rarely provide a positive identification, that the profession has not accepted the premise of the uniqueness of bite marks to prove identity, and that the evidence in the *Milone* case positively excluded the defendant as having made the impression.[15] In view of this, it is rather surprising that the Illinois court held the *Frye* case's "general acceptance" test to have been met. The court relied on some doubtful quotes in the literature and on a few other cases. One of these was People v. Johnson,[16] also an Illinois Appellate Court decision where testimony by an oral pathologist was admitted, based on his comparison of a bite mark photograph with a cast of defendant's teeth, to the effect that it was highly probable the teeth marks on the victim were made by the defendant. A more unscientific analysis could hardly have been done, but there was plenty of other incriminating evidence in the case. In a Texas case, a dentist's opinion that the defendant's teeth had made bite marks in cheese was also relied upon, along with other incriminating

tests on the basis of which a defendant was convicted.

13. The case was written up by the experts in an article: Vale, et al., "Unusual Three–Dimensional Bite Mark Evidence in a Homicide Case," 21 *J.For.Sci.* 642 (1976).

14. 43 Ill.App.3d 385, 2 Ill.Dec. 63, 356 N.E.2d 1350 (1976).

15. The defense odontologist, who later became a President of the American Academy of Forensic Sciences, by accident was shown a bite mark recovered from a woman's breast who had been found murdered in the same area where the Milone victim had been found. A suspect, Macek, was arrested for that crime, but the odontologist claimed that the bite mark supposedly made by Macek was in fact identical to the one in the Milone case. See, "Levine, Forensic Dentistry: Our Most Controversial Case," in *1978 Legal Medicine Annual* (Wecht, ed.) 73, 77.

It was reported that Macek in fact tendered a written confession, later repudiated, to having killed the victim for whose killing Milone was convicted. State v. Sager, 600 S.W.2d 541, 571 (Mo.App.1980), cert. de-

nied 450 U.S. 910 (1981), quotes Levine's writing to that effect.

It is clear that some serious questions are raised by the Milone trial and conviction, and some possibilities are here suggested: (1) the prosecution witnesses were wrong in identifying Milone, which raises questions about the ability to make positive identifications from bite marks; (2) the defense witness was wrong in excluding Milone and in identifying Macek as having placed the bite impression on the Milone victim, which raises the same question as in (1); (3) bite marks are not unique and Milone and Macek exhibit identical bite impressions, which takes away a fundamental premise upon which odontologists rely in the making of identifications from bite marks. In view of the unimpeachable background in forensic dentistry on both sides, we do not consider, as a fourth possibility, that one or more of the experts were incompetent. But the case presents some knotty problems for bite mark identification.

16. 8 Ill.App.3d 457, 289 N.E.2d 722 (1972). Dental evidence not made an issue on appeal.

evidence.[17] Finally, the appellate court relied on Patterson v. State,[18] a Texas appellate decision in which the fact that there was opposing expert opinion was said to go only to the weight of the evidence. None of these cases had the quantum of scientific evidence in its record that either *Marx* or *Milone* had.

The Illinois court, however, relied on *Marx* as well, comparing the dental identification evidence in *Milone,* which was variously reported to be of either good or poor quality, to that in *Marx,* which was admittedly of a highly unusual and exceptional nature. Though the *Marx* court, having before it exceptionally clear and distinctive evidence, could not decide that the "general acceptance" test was met, the *Milone* court, confronted by less distinctive evidence, had no such problem. Ignoring defense evidence, it called the evidence to be of "excellent" quality and had no difficulty at all calling the "concept of identifying a suspect by matching his dentition to a bite mark found at the scene of a crime … a logical extension of the accepted principle that each person's dentition is unique." [19]

In the years since the *Marx* and *Milone* decisions, other courts have eagerly followed suit, and challenges to admissibility have largely been unsuccessful, even though in the early years there had been no general acceptance of standards for comparison of bite marks. This did not stop courts from finding, on the testimony in the record of experts who were proponents of the evidence, that such a general acceptance had already

---

17. Doyle v. State, 159 Tex.Crim.R. 310, 263 S.W.2d 779 (App.1954).

18. 509 S.W.2d 857 (Tex.Cr.App.1974).

19. The Milone trial had a sequel. Following the trial but before the appeal was decided, the forensic odontologists in the American Academy of Forensic Sciences, at an annual meeting of its members, put on a rare performance. In a mock trial the evidence in People v. Milone was read from the transcripts—though one proponent contends it was an edited and shortened version—several of the original experts who testified at the trial reading their own testimony. The visual evidence was also presented, and the leading proponents and opponents had an opportunity to comment after the presentation. The session was open to all Academy members. It was attended by several hundred forensic scientists. At the conclusion, upon leaving the hall, many of them expressed unabashed astonishment that a fact finder could possibly have believed that the defendant's identity had been positively established by the bite mark, upon the evidence presented. The session sparked several soul-searching sessions among the forensic odontologists. At the February, 1977, meeting of the Academy's Forensic Odontology section, a "bite mark committee" was formed to engage in research on the reliability of such evidence as well as to investigate methods and nomenclature, none of which had received any approval by the practitioners in forensic odontology. In the ensuing years, the odontologists worked diligently to agree on terminology, set standards for forensic examinations, and devise protocols, culminating, in 1984, in the adoption of "The Guidelines for Bite Mark Analysis," by the American Board of Forensic Odontology. In 1992 Mr. Milone petitioned for a writ of habeas corpus on the grounds that the failure to grant a new evidentiary hearing would constitute a fundamental miscarriage of justice. He unsuccessfully argued that the combination of new bite mark expert testimony and the fact that a convicted serial killer confessed to the crime constituted newly discovered evidence which demonstrated his innocence. The court denied the petition, stating that the new expert opinion would only add to a myriad of expert opinion evidence already introduced (1,300 pages of trial transcript) and would not change the outcome of the case. The court reasoned that judicial economy and concern over finality of judgments outweigh the value additional expert opinion evidence can add to a case already full of conflicting expert testimony. United States ex rel. Milone v. Camp, 1992 WL 253147 (N.D.Ill. 1992).

been conferred,[20] or that general acceptance was not necessary as long as the testimony was based on "established scientific methods," [21] or, like in *Marx,* permitting such testimony as an exception to the stricter general acceptance test.[22]   Other cases held bite mark evidence admissible because other states had done so,[23] or for a combination of several reasons.[24]

In various cases, experts have expressed their opinions that the bite mark on the victim was "consistent with" those which would be made by the defendant's teeth,[25] or they have expressed suggestions that the identification was "highly probable," [26] which was said to be the same as "with reasonable dental certainty." [27]   However, where the expert testified that "he could not exclude these dentures [of the defendant] as being the mechanism for perpetrating these bite marks," [28] the court found the testimony insufficient to support a conviction and reversed.

In Bludsworth v. State,[29] the expert was asked to examine a bite mark on the scrotum of a two-year-old boy. The pliability of the scrotal tissue was said to be such as to disable the expert from making a positive identification with the dental impressions taken from the mother and the stepfather. The expert was, however, permitted to say that the bite mark was not made by the mother and that the stepfather's dentition was "consistent with the mark." The reviewing court held testimony to have been properly admitted since it tended to prove the intentional

20.   State v. Sager, 600 S.W.2d 541 (Mo. App.1980), cert. denied 450 U.S. 910 (1981)—the court included large segments of the defense odontologist's testimony who found a number of discrepancies between the defendant's dentition and the bite marks on the victim, but the court held that this went only to the weight and not admissibility; State v. Kleypas, 602 S.W.2d 863 (Mo.App.1980); People v. Middleton, 54 N.Y.2d 42, 444 N.Y.S.2d 581, 429 N.E.2d 100 (1981); Bundy v. State, 455 So.2d 330 (Fla.1984).

21.   State v. Temple, 302 N.C. 1, 273 S.E.2d 273 (1981).

22.   State v. Jones, 273 S.C. 723, 259 S.E.2d 120 (1979); State v. Peoples, 227 Kan. 127, 605 P.2d 135 (1980).

23.   Kennedy v. State, 640 P.2d 971 (Okl.Cr.1982): "Bite-mark comparison has received evidentiary acceptance in all eight of the jurisdictions in which its admission was sought."

24.   State v. Garrison, 120 Ariz. 255, 585 P.2d 563 (1978); Niehaus v. State, 265 Ind. 655, 359 N.E.2d 513 (1977), cert. denied 434 U.S. 902 (1977); State v. Routh, 30 Or.App. 901, 568 P.2d 704 (1977); State v. Green, 305 N.C. 463, 290 S.E.2d 625 (1982); People v. Smith, 110 Misc.2d 118, 443 N.Y.S.2d 551 (1981).

25.   People v. Middleton, supra note 20. The expert found the possibility of someone

else's having the same individual characteristics that were represented in the defendant's dentition to be "astronomical."

26.   People v. Slone, 76 Cal.App.3d 611, 143 Cal.Rptr. 61 (1978).   The expert also thought it "very highly improbable" that some individual other than defendant had inflicted the bite."

27.   People v. Slone, supra note 26.   The possibility of someone else having made the bite was "extremely slight." In Bradford v. State, 460 So.2d 926 (Fla.App.1984), the expert testified "to a reasonable degree of dental certainty and/or probability."

In Bundy v. State, supra note 20, the identification was made "to a high degree of reliability."

28.   People v. Queen, 130 Ill.App.3d 523, 85 Ill.Dec. 826, 474 N.E.2d 786 (1985).   After stating his opinion the expert was asked if the dentures *could* have made the bitemarks; he responded that his opinion, as expressed, meant the same thing.

In Jackson v. State, 511 So.2d 1047 (Fla. App.1987), the court held that even though evidence of a bite mark consistent with the defendant's teeth was found on the victim the evidence was insufficient to uphold the conviction.

29.   98 Nev. 289, 646 P.2d 558 (1982).

infliction of injuries on the child, which would tend to disprove the defendant's claim that the infant's death resulted in an accident when the stepfather dropped the child.

The wholesale acceptance, by the courts, of testimony on bite mark identifications has transformed the profession. Whereas prior to 1974 the main thrust of forensic dentistry was to prove identity of persons by means of a comparison of postmortem and antemortem dental records in mass disasters, the profession has changed direction and is now heavily involved in assisting prosecutors in homicides and sex offense cases. Having received judicial approval of bite mark comparisons, there seems to be no more limit on the extent of forensic odontological conclusions.

Thus, in People v. Jordan et al.,[30] the defendant was convicted upon proof, in part, that his victim had been strangled by him in view of her skeletonized remains having been discovered with signs of pink teeth. Though no bitemarks were involved here, four forensic odontologists testified regarding the "pink tooth phenomenon." Two testified for the state and agreed that while there are numerous causes of "pink teeth," one of which is strangulation, and while they also testified that forensic dentists were not qualified to determine the cause of death, they nevertheless concluded by process of elimination that, in this case, the victim's "pink teeth" were probably caused by strangulation. With two experts for the defense testifying to the other causes for "pink teeth," the defendant was nevertheless convicted. On appeal, the Supreme Court of Illinois affirmed. While it recognized that the odontologists could not testify to cause of death for lack of qualifications—though that is exactly what they did—and recognizing also that their opinions as to strangulation could not be stated positively, the court nevertheless found the experts competent to testify as experts on the "pink tooth phenomenon."

At times courts have allowed experts to testify beyond what many in the field would state an odontologist is able to opine. A recent example is Commonwealth v. Henry[31] in which the court held the dentist was qualified to testify that bite marks on the victim's body were attacking or sadistic in nature since he had done research in categorizing human bite marks and could distinguish lunatic and fighting bite marks from attacking or sadistic bite marks and from sexually oriented bite marks. This opinion was roundly criticized by the forensic odontological community.[32]

----

30. 103 Ill.2d 192, 82 Ill.Dec. 925, 469 N.E.2d 569 (1984).

31. 524 Pa. 135, 569 A.2d 929 (1990).

32. See, Letters to the Editor, 14 *Scientific Sleuthing Rev.* 2 (Fall 1990); 15 *Scientific Sleuthing Rev.* 3 (Winter 1991).

IV. MISCELLANEOUS

§ 16.08 Qualifications of the Forensic Odontologist

Like tool mark and fingerprint identification, bite marks have no accepted minimum number of points required for a match. Therefore, a forensic odontologist's opinion is subjective even though the foundation for his opinion must be based on objective criteria.[1] Knowledge of the expert's qualifications and his level of experience and expertise is critical to evaluate his opinion.

Challenges to an expert's qualifications in bite mark cases have usually failed.[2] It has been held to be error for a trial court to admit testimony by a medical examiner that marks on a victim's wrist were consistent with bite marks when the doctor was not an expert in forensic dentistry.[3]

The forensic dentist or forensic odontologist is to the ordinary dentist essentially what the forensic pathologist is to clinical (hospital) pathologists: he is a specialist dealing primarily with issues involving the identification of human beings by dental evidence.

Within the American Academy of Forensic Sciencies, a new section was established in the early 1970s for forensic odontologists. The Section thereafter sponsored the formation of the American Board of Forensic Odontology which set up requirements for certification in forensic odontology. While the requirements are fairly complex, in essence they require preliminarily a dental degree (D.D.S. or D.M.D.) from an accredited institution, and have attended a minimum of four annual meetings of a national forensic/forensic dental organization and participated in a minimum of two annual programs of a national forensic/forensic dental organization.

There is also a requirement that the applicant be "currently active and formally affiliated with a medical/legal agency such as a medical examiner's or coroner's office, law enforcement agency, insurance company, or federal dental service for at least one year."[4] This would seem to exclude dentists in private practice, regardless of their past education and experience, unless they are affiliated, at least part-time, with one of the above agencies. Applicants for certification must also have observed at least five autopsies, submit evidence of twenty-five significant forensic dental cases in which they have been involved, and present evidence of having accumulated 350 qualification points in a great variety of ways.[5]

§ 16.08

1. Sopher, *Forensic Dentistry* (1976) at 140.

2. People v. Williams, 128 Ill.App.3d 384, 83 Ill.Dec. 720, 470 N.E.2d 1140 (1984); Niehaus v. State, 265 Ind. 655, 359 N.E.2d 513 (1977); State v. Peoples, 227 Kan. 127, 605 P.2d 135 (1980); Commonwealth v. Cifizzari, 397 Mass. 560, 492 N.E.2d 357 (1986).

3. State v. Adams, 481 A.2d 718 (R.I. 1984) (In that case the prosecution also failed to disclose to defense a report by another medical examiner and the cast impression of the bite mark. This was held to be a discovery violation).

4. Pamphlet, American Board of Forensic Odontology Inc., 1990.

5. Qualification points, in varying quantities, are awarded for attendance at Board recognized scientific sessions in forensic odontology, presenting lectures or laboratory sessions at recognized meetings, publishing papers on forensics, holding office in recognized organizations, participating in depositions or appearing in court in dental identification cases, attending certain specialty courses at recognized institutions,

After meeting all of these criteria, the applicant must also pass an examination administered by the Board. Waiver provisions were provided for all the people who were in the field and who applied before a stated time. Certification is for a period of five years and must then be renewed under other criteria set by the board.

§ 16.09 Constitutional Issues

Dental examinations and dental impressions have been held not to be a search since teeth are fixed characteristics of the body, like fingerprints, and therefore the taking of an impression does not violate an accused's right to privacy or his Fifth Amendment privilege against self-incrimination.[1]

The Supreme Court of Georgia has held that an indigent defendant was entitled to state funds to pay for a court-appointed expert where dental impression evidence was the only evidence linking him to the murder.[2]

§ 16.10 Bibliography of Additional References

Anno., "Admissibility of Evidence Tending to Identify Accused by his own Bite Marks," 77 A.L.R.3d 1122 (1977).

Bang, "Factors of Importance in Dental Identification," 1 *For.Sci.* 91 (1972).

Barbenel & Evans, "Bite Marks in Skin—Mechanical Factors," 14 *J.For. Sci.Soc.* 235 (1974).

Bernstein, "Two Bite Mark Cases with Inadequate Scale References," 30 *J.For.Sci.* 958 (1985).

Cameron & Sims, *Forensic Dentistry,* 1974.

Carpenter, "Dental Identification of Plane Crash Victims," 51 *J.N.Car. Dent.Soc.* 9 (1968).

Comment, "Bite Mark Evidence: Hocus Pocus or Science," 16 *Cumb. L.Rev.* 127 (1985).

Comment, "Evidence: The Erosion of Legal Safeguards on the Admissibility of Bitemark Evidence in Criminal Trials: *Bradford v. State,*" 37 *U.Fla.L.Rev.* 880 (1985).

Cottone & Standish, *Outline of Forensic Dentistry* (1982).

Dorion, "Dental Nomenclature," 8 *Canadian Soc.For.Sci.* 107 (1975).

documenting routine identification cases or bite mark cases. Qualification points are also awarded for each formal affiliation with a board recognized institution "such as Medical Examiner, Coroner, Law Enforcement Agency, Federal dental service, or Insurance Company"—the same institutions to which one must be affiliated in order to be permitted to apply in any event. See text at preceding footnote.

§ 16.09

1. See, United States v. Holland, 378 F.Supp. 144 (E.D.Pa.1974); People v. Milone, 43 Ill.App.3d 385, 2 Ill.Dec. 63, 356 N.E.2d 1350 (Ill.1976); Patterson v. State, 509 S.W.2d 857, 862 (Tex.Cr.App.1974); State v. Asherman, 193 Conn. 695, 478 A.2d 227 (1984).

2. Thornton v. State, 255 Ga. 434, 339 S.E.2d 240 (1986).

Dorion, "Denture Teeth Identification," 8 *Canadian Soc.For.Sci.* 111 (1975).

Furness, "A General Review of Bite–Mark Evidence," 2 *Am.J.For.Med. & Path.* 49 (1981).

Furuhata & Yamamoto, *Forensic Odontology,* 1967.

Gladfelter, *Dental Evidence: A Handbook for Police,* 1975.

Glass, et al., "Multiple Animal Bite Wounds: A Case Report," 19 *J.For.Sci.* 305 (1974).

Haines, "Racial Characteristics in Forensic Dentistry," 12 *Med.Sci. & Law* 131 (1972).

Harvey, *Dental Identification & Forensic Odontology,* (England) 1976.

Hill, "Dental Identification In A Light Aircraft Accident," 19 *Med.Sci. Law* 82 (1979).

Holt, "Forensic Odontology–Assistance in a Problem of Identity," 21 *J.For.Sci.Soc.* 343 (1981).

Jakush, "Forensic Dentistry," 119 *J.Am.Dental Ass'n.* 355 (1989).

Jonason, et al., "Three Dimensional Measurement of Tooth Impressions in Criminal Investigations," 2 *Internat.J.For.Dentistry* 70 (Oct. 1974).

Karazulas, "The Presentation of Bite Mark Evidence Resulting in the Acquittal of a Man After Serving Seven Years in Prison for Murder," 29 *J.For.Sci.* 355 (1984).

Krauss, "Forensic Odontology in Missing Persons Cases," 21 *J.For.Sci.* 959 (1976).

Krauss, "Photographic Techniques of Concern in Metric Bite Mark Analysis," 29 *J.For.Sci.* 633 (1984). Letter to the editor in answer to this article at 30 *J.For.Sci.* 599 (1985).

Krauss & Warlen, "The Forensic Science Use of Reflective Ultraviolet Photography," 30 *J.For.Sci.* 262 (1985).

Luntz & Luntz, *Handbook for Dental Identification* (1973).

Manual of Forensic Odontology (Averill, ed. 1991).

Maples, "Some Difficulties in the Gustafson Dental Age Estimations," 24 *J.For.Sci.* 168 (1979).

Note, "Forensic Dentistry and the Law: Is Bite Mark Evidence Here to Stay?," 24 *Am.Crim.L.Rev.* 983 (1987).

Owsley & Webb, "Misclassification Probability of Dental Discrimination Functions for Sex Determination," 28 *J.For.Sci.* 181 (1983).

Proceedings of the First National Symposium on Dentistry's Role and Responsibility in Mass Disaster Identification, Am. Dental Ass'n. (1988).

Rao & Souviron, "Dusting and Lifting the Bite Print: A New Technique," 29 *J.For.Sci.* 326 (1984).

Rawson, et al., "Radiographic Interpretation of Contrast–Media–Enhanced Bite Marks," 24 *J.For.Sci.* 898 (1979).

Rawson, et al., "Incidence of Bite Marks In a Selected Juvenile Population: A Preliminary Report," 29 *J.For.Sci.* 254 (1984).

Rothwell, Hagland & Morton, "Dental Identification in Serial Homicides: The Green River Murders," 119 *J.Am.Dental Ass'n.* 373 (1989).

Rudnick, "The Identification of a Murder Victim Using a Comparison of the Postmortem and Antemortem Dental Records," 29 *J.For.Sci.* 349 (1984).

Simon, et al., "Successful Identification of a Bite Mark in a Sandwich," 2 *Internat.J.For.Dentistry* 17 (Jan. 1974).

Sims, et al., "Bite-marks in the 'Battered Baby Syndrome'," 14 *Med.Sci. & Law* 207 (1973).

Sognnaes, "Eva Braun Hitler's Odontological Identification—A Forensic Enigma?," 19 *J.For.Sci.* 215 (1974).

Sopher, *Forensic Dentistry* (1976).

Sperber, "Forensic Odontology," *Scientific and Expert Evidence* (Imwinkelried, ed. 1981).

Sperber, "The Whole Tooth and Nothing but the Tooth," *F.B.I.Law Enf.Bull.*, June 1982, p. 22.

Symposium on Forensic Odontology (series of articles by various authors) 14 *J.For.Sci.Soc.* 201–258 (1974).

Tesdahl, "Bite Mark Evidence: Making an Impression in Court," *Army Law.* 13 (July 1989).

Vale, "Bite Mark Evidence in the Investigation of Crime," 14 *Cal.Dental Ass'n J.* 36 (1986).

Vale & Noguchi, "Anatomical Distribution of Human Bite Marks in a Series of 67 Cases," 28 *J.For.Sci.* 61 (1983).

Wagner, "Bitemark Identification in Child Abuse Cases," 8 *Pediatric Dent.* 96 (1986).

Weigler, Note, "Bite Mark Evidence: Forensic Odontology and the Law," 2 *Health Matrix* 303 (1992).

Wilkinson & Gerughty, "Bite Mark Evidence: Its Admissibility Is Hard To Swallow," 12 *Western St.U.L.Rev.* 519 (1985).

Woolridge, "Legal Problems of the Forensic Odontologist," 18 *J.For.Sci.* 40 (1973).

Woolridge, "Significant Problems of the Forensic Odontologist in the U.S.A.," 1 *Int'l.J.For.Dentistry* 6 (Oct. 1973).

Yano, "Experimental Studies on Bite Marks," 1 *Internat.J.For.Dentistry* 13 (Oct. 1973).

Zarkowski, "Bite Mark Evidence: Its Worth in the Eyes of the Expert," 1 *J.L. & Ethics Dentistry* (1988).

Chapter 17

FORENSIC ANTHROPOLOGY

I. Introduction

I.　INTRODUCTION

§ 17.01　Scope of the Chapter

The objective of this chapter is to introduce the reader to the fast emerging field of forensic anthropology, defined by Kerley as "the specialized subdiscipline of physical anthropology that applies the techniques of osteology and skeletal identification to problems of legal and public concern." [1] The focus of the materials in this chapter is on the skeletal structure of human beings and the ways in which it can be instructive in various legal settings.　Although forensic anthropologists are most recurrently called upon to give their opinions on issues of criminal law cognizance, still they have a decided place in civil litigation, especially in the identification of mass disaster victims.

　　　　　§ 17.01　　　　　　　*For.Anthro.* 160 (1978).
　1.　Kerley, "Recent Developments in Forensic　Anthropology,"　21　*Yrbook　of*

This chapter provides a systematic overview of the most accepted means by which forensic anthropologists arrive at an identification of unknown human remains.   It is also designed to demonstrate the strengths and the weaknesses of forensic anthropology in subjects of legal concern outside those relating to the identity of a deceased person. It should be noted that forensic anthropologists serve a collaborative function assisting other forensic scientists, such as forensic pathologists or forensic odontologists, to make correct judgments on issues of legal significance.

The basic theory upon which the structure of forensic anthropology is premised is that each adult's skeletal configuration is distinct to that individual and to no one else.   From the skull to the feet there will be anomalies and defects in bones resulting from usage, aging or trauma which, to the trained eye of the forensic anthropologist, will permit the differentiation of one individual from another.   However, the forensic anthropologist rarely relies upon a single distinguishing characteristic in the identification of the skeletal features of a particular person.   Commonly his or her scientific task is to assemble notable attributes or anomalies which, when taken in the aggregate, will permit an identification to be made of unknown remains or will assist in determining the cause or manner of death.

The role of the forensic anthropologist is not simply to be the passive recipient of skeletal materials submitted to the laboratory for analysis.   The place of the forensic anthropologist is in the field as well giving a guiding hand and direction to the recovery of skeletal and artifactual material and to the assessment of taphonomic and other considerations in situ.

§ 17.02 The Origins of Forensic Anthropology

The history of the scientific discipline of forensic anthropology is recent and illustrious.   Most commentators[1] count the start of the currently well-established phase of forensic anthropology from the inauguration of the section on forensic anthropology within the American Academy of Forensic Sciences in 1972.   Since 1972 there have been fifty-three appellate court decisions referring to the testimony of anthropologists in Federal and state courts.[2]   Prior to 1972, there were only four occasions[3] when forensic anthropologists were similarly mentioned, the earliest of which was in 1949.

Prior to 1972, however, testimony about the analysis of human skeletal remains was given by persons with degrees in medicine or in anatomy rather than from persons within the subspecialty of physical

---

§ 17.02

1. Id. at 161. Snow, "Forensic Anthropology," 11 *Ann.Rev.Anthro.* 97 (1982).

2. See, *Scientific Sleuthing Review*, vol. 17, # 3 (1993) and vol. 18 # 1 (1994) for an analysis of these appellate court decisions.

3. People v. Dewey, 42 Ill.2d 148, 246 N.E.2d 232 (1969); Reed v. Commonwealth, 261 S.W.2d 9 (Ky.App.1953); Parker v. State, 228 Ind. 1, 88 N.E.2d 556 (1949); People v. Nischt, 23 Ill.2d 284, 178 N.E.2d 378 (1961).

anthropology. George A. Dorsey, Ph.D. (1868 to 1931) was the most notable exception.[4] After receiving his Ph.D. in 1894 in anthropology (Stewart says "actually archaeology") from Harvard, said to be the first awarded by that institution, Dorsey travelled to Chicago where he was named curator of the Field Museum in 1898.

While on the Field Museum staff in 1897 Dorsey testified as an expert witness for the prosecution in the trials of Adolph Luetgert for the murder of his wife, Louisa. The Illinois prosecutor sought to prove that Luetgert, a successful sausage manufacturer, had reduced his wife to a "foul-smelling sludge"[5] in one of his sausage vats through the medium of hot potash. According to Snow,[6] "unable to dissolve his marriage, he decided to dissolve his wife" but four bits of bone were retrieved from the bottom of the vat. The defense argued that these bone fragments were animal not human in origin and that therefore the proof of the death of Louisa, an essential ingredient of the corpus delicti, was wanting.

The prosecution relied upon Dorsey to show that the minute particles of bone were both human and female. Dorsey satisfied the prosecutor's every expectation and went further to identify the bone fragments as a metacarpal, the head of a rib, the phalanx of a toe and a sesamoid (foot) bone. Almost immediately after Luetgert's second trial and conviction in 1898 Dorsey was attacked by an expert for the defense at a regular meeting of the Medico–Legal Society of Chicago.[7] Some years later, Stewart would describe Dorsey as having "tripped up badly"[8] in his identifying testimony. But in 1978[9] Stewart apologized for his earlier criticism of Dorsey without, however, stating how Dorsey arrived at his species and gender determinations.

Much more generally well-known for its reliance upon the evidence of human skeletal remains than the Luetgert case was the murder of Boston physician, Dr. George Parkman, in 1849 by his debtor, Professor John Webster. Webster, at the time of the crime a Professor of Chemistry at the Harvard Medical School, was said to have incinerated his victim except for a "calcined skull and some heat-damaged dentures".[10]

The experts for the prosecution, including Harvard's Dr. Oliver Wendell Holmes, examined the remains and identified them as from "a white male, aged 50 to 60 years at death, whose ante-mortem stature was about 5 foot 10½ inches." [11] Parkman was known to be 60 years old and 5 foot 11 inches tall when he disappeared. In addition to the non-

---

4. Stewart, "George A. Dorsey's Role in the Luetgert Case: A Significant Episode in the History of Forensic Anthropology," 23 *J.For.Sci.* 786 (1978).

5. Snow supra note 1 at 100.

6. Id.

7. 16 *Chic.Med.Rptr* 172 (1899).

8. Stewart, "History of Physical Anthropology," in *Perspectives in Anthropology*, ed. Wallace et al, p. 70 (1977).

9. Supra note 1.

10. Snow, supra note 1 at 103. The murder conviction of Professor Webster was affirmed by the highest court of Massachusetts in Commonwealth v. Webster, 59 Mass. (5 Cush.) 295, 52 Am.Dec. 711 (1850).

11. Id.

specific identification from the bones, the dentures were positively matched to the missing Dr. Parkman. Among forensic anthropologists the medical testimony at the Webster trial has not been looked upon in later years with the same skepticism as that of Dorsey in the Luetgert trials.[12]

Some thirty years after the Webster trial, the Parkman Professorship in Anatomy at Harvard was passed from Oliver Wendell Holmes to Thomas Dwight. Although Dwight is reputed to have appeared "in several medico-legal cases," no details of these cases are known. It is known about Dwight that he had laid just claim to a thirty year career in which he produced many far-sighted research papers "on various aspects of skeletal identification."[13] For this, Stewart credits Dwight as "the father of American forensic anthropology."[14]

The modern era in forensic anthropology is said to have emerged with the publication of Krogman's "Guide to the Identification of Human Skeletal Material" in 1939.[15] That article, although written for non-scientist law enforcement personnel, was a general primer on the place of anthropology in the legal system.

§ 17.03 The Purposes of Forensic Anthropology

The primary role of the forensic anthropologist is to collect as much information as possible from skeletal features to assist in the identification of an individual. The data contributed by the anthropologist are compared to information on known persons in seeking to effect a positive identification. The anthropologist can also discover details concerning the cause and possibly the manner of death of persons from their skeletal remains. While it may be the statutory duty of the medical examiner to certify the cause and manner of death, the forensic anthropologist may be the only person who can determine an estimated time of death when skeletal remains are found with little or no soft tissue intact.

Apart from depicting the forensic anthropologist as one ministering to the dead only, a much more expansive approach to forensic anthropology has been advanced. According to Snow[1] forensic anthropologists should "come out of their bone closets" and conduct themselves "to their fullest as *human biologists*." In doing so forensic anthropology will be "no less a science of the living than of the dead."[2] More recently Lovis proposed[3] the amalgamation of a number of subdisciplines, like archaeology, in a holistic approach to what he terms "mortuary anthropology," and defined his new, more generic discipline as focusing not alone on "the death and disposition of individuals" but on "the circumstances of life" as well.

12. Berryman, "Anthropology as Applied to Forensic Science," 13 *Crime Lab. Digest* 38 (1986).

13. Supra note 8 at 72.

14. Id. Snow concurs. See supra note 1.

15. 8 F.B.I. Law Enf.Bull. 3–31 (1939).

§ 17.03

1. Supra note 1, section 17.02, at 129.

2. Id. at 128.

3. "Forensic Archaeology as Mortuary Anthropology," 34 *Soc.Sci.Med.* 113 (1992).

Recent court decisions reveal that this revisionist attitude to forensic anthropology has made significant inroads. Forensic anthropologists have been summoned to identify the fully-fleshed hands and feet of living persons who are suspected of involvement in criminal events.[4] Other extended uses are sure to follow.

II. IDENTIFICATION

§ 17.04 The Process of Identification: In General

In seeking to identify submitted specimens, the forensic anthropologist addresses a series of questions in a logical order, to wit:

1. Is the specimen bone?

2. Is the bone of human origin?

3. Is the bone of such an age to be of forensic significance?

If these questions are answered in the affirmative, then the process of identifying the skeletal remains of a particular person begins. In that effort the following are the major identifying traits to which the forensic anthropologist directs his or her scientific and analytical skills.

I. General or Class Characteristics:

   1. The determination of the age of the person at death

   2. The determination of the sex of the remains

   3. The determination of the race of the remains

   4. The estimation of the stature of the person during life

II. Individual Features:

   1. Ante-mortem bone trauma

   2. Bone variability

   3. Photographic superimposition

   4. Facial Reconstruction

1. IS IT BONE?

In the usual situation skeletal material is readily identified as such by the naked eye, even by the non-professional. However, in some cases, as where there is extreme fragmentation or extensive burning, other substances may resemble skeletal material. In such cases, the forensic anthropologist uses a dissecting microscope to examine the questioned material.

Skeletal material has distinctive observable characteristics which enable the expert to determine that it is indeed bone. These microstructures, particularly osteons (Haversian systems), the structural units of

---

4. See the discussion in "Identifying the Perpetrator" infra at sec. 17.11(5).

the compact bone's matrix [1] are identifiable even after extensive burning [2] or decomposition. For example, Dr. Douglas H. Ubelaker [3] reports receiving a sample of material retrieved from the debris of a house fire and believed to resemble burned skeletal remains. They were viewed through a microscope and found not to be bone but, in fact, the residue of a garden hose which had burned in a fire. [4]

2. IS IT HUMAN?

Once the material is identified as skeletal material, the species of origin must be determined. Where complete bones in good condition are recovered, the anthropologist can determine the species from its morphology if it is human. However, if the bone is fragmented due to trauma, fire, environmental effects, or deformity in life, its identification as human is more difficult. When the bone is not readily identifiable as human, two procedures can be used.

A. MACROSCOPIC METHOD

If the fragments are sufficiently large they can be compared to collections of different types of animal bones to see if they are consistent with any other animal. [5] In 1988, Dr. Douglas H. Ubelaker received two small calvaria [6] of unknown origin. The vaults of the calvaria were high and bulbous resembling human calvaria. However, the occipital area and several other features did not appear to be human. The calvaria were compared with collections of animal calvaria. No match was found, but a similarity was noted to the shape of a calf's calvarium. Immunological studies were performed on tissue that still adhered to the bones to determine the species.

These tests enabled it to be said that the source of the tissue was bovine. In addition, analysis of hair from the tissue associated it with bovine hair. Still, it could not be definitively stated that the calvaria originated from calves because the vaults possessed such a human-like character.

§ 17.04

1. The osteon includes the canals through bone that house nourishing blood vessels and lymphatic vessels, small spaces that contain bone cells, and concentric layers of matrix around the vertical canals. (Thibodeau, *Anatomy and Physiology* 144 (1987)) (see "Determination of Age, Microscopic Method" infra Sec. 17.05(1)(b) for a more complete description of microstructures).

2. Bradtmiller and Buikstra, "Effects of Burning on Human Bone Microstructure:

A Preliminary Study," 29 *J.For.Sci.* 537 (1984).

3. Curator, Department of Anthropology, National Museum of Natural History, Smithsonian Institution, Washington, D.C.

4. Personal communication, 1993.

5. Collections of animal skeletons are available for comparison at most museums of natural history.

6. The calvarium is the portion of the skull termed the "brain-case" or the dome.

The possibility of congenital hydroencephaly,[7] with associated enlargement of the cranial vault, was investigated. A documented sample of a hydrocephalic calf was located in a collection in Germany. The specimen was donated for comparison purposes.[8] The two calvaria in question closely resembled the sample from Germany. The morphological comparison, supported by the immunological and hair analyses, proved that the calvaria were those of hydrocephalic calves.[9]

B.   MICROSCOPIC METHOD

If the macroscopic method is not successful, or if the bone is too fragmented for this type of comparison, a thin section of the bone can be examined under a microscope. There is a type of bone termed plexiform bone which is not found in adult humans, and is found only infrequently in very young humans. It is considered characteristic of animal bone. Plexiform bone is "a primary bone tissue in which regular planes of longitudinal, radial, and circumferential primary canals form a symmetrical network of bone." [10] In plexiform bone, osteons are packed tightly with no bone between them, while in human bone osteons are scattered in an evenly spaced manner with bone between them.[11]

Unfortunately not all animal bone is completely distinct from human bone. Other primate, bear, and cat bone, for example, resemble human bone microscopically. Therefore, the positive determination of human origin microscopically is not always possible, but it may be possible to exclude a bone as not of human origin based on comparison of osteon configuration.[12]

In one reported investigation, several small bone fragments were received at a laboratory after having been retrieved from the vehicle of a murder suspect at a gas station. The suspect claimed these fragments were from a deer that he had poached and placed in his vehicle. A histological comparison was made with the known forelimb of a deer and a humerus from the remains of a middle-aged woman whom the suspect was thought to have murdered. The deer bone, as expected, contained a large amount of plexiform bone, and the osteons observed were packed together. The unknown fragments, on the other hand, consisted of no plexiform bone. The number of osteons per mm2 (2 square millimeters)

Brothwell, *Digging Up Bones* 36 (2d Ed. 1972).

7. Congenital hydroencephaly occurs when the ventricles of the brain are enlarged with excessive amounts of cerebrospinal fluid, the fluid that cushions the brain and spinal chord. When the condition occurs before the cranial sutures have fused, the head enlarges greatly. See, Ubelaker et al, "Differentiation of Hydrocephalic Calf and Human Calvariae," 36 *J.For. Sci.* 801 (1991).

8. The specimen was donated by of Professor G.W. Reick of the Institut for Tierzucht un Haustiergenetik in Geissen, Germany. Ibid, 810.

9. Ibid. at 811.

10. Owsley, "Case Involving Differentiation of Deer and Human Bone Fragments," 30 *J.For.Sci.* 572 (1985).

11. Ubelaker, *Human Skeletal Remains: Excavation, Analysis, Interpretation* 51 (1989).

12. Supra note 10 at 576.

in the unknown fragments was consistent with the count found in a known sample of bone taken from the victim. Other measurements of microscopic structures in the unknown fragments, including the thickness of the bone, and the diameter of canals within the osteon were consistent with the known fragments taken from the victim. Although, it could be determined that the bone fragments were not from a deer, it could not be said they were human, nor could it be confirmed that they came from the victim of the crime.[13] This evidence would not have been so compelling had the suspect claimed that he had poached a bear, a cat, or a chimpanzee since the microanatomy of the bones of those animals structurally resemble that of humans.[14]

3. IS THE BONE'S AGE OF FORENSIC VALUE?

To the forensic anthropologist the age of bones has two faces. One is to find the age at death of the person whose bones they are. Another is to determine the time during which the bones have gone undiscovered. It is the answer to the latter question which will decide whether or not the bones under examination have value for forensic purposes.

As a working thumb rule it is said that remains which are from a person dead for more than fifty years at the time of discovery are solely of archaeological interest and, therefore, excluded from the realm of forensic anthropology. The theory underlying the choice of a fifty-year cut-off date is that if the person whose remains are in question has been dead for that long a period then, if homicide was the manner of death, the culprit too would be either dead or of such advanced age as to make a prosecution a futile gesture.

Forensic scientists have quested long and hard for a method to date human skeletal remains. Carbon dating is valuable in this regard only when the remains are not only old but generally only of palaeontological interest. Morphological means, including those that rely on bone histology, have been investigated but it is well-recognized that the value of these techniques depends more on what effect environment has had on bone than the mere passage of time. Very ancient bones in a dry environment will appear misleadingly to be less ancient than bones from a grave where water has taken its persistent toll on the bones.

Knight[15] studied the changes in the bones of sixty-eight persons of documented age. His tests included an evaluation of nitrogen content, including the presence of proline and hydroxy-roline, amino-acid content, the strength of ultra-violet fluorescence of freshly cut bone, anti-human serum reaction and benzidine testing. Knight reported some success in his effort to correlate his findings to the known age of these bones.

---

13. Supra note 10 at 577.

14. Id.

15. Knight, "Methods of Dating Skeletal Remains," 9 *Med.Sci. & the Law* 247 (1969).

In a later effort Knight and two others [16] unsuccessfully sought to date remains using the scanning electron microscope. In another study [17] a statistical analysis using multivariate parameters, like total lipids, triglycerides etc., was said to have some limited promise. There remains a great need for further research into the subject of time dating human skeletal remains since all of the currently attempted dating processes have shortcomings and none permits accurate and precise estimates of the time since death of human skeletal remains.

4. ESTIMATING THE POST–MORTEM INTERVAL

Unlike the need to date human skeletal remains to demonstrate whether or not they are of forensic significance or only of value for archaeological purposes, the forensic anthropologist regularly encounters requests to determine the post-mortem interval or time since death of human skeletal remains known to have possible forensic import since their dating puts them at being fifty years or less old from death to the time of discovery. If the remains are within the fifty year window then further narrowing the post-mortem interval to a more precise time since death could aid in the identification of the remains through a search of the records of missing persons or otherwise.

The most important method of estimating the time since death is the observation of the extent of decomposition of the soft tissue and the estimation of the amount of time necessary for the body to decompose to that extent. Decomposition begins upon death and continues until the body is completely skeletonized. That period of time may be as short as two weeks, or may never be complete depending on many factors.[18] The forensic anthropologist will consider all of these factors in estimating the time since death.

"Variability of the decay rate of the human body is the rule." [19] These variables include environmental factors such as access by insects, temperature, humidity, and access by carnivores and other animals. Also influencing the rate of decomposition are the circumstances of the death, the location of the body after death, rainfall, the presence of clothing, and soil pH.[20]

16. "Knight, et al., The use of scanning electron microscopy in the dating of human skeletal remains," 27 *J.For.Sci.Soc.* 413 (1987).

17. Castellano et al, "Estimating the Date of Bone Remains: A Multivariate Study," 29 *J.For.Sci.* 527 (1984).

18. Ubelaker, *Human Skeletal Remains: Excavation, Analysis, Interpretation,* 130 (1989).

19. Mann, "Time Since Death and Decomposition of the Human Body: Variables and Observations in Case and Experimental Field Studies," 35 *J.For.Sci.* 103, 110 (1990).

20. Ibid at 104; Krogman & Iscan, *The Human Skeleton In Forensic Medicine* 30 (1986).

Access by insects

Flesh-eating insects play a large role in the decomposition of the human body.[21] The greater the access by insects, the faster decomposition occurs.[22] In addition, a method of estimation of time since death is based on the stage in the life cycle of the insects present upon discovery of the remains.

When the decomposing body is found, all insect larvae, pupae, pupal cases, and adult insects are observed. Each identified species in each stage of development present is counted. Samples of larvae and pupae are taken alive and allowed to grow into a more mature stage. This is done for two reasons, an insect species in its immature stages is difficult to identify, and the amount of time needed for the immature insects to become adults is important in the estimation of time since death. Some insects are also preserved to document for future reference the stages that were present at the time of discovery of the body.

The method for estimating time since death from insects is based on the fact that all insects have predictable intervals in each stage of their life cycles. By determining the species and the life cycle stage at the time of discovery, and the amount of time necessary for the immature stages to become adults, the approximate time of the laying of eggs may be extrapolated. Insects only lay eggs on dead tissue. Additional studies have estimated the time between death and the time that different insects are attracted to the body. For example, the blowfly and the common housefly are attracted to the body just after death while the fresh fly is only attracted after an odor has formed.[23] This information assists in approximating how long after death the eggs of a certain species may have been laid on the remains.

Temperature

Generally, colder temperatures decelerate the rate of decomposition, partly because insects are less active and larvae die when exposed to cold air preventing insects from contributing significantly to decomposition. During warmer temperatures, near or complete skeletonization may occur in two to four weeks, while cold temperatures may completely arrest decomposition. Fluctuating temperatures make the determination of time since death extremely difficult.[24]

Humidity

Higher humidity is correlated with higher levels of insect activity, and therefore, an increased rate of decomposition.[25] In the dry desert environment soft tissue has been found mummified but intact after thousands of years.[26]

---

21. Rodriguez and Bass, "Insect Activity and Its Relationship to Decay Rates of Human Cadavera in East Tennessee," 28 *J.For.Sci.* 423 (1983).

22. Supra note 19 at 106.

23. Krogman & Iscan, op. cit. supra note 20 at 23.

24. Supra note 19 at 105.

25. Id.

26. Supra note 19 at 130.

Access by carnivores and other animals

Carnivores and rodents will eat flesh and bone, and carry bones away accelerating the rate of decomposition.[27]

Circumstances of death

In remains that have sustained trauma with penetrating wounds decomposition occurs more rapidly than the intact body.   Insects and carnivores are attracted to the open wounds and their activities will accelerate decomposition.[28]

Location of body after death

Remains found lying directly on the ground decompose more rapidly than those found buried in the ground, wrapped in plastic, or on concrete.   Deeper burial slows decomposition more than a shallow burial.[29]   The more the body is shielded from environmental factors which will quicken decomposition, the slower the decomposition.

Rainfall

Rainfall slows decomposition to an extent because it reduces or stops the egg-laying activity of flies.   However, larval activity within the body is not affected.   Consequently, rainfall does not slow decomposition to a marked degree.[30]

Presence of clothing

The presence of clothing accelerates decomposition because it protects the body from sunlight which larvae avoid.[31]

Soil pH

Acidic soil accelerates decomposition while alkaline soil slows decomposition.[32]

§ 17.05 General or Class Characteristics of Human Bone

Once the specimen is identified as human bone and of relatively recent vintage, the anthropologist begins the process of seeking to identify the individual from whom the bone came.   The skeletal material is first classified according to general features such as age at death, sex, race, and stature of the individual.   The anthropologist distinguishes these features based on the analysis of traits that are similar within a subgroup, such as males, or individuals of the same race, but are distinct when comparing different subgroups.   Many of these traits, for example, the wide pelvis of the female, or the longer arms and legs of taller individuals, are outwardly visible traits that are reflected in the skeletal material.

27. Supra note 19 at 106.

28. Id. at 106.

29. Ibid.

30. Supra note 19 at 105.

31. Ibid. at 107.

32. Supra note 22 at 31.

Because every member of a subgroup does not exhibit exactly the same features, a range of variability within the subgroup is established either by careful examination of features or statistical analysis of the features of large numbers of skeletons of known subgroups. Several collections of documented skeletons have been studied to establish these ranges of variation. One of the most widely used collections is the T. Wingate Terry collection, housed at the Smithsonian Institution in Washington, D.C. It consists of skeletons of turn-of-the-century male and female skeletons of the Black and White races.

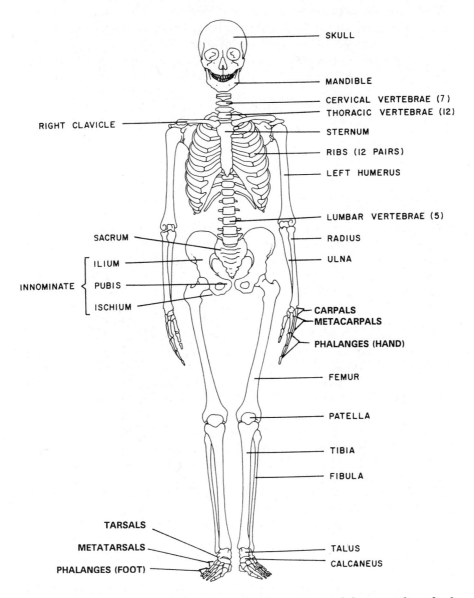

Fig. 1. The human skeleton, with the principal bones identified. Ubelaker, D.H. *Human Skeletal Remains: Excavation, Analysis, Interpretation.*

1.   ESTIMATION OF AGE AT DEATH

In the determination of the age at death of unidentified human remains, the medical examiner may require the assistance of a physical anthropologist. The methods used to determine age at death differ for sub-adults (children) and adults. The techniques for sub-adults are based on changes in bone related to growth, while the methods used for adults are based on changes due to degeneration of the bone. In the case of a sub-adult, it is particularly the distinctive features of the teeth and long bones (bones of the arms and legs) that are used to estimate age at death. As for adults, the most reliable methods used to estimate age at death include microscopic features of the long bones, macroscopic features of the pubic symphysis or the ribs, or a combination thereof.

A. SUB-ADULTS

The most accurate method of determining age at death in sub-adults depends upon an assessment of the degree of formation (in the gum) and eruption (emergence from the gum) of teeth until all permanent teeth have erupted.[1] Each tooth is usually formed, and erupts, and roots of deciduous (temporary) teeth are resorbed at predictable ages within a population, barring rare diseases or disorders. Charts have been devised that show the progression of formation, eruption, and resorption for many different populations. Some of these charts separate males and females as well because the rate differs between them. The range of error is smaller in charts that separate males from females.[2] To use this method, x-rays are taken of the maxilla and mandible. Each tooth is examined to determine presence and/or degree of formation of the crown and root. The degree of resorption of the roots of the deciduous teeth is also examined in older sub-adults who are losing these teeth. The results of these examinations are compared to the charts to determine an accurate age from the x-rays.

Using the same developmental theory, sub-adults who are still growing may be aged by x-raying the long bones. During the early stages of growth, each long bone consists of the diaphysis (the long shaft of the bone) and the epiphysis (the ends of the bone) which gradually fuse together at the metaphysis (the growth plate) as the individual grows.[3] Growth stops when union of the epiphysis and the diaphysis is complete in that bone. Females exhibit complete union at earlier ages than males. Because complete union of each bone is complete at its own individual and predictable age, the degree of union of different bones is compared to estimate age. For example, union of the bones of the ankle can be observed between age 14 and 18 in males, while union of the bones of the wrist is observed between the ages of 16 and 20.[4]

B. ADULTS: MICROSCOPIC METHODS

Determination of age at death in adults can also be achieved using long bones. In the case of adults, however, a microscopic examination of

§ 17.05

1. Ubelaker, op. cit supra note 18, section 17.04, at 63.

2. El-Nofely, "Dental Aging for Egyptian and Other Middle Eastern Children," 22 *Can.Soc.For.Sci.J.* 130 (1989).

3. Bass, *Human Osteology: A Laboratory and Field Manual* 16 (1987).

4. Supra note 18, section 17.04 at 75.

the long bones of the legs is necessary. The microscopic method of determining age was first devised by Kerley in 1965[5] and has been updated[6] several times.[7] The method involves taking a thin section of the femur, tibia, or fibula and microscopically examining it in four small circular areas (the diameter being approximately 1.62mm)[8] from the outer section of the bone. The number of primary osteons (formed when the surrounding bone was formed), secondary osteons (formed when the bone is remodelled) osteon fragments (results from remodelling), and the percentage of compact lamellar bone (evenly-spaced bands of bone that are parallel to each other and appear as long, parallel fibers under the microscope) present in the sample are calculated. The numbers are used in regression equations that determine the age at death of the individual. Kerley found that this method is accurate for fragmented bones, even if the entire cross-section is not present. The method is accurate for all ages. However, greater certainty is achieved for individuals under thirty years of age. Sex and race have not been found to affect the accuracy of the method.[9]

In 1969, Alquist and Damsten reported on a method utilizing square samples of the outer cortex of the bone in which only osteons and osteon fragments were counted. However, the Kerley method has been said to be more accurate than this new approach to bone aging.[10]

C. ADULTS: MACROSCOPIC METHODS

(i) Pubic Symphysis

Several macroscopic methods of determining age in adults are in use. The most widely used method involves the examination of the pubic symphysis. The pubic symphysis is located at the center of the pelvic girdle where the left and right pubic bones join. The left and right pubic bones have a small amount of cartilage between them that allows for a small amount of movement between the bones. (Figures 2 and 3) The area examined is that which is revealed when the pubic bones are separated and the cartilage is removed. The appearance of this area changes in a predictable manner as a person ages. A phase number and a corresponding age range is assigned to the individual based on the shape of the pubic symphysis and the relative roughness of different parts of the surface. The examination of the surface is complex, but generally, the rougher the surface, the younger the individual.

5. Kerley, "The Microscopic Determination of Age in Human Bone," 23 *Am.J.Phys.Anthro.* 149 (1965).

6. Singh & Gunberg, "Estimation of Age at Death in Human Males from Quantitative Histology of Bone Fragments." 33 *Am.J.Phys.Anthro.* 373 (1970).

7. Kerley and Ubelaker "Revisions in the Microscopic Method of Estimating Age at Death in Human Cortical Bone," 49 *Am.J.Phys.Anthro.* 545 (1978).

8. Stout & Gehlert, "Effects of Field Size When Using Kerley's Histological Method for Determination of Age at Death," 58 *Am.J.Phys.Anthro.* 123, 125 (1982).

9. Supra note 5 at 164.

10. Bouvier and Ubelaker, "A Comparison of Two Methods for the Microscopic Determination of Age at Death," 46 *Am.J.Phys.Anthro.* 391, 394 (1977).

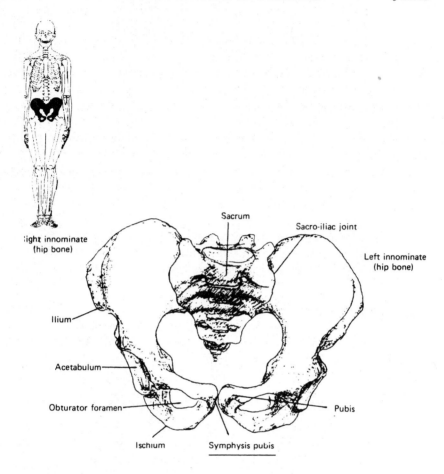

Fig. 2. The human pelvis, anterior view. Pubic symphysis identified. Bass, W.M., *Human Osteology: A Laboratory and Field Manual* 186, 1987.

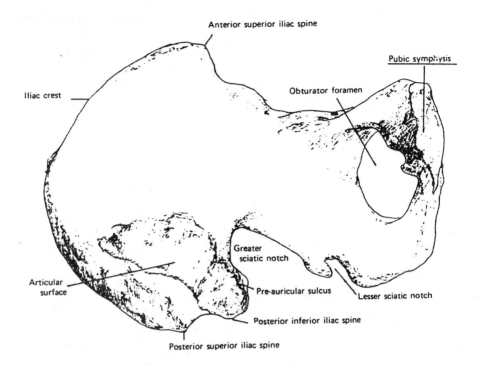

Fig. 3.   View of the face of the pubic symphysis, used in the estimation of age. Bass, W.M., *Human Osteology: A Laboratory and Field Manual* 190, 1987.

The changes in the pubic symphysis and their relationship to the aging of individuals were first documented by Todd in 1920 [11] using ten phases.   In 1955,[12] Brooks modified Todd's method, changing some of the morphological pattern for some ages and shifting the ages assigned to the different phases.   McKern and Stewart, proposed a method in 1957 which utilized only three components of the pubic symphysis in the determination of age.[13]   At a 1986 conference, Suchey and Brooks introduced a technique including six phases of changes and their corresponding ages.[14]   Changes in the pubic symphysis are sexually dimorphic, therefore many methods have separate guidelines for males and

11. Todd, "Age Changes in the Pubic Bone I The Male White Pubic." 3 *Am.J.Phys.Anthro.* 467–470 (1920).

12. Brooks, "Skeletal Age at Death: Reliability of Cranial and Pubic Age Indicators" 13 *Am.Jour.Phys.Anthro.* 567 (1955).

13. McKern and Stewart, "Skeletal Age Changes in Young American Males: Analyzed from the Standpoint of Age Identification." *Tech.Rep.* 1957; ep–45.

14. Brooks and Suchey, "Skeletal Age Determination Based on the Os pubis: A Comparison of the Acsadi–Nemeskeri and

females.[15] However, the Brooks and Suchey six-phase technique avoids the necessity for such discriminations. The phases are defined by characteristics found in both males and females in the same progression. However, the age range assigned to each of these phases is different for males and females. For example, a public symphysis from a male classified as phase III under this method would be aged within a range of 21 years to 46 years, while a female would be aged from 21 years to 53 years.[16]

Changes attributable to race have been shown to result in greater age-related changes in the pubic symphysis in Blacks and Mexicans in younger age ranges. Thus, under the Brooks and Suchey progression formula, if the race of the individual is known, the pubic symphysis is assigned a phase (using the six phases of the Suchey–Brooks method), and compared to a statistical table to determine the age range for the specific race. For example, a pubic symphysis that is in phase V is aged as 52.9 ± 13.7 years for a white male, but will be aged as 43.2 ± 10.9 years if the individual is a Black male, and younger still at 40.4 ± 8.5 years if the individual is a Mexican male.[17] A recent study suggests that the Suchey–Brooks approach is much more reliable than other methods and that their chart of racial differences provides defensible results.[18]

(ii) Sternal Ends of Ribs

The sternal ends of the ribs, the ends of the ribs that articulate with the costal cartilage in the front of the body, also change in a predictable manner as a person ages. Iscan, Loth, and Wright first introduced a method of determining age from the ends of the ribs in 1984 and have continually updated their system.[19] The theory underlying this approach is the same as the theory supporting the estimate of age from the changes in the pubic symphysis. The morphological features of the rib that are examined are the amount of billowing or depth and shape of pitting of the articular surface, the appearance of the rim around the articular surface, the quality of the bone, and the presence or absence of bony projections.

The sternal rib end is assigned to one of nine phases based on its morphology. Each phase is representative of a range of ages. The analysis of the morphological features is complex, but generally, the

Suchey–Brooks Methods." 5 *Human Evolution* 227 (1990).

15. Suchey, "Problems in the Aging of Females Using the Os pubis." 51 *Am.J.Phys.Anthro.* 467 (1979).

16. Supra note 14 at 233.

17. Katz and Suchey, "Race Differences in Pubic Symphyseal Aging Patterns in the Male," 80 *Am.J.Phys.Anthro.* 169 (1989).

18. Klepinger, "Evaluation of Cast Methods for Estimating Age from the Os Pubis," 37 *J.For.Sci.* 763 (1992).

19. Iscan, Loth, and Wright, "Age Estimation from the Rib by Phase Analysis: White Males," 29 *J.For.Sci.* 1094 (1984); Iscan, Loth, and Wright, "Age Estimation from the Rib by Phase Analysis: White Females," 30 *J.For.Sci.* 853 (1985); Iscan and Loth, "Determination of Age from Sternal Rib in White Males: A Test of the Phase Method," 31 *J.For.Sci.* 122 (1986); Iscan and Loth, "Determination of Age from the Sternal Rib in White Females: A Test of the Phase Method," 31 *J.For.Sci.* 990 (1986).

deeper the pitting, the more irregular the rim, and the poorer the quality of the bone, the older the individual is. The morphological features characteristic of each phase and the consequent age range assigned to each phase are different for males and females. For example, Phase 3 for the male rib is described as:

> The deepening pit has taken on a narrow to moderately U-shape. Walls are still fairly thick with rounded edges. Some scalloping may still be present but the rim is becoming more irregular. The bone is still quite firm and solid.[20]

The age range assigned to Phase 3 for males is 24.1 years to 27.7 years. Phase 3 for the female rib is described as:

> There is only slight if any increase in pit depth, but the V-shape is wider, sometimes approaching a narrow U as the walls become a bit thinner. The still rounded edges now show a pronounced, regular scalloping pattern. At this stage, the anterior or posterior walls of both may start to exhibit a central, semicircular arc of bone. The rib is firm and solid.[21]

The age range assigned to Phase 3 in females is 20.5 years to 24.7 years.

(iii) Other Macroscopic Methods

Other methods of determining age at death, such as degree of fusion of the endocranial sutures or of the maxillary sutures of the hard palate [22] may be used in conjunction with the foregoing methods. Nonetheless, these additional methods are not considered reliable enough to be used alone. In addition, if the skull is the only skeletal element submitted for examination, an age estimate stated in decades based on endocranial suture closure and in the general categories of child, adolescent, or young, middle-aged or old adult in the case of maxillary suture closure may be assigned.[23]

In order to estimate age or any other characteristic from skeletal remains, the skeletal features examined must be in good condition. Environmental conditions can change the appearance of the pertinent macroscopic and even microscopic characteristics of bone. This is especially true when bones are exposed to the environment for long periods of time. In order to obtain the best assurance of an accurate estimate of the age at death, the maximum number of methods should be used. The age ranges estimated by different methods should be integrated (not averaged) appropriately so that the narrowest, most accurate age range

20. Id. at 1096.

21. Supra note 19 at 855.

22. Mann, et al. "Maxillary Suture Obliteration: Aging the Human Skeleton Based on Intact or Fragmentary Maxilla," 32 *J.For.Sci.* 148 (1987); Gruspier and Mullen, "Maxillary Suture Obliteration: A Test of the Mann Method," 36 *J.For.Sci.* 512 (1991); Mann, et al. "Maxillary Suture Obliteration: A Visual Method for Estimating Skeletal Age," 36 *J.For.Sci.* 781 (1991).

23. Supra note 22, Mann et al at 790. (1991).

can be achieved. No one method should be used as the single criterion for judging the skeletal age in forensic cases."[24]

2. DETERMINATION OF SEX

Determination of sex in adults can be made with one hundred percent accuracy if the entire skeleton is present. The determination is based on visual examination of sexually dimorphic features by the experienced eye of the forensic anthropologist or mathematical assessment of sexually dimorphic bones of the skeleton. Determination of sex in sub-adults, however, is more difficult because secondary sexual characteristics have not become fixed in such persons.

A. PELVIC FEATURES, GROSS MORPHOLOGICAL ASSESSMENT (ADULT)

The most sexually dimorphic feature of the skeleton and, therefore, the bone structure from which the most accurate determination of sex can be made is the pelvis. The adult female pelvis is morphologically very different from the adult male pelvis because the adult female pelvis is adapted to permit the passage of an infant. The points of particular reference on the adult pelvis are the sciatic notch, the subpubic angle, the auricular area, the pre-auricular sulcus, the ventral arc, the pubis, and the subpubic concavity.[25] (Figure 4, and Table 1).

---

24. Saunders, "A Test of Several Methods of Skeletal Age Estimation Using A Documented Archaeological Sample," 25 *Can.Soc.Forens.Sci.J.* 97, 116 (1992).

25. Suri and Tandon. "Determination of Sex from the Pubic Bone," 27 *Med.Sci. Law* 294 (1987).

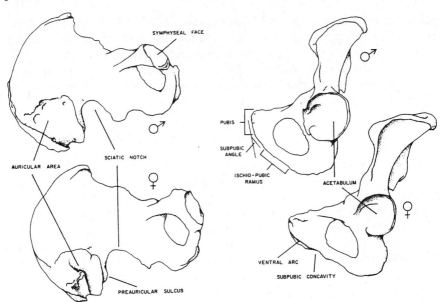

Fig. 4. The human pelvis with features used to determine sex identified. Ubelaker, D.H., *Human Skeletal Remains: Excavation, Analysis, Interpretation* 53, 1989.

Table 1*   Sex Determination

Morphological Feature	Male	Female
sciatic notch	narrow	wide
subpubic angle	more acute	more obtuse
auricular area	smooth	rough
pre-auricular sulcus	absent	present
ventral arc	absent	present
pubis	shorter	longer
subpubic concavity	absent/slight	large

*Derived from Ubelaker, D.H., *Human Skeletal Remains: Excavation, Analysis, Interpretation* 53–54, 1989.

The assignment of sex based on morphological features of the pelvic bones is very reliable for adults even when some of the features to be studied are not found or are too fragmented for analysis. Examination of only three gross macroscopic features of the pelvis, i.e. the subpubic concavity, the ventral arc, and the ischiopubic ridge, has been found sufficient to determine sex with an accuracy of 95%.[26] Several researchers have tested the accuracy of the so-called Phenice characters resulting in varying degrees of accuracy from approximately 66% to the 95% accuracy claimed by Phenice [27]. One study which used only one characteristic of the pelvis, the ventral arc, as a determinant of sex reported achieving an accuracy of 96%.[28]

B. OTHER FEATURES, GROSS MORPHOLOGICAL ASSESSMENT

In the absence of the pelvis, gross morphological features of other skeletal material can be examined. However, such examinations are considered less reliable indicators. Facial features or long bones are among those to be considered. Generally, the facial features, such as the supraorbital ridge and the mandible, and long bones are more prominent in males than in females. In addition, a bony projection on the skull just below the opening for the ear canal, called the mastoid process, is more prominent in males than in females. These comparisons are generalizations because human populations show great variations. Gracile males may appear to be female, while robust females may appear to be male, even to the eye of an experienced anthropologist.

Gross morphological examination is a relatively subjective method of determining the sex of an individual based on skeletal remains. The accuracy of the determination relies largely on the level of experience of the anthropologist.

C. MATHEMATICAL ASSESSMENT

Several mathematical means for determining the sex of skeletal remains have been devised. Such methods provide more objectivity because they rely less on the experience of the anthropologist and more on statistical analysis. These methods consist of measuring specific morphological features, such as the head of the femur, the length of the ischium and the pubis, or certain features of the cranium. A number is then calculated using an equation generated by statistical analysis of equivalent measurements of large numbers of skeletons of known sex. The number calculated will then be associated with a range of numbers calculated from the skeletons of known sex, resulting in a male or female determination.

D. FACIAL BONES

In 1963, Giles and Elliot published their discriminant function method of determining sex from measurements of certain morphological

26. Phenice. "Newly Developed Method of Sexing the Os pubis," 30 *Am.J.Phys.Anthro.* 297, 301 (1969).

27. MacLaughlin, and Bruce, "The Accuracy of Sex Identification in European Skeletal Remains Using the Phenice Characters," 35 *J.For.Sci.* 1384, 1389 (1990).

28. Sutherland, and Suchey, "Use of the Ventral Arc in Pubic Sex Determination," 36 *J.For.Sci.* 501, 510 (1991).

features of the cranial bones.[29]　Statistical analysis of five measurements of crania of three general races, "White," "Black," and "American Indian" was performed.　The five measurements are the cranial length, the basion-nasion length, the bizygomatic breadth, the basion-prosthion length, and the prosthion-nasion height.　The equation generated was:

Discriminant Function = 1.16x(cranial length) + 1.66x(basion-nasion length) + 3.98x(bizygomatic breadth) − 1.00x(basion-prosthion length) + 1.54x(prosthion-nasion height) [30]

The deciding line for the equation is 891.12, that is, if the DF of a cranium is greater than 891.12, it is considered male.　If the DF is less that 891.12, it is considered female.　Giles and Elliot found that this equation was 82.9% correct when used for 1022 crania of white, black, and American Indian background.　A later test of this discriminant function equation found the equation to be 88% accurate in a smaller sample of 52 crania of the different races.[31]

E.　POST-CRANIAL BONES

The type of statistical analysis based on measurements of skeletons of known sex has been used for other bones as well.　Equations have been generated for assigning the sex of an individual by measuring features of the pelvis,[32] long bones,[33] and metacarpals and the first proximal phalanx [34] with varying degrees of success.

F.　THE IMPORTANCE OF QUANTUM OF SKELETAL REMAINS

If the entire skeleton is recovered, the determination of sex using a combination of gross morphological examination and mathematical analysis is considered one hundred percent accurate.　Unfortunately, the recovery of a full skeleton is extremely rare in most forensic situations. If the skull and pelvis are complete, a combination of methods achieves a 98% accuracy, the pelvis alone or the pelvis and long bones a 95% accuracy and the skull alone 90% accuracy.　The skull and long bones result in a 90–95% accuracy, and the long bones alone an 80–90%

29.　Giles and Elliot, "Sex Determination by Discriminant Function Analysis of Crania" 21 *Am.J.Phys.Anthro.* 53 (1963).

30.　Snow, et al., "Sex and Race Determination of Crania by Calipers and Computer: A Test of the Giles and Elliot Discriminant Functions in 52 Forensic Science Cases," 24 *J.For.Sci.* 448, 451 (1979).

31.　Ibid at 449.

32.　Schulter–Ellis, et al., "Determination of Sex with a Discriminant Analysis of New Pelvic Bone Measurements. Pt. I," 28 *J.For.Sci.* 169 (1983); Schulter–Ellis, et al., "Determination of Sex with a Discriminant Analysis of New Pelvic Bone Measurements. Pt. II," 30 *J.For.Sci.* 178 (1985);

MacLaughlin, and Bruce, "The Sciatic Notch/Acetabular Index as a Discriminator of Sex in European Skeletal Remains," 31 *J.For.Sci.* 1380 (1986); Fernandez Camacho, "Osteometry of the Human Iliac Crest: Patterns of Normality and Its Utility in Sexing Human Remains," 38 *J.For.Sci.* 779 (1993).

33.　Tagaya, A., "Development of a Generalized Discriminant Function for Cross–Population Determination of Sex from Long Bones of the Arm and Leg," 22 *Can.Soc. For.Sci.J.* 159 (1989).

34.　Scheuer and Elkington, "Sex Determination from Metacarpals and the First Proximal Phalanx," 38 *J.For.Sci.* 769 (1993).

accuracy.[35]

G. SUB-ADULTS

Estimation of sex is much more difficult in sub-adults, especially before puberty.[36] The male and female pelvis look very much alike until distinctive sexual characteristics, including the adaptive changes in the female pelvis and increased robustness in the male, develop during adolescence.

A mathematical method of assessing the pelvis that consisted of the analysis of measurements of the pelvis has been explored with little success.[37] A visual assessment of the auricular surface, categorizing those with a raised or rough surface as female and those with nonraised or smooth surface as male, is accurate in sub-adult ages over 9 years of age. In those under 9 years of age, however, this method has been found unreliable.[38]

A more accurate method of determining the sex of sub-adult skeletal remains is based on the established fact that the male post-cranial skeleton comes to full maturation at a later age than the female post-cranial skeleton, while the formation and eruption of teeth occurs at about the same rate in males and females. The age of the individual is first estimated based on the degree of formation and eruption of the teeth. The results are then compared to the age estimated by examination of the maturation of the post-cranial skeleton based on the standard for males. If the two age estimates agree, the individual is probably a male, if they are very different, the individual is probably a female.[39]

3. DETERMINATION OF RACE

Like the determination of sex, the determination of race from skeletal material is based on either gross morphological examination or mathematical analysis of different measurements of morphological features. The most reliable measurements are based on morphological features of the skull. Other bones may be used, although with less certainty, if the skull is not recovered. Race is categorized broadly as caucasoid, negroid, or mongoloid. Generally, the caucasoid category includes individuals of European ancestry, negroid includes individuals of African ancestry, and mongoloid includes individuals of Asian, American Indian, and Eskimo ancestry. Some methods have even been shown

35. Krogman & Iscan, op cit. supra note 20, section 17.04, at 259.

36. Kerley, "Forensic Anthropology and Crimes Involving Children," 21 *J.For.Sci.* 333 (1976).

37. Ubelaker, op. cit. supra note 18, section 17.04, at 52.

38. Mittler, and Sheridan, "Sex Determination in Subadults Using Auricular Surface Morphology: A Forensic Science Perspective," 37 *J.For.Sci.* 1068, 1073 (1992).

39. Hunt, and Gleiser, "The Estimation of Age and Sex of Preadolescent Children from Bone and Teeth," 13 *Am.J.Phys.Anthro.* 479 (1955).

to distinguish different sub-groups of the American Indian race.[40] Each population exhibits a wide range of variability into which the individuals of the population fall. Racial admixture results in morphological features that resemble the different races of ancestry, complicating, but not making unresolvable, the question of race.

A. Gross Morphology of Skull

The morphological features examined in the bones of the skull are summarized in the attached chart and drawings. (Table 2, Figs. 5, 6, 7)

Table 2*   Race Determination

Morphological Feature	Caucasoid	Negroid	Mongoloid
zygomatic bones	retreating (no projection)	little projection	marked projection
eye orbits	triangular	rectangular	circular
nasal aperture shape lower margin	narrow nasal sill	wide nasal guttering	moderate slightly pointed
palate	narrow	broad	moderate
mouth region	flat	prognathous	flat

*Derived from Ubelaker, D.H., *Human Skeletal Remains: Excavation, Analysis, Interpretation* 119, 1989.

Bass, W.M., *Human Osteology: A Laboratory and Field Manual* 83–88, 1987.

40. Ossenburg, "Within and Between Race Distances in Population Studies Based on Discrete Traits of the Human Skull," 45 *Am.J.Phys.Anthro.* 701, 707 (1976).

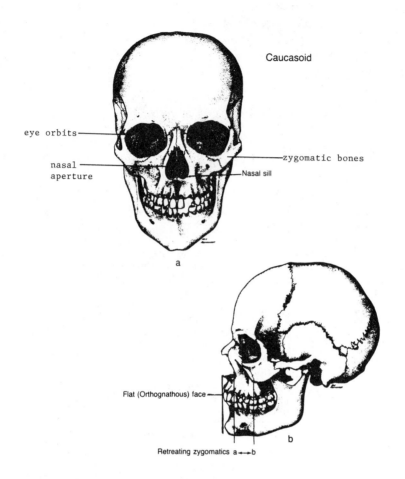

Fig. 5. The Caucasoid cranium. Bass, W.M., *Human Osteology: A Laboratory and Field Manual* 84, 1987.

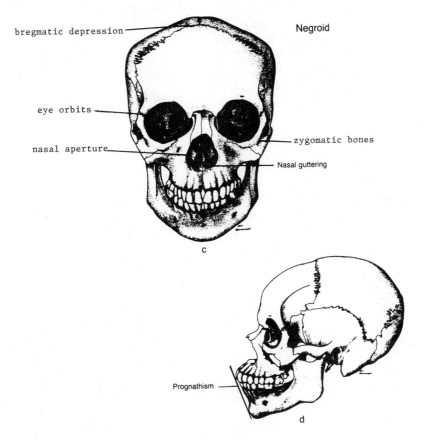

Fig. 6. The Negroid cranium. Bass, W.M., *Human Osteology: A Laboratory and Field Manual* 85, 1987.

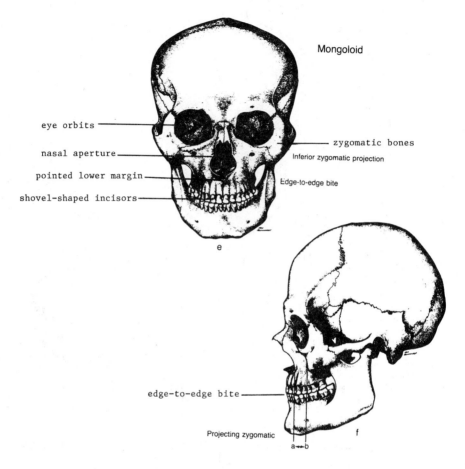

Fig. 7. The Mongoloid cranium. Bass, W.M., *Human Osteology: A Laboratory and Field Manual* 86, 1987.

B. GROSS EXAMINATION OF OTHER SKELETAL ELEMENTS

The only other bone that shows racial variation upon visual examination is the femur. The femur that is curved is more likely to be Indian, the straight femur tends to be Black, and the femur that is of medium curvature is considered White. These descriptions are only generalities since there is considerable overlapping between races. Femoral curvature combined with other features of the femur will permit a fairly accurate determination of race.[41] This method has been shown reliable for American Negroes, North American Indians and Whites, but unreliable for South American Indians from Peru and Ecuador.[42]

41. Stewart, "Anterior Femoral Curvature: Its Utility for Race Identification," 34 *Human Biology* 49, 53 (1962).

42. Gilbert, "Anterior Femoral Curvature: Its Probable Basis and Utility as a Criterion of Racial Assessment," 45 *Am.J.Phys.Anthro.* 601, 604 (1976).

C. MATHEMATICAL ASSESSMENT OF RACE: DISCRIMINANT FUNCTIONS

The most reliable method of mathematically assessing race from skeletal remains is the measurement of features of the skull. The method was introduced, along with a similar method for the sex typing of bones, in 1962.[43] The equations have been found to be 83% accurate in distinguishing White and Black skulls. However, they were not nearly so conclusive in distinguishing American Indian skulls.[44]

This discrepancy illustrates one of the major problems with discriminant functions. They are highly regarded when used for the population from which they were derived, but must be employed ever so cautiously when applied to other populations. The Snow study analyzed American Indian skeletons from a prehistoric site to establish the discriminant function equations, while the test applied the equations to American Indian skeletons from modern forensic cases. In another study, discriminant function analysis of Black American skeletons using equations generated from a collection of West African Black skeletons was found inaccurate. Differences may be due to changes in the culture or because of racial admixture in the modern United States.[45]

The Giles–Elliot method uses measurements that can only be taken from complete skulls. Unfortunately, forensic cases rarely provide the luxury of complete skulls. Therefore, a compromise method can be used that utilizes between three and six measurements of just the base of the skull.[46] Measurements of the bones of the midface,[47] and x-rays of the tympanic plate [48] have also given promise in distinguishing races.

Often, even small portions of cranial bones needed to determine race are not recovered. In such cases, discriminant functions developed for the pelvis can be used. However, these equations only distinguish between Black and White races. Nine measurements of the pelvis have achieved an 83% accuracy in males and an 88% accuracy in females, regardless of age.[49] If the femur is recovered, discriminant function equations are available that enable the inclusion of pelvic with femur measurements to determine race.[50]

43. Giles and Elliot, "Race Identification from Cranial Measurements," 7 *J.For. Sci.* 147 (1962).

44. Snow et al., op. cit supra note 30 at 452.

45. Id. at 459.

46. Holland, "Race Determination of Fragmentary Crania by Analysis of the Cranial Base," 31 *J.For.Sci.* 722 (1986).

47. Gill, et al, "Racial Identification from the Midfacial Skeleton with Special Reference to American Indians and Whites," 33 *J.For.Sci.* 92 (1988).

48. Finnegan, and Schulter–Ellis, "The Tympanic Plate in Forensic Discrimination Between American Blacks and Whites," 23 *J.For.Sci.* 771 (1978).

49. Iscan, "Assessment of Race from the Pelvis," 62 *Am.J.Phys.Anthro.* 205, 207 (1983); Iscan, and Cotton, "The Effect of Age on the Determination of Race from the Pelvis," 14 *J.Hum.Evol.* 275, 281 (1985).

50. DiBennardo, and Taylor, "Multiple Discriminant Function Analysis of Sex and Race in the Postcranial Skeleton," 61 *Am.J.Phys.Anthro.* 305 (1983).

4. DETERMINATION OF STATURE

Attempts to determine the stature of individuals from their skeletal remains have been long-standing. Dwight in 1894, discussed efforts to estimate stature that had been advanced in the scientific literature. He designated those proposals that resembled the full skeleton from head-to-toe as anatomical and those that were based on computations from the known length of individual bones as mathematical. His own method was based on the estimation of height "from the length of the spine measured in a straight line from the top of the atlas to the promontory of the sacrum."[51]

Dwight took due note of the fact that "there are persons with short legs and persons with long legs, and therefore no single rule of proportion can be true for both."[52] His ideas, although not controlling today, were the forerunners of current methods that have received considerable scientific accreditation. The determination of stature is more appropriately termed an "estimation" because stature is statistically extrapolated from defleshed skeletal remains, whereas soft tissue adds to an individual's stature in life.

A. LONG BONE MEASUREMENT: REGRESSION EQUATIONS

The most practical and reliable method of stature estimation utilizes mathematical regression from the length of long bones, or even well-defined, easily identified fragments of long bones. The long bones consist of the bones of the arms (the humerus, radius, and ulna) and legs (the femur, tibia, and fibula). The lengths of all of these bones show a linear relationship to the overall stature of the individual. The relationship is more reliable for some bones than others, and the more long bones that are able to be measured, the more accurate the estimation of stature during life will be.

Studies performed by Trotter and Gleser in 1952 and 1958[53], are the basis of methods in use today. These studies showed that the numerical relationship between length of specific long bones differs in different populations. Trotter and Gleser measured long bone lengths from the remains of servicemen from World War II and the Korean conflict and from another collection. The measurements of the long bones of the individual were then compared to his or her known stature during life obtained either from extant military-service records or measurements taken soon after death, in the case of the individuals in the other collection. Equations used to estimate stature during life from each different long bone and combinations of long bones were formulated for black males, white males, black females, and white females. The fact

51. Dwight, "Methods of Estimating the Height from Parts of the Skeleton," 46 *Medical Record,* 291, 294 (1894).

52. Id.

53. Trotter and Gleser, "Estimation of Stature from Long Bones of American Whites and Negroes," 10 *Am.J.Phys.Anthro.* 463 (1952); Trotter and Gleser, "A Reevaluation of Estimation of Stature Based on Measurements of Stature Taken During Life and of Long Bones After Death," 16 *Am.J.Phys.Anthro.* 79 (1958).

that the method is based on these different subgroups indicates that the evaluation of sex and race must precede the estimation of stature. An example of Trotter and Gleser's regression equations follows:

Negro males

3.26 × length of humerus	+ 62.10	± 4.43
3.42 × length of radius	+ 81.56	± 4.30
3.26 × length of ulna	+ 79.29	± 4.42
2.11 × max. length of femur	+ 70.35	± 3.94
2.19 × max. length of tibia	+ 86.02	± 3.78
2.19 × length of fibula	+ 85.65	± 4.08

and multiple regression equations:

1.15 × (max. length of femur + max. length of tibia)	+ 71.04	± 3.53
0.66 × max. length of femur + 1.62 × max. length of tibia	+ 76.13	± 3.49
0.90 × length of humerus + 1.78 × max. length of tibia	+ 71.29	± 3.49

0.89 × length of humerus
    − 1.01 × length of radius
    + 0.38 × max. length of tibia
	+ 74.56	± 3.38 [54]

(All measurements and the resultant statures are in centimeters.)

If no long bones are recovered, the second metacarpal bone can be used in the same manner as long bones. Second metacarpal lengths, determined radiographically, have been reported as reliable in stature approximations.[55] Of course, the equations for metacarpals include different numbers, but are of the same form as the equations used to estimate stature from long bones.

B. Long Bone Fragment Measurement: Regression Equations

Frequently not even intact long bones are recovered. The Steele and McKern method for estimating stature from long bone fragments includes data for several different fragments on each long bone. Using these measurements, the length of the long bone can be extrapolated, and the stature estimated using the length of the long bone.[56] Bass reported that it is "difficult to locate the necessary anatomical landmarks on fragmentary bones" using the Steele and McKern method.[57] Therefore, later studies were performed to identify easily located and

54. First Trotter & Gleser study, supra note 53 at 495.

55. Himes, et al., "Estimation of Stature in Children from Radiographically Determined Metacarpal Length," 22 *J.For.Sci.* 452 (1977); Musgrave and Harneja, "The Estimation of Adult Stature from Metacarpal Bone Length," 48 *Am.J.Phys.Anthro.* 113 (1978).

56. Steele and McKern, "A Method for Assessment of Maximum Long Bone Length and Living Stature from Fragmentary Long Bones," 31 *Am.J.Phys.Anthro.* 215 (1969).

57. Bass, "Development in the Identification of Human Skeletal Material (1968–1978)," 51 *Am.J.Phys.Anthro.* 555, 559 (1979).

measured landmarks on different long bones. These measurements are used to directly estimate height. Simmons established three easily located [58] measurements on the femur, i.e. the vertical diameter of the femur head, the proximal femur breadth, and the posterior height of the fibular condyle, that are proportional to living stature. Holland developed five measurements of the lateral and medial condyles of the tibia, their articular surfaces, and their relationship to each other that are proportional to height as well.[59] These studies include both population specific equations of proportionality and general equations which are not population specific. The non-population-specific equations are not as accurate as the population specific equations but still a range of statures can be reasonably calculated. These methods are helpful when fragments of the tibia or femur are the only long bones present.[60]

§ 17.06 Individualization of Human Bone

The evaluation of age, sex, race, and stature from skeletal remains relies on characteristics that individuals of the same subgroup have in common. Positive identification of an individual based only on a general description, for example, a 42–year–old black female approximately 5 feet 4 inches in height, is impossible. However, these characteristics may suffice for a tentative identification based on a comparison with missing persons data. Once this tentative identification is made, the task of positive identification based on characteristics unique to the individual (rather than the subgroup) can begin.

The process of individualizing skeletal material begins with gathering as much information as possible concerning the tentatively identified individual in life, primarily medical records. Positive identification can be based on the comparison of unique features that appear in antemortem radiographs with radiographs of the skeletal material. In addition, if the facial elements of the skull are found intact, a comparison to a photograph, or a reconstruction of the soft tissue of the face can also lead to a more positive identification.

1. ANTEMORTEM BONE TRAUMA

While the history for example, of a fractured long bone of the leg is helpful as corroborative evidence for an identification, antemortem radiographs of the fracture can lead to positive identification if the location and type of fracture, and the pattern of healing match a radiograph taken of the same area of the skeletal material. As with fingerprints, each fracture and healing pattern is unique.

Bones that are traumatized during life will show some degree of healing. The degree of healing is proportional to the amount of time

---

58. Simmons, "Stature Estimation from Fragmentary Femora: A Revision of the Steele Method," 35 *J.For.Sci.* 628, 633, 635 (1990).

59. Holland, "Estimation of Adult Stature from Fragmentary Tibias," 37 *J.For. Sci.* 1223 (1992).

60. See also, Snow & Williams, "Variations in Premortem Statural Measurements Compared to Statural Estimates of Skeletal Remains," 16 *J.For.Sci.* 455 (1971).

between the injury and the death. Even after years of healing, some noticeable remodelling or deformity of the bone is present. Based on this evidence, the anthropologist can determine with certainty that an antemortem bone injury occurred. The greater the number of skeletal injuries documented by a personal history or by radiographs, the more positive the identification will be.[1]

2. VARIABILITY OF CERTAIN BONES

The human skeleton shows great variation among individuals especially on radiographic examination. Certain areas of the skeleton, such as the frontal sinuses, the mastoid sinus and arterial patterns on the skull,[2] the scapula,[3] and the abdomen and pelvis,[4] have been found sufficiently variable to allow for a positive identification of an individual from them. In fact, a classification system for frontal sinuses, much like the system of classifying fingerprints, has been devised based on an evaluation of Japanese skulls.[5]

When using areas of variability to identify skeletal remains, the radiograph of the skeletal material is not only compared to the antemortem radiographs of the tentatively identified individual, but to radiographs of many skeletons of other individuals of the same sex and race. A positive identification is only achieved if the antemortem radiograph matches the radiograph of the skeletal material, but does not match any of the radiographs of other skeletons. This procedure is used as a control to ensure that the area of the skeletal material in each individual is unique.

3. PHOTOGRAPHIC SUPERIMPOSITION

If the entire skull, or sizeable portions of it, is found, a photographic superimposition can be performed. The procedure involves a comparison of a photograph of the individual the skull is purported to belong to with a photograph of the skull in question. Points of comparison between soft tissue landmarks and their related skeletal features are examined. If all points are congruent, the skull is considered to belong to the individual in the photograph. However, if any inconsistencies are found, the skull in question will be excluded as not the same as that in a photograph.

§ 17.06

1. For a report of a positive identification in Sri Lanka, see, Salgado et al., "Identification from Skeletal Remains," 36 *For. Sci.Int'l* 73, 80 (1988).

2. Rhine and Sperry, "Radiographic Identification by Mastoid Sinus and Arterial Pattern," 36 *J.For.Sci.* 272 (1991).

3. Ubelaker, "Positive Identification of American Indian Skeletal Remains from Radiographic Comparison," 35 *J.For.Sci.* 466 (1990).

4. Owsley and Mann, "Positive Personal Identity of Skeletonized Remains Using Abdominal and Pelvic Radiographs," 37 *J.For. Sci.* 332 (1992).

5. Yoshino, M. et al., "Classification System of Frontal Sinus Patterns by Radiography. It's Application to Identification of Unknown Skeletal Remains," 34 *For.Sci. Int'l.* 289 (1987); Yoshino, M. et al., "Classification System of Frontal Sinus Pattern," 22 *Can.Soc.For.Sci.J.* 135 (1989).

The early methods of identifying an individual based on a photograph involved simply tracing a photograph of the skull over a photograph of the individual.[6] Today technological advances have aided in producing more reliable, objective results. First, the photograph is enlarged to life size using the original negative if it is available.[7] Life size is usually determined by measuring an object in the same focal plane as the individual in the picture that is still able to be measured and enlarging the picture until that object is life size. Objects such as furniture,[8] or clothing[9] have been used, or physical characteristics such as the interpupil breadth of other people's eyes in the photograph if both individuals are facing the camera,[10] or the size of the dentition of the individual that can be seen in the photograph and measured in the skull.[11]

Once the photograph of the known individual is enlarged, the skull is mounted in the exact same position as the head is shown in the photograph and a photograph is taken of the skull. Several types of mounting media have been designed to hold a skull in a myriad of different positions. A variety of techniques of superimposing the photograph of the skull and the antemortem photograph have been advanced. Whatever method is used, significant features are marked and observed for consistencies and inconsistencies between the skull and the individual.[12] Newer methods involve the use of videotapes and computers.

One method takes advantage of two videocameras to tape the skull and the photograph and superimpose the images. The videotapes are useful because they can provide fading or sweep effects that show the skull and the photograph in various combinations together on the screen.[13] Computers can also be used to analyze and compare the skull and photograph. The images of the skull and the photograph are projected onto the monitor and the computer determines if the skull and photograph are from the same individual. This method is considerably more objective than an examination by an expert.[14]

6. Dorion, "Photographic Superimposition," 28 *J.For.Sci.* 724 (1983).

7. Id. at 724.

8. Sekharan, "A Revised Superimposition Technique for Identification of the Individual from the Skull and Photograph," 62 *J.Crim.L., Crim., and Pol.Sci.* 107 (1971).

9. Prinsloo, "The Identification of Skeletal Remains in Reginal versus K and Another: The Howick Falls Murder Case," 1 *J.For.Sci.* 11, 12 (1953).

10. Chee, and Cheng, "Skull and Photographic Superimposition: A New Approach Using a Second Party's Interpupil Distance to Extrapolate the Magnification Factor," 34 *J.For.Sci.* 708, 709 (1989).

11. McKenna, "A Method of Matching Skulls with Photographic Portraits Using Landmarks and Measurements," 29 *J.For. Sci.* 787, 794 (1984).

12. Lan, "Development and Current Status of Skull–Image Superimposition—Methodology and Instrumentation," 4 *For. Sci.Rev.* 125 (1992).

13. Iten, "Identification of Skulls by Video Superimposition," 32 *J.For.Sci.* 173 (1987); Koelmeyer, "Videocamera Superimposition and Facial Reconstruction as an Aid to Identification," 3 *Am.J.For.Med. and Path.* 45 (1982).

14. Delfino, "Computer–Aided Skull/Face Superimposition," 7 *Am.J.For.Med. and Path.* 201 (1986).

4.　FACIAL RECONSTRUCTION

Facial reconstruction also requires the entire skull or large portions of it in good shape. This method involves the actual three-dimensional reconstruction in clay of the soft tissues (fatty tissue, muscle, and skin) of the face. The thickness of soft tissue in different areas of the face differs for each sex and race.[15] Therefore, the sex and race of the individual must be determined before the facial reconstruction can begin. The skull, with the mandible if recovered, is mounted on a stand. Small depth markers are placed at designated points of the face to indicate the calculated soft tissue depth at that point. The facial contours are reconstructed in clay using the markers as guides. The size and location of the eyes, mouth, nose, and ears are based on the dimensions of the individual skulls, not charts. Prosthetic eyes are carefully placed in the eye sockets. The position of the eyes is based on the relative location of the cornea to the orbit, and measurements of muscles within the orbit.[16] Finally, hair and clothing are added based either on samples recovered with the skull or on generic hair appropriate for the race and sex of the skull.

The same principles utilized in the three-dimensional reconstruction can be applied in developing a two-dimensional sketch of the individual. The markers are placed as in the three-dimensional reconstruction, and the anthropologist works with either an artist or a computer[17] to develop a sketch of the individual based on the markers and the other principles used in three-dimensional reconstruction.

III.　CAUSE AND MANNER OF DEATH

§ 17.07　Signs of Trauma

Thus far, the focus of attention has been on the ability of the forensic anthropologist to identify an individual from skeletal remains. The forensic anthropologist, however, can also contribute information concerning the cause and manner of death of an individual where bone trauma is involved. Any trauma to bone, such as gunshot wounds, blunt trauma, and sharp trauma, including cut marks from dismemberment may be detectable on the skeletal remains even when there has been extreme destruction of the body.

1.　ANTEMORTEM, PERIMORTEM, OR POSTMORTEM TRAUMA

The anthropologist is able to distinguish antemortem from perimortem and postmortem bone trauma. The hallmark of antemortem bone trauma is signs of healing. Such signs are absent in peri- and postmor-

15. Dumont, "Mid–Facial Tissue Depths of White Children: An Aid in Facial Feature Reconstruction," 31 *J.For.Sci.* 1463 (1986); Macho, "An Appraisal of Plastic Reconstruction of the External Nose," 31 *J.For.Sci.* 1391 (1986).

16. Stewart, "The Points of Attachment of the Palpebral Ligaments: Their Use in Facial Reconstructions on the Skull," 28 *J.For.Sci.* 858 (1983).

17. Ubelaker and O'Donnell, "Computer–Assisted Facial Reproduction," 37 *J.For. Sci.* 155 (1992).

tem bone trauma. In addition, many postmortem changes that may appear to be antemortem trauma to the untrained eye are readily identified by the anthropologist. These changes, constituting postmortem artifacts, such as concretions or fractures, can result from chemical or mechanical erosion, sun or marine exposure, animal activity, or alterations made intentionally, or through the use of the skeletal remains ceremonially. In addition, many antemortem pathological conditions that may resemble perimortem trauma can also be identified by the anthropologist.

2. GUNSHOT–INDUCED TRAUMA TO BONE

The analysis of gunshot wounds which either penetrate (enter without exiting) or perforate (enter and exit) bone can be most informative. When gunshot wounds are identified on skeletal remains, the main issues for the forensic anthropologist concern the distinction between entrance and exit wounds, the sequence of the shots when more than one have left their marks on bone and the directionality of projectiles striking bone.

In the case of high velocity gunshot wounds, the entrance wound in bone which is not paper-thin, as in sub-adults, is a characteristic circular wound that usually approximates the size of the bullet, although not predictably. The exit wound is quite different, consisting of fragmented bone in a larger area.[1]

Entrance and exit wounds created by a low velocity gunshot wound more closely resemble each other; often, both are circular, approximating the size of the bullet. The first characteristic examined is the bevelling of the bone around the defect. As the bullet travels through the bone, it takes tiny fragments with it. Therefore, the entrance wound creates an internal bevel while the exit wound creates an external bevel.[2]

When examining gunshot defects of the skull, if the bevelling characteristics are obvious and discretely different from each other, they may be used alone to distinguish between entrance and exit wounds. However, if they are not, the fractures in the skull around the defects may reveal the origin of the defect. When the bullet enters the bone, two different types of fractures can be formed. The first fractures are radial fractures that extend out from the defect. The second fractures, if the force of the bullet suffices, are concentric fractures that arc around the defect between the radial fractures.[3] The entrance defect exhibits more fractures than the exit defect because the bullet loses some energy as it travels through bone and tissue.

§ 17.07

1. DiMaio, *Gunshot Wounds* 92–94 (1985).

2. Smith, "Cranial Fracture Patterns and Estimate of Direction from Low Velocity Gunshot Wounds," 32 *J.For.Sci.* 1416, 1417 (1987).

3. Ibid. at 1417.

In addition, the fact that none of these fractures can traverse another fracture aids in distinguishing entrance from exit defects in the skull. Although the concentric fractures appear to traverse radial fractures, each concentric fracture between radial fractures is actually separate, but of an equal radius as the concentric fracture on the other side of the radial fracture. Therefore, radial fractures associated with the entrance defect are long and not arrested. Radial fractures associated with an exit defect, formed after the entrance fractures, are shorter, in general, than entrance fractures due to the loss of energy in the bullet, and because the fracture lines may be arrested by entrance fractures.[4]

The sequence of gunshot wounds to the skull may be revealed in the examination of fractures associated with defects caused by a projectile. Recognizing that one fracture cannot traverse another fracture, if fracture A arrests fracture B, gunshot wound A was inflicted before gunshot wound B. Even in the event of multiple gunshot wounds to the head, this method will indicate the sequence of gunshot wounds. For example, if fracture A arrests fracture B, and fracture C arrests fracture A, gunshot wound C was inflicted first, followed by gunshot wound A, and then gunshot wound B.[5] In the absence of an exit wound, or in cases of multiple gunshot trauma to bone, the bevelling of the entrance defect or cone-like excavation of the exit wound may be used to indicate the direction of fire. If the bevelled entrance area is round, the bullet entered the skull at a right angle. Otherwise, the elongated portion of the bevel indicates the direction of fire.[6]

The combination of distinguishing entrance from exit wounds, determining direction of fire, and sequencing of events enables extensive analysis of gunshot defects of the skull and other bones. The sequencing of bullet trauma to bone, other than the skull, is decidedly difficult but not impossible, in the presence of unique circumstances.[7]

3. CASE STUDY: THE BONES OF CARL AUSTIN WEISS, M.D.

The possibilities for new and unexpected revelations from a forensic anthropologist's examination of bones which have been struck by bullets was amply proven in the scientific aftermath of the exhumation of Carl Austin Weiss, M.D., the purported assassin of populist United States Senator Huey P. Long of Louisiana, self-styled "the Kingfish". It is undisputed that Senator Long was shot at least once late Sunday night, September 8, 1935 while walking in a corridor of the Louisiana State Capitol in Baton Rouge during a state legislative session. Senator Long died from his wounds, possibly exacerbated by flawed surgical intervention, not two days later. Dr. Weiss died in the hallway of the capitol from a burst of gunfire from Senator Long's bodyguards.

---

4. Ibid. at 1417.

5. Rhine & Curran, "Multiple Gunshot Wounds of the Head: An Anthropological View," 35 *J.For.Sci.* 1236, 1237 (1990).

6. Ibid. at 1243.

7. Mann and Owsley, "Human Osteology: Key to the Sequence of Events in a Postmortem Shooting," 37 *J.For.Sci.* 1386 (1992).

At first blush the death of Huey Long seemed not to need an intensive investigation, being the quintessential open-and-shut case. But doubts as to the accountability of Dr. Weiss emerged almost immediately. Why would a sane and sober 29 year old rising physician, with a wife and infant child at their nearby home, want to throw away his life and the prospects for a certain future of distinction in the medical profession? The exhumation of the remains of Dr. Weiss on October 20, 1991 was conscientiously undertaken to seek to shed new light on this perplexing chapter in American history.

Under the leadership of Professor James E. Starrs, co-author of this text, a team of renowned scientists was assembled to conduct the autopsy and to analyze the remains. Douglas H. Ubelaker, Ph.D. was the forensic anthropologist member of the scientific team. Dr. Ubelaker's report [8] on his examination of the bones of Dr. Weiss, when compared to the testimony of Senator Long's bodyguards given at an inquest in Baton Rouge in September 1935, presented new and tangible evidence that Dr. Weiss' being the *deus ex machina* in this tragic event was subject to doubt.

After a laborious reconstruction of many of the bones of Dr. Weiss which had suffered trauma and fracturing from bullet strikes, Dr. Ubelaker reported that a minimum of twenty projectiles had left their marks on Dr. Weiss' bones. The number of separate bullet caused trauma could rise to as many as twenty-four depending on whether or not multiple bullet strikes were caused by the same projectile. The direction from which the projectiles struck Dr. Weiss was also appraised by Dr. Ubelaker. It was his judgment that "of the twenty-four likely trajectories 12 (50%) were directed from the posterior. Seven (29%) trajectories originated from the anterior direction, 3 (13%) from the right lateral and 2 (8%) from the left lateral." [9] The short of this extensive report was that Dr. Weiss was shot in the back twelve out of twenty-four times and shot from right and left sides 21% of the time while only seven of the twenty-four trajectories indicated entry from the front.

To bear weight on the question of the guilt or innocence of Dr. Weiss as the assassin rather than as one who was felled by over-reacting, trigger-itching bodyguards, Dr. Ubelaker's findings must be set against the testimony of the witnesses to the affray as they related it on September 16, 1935 before an inquest into the death of Dr. Weiss conducted by Thomas B. Bird, M.D., Coroner for East Baton Rouge Parish. All of the bodyguards who gave evidence asserted that Dr. Weiss was at all times menacing them as they were firing their guns at him. As a result there was more than a plain implication that Dr. Weiss was facing the bodyguards as their bullets rained down on him directly from the front.

8. The report was presented to the annual meeting of the American Academy of Forensic Sciences in New Orleans in February 1992.

9. Id. at page 34 of the report.

Dr. Ubelaker's findings just did not concur with the recollections of the bodyguards. One or the other must be in error. Since recollections of emotionally charged and transient events are readily suspect, it would appear that the bodyguards' recall of the tragedy was faulty. And if it was erroneous on the matter of whether they shot Dr. Weiss in the back, the genuine possibility surfaces that it was in error too when they said they remembered seeing Dr. Weiss shoot Senator Long. The analysis of the bone trauma to Dr. Weiss may not have entirely exonerated him but it certainly cast a long shadow of skepticism over his being an assassin. And when considered together with other new and startling findings resulting from Starrs' investigations [10] Dr. Weiss looks more like a scapegoat than an assassin.

4. BLUNT–FORCE TRAUMA

Blunt trauma inflicted at or about the time of death will result in unhealed fractures. In some cases, especially blunt trauma to the skull, the fractures will be depressed in the shape of the instrument used to inflict the trauma.[11]

5. SHARP–FORCE TRAUMA

Stab wounds are usually found in the rib cage or adjacent bones. If the stab wound was inflicted on living bone, the portion of the bone separated by the sharp instrument will bend away from the rest of the bone. If this condition is found, the stab wound was inflicted at or about the time of death and is forensically significant. If the wound was inflicted well before the time of death, healing would be present. After death, a stab wound causes the bone to fracture because the elastic property of the bone is lost after death. Cut marks near the ends of long bones are associated with dismemberment or defleshing of the body.[12]

IV. EVIDENCE OF ANTHROPOLOGICAL EXAMINATIONS

§ 17.08 The Current State of the Art

From all reports [1] the caseload of forensic anthropologists over the past few years has risen phenomenally. In the five year period from 1977 to 1981 Bass reports that his examination of skeletal remains

10. See, *True Crime: Assassination* 120 *(Time–Life Books, 1994).*

11. Ubelaker, *Human Skeletal Remains: Excavation, Analysis, Interpretation* 109 (1989).

12. Id. at 106 and 111.

§ 17.08

1. Galloway et al., "Physical Anthropology and the Law: Legal Responsibilities of Forensic Anthropologists," 33 *Yrbk. Phys.Anthro.* 39 (1990); Wienker & Rhine, "A Professional Profile of the Physical Anthropology Section Membership, American Academy of Forensic Sciences," 34 *J.For. Sci.* 647 (1989); Bass, "Summary of Skeletal Identification in Tennessee: 1971–1981," 28 *J.For.Sci.* 159 (1983).

doubled over the previous five year period. Wienker and Rhine, in a 1989 article reporting on a nationwide study, state that the total number of cases handled in 1986 by forensic anthropologists who responded to their questionnaire "surpassed the total reported from 1967 to 1978 by more than 12%." [2]

With the increase in the caseload of forensic anthropologists there has been a significant upsurge in their court appearances as expert witnesses.[3] However, the increase in court appearances by them has not kept pace with the caseloads they carry, even where the case has some juridical importance. This disparity has been explained either by the fact that lawyers may not be sufficiently familiar with forensic anthropology or by the forensic anthropologist's report being subsumed into the final opinion of a medical examiner or a coroner.

This unexpected growth in the caseload of forensic anthropologists and their concomitant greater involvement in the legal process, both civil and criminal, has resulted in efforts to educate members of this scientific discipline to an awareness of their responsibilities within the legal system.

A compilation and analysis of all reported decisions from both state and federal courts up to 1993, tallying more than fifty in all,[4] in which the testimony of physical anthropologists was mentioned confirms the more widespread and more crucial involvement of such experts in the courtroom in recent years. These decisions reveal, in general, a ready approval by the courts of the scientific standing of the opinions of anthropologists, termed by the courts either physical or forensic anthropologists.

The decisions also portray the testimonial relevance of such experts as encompassing more than opinions on the identity of fresh, decomposed, burned, disarticulated, dismembered or skeletonized human remains. More novel, well-nigh ingenious, ways have been found for the talents of physical anthropologists to be employed in identifying the perpetrators of crimes from distinctive musculoskeletal features of various parts of the human anatomy. It would appear that the courts have accepted the premise that the skeletal configurations of every human being provide a legitimate basis for individualizing one person from another, although no court has put it so forthrightly thus far.

This greater courtroom approval of forensic anthropologists, it is not at all farfetched to say, may be somewhat explained by the emergence of books by or about physical anthropologists, like Ubelaker [5] and Snow,[6] which have popularized, in captivating detail, the values of a steadfast

2. Wienker & Rhine, supra note 1 at p. 652.

3. Courtroom appearances increased "fourfold" from 1967 to 1986 while "caseloads increased tenfold" over the same period. Wienker & Rhine, supra note 1 at p. 652.

4. See, Starrs, "The Erumpent Quality of Bones in Forensic Science," 17 *Sci. Sleuth.Rev.* 1 (Fall 1993).

5. Ubelaker & Scammell, *Bones: A Forensic Detective's Casebook* (1992).

6. Joyce & Stover, *Witnesses from the Grave: The Stories Bones Tell* (1991).

reliance upon the established skills of such scientists. And the mass media, both broadcast and print, have given prominence and prestige to the work of forensic anthropologists in tracking their every move in the exhumations of notable persons in historic mysteries from beyond the grave, including Lee Harvey Oswald, President Zachary Taylor, Carl Austin Weiss M.D., Alfred Packer and the family of Czar Nicholas II. That bones can be telling and in the telling can speak volumes has become a staple of public recognition, in and out of the courts.

§ 17.09 Qualifying the Expert

1. THE NON-FORENSIC ANTHROPOLOGIST

As is true with expert witnesses in general, the trial courts are accorded great latitude, either by court rules or by the deference of appellate courts, in deciding whether a person possesses the qualifications to identify skeletal remains. It would be comforting to learn that only those whose special field of experience and knowledge has been devoted to physical anthropology would qualify as experts in that specialized and unique field. Such a limitation has not, however, found general favor with the reviewing courts.

In one of the earliest appellate court decisions reviewing an identification of skeletal remains, a Texas reviewing court in 1874 [1] proved itself a stickler for expert testimony, but not necessarily of an anthropologist, in the identification of skeletal remains. Lewis Wilson had been convicted of murdering his wife. The trial court had allowed the testimony of lay persons that the skeletal remains, the nature of which was not specified, were those of a woman. Without some demonstration that the lay persons had "knowledge of anatomy or human psychology" it was said to be reversible error for the trial court to allow testimony giving the gender of the person whose skeletal remains were in question.

On a retrial of Wilson, medical experts testified that the skeletal remains were those of a woman about 5'4" tall. The teeth were said to indicate an age between 20 to 25 years. The "facial angle" enabled the experts to say that she was of "mixed blood" for the caucasian facial angle, so it was said, ranged from 75 degrees to 85 degrees while that of a negro would be 65 degrees to 70 degrees. Nothing was said as to the facial angle of the skull under examination. On a further appeal from Wilson's second conviction for murder no fault was found in the medical evidence introduced at the retrial.[2]

Even though expert testimony would clearly be preferable to that of lay evidence in the identification of skeletal remains, lay persons with special knowledge of identifying anatomical features exhibited by a missing person have been permitted to assert that the unknown skeletal remains reveal those same distinctive traits, convincing them that the

---

§ 17.09   **2.** Wilson v. State, 43 Tex. 472 (1875).
1. Wilson v. State, 41 Tex. 320 (1874).

bones are those of a familiar of theirs. In a Georgia trial [3] a brother was seen fit to identify a skull, which had been buried and soaked in lime, as that of his brother. The brother had no doubt that a dental filling in one of the teeth in the skull matched one he knew his missing brother had since he had seen a dentist fill that tooth.[4] The brother was corroborated by a dentist who compared the entries on the missing brother's dental chart to the teeth in the skull. The murder conviction survived an appeal without any reference to the propriety of these identifications.

In a rare and unsatisfactory instance a Kentucky appeals court in 1909 [5] saw no merit in an objection to the testimony of a grandmother who had identified each of her two grandchildren from fire-charred commingled skeletal remains. In support of her testimony she had made an in-court identification of the skeletal remains which were presented to her for her inspection in the presence of the court and the jury. As can be seen, the quantum of specialized knowledge necessary to permit a person to identify skeletal remains has not consistently been held to a rigorously high standard by the appellate courts. A Texas Justice of the Peace in 1891 who said "he had seen several human skeletons" was permitted to examine small fragments of bones discovered at a burial site and to give his opinion that they were human, not animal, and that they resembled those of a child. In approving this testimony a Texas appeals court went on record with the insupportable remark that "there are thousands of men who have seen human skeletons and the bones of human beings, who are as competent to give a correct opinion as to whether the skeleton and bones are such as many of the so-called expert scientists." [6]

Seemingly one possessed of a degree in medicine automatically qualifies, in the view of the appellate courts, to identify skeletal remains.[7] In Gray v. Commonwealth [8] a Dr. William McBriar, described as one of the "medical witnesses", was permitted to infer from the strands of ten inch long hair adhering to a river-soaked skull that the skull was that of a female due to "the custom and habit of wearing the hair nowadays." Regardless of the "non sequitur" nature of the conclusion, a medical doctor was out of his depth in asserting it.

In an Alabama murder prosecution [9] of a father for killing his 14 year old adopted daughter, a toxicologist, although without a medical degree, was found qualified to identify "the skull, rib, leg and pelvis bones" discovered at a burial place as those of a "human being." The expert was even allowed to state the person's "approximate height" and the fact that the bones were of a "young person." The toxicologist had

3. McVeigh v. State, 205 Ga. 326, 53 S.E.2d 462 (1949).

4. Id. at 464.

5. Sprouse v. Commonwealth, 132 Ky. 269, 116 S.W. 344 (1909).

6. Jackson v. State, 29 Tex.App. 458, 16 S.W. 247, 248 (1891).

7. Infra note 3, section 17.10; infra note 5, section 17.10; ibid.

8. 101 Pa. 380 (1882).

9. DeSilvey v. State, 245 Ala. 163, 16 So.2d 183 (1943).

"made many investigations of death" and had made "a study of the human anatomy." Such specialized experience and study convinced the Alabama reviewing court that the toxicologist's lack of a medical degree did not disable him from offering an opinion on the identification of the skeletal remains.

Commonly the functions of a forensic anthropologist are performed by a pathologist whose training will include the study of the human anatomy but who will lack the degree of skilled sophistication of the anthropologist. In the view of the courts specialization in anthropology is not the *nec plus ultra* which enables a medical doctor to identify human skeletal remains.

In Voyles v. State [10] a body was found on July 13 or 14, 1976 in Bucy Bottom creek with a hand protruding out of water-covered debris. It was known that 40 year old Bernice Griggs had disappeared on March 12, 1976. A pathologist was called to the task of identifying the remains. He testified that "several bones were broken and that the remains were of a human, 'probably' of the female species." [11] That evidence together with the testimony of Mrs. Griggs daughter that the polka dot jacket found on the remains was the daughter's jacket which her mother had borrowed on the day she vanished sufficed to identify the remains.

In State v. Petree [12] one high school student was charged with killing another high school student during an impassioned and violent outburst. However it was not until two and a half years after the alleged victim had disappeared that a skeleton was found "about 30 inches below the surface of the ground in an old carrot pit beneath a wooden trap door covered by a mound of earth." The reverse fetal position in which the skeleton was observed to have been forced into the carrot pit signed the death as a homicide. The identity of the deceased was demonstrated by a medical examiner's opinion that the skeleton was that of a 14 to 17 year old female who was 5'2" tall (give or take 2 inches) bearing a healed fracture of the left forearm. These physical details corresponded to those of the missing girl and were corroborated by items of clothing on the skeleton which belonged to the girl. A forensic anthropologist might have added more specifics to the identification but, under all the circumstances, the identification was a done deed.

2. THE FORENSIC ANTHROPOLOGIST

One of the most remarkable aspects of the testimony of forensic anthropologists which stands out in the reported appellate court decisions is the rarity of the occasions when their qualifications or their opinions have been contested. That is most particularly the case when these experts stay within the traditional boundaries of their discipline and concentrate their attention on opinions of and about the identification of human remains. Contests are more frequent, more vigorous and

10. 362 So.2d 1236 (Miss.1978), cert. denied 441 U.S. 956 (1979).

11. Ibid. at p. 1238.

12. 659 P.2d 443 (Utah 1983).

more often well-made when forensic anthropology is utilized as a process for the identification not of deceased persons but of the living perpetrators of crimes.

It is justifiable to interpret this void in the ardor of an opposing attorney's advocacy as an implicit recognition of the stature of both the persons and the judgments of forensic anthropologists. It is equally possible that attorneys, mainly defense attorneys, do not have their thinking caps squarely in place when confronted by the expert testimony of forensic anthropologists speaking ex cathedra on matters right up their scientific alley.

Occasionally attorneys will stipulate to the qualifications of forensic anthropologists.[13] However, such a profferred stipulation need not be accepted since it deprives the expert of the opportunity to have his or her qualifications predispose the jury to decide that his or her opinions must be as august as his or her credentials. There are no harmful consequences, however, for the expert or the attorney when a stipulation accepting the expert's opinion as soundly based is interposed. In Fred v. State[14] the defense stipulated that Clyde Snow would testify that the remains in question were those of a female Caucasian, 55 to 70 years of age, 5'6" tall with osteoarthritis and gap in her front teeth. Possibly the stipulation can be explained by the fact that the stipulating attorney saw no adverse effects from Snow's testimony.

Just as unaccountable as the stipulation in *Fred* was the rejected opposition to the qualifications and testimony of the respected and even revered Wilton Krogman in the Massachusetts murder trial of *Gilbert*.[15] Dr. Krogman's sole purpose in testifying was to confirm the x-ray matching determination of radiologist Dr. Sosman. On that issue his expertise and credentials should have been not only unimpeachable but unchallengeable.

When Dr. William M. Bass III, state anthropologist for Tennessee, testified in *State v. Oody*[16] that the deceased's skeletal remains evidenced his having sustained defense wounds, his authority and capability to draw such an inference was unsuccessfully disputed. And when Dr. Bass averred in *State v. Shepherd*[17] that a sixteen year old mentally deficient woman's manner of death was "inconsistent with suicide or accident, given the fact of burial, the obvious involvement of another person in the burial and the remoteness of the area in terms of lack of detection" the defense let that opinion pass unopposed.

In *Oody* the objection was at best spurious, for forensic anthropologists are well-fortified by training and experience to define trauma to bones as resulting from defensive gestures. But, on the contrary, in *Shepherd* an objection would have been expected since opinions on the

13. State v. Abbott, 654 S.W.2d 260 (Mo.App.1983).

14. 531 P.2d 1038 (Okl.Cr.1975).

15. Commonwealth v. Gilbert, 366 Mass. 18, 314 N.E.2d 111 (1974).

16. 823 S.W.2d 554 (Tenn.Cr.App.1991).

17. 862 S.W.2d 557 (Tenn.Cr.App.1992).

manner of death are more characteristically the appropriate function of a forensic pathologist. But, on occasion, forensic anthropologists have been known to be at their best in giving firm support to manner of death decision-making. These Tennessee cases affirm that it is hard as hard tack to fathom from a distance the strategy of an attorney in making or neglecting an objection to the receipt of evidence.

As a result of the ineffectiveness or the failure of objections to the testimony of forensic anthropologists there are a dearth of decisions in which the factual basis for their expert opinions are explicated by the appellate courts. Consequently one can only guess how Dr. Bass in *State v. Phillips* [18] knew that the murder victim had been dead "between two months and one year," a matter well within his competence, or how he concluded that the order of the two shots to the deceased's head was "first from behind and then in the right side." It would be a reasonable surmise that the latter conclusion derived from his observation of the intersecting fracture lines radiating outward from the bullet entry wounds, the fracture line which stops at an intersecting fracture line having resulted from a later bullet strike.

Less readily unpuzzled is how the expert in *State v. Hollis* [19] determined that the deceased's bones had been "moved around in the fire as they burned" [20] or how the expert in another Kansas murder case, *State v. Cooper*,[21] knew from the "cracking pattern in the skull" that the bullet wound had been inflicted peri-mortem or how the expert in *State v. Teel* [22] arrived at the conclusion that the murder victim's neck trauma had been inflicted at the time of the victim's death.

Whereas the qualifications of forensic anthropologists are rarely put in issue, the status of forensic anthropology as an accepted scientific discipline is in most cases assumed without the necessity for argument or proof. State v. Klindt [23] was a singular instance in which the defense chose to charge the discipline of forensic anthropology with a lack of reliability while at the same time raising no objection to the qualifications of forensic anthropologist Clyde Snow. The Iowa Supreme Court in a terse paragraph agreed with the trial court that "forensic anthropology is a recognized scientific discipline" crediting it with the ability to determine the "time, cause, and manner of death of decomposed victims of homicides." [24]

§ 17.10 Demonstrative Evidence: Bones in the Courtroom

The trial court is presumptively the master of its own fate in another matter as well as in that of qualifying an expert on skeletal

18. 728 S.W.2d 21 (Tenn.Cr.App.1986).

19. 240 Kan. 521, 731 P.2d 260 (1987).

20. Ibid. at 265.

21. 794 P.2d 1164 (Kan.1990).

22. 793 S.W.2d 236 (Tenn.1990).

23. 389 N.W.2d 670 (Iowa 1986). See also, State v. Miller, 429 N.W.2d 26, 39

(S.D.1988). On federal habeas corpus, the district court's granting the petition has been reversed, *Miller v. Leapley, 34 F.3d 582 (8th Cir. 1994)*.

24. State v. Klindt, 389 N.W.2d 670, 673 (Iowa 1986).

remains. When bones are brought into the courtroom presumably to inform and enhance the testimony of the expert and to give the jury a more compelling basis to credit the opinion of the expert it will take more than an objection to prevent this dramatic use of demonstrative evidence. Inflammatory though this tactic certainly is, the appellate courts have not been constrained to balk at a trial court's allowing such a courtroom display.

As a strategic manoeuver it is sometimes desirable for an attorney to put before the observant and expectant eyes of a jury the physical evidence upon which a forensic anthropologist has relied in making an identification. The real possibility exists, however, that, in a criminal case, such a tactic will be criticized by defense counsel as having no other purpose than to arouse the jury to a hanging frenzy.

In deciding the merits of such a challenge the courts follow the usual rules for the admission of demonstrative evidence. In the first place, the proffered evidence must be germane to some matter in issue in the litigation. In the second, the item tendered must bear upon and assist in delineating the evidence of some testifying witness. Furthermore the display must not be so gruesome that it must necessarily distract the fact-finder from a careful and deliberate consideration of the factual matters in controversy.

The appellate court decisions reflect a ready and rather uncritical acceptance of the use of physical evidence, generally skeletal remains, in conjunction with the testimony of a forensic anthropologist so long as that evidence has some, even barely, tangential relation to the opinions stated by the expert. The appellate courts apparently give the jury credit for a degree of even-tempered objectivity and level-headed detachment that one would be hard-pressed to say they would have under the same circumstances out of the confines of the courtroom.

In Dutton v. State,[1] for example, both Dr. Angel, the forensic anthropologist and Dr. Hameli, the Delaware Medical Examiner, had noted fractures of the mandible and the sixth cervical vertebra of the homicide victim. To put the actual skeletal parts before the jury was said to be appropriate since their presence would enable the jury better to comprehend the experts' opinions that the fractures had occurred "at or about the time of the death of the victim."

Gruesomeness alone will not serve to prohibit the introduction into evidence of a human skull,[2] probably the most unsettling and frightening of all skeletal remains. It is a little known fact that at the trial of Lizzie Borden (a case brimming with and overpowered by more retrospective fiction than fact) in New Bedford, Massachusetts in 1893 for the hatchet murders of her father and stepfather, the skull of her father, Andrew

§ 17.10

1. 452 A.2d 127 (Del.1982).

2. In State v. Cazes, 875 S.W.2d 253, 263 (Tenn.1994) the victim's "cleaned and reconstructed skull" was used to illustrate the testimony of a forensic anthropologist who found a "signature" for the murder weapon in the trauma to the skull.

Jackson Borden, became the most florid centerpiece of the prosecution's case on June 13, the eighth day of Ms. Borden's trial.

During the direct testimony of Frank W. Draper, M.D.,[3] the Medical Examiner for Suffolk County and the first Medical Examiner in the Commonwealth of Massachusetts, prosecutor Hosea M. Knowlton interrupted his questioning to ask of Draper

Q: "Would the skull itself be of assistance in pointing out such things as occur to you to be important?"[4]

Upon Draper's replying that "it would," Knowlton, "very much [regretting] the necessity of doing it,"[5] asked Dr. Dolan, the local Medical Examiner, to produce the skull of Andrew Borden. Dr. Dolan "retired from the courtroom and returned with the skull of Mr. Borden,"[6] a skull, along with that of Abby Borden, that he admitted to "decapitating" in the presence of Dr. Draper at the Oak Grove Cemetery on August 11, 1892, one week after the Bordens had been murdered. According to one newspaper account the skull of Andrew Borden, as it appeared in the hands of Dr. Dolan, "was done up in a white handkerchief and looked like a bouquet, such as a man carries to his sweetheart."

The jury's eyes must have been rivetted solidly and solely on this "ghastly relic"[7] and not upon Lizzie Borden's reaction to its appearance. By happenstance Ms. Borden was not present at the time, having "complained of feeling poorly, and gone out"[8] shortly prior to the skull's making its entry into the courtroom. Strangely, in a case overcome with strange incidents, Melvin O. Adams, defense counsel, raised no objection to the presence of the skull in the courtroom. Indeed, with a nod of assent, he stipulated to its being the skull of Andrew Borden,[9] thereby obviating the need for Dr. Dolan to return to the witness stand for the purpose of identifying it.

The prosecutor then had Dr. Draper carry out various demonstrations with the skull using a tin plate to simulate the hatchet blade of the "handleless" hatchet which purported to be the murder weapon. The skull of Andrew Borden did not leave the courtroom upon the conclusion of Dr. Draper's testimony but it reemerged during the testimony of the next medical witness, Dr. David W. Cheever. Dr. Cheever, a professor of surgery at Harvard Medical School since 1882, concurred with the assertions of the prior medical witnesses concerning the time the murders were thought to have occurred, the amount of blood splattering there would have been and the nature of the murder weapon. When prosecutor Knowlton came to question the size of the blade which caused the wounds in the skull of Andrew Borden, he asked Dr. Cheever

---

3. Porter, The Fall River Tragedy 128, 195 (1985).

4. Trial Transcript 1046.

5. Trial Transcript 1046–1047.

6. Trial Transcript 1047.

7. Sullivan, *Goodbye Lizzie Borden* 121 (1974).

8. Kent, ed., *The Lizzie Borden Sourcebook* 269 (1992).

9. Trial Transcript 1047.

"Can you tell whether that shape of a hatchet accurately fits those wounds?" [10]

After trying the "handleless" hatchet in the non-perforating wounds in Andrew Borden's defleshed skull, Dr. Cheever responded

"I have tried this, and I thought it did accurately ... Yes, sir." [11]

Still no cry of foul and no remonstrance, not even to the wholly unscientific method utilized by Dr. Cheever, from the team of defense attorneys for Ms. Borden, not, that is, until the prosecutor remarked,[12] at the conclusion of Dr. Cheever's testimony, that he wanted the skull of Andrew Borden "to go to the jury" during its deliberations. Defense attorney Adams objected, ever so politely, in saying "I do not understand that that is going to the jury." [13]

With all the prosecutorial parrying and the slight defense thrusting in response on the question of the use of Mr. Borden's skull in court, the jury was not taken in by the melodrama of the moment. On June 20, the twelve male jurors, after deliberating but one and a half hours, returned their verdict acquitting Lizzie Borden of the murders. The acquittal effectively denied any appellate court from reviewing the propriety of the showing of Borden's skull before the jury. But later decisions from other courts have solidly confirmed the legitimacy of this use of skeletal parts in the courtroom.

In Reed v. Commonwealth [14], however, a Kentucky appeals court in 1953 did pass on the legitimacy of such a display and found it to be entirely in order. The skull of a female had been produced at the trial to prove from "the peculiarities of the teeth" that the skull was that of the deceased, Louise Young, for whose murder Reed was on trial.

Some courtroom displays of funereal artifacts have gone beyond the gruesome to the grisly but even then the appellate courts have not interfered with the trial court's exercise of discretion in authorizing the exhibition before the jury. The late Kentucky state anthropologist, David Wolfe, was permitted in the trial of Roy Lee Scott for the murder of his wife, Joyce, to produce a can containing insect larvae he had retrieved from the decomposed remains of a female human found disposed of in a sinkhole.[15] What exact connection such a viscerally upsetting display, combined with the showing of slides of the remains as first seen in the sinkhole, would have in assisting the jury to have a fuller understanding of the anthropologist's estimate of the time of death requires more proof than the Kentucky appeals court demanded in affirming the murder conviction.

10. Trial Transcript 1092.

11. Trial Transcript 1092.

12. Trial Transcript 1109.

13. Trial Transcript 1109.

14. 261 S.W.2d 9 (Ky.App.1953).

15. Scott v. Commonwealth, 685 S.W.2d 184 (Ky.1984). In State v. Klafta, 73 Hawaii 109, 831 P.2d 512 (1992) an objection to the admission of two vials containing maggots taken from the body of a live 16 month old infant was overruled and affirmed on appeal in an attempted murder prosecution of the mother.

Even dismembered and fire-charred human skeletal remains have not been considered too distracting to be admissible at a murder trial. The question of the identification of the remains was of paramount importance in State v. Hollis,[16] particularly whether the bones were "of the same person" or the commingled bones of more than one person. The Kentucky high court saw no reasonable objection to the trial court's giving the glad hand to the use of two buckets of such bones to illumine the identification testimony of physical anthropologist, Dr. Schneider.

All in all, bones and other physical evidence appertaining to the testimony of a forensic anthropologist may be subjected to the jury's viewing without the rebuke of an appellate court unless there are as yet undefined exceptional circumstances impinging upon such use. Seemingly a trial court's discretion in such matters is all but unreviewable.

§ 17.11 Legal Uses for the Forensic Anthropologist.

1. THE ANTHROPOLOGIST AS A TEAM PLAYER

Rarely is the opinion of a forensic anthropologist the mainstay of a legal determination. Most frequently the forensic anthropologist serves in a collaborative capacity, confirming and supplementing the opinions of experts in other scientific specialties, such as an odontologist,[1] a pathologist,[2] a radiologist,[3] a statistician[4] or, in an exceptional instance, a serologist.[5] This confirmatory role also acts on occasion to support an identification based on artifacts of known ownership found in proximity to human remains. It is not always a sure or sound investigative policy to make an identification on personal belongings alone especially where burned or dismembered remains suggest the real possibility that an attempt has been made to hide the true identity of the deceased.

In Roberts v. Wabash Life Insurance Co.,[6] suspicions had been raised that Clarence Roberts, the named insured on a $640,000 life insurance policy, was not in fact dead. Geneva Roberts, Clarence's wife, had sued the life insurance carrier to recover the face amount of the policy but the trial court denied her recovery on account of very tangible proof that her husband had fabricated a fiery death scene where he had planted the dead body of a look-alike stranger beneath whom he had placed his own Masonic ring.

Rather than accepting the ring as positive proof of the identity of the charred remains, the insurance company had sought the independent opinion of a fire investigator, a radiologist, an anthropologist, a patholo-

---

16. 240 Kan. 521, 731 P.2d 260 (1987).

§ 17.11

1. State v. Hartman, 703 S.W.2d 106 (Tenn.1985); State v. Goodman, 643 S.W.2d 375 (Tenn.Cr.App.1982).

2. People v. Kokoraleis, 132 Ill.2d 235, 138 Ill.Dec. 233, 547 N.E.2d 202 (1989).

3. State v. Hollis, 240 Kan. 521, 731 P.2d 260 (1987); State v. Hartman, supra note 1.

4. State v. Klindt, 389 N.W.2d 670 (Iowa 1986).

5. Roberts v. Wabash Life Ins. Co., 78 Ind.Dec. 731, 410 N.E.2d 1377 (Ind.App. 1980).

6. Supra note 5.

gist and other kindred experts. The differing opinions offered by these specialists together with the fact of Roberts' financial reversals and his guilty behavior prior to the fire convinced the Indiana appellate court that the judgment of the trial court was sound. The Masonic ring, supplemented by the suspicions aroused by the experts including the anthropologist, did not have the ring of truth.

In numerous other instances, forensic anthropologists have played a supporting role with other scientific disciplines in the identification of human remains. Anthropologists have been summoned to confirm the X-ray interpretations of radiologists who have compared ante-mortem with post-mortem X-rays for the purpose of declaring that both are of the same person.[7] When a pathologist declares neck trauma to be the cause of a death, an anthropologist may find that a fractured hyoid bone gives added credence to the pathologist's judgment.[8] Odontologists and anthropologists often work in tandem to effect an identification of human remains, the odontologist evaluating the teeth and the anthropologist assessing other skeletal features.[9]

2. CORROBORATING A CONFESSION

An anthropologist serves a highly esteemed function in adding evidence to corroborate the truthfulness of a confession. As a general rule, confessions cannot be the sole basis for a finding of guilt in a criminal trial.[10] Corroboration, from whatever source, is therefore imperative.[11]

In State v. Hollis,[12] the defendant had lived with the alleged victim who disappeared without a trace. Two buckets with ominous contents were found on the premises jointly occupied by Hollis and the missing person. The burned bones in the buckets were identified by anthropologist Dr. Schneider as those of a Caucasian male over 50 years of age who was about the same height as the missing person. Even more telling for the prosecution was Dr. Schneider's testimony that the bones had been "moved around in the fire as they burned." Dr. Schneider's testimony in this regard corroborated Hollis' confession in which he admitted having moved the bones of his erstwhile co-lodger as he sought to cremate them. The Kansas appellate court in affirming Hollis' murder conviction in 1987 did not pause to explain how Dr. Schneider knew the bones had been moved about during the failed attempt to consume them.[13]

---

7. Shipley v. State, 570 A.2d 1159 (Del. 1990).

8. State v. Crowley, 475 So.2d 783 (La. App.1985).

9. Matthews v. Superior Court, 201 Cal. App.3d 385, 247 Cal.Rptr. 226 (1988).

10. State v. Vangerpen, 71 Wash.App. 94, 856 P.2d 1106 (1993).

11. But the corroborative evidence need only be sufficient to give prima facie evidence of the corpus delicti. Ibid.

12. Supra note 19, section 17.09.

13. For another case involving a murder conviction based solely on a confession, wherein the anthropologist's testimony was insufficient to prove the corpus delicti, see, Parker v. State, 228 Ind. 1, 88 N.E.2d 556 (1949).

3.　AVOIDING A SPECULATIVE OPINION

The decisions reveal that positive identifications by anthropologists of individuals from their skeletal remains is a rarity in homicide prosecutions. The likelihood of such positive identifications increases in proportion to the amount and kind of skeletal material available for analysis. In one case an unqualified positive identification was asserted due to ante-mortem and post-mortem X-rays of both the skull and the dentition which anthropologist William Bass compared and concluded that they matched.[14]

More commonly anthropologists are remitted, for lack of adequate or sufficient skeletal material, to stating their conclusions in rather free-floating approximations. With the exception of Parker v. State,[15] all the appellate courts have been unreproving of these rather speculative and far-reaching estimations. It would seem, however, to be of little or no probative value and therefore inadmissible to declare as the expert did in Fisher v. State [16] that the ten fingers submitted for analysis all came from one person (race and sex unspecified) of the minimum age of 14. Yet the Texas appeals court found no fault with this quite nebulous scientific opinion. Other decisions from other states' courts have revealed an equally tolerant and acquiescent attitude toward similarly vague and sweeping statements of individuation by anthropologists.

Anthropologists are by the exigencies of their training and by the fact of their experiences skilled in a number of other scientific disciplines which are necessarily related to the performance of their primary tasks in the interpretation of musculo-skeletal quiddities. It is not beyond the competence of an anthropologist to read radiographs or to make assessments of the condition or the ante- or post-mortem loss of teeth. And appellate court decisions have unhesitatingly given anthropologists the latitude to present their opinions on such matters.[17]

When anthropologists stray beyond the disciplines of radiology and odontology, there should be a fixed requirement of specialized knowledge as a pre-condition to giving an expert opinion on such matters which are outside the usual reach of their experience and training. The decisions reveal that anthropologists have performed autopsies,[18] more properly the function of a pathologist, at least where tissues are present. In such cases the behavior of the anthropologists has not been challenged by attorneys nor rebuked by the courts. A challenge, if made, however, would certainly have prima facie merit.

Probably the most exceptional instance of a forensic anthropologist's going beyond the precise boundaries of his anthropological expertise is

---

14. Bass, op. cit. supra note 1, section 17.08, at 161.

15. Supra note 14.

16. 827 S.W.2d 597 (Tex.App.1992), affirmed Fisher v. State, 851 S.W.2d 298 (Tex.Cr.App.1993).

17. State v. Goodman, supra note 1, section 17.11 (teeth); State v. Hartman, supra note 1, section 17.11 (x-rays).

18. Scott v. Commonwealth, supra note 15, section 17.10.

Scott v. Commonwealth.[19] In *Scott*, Dr. David Wolfe, the late State Anthropologist for Kentucky, testified as to the time of the murder victim's death from insect larvae, as to the cause and manner of the individual's death from buck shot wounds and the identity of the victim from a comparison of ante- and post-mortem x-rays. All of this testimony, which was deemed "the principal evidence against the defendant," was uncontested in the trial court and survived attack on the appeal. In this instance the anthropologist had apparently been accepted as a scientific factotum with qualifications in radiology, pathology, entomology and his parent discipline of anthropology.

4. PROVING THE CORPUS DELICTI

Loosely and literally translated for legal purposes, the corpus delicti is the body or subject of the crime.[20] Every crime has its corpus delicti but in none, as a general rule, is it necessary to offer proof of the accused's wrongdoing as an essential element in establishing the existence of the corpus delicti.[21]

The assistance of a forensic pathologist is most often solicited in proving the corpus delicti of homicide. In such circumstances there are two primary concerns. First, can a particular person whom the accused is charged with killing be shown to be dead? Second, can the deceased person be proved to have died as a result of a criminal agency rather than from an accident, a suicide or natural causes? On these two matters the unique talents of forensic anthropologists have had inestimable value in the legal system.

It should be noted that an individual's death from criminal causes can be proved by circumstantial evidence even in the absence of the body of the victim itself. At one time a Texas statute [22] did require the production of the body of the victim to prove a person's death. But in 1973 that statute was repealed and its repeal has been construed as no longer mandating the discovery of a body to affirm the death of an individual.[23] However, the necessity of having a body, in whole or in parts, is imperative to the functioning of a physical anthropologist, if only as a factual predicate to the statement of his or her opinions.

A. IDENTIFYING THE DECEASED

Identifications of deceased individuals are contingent affairs. The more abundant the remains, and the more artifacts associated with

19. 685 S.W.2d 184 (Ky.1984); [also supra at note 15, section 17.10].

20. *Black's Law Dictionary* 310 (5th ed. 1979). According to general acceptance, "the corpus delicti embraces the fact that a crime has been committed by someone." LaFave & Scott, *Criminal Law* 18 (2d ed. 1986).

21. In general, see, Perkins, "The Corpus Delicti of Murder," 48 *Va.L.Rev.* 173 (1962). The identity of the perpetrator is not a part of the corpus delicti. People v. Ott, 84 Cal.App.3d 118, 148 Cal.Rptr. 479, 487 (1978).

22. Tex. Penal Code art. 1204, repealed 1973 Tex.Gen.Laws 995.

23. Fisher v. State, supra note 16.

them, the greater the possibility of an identification. But even fragments of bones can provide some meager support for an identification. In State v. Marra,[24] for example, a fifteen year old boy was said to have been killed by a gang, shut up in a refrigerator and dumped into a river. Some time later, two miles down stream from the site where the refrigerator was discarded a sneaker and a sock containing a left heel bone and left toe bone were found. Dr. Rodriguez testified for the prosecution that the bones were those of a Caucasian male aged fifteen to fifty years. Fortunately for the prosecution there was substantial and more specific other evidence of the fifteen year old's death to support a finding of the identity of the deceased fifteen year old.

In a 1969 Illinois appellate court decision [25] an anthropologist at the Smithsonian Institution was asked to give his opinion on the identity of the person whose first cervical vertebra, skull fragment, fingers, toes and teeth had been forwarded to him for his analysis. After his inspection the bones were said to be those of a child of either ten to twelve years of age.

Anthropologists are quite frequently asked to estimate the time that has elapsed between the death of an individual and the discovery of his or her remains. This estimate, an approximation though it must be, can be highly relevant to the identification of an individual who is known to have disappeared on a particular day. It can also have a considerable bearing on the veracity of a suspect's claimed alibi for the period during which it is said the deceased died. Clearly the wider the window of the anthropologist's estimate of the time since death the less the likelihood that it will be acceptable in court. To say that remains have been buried anywhere from two years to twenty-five or thirty years was decided to be too speculative to warrant the opinion's admission into evidence in an Indiana prosecution.[26] The opinion was said to lack any tangible value in proving the death of one individual to the exclusion of any other.

A positive identification of skeletal remains by an anthropologist is not often reflected in the appellate court decisions. But in the presence of ante-mortem x-rays of a known individual's bones, especially the dentition, and the existence of the same bones with the same distinctive features on the remains of an unknown person a positive identification is more than a hunch or scientific wool-gathering. Such was the fortuitous situation in the Tennessee murder trial of Hartman v. State.[27]

Although the varied methods of skull superimposition and reconstruction are being lauded as techniques which have gone beyond the experimental stage, still the appellate court decisions have not yet had the opportunity to weigh and to expostulate on the juridical value of these new techniques. Most forensic anthropologists have approached this development in identification warily and without any great convic-

24. 222 Conn. 506, 610 A.2d 1113 (1992).

25. People v. Dewey, 42 Ill.2d 148, 246 N.E.2d 232 (1969).

26. Parker v. State, supra note 13.

27. State v. Hartman, supra note 1.

tion in the certainty of identifications made by these methods, photographic, computer-assisted or otherwise. The testimony of the physical anthropologist in United States v. Webb [28] typifies this restrained reception. Six year old Steve Wilson was missing when an unidentified skull of a child was found in a grave to which the authorities were directed by Wilson's father, his suspected murderer. A physical anthropologist superimposed a photograph of Steve Wilson over a photograph of the unidentified skull. According to the expert's testimony no more could be said than that they "had a good fit."

B. IDENTIFYING THE CRIMINAL CAUSE OF DEATH

Once the first prong of the corpus delicti has been demonstrated by evidence of the death of a particular individual, it is incumbent on the prosecution on a charge of homicide to prove the death of the person came about by criminal means as opposed to accident, suicide or natural causes.[29] Anything short of that leaves the second prong of the corpus delicti unproved and the dismissal of a prosecution for homicide the inexorable outcome.[30]

To assist in proving a criminal agency's causal connection to the death, a forensic anthropologist looks at the skeletal remains for tell-tale signs of trauma which may be implicated in the person's death. In this quest four questions will be propounded to the expert:

1. Is there evidence of trauma on the skeletal remains?

2. What instrumentality or event produced the trauma?

3. Did the trauma occur ante-, peri- or post-mortem?

4. Was the trauma sufficient to have resulted in death?

(i) Evidence of Trauma to Bone

Even though a forensic anthropologist can testify to the existence of trauma to bone, that, in itself, may be unavailing as proof that death resulted from criminal causes. The ambiguity in assigning a criminal agency to the trauma revealed on bone can be dispelled by other, non-skeletal factors pointing to a death by criminal means.

---

28. 796 F.2d 60 (5th Cir.1986).

29. Chief Justice Shaw of Massachusetts explained this in Commonwealth v. Webster, 59 Mass. (5 Cush.) 295, 309 (1850): "When the dead body of a person is found, whose life seems to have been destroyed by violence, three questions naturally arise. Did he destroy his own life? Was his death caused by accident? Or was it caused by violence inflicted on him by others?"

30. This deficiency in proof is most marked in the death of infants where the difference between a foul play death and one from natural causes can be the difference between a meritorious prosecution and one that will fail. In re Flodstrom, 134 Cal.App.2d 871, 277 P.2d 101 (1954) (a mother's habeas corpus petition was granted for lack of corroboration of her confession of smothering her child).

In State v. Ellis [31] an anthropologist removed the skeletonized remains of a female university student from an antique water wagon where the body had apparently lain for four years. "No signs of trauma or force" were found on the remains except defects on the right thumb and the distal end of the right radius. Such defects were deemed not to be mortal in the usual case. Neither the cause of death nor the cause of these defects could be determined with any degree of certainty even though a lead object, which "exhibited characteristics" of a .22 caliber bullet, was discovered beneath the abdomen of the skeleton.

Clearly this woman's death could only be ascribed to suicide or homicide. A clash of psychiatric views was expressed on the deceased's mental state at the time of her disappearance. There was no disagreement, however, that "no clothing, jewelry, or articles of adornment" were found in the water wagon with the skeletal remains. This factor tipped the scales in favor of homicide as the manner of death in the opinion of the Nebraska Supreme Court.

(ii) The Wounding Instrumentality

When the instrument causing the trauma to bone can be ascertained there is a much greater likelihood of proving that the death resulted from homicide, especially if the defect is found in a bone from a vital area of the body not generally accessible to one bent on suicide.

The trial of Andrew Kokoraleis for murder in Du Page County, Illinois was the prosecution of one of four persons [32] who went on a rape, mutilation and murder rampage in the early 1980s against women in the suburban Chicago area. Frank Orlosky, a Professor of Physical Anthropology at Northern Illinois University, examined the remains of one of the victims, a 21 year old. Orlosky discovered a number of injuries to the victim's bones. Three "small and circular" stab wounds were found in the upper anterior chest which were consistent with an ice pick. There were three stab wounds in the victim's posterior upper body which also were said to be of the ice pick variety. Such evidence was so dispositive of the homicidal nature of the victim's death that the defendant did not dispute that fact on his unsuccessful appeal from his conviction for murder and his sentence to death.

The observation of trauma to bone can lead assuredly and justifiably to homicide as the mode of death. Cutmarks in bone attributable to dismemberment are more than strongly suggestive of homicide, although in one instance it was alleged that the dismemberment was designed to dispose of the remains of a victim of an automobile accident occurring through negligence not the deliberate fault of the accused. [33]

31. 208 Neb. 379, 303 N.W.2d 741 (1981).

32. People v. Spreitzer, 123 Ill.2d 1, 121 Ill.Dec. 224, 525 N.E.2d 30 (1988); People v. Kokoraleis, 149 Ill.App.3d 1000, 103 Ill. Dec. 186, 501 N.E.2d 207 (1986); and one Gecht.

33. People v. Dewey, 42 Ill.2d 148, 246 N.E.2d 232 (1969).

A bullet wound to the skull[34] particularly in the occipital region, is very likely to be a homicide rather than an accidental or suicidal shooting since the back of the head is not the usual site of entry for anything but a homicidal shooting. And if a bone sustains a defensive wound, as for example an ax wound to the hip while the leg of the person struck is drawn up to ward off the blow, then the death can reasonably be said to have resulted from homicide even though the defensive wound itself may not be fatal.

(iii) Peri–, Ante– or Post–Mortem Trauma to Bone

Anthropologists with great regularity have testified that injuries to bone were inflicted at or about the time of death.[35] The fact that such testimony is admitted without objection is suggested by the fact that the appellate courts have chosen not to describe the scientific basis for the anthropologist's testimony on this matter at the trial nor to oppose its admission on any basis. Consequently forensic anthropologists have given evidence that fractures were sustained "at or about the time of death."[36] A bullet wound to the skull was peri-mortem due to the discernible "cracking pattern" in the area of the entrance wound[37] and trauma to the neck was also said to be peri-mortem although the expert's reason for this conclusion was not explained by the appellate court in this instance.[38]

(iv) Bone Trauma as the Cause of Death

Although forensic anthropologists themselves have cautioned against members of their profession declaiming on the subject of the cause of death,[39] still the decisions disclose this is an admonition more to be stated than observed. Trauma to the skull from a hammer[40] has been stated by anthropologists to be fatal in nature. And in the New York murder trial of Jerry Ellis for killing a woman whose body was discovered four years after her disappearance a forensic anthropologist was permitted to testify that "the victim died from stab wounds to the neck."[41] That evidence and the defendant's incriminating admissions to a relative sufficed to support his guilt of murder in the second degree.

In State v. Oody,[42] where the cause of death was uncertain, the anthropologist was allowed to say the death result either from knife or

---

34. State v. Cooper, 794 P.2d 1164 (Kan.1990).

35. People v. St. Pierre, 122 Ill.2d 95, 118 Ill.Dec. 606, 522 N.E.2d 61 (1988); Bassett v. State, 449 So.2d 803 (Fla.1984); supra note 10; supra note 6.

36. State v. Cooper, 794 P.2d 1164 (Kan.1990); Dutton v. State, 452 A.2d 127 (Del.1982).

37. State v. Cooper, supra note 36.

38. State v. Teel, 793 S.W.2d 236 (Tenn. 1990).

39. Mann & Ubelaker, "The Forensic Anthropologist," *FBI Law Enf.Bull.* 20 (Jul. 1990); Sauer & Simson, "Clarifying the Role of Forensic Anthropologists in Death Investigations," 29 *J.For.Sci.* 1081, 1086 (1984).

40. Supra note 35.

41. People v. Ellis, 188 A.D.2d 1043, 592 N.Y.S.2d 200 (1992).

42. 823 S.W.2d 554 (Tex.Cr.App.1991).

ax wounds evidenced by trauma to bone. But when only fragmentary skeletal remains are found and they do not evidence any trauma, it is entirely appropriate for the anthropologist to profess himself unable to determine how the person died.[43]

5. IDENTIFYING THE PERPETRATOR

Forensic anthropologists have been permitted to identify the perpetrators of crimes through anatomical features said to be distinctive to a particular suspect[44] or to a limited class of suspects.[45] The decisions reflect the use of forensic anthropologists for these purposes in the identification of hands[46] or feet[47] that have left their mark at a crime scene or on an incriminating object. The testimony of forensic anthropologists on these occasions patently constitutes a novel application of this scientific discipline to legal questions. There is a significant danger that a permissive judicial attitude towards such testimony will not only allow individual forensic anthropologists to stray beyond the demonstrable limits of their field[48] but that it will also result in the conviction of innocent persons.[49]

A. THE ANALYSIS OF HANDPRINTS

The identification of a perpetrator's hand has drawn the attention of forensic anthropologists in two quite disparate and unique criminal trials, both from Illinois. People v. Hebel[50] was a prosecution for aggravated sexual assault upon a female child of ten. Hebel came to the attention of the authorities through photographs he had retrieved from a processing laboratory which had notified police that a number of the photographs might be pornographic, indicating the occurrence of child abuse. One photograph in particular pictured the thumb and forefinger of a hand spreading open the vaginal orifice of a child identified by marks on her buttocks and thigh as a ten year old house guest of the defendant's daughter. The prosecution sought to connect the defendant to this photograph by expert testimony identifying the hand in the photograph as belonging to the defendant, Hebel.

To accomplish its purpose the prosecution called two experts to testify. One was an expert in photography employed by the F.B.I. He compared the questioned pornographic photograph to a known photo-

---

43. State v. Harris, 1990 WL 171507 (Tenn.Cr.App.1990).

44. People v. Hebel, 174 Ill.App.3d 1, 123 Ill.Dec. 592, 527 N.E.2d 1367 (1988).

45. People v. Columbo, 118 Ill.App.3d 882, 74 Ill.Dec. 304, 455 N.E.2d 733 (1983).

46. Supra notes 44 and 45.

47. People v. Puluti, 120 Cal.App.3d 337, 174 Cal.Rptr. 597 (1st Dist.1981) (op. withdrawn by order of court); State v. Bullard, 312 N.C. 129, 322 S.E.2d 370 (1984).

48. State v. Johnston, Slip Op. (Ohio App. 4th 8/6/86); State v. Harvey, 121 N.J. 407, 581 A.2d 483 (1990).

49. As in the trials of those wrongly charged for the rape/murder of a ten-year old. See details in Buckley v. Fitzsimmons, 919 F.2d 1230 (7th Cir.1990), reversed 113 S.Ct. 2606 (1993).

50. Supra note 44.

graph of Hebel's hand. It was this expert's unopposed opinion that there were a "number of fairly unique characteristics in common" in the photographs but he could not "positively identify both hands to the exclusion of all other people in the world." [51] He summed up his position as being that there were sufficient common features in the photographs of the hands he compared to "strongly suggest" that the hands were of the same person.

However, the second expert for the prosecution, Ellis Kerley, Ph.D., a forensic anthropologist, was considerably more certain that the hands matched. He too compared the known and questioned photographs, making a photocopy of the questioned photograph on which he had red-inked twenty-two points of similarity with the photograph of Hebel's hand. [52] He found no points of dissimilarity. It was his opinion that the "same hand" appeared in both photographs but he admitted that it was "possible" the hands were different. The defense did not object to Dr. Kerley's testimony nor did it introduce contrary expert testimony, but waited to argue on the appeal from Hebel's conviction that the prosecution's evidence was insufficient to prove his guilt. The Illinois appellate court disagreed and affirmed Hebel's conviction.

A much more aggressive and multi-layered defense against the testimony of an anthropologist was lodged in the joint trial of Patricia Columbo and Frank DeLuca for the murders of Columbo's mother, father and thirteen year old brother. [53] In seeking to connect DeLuca to the crime scene the prosecution introduced evidence that a number of gloved handprints were discovered on the Columbo family's car. Since such evidence alone would be a most speculative and tenuous link to DeLuca, the prosecution called Professor Eugene Giles, a University of Illinois anthropology professor, to give his opinion on the identity of the person who had left the gloved-"handprint smudges" on the Thunderbird automobile.

Much to the satisfaction of the prosecution Giles testified that "the handprints on the trunk of the Thunderbird were made by someone missing the index finger of his left hand." [54] Further Giles opined that the handprints were not made by person whose index finger was just raised at the time, rather than missing entirely. It was the presence of "the underlying bone in the palm of the hand" [55] which led him to that conclusion.

Not only did the expert say that the hand was gloved when it left its imprint on the car but he also stated that the hand could have been in a flex position when it touched the car. He reached the latter conclusion from the measurements he made of the gloved handprint and prints "on record." There was a "slight difference in size from the axial tri-radius

51. Supra note 44 at p. 1375.

52. Supra note 44 at p. 1376.

53. Supra note 45.

54. Supra note 45 at p. 787.

55. Supra note 45 at p. 787.

to the tri-radius on the fourth digit and from the central part of the thenar-hypothenar area to the pad area of the fourth digit." [56]

There was much in the terminology in which Giles' opinion was framed that convinced the Illinois reviewing court on DeLuca's appeal from his murder conviction that the subject matter of Giles testimony was "beyond the common experience of the ordinary lay person" requiring and permitting the evidence only of "persons of skill or experience."

The defense also argued that the testimony was novel, untried and lacked the foundational requirement of general acceptance in the scientific community. Without directly replying, the Illinois court said that even if all of this were true, nevertheless Giles' views were admissible in court. Since Giles' opinions were derived from observations without recourse to "high-tech" instrumentation, or in the words of the court, without "intermediate mechanical stages," it would be considered according to a more permissive and favorable legal standard than that which burdens, say for example, the results of polygraph testing.

The defense's last argument that Giles was not qualified as a gloved-handprint expert was equally rejected. Even though Giles had never given court testimony before on that issue and had admitted not knowing of anyone or any literature on any previous testimony of a kindred nature, the Illinois reviewing court held that Giles had the "skill, training and experience" [57] as an expert in handprint measurements and comparisons!

The *Columbo* case was the rare situation when a sturdy and well-orchestrated assault was launched on a forensic anthropologist's testimony. The only item lacking in the defense arsenal was a forensic anthropologist willing to speak out against the methods or the conclusions of Professor Giles.

B. THE ANALYSIS OF FOOT AND SHOE PRINTS

Starting in the early 1980s a pernicious fad took hold among a few forensic anthropologists [58] in which a number of courts promptly became acquiescent complicitors due to their all-too-eager acceptance of this new, untried and unproven pseudo-scientific evidence relating to the identification of footwear or bare feet. A California appeals court dubbed one form of this extension of forensic anthropology "Cinderella analysis" [59] because it was founded on a matching of a suspect, through

---

56. Id.

57. Supra note 45 at p. 790.

58. The late Louise Robins, Ph.D. was the chief proponent of this mephitic fashion. Supra note 270 and State v. Maccia, 311 N.C. 222, 316 S.E.2d 241 (1984). United States v. Ferri, 778 F.2d 985 (3d Cir. 1985). See, Robbins, *Footprints: Collection, Analysis and Interpretation* (1985). For additional discussions on "Shoewear

and Footprint Comparisons," involving some of the same protagonists discussed here, see also § 9.31(3), in Chapter 9 on Trace Evidence. Apart from forensic anthropologists, crime laboratory trace analysts have also been known to testify about such comparisons.

59. People v. Puluti, (op. withdrawn by order of court) supra note 47 first used this appellation.

his bare feet or footwear, to footwear left at a crime scene. In other instances forensic anthropologists have appeared to testify on comparisons between crime scene outsole impressions and a suspect's foot or the insole wear patterns of the footwear of a suspect which concededly did not leave the questioned impression at the crime scene [60] or even to the outsole wear patterns on a shoe, the normal and standard fare of footwear analysts.

Raymond Puluti was accused of murdering his wife in their home and disposing of her body and her personal belongings in a remote area in Northern California. Nearly two years after the unexplained disappearance, her remains were found and identified from dental comparisons. The state's case against Puluti relied on circumstantial evidence. The Cinderella analysis resulted from the finding of a pair of men's shoes with tied laces at the wife's gravesite and a comparison with a number of shoes seized from Puluti's lodging as well as with inked foot impressions obtained from Puluti. These items, of known and unknown origin, were used by the late Louise Robbins, a physical anthropologist then on the faculty of the University of North Carolina, in reaching her conclusion that "the same person who wore defendant's shoes wore the gravesite shoes," and that "the probability of another person being in that location at that time, and the person having those particular combination of features in the foot, would be of an astronomical order." [61]

Dr. Robbins explained her methodology as using a "grid system consisting of points of measurements devised to analyze the pressure points of the feet." This enabled her to examine 68 "points of shape" within 13 major categories of the toe, ball of foot, heel and arch, and to take 46 points of measurement and "7 rations" of measurement (explained as length-to-width). [62] The defendant objected to this testimony as based on a novel scientific theory of an unfounded nature. He also introduced the testimony of his own expert, a podiatrist, to refute it.

The appellate court upheld the admission of the testimony of Dr. Robbins but did not seem persuaded that there was one overriding rationale to do so. After finding that no new experimental techniques were involved since Robbins' analysis was predicated on "accepted techniques, observations, simple measurements and deductive reasoning," the court stated that even if it were a new technique, it fulfilled the requirements of reliability of the methodology, accuracy of the procedures, and competence of the expert. But, said the court, even if the trial court had improperly admitted the evidence, the error in doing so had not prejudiced the defendant who had been linked to the murder by other compelling circumstantial evidence.

Not content to restrict her opinions identifying the wearer of a shoe to situations involving a "Cinderella analysis," Robbins was permitted

---

60. Bird v. State, 594 So.2d 644 (Ala.Cr. App.1990), reversed on other grounds 594 So.2d 676 (Ala.1991).

61. People v. Puluti, supra note 47 (op. withdrawn by order of court).

62. Ibid.

by an Ohio court [63] to say that a boot belonging to a suspect "possibly made" a bootprint at a crime scene even though a leading footwear analyst with the F.B.I. "was not able to determine whether the impression (at the crime scene) was made by any of the (accused's) boots, or whether the print was that of a boot or a bare foot." In this instance Robbins was directly challenged by another forensic anthropologist, Dr. Clyde Snow, who viewed bootprint analysis a la Robbins to be "beyond the field of forensic anthropology." He even questioned the scientific basis for Robbins' opinion. Espousing the incredible view that Robbins' testimony was "relevant and helpful to the finders of fact," the Ohio appellate court sanctioned its admission.

Notwithstanding the fact that Robbins' evidence was all too warmly endorsed by the courts in general, she did suffer occasional setbacks. In People v. Ferguson [64], her opinion that the footwear impression at the crime scene was made by the accused's foot to the exclusion of all others was rejected at the appellate level. And, in an Alabama case,[65] a podiatrist whose technique of comparison relied on the Robbins' approach was found to be unqualified to state his opinion excluding the three defendants' feet as having worn the shoe which made the outsole impressions at the crime scene.

Whereas prints originating from bare feet or footwear are the impressions most often detected at crime scenes, on occasion bloody sockprints are observed. The appellate courts are split as to the acceptability of a forensic anthropologist's identifying a bloody sockprint to an accused's foot. California, in the presence of Dr. Robbins' testimony, allowed such evidence [66] but a New Jersey court [67] would not credit Kent State University Professor Owen Lovejoy with the ability to include a suspect's foot as likely to have created a questioned sockprint even though it did see him as qualified to exclude the suspect by the same process of analysis. The court's unarticulated premises was apparently that a false positive was more to be shunned than a false negative.

Even though the appellate courts have not generally scrutinized the footprint or footwear evidence of forensic anthropologists in as punctilious or as critical a way as they should, the New Jersey Supreme Court in 1990 [68] turned thumbs-down on the tender of the opinion of forensic anthropologist Owen Lovejoy concerning his sex and stature determinations derived solely from his analysis of a bloody sneaker print on a pillow case. Lovejoy had concluded that the print was from a man wearing a shoe size 6½ plus or minus one half or a woman's size 8 to 8½. Aside from the fact that the New Jersey court was unimpressed by Dr. Lovejoy's being the only one in his profession who could vouch for his methods, it was not convinced that his methodology was of "sufficient scientific reliability." It did not aid Dr. Lovejoy's cause that he had

63. State v. Johnston, supra note 48.

64. 172 Ill.App.3d 1, 122 Ill.Dec. 266, 526 N.E.2d 525 (1988).

65. Bird v. State, supra note 60.

66. People v. Knights, 166 Cal.App.3d 46, 212 Cal.Rptr. 307 (1st Dist.1985).

67. State v. Prudden, 212 N.J.Super. 608, 515 A.2d 1260 (1986).

68. State v. Harvey, supra note 48.

examined 31 pairs of sneakers submitted by the Pony Sneaker Company, all of which ranged from size 7 to 11, and then concluded that the print in question was size 6½.

If Lovejoy's testimony had been approved, then the next step might have been for him or another expert to seek to state an opinion on the stature of the individual who had left the bloody shoeprint on the pillow case. The relation between shoe size or foot size and stature has long been accepted among physical anthropologists.[69] Aside from the "idiosyncratic views" of the late Louise Robbins[70] on this matter, the differences among forensic anthropologists on this subject stem from the divergent models they employ in reaching their stature determinations[71] rather than in any fundamental conflict among them on the scientific validity of deriving height from shoe or foot size.

6. THE EVIDENTIAL VALUE OF INSECTS

Entomology is a scientific discipline which is collateral to and complementary of anthropology. Many forensic anthropologists have given in depth study to and engaged in exacting research into the effects of insect activity on human remains and are therefore qualified to testify on such matters.

The subject of insect colonization of human remains has served a variety of purposes in the courts, mainly in criminal law enforcement. A principal, although not an exclusive,[72] use has been in estimating the time that has elapsed since the death of an individual. The decisions have uniformly agreed that estimating the time since death through the deposition and growth of insects on the remains is a proper subject for expert testimony.

The manner in which the opinion on the time of death is stated does not seem to be a matter of concern to the courts. It would appear that vagueness in gauging the time since death[73] as well as rather wide estimates[74] of the time since death are acceptable methods of expressing

---

69. Giles & Vallandigham, "Height Estimation from Foot and Shoeprint Length," 36 *J.For.Sci.* 1134 (1991).

70. Ibid.

71. Ibid.; Gordon & Buikstra, "Linear Marks for the Prediction of Stature From Foot and Boot Dimensions," 37 *J.For.Sci.* 771 (1992); Gordon et al., "Forensic Identification of Height and Weight Using Applied Anthropometry of the Foot," 78 *Am.J.Phys.Anthro.* 230 (1989).

72. Insects can carry traces of the blood or the drugs of the human host upon whom they feed. This recognition has given toxicologists a new approach to detecting toxins and drugs in human remains. McCarthy, "Forensic Entomology," 27 The Prosecutor 10 (Nov./Dec. 1993); Beyer, "Drug Identifi-

cation Through Analysis of Maggots," 25 *J.For.Sci.* 411 (1980). Nolte, "Insect Larvae Used to Detect Cocaine Poisoning in a Decomposed Body," 37 *J.For.Sci.* 1179 (1992). In addition "maggots tend to concentrate in areas of tissue damage" enabling an expert to say that force had been applied to that part of the body. State v. Benner, 40 Ohio St.3d 301, 533 N.E.2d 701, 711 n. 3 (1988).

73. The expert testified that insect larvae made it "quite possible" that the person had died seven months prior to its discovery. State v. Abbott, 654 S.W.2d 260, 266 (Mo.App.1983).

74. The time of death was estimated to be "15 to 19 days prior to (the expert's) examination of the corpse." Wilson v.

an expert's opinion on the significance of insect infestation of human remains.

The qualifications of the expert whose testimony is tendered on the subject of insects have been a matter of some dispute. In People v. Vernon,[75] a police officer was permitted to state that a murder victim had been in a park for at least 24 hours when found by the police. The police officer mentioned such things as the number of insects about the body of the victim as a basis for his opinion. This statement of opinion was approved not as the opinion of a scientific expert but as that of a lay person whose experience had given him a singular knowledge on the matter.

The qualifications of persons appearing as experts on entomology have been questioned even when the expert is not asked for an opinion on the time of death of a person from insect activity on the remains. In Pasco v. State,[76] it was entomologist Neal Haskell's assistant who analyzed the samples of insects submitted by a pathologist. Haskell, not having participated in the actual casework, was called to testify in general to the time necessary for fly larvae to appear. An objection to his qualifications was rejected when he was shown to be matriculating for a master's degree in entomology and that he had conducted ninety forensic entomological examinations as well as that he had written and lectured extensively in the field.

But another court [77] was skeptical of the claims of an anthropologist who, it felt, had dabbled beyond judicial or even scientific acceptance in entomological affairs. Michael Kinney had disappeared on May 8, 1985 while en route to his college classes in Aberdeen, South Dakota. Two days later a demand for $200,000 for the return of Kinney was received. Upon the payment of the ransom money to Michael Miller, he was arrested by police who had kept the ransom exchange site under surveillance. Thereafter the body of the victim, exhibiting trauma from bludgeoning and bullet strikes, was discovered in an abandoned local icehouse. Dr. Rodriguez, an anthropologist, was called to testify on the time that the body had been in the icehouse since death. His estimate, based on insect larvae infestations of the body and photographs of the decomposing body, was 18 to 20 days.

On Miller's appeal from his murder conviction, the South Dakota Supreme Court deprecated Rodriguez' testimony as based on extrapolations from a "unique study" in which "his methodology (was) completely untested by other scientists." The *Frye* rule of general acceptance, which governed the admissibility of such scientific testimony in South Dakota, was held not to have been satisfied, but the murder conviction was upheld by force of other, overwhelming evidence of Miller's guilt.

Commonwealth, 836 S.W.2d 872, 877 (Ky. 1992). The victim was said to have died "at least twelve hours" prior to the autopsy "due to the large number of maggots detected." State v. Pridgen, 313 N.C. 80, 326 S.E.2d 618, 621 (1985).

75. 89 Cal.App.3d 853, 152 Cal.Rptr. 765 (3d Dist.1979).

76. 563 N.E.2d 587, 594 (Ind.1990).

77. State v. Miller, supra note 23 (see comment there).

Whether the South Dakota court had been apprised of, or whether it would have given weight to, the two published reports of Rodriguez's studies of insect infestation of cadavers is unknown.[78] The court might also have noted the unchallenged receipt of the evidence of one David Faulkner, an entomologist, in the California decision of People v. Hamilton.[79] Faulkner there described an experiment he conducted in order to gauge the onset of insect infestation in a human cadaver left unburied, without its head or hands. He took a rabbit, severed its head and paws (to mimic the crime victim's condition) and in the dead of night (at midnight) put it where the victim had been discovered. This innovative and grisly experiment enabled Faulkner to assert the earliest time when the body would have been put where it was found. He did, however, admit to "a great deal of variation" in the matter.

The decisions reflect that experts have based their opinions on the time of infestation upon a number of factors. Generally it is the size of the larvae that will be used to determine their stage of development [80] but the number of them has also been said to be an important determinant.[81] In the *John* case [82] F.B.I. entomologist Wayne Lord indicated that the "mouth parts" of maggots depicted in photographs of their presence on a dead body were an aid to his identification of their stage of development. And in Scott v. Commonwealth,[83] the state anthropologist premised his time of death opinion upon his knowledge that the insects observed on the remains were present only in the summer.

There is no doubt from the decisions that experts consider the weather to be of signal import in deciding upon the developmental life cycle of insects discovered on human remains.[84] In Earhart v. State,[85] when the time of death determination of an expert was challenged as not having taken into account the influence of weather conditions on the generation of maggots the expert hastened to change her opinion. And in Taylor v. State,[86] when a forensic entomologist used the climate of Salina, Kansas, the city where the remains of a deceased wife had been found, for his aging predictions from maggot development, a forensic anthropologist contested these conclusions since they were said to be based on the wrong climate. It was "the micro-climate scene where the flies were actually feeding and laying their eggs on the body" [87] which should have been the weather standard, this opposing expert said. And

78. Rodriguez & Bass, "Decomposition of Buried Bodies and Methods that May Aid in Their Location," 30 *J.For.Sci.* 836 (1985); Rodriguez & Bass, "Insect Activity and Its Relationship to Decay Rates of Human Cadavers in East Tennessee," 28 *J.For.Sci.* 423 (1983).

79. 41 Cal.3d 408, 221 Cal.Rptr. 902, 710 P.2d 981 (1985), petition for habeas corpus denied 45 Cal.3d 351, 247 Cal.Rptr. 31, 753 P.2d 1109 (1988).

80. State v. John, 210 Conn. 652, 557 A.2d 93, 106 (1989).

81. Lee v. State, 545 N.E.2d 1085 (Ind. 1989); State v. Pridgen, supra note 74 at 621.

82. Supra note 80.

83. 685 S.W.2d 184 (Ky.1984).

84. Taylor v. State, 251 Kan. 272, 834 P.2d 1325, 1337 (1992).

85. 823 S.W.2d 607, 613 (Tex.Cr.App. 1991). On remand from 113 S.Ct. 3026 (1993), affirmed 877 S.W.2d 759 (Tex.Crim. App.1994).

86. Supra note 84.

87. Supra note 84 at p. 1337.

assuming the accuracy of this assertion, the fact that reliance on the "micro-environmental conditions" [88] might render the expert's opinion somewhat less precise has not been held to be an obstacle to the admission of conclusions founded on such guesstimates. [89]

In the absence of an actual specimen, either alive or dead, of a maggot taken from a dead body, one court [90] authorized an expert to judge its stage of development from a photograph of maggots feeding on the remains. Photography has also been important where the prosecutor wishes to quicken the pulse and disturb the viscera of the jury by the sight of maggots devouring a dead body. The obvious prosecutorial strategy is to use such pictorial representations to harden the jurors' minds and hearts against the person accused of killing the victim.

Even though such photographs "are gruesome and tend to incite the passions" [91] of the jury, they are admissible if they are employed to explain and illustrate the basis for an expert's opinion when it is contingent on an analysis of the maggots depicted in the photographs, [92] or when the maggot infestation supports an expert's opinion on the time of death. [93]

A worst case scenario in the utilization of visual depictions of maggots leeching on human remains is reported in State v. Klafta. [94] Sharon Anne Klafta was charged with attempted murder for the abandonment of her 16 month old daughter, Heather. The bruised, dehydrated and maggot-rife body of the child was found on the bank of a lake. Despite the battered condition of the child she survived the tragic incident.

On the trial of the mother, Dr. Goff, an entomologist, testified to the life cycle of the maggots found on Heather and their importance in appraising the time of her abandonment. Even though the Hawaii Supreme Court recognized that "evidence of maggot infestation is revolting to a person of ordinary sensibilities," it did not find the visual evidence received at the trial to have been out of order. The state's "horrific" [95] presentation included several photographs of Heather's naked body being consumed by maggots, revealing red sores created by the burrowing maggots in her vaginal area. The photographs showed the baby's body in a number of different positions with the maggots actively feeding on her.

In addition to these "horrific" photographs the state's expert gave a slide show of the life cycle of a fly with "color magnifications" of the fly in its various stages of worm, larva and fly development. The slides included close-ups of the "incisor-like cutting edges" in the mouth of the larvae. To further complement its presentation on this matter and to

88. People v. Clark, 6 Cal.App.3d 658, 86 Cal.Rptr. 106, 109 (5th Dist.1970).

89. Ibid.

90. Taylor v. State, supra note 84.

91. Bond v. State, 273 Ind. 233, 403 N.E.2d 812, 817 (1980).

92. Ibid.

93. Knoppa v. State, 505 S.W.2d 802, 803 (Tex.Cr.App.1974).

94. 73 Hawaii 109, 831 P.2d 512 (1992).

95. Id. at 521.

cement its case against the abandoning mother "two vials of maggots" and two slides of maggots which had been removed from Heather's body were put into evidence for the jury's attentive consideration. None of this was perceived on review to warrant either a retrial or an admonition to the prosecutor for this over-indulgence in graphic and lurid details.

7. THE FORENSIC ANTHROPOLOGIST IN CIVIL TRIALS

Civil actions, unlike criminal prosecutions, are designed to provide relief, generally monetary, to aggrieved individuals. The number of possible applications of forensic anthropology in such civil actions is much more limited than in criminal proceedings since the death of a person tends to generate more criminal than civil law investigative interest. Consequently it is not at all surprising to find only a handful of appellate court decisions on the use of forensic anthropologists in civil suits in contrast to their vast usage in criminal trials.

It is particularly in tort actions concerning the mishandling of the dead either "by multilation (sic), disinterment, interference with proper burial or other forms of intentional disturbance" [96] that the services of a forensic anthropologist have been sought. So when a land developer bought a tract of land upon which a cemetery was located and his excavations jeopardized the graves of those buried there, a suit was brought [97] by the relatives of those interred in the cemetery plots to forestall the development. The defense countered with the testimony of a forensic anthropologist that "he had discovered no evidence of graves in the excavated area" and that "he was of the opinion that no graves had been destroyed or removed" by the excavation. In spite of such persuasive testimony, unrefuted by any opposing expert, the court granted an injunction against the land development unless certain protective conditions were fulfilled.

Those who are charged with wrongdoing in the mishandling of dead bodies tend to be those obliged, by contract or by law, with the disposition of deceased persons. Morticians and crematoriums lead the list of those who have been sued by distraught relatives of a deceased person. [98] In one such action [99] a neonate died on the day of birth and was cremated. Apparently the cremation occurred as stipulated but the child's parents refused to accept the ashes, saying they were not those of their deceased child. When the crematorium conceded that the wrong cremated remains had been delivered to the parents, a court order was sought requiring the disclosure of the record of cremations of a number

---

96. Prosser and Keeton, *The Law of Torts* 63 (5th Ed.1984).

97. *Westmoreland v. Goldston,* slip op., Tenn.Ct.App., 1/20/84.

98. Ruth Wiese sued a mortuary for not cremating her husband in a timely fashion. L.A. Times, part 2, p. 3, col. 1 (1/21/87). A Seattle woman sued a funeral home for returning her husband's clothing along

with some of his body parts. A class action was certified in Los Angeles when eight people complained that a crematory had mixed cremated remains. *L.A. Times,* part B, p. 6, col. 1, 5/8/93.

99. Mangialino v. White Haven Memorial Park, 132 A.D.2d 970, 518 N.Y.S.2d 532 (4th Dept.1987).

of other individuals at or about the same time as the cremation of the plaintiff's daughter. The defense successfully argued against this disclosure with the support of the opinion of a "professor of forensic anthropology" that "it is not scientifically possible to determine from examination of cremated remains that they are the remains of a particular individual." [100] Of course if the cremated remains had included intact artifacts associated with the deceased and no one else, such as a dental post or surgical clips, say from a mastectomy, then the remains would bear the stamp of a recognizable and identifiable person.

As in the case of criminal prosecutions, civil proceedings most often involve the purported identification of a particular person whose identity is in question. Mass disasters resulting from airplane crashes, terrorist attacks or the like can produce perplexing problems of identification of the dead. And when a misidentification is asserted to have occurred, then a tort action may follow for compensation for the grief of those nearest to the person misidentified. One such case occupied the attention of the government, the Federal courts, and a slew of forensic anthropologists over many years in the recent past.[101]

Anne Hart was the wife of Lt. Col. Thomas Hart who was a member of a crew of sixteen aboard a U.S. Air Force plane shot down in Laos on December 21, 1972. The incident became known as the Pakse crash. Until 1973 only two members of the sixteen persons aboard were known to have survived the crash. The others were listed as M.I.A.s. In 1973, an American reconnaisance plane photographed an area in Northern Laos, some three hundred miles from the Pakse crash site, which revealed a signal which gave rise to the hope that Lt. Col. Hart was still alive. But in 1978 without having notified Mrs. Hart of the aerial photography the Army changed Lt. Col. Hart's status from missing to killed in action.

Not until Mrs. Hart and others on a visit to the Pakse crash site in September 1982 discovered two bone fragments did the Army institute a thorough canvassing of the area for other marks of the crew members of the downed plane. When an excavation disclosed 50,000 bone and dental fragments along with personal effects, including dog tags, the Army's Central Identification Laboratory in Hawaii was called to the task of sorting out these items to effect the needed identifications. Upon the completion of the C.I.L.'s analysis Lt. Col. Hart was said to have been identified, through the process of exclusion, as one of the casualties whose bones were among those submitted for examination.

Mrs. Hart obtained her own analysis of the seven bone fragments said to be from her husband from an independent forensic anthropologist. That expert concluded that these fragments could not be said to be those of Lt. Col. Hart nor could they be said to be from one person or several.

---

100. Id. at 533.

101. Hart v. United States, 681 F.Supp. 1518 (N.D.Fla.1988), reversed Hart v. United States, 894 F.2d 1539 (11th Cir.1990).

The Army's rejoinder was to hire its own forensic anthropologists to revisit the bone identifications by the C.I.L. The upshot was that eleven of the thirteen supposed identifications could not be confirmed. One of the forensic anthropologists, Dr. William Maples, called the Army's Hawaii laboratory's misuse of proper identification standards "blatant." As a result the identification of Lt. Col. Hart was rescinded but his name was not returned to the unaccounted for list.

Mrs. Hart and other surviving relatives of Lt. Col. Hart commenced suit in a Federal court in Florida to recover money damages for the Army's conduct in its flip-flopping over the identification of Lt. Col. Hart. The claim was based on the Federal Tort Claims Act. Whereas the Federal trial court agreed with the Harts' claim and awarded them one million dollars in damages, that verdict was overturned on appeal.

In reversing, the Federal appeals court failed to find anything but discretionary acts performed by the military in connection with the identification of Hart's remains. And the untoward suffering caused by discretionary acts is outside the allowable bases for a Federal Tort Claims Act suit by the explicit terms of the act.

The fact that the Army's own reviewing team of forensic anthropologists had reported that the Hawaii laboratory had no standard protocol for such a mass disaster identification proved the discretionary nature of the Army's undertaking, so the Federal appeals court said. Each "individual forensics examiner" was given the latitude to decide how much to rely upon any standards of any kind. Indeed "ordinary forensic standards" were deemed "inappropriate in cases such as the Pakse crash, when the remains of a number of persons are commingled, severely burned and shattered." [102]

The arbitrariness of the Army's scientific investigation, rather than buttressing Mrs. Hart's claim of outrageous governmental behavior, was a petard, not of her own doing, upon which she was hoisted. The appeals court viewed the individual examiner's right to choose whatever method of identification he wished under the circumstances to be clear evidence of the discretionary, unregularized nature of the C.I.L.'s identification process. And the emotional fallout to the Hart relatives from this discretionary action was said not to be recoverable in damages from the government.

For the purpose of recovering the proceeds of life insurance policies, the identification of the insured as deceased is fundamental. Regardless of whether the insured died from accidental, homicidal, suicidal or natural causes or even from an undetermined event, the fact of death is of overarching importance to the beneficiaries' recovery on a life insurance policy. In this regard, the expert services of a forensic anthropologist or even those whose talents are deemed equivalent to those of a

---

102. Hart v. United States, 894 F.2d 1539, 1545 (11th Cir.1990).

forensic anthropologist can be paramount as was proved in Roberts v. Wabash Life Ins. Co.[103]

Clarence Roberts had disappeared in November 1970 under mystifying conditions. On the 18th of that month his rural Indiana barn burned to the ground destroying all but his pick-up truck within it. The charred remains of a body was found outside the barn with a shotgun lying athwart it. Although the shotgun had been discharged, its position across the body did not comport with that expected from its deliberate discharge, if suicide was the intent. Strangely, the body bore no evidence of having been shot.

Investigation revealed that Roberts, prior to his disappearance, had suffered cataclysmic financial losses. When lawsuits were filed against him he became morose and despondent, even hinting of suicide. The possibility of suicide could not be discounted.

On the suspicious side, Roberts had spoken of having substantial sums deposited in a Swiss bank account. Several persons recalled seeing Roberts in the company of an unidentified man on the day of the barn fire. That man was a Roberts look-alike in stature and size and was known to have suffered a seizure of sorts while with Roberts, necessitating Roberts' putting the man into his car.

The autopsy on the charred remains disclosed the presence of 80 to 86% carbon monoxide in the blood but no fire residues in the respiratory passage. The pick-up truck which had been salvaged from the barn had "thirty or more" mighty questionable, apparently deliberately-inflicted holes in its exhaust system.

Various scientific tests, such as blood typing and dental identification, gave force to the suggestion that Roberts had killed a stranger, substituted him for himself and then vanished on the expectation that his family would have the benefit of his $640,000 in life insurance proceeds.

But the life insurance carrier balked at paying without firmer proof that this was not a concocted swindle being foisted on it by the alive but unlocated Roberts. At the trial on the action of Mrs. Roberts to recover on the life policies, opposing views were presented by a profusion of experts including radiologists, anthropologists, pathologists, dentists and others. An anthropologist retained by the claimant-wife submitted a most equivocal opinion, one almost as impenetrable as the question of whether Roberts was dead or alive. According to this expert [104] "there has been nothing discovered in a morphological comparison that would be incompatible with the identification of the cadaver as that of Clarence Roberts."

John Kennedy, a high profile arson investigator and author of writings on arson, examined both the scene of the fire and the charred bones. He was permitted to express his opinion that the limbs had first

---

103. 78 Ind.Dec. 731, 410 N.E.2d 1377 (1980).   **104.** Id. at 1386 footnote 4.

been removed and then the body had been doused with a flammable liquid and ignited. The introduction of that opinion at the trial was upheld by the Indiana appellate court since Kennedy professed to having investigated many fires "in which burned bodies were found" and to have researched the matter of burned bodies for a book he had authored. Neither trial nor appellate court was convinced that the charred remains had proven to be those of Roberts. Consequently the life insurance company's disclaimer of liability was upheld.

V.   TRIAL AIDS

§ 17.12   Locating and Selecting a Forensic Anthropologist

Unlike other scientific specialties in the forensic sciences, forensic anthropologists tend to be available to all who seek their professional assistance. Rarely are forensic anthropologists full-time employees of law enforcement-staffed or funded laboratories. Sometimes there is an affiliation with the office of a medical examiner but more commonly these experts are positioned in the academic departments of universities or in natural history museums in the various states. The anthropology program at the University of Tennessee at Knoxville, under the tutelage of its former chairman, William Bass, Ph.D., has been in the forefront of training forensic anthropologists. Anyone who has matriculated from that program is blessed with very special talents and credentials. As a consequence of the employment of forensic anthropologists in neutral and impartial pursuits they are regularly available to both prosecution and defense in criminal cases and to both sides in civil litigation.

The American Academy of Forensic Sciences[1] lists about 160 persons as being affiliated in various categories of membership in its Section of Physical Anthropology. About forty of those listed are student members. Another forty or so have successfully completed the professional and examination requirements of the American Board of Forensic Anthropology, an arm of the Forensic Sciences Foundation, and have the privilege of describing themselves as Diplomates. Presumptively these persons are the most qualified.

Forensic anthropologists are a close-knit confraternity of persons. Thus they are able to give frank and candid evaluations of the positions taken by fellow forensic anthropologists on matters of a legal import as well as on the research accomplishments of others in the field. It is well to recall that forensic anthropologists are well-schooled in radiology and allied disciplines so that they may provide informed judgments on many issues on the periphery of forensic anthropology properly so called.

§ 17.12

1.   P.O. Box 669, Colorado Springs, Colo. 80901–0669. Tel: 719–636–1100.

VI. MISCELLANEOUS

§ 17.13   Bibliography of Additional References

Anderson, *The Human Skelton: A Manual for Archaeologists* (1962).

Angel, "Bones Can Fool People," 43 *F.B.I.Law Enf.Bull.* 17 (1974).

Anno, "Admissibility of expert opinion testimony concerning identification of skeletal remains," 18 A.L.R.4th 1294.

Arensburg, "Methods for Age Identification on Living Individuals of Uncertain Age," 22 *Can.Soc.Forens.Soc.J.* 147 (1989).

Bass, "Forensic Anthropology: The American Experience" in Boddington, et al., editors, *Death, Decay and Reconstruction* (1987).

Berryman, "Anthropology as Applied to Forensic Science," 13 *Crime Lab.Dig.* 38 (Apr. 1986).

Boyd, "Buried Body Cases," 48 *F.B.I.Law Enf.Bull.* 1 (1979).

Buickstra, "A for Odyssey," 7 *Crim.Just.Rev.* 7 (1982).

Catts & Haskell, *Entomology and Death: A Procedural Guide* (1990).

Dorsey, "A Sexual Study of the Size of the Articular Surfaces of the Long Bones in Aboriginal American Skeletons," 137 *Boston Med. & Surg.J.* 80 (1897).

Dorsey, "The Skeleton in Medico–Legal Anatomy," 16 *Chicago Med. Rptr.* 172 (1899).

Dwight, "Methods of Estimating the Height from Parts of the Skeleton," 40 *Med.Rec.* 293 (1894).

Easton & Smith, "The Entomology of the Cadaver," 10 *Med.Sci. & L.* 208 (1970).

Erzinclioglu, "On the Interpretation of Maggot Evidence in Forensic Cases," 30 *Med.Sci. & L.* 65 (1990).

Erzinclioglu, "Te Entomological Investigation of a Concealed Corpse," 25 *Med.Sci. & L.* 228 (1985).

Evans, *Studies on the Anatomy and Function of Bones and Joints* (1966).

Iscan & Kennedy, editors, *Reconstruction of Life from the Skeleton* (1993).

Iten, "Identification of Skulls by Video Superimposition," 32 *J.For.Sci.* 173 (1987).

Kania, "Joining Anthropology and Law Enforcement," 11 *J.Crim.Jus.* 495 (1983).

Kennedy, "Morphological Variations in UlnarSupinator Crests and Fossae as Identifying Markers of Occupational Stress," 28 *J.For.Sci.* 871 (1983).

Kerley, "Forensic Anthropology: Increasing Utility in Civil and Criminal Cases," *Trial* 66 (Jan. 1983).

Krogman, *The Human Skeleton in Forensic Medicine* (1966).

Krogman, "Role of the OPhysical Anthropologist in the Identification of Human Skeletal Remains," 12 *F.B.I.Law Enf.Bull.* 17 (1943).

Lan, "Development and Current Status of Skull–Image Superimposition—Methodology and Instrumentation," 4 *For.Sci.Rev.* 126 (Dec. 1992).

Lovis, "Forensic Archaeology as Mortuary Anthropology," 34 *Soc.Sci. Med.* 113 (1992).

Mann, "Time Since Death and Decomposition of the Human Body: Variables and Observations in Case and Experimental Field Studies," 35 *J.For.Sci.* 103 (1990).

Maples, *Dead Men Do Tell Tales* (1994).

Ortner, "Description and Classification of Degenerative Bone Changes in the Distal Joint Surfaces of the Humerus," 28 *Am.J.Phys.Anthro.* 139 (1968).

Reichs, "Quantified Comparison of Frontal Sinus Patterns by Means of Computed Tomography," 61 *For.Sci.Internat'l.* 141 (1993).

Reichs, "The Use of Computed Tomography (CT) Scans in the Comparison of Frontal Sinus Configurations," 25 *Can.Soc.Forens.Sci.J.* 1 (1992).

Robbins, "Anthropological Methodologies Applied to Medico-legal Problems," 7 *Crim.Just.Rev.* 2 (1982).

Robbins, "The Individuality of Human Footprints," 23 *J.For.Sci.* 78 (1978).

Saunders et al., "A Test of Several Methods of Skeletal Age Estimation Using a Documented Archaeological Sample," 25 *Can.Soc.Forens.Sci.J.* 97 (1992).

Snow, "Forensic Anthropology," 11 *Ann.Rev.Anthro.* 97 (1982).

Snow et al., "The Reconstruction of Facial Features from the Skull: An Evaluation of Its Usefulness in Forensic Anthropology," 33 *Am.J.Phys.Anthro.* 221 (1970).

Stewart, "The Growth of American Physical Anthropology Between 1925 and 1975," 48 *Anthropological Q.* 193 (1975).

Stewart, "History of Physical Anthropology," in *Perspectives on Anthropology,* ed. A.F.C. Wallace et al. (1977).

Stewart, *Essentials of Forensic Anthropology* (1979).

Stewart, "Background of American Forensic Anthropology," 7 *Crim. Just.Rev.* 4 (1982).

Stewart, "George A. Dorsey's Role in the Luetgart Case: A Significant Episode in the History of Forensic Anthropology," 23 *J.For.Sci.* 786 (1978).

Tagaya, "Development of a Generalized Discriminant Function for Cross–Population Determination of Sex from Long Bones of the Arm and Leg," 22 *Can.Soc.Forens.Sci.J.* 159 (1989).

Ubelaker et al., "Computer–Assisted Photographic Superimposition," 37 *J.For.Sci.* 750 (1992).

Wecht, editor, "Forensic Anthropology" as Chapter 27 in *Forensic Sciences* (1993).

Wigmore, "The Luetgart Case," 32 *Am.Law.Rev.* 187 (1898).

Yoshino, et al., "Classification System of Frontal Sinus Patterns by Radiography: Its Application to Identification of Unknown Skeletal Remains," 34 *For.Sci.Internat'l* 289 (1987).

Yoshino & Seta, "Personal Identification of the Human Skull: Superimposition and Radiographic Techniques," 1 *For.Sci.Rev.* 24 (June 1989).

Yoshino et al., "Classification System of Frontal Sinus Patterns," 22 *Can.Soc.Forens.Sci.J.* 135 (1989).

*

PART IV

BEHAVIORAL SCIENCE EVIDENCE

The ever more pervasive use of experts in the behavioral sciences, while a topic for many books, cannot be ignored in a text on expert testimony in civil and criminal cases. Within the confines of this single volume, we have chosen to discuss selected topics dealing with testimony generated by mental health professionals testifying as experts in criminal and civil cases. The difficult selection process in deciding what aspect of psychologists' and psychiatrists' legal interactions ought to be discussed required making choices between a number of competing options.

In Chapter 18, we chose to deal with psychiatric and psychological evidence in a general way, explaining for the reader the broad fields of psychiatry, psychology and neurology. In Chapter 19 we addressed specific types of cases where use of mental health practitioners' expertise is often required at trial. The ever important insanity defense could, of course, not be ignored. This also encompasses a variety of related topics, such as the proliferation of "syndrome" testimony, the issues of competency to stand trial, including the synthetic creation of "competency" by the use of psychotropic drugs. Involuntary civil commitment is an important component of behavioral scientists' legal interactions and was also briefly explored. In both civil and criminal arenas, testimony on the unreliability of event witnesses' recollections could not be ignored, and use of mental health experts in litigation involving child custody, child abuse, and other family matters is widespread.

The section on the behavioral sciences would be woefully incomplete without some discussion on the detection of deception by various methods, including use of the polygraph, hypnosis, narcoanalysis and voice stress analysis. These topics comprise the final chapter of the book.

Chapter 18

PSYCHIATRY, PSYCHOLOGY
AND NEUROLOGY

I. INTRODUCTION

VI.   MISCELLANEOUS MATTERS

I.   INTRODUCTION

§ 18.01   Scope of the Chapter

The concepts of mental illness and mental impairment frequently engender legal sequelae in the lives of patients. These sequelae bring these patients in contact with the courts in civil as well as in criminal cases, and the purposes of therapists and lawyers are frequently at odds. The legal concept of insanity as a criminal defense, for instance, is predicated on responsibility for acts committed by free will. Psychiatric theory, on the other hand, is based on determinism which perceives causation scientifically in terms of mental illness or impairment. The concept of legal insanity has as its premise the belief that normal human beings are rational beings with the power to choose between right and wrong conduct. Thus, society will exempt from criminal responsibility those persons whose state of mind at the time of an offense conforms to the definition of insanity adopted by the jurisdiction where the crime occurred.

Mental health practitioners' purposes may also be at odds with those of the legal system when courts require them to perform tasks which they are ill equipped to undertake. In civil actions to commit involuntarily an incompetent person, for instance, psychiatrists and psychologists are frequently asked to predict the future behavior of such an individual. Yet, the mental health practitioners profess no special expertise in that field, as may also be seen in the next chapter's section on Predicting Future Dangerousness. The healing responsibilities of mental health practitioners may be compromised in yet other ways by the demands the courts place upon them. Thus, when a psychiatrist is required by law to inform potential victims of a patient's threats to that person,[1] it may well be doubted whether the relationship of trust

---

§ 18.01

1. In 1976, the California Supreme Court held that a mental health professional who had reason to believe a patient intended to kill or seriously injure a third person, had a duty to take whatever steps were reasonably necessary to protect those identifiable persons. See, Tarasoff v. Regents of the University of California, 17 Cal.3d 425, 131 Cal.Rptr. 14, 551 P.2d 334 (1976). Failure to warn intended victims may expose the professional to a negligence action. Since then, many states have adopted some version of the "duty to warn" either by case law or statute. See, e.g., McIntosh v. Milano, 168 N.J.Super. 466, 403 A.2d 500 (1979); Lipari v. Sears, Roebuck and Co., 497 F.Supp. 185 (D.Neb. 1980); Petersen v. State, 100 Wash.2d 421, 671 P.2d 230 (1983); Peck v. Counseling Service of Addison County, 146 Vt. 61, 499 A.2d 422 (1985). See also, Crocker, "Judicial expansion of the Tarasoff doctrine: doctor's dilemma," 13 *J. Psychiatry & Law* 88 (1985). Even where no law exists requiring such warning, mental health per-

between therapist and patient can ever be repaired by what the patient may see as a serious betrayal of confidence.

It is not the purpose of this chapter, and its succeeding one, to fully explore the broad scope of psychiatric, psychological, and neurological principles, and document all interactions with the legal system. Instead, it is the purpose of this chapter to explore general concepts about the mental health professions and to attempt to bridge the gap between lawyers and behavioral scientists by increasing the understanding of lawyers about mental health practitioners. In the next chapter, we will discuss more specific applications of the behavioral science professions; the selection of these topics included was made because of the frequency with which they feature as issues in civil and criminal litigation.

In exploring psychiatry, psychology, and neurology in this chapter and the next, it will come as no surprise that lawyers generally do not view the professionals in the behavioral sciences as being "scientists." They are frequently portrayed as individuals whose opinions are for sale to the highest bidder or who are easily duped by clever malingerers, pretenders, or criminals.[2] Such exaggeration bespeaks of a lack of understanding of the differences between law and the healing arts. Sweeping condemnations of the roles of psychiatrists and psychologists as obstructing rather than promoting justice ignore the fact that a serious body of empirical research and clinical experience underlies most expert testimony in these fields. There is also a much higher level of agreement among mental health professionals in making psychiatric diagnoses than lay persons, such as lawyers, suspect.

Despite these concerns, psychiatric expert testimony has long been accorded admissibility in a wide variety of legal disputes. The primary and adjunctive roles of the clinical psychologist in administering psychological tests which are used as diagnostic aids in determining the mental status or capacity of a patient are of a more recent vintage, though today, most states now recognize the psychologist as an independent expert in diagnosing, describing, and evaluating mental illness by psychological testing.[3] This chapter also explores the role of the neurologist in assessing competency and insanity through medical investigation for organic dysfunction of the brain. Since one of the more common

---

sons prudently ought to behave as if such a duty existed.

2. Weinstock, "Ethical Concerns Expressed by Forensic Psychiatrists," 31 *J.For.Sci.* 596 (1986).

3. In Jenkins v. United States, 307 F.2d 637 (D.C.Cir.1962), a federal appeals court held that a properly trained psychologist is competent to render an expert opinion based on findings as to the presence of mental disease or defect. Among the state cases are: People v. Davis, 62 Cal.2d 791, 44 Cal.Rptr. 454, 402 P.2d 142 (1965); State v. Donahue, 141 Conn. 656, 109 A.2d 364 (1954), app. dismissed and cert. denied

349 U.S. 926 (1955); People v. McDarrah, 175 Ill.App.3d 284, 529 N.E.2d 808 (1988); State v. Tull, 240 Md. 49, 212 A.2d 729 (1965); People v. Hawthorne, 293 Mich. 15, 291 N.W. 205 (1940); In re Masters, 216 Minn. 553, 13 N.W.2d 487 (1944); Knoeppel v. State, 382 S.W.2d 493 (Tex.Cr.App. 1964); Decker v. Hatfield, 798 S.W.2d 637 (Tex.App.1990); Rollins v. Commonwealth, 207 Va. 575, 151 S.E.2d 622 (1966), cert. denied 386 U.S. 1026 (1967); Schindler v. Schindler, 776 P.2d 84 (Utah App.1989). But see, State v. Alexander, 252 La. 564, 211 So.2d 650 (1968). See also the authorities cited, infra.

neurologically demonstrable species of mental impairment is psychomotor epilepsy, the major part of the discussion of organic neurological disorders is devoted to a consideration of the neurologist's role in diagnosing epilepsy.

§ 18.02 Some Common Psychiatric and Psychological Terms and Their Meaning

The following glossary of terms was compiled from numerous medical texts. Its purpose is to make some of the terminology used in psychiatric, psychological and neurological reports and testimony more understandable to attorneys who often must translate them into language the jury can understand. Some of the terms are no longer considered proper terminology by the mental health profession, but are nevertheless still used by its practitioners and by lawyers. The glossary that follows should not be viewed as a complete "dictionary" of the professional terminology that exists in the behavioral sciences, but only a listing of some commonly used terms.

Affect: Observable behavior pattern caused by subjectively experienced emotion or mood, which may be characterized by a reduction in the range of expressions deemed normal within a society, or in their intensity, or in their inappropriateness. Examples are euphoria, sadness, anger. Blunted affect is the lack of an affective reaction when one would be expected. Inappropriate affect is one that is discordant with the content of speech, i.e., laughing while discussing a family member's death. Labile affect is when there is a frequent shift from one mood to an opposite mood expression, without an apparent reason for the shift.

Affective Disorders: Group of mental disorders, also called mood disorders, affecting emotions ranging from severe depression to uncontrolled elation and mania, among them: (1) *Bipolar Disorder.* Patient has history of episodes of elation with or without a history of depression. Manic depressive illness. Cyclothymic disorder; and (2) *Unipolar Disorder.* Illness characterized by a history of depression without any history of elation. Major depressive disorder. Dysthymic disorder.

Aggressive Reaction: Personality disorder (not a neurosis or psychosis) characterized by resentment, irritability, or temper tantrums from inability to cope with inner frustrations, manifesting itself in a forceful, physical, verbal or symbolic attack.

Alcoholic Hallucinosis: A condition produced by excessive alcohol intake in which the subject hears voices which appear to persecute and abuse him.

Alcoholism, Acute: Drunkenness caused by the absorption of an amount of alcohol that impairs control of motor, speech, and other skills.

Alcoholism, Chronic: Condition attributable to absorption of excessive alcohol over an extended interval of time.

Alpha Waves: Normal electric discharges of the frontal and occipital parts of the brain obtained by measurement with an electroencephalograph machine.

Amnesia: Loss of memory resulting from organic trauma, delirium, lesions of the brain, hysteria, or epilepsy. Functionally, identity loss can represent a means of coping with neurotic conflict. Common types of amnesia are: (1) Anterograde: inability to retain new impressions; may be a feature of senility; and (2) Retrograde: inability to recall prior experiences.

Antisocial Personality: A personality disorder, not amounting to a psychosis or neurosis, featuring chronic antisocial behavior, unresponsiveness to punishment and inability to profit by experience.

Anxiety: An unpleasant affective state with the expectation but not the certainty of impending danger; sometimes manifested as a sense of fear that is poorly understood by the subject and which arises without justifiable cause. The anxious state may have overtones of "impending" danger rather than present danger.

Anxiety Neurosis: Neurosis in which anxiety is the predominant symptom.

Aphasia: Inability to utter, write or understand once familiar language, words, or objects; often caused by organic brain disorder.

Apoplexy: Syndrome resulting from sudden hemorrhage within the brain or from an abrupt blocking of a blood vessel in the brain.

Arteriosclerosis: Abnormal thickening and hardening of arterial walls.

Ataxia: Condition involving impaired coordinative control over the extremities; power is present in the extremities, but control is lacking.

Atrophy: Degeneration or wasting away of tissues, organs or parts due to lack of use, disease, or interference with nerve supply.

Automatism: Behavior performed in a state of mental dissociation without full awareness, i.e., somnambulism, fugues.

Battered Child Syndrome: Physical injury to a child resulting from excessive beating, usually by a parent or parents and ordinarily repeated over an extended period of time, which may suddenly cause the child to react violently toward the abuser. Mental illness in parents may be present. See Chapter 19.

Battered Spouse Syndrome: Physical and/or psychological injury to a spouse resulting from prolonged and excessive abuse by the other spouse that engenders certain stress symptoms which may culminate in a sudden act of violence toward the abuser by the abused spouse, at a moment when no immediate violence against the abused is threatened. See Chapter 19.

Beta Waves: Graphically recorded frequency of brain waves on the electroencephalograph which have a frequency of from 15 to 60 cps (cycles per second), and a lower voltage than the alpha waves; also called beta rhythm.

Brain Stem: Upward continuation of cervical portion of spinal cord, consisting of the medulla oblongata, pons, and midbrain.

CAT Scan: Computerized Axial Tomography. A method of studying the brain by using a series of X-rays.

Catatonic: A state found in some forms of schizophrenia, in which energy seems maintained either at a very high (catatonic excitement) or very low level; changes in muscle tone allow subject to display the ability to maintain for hours either a fixed statuesque pose (catatonic rigidity) or a catatonic waxy flexibility of the limbs; during catatonic excitement, subject exhibits wild, blind, apparently purposeless overactivity; in catatonic stupor, subject fails to respond to, or pay attention to, external stimuli; in catatonic negativism, subject resists all instructions or attempts to be moved without apparent motive; catatonic posturing involves a subject who voluntarily assumes an inappropriate or strange position for a long period of time.

Catalepsy: Generalized condition of diminished responsiveness usually characterized by trance-like states; may occur in organic or psychological disorders or under hypnosis.

Cerebellum: Lower portion of the brain below back of cerebrum concerned with muscular coordination and body equilibrium.

Cerebral Arteriosclerosis: Hardening of the arteries of the brain with a decrease in the blood flow to the brain from lessening of the diameter of the arteries servicing it; results in an organic brain syndrome manifested neurologically in convulsions, aphasia, chorea, parkinsonism, etc., or functionally in the form of intellectual dulling, memory defects, paranoid delusions, confusion, dementia, etc.; occurs, usually, only in persons over 50.

Cerebrum: The major frontal and upper parts of the brain which are centers of the high functions such as memory, intellect, speech, movement, sensation, etc.; consists of two hemispheres of nerve matter.

Child Sexual Abuse Accommodation Syndrome (CSAAS): a series of symptoms observed in children who have been subjected to sexual abuse, consisting of some or all of (1) learned pattern of secrecy and shame induced by threats made by the abuser; (2) a pattern of learned helplessness from child's inability to stop the abuse; (3) self-blame for the abuse; (4) behavioral changes such as withdrawal, over-achievement, or self-destructive tendencies; (5) delayed disclosure of the abuse; and (6) retraction.

Cognitive: The mental process of comprehension, judgment, memory and reasoning, as opposed to emotional and volitional processes.

Confabulation: The process of creating facts or events in response to questioning because of failure to recall these events factually due to memory impairment. Very common on amnesia or amnestic disorder.

Conversion Hysteria: A neurosis in which there is gross loss or impairment of some somatic or physical function caused by emotional conflicts, such as hysterical blindness, hysterical paralysis, hysterical tremors, hysterical limping. Used by sufferer to protect self from anxiety.

Countertransference: Unconscious emotional feelings of a therapist, originating in the therapist's youth experiences, toward the patient.

Defense Mechanism: Pattern of involuntary behavior, manifested through feelings, thoughts, or conduct, arising as a result of perceptions of psychic danger, designed to conceal or diminish the stressors that produced the anxiety. Some defense mechanisms are maladaptive, such as spitting and acting out; others may be either maladaptive or adaptive, such as suppression and denial, depending on the degree of the anxiety and the context in which it occurs. Some other defense mechanisms include: autistic fantasy, devaluation, displacement, dissociation, idealization, intellectualization, isolation, passive aggression, projection, rationalization, reaction formation, repression, somatization, and undoing.

Delirium: Disturbed mental state characterized by a combination of motor restlessness displaying excitement, confusion, incoherence, perplexity, and disorientation, in combination with a dream-like state and some sensory disturbance, such as hallucinations and delusions.

Delirium Tremens: A delirium due to alcohol (also called Korsakow's Syndrome) or other drug poisoning or withdrawal, or to dietary metabolic deprivation resulting from sudden abstinence from the substance that was abused.

Delusion: False, unshakable belief which is (1) contrary to fact, (2) inappropriate to the person's education, intelligence or culture, and (3) adhered to in spite of tangible evidence that it is false. A reality judgment which cannot be accepted by people of the same class, education, race and period of life as the person who expresses it and which cannot be changed by logical argument or evidence against it. Some common delusions: delusions of being controlled; delusions of grandeur (grandiose delusion); delusions of personal unworthiness; mood-congruent or mood-incongruent delusions; delusions of being persecuted; nihilistic delusions; somatic delusions; jealousy delusions; etc.

Dementia: Form of mental disorder in which cognitive and intellectual functions of the mind are prominently affected; impairment of memory is an early sign; total recovery is not possible since organic cerebral disease is involved.

Depersonalization Disorder: Alteration in the perception of the self so that the feeling of one's own reality is lost temporarily. Occurs also in schizotypal personality disorders and in schizophrenia.

Depression: Syndrome manifested by a sense of self-depreciation, self-doubt, melancholy, and guilt feelings. A Depressive Reaction is a syndrome describing a mental or emotional condition, precipitated by some external factor which may also result in psychomotor retardation, dejection and/or sense of inadequacy.

Disorientation: Failure to identify time, place, or surroundings.

Displacement: Shifting of emotional emphasis from one object or person to another as a means of disguising the true nature of the patient's illness.

Dissociation: Splitting of consciousness whereby inconsistencies in thought and conduct are overlooked. Dissociative reactions are sometimes characterized by fugues, amnesia, or other forms of dissociation. As in Dissociative Identity Disorder (formerly Multiple Personality Disorder).

Dura Mater: The tough, membranous, outer covering of the brain and spinal cord.

Ego: The part of the conscious personality which balances the demands of the real world and maintains harmony between the *id* (instinctual drives) and the *superego* (morality of the conscience); that portion of the total personality noticeable to others which maintains contact with the environment of the outer world.

Electroconvulsive Therapy (ECT): Use of a small amount of electricity to induce a major seizure in a patient who has a severe psychiatric illness, notably severe depression, delivered by a machine sophisticated enough to elicit a controlled seizure under precise conditions using low amounts of electricity.

Electroencephalogram (EEG): Recorded graph of the electrical activity of the brain cells made by an electroencephalograph.

Electroencephalograph: Instrument for picking up and recording the electrical activity of the brain cells, consisting in part of a number of electrodes (small silver disks) which are pasted to the scalp; the electrical potential of the brain is picked up by these electrodes and is amplified by the instrument, and recorded onto a chart by styluses writing in ink on a continuous roll of paper. Rhythm abnormality may be transient, abnormally slow, abnormally fast, or focally abnormal in a specific brain area.

Epilepsy: Syndrome characterized by recurrent periods of unconsciousness as the result of occasional, sudden, excessive, rapid and local electrical discharges of the brain cortex. If episodes are very brief, with temporary loss of consciousness and no convulsion, condition is called *petit mal;* if attacks are accompanied by convulsions, unconscious condition is called *grand mal.* In *grand mal,* convulsions are usually generalized, involving primarily the limbs and back muscles. In psychomotor epilepsy, the subject passes into a state of altered consciousness in lieu of convulsions, a state which is sometimes called automatic behavior. In psychomotor epilepsy, subject has total amnesia of the occurrences that transpire during seizure.

Euphoria: Exaggerated feeling of physical and emotional well-being non-consonant with apparent stimuli or events; usually of psychological origin, but also seen in organic brain diseases, or toxic and drug induced states.

Exhibitionism: Compulsion to display the sexual organs.

Fetishism: Sexual stimulation and gratification achieved by male through exposure to articles of female clothing such as lingerie or shoes.

Flight of Ideas: A continuous flow of accelerated speech wherein the subject makes abrupt changes of topics, often based on perceived associations, stimuli which distract, or plays on words. In extreme states, the speech may become incoherent. Often seen in manic episodes, though it also occurs in some cases of organic mental disorders and schizophrenia, psychotic disorders, and even as an acute reaction to stress.

Fugue: Period of memory loss during which the subject functions almost as if normal, but concerning which there is no subsequent recollection; as in dissociative disorders.

Grand Mal: A form of epilepsy characterized by periods of unconscious coma and true convulsions. The unconscious subject falls to the ground, undergoing a stiffening of the muscles (short tonic phase), followed by jerking and relaxation (clonic phase) and continued unconsciousness. During the *tonic* phase there is no respiration; during the *clonic* phase there is respiration and possible tongue biting, followed by exhaustion and stupor.

Grandiosity: Inflated estimate of one's own worth, importance, knowledge, or person. Is of delusional proportions when extreme. Example: teacher who regularly puts his students to sleep during lectures but who nevertheless is convinced of being the most exciting and dynamic instructor in the school.

Hallucination: an apparently real sensory perception, auditory or visual, without any real external or internal stimuli that cause it. Should be distinguished from illusions, during which external stimuli are misperceived or misinterpreted, and from normal vivid thought processes. Types of hallucinations: auditory, gustatory, mood-congruent, mood-incongruent; olfactory; somatic; tactile, and visual. In its serious form, hallucinations are commonly experienced by psychotics. Transient hallucinations are experienced at times by persons without mental disorders.

Hebephrenia: Psychotic form of schizophrenia featuring regression into silly, deteriorated, or infantile behavior and mannerisms. The term "hebephrenic" is no longer being used in psychiatry.

Hindbrain: Also rhombencephalon. Part of the brain developed from the posterior of the three primary brain vesicles of the embryonic neural tube.

Hypnosis: The inducement of a sleep-like trance or amnesia by means of psychological suggestion.

Hypochondria: Neurotic, morbid overconcern about disease.

Hysteria: Neurotic disorder characterized by anxiety, hypersensitivity, self-consciousness, immaturity and dependency. In the conversion form there is sometimes displayed the physical symptoms of gross loss, or impairment, of the function of one or more organs, i.e., hysterical blindness or hysterical convulsion. In the anxiety form, anxiety appears consciously but its cause is repressed. The hysteric patient is usually emotionally and sometimes physically immature.

Id: Psychoanalytic term for that portion of the mind containing an unconscious reservoir of primitive instincts, urges and drives. It includes the sex and aggressive drives for fulfillment in which morality and discipline are not involved.

Identity Disorder: A loss of the sense of sameness and historical continuity of one's self, and the inability to accept or adopt the role the subject perceives to be expected of him/her by society; often expressed by isolation, withdrawal, extremism, rebellion, and negativity, and typically triggered by a combination of sudden increase in the strength of instinctual drives in a milieu of rapid social evolution and technological change.

Illusion: A distorted or misinterpreted sensory impression which, in contrast to hallucinations, arises from an actual stimulus, i.e., shadow is taken to be a person, specks on window are seen as swarm of mosquitos. Prevalent in delirious states.

Imbecile: In the psychological sense, a mental defective with an I.Q. between 20 and 50, an adult with a mental age between 3 and 7, possessed of a faculty for self-preservation but requiring custodial or protective care. The term is no longer used clinically.

Intelligence: Aggregate capacity of the individual to act purposefully, think rationally and deal effectively with his environment, expressed in terms of I.Q.; a psychological determination of the relationship of a person's mental age to his chronological age.

Inversion: Exaggeration of tendencies opposite to those which are repressed, i.e., elder person's inversion of repressed sexual desires manifested by overt revulsion to sex.

Kleptomania: Compulsion to steal, which the subject tries to resist unsuccessfully.

Korsakow's Syndrome: Psychosis, usually due to alcohol or dietary deficiency, manifested by confusions, confabulation and suggestibility; occurs often as a sequel to delirium tremens. Physical signs: neuritis, muscle paralysis.

Malingerer: Person who consciously feigns or simulates mental illness or disorder for gain or other personal motives (i.e., acquittal on insanity in criminal prosecution).

Manic: Phase of manic-depressive psychosis in which the mood of the patient is overactive and expansive; characterized by excessive ego valuation and over-estimation of personal importance. Manic moods may include boisterousness, joviality, anger, joyousness. As in manic episode.

Manic–Depressive Psychosis: Also bipolar disorder; major depressive episode. Severe mood or affective disorder characterized by periods of cyclical swings between mania and depression. The manic phase is characterized by overactivity, euphoria with flight of ideas, excitement, lessening of sleep needs, impaired judgment and pressured speech. The depressive phase is often prolonged and is also characterized by moodiness, slowed thinking, movement, and eating processes, guilt feelings, decreased self-esteem, inability to sleep, general lack of interest.

Melancholia: Depressed phase of manic-depressive psychosis, the intensity and duration of which is out of proportion to any apparent precipitating factors.

Memory: Images which occur with the consciousness that they represent former perceptions and that their content has already been experienced in the past; comprised of four distinct elements, i.e., grasp, retentiveness, recall, and recognition.

Meninges: Three membranous tissues covering the brain and spinal cord: (1) pia mater, internal layer; (2) arachnoid, middle layer; and (3) dura mater, external layer.

Mental Disorder: A disorder conceptualized as a clinically significant psychological, biological or behavioral syndrome, or a pattern of conduct, that causes a person present distress, pain, disability, or impairment in an important area of functioning that is not merely an expectable response to particular events (i.e. grief upon losing child) but is caused by a behavioral, psychological, or biological dysfunction of the person. If the disorder is widely known and accepted in the mental health profession under a particular label, it is listed in DSM–IV along with suggested treatment.

MMPI: Minnesota Multiphasic Personality Inventory, a psychological test measuring personality structure and assisting in psychiatric diagnosis. The test currently used is MMPI–2.

Mood: A pervasive and sustained emotion which significantly influences a person's perception of his environment. Common mood disorders include depression, elation, anxiety and anger. Mood-congruent psychotic features are delusions or hallucinations whose content is totally consistent with depression or manic behavior. Mood-incongruent psychotic features, by contrast, involve delusions or hallucinations which are neither consistent with depressed nor manic moods.

Moron: Obsolescent term describing a person with an inferior intellect who can be trained and guided to become a self-supporting member of society; a mental defective with an I.Q. between 50 and 70; an adult with a mental age between 7 and 12.

MRI: Magnetic Resonance Imaging. A relatively new diagnostic tool used in studying brain activity by using magnetic field imaging. Is also used on other parts of the body.

Multiple Personality Disorder (MPD). Now called Dissociative Identity Disorder. See, Dissociation.

Mutism: Failure to speak or refusal to answer questions because of conscious or unconscious reasons.

Myelograph: X-ray examination of the spinal column and outer brain after injection of a radiopaque medium.

Narcoanalysis: Process whereby a subject is put to sleep, or into a semi-somnolent state by means of chemical injections and then interrogated while in a dream-like state.

Negativism: The process of doing the opposite of what is asked or demanded.

Nervous System: Composed of (1) central nervous system—brain and spinal cord controlling mental and voluntary muscular acts; (2) autonomic nervous system—nerves which control acts of organs and smooth muscle tissue.

Neurology: The branch of medicine dealing with the nervous system and its disorders.

Neuroses: Set of symptoms due essentially to unresolved emotional conflict resulting usually in anxiety; psychoses are more debilitating that neuroses.

Nymphomania: Excessive sexual desire in a female; corresponding desire in the male is called satyriasis.

Obsession: Morbid, absurd, or simply unwanted, persistent idea which obtrudes into one's mind and preoccupies the person recurrently even though it is recognized that such preoccupation is foolish and alien; it dominates the subject's consciousness against his desire and to the distress of the rest of the personality, i.e., perfectionism. The individual suffering from obsession recognizes the nonsensical nature of the compulsion but is powerless against it; may be motivated by repressed factors which fragmentarily break through the conscious attitudes, codes and virtues. Characteristic of Obsessive Compulsive Disorder, but is also seen in Schizophrenia.

Oedipal complex: In psychoanalytic theory, the attachment for the opposite sex which develops in children between the ages of 3 to 5 years along with envious and aggressive feelings toward the same sex person. As the child grows up, these feelings become suppressed.

Organic: A detectable alteration in the structure, integrity or mechanics of a diseased organ. Modern psychiatry no longer classifies disorders as "organic" because this implies that other disorders cannot have an organic origin.

Organic Brain Syndrome (OBS): Not currently used, but refers to a constellation of symptoms of disorders caused by or associated with impairment of brain tissue function. May be manifested by disorientation, loss of memory and impairment of the ability to learn, comprehend, calculate and exercise judgment. May be psychotic or nonpsychotic, mild, moderate, or severe.

Panic Attack: Attack of acute, intense, and overwhelming anxiety, accompanied by a considerable degree of personality disorganization. While they are characteristic of Panic Disorder, they may also occur in somatization disorder, major depression, and schizophrenia.

Paranoia: Rare chronic psychosis without hallucinations in which the subject has a fixed unshakable delusion, but reasons logically and in a systemized way from that false premise and has perfect preservation of clear and orderly thinking. As in paranoid personality disorder; paranoid type of schizophrenia.

Paroxysmal Cerebral Dysrhythmia: The underlying electrical disturbance in the EEG rhythm of epileptics.

Passive–Dependency Reaction: Personality disorder not amounting to a psychosis or neurosis that is characterized by feelings of inadequacy, tendencies to lean on others, and indecisiveness. Also, passive-aggressive personality disorder or negativistic personality disorder.

Peripheral Nervous System: That portion of the nervous system found outside of the brain and spinal cord.

Personality Disorders: Group of mental disorders characterized by maladaptive patterns of behavior, often recognizable during adolescence or earlier. Affect the personality of the individual. Among the disorders are:

Antisocial Personality. Personality disorder characterized by basic lack of socialization and by behavior patterns that bring the individual repeatedly into conflict with society. Sufferers are incapable of significant loyalty to individuals, groups or social values and are also grossly selfish, callous, irresponsible, impulsive and unable to feel guilt or to learn from experience or punishment.

Avoidant Personality. A disorder manifested by a pattern of social inhibition, a feeling of inadequacy, and an over-sensitivity to negative evaluation.

Borderline Personality. Disorder which manifests itself in a pervasive instability in interpersonal relationships, self-image, and affects, and marked impulsivity.

Dependent Personality. Disorder manifested by a pervasive and excessive need to be taken care of leading to excessively submissive and clinging behavior and fears of separation.

Histrionic Personality. Disorder characterized by excitability, emotional instability, over-reactivity, and self-dramatization that is attention seeking and often seductive, notwithstanding that the individual is unaware of its presence.

Narcissistic Personality. Disorder manifested by acting in a grandiose manner, exhibiting a need for admiration, and lack of empathy.

Obsessive Compulsive Personality. Disorder characterized by excessive concern with conformity and adherence to standards of conscience.

Paranoid Personality. Disorder characterized by hypersensitivity, rigidity, unwarranted suspicion, jealousy, envy, excessive self-importance and a tendency to blame others and ascribe evil motives to them.

Passive–Aggressive Personality. Also, Negativistic Personality. Disorder characterized by aggressive behavior manifested in passive ways, such as obstructionism, pouting, procrastination, intentional inefficiency or stubbornness.

Schizoid Personality. Disorder manifested by shyness, over-sensitivity, seclusiveness, frequent day-dreaming, avoidance of close or competitive relationships and often eccentricity.

Schizotypal Personality. Disorder manifested by a strong sense of discomfort in close relationships, cognitive or perceptual distortions and eccentricities of behavior.

PET Scan: Positron Emission Tomography. Examination of brain-cell activity by recording how radioactive glucose is utilized.

Petit Mal: Form of Epilepsy displaying transient spells of unconsciousness without convulsions; comes abruptly without aura and lasts a few seconds; may be twitching of the eyelids, face, shoulder and arm muscles; subject may continue what he was doing in a "black out"; rhythm of the brain may drop to 3 cps on the EEG.

Phobia: A compelling, morbid fear of a specific situation, object or activity, which the subject knows is groundless, but which the individual is unable to resist with success; compulsion to avoid something, a very ordinary activity, in order not to arouse anxiety;

usually the sufferer can give an apparently rational explanation of the avoidance. Some phobias are:

Acrophobia. Fear of heights.

Agoraphobia. Fear of open spaces.

Ailurophobia. Fear of cats.

Algophobia. Fear of pain.

Claustrophobia. Fear of closed spaces.

Erythrophobia. Fear of blushing.

Mysophobia. Fear of dirt and germs.

Panphobia. Fear of everything.

Xenophobia. Fear of strangers.

Post-traumatic stress syndrome: Group of disorders which occurs in some people who have survived or been subjected to a serious traumatic event outside the common experience of human beings.

Pre–Menstrual Syndrome (PMS) (also called Late Luteal Phase Dysmorphic Disorder): Not officially categorized in DSM–IV, but listed as a disorder "for further study," PMS is a disorder of physical and emotional changes associated with specific phases of the menstrual cycle, specifically beginning during the last week of the luteal phase which remit within a few days of the onset of the follicular phase.

Psychiatrist: A physician (doctor of medicine) who specializes in the diagnosis and treatment of individuals suffering from mental disturbances or diseases. The educational requirements are, at least, four years of medical school, one year of internship, and a three-year residency in psychiatry.

Psychoanalysis: Concept of human development and behavior devised by Freud and amplified by his followers, and, subsequently, by those who dissented from and varied his original technique; based on the belief that emotional disorders are due to unconscious conflicts, most of them dating back to childhood. It is used to cure people of emotional disturbances by ascertaining the subconscious basis of the emotional conflict underlying personality dysfunction, and by allowing the individual to elicit these factors into consciousness, to react to them, to release repressed emotions, or to live through, emotionally or in fantasy, the repressed problems; the theory is that making the subject aware of the origin of the conflicts, he will be better able to overcome them. Psychoanalysis is also used as a diagnostic tool to explain bizarre conduct in terms of psychoanalytic rules.

Psychologist: A non-physician trained in the understanding of mental mechanisms. The field includes testing of mental capacities, determinations of personality structures, vocational and personal guidance, experimental and animal psychology, and attempts at the correction of intellectual and emotional disabilities by use of psychological methods.

Psychomotor Epilepsy: An epileptic seizure without convulsions in which the consciousness is so impaired that the subject is amnesic; during attack patient is belligerent and irritable and may commit an act of violence; less common than grand mal or petit mal and rarely suffered without one of these two types also being manifested at other times; disturbance is localized in the temporal lobe of the brain.

Psychosis: Severe mental disturbance of organic or emotional origin characterized by asocial behavior, loss of contact with reality and deterioration of the personality, such as schizophrenia, manic-depressive affective disorder.

Psychosomatic: Combined influence of emotional and physical factors.

Psychotropic: Term used to describe drugs that act specially on the psyche.

Pyromania: Compulsion to set fires.

Regression: Reversion to modes of thought, feeling and behavior which are more appropriate to an earlier stage in individual and social development.

Repression: Unconscious, involuntary process of thrusting out of consciousness of ideas or urges to action which are incompatible with ideals, conscience, and perception of what is right or wrong.

Retrograde amnesia: see Amnesia.

Retrospective Falsification: Unconscious distortion of past experiences to conform to present emotional needs.

Rorschach Test: Projective method of determining the structure of personality by noting the patient's reaction to a set of cards containing standardized ink blots; used in detecting neurotic and psychotic traits.

Schizophrenia: Severe psychosis characterized by various degrees of withdrawal from reality into a private isolated world, thought disorder, autistic thinking, delusion formation, bizarre behavior and/or hallucinations often of an auditory nature, such as hearing thoughts spoken aloud or hearing voices.

Senile Psychosis: Mental illness developing in elderly persons characterized by progressive loss of memory, irritability, delusion formation, eccentricity, and confusion.

Sociopath: A person who has trouble getting along with others because of some long-standing personality problem.

Somatoform Disorders: Group of mental disorder that assumes the form of a somatic illness. Principal somatoform disorders are: somatization disorder, conversion disorder, psychogenic pain disorder, and hypochondriasis.

Subarachnoid Space: Area between the middle and internal membranes covering the brain and spinal cord.

Subdural Space: Area between external and middle membranes covering the brain and spinal cord.

Superego: Conscience; part of the personality which represents ideals, goals and self-judgment; the judge, the censor and the punisher as well as the ideal for each personality.

Synapse: The location of functional apposition between neurons, where one neuron transmits an impulse to another neuron by electrical or chemical means.

Syndrome: When a relatively large number of persons, having the same symptoms, exhibit a combination or variation of functional psychiatric disorders that leads to emotional anguish or distress and severe emotional trauma, psychiatrists classify those persons under one or more labels. See, e.g., battered spouse syndrome, Holocaust syndrome, post-traumatic stress syndrome, rape trauma syndrome, premenstrual syndrome, etc.

Tardive Dyskinesia: Involuntary movements of the body consisting of one or more of the above: leg twitching or spastic movements of neck, body, and pelvis, finger, toe and/or ankle movements, facial distortions such as tongue twisting or protrusion, masticating and chewing, or lip movements.

Thematic Apperception Test (TAT): Projective personality test requiring subject to make make up a story about people illustrated in pictures shown to the subject.

Transference: The unconscious transference to one person (frequently a therapist) of feelings of affection and love developed in early life toward persons who had great influence in the patient's early life (e.g. parents).

Trauma: A physical injury caused by a blow, or fall, or a psychologically damaging emotional experience.

Wechsler Adult Intelligence Scale–Revised (WAIS–R): Psychological diagnostic test to measure intelligence and mental retardation in adults, consisting or standardized verbal and performance subscales.

II. FORENSIC PSYCHIATRY

§ 18.03   The Profession of Psychiatry.

A psychiatrist is a medical doctor (MD) who, after completing the requirements of the medical degree, has conducted further studies in psychiatry. A psychiatrist, today, must first become a licensed medical doctor by completing medical school and passing the United States Medical Licensing Examination (USMLE) through the National Board of Medical Examiners. This test has three parts: the first part is taken upon completion of the second year of medical school; the second part is taken during fourth year of medical school, and the final part is taken toward the end of the first year of post-graduate residency.

After medical school, the individual desiring to become a psychiatrist must enter into a psychiatric residency for four years during which the student is exposed to all aspects of psychiatry. Upon completion of the residency, the student becomes a Board-eligible psychiatrist, and is allowed to sit for the board test administered by the American Board of Psychiatry and Neurology. This test consists of two parts, written and oral. The written test must be passed before the candidates can take the oral examination. Being board-eligible entitles the doctor to practice psychiatry; being board certified makes the individual more marketable and is essentially a pre-requisite in academia. There are further specialty boards, such as the American Board of Forensic Psychiatry.

The leading professional organization, The American Psychiatric Association, was founded in 1844. It is a national membership association of doctors of medicine who specialize in the diagnosis, treatment, and care of mental illnesses.[1]

§ 18.04   Types of Psychiatric Disorders

To deal adequately with psychiatric issues, the attorney must become familiar with the medical dialogue of the psychiatrist. When law students initially confront the concept of psychiatry and law, it is typically in a first year course in criminal law where the insanity defense is discussed. Yet, while psychiatrists, psychologists or neurologists may be called upon to testify whether a person is sane or insane, insanity as such is a purely legal concept (as will be explored in Chapter 19); the term has no medical equivalent. To mental health professionals, the legal concepts of "insanity," "incompetency," and "diminished responsibility," can be reached only by connecting the law with identifiable mental illness. Sickness or impairment of the mind is medically defined by certain diagnostic labels, which do not remain constant. The American Psychiatric Association officially adopts a system of classification of mental disorders, a system that is subject to periodic revisions as the state of knowledge expands, and published in a Diagnostic and Statistical Manual of Mental Disorders, the current version of which is referred to as *DSM–IV.*[1]

§ 18.03

1. Its address is: American Psychiatric Association, 1400 K Street, N.W., Washington, D.C. 20005.

§ 18.04

1. The current edition is DSM–IV (*Diagnostic and Statistical Manual of Mental Disorders—Fourth edition,* 1994). The first edition appeared in 1952; DSM–II went into effect in 1968, and DSM–III in 1974. In 1983, the American Psychiatric Association appointed a working group to revise DSM–III which resulted in the publication

of DSM–III–R in 1989. The current text, DSM–IV, which was in the works for more than a dozen years, is the product of more than 1,000 professionals. As a practical matter, psychiatrists working to produce this volume were organized in 13 work groups, each of which was given primary responsibility for one section of the manual and reported to the "Task Force on DSM–IV." Extensive inter-group consulting occurred as well. While cautionary notes, which were included in the former editions as well, indicate DSM–IV is to be used for diagnosis and treatment by mental health

Apart from the DSM compilations of the American Psychiatric Association which are well known to trial attorneys, and other mental health nomenclature compilations that were developed at different times in the past, there also exists an International Classification of Diseases (ICD) developed by the World Health Organization (WHO), which has gone through a number of different editions. The current edition of the *International Statistical Classification of Diseases and Related Health Problems,* more popularly known as ICD–10, reflects the close cooperation between the drafters of ICD–10 and DSM–IV, and shows that each exerted much influence on the other's end product.

The use of the very term "mental" disorder has come under some criticism. The professionals in the field of mental health know that much mental disease has physical underpinnings, just as many physical disorders have roots in the mind. The drafters of DSM–IV were aware of this, but retained the term "mental disorders" because no adequate substitute was found.

While it is beyond the scope of this chapter to summarize the voluminous diagnostic literature on mental disorders, it remains useful for the attorney to be aware at least of the scheme whereby diseases or disorders of the mind are categorized. DSM–IV uses the following classification of principal mental disorders.[2]

I. Disorders Usually First Diagnosed in Infancy, Childhood, or Adolescence

In this category, DSM–IV lists mental retardation; learning, motor skills, and communication disorders; pervasive developmental disorders; attention deficit and disruptive behavior disorders; feeding and eating disorders of infancy and early childhood; Tourette disorders as well as tic disorders; elimination disorders. The category concludes with various other conditions of infancy, childhood or adolescence, such as separation anxiety, selective mutism, and other conditions.

II. Delirium, Dementia, and Amnestic and Other Cognitive Disorders

These diseases, some of which were, in DSM–III–R categorized as "Organic Mental Syndromes and Disorders," include delirium due to various conditions such as general medical condition, substance abuse, or multiple etiologies; dementia of the Alzheimer's type as well as with delirium, delusions or depressed mood; dementia due to other diseases or trauma, such as HIV infection, head trauma, Parkinson's disease, and

professionals, and not for legal purposes, no litigator using or opposing forensic experts in this field can afford to be unfamiliar with this Manual.

2. The principal categories are listed only; some subgroups are also omitted, other subgroups listed individually in DSM–IV are here combined. Consult DSM–IV for the officially adopted classification system. The numbering of the categories in this text was done by the authors, not by the American Psychiatric Association, and therefore does not constitute an official classification system.

other etiologies. Also included here are amnestic disorders and some other cognitive disorders that are not otherwise specified.

III.   Mental Disorders Due to Other General Medical Conditions

This group lists catatonic disorders due to a variety of circumstances, and personality changes due to a general medical condition rather than due to separately listed causes, i.e. substance dependency.

IV.   Substance–Related Disorders

Undoubtedly, substance-related disorders comprise the largest group of dysfunctions that relate to the taking of drugs of abuse, including the consumption of alcohol and side effects of medically prescribed drugs, and to the exposure to various toxins. Some of the important subgroups are: drug or alcohol dependency, abuse, intoxication, and withdrawal; amphetamine or similarly acting sympathomimetic dependency or abuse; disorders related to use and abuse of caffeine, cannabis, cocaine, hallucinogens, inhalants, nicotine, opioids, phencyclidine (PCP) or phencyclidine-like substances, sedatives, hypnotic drugs, and disorders related to use and abuse of a combination of various substances.

V.   Schizophrenia and Other Psychotic Disorders

In this category, the disorders have psychotic symptoms as the major defining feature. Included herein are schizophrenia in its various types (paranoid, disorganized, catatonic, undifferentiated, residual); schizophreniform, schizoaffective, and delusional disorders; and various other problems related to the thinking process.

VI.   Mood Disorders, Also Called Affective Disorders

Here, the disorders deal primarily with problems of feelings. The main subgroups deal with depressive disorders, which are very common in society, bipolar disorders (manic-depressive, hypomanic and cyclothymic); dysthymic disorders; and other mood disorders, whether due to a general medical condition, substance-induced, or not otherwise specified.

VII.   Anxiety Disorders

This category includes a number of conditions that are sought to be used as excuses or defenses in criminal cases. Among the conditions are: various panic attacks, agoraphobia, and panic disorders; specific phobias (formerly called "simple phobias"); social phobia; obsessive compulsive disorder; post-traumatic stress disorders caused by a great variety of stimuli or experiences (battered spouses, rape-trauma, child sexual abuse, Stockholm syndrome); acute stress disorder; as well as anxieties caused by a general medical condition, or substance-abuse induced.

VIII.   Somatoform Disorders

This category includes conditions where involuntarily produced physical symptoms suggest general medical problems that cannot be explained by the general medical condition of the person. Included in this category are: hysteria (also called Briquet's syndrome), now referred to a somatization disorder; conversion and pain disorders; hypochondriasis (or hypochondriacal neurosis); and body dismorphic disorder (formerly called dysmorphophobia).

IX. Factitious Disorders

Here listed is a disorder characterized by physical or psychological symptoms that are either intentionally produced or feigned, in order to assume the role of a sick person, without there being an obvious external incentive for it. It is to be distinguished from malingering in that in malingering a specific purpose is sought to be accomplished, such as avoiding jury duty, military service, or standing trial. The factitious disorder may be associated with either predominantly psychological or predominantly physical signs and symptoms.

X. Dissociative Disorders

This category lists disorders characterized by a disruption in functions that are normally integrated in the healthy individual, namely the functions of consciousness, memory, identity, or perception of one's surroundings. Among the subgroups are: dissociative amnesia, formerly called psychogenic amnesia; dissociative fugue (formerly psychogenic fugue); dissociative identity disorder, a condition that was formerly categorized as multiple personality disorder (or MPD), a label that will long be continued in use in legal proceedings as well as popular use; and depersonalization disorder.

XI. Sexual and Gender Identity Disorders

Here included are three distinct groups of disorders: sexual dysfunctions, paraphilias, and gender identity disorders. The sexual dysfunctions include sexual desire disorders (hypoactive, aversion, female sexual arousal, male erectile disorders), orgasmic disorders (female orgasmic, formerly called inhibited female orgasm; male orgasmic, and premature ejaculation disorders); sexual pain disorders (dyspareunia, vaginismus, or substance induced). The paraphilias subgroup includes exhibitionism, fetishism, frotteurism, pedophilia, sexual masochism, sexual sadism, transvestic fetishism, and voyeurism. The gender identity disorders relate to conditions where there is a persistent cross-gender identification, motivated by a strong discomfort about one's assigned sex or gender role, without concurrent physical intersex conditions (such as androgen insensitivity syndrome), which impair substantially the person's functioning on social or occupational settings.

XII. Eating Disorders

This group of disorders includes anorexia nervosa, manifested by disturbances in the perception of the size and shape of the patient's body coupled with intense fear of gaining weight and consequent loss of appetite; and bulimia nervosa or binge eating of larger quantities of food at one setting than is normal under the circumstances, coupled with inappropriate methods to prevent gaining weight.

XIII. Sleep Disorders

Here the division is first into primary sleep disorders, and next disorders that are related to some other mental condition. Among the primary sleep disorders are dyssomnias (difficulties that pertain to the length of time one sleeps, how deep or shallow the sleep is, and when one can sleep—these disorders seldom have legal sequelae), and parasomnias (conditions wherein the difficulties with sleeping result in other abnormal behavior patterns such as nightmares, previously called dream anxiety disorders, sleep terror, and sleepwalking). The disorders that are related to other mental conditions are usually defined in conjunction with the event that causes insomnia; they also include excessive sleepiness (hypersomnia) due to causes such as substance abuse and other mental deviations from what is assumed to be normal conduct.

XIV. Impulse–Control Disorders Not Elsewhere Classified

While this section is a fairly brief one in DSM–IV, it deals with a number of disorders that are manifested by criminal or otherwise antisocial behavior. Among these conditions are: intermittent explosive disorder, characterized by failing to resist aggressive impulses that result in assaults and batteries upon other individuals or in the destruction of another's property; kleptomania (compulsive stealing); pyromania (setting of fires to satisfy impulses); pathological gambling; compulsive hair pulling so that noticeable hair loss results, called "trichotillomania"; and other non-specified impulse-control disorders.

XV. Adjustment Disorders

This category of disorders is also a brief one, because it appears to overlap with other disorders. Adjustment disorders are characterized by the development of symptoms that deal with emotions or behavior that result from specific and identifiable psychological stress.

More important, in terms of impact on the legal system, is the next category.

XVI. Personality Disorders.

Here we deal with conditions that frequently result in severe antisocial and/or criminal behavior. Among the disorders listed here are: paranoid personality; schizoid personality; schizotypal personality; antisocial personality; borderline personality; histrionic personality; narcissistic personality; obsessive compulsive personality; and some others less likely to result in disruption of societal interests.

In the remainder of the DSM–IV classification system, some other conditions are identified that may require clinical attention, but seldom involve the legal system, except in connection with other conditions.

It is obviously beyond the scope of this chapter to define and describe in detail all of the named disorders. In this chapter, we will only discuss some of the broad categories and how the disorders identified therein are distinguished from other groups of disorders. The reader who is in need of more in depth information, is referred for that purpose to the official manual of the American Psychiatric Association or to the excellent and fairly current textbooks listed in the bibliography at the end of this chapter, some of which are written especially for lawyers.

It should also be noted that at the time DSM–IV was published, certain disorders and syndromes that have featured in civil and criminal litigation in recent years were still under study and are not included in its diagnostic manual. Among them are the Late Luteal Phase Dysmorphic Disorder, better known to lawyers as the Pre–Menstrual Syndrome, and many of the subgroups of Post Traumatic Stress Syndrome, such as the rape-trauma syndrome, the child sexual abuse accommodation syndrome, the battered spouse syndrome, the Holocaust syndrome, the battle-fatigue syndrome, etc.[3] The psychiatric and psychological literature continues to report on ongoing studies which may describe disorders that are becoming well known in the mental health field even though they are not yet described in the official diagnostic literature. The relative novelty of such disorders, and the lack of widespread adoption of its diagnostic and treatment criteria, exposes expert witnesses testifying in these areas to searching cross-examination.

§ 18.05   Summary of the Main Categories of Psychiatric Disorders

While in the previous section an attempt was made to follow, by and large, the classification system of mental disorders as characterized and catalogued in the standard psychiatric manual DSM–IV, this section contains a more general discussion of the principal categories of mental disorders which have frequent legal sequelae.

Mental retardation, characterized by a delayed or disturbed development in intelligence and other language, motor, or social skills, is considered a disorder in psychiatric terms although it is generally lifelong. The onset is before the age of 18, and the disorder is often congenital in that it results from arrested development of the brain by reason of some germinal effect. It may also be caused by infection or injury to the brain.

The various organic brain syndromes have one thing in common. Each is detectable as a physical or structural dysfunction of the brain that is either permanent or transient. For example, the disorder associated with cerebral arteriosclerosis, often found in the aged, is caused by the hardening of the blood vessels supplying the brain with oxygen. Syphilis of the nervous system is also an organic brain disorder with an incubation period of eight to ten years; it involves the degeneration of the nerve cells of the brain and spinal cord, with progressive loss of

---

3. Some of these are discussed in Chapter 19, infra.

mental power. Epilepsy and encephalitis (sleeping sickness) are also considered organic brain disorders.

There is a group of disorders which is not known, as of now, to be caused by any identifiable physical defect. There may be no detectable physical or chemical change in the brain which can be related to abnormal behavior patterns of the individual suffering from the particular psychoses. Disorders of this type are seen as functional (i.e. non-organic) disorders because medical science has not as yet been able to demonstrate that they are organically caused. The medical explanation for the existence of these disturbances was originally propounded by Dr. Sigmund Freud and is still adhered by to a sizable number of today's psychiatrists. The functional mental illness in the Freudian sense is considered the result of a complex interplay of instinctual, acquired and environmental forces which intersect with the adaptive and defense forces of the subconscious mind. Differentiating these functional disorders from organic brain syndromes should not be understood as meaning that these disorders are, somehow, independent of brain function. Indeed, it is accepted that all psychological behavior patterns, normal as well as abnormal, depend upon brain functioning.

Schizophrenic disorders, a major subcategory of functional psychoses, involve an individual's inability to conceive reality, to build relationships, or to fashion concepts. Delusions or hallucinations also occur. One afflicted with schizophrenia loses interest in human relationships. For example, in one form of schizophrenia, the afflicted party may display shallow, silly behavior, often in the form of unpredictable giggling. Delusions may also occur. In the paranoid form the schizophrenic has delusions of persecution, or grandeur, and a suspicion that the world is hostile. Schizophrenia, as a thinking disorder, is equally common in both sexes.

The affective (or mood) disorders comprise another major subcategory of the functional psychoses. One of the most common of the affective psychoses has long been referred as manic-depressive disorder. This disorder is symptomized by mood swings, illusions, delusions, and hallucinations. Mood change can be precipitated by events which would have little effect on the normal person. There are several phases to this disorder. In the manic phase, the individual is hyperactive, his/her mood is abnormally optimistic and decisions are likely to be made impulsively. Other symptoms of the manic phase are overtalkativeness, distractibility, irritability and overinterest. To the contrary, in the depressed state, things look very bleak. The individual ceases to communicate with the world and loses interest in it. Physical activity often slows.

The third major subcategory of functional psychoses is the paranoid state. Psychiatric sources indicate that this condition is extremely rare. In this state, the afflicted party conceives an intricate and internally logical system of persecutory and/or grandiose delusions with accompanying hallucinations. The individual's emotional response and behavior are consistent with the delusion. The delusion is independent, in the sense that it does not appear to interfere with the remainder of the personality and intelligence, which continues essentially as if the individual were normal.

The neuroses are the result of the individual's attempt to resolve unconscious emotional conflicts in a manner which handicaps the achievement of normal living patterns. The chief symptom of the neuroses is anxiety. To some extent everyone experiences some of the symptoms of neuroses, but the truly neurotic person displays a consistent recurrent or constant maladjustment from early life.

The various types of personality disturbances have a common element in that the individual acts in a manner that reveals an inability to adjust to the world. The antisocial personality is one type of personality disorder that is often said to be prevalent among the so-called "criminal" population; the antisocial personality is unable to conform to prevailing social norms. It is also said that such a person suffers from the inability to form any lasting and satisfying relationships. Psychiatrists tell us that this type of personality displays superficial charm, unreliability, untruthfulness, lack of remorse, absence of any sense of responsibility, recidivism of improper conduct, inability to learn from experience, little insight, incapacity for love, and an unintegrated sex life.

§ 18.06 Examination of the Patient/Client

An examination of a person for the purpose of assessing whether the person suffers from any of the disorders described before is called a Mental Status Examination. It remains important for the attorney to become aware of all of the conditions under which the mental status examination was conducted, since errors in diagnosis can result from omissions or faulty observations by the examiner. The unexplained absence of any of the following elements in a psychiatric inquiry and/or report may connote an abbreviated and possibly inadequate mental status examination.

1. GENERAL CLINICAL OBSERVATIONS

(1) The circumstances of the examination—date, place, setting, presence of third parties, reason for making the examination.

(2) The general appearance of the patient—clothes, sex, race, age, demeanor, posture, gait, facial expressions, nutritional status, eyes, skin.

(3) The behavior of the patient—intelligence (abstract thinking tested by mathematics such as serial sevens, subtracting by sevens, or interpreting proverbs such as "a bird in the hand is worth two in the bush"), memory (tested by telling a story and asking subject to repeat it, or by showing a span of digits and asking subject to recall them), orientation (in time and personal identity), mannerisms, non-verbal motor or sensory perception (tremors, response to stimulation, consciousness, rigidity), speed of thought, vocabulary, judgment, insight,

clarity of expression, garrulousness (stream of talk or hyperactive conduct).

(4) The emotions of the client [1]—anger, depression, elation, anxiety, hallucinations, delusions, suppression of emotion, appropriateness of emotion, cause of abnormal emotion.

2. HISTORY—PAST AND PRESENT [2]

(1) Family history—father, mother, siblings, family prior history of mental illness, home atmosphere, dysfunctional home environment.

(2) Personal history—birth, health, school record, play record, work record, military history, medical history, diseases, court and criminal records, interests, habits, marital data, children, menstrual history, sex development, previous antisocial or dysfunctional behavior, complaints and symptoms elicited from the patient.

3. PHYSICAL AND NEUROLOGICAL EXAMINATION

The examiner may conduct a physical examination including such factors as weight, height, pulse, blood pressure, eyesight, ears, head and neck, skin, nose, mouth, chest and lungs, abdomen, extremities and genitalia. A neurological examination may also be conducted if the examiner suspects problems of organic nature. Lab tests of blood, urine, spinal fluid, as well as a CAT Scan, MRI or an EEG may be ordered.

4. PSYCHOLOGICAL TESTING

The examiner may order psychological tests to supplement other clinical observations. In this connection, see § 18.09, infra.

5. DIAGNOSTIC CLASSIFICATION

Here, the examining psychiatrist states the diagnostic opinion of the patient's mental condition in terms of the presence of specific mental disorders, if any, as discussed in § 18.04, supra. The examiner may also make recommendations for treatment and a prognosis of future development.

———

In exploring whether the report (whether oral or written) of a psychiatrist can be safely relied upon, it must be taken into account that psychiatric knowledge is constantly in a state of flux. What was accepted in earlier editions of the Diagnostic and Statistical Manual may have

---

§ 18.06

1. Members of different ethnic or national origins may display different comparative emotions.

2. Technically, an opinion founded in part on case history is based on hearsay.

Under modern principles of evidence law, however, such opinion will be admissible because in the professional disciplines such hearsay is relied upon for the purpose of making clinical judgments.

been modified. Similarly, new experiments are being conducted and findings evaluated that may lead practitioners of psychiatry to espouse conclusions that are not yet shared by the profession at large.[3]

While general clinical observations, as stated above, are necessary to arrive at a proper expert opinion, the manner in which the data is conducted or the nature of the instructions given to the patient may very well influence what reactions or responses are perceived by the examiner. The data may thus be distorted and contribute to an opinion to which other qualified mental health professionals would not subscribe.[4] Whether a person is seen as belonging to a lower socio-economic class, or to the middle class, may result in diagnoses that are significantly different. Thus, attorneys attempting to evaluate whether data produced by a mental status examination properly supports the expert's testimony must be aware of a multitude of factors that require familiarity with and sophistication in evaluating the psychiatric and psychological literature.[5]

§ 18.07 The Psychiatrist as an Expert Witness in Litigation

That the opinions of psychiatrists, generally, are admissible in evidence, providing the other requirements for the admission of expert opinion testimony are met,[1] is so well established as to require no citation of authority. The nature of specific types of testimony may be the subject of some objection, but where these types of evidence are covered specifically in this treatise, decisions relating to those issues are included within the discussion of these topics.[2] We discuss here some general legal principles that apply to psychiatric evidence.

1.   QUALIFICATIONS OF THE EXPERT WITNESS

Before a witness will be allowed to give opinion evidence as an expert, it must be shown that the witness is qualified. It should be

---

3. An indispensable tool for the practicing lawyer confronting psychiatric or psychological testimony are the books authored by Jay Ziskin and Faust. Dr. Ziskin is a psychologist and attorney. Their primary work is titled *Coping with Psychiatric and Psychological Testimony*, a three-volume treatise currently in its 4th edition (1988) with 1990 Supplement.

4. See, Rosenthal, *Experimenter Effects on Behavioral Research*, 1966. The author cites research showing that the expectations or characteristics of examining mental health professionals exert significant influence on the opinion the data generates. Thus, a professional with a particular attitude, outlook, or personality, will produce data, and consequently an expert opinion, that differs from those obtained by other professionals.

5. For a discussion on the problems and limitations mental health professionals face in making clinical evaluations and judgments, see, Borum, Otto, & Golding, "Improving clinical judgment and decision making in forensic evaluation," *The Journal of Psychiatry & Law* (Spring 1993) at 35.

§ 18.07

1. See Chapter 1, supra.

2. E.g., in Chapter 19, court decisions dealing with the admissibility of evidence relating to special mental health issues are included in the various subsections. Thus, the case of Brunner v. Brown, 480 N.W.2d 33 (Iowa 1992), holding that hearsay evidence on which a psychiatrist relied to form an opinion about a testator's mental state was admissible will be discussed in the section on Proof of Testamentary Capacity, infra § 19.___.

noted that, in the broad field of medicine, any person who has obtained the M.D. degree will be permitted to testify on any issue involving medicine. This is true also with respect to mental health. Any physician will typically be qualified to offer an opinion about the mental state of a person, if that opinion is relevant to disputed issues in the case. While the opinion may be admissible, it will of course not be very persuasive in the case of any evidence to the contrary, unless the witness can show the special qualifications of a psychiatrist. This is explored in more detail in the specific applications of psychiatry discussed in Chapter 19.

2.   SCOPE OF PSYCHIATRISTS' TESTIMONY

In Chapter 19, we will discuss the use of psychiatric testimony in a variety of civil and criminal cases. In the criminal area, one of the main topics of mental health professionals' testimony is on issues of insanity and competence to stand trial. There is, however, a definite trend toward admitting expert testimony on a variety of issues not related to sanity and competence. Despite the fact that many courts have said that psychiatric testimony on the issue of specific intent or motive is not admissible,[3] some courts now do allow experts to testify to defendants' lack of specific intent.[4] There are few cases on defendants' right to use psychiatric testimony in support of a claim of self defense.[5] In regard to evidence that defendant showed no evidence of sexual deviation, also see Chapter 19 on child sexual abuse cases and prosecutions involving sex offender profiles.

Courts generally do not permit experts to state that a witness is truthful or lying.[6] This has led to a rule prohibiting the courts to order witnesses to submit to psychiatric examinations.[7]

---

3. E.g., United States v. West, 670 F.2d 675 (7th Cir.1982); State v. Brom, 463 N.W.2d 758 (Minn.1990): expert testimony on premeditation not permitted; State v. Christensen, 129 Ariz. 32, 628 P.2d 580 (1981): expert may not testify to lack of premeditation, but may state that accused is generally impulsive. The prosecution also may not use such testimony. See, State v. Mitter, 168 W.Va. 531, 285 S.E.2d 376 (1981): improper to show accused acted for gratification.

4. E.g., State v. Vosler, 216 Neb. 461, 345 N.W.2d 806 (1984); Commonwealth v. Garcia, 505 Pa. 304, 479 A.2d 473 (1984): admissible in murder prosecutions but not for robbery; State v. Miller, 677 P.2d 1129 (Utah 1984); United States v. Hill, 655 F.2d 512 (3d Cir.1981): accused susceptible to inducement and easily entrapped. Accord, United States v. Newman, 849 F.2d 156 (5th Cir.1988).

5. The decisions are mixed. Thus, in Commonwealth v. McCusker, 448 Pa. 382,

292 A.2d 286 (1972) testimony on accused's mental condition in a self-defense case was admitted, but in Jahnke v. State, 682 P.2d 991 (Wyo.1984), it was held expert cannot explain why accused believed he had to kill his father in self defense though the father was neither attacking or threatening to attack. See also, Chapter 19, infra., in section on battered spouse syndrome.

6. State v. Myers, 382 N.W.2d 91 (Iowa 1986): witness may not state that children generally tell the truth about sexual abuse; State v. Woodburn, 559 A.2d 343 (Me.1989): improper to state six-year old cannot distinguish truth from falsity. On unreliability of eyewitness identifications, see Chapter 19.

7. E.g., State v. D.R.H., 604 A.2d 89 (N.J.1992); State v. Keen, 309 N.C. 158, 305 S.E.2d 535 (1983); United States v. Eschweiler, 745 F.2d 435 (7th Cir.1984); People v. Manson, 61 Cal.App.3d 102, 132 Cal.Rptr. 265 (1976).

While most testing of patients is done by psychologists, psychiatrists nevertheless are permitted to express opinions based on standardized psychological test results. Thus, in Byrd v. State,[8] the defendant was accused of beating his girlfriend to death. The court held that the defense psychiatrist should have been permitted to testify at the murder trial that there was an inconsistency between the defendant's psychological profile as indicated by the MMPI (Minnesota Multi–Phasic Personality Inventory) and the "knowingly killed" element of the murder charge levied against him.

3. THE WEIGHT OF PSYCHIATRIC EVIDENCE

In instructing the jury, courts frequently use a fairly standard instruction that the jury is free to weigh the testimony of experts and accept or reject such portions of it as they feel the evidence warrants. Such an instruction sometimes comes as a surprise to psychiatrists, who believe that after having been asked to give testimony, their opinion will have some decisive weight in the outcome of the case. This is not generally the case. Even when the expert testimony is not contradicted, the jury will be permitted to disregard it in the face of contrary lay witness testimony about the mental condition of the person whose status is in issue. It has been held, however, that a trier of fact cannot reject unimpeached psychiatric expert testimony that defendant suffered from a serious mental disorder rendering him incapable of conforming his conduct to the law when he murdered his parents.[9]

4. THE ANTICIPATION OF A PSYCHIATRIC DEFENSE IN CRIMINAL CASES

In many states, defendants in criminal cases who intend to present an insanity defense must give notice of such an intent to the state. The constitutionality of such requirements is well established.[10] Failure to comply with this requirement may result in exclusion of the defense.[11] Where no such statutory requirement exists, prosecutors are limited to traditional investigative techniques to discover the likelihood and scope of an anticipated psychiatric defense.

5. THE PROSECUTION'S RIGHT TO COMPEL PSYCHIATRIC EXAMINATIONS

In criminal cases where the mental condition of a defendant is raised, it has been held that even in the absence of statutory authority, a trial court can order the defendant to submit to an examination by a

---

8. 579 N.E.2d 457 (Ind.App.1991).

9. People v. Baker, 253 Ill.App.3d 15, 192 Ill.Dec. 564, 625 N.E.2d 719 (1993).

10. See, Williams v. Florida, 399 U.S. 78 (1970); Fed.R.Crim.Pro. Rule 12.2(a). See also, Taylor v. Illinois, 484 U.S. 400 (1988).

11. United States v. Winn, 577 F.2d 86 (9th Cir.1978). But see, Ronson v. Commonwealth, 604 F.2d 176 (2d Cir.1979), reversing exclusion of the defense.

state designated psychiatrist, even where an insanity defense is not involved.[12] Today, such examinations may be compelled even before an insanity or mental condition defense has been raised.[13] If defendant fails to permit the examination and refuses to cooperate, the sanctions can be three-fold: (1) exclusion of the defense,[14] (2) exclusion of the defense's expert witness testimony,[15] (3) and comment to the jury upon the refusal of the defendant to cooperate in an examination.[16] When a state psychiatric examination has been conducted to determine whether defendant is competent to stand trial, the state's examiner can also testify on the issue of insanity.[17]

When a court ordered examination is to take place, defense counsel must be notified of the examination.[18] This does not mean, however, that defense counsel has a right to be present during the examination.

6. PHYSICIAN–PATIENT PRIVILEGE NOT APPLICABLE

At common law, the physician-patient privilege did not exist; it is not constitutionally required.[19] Privileges are purely a matter of local law. By the weight of authority, neither a physician-patient, a psychiatrist-patient, or a psychologist-patient privilege applies when examinations have been conducted purely for the purpose of litigation.[20] Some courts have held that the privilege is waived where a defendant raises an insanity defense.[21]

7. THE DEFENDANT'S PRIVILEGE AGAINST SELF–INCRIMINATION

Where insanity is raised as a defense, the attempted introduction of incriminating oral statements made to the psychiatrist by the accused while the latter was in custody raises questions of the voluntariness of the statement, whether the privilege against self-incrimination has been

12. There is an inherent power for a court to order a mental examination when the accused enters a plea of insanity. State v. Whitlow, 45 N.J. 3, 210 A.2d 763 (1965). See also, United States v. Cohen, 530 F.2d 43 (5th Cir.1976); State v. Johnson, 383 A.2d 1012 (R.I.1978). But see, State v. Hennum, 441 N.W.2d 793 (Minn.1989).

13. State v. Manfredi, 213 Conn. 500, 569 A.2d 506 (1990).

14. State v. Parker, 19 Ariz.App. 204, 505 P.2d 1095 (1973): proper to exclude insanity defense when it was offered too late for examination by state to be conducted. Also, People v. Hayes, 421 Mich. 271, 364 N.W.2d 635 (1984).

15. State v. Whitlow, 45 N.J. 3, 210 A.2d 763 (1965); Parkin v. State, 238 So.2d 817 (Fla.1970).

16. Johnson v. People, 172 Colo. 72, 470 P.2d 37 (1970); State v. Schantz, 98 Ariz.

200, 403 P.2d 521 (1965), cert. denied 382 U.S. 1015 (1966).

17. See, Buchanan v. Kentucky, 483 U.S. 402 (1987).

18. Satterwhite v. Texas, 486 U.S. 249 (1988).

19. Noggle v. Marshall, 706 F.2d 1408 (6th Cir.1983).

20. E.g., State v. Toste, 178 Conn. 626, 424 A.2d 293 (1979); State v. Gonzales, 111 Ariz. 38, 523 P.2d 66 (1974); Granviel v. State, 552 S.W.2d 107 (Tex.Cr.App.1977).

21. E.g., Haynes v. State, 739 P.2d 497 (1987). But see, United States v. Alvarez, 519 F.2d 1036 (3d Cir.1975). In People v. Knuckles, 226 Ill.App.3d 714, 168 Ill.Dec. 680, 589 N.E.2d 1080 (1992), the court held there was no waiver because the privilege asserted was that of the attorney-client where the lawyer retained the psychiatrist.

violated, whether the accused had been offered the rights guaranteed by *Miranda* and whether (s)he made an effective waiver of these rights.[22]

8. DEFENDANT'S RIGHT TO COURT-APPOINTED PSYCHIATRIST

Today, an indigent defendant is entitled, constitutionally, to a court-appointed defense psychiatrist as long as the defendant makes a threshold showing that psychiatric issues are likely to be significant issues in the case.[23] As a general rule, it is held that defendant does not have a right to select the psychiatrist and it is the function of the trial court, however, to appoint the defense psychiatrist.[24] While earlier case law held that an accused did not have a right to have a defense-oriented expert,[25] there seems to be trend toward permitting a defendant to have the services of an expert-advocate.[26]

III. FORENSIC PSYCHOLOGY

§ 18.08 Psychology and Its Professionals

Psychology is the science of mind and behavior. It involves the principles, methods and procedures that are involved in understanding, predicting, and influencing behavior. A psychologist must be knowledgeable about the principles that pertain to such broad human activities as learning, perception, motivation, thinking, emotions, and interpersonal relationships. Psychology also is heavily involved in studying the methods and procedures of interviewing and counseling, and its practitioners must be trained in the methods and procedures of psychotherapy. It also involves the use of methods of assisting persons to modify feelings, attitudes and behavior which are intellectually, socially or emotionally maladjustive or ineffectual. Further, psychology also deals with the constructing, administering and interpreting of tests of intelligence, special abilities, aptitudes, interests, personality characteristics,

---

22. The courts have generally held that the self-incrimination privilege applies to state required psychiatric examinations: Williams v. Director, Patuxent Institution, 276 Md. 272, 347 A.2d 179 (1975); Commonwealth v. Pomponi, 447 Pa. 154, 284 A.2d 708 (1971). Similarly, *Miranda* requirements apply and the psychiatrist must warn the patient/accused of his rights under that decision prior to commencing an interrogation for diagnostic purposes. See, Estelle v. Smith, 451 U.S. 454 (1981). Even before this decision, some states recognized by statute that no statements made by an accused in cooperating with a psychiatrist in a compulsory examination to determine competency or sanity may be admitted in evidence on the issue of guilt in any criminal proceeding.

23. Ake v. Oklahoma, 470 U.S. 68 (1985).

24. See v. State, 296 Ark. 498, 757 S.W.2d 947 (1988). But see, United States v. Matthews, 472 F.2d 1173 (4th Cir.1973): accused may select his own psychiatrist; United States v. Schultz, 431 F.2d 907 (8th Cir.1970): trial court should be generous in appointing defense psychiatrists.

25. E.g., Proctor v. Harris, 413 F.2d 383 (D.C.Cir.1969).

26. Smith v. McCormick, 914 F.2d 1153 (9th Cir.1990). See also, De Freece v. State, 848 S.W.2d 150 (Tex.Cr.App.1993).

emotions and motivation. It further pertains to the psychological evaluation, preventing and improvement of adjustment problems of individuals and groups, and the resolution of interpersonal and social conflicts.

Clearly, such a broad field of study has many facets and novel applications. Forensic psychology, that part which deals in the legal applications of psychology, has gained great prominence in the last fifty years. Psychologists are now called upon to assist attorneys in pretrial preparation and to testify at trial in both civil and criminal cases. Clinical psychologists—as opposed to academic psychologists—are most effective as legal consultants and expert witnesses because they deal with patients on a regular basis delivering psychological services to the public.

A clinical psychologist is one who studies the abnormal behavior of humans. To qualify as a clinical psychologist in most states, one must study four years beyond the bachelor's degree, obtaining a Ph.D. in psychology, and then serve a period of time as an intern in a hospital doing diagnostic and treatment work with the mentally handicapped. A final two-year period must be spent in a residency.

Since persons can hold themselves out as "psychologists" with a mere bachelor's degree in that field, if they are employed and work under the supervision of a properly licensed professional, and can be employed in various job designations that include psychologist, counselor, advisor, family consultant, diagnostician, clinical social worker, psychiatric social worker, psychosocial worker, marriage counselor, mental health therapist, and other designations, attorneys must determine exactly what the credentials are of the individual who purports to be a psychologist before retaining an individual for forensic consultation.

Today, in most states, in order to operate an independent practice, psychologists must not only complete a prescribed educational program, but they must also pass a state licensing examination. Licensing requirements vary from state to state; in turn, educational standards also vary from state to state. Candidates for licensure in psychology generally must hold a doctorate in psychology and possess a minimum of one year postgraduate experience. Some states, in contrast, permit candidates with a master's degree in psychology and five years supervised postgraduate experience to sit for the licensing exam.[1]

Reciprocity of licensure exists between most states where the licensing requirements are substantially equivalent. Such statutes pose difficulties for psychologists from the few states not requiring Ph.D. degrees who seek licensure in other states. However, state licensing boards

§ 18.08

1. E.g., W.Va.Code, 30–21–7(a)(3). West's Fla.Stat.Ann. § 490.001 et seq., requires a doctoral degree in psychology from an approved program, passing the examination, and having two years or 4,000 hours of experience in the field of psychology in association with or under the supervision of a licensed psychologist. See, Abramson v. Gonzalez, 949 F.2d 1567 (11th Cir.1992), for a dispute dealing with the regulation of entry to the profession.

typically have discretion to waive the licensing exam in whole or in part and may exercise this discretion in favor of psychologists that have gained extensive experience in a state whose requirements are not "substantially equivalent."

Educational programs in psychology are accredited by the American Psychological Association. At present, many psychology programs are not accredited for one reason or another. Therefore, licensure candidates need not graduate from an accredited program. In such cases, the licensing board must compare the applicant's educational credentials to the standards set by the American Psychological Association.

State licensing exams typically consist of a nationally standardized written portion and an oral part designed by the state licensing board. In addition, some state licensing boards prepare and implement a supplementary written portion. Once licensed, psychologists are bound by a code of professional ethics; [2] complaints are generally directed to the state licensing boards. In turn, the state boards investigate the charge and may take such action as is permitted by statute and deemed appropriate by the board.

Psychologists that are called upon to perform services relating to the legal system are known as forensic psychologists, a designation that does not require separate licensing. Trial lawyers often call upon licensed psychologists to assist in trial preparation and to testify at trial. In the period before trial, psychologists typically participate in jury selection and witness preparation, advise on the timing and sequencing of evidence, educate attorneys on the psychological aspects of courtroom strategy and nonverbal communication, and make competency determinations.

Participation by psychologists in jury selection involves detecting the emotional makeup, longstanding attitudes, and ingrained values which may predispose potential jurors in one direction or another. Typically, attorneys detect these traits while interviewing jurors with a questionnaire prepared by the advising psychologist.[3] Psychologists also train attorneys on scoring juror responses to the questionnaire. Ultimately, the attorney uses this information when making juror objections for cause or otherwise.

Today, psychologists are often involved in legal matters which heretofore were believed to be within the special experience and knowledge of psychiatrists. In that sense, the two professionals frequently overlap in their functions. Thus, psychologists often make competency

---

2. It is very important for attorneys employing psychologists to become aware of the ethical constraints of the psychological profession. The American Psychological Association, in 1990, formulated Ethical Principles for forensic psychologists. See, "Specialty Guidelines for Forensic Psychologists," 15 *Law and Human Behavior* 655 (1991).

3. The preparation of such questionnaires requires special skills because the ease with which answers obtained may be influenced by the manner in which the questions are phrased. It is for that reason that psychologists frequently consult with persons drafting public opinion polls. See, Coleman, "Pollsters Enlist Psychologists In Quest for Unbiased Results," *The N.Y. Times* [Nat. ed.], Sept. 7, 1993, at B5.

determinations for the legal system.[4] In this regard, psychologists implement the Competency Screening Index. The Competency Screening Index was developed by the Laboratory of Community Psychiatry in conjunction with the National Institute of Mental Health. The test consists of a series of sentence completion exercises and screens defendants as to their competency to stand trial. In this manner, psychologists are able to make timely and believed reasonably accurate competency determinations.

The psychologist's role at trial is dictated by the nature of the case, criminal or civil. In criminal cases, psychologists often testify on the defendant's probable state of mind during the commission of the crime. Defendant's state of mind testimony includes insanity, diminished responsibility, mental disorder, severe depression, confusion and automatism. If unsuccessful at the trial stage, attorneys may use the psychologist's testimony at the sentencing stage to either reduce the convicted defendant's sentence, or to prove future dangerousness for enhancement of sentence purposes. Increasingly, psychologists also testify on the presence or absence of a required mental state for specific crimes, and on victim mental states in cases involving the battered woman syndrome, child abuse syndrome, child sexual abuse accommodation syndrome, and rape trauma syndrome.

In civil cases, the psychologist's role is much more extensive than in criminal cases. In domestic relations cases, psychologists often testify on which parent should receive child custody and visitation; they also testify in cases involving child abuse and neglect, paternal fitness, psychological damage and neurological impairment, civil commitment of the retarded, employment discrimination, juvenile placement, special education assignments, and trademark infringements to name but a few. Psychologists also interpret intellectual/personality tests such as MMPI–2 and MMPI, MCMI, WAIS and WAIS–R, Rorschach, Bender, and Gestalt. Simply put, the psychologist's role in the legal system is ever growing.

The psychological examination is similar to the mental status examination of psychiatrists, and must be geared to the specific purpose that is sought to be served. It would differ greatly, depending on whether the psychologist seeks to determine competency to stand trial, competence to take care of life's daily tasks, capacity to make a will or enter into contracts, insanity at a particular moment in the past, or whether the person is likely to be a danger to self or others in the future. In addition to mental status examinations, psychologists depend greatly in their diagnoses on the outcome of various testing devices.

§ 18.09 Psychological Testing Devices

The tools of the clinical and forensic psychologists consists in essence of the Mental Status Examination, complemented by the use of diagnostic, standardized tests that have been validated.

---

4. Psychologists' examinations are often helpful because their testing procedures are more objective than psychiatric examina- tions. See, State v. Gardner, 616 A.2d 1124 (R.I.1992).

A Mental Status Examination would consist of an observation and evaluation of the subject during a clinical interview where the analyst may pay attention to such factors as the subject's appearance, grooming, behavior, posture, gait, facial expressions, eye contact, motor activity, rate of speech and pitch, emotions, verbal associations, and other factors. The tests which a psychologist might well use in forensic testing include the Wechsler Adult Intelligence Scale, currently the "WAIS–R", the Minnesota Multiphasic Personality Inventory, either the older and extensively validated "MMPI" or the newer "MMPI–2"; and a Rorschach Test.

Psychological tests are diagnostic aids in measuring the range and nature of intellectual ability and emotional response. The tests are not conclusive means of determining the mental status of a subject, and are used in combination with the mental status examination. Their value is no greater than the skill, training, and practical experience of the clinician who employs them. The tests have proved of particular assistance in a wide variety of diagnoses. Devising, standardizing, refining, and validating psychological tests continues to be a major research activity of psychologists. One of the main concerns when selecting a test is always its reliability, which is whether it obtains the same results consistently, and its validity, which is whether it actually measures what it is purported to assess. Since there exist literally hundreds of psychological tests, our discussion will be limited to some of the most frequently and widely used.

1. PERSONALITY TESTS

Personality tests, designed to help identify abnormal tendencies in the individual personality, are of two types: (a) the self-report personality inventory (also referred to as psychometric tests), which are objective tests wherein the subject is given a prepared list of answers to questions and is asked to agree or disagree or pick the correct answer, the response then being measured by a previously established scale; (b) the projective tests, which consist of subjective stimulus-response tests whereby the subject is given ambiguous stimulus material that prevents him or her from knowing what the right answer should be when asked to relate its meaning and organization. The aim of these tests is to reveal the subject's quality of personality. These two distinguishable approaches are complementary to each other; neither is used to the exclusion of the other.

The essence of projective personality tests is that they are unstructured. That is, there is no rigidly agreed-on public meaning for the stimulus configurations to which the subject is asked to respond. *Projection* —the tendency of a person to attribute his own unwanted motives and social traits to others—is, in the technical sense of the term, only one of the mechanisms involved. The idea is to be able to observe how the subject experiences and deals with life situations. The test responses are really being used as substitutes for observed behavior in daily activities of the subject, since this is generally inconvenient or impossible.

(a) Self-report personality inventory test: The most popular of the self-report inventories is the Minnesota Multiphasic Personality Inventory (MMPI), developed during research in the Department of Neuropsychiatry at the Medical School of the University of Minnesota. In the still commonly used test, the subject is given some 566 true-false questions. A "normal" person supposedly will answer a given number as false, but it is not so much the total number of false answers that matters, than the pattern in which false or true answers are given. Since it is a true-false test, the MMPI does not require clinical observation of the subject during the test, and his personality is judged almost exclusively from the true-false response. The wording of the questions is simple; however, the use of double negatives in some of the original questions has had a tendency to confuse a subject and induce an abnormal answer solely because of misperception of the question.

The aim of the test is to identify psychopathological characteristics demonstrated by the subject's choices on the test. The questions are structured to prevent fabrication or an attempt by the subject to present himself favorably. In determining the personality type of the subject, the answers obtained are compared with the established group responses of mentally ill persons. These established scale patterns were determined by giving the MMPI test to a large number of clinical mental patients who represented all of the major psychiatric diagnostic categories being utilized at the time of the test construction, and a similar number of normally adjusted subjects selected mainly of relatives and visitors of patients in the University of Minnesota hospitals. The subject's personality is diagnosed by the degree to which the answers resemble one of the criteria groups. Obviously, then, the accuracy of the test depends greatly upon the adherence to scientific psychological principles in fashioning the various criteria groups. If these are chosen without reliable clinical support, the whole test is worthless.

Because the MMPI test was developed on the basis of empirical findings, and has been widely validated by controlled studies, it is deemed generally unimpeachable statistically. The major criticism which has been made is the need for new validation since "normality" was defined on the basis of responses obtained about a half century ago. Related to this is the potential cultural bias involved in using a test developed from the responses of American adults. Because of trend toward automation, there is the danger that "interpretation of MMPI profiles by inadequately trained users" may be encouraged where, in fact, a proper interpretation calls for "considerable sophistication." [1] Despite these potential problems, the MMPI is probably the most carefully researched test ever devised. It has a high degree of reliability,

§ 18.09

1. See, Anastasi, *Psychological Testing*, (3d. ed.) 1988. Cronbach & Cronbach, *Essentials of Psychological Testing*, 1970;

Deese, *Psychology as Science and Art*, 1972; Dahlstrom, et al., *MMPI Handbook*, 1972, Vol. 2; and other sources in the Bibliography at § 18.16, infra.

though perhaps not quite as high as the Wechsler's Adult Intelligence Scale–Revised (WAIS–R) discussed under the subsection of Intelligence Tests.

To remedy some of the objections raised to the original test, in 1992 a new MMPI–2 was published. One of the problems attendant to the use of the MMPI–2 is that there are few if any validation studies currently available, while over 8,000 studies have been done on the original MMPI.[2] It is for that reason that psychologists, especially those engaged in forensic work, prefer to keep using MMPI in addition to MMPI–2.

There are, of course, various other personality tests. Among those fairly widely used are: the California Psychological Inventory (CPI), an objective personality test; the Myers–Briggs Type Indicator (MBTI), an objective personality test based on Dr. Jung's type theory; and the NEO Personality Inventory (NEO–PI), an objective personality test consisting of 181 questions designed to measure the five major personality factors.

(b) Projective tests: The Rorschach Inkblot test, developed in 1921 by Swiss psychiatrist Hermann Rorschach, is perhaps the best known projective test. His *Psychodiagnostics,* published in 1921 and translated into English in 1942, symbolized the beginning of projective testing. The technique became the favorite clinical tool of psychologists after World War II. The test's value is derived from the fact that the subject cannot feign illness by tailoring the responses, because, in this test, there are no right or wrong answers. The subject is shown singularly ten distinctive inkblots of bilateral symmetry. The blots are contained on square cards. Some are colored; all have slightly different intensities of shading. The subject is asked to relate what he or she sees in the inkblot pictures. Responses are scored on the basis of content, location, color, shading, motion, form, etc. The result is dependent on the subjective observation of the clinical examiner. Indeed, the scoring of the subject's responses may vary with the examiner.

The Rorschach test and all projective unstructured tests are founded on the hypothesis that not only what the person selects to perceive among the multitudinous stimuli which present themselves, but also how the perceptions are organized and the manner in which the responses are made, reveal important signs of character and pathology. The purpose is to discover the subject's inner attitudes. The Rorschach test by its nature cannot be standardized. Primary reliance is placed on the examiner's expertise in sifting, sorting, weighing, and organizing the observations that are made.

Some clinical psychologists believe the Rorschach test is the most effective test in making neuropsychiatric diagnoses, despite evidence that

---

2. The wide use of MMPI and variety of validations studies may be illustrated by such studies as: Hargrave, Hiatt & Gaffney, "A Comparison of MMPI and CPI Test Profiles for Traffic Officers and Deputy Sheriffs," 14 *J.Pol.Sci. & Admin.* 250 (1986); and Shusman, Inwald & Knatz, "A Cross–Validation Study of Police Recruit Performance as Predicted by the IPI and MMPI," 15 *J.Pol. Sci. & Admin.* 162 (1987).

in some cases different tests provided the proper diagnosis which was missed in use of the Rorschach. Yet, one of the special aspects of Rorschach is that the test gives information about the manner in which the subject may react to mental illness and the efforts the subject makes to conceal or hide the effects of that illness.[3]

The Rorschach, like most tests, is only a tool to gather information. Certain responses may influence the examiner's diagnosis, i.e., neurotics reportedly see "blood" in certain of the inkblots; people suffering from schizophrenia reportedly show a drop in perception of form quality, fragmentary perception of only part of the blot and/or confusion of two different perceptions of the same area of a blot into a third unintelligible perception. Rorschach scores are determined with reference to reception of (1) form, shape, color and shading; (2) content, i.e. plant, animal, movement; and (3) location, i.e., whole card or only a segment.

Clinical psychologists recognize the following as Rorschach axioms: (1) the higher the intelligence, the more responses to the whole and the more meaningfully organized the whole response; (2) the clearer the perception, the more popular and standard the response; (3) the more divorced from reality, the greater the perception of movement where others do not normally see it. Other axioms are recognized, but because of the complexity of the material, its assumptions are not readily abstracted in summary form.

Apart from being the most widely used, the Rorschach test is probably also the most widely criticized of all psychometric techniques. A body of research findings has raised questions about even the most basic elements of scoring. For example, the subject's use of color in formulating a response is important, yet, comparative studies with standard and achromatic series of Rorschach cards have demonstrated that "color itself has no effect on most of the response characteristics customarily attributed to it."[4] Despite the inherent limitations of all projective tests, they remain popular.

The Thematic Apperception Test (TAT) is a projective test which had its origins in studies at Harvard University. It was first published and marketed as a test in 1943, and attempts to determine the interpersonal reactions of the subject through the narration of consecutive stories by the subject when shown a set of 20 ambiguous pictures, mostly drawings, which contain people of both sexes and different ages in situations designed to trigger stories of psychological significance. Because of the time involved in conducting the test, it is often abbreviated with the subject only viewing ten or twelve pictures. The full set contains 30 pictures, including some alternative versions for males and females or adolescent and adults. In construing the story of each picture, the subject is instructed to narrate what is happening at the

---

3. Rabian, *Projective Techniques in Personality Assessment* (1968) at p. 115.

4. For some of the early analyses of various tests, and an examination of criticisms, see, Anastasi, *Psychological Testing* (1968); Nunnally, *Psychometric Theory* (1965); Allen, *Elements of Rorschach Interpretation* (1954); Kopter & Davidson, *The Rorschach Technique* (1962).

moment, what led up to it, how the people feel, and what the outcome of the situation will be. The diagnostician then analyzes the 20–story responses for pervasive personality patterns. Psychologists believe that the subject is less likely to conceal his or her true motivation and feelings when protected by the anonymity of explaining the actions of third persons—the people in the photographs. This test is believed to be appropriate in diagnosing fantasies, motives, drives, ambitions, preoccupations, attitudes and interpersonal relationships.[5]

The assumptions made in TAT interpretation are that in completing the situation or story the individual's own striving, conflicts, and dispositions will be revealed; in telling the story, the subject is likely to identify with the persons depicted and thus reflect the story teller's own wishes and conflicts by relating stories which are very revealing and others which are of no diagnostic value. The revelation of inner psyche motivations will be greater when the picture is ambiguous. Variables which may affect the responses include the presence or absence of the examiner, the way in which the test is administered, the instructions given to the subject, the attitude of the examiner, the physical conditions of the test surroundings, and the differences in color brightness and background of the pictures. Formal scoring systems are not typically used while assembling TAT results, instead, a clinical analysis consists of carefully developed hypotheses from each story on the basis of the experience of the examiner and aided by published works on the major themes brought out by each picture. Obviously, the knowledge, experience, skill, and thoroughness of the examining clinician will determine the worth of the test in a particular case.

To permit the test to be used for the diagnosis of pre-puberty children, a different but similar test, called the Children's Apperception Test (CAT) was created. This test uses pictures of animals, which reveal as much useful information about their mental processes to the examiner while telling stories about animals as may be discovered when adults describe the photographs containing humans.

There are many other types of projective tests, such as those involving word association or sentence completion. For further information on these the reader is referred to the authorities listed in footnotes throughout this section or in § 18.16, *infra*.

2. INTELLIGENCE TESTS

Intelligence tests are utilized to determine the degree of an individual's intelligence—his I.Q., or intelligence quotient. They are reliable enough to play a primary role in the assessment of minimal intelligence on the various issues of capacity, responsibility, competence, and credibility. While most clinical psychologists will readily concede that I.Q. is not a mathematical absolute, it is a useful tool in diagnosing the mental

---

5. See, Bellak, *The T.A.T. and C.A.T. in Clinical Use,* 1970; Kagan & Lessner, *Con-* *temporary Issues in Thematic Apperception Methods* (1961).

state of a subject. Some I.Q. tests such as the Otis Quick Score Test could be given to groups of people with only the necessity of a monitor, pencils, and paper. If the circumstances suggest a mental deficiency, an individually administered test could then be given by an expert.

The Stanford–Binet Test is an individually administered test to determine children's I.Q. and might be employed to test a prospective child witness. In most instances, however, the psychologist will be using the Wechsler Adult Intelligence Scale–Revised (WAIS–R). The WAIS–R is an individually administered standardized adult intelligence test with separate norms for various age levels from adolescence to old age. The I.Q. under WAIS–R is determined from a combination of Verbal Tests and Performance Tests. The verbal tests consist of oral subjects covering common sense, judgment, general information, mathematics, digit span, word similarity and vocabulary. The performance tests consist of visual or visual-manipulative tests of digit-symbol pairing, picture completion, block design, picture arrangement, and object assembly. As with all psychological tests, variables such as anxiety, ill health, distraction, uncooperativeness, mental illness, inattentiveness, lack of education, influence of the examiner and divergent cultural background can affect the validity of an adult I.Q. test. However, the tests attempt to minimize cultural differences and educational gaps, and WAIS–R is a very reliable test with some very good validation studies.

I.Q. scores are used to classify subjects according to the following nomenclature: mild mental retardation (I.Q. of 50–70); moderate mental retardation (I.Q. of 30–49); and severe mental retardation (I.Q. scores of 29 and below).

3. PSYCHOMOTOR TESTS

Psychomotor tests are tests of retention, memory, and conceptual thinking. Although particularly prevalent as a tool for diagnosing organic brain damage, the tests are not confined to the sphere of neuropsychology and are also used by psychologists to diagnose functional mental illness.

The Bender–Gestalt Test is a psychomotor test used to estimate maturation and intelligence and to determine the presence of organic cerebral disease. Under this test, designs which are exhibited are then copied by the test subject. The evaluation of the subject's linear design perception and visual motor functions are used to diagnose possible organic brain impairment. Other older psychomotor tests are: the Porteus–Maxes Test which tests for common sense, impulsiveness and mental deficiency; the Graham–Kendall Memory for Design Test, which tests for visual motor memory resulting from brain damage; the Wechsler Digits Test which tests visual and oral memory functioning; and the Goldstein–Scheere Cube Test, which tests for flexibility in thinking, mental deficiency, and brain damage. More recently, psychologists have developed extensive new test batteries to assess neuropsychological performance. These include the Halstead–Reitan Neuropsychological Test Battery and the Luria–Nebraska Neuropsychological Battery.[6]

§ 18.10 The Psychologist as an Expert Witness

Like opinion testimony of psychiatrists, psychologist expert evidence today gains widespread acceptance. The particularities of specific cases wherein examinations and testing were done may at times be challenged, as will be seen in Chapter 19. Overall, however, psychologists have been permitted to qualify as experts on a wide variety of topics relating to mental health.

The courts' attitudes were not always that way. Whether a psychologist may testify as an expert on insanity and competency was, for a long time, a subject of much debate.[1] Indeed, it has been asserted that studies show psychiatrists and psychologists are no better than lay people at making clinical judgments.[2] Nevertheless, most jurisdictions permit such testimony today.[3] Psychologists have also been permitted to testify to opinions about the mental status of subjects based on the results of psychological tests they administered.[4] They have been permitted to testify about the behavioral traits of child abuse victims,[5] on the battered spouse syndrome,[6] and on the psychological factors undermining the accuracy of eyewitness identifications.[7] Psychologist's testimony to the effect that a complaining witness was telling the truth, however, was held improper as invading the responsibility of the jury.[8]

---

6. For a detailed description of these tests, see, *Handbook of Clinical Neuropsychology,* Filskov & Bole, eds., 1981.

§ 18.10

1. See the cases collected in 78 A.L.R.2d 919.

2. See, Coleman, "Psychologists' Expert Testimony Called Unscientific," *The New York Times,* Oct. 11, 1988, p. 19.

3. E.g., People v. Lyles, 186 Colo. 302, 526 P.2d 1332 (1974); Henderson v. State, 159 Ind.App. 621, 308 N.E.2d 710 (1974); People v. Noble, 42 Ill.2d 425, 248 N.E.2d 96 (1969).

4. People v. Stoll, 49 Cal.3d 1136, 265 Cal.Rptr. 111, 783 P.2d 698 (1989) [MMPI and MCMI]; People v. Coleman, 38 Cal.3d 69, 211 Cal.Rptr. 102, 695 P.2d 189 (1985) [MMPI and Rorschach]; but see, Bertsch v. Brewer, 97 Wash.2d 83, 640 P.2d 711 (1982) [MMPI-based opinion testimony improperly admitted without proper foundation]. The tests must also be generally accepted as validated in the psychological profession. Thus, in People v. John W., 185 Cal.App.3d 801, 229 Cal.Rptr. 783 (1986), it was proper to exclude opinion testimony based on an administration of "an electronic physiological test known as a penile plethysmograph." In Byrd v. State, 593 N.E.2d 1183 (Ind.1992), reversing in

part 579 N.E.2d 457, the court held that expert testimony on the MMPI which suggested that a murder defendant's personality was inconsistent with the alleged offense was properly excluded at trial. Also, a man tried for sex abuse crimes was not entitled to have a psychologist testify to his MMPI scores for the purpose of establishing he did not conform to the profile characteristics of sex offenders, said the court in State v. Elbert, 831 S.W.2d 646 (Mo.App.1992). Such evidence has been "almost universally rejected," said the court.

5. Kirkpatrick v. State, 747 S.W.2d 833 (Tex.App.1987). On the child sexual abuse accommodation syndrome, see Chapter 19, infra.

6. Commonwealth v. Rose, 725 S.W.2d 588 (Ky.1987), cert. denied 484 U.S. 838 (1987). On the battered spouse syndrome, see Chapter 19, infra.

7. People v. McDonald, 37 Cal.3d 351, 208 Cal.Rptr. 236, 690 P.2d 709 (1984). See Chapter 19, infra.

8. E.g., State v. Moreland, 50 Ohio St.3d 58, 552 N.E.2d 894 (1990); State v. Schimpf, 782 S.W.2d 186 (Tenn.Cr.App. 1989); Garcia v. State, 712 S.W.2d 249 (Tex.App.1986). See also, Commonwealth v. O'Searo, 466 Pa. 224, 352 A.2d 30 (1976):

In civil cases, it was proper to admit expert testimony on the psychological effects of marriage on the wife.[9] Psychologists also testify frequently in employment discrimination cases flowing from sexual harassment, and in child custody disputes regarding the best interests of the child.[10] Psychologists also are asked to conduct "psychological autopsies"[11] in insurance disputes and worker's compensation cases, to resolve the issue of suicide, accident, or natural death in equivocal deaths.

Because so many unlicensed psychologists, or persons who lack doctoral degrees in psychology, take the witness stand to testify to symptoms that deal with mental dysfunctions, lawyers must carefully scrutinize the credentials of the witnesses and, if necessary, oppose the testimony for lack of expert qualifications. Depending upon the type of testimony sought to be elicited, the courts have been remarkably inconsistent in the degree to which courts insist on extensive professional qualifications when an expert proffers psychological opinions. Thus, in some jurisdictions, an investigator and social worker employed by the state's department of human services might be permitted to testify on the psychological phenomenon known as the "child sexual abuse syndrome,"[12] or a rape counselor might be permitted to state that a victim suffered from the rape trauma syndrome,[13] whereas in other jurisdictions the court might reject such testimony even when offered by a licensed clinical psychologist.[14] Thus, a person who professes to be knowledgeable in a subject by virtue of his employment in a child welfare

clinical psychologist cannot substantiate and corroborate defendant's version of critical events.

9. McKilligan v. McKilligan, 156 A.D.2d 904, 550 N.Y.S.2d 121 (3d Dept.1989).

10. In Chris D. v. Montgomery County Board of Education, 753 F.Supp. 922 (M.D.Ala.1990), the child psychologist was deemed unqualified by virtue of the fact her master's degree was obtained more than 10 years prior to her testimony and there was no indication she had remained current with developments in the field.

11. A "psychological autopsy" is not truly a test or a technique, but a process or a way of looking at data. The term was coined by Dr. Schneidman in the early 1950s, but it would be more accurate to use the terminology: psychological reconstruction. The reliability of such psychological reconstructions is subject to some doubt; the psychologist testifies about a patient he/she has never met or tested while alive. It is somewhat similar to a psychologist who determines whether an unknown testator had the capacity to make a will when

that capacity is disputed after the testator's death. For judicial use of such an "autopsy," see, Jackson v. State, 553 So.2d 719 (Fla.Dist.Ct.App.1989); In re Estate of Hoover, 155 Ill.2d 402, 185 Ill.Dec. 866, 615 N.E.2d 736 (1993). See also, Ogloff & Otto, "Psychological Autopsy: Clinical and Legal Perspectives," 37 *St. Louis U.L.J.* 607 (1993); Harris, "The Psychological Autopsy: A Retrospective Study of Suicide," 20 *Stetson L.Rev.* 289 (1990).

12. E.G., Duckett v. State, 797 S.W.2d 906 (Tex.Cr.App.1990). See also Chapter 19, infra.

13. See, People v. Bledsoe, 36 Cal.3d 236, 203 Cal.Rptr. 450, 681 P.2d 291 (1984): testimony held improper, though conviction affirmed because of strong evidence apart from the expert's testimony.

14. Hall v. Arkansas, 15 Ark.App. 309, 692 S.W.2d 769 (1985): expert testimony by a psychologist on the dynamics of child sexual abuse was prejudicial enough to require reversal of the conviction. See also, People v. Bledsoe, supra note 13.

department may qualify as an expert on a topic which is still highly controversial within the health care profession.[15]

IV. FORENSIC NEUROLOGY AND NEUROPSYCHOLOGY

§ 18.11   The Professions of Neurology and Neuropsychology

The neurologist is a physician concerned with the specialized study of the nervous system and the anatomical and physiological functions of its different parts. The study is a branch of internal medicine. The neurologist assists in the diagnosis of organic brain disorder involving structural defect or impairment of brain tissue function, i.e., trauma, cerebral embolism, senile deterioration of the brain, toxic brain poisons (drugs, carbon monoxide), central nervous system syphilis, cardiac disease, arterial hypertension, alcoholic hallucinosis, delirium tremens, cerebral arteriosclerosis, brain tumor, metabolic defect, infection, degenerative brain disease, and convulsive disorders such as epilepsy. The neurologist is also often asked to declare a person legally dead when extraordinary life-prolonging methods have been used and a consideration is given to organ transplantation. To achieve their purpose, practitioners of neurology "search for structural nervous system pathology based upon clinical and laboratory evidence (for example the physical neurological examination and such diagnostic methods as cerebrospinal fluid studies, the computerized axial tomography [CAT scan], magnetic resonance imaging [MRI] and the [EEG] electroencephalogram.)"[1] The neurologist's field of endeavor overlaps that of the neuropsychologist and psychiatrist when study of the complex upper level mental functions is appropriate.

In the modern medical world it is impossible for one person to thoroughly cover both the fields of neurology and psychiatry. Neurologists do not attempt, as a rule, to diagnose or treat functional mental illness; rather, they concentrate on treating diseases of organic etiology. Organic mental illness may be acute or chronic. A cure may be effected in the case of acute illness by that branch of neurology known as neurosurgery, i.e., removal of a tumor.

Neuropsychology, by contrast, is not a medical practice and neuropsychologists are not physicians. Rather, neuropsychology is a system of psychology based upon neurology, and is concerned with the behavioral consequences of brain damage. The neuropsychologist is first a clinical psychologist, but has also received advanced training in neuroanatomy and neurology. The specialty has become, over the past several decades, one of the fastest growing division of clinical psychology. Neuropsychol-

---

15. See, Chapter 19, infra., on the subject of the Child Sexual Abuse Accommodation Syndrome.

§ 18.11

1. Gilandas & Touyz, "Forensic Neuropsychology: A Selective Introduction," 28 *J.For.Sci.* 713 (1983).

ogy came of prominence largely "in response to the need of the medical profession for additional diagnostic aids to assist doctors in the diagnosis and location of brain damage." [2] There are two different categories of neuropsychologists, the locationalists, and the functionalists.

Neuropsychologists are specially concerned with monitoring human higher intellectual functioning; they pay less attention to basic physiological processes such as reflexes, concentrating instead, on measuring tactile, visual-spacial, word usage, memory, and intellectual processes. The tools of the neuropsychologists are psychological tests chosen for their significance in determining the mental status of patients. Thus, neuropsychologists interact with the legal system increasingly in finding the causal connection between certain traumatic events and subsequent neuropsychological deficits. In general, neuropsychologists have an excellent performance rate in finding impairment of the brain. But when it comes to determining the cause of the impairment, their performance is not quite as good.

§ 18.12 Some Organic Neurological Disorders

Brain tissue malfunction resulting from organic brain disorder is characterized by impairment of orientation, memory, intellectual function and judgment. The victim of such a disorder is apt to act in an abnormal manner. Since personality is dependent upon brain function, it follows that changes from normal personality may be expected to accompany organic brain disorder.

One of the major brain dysfunctions is epilepsy. There are three different forms: (1) grand mal; (2) petit mal; and (3) psychomotor epilepsy.

The grand mal form of epilepsy involves, generally, a convulsive state and loss of consciousness, virtually precluding knowing conduct.[1] The petit mal form involves only an unconscious state. One undergoing a petit mal seizure rarely exhibits elaborate acts of purposeful movement. Hence, this form is also unlikely to be associated with purposeful conduct or criminal activity.

Proof that the accused suffers from the psychomotor form of epilepsy is sometimes offered on insanity issues.[2] During a psychomotor

2. Wren & Greenfield, "Dealing with Neuropsychological Evidence," *For The Defense,* July, 1989, p. 11.

§ 18.12

1. People v. Freeman, 61 Cal.App.2d 110, 142 P.2d 435 (1943); unconscious epileptic attack sufficient to absolve defendant of homicide by auto; but see, Smith v. Commonwealth, 268 S.W.2d 937 (Ky.1954) and 282 S.W.2d 840 (Ky.1955): epilepsy not sufficient to negate responsibility for manslaughter; People v. Eckert, 2 N.Y.2d 126, 157 N.Y.S.2d 551, 138 N.E.2d 794 (1956),

affirming conviction for criminal negligence when defendant lost control of his vehicle while unconscious during epileptic seizure, the court holding defendant knew he was subject to attacks and was negligent in driving at all.

2. People v. Gambacorta, 197 N.Y. 181, 90 N.E. 809 (1910); Oborn v. State, 143 Wis. 249, 126 N.W. 737 (1910). Reversible error to deny an indigent defendant who asserts an insanity defense an EEG examination at government expense: United States v. Hartfield, 513 F.2d 254 (9th Cir. 1975). See also § 19.03 et seq., infra.

episode, the victim of the seizure may commit a violent act involving fairly elaborate motor acts without awareness or recall. Amnesia for the events transpiring during the seizure episode is permanent and originates contemporaneously with the seizure rather than subsequent to it, There is no moral consciousness of guilt for acts committed during the seizure. Psychomotor epilepsy does not of itself imply insanity or incompetency unless there is evidence that the accused suffered a seizure at the time of the act or at trial.[3]

During the seizure state there is a profound disturbance in the electrical brain patterns. The examining neurologist who suspects a patient may suffer from psychomotor epilepsy may order an electroencephalograph (EEG) test of the brain waves, CAT scan (x-rays) and/or MRI, a procedure that utilizes a magnetic flux field in conjunction with radio frequency pulses to create an image on film.[4] The older and better known popularly, remains the EEG test, though it is being displaced rapidly by the newer diagnostic instruments. The EEG can yield conclusive objective evidence that a subject is suffering from organic brain disorder (epilepsy, hematoma—blood clot on the brain, tumor) even though all other physical tests are negative. It should be noted that it is accepted fact among neurologists that a negative EEG is not conclusive evidence of normality. From the seizure discharge, in the case of epilepsy, it is possible for the neurologist to identify the particular form of epilepsy involved. Abnormality is reflected by the electrical brain waves measured by the electroencephalograph and recorded on the electroencephalogram. The brain waves (electrical discharges of the cerebral cortex) during an epileptic seizure have a particular, identifiable pattern. When the discharges are in the abnormal state, the individual is undergoing an epileptic seizure.

The electroencephalograph is a delicate electronic recording instrument that monitors, magnifies, and graphically charts the cortical electrical discharges. The instrument amplifies brain electric potential several million fold. It is attached to the head of the subject by pasting a series of electrodes to particular areas of the scalp. Voltage occurring between these electrodes is recorded in chart form by styluses writing in ink on a continuous paper roll. The chart which depicts the brain rhythm is the electroencephalogram (EEG). A very slow or fast brain wave cycle, in terms of predetermined standards of discharge, suggests organic disorder.

If an EEG test has been made by the neurologist as part of his diagnostic examination, it may be introduced in evidence and explained by the expert.[5] The graphic chart of abnormal brain waves furnishes an

3. U.S. ex rel. Wiggins v. Pennsylvania, 302 F.Supp. 845 (E.D.Pa.1969), affirmed 430 F.2d 650 (3d Cir.1970).

4. Magnetic Resonance is being used to evaluate a range of neural diseases, from brain tumors to multiple sclerosis. It is also used to evaluate other organs in the body, such as the liver, pancreas, kidneys, genito-urinary tract, the heart and extremities. MR spectroscopy also is being used as a diagnostic tool for brain disorders.

5. Frey v. State, 171 Tex.Crim. 100, 345 S.W.2d 416 (1961), cert. denied 368 U.S. 865 (1961). The same principle would also

excellent source of demonstrative evidence where the defense seeks to persuade the trier of fact on the issue of insanity.[6]

The instrument is of significant importance in differentiating true psychomotor epileptics from would-be malingerers. A single normal EEG charge does not preclude the presence of recurring seizure. Repeated EEG examinations may be necessary to demonstrate the presence of electrical abnormality. While the EEG is a vital diagnostic aid in proving organic brain disorder in litigation, it is of value only in the light of a clinical examination. Some apparently normal persons have abnormal EEGs, and there have been reported cases of epileptics with normal EEGs. The accuracy of the EEG depends largely on the technician's skill. For example, unless the electrodes are placed in precisely the correct area of the scalp, they may fail to record the activity of the necessary portion of the cerebrum.[7]

§ 18.13   Neurological and Neuropsychological Examinations

Whenever an expert is utilized in court, the credibility of the witness is highly dependent upon the thoroughness of the examination. In the case of a neurologist, a complete neurological examination involves an assessment of the status of the nervous system, including the sensory nerves, the motor nerves, and the central aspects (brain and spinal cord), which integrate behavior and perception. The neurological examination should be performed by a neurological specialist. Diagnostic information as to the organic state of the nervous system is gleaned largely by inferential means, since direct access to the nervous system is not feasible. The examination consists of the following: taking the neurological history, testing and recording coordination; study of muscle tone (size, response, strength, and atrophy); testing involuntary reflexes (Babinski response), hearing, sight, sensation and balance (Romberg test); observing and testing the emotional reactions, the level of consciousness, thought content, language and speech; X-rays of the skull and spinal column and myelography (introduction of radio-opaque substance into the area of the spinal cord and dorsal brain membrane to detect lesions), if necessary; electroencephalography (EEG); CAT scan; MRI; and the examination of the cerebrospinal fluid by puncture of the vertebral column which contains the spinal cord and the fluid.

By contrast, the neuropsychologist's examination is directed toward four different purposes. Initially, it must be determined whether the patient exhibited behavior that deviates from the norm. Such abnormal behavior is called a dysfunction or impairment. Assuming there is

permit introduction of CAT Scan and MRI diagnostic results.

6. See, Gibbs, *Medical Electroencephalography,* 1967. This explanatory book is a must for any attorney seeking to prove that epilepsy is a form of insanity. Gibbs indicates that no more than one-third of persons suffering from epilepsy show seizure activity while awake and that a considera-

ble proportion of epileptics feature a normal "awake" EEG.

7. The EEG is subject to the following variables which may obscure the pattern: placement of the electrodes, age, brain metabolism, blinking, swallowing, coughing, movement, level of consciousness, and intake of stimulants or sedatives.

abnormal behavior, the extent or degree of the behavioral abnormality must be established and characterized as either constituting a mild or a severe impairment. Having determined there is abnormal behavior, it must then be determined whether its cause is organic in origin.[1] If there is organic trauma, the neuropsychologist seeks to determine where the injury is located and of what nature it is. To achieve these results, the neuropsychologist has recourse to noninvasive and psychological tests that permit a diagnosis of brain damage to be made, and is also heavily dependent upon a past "history" of the patient which, in the case of forensic examinations, it is the duty of the employing attorney to gather. Neuropsychologists may also examine EEGs, CAT scans and MRIs.

Perhaps the most widely used group of neuropsychological tests is the Halstead–Reitan Battery,[2] which measures a wide spectrum of behavior manifestations, ranging from motor coordination to attentiveness. The test manuals identify performance criteria of "normal" persons and of those who are suspected to have suffered brain damage. The battery of tests also typically includes several other tests, some of which have already been mentioned.[3] On the basis of the totality of the test results, the neuropsychologist will arrive at an evaluation of whether brain damage caused certain behavioral patterns, and what its cause is. Finally, the diagnosis of the neuropsychologist may include the probable connection of the dysfunction to trauma related to a particular brain area.

§ 18.14   The Neurologist and Neuropsychologist as Expert Witness

A neurologist, by virtue of the fact that the profession requires a medical doctorate, will be readily permitted to qualify as an expert witness in any court. As previously discussed, the general rule is that anyone who is shown to possess a medical degree permitting the person to diagnose and treat human ailments, will be permitted to give opinion testimony on any medical issue. Thus, a general practitioner/doctor is permitted to testify on matters that pertain to a medical specialty.[1]

---

§ 18.13

1. "Organic" means that it arises from a physical injury to the brain. Non-organic causes would be abnormalities that are precipitated by emotional or other mental problems.

2. See, Lundstrom v. Brekke Enterprises, Inc., 115 Idaho 156, 765 P.2d 667 (1988).

3. The most often used intelligence test is the Wechsler Adult Intelligence Scale–Revised (WAIS–R), which is complemented by the Minnesota Multiphasic Personality Inventory II (MMPI–II). See § 18.09, supra. Other tests frequently used by neuropsychologists include the Wechsler Memory Scale, which shows how the subject's "memory quotient" compares to the "intel-ligence quotient"; and the Wide Range Achievement Test (WRAT), which measures previously acquired skills such as reading ability, spelling proficiency, rudimentary arithmetic skills. At one time, the Bender–Gestalt test was widely used by neuropsychologists, but, today, that test is in disfavor because it is hard to obtain an accurate base rate.

§ 18.14

1. Sher v. De Haven, 91 U.S.App.D.C. 257, 199 F.2d 777 (1952), cert. denied 345 U.S. 936 (1953). Of course, the credibility of such a generalist medical doctor may not be very high, especially when opposed by a board certified specialist.

Much like when dealing with evidence offered by clinical psychologists, the courts have not always been in agreement on whether neuropsychologists will be permitted to testify on neurological defects. Thus, a court said that there was "no authority permitting a psychologist to give expert testimony as to the future condition of a brain as a result of an accident ... [or] whether existing brain damage was the result of a particular accident."[2] Other courts, however, have freely admitted neuropsychological expert evidence when relevant and upon laying the proper foundation.[3]

V. TRIAL PRACTICE

§ 18.15 Locating the Expert

1. THE PSYCHIATRIST

In large metropolitan areas there are typically a number of highly qualified forensic psychiatrists available for retention by private attorneys. In rural areas, attorneys must typically call upon private psychiatrists who are perhaps not forensically trained. Medical schools, clinics, and hospitals may have psychiatrists on their staffs. The American Psychiatric Association publishes a biographical and geographical index by state and city of the membership of that association.[1] This source is especially valuable as a source of names and locations of potential witnesses, and it can be found in the library of city, county, and state medical societies. National societies and certification boards of psychiatrists and psychoanalysts may be able to supply the names of local members.[2] The names of local forensic psychiatrists may also be sought

---

2. GIW Southern Valve Co. v. Smith, 471 So.2d 81, 82 (Fla.App.1985). The same court added that "a witness who is a psychologist and not a medical doctor lacks the qualifications to trace retrospectively what would occur to the brain from a given trauma."

3. Admitting neuropsychological evidence, see, e.g., Beecher Wholesale Greenhouse, Inc. v. Industrial Commission, 170 Ill.App.3d 184, 120 Ill.Dec. 720, 524 N.E.2d 750 (1988). Reversing the trial court's exclusion of the neuropsychologist, see Sanchez v. Derby, 230 Neb. 782, 433 N.W.2d 523 (1989). It was error, however, to permit a neuropsychologist who was not shown to have expertise in the area to testify that the plaintiff's diabetes could have resulted from the accident, in Levin v. Welsh Brothers Motor Service, Inc., 164 Ill.App.3d 640, 115 Ill.Dec. 680, 518 N.E.2d 205 (1987). Refusal of the trial court to strike the evidence was deemed harmless error in view of

the vigorous cross-examination which fully disclosed the neuropsychologist's lack of expertise.

§ 18.15

1. The address of the American Psychiatric Association is 1400 K. Street, N.W., Washington, D.C. 20005.

2. Certified members of the American Board of Psychiatry and Neurology practicing in cities of the United States are listed in the *Directory of Medical Specialists* which is published, periodically, by Marquis–Who's Who of Chicago, Ill. The American Board of Forensic Psychiatry, and the American Academy of Forensic Sciences (Psychiatry and Behavioral Sciences Section) have offices at Colorado Springs, Colo. Persons holding a valid, unrevoked certificate of qualification are entitled to use the designation, "Diplomate of the American Board of Forensic Psychiatry."

through various medico-legal societies and medical associations. An important resource in locating psychiatrists are other trial attorneys who have made use of such experts, and who are ordinarily willing to share their experiences with interested colleagues.

In criminal cases, prosecutors typically can call upon full-time state employed psychiatrists who conduct psychiatric examinations at the behest of the courts or local prosecuting attorneys. Although the right to a psychiatric examination in criminal cases is not absolute, it has been recognized that a court must appoint a psychiatrist to conduct a psychiatric examination at state's expense for an indigent defendant when there is some showing which would indicate that the defendant's insanity or incompetency is a substantial issue.[3]

If a patient has a prior history of hospitalization for mental disorders, psychiatric testimony regarding the nature of the illness should be sought from the examining or treating physician or from the patient's medical records properly identified by the hospital's medical records librarian. The statutes of most states provide for the admissibility of medical records as a statutory exception to the hearsay rule. Usually, such records are made available only upon presentation of a signed, acknowledged authorization from the patient. Most hospitals also require payment for copying the record.

2. THE PSYCHOLOGIST AND NEUROPSYCHOLOGIST

Clinical psychologists will sometimes be consulted by the forensic psychiatrist who wishes to use diagnostic psychological test results as a means of corroborating a psychiatric diagnosis.

It is not difficult to locate and engage a clinical psychologist as an expert mental diagnostician. All large universities and most smaller colleges have clinical psychologists who teach and do research. Mental hospitals and mental health clinics often have such professionals on staff also. Every metropolitan district will contain numerous private practitioners. Local and national societies may be contacted for information regarding the names and addresses of local clinical and/or forensic psychologists and neuropsychologists.[4] Compilations containing the names of practicing clinical and forensic psychologists, and of neuropsychologists, including biographical data concerning their educational background, specialty, and address, are readily found in the directory sections of medical, public, college and university libraries. As with psychiatrists, not to be overlooked are other attorneys who may share with you their past experiences with psychologists as expert witnesses.

---

3. See, Ake v. Oklahoma, 470 U.S. 68 (1985): indigent defendant has a constitutional right to psychiatric evaluation and assistance in preparing a defense when defendant's mental state is a critical issue, or at capital sentencing hearings where the prosecution produces psychiatric evidence of defendant's future dangerousness.

4. The American Psychological Association has offices at 750 First St., N.E., Washington, D.C. 20002–4242. The group also has divisions of clinical psychology.

3.   THE NEUROLOGIST

The staffs of local medical schools and hospitals will usually include one or more trained neurologists. Local city, county, and state medical societies also maintain lists of members who specialize in neurology and neurosurgery. National societies of neurologists may be consulted to obtain the names of local members.[5] Most state hospitals, medical schools, and mental health institutes have extensive EEG, MRI, and CAT scan facilities available.

VI. MISCELLANEOUS

§ 18.16   Bibliography of Additional References

Consult also the sources cited in the footnotes to this chapter, most of which are not repeated here.

1.   BOOKS

Ackerman & Kane, *How to Examine Psychological Experts in Divorce and Other Civil Actions,* 1990.

Aiken, *Assessment of Personality,* 1989.

Amchin, *Psychiatric Diagnosis: A Biopsychosocial Approach Using DSM–III–R,* 1990.

Anon., *Innovations in Clinical Practice: A Source Book* [Vols. 1–11] 1982–1992.

Anon., *1993 Cue Book,* 1993. This manual was developed for use by mental health professionals when testifying in court, but is of interest to litigators as well.

Anon., *Diagnostic and Statistical Manual of Mental Disorders (DSM–IV),* 4th ed., 1994. This book, published by the American Psychiatric Association, is the official manual listing all recognized mental disorders, and is a must for lawyers confronting psychiatric or psychological issues in court.

Applebaum & Gutheil, *Clinical Handbook of Psychiatry and the Law,* 2d ed. 1991.

Blau, *The Psychologist as Expert Witness,* 1984.

Blau, *Psychological Examination of the Child,* 1991.

Blinder, *Psychiatry in the Everyday Practice of Law,* 2d ed. 1982.

---

5. American Neurological Association, 2221 University Ave., S.E., Suite 350, Minneapolis, MN 55414.

Brammer, Shostrum & Abrego, *Therapeutic Psychology: Fundamentals of Counseling and Psychotherapy,* 5th ed. 1989.

Carson, *Abnormal Psychology and Modern Life,* 9th ed. 1992.

Cooper, Bloom & Roth, *The Biochemical Basis of Neuropharmacology,* 5th ed. 1986.

Dalton, *Premenstrual Syndrome and Progesterone Therapy,* 2d ed. 1984.

Davison & Neale, *Abnormal Psychology: An Experimental Clinical Approach,* 5th ed. 1990.

Ewing, *Psychology, Psychiatry, and the Law,* 1985.

Goodwin & Guze, *Psychiatric Diagnosis,* 4th ed. 1989.

Graham, *The MMPI: A Practical Guide,* 1977.

Gravetter & Wallnau, *Statistics for the Behavioral Sciences,* 3rd ed. 1992.

Hood & Johnson, *Assessment in Counseling: A Guide to the Use of Psychological Assessment Procedures,* 1991.

Kermani, *Handbook of Psychiatry & the Law,* 1989.

Kutash & Wolf (Eds.), *Psychotherapists' Case Book,* 1986.

Levinthal, *Introduction to Physiological Psychology,* 3rd ed. 1990.

Loftus, *Eyewitness Testimony,* 1979.

Loftus & Doyle, *Eyewitness Testimony: Civil and Criminal,* 2d ed., 1992.

Matarazzo, *Wechsler's Measurement and Appraisal of Adult Intelligence,* 5th ed. 1972.

Monahan, *Predicting Violent Behavior: An Assessment of Clinical Techniques,* 1981.

Morris, *Contemporary Psychology and Effective Behavior,* 7th ed. 1990.

Morse, *Commentary on Legal Psychiatry,* 1989.

Othmer, *The Clinical Interview Using DSM–III–R,* 1989.

Perlin, *Mental Disability Law: Civil and Criminal* (3 vols.) 1989.

Perlin, *Law and Mental Disability,* 1994.

Phares, *Clinical Psychology: Concepts, Methods, and Profession,* 4th ed. 1992.

Rorschach, *Psychodiagnostics,* 1921.

Sadoff, *Forensic Psychiatry: A Practical Guide for Lawyers,* 2d ed., 1988.

Shuman, *Psychiatric and Psychological Evidence,* 1986.

Skodol, *Problems in Differential Diagnosis,* 1989.

Spitzer, ed., *Diagnostic and Statistical Manual of Mental Disorders (DSM–III–R),* 3d rev' ed. 1987. This book, published by the American Psychiatric Association, is now superseded by DSM–IV, published in 1994. See, Anon., supra.

Spitzer, *et al., DSM–III–R Casebook,* 1988.

Szasz, *The Myth of Mental Illness,* 1961.

Szasz, *Law, Liberty and Psychiatry: An Inquiry Into The Social Uses of Mental Health Practices,* 1963.

Turkat, *The Personality Disorders: A Psychological Approach to Clinical Management,* 1990.

Waldinger, *Psychiatry for Medical Students,* 1984. The book is excellent for lawyers as well!

Waldinger, *Fundamentals of Psychiatry,* 1986.

Walker, *Terrifying Love: Why Battered Women Kill and How Society Responds,* 1989.

Ziskin & Faust, *Coping With Psychiatric and Psychological Testimony* [3 Vols.], 4th ed. 1988, with 1990 supplement. This work has featured prominently on lists of need-to-have books for trial attorneys.

Ziskin, Faust & Hiers, *Brain Damage Claims: Coping With Neuropsychological Evidence,* 1991.

2. ARTICLES

Because the literature in psychiatry, psychology, neurology and law is so voluminous, the authors have not attempted to list herein selected articles from the mental health literature. Significant legal sources, however, have been listed here. Among the many professional periodicals in the mental health field that published articles on forensic psychiatry, psychology, and neurology that can be consulted by lawyers, we note:

American Academy of Psychiatry and Law Bulletin

American Journal of Orthopsychiatry

American Journal of Psychiatry

American Psychologist

Archives of Clinical Neuropsychology

Archives of Physical Medicine and Rehabilitation

Behavioral Sciences and the Law

[The] Bulletin of the American Academy of Psychiatry and Law

[The] Clinical Neuropsychologist

International Journal of Clinical Neuropsychology

Journal of the American Psychiatric Association

Journal of Clinical Psychology

Journal of Consulting and Clinical Psychology

Journal of Consulting Psychology

Journal of Experimental Psychology: Human Perception and Performance

Journal of Nervous and Mental Disorders

Journal of Personality Assessment

Journal of Projective Techniques and Personality Assessment

Journal of Psychiatry and Law

Law and Human Behavior

Professional Psychology: Research and Practice

Psychiatry

Psychological Bulletin

Psychological Review

Faust & Ziskin, "Expert Witness in Psychology and Psychiatry," 241 *Science* 31 (1988).

Gilandas & Touyz, "Forensic Neuropsychology: A Selective Introduction," 28 *J.For.Sci.* 713 (1983).

Goldman & Jacob, "Anatomy of a Second Generation Tarasoff Case," 36 *Can.J.Psychiatry* 35 (1991).

Goldstein, "Litigious Paranoids and the Legal System: The Role of the Forensic Psychiatrist," 32 *J.For.Sci.* 1009 (1987).

Goldstein, "When Doctors Divulge: Is There a 'Threat From Within' to Psychiatric Confidentiality," 34 *J.For.Sci.* 433 (1989).

Graham & Babacy, "Expert Testimony by Psychologists: Novel Scientific Evidence," 14 *Law & Psych.Rev.* 71 (1990).

Guilmette & Giuliano, "Taking the Stand: Issues and Strategies in Forensic Neuropsychology," 5 *Clinical Neuropsychologist* 197 (1991).

Loftus & Loftus, "On the permanence of stored information in the human brain," 35 *Am.Psychologist* 409 (1980).

Loftus, "Eyewitness: Essential but Unreliable," *Psychology Today,* Feb. 1984, p. 22.

Mosteller, "Legal Doctrines Governing the Admissibility of Expert Testimony Concerning Social Framework Evidence," 52 *Law & Contemp.Probs.* 85 (1991).

McCrae & Costa, "Validation of the Five–Factor Model of Personality Across Instruments and Observers," 52 *J.Personality and Soc. Psychol.* 81 (1987).

McCrae & Costa, "Reinterpreting the Myers–Briggs Type Indicator From the Perspective of the Five–Factor Model of Personality," 57 *J. of Personality* 17 (1989).

Reynolds, et al., "Demographic Characteristics and IQ Among Adults: Analysis of WAIS–R Standardization Sample as a Function of the Stratification Variables," 25 *J.School Psychol.* 323 (1987).

Rogers, et al., "Psychiatrists and the Parameters of Expert Testimony," 15 *Int'l J.L. & Psychiatry* 387 (1992).

Roman & Wagar, "Assessing Competence to Stand Trial—The Clash Between Legal and Psychiatric Standards," *Criminal Justice,* Fall 1989, p. 15.

Saks, "Expert Witnesses, Nonexpert Witnesses, and Nonwitness Experts," 14 *Law & Hum.Behavior* 291 (1990).

Shusman, *et al.,* "A Cross–Validation Study of Police Recruit Performance as Predicted by the IPI and MMPI," 15 *J.Pol.Sci. & Admin.* 162 (1987).

Tanay, "Money and the Expert Witness: An Ethical Dilemma," 21 *J.For.Sci.* 769 (1976).

Taslitz, "Myself Alone: Individualizing Justice Through Psychological Character Evidence," 52 *Md.L.Rev.* 1 (1993).

Wren & Greenfield, "Dealing With Neuropsychological Evidence," *For The Defense,* July 1989, p. 11.

3. LAW REVIEW NOTES AND COMMENTS

"Mens Rea: The Impasse of Law and Psychiatry," 26 *Gonzaga L.Rev.* 613 (1991).

"Professional Obligation and the Duty to Rescue: When Must a Psychiatrist Protect His Patient's Intended Victim?," 91 *Yale L.J.* 1430 (1982).

Chapter 19

SPECIFIC TYPES OF BEHAVIORAL
EXPERT EVIDENCE

---

§ 19.01   Introduction and Scope of Chapter

The behavioral sciences have had a long and difficult path into the courtrooms of the United States. Criticism of these "mind sciences" comes from scholars and legal practitioners alike, who attempt to compare behavioral science to the more concrete and structured physical sciences, and find it wanting. However, evidence and expert testimony on mental health and abnormality is becoming increasingly popular in the modern courtroom, as the legal system struggles to maintain equitable standards for both plaintiffs and prosecutors, and defendants.

After having discussed, in the previous chapter, the most prominent of the branches of the behavioral sciences in a general way, we move in the following sections to a discussion of specific applications of the use of experts on mental health to legal issues that are of prominence in today's courtroom. In doing so, attention was given to psychiatrists and psychologists who testify in both criminal and civil cases.

I. THE DEFENSE OF INSANITY AND RELATED CONCEPTS

§ 19.02 Insanity as a Defense to Crime

The concept of criminal insanity is based on two premises. First, most crimes require intent. If one's acts are in some way caused by mental impairment, then that person will be said to lack the ability to form the requisite intent. Second, criminal responsibility is based on a belief that human beings possess free will. An individual whose mental state precludes free will is not legally responsible for that person's conduct. Thus, it has become accepted to varying degrees in western civilization that a person who is insane at the time of the commission of a criminal act cannot be held responsible for that crime. Insanity, thus, is a defense to criminal action.

While this latter concept is easily stated, its application to specific fact situations causes innumerable problems, for a variety of reasons. First, "sanity" and "insanity" are purely legal concepts, which mental health experts must relate to their medical and clinical language that has no exact equivalent for them. Second, what constitutes insanity is not easily determined by a uniform standard, since various jurisdictions define insanity differently. We will consider five major tests whereby insanity at the time of the offense is measured. Each one of these tests determines what type of evidence is relevant in the particular jurisdiction on the issue of insanity.

Even when different jurisdictions follow the same test, their courts may differ in their interpretation or application of the test. The fact that there are multiple rules of differing, and at times changing, content is an indication that this area of the law remains in a state of flux.

1. THE M'NAGHTEN TEST

Perhaps the oldest and best known test for insanity is the M'Naghten Test, formulated by the House of Lords in 1843,[1] long before the advent of the Freudian theory of functional mental disorder. The M'Naghten test is also popularly referred to as the "right/wrong" test. In order to establish an insanity defense under this test the lawyer must prove that the accused, because of mental disease or defect, failed to understand either the nature and quality *or* the wrongfulness of his or her act.

M'Naghten, then, essentially consists of two different tests, either one of which may serve to exonerate a defendant on the ground of insanity. The decisions indicate that even the courts may often forget the dichotomy. It raises the following three questions upon which proof should be presented:

§ 19.02
1. Daniel M'Naghten's Case, House of Lords, 10 Cl. & F. 200, 8 Eng. Reprint 718 (1843).

(1) Was the accused suffering from a defect or reason resulting from disease of the mind?

(2) Did the accused know the nature of the act? [2]

(3) Did the accused know the quality of the act? [3]

Even if the defense should receive an unfavorable answer to the foregoing questions, there remains a second test, namely:

Did the defendant, at the time of committing the unlawful act, know that he was doing wrong?

The word "wrong" is susceptible of two connotations: legal wrong, and moral wrong. Legal wrong would be one condemned as such by the criminal law; a moral wrong is one that is violative of the norms of society. In the context of the insanity defense, most courts choose the "morally wrong" connotation, but the courts are by no means unanimous on that point. [4]

Of all of the tests for insanity, the M'Naghten test is considered to be the strictest test—hardest for the defense to satisfy. At one time, M'Naghten was clearly the majority test in American jurisdictions. With the advent of the Product Test, its importance waned somewhat, and when the American Law Institute (A.L.I.) formulated its Model Penal Code test, to be discussed later, the latter test actually became the majority test, relegating M'Naghten to a strong minority position among the states. In the aftermath of the acquittal of John W. Hinckley, Jr. in the 1982 attempted assassination of President Reagan, several states that had adopted the more lenient A.L.I. test responded to the public outrage over the acquittal by returning to M'Naghten, which has, once again, become the majority test.

2. THE IRRESISTIBLE IMPULSE TEST

As a supplement to the M'Naghten test, the "irresistible impulse" test is also used in a number of jurisdictions. Under this test, one who

---

2. This would apply to intellectual comprehension of the physical effect of the act. An expansive view of this issue would also include consideration of the defendant's ability to evaluate the effect of his conduct.

3. This encompasses the ability to understand and evaluate the probable consequences of one's act.

4. In Harrison v. State, 44 Tex.Crim. 164, 69 S.W. 500 (1902), the court said that the M'Naghten "wrong" means a legal wrong and not a moral wrong. The case indicates that knowledge of the unlawfulness of an act is sufficient to render the defendant criminally responsible for committing the act, and that an insane delusion that the unlawful act was commanded by God, though it was known to violate the temporal law, was no defense.

But compare Cardozo's statement in People v. Schmidt, 216 N.Y. 324, 331, 110 N.E. 945, 949 (1915): "If, however, there is an insane delusion that God has appeared to the defendant and ordained the commission of a crime, we think it cannot be said of the offender that he knows the act to be wrong." See also, Merritt v. State, 39 Tex. Crim. 70, 45 S.W. 21 (1898), where the defendant's insane delusion that the deceased was the leader of the mob trying to kill him and the killing of the deceased in defense of his life based on such a delusion was held sufficient to exempt the defendant from criminal responsibility.

For commentaries on the issue, compare Hall, *General Principles of Criminal Law*, 2d ed. 1960, at 488, and Weihofen, *Mental Disorder as a Criminal Defense* (1954) 96.

knows the type of conduct and who knows it is wrong, may still have an insanity defense available if, because of mental illness, the person was unable to avoid doing that which is wrong.[5]

The motivation for formulating the irresistible impulse rule arose from the psychiatrist's difficulty in perceiving the various forms of compulsive behavior within the M'Naghten definition of legal insanity. Compulsive behavior such as kleptomania, pyromania, and dipsomania occurs when the actor does know right from wrong and does contemplate the consequences of the normative violation, knowing it is wrong, but nevertheless persists in the prohibited conduct because of an inner force the actor is powerless to resist. Psychiatrists might not categorize this individual as insane in the right-wrong sense; consequently, if such behavior is to be exempted from responsibility, the irresistible impulse is a necessary adjunct to M'Naghten. It should also be observed that if the named dysfunctions do not qualify as an irresistible impulse, they would under the next test.

3. THE DURHAM TEST

The "Durham" test, named after an individual who had featured in several District of Columbia mental illness litigation matters, attempted to narrow the insanity defense inquiry to the simple issue of whether the criminally accused person's act was or was not the "product" of a mental disease. For that reason, the Durham test is also referred to as the Product Test.

In adopting the concept in the 1954 decision,[6] the Court of Appeals for the District of Columbia did not fashion a brand-new test. In earlier cases, the New Hampshire Supreme Court had adopted this same concept,[7] which had also been advocated in the United States in 1917 by a Committee of the American Institute of Criminal Law and Criminology.[8] The Durham test never gained acceptance by other modern jurisdictions and encountered a rocky course even within the District of Columbia, where it was finally abandoned in favor of the next test up for discussion.[9]

4. THE A.L.I. TEST

Under this test of a more recent vintage, formulated by the American Law Institute, a person is not responsible for unlawful conduct if at

---

5. Illustrative cases are State v. White, 58 N.M. 324, 270 P.2d 727 (1954), and Commonwealth v. Rogers, 48 Mass. (7 Metc.) 500 (1844).

6. See, Durham v. United States, 94 U.S.App.D.C. 228, 214 F.2d 862 (1954). The defense attorney who succeeded in convincing the District of Columbia Circuit to adopt the new test was Abe Fortas, later to become a Justice on the Supreme Court.

7. State v. Pike, 49 N.H. 399 (1869), and State v. Jones, 50 N.H. 369 (1871).

8. See, Weihofen, *Mental Disorder as Criminal Defense* (1954) 115.

9. The Durham test was modified considerably in McDonald v. United States, 114 U.S.App.D.C. 120, 312 F.2d 847 (1962), and abandoned in United States v. Brawner, 471 F.2d 969 (D.C.Cir.1972).

the time of such conduct, as a result of mental disease or defect, the individual lacked substantial capacity either to appreciate the criminality of his conduct or to conform his conduct to the requirements of law.[10]

The A.L.I. test, sometimes with slight modifications, was adopted in a number of states, either by statute or court decision, and also became the test used in all federal circuits. It became the majority test in the 1970s,[11] but after Congress, in 1984, passed a new Federal Test for insanity, and some states abandoned it to return to a M'Naghten-type test,[12] the A.L.I. became a minority position. Today, while still the law in a number of states, its primary importance lies in the manner in which it influenced the development of the criminal law on the issues of the insanity defense.

5. THE FEDERAL TEST

In the aftermath of the acquittal, in 1982, on grounds of insanity, of Hinckley for the attempted assassination of President Reagan, Congress, for the first time, passed a statute to formulate a uniform test for insanity for use in federal criminal trials. The Insanity Defense Reform Act of 1984 (18 USCA § 20) provides:

> "(a) Affirmative Defense. It is an affirmative defense to a prosecution under any Federal statute that, at the time of the commission of the acts constituting the offense, the defendant, as a result of *severe* mental disease of defect, was unable to appreciate the nature and quality or the wrongfulness of his acts. Mental disease or defect does not otherwise constitute a defense. [Emphasis supplied.]
>
> (b) Burden of Proof. The defendant has the burden of proving the defense of insanity by clear and convincing evidence."

Under previous federal practice, once the evidentiary presumption of sanity had been overcome by evidence of insanity produced by the defendant, the burden of proving sanity beyond a reasonable doubt then

---

10. American Law Institute, Tentative Draft No. 4, Model Penal Code, § 4.01. A subsection also provided that "The terms 'mental disease or defect' do not include an abnormality manifested only by repeated criminal or otherwise antisocial conduct." For a critical comment on the use of the word "criminality" instead of "wrongfulness," see, Weihofen, 58 *J.Crim.L., C. & P.S.* 27 (1967). See also, United States v. Freeman, 357 F.2d 606 (2d Cir.1966), wherein the court adopted the A.L.I. test but substituted "wrongfulness" for "criminality," as suggested by Professor Weihofen.

11. A 1981 annotation listed 29 states, in addition to the federal circuits, as having adopted the A.L.I. test, as against 15 states adhering to M'Naghten and 5 states following the M'Naghten rule augmented by the irresistible impulse test. See, 9 A.L.R.4th 526.

12. After the California Supreme Court, in People v. Drew, 22 Cal.3d 333, 149 Cal. Rptr. 275, 583 P.2d 1318 (1978) discarded M'Naghten in a 4–to–3 decision and adopted the A.L.I. test, the decision was in effect nullified as a result of the passage, by California voters, of Proposition 8 in 1982, which then resulted in passage of a new statute that is said to return to the M'Naghten rule. See, People v. Skinner, 39 Cal.3d 765, 217 Cal.Rptr. 685, 704 P.2d 752 (1985).

shifted to the prosecution. The Insanity Defense Reform Act shifts the burden of proving insanity to the defendant.[13]

6. MODERN CONCEPTUAL CHANGES

When, as discussed earlier, Hinckley was acquitted, on ground of insanity, of a charge of violating the federal presidential assassination statute, the public outcry which resulted in the Insanity Defense Reform Act, discussed above, had national repercussions. Over thirty bills were introduced in Congress and in the states, some of which advocated the abolishing of the insanity defense altogether.

After the American Bar Association House of Delegates, in 1983, repudiated the A.L.I. test which it had publicly supported since 1975 and turned to the "cognitive" approach which was an outgrowth of M'Naghten, some states abolished the defense of insanity altogether.[14] Other states retained the insanity defense but combined it with a sentencing scheme that permits a finding of guilty by reason of insanity, which leads to civil commitment, or a finding of guilty but mentally ill (GBMI) [15] which leads to a sentencing procedure that is not very different from that adopted in Montana, where the defense was abolished.[16]

§ 19.03 Psychiatric and Psychological Evidence of Insanity

Depending on where the burden of proof lies,[1] an acquittal on grounds of insanity cannot occur unless it is either shown by the prosecution that the accused was sane at the time of the commission of the criminal act, or unless the defense established the existence of a mental disease or disorder that qualifies as "insanity" under the legal test existing in the jurisdiction. Courts have to determine, at times,

---

13. In Leland v. Oregon, 343 U.S. 790 (1952), the Supreme Court upheld a state statute that placed the burden of proving insanity *beyond a reasonable doubt* upon the defendant.

14. E.g., Mont.Rev.Codes § 40–14–201, held constitutional in State v. Korel, 213 Mont. 316, 690 P.2d 992 (1984); Idaho Code § 18–207.

15. Creating a "guilty but mentally ill" disposition and other changes in the Illinois statutory scheme on insanity led the court to strike down a GBMI verdict in People v. Fierer, 124 Ill.2d 176, 124 Ill.Dec. 855, 829 N.E.2d 972 (1988). See also, Loeb, "Let's Abolish the Guilty But Mentally Ill Verdict," *Ill.Bar J.*, Nov. 1989, p. 802.

16. Kermani, in *Handbook of Psychiatry and Law*, 1989, at 174, argues that retention of the insanity defense is essential to the moral integrity of the law, and that this is the official position of the American Psychiatric Association (APA). The APA was

also said to be "extremely skeptical" about GBMI and similar indeterminate verdicts. By contrast, the House of Delegates of the American Medical Association (AMA) voted to support the abolition of the defense of insanity on Dec. 6, 1983.

§ 19.03

1. Traditionally, the prosecution is aided by the common law presumption of sanity and does not have to prove the defendant's sanity in its case in chief. When the defense has presented sufficient evidence of insanity to destroy the presumption, then, under the A.L.I. test and the procedure followed in states that adhere to "affirmative defense" standards, the burden of proving defendant's sanity beyond a reasonable doubt would revert back to the prosecution. In the aftermath of recent changes, the burden of proving insanity now is placed upon the defendant in federal and many state courts. See, § 19.02 at (5) and (6), supra.

whether the fact a defendant suffers from a specific mental disorder or dysfunction satisfies the legal test for insanity.

While it is customary to present expert testimony on the issue of sanity or insanity, it is clear that the courts freely admit lay opinion testimony on defendant's behavior from witnesses who are shown to have had a close acquaintance with the accused over a reasonable period of time.[2] It is entirely up to the jury to decide what weight they will give to the psychiatric/psychological and the lay testimony, and courts have said that the jury need not believe the expert witnesses and may find against the expert opinions.[3] Here are some representative cases in which courts dealt with specific mental disorders in insanity defense cases.

1. DISSOCIATIVE IDENTITY DISORDER, FORMERLY MULTIPLE PERSONALITY DISORDER (MPD)

The occurrence of multiple personalities taking control of the same person is a rare condition. It has long been called the Multiple Personality Disorder, although the newest *Diagnostic and Statistical Manual of Mental Disorders—Fourth Edition* (DSM–IV) has renamed the condition "Dissociative Identity Disorder."[4] It may be defined as a condition wherein several people occupy the same body. The MPD victim's "primary" or "host" personality is "the personality that has executive control of the body for the greatest percentage of time during a given period."[5] All other personalities that may take control of the body's functions at times other than when the "host" personality is in control, are called "alter" personalities. DSM–IV describes the condition as:

> "Each personality state may be experienced as if it has a distinct personal history, self-image, and identity, including a separate name. Usually there is a primary identity that carries the individual's given name and is passive, dependent, guilty, and depressed. The alternate identities frequently have different names and characteristics that contrast with the primary identity (e.g. are hostile, controlling, and self-destructive). Particular identities may emerge in specific circumstances and may differ in reported age and general knowledge, or predominant effect."[6]

Each state also, at some time, and recurrently, takes full control of what the individual does. There are cases of MPD in which the *alters* are

---

2. E.g., State v. Walls, __ W.Va. __, 445 S.E.2d 515 (1994); United States v. Hartfield, 513 F.2d 254 (9th Cir.1975). It is reversible error to refuse to permit testimony of lay witnesses to prove insanity: Hunter v. State, 335 So.2d 194 (Ala.Crim. App.1976), cert. denied 335 So.2d 203 (Ala. 1976). See also, Edwards v. State, 540 S.W.2d 641 (Tenn.1976).

3. See, e.g., Fitch v. State, 160 Ind. 697, 313 N.E.2d 548 (1974); Byrd v. State, 297 So.2d 22 (Fla.1974); United States v. Coleman, 501 F.2d 342 (10th Cir.1974).

4. DSM–IV (1994) at 484.

5. Braun, *Treatment of Multiple Personality Disorders* (1986), quoted in United States v. Denny–Shaffer, 2 F.3d 999, 1006 (10th Cir.1993).

6. DSM–IV (1994) at 484.

entirely separated with respect to memory, perceptions, emotions, and identity, so that no one personality knows about any of the others. In fact, the personalities can be so different that the differences may show up through physical symptoms. Different *alters* often require different eyeglass prescriptions, speak different languages, will score significantly different on personality tests, and will even respond differently to medications." [7]

In the *Denny–Shaffer* case, the psychiatrists agreed that Bridget Denny–Shaffer, who had been charged with kidnapping an infant from a hospital while posing as a nurse, was suffering from a multiple personality disorder (MPD) and that one of Bridget's alter personalities, "Rina," was controlling Bridget's conduct. They also agreed that the defendant's dominant or host personality, "Gidget," did not consciously participate in the abduction. The experts could not, however, establish positively that the alter personality in control of defendant at the time of the offense was legally insane, i.e., "unable to appreciate the nature and quality or the wrongfulness" of her acts under the Federal Insanity Defense Reform Act of 1984.[8]

The legal issue when an insanity defense is pursued is whether the "host" personality can be said to be insane when the crime was committed while an "alter" personality, who knew the nature and quality of the acts that were being committed, was in control and at the same time the "host" personality was unaware of what conduct was occurring. In that sense, MPD presents a unique legal issue. One of the experts testifying in the *Denny–Shaffer* case recognized there are two possible views of what the legal standard of insanity requires, and articulated the problem:

> "If the [insanity] standard is taken to mean that all alters, or at least the host personality, must be fully aware of the nature, quality, and wrongfulness of an act, then Bridget Denny–Shaffer was not responsible at the time of the [abduction.] Such an application would probably mean that no one suffering from Multiple Personality Disorder could be held responsible for anything unless all alters were co-conscious at all times. Such is almost never the case. If, on the other hand, a MPD [victim] is viewed as a single individual with varying personality components and not divided as though he or she were a group of separate people, the ... question would be whether, at the time of the instant offense, the personality in control suffered from a mental disease or defect such as to be unable to understand the nature, quality, and wrongfulness of their acts. If this is the appropriate application of the standard, then ... at the time of the instant offense, Bridget Denny–Shaffer did suffer from a significant

7. United States v. Denny–Shaffer, 2   **8.** Supra § 18.02(5).
F.3d 999, 1009 (10th Cir.1993).

mental illness, but it was not such as to render her unable to understand the nature, quality, and wrongfulness of her act." [9]

In determining whether defendant's condition satisfied the insanity standard of the federal statute, the court held that if defendant suffered from multiple personality disorder and that her "host" or dominant personality was not in control at the time of the crime, that would suffice to entitle her to jury instructions on insanity under the 1984 Insanity Defense Reform Act, 18 USC 17(a).[10]

Earlier cases have not agreed with the view of the Denny–Shaffer court. Thus, courts have held that evidence of MPD alone is not a defense since the court will not parcel out criminal responsibility among various "alters" who may occupy defendant's mind.[11] Most of these cases did not squarely address the unique problems presented by an MPD victim. It is likely that the Denny–Shaffer rationale will gain wider acceptance in the future, since it considered in greater detail the current state of psychiatric and psychological knowledge about this highly unusual and rare condition.

Somnambulism, now catalogued as "sleepwalking disorder," [12] may also be viewed as a dissociative state like MPD, wherein the primary personality sleeps and the individual acts under some latent aspect of the personality without awareness of the primary personality. In Bradley v. State,[13] the court stated that somnambulism was a species of insanity, and that it was error to withhold an instruction to the jury regarding the accused's somnambulism.[14] Other cases have followed the same path.[15]

---

9. Testimony of Dr. Mary Alice Conroy, quoted in United States v. Denny–Shaffer, supra note 7 at 1008.

10. U.S. v. Denny–Shaffer, supra note 23 at 1017. On MPD generally, see also, Lasky, *Evaluation of Criminal Responsibility in Multiple Personality and Related Dissociative Disorders,* 1982.

11. In Kirkland v. State, 166 Ga.App. 478, 304 S.E.2d 561, 564 (1983) the bank robbery defendant had been diagnosed as having a "psychogenic figure," which is similar to MPD. The court rejected a M'Naghten-type insanity defense, and said there was only one person who committed the act and one person accused of it, and it was "immaterial whether she was in one state of consciousness or another, so long as in the personality then controlling her behavior, she was conscious and her actions were the product of her own volition" [relying on State v. Grimsley, 3 Ohio App.3d 265, 444 N.E.2d 1071 (1982)]. The recent case of Commonwealth v. Roman, 414 Mass. 235, 606 N.E.2d 1333 (1993) also followed the Grimsley opinion's rationale without offering a careful analysis of the

various views. See also, State v. Darnall, 47 Or.App. 161, 614 P.2d 120 (1980); State v. Rodrigues, 67 Haw. 70, 679 P.2d 615 (1984), cert. denied 469 U.S. 1078 (1984)— no persuasive analysis was made of the precise MPD issue.

12. See, DSM–IV (1994) at 587, listed under the Sleep Disorders.

13. 102 Tex.Crim. 41, 277 S.W. 147 (1925).

14. The instruction asked the jury to acquit if a reasonable doubt existed as to whether defendant was conscious when he shot the victim.

15. E.g., Tibbs v. Commonwealth, 138 Ky. 558, 128 S.W. 871 (1910): evidence showed defendant was somnambulist and would not recall what acts he committed while in that state; Lewis v. State, 196 Ga. 755, 27 S.E.2d 659 (1943), implying that somnambulism is an insane mental condition; Fain v. Commonwealth, 78 Ky. 183 (1879): evidence that loss of sleep and mental anxiety tend to result in somnambulism should have been admitted.

2. POSTPARTUM PSYCHOSIS

Most mothers find that the hours after the birth of a child are happy and joyful, filled with love and dreams for a bright future for the newborn. But for some, the happy thoughts depart in a nightmare of postpartum psychosis, which may cause an otherwise normal mother to snap and, in one horrible moment, kill the infant.

Postpartum psychosis, sometimes incorrectly called "baby blues," [16] is a serious but treatable psycho-medical mood disorder with major depressive tendencies suffered by some women shortly after they have given birth, and which disappears within three to seven days after delivery.[17] There is little agreement on the causes of the disorder. Some medical authorities believe the depression is physiologically-based as a result of hormonal imbalances following delivery, while others believe the dysfunction is caused by pre-existing psychological factors that become magnified as a result of the stresses of childbirth. Neither opinion on the origin of the condition has been empirically validated. Persons who kill while experiencing a severe postpartum episode are ordinarily individuals who have no prior criminal record and were looking forward to the impending birth and motherhood. In that sense, they are different from ordinary infant killers who perpetrate the act out of economic reasons, because of shame, or because of believed inability to take care of the infant, or for other identifiable motives. How prevalent postpartum psychosis impelled killings are is likewise difficult to assess. There are probably many cases where deaths diagnosed as sudden infant death syndromes (SIDS), infant kidnapings, and child deaths due to abandonment or being "dropped," are actually postpartum psychosis killings. While efforts are ongoing to increase the understanding of this major depressive episode among medical and hospital personnel, law enforcement officials, lawyers, courts, and public health authorities, much remains to be done in this regard.

Postpartum disorders are characterized by varying physical and psychological discomforts and pains that range from mild to very severe. While mild depression in new mothers is very common,[18] in a few cases,[19] the postpartum psychosis may be so severe that it can cause some mothers to commit infanticide.[20] A woman suffering from the psychosis

---

16. The term "baby blues" is probably a very mild form of postpartum depression that disappears within 24 hours of birth, and is not likely to lead to serious psychotic episodes and infanticide.

17. Burkow & Fletcher, *The Merck Manual of Diagnosis and Therapy* (15th ed.) 1987, at 1788. See also, *Diagnostic and Statistical Manual of Mental Disorders—Fourth Edition* [hereinafter DSM–IV] (1994) at 386, on Postpartum Onset Specifiers, which is listed under "Mood Disorders Not Otherwise Specified." Thus, postpartum psychosis is not recognized as a separate mental disorder.

18. Lee, "Postpartum Emotional Disorders," *1984 Med. Trial Tech.* 286 (1984): up to 50% of all women experience some emotional dysfunction within 24 hours of delivery; Pitt," 'Atypical' Depression Following Childbirth," *114 Brit.J.Psychiatry* 1325 (1968): up to 80% of new mothers suffer the "blues" after delivery.

19. Murray & Gallahue, "Postpartum Depression," 113 *Genetic Soc. & Gen. Psychology Mon.* 193, at 197 (1987), suggests that the severe form of the psychosis occurs only in one or two per thousand births.

20. Infanticide is not typically defined as a separate offense in the United States.

can no longer distinguish reality from fiction and is subject to incoherence, illogical thinking, behavior that is grossly disorganized or catatonic, delusional and hallucinating, while suffering anxieties that threaten both the woman and child. If an infant killing occurs while a person is suffering such an episode, this then raises the question as to whether the mental condition ought to be considered a defense to the crime. While there is sparse legal authority, legal commentaries on the issue abound.[21]

The defense has reportedly been used in over thirty trials, and, in the period between 1985 and 1990 is said to have resulted in acquittals by reason of insanity in half of the cases, with the other half resulted in convictions of some form of homicide with sentences that ranged from probation to twenty years.[22] England's Infanticide Act of 1938 recognizes the defense specifically in mitigation of offense.[23]

The lack of precision in medical as well as legal terminology[24] causes difficulties in questioning experts. A further complication in assessing the degree of acceptance of the defense in the criminal justice system is the fact that where use of the defense resulted in an acquittal, and also in cases where the defense has been used in mitigation of sentence following a guilty plea to a lesser charge, there is no appellate decision exploring whether an insanity defense is properly supported by evidence that the defendant suffered from a postpartum psychotic episode when committing the crime. Whatever information is available about such instances and subsequent court proceedings comes from the occasional literature and accounts in the news media.[25]

Few appellate decisions refer to postpartum psychosis in the context of an insanity defense or on the issue of diminished responsibility.[26]

It is considered either murder or manslaughter.

21. See, e.g., Reece. "Mothers Who Kill: Postpartum Disorders and Criminal Infanticide," [hereafter "Mothers Who Kill"] 38 *UCLA L.Rev.* 699 (1991); Gardner, "Postpartum Depression Defense: Are Mothers Getting Away With Murder?" 24 *New Eng.L.Rev.* 953 (1990); Rosenberg, "Postpartum Psychosis As a Defense to Infant Murder," 5 *Touro L.Rev.* 287 (1989); Brusca: "Postpartum Psychosis: A Way Out for Murderous Moms? 18 *Hofstra L.Rev.* 1133 (1990); Comment, "A Postmortem of the Postpartum Psychosis Defense," 18 *Cap.U.L.Rev.* 525 (1989); Moss, "Postpartum Psychosis Defense," *A.B.A.J.* 22 (Aug. 1988).

22. Reece, "Mothers Who Kill," supra note 21 at 702.

23. "Where a woman by any wilful act or omission causes the death of her child ... but at the time of the act ... the balance of her mind was disturbed by reason of her not having fully recovered from the effect of giving birth to the child ...,

then, notwithstanding ... the offence would have amounted to murder, she shall be guilty of ... infanticide ..." The Infanticide Act of 1938, reprinted in 8 *Halsbury's Statutes of England* 334 (3d. ed. 1968).

24. Some authors and courts use the terms "baby blues," maternity blues, postpartum depression, postpartum psychosis, psychotic postpartum syndrome, postpartum dissociative syndrome, as synonymous, or use different terms interchangeably. The situation is not ameliorated by *DSM-IV*'s failure to recognize and catalogue postpartum disorders in various categories depending upon severity.

25. Many instances of postpartum psychotic killings resulting in acquittals or gleaned from the occasional literature are described in the articles cited in footnote 21, supra.

26. See: State v. White, 93 Idaho 153, 456 P.2d 797 (1969), which resulted in an acquittal after jury was instructed on volitional prong of the A.L.I. test for insanity.

Because of this sparsity of legal authority, no clear view on the degree of acceptance within the legal system exists.

At this time, it is unclear whether the postpartum psychosis defense will receive careful attention in the criminal justice system, or whether it will go the way of some other seldom used and little regarded defenses such as the "involuntary subliminal television intoxication" defense [27] and the "twinkie" defense. It ought to be clear that evidence the defendant suffered from postpartum psychosis at the time of the killing ought to be admissible on the issue of whether the defendant had the ability to formulate the intent required for the offense charged. In that sense, postpartum psychosis is not any different from other mental disorders that preclude a required *mens rea*. Even when not able to excuse the conduct, the defendant's condition should be a significant factor in assessing whether criminal responsibility ought to be diminished or mitigated in jurisdictions where the diminished capacity concept is viable.

§ 19.04   The Diminished Responsibility Concept

The concept of diminished responsibility recognizes, to a limited extent, varying degrees of responsibility with, on the one hand, full responsibility for crime for sane individuals, and partial or diminished responsibility for some individuals who are not insane under the traditional tests for insanity, and yet are not fully sane either. The purpose of such a rule is to give consideration to the mental dysfunction in diminishing the punishment or finding an accused guilty of a lesser offense.[1] The concept exists in some form in a number of states,[2] but has not received universal acceptance. It was rejected by the United States Supreme Court in Fisher v. United States.[3] Even though it once

---

The Idaho Supreme Court held inclusion of the volitional prong was proper. But see, Clark v. State, 95 Nev. 24, 588 P.2d 1027 (1979), where the court upheld a conviction after defendant showed "postpartum depression" evidence in a M'Naghten cognitive-prong state. In Mitchell v. Commonwealth, 781 S.W.2d 510 (Ky.1989) and in State v. Holden, 321 N.C. 689, 365 S.E.2d 626 (1988) postpartum depressed defendants' convictions of murder were affirmed. In Commonwealth v. Comitz, 365 Pa.Super. 599, 530 A.2d 473 (1987), the trial judge's decision that defendant's postpartum psychosis did not constitute sufficient grounds for excusing her act was upheld—the case also discussed other instances where a postpartum defense was raised.

27. In Zamora v. State, 361 So.2d 776 (Fla.App.1978), the court rejected defendant's arguments that his involuntary subliminal television intoxication caused by exposure to an inordinate number of hours of viewing media violence should be considered a form of insanity under M'Naghten. The nature of the purported defense may be gleaned from the transcript of the psychologist—expert at the trial, which is reprinted in Moenssens, et al., *Criminal Law—Cases and Comments* (5th ed. 1992) at pp. 1049–1053.

§ 19.04

1. See 22 A.L.R.3d 1228 for an extensive collection of cases where the concept was used in mitigation of punishment.

2. In State v. Simmons, 172 W.Va. 590, 309 S.E.2d 89 (1983), the court listed as the states that recognize it: Colorado, Massachusetts, and New York. The opinion also listed the following states as having refused to recognize the concept: Arizona, Maryland, Ohio. Other states refusing to adopt the concept include Rhode Island and Wisconsin.

3. 328 U.S. 463 (1946), refusing to impose the concept on the District of Columbia. Also rejecting diminished responsibility, see, Johnson v. State, 292 Md. 405, 439 A.2d 542 (1982).

flourished in California,[4] the "defense" of diminished capacity was abolished by statute in 1982 in response to the passage of Proposition 8, alluded to earlier.[5]

Professor Morse makes the point that two variants of the concept are revealed in the case law: (1) the "mens rea variant" which is not a true defense but where it is attempted to create a reasonable doubt as to the ability of an accused to possess the mental state required for conviction of the charged offense by the introduction of expert testimony on the accused's defective or substandard mental functioning, and (2) the "true" diminished capacity, which Morse calls the defense of "partial responsibility," wherein an accused possesses the required mental state for conviction but is adjudged guilty of a lesser offense because of a mental dysfunction which quantitatively diminishes moral responsibility. He advocates abolishing the second branch.[6]

Expert opinion evidence of the existence of specific psychiatric disorders as impairing an individual's ability to possess the mental state required for commission of an offense is widely accepted.[7]

§ 19.05   The Battered Spouse Syndrome as Defense or Diminished Capacity

One of the most publicized issues of the last two decades has been that of wife or spouse battering and how the legal system has dealt with the repeatedly battered person who murders her or his mate. Until recently, courts were unwilling to allow mental health expert testimony concerning the effects of domestic violence on women who eventually, and fatally, lash out at an abuser.[1] However, this attitude is changing

---

4. People v. Wolff, 61 Cal.2d 795, 40 Cal.Rptr. 271, 394 P.2d 959 (1964). For comments on the opinion, see, "Keeping Wolff From the Door: California's Diminished Capacity Concept," 60 *Cal.L.Rev.* 1641 (1972); and "Diminished Capacity: Its Potential Effect in California," 3 *Loyola L.A.L.Rev.* 153 (1970).

5. Supra, § 19.02(4) at footnote 12.

6. See, Morse, "Undiminished Confusion in Diminished Capacity," 75 *J.Crim.L. & Criminology* 1 (1984). Criticizing Morse's views, see, Dressler, "Reaffirming the Moral Legitimacy of the Doctrine of Diminished Capacity: A Brief Reply to Professor Morse," 75 *J.Crim.L. & Criminology* 953 (1984).

7. E.g. State v. Breakiron, 108 N.J. 591, 532 A.2d 199 (1987): mental disease may negate malice needed for murder. But, in United States v. Cebian, 774 F.2d 446 (11th Cir.1985), the court's refusal to instruct the jury that they should consider whether defendant's suffering from post traumatic stress disorder (PTSD) as a result of spousal abuse affected his ability to formulate specific intent was upheld, reasoning that

the "diminished capacity" defense based on PTSD was already adequately conveyed by the judge's other instructions on specific intent.

§ 19.05

1. For discussions on the development of using expert testimony on the battered spouse syndrome, see, "Battered Women and Self–Defense: Myths and Misconceptions in Current Reform Proposals," 140 *U.Penn.L.Rev. 1* 379 (1991); "Ohio Joins the Majority and Allows Expert Testimony on the Battered Woman Syndrome: State v. Koss, 551 N.E.2d 970 (Ohio 1990)," 60 *U.Cinc.L.Rev.* 877 (1992); Thar, "The Admissibility of Expert Testimony on Battered Wife Syndrome ... An Evidentiary Analysis," 77 *N.W.L.Rev.* 348 (1982); "The Battered Wife's Dilemma: To Kill or To Be Killed," 32 *Hastings L.J.* 895 (1981); Rosen, "The Excuse of Self–Defense: Correcting a Historical Accident on Behalf of Battered Women Who Kill," 36 *Am.U.L.Rev.* (1986); Morse, "The Misbegotten Marriage of Soft Psychology and Bad Law: Psychological Self–Defense as a Justification for

radically as society becomes more aware of this overwhelming problem. If anything, the homicide charges brought against sports celebrity O.J. Simpson in 1994, and the news media revelations of past spousal abuse during his marriage to one of the murder victims, have served to project the issue of family violence into the national consciousness.

Historically, wife battering was an accepted form of punishment for the deviant or uncontrollable wife.[2] Even in early America, wife beating was legally permissible.[3] Today, although not legal, wife or spouse battering is one of the most socially disturbing problems faced by our culture, perhaps in part because the historical beliefs are still entrenched in the attitudes of many people. Yet, the problem presented by spousal battering ranks high on the list of social ills. One source claimed that women are more likely to be battered than to be raped, mugged or involved in a car accident.[4] And, it is important to note, although most victims of family violence are women, at least one study shows that 16% of domestic violence injury victims were men.[5]

1. DEVELOPMENT OF THE SYNDROME

1. Cycles of Abuse

Dr. Lenore Walker is one of the leading clinical psychologists in the field of domestic violence. It is her theory of the cycles of abuse which has been most commonly accepted by her peers and the judicial system.[6] Walker defines three phases typical to an abusive relationship: 1) the tension building phase, characterized by slight instances of physical or emotional abuse; 2) the acute battering phase, characterized by more frequent, and escalated instances of violence, and; 3) the loving contrition phase, characterized by the batterer's apologies and repeated promises to change his behavior.[7] The term battered spouse refers to a woman who has been through the cycle at least twice.[8]

The phases in the cycles tend to elicit specific behavior from the battered spouse. For example, during stage one, women tend to try to

---

Homicide," 14 *L. & Human Behav.* 595 (1990).

Originally, the disorder herein discussed was referred to as the "battered wife syndrome." While spousal abuse may also involve a battered husband, the reverse is more common and, therefore, in this section, "she" may be used more often when referring to the victim.

2. Rosen, "The Excuse of Self–Defense: Correcting a Historical Accident of Behalf of Battered Women Who Kill," 36 *Am. U.L.Rev.* 11, 11–12 (1986); Angela Browne, in *When Battered Women Kill,* 1987, at 167, refers to the rule-of-thumb cases where a man was legally able to beat his wife, "with a stick as large as his finger but not larger than his thumb."

3. Id.

4. Fact Sheet, Maryland Battered Spouse Syndrome Bill (H.B. 49, S.B. 141, 1991 Sess.)

5. Campbell, J., Abuse of Female Partners, *Nursing Care of Victims of Family Violence,* p. 76 (1984). The widely reported case of John Wayne Bobbitt in Virginia, whose penis was cut off by his spouse in 1994, is one of the better publicized examples.

6. Schneider, Elizabeth, Describing and Changing: Women's Self–Defense Work and the Problem of Expert Testimony on Battering, 9 *Women's Rts. L.Rep.* 195, 207 (1986).

7. Walker, Lenore, *The Battered Woman Syndrome,* 95–104 (1985); Walker Lenore, *The Battered Woman,* 16, 42–55 (1979).

8. Id. at 45.

avoid the batterer, which may in fact, reinforce the pattern of abusiveness.[9] Women in phase two tend to cope with frenzies of violence and wait for an ebb in the flow of abuse.[10] Relief and dread are common to women in phase three and it is this lull in the abuse which is said to inflict the most severe psychological trauma on the woman.[11]

2. Learned Helplessness Theory

One of the most puzzling aspects of the battered woman syndrome is the fact that the woman stays in an abusive relationship. Dr. Martin Seligman formulated a theory which explains the battered woman's responses to the cycle of violence, termed learned helplessness.[12] Seligman's explanation for the woman's passivity is that she begins to develop coping devices to deal with her abuse. The battered spouse is not helpless but simply becomes homogenized to the violence and, rather than trying what she sees as an impossible attempt to escape, the woman puts all of her energies into coping.[13] Dr. Walker, in her work, further points out that there are generally other factors, besides physical abuse, operating in an abusive relationship. Sexual abuse, extreme spousal jealousy, repeated threats on the woman, and alcohol or drug abuse by the batterer can all be factors leading up to the development of learned helplessness.[14]

2. SELF DEFENSE AND THE BATTERED SPOUSE

Most jurisdictions require that a defendant claiming self defense show: (1) an honest belief that he/she was under threat of serious danger of imminent bodily harm or death; (2) that his/her acts were a necessity; (3) he/she used no greater force than necessary for his/her defense, and; (4) that the defendant was not the aggressor.[15]

In the early battered spouse cases where use of self defense was attempted, these elements proved to be almost insurmountable for the defendant to overcome. Women were foreclosed altogether from using a self defense claim because the killing was not committed during an abusive attack.[16] The general view of courts and opponents of battered spouse syndrome evidence was that woman who used deadly force against a non-aggressor spouse could not take advantage of a traditional self-defense plea because her attack was not necessary, her use of deadly force was excessive, and she was the aggressor in the events immediately

---

9. Walker, Lenore, *Terrifying Love: Why Battered Women Kill and How Society Responds*, 43 (1979).

10. Id. at 61–62.

11. Id. at 45.

12. Seligman, Martin, *Helplessness: On Depression, Development, and Death* (1975).

13. *Terrifying Love* at 50–51.

14. Id. at 50–51.

15. LaFave, W. & Scott, A., *Criminal Law*, 454–63 (2d ed. 1986). See also, in spousal violence cases, People v. Evans, 259 Ill.App.3d 195, 197 Ill.Dec. 278, 631 N.E.2d 281 (1994) restating the general requirements for self defense in the context of a battered woman killing her husband.

16. State v. Nunn, 356 N.W.2d 601 (Iowa App.1984).; Commonwealth v. Grove, 363 Pa.Super. 328, 526 A.2d 369 (1987).

prior to the killing of her spouse.[17]   Without testimony to explain the syndrome, self defense could not be established.   Yet, the early courts saw no need to hear the syndrome testimony because the woman, from the very onset, did not fall within the traditional boundaries of a self-defense claim because there was no imminent threat to her own life at the time of the killing.[18]

Some courts rejected the evidence because the battered woman syndrome was not sufficiently developed, as a matter of commonly accepted scientific knowledge, to warrant testimony on it under the guise of expertise.[19]

When courts began to accept that the reason that such killings occurred at a moment when the victim was making no threats, in fact might have been sleeping, was an integral part of the psychological trauma of wife beating, the trend of foreclosing the defense rapidly changed,[20] even in the nontraditional cases, because of the growth in and increased judicial recognition of the battered spouse syndrome began to be noted.   Some courts still require a showing of abuse, however, before the testimony on the syndrome is admissible.

3. JUDICIAL ACCEPTANCE

Jurisdictions do not handle expert testimony on battered spouse syndrome in a coherent, uniform way.   Courts and legal scholars have tried to sort out the specific role, if any, that expert testimony should play in the trial process, resulting in heated debate and inconsistency in application.[21]   Opposition to admission comes in several forms.   Many critics argue that expert testimony on battered spouse syndrome invades the fact finding function of juries and overtakes their deliberations. Some opponents submit that the testimony is unnecessary because self defense claims and the motivations of a battered spouse are well within jury understanding and, that being the case, testimony ought to be inadmissible.   Critics have also argued that the credibility of the experts in this field is suspect,[22] an argument that had more credibility at a time when psychologists and psychiatrists had not fully embraced the battered spouse syndrome.

17.   Id.   See, e.g., People v. Aris, 215 Cal.App.3d 1178, 264 Cal.Rptr. 167, 174 (1989); State v. Stewart, 243 Kan. 639, 763 P.2d 572, 578 (1988).

18.   Dahl, Peter, Comment, Legal and Psychiatric Concepts and the Use of Psychiatric Evidence in Criminal Trials, 73 *Cal. L.Rev.* 411 (1985).

19.   State v. Thomas, 66 Ohio St.2d 518, 423 N.E.2d 137 (1981): the testimony proffered was that of a psychiatric social worker.   Also holding the evidence inadmissible, see, State v. Necaise, 466 So.2d 660 (La. App.1985); State v. Martin, 666 S.W.2d 895 (Mo.App.1984); State v. Moore, 72 Or.App. 454, 695 P.2d 985 (1985); Fielder v. State,

683 S.W.2d 565 (Tex.App.1985)—defendant not shown to be a battered woman; Buhrle v. State, 627 P.2d 1374 (Wyo.1981); State v. Griffiths, 101 Idaho 163, 610 P.2d 522 (1980).

20.   See, supra note 1 for sources listing the standing of most every state on the expert testimony issue.

21.   See generally, Anno. "Admissibility of Expert or Opinion Testimony on Battered Wife or Battered Woman Syndrome," 18 A.L.R.4th 1153.

22.   Ibn–Tamas v. United States, 407 A.2d 626 (D.C.App.1979); but see the decision on remand 455 A.2d 893 (D.C.App. 1983).

Another problem in admitting testimony based on the syndrome was the requirement in many states that before novel expert testimony could be admitted, it ought to have been generally accepted in the field in which it belongs.[23] This requirement was a stumbling block to admissibility at a time when the battered spouse syndrome had not yet been "generally accepted" in the behavioral sciences. However, with the advent of *Daubert*,[24] and the explosive reception of the theory since the early cases, these concerns are less relevant.

Having passed the "general acceptance" hurdle, proponents of the admission of such testimony still can prevail only if given an opportunity to educate the factfinder in the symptoms and effects of battered spouse trauma, to demonstrate that defendant's perceptions of the seriousness of the posed threat were founded on reasonable assumptions. Further, experts are able to show that the defendant acted reasonably under her particular circumstances. Expert testimony can also show that only the abused defendant is privy to the specific behaviors of the victim and she most likely knows, through voice patterns or intonations or gestures, when the next violent attack is to occur and how serious it might be.

Expert testimony of battered spouse syndrome is, of course, limited by general rules that apply to all cases involving opinion testimony: it is limited to relevant matters; the scope of a witness' testimony is also limited by the scope of the person's expertise in the field in which they are testifying; and the testimony's probative value into the defendant's perceptions must outweigh its prejudicial effect upon the factfinder. Even where the evidence is readily recognized, some states differ as to the allowable scope of the testimony presented by the expert.

Courts that are more liberal on the issue of admission[25] seem to allow a broad scope of testimony by the expert, finding that the syndrome relates directly to the self defense claim and whether or not the defendant's belief of imminent harm was reasonable. Other courts allowing the testimony do so for other reasons[26] or restrict it in certain ways. For example, one court limits the testimony to general information about battered spouse syndrome but does not permit specific testimony concerning whether or not the defendant actually suffered from

---

23. This test for admissibility, discussed extensively in Chapter 1, was derived from the holding in Frye v. United States, 293 Fed. 1013 (D.C.Cir.1923).

24. See, supra Chapter 1 for a full discussion of Daubert v. Merrell Dow Pharmaceuticals, Inc., 113 S.Ct. 2786 (1993). *Daubert* substituted proof of "reliability" of a novel form of evidence for proof of its "general acceptance."

25. E.g., State v. Kelly, 97 N.J. 178, 478 A.2d 364 (1984); State v. Anaya, 438 A.2d 892 (Me.1981); State v. Allery, 101 Wash.2d 591, 682 P.2d 312 (1984); People

v. Torres, 128 Misc.2d 129, 488 N.Y.S.2d 358 (1985); State v. Hickson, 630 So.2d 172 (Fla.1993); State v. Hill, 287 S.C. 398, 339 S.E.2d 121 (1986); State v. Hodges, 239 Kan. 63, 716 P.2d 563 (1986); State v. Leidholm, 334 N.W.2d 811 (N.D.1983); State v. Middleton, 294 Or. 427, 657 P.2d 1215 (1983).

26. E.g., People v. Minnis, 118 Ill. App.3d 345, 74 Ill.Dec. 179, 455 N.E.2d 209 (1983); State v. Baker, 120 N.H. 773, 424 A.2d 171 (1980); Fultz v. State, 439 N.E.2d 659 (Ind.App.1982).

the syndrome.[27] This court said that general battered spouse syndrome testimony did not mandate the need for a state medical examination of the defendant, as specific testimony would, and therefore the testimony would not disadvantage the prosecution.[28] In New Mexico, the trial court in *State v. Gallegos* admitted testimony but did not allow the term battered wife syndrome to be used.[29] The Maryland Court of Special Appeals stated that even if the court were to allow the testimony, it would only be used to determine the defendant's state of mind.[30]

Several courts have altogether precluded the use of expert testimony on the battered spouse syndrome in cases where the defendant attacks her abuser during a lull in the violence. The rationale behind such decisions rests upon the courts' belief that the defendant cannot avail herself of self-defense at all and the testimony is therefore, irrelevant. In both State v. Martin[31] and Buhrle v. State,[32] the respective courts held that too much time had elapsed between the last incident of abuse and the killing, and the defendant was not, therefore, in imminent danger, she could not assert a self-defense plea and, thus, testimony on battered spouse syndrome was irrelevant.[33]

In Maryland, two cases exemplify the courts' treatment of battered spouses. In Kriscumas v. State,[34] the court would not allow jury instruction on either traditional or imperfect self-defense because the defendant was the aggressor in the attack. The defendant's aggressor status effectively foreclosed self-defense, therefore the court had no reason to hear expert testimony on the battered spouse syndrome.[35]

However, cases refusing to admit the testimony are becoming much less frequent.[36] In State v. Kelly,[37] a landmark New Jersey case, the New Jersey Supreme Court held that evidence of the battered spouse syndrome was relevant to the defendant's claims of an honest and reasonable belief that she was in danger of imminent death or severe harm and that the testimony held up to the scrutiny under New Jersey principles of scientific evidence. Similarly, in State v. Gallegos,[38] the New Mexico Court of Appeals allowed a self-defense instruction for a defendant who killed her mate during an ebb in violence saying that past abuse is relevant to the defendant's perception of "immediacy of dan-

---

27. State v. Hennum, 441 N.W.2d 793 (Minn.1989).

28. Id. at 799.

29. 104 N.M. 247, 253, 719 P.2d 1268, 1274 (1986).

30. Kriscumas v. State, 72 Md.App. 721 (1987) (unreported case). The court never decided that point because the testimony had not been admitted.

31. 666 S.W.2d 895 (Mo.App.1984).

32. 627 P.2d 1374 (Wyo.1981).

33. To the same effect, see, State v. Stewart, 243 Kan. 639, 763 P.2d 572 (1988): battered wife can't claim self defense when she kills sleeping spouse. Fact she had suffered years of abuse no reason to overlook the "imminent danger" rule.

34. 72 Md.App. 721 (1987).

35. Followed in Friend v. State, 77 Md. App. 788 (1988).

36. For a more comprehensive listing of the jurisdictions which allow the use of battered spouse testimony, see, Battered Women and Self–Defense: Myths and Misconceptions in Current Reform Proposals, 140 *U.Penn.L.R.* 379 (1991).

37. 97 N.J. 178, 478 A.2d 364 (1984).

38. 104 N.M. 247, 719 P.2d 1268 (App. 1986).

ger." The trial court had allowed the testimony originally but refused the jury instruction on self-defense.[39]

Pennsylvania gave a different rationale for allowing battered spouse syndrome testimony in Commonwealth v. Stonehouse.[40] This court justified admission of the expert testimony by pointing out that it was important to dispel certain common myths about battered women. The court rebuffed the idea that women who defend themselves with weapons are not passive and are, therefore, not within the realm of the battered spouse syndrome.

Finally, the Ohio Supreme Court overruled a prior decision with its landmark opinion in State v. Koss.[41] The court distinguished its prior decision by saying that the science involved in the battered spouse syndrome had gained the requisite acceptance in the field and by pointing out that the testimony would assist the factfinder because certain myths about battered women needed to be explained.[42] However, this court also noted that a prerequisite to the testimony was the showing that the defendant was, in fact, a victim of abuse.[43]

While evidence of the battered spouse syndrome is typically in support of the defense, there is at least one case in which expert battered spouse evidence was used against the defendant, by the prosecution. In Arcoren v. United States,[44] defendant was accused of rape and assault and battery of his estranged wife, who had fled the apartment where the events occurred to alert the police. Some months later, at the trial, the woman recanted her story and sought to explain away her injuries. The government thereupon called an expert witness who testified that the wife was likely suffering from the "battered spouse" syndrome which caused her to alter her testimony because of an unwillingness to hurt her husband. After conviction, defendant argued the trial court had erred in admitting the battered woman syndrome evidence, but the Circuit Court of Appeals, in affirming the conviction, held that Federal Rule of Evidence 702, which provides that qualified expert testimony is proper where it "will assist the trier of fact to understand the evidence or to determine a fact in issue," encompasses the use of psychiatric and psychological evidence. The court said:

> "Rule 702 is one of admissibility rather than exclusion.... The concept expressed by the Rules is sufficiently broad to embrace psychiatric and psychological testimony from those who possess specialized knowledge concerning mental aberrations in human be-

---

39. Id.

40. 521 Pa. 41, 64, 555 A.2d 772, 784 (1989).

41. 49 Ohio St.3d 213, 551 N.E.2d 970 (1990). The court had previously held, in State v. Thomas, 66 Ohio St.2d 518, 423 N.E.2d 137 (1981), that the testimony was irrelevant to a plea of self-defense, was within the jury's scope of understanding,

that the science in the field was underdeveloped and that the prejudicial effect of the testimony outweighed the probative value.

42. Id.

43. Id. at 974.

44. 929 F.2d 1235 (8th Cir.1991), said to be a case of first impression.

havior, when such knowledge will help the jury to understand relevant issues in the case."[45]

Although some legislatures have recognized the seriousness of the spousal violence problem [46] and mandated admission of battered spouse syndrome evidence, and courts are becoming more receptive to such opinion testimony, it remains essential that the practitioner be aware of the jurisdiction's peculiarities during case preparation, expert selection, argument and jury instruction preparation. Even where the evidence is not admitted on the defense of self-defense, or as going to the issue of whether the defendant possessed the necessary mental state for a given offense, use of the syndrome may serve pleas in mitigation for diminished responsibility considerations.

§ 19.06   Evidence of Other "Mental" Abnormalities

There are a multitude of so-called "mental" abnormalities or disorders that arise as evidential issues in civil and criminal cases on rare occasions. It is impossible to catalogue them all herein, but a few deserve special mention because the issues have recurred or are still debated.

1.   XYY CHROMOSOMAL DEFECT AS INSANITY EVIDENCE

The XYY chromosomal defect found in some members of the human population has, at times, been urged as a defense to criminal responsibility. The XYY theory is that certain individuals, due to their genetic make-up, are unable to control their cognitive and/or volitional functions, and, hence, should not be held responsible for their unlawful acts. Unlike most testimony based on profiles and syndromes, the so-called XYY defense has a purely physical basis and is not dependent upon psychologically induced conditions.

Genetically speaking, the normal human cell is made up of 46 chromosomes, comprised of 22 pairs of autosomal chromosomes (22 Xs and 22 Ys), plus the 45th and 46th chromosomes, which are either X or Y sex chromosomes. XX is female and XY is male. The X chromosome has been thought by some scientists to be responsible for the passive attitude in one's personality makeup, while the Y chromosome is believed to control aggressive potential, although other scientists dismiss this theory as a chauvinistic gratuity unfounded in medical or biological science. When a male has an extra Y chromosome constituting a XYY chromosomal makeup, it is theorized that he may become intensely

---

45. Id. at 1239–40.

46. See, e.g., People v. Evans, *supra* note 15 at 205, in footnote 1: "The Illinois Domestic Violence Act of 1986 provides that its underlying purposes are: '(1) Recognize domestic violence as a serious crime against the individual and society which produces family disharmony in thousands of Illinois families, promotes a pattern of escalating violence which frequently culminates in intra-family homicide . . .; (3) Recognize that the legal system has ineffectively dealt with family violence in the past . . . and . . . that, although many laws have changed, in practice there is still widespread failure to appropriately protect and assist victims.' " 750 I.L.C.S. 60/102. (1992).

aggressive, display anti-social behavior, and also have a relatively low intelligence.[1] It has also been theorized the XYY individual may be unable to control his behavior.

To date, there is an absence of any reliable scientific proof that a person with an XYY chromosomal makeup will develop criminal or anti-social behavior. Research has been hindered by virtue of the fact there is an inadequate cross-section of XYYs in the general population who are available for testing. The majority of research, thus far, has been done on prison inmates. It is possible that the XYY concept will develop to the point where it is generally accepted by the scientific community. When this point is reached, the XYY defect may be of some evidentiary use in criminal justice litigation. At present, however, the fact that persons with an extra Y chromosome may be prone to aggressiveness and are antisocial is deemed insufficient to rebut the presumption of sanity.

People v. Tanner[2] is an example of an early judicial response to the problem presented by the XYY "criminal type" issue. *Tanner* held that a trial judge did not abuse his discretion in finding the evidence insufficient to establish legal insanity of an XYY individual charged with assault with intent to murder in a state where the M'Naghten "right-wrong" test had to be met in order to establish legal insanity.

Two geneticists, in *Tanner,* presented lengthy and complex evidence on the XYY syndrome and attempted to show that XYY individuals are excessively aggressive because of their chromosomal makeup. In ruling the evidence deficient, the trial judge notes these reasons: First, only few and relatively small studies had been done, which were inconclusive in that they did not state that all XYY individuals act aggressively, but only that aggressiveness could be one consequence of the chromosomal makeup. Second, the expert were unable to state that it was defendant's XYY chromosomal makeup that caused them to be make the assault in the instant case. And third, the experts could not state that possessing an extra Y chromosome prevented the defendant from knowing the nature and quality of his act or that it was wrong—the M'Naghten criteria for the insanity defense.[3]

§ 19.06

1. See, Farrell, "The XYY Syndrome in Criminal Law: An Introduction," 44 *St. Johns L.Rev.* 217 (1969); Housley, "Criminal Law: The XYY Chromosome Complement and Criminal Conduct," 22 *Okla. L.Rev.* 287 (1969); Money, Gaskin & Hull, "Impulse, Aggression, and Sexuality in the XYY Syndrome," 44 *St. John's L.Rev.* 220 (1969); Note, "The XYY Chromosomal Abnormality: Use and Misuse in the Legal Process," 8 *Harv.J.Legis.* 469 (1972); Montague, "Chromosomes and Crime," 2 *Psy-*chology Today 5 (1968); Comment, "The XYY Supermale and the Criminal Justice System: A Square Peg in a Round Hole," 25 *Loyola L.A.L.Rev.* 1343 (1992).

2. 13 Cal.App.3d 596, 91 Cal.Rptr. 656 (1970).

3. See also, Millard v. State, 8 Md.App. 419, 261 A.2d 227 (1970); People v. Yukl, 83 Misc.2d 364, 372 N.Y.S.2d 313 (1975); and State v. Roberts, 14 Wash.App. 727, 544 P.2d 754 (1976).

2. AUTOMATISM

Since one of the essential elements of criminality is the ability to engage in willed conduct, it follows that individuals who do not know what conduct they are engaged in cannot be guilty of a crime. That principle underlies, in part, the insanity defense. It has also been applied to the circumstance wherein an individual acts unknowingly because of "automatism,"[4] sometimes also called "unconsciousness" or even "black-out."[5] From a legal standpoint, there is a great deal of similarity between the defense of unconsciousness and the dissociative state discussed earlier in multiple personality disorders.[6]

Traumatic automatism is a "state of mind in which a person does not have conscious and willful control over his actions, and lacks the ability to be aware of and perceive his external environment."[7] It is an abnormal condition of the mind which is capable of being designated a mental illness or deficiency.[8] Clinicians have causally linked automatism to a wide variety of conditions including: epilepsy,[9] organic brain disease, concussional states following head injuries, drug abuse, hypoglycemia and acute emotional disturbance,[10] unconsciousness due to hypnotism,[11] somnambulism,[12] and "emotional trauma."[13] One court added, "While in an automatistic state, an individual performs complex actions without an exercise of will. Because these actions are performed in a state of unconsciousness, they are involuntary. Automatistic behavior may be followed by complete or partial inability to recall the actions performed while unconscious."[14]

Automatism is different from insanity, in that the alleged criminal act does not have to be a consequence of mental disease or defect. The defendant who acted unconsciously may have suffered a difficult-to-define mental deficiency or a simple brain trauma that leaves no permanent aftereffects. A defendant found not guilty by reason of automatism will be exonerated from all legal consequences of his act,[15] whereas a

4. E.g. People v. Froom, 108 Cal.App.3d 820, 166 Cal.Rptr. 786 (1980).

5. Unconsciousness through epilepsy recognized as a defense in Virgin Islands v. Smith, 278 F.2d 169 (3d Cir.1960). If, however, a person has repeatedly suffered blackouts so as to be on notice of the possibility of recurrence, then the defense is not available: People v. Decina, 2 N.Y.2d 133, 157 N.Y.S.2d 558, 138 N.E.2d 799 (1956).

6. See, supra § 19.03(1).

7. Fulcher v. State, 633 P.2d 142, 143 (Wyo.1981)—testimony of Dr. LeBegue.

8. DSM–IV, at 477, lists dissociative conditions as "a disruption in the usually integrated functions of consciousness, memory, identity or perception of the environment," but makes no mention of what the law calls "automatism." At 846, in an Appendix to the main volume, it mentions briefly "blacking out" among the Glossary of Culture Bound Syndromes.

9. Virgin Islands v. Smith, 278 F.2d 169 (3d Cir.1960); *cf.* People v. Decina, supra note 5.

10. People v. Grant, 46 Ill.App.3d 125, 4 Ill.Dec. 696, 360 N.E.2d 809 (1977).

11. People v. Marsh, 170 Cal.App.2d 284, 338 P.2d 495 (1959).

12. Fain v. Commonwealth, 78 Ky. 183 (1879).

13. People v. Lisnow, 88 Cal.App.3d Supp. 21, 151 Cal.Rptr. 621 (1978).

14. Fulcher v. State, supra note 7.

15. Unconsciousness is a complete defense if not self-induced: Greenfield v. Commonwealth, 214 Va. 710, 204 S.E.2d 414 (1974), habeas relief denied *sub nom.* Greenfield v. Robinson, 413 F.Supp. 1113 (W.D.Va.1976).

person found not guilty by reason of insanity, or found guilty but mentally ill, will ordinarily be committed to a mental institution.[16]

While the cited cases seem to treat the terms "automatism" and "unconsciousness" as synonymous, Professor Michael Corrado vehemently rejects that idea. He stated that "If automatism is a defense, it is not because of unconsciousness; the actors in these cases are not unconscious in any ordinary sense. * * * If automatism is a defense, it is because the action involved, while conscious and purposive, is not voluntary ... because ... the act of will is itself caused by something beyond the actor's control—a blow on the head, a sleep disorder, epilepsy, hypnotic suggestion...." [17]

It has been argued that the defense of automatism ought to be available also when a defendant has been brainwashed,[18] though that view has been strongly criticized.[19] The fact that very few cases have adequately dealt with this mental abnormality may be due to either a lack of agreement within the mental health professions or a difficulty of finding witnesses who possess the required expertise in dealing with the condition.

3. PREMENSTRUAL SYNDROME (PMS)

Premenstrual Syndrome (PMS) evidence represents a fairly novel legal phenomenon which has been utilized in several criminal and civil cases, usually unsuccessfully when argued as a defense to criminal responsibility, often successfully when argued in mitigation of sentence or disposition. In civil cases and at the trial level, success in using PMS evidence has perhaps been greater. In earlier psychiatric terminology, it was referred to as the Late Luteal Phase Dysphoric Disorder. Currently, it is mentioned in DSM–IV as "Premenstrual Dysphoric Disorder" among the mental conditions classified for further study.[20] According to medical research, there is no known cause for PMS syndrome. Although it is suggested that PMS is hormone-related, investigators were unable to document specific hormone level changes relating to PMS symptoms, or confirm the increasingly widely held belief that there is a close

---

16. State v. Caddell, 287 N.C. 266, 215 S.E.2d 348 (1975); followed in Fulcher v. State, supra note 7. Agreeing that automatism is not insanity, see, People v. Grant, supra note 10: the court stated that a defendant who suffered from psychomotor epilepsy could avail himself either of the defense of insanity if he could prove a causal connection between the mental disorder and the conduct, or of the defense of automatism if he could show that his conduct consisted of involuntary or automatic actions of a sane person.

17. Corrado, "Automatism and the Theory of Action," 39 *Emory L.J.* 1191 (1990).

18. Delgado, "Ascription of Criminal States of Mind: Toward a Defense Theory for the Coercively Persuaded ('Brainwashed') Defendant," 63 *Minn.L.Rev.* 1 (1978).

19. Dressler, "Professor Delgado's 'Brainwashing' Defense: Courting a Determinist Legal System," 63 *Minn.L.Rev.* 335 (1970).

20. In current psychiatric classification, PMS is mentioned under "Depressive Disorder Not Otherwise Specified." See, *DSM–IV* (1994) at 716.

relation between PMS and family violence.[21]

Dr. Katherine Dalton, the prominent British researcher and the world's most prominent advocate for PMS sufferers, defines PMS as "the presence of monthly recurring symptoms in the premenstruum or early menstruation with a complete absence of symptoms after menstruation" which results in such behavioral manifestations as "irritability, anger, confusion, depression, amnesia and uncontrollable impulses resulting in violence."[22]

In 1982, the defense was raised in the unreported case of *People v. Santos.* The defendant was charged with battery of her infant daughter and raised PMS as a defense in a pretrial hearing, asserting that she was unaware of what she was doing because she had blacked out and did not know what she was doing. There never was a ruling on the merits of the PMS defense, but after lengthy negotiations, the defendant pleaded guilty to a misdemeanor and felony charges were dropped.[23] In a more recent case, a forty-two-year-old surgeon in Virginia was charged with drunk driving and abusive behavior to a police officer when she tried to kick the officer and refused sobriety testing. When defendant told the judge it was because of PMS, he agreed and found her not guilty.[24]

There were three early English cases in which the merits of PMS were considered and, to some extent, recognized by the courts, though not as a defense to crime, but rather in mitigation of punishment. In the case of Sandie Craddock, the 29-year-old defendant had a record of more than thirty prior convictions for violent acts and had attempted suicide at least 25 times. She had been in and out of mental hospitals, but doctors were unable to diagnose a precise ailment or condition. After she was charged with murder in the stabbing to death of a woman bar attendant, her counsel, in studying her past record, discovered that all of the offenses and suicide attempts had occurred at approximately the same time in her monthly menstrual cycle. He then sought Dr.

---

21. Robinson, "Premenstrual Syndrome: Current Knowledge and Management," 140 *CMAJ* 605, at 606–607 (Mar. 15, 1989).

22. In Britain, the terminology used is Premenstrual Tension or "PMT." On the subject, generally, see, Dalton, *Premenstrual Syndrome and Progesterone Therapy,* (2d. ed.), 1984. See also: Norris, *PMS: Premenstrual Syndrome,* 1983; Dalton, "Premenstrual Syndrome," 9 *Hamline L.Rev.* 143 (1986)—the same law review volume also contains the following related articles: Keye & Trunnell, "Premenstrual Syndrome: A Medical Perspective," (at 165); Riley, "Premenstrual Syndrome as a Legal Defense," (at 193); Heggestead, "The Devil Made Me Do It: The Case Against Using Premenstrual Syndrome As A Defense In a Court of Law," (at 155). Also see, Chait, "Premenstrual Syndrome and Our Sisters in Crime: A Feminist Dilemma," 9 *Women's Rts.L.Rep.* 267 (1986); Vanesis, "Women, Violent Crime and the Menstrual Cycle," 31 *Med.Sci. & L.* 11 (1991).

Other symptoms of PMS that have been suggested are, abdominal bloating, backache, weight gain, breast tenderness, acne, constipation, fatigue, lethargy. See, Mulligan, "Premenstrual Syndrome," 6 *Harv.Women's L.J.* 219, 220 (1983).

23. No. 1K046299 (N.Y.Crim.Ct., Nov. 3, 1982). See, in this regard, Oakes, "PMS: A Plea Bargain in Brooklyn Does Not A Rule Of Law Make," 9 *Hamline L.Rev.* 203 (1986).

24. See, *The Washington Post,* Jul. 7, 1991, at A1; Note, "Has The PMS Defense Gained A Legitimate Toehold in Virginia Criminal Cases?—*Commonwealth v. Richter,*" 14 *Geo.Mason U.L.Rev.* 427 (1991). Unreported case.

Dalton's help and Craddock was diagnosed a PMS sufferer and treated with massive doses of the hormone progesterone. Ms. Craddock's behavior altered drastically and she became more stable. The prosecution agreed to reduce the charge to manslaughter because of her diminished responsibility. She was placed on probation on the condition that she continue the progesterone treatments.[25]

Ms. Craddock then changed her name to Sandie Smith and her probation officer was satisfied that the treatment permitted "Smith" to lead a normal life. Thereafter, Dr. Dalton gradually began to reduce the dosage and the frequency of progesterone treatments, and at the time when Ms. Craddock/Smith was receiving her smallest dose of the hormone and while she was in her premenstruum, she went berserk. Wielding a knife, she twice threatened to kill a peace officer. Placed under arrest and charged, she was convicted but was placed on three years' probation because of the PMS evidence. On appeal, her counsel (who had also represented her in the earlier trial) asked the court of appeals to recognize PMS as a complete defense. The court refused to recognize her medical condition as a substantive defense and found it more appropriate to use PMS as a mitigating factor in sentencing.[26] There was a third case in England where a woman deliberately killed her lover by smashing him against a utility pole with her car. Again, PMS was recognized as a mitigating factor, though not as a substantive defense.[27] In 1988, in Regina v. Reynolds,[28] an appeals court refused to set aside a verdict of murder committed upon the mother of the 18–year-old defendant and reduce it to manslaughter because the trial judge refused to give consideration to the PMS evidence. Thus, in none of the cited cases was PMS recognized as a complete defense.

PMS has been raised as an issue in several civil cases in the United States, including cases involving wrongful death, custody, bankruptcy, and abuse of the regulatory process.[29] It has been used, with varying degrees of success, in numerous unreported civil and criminal trials.

25. See, Regina v. Craddock, 1 C.L. 49 (1981); see also sources cited in note 22, supra. See also, "Criminal Law—Premenstrual Syndrome: A Criminal Defense," 59 *Notre Dame L.Rev.* 253 (1983).

26. Regina v. Smith, 1/A/82 (Crim.App. Apr. 27, 1982).

27. Id. Regina v. English is an unreported case decided on Nov. 10, 1982, by the Norwich Crown Court.

28. Crim.App., Apr. 22, 1988.

29. E.g., Crockett v. Cohen, 299 F.Supp. 739 (W.D.Va.1969)—review of HEW decision disallowing disability benefits to a woman suffering from premenstrual tension; Hoffmann–LaRoche v. Kleindienst, 478 F.2d 1 (3d Cir.1973)—review of federal order to control distribution of drug to woman suffering PMT; Reid v. Florida Real Estate Commission, 188 So.2d 846 (Fla. App.1966)—reversing Commission's order suspending broker's license of woman arrested for shoplifting while suffering from premenstrual tension; Tingen v. Tingen, 251 Or. 458, 446 P.2d 185 (1968)—evidence of PMS introduced on issue of mother's competency in child custody action; In re Irvin, 31 B.R. 251 (Bkrtcy.D.Colo.1983)— expert evidence that woman suffered from a borderline personality disorder and from moderately severe PMS considered on issue whether a judgment for damages for having stabbed defendant's homosexual lover with a steak knife could be discharged in bankruptcy. In re Irvin was followed in In re Borste, 117 B.R. 995 (Bkrtcy.W.D.Wash. 1990), where the judge compared defendant's obsessive-compulsive disorder (OCD) with PMS, holding that while she lacked the intent to overcharge her credit cards she was not relieved of responsibility.

The scientific community has not been unanimous in approving the effects of progesterone treatment. Some studies suggest that progesterone has no more therapeutic value than a placebo. These studies in turn were criticized as spurious because the clinical subjects were suffering from conditions other than PMS or the progesterone dosages were inadequate.[30]

Can PMS be raised as a form of insanity defense? Probably not, since it is not a disease or defect of the mind, but a physiological disorder which would not seem to fit under the any of the tests for insanity.[31] It might be possible, however, to raise PMS as a form of automatism defense. While there are some forms of automatism which may be caused by mental disease or defect, persons with a healthy mind can be just as susceptible to automatism because of such physiological disorders as somnambulism, delirium from fever or drugs, diabetic shock, or epileptic seizures.[32] Critics of this approach fear that acceptance of PMS in the legal arena offers too great a potential for abuse. Clearly, if PMS is admitted by a court, establishing the existence of the condition ought to be subjected to a high standard of proof.

4. EVIDENCE OF OTHER "SYNDROMES"

There has been a veritable proliferation of cases in which psychiatrists and psychologists have testified that individuals acted in accordance with certain "syndromes" or "profiles" acquired as a result of some mental or physical trauma. One jurist described the proliferation phenomenon in these words:

> "When a relatively large number of persons, having the same symptoms, exhibit a combination or variation of functional psychiatric disorders that leads to purely emotional stress that causes intense mental anguish or emotional trauma, i.e., trauma having no direct physical effect upon the body, psychiatrists put those persons under one or more labels. Today, we have the following labels: 'The Battered Wife Syndrome,' ...; 'The Battered Child Syndrome;' 'The Battered Husband Syndrome;' ... 'The Battered Patient Syndrome;' 'The Familial Child Sexual Abuse Syndrome,' ...; 'The Rape Trauma Syndrome,' ...; 'The Battle Fatigue Syndrome;' 'The Viet–Nam Post–Traumatic Stress Syndrome,' ...; 'The Policeman's Syndrome,' ...; 'The Whiplash Syndrome;' 'The Low–Back Syndrome;' 'The Lover's Syndrome;' 'The Love Fear Syndrome,' ...;

---

30. See, Keye & Trunnell, "PMS: A Medical Perspective," op. cit. supra note 22, at 180; Van Der Meer, et al., "Effect of High-dose Progesterone on the Premenstrual Syndrome: A Double–Blind Crossover Trial," 2 *J. Psychosomatic Ob.Gyn.* 229 (1983).

31. It is reported that, in France, an affirmative showing of PMS is considered a form of legal insanity which may constitute a complete defense. See, Pahl–Smith, "Premenstrual Syndrome as a Criminal Defense: The Need for Medico–Legal Understanding," 25 *N.C.Central L.Rev.* 246, 252 (1985).

32. In Edwards v. Ford, 69 Ga.App. 578, 26 S.E.2d 306 (1943), a wrongful death action, the defense attributed the driver's unconsciousness to PMS symptoms.

'The Organic Delusional Syndrome;' 'The Chronic Brain Syndrome,' ...; and 'The Holocaust Syndrome.' Tomorrow, there will probably be additions to the list, such as 'The Appellate Court Judge Syndrome.' " [33]

The opinion evidence in civil and criminal cases is offered either to provide an excuse or a mitigation for conduct of one of the litigants, usually the defendant. So far, courts have been somewhat restrained in admitting evidence on the newer and lesser known "syndromes."

A "syndrome" or a "profile" is a set of behavioral indicators forming a very characteristic pattern of actions or emotions that tend to point to a particular condition. The existence of such a condition is most often based upon clinical psychological observations in case studies that, because of the constant presence of common events, are said to be statistically related. Expert testimony by a psychiatrist or psychologist will always be needed if any hope of admission of the evidence is to be entertained. The expert witness will need to identify not only the existence of a particular syndrome, but also explain why, and to what probabilistic degree, the syndrome affected a person's past behavior as well as to forecast how such a person may act in the future.

Courts that are critical of such evidence often see it as disguised inadmissible character testimony,[34] or question the reliability of the psychiatric or psychological opinion because it involves statistical data used to calculate probabilities the reliability or sufficiency of which cannot be adequately demonstrated.

The literature on syndrome or profile defenses is voluminous and we leave it to other authors to provide both extensive listing of authorities and thorough analysis of the innumerable issues generated by syndrome evidence proffers.[35] Limiting our coverage to a brief description of the mental conditions and experiences which have featured in recent cases,

---

33. Werner v. State, 711 S.W.2d 639 (Tex.Cr.App.1986)—Teague, Judge, dissenting. The case involved the admissibility of evidence on "The Holocaust Syndrome," offered in support of a self defense. The syndrome is one exhibited by children of survivors of the Nazi Holocaust, who grew up hearing the stories from their parents that entire Jewish families perished in the concentration camps in Germany during World War II without resisting, and who have formed a firm determination that if their lives are ever threatened, they will immediately resist forcibly and not permit injustice to be foisted upon them. This mind-set makes them vulnerable to precipitous use of deadly force in what they believe is self defense when confronted with assaultive behavior.

34. See also § 19.08, infra, in discussions on the Rape Trauma Syndrome, and the Child Sexual Abuse Accommodation Syndrome, where several courts have taken that approach.

35. Perhaps one of the most thorough review of syndrome defense is the article by Professor David McCord. See, McCord, "Syndromes, Profiles and Other Mental Exotica: A New Approach to the Admissibility of Nontraditional Psychological Evidence in Criminal Cases," 66 *Ore.L.Rev.* 19 (1987). It also contains innumerable references to the legal and mental health literature. It will be hereafter referred to as "McCord on Syndromes." Consider also the monumental treatise (3 volumes) by Professor Michael L. Perlin—see, Perlin *Mental Disability Law: Civil and Criminal* (1989), and his more abbreviated treatment in Perlin, *Law and Mental Disability* (1994), as well as Professor Andrew Taslitz's well researched article: Taslitz, "Myself Alone: Individualizing Justice Through Psychological Character Evidence," 52 *Md.L.Rev.* 1 (1993).

we note that many of them fit within the psychiatric classification of the Post–Traumatic Stress Disorder (PTSD). The term is a general one, describing a constellation of syndromes with different origins, all of which involve exposure by the patient to a traumatic event which patients later reexperience involuntarily through painful, intrusive recollections of nightmares and dissociative states similar to blackouts under particularly stressful conditions. It is a recognized psychiatric syndrome falling among the Anxiety Disorders.[36]

When the traumatic event is one that has occurred in many individuals, the symptoms may be referred to by its own peculiar circumstance. Thus, PTSD is sometimes identified by different labels in the literature and cases as, for instance: (1) The Vietnam Veteran Syndrome, also referred to as Combat Syndrome or Battle Fatigue Syndrome;[37] (2) The Holocaust Syndrome, described earlier;[38] (3) The Love–Fear Syndrome;[39] (4) The Policeman's Syndrome;[40] (5) The Chronic Brain Syndrome[41]; The Munchausen's Syndrome By Proxy[42]; The Captivity Syndrome[43]; The Battered Child Syndrome[44]; The Episodic Dyscontrol Syndrome" and "Intermittent Explosive Disorder"[45]; The Pathological Gamblers' Syndrome;[46] and The Male Sexual Victimization Syndrome.[47]

36. See, "Posttraumatic Stress Disorder," *DSM–IV* (1994) at 424. See also, Harry & Resnick, "Posttraumatic Stress Disorders in Murderers," 31 *J.For.Sci.* 609 (1986). In United States v. Cantu, 12 F.3d 1506 (9th Cir.1993), PTSD evidence justified downward departure from sentencing guideline.

37. E.g. Miller v. State, 338 N.W.2d 673 (S.D.1983) (dissenting opinion). See also, Ford, "In Defense of the Defenders: The Vietnam Vet Syndrome," 19 *Crim.L.Bull.* 1983); "Vietnam Veterans and the Veteran's Stress Disorder," 68 *Marq.L.Rev.* 647 (1985). In State v. Korell, 213 Mont. 316, 690 P.2d 992 (1984), Justice Sheehy, in the context of a classic Vietnam Veteran's Syndrome case, would have held unconstitutional the state's statute abolishing the insanity defense. Professor David McCord reports the syndrome encompasses no less than eight separate harmful syndromes; see, McCord on Syndromes, supra note 35, at 64–66.

38. See, Werner v. State, supra at note 33.

39. See, People v. Terry, 2 Cal.3d 362, 85 Cal.Rptr. 409, 466 P.2d 961 (1970).

40. Binder, *Psychiatry in the Every Day Practice of Law* (2d ed.) 1982).

41. People v. Reed, 8 Ill.App.3d 977, 290 N.E.2d 612 (1972).

42. People v. Phillips, 122 Cal.App.3d 69, 175 Cal.Rptr. 703 (1981)—proper to admit evidence of a disorder characterized by a woman allowing her child to become ill so that mother will receive the attention and sympathy of others, even though disorder not recognized in DSM.

43. United States v. Kozminski, 771 F.2d 125 (6th Cir.1985), initially admitted psychologist testimony to explain why two men held in captivity did not seek to escape when an opportunity presented itself and remained compliant, but then holding testimony was improperly admitted because underlying theory was not generally accepted: 821 F.2d 1186 (6th Cir.1987). But in United States v. Winters, 729 F.2d 602 (9th Cir.1984), testimony explaining why women transported across state lines for immoral purposes had not sought to escape over long period of time was properly admitted and did not need to pass the "general acceptance" test.

44. Syndrome similar in its effects to Battered Spouse Syndrome—§ 19.05, supra. See, Jahnke v. State, 682 P.2d 991 (Wyo.1984). Psychologist testimony for defense held properly excluded for failure to show general acceptance.

45. See, McCord on Syndromes, supra note 35 at 63.

46. McCord on Syndromes, supra note 35 at 66.

47. State v. Borchardt, 478 N.W.2d 757 (Minn.1991)—Syndrome had not reached a sufficient level of acceptance in the medical community to be admissible.

Professor McCord criticizes the approaches used by courts or advocated by other evidence authors in dealing with the admissibility of "soft science" psychological evidence,[48] and suggests courts discard older standards or suggestions for admissibility and use a four-factor balancing approach in determining whether nontraditional psychological evidence ought to be admitted. Taking as a starting point the Federal Rule 702 concept that the evidence is admissible if it will assist the trier of fact to understand the evidence or to determine a fact in issue, he suggests that courts explore whether this standard has been met by looking at (a) the necessity for the evidence, (b) its reliability, (c) its understandability, and (d) its importance, and by balancing the outcomes if some factors "cut different ways." [49] In a real sense, his suggestions closely approach the standards for interpreting Rule 702 admissibility requirements which the Supreme Court would announce some eight years later in Daubert v. Merrell Dow Pharmaceuticals.[50] McCord's explanation of how these four factors ought to be looked at [51] is highly recommended reading for persons seeking to seriously argue to a court that such nonconventional psychological evidence ought to be either admitted or rejected.

§ 19.07 Consequences of an Acquittal by Reason of Insanity

When a person has been acquitted by reason of insanity, the defendant does not necessarily go free. Statutes usually require that acquittees be committed in accordance with the constitutional requirements for civil commitment as announced by the United States Supreme Court in Addington v. Texas.[1] In Jones v. United States,[2] a decision that came close on the heels of the acquittal of John W. Hinckley Jr. on grounds of insanity for the attempted assassination of President Reagan and no doubt influenced by the furor going on in the media and legislatures to "do something" about the insanity defense, the Supreme Court recognized that insanity acquittees might be placed under a greater burden than ordinary civil committees, and approved a post-acquittal re-commitment procedure mandated by Congress which placed upon the defendant the burden of proving a lack of mental illness or dangerousness, and also permitted involuntary commitments of such acquittees for periods longer than the maximum sentence the detainee could have received had he been convicted of the offense.

The Court also acknowledged that it was reasonable for Congress to provide for hospitalization and detention on the assumption that the defendant's mental illness which had lead to his acquittal continued past his acquittal and would require continued treatment. The Court reached that result despite the fact defendant's crime, of which he was acquitted, was attempted shoplifting. Upholding Congress' commitment

---

48. McCord on Syndromes, supra note 35 at 70 ("Five Approaches That Are Wrong").

49. Id. at 94.

50. See Chapter 1, supra, at § 1.03.

51. McCord on Syndromes, supra note 35 at pp. 95–192.

§ 19.07

1. 441 U.S. 418 (1979), requiring at least proof by clear and convincing evidence that the acquittee would be a danger to self or others.

2. 463 U.S. 354 (1983).

scheme for persons acquitted by reason of insanity perhaps also saved the insanity defense, very much under legislative siege at that time, from being abolished in more states, by making it clear to the public that a person acquitted on grounds of insanity would not be released, and could in fact be detained for a period of time longer than the maximum sentence he might have otherwise received.[3] Professor Michael L. Perlin calls the *Jones* decision a political one, "reflecting the Court's reluctance to contradict what it perceives as public sentiment."[4] Following the *Jones* decision, most state courts adopted the proof standards in that decision as consonant with state constitutional requirements as well.[5]

There is a limit, however, on how long insanity acquittees can be detained following a showing that they are no longer mentally ill. In *Foucha v. Louisiana*,[6] the state statute provided that the detainee who has recovered from his mental illness will be released only when he proves he will not be a danger to himself or others when released. Foucha was detained because psychiatric evaluations suggested that he had an anti-social personality and, previously, had suffered a "drug-induced psychosis." The Court held that the provisions permitting continued detention violated due process when the person was no longer mentally ill. Once the reason for involuntary commitment had disappeared, the acquittee could no longer be institutionalized, said the Court.[7] The Court, however, was badly split and four dissenters would have permitted the continued detention.[8]

§ 19.08   "Syndrome" Evidence to Bolster the Prosecutor's Case

Most of the psychological evidence is typically introduced or proffered by defendants. In this section, we discuss two types of syndrome evidence that prosecutors seek to use to bolster the testimony of victims of rape and of child sexual abuse.

1. THE RAPE–TRAUMA SYNDROME (RTS)

The prosecution of rape cases has changed much in the last generation. Most of the common law elements of the offense have been modified; indeed, the very name of the offense has been changed in many jurisdictions to "criminal sexual assault." To dispel some of the myths perpetuated since Sir Matthew Hale asserted, in connection with

---

3. Criticizing the decision, see, e.g., Note, "Throwing Away the Key: Due Process Rights of Insanity Acquittees in Jones v. United States," 34 *Am.U.L.Rev.* 479 (1985); Note, "Automatic and Indefinite Commitment of Insanity Acquittees: A Procedural Straightjacket," 37 *Vand.L.Rev.* 1233 (1984).

4. Perlin, *Law and Mental Disability* (1994) at 612.

5. E.g., State v. Field, 118 Wis.2d 269, 347 N.W.2d 365 (1984); Benham v. Ledbetter, 609 F.Supp. 125 (N.D.Ga.1985), af-

firmed 785 F.2d 1480 (11th Cir.1986); State v. Ross, 795 S.W.2d 648 (Mo.App. 1990); Tulloch v. State, 237 Neb. 138, 465 N.W.2d 448 (1991). For a detailed analysis of these issues, see, Perlin, *Law and Mental Disability* (1994) at pp. 602–617.

6. 112 S.Ct. 1780 (1992).

7. Id. at 1784, relying for that proposition on its former decision in O'Connor v. Donaldson, 422 U.S. 563 (1975).

8. Justices Kennedy, Thomas, Scalia, and the Chief Justice.

the crime of rape, that it was a charge easy to make and difficult to disprove, rape-shield statutes have been enacted that restrict the scope of examination of the complainant's past sexual behavior, the corroboration requirement has been done away with, as has the prompt reporting requirement. Nevertheless, in most cases where the defendant contends the intercourse was consensual, a successful prosecution for rape still hinges very much upon the credibility of the victim. That credibility is diminished when it is shown that the victim either did not promptly report the offense or acted otherwise in a manner inconsistent with the stereotypical image society has of the "true" rape victim, and defense attorneys continue to point to the post-rape behavior of the victim to suggest the alleged sexual assault did not occur.

In recent years, psychologists have come to the aid of prosecutors by offering testimony on the rape-trauma syndrome, a condition not separately catalogued in DSM–IV but nonetheless mentioned, and well known to the mental health profession, as a form of PTSD behavior. The syndrome purports to describe the mental state and behavior characteristics of a victim of sexual assault, in terms of both her conduct immediately following the offense and the long-term aftermath of the experience. The general public is not generally aware of the many effects that the traumatic event of a sexual assault has upon the victim's psyche, and mistakes victim behavior such as failing to promptly report the offense as evidence that the rape did not occur and that the intercourse was consensual as contended by defendant.[1]

Just as PMS had Dr. Katherine Dalton as its primary researcher, so is acceptance of the rape trauma syndrome largely the result of the work of Dr. Ann W. Burgess and her co-worker Dr. Lynda Holmstrom. Dr. Burgess has frequently testified on RTS and in one case she described the two stages that follow a criminal sexual assault: "The first is the acute phase, lasting days or weeks, during which the victim is emotionally overwhelmed and has difficulty performing ordinary functions; this is followed by a long time reorganization phase, lasting months or years, during which the victim deals with the symptoms specific to the rape which must be integrated into the victim's psychological experience to enable her to function at a pre-crisis level."[2] The recovery period may take a long time, and research established that four to six years after the traumatic event, 25% of the victims were still symptomatic of RTS. The traumatic event recurs in the memory of the victim in what is called "flashback" when some emotional trigger is pushed, which may be almost anything. According to Dr. Burgess' testimony in *Commonwealth v. Gallagher*, "the victim's failure to identify [her assailant] two

§ 19.08

1. On the many rape myths and their effect on juror and judicial attitudes and decision-making in rape prosecutions, see the impressive study of Torrey, "When Will We Be Believed? Rape Myths and the Idea of a Fair Trial in Rape Prosecutions," 24 *U.Cal.Davis L.Rev.* 1013 (1991).

2. Commonwealth v. Gallagher, 519 Pa. 291, 547 A.2d 355 (1988), describing the testimony of Dr. Burgess. See the follow-up study by Burgess & Holmstrom, "Rape: Sexual Disruption and Recovery," 49 *Am.J.Orthopsych.* 648 (1979).

weeks after the rape is unremarkable, as she was in the acute phase of RTS in which a victim has difficulty performing even normal functions, and the in-court identification five years later is particularly credible, as it results from a flashback, with the mind operating as a computer."[3]

According to psychologists, it is also not uncommon for victims of sexual assaults to delay reporting the abuse while they are in the acute stage following the traumatic event.[4] A whole host of other normal and logical consequences of the severe trauma of having been raped have been noted.[5]

The courts have not been consistent in admitting RTS testimony. Some courts refused to admit the testimony because it was seen as an attempt to bolster the credibility of the victim,[6] which is said to be an impermissible encroachment on the jury's function of determining credibility. Nevertheless, in the majority of jurisdictions, expert testimony that relates to the ability of a sexual assault victim to perceive, recall or relate is freely admissible.[7] Professor McCord reports that "there is unanimous agreement among the courts which have considered the issue that rape trauma syndrome testimony ... is properly admissible to explain what might otherwise seem to be unusual complainant behavior."[8]

Some courts have admitted RTS evidence to explain the post-rape behavior of alleged victims but not to show that such behavior is consistent with sexual abuse. In State v. Alberico,[9] the court saw no logical difference between the two, stating: "Both of these purposes for which PTSD is offered rest on the valid scientific premises that victims

---

3. Id.

4. See, Commonwealth v. Garcia, 403 Pa.Super. 280, 588 A.2d 951 (1991).

5. See, e.g., Burgess & Holmstrom, "Rape Trauma Syndrome," 131 *Am.J.Psychiatry* 981 (1974)—the authors coined the term "rape trauma syndrome"; Ross, "The Overlooked Expert in Rape Prosecutions" 14 *U.Toledo L.Rev.* 707 (1983); and the following comments: "Expert Testimony on Rape Trauma Syndrome: Admissibility and Effective Use in Criminal Rape Prosecutions," 33 *Am.U.L.Rev.* 417 (1984); "Checking the Allure of Increased Conviction Rates: The Admissibility of Expert Testimony on Rape Trauma Syndrome in Criminal Proceedings," 70 *Va.L.Rev.* 1657 (1984); " 'Rape Trauma Syndrome' and Inconsistent Rulings on its Admissibility Around the Nation," 24 *Willamette L.Rev.* 1011 (1988). For a perceptive analysis of the legal issues, see, Massaro, "Experts, Psychology, Credibility, and Rape: The Rape Trauma Syndrome Issue and Its Implications for Expert Psychological Testimony," 69 *Minn.L.Rev.* 395 (1985).

6. Commonwealth v. Gallagher, supra note 2 at 293, 547 A.2d at 357: "The testimony of Burgess regarding RTS was introduced for the sole purpose of shoring up the credibility of the victim on the crucial issue of identification" which invades the province of the jury. See also, State v. Alberico, 116 N.M. 156, 861 P.2d 192 (1993), wherein the court held PTSD testimony was held admissible because it was listed in DSM-III-R, but RTS was not because it was not so listed, even though the record shows that RTS was as acceptable to psychologists as PTSD was!

7. E.g. State v. Staples, 120 N.H. 278, 415 A.2d 320 (1980); State v. Harwood, 45 Or.App. 931, 609 P.2d 1312 (1980); State v. Pettit, 66 Or.App. 575, 675 P.2d 183 (1984); State v. Middleton, 294 Or. 427, 657 P.2d 1215 (1983); Smith v. State, 100 Nev. 570, 688 P.2d 326 (1984); People v. Eiskant, 253 Ill.App.3d 773, 192 Ill.Dec. 863, 625 N.E.2d 1018 (1993); State v. Freeney, 228 Conn. 582, 637 A.2d 1088 (1994).

8. McCord, "The Admissibility of Expert Testimony Regarding Rape Trauma Syndrome in Rape Prosecutions," 26 *B.C.L.Rev.* 1143, 1177–78 (1985).

9. 116 N.M. 156, 861 P.2d 192 (1983).

of sexual abuse exhibit identifiable symptoms. Either the PTSD diagnosis is a valid scientific technique for identifying certain symptoms of sexual abuse or it is not. Expert testimony in these two cases show that it is valid." [10]

In jurisdictions that admit RTS evidence on behalf of the state to explain the conduct of rape victims, logic dictates that defendants also be permitted to introduce RTS expert testimony to show that an alleged victim of forcible rape acted inconsistently with expected victim behavior. Thus, in Henson v. State,[11] the defense presented testimony that the complainant went dancing and drinking at the same bar where she had met the alleged rapist on the night after the attack. The defense subsequently sought to present expert testimony of a psychologist who was an expert in the treatment of post-traumatic stress syndrome, that the complaining witness' behavior was inconsistent with that of a person who had been the victim of a traumatic forcible rape. The trial court's ruling not to permit such expert testimony was held to be reversible error.

Of course, before RTS evidence can be admitted, certain general requirements must be fulfilled. According to one court: (1) the expert must be properly qualified; (2) the jury should be admonished and instructed that the evidence is for the purpose of explaining the other evidence in the case and cannot serve as the ultimate basis of the jury's verdict; and (3) the court must not permit the expert to give an opinion, explicitly or implicitly, as to whether the alleged victim was raped.[12]

Lawyers should carefully explore the issue of the witness' qualifications. RTS is an area in which many of the so-called expert witnesses are not clinical psychologists or psychiatrists, but, indeed may be social workers,[13] investigators for public agencies, or other skilled witnesses who have attended some workshops and training seminars on RTS but may lack the educational requirements expected of true scientific examiners. Some of these "experts" are undoubtedly qualified; there is, however, a great risk that well meaning but insufficiently trained investigators may be permitted to qualify as experts by courts who ordinarily have a low threshold in their requirement of expertise of witnesses who proffer opinion testimony.

2. THE CHILD SEXUAL ABUSE ACCOMMODATION SYNDROME (CSAAS)

The Child Sexual Abuse Accommodation Syndrome (CSAAS), or simply the Child Sexual Abuse Syndrome, is similar to RTS and is based on the concept that sexually abused children exhibit a series of symptoms that fall within the broad scope of post-traumatic stress disorder (PTSD). The syndrome is not separately listed in DSM–IV but is

---

10. Id. at 210.

11. 535 N.E.2d 1189 (Ind.1989).

12. State v. Jackson, 181 W.Va. 447, 383 S.E.2d 79, 83 (1989).

13. See, People v. Eiskant, supra note 7.

broadly discussed within the psychiatric and psychological professions, as the considerable legal and behavioral literature attests.[14] Some of the typical reactions of CSAAS victims are (1) secrecy, (2) helplessness, (3) entrapment and accommodation, (4) delayed reporting, sometimes with conflicting stories that fail to convince, and (5) a retraction of the accusation that follows disclosure of what happened.[15]

When it comes to expert testimony on CSAAS, the courts have not been as generous toward admissibility of the evidence, largely because there continues to be serious disagreement within the behavioral sciences on the reliability of the expert's conclusions. At the 1991 American Bar Association meeting in Atlanta, a special program was titled, "The Children's Hour—Perils in Litigating Cases Involving Children." Dr. Harry Krop, the director of Community Behavioral Services in Gainesville, Florida, stated that the "system" in which he works has not caught up with how to treat and detect possible false allegations by children. He also faced doubts about the basic premises underlying CSAAS in that there is no empirical data to support the identification of abused children on the basis of the five factors listed in the preceding paragraph.[16] In fact, Dr. Krop reportedly said, the authority who first described CSAAS, Dr. Roland Summit, said himself in a deposition that he doesn't consider himself qualified to treat and evaluate abuse victims. Dr. Krop concluded his remarks by stating that "the vast majority of experts who testify in such cases are overreaching the data, and should not be used to say that children are or are not abused." [17]

Problems of competency of the investigators (not scientists) of child abuse reports and their "techniques" in interviewing purported child victims and their relatives by using blatantly leading questions, use and potential misuse of anatomically correct dolls in the interviewing process, and incompetent assessments of truthfulness or lying by child victims, have raised serious questions about the reliability of the witness' findings of child abuse, and have suggested that the investigators' incorrect examination techniques may actually implant ideas in victims that they then report as fact.*

14. See, e.g., Roe, "Expert Testimony in Child Sexual Abuse Cases," 40 *U.Miami L.Rev.* 97 (1985); Gardner, "Prosecutors Should Think Twice Before Using Experts in Child Abuse Cases," 3 *Crim.Just.* 12 (1988); Comment, "The Admissibility of Expert Testimony in Intrafamily Child Sexual Abuse Cases," 34 *U.C.L.A.L.Rev.* 175 (1986); Comment, "Syndrome Testimony in Child Abuse Prosecutions: The Wave Of the Future?," 8 *St. Louis U.Pub.L.Rev.* 207 (1989); Summit, "The Child Sexual Abuse Accommodation Syndrome," 7 *Int'l J.Child Abuse & Neglect* 177 (1983); McCord, "Expert Psychological Testimony About Child Complaints in Sexual Abuse Prosecutions: A Foray into the Admissibility of Novel Psychological Evidence," 77 *J.Crim.L. & Criminology* 1 (1986).

15. See, Summit, op. cit. supra note 14.

16. See, "ABA Meeting Features Programs on Child Witnesses, Sentencing of Organizations," in 49 [BNA] *CrL.* 1452 (Aug. 26, 1991).

17. Id. at 1454.

* In State v. Delaney, 187 W.Va. 212, 417 S.E.2d 903 (1992), the court admitted opinion evidence of a "sexual assault counselor" who was not a trained psychologist or psychiatrist and who admitted that she was not neutral, being a self-proclaimed "advocate for victims," whose testimony proved to be the "damning" evidence. See, Wilt v. Buracker, 443 S.E.2d 196, 212 (W.Va.1993) [Neely, J., concurring]. Thus, relatively unskilled persons are permitted to make

Despite these misgivings and Dr. Krop's opinion,[18] many prosecutors are eager to bolster the testimony of child witnesses by calling CSAAS "expert" witnesses. And there are a number of courts that have admitted CSAAS evidence.[19] In recent years, however, there have been a number of cases in which courts held that the prosecution overstepped its boundaries by offering expert testimony on CSAAS. Thus, in 1993, in United States v. Whitted,[20] it was held that a doctor's testimony that sexual abuse occurred was error in that it implicitly vouched for the truth of the complainant's story, which impermissibly invaded the province of the jury. Four days after *Whitted,* the Kansas Supreme Court overturned a conviction for killing in the perpetration of child abuse, because the prosecution's expert had improperly used "profile" evidence and pretended to act, in the words of the court, as a "human lie detector" by telling the jury who to believe.[21] Another three days later, the North Carolina Court of Appeals, in State v. Hutchens,[22] also held the prosecution overstepped its boundaries in offering expert testimony that the emotional state of the victim was consistent with the type of behavior exhibited by child abuse victims.

Perhaps less surprising, in view of its decisions on RTS, was the decision of the Pennsylvania Supreme Court in Commonwealth v. Dunkle,[23] holding that CSAAS testimony was inadmissible because it is something that is not generally accepted as reliable in the fields of psychiatry and psychology and constituted improper bolstering of the victim's credibility.[24] In surveying the literature in the field, the court came to the conclusion that there is no classical or typical personality profile for abused children. "Researchers have been unsuccessful in their attempts to find common reactions that children have to sexual abuse. In fact, research has indicated that children act in incredibly diverse ways to sexual abuse," concluded the Pennsylvania court.[25]

It is clear, then, that the admissibility of CSAAS evidence is not one on which the courts agree, and which must remain dependent upon the

difficult clinical diagnoses on behalf of the prosecution which the same individual would not be permitted to make in the private practice of clinical psychology or psychiatry, with its rigorous educational mandates, completion of supervised internships and required passage of a rigorous examination before a peer-review licensing board as required by law in the state: State v. Delaney, supra, at 218, 417 S.E.2d at 909 [Neely, J., dissenting].

18. See, supra notes 16–17.

19. E.g., State v. Delaney, 187 W.Va. 212, 417 S.E.2d 903 (1992); State v. Edward Charles L., 183 W.Va. 641, 398 S.E.2d 123 (1990); People v. Nelson, 203 Ill.App.3d 1038, 149 Ill.Dec. 161, 561 N.E.2d 439 (1990)—listing cases in other jurisdictions on both sides of the issue.

20. 994 F.2d 444 (8th Cir.1993). Conviction reversed.

21. State v. Cheeks, 253 Kan. 93, 853 P.2d 655 (1993).

22. 110 N.C.App. 455, 429 S.E.2d 755 (1993).

23. 529 Pa. 168, 602 A.2d 830 (1992) (over three dissents).

24. Some of the factors the expert relied upon to conclude the victim was an abused child included: drug and alcohol abuse, eating disorders, low self-esteem, not doing school work. The court said these manifestations are common among children and not related solely to child abuse. To admit such evidence invites the purest of speculation and conjecture and is neither scientifically nor legally supportable. Commonwealth v. Dunkle, supra note 23.

25. Commonwealth v. Dunkle, supra note 23.

degree of consensus that may develop on this issue in the professions that study human behavioral characteristics.

If the evidence is not admitted on behalf of the prosecution, the courts should also be consistent and not admit it on behalf of the defense either. Thus, in State v. Hulbert,[26] the Iowa Supreme Court held that expert testimony, on behalf of the defense, that the accused did not fit the profile of the typical child molester was properly excluded, because it would not have been of assistance to the decision-making function of the jury. And where the prosecution is permitted to use its expert testimony, the defense may have a constitutional right to have its own psychologist explain the complaining witness, said a Wisconsin court in 1993.[27] The court relied on a recent Illinois Supreme Court decision [28] which stated:

> "While it may be possible for an expert to form an opinion regarding [rape trauma syndrome] based only on a review of reports and trial testimony, this is clearly not the preferred method. An expert who has personally examined a victim is in a better position to render an opinion than is an expert who has not done so.... Defendant argues that in-court observation by an expert would provide an inadequate basis for expert opinion ... because defendant's expert would be unable to ask follow-up questions. Moreover, defendant points out that he would be placed in a strategic disadvantage if he were forced to wait until trial before his expert could evaluate the evidence of rape trauma syndrome ..." [29]

These and other considerations led the court to conclude it would be fundamentally unfair to permit the state to present the testimony of an examining expert but to limit the defendant to a nonexamining expert.[30]

§ 19.09 Determining Competency to Stand Trial

There are very few rights that are firmer established in our legal heritage than the right not to be tried for a crime while incompetent. It is a right that was recognized in Blackstone's days. The rules that existed in Great Britain, that an incompetent person could not be tried for an offense, were transposed into our American legal system. The contemporaneous development of the fields of psychiatry and psychology and the imposition of constitutional guarantees of fairness and due process upon the criminal justice system by the Supreme Court, combined to create a legal framework for determining competency of a criminal defendant to be tried for an offense.

---

26. 481 N.W.2d 329 (Iowa 1992).

27. State v. Maday, 179 Wis.2d 346, 507 N.W.2d 365 (App.1993)—decided in the context of RTS evidence.

28. People v. Wheeler, 151 Ill.2d 298, 176 Ill.Dec. 880, 602 N.E.2d 826 (1992).

29. People v. Wheeler, supra note 28 at 309–310, 602 N.E.2d at 833.

30. Relying on the statement in Ake v. Oklahoma, 470 U.S. 68, 79 (1985) that "a State may not legitimately assert an interest in maintenance of a strategic advantage over the defense, if the result of that advantage is to cast a pall on the accuracy of the verdict obtained."

Competency to stand trial is different from insanity in several ways. First, insanity looks to the condition of defendant's mental state at the time of the commission of the criminal act with which he is charged, whereas competency to stand trial looks toward the defendant's mental condition at the time a trial is contemplated. Second, insanity at the time of trial, if established by the evidence, is a defense to criminal responsibility, whereas establishing the incompetence of an accused merely postpones the trial until such time as the defendant regains his competency. Thus, in proceedings against a defendant, competency to stand trial would chronologically be raised first. If the defendant is found incompetent, no trial will be commenced. If, on the other hand, defendant is found competent, then a trial will commence at which time defendant may raise, as a defense, the fact of his insanity at the time of committing the crime.

1.   THE STANDARD FOR DETERMINING COMPETENCE

"Competency to Stand Trial" is a legal concept superimposed upon all criminal trials. The legal standard for determining competence derives from the landmark decision of Dusky v. United States [1] wherein the Supreme Court held that prior to a criminal trial a defendant must be shown to have "sufficient present ability to consult with his attorney with a reasonable degree of rational understanding" and that "he has a rational as well as factual understanding of the proceeding against him." [2] While states may set a higher standard, the constitutional minimum is the *Dusky* rule below which states may not go. While there are no fixed rules on how the issue may arise, it is clear that it is not only an issue that can be raised by the defense, but, in fact either the prosecutor or the court must raise the competency issue on their own motion if information of defendant's irrational behavior is either transmitted to them, or observed in court. Whenever defendant's behavior raises doubts as to his competency and ability to assist his/her attorney in the preparation of a defense, a competency hearing must be held.[3] The competency hearing is an adversary proceeding, where witnesses will be heard and may be cross-examined.

In earlier years, states did not agree on who had the burden of proof, and what the required quantum of proof was. Some states placed the burden of proof of incompetency on the prosecution, some placed it on the defendant, and some simply gave the burden to the moving party. The same dichotomy was seen in the allocation of the required quantum of proof. In some states the prosecution had to prove competency by a preponderance of the evidence, other states required the same quantum of evidence but asked defendant to prove incompetency. A few states

§ 19.09

1.   362 U.S. 402 (1960).

2.   Id.

3.   Pate v. Robinson, 383 U.S. 375 (1966) held that due process is violated if an in-

competent person is convicted, and Drope v. Missouri, 420 U.S. 162 (1975), supplemented Dusky in requiring defendant must be able to "assist in his defense."

required a greater quantum of proof by clear and convincing evidence. The constitutional standard was set in Medina v. California,[4] where state law required defendant to prove his incompetency by a preponderance of the evidence. He failed to rebut, by sufficient evidence, the presumption of competency which had aided the prosecution, and was subsequently tried, convicted and sentenced to death. The United States Supreme Court affirmed, holding that fundamental fairness did not require that the state be assigned the burden of proving competency. To place the burden of proving incompetency by a preponderance of the evidence upon the defendant did not violate due process.[5]

2. THE DETERMINATION OF COMPETENCY

In the ordinary case, the examination into the competency of an accused to stand trial may take place in a maximum security hospital of forensic psychiatric evaluation unit of a state mental hospital, though some states permit out-patient examinations. While lay testimony alone is sufficient to meet the legal standard of proof, expert evaluations are more often relied upon. When a professional assessment of competency is made, it is often done pursuant to a single interview, though supervision for a period of days, or even weeks, is becoming more commonplace.

Courts seem to require less proof of competency than that which will satisfy psychiatrists.[6] Typically, an expert determination of competency or incompetency will be the result of a mental status examination, supplemented at times by psychological testing.[7] A finding of incompetency can be determined upon the basis of discovering that the accused suffers from a significant psychiatric disorder, or suffers from a physiological disorder that prevents the patient from satisfying the *Dusky* test. Such neurological disorders might be a case of advanced epilepsy, cerebral tumor, arteriosclerosis, and other serious physiological impairments. While mental retardation or a suffering from amnesia is not ordinarily sufficient to be incompetent to stand trial,[8] there is at least one case in which incompetency was based on the defendant being a deaf-mute who had never learned to communicate.[9] Less severe neurological impediments had been found to be sufficient to establish incompetency.[10]

According to Kermani, the Harvard Laboratory of Community Psychiatry has devised two standard tests for the purpose of providing an accurate and comprehensive assessment of competency. The tests are called (1) the Competency Screening Test (CST), and (2) the Competency

---

4. 112 S.Ct. 2572 (1992).

5. Id.

6. See, Perlin, *Law and Mental Disability*, 517 (1994).

7. See Chapter 18, supra.

8. If, for example, the attorney can reconstruct from other witnesses what evidence for the defense can be raised or discovered.

9. The case of Donald Lang, about whose experience the book titled *Dummy* was written, began its legal/appellate journey as People v. Lang 26 Ill.App.3d 648, 325 N.E.2d 305 (1975), but resulted in numerous subsequent appellate decisions.

10. See, Perlin, op. cit. supra note 6 at 518–519 for authorities.

Assessment Instrument (CAI).[11] Other tests have also been constructed, and many evaluations of competency are made on the basis of mental status examinations that do not include formalized testing. Some medical examinations have included examinations by injections with sodium pentothal and sodium amytal.[12]

3.   RESTORING THE DEFENDANT'S COMPETENCY

Pharmacological advances have created antipsychotic drugs which, if administered to persons who are determined to be incompetent to stand trial, may restore these individuals to competence. The administration of such medication can be commenced even during the evaluation process if a person is committed for forensic evaluation under an appropriate state statute. At the conclusion of such evaluation period, it is possible that the accused may be reported out as "competent," so that a trial can be scheduled. When an accused has been found incompetent to stand trial at the conclusion of the evaluation process, involuntary commitment proceedings must be instituted if the accused is to remain institutionalized.[13] The question that then arises is whether the accused can be compelled to undergo forced medication so that his competency will be restored, or whether he/she has a constitutional right to remain unmedicated. There have been two Supreme Court cases that touch tangentially on this issue.

In the first of the two cases, competency to stand trial was not involved. In Washington v. Harper,[14] the accused was incarcerated in a state correctional facility for violating parole. He was diagnosed as suffering from a manic-depressive disorder and initially agreed to take anti-psychotic medication of a type ordinarily administered in the treatment of mental disorders such as schizophrenia. The medication was prescribed by the prison psychiatrist, but thereafter Harper refused to continue. The psychiatrist then sought a hearing before the mental health prison committee,[15] which held a hearing and determined he was violent and a danger to others as a result of mental disease. Involuntary medication was thereupon ordered. Harper then brought a Section 1983 action for an injunction and damages. The trial court held his protected liberty right in refusing medication was adequately protected by the in-prison hearing and a finding he was a danger, but the state supreme court disagreed, holding that due process required an adversary judicial hearing prior to the involuntary forced medication of an inmate, at which hearing the state would have to prove by "clear, cogent, and

---

11. See, Kermani, *Handbook of Psychiatry and The Law* 139 (1989).

12. See, in this regard, Chapter 20, infra at § 20.19 et seq. on Narcoanalysis.

13. Such proceedings may be required as a result of Jackson v. Indiana, 406 U.S. 715 (1972). See also, infra § 19.11 et seq. on Involuntary Civil Commitment.

14. 494 U.S. 210 (1990).

15. Composed of a non-treating psychiatrist, a psychologist, and the prison's associate superintendent, none of whom may have been involved in the prisoner's prior medication decision.

convincing evidence" that the medication was both necessary and effective for furthering a compelling state interest.

The United States Supreme Court disagreed and reversed, addressing first the issue of substantive rights of the prisoner, and the procedural steps taken in this case. First the Court held that a state may override a prisoner's decision to be free from involuntary medication. The procedure set out in the prison regulations, requiring the full panoply of procedural rights at a hearing where a medical finding of a mental disorder that will likely cause danger if not treated must first be made, satisfy the requirement that the needs for institutional safety and security can outweigh Harper's individual rights. The proper standard for making that decision was a finding whether the regulation requiring forced medication is reasonably related to legitimate penological interests, and the Court found that the instant regulation met that requirement. The Court said that "Prison administrators have not only an interest in insuring the safety of prison staffs and administrative personnel, but the duty to take reasonable measures for the prisoners' own safety." [16] The Court also disagreed with defendant's contention that he should first have been found incompetent because his wishes could be overridden.

The Court then also decided that the Washington procedure comported with due process, and that a full-scale adversary judicial hearing was not required. While the rights of the individual in refusing medication are substantial, since forced medication may lead to undesirable and unpleasant side effects, these rights must be considered in the light of hospital and prison realities. The Court held that the inmate's rights are perhaps even more adequately protected by a hearing where an impartial panel of medical professionals decides whether to involuntarily medicate than when the decision is made by a judge. Thus, the regulation that was before the Court was held permissible under the Constitution. [17]

The second Supreme Court decision dealt directly with involuntarily medicating a detained person who intended to raise an insanity defense. The case is Riggins v. Nevada. [18] Here, Riggins was institutionalized pending trial at which he intended to raise an insanity defense, and moved the court to terminate use of the drug Mellaril which, he argued, would deprive him of letting the jury see his true condition. At the hearing, the experts disagreed on whether Riggins would be competent to stand trial without the drug, and they also disagreed on the effects of the drug upon Riggins' demeanor and on his ability to assist in his defense. The trial denied his motion. Riggins testified while under medication, was convicted and sentenced to death. On appeal, the United States Supreme Court reversed. Relying upon *Harper,* the Court held that while the state could compel medication under some circum-

---

16. Id. at 225.

17. The dissent by Justice Stevens, wherein Brennan and Marshall joined, disagreed that a "mock trial before an institu- tionally biased tribunal" constituted "due process of law."

18. 112 S.Ct. 1810 (1992).

stances, as where the person is a danger to self or others, in this case the court erred by ordering a continuation of medication without making a finding that there was a need for it or that there were no reasonable alternatives.   The failure of the court to make a finding and conduct a balancing test ignored Riggins' rights altogether, and the effects of the medication created a "strong possibility that Riggins' defense was impaired due to administration" of the drug.[19]   It was the lack of a finding that forced medication was necessary to accomplish an essential state policy which caused the prejudice to the defendant.

This leaves the issue of whether compelled medication to force competency to stand trial is constitutionally undecided.   While the Court's opinion suggested, in dictum, that forced medication to make someone competent to stand trial might be an adequate state interest, it should be noted that in a concurring opinion by Justice Kennedy, he concluded that "if the State cannot render the defendant competent without involuntary medication, then it must resort to civil commitment, if appropriate, unless the defendant becomes competent through other means."[20]

§ 19.10   "Competency" for Other Purposes

The competency of an accused is featured in contexts other than competency to stand trial.

1.   COMPETENCY TO ENTER A GUILTY PLEA AND WAIVE COUNSEL

In Godinez v. Moran,[1] a split Court had to decide whether different standards are applied for competency to enter a guilty plea from that required to stand trial.   The defendant in a multiple murder prosecution, had been found competent to stand trial, but hereafter dismissed his lawyer, whereupon he decided to plead guilty.   After his conviction, the Court of Appeals held, however, that to plead guilty "requires a higher level of mental functioning than that required to stand trial," and requires that the defendant have "the capacity for 'reasoned choice' among the alternatives available to him."[2]   The Supreme Court disagreed.   A defendant who is found competent to stand trial under the standard of Dusky v. United States,[3] but who does not plead guilty, has

---

19. Id. at 1816.

20. Id. at 1820 [Concurring opinion.] See also, Sullivan v. Flannigan, 8 F.3d 591 (7th Cir.1993), holding that Illinois' statutory scheme that provides for administrative review of a prison physician's decision to order medication comports with due process, and that an inmate has no right to have prison authorities cease administration of psychotropic drugs so he can show he can function without them.   The same court held, in Felce v. Fiedler, 974 F.2d 1484 (7th Cir.1992), that Wisconsin failed

to comply with Riggins in requiring a parolee candidate to undergo involuntary medication as a condition of what would otherwise be release under a mandatory parole system without a prior finding of medical necessity.

§ 19.10

1. 113 S.Ct. 2680 (1993).

2. See, Moran v. Godinez, 972 F.2d 263 (9th Cir.1992).

3. Supra § 19.09(1) at note 1.

several weighty decisions to make, such as whether to accept a bench trial instead of a jury, put on evidence in support of a defense, raise affirmative defenses, and whether to testify. No higher standard should be required to enter a guilty plea, said the Court. Justice Thomas, writing for the Court, also added that the waiver of the right of counsel equally does not require a higher level of competency, as long as the waiver is also voluntary. The competency needed, he pointed out, was competency to voluntarily and knowingly waive a right—not competency to adequately represent himself.

2. COMPETENCY TO BE EXECUTED

Just as an incompetent person cannot stand trial, a person who has been convicted of an offense and sentenced to death, and who thereafter becomes incompetent, cannot be executed, said the Court in Ford v. Wainwright.[4] Ford, a Florida inmate awaiting execution, had become psychotic about eight years after first being incarcerated. Because there was no evidence of malingering, dissembling, or otherwise putting on a performance, Ford's counsel sought a determination of competency to be executed under Florida law. The three psychiatrists ordered by the Governor to examine Ford each came up with different psychiatric diagnoses. They all agreed that Ford did know and understand all the implications of the death penalty, whereupon the Governor signed the death warrant. When the case ultimately reached the United States Supreme Court, that tribunal reversed, finding impressive precedent in the common law and the law of all fifty states that an incompetent person cannot be executed. While the State of Florida had conducted some sort of process to determine competency, the Supreme Court struck down that procedure as not satisfying due process in three different regards: (1) the failure to include the inmate and counsel in the truth-seeking process; (2) denial of the right to challenge or impeach the state-appointed psychiatrists' opinions through cross-examination; (3) that the decision-making process was entirely in the executive branch without the neutrality of an impartial tribunal. The Court thereupon reversed and remanded to allow Ford an evidentiary hearing.[5]

Thereafter, in Penry v. Lynaugh,[6] the Court decided that execution of a mentally retarded person was not barred by the Eighth Amendment, but remarked that whether a particular criminal penalty was cruel and unusual punishment is a concept that changes in accordance with "evolving standards of decency that mark the progress of a maturing society," thereby leaving open the door for a later change of law.

4. .477 U.S. 399 (1986), rehearing denied Ford v. State, 522 So.2d 345 (Fla.1988)— denying habeas relief, cert. denied sub nom. Ford v. Dugger, 489 U.S. 1071 (1989). For a medical perspective on psychiatrists' participation in death penalty cases, see, Mossman (M.D.), "The Psychiatrist And Execu-

tion Competency: *Ford* ing Murky Ethical Waters," 43 *Case West.Res.L.Rev.* 1 (1992).

5. The decision was badly splintered, with no less than four different opinions by various Justices concurring, concurring in part, and dissenting.

6. 492 U.S. 302 (1989).

The question of whether an incompetent incarcerated person could be involuntarily medicated with psychotropic drugs so as to make him competent to be executed, presented itself before the Court first in Perry v. Louisiana,[7] wherein Perry had been convicted of murdering five family members.[8]   He had been found competent to stand trial, but after conviction became psychotic.   At the hearing on competency to be executed, the four state mental health specialists agreed on the issue of mental illness and also that he could be made competent if properly medicated.   An order to that effect was entered and, some months later, when a new report from the prison hospital was received declaring that Perry now understood why he was going to be executed, the court held a hearing at the conclusion of which it decided Perry was competent to be executed, and could be kept competent by forced medication until executed.   The Supreme Court decided not to resolve the precise issue before it, but send the case back to the state court for further proceedings in the light of Washington v. Harper,[9] which had been decided in the interim.   Since *Harper* did not precisely answer the question, the reason for the remand is unclear.

The federal constitutional issue will not be resolved in Perry's case, however, since on remand, the Louisiana Supreme Court decided, in State v. Perry,[10] that the state constitution prohibited the forced medication to make an insane person competent for execution.   Perhaps the most important concept in the Louisiana decision was that the court decided that administering medication to restore competency did not constitute "medical treatment" but was simply a procedural step in implementing a death sentence.

II.   INVOLUNTARY CIVIL COMMITMENT AND THE CONCEPT OF "FUTURE DANGEROUSNESS"

§ 19.11   Introduction

The subject matter of coerced civil commitment, with its important sub-topic of the prediction of future dangerousness and the related issues that deal with the rights of institutionalized patients is a vast one, on which many books have been written.   In the context of this multi-discipline textbook, we can but deal with it in abbreviated form and suggest lawyers involved in the representation of persons about to be compelled into joining the ranks of the institutionalized against their will study the matter in greater depth by referring to specialized sources.   Perhaps the best and most up to date treatment of the subject, both with

---

7.   494 U.S. 1015 (1990).

8.   Against advice of his counsel, he had withdrawn a plea of not guilty by reason of insanity and entered a not guilty plea at trial.

9.   Supra note 14, § 19.09.

10.   610 So.2d 746 (La.1992).

respect to exploration of the mental health literature and the legislative and case law is that by Professor Michael L. Perlin.[1]

Involuntary institutionalization involves a serious deprivation of a person's liberty rights. Historically, when a person was to be committed against his will to a hospital for the insane, commitment procedures were very simple matters. An interested party, often a close relative, made the arrangements through a physician or public agency with a hospital and that might be the last one ever heard of the institutionalized person. The commitment was for an indefinite period of time, often life, and entailed no procedural guarantees since the commitment process was viewed as "civil." Under the impetus of United States Supreme Court decisions striking down these historical practices, legislatures passed statutes regulating the commitment process in such a manner as to preserve, safeguard, and respect to the widest extent possible, the committee's rights as an individual.

While state civil commitment laws vary from jurisdiction to jurisdiction, they all have superimposed upon them a provision that the person to be committed has the right to counsel, the right to present evidence on the issue of that individual's mental status, and rights after institutionalization to treatment and, perhaps, a release from confinement in the mental hospital. Modern statutes and practices also seek to avoid potential constitutional problems by encouraging strongly the process of voluntary hospital commitment, or outpatient treatment.

§ 19.12 Principal Concepts

At the very center of the commitment process lie the constitutional guarantees to which a person sought to be institutionalized involuntarily is entitled. These guarantees are expressed in terms of the standard of proof that is required to justify commitment, and the manner whereby an institutionalized person may seek release from confinement.

1. RIGHT TO HEARING AND STANDARD OF PROOF

Statutes recognize that the process of involuntary institutionalization can receive its impetus in different ways: a person may need to receive psychiatric and supervisory care on an emergency basis; or a person may need to be committed for a limited purpose and duration, such as for evaluation and observation; or a person may need to be institutionalized involuntarily for an indefinite period of time. While laws set out conditions under which each of these purposes can be accomplished, we will concentrate on the third purpose: that of a commitment process for an indefinite period of time.

The process whereby involuntary institutionalization may be commenced depends upon state statute, but it typically envisions the filing of

§ 19.11
1. See, Perlin, *Law and Mental Disability*, 1994. The author devotes the first 396   pages of his text to these issues.

a petition by an interested person. The petitioner may be a relative, friend, associate, physician, counselor, social worker, police officer, a member of the general public, or a combination of several of these. Upon the filing of the petition, the person to be institutionalized, called the "committee" in many jurisdictions, is entitled to an early hearing. In fact, under many state statutes the committee may have a right to a preliminary hearing if he or she has already been institutionalized on an emergency basis pending the "final" hearing.[1]

At the hearing to determine involuntary commitment for an indefinite period, the patient is entitled to certain constitutional rights that were first set out in Addington v. Texas,[2] and thereafter provided by statutes or local court decisions. The hearing must be scheduled within a relatively short period of time after temporary institutionalization has occurred; it must be conducted before a judicial officer, rather than hospital staff or executive branch public officials, but often can be conducted in a hospital setting; the hearing can be closed to the public unless the patient wants a public one; the patient has a right to a complete record of the hearing so that an appeal process will be possible; the patient has the right to be present (though that right can be waived), and to prior notice of the scheduled hearing.

While statutes provide specifically for assistance by counsel at the commitment hearing, no United States Supreme Court decision has held, to date, that an indigent person about to be committed has the right to be assisted by an attorney. The Court has said, however, in Vitek v. Jones,[3] that a prisoner is entitled to all of the procedural due process rights, including "qualified and independent assistance," prior to a transfer to a mental hospital. Similarly, many statutes provide for independent expert psychiatric or psychological assistance for the patient at the hearing. Most cases dealing with the issue also hold that the patient has the right of confrontation, though courts take different approaches to the extent to which the rules of evidence (and against hearsay) are applicable in commitment hearings. There is also no definitive pronouncement on (1) whether the privilege against self-incrimination applies to commitment hearings, some courts relying on Application of Gault,[4] and others on Allen v. Illinois,[5] or on (2) the right to a jury trial.[6]

§ 19.12

1. In Mathews v. Eldridge, 424 U.S. 319 (1976), the Court struck down a state procedure for institutionalizing a person for up to 72 hours of observation, holding due process was violated by not interposing the requirement of a judicial finding of probable dangerousness.

2. 441 U.S. 418 (1979).

3. 445 U.S. 480, 497 (1980). [Concurring opinion of Powell, J.]

4. 387 U.S. 1 (1967), holding that the full panoply of rights afforded defendants in adult criminal trials are also available to the adjudicatory hearing in (supposedly "civil") juvenile proceedings.

5. 478 U.S. 364 (1986), holding that the privilege against compelled self-incrimination is not available in (equally "civil") proceedings under a dangerous sexual offender statute.

6. Most state cases dealing with that issue did not find such right, probably influenced strongly by the Supreme Court's decision in McKeiver v. Pennsylvania, 403 U.S. 528 (1971) which held that jury trials are not constitutionally required in juvenile proceedings.

Perhaps the most significant constitutional issue is the quantum of proof and burden of proof requirements for involuntary institutionalization. States ranged from "mere preponderance" to "beyond a reasonable doubt." The issue was settled in Addington v. Texas,[7] where the Court predictably placed the burden upon the petitioner moving for institutionalization and, on the issue of quantum, chose the middle ground of proof by clear and convincing evidence, recognizing that proof beyond a reasonable doubt might be difficult to achieve in commitment cases when the proof depended so strongly on a prediction of future dangerousness to self or others. However, the Court also approved, recently, a state statutory scheme which required proof beyond a reasonable doubt when commitment was sought for mental illness, but only proof by clear and convincing evidence if based on mental retardation.[8]

The reasons for the hospitalization must, of course, also be established at the hearing. Constitutionally and/or by statute, persons may be involuntarily committed upon a finding that they are unable to care for themselves, that there is no reasonable less restrictive alternative, and that if not institutionalized they will be a danger to themselves or to others. The linchpin is the latter requirement: the determination of future dangerousness, which is dealt with separately.[9]

2. DURATION AND NATURE OF THE CONFINEMENT

When a patient has been committed following a constitutionally and statutorily sanctioned hearing, confinement can be for an indefinite period of time. The Supreme Court has held, however, that when the basis for confinement no longer exists, it must be terminated.[10] This ended indeterminate involuntary hospitalizations and, as recognized in most state statutes, provides that an institutionalized person has a right to periodic review. At these periodic reviews, new hearings must be held wherein the patient has essentially the same rights as attached to the initial commitment hearing.

During confinement, the patient has certain rights that evolved over a long period of time but have culminated in the passage by many states, of Patients' Bills of Rights, and other legislative or executive branch initiatives providing for a right to treatment during involuntary hospitalization.[11] United States Supreme Court authority in the area derives

---

7. Supra note 2.

8. See, Heller v. Doe, 113 S.Ct. 2637 (1993), holding there was a rational basis for distinguishing between handicapping conditions, because the mentally ill were subject to more invasive types of treatment (psychotropic drugs) than the mentally retarded, and such different treatment did not violate the equal protection clause.

9. See § 19.14, infra.

10. See, O'Connor v. Donaldson, 422 U.S. 563 (1975).

11. See, for instance, the Task Panel on Legal and Ethical Issues of the President's Commission on Mental Health. The historical development of the rights of institutionalized patients, and its current status, is explored in great detail by Professor Perlin in Chapter 2 of his treatise. See, Perlin, op. cit. note 4, Sec. 19.08, at pp. 161–396.

from several cases, some of which have already been explored earlier.[12] In Youngberg v. Romeo,[13] The Supreme Court determined that institutionalized patients have a constitutionally protected right under the Fourteenth Amendment to adequate food, shelter, clothing, medical care, conditions of reasonable care and safety, and freedom from bodily restraint. Whether these rights are violated is to be determined on the basis whether the conditions of confinement were made by professionals exercising sound judgment, in which case the conditions are presumptively valid, or whether the decision by the professional was in substantial departure from accepted professional practices. No later United States Supreme Court cases have dealt with the conditions under which confinement can be lawfully conducted.

There is considerable state and lower federal court case law on the conditions of confinement, the right to refuse medication or to refuse alternative treatments,[14] rights in regard to the exercise of First Amendment rights, and so on, all of which is beyond the scope of this overview of the subject matter.

3. JUVENILE CONFINEMENTS

Historically, all states recognized the rights of parents to commit their children to a mental hospital virtually without providing any justification therefor. Since the unfettered parental discretion created a real danger to arbitrary action and abuse, especially among poorer families, courts interjected themselves at different levels seeking to provide a modicum of due process for juveniles and legislatures responded by regulating the procedure. In dealing with the adequacy of such state schemes, the United States Supreme Court recognized that the questions involved in juvenile commitments were essentially "medical in character," but also enunciated standards for juvenile commitments in Parham v. J.R.,[15] holding: (1) that juveniles were entitled to an independent fact finding by a neutral factfinder, such as a trained physician, but not an adversary hearing, that the statutory conditions for institutionalization were met; (2) that the hearing must carefully explore the causes and background of the child and family involved; (3) that the decisionmaker must be free to refuse to admit a juvenile who does not meet the

---

12. See, e.g., the decisions on restoring a criminal defendant's competence through the use of psychotropic medication in § 19.-09(3), supra, and on competency to be executed in § 19.10(2).

13. 457 U.S. 307 (1982).

14. E.g., the fairly common electro-convulsive shock therapy (ECT): "ECT is the use of a small amount of electricity to induce a major seizure in a patient who has a severe psychiatric illness, notably severe depression. The use of anesthetic medication, muscle relaxants, and oxygen with the treatment has resulted in a minimal amount of medical risk to patients receiving ECT. While the medical profession does not know exactly 'why ECT works' to improve illness, it is known that ECT, as well as anti-depressant medications, affect a number of brain functions. Shalih v. Lane, 423 S.E.2d 192 (Va.1992)—a malpractice action brought by a nurse who had claimed injury due to electroshock that was being administered to a patient. The case explains how ECT is used in the treatment of mental disorders.

15. 442 U.S. 584 (1979).

conditions set out in the law; and (4) continued commitment must be subject to periodic review. Of all the Supreme Court cases dealing with commitment and institutionalization, *Parham v. J.R.*, perhaps has been most resoundingly criticized in both dissents and in the legal literature.[16]

§ 19.13 Commitment After Successful Insanity Plea

After a defendant in a criminal trial has been acquitted of the offense charged on the ground of insanity, further detention of the individual is to occur on the basis of involuntary civil commitment proceedings discussed in § 19.11, but with some modifications. In Jones v. United States,[1] the Court agreed that insanity acquittees could be treated differently from ordinary committees, and approved a post-acquittal commitment scheme that cast upon the patient the burden of proving lack of mental illness or dangerousness, and that also permitted post-acquittal commitments that were of a duration longer than the maximum sentence permitted under the statute had the defendant been convicted. If defendant was found by the fact finder to have been insane, and therefore acquitted, it was reasonable to assume that "someone whose mental illness was sufficient to lead him to commit a criminal act is likely to remain ill and in need of treatment."[2]

Legislatures have reacted to the *Jones* decision and to the post-Hinckley acquittal furor by enacting a wide variety of statutory schemes to deal with the criminal defendant who is acquitted on grounds of insanity, and on what the standards ought to be in making subsequent decisions involving release, that are beyond the scope of this overview. It should be noted, however, that in 1992 the Court did hold that an insanity acquittee's retention following the acquittal in a forensic mental hospital, could not be justified following a determination that the patient was no longer mentally ill, though he might still be considered dangerous.[3]

§ 19.14 The Prediction of Future Dangerousness

The linchpin justifying involuntary hospitalization and commitment, especially when dealing with persons charged with crimes, has been a determination that, if released, the persons would be a danger to themselves or to others. But the concept of future dangerousness has had wider application in the law; it is frequently the basis upon which enhanced punishment, indeed imposition of the death penalty, has been premised. It is important, therefore, to explore the degree of accuracy with which such predictions can be made.

16. See, on this subject, Perlin, op. cit. note 4, Sec. 19.08, at 140.

§ 19.13

1. 463 U.S. 354 (1983).

2. Id. at 366.

3. The case is Foucha v. Louisiana, 112 S.Ct. 1780 (1992), wherein a sharply divided court held that since the basis for Foucha's continued detention had been mental illness, a continuation of the hospital confinement violated due process after the reason for the commitment had disappeared.

The official statement of the American Psychiatric Association (APA) on the prediction of future dangerousness is that psychiatrists have no special knowledge or ability with which to predict dangerous behavior.[1] According to studies, psychiatrists fail to accurately predict dangerousness for two out of every three patients, even where those patients have a history of violent behavior.[2] Despite this blanket disavowal psychiatrists and psychologists regularly assess the dangerousness of people and are regularly called upon by the courts to testify regarding dangerousness in numerous and varied cases. Decisions involving the determination of dangerousness arise when considering bail, sentencing, the death penalty, parole, sexually dangerous persons, protective services to children and adults, involuntary commitments, deinstitutionalization and hospitalization of insanity acquittees. Clearly, the need for accurate predictions as to whether a person is likely to commit a violent act is one felt very strongly by society which seeks to protect its citizens from violence. On the other hand, and equally important, is the need to protect the rights and freedom of the individual. It is between these two differing objectives that courts struggle.

By no possible standard for the admissibility of expert opinion testimony can the admission of psychiatric testimony on future dangerous pass the test. The concept of predicting dangerous is not one generally accepted as accurate in the psychiatric profession if the *Frye* test is used as the standard for admissibility,[3] much less can the testimony pass the "proof of reliability" test of Daubert v. Merrell Dow Pharmaceuticals.[4] Perhaps the courts permit the expert testimony to come in as a matter of last resort: inasmuch as the decision of future dangerousness needs to be made for legal purposes (i.e. continued detention or increased punishment), and inasmuch as lay testimony is permitted to talk about the violence of the person for the purpose of letting the jury infer that past violence means also future violence, it makes little sense to exclude the opinions of those experts who, though they disclaim expertise on the precise issue, nevertheless are supposed to be the professionals who study the human mind and behavior.[5]

§ 19.14

1. The APA's position that psychiatric predictions had a fundamentally low reliability and ought not to be used was set forth in an *amicus* brief filed in Barefoot v. Estelle, 463 U.S. 880 (1983), but rejected by the Supreme Court, which held that since the issue of future dangerousness was one that had to be resolved in legal controversies, there was "little sense" in excluding mental health experts from the "entire universe of persons who might have an opinion on this issue." Id. at 896. See also, APA, News Release, "Statement of the American Psychiatric Association on Prediction of Dangerousness" 3–18–83.

2. Monohan, *Community Mental Health and the Criminal Justice System* (1976) at 20.

3. See the "general acceptance" test of Frye v. United States, supra Chapter 1 at § 1.03.

4. 113 S.Ct. 2786 (1993), also discussed in Chapter 1, supra, at § 1.03.

5. Not all psychiatrists admit to an inability to predict future dangerousness. A Texas doctor, James Grigson, has been at the center of long-standing controversies for his self-professed ability to predict future dangerousness infallibly. The great demand upon his services as a state expert in capital sentencing cases earned him the nickname "Dr. Death," a name he accepted with "pride" on a CBS 60 MINUTES segment devoted to his witness exploits. Medical schools psychiatry departments regularly show videotapes of Dr. Grigson's testimo-

The reliability and validity problems associated with predictions of dangerousness stem from the lack of a legal definition of dangerousness. It is an imprecise, vague concept. The two methods generally used in predicting violence are clinical and actuarial. The clinical method utilizes patient histories as obtained during a mental status examination and a thorough social history, psychological testing, and clinical observations of the patient from which the therapist draws a conclusion on whether this patient will commit future acts. Most often it is the clinical-based impression that is heard in judicial proceedings.[6] Predictions made on the basis of clinical data is unreliable and invalid largely because psychiatric interviews and procedures are not standardized. Psychiatrists may observe the same behavior and symptoms but interpret their meaning differently or assign different weights or values. Furthermore, physicians are trained to identify and diagnose mental disorders. Even assuming they are accurate in their diagnosis of mental illness, it would not improve the accuracy of predictions of dangerousness because no correlation has been shown between mental illness and dangerous behavior.[7] The level of error in the clinical method has been assessed as between 50 and 90 percent.[8]

The actuarial method bases its predictions on a number of variables such as sex, race, age, IQ, prior arrests, substance abuse and marital status. The predictions are based on demographic data already shown to correlate with dangerousness. Statistical probabilities are assigned to each variable based on its correlation with dangerous behavior. The aggregate of these statistics results in a numerical probability, which casts such predictions in a cloak of scientific accuracy. This method has shown an error rate of about 86 percent,[9] which is not very different from the high error rate found to exist in clinical predictions.

The dangerousness standard has evolved from the balancing of the state's interest in protecting both society and the mentally ill individual and protecting the individual's interest in personal liberty. When based

ny in death cases for critical comment. He has been referred to by Dr. Kermani as an individual "wearing the compassionate demeanor of a Marcus Welby stereotype over a 'hangman' mentality lacking all empathy and concern." See, Kermani, *Handbook of Psychiatry and Law* 195 (1989).

6. The actuarial method was not allowed in Lockett v. Ohio, 438 U.S. 586, 608 (1978) because it was the sole basis for the expert's prediction of dangerousness and failed to take into account the characteristics of the individual involved.

7. Studies show psychiatrists tend to overpredict dangerousness. In one study, researchers correctly predicted 50 percent of those who would behave violently, but at the same time the same factors used indicated a twice as large group would be violent who were not. See, Cocozza & Steadman, "Some Refinements in the Measure-

ment and Prediction of Dangerous Behavior," 131 *Am.J.Psychiatry* 1012 (1974); Kozal, Boucher & Garofalo, "The Diagnosis and Treatment of Dangerousness," 18 *Crime & Delinquency* 371 (1972); Wenk, Robison & Smith, "Can Violence Be Predicted?" 18 *Crime & Delinquency* 393 (1972).

8. Shuman, *Psychiatric and Psychological Evidence* 181 (1986). Minimal empirical evidence exists in predicting dangerousness. The deliberate release of suspected dangerous people for the sake of experimentation is unthinkable. Further, despite the extensive use of "dangerousness" in the legal system, the concept is very poorly defined; it is neither a psychiatric nor a medical diagnosis.

9. Wenk, Robinson & Smith, "Can Violence Be Predicted," 18 *Crime & Delinquency* 393 (1972).

on being mentally ill and dangerous to oneself or others, the standard is both underinclusive and overinclusive. As a result, people who need treatment and protection from themselves do not get committed, whereas others who are not a threat to anyone can find themselves institutionalized. Actual past criminal conduct is considered to be the most important variable in accurately predicting future dangerousness and the sole reliable predictor. The offense that brings a person to the attention of the court may be strong evidence of dangerousness, especially if there was no rational motive or the offense was calculated, or the accused was remorseless. However, even brutal offenses have not been shown to have any correlation with the probability of committing future violent acts.[10]

Psychiatrists' expertise in predicting dangerousness is limited in its value and reliability. Nevertheless, knowledgeable, well-balanced, experienced and objective clinicians can make predictions regarding future dangerousness considerably better than a flip of the coin. The courts' reliance on mental health experts on this issue should be a cautious one. Until precise definitions of dangerousness and standard protocols for evaluating dangerousness are developed, courts ought to subject dangerousness testimony to the strictest of scrutiny.

III. EXPERTS ON THE UNRELIABILITY OF EYEWITNESSES

§ 19.15 The Inherent Unreliability of Eyewitnesses—True or False?

The chronicles of legal history are filled with tragic cases of mistaken identity.[1] The tale of Berson and Morales echoes that of hundreds of thousands of others. In the 1970s, Lawrence Berson was accused of several rapes and George Morales was accused of robbery. Both men were picked out of police lineups by victims of the respective crimes and both men were innocent. Berson was cleared when another man, Richard Carbone, was arrested and implicated in the rapes. Carbone was convicted on the rape charges and later confessed to the robbery, clearing Morales.[2]

Regrettably, it is impossible to know how many innocent men and women have been sentenced to prison or death on the basis of faulty eyewitness testimony. However, it has been estimated that more than

---

10. See, Braley, "Estelle v. Smith and Psychiatric Testimony: New Limits on Predicting Future Dangerousness," 33 *Baylor L.Rev.* 1033 (1981); Zenoff, "Controlling the Dangers of Dangerousness: The ABA Standards and Beyond," 53 *Geo.W.L.Rev.* 585 (1985).

§ 19.15

1. "The vagaries of eyewitness identification are well known, the annals of criminal law are rife with instances of mistaken identification." United States v. Wade, 388 U.S. 218 (1967).

2. Id.

4,250 Americans per year are wrongfully convicted due to sincere, yet woefully inaccurate eyewitness identifications.[3] Over the past fifty years, scientific research has revealed that eyewitness testimony is often an incorrect account of what actually took place.[4] Scientists now know that the human mind does not act as a video camera meticulously recording and replaying everything within its viewfinder.[5] Rather, human memory is a complex process which is vulnerable at every stage.[6] This knowledge, in turn, has led attorneys to invite psychologists who have done studies on these issues to testify to their conclusions when the critical evidence was that of occurrence witnesses. Most of the cases wherein this testimony has been offered have been criminal prosecutions involving eyewitness identifications of a defendant, though the principles of perception, memory, and recollection are applicable equally to event witnesses in civil litigation.

§ 19.16 Perception, Memory, and Recollection

The acquisition of information into memory involves a three-step process. At each stage of the process, errors are possible. During acquisition, the first step in the memory process, an event is perceived and information "bits" are initially stored in memory. In the second stage, information is held or retained in memory. In the final stage, memory is searched and pertinent information is retrieved and communicated. In the acquisition stage, information is "encoded" into a person's memory system. However, every detail of an experience is not encoded; the human mind can only process a fraction of the rapidly incoming physical stimuli. Both consciously and unconsciously, the observer determines which details are actually encoded according to where his or her attention is focused.[1]

The physical aspects of an event are obviously compromised by the selective nature of the acquisition stage of memory. However, matters are further complicated by the fact that acquisition also involves a social component. Thus, a witness' ability to perceive accurately is affected by both event factors—those inherent to the event itself—and witness factors—those inherent to the witness.

1. INFLUENCE OF THE EVENT FACTORS

Event factors include duration of the event, complexity of the event

---

3. Id.

4. See, Brigham & Barkowitz, "Do 'They All Look Alike?:' The Effect of Race, Sex, Experience, and Attitudes on the Ability to Recognize Faces," 8 *J. Applied Social Psychology*, 1978, p. 306; Buckhout, "Nobody Likes a Smartass: Expert Testimony by Psychologists," 3 *Social Action and the Law Newsletter*, 1976, (4), p. 41; Goldstein, "The Fallibility of the Eyewitness: Psychological Evidence," D.B. Sales (ed.), *Psychology in the Legal Process* (1977).

5. See generally, Loftus & Doyle, *Eyewitness Testimony: Civil and Criminal* (1987).

6. Id.

§ 19.16

1. Penrod, Loftus, & Winkler, "The Reliability of Eyewitness Testimony: A Psychological Perspective," in *The Psychology of the Courtroom* 155 (Kerr & Bray, eds., 1992).

and violence of the event witnessed.[2]   Common sense and science show that increased exposure time improves the accuracy of witness perception.[3]   However, witnesses generally overestimate time and have great difficulty gauging the duration of an event.   For example, Professor Buckhout, a cognitive psychologist, staged an assault during one of his classes.   The assault actually lasted 34 seconds, but the average estimate of time by 141 witnesses to the event was overestimated by a factor of almost two and one half to one (2.5:1).[4]

Complexity of the event witnessed has a direct effect on the encoding of information.[5]   Psychological research has shown that complex events are more difficult to recognize and encode into memory than more basic events.[6]   For example, a street fight among multiple parties is less likely to be recollected with accuracy than a fight between two parties.

Violence also affects a witness' acquisition of information.   In 1978, an experiment was conducted in which subjects viewed violent and non-violent tapes of an event.   The subjects who viewed the violent version of the event had more difficulty perceiving and recalling the event than those subjects who had seen the non-violent version.[7]

2. INFLUENCE OF PERSONAL FACTORS

In addition to event factors, perception is also affected by witness factors.   Witness factors include stress, weapon focus, and expectation.   Lay persons believe that stressful events accentuate memory, that what is seen or heard during periods of high stress is more accurately recorded and recalled.   However, empirical data indicates that stress, anxiety and fear disrupt the normal perception process and distort subsequent memory.[8]   Thus, a witness' statement that he was "so frightened that his (the criminal's) face is etched in my memory forever" is a psychological oxymoron.

Psychologists term the relationship between stress and memory as the Yerkes–Dodson Law.   The Yerkes–Dodson Law depicts the relationship between stress and memory as an inverted "U" curve.   At low arousal, memory is low.   Memory improves with increased stress levels to a point (optimal performance).   After the point of optimal performance, memory decreases with increased stress levels.   Thus, it is not

2.   Id. Lighting changes and salience of fact are also event factors which can affect witness perception. For a complete catalog and discussion of event factors see, Penrod et al., op. cit. supra note 1.

3.   Id.

4.   Buckhout, "Psychology & Eyewitness Identification," 2 *L. & Psychology Rev.* 75 (1976).

5.   Penrod, supra note 1.

6.   Langer, Wagner, & Werner, "The Effect of Danger Upon the Experience of Time," 74 *Am.J.Psych.* 94 (1961).

7.   Clifford & Hollin, "Effect of the Type of Incident and the Number of Perpetrators on Eyewitness Memory," 66 *J.App.Psy.* 3 (1981).

8.   But see, Bruner, "Social Psychology and Perception," in *Readings in Social Psychology* 91 (3d ed. MacCoby, Newcomb & Hartley, eds., 1958).

uncommon for a witness to recall the details of crime less accurately than they recall routine events.

Psychological research has also shown that people under stress tend to concentrate on those aspects of an event or experience which they feel are most important.[9] Weapon-focus is an example of this psychological phenomenon. An individual faced with a gun held to their head is likely to concentrate on the gun to the complete exclusion of the attacker's face or physical characteristics.

As early as 1909, it was noted that expectation has a profound effect upon perception: "observation is peculiarly influenced by expectation, ... we tend to see and hear what we expect to see and hear."[10] Modern science can now account for the relationship between expectation and perception. As noted earlier, the human mind can only process a fragment of the physical stimuli digested by the senses. The mind compensates by integrating the stimuli with concepts based upon a fund of general knowledge acquired over time or, put more simply, with expectation.[11] In this manner, individuals subconsciously reconstruct events from what they assume must have occurred.

Expectation includes personal biases, cultural biases, temporary biases, latent prejudices, and stereotypes each of which have the ability to influence acquisition. For example, a group of subjects were shown a photograph of several people standing in a subway train, including a white man holding a razor and apparently arguing with a black man.[12] When asked to describe what they had seen, over half of the participants reported that the black man had been wielding the razor.

3. INFLUENCE OF STORAGE FACTORS

Memory is also susceptible to extraneous influences during storage, the second stage of the memory process. Memory of events decays over time.[13] Although an individual may accurately perceive an event, its representation in the observer's memory system will not remain intact for very long.[14] Considerable memory loss is likely to occur between an event and an eyewitness' actual identification of a suspect in a criminal case. The human mind actively fills the gaps created by long-term memory loss; this gap-filling process introduces inaccuracies into memory for the sake of a "complete" picture.[15] Obviously, this process has great implications for the criminal defendant.

9. See, Ittleson, "The Constancies in Visual Perception," in *Explorations in Transactional Psychology* 339–51 (Kilpatrick ed. 1961).

10. Whipple, "The Observer as the Reporter: A Survey of the 'Psychology of Testimony,'" 6 *Psychol.Bull.* 153 (1909).

11. Penrod, supra note 1.

12. Allport & Postman, The Psychology of Rumor 75 (1965).

13. Crumbaugh, "Temporal Changes in the Memory of Visually Perceived Form," 67 *Am.J.Psych.* 647 (1954).

14. Allport, "Change and Decay in Visual Memory Image," 21 *Brit.J.Psych.* 133 (1931).

15. See, Sussman, Sugarman, & Zavala. "A Comparison of Three Media Used in Identification Procedures," in *Personal Appearance Identification: Psychological*

Lay persons tend to believe that there is a positive correlation between witness confidence and memory accuracy—that the more conviction a witness has the more likely his or her testimony is to be an accurate depiction of the event.   However, psychological research indicates that there is in fact a negative correlation between a witness' confidence in his or her memory and the accuracy of that memory.[16] Thus, the more confidence a witness has in his or her memory, the more likely the witness' memory of the event is inaccurate.   Again, this counter-intuitive psychological principle has far reaching ramifications for litigants.

An individual's memory system may also be augmented or altered during the storage stage by intervening occurrences.[17] For example, a witness may read or hear about an incident he or she observed.   The mind tends to incorporate post-event information such as that conveyed by the article or discussion with that previously encoded from the incident itself.[18]

In 1976, Dr. Elizabeth Loftus conducted an experiment to demonstrate how post-event information in the form of questioning can affect memory.   In this experiment, subjects viewed a videotaped auto accident and were questioned about what they observed.   The question about how fast the cars were going when they *smashed* into each other elicited significantly higher estimates of speed than those questions posed with words such as "collided," "bumped," "hit" and "contacted" instead of "smashed."

A week later the subjects were again questioned.   They were asked "did you see any broken glass?"   The videotaped accident in fact did not involve broken glass, but those subjects who had been questioned earlier with the verb "smashed" were more likely to assert that they had seen broken glass in the video tape.   A memory was formed when the subjects viewed the tape, but it was later augmented and altered by the suggestive questions of the interviewers.[19]   The implications of this study on police questioning techniques and general investigative procedures is obvious.

4.   INFLUENCE OF RECALL FACTORS

The final stage of memory, retrieval, is also vulnerable to outside influences.   For example, social factors may influence the witness' recollection of events, especially in the criminal identification setting.[20]

Studies of Human Identification and Recognition Processes XI–8 (A. Zavala ed. 1970).

16. See, Buckhout, Figueroa, & Hoff. "Eyewitness Identification: Effect of Bias in Identification from Photographs," 6 *Bull Psychonomic Soc.* 71 (1974).

17. Allport, supra note 14.

18. Loftus & Loftus, *Human Memory The Processing of Information*, (1976).

19. The subjects were also influenced by their expectation that a car accident would involve broken glass.

20. Levine & Tapp. "The Psychology of Criminal Identification: The Gap From Wade to Kirby," 121 *U.Pa.L.Rev.* 1079 (1973).

Eyewitnesses, like other people, do not want to appear foolish. By arranging a line-up, police officials suggest to an eyewitness that they have apprehended the culprit. Consequently, the eyewitness may select an individual despite his or her lingering uncertainty, to avoid "letting the criminal go free" and to avoid looking foolish.[21]

All of these factors have been stressed by psychologists who advocate admission of expert testimony on the unreliability of event witnesses as reasons for their advocacy. However, opponents have been no less vocal, and thus the legal literature abounds with writings on the issue.[22]

Modern psychological science has revealed much about human memory and the fallibility of eyewitness testimony in the 200 years since T. Reid, an influential scholar of his day, wrote:

> . . . and if a skeptical counsel should plead against the testimony of the witness, that they had no other evidence for what they declared than the testimony of their eyes and ears, and that we ought not to put so much faith in our senses as to deprive men of life or fortune upon their testimony, surely no upright judge would admit a plea of this kind. I believe no counsel, however skeptical, ever dared to offer such an argument; and, if it were offered, it would rejected with disdain[.] [23]

Unfortunately, in this area of endeavor, the American legal system has not embraced the teachings of modern psychology wholeheartedly.

§ 19.17 What Can Experts Say?

In a jurisdiction where the expert is permitted to testify on the issue, the witness can explain the mechanism of perception, processing, memory, and recollection, and describe what empirical research has been conducted on the subject and what the results are. The expert will ordinarily not be permitted to testify on the accuracy of a particular witness. In a child sexual abuse case, in a jurisdiction that accepts opinion evidence in this area of the law, the expert typically can testify on the problems child victims of abuse have remembering and describing the incidents of which they complain, but cannot state whether a

---

21. Marshall, Marquis, & Oskamp, Comment, "Effects of Kind of Question and Atmosphere of Interrogation on Accuracy and Completeness of Testimony," 84 *Harv. L.Rev.* 1620 (1971). Another social factor which can influence the eyewitness identification process is a human being's need to behave like those around him. The need to conform increases the eyewitness' desire to select an individual to show the police that they, too, feel that the criminal is in the line-up. Id.

22. E.g., Loftus & Schneider, " 'Behold with Strange Surprise': Judicial Reactions to Expert Testimony Concerning Eyewit-

ness Reliability," 56 *U.M.K.C.L.Rev.* 1 (1987); Westling, "The Case for Expert Witness Assistance to the Jury in Eyewitness Identification Cases," 7 *Ore.L.Rev.* 93, 99–100 (1992)—listing all of the writings on the issue since 1979; Comment, "Expert Testimony on Eyewitness Identification: The Constitution Says, 'Let The Expert Speak'," 56 *Tenn.K.Rev.* 735 (1989); Fassett, "The Third Circuit's Unique Response to Expert Testimony on Eyewitness Perception: Is What You See What You Get?," 19 *Seton Hall L.Rev.* 697 (1989).

23. Reid, *Essays on the Intellectual Powers of Man* (1969).

particular child was abused on the basis of psychological evidence, or that the child was truthful when complaining.[1]

§ 19.18   Admissibility of Eyewitness Expert Testimony

Trial courts and appellate courts in America have taken decidedly different positions on the issue of expert testimony addressing eyewitness reliability.[1] The majority of jurisdictions continues to exclude eyewitness expert testimony.[2] However, a growing number of courts have upheld exercise of the discretionary power of trial judges who exercised discretion in favor of admitting expert opinion testimony on eyewitness reliability.[3]

State v. Chapple was the first appellate decision to admit expert testimony on eyewitness reliability over the ruling of a trial court.[4] The defendant in *Chapple* was picked from a photo display by two participants in a drug transaction. One of the identifiers had previously failed to select the defendant, and instead identified the photograph of someone else.[5] Seven defense witnesses testified that the defendant was out of state in Illinois on the day of the crime.[6] *Chapple* held that the trial court had abused its discretion by rejecting the proffered testimony of an expert on eyewitness identification under these circumstance.[7]

Shortly after *Chapple,* the California Supreme Court decided People v. McDonald.[8] McDonald was convicted of murder after seven eyewitnesses identified him, with varying degrees of certainty. An eighth eyewitness "categorically testified" that McDonald was not the murderer.[9] Further, six defense witnesses testified that McDonald was in another state on the day of the crime. The *McDonald* court considered and rejected each of traditional reasons for excluding expert testimony on eyewitness reliability.[10] The court cited *Chapple* with approval and concluded, "Like the Arizona Supreme Court, we decline to assume that the subject matter of [the expert's] testimony would have been fully

§ 19.17

1. See, People v. Wilson, 246 Ill.App.3d 311, 186 Ill.Dec. 226, 615 N.E.2d 1283 (1993).

§ 19.18

1. Westling, op. cit. note 22, sec. 19.16, supra.

2. Id. Traditional justifications for rejecting expert testimony include: 1) Such testimony would invade the province of the jury, 2) Such testimony is not needed because eyewitness testimony is within the experience of the average juror, and 3) Such testimony fails to meet contemporary scientific standards of acceptance, and thus is not a proper subject for expert testimony. See Westling for a refutation on each of these arguments.

3. Doyle, *Trial Strategy in Identification Cases: The Eyewitness Without the Expert,* 1991.

4. State v. Chapple, 135 Ariz. 281, 660 P.2d 1208 (1983).

5. Id. at 1222.

6. Id. at 1212.

7. Id. at 1223–1224. The *Chapple* decision rests in part on Arizona Rule of Evidence 702 and in part on the *Amaral* factors. Id. at 1218–1219.

8. 37 Cal.3d 351, 208 Cal.Rptr. 236, 690 P.2d 709 (1984).

9. Id. at 238, 690 P.2d at 711.

10. Id. at 246–251, 690 P.2d at 719–723.

known to the jurors; rather, the professional literature persuades us to the contrary.[11]

In *United States v. Downing,* the Third Circuit surveyed the traditional cases and the recent cases addressing expert testimony on eyewitness reliability and concluded: "[W]e find persuasive more recent cases in which courts have found that, under certain circumstances, this type of expert testimony can satisfy the helpfulness of Rule 702." [12]

The Sixth Circuit has also addressed the issue. In *United States v. Smith* the court held that expert testimony should have been admitted, but it was harmless error to exclude under the facts of the case.[13] In comparing *Smith* with an earlier case, the court noted that the "science has gained reliability" and that the discipline has the "exactness, methodology and reliability of any psychological research." [14]

In *State v. Buell* the Ohio Supreme Court held that "the expert testimony of an experimental psychologist concerning the variables and factors that may impair the accuracy of a typical eyewitness identification is admissible under [Rule] 702." [15] The Ohio court expressly limited its holding to general testimony; the experts were not to comment on the reliability or accuracy of particular witnesses involved in the case at hand.[16]

Alaska addressed the issue of eyewitness expert testimony favorably in Skamarocius v. State.[17] The case involved a single witness and marginal corroborating evidence. The court reasoned that:

> "... [the expert's] testimony was sufficiently within the mainstream of current psychological theory to satisfy the *Frye* test.... The prosecutor supported the accuracy of [the victim's] identification by relying heavily on the common sense assumptions that [she] was confident in her identification and that a person subject to a sexual assault would have her assailant's image branded into her memory. [The expert's] testimony could have undermined both of these common sense assumptions." [18]

The court held that the trial court had abused its discretion in excluding the proffered expert testimony.[19] In at least one case, the decision

---

11. Id. at 253, 690 P.2d at 726.

12. United States v. Downing, 753 F.2d 1224 (3d Cir.1985). See also, United States v. Sebetich, 776 F.2d 412 (3d Cir.1985), cert. denied 484 U.S. 1017 (1988).

13. United States v. Smith, 736 F.2d 1103 (6th Cir.1984), cert. denied 469 U.S. 868 (1984).

14. Id. at 1106.

15. State v. Buell, 22 Ohio St.3d 124, 489 N.E.2d 795 (1986), cert. denied 479 U.S. 870 (1986).

16. Id. at 804.

17. 731 P.2d 63 (Alaska App.1987).

18. Id. at 66. Note, however, that the *Frye* test mentioned by the court has been replaced in federal civil and criminal trials by a "proof of reliability" concept in Daubert v. Merrell Dow Pharmaceuticals, 113 S.Ct. 2786 (1993). After *Daubert*, the linchpin for admission of relevant expert evidence is whether it is "scientific, technical, or other specialized knowledge" which "will assist the trier of fact to understand the evidence or to determine a fact in issue...." Fed.R.Evid. 702.

19. Id.

whether to admit or deny admission of the testimony was simply left to the sound discretion of the trial court.[20]

Despite these cases, in the majority of jurisdictions that have faced the issue, expert opinion evidence on the unreliability of event witnesses has been excluded. Most of the decisions to prohibit the testimony used as their rationale that the credibility of any witness is an issue for the jury to determine,[21] and that to permit such testimony impermissibly invades the province of the jury.[22] The reasons for exclusion are perhaps best reflected by People v. Enis,[23] wherein the Illinois Supreme Court said:

> "We caution against the overuse of expert testimony. Such testimony, in this case concerning the unreliability of eyewitness testimony, could well lead to the use of expert testimony concerning the reliability of other types of testimony and, eventually, to the use of experts to testify as to the unreliability of expert testimony. So-called experts can usually be obtained to support most any position. The determination of a lawsuit should not depend upon which side can present the most or the most convincing expert witnesses. We are concerned with the reliability of eyewitness expert testimony, whether and to what degree it can aid the jury, and if it is necessary in light of defendant's ability to cross-examine eyewitnesses. An expert's opinion concerning the unreliability of eyewitness testimony is based on statistical averages. The eyewitness in a particular case may well not fit within the spectrum of these averages. It would be [inappropriate] for a jury to conclude, based on expert testimony, that all eyewitness testimony is unreliable." [Citations omitted.]

§ 19.19   Path of the Future

Since the advent of the Daubert v. Merrell Dow Pharmaceuticals,[1] which did away with the "general acceptance" rule for the admission of novel scientific or expert testimony and replaced it with a standard of evidentiary reliability, which must be determined by the trial judge prior to admission, courts, whether they admitted or denied admission to evidence on the factors affecting the reliability of event witnesses, may have to revisit the issue and explore whether the "reasoning or methodology underlying the testimony is scientifically valid and . . . whether the reasoning or methodology properly can be applied to the facts in issue." That was in fact the reason for remanding the case to the trial court in

---

20. State v. Whaley, 305 S.C. 138, 406 S.E.2d 369 (1991).

21. E.g. Criglow v. State, 183 Ark. 407, 36 S.W.2d 400 (1931); Utley v. State, 308 Ark. 622, 826 S.W.2d 268 (1992). See also, State v. Kemp, 199 Conn. 473, 507 A.2d 1387 (1986); State v. Reed, 226 Kan. 519, 601 P.2d 1125 (1979); State v. Gurley, 565 So.2d 1055 (La.App.1990); State v. Fox, 98 Or.App. 356, 779 P.2d 197 (1989); United States v. Hudson, 884 F.2d 1016 (7th Cir. 1989); United States v. Curry, 977 F.2d

1042 (7th Cir.1992); United States v. Langford, 802 F.2d 1176 (9th Cir.1986).

22. E.g., Caldwell v. State, 267 Ark. 1053, 594 S.W.2d 24 (1980); Perry v. State, 277 Ark. 357, 642 S.W.2d 865 (1982).

23. 139 Ill.2d 264, 289–90, 151 Ill.Dec. 493, 503, 564 N.E.2d 1155, 1165 (1990).

§ 19.19

1. 113 S.Ct. 2786 (1993)—see Chapter 1, supra, at § 1.03.

U.S. v. Amador–Galvan,[2] and the reason why the Supreme Court remanded U.S. v. Rincon [3] for further consideration.

Though the American judicial system has been slow to accept the lessons of modern psychology, there does appear to be a growing group of judges willing to accept the logic of the premise of the unreliability of event witnesses and permit expert testimony on that topic. Whether these recent cases signal a trend which will grow, only time will tell. We can only hope that the legal community will, in this case, be as receptive to opinion testimony that has a sound basis in experimental science, as it has been in other novel fields. If so, perhaps one, two, or more innocent people who otherwise would have been convicted of crimes they did not commit will be set free; after all, it is better to acquit 10 guilty persons than to convict one innocent person.[4]

IV. MENTAL HEALTH EVIDENCE IN CHILD CUSTODY CASES

§ 19.20 Relevance of Behavioral Sciences to Child Custody

The generalizations currently used by the courts in child custody cases reveal there is a strong need for evidence that will explain how a child's best interests will be better served in one placement as opposed to another. Behavioral scientists have been playing an increasingly important role in furnishing relevant information on that issue to the courts. Their most valuable contribution to the issues is in assisting the courts in articulating a sound basis for their placement decisions.[1]

The legal concepts on child custody are unlike those in areas of the law such as contracts or property, where the court applies objective facts to establish rules of law. The essence of child custody lies in human relationships, comprised of the thoughts, feelings, and behavior of the people involved. The very nature of domestic relations law is colored by many shades of gray. Child custody questions do not lend themselves to easily decided, objective answers. It is in this field of uncertainty that courts often turn to the expertise of psychologists, psychiatrists, social

---

2. 9 F.3d 1414 (9th Cir.1993) (the court said that testimony attacking the reliability of witnesses who identified the defendant as a marijuana smuggler was relevant to his defense, but it needed to be determined whether the theories underlying eyewitness identification are scientifically valid, helpful, and reliable).

3. 984 F.2d 1003 (9th Cir.1993), vacated by 114 S.Ct. 41 (1993).

4. Blackstone, W., *Commentaries on the Laws of England*, Boston, Beacon (1765, 1962).

§ 19.20

1. Not everyone agrees with this premise. See, e.g., Bradbrook, "Relevance of Psychological and Psychiatric Studies to the Future Development of the Laws Governing the Settlement of Inter–Parental Child Custody Disputes," 11 *J.Fam.L.* 572 (1972). See also, Okpaku, "Psychology: An Impediment or Aid in Child Custody Cases?," 29 *Rutg.L.Rev.* 1117, 1149 (1978).

workers, and child protective services specialists.[2] Applying their expertise to the facts regarding a particular child is the most direct form of aid
that can be expected from these professionals. Indirectly, however, they
provide assistance through shared information about child development
and family dynamics in laying a basis upon which judges can draw in
making reasoned decisions.

Custody issues arise in either divorce (disputes between parents) or
child placement (disputes between parents and third parties) cases.[3]
Incident to a divorce, several forms of custody may be encountered: sole,
split, divided, or joint. Child placement cases typically involve foster
care, adoption, and adjudication of the status of juveniles.

That one group or type of case is easier for the judge to decide is
doubtful; custody disputes are difficult for all involved. Often the child
is the prize between its parents who engage in custody battles for a
number of reasons: (1) as an expression of anger and hatred for the
spouse; (2) as a means of holding onto the other spouse; (3) to reduce
support payments; (4) in a good faith belief that the child will be better
cared for by themselves; or (5) to keep the marital home. Consequences
for the child may be confusion, divided loyalties, insecurity, fears of
rejection, and possibly even guilt for some sense of responsibility for the
marital breakup.[4] The judge, too, frequently agonizes over competing
factors, cognizant that the decision will set the stage for the child's
future development.

The legal criteria by which custody disputes are to be decided have
seen considerable development over the years. Before the nineteenth
century, courts considered children the property of the father. The
"tender years doctrine" then shifted custodial preference to the mother
as long as she was considered a "fit" person. The past legalistic,
punitive, and/or moralistic approaches to determining parental fitness
were then upgraded to require "... that alleged unfitness be directly or
meaningfully related to child rearing."[5] Still, many custody cases are
fought over charges of one parent being unfit as opposed to the other
parent being more fit. In the heat of anger or hatred, these parents
become oblivious to the suffering their fighting causes the child. It is in
these cases, especially, that mental health professionals are needed to

2. Shepherd, "Solomon's Sword: Adjudication of Child Custody Questions," 8
U.Rich.L.Rev. 151 (1974).

3. See, Goldzband, *Custody Cases and
Expert Witnesses: A Manual for Attorneys* 4
(1980). Specific case types can be broken
down into parent v. parent, parent v. other
relatives (grandparents), parent v. non-rela-
tives (foster parents and adoptive parents),
unwed father v. mother or others, and the
state v. parent or others (neglected or
abused children).

4. Batt, "Child Custody Disputes: A De-
velopmental–Psychological Approach to
Proof and Decisionmaking," 12 *Willamette
L.J.* 491 (1976).

5. Group for the Advancement of Psychiatry, *New Trends on Child Custody Determinations,* 24 (1980). On the issue, generally, see also, Lowery, "Child Custody Decisions in Divorce Proceedings: A Survey of
Judges," 4 *Professional Psychology* 492
(1981); Goldstein, Freud & Solnit, *Beyond
the Best Interests of the Child* (1973); Goldstein, Freud & Solnit, *Before the Best Interests of the Child* (1979); Batt, op. cit. supra
note 306; Watson, "The Children of Arma-
geddon: Problems of Custody Following Divorce," 21 *Syracuse L.Rev.* 55 (1969).

impart not only to the court, but also to the parents, the consequences to the child of such conduct. In recent years, some parents have sought to fight the custody battle by accusing one parent of improper sexual conduct with children. While these charges are undoubtedly justified in many cases, most family law practitioners know false charges are sometimes leveled solely to gain the prize that will undoubtedly result: namely custody of the children.

In making custody determinations, some courts continue to rely upon traditional concepts that have been questioned by family health specialists, such as: (1) that siblings should not be separated; (2) that older boys belong with their father; and (3) that adolescents are capable of choosing their custodial parent. Despite the fact the great majority of states reject the tender years presumption by statute or case decision, these and other presumptions persist. The most effective rebuttal to the use of improper or unjustified criteria whereupon to base custody decisions is use of qualified, thoughtful, considerate, and empathic mental health professionals who are, themselves, free from personal or institutional bias.

The modern standard for deciding to whom custody will be awarded is the "child's best interest," which calls also into consideration any of the traditionally held presumptions as well as the issue of parental fitness. In fact, the term is broad enough to incorporate any factor or approach appropriate to any particular case. For example, in the areas of adoption and foster care, two influential, although sometimes criticized, books, *Beyond the Best Interests of the Child* and *Before the Best Interests of the Child* [6] propose that a child's best interests are met by placement with its psychological parent. Another concept therein advanced interjects within the "best interests" standard also the "least detrimental alternative" thought. All of these concepts may be evaluated and studied in a particular case. Lawyers and judges are unable to make an informed decision on such issues without the assistance and enlightenment that qualified professionals can provide in the fact finding process.

§ 19.21 Role of Mental Health Experts

Defining the legal standards, vague as they are, does not remove the necessary subjectiveness of the court's assessments. It is for that reason that courts and attorneys need the expertise of psychiatrists and psychologists who are specialists in the fields of child development and family relations. Judges need guidance in assessing the significance of past behavior patterns, present circumstances, and in anticipating how, when, and by whom a child's "best interests" will be met. Out of court, psychologists and psychiatrists can assist the attorney in case preparation such as interviews of the client, developing possible alternatives to present to the court (as in juvenile sentencing or dependent child

---

6. See the Goldstein, Freud & Solnit works cited at note 5, supra.

placement questions) or in preparing to meet the testimony of opponent's expert witness.

1. CRITICISMS OF USE OF EXPERTS

The "best interests" standard is a functional one that incorporates community values, parental experience, and common sense that, on the surface, does not dictate a need for expert assistance.[1] Okpaku discounts the use of mental health specialists arguing there should be "a more honest reliance on the experientially based discretion of the judges."[2] She suggested that judges generally defer to expert psychological testimony in three instances: (1) to justify an unconventional custody award; (2) to circumvent decisional guidelines; and (3) to provide a seemingly "easy" answer for a difficult case. Okpaku states that psychologists employ a two-step approach of first predicting future behavior of parents based on assessments of their emotional states, and then predicting how the behavior of the parents will affect the child. The predictions are alleged to be flawed because of reliance on clinical interviews and psychological tests for the base data of their predictions. In the view of Okpaku, the behavioral science field lacks empirical data that demonstrates psychological theories and therefore does not provide the courts valid assistance in custody determinations.

Despite this strong criticism, behavioral science experts *can* supply courts with information that might not otherwise be available to the decision-maker. At times, children are not or cannot be interviewed by the court. Guardians ad litem are not always appointed to represent children during the proceedings. Often court proceedings are adversarial, name-calling contests that lose focus of the child. Information from an expert regarding the characteristics of the parties can assist the judge in understanding the dynamics of what is transpiring out of court. Judges should, of course, not rely blindly on the testimony of psychologists and psychiatrists, nor use their testimony as an excuse for the making of a decision they are unwilling to make themselves. Continuing research in the areas of child development and family interactions confirms some widely held concepts and rejects others as unfounded. Judges need to require those qualifying as experts to testify based on recent empirical data and thorough evaluations; only then can the expert opinions be of any value in decision-making.

When mental health experts are retained by attorneys representing the parties, their role becomes extremely crucial. A tendency to take sides in an adversarial context may cause the expert retained by one party to lose sight of the "best interests" concept. Thus, the stage is set for the battle of the experts. For that reason, attorneys appointed to act as guardian ad litem for the child should ask for an independent expert

§ 19.21

1. Shuman, *Psychiatric and Psychological Evidence*, 303 (1986).

2. Okpaku, "Psychology: Impediment or Aid in Child Custody Cases?," 29 *Rutg. L.Rev.* 1117, 1153 (1976).

evaluation. In that case, the expert's testimony should be limited to the appropriateness of custody with the examined party, and not as to whether custody is preferred over the competing parent. The most important use of privately retained experts may well be where the request for custody is one outside the community norm, such as one involving a homosexual parent, of mixed race, or within an interracial marriage. In these situations, a thoughtful expert can be used to educate the court about consequences to the child.

Recognizing that the truth lies somewhere in between the warring factions, courts frequently resort to court-ordered examinations of the parties. After conducting such an examination, the expert is expected to furnish the report directly to the court, with copies to the opposing parties. In such a case, the expert is to present a report that reflects the expert's recognition of a duty to remain neutral in assessing the parties—an obligation that rests as well on professionals retained by the parties, but which is often forgotten. The result is usually a complete, objective report which truly focuses on the best interests of the child. A bonus benefit of the court-appointed expert may be saving the parties the expense of retained experts and saving the courts the time to hear conflicting expert testimony. The danger involved here is that the court-appointed expert's report, presumably objective and untainted by party bias, is often given too much weight and used by the court as the linchpin that removes the responsibility from the judge in making the decision personally. Also, the so-called impartiality of the expert may be entirely fictitious for a variety of reasons, not least of which may be the personal bias of the expert.[3]

2. USE OF PSYCHIATRIC AND PSYCHOLOGICAL TESTS

To assist the court in determining the best interests of the child, information is needed from three major areas—the relation between the parent and child, the child's needs and the parent's capacities to meet those needs, and relevant family dynamics. The sources of this information include the child, the parents, and third parties such as school teachers, doctors, babysitters, and the like. Failure to address every appropriate area lessens the reliability of the evaluation and provides ammunition to the cross-examining attorney. Methods for gathering this historical data include clinical interviews and psychological testing.

Examination of the child should generally include thorough evaluations of intellectual performance and ability, neuropsychological factors, academic achievement, personality and emotional adjustments.[4] Particularly helpful in assessing learning problems and intellectual disorders in children are the Wechsler Preschool and Primary Scales of Intelligence (WPPSI). The Wechsler subtests address verbal and performance

---

3. See, Moenssens, "The 'Impartial' Medical Expert: A New Look at an Old Issue," Ch. 19 in *1974 Legal Medicine Annual* (C. Wecht, ed., 1974).

4. Ollendick, *Child Behavior Assessment: Principles and Procedures,* 206 (1984).

skills and result in a verbal quotient, a performance quotient, and a summary quotient. A personality test frequently used with children has been the Children's Apperception Test (CAT). Picture cards are presented about which the child is to tell a story.[5] The Make-a-Picture-Story-Test (MAPS) is another projective test used to evaluate children. The child is given human and animal figurines to create a picture after viewing a series of scenes.[6] The fact that some children resist talking openly about their problems prompted Richard Garner to develop the "Talking, Feeling and Doing Game."[7] The game assesses the cognitive, emotional, and physical orientations of the child. The questions are designed to elicit the child's feelings about the parents.

Clinical interviews with children may be totally conversational or may be a combination of talking and playing, depending on the child's age and abilities. The use of toys and dolls is appropriate for very young children. Anatomically correct dolls are often used with children suspected of having been sexually abused.

Examinations of parents are also undertaken to assess basic mental health and their personality function in regards to parenting ability. Particular areas addressed include issues of dependency, power, anger, sexuality, or defending against unhappiness by using the child. Other mental health issues to explore in the parents are psychosis, substance abuse, and character disorders. It is important to gather past personal history, including childhood experiences. Assessing the degree of flexibility of parents to accept feedback regarding their parenting responsibilities and the parents' abilities to form treatment alliances regarding their children will provide indicia of the maturity of the parents.

Cognitive abilities as adults as they relate to parenting is another factor to consider in custody assessments. The Wechsler Adult Intelligence Scale–Revised (WAIS–R) is the most widely administered adult intelligence test in the United States. Other tests are Stanford–Binet, MMPI and/or MMPI–2, Rorschach, etc.[8] When using psychological tests, it should be remembered that some cultural bias potentially exists in every test, either as designed or interpreted. Failure to administer the test according to standard instructions may invalidate or skew the test. Test performance is also sensitive to the setting in which the test is administered, and those drawing conclusions from tests results need to remain aware that, regardless of circumstances, cognitive abilities remain the same but individual behavior frequently varies according to the situation. It is, thus, not enough for a mental health professional to report a behavior without uncovering and explaining what motivates it.

---

5. It is said, however, that conclusions about a parent's capacity drawn from the child's story are considered "highly speculative and are not likely to hold up well in court." See, Gardner, *Family Evaluation in Child Custody Litigation* 182 (1982).

6. A cross-examiner will likely argue that expert opinions based solely on projective, subjective tests like these are the child's fantasy.

7. Gardner, op. cit. supra note 5, at 189.

8. See, in this regard, Chapter 18 on Psychological Testing, supra § 18.09.

A crucial factor in conducting child-custody studies in determining which parent is more "fit" is the timing of the tests. Studies indicate that people return to their usual state of functioning about 6 to 12 months following a divorce.[9] Once the decision to divorce is made, some people may readjust sooner. The level of stress divorcing parents may be experiencing at the time the study is performed should be considered a contributing factor.

Examination of family interaction, particularly the child with the parent, is most often accomplished by personal observation or by viewing videotapes of such interaction. These videotapes can be used to educate parents about the dynamics of what is occurring in the family. Clinicians watch for spontaneity between the child and parent and the level of sensitivity displayed. Other signals relating to parent-child interaction are whether the parent listens to the child, touches the child, and encourages the child in play and conduct.

Interviews with third parties are also important. School teachers, bus drivers, day care providers, doctors and nurses, relatives and neighbors are among the many individuals who can provide a wealth of information. No source of relevant information should be overlooked.

3. REPORTING CONCLUSIONS

Once reduced to writing, the expert's evaluation is sent to the court, if court-appointed, or to the retaining attorney. The report should be extensive, listing all of the circumstances under which information was gathered, including the referral, the background information, the examination procedures, impressions of the persons, the results of the examination, a summary and recommendations. Recommendations should address the needs of the child. There is disagreement in the profession on whether the report should include a recommendation as to who should have custody, most clinicians agreeing that this is not an appropriate part of the report.

§ 19.22 Admissibility of Expert Testimony

Recognizing that traditional adversarial procedures do not supply the judge with the kind of information and professional advice needed for a custody determination, courts mostly welcome psychiatric and psychological expert testimony in child custody cases. It is within the judge's discretion whether the expert evidence is helpful, how many experts are permitted to testify, what the needed qualifications are, and the admissibility of specific forms of expert testimony. Most of these issues and precedents have already been addressed elsewhere in this chapter.

---

9. Ollendick & Otto, "MMPI Characteristics of Parents Referred for Child–Custody Studies," 117 *J.Psychology* 227, 229–231 (1984), citing Hackney & Ribardy, "An Empirical Investigation of Emotional Reactions to Divorce," 36 *J.Clin.Psychol.* 105–110 (1980).

Once the judge determines that expert testimony will be helpful, it must be decided whether the witness qualifies as an expert. One of the minimal requirements to qualify as an expert in psychiatry or psychology is an academic degree in the field and a state license. Graduation and licensing, however, is only a starting point, since it reveals very little about a mental health professional's experience and specialized study. Courts often seem to believe that a degree and license are not controlling factors. In fact, in the area of child custody, courts often permit unlicensed individuals to qualify to give opinion testimony, such as social workers, child protective services investigators and the like. In all cases, the attorney should explore in great detail the extent of the person's education, training, speciality education, professional practice, professional affiliations, and actual experience in investigating the issues that are before a court.

If a witness is qualified, the next question of admissibility relates to whether the subject matter about which the expert professes to testify is reliable. Reliability of evidence derived from a scientific principle generally depends on the following factors: (1) the validity of the underlying scientific principle; (2) validity of the technique or process that applies the principle; (3) the condition of any instrumentation used in the examining process; (4) adherence to proper procedures; (5) the examiner's qualifications; and (6) the qualifications of the person who interprets test results. These general tests for admissibility of novel expert opinion testimony were discussed earlier in Chapter 1, and specific applications of mental health professionals' evidence have been referred to in previous sections of this Chapter.[1]

Judges for the most part recognize the value of testimony by mental health professionals and their expertise in the areas of child growth and development, personality assessment and family dynamics. Even so, there are exceptions and judicial receptiveness to psychological expert testimony may range from total disregard to selective acceptance and total reliance. There are judges who are reluctant to give credence to expert testimony if the expert has not personally observed and studied the child. This may present a dilemma for the professional if the situation is one where further examination may be detrimental to the child. Such a situation often arises in child sexual abuse cases where the child has been repeatedly interviewed by parents, teachers, doctors, social workers, and police officers. It may be the expert's opinion that the reports of the third parties provide the needed information and that another examination is not necessary and would be harmful to the child. Judges are not insensitive to concerns about the child, but feel generally that the "expert who has first-hand knowledge is better than one who does not."[2]

§ 19.22

1. See, e.g., §§ 19.03, 19.06, and 19.08.

2. Ellis, "Evaluating the Expert: Judicial Expectations of Expert Opinion Evidence in Child Placement Adjudications," 5 *Cardozo L.Rev.* 582, 596 (1984).

There are three perspectives from which a judge may evaluate an expert. First, the evaluation of the expert may focus on the facts and reasonings upon which the opinion is based. Secondly, the judge may weigh the professional's credentials and experience. Thirdly, the expert may be viewed merely as a representative of a particular field.[3] Since the credentials of experts are ordinarily above reproach, judges frequently challenge the experts on the bases for their opinions. Accordingly, experts should expect to be prepared to explain conclusions, opinions, and underlying reasoning in clear language and be able to support their testimony with corroborative evidence from other authorities.

There are two standards of proof in custody determinations. The first is proof by a preponderance of the evidence, which shows that the fact sought to be proved is more probable than not. This is the usual burden of proof in civil cases and is sufficient unless custody is to be awarded to a nonparent. The second standard is clear and convincing proof, the intermediate standard between preponderance of the evidence in civil litigation and the beyond-a-reasonable-doubt standard that is required in criminal prosecutions. Clear and convincing evidence is ordinarily seen as the degree of proof which produces a firm belief the allegations are true.[4] The Supreme Court has held that due process requires clear and convincing evidence before the residual rights of a parent may be terminated.[5]

§ 19.23 Determining Need for and Use of Expert

1. CUSTODY AND VISITATION PROCEEDINGS

The nature and intensity of children's needs vary with each individual child and with that child's age at a given point in time. Presenting the judge with objective information about the particular child in an understandable manner is a valuable service provided by the mental health practitioner. The expert may be the only objective source since parents all too often are preoccupied with agendas of their own. Psychologists and psychiatrists are asked to participate in custody cases considered to be difficult cases. It may be a situation where the competing parents are equally fit or unfit. It may be a case where the child has special needs such as a physical, mental, or emotional handicap. Or the case may involve a parent whose lifestyle is non-traditional, for example, a migrant farm worker father or a mother who tends bar at night. Such lifestyles may or may not harm a child. What's best for the child requires a thorough evaluation of all the relevant factors.

Another important service provided by mental health practitioners is an evaluation needed in the determination of visitation for the non-

---

3. The key here is the level of regard the judge has for the usefulness of that field.

4. *Black's Law Dictionary* 251 (6th ed. 1990).

5. Santosky v. Kramer, 455 U.S. 745 (1982)—State termination of parental rights of abused and neglected children.

custodial parent. Parenting via visitation may be superficial as well as artificial. Often visits are for brief periods and in public places such as parks. Visitation plans that keep both parents actively involved with the child's life are preferred as they will help relieve the sense of loss children feel following a divorce. Parents frequently are too threatened or resentful of the non-custodial parent to see the situation through the eyes of the child. Unfortunately, judges often fail children in this respect as well. Visitation plans that focus on holidays and vacations invariably have the parents' convenience and interests at heart, not the needs of the child. The expert may be the only person who can effectively promote the best interests of the child in this area. A psychologist or psychiatrist may also be needed to explain the negative consequences of forced visitation,[1] and to support requests for modifying visitation that is not currently acceptable to the parties.

2. CHILD ABUSE PROCEEDINGS

Public recognition of widespread physical abuse and neglect of children has resulted in the establishment of child protective services in every state. Operating typically on a 24–hour basis, complaints are received, investigated, and reported. Acute and/or chronic cases of dependent children frequently come before the court. Remedies range from court ordered services for the parents to temporary foster care placements or termination of all residual parental rights with the right to place for adoption. Judges must weigh the parents' right to their children against the child's well-being. Heavy reliance is often placed on the reports of mental health specialists in these matters.

In situations where a child has been severely injured or sexually abused, criminal prosecution may result as well as the civil remedies listed above. Special litigation problems arise when the victim is a child. The child may be the only witness. As such, the child may be physically unable to testify or may be legally incompetent to testify. Where the child is not capable of testifying, valuable evidence can be gleaned from the child's behavior. Both parties would then have a need for expert assistance to analyze the behavioral evidence.

Expert testimony in both the criminal and civil proceedings that follow child abuse or neglect is used to establish whether the abuse occurred as well as the identity of the abuser. Mental health professionals can use their knowledge of the battered child syndrome and the child sexual abuse accommodation syndrome[2] in jurisdictions that admit the evidence to answer these questions. Children who change their stories

---

§ 19.23

1. Negative consequences may be: child-focus conflicts between parents; impossible loyalty choices for the child; disruption of the parenting by the psychological and biological father; disruption of the routine and schedule of the child's home and peer environment; increased awareness of the original spousal conflict for the child; consequent symptoms of social, academic and personal maladjustment. See, Blau, *The Psychologist as Expert Witness* 155 (1984).

2. See § 19.08, *supra*.

or who claim the injury was accidental can be compared to the traits of abused children. Likewise, if the adult claims the injury was accidental, or if more than one person could have abused the child, traits of batterers may be useful in identifying the responsible person. Use of these syndromes as indicators of character may be helpful to the evaluator even if testimony on the syndrome cannot be introduced in a particular jurisdiction.

Another possible use for expert assistance may be to assess the credibility of the child witness. While few courts may admit such testimony, its exploration may assist the expert in determining a causal connection between behavior and resulting harm. Impeachment attempts of the child may suggest fabrication by the child, that the child has been brainwashed by authorities, or that the allegation is an attempt at retaliation against an authority figure.

3. JUVENILE ADJUDICATIONS

In the court's dealings with juvenile offenders, judges are ordinarily very responsive to psychological reports. They deal not only with criminal conduct, but also with status offenses such as juvenile truancy, running away, and promiscuity. First offenses generally result in probation and/or remedial services. Repeat offenders, however, require consideration of alternative placement. At this point, the adolescent becomes a ward of the state and is subject to commitment to state "learning centers," group homes or specialized foster care. Mental health professionals may be called upon for evaluations as to what type of placement would best meet the child's needs. Once placements have been made, courts continue to rely on psychologists and psychiatrists to evaluate the services provided in state facilities.

§ 19.24 Use of the Expert in Court

The mental health practitioner's courtroom appearance in child custody and intra-family conflict cases, and the permissible scope of the expert's evidence, is not appreciably different from that which has already been discussed in earlier portions of the book, and, therefore, reference is made to such treatment of the subject. Chapter 1 deals with the general approaches to direct and cross-examination of expert witnesses in general, and earlier sections of this chapter and the previous one have addressed specific evidentiary problems related to psychiatric and psychological evidence.

————

V. MISCELLANEOUS

§ 19.25 Bibliography of Additional References

References contained in the footnotes are generally not repeated here. The reader is also referred to the additional references following Chapter 18.

1. BOOKS

Barber, *Hypnosis: A Scientific Approach,* 1969.

Caplan, *The Insanity Defense and the Trial of John W. Hinckley, Jr.,* 1984.

Hilgard & Hilgard, *Hypnosis in the Relief of Pain,* 1983.

Loftus, *Eyewitness Testimony,* 1979.

Low, Jeffries & Bonnie, *The Trial of John W. Hinckley: A Case Study in the Insanity Defense,* 1986.

Perlin, *The Jurisprudence of the Insanity Defense,* 1994.

Perlin, *Law and Mental Disability,* 1994.

Putnam, *Diagnosis and Treatment of Multiple Personality Disorder,* 1989.

Suman, *Psychiatric and Psychological Evidence,* 1986.

Weihofen, *Insanity as a Defense in Criminal Law,* 1933.

2. ARTICLES

Alberts & Alberts, "Unvalidated Treatment of Premenstrual Syndrome," 19 *Int'l J.Mental Health* 69 (1990).

Alexander & Szasz, "From Contract to Status via Psychiatry," 13 *Santa Clara L.Rev.* 537 (1973).

American Medical Association, "Scientific Status of Refreshing Recollection by the Use of Hypnosis," 253 *JAMA* 1918 (1985).

American Psychiatric Association Task Force Report 14, *Electroconvulsive Therapy* (1984).

Applebaum, "Confidentiality in the Forensic Evaluation," 7 *Int'l J.L. & Psychiatry* 286 (1984).

Applebaum, "The Right to Refuse Treatment with Antipsychotic Medications: Retrospect and Prospect," 145 *Am.J.Psychiatry* 413 (1988).

Applebaum, "Civil Commitment From a Systems Perspective," 16 *Law & Human Behavior* 61 (1992).

Applebaum, "Hospitalization of the Dangerous Patient: Legal Pressures and Clinical Responses," 12 *Bull.Am.Academy Psychiatry & L.* 323 (1984).

Arenelia, "The Diminished Capacity and Diminished Responsibility Defenses: Two Children of a Doomed Marriage," 77 *Colum.L.Rev.* 827 (1977).

Bagby, et al., "Decision Making in Psychiatric Civil Commitment: An Experimental Analysis," 148 *Am.J.Psychiatry* 28 (1991).

Ballinger, "Emotional Disturbance During Pregnancy and Following Delivery," 26 *J.Psychosomatic Res.* 629 (1982).

Bernstein, "Termination of Parental Rights on the Basis of Mental Disorder: A Problem of Policy and Interpretation," 22 *Pac.L.J.* 1155 (1991).

Bolton, "Testamentary Capacity," 3 *L. & Psych.Rev.* 107 (1977).

Bremner, et al., "Dissociation and Posttraumatic Stress Disorder in Vietnam Combat Veterans," 149 *Am.J.Psychiatry* 328 (1992).

Bricker, "Fatal Defense: An Analysis of Battered Woman's Syndrome Expert Testimony for Gay Men and Lesbians Who Kill Abusive Partners," 58 *Brook.L.Rev.* 1379 (1993).

Brooks, "A Comparison of a Mentally Ill Individual's Rights to Refuse Medication Under the United States and New York State Constitutions," 8 *Touro L.Rev.* 1 (1991).

Brotherton, "Post–Traumatic Stress Disorder—Opening Pandora's Box?" 17 *New Eng.L.Rev.* 91 (1981).

Callahan, et al., "The Volume and Characteristics of Insanity Defense Pleas: An Eight–State Study," 19 *Bull.Am.Acad.Psychiatry & L.* 331 (1991).

Davis, "Law, Science and History: Reflections Upon In the Best Interests Of The Child," 86 *Mich.L.Rev.* 1096 (1988).

Dybwab & Herr, "Unnecessary Coercion: An End to Involuntary Commitment of Retarded Persons," 31 *Stan.L.Rev.* 753 (1979).

Ewing, "Dr. Death and the Case for an Ethical Ban on Psychological Predictions of Dangerousness in Capital Sentencing Proceedings," 8 *Am.J.Law & Med.* 407 (1983).

Feinstein, "Posttraumatic Stress Disorder: A Descriptive Study Supporting DSM–III–R Criteria," 146 *Am.J.Psychiatry* 665 (1989).

Fentiman, "Whose Right Is It Anyway? Rethinking Competency to Stand Trial In Light of Synthetically Sane Insanity Defendants," 40 *U.Miami L.Rev.* 1109 (1986).

Friedman, "Toward Rational Pharmacotherapy for Posttraumatic Stress Disorder: An Interim Report," 145 *Am.J.Psychiatry* 281 (1988).

Gobert, "Psychosurgery, Conditioning, and the Prisoner's Right to Refuse Rehabilitation," 61 *Va.L.Rev.* 155 (1975).

Goldstein, "The Psychiatrist's Guide to Right and Wrong: Part III: Postpartum Depression and the 'Appreciation' of Wrongfulness," 17 *Bull.Am.Acad.Psychiatry & L.* 121 (1989).

Green, "The Operative Effect of Mental Incompetency in Agreements and Wills," 21 *Tex.L.Rev.* 554 (1943).

Green, et al., "Risk Factors for PTSD and Other Diagnoses in a General Sample of Vietnam Veterans," 147 *Am.J.Psychiatry* 729 (1990).

Haddad, "Predicting the Supreme Court's Response to the Criticisms of Psychiatric Predictions of Dangerousness in Civil Commitment Proceedings," 64 *Neb.L.Rev.* 190 (1988).

Hermann et al., "Sentencing of the Mentally Retarded Criminal Defendant," 41 *Ark.L.Rev.* 765 (1988).

Hiday, "Are Lawyers Enemies of Psychiatrists? A Survey of Civil Commitment Counsel And Judges," 140 *Am.J.Psychiatry* 343 (1983).

Hiday, "Coercion in Civil Commitment: Process, Preferences and Outcome," 15 *J.L. & Psychiatry* 359 (1992).

Hilgard, "Research Advances in Hypnosis: Issues and Methods," 38 *Int'l J.Clin. & Experim.Hypnosis* 248 (1987).

Hinds, "Involuntary Outpatient Commitment for the Chronically Mentally Ill," 69 *Neb.L.Rev.* 346 (1990).

Jackson, "The Clinical Assessment and Prediction of Violent Behavior: Toward A Scientific Analysis," 16 *Crim.Just. & Behavior* 114 (1989).

Jackson, "Psychiatric Decision–Making for the Courts: Judges, Psychiatrists, Lay People," 9 *Int'l J.L. & Psychiatry* 507 (1986).

Larkin & Collins, "Fitness to Plead and Psychiatric Reports," 29 *Med. Sci. & Law* 26 (1989).

Loftus & Loftus, "On the Permanence of Stored Information in the Human Brain," 35 *Am.Psychologist* 409 (1980).

Loftus, "Eyewitness: Essential But Unreliable," *Psychology Today,* Feb. 1984, p. 22.

McConkey & Kinoshita, "The Influence of Hypnosis on Memory After One Day and One Week," 97 *J.Abnormal Psychol.* 48 (1988).

Menzies, et al., "Female Follies: The Forensic Psychiatric Assessment of Women Defendants," 15 *Int'l J.L. & Psychiatry* 179 (1992).

Miller & Germain, "The Retrospective Evaluation of Competency to Stand Trial," 11 *Int'l J.L. & Psychiatry* 113 (1988).

Mossman, "Assessing and Restoring Competency to Be Executed: Should Psychiatrists Participate?" 5 *Behav.Sci. & L.* 397 (1987).

Mossman, "The Psychiatrist and Execution Competency: Fording Murky Ethical Waters," 43 *Case W.Res.L.Rev.* 1 (1992).

Mueser, "Auditory Hallucinations in Combat–Related Chronic Posttraumatic Stress Disorder," 144 *Am.J.Psychiatry* 299 (1987).

Perlin, "Unpacking the Myths: The Symbolism Mythology of Insanity Defense Jurisprudence," 40 *Case W.Res.L.Rev.* 599 (1990).

Perlin, "Are Courts Competent to Decide Competency Questions? Stripping the Facade from United States v. Charters," 38 *U.Kan.L.Rev.* 957 (1990).

Perlin, "Psychodynamics and the Insanity Defense: 'Ordinary Common Sense' and Heuristic Reasoning," 69 *Neb.L.Rev.* 3 (1990).

Pitman, et al., "Prevalence of Posttraumatic Stress Disorder in Wounded Vietnam Veterans," 146 *Am.J.Psychiatry* 667 (1989).

Redmond, "Testamentary Capacity," 15 *Bull.Am.Acad.Psychiatry & L.* 247 (1987).

Reed, "An Analysis of the Law of Testamentary Capacity," 1 *W.New Eng.* 429 (1979).

Ross, et al., "Sleep Disturbance as the Hallmark of Posttraumatic Stress Disorder," 146 *Am.J.Psychiatry* 697 (1989).

Saks, "Multiple Personality Disorder and Criminal Responsibility," 25 *U.C.Davis L.Rev.* 383 (1992).

Schopp, "Wake Up and Die Right: The Rationale, Standard, and Jurisprudential Significance of the Competency to Face Execution Requirements," 51 *La.L.Rev.* 995 (1991).

Schreiber, et al., "An Evaluation of Procedures for Assessing Competency to Stand Trial," 15 *Bull.Am.Acad.Psychiatry & L.* 187 (1987).

Showalter, "Psychiatric Participation in Capital Sentencing Procedures: Ethical Considerations," 13 *Int'l J.L. & Psychiatry* 261 (1990).

Slobogin, "Dangerousness and Expertise," 123 *U.Pa.L.Rev.* 97 (1984).

Slobogin, "The Guilty But Mentally Ill Verdict: An Idea Whose Time Should Not Have Come," 53 *Geo.Wash.L.Rev.* 494 (1985).

Smith & Hager, "The Senile Testator: Medicolegal Aspects of Competency," 13 *Clev.Mar.L.Rev.* 397 (1964).

Sparr & Boehnlein, "Posttraumatic Stress Disorder in Tort Actions: Forensic Minefield," 18 *Bull.Am.Acad.Psychiatry & L.* 283 (1990).

Stout, "Premenstrual Symptoms in Black and White Community Samples," 143 *Am.J.Psychiatry* 1436 (1986).

Weihofen, "Mental Incompetency to Contract or Convey," 39 *S.Cal. L.Rev.* 211 (1966).

Wilsey, "Testamentary Capacity and Undue Influence," *Fla.Bar J.,* May, 1987, at 13.

Winick, "The Right to Refuse Mental Health Treatment: A First Amendment Perspective," 44 *U.Miami L.Rev.* 1 (1989).

Worrell, "Psychiatric Prediction of Dangerousness in Capital Sentencing: The Quest for Innocent Authority," 5 *Behav.Sci. & L.* 433 (1987).

Chapter 20

THE DETECTION OF DECEPTION

I. INTRODUCTION

I. INTRODUCTION

§ 20.01 Purpose and Scope of the Chapter

The purpose of this chapter is twofold: (1) to acquaint the reader with the nature, potential, and limitations of attempts by various scientific means to detect deception; and (2) to present a discussion of the legal aspects of the reported results.

Perhaps the best known of the techniques to detect deception is that known as the polygraph technique, also referred to, inaccurately, as the "lie detector." It is for that reason that most of the chapter is devoted to that part. In addition, we also explore the use of hypnosis and narcoanalysis, used clinically by physicians and psychologists, and, finally, the process known as voice stress evaluation.

It would not be possible in the space of a portion of a book chapter to explain adequately the intricacies of the polygraph technique, a technique that has developed independently of the mental health specialists about whom we reported in Chapters 18 and 19, nor to fully cover the many attending legal issues. For that reason, our objective has been to accommodate the general interests and ordinary needs of the legal profession in the treatment of that subject.[1]

II. THE POLYGRAPH TECHNIQUE*

§ 20.02 The Instruments for Diagnosis of Truth or Deception

To many persons the polygraph is thought of as a "lie-detector," and all too often they perceive it to be a mechanical device that will somehow alert the operator whenever a question is answered untruthfully. Or they may have an entirely different viewpoint and discount altogether the notion that deception can be inferred from the use of any kind of instrumentation. Both positions are unsupportable.

Although no mechanical device exists that will in and of itself detect deception, it is a demonstrable fact that there are instruments capable of recording physiological changes that may serve as the basis for a reliable

---

§ 20.01

1. For the attorney or judge who is confronted with actual case situations requiring more detailed information with regard to either the scientific or legal aspects of the technique, see, Reid and Inbau, *Truth and Deception: The Polygraph ("Lie Detector") Technique* (2d ed. 1977). A successor text is scheduled for publication in 1995 under the title of *The Polygraph Technique*.

One of the new co-authors is Brian C. Jayne, who assisted in the preparation of the present discussion of the technique.

* A very similar presentation of this subject will appear in the forthcoming new editions of *Protective Security Law* and *The Polygraph Technique*, both co-authored by Fred E. Inbau.

diagnosis of truth or deception, provided certain procedures are followed. The instruments are technically known as polygraphs, and the procedure by which they are utilized for diagnostic purposes is known as the polygraph technique.

The standard polygraph instrument is designed to make a permanent and simultaneous recording of a subject's respiratory rate and volume, relative changes in electrodermal resistance (the ability of the skin to conduct electricity), as well as changes in the subject's blood pressure and heart rate. These physiological systems have been selected for monitoring because they each reflect activity within the subject's autonomic nervous system. While some instruments may make additional recordings (muscle movement recorder, cardio tachometer, cardio activity monitor) any instrument that does not record, at a minimum the three aforementioned physiological systems is inadequate for actual case testing.

The body attachments by which respiration, pulse, blood pressure and electrodermal resistance are recorded are as follows:

1. Pneumograph tubes, with the aid of beaded chains, are fastened around the chest and abdomen of the person being tested.

2. A blood pressure cuff, of the type used by physicians, is fastened around the subject's upper arm.

3. Two electrodes are affixed to the subject's fingers, and an imperceptible amount of electric current is passed from one to the other for the purpose of measuring electrodermal resistance.

All of the foregoing units, as well as the entire polygraph itself, are shown in Figure 1, which also illustrates the relative positions of the subject and examiner during the chart recording phase of the examination.

Fig. 1. Reid Polygraph in Operation. Observe the pneumograph tubes around the subject's chest and abdomen, the blood pressure cuff around the right arm, and the electrodes attached to two fingers of the left hand.

The examiner is Joseph P. Buckley, President of John E. Reid and Associates; the subject is posed by Michael Adamec, a staff examiner.

In the polygraph tracings that follow, only Figure 7 contains the full complement of polygraph recordings, with the top two monitoring the subject's respiration, and the bottom one monitoring cardiovascular changes. The tracing between the cardiovascular and respiratory channels monitors electrodermal resistance. To better illustrate significant changes in chart responses, all but one of the following figures contain only two of the four standard polygraph channels.

§ 20.03   Examiner Qualifications and Training

Because the polygraph technique involves a diagnostic procedure rather than the mere mechanical operation of an instrument, a prime requisite to its effectiveness and reliability is examiner competence.

An examiner must be a person of intelligence, with a good educational background—preferably a college degree. And since the examiner will be dealing with persons in delicate situations from a myriad of different backgrounds, he or she must also possess suitable personality characteristics, which might be summarized as the ability "to get along" well with others and to be confident and persuasive during interpersonal relationships.

Adequate training for a polygraph examiner should consist of both classroom instruction as well as an internship conducted under the guidance of a competent, experienced examiner. During training the student should be exposed to a sufficient volume of actual cases to permit frequent observations of polygraph examinations. Classroom instruction should include lectures relating to polygraph instrumentation and procedures as well as the relevant areas within psychology, psychopathology, physiology, pharmacology and law. Attention must also have been given to the detailed study and analysis of a considerable number of polygraph test records in actual cases in which the true facts of truthfulness or deception were later established by corroborated evidence.

There are, unfortunately, relatively few persons holding themselves out as polygraph examiners who have received this recommended level of training, particularly with respect to the fully supervised internship during which the trainee examines subjects in actual case situations.

§ 20.04   Examination Room Requirements

The examinations must be conducted in a quiet, private room. Extraneous noises, or the presence of a third party, except for an interpreter when needed, would produce distractions that could seriously affect the examination and diagnosis.

§ 20.05   Test Procedures

A polygraph examination consists of three separate phases, (1) a pretest interview, (2) a chart recording phase, and (3) the diagnosis of truth or deception. Once the examiner has rendered a diagnostic opinion of the subject's truthfulness based on chart recordings the examination is complete.

1.   ISSUE SELECTION FOR PRE-TEST INTERVIEW AND TEST

Before an examination is administered the examiner must be provided with all relevant investigative data. This will provide the basis for conducting a proper pretest interview and is also necessary to establish the issue of the examination.

The polygraph technique is most valid when a single issue (incident) is addressed. Furthermore, there are certain limitations in selecting a proper issue. The first of these is that the issue must be based on a disputed physical action or statement, such as stealing a car, shooting a gun, or saying to a woman, "If you scream I'll hurt you".

It is highly improper to conduct a test upon an issue investigating a subject's opinions or beliefs that can change with time and motivation. Examples of such issues include, "Did you hurt (victim) when you had sex with her?"; "Did the police threaten you in any way?"; and, "Did you touch (child) for sexual gratification?" Each of these issues allows the subject to place his own interpretation on the key words: hurt, threaten, or gratification.

Issues investigating a subject's intentions at the time something was done or said can create similar problems. For example, testing whether or not a subject who wrote a threatening note is telling the truth when he now claims that the note was written in jest, would be inappropriate. In retrospect, the subject could certainly convince himself that his intentions were not serious at the time the note was written.

A proper polygraph issue will attempt to address an action or statement as specifically as possible and avoid all-encompassing issues such as, "Did you lie at all during your court testimony?", or, "Are you telling the complete truth about what that man did to you?" If a subject exhibits deceptive response criteria to such broad inquires, it is not possible to determine whether the responses are from a person essentially telling the truth but uncertain as to a minor detail, or from a person who is knowingly withholding or fabricating significant information. In these situations much greater reliance can be placed on polygraph opinions if the issue being investigated is more narrow, e.g., "Did John Smith tell you that he shot Bill Jones?", "Did Larry Miller have sexual intercourse with you?"

In summary, the issue should focus on:

(1) A single incident, not multiple, unrelated incidents;

(2) Factual events, not matters of opinions;

(3) Disputed physical actions or statements, not intentions; and

(4) Narrowly defined issues, not broad inquiries.

2. PRETEST INTERVIEW

There are a number of reasons for conducting a pretest interview. These include defining and discussing the issue of the examination, explaining the instrument and procedures to the subject, evaluating the subject's physical and emotional suitability for the examination, and developing test questions with the subject. During the pretest interview the examiner will seek to properly condition the subject for the subsequent tests which may involve alleviating a subject's apprehensions, reassurances of the objectivity of the diagnostic process, or carefully defining specific terms used in formulating test questions. Also, during the interview, one of the most important areas of subject conditioning is the proper selection and development of control questions.

At the time of the pretest interview the examiner must be perceived by the subject as being completely objective and unbiased with regard to the subject's truthfulness or deception. Under no circumstances should the examiner indulge in an interrogation during a pretest interview. To do so could seriously impair the validity of the subject's subsequent responses to test questions.

3. CONTROL QUESTIONS

Indispensable to a valid polygraph examination is the development and use of proper control questions. A control question is unrelated to the issue under investigation but it addresses a behavior or motivation similar to that concerning the matter under investigation. Of utmost importance, the control question must be one to which the subject will either lie or be uncertain of his answer. For instance, in a manslaughter investigation where the killing appeared to occur as the result of an argument, the examiner may develop a control question centered around the subject losing his temper, or doing things he regrets. The final wording of the control question may be something like, "Besides what you told me, did you ever do anything else that you regretted?"

4. RELEVANT QUESTIONS

Questions designed to specifically address the issue under investigation are termed relevant questions. The proper formulation of relevant questions is critical to the final inferences drawn from a subject's polygraph chart responses.

Relevant questions should not address multiple conduct. For example, "Did you strike a woman and steal her purse?" is an improper relevant question because the subject may have hit the woman but not stolen her purse, or vice versa.

Relevant questions should not be assumptive. Therefore, in a rape case where the suspect is denying having intercourse with the victim, it is improper to ask as a relevant question, "Did you force Mary Johnson to have sex with you?" because the question assumes that the subject had sex with the victim. Assumptive questions of this nature could result in deceptive chart indications from a truthful subject.

Relevant questions should be worded in simple language and be as succinct and direct as possible. For example, in a sexual harassment case where a supervisor denied ever talking to his secretary about the possibility of having a sexual relationship it would be improper to ask the secretary the following relevant question, "Are you fabricating the allegation that Tom Smith offered you a raise based on the contingency that you have sexual intercourse with him?" The way to formulate this question would be, "Did Tom Smith ask you to have sexual relations with him?"

5. IRRELEVANT QUESTIONS

An irrelevant question is one that has no bearing whatsoever on the issue under investigation and also one to which the subject will be telling the truth. An example of such a question is one regarding the place where the examination is being conducted—for instance, "Are you in Chicago right now?"

Irrelevant questions serve several important procedural functions during chart recording. Each polygraph test begins with the asking of irrelevant questions in order to acclimate the subject to the testing procedure so that normal physiology can be recorded before relevant or control questions are asked. These questions are also used to separate or terminate an emotional response that occurred to relevant or control questions. They provide a non-critical period of chart time during which the examiner can make instrument adjustments if needed. Finally, in some instances, a subject's physiological response to an irrelevant question can enter into the diagnosis of truth or deception. For example, some deceptive subjects will purposefully distort chart recordings when these questions are asked.

6. CONSTRUCTION AND NUMBER OF QUESTIONS

Prior to a test the subject is told precisely, word for word, what questions will be asked. Assurance is also given that no questions will be asked that have not been specifically reviewed. *Surprise has no part in a properly conducted polygraph examination.*

Following is a list of the types and arrangement of questions which should be asked during a polygraph test and to which the subject is to answer with either a "yes" or a "no" response. (Any other talking would distort the recordings.) The questions are based on a hypothetical murder case in which the victim is Paul Joseph and the suspect is Randy Lawrence.

1. Do some people call you Randy? (irrelevant)

2. Are you over 21 years old? (irrelevant)

3. Last Saturday night did you shoot Paul Joseph? (relevant)

4. Are you in Chicago right now? (irrelevant)

5. Did you kill Paul Joseph? (relevant)

6. Besides what you told me about did you ever do anything else in your life that was against the law? (control)

7. Is today Wednesday? (irrelevant)

8. Last Saturday did you fire a gun at Paul Joseph? (relevant)

9. Besides in the two fights you told me about, did you ever hurt anyone else in your life? (control)

§ 20.06 Required Chart Recordings

A single polygraph test consists of the examiner asking each of the 9 or 10 prepared test questions, allowing about 10 seconds following an irrelevant question and 15 to 20 seconds following a relevant or control question.

One such test does not constitute a polygraph examination; a minimum of three is considered standard before a diagnosis can be attempted. Depending on the technique utilized, there could be as many as five separate tests conducted during an examination. There are a number of different test designs an examiner can use, depending on the specific circumstances of each examination.

§ 20.07 The Diagnosis

At the risk of oversimplification, it may be said that a subject who is telling the truth to the issue under investigation will focus emotional attention (as identified through chart responses) toward the control questions and away from relevant questions. Conversely, a deceptive subject's focus of emotional attention will be directed toward relevant questions and away from control questions.

In order for a subject's recordings to produce sufficient criteria to formulate a definite opinion of truth or deception he must be (1) capable of exhibiting autonomic arousal, and (2) able to form perceptual distinctions between relevant and control questions. Consequently, a subject who is not capable of exhibiting arousal or forming perceptual distinctions because of psychological or medical problems, ingestion of chemical agents, or other reasons, will produce inconclusive polygraph recordings (those with no significant differences between relevant and control question responses).

The following reproductions of polygraph chart tracings are illustrative of the emotional focus that would lead to an inference of (a) truthfulness (Figures 2, 3, and 4) or (b) deception (Figures 5–10) regarding the issue under investigation.

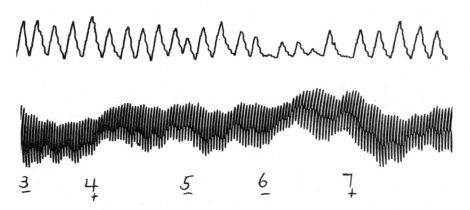

Fig. 2. Record of truth-telling embezzlement suspect, indications of truthfulness in both respiration and cardiovascular responses.

Questions 3 and 5 pertained to the embezzlement of a large sum of money, 3 being "Do you know who stole the missing money?" and 5 being "Did you steal the missing money?". Questions 4 and 7 were irrelevant. Observe the suppression in respiration and the blood pressure rise at control question 6, when the subject was asked: "Did you ever steal anything?" The subject's emotional focus to this control question provides criteria to support an opinion of truthfulness to the relevant questions.

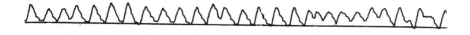

Fig. 3. Record of truth-telling complainant in rape case. Indications of truthfulness in respiration alone.

Questions 4 and 7 were irrelevant. At 3 and 5 the subject was asked whether she had consented to the acts (as alleged by the two accused young men). Her "no" answers did not produce significant responses, whereas 6, the control question, did. At 6 she was asked whether she had ever had sexual intercourse with anyone prior to the date of the alleged rape. Her response in respiration at that point clearly indicates a stronger emotional focus to the control question than the relevant questions. This allowed the examiner to conclude that the accusation of rape was truthful.

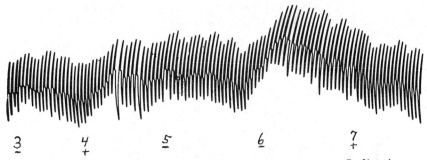

$\underline{3}$ $\underset{+}{4}$ $\underline{5}$ $\underline{6}$ $\underset{+}{7}$

Fig. 4. Record of a truth-telling arson suspect. Indications of truthfulness in blood pressure-pulse alone.

Questions 3 and 5 pertained to an arson for which the motive was destruction of the employer's books and records in order to conceal an embezzlement; 4 and 7 were irrelevant; 6 was the control question: "Did you ever steal anything?" The only significant response appeared in the blood pressure tracing at control question 6, a known lie reaction, since shortly after the test the subject admitted having stolen money at various times and places. In view of the reaction to the known lie at 6 and the lack of any response at arson questions 3 and 5, the proper interpretation was one of truth-telling regarding the arson.

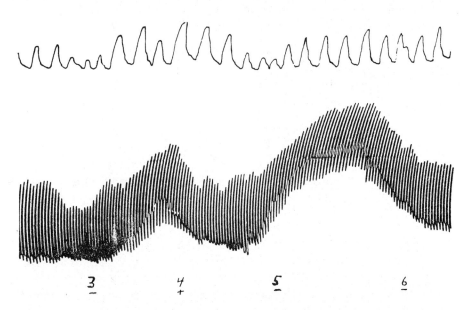

$\underline{3}$ $\underset{+}{4}$ $\underline{5}$ $\underline{6}$

Fig. 5. Record of a lying burglary suspect. Indications of lying in both respiration and cardiovascular responses.

Questions 3 and 5 pertained to a burglary; 4 was irrelevant; 6 was the control question: "Did you ever steal anything?", to which the subject's answer of "no" was a known lie.

Significant responses appear in both respiration and blood pressure at 3 and 5—because of the fact that the subject's lying regarding the burglary was of paramount concern, whereas his general stealing, and a lying about it at 6 was of no consequence.

This is the reverse of the situation of a person who is telling a truth regarding the main issue; his principal concern on the test is the control question lie.

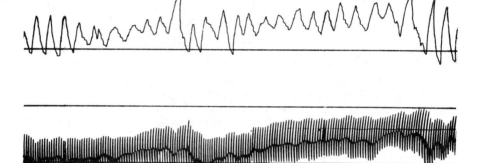

2+   3−   4+   5−   6−   7+

Fig. 6. Record of lying male suspect in aggravated assault upon a woman. Indications of lying in respiration alone.

Questions 3 and 5 were relevant; 2, 4, and 7 were irrelevant; 6 was the control question: "Since November, did you think of dating any other woman than your wife?".

In the respiration tracing, observe the normal breathing at 2, the rise in the base line of the tracing beginning at 3, the relief in respiration at 4, a further base line rise at 5, then the descent shortly after 6 and a return to the original level at 7. Specific, as well as general base line changes such as these are very reliable indications of the subject's emotional focus to relevant questions 3 and 5.

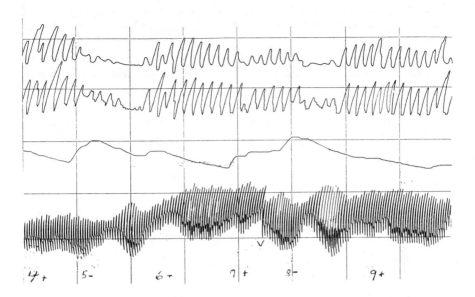

Fig. 7. Record of a deceptive rape suspect. Indications of deception are apparent from the much more significant responses in all three parameters to relevant questions 5 and 8, in stark contrast to the lack of arousal to control questions 6 and 9.

The top two tracings record respiratory changes, one thoracic and the other from abdominal breathing. The third tracing monitors the electrodermal resistance. The bottom one monitors cardiovascular changes.

The subject denied ever having sexual intercourse with the victim. Consequently relevant questions 5 and 8 addressed the issue of whether or not the subject had sexual intercourse with the victim, whereas control question 6 asked, "Besides speeding, did you ever do anything else that was against the law?" and control question 9 was phrased, "Did you ever lie about anything sexual you've done in your life?"

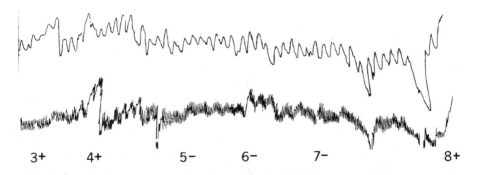

Fig. 8. Record of a murderer's deliberately distorted tracings.

During the examination of this subject, who was being questioned concerning the death of his wife, the examiner observed a flexing of the biceps muscle and some abnormally heavy breathing at various times throughout his first test. A repetition of the test was accompanied by the same behavior on the part of the subject. The records contained erratic respiratory and blood pressure tracings, and there was little doubt that they represented a deliberate effort to evade detection. Subsequently, the subject admitted that he had attempted to distort his record in order to confuse the examiner.

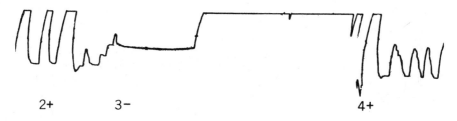

2+   3−   4+

Fig. 9. The deliberately distorted respiratory tracing of a child molester.

The subject was a university graduate student who had been accused of taking indecent liberties with a child. At relevant question 3 he held his breath for a full 60 seconds!

Although respiratory blocks of from 5 to 15 seconds may represent true, natural emotional arousal responses, the duration of this respiratory block was clearly indicative of deliberate distortion, which the subject later admitted to be the case.

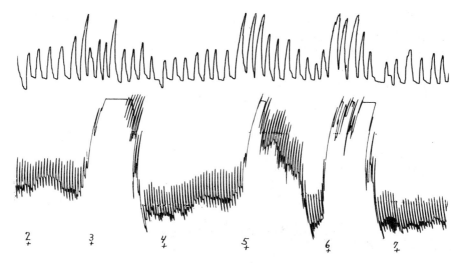

2   3   4   5   6   7
+   +   +   +   +   +

Fig. 10. An Attempt to Mislead the Examiner During Test. Observe, in this record of a bribery suspect, the obvious efforts to distort both the blood pressure and respiration tracings, by arm muscular movements and by heavy breathing, in response to relevant questions 3 and 5, and to control question 6. Questions 2, 4 and 7 are irrelevant. A record of this type may be considered a very reliable indication of deception. It is extremely rare for this to happen in the case of a truth-telling person.

§ 20.08   Effect of Nervousness Upon Diagnosis

One of the most frequently asked questions about the polygraph technique is the effect of extreme nervousness. First of all, a proper pretest interview lessens the apprehensions of a truthful though tense or nervous subject. Secondly, a subject whose nervousness persists will reveal that factor by the uniformly irregular nature of his polygraph tracings; in other words, physiological changes or disturbances induced only by nervousness usually appear on the polygraph record without relationship to any particular question or questions. They are usually of no greater magnitude—or, in any event, not consistently so—when relevant questions are asked than when irrelevant or control questions are asked. Finally, and most importantly, the employment of control questions offers considerable security against a misinterpretation of reactions caused by nervousness.

§ 20.09   The "Friendly Examiner" Syndrome

The "friendly examiner" syndrome describes a theoretical concern in which it is hypothesized that a deceptive subject who takes a polygraph examination at the request of his attorney will produce truthful results. The basis for this theory is the conjecture that because the subject knows the attorney will not use deceptive polygraph results against him the subject will not exhibit deceptive response criteria during the examination. This concern is unsupported both on theoretical and statistical grounds.

A subject who fails to exhibit emotional responses during a polygraph examination for whatever reason (low motivation, ingestion of drugs, fatigue, etc.) will be equally unresponsive to relevant and control questions. Under this circumstance, the subject's results would be reported as inconclusive, rather than truthful. Secondly, studies comparing polygraph chart responses from subjects who took the examination on behalf of a law enforcement agency to subjects who took the examination on behalf of a defense attorney showed no significant differences in responsivity.[1]

Basic to the foregoing comments about the friendly examiner syndrome is the impartial manner that the examiner portrays to the subject throughout the examination process.

§ 20.09

1. See, Raskin, et al., "Validity and Reliability of Detection of Deception," *Polygraph* 6(1) 1–39 (1977); and Matte & Reuss, "A Field Study of the 'Friendly Polygraphist' Concept," *Polygraph* 19(1) 1–8 (1990).

§ 20.10   Reliability of Diagnosis

Reliability refers to the consistency of test findings. This is an important measure within the polygraph technique field because it reflects on the objective manner in which examination results are interpreted, i.e., is the examiner's opinion supported by the polygraph data?

One measure of reliability within the polygraph technique is the extent to which examiners agree upon their diagnosis based upon evaluation of polygraph charts. As in any clinical procedure, the reliability of polygraph findings will depend to a great extent on the competency of the examiner as well as inherent characteristics within the subject of the examination.

In approximately twenty-five percent of subjects presented to a competent polygraph examiner, truthfulness or deception may be so clearly disclosed by the nature of the reactions to relevant and control questions that the examiner will be able to point them out to a lay person and satisfy him or her of their significance. In approximately sixty-five percent of the cases, however, the indications are not that obvious; they are sufficiently subtle in appearance and significance as to only be ascertained through expert interpretation. In approximately ten percent of cases even a competent examiner will be unable to arrive at a conclusive diagnosis because of a subject's physiological or psychological characteristics or because of other extraneous factors.

The director of the Unit for Experimental Psychiatry at the University of Pennsylvania, Martin T. Orne, M.D., Ph.D., who has devoted considerable attention to the polygraph technique and conducted many experiments with it, has expressed the view that a scientific evaluation of the polygraph technique has been unobtainable because of the inherent limitations upon actual case studies. Nevertheless, he is of the opinion that "in appropriate hands the reliability of the polygraph is far greater than what one could expect from accounts of eyewitnesses who briefly observe a stressful and arousing event", and, "certainly it would be more reliable than the available techniques of ascertaining truth such as psychiatric evaluations or the more esoteric procedures like the use of hypnosis or 'truth serum' ".[1]

The vast majority of field research utilizing experienced examiners and standard field procedures indicates that the reliability of examiner diagnosis based upon blind interpretation of polygraph charts has been estimated at approximately 90%. Excluded from this statistic, of course, are studies which utilized student examiners to collect or interpret the charts[2] or studies in which standard field procedures were not followed.[3]

§ 20.10

1. Orne, "Implications of Laboratory Research for the Detection of Deception," in Ansley (ed.), *Legal Admissibility of the Polygraph* (1975) at pp. 110–111.

2. See, for example, Horvath, "The Effect of Selected Variables on Interpretation of Polygraph Results," *Journal of Applied Psychology* 127–136 (1977). The results of this study were based, in part, on the analy-

3. See note 3 on page 1211.

§ 20.11 Accuracy of Diagnosis

The accuracy of the polygraph technique represents a measure of how often an examiner is correct in his final diagnosis of a subject's truthfulness. In many cases, the truth about who committed an offense may never be learned from confessions or from subsequently developed factual evidence. Proof is often lacking, therefore, that the examiner's diagnosis in any given case is either right or wrong. This situation precludes the possibility of making any absolute statement with respect to the accuracy of an examiner's diagnosis.

It is important to understand that an examiner's diagnosis is based, in part, on evaluation of investigative findings and the subject's verbal and nonverbal behavior during the pretest interview, in conjunction with the evaluation of polygraph chart responses. When all three of these criteria are consistent, e.g., investigative findings supporting probable truthfulness; the subject's demeanor and behavior during the pretest interview appearing truthful; and the polygraph chart responses indicating truthfulness, a very high degree of confidence can be placed upon the accuracy of the final diagnosis. (It should be noted that this same diagnostic approach is involved in rendering opinions of deception as well).

On the other hand, when inconsistencies within these detection of deception criteria exist, and cannot be resolved, a competent examiner is taught to render an inconclusive opinion, or otherwise exercise considerable caution in making his final diagnosis.

Dozens of studies that have been conducted on the accuracy of polygraph chart responses under various circumstances provide a range of different findings.[1] These studies, however, focus on the narrow issue of chart analysis, and do not take into consideration the aspects of investigative findings or the subject's behavior symptoms which are believed to contribute to, and enhance the accuracy of the final diagnosis of truthfulness or deception.

When a competent examiner administers and interprets the results of a polygraph examination, the accuracy of his diagnosis compares very favorably to other similar testimonial evidence such as that offered by a physician, psychiatrist, or psychologist.

§ 20.12 Polygraph Fallacies

Over the past couple of decades, psychophysiologists have exerted greater dominance and influence within public perceptions relating to

sis of field cases conducted by student examiners still in training.

3. As an example of research that does not parallel field procedures see, Klienmuntz & Szucko, "On the fallibility of lie detection," *Law and Society Review,* 17:84–104 (1982). Contrary to accepted field practice, evaluators were forced to render opinions upon viewing only one out of the 4 or 5 tests administered to the subject.

§ 20.11

1. In a review of 11 such field studies conducted between 1980 and 1990 involving a total of 920 suspects, Ansley reported that examiners were correct in 90% of their diagnoses based on the limited analysis of chart responses alone. See, Ansley, "The Validity and Reliability of Polygraph Decisions in Real Cases," *Polygraph* 19(3) 169–181 (1990).

the polygraph technique, arguing that it falls primarily within their domain of expertise. These individuals, while knowledgeable about psychophysiology, often have no formal training in applying those principles to the detection of deception in field practice. This narrowly focussed perspective has propagated a number of fallacies with respect to the polygraph technique. Furthermore, because many such psychophysiologists come from a purely academic background, they are quick to announce how things "ought" to be, rather than the more realistic assessment of what actually happens in field applications.

It is important to understand that the polygraph instrument does not record "deceptive" or "truthful" responses, but rather physiological changes that can be used as the basis for a diagnosis. However, what many psychophysiologists do not comprehend is that the accuracy of inferences drawn from the chart responses is directly related to the examiner's ability to conduct a proper pretest interview, properly formulate test questions, and identify intrinsic states within the subject or test environment. In other words, during a polygraph examination the validity of a subject's psychophysiological responses to test questions does not occur in isolation of the examiner's ability to properly administer the technique.

It may be somewhat confusing, therefore, to learn that computer software has been developed that purports to accurately render opinions of truth or deception from analyses of polygraph charts. While such programs would undoubtedly increase the reliability of polygraph chart diagnoses, they will not increase the accuracy of inferences made from analyses of those charts because the computer has no way of knowing whether or not a proper pretest interview was conducted, or proper test questions formulated; nor does the software consider intrinsic emotional states or the medical condition of the subject.

As another fallacy, there is a pervasive effort by some psychologists to treat polygraph results as if they are the product of a psychometric test.[1] A psychometric test represents a highly standardized procedure in which instructions, test questions, question sequence, and scoring are identical for all people. With a psychometric test, the only variable should be the person's response to a test item. With the polygraph technique, however, test questions must be individually formulated. The examiner must condition subjects in different ways. Examiner judgment is required to select appropriate tests or to employ specialized procedures during chart recordings. The validity of the subject's responses to test questions will be directly influenced by the examiner's ability to conduct a proper pretest interview, and each interview is unique.

§ 20.12

1. Lykken, in his book *A Tremor in the Blood, Uses and Abuses of the Polygraph Technique* (1980) makes reference to "Clinical vs. Statistical" lie detection, the latter of which describes a psychometric treatment of results. Ten years later another text written by yet two other psychologists approach the polygraph technique purely from a psychometric perspective, see, Ben-Shakhar & Furedy, *Theories and Applications in the Detection of Deception* (1990).

Rather than being a psychometric test, the polygraph technique represents a clinical evaluation similar to that made by a physician. A physician's diagnosis is based on taking a medical history from the patient, evaluating present symptoms, and ordering appropriate tests to confirm or refute a suspected diagnosis. This is a very similar process to that which a polygraph examiner uses to arrive at a diagnosis of truth or deception. Consequently, when opponents argue that the polygraph technique is flawed because it fails to meet standards of a psychometric test, one must appreciate that the polygraph technique does not purport to be a psychometric test.

As a final fallacy, it is common for polygraph opponents to consider inconclusive polygraph results as errors. In one study, researchers did not even permit examiners to render inconclusive opinions.[2] However, the inconclusive report is very important in any clinical procedure, in order to maintain a high level of validity. When a physician is unable to specifically diagnose a patient's symptoms, and therefore orders additional tests, performs exploratory surgery, or refers the patient to a different specialist, certainly the physician has not made a diagnostic error!

A significant portion of a polygraph examiner's training involves recognizing situations in which a subject's polygraph charts may not validly reflect their true status, as well as identifying those situations in which there is insufficient consistency or clarity of chart responses to support a conclusive opinion. Under this circumstance a competent examiner is trained to render an inconclusive opinion, and perhaps suggest a re-examination, rather than risk a possible erroneous conclusive opinion. A competent examiner's opinion should be inconclusive between 10 and 15 percent of the time.

§ 20.13　Preparing a Subject for a Polygraph Examination

The preparation of a subject for a polygraph examination requires that the examiner be provided with all case facts and investigative information. If the examination results are stipulated for admission as evidence at trial, the examiner will want to obtain similar information from all sides. From that background information the examiner will identify the principal issue for the examination. Reliance should be placed upon the examiner's expertise to help establish the best issue for the examination, as well as identify unsuitable issues.

The subject of the examination should be given as much notice as possible prior to the examination. In addition, the night before the examination he should be instructed to get a full night's sleep, avoid the use of illegal drugs, and use alcohol only in moderation. If the subject is

---

2. See, Szucko, J. & Kleinmuntz, B. "Statistical Versus Clinical Lie Detection," *American Psychologist* 36 May: 488–496 (1981). Another example of this is the Office of Technology Assessment's 1983 report on the *Scientific Validity of the Polygraph* *Technique,* Saxe, the principal author, recalculated existing field data to include inconclusive results as errors (Washington D.C.: US Congress Office of Technical Assessment, OTA–TM–11–15.)

taking prescribed medication, he should continue to take his normal dose of medication and inform the examiner of this. (Most examiners request that the subject complete a medical data sheet eliciting this type of information).

An attorney can increase the probability that the examiner will be able to form a definite opinion by speaking to the subject in positive terms about the benefit the examination results may have on his case, thereby enhancing the subject's motivation toward the examination. In addition, the subject should be reassured that the selected examiner is highly competent and has a reputation for reporting accurate results. The subject should not be told that the polygraph is a mere formality. To do so may increase the probability that the subject, whether truthful or deceptive, will produce inconclusive examination results.

III. THE LEGAL STATUS OF THE POLYGRAPH TECHNIQUE

A fundamental change in the legal status of the polygraph technique occurred in 1988 when Congress enacted the *Employee Polygraph Protection Act*.[1] It very significantly restricted the opportunity of private employers to avail themselves of the technique in their efforts to protect against employee thievery and other criminal actions committed against them.[2]

§ 20.14 Congressional Enactment

Although the title of the Act uses the word "polygraph", it is also directed at "lie-detectors," which, by the Act's definition, includes "polygraph, deceptograph, voice stress analyzer, psychological stress evaluator, or any other similar device ... that is used ... for the purpose of rendering a diagnostic opinion regarding the honesty or dishonesty of an individual." "Polygraph" itself is separately defined as an instrument that "records continuously, visually, permanently, and simultaneously changes in cardiovascular, respiratory, and electrodermal patterns as minimum instrumentation standards, ..."

With certain exceptions specified in the Act, it is "unlawful for any employer engaged in or affecting commerce or in the production of goods for commerce ..." to "require, request, suggest, or cause any employee or prospective employee to take or submit to any lie detector test ..."

---

1. 29 U.S.C.A. § 2001 et seq. It was enacted on June 27, 1988, and became effective 90 days thereafter.

2. The annual cost of employee theft in the U.S. has been estimated at $40 billion. That estimate is based upon the result of a three year federally funded research project involving a large state university, a research team of eight regular members, and 47 corporations. The study included a survey of 9,431 employees and 247 top executives from retail, hospital, and manufacturing firms. One third of the employees admitted thefts from employers. See the book by two of the principal researchers, Hollinger and Clark, *Theft By Employees* (1983).

Any auxiliary usage made of any test, or of its results or refusals to take a test, is also specifically prohibited.

An employer who violates any provision of the Act is subject to a civil penalty up to $10,000. Additionally, the Secretary of Labor is empowered to impose injunctive action. Also, a violator may be sued either in the federal or state courts by employees or applicants, and a class action is also available on behalf of persons similarly situated. The rights and procedures provided by the Act "may not be waived by contract or otherwise."

Despite the condemnation of the polygraph technique (along with all the other "lie detector" implements and procedures referred to in the Act), Congress provided a number of major exceptions to the prohibitions. A major one, insofar as criminal investigators are concerned, is testing by "the United States Government, any state, or local government, or any political subdivisions of a state or local government." Police usage, therefore, is permissible.

Among other exceptions from the Act's coverage are experts or consultants under contract with the various national intelligence agencies, or with the F.B.I.

With respect to non-governmental, private employers, exceptions are made for those whose primary business purpose consists of providing security systems or services, and whose functions include protection of public transportation, facilities such as electric or nuclear power plants, and authorized drug manufacturers, suppliers, and dispensers of controlled substances.

Upon compliance with the requirements of two specified sections of the Act, private employers may have polygraph tests conducted for "an ongoing investigation involving economic loss or injury to the employer's business, ...," provided the employee to be tested had access to the missing property and against whom there is reasonable suspicion of involvement. This is conditioned, however, upon the employer providing the employee a written statement revealing such facts and suspicion.

Because of the complexity of meeting the rigid requirements for any attempted utilization of the Act's exceptions and prescribed conditions, private employers are advised by the authors of this text to obtain the advice of legal counsel who may examine the Act himself and possibly contact a polygraph examiner or firm to avail himself of the various forms and documents that have already been used to guard against inadvertent non-compliance.

§ 20.15 Polygraph Case Law

Assuming the legality of a polygraph test in a particular case, civil or criminal, the issue may then arise as to the admissibility of the test results as courtroom evidence.

A guideline for admissibility was established in the 1923 case of Frye v. United States.[1] It held that before the results of any such test of a scientific nature could be used as evidence there must be proof that the test had gained "general acceptance" within the particular field of science to which it belonged. In applying that rule in *Frye,* the Court of Appeals for the District of Columbia affirmed the trial court's rejection of the testimony of a psychologist who had administered a "systolic blood pressure deception test" upon the accused defendant and concluded he was telling the truth.[2]

In the first chapter of the present text, under the subject of "Test of Admissibility" (Section 1.03), there is an extensive discussion of the legal developments from *Frye v. United States* through the more flexible "relevancy test" established in Rule 702 of the Federal Rules of Evidence (and in the equivalent rule in some states). It then analyzes the new federal court rule announced by the United States Supreme Court in the 1993 case of Daubert v. Merrell Dow Pharmaceuticals.[3] In *Daubert* the Court substituted for the earlier tests one based upon proof of "scientific reliability". It also submitted, for usage by the federal trial courts, procedures for determining "scientific reliability."

Although *Daubert* was a directive for federal courts, the Supreme Court's pronouncements are bound to have an impact upon the state courts. It is likely, however, that the determination of "scientific reliability" in any particular case, whether state or federal, will probably be no less onerous than when applying the "general acceptance" test of *Frye v. United States.*

Irrespective of the various guidelines of admissibility that the courts have applied, the prevailing judicial attitude had been a general unwillingness to admit in evidence the results of polygraph tests.[4] The principal exceptions to per se inadmissibility have been instances in which the opposing parties agree to have a designated examiner conduct a test upon a particular individual—plaintiff or defendant in a civil case; accuser or accused in a criminal case; or a witness for either side—with the understanding that the results would be admissible in evidence without objection. Upon that issue, there has been no consensus among the courts; in fact only a minority have favored such limited usage. One state appellate court, the Supreme Court of New Mexico, has held, however, that not only may stipulated test results be admitted, but that the defendant in a criminal case is also entitled, as a constitutional due

---

§ 20.15

1. Frye v. United States, 293 Fed. 1013 (D.C.Cir.1923).

2. For a long time the myth prevailed that Frye was actually innocent but it was dispelled in Starrs, "A Still-Life Water Color: Frye v. U.S.", 27 *J.For.Sci.* 684 (1982).

3. 113 S.Ct. 2786 (1993).

4. The many cases prior to 1977 are discussed in *Truth and Deception: The*

Polygraph ("Lie–Detector") Technique (2d ed. 1977), by John E. Reid and Fred E. Inbau. The legal aspects of the technique as of that date are discussed at pages 309–393. The preceding pages of that text are devoted to the technique itself, accompanied by illustrations of the instrument and of its recordings in actual cases.

A successor text was scheduled for publication in 1994, co-authored by Brian C. Jayne, Joseph P. Buckley, and Fred E. Inbau.

process right, to have his polygraph test results admitted into evidence, subject to proof of the test's reliability and the examiner's competency.[5]

Unique among the federal circuit courts, the Eleventh Circuit ruled, in the 1989 case of United States v. Piccinonna,[6] that polygraph test results could be admitted within that circuit's trial courts under either one of two conditions: upon stipulation by both parties, or for purposes of impeachment or corroboration of a witness at trial. The court prescribed certain precautions that must be taken to insure the reliability of the results and examiner competency, and in that respect it conferred "wide discretion" upon the trial judge.

Four of the court's judges dissented. In their lengthy dissenting opinion they expressed considerable doubt upon the validity of polygraph tests and concluded that the results should not be admissible under either Federal Rule of Evidence 702, which was earlier discussed, nor under Rule 608 with respect to impeachment of a witness. They also noted that in the instant case the government did not participate in the selection of the polygraph examiner.

The majority opinion in *Piccinonna* contains an extensive review of the polygraph case law in other federal circuits and in the state courts.[7]

On the negative side of the polygraph issue, is the 1989 decision of the Massachusetts Supreme Court in Commonwealth v. Mendes,[8] rendered very soon after the federal *Piccinonna* case. With only one justice in dissent, the court overruled its earlier cases and held that polygraph evidence, "with or without pretest stipulation, is inadmissible in criminal trials ... either for substantive purposes or for corroboration or impeachment of testimony." It also noted that although the courts of North Carolina, Oklahoma and Wisconsin had previously admitted polygraph evidence, on reexamination they too have concluded to disallow it.

As with the Eleventh Circuit in *Piccinonna,* the opinions in *Mendes* contain extensive reviews of the case law generally and, in part, also of the literature upon the subject of polygraph examinations.[9]

In rejecting polygraph test results as evidence, the courts have invoked various reasons other than concern over reliability. For in-

5. State v. Dorcey, 88 N.M. 184, 539 P.2d 204 (1975). The court also held that the results were admissible under one of its statutory rules of evidence similar to Rule 702 of the Federal Rules of Evidence. As of 1993, the *Dorcey* decision remains viable.

6. 885 F.2d 1529 (11th Cir.1989).

7. The majority noted that several circuits—the Third, Sixth, Seventh, Ninth, and Tenth—have admitted polygraph evidence for very limited purposes, such as to rebut the defendant's claim of interrogation coercion; in explanation of why the police did not conduct a more thorough investigation; or for some other limited purpose

"unrelated to the substantive correctness of the results of the polygraph examination." Also mentioned is the fact that the Eighth Circuit permits stipulation admissibility.

8. 406 Mass. 201, 547 N.E.2d 35 (1989).

9. The Wisconsin Supreme Court, in its 1981 case of State v. Dean, infra note 10, which rejected its earlier favorable polygraph decisions, gave much consideration to the standard 423 page text, with 325 illustrations, upon the polygraph technique (cited supra note 1, sec. 20.01); however, it was not even cited in either *Piccinonna* or *Mendes.*

stance, the 1981 Wisconsin Supreme Court case of State v. Dean [10] nullified its 1974 decision in State v. Stanislawski [11] which had approved admissibility when the opposing parties entered into a pre-test agreement and stipulated to the admission of the results in evidence. In doing so, however, the court, per Justice Shirley Abrahamson, stated that it was not prepared to say that polygraph test results are so unreliable as to preclude their admissibility under any circumstances. [12] The primary concern, as expressed by Justice Abrahamson, was that the previously approved stipulation procedure was "not operating satisfactorily to enhance the reliability of the polygraph evidence and to protect the integrity of the trial process as they were intended to do." [13]

§ 20.16 Essential Requirements for Usage of Test Results as Evidence

As the very title of the present section signifies, polygraph test results are not simply the product of an instrument's recordings of various physiological phenomena. They are based essentially upon a *technique* for diagnosing truth or deception from the recordings that are obtained.

Indispensably, the reliability of a polygraph examiner's diagnosis is dependent upon his competency. Unfortunately, as is true in some other professions and occupations, there are many professed experts who lack the essentials of competency. Most certainly, competency should be a prime requirement for an examiner's testimony in court, and particularly in a criminal case trial where life or liberty is at stake.

Following are the recommendations that have been submitted for the consideration of a court contemplating a favorable ruling on the admissibility of polygraph test results. They are contained in the previously referenced text upon the polygraph technique: [1]

"Before permitting polygraph test results to be admitted as evidence in any case, the court should require the following: (1) that the examiner possess a college degree, at least at the baccalaureate level; [2] (2) that he had received at least 6 months of internship training under an experienced, competent examiner or examiners, with a sufficient volume of case work to afford frequent supervised testing in actual case situations; (3) that the examiner has had at least 3 years' experience as a specialist in the field of polygraph examinations; (4) that the examiner produce in court the polygraph records that were obtained, so as to make

10. 103 Wis.2d 228, 307 N.W.2d 628 (1981).

11. 62 Wis.2d 730, 216 N.W.2d 8 (1974).

12. Supra note 10, at 646.

13. Id. at 653.

§ 20.16

1. Supra note 4, sec. 20.15.

2. Although a college degree is certainly no guarantee of the intellect required for examiner competency, this requirement will minimize the number of occasions when unqualified examiners testify. Moreover, the educated person is less reluctant to admit that his test results were of an indefinite nature; he will not view such a report as a reflection upon himself personally.

them available for cross-examination purposes;[3] and (5) with respect to any testimony explaining the records, all that the examiner may reveal about the 'control' question phase of the examination is that the question is one which concerns an unrelated but basically similar matter, and one to which the person being tested may give either an untruthful answer or else an answer which to him is of doubtful accuracy; and that the only purpose of the control question is to permit the examiner to compare the polygraph tracings at that point with those made when the specific case questions were answered.[4]

"In any jury trial where the test results are admitted in evidence the court should, of course, instruct the jury that they must not consider the polygraph examiner's opinion as conclusive, but that they are privileged to consider the opinion along with all the other evidence in the case and to give that opinion whatever weight and effect they think it reasonably deserves."

Comparable precautions should be taken by any person or agency seeking to obtain a valid polygraph test upon a client or anyone else for purposes other than courtroom usage.

IV. HYPNOSIS

§ 20.17   Nature and Limitations

Hypnosis has been defined as an artificially induced trancelike state, resembling somnambulism in which the subject is highly susceptible to suggestions, oblivious to all else, and responds readily to the commands of the hypnotist.[1]

In view of the frequency with which hypnosis had been used for police investigation purposes, and also in view of the many court decisions regarding the admissibility of the statements and testimony of persons who have been hypnotized, the American Medical Association, through its Council on Scientific Affairs, conducted a study on "The Scientific Status of Refreshing Recollection by the Use of Hypnosis." The Council, under the chairmanship of Martin T. Orne, M.D., Ph.D., Director of the Unit for Experimental Psychiatry of the University of Pennsylvania, submitted its report in August, 1984. It has been officially adopted by the A.M.A.[2]

---

3. This will present some difficulty because in many instances the recordings are not sufficiently indicative of truth or deception to be adequately explainable to nonexperts.

4. For a full explanation of the reason for this recommendation the reader should consult the text identified in supra note 4, sec. 20.15.

§ 20.17

1. *Stedman's Medical Dictionary* (25th ed. 1990).

2. The report appears in 253 *J.A.M.A.* 1918 (April, 1985).

The report states that there is no evidence to indicate an increase in *only accurate memory* during hypnosis; moreover, external corroboration does not necessarily establish that the subject's recollection is independent of suggestion by the hypnotist. In the panel's view, "there is no justification for the prosecution's use of hypnosis on a suspect," particularly when consideration is given to the constitutional protection accorded accused persons. However, where an accused person shows "clear evidence of amnesia," and defense counsel requests hypnosis, and it is conducted by a psychiatrist or psychologist, and he subsequently testifies, there is "an obligation to emphasize the need for independent corroborative evidence and the questionable reliability of memories that have not been so corroborated." With regard to the use of hypnosis on victims or witnesses in an effort to enhance recall, the report states that it should be limited to the investigative process. Even then there should be adherence to certain safeguards (which are discussed in the following paragraph).

The chairman of the A.M.A. panel, Dr. Orne, has conducted considerable research of his own upon the use of hypnosis. In one of his many publications he states that "hypnotized individuals are capable of wilfully lying."[3] He also cautions that in instances where hypnosis is conducted on a presumed witness who later becomes a suspect, there is a considerable risk of a false confession resulting from a post-hypnotic interrogation. It may stem from the interrogator's efforts to convince the suspect that he must have been at the crime scene, because otherwise there would have been no way to learn of the details discussed during the hypnotic session.

In Dr. Orne's opinion, "hypnotically induced testimony is not reliable and ought not to be permitted to form the basis of testimony in court." If, however, hypnosis is to be used for investigative purposes, and particularly on a subject who may subsequently testify in court, the hypnotic session should be conducted under circumstances that permit certain safeguards to be erected against erroneous interpretations of data and responses. It is recommended (1) that the hypnotist be a psychiatrist or psychologist who is not affiliated with either the prosecution (including the law enforcement community) or the defense; (2) the hypnotist should function in his task upon submission of essential factual information in writing, but without knowledge of the extent and details of the ongoing investigation; (3) the test be conducted by the hypnotist upon the subject without the presence of any other individuals; and (4) the session be videotaped in its entirety.[4]

In contrast to the negative conclusions in the A.M.A. report and in Dr. Orne's publications, some psychologists have reported that hypnosis has been very helpful in criminal investigations, with new information or

---

3. See the chapter on "Hypnotically Induced Testimony," by Dr. Orne and three of his colleagues, in Wells and Loftus, *Eye-* *witness Testimony: Psychological Perspective* (1984) 171–213, at p. 209.

4. *Id.*

valuable leads being obtained in 60 to 90 percent of the cases.[5] Also, over 1,000 officers of the Los Angeles Police Department have received training in hypnosis, and it has been estimated that over 5,000 police officers nationally have received such training.[6]

§ 20.18   General Legal Aspects

Of the many litigated hypnosis cases, the most significant of all is the 1987 decision of the Supreme Court of the United States in Rock v. Arkansas.[1] At trial defense counsel had unsuccessfully attempted to introduce in evidence the hypnotically refreshed testimony of the defendant who had been charged with the fatal shooting of her husband. Her attorney, without the court's permission or the knowledge of the prosecutor, arranged for Rock to submit to two hypnotic sessions. The avowed purpose was to have her recall the details of the event.

Although Rock did not recall any additional information during either of the tape-recorded sessions, she was reported to be able to recall, post-hypnotically, additional details of the shooting favorable to her defense.[2]

The Arkansas courts had refused to allow Rock's post-hypnotic testimony into evidence, adopting a per se inadmissible rule. In excluding the hypnotically refreshed testimony of the defendant, the Arkansas Supreme Court limited her testimony to memories of the event related prior to the hypnotic sessions.[3] The court held that the post-hypnotic testimony violated the rule established in the 1923 case of *Frye v. United States,* whereby evidence of a scientific nature cannot be admissible

---

5. See, Block, E.B., *Hypnosis: A New Tool in Crime Detection* (1976); Kroger and Douce, "Hypnosis in Criminal Investigation," 27 *Int. J. Clinical and Exp. Hypnosis* 358 (1979); Reiser, Martin, "Hypnoses as a Tool in Criminal Investigation," 43 *The Police Chief* 36 (1976), and "More About Hypnosis," 46 *The Police Chief* 10 (1979); Schafer, P.W. and Rubio, R., "Hypnosis To Aid the Recall of Witnesses," 26 *Int. J. Clinical & Exp. Hypnosis* 81 (1978); Statton, J.C., "The Use of Hypnosis in Law Enforcement Criminal Investigations," 5 *J. Police Sci. & Adm.* 399 (1977).

6. See, *Hypnotically Refreshed Testimony: Enhanced Memory or Tampering with Evidence* (1984), by Orne et al., prepared for the National Institute of Justice of the Department of Justice, under contract # J–LEAA–013–78, fn. 9.

The above report, in fn. 9, states that the most widely known training program for instructing police in the use of hypnosis is the Law Enforcement Hypnosis Institute of Los Angeles, directed by Martin Reiser, Ph. D., which offers a "comprehensive program" that lasts "four days, consisting of 32 class hours of theory, demonstration,

and practice." Shorter programs are conducted by various other organizations throughout the country.

The Federal Bureau of Investigation, the Department of the Treasury, and the criminal investigation branches of the military have adopted policies such as those recommended by Dr. Orne, whereby investigative hypnosis must be administered exclusively by individuals trained in medicine or psychology with special expertise in hypnosis. Moreover, investigators intimately familiar with the special problems of hypnosis but unfamiliar with the details of the case, should coordinate its use in interrogation.

§ 20.18

1. 483 U.S. 44 (1987).

2. Rock recalled that she "had her thumb on the hammer of the gun, but had not held her finger on the trigger." The gun, she said, had discharged after her husband grabbed her arm during the struggle, suggesting that the gun was in some way defective and had misfired.

3. Rock v. State, 288 Ark. 566, 708 S.W.2d 78 (1986).

unless it has been generally accepted in the scientific field to which it belonged.[4] Rock received a ten-year sentence in prison and a fine of $10,000.

The Supreme Court granted certiorari to consider the constitutionality of the Arkansas ruling. In its 5–4 decision in *Rock v. Arkansas* the Court held that the per se inadmissible approach to hypnotically refreshed testimony constituted an arbitrary restriction on Rock's right to testify in her own defense and was therefore unconstitutional under the due process clause of the Fourteenth Amendment.[5]

The Court acknowledged that many problems inherently exist in the hypnotic process, but stated that these inaccuracies could be lessened by instituting procedural guidelines, using corroborating evidence and effective cross-examination, and educating the jury as to the risks associated with hypnotically refreshed testimony.

Thus, the approach to hypnotically refreshed testimony outlined in *Rock* admits hypnotically received testimony where it is shown, through corroborating evidence or otherwise, that the testimony is reliable. Courts may no longer deny a criminal defendant the right to hypnosis evidence, but rather must look at each case to determine the admissibility of the testimony. While state courts can still exclude a criminal defendant's post-hypnotic testimony, they can now do so only after employing a case-by-case balancing test and weighing the unreliability of potential testimony against the criminal defendant's constitutional right to testify.

The opinion of the Court in *Rock* sets forth the general case law upon the subject—the cases that applied a per se rule of inadmissibility with regard to witnesses and victims of crime, as well as those upholding admissibility, usually under certain limitations. All courts, of course, must now comply with the Supreme Court's ruling in *Rock* with respect to defendants in criminal cases.

The *Rock* case was the subject of a 1990 article in a medical journal by Dr. Orne and two of his colleagues at the Institute of Pennsylvania Hospital and University of Pennsylvania, under the title of "Rock v. Arkansas: Hypnosis, the Defendant's Privilege."[6] In it, they accept, of course, the Court's ruling in *Rock,* but they express their grave concern with respect to court usage of hypnosis results involving witnesses and crime victims. They also call attention to the futility of cross-examination as a safeguard against the fallibility of hypnotically refreshed testimony. They report that hypnosis creates a "memory hardening" condition which gives the hypnotized person "great confidence in both

---

4. 293 Fed. 1013 (D.C.Cir.1923). The *Frye* case test has been replaced in federal cases by Daubert v. Merrell Dow Pharmaceutical, 113 S.Ct. 2786 (1993). For a detailed discussion of *Daubert,* see the preceding section on the Polygraph Technique.

5. 483 U.S. 44 (1987), the Court also noted the relevance of the Compulsory Process clause of the Sixth Amendment and the Fifth Amendment's Privilege Against Self–Incrimination.

6. 38 *Int'l J. Clinical and Experimental Hypnosis* 250 (1990).

true and false memories" and thereby greatly inhibits cross-examination.[7]

The authors formulated four points in support of their overall conclusion that "... hypnotically induced memories should *never* be permitted to form the basis for testimony by witnesses or victims in a court of law."[8] The points are: (a) the fundamental unreliability of recollections elicited in hypnosis; (b) the persistence of these recollections in the waking condition; (c) the difficulty the person has in retrospectively distinguishing memories that existed prior to hypnosis from those elicited in hypnosis; (d) the unwarranted increase or maintenance of confidence in the accuracy of hypnotically elicited recall which thereby reinforces its credibility.

In view of the favorable ruling established for the defendant, proponents for admissibility regarding witnesses and victims pose the question of "fairness." As to that, Orne and his colleagues submit that a miscarriage of justice is more likely to occur "by admitting the hypnotically altered testimony of witnesses and victims than that of defendants," because "the hypnotized witness's testimony often becomes part of the accusatory 'evidence' ...".[9]

V. NARCOANALYSIS ("TRUTH SERUM")

§ 20.19 Nature of the Test, and Its Limitations

Narcoanalysis consists of the interrogation of an individual placed under the influence of a drug such as scopolamine, sodium amytal, or sodium pentothal, all of which inhibit the subject's control over his nervous system. The effect of this reduced control is often to decrease inhibitions and to stimulate the expression of repressed information.

Administered by injection, proponents believe these drugs lead to the subject's inability to resist telling the truth. However, a significant number of writers and authorities have challenged the ability of any so-called "truth-serum" to reliably produce these results.[1]

Within the psychiatric profession itself, disagreement exists over the merits and reliability of narcoanalysis.[2] Some psychiatrists assert that

---

7. Id. at 257.
8. Id. at 257.
9. Id. at 261.

§ 20.19

1. A complete history of one of the drugs, scopolamine, is given in Geis, "In Scopolamine Veritas," 50 *J.Crim.L.C. & P.S.* 347 (1959). Comprehensive treatments of many aspects of narcoanalysis can be found in Despres, Legal Aspects of Drug Induced Statements, 14 *U. of C.L. Rev.* 601 (1947), and Dession, Freedman, Donnelly,

and Redlich, "Drug–Induced Revelation and Criminal Investigation," 62 *Yale L.J.* 315 (1953); Redlich, Ravits, and Dession, "Narco–Analysis and the Truth," 107 *Am.J.Psychiatry* 586 (1951); and in 41 A.L.R.3d 1369.

2. Gould, "An Analysis of the Limited Legal Value of Truth Serum," 11 *Syracuse L.Rev.* 64 (1959); Geis and Kamm, "Drug Induced Statements," 10 *Clev.Marsh.L.Rev.* 313 (1961); Hanscom, "Narco–Interrogation," 3 *J.Forensic Med.* 9 (1956); Gall,

the technique is overrated for the purpose of detecting deception.[3]

With regards to narcoanalysis for eliciting confessions from the guilty, some experienced investigators and interrogators have suggested that subjects will only confess if they are consciously or subconsciously inclined to confess anyway. Thus, the subjects who do confess under narcoanalysis would have done so anyway if they had undergone a competently conducted interrogation unaided by narcoanalysis. In addition, these experts believe that a person who will refrain from confessing to a competent interrogator will also be able to withhold the truth under narcoanalysis.

§ 20.20 Admissibility of Test Results

In general, courts refuse to admit narcoanalysis test results, finding that narcoanalysis has not received scientific recognition as a valid technique.[1]

The leading state case holding that narcoanalysis is not considered scientifically reliable for the purpose of ascertaining the truth is the 1989 New Jersey Supreme Court case, State v. Pitts.[2] In *Pitts,* the trial court conducted an extensive hearing on the admissibility of narcoanalysis testimony. The New Jersey Supreme Court upheld the trial court's disallowance of state-of-mind testimony based on the defendant's "beliefs" expressed during the sodium amytal interview. The court also disallowed expert testimony in the penalty phase that relied on factual conclusions derived from the sodium amytal interview.

There was one dissent in *Pitts* from the majority decision of the six other justices. Both the majority and dissenting opinions contain extensive discussions of the scientific as well as the legal aspects of narcoanalysis evidence.

Courts have rejected a defendant's narcoanalysis test results in a variety of case situations, including: 1) to obtain a new trial based upon exculpatory statements made while under narcoanalysis;[3] 2) to have a narcoanalysis test in order to corroborate the veracity of denials of guilt already made from the witness stand;[4] 3) to have the opinions of psychiatrists offered to establish that a pretrial narcoanalysis indicated the defendant was telling the truth;[5] and 4) to show videotaped sodium

"The Case Against Narcointerrogation," 7 *J.Forensic Sci.* 29 (1962).

3. MacDonald, "Truth Serum," 46 *J.Crim.L.Criminology & Police Sci.* 259 (1955).

§ 20.20

1. See, e.g., Archie v. Commonwealth, 420 S.E.2d 718 (Va.App.1992); State v. Ward, 712 S.W.2d 485, 487 (Tenn.Crim. App.1986); State v. Rosencrantz, 110 Idaho 124, 714 P.2d 93 (App.1986); Cain v. State,

549 S.W.2d 707 (Tex.Cr.App.1977); Marshall v. State, 620 P.2d 443 (Okla.Cr.1980).

2. 116 N.J. 580, 562 A.2d 1320 (1989).

3. United States v. Bourchier, 5 USCMA 15, 17 CMR 15 (1954).

4. State v. Lindemuth, 56 N.M. 257, 243 P.2d 325 (1952).

5. Merritt v. Commonwealth, 386 S.W.2d 727 (Ky.1965); Commonwealth v. Butler, 213 Pa.Super. 388, 247 A.2d 794 (Pa.1968).

amytal interviews of the defendant to the jury.[6]

In addition to the negative results regarding submitted evidence for or against an accused, the courts have not allowed the results of tests conducted on witnesses. For example, a court has held that the failure of two of the prosecution's witnesses to comply with a court order to submit to a narcoanalysis test did not entitle the defendant to a new trial.[7]

A federal court had held that it was error to admit a tape recording of a prosecution witness' statements under the influence of sodium pentothal even for the limited purpose of restoring his credibility after impeachment.[8]

Although narcoanalysis test results have not been considered probative of the substantive issues in trials, some courts have held that narcoanalysis "refreshed testimony" to be admissible.[9] For example, the Ninth Circuit has refused to disallow a witness' testimony at trial while under sodium amytal.[10] However, the court only allowed the testimony after deciding that specific guidelines regarding the use of testimony refreshed by narcoanalysis produced sufficient evidence of reliability to permit its admission.[11]

§ 20.21   Admissibility of Post–Narcoanalysis Statements

Although courts have held confessions and statements made under narcoanalysis inadmissible, they have not found subsequent confessions inadmissible if the evidence shows that the confession was not solely the product of the narcoanalysis.[1] For example, in a 1954 Illinois murder case,[2] an injured 17–year old murder suspect received an injection of sodium pentothal without consent after his arrest. Although the court termed this action a "flagrant violation" of his constitutional rights, it upheld the conviction because the defendant's confession came later and was not the result of the administration of the "truth serum." [3]

On the other hand, in 1963 the United States Supreme Court reversed, for an evidentiary hearing, an Illinois case in which a confession was obtained fifteen hours after scopolamine and other drugs were

---

6. State v. Alley, 776 S.W.2d 506 (Tenn. 1989).

7. Cross v. State, 136 Ga.App. 400, 221 S.E.2d 615 (1975).

8. Lindsey v. United States, 237 F.2d 893 (9th Cir.1956).

9. United States v. Solomon, 753 F.2d 1522 (9th Cir.1985) (allowing testimony of witness administered sodium amytal before testifying at trial); Sedgwick v. Kawasaki Cycleworks, Inc., 71 Ohio App.3d 117, 593 N.E.2d 69 (1991).

10. United States v. Solomon, supra note 9.

11. Id.

§ 20.21

1. Henson v. State, 159 Tex.Crim. 647, 266 S.W.2d 864 (1953).

2. People v. Heirens, 4 Ill.2d 131, 122 N.E.2d 231 (1954).

3. Id. at 237 ("[I]f it is reasonably found that there is no relationship of cause and effect, the fact that illegal acts were committed in order to extract information or confessions from the accused does not warrant setting aside the conviction.")

administered to a narcotic addict undergoing withdrawal symptoms.[4] The Court held that a further hearing was warranted regarding the confession's admissibility even though the drugs were not administered for the purpose of eliciting a confession. The defendant had made no allegation that he was under their influence at the time he signed the confession, and no evidence of suggestion or coercion existed.[5]

§ 20.22 Mental Condition Determinations

There is a conflict of authority in cases where a person's mental condition is at issue, as to whether expert witnesses can describe the narcoanalytic technique to the jury. If the court admits an explanation of narcoanalysis and a discussion of the statements made by the subject under the influence of the drug, it must be solely for the purpose of evaluating the expert's opinion of the subject's mental capacity or intent. Thus, the statements made under narcoanalysis cannot be accepted as proof of any other issue in the case. Even for this limited purpose, however, the case law is divided over the admissibility of narcoanalysis results.[1]

Courts have not allowed psychiatrists to testify about a defendant's "state-of-mind." For example, in a New Jersey Supreme Court case, the court found that permitting the psychiatrist to so testify would allow the narcoanalysis interview to establish the truth of the defendant's beliefs.[2] Moreover, substantial case law supports the view that psychiatric testimony based on narcoanalysis is inadmissible even as a basis for expert opinion concerning mental capacity.[3]

Psychiatrists have used hypnosis as an analytical procedure for ascertaining an accused person's competency to stand trial, as well as his mental condition at the time of the act for which he is criminally charged. For the expert's testimony on such issues to be admitted, however, proof must exist that hypnosis is reliable for that purpose, and

---

4. Townsend v. Sain, 372 U.S. 293 (1963).

5. For a discussion of the moral issues involved in this case, see, Sheedy, "Narcointerrogation of a Criminal Suspect," 50 *J.Crim.L.Criminology & Police Sci.* 118 (1959).

§ 20.22

1. People v. Jones, 42 Cal.2d 219, 266 P.2d 38 (1954), is the leading case in this area. See also, Lemmon v. Denver, 9 Utah 2d 195, 341 P.2d 215 (1959); People v. Myers, 35 Ill.2d 311, 220 N.E.2d 297 (1966), cert. denied 385 U.S. 1019 (1967); People v. Esposito, 287 N.Y. 389, 39 N.E.2d 925 (1942).

2. State v. Pitts, supra § 20.20, note 2, section 20.20 (disallowing expert testimony). See also, Commonwealth v. Stark, 363 Pa.Super. 356, 526 A.2d 383 (1987) (disallowing expert testimony because "to have

permitted the expert to state his opinions with regard to state-of-mind ... would have had the same practical effect as permitting the psychiatrist to testify to the test results"). But see, People v. Ford, 304 N.Y. 679, 107 N.E.2d 595 (1952); Brown v. State, 304 P.2d 361 (Okl.Cr.1956) (use of narcoanalysis as one of many tools used to determine the defendant's mental condition did not render the hospital superintendent's testimony relative to the defendant's sanity inadmissible).

3. See, for example, State v. Sinnott, 24 N.J. 408, 132 A.2d 298 (1957); State v. White, 60 Wash.2d 551, 374 P.2d 942 (1962), cert. denied 375 U.S. 883 (1963); State v. Cypher, 92 Idaho 159, 438 P.2d 904 (1968); People v. Hiser, 267 Cal.App.2d 47, 72 Cal.Rptr. 906 (Cal.Ct.App.1968); People v. Seipel, 108 Ill.App.2d 384, 247 N.E.2d 905 (1969), cert. denied 397 U.S. 1057 (1970).

that the psychiatrist is qualified as an expert in its psychiatric usage. Absent those conditions, a court may properly refuse to admit any testimony relating to a hypnotic interview.

§ 20.23 Legislation

One state legislature, Illinois, has declared that "[i]n the course of any criminal trial the court shall not require, request, or suggest that the defendant submit ... to questioning under the effect of thiopental sodium or to any other test or questioning by means of any mechanical device or chemical substance.[1] A similar prohibition exists with respect to trials or pre-trial proceedings in civil cases.[2]

Two states allow narcoanalysis use in limited circumstances. Colorado allows the use of narcoanalysis interviews on the issue of a defendant's sanity or eligibility for release from civil commitment.[3] Kentucky allows the use of truth serum in considering parole determinations.[4]

VI. VOICE STRESS ANALYSIS (PSYCHOLOGICAL STRESS EVALUATION)

§ 20.24 Nature of the Instruments

Several types of instruments have been developed for the purpose of analyzing stress in the human voice in order to determine whether the speaker is lying or telling the truth. A former manufacturer of one of them, the Psychological Stress Evaluator (PSE), is Dektor Counterintelligence and Security, Inc. of Savannah, Georgia. It was invented in the latter part of 1960 and placed on the market in 1970. Following is a description of the instrument and its underlying principles according to Dektor's promotional literature:

> The PSE (Psychological Stress Evaluator) is an instrument that detects, measures and graphically displays certain stress-related components of the human voice.

> Superimposed on the audible voice are inaudible frequency modulations. The FM quality of the voice is susceptible to the amount of stress that one may be under when speaking. To the human ear, a person may sound perfectly normal, free of tremors or "guilt-revealing" sound variations. The PSE senses the differences and records the changes in the inaudible FM qualities of the voice

§ 20.23

1. S.H.A. 725 ILCS 125/8b (1993). This prohibition extends to sentencing hearings after trial. People v. Ackerman, 132 Ill. App.2d 251, 269 N.E.2d 737 (1971).

2. 735 ILCS 5/2-1104 (Smith–Hurd 1993).

3. West's Colo.Rev.Stat.Ann. § 16–8–106 (1993).

4. Ky.Rev.Stat.Ann. § 439.335 (Michie/Bobbs–Merrill 1993).

on a chart. When the chart is interpreted by an experienced examiner it reveals the key stress areas of the person being questioned. * * *

The key to successful use of the PSE is the preparation of simple selected questions keyed to the individual and structured to reveal normal or truthful answers and answers that are false. Once the personal pattern has been established, any evasive or false answers reveal stress; if a person is not telling the truth, then analysis of his voice pattern will show it. * * * [1]

Other voice stress analysis instruments include: The Voice Stress Analyzer, produced by Decision Control Incorporated; the Mark II Voice Analyzer, manufactured by Law Enforcement Associates Incorporated; The Mark IX–P Voice Stress Analyzer, produced by the Communication Control System Incorporated; the Hagoth, produced by the Hagoth Corporation; and the Voice Stress computer, a pocket calculator-sized instrument, developed by John Welsh.

§ 20.25 Reliability Studies

A number of validation studies have been made regarding the voice analysis technique for the determination of truth and deception. One of them was conducted by Dr. Joseph Kubis of the Department of Psychology at Fordham University. He did it under a grant from the U.S. Army and submitted his report in August, 1973. At the time of the Kubis study only two of these instruments were available, The Decision Control's "Voice Stress Analyzer," and the Dektor "Psychological Stress Evaluator." His report concluded that neither instrument "may be accepted as valid 'lie detectors' within the constraints of an experimental paradigm." [1] In consequence of the Kubis study the Army abandoned its interest in either of the instruments tested by Kubis. [2] The Air Force and the National Security Agency also conducted tests which indicated unreliability. [3]

§ 20.24

1. The text was reproduced in the report of the June 4 and 5, 1974 Hearings before the Subcommittee of the Committee on Government Operations, House of Representatives on "The Use of Polygraphs and Similar Devices by Federal Agencies," U.S. Gov.Pr.Office # 37–843 0, at p. 242.

According to the author of an article favorable to the Dektor PSE, the instrument can also "aid psychiatrists in distinguishing fact from fancy in patient statements, and the physician in diagnosing brain damage in newborns." See, Cain, "The Psychological Stress Evaluator: Forensic Applications and Limitations," *Identification News*, Sept. 1977, 3 at p. 4.

§ 20.25

1. Technical Report No. LWL–CR–03B70, August 1973, U.S. Army Warfare Laboratory, Aberdeen Proving Grounds, Maryland. In the same study, which included experiments with the Polygraph Technique, Kubis found that, in contrast to the voice analysis technique, the polygraph technique possessed a high validity.

For a response by Dektor to the Kubis study and conclusion, see the Report, supra n. 1, at p. 301.

2. Link, "Lie Detection Through Voice Analysis," 3 *Military Police Law Enforcement Journal* 38, at p. 40 (1976).

3. Supra n. 2. The author concluded his article as follows:

"... hard evidence that the voice analysis lie-detection technique is effective has not been introduced. It further seems that, at a minimum, much further testing and refinement will be required

Studies conducted by Dr. Frank Horvath of the School of Criminal Justice of Michigan State University confirmed the Kubis conclusion of unreliability of the voice analyzer technique.[4]

Among several other studies upon the subject is one by Dr. Israel Nachshon of the Department of Criminology at Bar Ilan University in Israel, in which he, too, reached a similar conclusion to the ones reported by Kubis and Horvath.[5]

§ 20.26 Case Law

Federal and state courts have held PSE test results inadmissible as evidence in civil and criminal cases.[1] Most courts have considered the PSE test under the "general acceptance" standard first enunciated in *Frye v. United States.* They concluded that the PSE is not "sufficiently established to have gained general acceptance in the particular field to which it belongs." Courts note that few well controlled studies of the reliability of voice stress analysis exist, and that none of these studies have shown that voice stress analyzers effectively detect deception.

before voice analysis can be considered useful for military lie detection. Resolution of these problems does not seem to be enhanced by inconsistent statements made by the experts in voice analysis. Until a scientifically acceptable validity rate for voice analysis (that approaches the validity rate of the polygraph technique) is established and, until the boundaries are clearly established for what voice analysis can and cannot do, it does not seem reasonable that voice analysis for lie detection ought to be adopted by any of the military services."

4. See, Horvath, "An Experimental Comparison of the Psychological Stress Evaluator (PSE) and the Galvanic Skin Response (GSR) in Detection of Deception," a paper presented at the August, 1976 meeting of the American Polygraph Association; Horvath, "Effect of Different Motivational Instructions on Detection of Deception With the Psychological Stress Evaluator and the Galvanic Skin Responses," 64 *J.App.Psy.* 323 (1979); Horvath, "Detecting Deception: The Promise and the Reality of Voice Stress Analysis," 27 *J.Forensic Sci.* 340 (1982). Also see, VanDercar et al., "A Description and Analysis of the Operation and Validity of the Psychological Stress Evaluator," 25 *J.Forensic Sci.* 174 (1980).

5. Nachshon, Psychological Stress Evaluator: Validity Study (1977), which was supported by grant number 953-0264-001 from the Israel Police; Nachshon and Feldman, "Vocal Indices of Psychological Stress: A Validation Study of the Psychological Stress Evaluator," 8 *J.Pol.Sci. & Admin.* 40 (1980); Nachshon, et al., "Validity of the

Psychological Stress Evaluation: A Field Study," 13 *J.Pol.Sci. & Admin.* 275 (1985).

Compare the following opposing conclusion. In a report titled "Psychological Stress Evaluator: A Study," published in 1972, its author Michael P. Kradz, then of the Howard County Police Department in Elicott City, Maryland, concluded that "Using the PSE as instrumentation, 100% accuracy was produced in ... 36 subject examinations for which complete and concrete corroboration was, or later became, available." Kradz's conviction that the PSE was valid led him to join the staff of Dektor Counterintelligence and Security, and that company's 1984 literature lists him as Director of PSE Training & Services.

§ 20.26

1. See, Barrel of Fun v. State Farm Fire & Casualty Co., 739 F.2d 1028 (5th Cir. 1984); United States v. Traficant, 566 F.Supp. 1046, 1047 (N.D.Ohio 1983); State v. Arnold, 533 So.2d 1311 (La.App.1988); People v. Drake, 748 P.2d 1237, 1247 (Colo. 1988); Neises v. Solomon State Bank, 236 Kan. 767, 696 P.2d 372 (1985); Sabag v. Continental South Dakota, 374 N.W.2d 349 (S.D.1985); State v. Makerson, 52 N.C.App. 149, 277 S.E.2d 869, 872 (1981); Caldwell v. State, 267 Ark. 1053, 594 S.W.2d 24, 28 (1980); People v. Tarsia, 67 A.D.2d 210, 415 N.Y.S.2d 120, 122 (1979), affirmed 50 N.Y.2d 1, 427 N.Y.S.2d 944 (1980); State v. Ochalla, 285 N.W.2d 683, 684 (Minn.1979); State v. Schouest, 351 So.2d 462 (La.1977); Smith v. State, 31 Md.App. 106, 355 A.2d 527 (1976).

§ 20.27 Legislation

Legislation on voice stress analysis generally revolves around two areas: 1) employee protection from testing by employers, and 2) privacy concerns arising from testing without the individual's consent.

In 1988, Congress passed the Employee Polygraph Protection Act, making it unlawful for any employer "directly or indirectly, to require, request, suggest, or cause any employee or prospective employee to take or submit to any lie detector test." [1] The prohibition includes voice stress analysis.

A number of states have enacted similar statutes. For example, Michigan, Minnesota, Nebraska, Nevada, New York, and Wisconsin all have statutes forbidding employers from using voice stress analysis. [2]

Some of the ads by manufacturers of voice stress analysis devices brazenly stated the instrument could be used without the awareness of the subject, a practice that in many instances would be in clear violation of federal and state laws.

Among the various specific prohibitions upon surreptitious usage of such instruments are statutes in California, Pennsylvania, and Wisconsin. [3] In addition, a New York law prohibits a police officer from requiring a victim of a sexual crime to undergo a voice stress analysis. [4]

A couple of states nevertheless have licensing requirements specifically for voice stress analyzers. [5] An Arkansas law requires a voice stress analyzer to be a "person of honesty, truthfulness, integrity and moral fitness." [6] In addition, other more general laws require licensing for anyone who uses devices for the purpose of detecting deception.

§ 20.27

1. 29 U.S.C.A. § 2001 (1993).

2. Mich.Comp.Laws Ann. § 73.302 (West 1993); Minn.Stat.Ann. § 181.75 (West 1993); Neb.Rev.Stat. § 81–1902 (1993); Nev.Rev.Stat. 613.440 (1993); N.Y.—McKinney's Labor Law § 733 (1993); Wis.Stat.Ann. 111.37 (West 1993).

3. West's Ann.Cal.Penal Code § 637.3 (1993); 19 Pa.Cons.Stat.Ann. § 7507 (1993); Wis.Stat.Ann. 942.06 (West 1993).

4. N.Y.—McKinney's Crim.Pro.Law § 160.45 (1993).

5. See, for example, Neb.Rev.Stat. § 81–1917 (1993).

6. Ark.Code Ann. § 17–32–304(a)(2) (Michie 1993). The Arkansas law further provides that the test results are inadmissible as evidence. Ark.Code Ann. § 17–2–302.

INDEX

References are to Pages

---

†